Baseball Prospectus Futures Guide 2015

THE WORLD'S FINEST ANALYSIS OF BASEBALL'S FINEST MINOR-LEAGUERS

Featuring a cavalcade of hundreds of tomorrow's major league stars

Nick Faleris, Chris Mellen

*Mark Anderson, Tucker Blair, Ben Carsley, Mike Gianella, Craig Goldstein,
Jordan Gorosh, Jeff Moore, Jeff Quinton, Bret Sayre*

*CJ Wittmann, Chris Rodriguez, Ethan Purser, Ryan Parker, Chris King, Patrick Ebert,
Frankie Piliere, Todd Gold, David Rawnsley*

Geoff Young, Editor

Dave Pease, Publisher

Library of Congress Cataloging-in-Publication Data:
ISBN-13: 978-1508819363
ISBN-10: 150881936X

Printed in the United States of America
10 9 8 7 6 5 4 3 2 1

Header images public domain via Wikimedia Commons.

Cover: Mauricio Rubio

Design and layout by Bryan Davidson and Jon Franke

Table of Contents

Preface

by Geoff Young

Maybe you've heard of Felix Hernandez. Before he became a perennial All-Star and Cy Young Award candidate, he was a 16-year-old kid signed out of Venezuela by people who recognized his talent. He honed his craft across the United States, in places like Everett, Washington; Appleton, Wisconsin; and San Bernardino, California.

One May afternoon in 2004, my friend Jeff and I drove to Rancho Cucamonga to watch Hernandez pitch for the visiting Inland Empire 66ers. His status as one of baseball's best pitching prospects preceded him, and we hoped to catch a glimpse of greatness in the making. My notes from that game tell a different story:

> Hernandez featured a fastball that ran 91-94... occasionally touching 95. But his command was off, and the killer breaking ball I'd read about never materialized. Final line: 4 IP, 8 H, 7 R, 5 ER, 3 BB, 3 K, 2 HR. Not quite what I was expecting, but even the brightest talents have bad days.

The most important sentence there is the last. Hernandez looked bad when we saw him, but this was a rare event. In the larger context of his overall body of work, it gave an incomplete and misleading picture of the promising young hurler who was destined for bigger things.

I don't pretend to be a professional talent evaluator. Scouting is hard work that requires a keen eye and relentless dedication to the craft. Fortunately I know many people who have these qualities and are willing to share their knowledge with others. Some of their names grace these very pages.

Thanks to their accumulated wisdom in the form of reports gathered over multiple looks, we can differentiate between a bad pitcher and a good pitcher having a bad day. Statistics tell us *what* happened on the field. Scouting reports dig deeper and tell us *why* it happened, which is at least as important in trying to chart a course for the future.

There are no guarantees, but with a reliable guide, you at least give yourself a fighting chance. This book is that guide.

It starts with the Baseball Prospectus Top 101, a high-level view of baseball's brightest as judged by the BP prospect team. Past lists have included Clayton Kershaw, Andrew McCutchen, Evan Longoria, Joey Votto, David Price—look, this could take a while; the point is, you'll want to pay attention because tomorrow's stars are hiding in here.

Next come reports on the top 10 prospects from each of the 30 teams. Using information culled from their own eyewitness accounts, as well as from industry sources, they identify the strengths, weaknesses, and expected roles of 360 young players. With additional snapshots of guys who could make the list next year or help their team right now, the total number of prospects to dream on approaches 500. That's a lot of dreams.

You'll also find more detailed reports on 30 of those players—one per team—as viewed in person by the BP prospect team.

These are where you can learn why Dylan Bundy's 60-grade cutter could get even better and swoon over descriptions of Raimel Tapia's "very easy, well timed, and balanced" swing.

Then come the organizational rankings, which show how teams stack up against one another in terms of players on the rise, depth, and so forth. This is followed by Perfect Game's top 100 draft prospects list and their in-depth looks at how several current top prospects were viewed as amateurs.

Next, fantasy players will benefit from Ben Carsley's "Friends Don't Let Friends Draft Mid-Rotation Prospects," which reminds us that although you might end up with Jordan Zimmermann or Sonny Gray, you're far more likely to get stuck with Aaron Poreda, Alex White, Simon Castro, or someone else who is very important to his family but not so much to your fantasy team.

Jeff Quinton follows with "Defensive Decision Making and Prospect Valuation," which promises to help you "avoid inviting additional error into an already impossible task." He uses the ideas of great thinkers far removed from the realm of baseball to show us how we can improve our decision-making processes and evade common pitfalls before they come back to haunt our dreams of fantasy league glory.

Returning to the lists you crave, Bret Sayre gives his top 101 fantasy prospects, which is like the other list, only different. For example, Austin Hedges is a terrific major-league prospect, but his ability to handle a pitching staff and throw behind runners is useless in all but the strangest of fantasy formats.

Next up, Craig Goldstein's "The Ones Who Could Jump" provides insights into 20 players who could take a big step forward in 2015. Last year he identified Nomar Mazara, Ryan McMahon, and Marco Gonzales as ones to watch. Now they are on everyone's radar. Here's where you find that next batch of risers.

Mike Gianella follows with the 50 prospects most likely to pay immediate dividends in 2015. If your roster just needs a few minor tweaks, this is the list for you.

Sometimes more drastic actions are required. "The Top 50 2014 Signees for Dynasty Drafts" can help. Everyone knows about Yasmany Tomas and Carlos Rodon, but what about Touki Toussaint, Roberto Baldoquin, Michael Gettys, and a host of others? (Bonus: We got so excited, we threw in 10 honorable mentions at the end for no extra charge!)

Finally, we close with "The Top 40 Fantasy Prospects Outside of Major League Baseball," which examines the next wave of talent to come from, well, wherever. Some of these guys are in high school, some are in college. Others are in Japan or Cuba. Increasingly, baseball is being played all over the planet (maybe elsewhere, too, but that's a topic for another day), and if you're in a league where anything goes, you'll want to know these names sooner rather than later.

But the end isn't really the end. Rather, it's a launching point for further discovery. The learning process never ceases, and we'll bet that you find yourself referring to this book again and again.

Whether you work for a major-league organization, play fantasy, or just love baseball, the *Futures Guide* will help you navigate the vast rivers of information available today. It will enhance your understanding of and appreciation for the up-and-coming stars of this great game.

Is there another King Felix in these pages? He's a very large man and this is a very small book, so probably not. However, there's a strong chance that many of the names you read about here will be known throughout the lands in just a few short years. When that happens, won't you feel smart for having been "on them" back when they were in A-ball, learning how to be great? ■

Prospect Preamble

by Craig Goldstein

For the third consecutive year, Baseball Prospectus has opted to publish a book wholly dedicated to scouting, fantasy baseball and the minor leagues. Many more baseball fans thirst for information regarding the game's future superstars each year. We love prospects because they represent the future, sure, but we love them because they're the unknown. They put us all—novice and experienced scouts alike—on equal footing in some respects, because all it takes is having an opinion to be right. It's like gambling, but the only thing you invest is hope, and there's always another peg to hang your hat on if you happen to be wrong: something I'm intimately familiar with.

It was never a foregone conclusion that I would be writing this piece for the *Futures Guide*, talking about prospects. I'm not exactly a natural follow-up to Jason Parks. I don't have his grasp of language or hashtags, I've rarely been #Gerndt, my knees are structurally sound, the list goes on. While Parks introduced what scouting was from the perspective of a man who has spent the previous decade on the backfields, I can only tell you what it means to someone still trying to find their footing, and there's something symbolic in that. Parks was a finished product when it came to scouting, while I'm a work in progress. In writing the Prospect Preamble in back-to-back years, we can provide opinions from distinctly different vantage points along the same spectrum. So while I encourage you to revisit last year's Preamble, here's my take:

There's a lot made of the chasm between stats and scouts, and while BP-alum Dayn Perry said it best in his classic "beer *and* tacos" line, we often struggle to understand how they work together. What's important to remember about scouting and advanced analytics is that they're all working from the same concept: create a baseline of knowledge and compare what we're looking at now to what has worked (or hasn't) historically. Stat types can do this with row upon row of data, and algorithms that create something along the lines of a similarity score. Similarly, an older scout has player profile upon player profile indexed in his memory, with the ability to identify and compare what a prospect has or does to what he's seen before. He has an idea of which flaws are fixable and which are fatal. The more games, players, and levels seen, the larger the index, the larger the sample. Every game that we attend, every double play we see turned, and every swing we take in (and how these things are done) is another row of data logged. Hence the importance of going to games in person, and not scouting the stat line.

I joined Baseball Prospectus in August of 2013 as an intern on the fantasy side. While that may not seem so long ago, here are some things that will make you understand exactly how long a year and half can be: Robin Thicke was a thing, Dennis Rodman going to North Korea was breathlessly reported on multiple news outlets, the Cronut got more attention than Dennis Rodman in North Korea, and we were obsessed with "What Does The Fox Say?" Suffice it to say that when I started writing up major leaguers at BP, I didn't see a transition to the Prospect Team coming down the pipeline. My heart has always lurked below the surface when it comes to baseball: case in point, when I did write about big leaguers, those articles tended to skew toward rookies or U25 types. I was fortunate to be part of a team that encouraged the coverage of the minor leagues from a fantasy angle. More than that, I was fortunate to be in an organization that encouraged the cross-pollination of the teams in place. I did as much as I could to gather information from all sources, but relied heavily upon the Baseball Prospectus Prospect Team, who encouraged me to expand the number of games I saw in person, and always had time to discuss the evaluative process and exchange information with me.

Certainly, that team has suffered the loss of substantial institutional knowledge for the third straight year, with some of our most public—and trusted—voices receiving industry recognition for their efforts. This is a point of pride for the organization, to be sure, but also leaves a void to be filled. Fortunately, we have experience in that department, and we're going to continue to restaff and restock the BP Prospect Team with talented, hard-working individuals who can maintain and elevate our standards. Sure, we could trade on the goodwill generated by the industry-quality work generated by Parks and Kevin Goldstein before us, but without creating a high-end product of our own, the value of the product we've worked so hard to create would be diluted. And that's a good thing, because it keeps us motivated to match the level of excellence set by our fellow evaluators in the prospect community, as well as those who have come before us.

We're aware that the prospect-watching community can be exclusive, with a high bar to clear before one is accepted as a trustworthy source. While that's a positive in some respects, it can be easy to push a potential devotee away by dismissing them for the very lack of knowledge that they're trying to rectify. This guide's purpose is to reach anyone who has an interest in the future of baseball, be it real or fantasy, and to inform them through eyewitness accounts and scouting reports. Through essays on decision making and prospect valuation, and on the dangers of mid-rotation prospects. To take the same information and back-room discussions that I am privy to as a BP author, and turn them toward the public in a digestible and entertaining manner. Jason described last year's iteration of the *Futures Guide* as the beginning of a vision, and it's our hope that this year's *Guide* serves as a continuation of those same ideals. ■

Team Top 10 Prospects 2015

Welcome to the team top 10s. Before immersing yourself in what follows, you'll need to know a few things:

Terminology

20/80: Scouting scale; often used as the 2/8 scale; used to denote physical tool grades both in the present and the future. The scale can also indicate a future player role, i.e., future major league grade (overall) at tool maturity. This is the break-down:

- 20=Very poor
- 30=Well below-average
- 40=Below-average
- 50=Average; major-league regular
- 60=Above-average (plus); first-division
- 70=Well above-average (plus-plus); all-star
- 80=Elite; bacon

Big Raw: Power (or the power tool) is often just referred to as "raw."

Bore: A pitch that shows intense arm-side movement into the hitter standing in the arm-side box (RHP/RH; LHP/LH).

First-division: A player that could start for a playoff-caliber team.

Hittability: Put simply, the overall command and feel for the act of hitting. It's a broad term, but it's usually used to describe hitters who put the barrel of the bat on the baseball, command of the bat, the ability to make contact all over the zone against all types of offerings, etc.

Life: action/movement on a particular pitch; usually used to described the late movement on a fastball.

Makeup: Makeup is about work ethic and the desire to improve and maximize the potential suggested by the raw physical tools. Makeup is not about being a jerk or being likeable or being a sweetheart to fans in the stands. Makeup is a major component in a player's ability to respond and adjust to failure and setbacks on the field.

OFP (Overall Future Potential): The measure of all tool futures based on the projected growth and maturity of those tools. The individual grades are calculated and assigned proper weight, and the result of that division is the player's OFP, or projected ceiling.

Pitchability: Put simply, the overall command and feel for the act of pitching. It's a broad term, but it's usually used to describe pitchers with instincts for their craft, sequencing ability, understanding of how to get hitters out, how to pitch east, west, north, and south, etc.

Run: Another way of describing the speed tool; also used to describe a pitch that will show movement to the arm-side of the pitcher, hence running away from a hitter in the opposite box.

Secs: Secondary pitches.

#Want: The manifestation of human desire and physical yield; when the yearning for perfection becomes visible to the naked eye.

Toolbar

We've also included a graphical display of each player's future projected (i.e., *not* present) physical tools.
For hitters, it looks like this:

MLB ETA	Hit	Power	Run	Glove	Arm		OFP	Realistic
2014	–	55	50	65	80		60 1ST DIV PLAYER	45 BACKUP C/<AVG REG

These are the traditional five tools used to evaluate hitters. OFP is explained above, while "realistic" represents a less optimistic overall view of the future. Both come with number grades as well as descriptions to give you some idea of the type of player we're envisioning.
For pitchers, it looks like this:

MLB ETA	CT	FB	CH	CB	SL		OFP	Realistic
2016	–	65	60	60	–		65 NO.2 STARTER	55 NO.3 STARTER

CT = cutter, FB = fastball, CH = changeup, CB = curve ball, SL = slider.

Now you know how this chapter works. Read and enjoy.

1. Archie Bradley   RHP

Born: 8/10/92   **Age:** 22   **Bats:** R   **Throws:** R   **Height:** 6'4"   **Weight:** 235

MLB ETA		CT	FB	CH	CB	SL		OFP		Realistic
2015		**60**	**70**	**50**	**65**	**–**		**70** NO. 2 STARTER		**65** NO. 2/3 STARTER

YEAR	TEAM	LVL	AGE	W	L	SV	G	GS	IP	H	HR	BB	K	BB9	SO9	GB%	BABIP	WHIP	ERA	FIP	FRA	WARP
2014	RNO	AAA	21	1	4	0	5	5	24.3	26	0	12	23	4.4	8.5	46%	.373	1.56	5.18	3.78	4.40	0.9
2014	MOB	AA	21	2	3	0	12	12	54.7	45	2	36	46	5.9	7.6	44%	.285	1.48	4.12	4.23	6.15	-0.5
2014	DIA	Rk	21	0	0	0	1	1	4.0	5	0	1	6	2.2	13.5	75%	.417	1.50	4.50	1.78	2.88	0.2
2015	ARI	MLB	22	3	7	0	16	16	80.3	73	7	42	75	4.7	8.4	47%	.315	1.43	4.43	4.33	4.81	0.1
2016	ARI	MLB	23	10	10	0	32	32	203.7	166	16	92	205	4.1	9.1	47%	.302	1.27	3.61	3.62	3.92	2.0

Breakout: 0%   Improve: 0%   Collapse: 0%   Attrition: 0%   MLB: 0%   Upside: 19   *Comparables: Zack Wheeler, Jeurys Familia, Chris Archer*

Drafted/Acquired: 1st round, 2011 draft, Broken Arrow HS (Broken Arrow, OK)

Previous Ranking: #1 (Org), #9 (Top 101)

What Happened in 2014: It was a year of firsts for the large Sooner State product, as Bradley saw his first extended DL stint and hit his first developmental buzz saw between Double-A and Triple-A before bouncing back some in the Arizona Fall League and enjoying his first bout of success, adding a new weapon to his already potent arsenal in the process.

#11
BP Top
101
Prospects

Strengths: Big, sturdy workhorse; strong-man power through core and lower half; above-average arm speed; fastball can reach elite velocity, works comfortably in plus to double-plus velocity band with arm-side action; capable of pounding bottom of the zone on steep plane; curve can be a true hammer with violent bite and good depth at its best; cutter is potential impact offering with sharp, short slide and tilt, running 87-90 mph; upper-80s change will flash above average with soft fade; when right, shows high level of confidence and impressive mound presence; impact arsenal; solid athleticism off mound.

Weaknesses: Command and control below average at present; hard spike curve played soft and imprecise after missed time, often due to failure to get on top; change can get firm and flat, placing high level of import on sequencing to properly set up; below-average body control through mechanics; fails to repeat with regularity; slot can drift; arm speed can be negated by fickle timing; inconsistent landing ranges from straight line to slightly closed with a hint of crossfire; injury/discomfort further complicated work toward mechanical refinement.

Risk Factor/Injury History: Low; impact stuff will play to late innings at worst; achieved Double-A.

Bret Sayre's Fantasy Take: In fantasy leagues, Bradley is essentially playing Bill Murray's role in Groundhog Day—as he enters the 2015 with an outside chance for a rotation spot and angling for an early-season call-up. Despite the rough 2014, Bradley still has SP1 upside with 200-plus strikeout ability, but is more likely to settle in as a top-30 starter who gives back some of that ERA/strikeout-based value in his WHIP. He's still a top-five fantasy pitching prospect. Don't overthink it.

The Year Ahead: There is no sugarcoating the struggles the former first rounder endured from the spring through the fall. With a combination of inconsistent timing and overthrowing in the mix, Bradley scuffled through his first month of action with Triple-A Reno before an intercostal strain in his right elbow forced him to the disabled list. He returned to game action two months later with Double-A Mobile, where the power righty continued to battle his mechanics from a variable arm slot to inconsistent posture, timing, and landing, all of which combined to throw off his release and complicate his execution. Keep in mind, this is still some of the loudest stuff in the minors, and even under the best of circumstances loud stuff is not particularly easy to wield with precision. Bradley's situation is further complicated by a big body that he is still learning to control and that was forced to compensate for irregularities in the arm for a large portion of the year. In short, Bradley wasn't "right" for most of the summer, and when you loosen the bolts on a muscle car and drive it around for a while, it's going to take some time to work everything back into proper alignment. Provided a winter of rest sees Bradley at 100 percent this spring, he'll likely begin 2015 with a confidence-building assignment back in Double-A. There's the ever-present risk that he never gets his body to do what it needs to do pitch to pitch, but if everything clicks it's going to be some of the filthiest stuff in the game. He has the raw ability and potential to bridge that gap between forgettable 2014 to legit, front-end major leaguer in the blink of an eye.

2. Braden Shipley RHP

Born: 2/22/92 **Age:** 23 **Bats:** R **Throws:** R **Height:** 6'3" **Weight:** 190

MLB ETA	CT	FB	CH	CB	SL	OFP	Realistic
2016	–	70	70	65	–	65 NO. 2/3 STARTER	55 NO. 3/4 STARTER

YEAR	TEAM	LVL	AGE	W	L	SV	G	GS	IP	H	HR	BB	K	BB9	SO9	GB%	BABIP	WHIP	ERA	FIP	FRA	WARP
2014	MOB	AA	22	1	2	0	4	4	20.0	14	3	10	18	4.5	8.1	56%	.216	1.20	3.60	4.84	5.40	0.1
2014	VIS	A+	22	2	4	0	10	10	60.3	57	7	21	68	3.1	10.1	47%	.331	1.29	4.03	4.39	5.72	0.6
2014	SBN	A	22	4	2	0	8	8	45.7	46	1	11	41	2.2	8.1	47%	.336	1.25	3.74	2.83	3.92	0.6
2015	ARI	MLB	23	3	8	0	18	18	88.7	91	10	37	72	3.8	7.3	45%	.323	1.43	4.85	4.60	5.27	-0.3
2016	ARI	MLB	24	9	10	0	30	30	192.0	182	19	80	173	3.8	8.1	45%	.318	1.37	4.35	3.97	4.73	0.0

Breakout: 0%   **Improve:** 0%   **Collapse:** 0%   **Attrition:** 0%   **MLB:** 0%   **Upside:** 3   *Comparables: Dan Straily, Alex Colome, Aneury Rodriguez*

Drafted/Acquired: 1st round, 2013 draft, University of Nevada-Reno (Reno, NV)

Previous Ranking: #3 (Org), #62 (Top 101)

What Happened in 2014: Shipley showed steady progress working through the Midwest and California Leagues before capping a solid developmental year with a brief stint at Double-A Mobile.

Strengths: Good size and athleticism; strength projects to handle innings; low-mileage arm; fast arm with short circle; fastball comes with arm-side action and good bore; barrel-misser; pounds inner half against same-side bats; low- to mid-90s velo without losing life; change flashes double-plus at present with arm speed and slot deception; hard dive and fade; weapon down in the zone; low-80s, 11-to-5 curve shows hard bite and impressive depth; improved confidence working off the breaker, included early and behind in the count; improved proficiency in sequencing.

Weaknesses: Can become predictable in fastball/changeup use; upbeat tempo can cause arm drag and arm-side misses; still working to find uniform release on curve, resulting in flurries of 4, 5, and 6 grades on the 20-80 scale; can get deliberate in mechanics, leading to unnatural execution of changeup and decrease in effectiveness across the board; needs to continue to work toward second-nature motion where natural feel should take over; high-end arsenal with mid-level execution at present.

Risk Factor/Injury History: Moderate; limited Double-A exposure.

Bret Sayre's Fantasy Take: Shipley may not have Bradley's fantasy ceiling, but there's still plenty to like here. It's not ideal for strikeout potential that his change is his go to pitch, but if he can miss bats with the curve, he could reach that 200-strikeout plateau. Overall, he projects as a good SP3 with strong ratio contributions and the ability to throw a lot of innings.

The Year Ahead: Shipley accomplished a great deal in 2014, including increased proficiency with his breaking ball, a solid jump in workload without significant fall-off in performance, and increased comfort mixing and matching his offerings in variable game situations. A relative newcomer to pitching, Shipley has made tremendous progress over the past three seasons in putting together a system of mechanics that work for him and his repertoire, and his athleticism is an asset both in implementing tweaks via developmental staff suggestions and in self-correcting in-game when his motion slides slightly out of whack. With a chance for three plus or better offerings and the strength and arm to shoulder a major-league starter's workload, Shipley represents one of the more exciting profiles in the minors. He should head back to Mobile to start 2015, where Southern League hitters will demand of him more precision in execution, and the sheer quality of his stuff will be less effective in dissimulating his shortcomings. There is front-end upside if he can continue to tighten his consistency and build a more robust understanding as to how to best implement his weapons in concert with each other.

#22
BP Top 101 Prospects

3. Aaron Blair RHP

Born: 5/26/92 **Age:** 23 **Bats:** R **Throws:** R **Height:** 6'5" **Weight:** 230

MLB ETA	CT	FB	CH	CB	SL	OFP	Realistic
2016	–	60	60	60	50	65 NO. 2/3 STARTER	55 NO. 3/4 STARTER

YEAR	TEAM	LVL	AGE	W	L	SV	G	GS	IP	H	HR	BB	K	BB9	SO9	GB%	BABIP	WHIP	ERA	FIP	FRA	WARP
2014	MOB	AA	22	4	1	0	8	8	46.3	30	4	16	46	3.1	8.9	44%	.228	0.99	1.94	3.49	4.19	0.6
2014	VIS	A+	22	4	2	0	13	13	72.3	70	6	21	81	2.6	10.1	41%	.338	1.26	4.35	3.86	4.37	1.1
2014	SBN	A	22	1	2	0	6	6	35.7	25	2	14	44	3.5	11.1	42%	.258	1.09	4.04	3.01	3.81	0.7
2015	ARI	MLB	23	4	9	0	20	20	103.0	100	11	40	91	3.5	8.0	41%	.317	1.35	4.43	4.28	4.81	0.1
2016	ARI	MLB	24	10	10	0	31	31	198.7	189	20	58	175	2.6	7.9	41%	.313	1.24	3.99	3.67	4.34	0.9

Breakout: 0%   **Improve:** 0%   **Collapse:** 0%   **Attrition:** 0%   **MLB:** 0%   **Upside:** 23   *Comparables: Sean Nolin, Chad Bettis, Scott Barnes*

Drafted/Acquired: 1st round, 2013 draft, Marshall University (Huntington, WV)

Previous Ranking: #5 (Org)

What Happened in 2014: A developmental step forward with his curve helped the burly righty to climb three levels while logging over 150 innings and regularly missing bats and barrels alike.

#43
BP Top 101 Prospects

Strengths: Big, durable build; hard downward plane on all offerings, with particularly tough-to-square trajectory in the lower third; heavy, low-90s fastball can kiss 95 up in the zone; off-speed works with arm-side action and 8-10 mph velocity delta off heater; regularly slips off swing plane; upper-70s curve gives him third potential plus offering with two-plane action and good shape out of same slot as fastball and change; easy and repeatable motion and arm action; slight twist through leg lift and entering drive adds some deception; shows slider as different look breaker; can throw strikes with all offerings.

Weaknesses: Velocity can dip later in starts; can fail to finish, negatively impacting execution and placement of curve and change; fastball is plane reliant and hittable up in the zone; curve can come soft without power bite, limiting utility as swing-and-miss pitch in the zone; despite potential, fastball and curve could grade sub-plus at maturity, increasing need to leverage plane and sequencing; control outdistances command; arm slot lessens effectiveness of offerings up in the zone.

Risk Factor/Injury History: Moderate; limited Double-A exposure.

Bret Sayre's Fantasy Take: A lazier writer would copy what he wrote for Shipley and say "kinda like that." Blair has a little less ceiling and floor than the man he trails on this list, mostly due to the fact that he'll probably miss fewer bats, but the general hypothesis remains the same.

The Year Ahead: Blair's deception, size, and ability to create a sharp plane despite a low three-quarters slot proved too much for low-minors bats last summer, especially once the Marshall University product was able to tap into his two-plane breaker with regularity. While fellow 2013 draftee Braden Shipley's upside arsenal represents the pitching equivalent of an 8 1/2-inch MAC—dangerously sharp and ideal for carving with precision and style—Blair's stuff is more in the vein of a high-quality Wusthof dinner knife, with balance and utility the signature characteristics. His offerings are each expelled with uniformity, and the well-shielded release adds to hitters' difficulty in picking up and identifying the secondaries. Blair should be able to lean on this advantage to and through his major-league debut, giving his stuff a half-grade or so bump (playable to raw) and enabling him to continue to miss bats at rates that belie the natural quality of the repertoire. Blair took solid steps forward in improving the consistency of his curve, giving him a vertical weapon to pair with his already solid fastball/changeup combo. Evaluators want to see how the stuff plays against advanced lineups with multiple looks, which could come with Double-A Mobile or Triple-A Reno depending on how aggressively the Diamondbacks want to work. If the in-zone command tightens enough for Blair to avoid regular mistakes up in the zone, he could flirt with number-two production; otherwise he profiles as a dependable mid-rotation innings-eater.

---

4. Touki Toussaint   RHP

Born: 6/20/96   **Age:** 19   **Bats:** R   **Throws:** R   **Height:** 6'3"   **Weight:** 185

MLB ETA	CT	FB	CH	CB	SL	OFP	Realistic
2018	–	75	60	70	–	70 NO. 2 STARTER	50 NO. 4 STARTER/RP

YEAR	TEAM	LVL	AGE	W	L	SV	G	GS	IP	H	HR	BB	K	BB9	SO9	GB%	BABIP	WHIP	ERA	FIP	FRA	WARP
2014	DIA	Rk	18	1	1	0	7	5	15.0	14	0	12	17	7.2	10.2	33%	.111	1.73	4.80	4.56	10.61	-0.1
2014	MSO	Rk	18	1	3	0	5	5	13.7	24	5	6	15	4.0	9.9	44%	.422	2.20	12.51	8.35	8.24	-0.1
2015	ARI	MLB	19	1	4	0	8	8	33.3	39	5	20	18	5.4	4.9	44%	.326	1.77	6.44	6.31	7.00	-0.6
2016	ARI	MLB	20	5	8	0	27	27	165.3	169	20	78	110	4.2	6.0	44%	.306	1.49	5.12	4.95	5.56	-1.4

Breakout: 0%   Improve: 0%   Collapse: 0%   Attrition: 0%   MLB: 0%   Upside: 1   *Comparables: Mike Foltynewicz, Kyle Ryan, Jeurys Familia*

Drafted/Acquired: 1st round, 2014 draft, Coral Springs Christian Academy (Coral Springs, FL)

Previous Ranking: NR

What Happened in 2014: Toussaint displayed perhaps the highest upside of any prep arm in the 2014 draft class, parlaying strong performances on the showcase circuit with a solid spring into a first-round draft slot and over-slot bonus.

Strengths: Fresh arm; high-level athleticism; electric arm speed produces heavy spin and easy-plus velocity; broad, projectable build; arm works free and loose with good deceleration; fastball works regularly 90-94 mph and can climb to 97; mid-70s curve is guillotine-like in trajectory, a lethality; works in and out of zone and matches fastball release; improving changeup has shown both cut and fade; impressive progress with off-speed over past 18 months; high waist and wide wingspan help extension; elite upside stuff in projectable/malleable package.

Weaknesses: Descends into extreme bouts of wildness; mechanics more conceptual than dependable at present with inconsistencies throughout; can rush through motion where even impact arm speed cannot catch up; fastball velo can drop to 88-92 mph velocity band later in starts; impact offerings routinely play a grade or more below ceiling due to failure to execute; may need to rein in power stuff some to more effectively implement in zone.

Risk Factor/Injury History: High; short-season résumé; 28 2/3 total professional innings.

Bret Sayre's Fantasy Take: The ceiling is extremely high here, but Toussaint is a long way away from it mattering—both from an ETA standpoint and a performance standpoint. He's a surefire early second rounder in dynasty drafts this year, and he has the highest strikeout potential of any arm in this system. Drink that in for a second.

The Year Ahead: After a long year of showcases, travel ball, and a three-plus month high school season, it's perhaps no surprise that Toussaint started to wear down during his two-month pro stint. While control issues have been a constant for the precocious righty throughout his amateur career and have been a fixture in his file, the degree to which he saw his mechanics slip during his brief tour through the Arizona complexes and Pioneer League surprised evaluators getting their first look at the 2014 first rounder. During fall instructs Toussaint was able to slow things down and work more deliberately, resulting in an influx of quality strikes and soft contact without significantly sacrificing power. Whether in game or in a side session, the former Vandy commit has the ability to wow with his arsenal, and has proven adept at taking in direction and working to implement tweaks in his approach and execution. Toussaint won't turn 19 until the middle of this summer, though that shouldn't stop Arizona from challenging him with a Kane County assignment in 2015 provided the Diamondbacks do not elect to manage his innings in a more controlled environment via a return to the Pioneer League. Either way, Toussaint has the potential to progress aggressively through the system once he's able to locate the nexus between power and proficiency of execution, and if last fall was a harbinger of things to come, then this summer could establish Touki as one of the top minor-league arms in the game.

5. Brandon Drury   3B/2B

Born: 8/21/92 **Age:** 22 **Bats:** R **Throws:** R **Height:** 6'2" **Weight:** 190

MLB ETA	Hit	Power	Run	Glove	Arm	OFP	Realistic
2016	50	55	–	50	55	55 >AVG REGULAR	50 ML REGULAR

YEAR	TEAM	LVL	AGE	PA	R	2B	3B	HR	RBI	BB	SO	SB	CS	AVG/OBP/SLG	TAv	BABIP	BRR	FRAA	WARP
2014	MOB	AA	21	116	12	7	0	4	14	7	19	0	0	.295/.345/.476	.306	.321	0.8	3B(28): -1.8, 2B(2): -0.0	0.9
2014	VIS	A+	21	478	73	35	1	19	81	41	76	4	3	.300/.366/.519	.306	.326	-2.7	3B(84): 1.6, 3B(4): 1.6	3.5
2015	ARI	MLB	22	250	21	13	1	6	27	9	58	0	0	.233/.263/.366	.230	.280	-0.5	3B -0, 1B -0	-0.3
2016	ARI	MLB	23	424	45	21	2	10	44	26	98	0	0	.226/.277/.366	.239	.271	-0.9	3B -2	-0.2

Breakout: 0%   Improve: 0%   Collapse: 0%   Attrition: 0%   MLB: 0%   Upside: 48   *Comparables: Neil Walker, Josh Vitters, Blake DeWitt*

Drafted/Acquired: 13th round, 2010 draft, Grants Pass HS (Grants Pass, OR)

Previous Ranking: On The Rise

What Happened in 2014: Drury continued his steady climb through the organization with his bat leading the way through the Cal and Southern League and a growing band of evaluative supporters following in his wake.

Strengths: Solid feel for barrel over the white; compact cuts produce regular hard contact to the gaps; improved tracking; fluidity to swing with good extension through impact; capable of loading deep, dropping barrel, and driving over the fence; sturdy build; above-average raw derived more from strength than force generated from bat speed; solid hands and left-side arm; improved lower-half actions; has amassed solid portfolio of production through three full-season levels.

Weaknesses: Bat speed is average; can struggle with velocity up and at the fringes; will expand zone behind in count; inconsistent ability to spot spin and attack quality offerings; true kill zone skews to middle; at times reliant on mistakes to find balls to drive; variable load can lead to inconsistent barrel delivery and empty swings in zone; limited defensive profile; decrease in lower-half agility could push defensive production from adequate to liability; five-o'clock power outstrips in-game utility; production has come more despite approach than because of it.

Risk Factor/Injury History: Low; Double-A capable with solid Arizona Fall League showing.

Bret Sayre's Fantasy Take: Neither position that Drury is capable of manning is a strong point for fantasy owners or the Diamondbacks, giving him an additional reason to buy into the profile. That said, Drury will be helped by Chase Field, but not enough to be a top-10 producer at either position. He could hit .260 with 20 homers, and while that would be usable in all leagues, it wouldn't make him irreplaceable.

The Year Ahead: Drury lacks impact tools, but a solid aggregate profile and in-game feel has resulted in consistent production across multiple minor-league levels and led evaluators to consider Aristotelian paradigms when projecting an ultimate role. Indeed, with Drury the whole may be greater than the sum of the parts, which will be important since there isn't a particular skill that is likely to consistently drive his value. The swing is generally contact friendly, but he is still learning when to leverage up the load and lift. He's prone to give away at-bats when he locks on a zone or pitch type and will need to demonstrate better adaptability as he faces more advanced arms. There is a wide range of opinion as to where the hit and power tools ultimately settle, with some preferring he sell out a little more to tap into the raw power and others insisting the bat works best as a short-swing gap rider. The best outcome may be a more funneled approach, if Drury proves capable of implementing such a game plan, with enough barrel control to keep compact and reactive early in the count while slowly adding length and leverage and shrinking his pitch/zone focus as circumstances permit. The ceiling isn't sexy, but the bat could play above average at third or second base. With even a fringy glove, that should be enough to warrant regular big-league time, and if there is a developmental step up left in the plate approach, he could find himself flirting with a first-division label. Drury should start 2015 back in Mobile and could get his first taste of major-league action by late summer should the opportunity arise.

6. Jake Lamb 3B

Born: 10/9/90 **Age:** 24 **Bats:** L **Throws:** R **Height:** 6'3" **Weight:** 220

MLB ETA	Hit	Power	Run	Glove	Arm	OFP	Realistic
Debuted in 2014	50	60	–	55	55	50 ML REGULAR	45 PLATOON/RESERVE

YEAR	TEAM	LVL	AGE	PA	R	2B	3B	HR	RBI	BB	SO	SB	CS	AVG/OBP/SLG	TAv	BABIP	BRR	FRAA	WARP
2014	ARI	MLB	23	133	15	4	1	4	11	6	37	1	1	.230/.263/.373	.226	.291	0.4	3B(34): 0.4	0.0
2014	RNO	AAA	23	21	3	4	0	1	5	3	4	2	0	.500/.571/.889	.464	.615	0.1	3B(5): -0.2, 1B(1): -0.1	0.5
2014	MOB	AA	23	439	60	35	5	14	79	50	99	0	0	.318/.399/.551	.340	.389	-1.1	3B(97): 2.4	4.8
2015	ARI	MLB	24	250	27	13	1	7	31	20	70	1	0	.251/.315/.418	.269	.326	-0.2	3B 0, 1B -0	0.8
2016	ARI	MLB	25	615	71	28	2	18	70	48	169	3	1	.234/.298/.389	.257	.300	-0.9	3B 0	1.2

Breakout: 0%   Improve: 22%   Collapse: 26%   Attrition: 32%   MLB: 68%   Upside: 43   *Comparables: Mat Gamel, Alex Liddi, Chase Headley*

Drafted/Acquired: 6th round, 2012 draft, University of Washington (Seattle, WA)

Previous Ranking: #10 (Org)

What Happened in 2014: Lamb continued to defy doubters, slapping Southern League arms around to the tune of a .318/.399/.551 slash line over 103 games (ranking first, second, and second, respectively, among all qualifying Southern League bats), before logging his first 133 plate appearances with the Snakes.

Strengths: Good power from the left side; natural lift; solid bat speed; capable of turning on velocity; best working middle-in and ahead; solid strike zone awareness and comfortable working deep into counts; seeks out pitches to drive and limits offerings at pitchers' pitches; steady glove with athletic actions and above-average arm.

Weaknesses: Swing can get rigid in upper half; can extend early, limiting power utility on outer half; swing quirks lead to porous plate coverage and susceptibility to advanced sequencing and placement; barrel trajectory could limit regular contact and hit/power utility at highest level; contact issues magnified against same-side arms and particularly same-side spin away.

Risk Factor/Injury History: Low; reached majors; solid track record of offensive production; broken hamate in 2013 with no noticeable lingering effects.

Bret Sayre's Fantasy Take: From a fantasy standpoint, Lamb is a slightly lesser version of former third-baseman-of-the-future Matt Davidson. Given how well that's worked out, it's okay to be skeptical, but Lamb is close to the majors and will be helped out by playing half his games in a park that plays to his strength.

The Year Ahead: While evaluators have been slow to warm to the University of Washington product, his Double-A-tested ability to work for his pitches and square them up when presented has lengthened the leash some are willing to give him in determining whether he can put together an adequate major-league approach to account for his in-zone contact issues. To many, however, Lamb is still viewed as a flawed everyday player or solid bench/platoon bat whose swing simply won't allow for enough consistent contact for a power-centric profile to thrive. Though upstream injuries forced a premature promotion to the bigs last summer, his struggles with lefty arms and overall inability to unpackage the manner in which major-league arms attacked him reinforced the concerns scouts have expressed over the life of his professional career. Contact issues notwithstanding, if Lamb can tease out even average power and on-base production, the overall profile will play thanks to quality work with the leather and the inherent value in his plus raw power. He will get a chance to win the everyday job in Arizona this spring, but would be best served getting regular at-bats with Triple-A Reno if the Diamondbacks opt to go in a different direction with the 25-man.

7. Jimmie Sherfy RHP

Born: 12/27/91 **Age:** 23 **Bats:** R **Throws:** R **Height:** 6'0" **Weight:** 175

MLB ETA	CT	FB	CH	CB	SL	OFP	Realistic
2015	–	65	–	–	65	60 CLOSER	50 MID/LATE INN RP

YEAR	TEAM	LVL	AGE	W	L	SV	G	GS	IP	H	HR	BB	K	BB9	SO9	GB%	BABIP	WHIP	ERA	FIP	FRA	WARP
2014	MOB	AA	22	3	1	1	37	0	38.0	34	4	18	45	4.3	10.7	47%	.316	1.37	4.97	3.92	4.47	0.2
2014	VIS	A+	22	2	0	6	11	0	11.0	6	2	5	23	4.1	18.8	53%	.308	1.00	3.27	3.56	3.93	0.2
2015	ARI	MLB	23	2	1	2	39	0	39.0	34	4	16	44	3.7	10.2	45%	.325	1.27	3.84	3.78	4.17	0.3
2016	ARI	MLB	24	3	1	3	59	0	59.3	51	6	22	65	3.3	9.9	45%	.316	1.23	3.63	3.50	3.95	0.7

Breakout: 0%   Improve: 0%   Collapse: 0%   Attrition: 0%   MLB: 0%   Upside: 15   *Comparables: Heath Hembree, Tommy Kahnle, R.J. Alvarez*

Drafted/Acquired: 10th round, 2013 draft, University of Oregon (Eugene, OR)

Previous Ranking: NR

What Happened in 2014: In Sherfy's first full season of professional ball the former Oregon Duck flummoxed California, Southern, and Arizona League bats alike, averaging 11 strikeouts per nine innings pitched and flashing two borderline double-plus offerings in his fastball and slider.

Strengths: Lots of funk and deception to go with impactful fastball/slider combo; creates angles; mid-90s heater reaches as high as 98 and comes with dance and late jump; slider matches fastball slot and trajectory, allowing for utility as an in-zone freeze pitch and swing-and-miss offering; tilted breaker with big depth and bite; late-inning mentality and approach; abuses same-side bats.

Weaknesses: Nontraditional slot and arm action; high-effort delivery; stuff can vacillate up to a full grade due to high-maintenance mechanics and corresponding tendency to lose release; can battle control and execution; lacks effective weapon with which to attack lefty bats; can fixate on baserunners at the expense of execution of pitches; undersized and lacks durable physique; concerns body/arm won't withstand big-league workload and arm action; abrupt deceleration on fastball; shows heavy glove-side fall-off, primarily with breaking ball; bouts of wildness could limit ability to earn trust in high-leverage situations.

Risk Factor/Injury History: High; standard reliever volatility risk coupled with high-effort mechanics, stressful arm action, and below-average command profile.

Bret Sayre's Fantasy Take: The lack of a dominant option at the back of the Diamondbacks' 'pen may help Sherfy a bit, but there's no reason to invest heavily in a reliever with this much inconsistency. However, once he reaches the majors, he will be a name to keep an eye on.

The Year Ahead: Sherfy put together some of the most dominant relief appearances of the 2014 season, and particularly last fall as a member of an impressive 'pen for the Arizona Fall League champion Salt River Rafters. Between dominant appearances, however, evaluators were peppered with subpar performances that included out-of-whack timing, poor balance, and diminished stuff, including a less lively low-90s fastball and a slider that played soft and fringy. When everything is clicking for Sherfy the right-handed batter's box is an uncomfortable place to be, and there's so much life to the arsenal that even lefties can struggle to put barrel to ball despite his lack of an effective change piece to keep them honest. His ability to find that sweet spot with regularity will be the ultimate determinant of his future role, with potential outcomes ranging from situational righty to shutdown late-inning arm. After his strong Arizona Fall League showing, the Diamondbacks could be encouraged to push him aggressively, and while there's a robust collection of power relief arms populating the upper levels of the organization, Sherfy may be the best suited of the bunch to step in and provide immediate value.

---

8. Sergio Alcantara   SS

Born: 7/10/96   **Age:** 18   **Bats:** B   **Throws:** R   **Height:** 5'10"   **Weight:** 150

MLB ETA	Hit	Power	Run	Glove	Arm		OFP	Realistic
2019	**50**	**–**	**–**	**65**	**70**		**55** >AVG REGULAR	**45** UT/DEF SPEC

YEAR	TEAM	LVL	AGE	PA	R	2B	3B	HR	RBI	BB	SO	SB	CS	AVG/OBP/SLG	TAv	BABIP	BRR	FRAA	WARP
2014	MSO	Rk	17	320	48	11	0	1	18	48	62	8	4	.244/.361/.297	.257	.314	1.2	SS(70): 8.9	2.8
2015	ARI	MLB	18	250	22	8	1	1	15	23	72	0	0	.191/.268/.251	.199	.267	-0.3	SS 4	-0.1
2016	ARI	MLB	19	250	24	7	1	2	18	23	63	0	0	.214/.289/.283	.220	.281	-0.3	SS 3	-0.3

Breakout: 0%   Improve: 0%   Collapse: 0%   Attrition: 0%   MLB: 0%   Upside: 9   *Comparables: Ruben Tejada, Tyler Pastornicky, L.J. Hoes*

Drafted/Acquired: International Free Agent, 2012, Dominican Republic

Previous Ranking: #8 (Org)

What Happened in 2014: The young Dominican was advanced one developmental rung and held his own in the Pioneer League, setting him up for a full-season debut in 2015 at the age of 18.

Strengths: Advanced glovework and innate feel at the six-spot; arm grades consistently to fringe-double-plus or better and plays across zone; lower half works to set up delivery; pure first step; soft hands and instinctual transfer; works the bag; good feel at the plate; understands strike zone; solid basic approach and advanced for age/experience; glove, run, and hit all project well with normal course addition of strength.

Weaknesses: Lacks physicality at present; well-below-average power; fringy foot speed limits slash and slap utility at the plate; strike zone awareness will be less meaningful if bat doesn't grow into viable enough weapon to keep pitchers out of the middle of the zone; hit could top out as down-order producer with hollow average; limited value on the basepaths.

Risk Factor/Injury History: High; rookie-level résumé.

Bret Sayre's Fantasy Take: There's very little to see here from a fantasy standpoint, as he's a defense-first shortstop who is many years away. Alcantara is not worth rostering at all, unless you're in a deep sim league.

The Year Ahead: Alcantara's glove continues to push him through the system at an advanced rate, with a 2015 assignment to full-season Kane County likely to provide a huge test for the talented teen. The Midwest League is notoriously unwelcoming to bats, particularly in the frigid early months, and the voluminous rosters can limit the number of repeat looks available to hitters as the season unfolds. Alcantara should have no issue shining with the glove, but if he scuffles with the bat for an extended period Arizona will be forced to decide whether it makes more developmental sense for the youngster to fight his way through those struggles as one of the youngest players in the league, or return to a Pioneer League that he has already easily traversed. Alcantara's top developmental focus may be the need to become more physical in short order, not just to boost the stock in his lumber but to help him adjust to and handle the physical demands of a full pro season. It's a long-lead developmental project, but one that provides some foundational value in the glove and a nice offensive baseline to work with given the advanced tracking and strike zone awareness.

9. Marcus Wilson   OF

Born: 8/15/96   **Age:** 18   **Bats:** R   **Throws:** R   **Height:** 6'3"   **Weight:** 175

MLB ETA	Hit	Power	Run	Glove	Arm	OFP	Realistic
2019	50	50	60	55	55	60 1ST DIV PLAYER	45 4TH OF/PINCH RUN

YEAR	TEAM	LVL	AGE	PA	R	2B	3B	HR	RBI	BB	SO	SB	CS	AVG/OBP/SLG	TAv	BABIP	BRR	FRAA	WARP
2014	DIA	Rk	17	148	15	2	2	1	22	16	40	4	2	.206/.297/.275	.189	.289	-2.4	CF(30): 0.1	-0.7
2015	ARI	MLB	18	250	19	8	1	3	19	12	80	2	1	.188/.229/.265	.185	.267	-0.2	CF -0	-1.3
2016	ARI	MLB	19	250	23	8	2	4	21	13	74	2	1	.201/.248/.297	.206	.272	-0.1	CF 0	-1.8

Breakout: 0%   Improve: 0%   Collapse: 0%   Attrition: 0%   MLB: 0%   Upside: 18   *Comparables: Che-Hsuan Lin, Austin Jackson, Abraham Almonte*

Drafted/Acquired: 2nd round, 2014 draft, Junipero Serra HS (Gardena, CA)

Previous Ranking: NR

What Happened in 2014: The Diamondbacks popped Wilson in the second round of the 2014 first-year player draft and bestowed a seven-figure signing bonus upon the former Arizona State commit, sending him to the Arizona complexes for his first professional assignment.

Strengths: Broad set of potential average or better tools; good athleticism; solid present physicality and projectable frame and build; above-average bat speed; loose and whippy swing at its best generates hard contact gap to gap; power projects; plus speed can help outrun mistakes in the field; above-average arm strength with solid carry plays to right-center gap; potential above-average center-field profile; young for draft class.

Weaknesses: Raw reads on bases and in field cut into ability to fully leverage speed; can get tight in upper half, causing some choppiness in swing plane and complicating barrel delivery; swing can get long with some barrel drag; needs to log reps in field and at plate; approach across game still work in progress; spec profile with wide gap between present ability and minimal threshold for major-league skill set.

Risk Factor/Injury History: High; complex-level résumé.

Bret Sayre's Fantasy Take: Wilson is going to be an interesting sleeper at the end of dynasty drafts this year, as he could be a five-category contributor in time (and who doesn't love a good five-category contributor?). But he's only for owners who don't mind waiting on long-lead prospects.

The Year Ahead: Wilson is a potential five-tool player capable of providing value across his profile, but is more athlete than refined baseballer at present. As one of the younger members of the 2014 draft class, Wilson won't turn 19 until the end of August, giving the Diamondbacks the benefit of some extra developmental wiggle room on the front end. A return assignment to the complex league in 2015 could afford Wilson with the opportunity to continue to see low-pressure, in-game opportunities in an instructional environment, with the SoCal prep product still matching up favorably agewise with his competition. The upside is that of a first-division center fielder who stands out due more to a broad and balanced skill set than to any single game-changing tool. There is some level of safety inherent in the combination of athleticism and what should be a solid up-the-middle glove and positive value on the bases, but the overall game is raw enough to preclude true foundational value at present, leaving a hefty flameout risk to fill that vacuum. It will likely be a deliberate climb through the minor-league ranks, particularly at the outset, but establishing a firm foundation for the profile and building some core competencies will expand the band of potential outcomes and form a much higher floor than the profile currently presents. That should be all the incentive Arizona needs to take a methodical approach in its handling of such a valuable asset.

10. Kaleb Fleck   RHP

Born: 1/24/89   **Age:** 26   **Bats:** R   **Throws:** R   **Height:** 6'2"   **Weight:** 190

MLB ETA	CT	FB	CH	CB	SL	OFP	Realistic
2015	–	65	–	–	60	55 CLOSER	45 MID RP

YEAR	TEAM	LVL	AGE	W	L	SV	G	GS	IP	H	HR	BB	K	BB9	SO9	GB%	BABIP	WHIP	ERA	FIP	FRA	WARP
2014	MOB	AA	25	7	3	17	56	0	63.3	55	4	28	79	4.0	11.2	44%	.336	1.31	2.56	2.89	3.12	1.3
2015	ARI	MLB	26	2	1	2	48	0	54.0	51	5	23	51	3.8	8.5	46%	.325	1.38	4.24	4.03	4.61	0.1
2016	ARI	MLB	27	2	1	2	47	0	53.3	49	5	20	51	3.4	8.6	46%	.320	1.30	3.98	3.65	4.32	0.4

Breakout: 0%   Improve: 0%   Collapse: 0%   Attrition: 0%   MLB: 0%   Upside: 3   *Comparables: Yoel Hernandez, Neil Wagner, Jay Buente*

Drafted/Acquired: Undrafted Free Agent, 2011, University of Pittsburgh-Johnstown (Johnstown, PA)

Previous Ranking: NR

What Happened in 2014: Fleck reached the highest innings total of his professional career with 63 1/3 solid Southern League innings before wowing during the Arizona Fall League with a harder and sharper slider piece and improved ability to pound the zone.

Strengths: Mid- to upper-90s fastball with good arm-side run; can work both sides of the dish and elevate heater late in count without sacrificing life; 85-87 mph slider flashed wipeout action in fall with hard bite and impressive depth; at best, maintains consistent three-quarters slot with both fastball and slider, matching release and pitch trajectory; improved line to plate through fall aided in strike-throwing ability and greater consistency in execution; strong, durable build; creates solid downhill plane; recent success working the quadrants and pounding the strike zone.

Weaknesses: Can get upright in finish, limiting extension and driving fastballs up and out of the zone; generally fastball and slider each graded out a half-grade lower in-season, with greater fluctuations in control; has struggled historically to maintain tempo and balance, lapsing into periodic issues with release point and leading to walks; limited track record evidencing latest developmental improvements.

Risk Factor/Injury History: Moderate; standard relief volatility risk.

Bret Sayre's Fantasy Take: Unless your league rosters 500 prospects and counts holds, leave Fleck for the next guy.

The Year Ahead: Fleck's big velocity and developmental progress through the 2014 season already had him pointed toward a potential major-league debut at some point in 2015, but something as simple as eight impressive Arizona Fall League appearances may have accelerated that timeline, with the hard-throwing righty elevating his status in the eyes of several evaluators. The most important progress came in the emergence of his slider as a true plus offering last fall, giving him two fastball trajectory offerings with opposite finish, each capable of drawing empty swings and leading bats out of the zone. Further, Fleck showed a more direct line to the plate and improved ability to work effectively on the margins, helping his stuff to play up by limiting free passes and mistakes over the heart of the plate, alike. If these improvements remain fixtures in the profile come spring Fleck may have pushed his profile from pure arm-strength reliever to potential high-leverage, late-inning arm, adding to the Diamondbacks' already ample supply of cost-controlled arms vying for a spot in the back of the big-league bullpen.

Notable Omissions

RHP Jose Martinez: When healthy, Martinez boasts a dynamic fastball/curveball combo that rivals the top pitch pairings in the system. Unfortunately, the talented hurler hit a developmental bump in the road last summer, suffering a stress fracture in his right elbow and undergoing surgery in June. A healthy Martinez progressing on the trajectory on which he entered the season would have likely stood comfortably with Touki Toussaint in the above rankings. He should return to game action in 2015 and turns 21 in April.

OF Yasmany Tomas: The high-profile Cuban signee was not considered for inclusion in the top 10 prospect rankings due to his professional experience and the limited likelihood that he spends any significant developmental time in the minors. Tomas profiles as a power-first corner outfielder with a pronounced rotational uppercut that limits the overlap of swing plane and pitch trajectory and could complicate his ability to fully leverage his big

---

FROM THE FIELD

Braden Shipley

Team: Arizona Diamondbacks
Evaluator: Jordan Gorosh
Dates seen: May 26, 2014
Affiliate: South Bend Silver Hawks (Low-A, Diamondbacks)
OFP: 60
Realistic role: low no. 3 starter
Mechanics: Bigger than listed weight. Strong, athletic build. Over-the-head windup; high front elbow; high three-quarters; generates big time tilt. Good plane. Small hip turn. Very athletic. Pressure on back leg. Generates average hip torque. Drops arm low behind back knee, causing some deception.

Pitch type	Present grade	Future grade	Sitting velocity	Peak velocity	Report
FB	55	60	91-93	95	Four-seam fastballs, especially up, would straighten out. True pitch. Needed to throw more two-seam fastballs, which he would to arm side. Up to 94-95 when he needs it, but worked 91-93 with life down in the zone. Can add and subtract a tick or two. Strongest fastballs are down in zone, working top of knees to shins. Command needs some sharpening, especially arm side.
CH	60	65	81-85	86	True money pitch; deception low in the zone; fastball arm speed. Pitch dies at the plate, with some sink. Limited fade, but looks like a fastball until the last second. Touched every number on the gun from 81 to 86 with the offering, adding and subtracting. Threw two at 77 as well. Will throw to right-handed batters in addition to left-handed batters. Pitches backward, and often throws changeups in hitters counts. Trusts the pitch implicitly.
CB	45	50	77-79	80	Spike curve grip. Can throw pitch for a strike or as chase offering. Will get loose and hang, but flashed solid-average. Pitch is better on outer half of the plate to right-handed batters; won't use it much to lefties. Keeps hitters off his other offerings; used to set up other pitches. Can produce big break, often early out of the hand.

Overall: Shipley is newer to pitching, yet looks polished on the bump. Has good presence, fields the position well, and controls the game. His fastball could straighten out at times, but with more repetition, may use some finger pressure to run and cut. Fastball command could get a bit loose, but athleticism and overall repeatable delivery allow for improvement. Uses advanced sequencing, and played off his changeup. The change doesn't have big movement, but rather excellent deception and dying action at the plate—eight swinging strikes on in my viewing. The curveball lags behind the other two offerings, but should become major-league average. Shipley's stuff isn't overly loud, but the entire package—along with a swing-and-miss changeup—should allow him to become a mid-rotation starter.

raw pop against advanced major-league arms. His success at the plate could hinge on his natural bat-to-ball skills, as well as his ability to put together quality at-bats that help him sniff out offerings in his kill zone—two areas that evaluators are still split on, thanks to inconsistent showings on the international stage.

Prospects on the Rise

1. OF Matt Railey: The Diamondbacks' third-round selection in the 2014 first-year player draft utilizes a flat, line-drive swing plane to spray hard contact to all fields. While he generates good torque through his core, it isn't really an ideal swing for over-the-fence pop, making the overall profile that of an average or better hit tool to go with maybe average playable pop if his natural ability to backspin can provide a hefty enough extra-base tally. Railey has average straight-line speed but gets good jumps out of the box, clocking home-to-first times in the 4.07 to 4.14 range from the left side, and ramps up to a tick above average underway. He could fit well toward the top of the order as a contact-oriented two-hole hitter capable of working the gaps and advancing runners. The former FSU commit isn't a natural center fielder, but he runs and throws well enough to get an opportunity to stick up the middle, where his bat is a more traditional fit. After enjoying a strong spring from a performance standpoint leading up to the draft, Railey saw his professional debut cut short due to a torn hamstring. He was back in action during fall instructs and should be working full speed and unrestricted from the drop this spring. Railey is almost a year and a half older than fellow draftee Marcus Wilson, so there is slightly more urgency in getting the former moving through the system, but it's also a more refined profile at present than Wilson's, giving him a chance to hit the ground running this year.

2. 2B Isan Diaz: Diaz's shaky pro debut belies the advanced feel at the plate he had on display throughout the lead up to the 2014 draft. The northeastern product boasts good barrel acceleration, some pop to the pull side, and an ability to square up the ball across the quadrants. There is potential for an average or better hit tool to go along with low double-digit home-run power and plenty of gap coverage, which would fit well at the keystone, where he best profiles defensively. On the dirt, his hands are adequate and his nimble lower half and ability to throw from varying angles could amount to above-average production at second when all is said and done, though his fringy arm strength could limit his ability to finish at the margins up the middle and on negative and neutral momentum pivots working the bag. Diaz will be working with a clean slate this spring and could put up impressive numbers at the lower levels in short order.

3. 2B/SS Domingo Leyba: Leyba came to Arizona as part of the package received in the three-way trade that sent Didi Gregorius to the Bronx. A switch-hitter with a good feel for the barrel, Leyba comes with a quiet load and efficient path that keep the barrel on plane, and regularly produces quality contact across the diamond. There isn't much room in the frame for increased bulk, but the 19-year-old will add strength as his body matures, and his ability to square up balls across the quadrants should help him to develop enough pop to work the gaps and account for an aggressive approach that otherwise limits his on-base profile. He is a capable defender that fits best at second base but has the hands and lateral quickness to handle a limited utility role depending on how much value the bat ultimately provides. Leyba was impressive in his 2014 stateside debut, slashing a combined .323/.360/.423 as an 18-year-old splitting time between the New York-Penn and Midwest Leagues. Arizona could push him to High-A in 2015, where a strong offensive showing could place him firmly in next year's top 10.

Factors on the Farm

Prospects likely to contribute at the major-league level in 2015

1. SS Nick Ahmed: While Ahmed has been surpassed by Brandon Drury as the most valuable prospect piece obtained in the 2013 Justin Upton deal, the University of Connecticut product is poised to provide some major-league value in 2015 thanks to advanced glovework at the six-spot, above-average speed that could provide value in a pinch-run capacity, and the increased opportunities up the middle in Arizona resulting from Gregorius's departure. It's a light offensive profile that might limit the overall upside to that of a second-division regular, but the remainder of Ahmed's game plays above average and is major-league ready.

2. LHP Robbie Ray: After a rough major-league debut in Motown last summer, Ray will bring his heavy low-90s fastball and solid change piece to the desert, where Arizona will look for him to compete for a spot in the back of the big-league rotation. Ray's arsenal lacks impact, and he has yet to demonstrate enough precision to avoid getting into trouble when he works with too much of the white. He'll need to do a better job of working the bottom of the zone in the hitter-friendly confines of Chase Field to avoid the long ball, and even if everything snaps into place it's probably not more than a fourth-starter profile, which is valuable, but likely not impactful. One evaluator noted the potential for Ray to see an uptick in velocity with a shift to the 'pen, and given the upside arms converging on the 25-man roster over the next two years, such a shift could be in the cards. For now, however, there is no reason for Arizona not to continue to work on shaping Ray into a workhorse lefty capable of providing 175-plus cost controlled innings out of the back of the rotation.

3. C/1B Peter O'Brien: Were O'Brien a safer bet to stick behind the dish he would easily slot in as one of the top 10 prospects in the 'Zona system. But with first base the much more likely landing spot, and setting aside the fact that Arizona already has a pretty good stick currently manning the three-spot, the overall profile looks less impressive due to the negative impact his in-zone contact issues are likely to have on the playable power. That said, with power at a premium in today's game, O'Brien's plus or better raw should allow him to eventually carve out a spot on the 25-man as a bench bat, and that opportunity could come as early as this year. He'll likely break camp with a ticket to Triple-A Reno, where Arizona could continue to give him reps behind the plate in the hope that he'll develop enough feel to eventually serve in a backup capacity. If and when that experiment fails, he could be trade bait and would fit well with an American League club looking for an inexpensive lotto ticket at first base or DH.

ATLANTA BRAVES

1. Lucas Sims   RHP

Born: 5/10/94   **Age:** 21   **Bats:** R   **Throws:** R   **Height:** 6'2"   **Weight:** 195

MLB ETA	CT	FB	CH	CB	SL	OFP	Realistic
2016	–	65	60	60	–	65 NO.2/3 STARTER	55 NO.3/4 STARTER

YEAR	TEAM	LVL	AGE	W	L	SV	G	GS	IP	H	HR	BB	K	BB9	SO9	GB%	BABIP	WHIP	ERA	FIP	FRA	WARP
2014	LYN	A+	20	8	11	0	28	28	156.7	146	12	57	107	3.3	6.1	42%	.277	1.30	4.19	4.56	5.76	-0.5
2015	ATL	MLB	21	7	10	0	26	26	132.0	128	14	58	100	4.0	6.8	41%	.307	1.41	4.60	4.76	5.00	-0.7
2016	ATL	MLB	22	10	10	0	31	31	201.0	184	21	72	166	3.2	7.4	41%	.298	1.28	4.07	4.09	4.42	-0.1

Breakout: 0%   **Improve:** 0%   **Collapse:** 0%   **Attrition:** 0%   **MLB:** 0%   **Upside:** 24   *Comparables: Tyler Chatwood, Robbie Ray, Michael Pineda*

Drafted/Acquired: 1st round, 2012 draft, Brookwood HS (Snellville, GA)

Previous Ranking: #1 (Org), #40 (Top 101)

What Happened in 2014: Sims didn't have the most impressive overall line in High-A, but the 20-year-old logged 156 2/3 innings over 28 starts and showed he can hold up deep into a season.

Strengths: Easy delivery; smooth and fluid throughout motion; good balance; athletic; ability to repeat arm slot; fastball operates 91-94 with ease; can reach back for more when needs to; displays late life; excellent crispness to curveball; throws with loose wrist; creates hard snap; deep shape, with downward bend in high-70s; can change shape; legit bat-missing offering; flashes feel for change; bottom-dropping action in low-80s; projection for command growth; competes on mound.

Weaknesses: Can lose finish with delivery; will drift with landing; leaves him prone to working too elevated with heater; command on the loose side; needs improvement spotting into all four quadrants of strike zone; decent-sized fastball command gap to close; curve gets slurvy when wrist wraps upon release; loses good bite and rolls; change tends to float when thrown in mid-80s; more like a fastball pitcher is taking something off of; can get too amped up—loses rhythm and pace.

Risk Factor/Injury History: Moderate risk; yet to pitch in Double-A; command progression.

Bret Sayre's Fantasy Take: The fact that Sims' statistical trajectory isn't where it was last year doesn't make him less of a fantasy prospect this year. With two pitches that project as plus, he has the potential to be a 180-strikeout pitcher at the major league level, and while that isn't quite what it used to be in this high-K environment, it's fantasy worthy in all leagues.

The Year Ahead: Sims is all but set to get his first test in the upper minors. While on the surface 2014 looks like a mixed bag, the reports indicated that the arm took some nice strides. Sims found more consistency with his delivery later in the season and gained confidence using his changeup more in sequences, two big keys for the 21-year-old to make a smooth transition to Double-A. Sims' lively fastball and hard-breaking curveball give him two plus pitches, while the change has the potential to get to that level over the long run. The package here can develop into a pretty legit arm. To pass the near-term test this season and reach his full potential down the line he'll need to show progress throwing better strikes with his fastball. Sims has to learn to spot the pitch better in the lower tier and grab less white with the offering. His athleticism and ability to repeat point toward more command growth coming as he continues to mature, but if it only ends up the area variety, the profile plays down some despite the raw stuff.

> #54
> BP Top 101 Prospects

2. Jose Peraza   2B

Born: 4/30/94   **Age:** 21   **Bats:** R   **Throws:** R   **Height:** 6'0"   **Weight:** 165

MLB ETA	Hit	Power	Run	Glove	Arm	OFP	Realistic
Late 2015	55	–	70	60	60	55 >AVG REGULAR	45 UT/2ND DIV.

YEAR	TEAM	LVL	AGE	PA	R	2B	3B	HR	RBI	BB	SO	SB	CS	AVG/OBP/SLG	TAv	BABIP	BRR	FRAA	WARP
2014	MIS	AA	20	195	35	7	3	1	17	7	15	25	8	.335/.363/.422	.295	.361	5.2	2B(41): -2.9	1.4
2014	LYN	A+	20	304	44	13	8	1	27	10	32	35	7	.342/.365/.454	.302	.376	5.0	2B(58): -6.2, SS(7): 0.6	2.3
2015	ATL	MLB	21	250	31	8	2	1	15	6	47	21	5	.257/.278/.330	.234	.307	2.5	2B -3, SS 4	0.6
2016	ATL	MLB	22	505	51	17	6	4	45	20	82	48	13	.287/.318/.373	.256	.331	7.5	2B -10	1.3

Breakout: 0%   **Improve:** 0%   **Collapse:** 0%   **Attrition:** 0%   **MLB:** 0%   **Upside:** 53   *Comparables: Jose Altuve, Jean Segura, Luis Sardinas*

Drafted/Acquired: International Free Agent, 2010, Venezuela

Previous Ranking: #5 (Org)

What Happened in 2014: The Venezuelan infielder flashed impressive contact skills across two levels, including 44 games at Double-A, hitting .339 overall on the year while fanning only 47 times in 499 plate appearances.

Strengths: Extremely fluid in the field; highly athletic; excels at controlling body; light on feet; quick first step; excellent instincts; above-average range; soft hands; enough arm to make throw from deep in the hole; speed is an asset; double-plus runner; ability to impact the game on the bases; feel for getting barrel on the ball; short stroke; approaches the game with even-keeled mind-set.

Weaknesses: Aggressive approach; pitch selection needs tightening; expands zone often; will chase bad balls; tends to punch at offerings; hit tool can play down due to lack of consistent hard contact; well-below-average power; at times will needlessly rush throws; needs more strength to prevent body from wearing down.

Risk Factor/Injury History: Moderate risk; 44 games at Double-A; development of strike zone management skills.

Bret Sayre's Fantasy Take: The stats that Peraza has put up set an unrealistic expectation for his fantasy value, but the skill set provides enough value without getting carried away. He's run wild with 124 steals in 224 games over the past two years, but that is against minor-league catchers. The realistic best-case scenario here is a pre-breakout Jose Altuve: a .280ish average with 30-35 steals.

The Year Ahead: Peraza's rapid ascent into the upper minors has been carried by his innate ability to make contact and outstanding defensive chops. The 21-year-old is one of those natural players in the field, with a strong feel for controlling his actions and instincts to seemingly be moving into the correct position before the crack of the bat. A move to second base last season speaks more to Atlanta's infield landscape at the major-league level than to Peraza's ability at shortstop; in a different organization the prospect more than likely continues to track all the way up on the left side of the infield. While the infielder's ability to make contact is a strength, there are concerns about how the approach will shake out and whether the bat plays light when also factoring in the lack of power. Progression with toning things down at the plate and fine-tuning his pitch selection are big keys toward reaching his potential as a long-term regular in The Show. Even if the bat ends up playing down, this player brings plenty of value to a roster in a utility role. The developmental path has been aggressive for Peraza, but he's very advanced for his age and a debut sometime toward the end of 2015 is well within reach.

3. Michael Foltynewicz   RHP

Born: 10/7/91   **Age:** 24   **Bats:** R   **Throws:** R   **Height:** 6'4"   **Weight:** 200

MLB ETA	CT	FB	CH	CB	SL	OFP	Realistic
Debuted in 2014	–	80	–	55	–	60 NO. 3 STARTER	55 LATE INN RP/CL

YEAR	TEAM	LVL	AGE	W	L	SV	G	GS	IP	H	HR	BB	K	BB9	SO9	GB%	BABIP	WHIP	ERA	FIP	FRA	WARP
2014	HOU	MLB	22	0	1	0	16	0	18.7	23	3	7	14	3.4	6.8	29%	.333	1.61	5.30	4.87	4.43	0.1
2014	OKL	AAA	22	7	7	0	21	18	102.7	98	10	52	102	4.6	8.9	49%	.322	1.46	5.08	4.79	5.61	0.6
2015	ATL	MLB	23	5	7	0	23	18	102.3	108	12	52	75	4.6	6.6	46%	.302	1.56	5.10	5.35	5.54	-0.6
2016	ATL	MLB	24	8	10	0	26	26	155.3	161	21	63	127	3.7	7.4	46%	.325	1.44	4.96	4.76	5.40	-1.7

Breakout: 17%   Improve: 24%   Collapse: 3%   Attrition: 23%   MLB: 32%   Upside: 33

Comparables: Felix Doubront, Anthony Ranaudo, Carlos Carrasco

Drafted/Acquired: 1st round, 2010 draft, Minooka HS (Minooka, IL)

Previous Ranking: #4 (Org – HOU); 43 (Top 101)

What Happened in 2014: The Illinois native continued to showcase a borderline elite fastball while struggling to dial in his control over 102 2/3 Triple-A innings and 16 relief appearances, totaling 18 2/3 innings, in his first major-league call-up.

Strengths: Workhorse build; elite arm strength; routinely tops triple digits with the heater, sitting upper-90s, and maintains well into starts; some late arm-side action; curve flashes bite with 11-to-5 action; fully leverages body; good extension; shields ball through arm circle; big presence.

Weaknesses: Below-average control; fastball can catch a lot of plate, flattens up in zone; tendency to come around curve, causing slurvy shape and soft action; change is below-average; can tip with slow arm and come firm and flat with matching arm speed; high-effort finish.

Risk Factor/Injury History: Low risk; achieved major leagues; high-floor as late-inning option.

The Year Ahead: Foltynewicz continues to entice with top-shelf arm strength and one of the better fastballs in the minors, but through 104 starts and over 560 innings at the minor-league ranks the imposing righty has continually struggled to find the strike zone with consistency, leading to elevated pitch counts and problematic walk rates. His inability to spot his stuff within the four corners of the zone has additionally rendered Folty more hittable than the raw stuff would otherwise indicate. While the former Illinois prep product has his share of supporters who would like to see him continue to work out of a rotation, where his size, durability, and premium arm would all be assets, it is becoming increasingly likely that Foltynewicz finds an ultimate home in the 'pen. If Atlanta opts to continue to develop Folty as a starter he will head back to Triple-A to continue to work on finding some consistency in his mechanics and execution, as well as softening his off-speed. Should the Braves let him loose in relief he has a shot to break camp with the big club. Either way he should find his way to The Big Peach at some point in 2015.

4. Christian Bethancourt   C

Born: 9/2/91   **Age:** 23   **Bats:** R   **Throws:** R   **Height:** 6'2"   **Weight:** 205

MLB ETA	Hit	Power	Run	Glove	Arm	OFP	Realistic
Debuted in 2014	–	55	50	65	80	**55** >AVG REGULAR	**45** BACKUP C/<AVG REG

YEAR	TEAM	LVL	AGE	PA	R	2B	3B	HR	RBI	BB	SO	SB	CS	AVG/OBP/SLG	TAv	BABIP	BRR	FRAA	WARP
2014	ATL	MLB	22	117	7	3	0	0	9	3	26	1	1	.248/.274/.274	.210	.322	0.2	C(31): 0.3	0.0
2014	GWN	AAA	22	365	33	17	1	8	48	13	61	7	1	.283/.308/.408	.244	.318	0.3	C(80): 0.7	1.0
2015	ATL	MLB	23	250	26	10	0	5	22	5	55	4	2	.245/.261/.352	.235	.291	-0.2	C 1	0.4
2016	ATL	MLB	24	510	50	19	1	9	47	19	117	8	4	.238/.268/.335	.226	.290	-0.1	C 1	0.0

Breakout: 5%   **Improve:** 16%   **Collapse:** 2%   **Attrition:** 15%   **MLB:** 23%   **Upside:** 25   *Comparables: Wilson Ramos, Audry Perez, Tony Cruz*

Drafted/Acquired: International Free Agent, 2008, Panama

Previous Ranking: #2 (Org), #87 (Top 101)

What Happened in 2014: The strong-armed catcher took the next step up to Triple-A, where his bat continued to hold its own and his defensive prowess was on display. He then got a taste of The Show over 31 games.

Strengths: Fluid and athletic; body to withstand rigors of the position; good present strength; elite arm strength; quick release; ability to throw accurately at full power; catch-and-throw skills to control running game; improving footwork; firm glove; body to smother balls; solid-average bat speed; can control head of bat; raw power to tap into.

Weaknesses: Gets loose with defensive game; glove hand will drift; footwork can be choppy; at times comes up early; can be too casual getting body in front of ball; wild at times with approach; likes to swing early; prone to being pitched to—lacks a plan at the plate; strong chance hit tool plays below-to-fringe-average; power might end up as limited factor; concentration and focus tend to drift.

Risk Factor/Injury History: Low risk; achieved major-league level; limitations with bat.

Bret Sayre's Fantasy Take: Despite the flashes of power over the past two seasons in the upper minors, Bethancourt is still not a worthy stash in fantasy leagues, unless you're in a league where more than 20 catchers are owned. If he's a .240 hitter with 12 homers, that's great for the Braves, but not for fantasy owners.

The Year Ahead: Bethancourt's defensive ability gives him a strong chance at carving out a long major-league career, but there is still plenty of uncertainty as to what the overall body of work will look like. There are no questions that the 23-year-old's ability to control the running game and his well-above-average potential glove bring plenty of value to a club. The defense alone can keep Bethancourt in the lineup on a daily basis well into his peak years. Despite more consistency with his contact in the upper minors the past couple of seasons, the bat has the chance to fall into the more limited category against high-caliber arms. The lack of a plan at the plate is glaring, along with how susceptible he is to being fed breaking balls away. If the backstop can adjust more to sequencing and show growth with his strike zone knowledge, there is some offensive consistency that can be squeezed out. It's most likely a bottom-of-the-order hitter, with .235-.250 averages and 10-plus home runs. In 2015 Bethancourt should get a chance to establish himself at the highest level, and bring into focus whether he can sustain status as a regular or slides into more of a backup role over the long run.

5. Braxton Davidson   OF/1B

Born: 6/18/96   **Age:** 19   **Bats:** L   **Throws:** L   **Height:** 6'2"   **Weight:** 210

MLB ETA	Hit	Power	Run	Glove	Arm	OFP	Realistic
2019	55	65	–	50	55	**60** 1ST DIVISION PLAYER	**50** AVG ML PLAYER

YEAR	TEAM	LVL	AGE	PA	R	2B	3B	HR	RBI	BB	SO	SB	CS	AVG/OBP/SLG	TAv	BABIP	BRR	FRAA	WARP
2014	BRA	Rk	18	140	23	7	1	0	8	22	32	0	0	.243/.400/.324	.282	.342	1.0	LF(9): 0.3	0.3
2014	DNV	Rk	18	46	1	2	0	0	3	9	10	0	0	.167/.348/.222	.212	.231	-0.8	LF(10): 0.4	-0.2
2015	ATL	MLB	19	250	17	7	0	2	18	17	82	0	0	.182/.243/.241	.193	.268	-0.4	LF 2	-1.1
2016	ATL	MLB	20	250	24	6	1	4	21	18	77	0	0	.197/.261/.285	.209	.272	-0.4	LF 1	-1.7

Breakout: 0%   **Improve:** 0%   **Collapse:** 0%   **Attrition:** 0%   **MLB:** 0%   **Upside:** 1   *Comparables: Dalton Pompey, Caleb Gindl, Aaron Hicks*

Drafted/Acquired: 1st round, 2014 draft, T.C. Roberson HS (Asheville, NC)

Previous Ranking: NR

What Happened in 2014: The Braves selected the potential power-hitting left-handed hitter 32nd overall in the Rule 4 draft, and then Davidson played 50 games after signing to start his development journey.

Strengths: Well filled out body for age; excellent present strength; strong lower half; fluid swing from left side; quiet hitting mechanics; strong wrists and forearms; generates easy, above-average bat speed; controls head of the bat; swing already shows lift and postcontact extension; drives the ball with carry; taps into lower half; mature approach for age; good fastball hitter; willing to go deep into counts; arm to play a corner outfield spot.

Weaknesses: Below-average foot speed; actions in outfield aren't the most fluid; on the clumsy side; limited to first base if can't stick in a corner (left field); can drop back shoulder and sell out too much for power; hit tool could play down; front leg doesn't always get set on time; needs work against secondary stuff; backside tends to cave against arm-side pitching; defense not going to be focal point of profile.

Risk Factor/Injury History: High risk; limited professional experience; bat-first profile.

Bret Sayre's Fantasy Take: As the scouting report suggests, Davidson is all about the bat—and it has the potential to be fantasy relevant across all leagues, regardless of whether he sticks in the outfield. It's a deep year in dynasty drafts, but Davidson is a worthy second rounder in most formats, as a guy who could potentially hit 30 homers without killing you in batting average down the road.

The Year Ahead: Much of the talk leading up to the draft regarding the then-18-year-old centered on his in-game power, mature approach, and questionable defense. Davidson is already big and strong, with the type of bat speed and swing composition to hit the long ball to all fields. Toss in an early feel for hitting, and there's a lot to work with offensively. The reports on his defense since turning pro haven't been glowing, though. They've highlighted a lack of fluidity going after fly balls and slow reads off the bat. A couple of sources expressed thoughts that Davidson has a chance to get better in the outfield, but it would be left field all the way if he can stick. It'll be interesting to see how quickly things can start moving forward for the player in 2015 given his advanced mind-set at the plate upon entering the pro ranks. If it shows early, this is a power bat that can start to gain considerable traction.

6. Ricardo Sanchez LHP

Born: 4/11/97 **Age:** 18 **Bats:** L **Throws:** L **Height:** 5'10" **Weight:** 170

MLB ETA	CT	FB	CH	CB	SL	OFP	Realistic
2019	–	60	55	60	–	65 NO. 2/3 STARTER	50 NO. 4 STARTER

YEAR	TEAM	LVL	AGE	W	L	SV	G	GS	IP	H	HR	BB	K	BB9	SO9	GB%	BABIP	WHIP	ERA	FIP	FRA	WARP
2014	ANG	Rk	17	2	2	0	12	9	38.7	40	0	22	43	5.1	10.0	55%	.355	1.60	3.49	3.90	5.81	0.2
2015	ATL	MLB	18	1	2	0	9	6	31.7	37	4	19	16	5.4	4.5	48%	.307	1.79	6.09	6.30	6.62	-0.5
2016	ATL	MLB	19	5	6	0	33	21	155.0	156	15	69	104	4.0	6.0	48%	.288	1.45	4.51	4.73	4.91	-0.5

Breakout: 0%   Improve: 0%   Collapse: 0%   Attrition: 0%   MLB: 0%   Upside: 1   *Comparables: Jenrry Mejía, Roman Mendez, Brad Hand*

Drafted/Acquired: International free agent, 2013, Venezuela

Previous Ranking: #8 (Org – LAA)

What Happened in 2014: The six-figure J2 bonus baby eased into stateside action with 38 2/3 innings at the complexes, where he impressed evaluators with his creamy mechanics and projectable arsenal.

Strengths: Easy motion, smooth arm; low-90s fastball regularly touches 94-95 mph; shows some feel for spotting the pitch in-zone; 72-78 mph curve most effective at the higher end of the velo band, coming with average depth and above-average bite; low-80s changeup shows promise and displayed growth; projects to above-average command thanks to easy motion and solid athleticism; in-game poise belies age and experience level.

Weaknesses: Fastball lacks plane; pitch will be reliant on quality velocity and in-zone precision to avoid barrels at upper levels; changeup is consistently below-average offering at present; still developing feel across arsenal.

Risk Factor/Injury History: High risk; complex-level résumé.

The Year Ahead: Despite his diminutive stature, Sanchez packs enough oomph in his stuff and ease in his mechanics to project out as a future rotation stalwart. There is a wide delta between present profile and where he needs to be to turn over major-league lineups with regularity, but the precocious lefty has time on his side and is working with an advanced skill set compared to the majority of his contemporaries. This season will include a continued focus on building up arm strength and innings, while working to improve his feel and comfort level across each of his offerings. He should see time in Orem this summer, where he could push his innings totals as high as 70-plus, which would leave him well prepared for a full-season assignment in 2016.

7. Rio Ruiz 3B

Born: 5/22/94 **Age:** 21 **Bats:** L **Throws:** R **Height:** 6'2" **Weight:** 215

MLB ETA	Hit	Power	Run	Glove	Arm	OFP	Realistic
2016	55	55	–	50	60	55 >AVG REGULAR	50 AVG ML PLAYER

YEAR	TEAM	LVL	AGE	PA	R	2B	3B	HR	RBI	BB	SO	SB	CS	AVG/OBP/SLG	TAv	BABIP	BRR	FRAA	WARP
2014	LNC	A+	20	602	76	37	2	11	77	82	91	4	4	.293/.387/.436	.295	.335	-3.7	3B(105): -10.0, 3B(11): -10.0	3.1
2015	ATL	MLB	21	250	21	11	1	3	22	22	59	1	0	.219/.289/.315	.233	.279	-0.4	3B -4	-0.6
2016	ATL	MLB	22	250	26	12	0	3	22	23	57	1	0	.225/.295/.324	.234	.285	-0.6	3B -4	-0.7

Breakout: 0%   Improve: 0%   Collapse: 0%   Attrition: 0%   MLB: 0%   Upside: 19   *Comparables: Taylor Green, Jake Smolinski, Matt Dominguez*

Drafted/Acquired: 4th round, 2012 draft, Bishop Amat Memorial HS (La Puente, CA)

Previous Ranking: #9 (Org – HOU)

What Happened in 2014: Ruiz continued to grow his offensive game in the hitter's haven that is High-A Lancaster, showing signs of emerging power to go with a solid feel for the zone and improved feel for contact.

Strengths: Smooth lefty swing; bat path offers lengthy pitch plane/swing plane overlap, allowing for use of whole field; maturing body; added length to load and leverage to swing; firm front side at contact; puts together good at-bats; improving approach; strong left-side arm; capable of making the flashy finish on balls in range.

Weaknesses: Some trouble getting barrel to the inner half against same-side arms; infrequent hard contact against lefties; power may top out around average; swing geared to line-drive contact; still learning to lift; present pop skewed to pull side; range at third is fringe-average; still working to improve footwork; inconsistent setup can impact accuracy across the diamond; well-below-average run.

Risk Factor/Injury History: High; yet to reach upper minors.

The Year Ahead: Ruiz doesn't boast an impact profile, but there is potential for above-average offensive production to go with a solid-average glove at the hot corner. The former over-slot signee has made progress growing his approach and fine-tuning his swing mechanics, which has allowed him to form a firm foundation for an on-base skill set. Despite solid overall production in 2014, Ruiz can struggle against same-side arms, tracking less effectively and failing to regularly barrel up balls in the zone or adequately cover the inner half. Further, while Ruiz has made progress with the glove, he needs to further improve his footwork and lower-half actions to better aid him in finishing plays at the margins and more consistently deliver balls to first with precision. He should spend 2015 with Double-A Mississippi, arguably the most difficult offensive environment in the Southern League.

8. Garrett Fulenchek   RHP

Born: 6/7/96   **Age:** 19   **Bats:** R   **Throws:** R   **Height:** 6'4"   **Weight:** 205

MLB ETA	CT	FB	CH	CB	SL	OFP	Realistic
2019	–	65	55	–	60	60 NO. 3 STARTER	50 NO. 4 STARTER

YEAR	TEAM	LVL	AGE	W	L	SV	G	GS	IP	H	HR	BB	K	BB9	SO9	GB%	BABIP	WHIP	ERA	FIP	FRA	WARP
2014	BRA	Rk	18	0	7	0	12	10	37.7	34	2	22	29	5.3	6.9	59%	.329	1.49	4.78	4.65	6.11	0.0
2015	ATL	MLB	19	2	3	0	8	8	33.7	38	4	20	20	5.3	5.3	48%	.323	1.70	5.83	5.65	6.34	-0.6
2016	ATL	MLB	20	7	9	0	30	30	190.3	185	19	84	137	4.0	6.5	48%	.305	1.41	4.54	4.45	4.93	-1.2

Breakout: 0%   Improve: 0%   Collapse: 0%   Attrition: 0%   MLB: 0%   Upside: 1   *Comparables: Mike Foltynewicz, Kyle Ryan, Edwin Escobar*

Drafted/Acquired: 2nd round, 2014 draft, Howe HS (Howe, TX)

Previous Ranking: NR

What Happened in 2014: The Texan signed for a seven-figure, above-slot bonus after being drafted in the second round, then threw 37 2/3 innings in the Gulf Coast League with mixed results.

Strengths: Ideal frame; uses size to create leverage; fastball already works low-90s with sink; downward action makes it tough to square up in the lower tier; potential to add more velocity as physically matures; snaps slider with good spin; throws from same angle as heater; late cutting action to offering; potential to miss barrels; flashes feel for change; turns over with a loose wrist; strong projection for growth to overall arsenal.

Weaknesses: Can lose release point; command needs a grade improvement; leaves fastball in dangerous areas; tends to telegraph changeup; slider could use more depth to get chases; struggles throwing secondary stuff for strikes; needs emergence of true out pitch in repertoire.

Risk Factor/Injury History: High risk; limited professional experience; secondary stuff growth.

Bret Sayre's Fantasy Take: This is another long play, and with only moderate upside, he's not going to be a focus in dynasty leagues. However, Fulenchek makes for an interesting last-round flier in deeper dynasty leagues this offseason—beyond that, he's more just someone to monitor.

The Year Ahead: Fulenchek is the type of arm that can really grow over the course of the next three to four years as he continues to physically mature. The 19-year-old's fastball already works in the low-90s and displays solid sinking action in the lower tier of the strike zone. There's reason to believe the 6-foot-4 right-hander can add some more velocity, as the frame has plenty of room for size and strength. It could very well be a power arm sitting in the mid-90s when Fulenchek reaches his early-to-mid-20s. The development of the secondary arsenal will be a big key to giving the righty multiple options for putting hitters away. He shows feel for both a slider and changeup, but presently struggles throwing each for strikes, hardly uncommon for a pitcher of his age and experience level. There's a chance here for the perfect developmental storm, if the potential physical gains coincide with the command taking a step forward. It's more likely that things move more slowly early on, with this season marking the ramping up of his arm strength and stamina.

9. Ozhaino Albies   SS

Born: 1/7/97   **Age:** 18   **Bats:** B   **Throws:** R   **Height:** 5'9"   **Weight:** 150

MLB ETA		Hit	Power	Run	Glove	Arm		OFP	Realistic
2019		55	–	70	55	55		60	45
								1ST DIV PLAYER	UT/<AVG REGULAR

YEAR	TEAM	LVL	AGE	PA	R	2B	3B	HR	RBI	BB	SO	SB	CS	AVG/OBP/SLG	TAv	BABIP	BRR	FRAA	WARP
2014	BRA	Rk	17	78	16	3	0	0	5	11	6	7	2	.381/.481/.429	.212	.414	0.0	SS(1): 0.1	0.0
2014	DNV	Rk	17	161	25	4	3	1	14	17	17	15	3	.356/.429/.452	.331	.395	2.8	SS(29): 0.4	2.1
2015	ATL	MLB	18	250	24	8	1	2	15	10	71	6	2	.204/.240/.271	.200	.275	0.4	SS 1	-0.4
2016	ATL	MLB	19	250	22	8	1	2	20	7	61	7	2	.229/.254/.304	.208	.290	0.8	SS 0	-1.3

Breakout: 0%   Improve: 0%   Collapse: 0%   Attrition: 0%   MLB: 0%   Upside: 6   *Comparables: Eduardo Nunez, Danny Santana, Arismendy Alcantara*

Drafted/Acquired: International Free Agent, 2013, Curaçao

Previous Ranking: NR

What Happened in 2014: The shortstop out of Curaçao made his stateside debut, more than holding his own, hitting .364 and swiping 22 bags in 57 games.

Strengths: Very good athlete; fast-twitch muscles; well-above-average runner; likely to keep most, if not all, of speed; short, smooth stroke from left side; a bit longer with swing as a right-hander; controls head of bat through hitting zone well; generates good bat speed; can add more with physical maturity; shows ability to barrel ball with backspin; quick first step in the field; moves well to both left and right; mature approach to game for age.

Weaknesses: Slight build; frame is on the limited size; might be shorter than listed; needs more strength to enhance overall game; minimal present power; low power ceiling; tendency to cut swing off and punch; aggressive approach; can fish for stuff away; arm is presently on the fringe-average side; will need added strength to stick on the left side of the diamond; raw and unrefined overall game.

Risk Factor/Injury History: Extreme risk; 18 years old; physical projection of body.

Bret Sayre's Fantasy Take: If you're going to take a chance on either Albies or Fulenchek as a long-term hold, Albies is the guy you want. He could move himself on a Jose Peraza-type path, but with the potential for slightly more usable power. It's just a long, long way away.

The Year Ahead: It was impressive the way Albies handled himself as one of the youngest players in the Appalachian League. Not only did he have a mature aura on the field, but he went out and performed in a manner that suggested he was way out ahead of the curve. The reports have all been pretty favorable as well, with strong backing for the way the 18-year-old goes about his business, for his athleticism, and for his early feel for hitting. The switch-hitter has the loose hands to stay inside of the baseball, especially left-handed, while also being able to guide the head of the bat to go the other way. He has the defensive tools to potentially handle shortstop, and plenty of athleticism to move to the other side of the bag or potentially out to center. This is obviously a risky profile due to the age, and also because of the strength gains needed and questions about whether the frame can pack that much size. Moderate developmental progression likely points to a utility type, with the big payout, if everything clicks, being a first-division regular providing high contact, speed, and solid defense.

10. Alec Grosser   RHP

Born: 1/12/95   **Age:** 20   **Bats:** R   **Throws:** R   **Height:** 6'2"   **Weight:** 190

MLB ETA		CT	FB	CH	CB	SL		OFP	Realistic
2018		–	60	50	–	65		60	50
								NO. 3 STARTER	LATE INN RP

YEAR	TEAM	LVL	AGE	W	L	SV	G	GS	IP	H	HR	BB	K	BB9	SO9	GB%	BABIP	WHIP	ERA	FIP	FRA	WARP
2014	DNV	Rk	19	4	3	0	13	12	63.7	60	0	22	63	3.1	8.9	65%	.323	1.29	3.68	2.91	4.94	0.4
2015	ATL	MLB	20	2	4	0	13	9	48.3	53	5	28	30	5.2	5.6	55%	.321	1.69	5.79	5.44	6.29	-0.9
2016	ATL	MLB	21	6	8	1	38	22	160.7	159	17	74	133	4.1	7.4	55%	.319	1.45	4.82	4.40	5.24	-1.4

Breakout: 0%   Improve: 0%   Collapse: 0%   Attrition: 0%   MLB: 0%   Upside: 1   *Comparables: Chaz Roe, Bryan Mitchell, Brandon Maurer*

Drafted/Acquired: 11th round, 2013 draft, T.C. Williams HS (Alexandria, VA)

Previous Ranking: NR

What Happened in 2014: The right-hander pitched in 13 games at short-season, fanning a batter per inning for the year and flashing intriguing stuff in the process.

Strengths: Frame to continue adding size; clean arm action; creates angle on right-handed hitters due to low three-quarters arm slot; fastball operates 91-93; displays arm-side run with some sink; bears in on right-handed hitters; can occasionally cut to glove side; snaps slider off well; breaks hard across hitter's line of sight with late downward darting action; will change shape; potential bat-missing pitch; carries himself well on the mound; even-keeled approach.

Weaknesses: Light on the strength side; stuff presently drops off deeper into outings; fastball flattens out above middle of the thighs; command is loose; needs about a grade jump; slider can sweep and spin; inconsistent at throwing offering for a strike; changeup presently below average; tends to float; doesn't display a lot of trust in offering; needs to work into sequences more; learning how to pitch.

Risk Factor/Injury History: High risk; short-season résumé; command growth.

Bret Sayre's Fantasy Take: If you're taking a chance on Grosser, who is still most likely a reliever in the end, then your league must be extremely deep, both in teams and roster size. Otherwise, just another arm to monitor for now.

The Year Ahead: Grosser is an intriguing arm, with both a fastball and slider that can play as plus-to-better at peak. Despite a lower arm slot, the 20-year-old does a fairly good job keeping his arm consistently in slot and repeating his mechanics. The command presently needs work, but the hope is that as the right-hander adds more strength and gets further repetition with his arsenal it can take a step forward. The X factor is the changeup, the development of which will have a strong influence on whether he sticks in the rotation. He shows some feel for creating arm-side fading action, but is presently very unrefined with the pitch. The progression of the pitch will be a matter of interest in his likely full-season assignment. I don't expect it to grow leaps and bounds overnight, but if he shows trust in the pitch, it will be a positive sign.

Prospects on the Rise

1. OF Victor Reyes: The 20-year-old outfielder is the ultimate projection player, with impressive tool ceilings on paper and a body to dream on when it comes to filling out. The present is a much different picture. Reyes flashes a pretty left-handed stroke, with good bat speed and the ability to drive the ball the other way. There's raw power to tap into, too, and more strength to come. The overall game is fairly raw, especially the approach and outfield defense, but he has the type of raw talent to project as a first-division regular if everything clicks, and really emerge onto the scene in the process.

2. SS Johan Camargo: The 21-year-old flashes some promise with the bat, including loose hands that enable him to control the barrel and the type of power to plug both gaps, with occasional over-the-fence pop. It's an immature offensive profile right now, mainly because of the lack of present strength, which hinges on a lot of projected growth to achieve the utility that the offensive tools suggest. While Camargo presently patrols shortstop and possesses the arm to stick on the left side of the infield, his lack of foot speed and range point toward second base as things continue to progress. It's a player who can take a step forward in 2015, especially if the strength starts to come, and be in the discussion this time next year for a firm spot in the top 10.

FROM THE FIELD

Lucas Sims

Team: Atlanta Braves

Evaluator: Tucker Blair

Dates seen: April 14, 2014

Affiliate: Lynchburg Hillcats (High-A, Braves)

OFP: 60

Realistic role: no. 2 starter

Mechanics: Nice frame; strong legs; muscular top; mild room for growth; mechanics are very clean; stays compact and repeats his delivery; arm action is smooth; solid arm speed; big leg kick; good extension; solid plane; quick on the mound; quick to home plate; delivery times in 1.36-1.46 range.

Pitch type	Present grade	Future grade	Sitting velocity	Peak velocity	Report
FB	50	60	90-93	94	Good extension and drive; terrific plane; fastball shows late life with mild arm-side run; plays up due to tick stutter in delivery from high leg kick; commanded the pitch well most of the night; command becomes loose when overthrows; worked it quick and pounded all corners of the plate; not afraid to attack hitters inside; room for growth into frame could provide potential uptick in velocity; already sits comfortably at 90-93.
CB	60	60	74-78	78	Plus pitch; 12-to-6 break; great depth; tight spin; two-plane break; some struggles with release point but still effective; hitters struggled to pick up spin out of hand; strikeout pitch; true weapon; ability and braveness to throw in any count; ability to back-door and also wrap around hitters.
CH	45	60	81-84	86	Shows some fade; decent feel; arm-side run; really drops off the table at times; inconsistent currently; velocity fluctuates; becomes firm at higher velocity; ability to replicate fastball arm speed; command is loose; fringe-average currently; ability to throw against left- and right-handed hitters; refinement will come from more repetition; clearly working on this pitch in games; will occasionally flash plus.

Overall: Turns 20 shortly, but pitches like he is a 24-year-old; pitchability through the roof. I absolutely loved how he attacked hitters the entire night with a bulldog mentality. Sims was determined and pissed off on the mound, but in a controlled manner. He was in charge of the game the entire night. With three pitches that could be plus, Sims is one of those starters that every team dreams of. The change lags behind the plus curveball and the very underrated fastball, but the pitch flashes plus and gradually improved as the game went along. Sims is advanced for his age, and the only things holding him back could be his need to build stamina and his general inexperience in professional baseball.

3. RHP Wes Parsons: The big right-hander hit resistance after popping onto the radar, but the ingredients are still here to round into a big-league arm and push back up in this system. Parsons' fastball is in the low-90s, with the chance to tick up a bit with some strength gains. He also mixes in a slider that can play above average and an average changeup. The long pole is the overall refinement still needed with the secondary stuff, along with whether any piece of the arsenal will play as legit weapons against advanced hitters.

4. RHP Tyrell Jenkins: Shoulder woes kept Jenkins out of action until late June last season, but the former supplemental first rounder was able to slowly work his way back to effectiveness over the course of 13 Florida State League starts, capping off an encouraging 2014 with six strong Arizona Fall League starts spanning 24 1/3 innings. Jenkins worked consistently in the low- to mid-90s with his heavy fastball during his Arizona Fall League stint, with his upper-70s curve flashing its presurgery bite. The upside remains that of a solid mid-rotation arm, but to get there Jenkins will need to continue to grow his command profile and off-speed, while proving durable enough to handle a starter's load. He should see time with Double-A Mississippi in 2015 and could be ready to contribute in Atlanta as early as the following summer.

Factors on the Farm

Prospects likely to contribute at the major-league level in 2015

1. RHP Jason Hursh: The former first-round pick jumped right into Double-A in his first full professional season and was able to transition to the level relative smoothly. Hursh rides the strength of a heavy fastball that can get up into the mid-90s, along with working a slider and changeup into sequences. Both of the 23-year-old's secondary offerings lag behind his heater and might not be viable in a major-league rotation. This is an arm that can provide starting depth now if needed, or bolster a bullpen.

2. RHP Arodys Vizcaino: After battling injury for the past three seasons, including Tommy John surgery in 2012, Vizcaino was able to work his way back through three minor-league levels in 2014 before logging major-league innings for the first time since 2011. The arm still produces power stuff, including a mid-90s fastball and low-80s power curve, but Vizcaino still struggles with feel and consistency, currently lacking the command to be trusted with high-leverage situations. There is optimism that the 24-year-old has finally put his elbow woes behind him, and he'll enter 2015 with a chance to earn a spot in the Atlanta 'pen after returning to his organization of original acquisition in November 2014 as part of the deal that sent Tommy LaStella to the Cubs. Vizcaino has late-inning potential and is under control through the 2018 season, affording plenty of time for him to establish himself as a useful piece on a retooling Braves club.

BALTIMORE ORIOLES

1. Dylan Bundy RHP

Born: 11/15/92 **Age:** 22 **Bats:** B **Throws:** R **Height:** 6'1" **Weight:** 195

MLB ETA	CT	FB	CH	CB	SL	OFP	Realistic
Debuted in 2012	80	70	70	60	–	75 NO. 1 STARTER	60 NO. 3 STARTER

YEAR	TEAM	LVL	AGE	W	L	SV	G	GS	IP	H	HR	BB	K	BB9	SO9	GB%	BABIP	WHIP	ERA	FIP	FRA	WARP
2014	FRD	A+	21	1	2	0	6	6	26.3	28	0	13	15	4.4	5.1	47%	.318	1.56	4.78	3.97	4.81	0.3
2014	ABE	A-	21	0	1	0	3	3	15.0	10	0	3	22	1.8	13.2	55%	.323	0.87	0.60	1.10	1.32	0.7
2015	BAL	MLB	22	2	3	0	7	7	34.3	34	3	15	29	3.9	7.6	43%	.297	1.41	4.23	4.42	4.60	0.2
2016	BAL	MLB	23	9	10	0	30	30	188.7	182	23	77	156	3.7	7.4	43%	.288	1.38	4.38	4.59	4.77	-0.2

Breakout: 15%   Improve: 23%   Collapse: 5%   Attrition: 17%   MLB: 34%   Upside: 32   *Comparables: Alex Wood, Nick Tropeano, Jarrod Parker*

Drafted/Acquired: 1st round, 2011 draft, Owasso HS (Owasso, OK)

Previous Ranking: #2 (Org), #15 (Top 101)

What Happened in 2014: The 22-year-old right-hander made his return to the mound after missing all of 2013 due to Tommy John. The results were mixed, but eventually the stuff started to show a return to previous form.

Strengths: Extremely athletic; body put together well; near-elite arm strength; smooth arm action; crisp delivery; repeatable; fastball will work 94-97; exploding late life and finish; creates tight spin and rotation with curve; hard snap from high three-quarters arm slot; deep, bending break with teeth and heavy downward action; present plus offering; change shows good guise to fastball; solid arm-side fading action; crisp with cutter when throws in sequences; late glove-side break and slice; can both miss barrels and create weak contact; power-arm potential.

Weaknesses: Runs into ruts of not finishing delivery; command suffers as a result; fastball will work too elevated; can be loose with curveball; lacks finish and will drift into upper tier of zone; change gets too firm; inconsistent action; overall arsenal still in the stages of returning to form; fastball velocity yet to reach prior levels; refinding feel for cutter.

Risk Factor/Injury History: Moderate; Tommy John on résumé; continued return of feel for arsenal.

Bret Sayre's Fantasy Take: The combination of absenteeism and underwhelming statistical performance puts Bundy's perceived value at the lowest point since he was drafted. For shrewd owners who can see past that to the SP2 that Bundy can realistically progress into, this represents a great buying opportunity. He's a potential high contributor in all four categories, despite likely calling a bandbox home. He easily remains a top-five fantasy arm.

The Year Ahead: Bundy passed the initial marker in his return from injury last season as the right-hander showed that his health is trending in the right direction. Reports were clear that the 22-year-old is still finding his way in terms of feeling the stuff, but the flashes shown during his time on the mound were a very positive sign that things were coming back together. While the fastball velocity and crispness of the cutter were lacking, his curveball displayed the same prior shape and excellent bite. That's a good clue that Bundy is building the confidence and trust in his arm to let loose again. This is a player who has been universally praised for both his work ethic and makeup. The expectation is that with a strong foundation already built and another offseason at his disposal, there's a very strong chance the prospect will show big gains this year. While we must be prepared that things may not approach the previously identified potential outcome, the belief here is that Bundy will return to his prior form. Once his workload is built back up, it will be all systems go as he attempts to achieve his monster ceiling, with a legit chance to help at the major-league level during the stretch run this season.

> ### #8
> BP Top 101 Prospects

2. Hunter Harvey RHP

Born: 12/9/94 **Age:** 20 **Bats:** R **Throws:** R **Height:** 6'3" **Weight:** 175

MLB ETA	CT	FB	CH	CB	SL	OFP	Realistic
Late 2016	–	65	60	70	–	70 NO. 2 STARTER	55 NO. 3/4 STARTER

YEAR	TEAM	LVL	AGE	W	L	SV	G	GS	IP	H	HR	BB	K	BB9	SO9	GB%	BABIP	WHIP	ERA	FIP	FRA	WARP
2014	DEL	A	19	7	5	0	17	17	87.7	66	5	33	106	3.4	10.9	46%	.290	1.13	3.18	3.42	4.27	1.5
2015	BAL	MLB	20	3	5	0	13	13	61.7	60	7	31	57	4.5	8.3	45%	.302	1.47	4.55	4.92	4.95	0.1
2016	BAL	MLB	21	7	9	0	28	28	168.7	166	20	77	167	4.1	8.9	45%	.308	1.44	4.58	4.45	4.98	-0.5

Breakout: 0%   Improve: 0%   Collapse: 0%   Attrition: 0%   MLB: 0%   Upside: 11   *Comparables: Carlos Martinez, Shelby Miller, Robbie Ray*

Drafted/Acquired: 1st round, 2013 draft, Bandys HS (Catawba, NC)

Previous Ranking: #3 (Org), #58 (Top 101)

What Happened in 2014: The former first-round pick carved up A-Ball hitters in his full-season debut, firmly cementing his status as an upper-echelon prospect in the process. However, a scare with a shoulder strain ended his season early and cast somewhat of a cloud on an otherwise positive year.

Strengths: Ideal frame; plenty of room to add size and strength; very athletic on mound; loose arm; fastball works 91-95 with late finish; occasional glove-side cutting action; lively in lower tier of zone; aggressive and fearless with pitch; creates hard snap with curveball; power offering at 78-82; deep bend through zone; will change shape; bat-missing potential; changeup flashes strong parachuting action; high growth potential with repetition and trust; competitor on mound.

Weaknesses: Physical maturation needed to hold up over the long season and push arsenal; fastball velocity tends to yo-yo from outing to outing; can jerk head and body off target during delivery; heater works elevated as a result; command is presently fringe-average; can cast curve, which leads to early break; change is presently projection; on the firm side; still developing trust to work into sequences consistently; presently heavily fastball and curve dependent.

Risk Factor/Injury History: High; limited professional experience; shoulder strain (2014); emergence of true third offering.

Bret Sayre's Fantasy Take: With three pitches that can potentially miss bats at the major-league level, Harvey's strength as a fantasy asset is going to be his 200-strikeout potential. As with Bundy and everyone else in this system, the division and ballpark will work against him, but there's SP2 upside here, as Harvey could put up a 3.25 ERA, and 1.10 WHIP to go along with those big K numbers at peak.

The Year Ahead: Everything for Harvey on the mound flows off of an extremely athletic and loose delivery. The right-hander creates easy velocity, with the ball effortlessly coming out of his hand when delivering the heater. The offering explodes on hitters, often showing strong late finish that makes it difficult to square up and for hitters to gauge. The 20-year-old is also adept at staying above the baseball when spinning his curveball, which already plays around above average. The early feel at the young age bodes very well for a consistent plus-plus power breaker emerging in the near future. The athleticism and overall ease point to command growth being highly achievable as well. Toss in a competitive streak that stands out on the mound, and this profile has the makings of an impact starting arm. The near-term task at hand for Harvey is developing his changeup, which is imperative for reaching his full potential. Reports from the season and sources spoken to for this list pointed to increased comfort utilizing the offering as the year wore on. The other pieces of his arsenal will likely push him out of the lower levels before the change is fully progressed, but the view here sees further growth with the offering coming this season. If it occurs, it should lead to a strong chance the prospect closes out 2015 in Double-A, and will begin to put the righty on the radar for major-league consideration in the not-so-far-off future in the process.

---

3. Chance Sisco C

Born: 2/24/95 **Age:** 20 **Bats:** L **Throws:** R **Height:** 6'2" **Weight:** 193

MLB ETA	Hit	Power	Run	Glove	Arm	OFP	Realistic
Late 2017	55	50	–	50	50	60 1ST DIV PLAYER	50 AVG ML PLAYER

YEAR	TEAM	LVL	AGE	PA	R	2B	3B	HR	RBI	BB	SO	SB	CS	AVG/OBP/SLG	TAv	BABIP	BRR	FRAA	WARP
2014	DEL	A	19	478	56	27	2	5	63	42	79	1	2	.340/.406/.448	.311	.406	-1.2	C(74): -0.9	3.8
2015	BAL	MLB	20	250	20	10	0	3	22	15	62	0	0	.236/.288/.317	.232	.307	-0.5	C -0	0.0
2016	BAL	MLB	21	250	27	12	0	4	24	18	59	0	0	.250/.309/.356	.250	.316	-0.7	C 0	0.9

Breakout: 0% Improve: 0% Collapse: 0% Attrition: 0% MLB: 0% Upside: 71 *Comparables: J.R. Murphy, Hank Conger, Travis d'Arnaud*

Drafted/Acquired: 2nd round, 2013, Santiago HS (Corona, CA)

Previous Ranking: #9 (Org)

What Happened in 2014: Sisco put together a solid first full professional season, showing surprising advancement at the plate and the ability to create consistent, hard contact, but left opinions mixed when it comes to the defense.

Strengths: Athletic; good frame; solid-average arm strength; strong hands; plus bat speed; capable of adjusting to the path of the ball; extends well postcontact to use the whole field; present gap power; potential for more home-run pop as physically matures; has shown early improvement in transition to catching; body and athleticism to handle position; high baseball IQ.

Weaknesses: Choppy footwork; gets tangled when firing feet; glove hand will drift; needs a lot of work getting body in good position to block; questions as to whether there's enough to stick; swing on the flat side; power may ultimately play at fringe-average; will lunge at stuff with spin; below-average runner; lacks impact tools.

Risk Factor/Injury History: High; yet to reach upper minors; dual-threat development; some questions on ability to stick behind plate.

Bret Sayre's Fantasy Take: If Sisco stays behind the plate, his offensive potential will certainly put him above the mixed-league line of demarcation, but moving off the position would certainly be a blow to his value. On the other hand, sticking behind the plate will slow his ETA, so it's a double-edged sword. Either way, there's a .280 hitter with 15 homers in there, which is usable everywhere in this offensively challenged environment.

The Year Ahead: Sisco emerged within this system last season, during which he offered a glimpse at an offensive skill set that proved to be more advanced than previously thought. A fluid stroke and strong hands enable the backstop to create consistent contact along with good backspin into both gaps. The 20-year-old is more than willing to use the whole field at an early age and displays a level mind-set at the plate, which bodes well for consistent adjustments with each step up the ranks. While there are still improvements to be made in handling good breaking stuff, the hands play well and stay back when attacking offerings. The potential exists for .270s-.280s averages, with home-run power that can round out as average in peak seasons. However, opinions are mixed on the defense and ability to stick behind the plate; some see the athleticism and early progression of the skills as an indication that Sisco can reach an adequate defensive level as a backstop, while others feel there are key limitations and the gap is too large to close. The placement within this list and role grades speak to the belief that the player has taken some steps at closing the initial gap and that things can look very different down the line. This is a player who will need time to marinate on both sides of the ball, but can reward the developmental patience with a solid major-league player at full bloom.

4. Christian Walker   1B

Born: 3/28/91   **Age:** 24   **Bats:** R   **Throws:** R   **Height:** 6'0"   **Weight:** 220

MLB ETA	Hit	Power	Run	Glove	Arm		OFP	Realistic
Debuted in 2014	55	50	–	50	–		55 >AVG REGULAR	50 AVG ML PLAYER

YEAR	TEAM	LVL	AGE	PA	R	2B	3B	HR	RBI	BB	SO	SB	CS	AVG/OBP/SLG	TAv	BABIP	BRR	FRAA	WARP
2014	BAL	MLB	23	19	1	1	0	1	1	1	9	0	0	.167/.211/.389	.227	.250	0.0	1B(6): 0.1	0.0
2014	NOR	AAA	23	188	15	10	0	6	19	18	49	0	0	.259/.335/.428	.274	.327	-2.8	1B(44): -1.4, 3B(1): -0.0	0.0
2014	BOW	AA	23	411	58	15	2	20	77	38	83	2	1	.301/.367/.516	.315	.337	0.9	1B(91): 1.8	3.2
2015	BAL	MLB	24	250	26	10	0	8	30	16	63	0	0	.245/.299/.395	.264	.300	-0.5	1B 0	0.3
2016	BAL	MLB	25	460	54	19	0	14	53	31	125	0	0	.242/.299/.388	.260	.308	-1.2	1B 0	1.0

Breakout: 1%   Improve: 12%   Collapse: 12%   Attrition: 21%   MLB: 34%   Upside: 0   *Comparables: Jesus Aguilar, Neftali Soto, Brock Peterson*

Drafted/Acquired: 4th round, 2012 draft, University of South Carolina (Columbia, SC)

Previous Ranking: Factor on the Farm

What Happened in 2014: Walker continued to hit at a solid clip and prove himself at each stop. He handled Double-A arms to the tune of a .301 average with 20 bombs, but dropped off some at the highest level of the minors before a brief call to The Show.

Strengths: Sturdy build; good present strength; strong bat-to-ball ability; consistently barrels up pitches hard; keeps hands inside of offerings; recognizes ball quickly; all-fields approach; understanding of strike zone; grinds through plate appearances; has been learning how to muscle up and add lift to swing; punishes mistakes; improving around the bag; hard worker.

Weaknesses: Body is maxed out; can be on the passive side at the plate; swing flashes in-zone miss; can struggle keeping hands above high-velocity stuff; capable of being worked away with spin by good arms; questions on ultimate power translation; may have to sacrifice too much contact for power to translate; at times clunky at first; limited range.

Risk Factor/Injury History: Low; achieved major-league level; translation of power.

Bret Sayre's Fantasy Take: There's more pull here in deeper mixed leagues and AL-only formats, as Walker doesn't carry top-tier potential for a corner bat. At best, we're likely looking at an Adam LaRoche-type with slightly less power—and LaRoche was barely a top-15 fantasy first baseman in 2014. Think a .260 average with 20 homers, even with the park helping him. Though with Nelson Cruz moving on, Walker may see a healthy amount of playing time in 2015.

The Year Ahead: An oft-debated player with regards to the ultimate role, it should not be downplayed that the former fourth-round pick has hit his way onto the prospect landscape. Walker possesses the type of profile where there's more than initially meets the eye and requires a longer study before one warms up to the overall portfolio. This isn't an aesthetically pleasing player who's graceful on the field and oozes natural tools. But what the 24-year-old has proven to do well is hit, and players who do so consistently end up having careers in some capacity. There are questions about whether there's enough in the hit tool to keep the hard contact from plateauing against unforgiving arms who mercilessly exploit weaknesses, as well as concerns about how much of the power is going to translate. Sources spoken to for this list were uniform in that the outcome likely isn't a first-division talent, but things are very much trending toward an overall body of work that can include some productive seasons. Walker should get more seasoning in Triple-A at the onset of 2015, with the player in the driver's seat as to whether an extended chance is in the cards at some point before the year's end.

5. Josh Hart CF

Born: 10/2/94 **Age:** 20 **Bats:** L **Throws:** L **Height:** 6'1" **Weight:** 180

MLB ETA		Hit	Power	Run	Glove	Arm		OFP	Realistic
2018		55	–	65	65	–		55 >AVG REGULAR	45 4TH OF/<AVG REG

YEAR	TEAM	LVL	AGE	PA	R	2B	3B	HR	RBI	BB	SO	SB	CS	AVG/OBP/SLG	TAv	BABIP	BRR	FRAA	WARP
2014	DEL	A	19	353	22	5	1	1	28	21	86	11	5	.255/.301/.285	.225	.339	-0.6	CF(85): -5.8	-0.9
2014	ORI	Rk	19	25	2	0	1	0	0	1	2	2	0	.167/.200/.250	.197	.182	0.6	CF(4): -0.2	-0.1
2015	BAL	MLB	20	250	20	7	1	1	14	9	76	3	1	.194/.228/.245	.185	.275	-0.1	CF -3	-1.5
2016	BAL	MLB	21	250	22	7	1	2	19	10	69	3	2	.217/.255/.292	.209	.293	0.1	CF -3	-1.9

Breakout: 0%   Improve: 0%   Collapse: 0%   Attrition: 0%   MLB: 0%   Upside: 13   *Comparables: Desmond Jennings, Gregory Polanco, Aaron Altherr*

Drafted/Acquired: 1st round, 2013 draft, Parkview HS (Lilburn, GA)
Previous Ranking: #10 (Org)

What Happened in 2014: The former first-round pick's first full season of pro ball was fairly underwhelming and received mixed reviews, with the raw athleticism still having a ways to go to translate into polished baseball skills.

Strengths: Excellent athlete; wiry frame with some room for growth, especially in lower half; easy-plus runner; strong instincts in center; gets good jumps and reads; plus range into both gaps; routes have been rapidly improving; quick, efficient stroke; life in hands; capable of barreling up offerings hard; willing to use the whole field; can develop some power with more physical maturation.

Weaknesses: Offensive game is unrefined; in the early stages of learning strike zone; expands often; fooled by spin frequently, especially soft stuff away; contact tends to be hollow; falls back on slashing and slapping rather than driving; needs more comfort and confidence; power could play down to well below average; arm is fringe-average at best.

Risk Factor/Injury History: High; yet to reach upper levels; large gap between present and future; surgery for meniscus repair (2014).

Bret Sayre's Fantasy Take: Don't let the full-season résumé fool you, this one is going to take a while; however, the payoff could still be surprisingly valuable. Hart's biggest asset is going to be his potential 30-plus steals, and if he can somehow turn his hit tool and/or approach into a top-of-the-lineup hitter, he could get very interesting.

The Year Ahead: The speedy center fielder proved to be somewhat overmatched in his full-season debut, but a meniscus injury broke up his season and reports from later in the year highlighted some offensive improvement. Make no mistake, though, Hart is a long-term project, especially with the bat, where things may just be middle of the road for some time to come. However, the speed and potential with the glove give him a chance to be able to ride both tools up to the majors. A couple of evaluators spoken to for this list had extremely positive remarks about how quickly the defensive adjustments were implemented since signing and how the glove can impact the game down the line. Whether it's just sitting at his floor as a reserve or reaching his full potential, at some point, Hart will have to hit. Some suggested that with increased comfort and more confidence to be aggressive with his swing, the 20-year-old can display the hard contact he flashed at times last season on a more consistent basis as soon as 2015. The belief here is that a more subtle progression will take place this season following a repeat assignment in the South Atlantic League. Positive results there will aid in building confidence before a decision is made as to whether the player is ready for a bump to the next level at some point in the summer.

6. Zach Davies RHP

Born: 2/7/93 **Age:** 22 **Bats:** R **Throws:** R **Height:** 6'0" **Weight:** 150

MLB ETA		CT	FB	CH	CB	SL		OFP	Realistic
2015		–	50	55	50	50		50 NO. 4 STARTER	50 NO. 5 SP/LONG RP

YEAR	TEAM	LVL	AGE	W	L	SV	G	GS	IP	H	HR	BB	K	BB9	SO9	GB%	BABIP	WHIP	ERA	FIP	FRA	WARP
2014	BOW	AA	21	10	7	0	21	20	110.0	106	8	32	109	2.6	8.9	54%	.314	1.25	3.35	3.30	4.13	1.7
2015	BAL	MLB	22	5	7	0	18	18	97.0	104	11	36	72	3.3	6.7	50%	.303	1.44	4.61	4.79	5.01	0.0
2016	BAL	MLB	23	9	10	0	29	29	180.0	186	20	60	142	3.0	7.1	50%	.302	1.37	4.20	4.29	4.57	0.3

Breakout: 0%   Improve: 0%   Collapse: 0%   Attrition: 0%   MLB: 0%   Upside: 18   *Comparables: Patrick Corbin, Hector Rondon, Cesar Carrillo*

Drafted/Acquired: 26th round, 2011 draft, Mesquite HS (Gilbert, AZ)
Previous Ranking: #8 (Org)

What Happened in 2014: The former 26th-round pick logged 110 innings in Double-A, where he continued to show strong pitchability, and then more than held his own in the prospect-heavy Arizona Fall League to close out the year.

Strengths: Athletic; fluid delivery; easy arm action; fastball operates 88-91 with strong arm-side run and sink; can spot to all four quadrants of the zone; turns over solid-average change; good deception via consistent arm action to that of fastball; fades heavily to arm side; confident to use offering at any point in the count; flashes feel for both curveball and slider; above-average command profile.

Weaknesses: Very lean; needs added strength to maintain stuff; creates so-so plane out of delivery; fastball is merely average; must locate and hit spots in lower tier to be effective; extremely hittable when mislocated; will cast curve; command of offering is spotty; needs further sharpening to play at average; heavily relies on change to put hitters away; no plus pitch in repertoire.

Risk Factor/Injury History: Low; 21 appearances in Double-A; walks a fine line with stuff.

Bret Sayre's Fantasy Take: This is not the type of profile you want to use a roster spot on in mixed leagues. Davies will be a major-league pitcher, but he has limited stuff and he'll be pitching in a tough environment—and that could lead to underwhelming contributions in all categories.

The Year Ahead: Davies is an undersized right-hander with limited stuff who navigates through lineups by changing speeds often, working backward, and spotting on the corners. This arm operates with a razor thin margin of error, but possesses plus command and an understanding of how to execute within his means. The small body makes it tougher to see the arm being able to consistently handle the rigors of the long season and emerge into a workhorse. If Davies ends up growing a bit more into his body as he approaches his mid-twenties, the potential role becomes that much more attainable. However, the likely scenario is that the 22-year-old slides somewhere in as a fifth starter/swingman. The belief here is that the arm has a much better chance at being successful in the long run as a reliever, but the competitiveness and feel for the craft give the prospect a shot to stick around as a starter at the major-league level longer than expected. A placement in Triple-A to start 2015 will be yet another test of the arsenal against more advanced hitters, but if the previous ones are any indication, the small righty will pass it and get a chance in The Show in the process.

---

7. Mike Wright RHP

Born: 1/3/90 **Age:** 25 **Bats:** R **Throws:** R **Height:** 6'6" **Weight:** 215

MLB ETA	CT	FB	CH	CB	SL	OFP	Realistic
2015	–	55	50	–	55	50 NO. 4 STARTER	50 LATE INN RP

YEAR	TEAM	LVL	AGE	W	L	SV	G	GS	IP	H	HR	BB	K	BB9	SO9	GB%	BABIP	WHIP	ERA	FIP	FRA	WARP
2014	NOR	AAA	24	5	11	0	26	26	142.7	159	10	41	103	2.6	6.5	39%	.322	1.40	4.61	3.79	4.37	1.6
2015	BAL	MLB	25	6	9	0	23	23	124.0	139	14	34	85	2.5	6.2	43%	.311	1.40	4.63	4.65	5.04	-0.1
2016	BAL	MLB	26	8	9	0	25	25	148.7	165	13	41	107	2.5	6.5	43%	.315	1.38	4.40	3.99	4.78	-0.1

Breakout: 17%   Improve: 21%   Collapse: 8%   Attrition: 24%   MLB: 36%   Upside: 1   *Comparables: Rudy Owens, Simon Castro, Chris Rusin*

Drafted/Acquired: 3rd round, 2011 draft, East Carolina University (Greenville, NC)

Previous Ranking: #6 (Org)

2014 Stats: 4.61 ERA (142.2 IP, 159 H, 103 K, 41 BB) at Triple-A Norfolk

The Tools: 5+ FB; 5+ SL; 5 CH

What Happened in 2014: Wright struggled to make the transition to Triple-A, where he found plenty of barrels and failed to miss enough, but the big right-hander did put together a strong final month of the season and logged another heavy workload in the upper minors.

Strengths: Strong body; capable of withstanding rigors of position; clean delivery and arm action; fastball comfortably works 91-93; can reach for more; shows heavy, downward action and angle; snaps slider with tilt; tight, late break in mid-80s; can miss bats; turns over change with arm-side fade; deception between fastball; capable of throwing entire arsenal for strikes.

Weaknesses: Stuff is solid-average across the board; lacks strong chase pitch; works consistently around the plate; leads to a lot of contact against; slider gets slurvy in lower velocity band (low-80s); change more deception than action; limited overall growth potential.

Risk Factor/Injury History: Low; 43 starts in upper minors; mature arsenal.

Bret Sayre's Fantasy Take: The strikeouts are just not going to be there with Wright for him to be a viable mixed-league stash—given that he's unlikely to ever make it past waiver-wire material. The WHIP would be reasonable if he can avoid getting hit too hard, but that's really all you're hoping for.

The Year Ahead: Wright is likely to return to Triple-A to start 2015 and will look to prove that his final month of the season was more the norm than an anomaly against quality competition. This large right-hander offers promise as a workhorse starter who can take the ball every fifth day and give the ballclub more good performances than bad. The 25-year-old's bread and butter is a heavy low-90s fastball with which he likes to aggressively pound the zone. The pitcher isn't afraid to come right after hitters and understands the value of getting ahead in sequences. Wright's strike-throwing ability can be both a strength and a weakness, however. When he is consistently snapping off his slider in the mid-80s while mixing the changeup in sequences, there's enough to miss bats. The slider plays down with some frequency, mostly spinning and sweeping into the zone, which leaves the changeup and fastball prone to a lot of contact given their around-the-plate nature. The pressure of churning through lineups may ultimately be too much for this arm's stuff, but a rebound in the International League this season will at the very least get the player a call to The Show in some capacity sometime this summer.

8. Tim Berry   LHP

Born: 3/18/91   **Age:** 24   **Bats:** L   **Throws:** L   **Height:** 6'3"   **Weight:** 180

MLB ETA	CT	FB	CH	CB	SL	OFP	Realistic
2015	–	55	55	55	–	50 NO. 4 STARTER	50 NO. 5 SP/MID RP

YEAR	TEAM	LVL	AGE	W	L	SV	G	GS	IP	H	HR	BB	K	BB9	SO9	GB%	BABIP	WHIP	ERA	FIP	FRA	WARP
2014	BOW	AA	23	6	7	0	23	23	133.3	122	12	45	108	3.0	7.3	45%	.288	1.25	3.51	4.10	4.47	1.4
2015	BAL	MLB	24	5	9	0	21	21	109.0	123	14	46	70	3.8	5.8	44%	.306	1.55	5.29	5.44	5.75	-0.9
2016	BAL	MLB	25	2	1	0	42	0	44.0	48	5	17	32	3.5	6.5	44%	.306	1.47	4.86	4.64	5.29	-0.2

Breakout: 0%   Improve: 0%   Collapse: 0%   Attrition: 0%   MLB: 0%   Upside: 2   *Comparables: Alex Wilson, Yohan Flande, Rob Rasmussen*

Drafted/Acquired: 50th round, 2009 draft, San Marcos HS (San Marcos, CA)

Previous Ranking: #7 (Org)

What Happened in 2014: The southpaw put together a solid season in Double-A as a 23-year-old, often keeping batters off-balance, especially lefties, who he held to a .212 clip.

Strengths: Room for more physical growth; loose arm; low-energy-expending delivery; fastball works low-90s with tailing action; curveball flashes deep break when staying on top; can miss bats; turns over change with loose wrist; best action in low-80s; deceptive versus fastball; strike thrower; good feel for craft.

Weaknesses: Delivery can be inconsistent; body will open early; fastball tends to play down; loose within the strike zone and becomes very hittable; questions on whether stuff will start advanced bats early; can cast curve; change too firm on occasion; lacks overpowering arsenal.

Risk Factor/Injury History: Low; 133 1/3 Double-A innings; Tommy John on résumé (high school); questions on translation of stuff against elite hitters.

Bret Sayre's Fantasy Take: There's slightly more strikeout potential with Berry than with either of the two names ahead of him, but it also comes with a higher bullpen probability. However, like Davies and Wright, he's not a good use of a mixed-league roster spot.

The Year Ahead: While the stuff here isn't overpowering, Berry flashes a solid-average arsenal that he understands how to execute. The left-hander is easy with his release, which—combined with his longer limbs—allows the low-90s heater with some late, tailing action to sneak up on hitters. When the pitcher is spotting his fastball to both sides of the plate and moving it around the strike zone, both the curveball and changeup play up due to opposing hitters being more apt to get their bats started early. The inherent issue for Berry is that often his delivery becomes inconsistent and the command gets loose within the zone, especially when trying to spot to the arm side. Given that the fastball is a more hittable offering in general, and the lack of a legit putaway secondary pitch, opinions are mixed as to whether the prospect sticks as a starter in the long haul. In all likelihood Berry is the type of arm who can get a chance to start early in his career and then makes the transition to the bullpen. Don't rule out the pitcher having a chance to stick for longer than expected in the rotation if the command can take a slight step forward, but the smart money says the most successful portion of the career comes as a reliever. Triple-A is the next test for the lefty to begin 2015, where if all goes well, he can push for major-league look by the end of the year.

9. Mike Yastrzemski   OF

Born: 8/23/90   **Age:** 24   **Bats:** L   **Throws:** L   **Height:** 5'11"   **Weight:** 180

MLB ETA	Hit	Power	Run	Glove	Arm	OFP	Realistic
Late 2015	50	–	50	55	55	50 AVG ML PLAYER	45 4TH OF/<AVG REG

YEAR	TEAM	LVL	AGE	PA	R	2B	3B	HR	RBI	BB	SO	SB	CS	AVG/OBP/SLG	TAv	BABIP	BRR	FRAA	WARP
2014	BOW	AA	23	201	23	13	4	3	12	14	34	1	2	.250/.310/.413	.257	.293	-0.5	CF(38): 3.3, LF(4): -0.1	0.8
2014	FRD	A+	23	107	21	7	2	1	19	8	16	5	0	.312/.364/.462	.298	.350	0.5	LF(14): 0.0, RF(9): -0.6	0.7
2014	DEL	A	23	288	52	14	10	10	44	19	64	12	4	.306/.365/.554	.319	.371	4.3	RF(54): 1.9, CF(6): 0.1	3.3
2015	BAL	MLB	24	250	26	10	2	5	21	13	64	3	1	.225/.273/.349	.236	.286	0.1	RF 0, CF 2	0.2
2016	BAL	MLB	25	250	26	11	3	5	25	15	62	3	2	.240/.295/.373	.250	.303	0.2	RF 0, CF 2	1.1

Breakout: 0%   Improve: 0%   Collapse: 0%   Attrition: 0%   MLB: 0%   Upside: 23   *Comparables: Scott Van Slyke, Alfredo Marte, Chris Pettit*

Drafted/Acquired: 14th round, 2013 draft, Vanderbilt University (Vanderbilt, TN)

Previous Ranking: NR

What Happened in 2014: The outfielder from Massachusetts played at three levels last year, putting together a solid season overall, but hitting resistance in a 43-game stop in Double-A.

Strengths: Athletic build; good present strength; strong outfield instincts; fundamentally sound; takes excellent routes; solid-average arm; sets himself up well when making throws; compact stroke; up-the-middle approach; willing to use the whole field; brings a plan to the plate; gap power; smart runner; high baseball IQ; plays the game with enthusiasm.

Weaknesses: Maxed out body; little physical projection left; limited future tool growth; inconsistent balance at plate; swing on the flat side; back side tends to cave against arm-side pitching; questions on ability to consistently hit high-quality stuff; power likely to play fringe-average at best; more of a 'tweener in center field.

Risk Factor/Injury History: Moderate; limited Double-A experience; questions on profile.

Bret Sayre's Fantasy Take: There is admittedly very little fantasy upside here, but very deep leaguers could take some solace in knowing that he's likely going to make the majors in some capacity. With Nick Markakis and Nelson Cruz having moved on and little outfield depth in the upper minors, there is more opportunity for Yastrzemski in the organization.

The Year Ahead: Given the age and level of polish, it isn't surprising that Yastrzemski produced well in the low minors and proved worthy of an accelerated push into the upper levels during his first full year of professional ball. While there isn't a carrying tool in this profile and it is on the bland side overall, the 24-year-old brings a balanced skill set to the table, where he touches a piece of each aspect of the game. Tack on that the makeup and feel for the game draw high praise, and this is a player with a very good chance at achieving the major leagues. What things will look like in the long run is likely to be on the modest side, but Yastrzemski can carve out an extended career and provide value on a big-league roster. If things break right, mainly with proving that the bat can adjust and combat the jump in quality of competition, the outfielder can end up a second-division type who hits in the bottom third of a deeper lineup during peak seasons. The realistic outcome points to a fourth outfielder in the long haul who can spell all three regulars and fill in during extended stretches. This season will see Yastrzemski return to Double-A, where a few adjustments at the plate will go a long way toward putting him in position for a cup of coffee at summer's end.

10.   Jomar Reyes   3B

Born: 2/20/97   **Age:** 18   **Bats:** R   **Throws:** R   **Height:** 6'3"   **Weight:** 220

MLB ETA	Hit	Power	Run	Glove	Arm	OFP	Realistic
2019	**50**	**60**	–		**60**	**60** 1ST DIV. PLAYER	**45** BENCH/<AVG. REG.

YEAR	TEAM	LVL	AGE	PA	R	2B	3B	HR	RBI	BB	SO	SB	CS	AVG/OBP/SLG	TAv	BABIP	BRR	FRAA	WARP
2014	ORI	Rk	17	207	23	10	2	4	29	15	38	1	0	.285/.333/.425	.346	.329	0.7	3B(18): -1.8	1.1
2015	BAL	MLB	18	250	18	8	0	3	21	10	74	0	0	.198/.234/.281	.197	.267	-0.4	3B -3	-1.5
2016	BAL	MLB	19	250	26	11	0	6	26	10	65	0	0	.228/.263/.357	.230	.283	-0.5	3B -4	-0.9

Breakout: 0%   Improve: 0%   Collapse: 0%   Attrition: 0%   MLB: 0%   Upside: 29   *Comparables: Josh Vitters, Alex Liddi, Maikel Franco*

Drafted/Acquired: International free agent, 2014, Dominican Republic

Previous Ranking: NR

What Happened in 2014: Reyes made his stateside debut just months after signing, spending 2014 at the Florida complexes at the age of 17, impressing with his raw power and feel at the plate.

Strengths: Physically imposing; larger than listed by an inch or two and ten-plus pounds; big raw power; simple stroke and plenty of strength to carry the fence, pole-to-pole; tracks well; comes to battle with solid offensive approach for age, experience; enough feel to hit for some average despite long levers; strike zone command should help grow the on-base profile; plus arm with easy release; hands work at the hot corner.

Weaknesses: Body may quickly force Reyes across the diamond to first base; well-below-average runner, likely stretched in an outfield corner; lower half lags in the infield, limiting range and ability to convert at the margins; may have more difficulty limiting coverage holes against more advanced arms; chance for swing-and-miss to manifest.

Risk Factor/Injury History: High; complex-level résumé.

The Year Ahead: Reyes gives the Orioles a chance for some homegrown impact power—something that has been sorely missing from the organization affiliates in recent years. While he looks every bit the part of a bruising thumper, the swing is quicker and more compact than the presentation suggests. That, along with his strike zone awareness, leaves the door open for the big-bodied Dominican to hit for a little bit of average, and early signs indicate a willingness to lay off the close strike and allow arms to work around him, boding well for his future on-base ability. He seems destined for a defensive home at first base, though Reyes has soft enough hands and a strong enough arm to hang at third if he proves capable of cleaning up and quickening his lower-half actions as he continues to physically mature. Though he'll play all of 2015 at the age of 18, Baltimore could challenge Reyes with a full-season gig in Delmarva, where a strong showing could quickly catapult him onto the national prospecting scene.

Prospects on the Rise

1. C Jonah Heim: The defensive potential is the present calling card for the 20-year-old, with a game behind the dish that can develop into the above-average-to-better category and an arm designed to control the running game. Heim already shows solid footwork at a young age that enables him to fire quickly and move well laterally despite well-below-average speed. The body is also an asset when it comes to blocking and controlling offerings in the dirt. What will really establish the switch-hitting backstop is progress with the bat. There's plus bat speed and raw power to tap into, but the skills are presently very raw and lag behind the defense. The potential exists to ride the glove right up to The Show, while proving that the bat is more than an afterthought will push this prospect's status up another level.

2. RHP Pat Connaughton: The thinking is that the 22-year-old right-hander, known as a starting guard on Notre Dame's basketball team in other circles, can really blossom when fully focusing on baseball. Connaughton brings a lively fastball that comfortably sits in the low-90s and has the potential to tick up higher as the stamina builds. His 6-foot-5 frame also allows him to get good leverage and create solid plane when delivering offerings. The secondary arsenal needs some work, especially when it comes to sharpening the breaking ball, but

FROM THE FIELD

Dylan Bundy

Team: Baltimore Orioles

Evaluator: Tucker Blair

Dates seen: June 27, 2014

Affiliate: Aberdeen IronBirds (Short-Season, Orioles)

OFP: 70

Realistic role: 65; no. 2 starter

Mechanics: Extremely built frame; one of the most athletic pitchers I remember seeing; maxed frame; fluid mechanics; clean delivery with plenty to like; mild stab but not enough to warrant significant concern; excellent drive; arm stays high in three-quarters slot and body is able to stay low and drive toward home; excellent vertical axis with arm relative to the ground; creates a tremendous plane; drops and drives; excellent arm speed; hips stay proportionate throughout delivery; consistent delivery times in 1.38-1.41 range; the overall mechanics are impressive; body is in unison and he keeps balance throughout the entire start.

Pitch type	Present grade	Future grade	Sitting velocity	Peak velocity	Report
FB	60	60	91-93	94	Excellent command; able to spot the fastball in all quadrants at any time; mild arm-side run from an excellent plane; velocity is fine at this level; pitch is still above-average offering even without the velocity he possessed in the past; explosive offering with life; ball gets on hitters quicker than anticipated.
CT	60	70	87-89	89	Not the true weapon it was in the past; still a great pitch; acts as a fastball and then has late, hard cut; nearly a foot on the cut; excellent pitch and able to throw to both sides of the plate; throws at the hands of both left- and right-handed hitters; has multiple versions of horizontal movement from arm-side run and cut; vertical movement from plane; pitch is hard to track and hitters will generally struggle with this offering at any level; velocity and crispness of pitch have not returned quite yet; was an elite offering before; doubt it returns to full form, but slight tick in velocity and some general tightening of command will get this pitch back to plus-plus.
CB	60	65	73-75	75	12-to-6 offering; great depth; tight spin; will miss bats at any level; able to drop pitch into lower part of strike zone; pitch looks even deeper in its rotation because of excellent plane and high arm slot with low drive; will cast it occasionally; will release too late with arm out in front and ball will drift up in zone; not a large concern and can be tightened up; command of offering is plus and could improve more once he improves the occasional release point malfunction.
CH	50	60	86-88	88	Only threw a few of them; slight parachute action; fade toward arm side; the velocity difference from the fastball is not great; largely from the velocity a tick down since the surgery; able to replicate same arm speed and arm action; release points were fine; threw one that was firm at 88; good pitch if his fastball velocity ticks up again; pitch does not have enough differential without the velocity gain; still shows enough movement and fade to provide usefulness regardless.

Overall: Dylan Bundy has made the trek back from Tommy John surgery. It has been a long journey for the right-hander, but he looks to be mostly back in form. The velocity may never return to 94-98, but I do expect another slight tick in velocity from 91-94. It likely does not happen this season. Regardless, he still has a terrific arsenal.

Bundy is one of the most polished pitchers in the minors, displaying an extraordinary amount of pitchability, confidence, and cognizance on the mound. While many will look at the arsenal and say this is not the same pitcher, I still believe the intense makeup and pitchability boost Bundy up the charts. This is one of the most competitive players I have seen, even against competition like the New York-Penn League. Bundy did not care where he was, he wanted to annihilate every hitter with his arsenal.

Bundy is still an extremely talented arm regardless of whether the velocity returns, the cutter returns to its old form, and the changeup gains its full effectiveness. With his pitches still grading out as plus or potentially plus, Bundy has a deep arsenal that will help him work through a major-league lineup when one of his pitches is off for the night. The curveball is currently the best secondary offering, but the cutter has potential to be that pitch down the road if the velocity and crispness of it returns. Bundy is going to pitch—and pitch well—in the majors. However, there is some mild risk here simply because he has Tommy John on the record and the arsenal has not quite reached its past potential.

On the cutter, Bundy definitely threw it multiple times. Multiple eyes confirmed the same and the movement was nothing similar to the changeup.

he shows solid feel for the changeup. The Orioles are taking a patient route with Connaughton and allowed the prospect to return to school for his final season on the court. They could be rewarded for their strategy and hope that taking a chance on the arm in the fourth round last year will lead to a solid payout once he enters the system full time this season.

Factors on the Farm
Prospects likely to contribute at the major-league level in 2015

1. OF Dariel Alvarez: The 26-year-old Cuban import spent last season in Baltimore's upper levels, where he put together a solid campaign and showed that he's made the initial adjustment to professional ball. Feedback from sources indicated that the outfielder improved his pitch recognition and avoided frequent bouts of lunging out onto his front foot. The result was a steady output of consistent, hard contact and the ability to adjust his stroke to the path of the ball. Alvarez is more of a free-swinger at the plate, with a larger strike zone and higher margin of error for getting the bat on the ball against less experienced competition. The ante has now gone up with a step into Triple-A and potentially beyond. He should be able to help the big club at some point in 2015, whether it's in a reserve role or as a fill-in for an extended stretch.

2. RHP Tyler Wilson: The University of Virginia product has steadily risen up the ranks since signing in 2011 and took a step forward last season in the upper levels of the system. The 25-year-old right-hander has always shown to be able to handle a heavy workload, but also flashed more consistency with the command and crispness of his arsenal, especially in regards to missing more bats with his curveball. Wilson is capable of pounding the strike zone with his low-90s fastball and possesses good strike-throwing ability. He's around the plate often, but with continued consistency of the curve he can get good bats started early. The changeup plays inconsistently, often on the firm side and lacking strong separation to the heater. It may ultimately play better as a seventh-inning role at peak in the bullpen, but the arm provides good depth in 2015 wherever the organization chooses to utilize it.

3. RHP Logan Verrett: Baltimore scooped up Verrett in the 2014 Rule 5 draft, as the Mets' pitching depth precluded the Baylor product's addition to the 40-man. He brings to the table a four-pitch mix spearheaded by an upper-80s to low-90s fastball that he wields with aggression and confidence—sometimes to his detriment, as he can be susceptible to hard contact up in the zone and middle-in. His slider is a worthy second offering, hovering around 80 mph and flashing above-average bite, with an average changeup coming in the low-80s with some soft fade. He rounds out the repertoire with a fringy curve that can be useful as a change-of-pace offering and drop-in first-pitch strike getter. His above-average command allows the average stuff to play up, and he should get an opportunity to break camp with the big club as a swingman capable of providing innings out of the 'pen and insurance against having to rush some of the higher upside Triple-A arms should a need arise in the Orioles' rotation.

BOSTON RED SOX

1. Blake Swihart C

Born: 4/3/92   **Age:** 23   **Bats:** B   **Throws:** R   **Height:** 6'1"   **Weight:** 175

MLB ETA	Hit	Power	Run	Glove	Arm	OFP	Realistic
Late 2015	60	50	–	60	65	65 1ST DIV/OCC ALL STAR	55 >AVG REGULAR

YEAR	TEAM	LVL	AGE	PA	R	2B	3B	HR	RBI	BB	SO	SB	CS	AVG/OBP/SLG	TAv	BABIP	BRR	FRAA	WARP
2014	PAW	AAA	22	71	6	3	1	1	9	2	15	1	0	.261/.282/.377	.213	.321	0.1	C(16): 0.2	0.0
2014	PME	AA	22	380	47	23	3	12	55	29	65	7	1	.300/.353/.487	.303	.337	2.2	C(81): 0.7	4.2
2015	BOS	MLB	23	250	21	12	2	3	24	14	57	2	1	.242/.285/.351	.240	.302	-0.1	C 0	0.5
2016	BOS	MLB	24	405	39	19	2	5	35	28	96	3	1	.232/.286/.330	.232	.295	-0.3	C 1	0.3

Breakout: 7%   Improve: 19%   Collapse: 2%   Attrition: 18%   MLB: 27%   Upside: 55   *Comparables: Jonathan Lucroy, Austin Romine, Miguel Montero*

Drafted/Acquired: 1st round, 2011 draft, V Sue Cleveland HS (Rio Rancho, NM)

Previous Ranking: #6 (Org), #73 (Top 101)

What Happened in 2014: The backstop took a big step forward both offensively and defensively at Double-A, where he showed the ability to create a lot of solid contact and heavily control the running game, and he now sits one step from The Show.

Strengths: Athletic; fast-twitch muscle; good present strength; room to add a bit more; smooth, fluid stroke from both sides of the plate; loose hands; excellent bat control; works to keep weight back when unfolding; drives ball well into both gaps, especially left-handed; creates carry and loft right-handed; learning how to muscle up and tap into power as lefty; willing to use the whole field; quick feet; fires well out of crouch; excellent reflexes; firm glove hand; can pop 1.87-1.90 consistently; excellent makeup; high baseball IQ; driven to succeed.

Weaknesses: Body needs continued development to handle rigors of position and avoid nagging injuries; can be slow with release at times; inconsistent staying down when trying to smother offerings; ball control must improve to reach full defensive potential; left-handed swing a bit flat; can struggle to drop head and turn on offerings middle-in; will yank head of bat and roll over; backside can cave against spin away when hitting lefty; power strictly of the pull-side variety from both sides of plate; likely to lose some speed and athleticism into late-twenties due to demands of position.

Risk Factor/Injury History: Low risk; 18 games in Triple-A; bat playing down due to physical demands of position.

Bret Sayre's Fantasy Take: There's always risk investing in catching prospects in dynasty leagues, but Swihart's proximity, floor with the bat, and strong makeup help mitigate that as much as it's possible. The potential for a .280-hitting backstop with 15 homers is certainly worth the risk, though, and is what makes Swihart a top-three fantasy catching prospect.

The Year Ahead: The theme for the then-22-year-old in 2014, from both sources and our looks throughout the year, was "improvement." Swihart took some strong steps forward, really putting his skills together while also proving he was more than up to the difficult jump into the Eastern League. The backstop does a bit of everything and offers a well-rounded package that can impact both sides of the ball. His hit tool has continued to show tangible progress, as the loose hands and evolution of his approach have helped create hard contact to all fields and allowed him to tap into his power. Peak seasons for Swihart can very well approach .280s averages with 35ish doubles and 15-plus home runs. Along with the bat, the defense has also moved forward, with a steady game behind the dish highlighted by strong receiving skills and an arm that can control the running game. This is a player who can potentially hit as high as the two-hole in a contending team's lineup, while providing above-average defense and slotting in as a core contributor for a handful of seasons. There is risk that the bat plays down some due to the physical demands and nature of the position, but Swihart's makeup offers strong clues that adjustments and continued growth will be there as he builds major-league experience. This season will allow the switch-hitter to put the finishing touches on his minor-league career in Triple-A, with a debut likely at some point toward the end of the season.

#17

BP Top
101
Prospects

2. Henry Owens LHP

Born: 7/21/92 **Age:** 22 **Bats:** L **Throws:** L **Height:** 6'6" **Weight:** 205

MLB ETA	CT	FB	CH	CB	SL	OFP	Realistic
2015	–	55	65	55	–	60 NO. 3 STARTER	55 NO. 3/4 STARTER

YEAR	TEAM	LVL	AGE	W	L	SV	G	GS	IP	H	HR	BB	K	BB9	SO9	GB%	BABIP	WHIP	ERA	FIP	FRA	WARP
2014	PAW	AAA	21	3	1	0	6	6	38.0	32	4	12	44	2.8	10.4	44%	.301	1.16	4.03	3.59	4.58	0.1
2014	PME	AA	21	14	4	0	20	20	121.0	89	6	47	126	3.5	9.4	48%	.267	1.12	2.60	3.16	3.84	2.2
2015	BOS	MLB	22	8	7	0	24	24	125.7	113	11	61	132	4.4	9.5	42%	.301	1.39	3.98	4.17	4.32	1.2
2016	BOS	MLB	23	10	10	0	30	30	183.7	161	18	96	188	4.7	9.2	42%	.289	1.40	3.99	4.22	4.33	1.1

Breakout: 0% **Improve:** 0% **Collapse:** 0% **Attrition:** 0% **MLB:** 0% **Upside:** 38   *Comparables: Tommy Hanson, Gerrit Cole, Trevor May*

#46
BP Top 101 Prospects

Drafted/Acquired: 1st round, 2011 draft, Edison HS (Huntington Beach, CA)

Previous Ranking: #5 (Org), #69 (Top 101)

What Happened in 2014: The tall left-hander took the Eastern League by storm, where he missed plenty of barrels and limited hard contact in consistently cruising through opposing lineups, before hitting a bit of a bump after a late-season promotion to Triple-A.

Strengths: Loose, low-energy-expending delivery; easy release; creates good angle on hitters from first-base side of rubber with three-quarters arm slot; deceptive look; fastball jumps on batters; displays downward action and late tail when staying on top; improving ability to spot east/west; turns over change with loose wrist; seamless look to that of heater; quality, deep fading action; will bottom out when thrown glove side; bat-missing ability; confidence to use offering at any point in the count; curveball flashes deep break; will drop in for a strike; improving feel for craft; shows understanding of how to execute craft.

Weaknesses: Fastball can play average at 88-91; lacks explosiveness; command gets loose when reaching back (92-94); will work too elevated and in middle of the plate; mistakes can be masked against lesser hitters; heavily leans on fastball-changeup combo; reluctant at times to utilize curve when in trouble; offering can be too soft and allow hitters to wait back on it; lacks consistent chase look; curve needs push to take pressure off of other two pitches; some concerns on overall command profile; lot of body to control—delivery can drift during stretches.

Risk Factor/Injury History: Low risk; 159 innings in upper levels; emergence of consistent third offering.

Bret Sayre's Fantasy Take: In fantasy leagues, it's a risk to rely on pitchers whose carrying secondary pitch is a change—since it leads to fewer strikeouts—but it's not as big of a deal when the pitcher is left-handed like Owens. He will likely never be more than a pretty good SP3 with strong WHIP contributions and around 160 strikeouts, but the realistic floor is still a usable mixed-league starter—a rare trait in a pitching prospect.

The Year Ahead: Owens has taken considerable strides forward from his early career, when his delivery was fairly crude and often contributed to loose fastball command and inconsistent velocity from outing to outing. The 6-foot-6 left-hander has also shown strong improvement with his pitchability, transitioning in Double-A last year from more of a thrower trying to challenge with his heater in the low minors to a pitcher focusing on spotting up. The changeup is the offering that really shines, as Owens displays a high level of confidence in the pitch, with both the feel and ability to execute, driving it to a plus-to-better weapon at his disposal. Angle consistent to that of his fastball and excellent separation should continue to keep hitters off-balance against the change. The key to reaching the overall potential is how much further the curveball can progress. The 22-year-old flashes comfort with the pitch, but it often plays on the soft side and is typically more of an afterthought than a full-fledged complementary piece. With some further fine-tuning to the overall arsenal in Triple-A this season, the lefty has a good chance to get a look in The Show at some point. It's an arm that should be able to settle in as a third or fourth starter for the long haul, which provides good value for an organization when bolstering its rotation internally.

3. Manuel Margot CF

Born: 9/28/94 **Age:** 20 **Bats:** R **Throws:** R **Height:** 5'11" **Weight:** 170

MLB ETA	Hit	Power	Run	Glove	Arm	OFP	Realistic
Late 2016	55	50	70	60	55	65 1ST DIV/OCC ALL STAR	50 AVG ML PLAYER

YEAR	TEAM	LVL	AGE	PA	R	2B	3B	HR	RBI	BB	SO	SB	CS	AVG/OBP/SLG	TAv	BABIP	BRR	FRAA	WARP
2014	SLM	A+	19	56	4	5	0	2	14	2	5	3	2	.340/.364/.560	.313	.333	0.0	CF(16): -0.1	0.5
2014	GRN	A	19	413	61	20	5	10	45	37	49	39	13	.286/.355/.449	.283	.309	2.8	CF(96): 11.7	4.0
2015	BOS	MLB	20	250	28	10	1	4	21	15	54	13	6	.229/.277/.333	.230	.277	0.8	CF 6, RF 0	0.7
2016	BOS	MLB	21	250	26	11	2	4	24	18	47	15	6	.244/.303/.360	.249	.286	1.6	CF 6, RF 0	1.8

Breakout: 0% **Improve:** 0% **Collapse:** 0% **Attrition:** 0% **MLB:** 0% **Upside:** 57   *Comparables: Cedric Hunter, Aaron Hicks, Fernando Martinez*

Drafted/Acquired: International Free Agent, 2011, Dominican Republic

Previous Ranking: On The Rise

What Happened in 2014: The Dominican center fielder flashed impressive bat-to-ball ability and the legs to impact the game, while showing strong up-the-middle defensive potential while fully emerging onto the scene in his first foray into full-season baseball.

Strengths: Excellent athlete; lean and wiry muscle-type; fluid actions; improving strength; quick stroke; strong hands and wrists; ability to control head of the bat; good separation with hands during stride; attacks the ball; gap-to-gap approach; sneaky power; creates backspin when barreling offerings up; quick first step; strong defensive instincts; anticipates well at the crack of the bat; above-average range; excellent closing speed; takes good routes to the ball; improving arm with physical maturity; speed to impact the game on the bases; mature approach to the game.

Weaknesses: Will lunge at offerings with spin; swing at times comes up underneath the ball; still learning identity as a hitter; strike zone can be on the wide side; gets too aggressive early in the count; presently punches instead of driving to opposite field consistently; swing geared more to line-drive contact; power may ultimately play below average; reads off pitchers need work to fully maximize base-stealing ability; presently relies on raw speed; throws can die on approach to bases; arm not geared for corner.

Risk Factor/Injury History: High risk; yet to reach upper levels; full development of hit tool.

Bret Sayre's Fantasy Take: Despite being a better real-life prospect than fantasy one, Margot brings plenty to get dynasty leaguers excited about. The speed will carry his value, at least initially, but with the potential to hit .270 and slug 15-18 homers at peak, he could provide Brett Gardner-type fantasy value (the 30-steal version, not the 50-steal version) if it all comes together.

The Year Ahead: Margot is the type of player who can bring considerable value to a roster at full potential, with a blend of high contact skills, some pop, speed, and above-average defense at a premium position. The vision is a top-of-the-order table setter who can set the tone and impact the game in multiple ways. The 20-year-old is still a ways off and needs ample seasoning, but should the bat not play all the way, he offers a solid floor due to the strong up-the-middle defensive profile. With that in mind, the overall feel is that things have a good chance to reach the potential role at peak. Margot flashes the loose hands and separation during his stride that lead one to believe that consistent, hard contact against high-quality stuff will show with continued experience. The prospect took a nice step forward last year with that experience starting to build, showing much more comfort and confidence in his skills at the plate. Even if the power ends up playing a bit lower than the on-paper grade, there's still good potential extra-base ability given the gap-to-gap approach and legs to stretch hits. After a brief tour to close out 2014, an assignment in High-A this year will be an opportunity for Margot to prove he possesses the ability to adjust. There's a strong chance that he finishes out the season in the Eastern League, with chatter on his future as an above-average regular likely getting much louder in the process.

4.   Eduardo Rodriguez   LHP

Born: 4/7/93   **Age:** 22   **Bats:** L   **Throws:** L   **Height:** 6'2"   **Weight:** 200

MLB ETA	CT	FB	CH	CB	SL	OFP	Realistic
2015	–	60	55	–	55	55 NO. 3/4 STARTER	50 NO. 4 STARTER

YEAR	TEAM	LVL	AGE	W	L	SV	G	GS	IP	H	HR	BB	K	BB9	SO9	GB%	BABIP	WHIP	ERA	FIP	FRA	WARP
2014	BOW	AA	21	3	7	0	16	16	82.7	90	5	29	69	3.2	7.5	46%	.328	1.44	4.79	3.52	3.61	1.8
2014	PME	AA	21	3	1	0	6	6	37.3	30	1	8	39	1.9	9.4	47%	.299	1.02	0.96	2.42	2.62	1.2
2015	BOS	MLB	22	6	7	0	20	20	103.3	112	9	41	71	3.6	6.2	46%	.310	1.48	4.73	4.62	5.14	0.0
2016	BOS	MLB	23	9	10	0	29	29	180.7	171	16	76	139	3.8	6.9	46%	.286	1.36	4.13	4.31	4.49	0.7

Breakout: 15%   Improve: 26%   Collapse: 5%   Attrition: 23%   MLB: 38%   Upside: 2   *Comparables: David Holmberg, Patrick Corbin, Casey Kelly*

Drafted/Acquired: International Free Agent, 2010, Venezuela

Previous Ranking: #4 (Org- BAL), #61 (Top 101)

What Happened in 2014: An early-season injury slowed down the first half of the year for the then-21-year-old left-hander in Double-A, but he picked up steam midseason and adjusted seamlessly after a deadline deal sent him from Baltimore's to Boston's organization.

Strengths: Easy, repeatable delivery; sturdy build; gets on top of ball; fastball operates 90-93 comfortably with occasional arm-side tail; can reach for more in stretches; capable of throwing downhill; slider flashes tilt and depth; will throw for strikes; potential to miss bats with further tightening; change fades arm side with some sink; effective in lower band of velocity (82-83); can spot entire arsenal around the strike zone.

Weaknesses: Fastball can be flat; will work too elevated with offering and grab a lot of white; command needs work; inconsistent finishing delivery; change can be too firm and lose action in upper-velocity band (85-86); slider gets loose and sweeps; lacks consistent secondary offering batters will chase; stuff can be very bland on nights it plays down.

Risk Factor/Injury History: Low risk; 33 Double-A starts; secondary arsenal growth.

Bret Sayre's Fantasy Take: Shallow mixed leaguers will probably shoot for someone with more upside than the 22-year-old lefty, but those in deeper leagues would be wise to invest here. At best, he's likely a fringe top-50 candidate, but he should be able to throw a lot of innings with respectable ratios—and that's an undervalued trait in 16-team leagues and deeper.

#61
BP Top
101
Prospects

#65
BP Top
101
Prospects

The Year Ahead: Rodriguez overcame early-season struggles and a groin injury—causing him to miss a month—to really close 2014 out strong. When on, the left-hander flashes an above-average three-pitch mix that he displays confidence in, as well as the ability to vary through sequences while spotting around the zone. The stuff is capable of keeping opposing hitters off-balance, thus inducing weak contact and missing bats in key situations. The 22-year-old's strike-throwing ability also plays to his advantage by forcing batters to get aggressive early. However, at present, neither secondary offering is consistently plus, and Rodriguez can really struggle in outings when his stuff is lacking. There's a finer margin of error overall for the pitcher. The potential exists for the command to take a step forward, as the delivery is loose and athletic, a development that bears watching this season in Triple-A, as he showed improvement locking into his delivery to finish out 2014. If the trend continues, Rodriguez can prove to be ready for a legit look as a starter at some point in 2015. This is an arm that likely slots toward the back of a rotation in the long run, but could eat innings and serve as a solid complementary piece.

5.   Rafael Devers   3B

Born: 10/24/96   **Age:** 18   **Bats:** L   **Throws:** R   **Height:** 6'0"   **Weight:** 195

MLB ETA	Hit	Power	Run	Glove	Arm	OFP	Realistic
2019	55	65	–	50	55	65 1ST DIV/OCC ALL STAR	50 AVG ML REGULAR

YEAR	TEAM	LVL	AGE	PA	R	2B	3B	HR	RBI	BB	SO	SB	CS	AVG/OBP/SLG	TAv	BABIP	BRR	FRAA	WARP
2014	DRS	Rk	17	128	26	6	3	3	21	21	20	4	1	.337/.445/.538	.345	.386	0.0		0.0
2014	RSX	Rk	17	174	21	11	2	4	36	14	30	1	0	.312/.374/.484	.270	.363	-0.2	3B(11): 1.9	0.4
2015	BOS	MLB	18	250	17	9	1	3	21	10	75	0	0	.198/.234/.278	.194	.273	-0.4	3B 4	-0.8
2016	BOS	MLB	19	250	25	12	1	5	24	11	67	0	0	.224/.264/.345	.228	.286	-0.5	3B 4	-0.2

Breakout: 0%   Improve: 0%   Collapse: 0%   Attrition: 0%   MLB: 0%   Upside: 9   *Comparables: Josh Vitters, Maikel Franco, Alex Liddi*

Drafted/Acquired: International Free Agent, 2013, Dominican Republic

Previous Ranking: On The Rise

What Happened in 2014: The 18-year-old 2013 international signee quickly assimilated into the professional ranks, where he forced an earlier-than-expected arrival stateside and kept right up by ripping in the Gulf Coast League to the tune of an 858 OPS.

Strengths: Already filling into frame with good present strength; strong lower half; generates plus bat speed; easy, fluid swing from left side; strong hands and forearms; creates postcontact extension and lift; drives the ball with authority to all fields; contact is loud; plus-plus raw; demonstrates the makings of a patient approach; 25-plus home-run potential; arm for left side of infield; shows maturity for age and experience level.

Weaknesses: In the early stages of learning strike zone; will get out in front of and chase stuff with spin; comes up under ball when elevated; swing can get loose; will need time to adjust to better competition; concerns on how body will eventually look; added weight will likely affect mobility and range; below-average speed; footwork can be choppy; needs work gauging angles at hot corner more effectively; may ultimately end up at first base.

Risk Factor/Injury History: Extreme risk; complex-league résumé; 18 years old; large gap between present and future.

Bret Sayre's Fantasy Take: There is going to be no shortage of hype around Devers in dynasty leagues (and if your league is competitive and/or deep, that's likely already started), but despite the need to pump the brakes slightly, he's worth the hype. If the bat does what it's capable of, it won't matter what position he's eligible at, as no one's turning down a .280-hitting first baseman with 25-plus homers.

The Year Ahead: Devers is clearly advanced for his age, as seen by his stateside debut, but it's also important to remember that he's a relative baby when it comes to the developmental journey and present stage of the overall skills. There's a lot to like here, especially with the potential middle-of-the-order power the 18-year-old can grow into. His swing already shows the ability to drive offerings with carry and tap into the lower body strength. The ease with which the third baseman creates bat speed jumps out as well, along with how the swing unfolds to power the ball to all fields. The raw offensive tools point to a bat that can be special if the secondary skills progress with experience. That aspect is what creates the role variability, and it's expected that Devers will need some time to marinate early in his career. The maturity level leads one to believe the prospect will be able to handle what's going to be an aggressive assignment in 2015, regardless of whether it is at short- or full-season. It's very early in the overall process, but by this time next year, there's a strong chance this player is pushing for status closer to the front of this list and emerging as a top power-hitting corner infield prospect in the lower levels of the minors.

#90

BP Top
101
Prospects

6. Michael Chavis   INF

Born: 8/11/95   **Age:** 19   **Bats:** R   **Throws:** R   **Height:** 5'10"   **Weight:** 190

MLB ETA	Hit	Power	Run	Glove	Arm		OFP	Realistic
Late 2018	65	55	–	50	55		60 1ST DIVISION PLAYER	50 AVG ML REGULAR

YEAR	TEAM	LVL	AGE	PA	R	2B	3B	HR	RBI	BB	SO	SB	CS	AVG/OBP/SLG	TAv	BABIP	BRR	FRAA	WARP
2014	RSX	Rk	18	150	21	12	3	1	16	15	38	5	3	.269/.347/.425	.365	.368	-1.4	3B(9): -0.1, SS(4): 0.3	1.0
2015	BOS	MLB	19	250	18	10	1	2	19	12	77	3	2	.198/.239/.271	.194	.279	-0.2	3B -0, SS 0	-1.1
2016	BOS	MLB	20	250	24	12	1	4	23	12	68	3	2	.225/.268/.337	.227	.294	-0.1	3B 0, SS 0	-0.6

Breakout: 0%   **Improve:** 0%   **Collapse:** 0%   **Attrition:** 0%   **MLB:** 0%   **Upside:** 8   *Comparables: Maikel Franco, Josh Vitters, Matt Davidson*

Drafted/Acquired: 1st round, 2014 draft, Sprayberry HS (Marietta, GA)
Previous Ranking: NR

What Happened in 2014: The highly touted prep bat had a monster high school season before getting snagged by Boston 26th overall, and then quickly enrolled in his intro to professional baseball course in the Gulf Coast League.

Strengths: Explosive hands; easy swing; drives bat head through zone; plus bat speed; barrels offerings up with backspin; contact is loud; can put a charge into ball to both gaps; natural power to tap into; good athlete with fluid actions; quick first step; arm for left side of diamond; approaches game with enthusiasm.

Weaknesses: Approach and plate discipline in the infancy stages of development; presently overcommits hands against spin; some moving parts to get load and timing started; can leave him prone to getting under the ball; will have to balance hit and power; either tool can play down in the favor of the other; lacks ideal size; questions on defensive landing place (third or second).

Risk Factor/Injury History: High risk; limited professional experience; big gap between present and future.

Bret Sayre's Fantasy Take: The average will drive Chavis' fantasy value, but he can contribute in all five categories. Having slid to 26th overall in the draft, he may be overlooked in the early second round of dynasty drafts this spring, but he should comfortably be off the board in the 15-20 range.

The Year Ahead: The 19-year-old infielder rightfully drew strong praise all spring for the potential of his hit tool. Chavis flashes impressive bat speed driven by loose, lively hands that allow him to rifle the head of the bat efficiently to the point of contact, resulting in the ball really popping off the barrel. Good hitters typically develop some sort of power in the long run, and if that trend continues, this righty has the potential to develop average power. The more telling clues, along with the application in game action, are likely a few seasons off, but the raw power and ability to backspin offerings point to home-run totals that can eventually approach the upper teens. Though Chavis is a better athlete than his more modest frame would lead on, the body itself doesn't leave much physical projection. On the positive side, it lends strong credence to his sticking on the infield with defensive progression, but doesn't offer any expectations of development into a legit thumper. Reaching his ceiling keys on the hit tool fully playing up, which will be driven by both his approach and pitch selection taking the appropriate strides. An assignment in full-season ball should be Chavis' path in 2015, where the bat has a good chance to show as advanced in the South Atlantic League and push this prospect to greater status in the process.

7. Matt Barnes   RHP

Born: 6/17/90   **Age:** 25   **Bats:** R   **Throws:** R   **Height:** 6'4"   **Weight:** 205

MLB ETA	CT	FB	CH	CB	SL		OFP	Realistic
Debuted in 2014	–	70	50	55	–		55 NO. 3/4 STARTER	50 LATE INN RP (SETUP)

YEAR	TEAM	LVL	AGE	W	L	SV	G	GS	IP	H	HR	BB	K	BB9	SO9	GB%	BABIP	WHIP	ERA	FIP	FRA	WARP
2014	BOS	MLB	24	0	0	0	5	0	9.0	11	1	2	8	2.0	8.0	34%	.357	1.44	4.00	3.49	2.72	0.2
2014	PAW	AAA	24	8	9	0	23	22	127.7	119	8	46	103	3.2	7.3	44%	.294	1.29	3.95	3.71	4.45	1.0
2015	BOS	MLB	25	7	7	0	22	22	111.0	114	10	44	100	3.6	8.1	45%	.315	1.42	4.31	4.22	4.68	0.6
2016	BOS	MLB	26	5	4	0	63	9	110.3	119	12	41	97	3.3	7.9	45%	.320	1.46	4.79	4.20	5.20	-0.3

Breakout: 24%   **Improve:** 43%   **Collapse:** 13%   **Attrition:** 36%   **MLB:** 65%   **Upside:** 6   *Comparables: Brad Peacock, Brad Mills, Scott Barnes*

Drafted/Acquired: 1st round, 2011 draft, University of Connecticut (Storrs, CT)
Previous Ranking: #4 (Org), #64 (Top 101)

What Happened in 2014: The then-24-year-old was on the inconsistent side overall in Triple-A, but found a groove with his heavy fastball down the stretch, missing more bats and churning through lineups deeper into outings, before a brief call to the bigs to finish off the year.

Strengths: Sturdy frame; body to withstand the rigors of the long season; easy delivery; strong arm; fastball works 92-95 consistently; shows hard arm-side run and heavy action; can reach back for more in bursts (96-97); heater difficult to square up in lower tier of zone; can spot east/west with offering; curveball flashes deep two-plane break; shows power in high-70s; capable of turning over changeup with arm-side fade; action has improved since early pro career.

Weaknesses: Can drift with landing of delivery; will open early, leading to inconsistent command and lack of finish; tends to wrap wrist with curve; offering gets loose and slurvy; fastball flattens out above middle of the thighs; needs to be selective when elevating; works a bit too much in middle of the plate; change can be on the firm side (86-87); loses fading action; more of a contact-inducing pitch than bat-misser.

Risk Factor/Injury History: Low risk; achieved majors; curveball consistency.

Bret Sayre's Fantasy Take: For a pair of reasons, Barnes, with his volatility, is still a better use of a roster spot in a fantasy league than a back-end starter. First, if he makes it as a starter, he'll put up better numbers, including more strikeouts. Second, if he doesn't, he has high-leverage potential in the bullpen—in fact, Barnes has more upside right now as a potential closer than as a potential starter.

The Year Ahead: Barnes has been something of an enigma the past couple of seasons. His overall stuff has often looked stuck in neutral, but has shown flashes of being able to dominate in stretches, leading to hopes that a breakthrough is around the corner. The right-hander's fastball is a legit weapon, with strong arm-side run and late life to complement velocity that can sit 94-95 deep into outings. The 25-year-old will run into trouble when he works up in the zone with too much frequency, which gets exacerbated when his delivery falls out of whack. When on, Barnes' curve can play as an above-average offering and flash deep, late break to miss bats. It pairs well with an average changeup that keeps hitters out in front. Consistency has been his Achilles' heel, though, especially for the curve and command of the entire arsenal. There's still promise to iron out some of the kinks and emerge as a fringe third-to-fourth starter type, but the sounds of a future relief role in the long run have grown louder. There's a good chance that he sticks around for an extended major-league career, especially given the effectiveness of the fastball. At the very least, he'll get a chance to prove he can start at the highest level during 2015. If the stretch to close out 2014 is more reality than tease, Barnes very well might stick in the rotation for a handful of seasons.

8.   Garin Cecchini   3B/OF

Born: 4/20/91   **Age:** 24   **Bats:** L   **Throws:** R   **Height:** 6'3"   **Weight:** 220

MLB ETA	Hit	Power	Run	Glove	Arm		OFP	Realistic
Debuted in 2014	60	50	–	50	55		55 >AVG REGULAR	50 AVG ML REGULAR

YEAR	TEAM	LVL	AGE	PA	R	2B	3B	HR	RBI	BB	SO	SB	CS	AVG/OBP/SLG	TAv	BABIP	BRR	FRAA	WARP
2014	BOS	MLB	23	36	6	3	0	1	4	3	11	0	0	.258/.361/.452	.313	.368	-0.5	3B(9): -0.5	0.3
2014	PAW	AAA	23	458	52	21	1	7	57	44	99	11	1	.263/.341/.371	.257	.331	2.0	3B(84): -3.4, LF(26): -0.0	1.0
2015	BOS	MLB	24	250	25	13	1	2	22	25	58	6	1	.251/.333/.345	.259	.327	0.4	3B -2, LF 0	0.4
2016	BOS	MLB	25	509	60	26	2	9	51	52	133	12	2	.252/.337/.381	.270	.336	1.0	3B -6	0.5

Breakout: 2%   Improve: 10%   Collapse: 9%   Attrition: 16%   MLB: 30%   Upside: 15   *Comparables: Zach Lutz, James Darnell, Eric Campbell*

Drafted/Acquired: 4th round, 2010 draft, Alfred M. Barbe HS (Lake Charles, LA)

Previous Ranking: #4 (Org), #51 (Top 101)

What Happened in 2014: The smooth swinging left-handed hitter took a bit of a step back in Triple-A, but showed more comfort later in the year, including during a brief call to The Show to close out the year.

Strengths: Physically maturing frame; improving strength; body to withstand the rigors of season; loose hands; capable of staying inside of ball well; mechanically sound swing; all-fields approach; drives ball well into opposite field gap; not afraid to work deep into counts; learning how to muscle up; raw strength and power to tap into; has made defensive strides; improving hands; arm for left side of the diamond; excellent work ethic; strong appetite for the game.

Weaknesses: Actions can be stiff and robotic at third; footwork needs work; reactions can lag and limit range; runs into ruts of too much top hand in swing; inconsistent backspin; can chop or roll over, especially stuff with spin; power may ultimately play at fringe-average; pressure on bat to perform consistently with move to corner outfield spot; backside caves often against arm-side pitching.

Risk Factor/Injury History: Low risk; achieved major leagues; questions on ultimate defensive home.

Bret Sayre's Fantasy Take: Despite the rough 2014, there's still plenty of reason to own Cecchini in dynasty leagues. And while the Hanley Ramirez and Pablo Sandoval signings block him through and through in Boston, he can still be a .280 hitter with 15-plus homers and strong on-base skills. He's a strong buy-low target in deeper leagues right now.

The Year Ahead: Cecchini is a prospect who draws a considerable range of views. On one hand, there's a strong control of the strike zone and solid bat-to-ball ability that bode well for producing contact. On the other hand, the lack of consistent power and defensive limitations cast some doubts as to what the overall profile is going to look like in the long run. For those who have seen the 24-year-old over the course of his pro career, there is little doubt of his consistent development, work ethic, and passion. The question is where the leveling point resides. A big boost for Cecchini offensively would be tangible progression with his power. The raw strength is there, but at times the swing is inconsistent in producing loft and has some hooking nature, leading to more topspin than backspin when he tries to muscle up. The final profile might ultimately be a doubles hitter with occasional over-the-fence pop, which puts even more focus on the defensive home. It's never going to be overly flashy or pictur-esque at the hot corner, but there's room for enough growth to make things work. Ultimately, Cecchini's future is likely that of an average regular who can have things play up higher for a few career-type seasons at peak. An extended look can come as early as 2015, depending on the organization's needs, but a return to Triple-A is likely in the cards.

9. Brian Johnson   LHP

Born: 12/7/90   **Age:** 24   **Bats:** L   **Throws:** L   **Height:** 6'3"   **Weight:** 225

MLB ETA		CT		FB		CH		CB		SL		OFP		Realistic
2015		–		**55**		**50**		**55**		–		**50** NO. 4 STARTER		**50** NO. 5 STARTER/MID RP

YEAR	TEAM	LVL	AGE	W	L	SV	G	GS	IP	H	HR	BB	K	BB9	SO9	GB%	BABIP	WHIP	ERA	FIP	FRA	WARP
2014	PME	AA	23	10	2	0	20	20	118.0	78	6	32	99	2.4	7.6	48%	.229	0.93	1.75	3.15	3.69	2.1
2014	SLM	A+	23	3	1	0	5	5	25.7	23	0	7	33	2.5	11.6	41%	.333	1.17	3.86	1.76	2.52	1.0
2015	BOS	MLB	24	7	6	0	21	21	105.0	100	9	43	84	3.7	7.2	46%	.291	1.36	4.00	4.39	4.34	1.0
2016	BOS	MLB	25	10	9	0	31	31	194.3	182	15	68	163	3.1	7.6	46%	.293	1.28	3.66	3.78	3.98	2.0

Breakout: 15%   **Improve:** 32%   **Collapse:** 13%   **Attrition:** 28%   **MLB:** 50%   **Upside:** 30   *Comparables: Adam Warren, Lance Lynn, Anthony Ranaudo*

Drafted/Acquired: 1st round, 2012 draft, University of Florida (Gainesville, FL)
Previous Ranking: NR

What Happened in 2014: The former first-round pick out of the University of Florida showed what he can do when healthy for the entire season, effectively churning through lineups at Double-A while logging a robust 143 2/3 innings for the year.

Strengths: Strong body; proportionately filled out; sturdy lower half; smooth, repeatable delivery; stays balanced; fastball works 89-92, with some downward movement and late tail; executes offering well; spots in lower tier and on corners frequently; plus command; good shape to curve in upper-velocity band (76-77); flashes late break with bite; has feel for change; separates well at 79-81; arm-side fading action; can spot well; strong pitch-ability and command profile; demonstrates excellent knowledge of craft; high baseball IQ.

Weaknesses: Fastball can be on the pedestrian side; will flatten out when elevated; body at times restricts delivery and slows down arm; can cast curve; on the soft and loopy side in lower-velocity band (73-74); hitters have easier time waiting back on it; quality of action with changeup goes in and out; lacks true knockout offering; walks fine line against high-caliber hitters.

Risk Factor/Injury History: Low risk; 20 starts at Double-A; mature arsenal.

Bret Sayre's Fantasy Take: Johnson will be a major-league starter, but he's not someone you're going to want to roster in mixed leagues, outside of incredible desperation. It's possible that he'll run into stretches of fantasy usefulness, à la Joe Saunders, but he's the last guy on this list I'd own for fantasy, and it's not that close.

The Year Ahead: Johnson's ceiling is on the more limited side and there isn't a ton of growth left in the stuff, but the left-hander knows how to go about his craft and shows the type of cerebral approach to the game that bodes well for maximizing every ounce of his talent. The 24-year-old is adept at spotting his fastball on the corners and in the lower tier of the strike zone, where opposing batters tend to get on top of the offering due to the downward action. He becomes very hittable when his fastball is operating above the thighs, which bears watching in Triple-A and beyond. Despite lacking a consistent bat-missing secondary piece, Johnson utilizes both his curveball and changeup to his advantage by mixing them in at any point in sequences, along with being able to throw each easily for strikes. His chances of sticking in the rotation over the long haul hinge on the command continuing to stay at current levels. Any regression or inability to maintain it in long stretch-es likely pushes him to the bullpen, but the belief is that the feel for and approach to the game will allow the overall profile to play up. Look for Johnson to get a taste of what it takes to navigate through major-league lineups before summer's end.

10. Michael Kopech   RHP

Born: 4/30/96   **Age:** 19   **Bats:** R   **Throws:** R   **Height:** 6'3"   **Weight:** 195

MLB ETA		CT		FB		CH		CB		SL		OFP		Realistic
Late 2018		–		**70**		**55**		**60**		–		**65** NO. 2/3 STARTER		**50** LATE INN RP (SETUP)

YEAR	TEAM	LVL	AGE	W	L	SV	G	GS	IP	H	HR	BB	K	BB9	SO9	GB%	BABIP	WHIP	ERA	FIP	FRA	WARP
2014	RSX	Rk	18	0	1	0	8	8	13.7	11	0	9	16	5.9	10.5	45%	.300	1.46	4.61	3.14	3.96	0.2
2015	BOS	MLB	19	2	3	0	7	7	31.0	38	4	21	16	6.1	4.6	45%	.317	1.89	6.51	6.56	7.08	-0.5
2016	BOS	MLB	20	4	7	0	28	28	173.0	184	16	88	110	4.6	5.7	45%	.299	1.57	5.10	4.94	5.54	-1.3

Breakout: 0%   **Improve:** 0%   **Collapse:** 0%   **Attrition:** 0%   **MLB:** 0%   **Upside:** 1   *Comparables: Mike Foltynewicz, Edwin Escobar, Jenrry Mejia*

Drafted/Acquired: 1st round, 2014 draft, Mount Pleasant HS (Mount Pleasant, TX)
Previous Ranking: NR

What Happened in 2014: The athletic right-hander absolutely dominated the high school competition in Texas before being selected 33rd overall, and then got a brief taste of professional ball down in Florida.

Strengths: Very athletic; room to add more strength and muscle onto frame; elite arm strength; fastball comfortably sits 93-95; can reach for more (98); heater shows late arm-side run in low-90s; explosive offering in mid-90s; throws secondary stuff with loose wrist; curve flashes teeth and depth; power element to pitch; can turn over change; throws with consistent arm action; flashes late arm-side fade; power-arm potential.

Weaknesses: Jerk and timing to his mechanics; some smoothing out is necessary; arm can get late into slot; leads to inconsistent control; footwork drifts on landing, leading to early opening; curve gets soft and loopy; will wrap wrist; in the early stages of refining changeup; learning how to consistently grip and bury in back of hand; will slow body down when delivering; overall package is on the raw side.

Risk Factor/Injury History: Extreme risk; limited pro experience; 19 years old; delivery improvements needed.

Bret Sayre's Fantasy Take: Kopech has the upside to warrant the complex-league arm fishing that's too often a bad investment. He should be taken within the first 30 picks in dynasty drafts this year, and his fastball/curve combo has the potential for big strikeout numbers in the majors. Plus, he's a Texan.

The Year Ahead: When gazing off into the distant horizon with this arm, it's hard not to get overly excited about what the raw talent could round into. Kopech possesses the arm strength and frame that seem to be prerequisites when discussing prototypical power pitchers. The heater explodes out of his hand, showing both arm-side life and hop. It's an offering that can eventually be downright nasty on opposing hitters. Both the curveball and changeup show the potential to be above-average or better pitches, with an element of ease when delivered and strong clues that each can eventually be very crisp. The short-term plan is all but assured to be focused on ironing out the right-hander's delivery, which likely means the stuff plays down some in the near term as he gets comfortable with inevitable changes. Gradual improvement with the command and control of the arsenal early on will be a good sign that things are beginning to take. There's a big gap between the present and future, along with a lot of variability in the future projection. It's important to be mindful that this isn't going to be a rapid process and the risk is high, but 2015 is the start of the journey and by the end of the season he could gain good developmental traction.

Notable Omission

OF Rusney Castillo: Despite some brief minor-league time prior to a call-up at the end of last season, Castillo falls into the category of players that we've traditionally decided to omit, due to the straight-to-majors appearance and the bypass of the developmental process. However, the 27-year-old Cuban would rank third in this system had he been eligible under our standard. He has a chance to attain legit first-division status once he gets back up to speed, after having considerable time off from baseball prior to signing with Boston. The expectation is that Castillo will break camp in 2015 as a member of the 25-man roster, where he has a strong shot at manning the outfield regularly and flashing a power and speed combination that can carry him as a contributing member of the lineup on a daily basis.

Prospects on the Rise

1. 2B Wendell Rijo: There's a case for the Dominican second baseman to be included in this top 10 after he more than held his own as an 18-year-old in the South Atlantic League, generating good reports on the progress of the overall game. But the gap between the present and future is still rather large. Despite some moving parts in his prepitch setup, Rijo shows bat speed and innate bat-to-ball ability, with the hit tool capable of playing to above-average down the line. The power projects as below average, but he can drive offerings into both gaps, which when combined with his plus wheels can lead to solid extra-base output. The plate discipline and pitch selection, and a commitment to defensive fundamentals, are what need the most overall work in the game. Rijo is a player who's going to be considerably age-advanced, with a step up into High-A this season likely a big challenge. But if the signs are there that he's polishing up, he's a definite top-10 prospect this time next season.

2. SS Javier Guerra: The 19-year-old drew strong reviews for his defensive potential in his stateside debut last season. Guerra is loose and agile at short, with smooth actions, plus range, and a plus-to-better arm. The instincts and reads off the bat are also there. The 2012 international signee has the makings of a defender who can impact the game in the field, with the glove alone possibly carrying him all the way up. He flashes solid-average or better bat speed and the ability to keep his hands inside the ball. Presently, the approach needs a lot of toning down for the bat to keep moving, and the 5-foot-11 Panamanian could stand to further fill into the frame to enhance his overall game. It's a long-lead player who will require offensive marinating, but a step in the right direction with the bat and signs of more strength in 2015 will push him up quickly.

3. OF Nick Longhi: The 19-year-old outfielder was inked to a mid-six-figure bonus as a 30th-round selection a year ago, and was starting to show the makings of a solid first year in short-season ball before a thumb injury curtailed things. Longhi is already well filled out for his age, with a strong upper body and solid trunk that lead to plus-to-better raw power. The stroke already generates solid postcontact extension and loft, which bodes well for the game power beginning to manifest over the next season or two. There are some concerns about the nature of his swing, mainly in regards to the length and present path of his hands, which puts some strain on how well the contact can translate in higher levels. The defense isn't going to be a carrying tool as the likely destination is left field, but this is a right-handed, potential power bat that can emerge and rise within the system as early as next offseason.

FROM THE FIELD

Blake Swihart

Team: Boston Red Sox

Evaluator: Chris Mellen

Dates seen: April 10; May 8, 24, and 26; and July 19, 2014

Affiliate: Portland Sea Dogs (Double-A, Red Sox)

Physical/health: Medium frame, with a little bit more room to fill into; lean muscle; well-defined forearms; athletic; takes care of himself; a bit small in the legs for position; needs to continue to focus on training to limit nagging injuries; demands of position will take toll on body and athleticism.

Makeup: Elite; driven to succeed; constantly working when on the field; engages with teammates well; plays the game with passion; shows ability to adjust; takes the highs with the lows—has a good perspective on the game.

MLB ETA	Risk factor	OFP	Realistic role
2015	Low	60	55; major-league regular

Tool	Future grade	Report
Hit	60	Smooth, fluid swing from both sides of the plate; loose hands, especially left-handed; shows ability to adjust hands to stay inside of the ball; goes up the middle and the other way with authority left-handed; needs some work improving fluidity when dropping head of the bat on the ball; can yank head of the bat and roll over; more of a pull hitter from the right side; patient and methodical in the box; willing to work counts/take strikes; solid pitch recognition—does cave some against breaking stuff away left-handed; excellent bat control; high contact potential, with chance to hit .290s in peak.
Power	55	60 raw power—more power from right side than left side; leverage in swing right-handed; knows how to lift ball and create carry as a righty; bit more flat swing as a lefty, but showed ability to muscle up over the course of looks; bat control enables hitter to take some chances; mostly pull-side power from both sides of the plate; sweet spot for plugging opposite field gap as a lefty; 35-40 doubles potential; home park will have impact on home-run totals; see 15 or so home runs annually during peak.
Baserunning/ speed	40	4.42-4.58 down the line left-handed; slower out of box, but presently accelerates well; makes the turn at first fluidly; capable of stretching a hit or taking an extra base; smart on the bases—always see being a heady runner; will lose some speed into late twenties; will be area of game with least impact.
Glove	55	Firm glove when receiving; quick feet; fires quickly; above-average range behind the dish; excellent reflexes—reacts well to changes in the ball; works to smother pitches in the dirt; inconsistent staying down at times, however; will get big and front the ball; next step to reach defensive potential is to further polish ball control skills; leader out on the field; handles rhythm of the game well; learning the finer points of the position—so far has shown to be up to the transition.
Arm	65	Plus-to-better arm strength; 1.86-1.97 pop times to second base on stolen-base attempts; can be a little slow with release; pounces out of crouch with very quick feet; above-average accuracy; throws on a line and down into runner for the tag; with continued work smoothing out release has potential to highly impact an opponent's running game.

Overall: Definition of a baseball player; does a bit of everything well; high chance to maximize every ounce of talent due to makeup; see a first-division regular here; can hit as high as the two-hole in a deep lineup; type of bat control and contact ability to approach .300 in the majors; see .280-.295, with 35-40 doubles and 15-17 home runs as peak season potential; add in defense at a premium position, and this is a core contributor on a contender.

Factors on the Farm

Prospects likely to contribute at the major-league level in 2015

1. SS Deven Marrero: The former Arizona State standout has steadily risen up the ranks since signing and brings strong defense to the diamond. Marrero flashes a soft glove at shortstop, with a quick first step and the ability to range well to both sides. The 24-year-old controls his body well when making off-balance plays, while also possessing plenty of arm for the position. It's easy-plus defense. Depending on a need within the middle infield over the course of the season, the glove alone gives the prospect a leg up at contributing. The light nature of the bat does raise questions as to whether the profile is more of a bench type than consistent regular. Despite quick hands and an efficient swing, the contact isn't overly loud and the approach is inconsistent. The clues point to more of a fringe-average hitter, but when factoring in the defense it's a player who can keep a spot on a roster for a good stretch of seasons.

2. LHP Edwin Escobar: Acquired in the deal that sent Jake Peavy to San Francisco, the left-hander will look for more consistency in Triple-A during 2015 to start regaining traction. The Venezuelan features a three-pitch mix highlighted by a low-90s fastball and changeup with late, fading action. Escobar also typically finishes his delivery well, which enables him to effectively pound the strike zone. The heater does play down in stretches, where the velocity can get light and leaves it prone to hard contact. The arm's breaking ball also remains inconsistent where it can get slurvy over showing true curveball action. There's room for growth here for the 23-year-old, especially if the breaking ball can tighten a bit further. It's a likely back-end starter or reliever, who can get a shot in either role this season with a good showing in the International League.

CHICAGO CUBS

1. Addison Russell   SS

Born: 1/23/94   **Age:** 21   **Bats:** R   **Throws:** R   **Height:** 6'0"   **Weight:** 195

MLB ETA	Hit	Power	Run	Glove	Arm		OFP	Realistic
2015	**60**	**60**	**50**	**55**	**60**		**70** ALL STAR	**60** 1ST DIVISION PLAYER

YEAR	TEAM	LVL	AGE	PA	R	2B	3B	HR	RBI	BB	SO	SB	CS	AVG/OBP/SLG	TAv	BABIP	BRR	FRAA	WARP
2014	MID	AA	20	57	7	3	1	1	8	8	8	3	2	.333/.439/.500	.293	.385	-0.3	SS(11): -1.1	0.3
2014	TEN	AA	20	205	32	11	0	12	36	9	35	2	2	.294/.332/.536	.309	.306	0.2	SS(47): 4.6	2.6
2014	STO	A+	20	18	0	0	0	0	1	2	6	1	0	.188/.278/.188	.168	.300	-0.1	SS(4): 0.3	-0.1
2015	CHN	MLB	21	250	30	11	2	7	25	17	66	5	2	.240/.299/.388	.262	.304	0.2	SS -0	1.1
2016	CHN	MLB	22	250	29	11	2	7	28	19	61	5	2	.246/.310/.394	.266	.307	0.4	SS -1	2.2

Breakout: 4%   **Improve:** 14%   **Collapse:** 7%   **Attrition:** 11%   **MLB:** 35%   **Upside:** 71   *Comparables: Xander Bogaerts, B.J. Upton, Reid Brignac*

#2
BP Top 101 Prospects

Drafted/Acquired: 1st round, 2011 draft, Pace HS (Pace, FL)

Previous Ranking: #1 (Org - OAK), #7 (Top 101)

What Happened in 2014: After losing April and May to a torn hamstring, Russell spent the bulk of his age-20 season at Double-A between Midland and Tennessee, where he continued to shine on both sides of the ball while surrounded by players several years his senior.

Strengths: Impact potential with the stick; strong hands and barrel control; good bat speed; improved approach; should grow into high-contact MLB bat that will hit for average and power; solid actions at short; good hands with left-side arm; solid run paired with baserunning acumen; clocks plus times out of the box and should settle in as average run at maturity.

Weaknesses: Still working to slow down game in the field; setup and footwork can get loose, particularly at the margins, leading to drift in throws; can slip into overly aggressive approach at plate.

Risk Factor/Injury History: Low; advanced skill set and feel; success as a 20-year-old in Double-A; missed two months early in 2014 season due to hamstring tear, but no long-term concerns.

Bret Sayre's Fantasy Take: Despite topping this list, Russell isn't number one fantasywise in this system, but he's still a slam-dunk top-10 fantasy prospect, and moving from Oakland to Chicago only helps his future value. Russell could be a .280-plus hitting shortstop with 20-25 homers and double-digit steals in his prime—which could make him a top-three option at the position—but the presence of Starlin Castro will slow his arrival. For now.

The Year Ahead: Russell is close to major-league ready and possesses the skill set, makeup, and natural ability to make an immediate impact as soon as he is called upon. The profile is an elite blend of offensive upside, defensive stability at a high-worth position, athleticism, and strength, the aggregate of which could produce a perennial all-star capable of impacting the game in all facets. Not only might this be the best collection of tools, upside, and probability from a talented crop of minor-league shortstops, but there's a case for top prospect in the game. He should debut in Chicago in 2015 and it won't be long before Russell surpasses the "L" stop as the best known Addison in Wrigleyville.

2. Kris Bryant   3B

Born: 1/4/92   **Age:** 23   **Bats:** R   **Throws:** R   **Height:** 6'5"   **Weight:** 215

MLB ETA	Hit	Power	Run	Glove	Arm		OFP	Realistic
2015	**55**	**70**	**–**	**50**	**65**		**70** ALL STAR	**60** 1ST DIVISION PLAYER

YEAR	TEAM	LVL	AGE	PA	R	2B	3B	HR	RBI	BB	SO	SB	CS	AVG/OBP/SLG	TAv	BABIP	BRR	FRAA	WARP
2014	IOW	AAA	22	297	57	14	1	21	52	43	85	7	2	.295/.418/.619	.358	.367	-2.2	3B(67): 5.3	4.4
2014	TEN	AA	22	297	61	20	0	22	58	43	77	8	2	.355/.458/.702	.405	.440	0.1	3B(62): 1.5	6.0
2015	CHN	MLB	23	250	37	10	0	14	41	27	79	4	1	.261/.351/.514	.321	.336	0.0	3B 4	2.5
2016	CHN	MLB	24	627	96	27	1	32	97	74	195	10	3	.264/.363/.499	.315	.349	0.1	3B 8	4.1

Breakout: 1%   **Improve:** 34%   **Collapse:** 2%   **Attrition:** 13%   **MLB:** 73%   **Upside:** 275   *Comparables: Giancarlo Stanton, Chris Carter, Chris Davis*

#5
BP Top 101 Prospects

Drafted/Acquired: 1st round, 2013 draft, University of San Diego (San Diego, CA)

Previous Ranking: #2 (Org), #17 (Top 101)

What Happened in 2014: A Shermanesque march through the Southern League and equally impactful stint with the Triple-A Iowa Cubs left Bryant knocking on the door at Wrigley as the 2014 season drew to a close.

Strengths: Elite raw power; big leverage and big boy present strength; ability to produce regular hard contact;

good plate coverage allowing for wide kill zone on mistake pitches; borderline double-plus arm; solid athleticism and coordination for a big man; strong grades for makeup.

Weaknesses: Long levers produce holes in swing that could be attacked by major-league arms; limited swing plane/pitch plane overlap narrows contact margin; some issues with velocity on inner half; capable at third base but may lack lower-half agility to excel; run could settle a tick below average at maturity.

Risk Factor/Injury History: Low risk; success at all minor-league levels.

Bret Sayre's Fantasy Take: The argument is there to make Bryant the top fantasy prospect in all of baseball, as only Byron Buxton has much of a case to challenge him. Whether he ends up at third base or in the outfield shouldn't matter to fantasy owners if he comes anywhere close to his offensive potential, which is someone who can hit 35-plus bombs a year and drive in 100-plus runs, while still helping your batting average (slightly).

The Year Ahead: Through his minor-league career, which totals just a shade over a full major-league season's worth of plate appearances, Bryant has posted pornographic numbers at the plate, including a slash line of .327/.428/.666 while averaging nearly a home run every three games. He's ready to bring his act to The Show, where he should eventually settle in as a fixture in the middle of the Cubs lineup. This season could be choppy at times due to the potential for major-league arms to exploit shortcomings in a swing. But the approach, work ethic, and IQ should aid Bryant in making his adjustments, and the raw power will be a legit threat from day one. Depending on the organization's needs, Bryant could remain at third or transition out to right field, where his arm and athleticism could make him a solid defender. Either way, he will join Russell as the foundation of a talented, young Cubs lineup for years to come, with 2015 likely to serve as the coming-out party.

3. Jorge Soler   RF

Born: 2/25/92   **Age:** 23   **Bats:** R   **Throws:** R   **Height:** 6'4"   **Weight:** 215

MLB ETA	Hit	Power	Run	Glove	Arm		OFP	Realistic
Debuted in 2014	50	70	–	50	65		65 1ST DIV/ALL STAR	55 >AVG ML PLAYER

YEAR	TEAM	LVL	AGE	PA	R	2B	3B	HR	RBI	BB	SO	SB	CS	AVG/OBP/SLG	TAv	BABIP	BRR	FRAA	WARP
2014	CHN	MLB	22	97	11	8	1	5	20	6	24	1	0	.292/.330/.573	.325	.339	-0.2	RF(24): -0.8	0.6
2014	IOW	AAA	22	127	22	11	1	8	29	17	26	0	1	.282/.378/.618	.320	.303	-0.1	RF(27): 1.3	1.1
2014	TEN	AA	22	79	13	9	1	6	22	12	15	0	0	.415/.494/.862	.461	.457	-0.3	RF(16): -1.3	1.6
2014	CUB	Rk	22	30	7	3	0	1	6	4	7	0	0	.400/.500/.640	.415	.529	-0.6	RF(6): -0.5	0.4
2015	CHN	MLB	23	250	29	13	1	10	35	19	57	2	1	.258/.316/.457	.287	.299	-0.2	RF -2	0.9
2016	CHN	MLB	24	616	78	33	3	23	82	47	138	4	1	.257/.315/.450	.281	.299	-0.6	RF -4	1.9

Breakout: 2%   **Improve:** 33%   **Collapse:** 5%   **Attrition:** 13%   **MLB:** 69%   **Upside:** 112   *Comparables: Wil Myers, Wladimir Balentien, Domonic Brown*

Drafted/Acquired: International Free Agent, 2012, Cuba

Previous Ranking: #4 (Org), #45 (Top 101)

What Happened in 2014: Injuries continued to plague Soler through the first half of the season, but once healthy the Cuban slugger torched Double- and Triple-A arms over 54 games before finishing 2014 with a solid 24-game stint with the Cubs.

Strengths: Impact power potential; leveraged swing; punishes middle-in; good bat speed and foundation for solid hit; right-field profile with easy-plus arm and adequate feel/reads; natural strength and physicality.

Weaknesses: Hit tool could limit playable power; in limited exposure has struggled to adjust to spin, particularly away; lacks significant pro reps, experience; failed to adjust to major-league arms as holes in approach were exploited; tight musculature with questions about durability; effort concerns have lessened but linger.

Risk Factor/Injury History: Moderate; lacks significant pro reps, experience; injury issues over past two seasons; long-term durability questions.

Bret Sayre's Fantasy Take: The time continues to be at hand for Soler, who is likely to patrol right field for the Cubs on Opening Day. Fantasy owners saw both the good and the bad in his brief 2014 debut, but in the long term it's a strong Rotisserie profile as even his RBI totals should be helped by his aggressiveness. In fact, the overall production could look like that of fellow Cuban defector Yoenis Cespedes.

The Year Ahead: After a solid but checkered September showing, Soler should be ready to step in full time for the Cubbies on Opening Day. The upside is a true middle-of-the-order masher, but to reach those heights Soler will need to prove capable of adjusting to major-league arms with a book and a game plan. Even if the hit tool never fully materializes, Soler could prove a dangerous five- or six-hole bat capable of punishing mistakes. The Cubs will continue to work with him on varying his workout regimen to help increase flexibility and hopefully avoid the strains and muscle tears that have limited his availability over the past two summers. With limited value in the field and on the bases, much will be riding on the progress Soler makes in 2015 tightening his game at the plate.

#19
BP Top
101
Prospects

4. Albert Almora   CF

Born: 4/16/94   **Age:** 21   **Bats:** R   **Throws:** R   **Height:** 6'2"   **Weight:** 180

MLB ETA	Hit	Power	Run	Glove	Arm	OFP	Realistic
2016	60	55	50	65	55	65 1ST DIV/ALL STAR	55 >AVG ML PLAYER

YEAR	TEAM	LVL	AGE	PA	R	2B	3B	HR	RBI	BB	SO	SB	CS	AVG/OBP/SLG	TAv	BABIP	BRR	FRAA	WARP
2014	TEN	AA	20	144	20	7	2	2	10	2	23	0	1	.234/.250/.355	.214	.267	-0.1	CF(32): -1.1	-0.4
2014	DAY	A+	20	385	55	20	2	7	50	12	46	6	3	.283/.306/.406	.254	.305	0.9	CF(87): 4.3	1.7
2015	CHN	MLB	21	250	22	12	1	3	20	5	51	1	1	.237/.255/.336	.225	.285	-0.4	CF 3	0.1
2016	CHN	MLB	22	250	24	11	1	3	22	12	54	1	1	.237/.279/.335	.235	.291	-0.5	CF 3	0.3

Breakout: 0%   **Improve:** 0%   **Collapse:** 0%   **Attrition:** 0%   **MLB:** 0%   **Upside:** 23   *Comparables: Engel Beltre, Rafael Ortega, Xavier Avery*

#38
BP Top
101
Prospects

Drafted/Acquired: 1st round, 2012 draft, Mater Academy Charter School (Hialeah, FL)

Previous Ranking: #3 (Org), #25 (Top 101)

What Happened in 2014: Almora continued to bemuse and befuddle evaluators, working hot and cold at the plate with High-A Daytona before catching fire in July and finishing the year at Double-A Tennessee.

Strengths: Near-elite bat-to-ball ability; added strength with plus raw power showing in BP; preternatural reads off the bat; efficient routes; solid arm and IQ should produce holds and kills at highest level; savvy reads and selective aggressiveness on the bases; high grades for makeup; swagger.

Weaknesses: Rudimentary approach at present; overly aggressive at the plate, too often leading to soft contact and limiting utility of pitch identification and strike zone awareness; without refinement in approach could struggle to fully realize hit-tool potential; inconsistent day-to-day play; added strength could negatively impact speed and limit ultimate range at maturity.

Risk Factor/Injury History: Moderate; young for level but has been slow to adjust at each level; yet to show success at Double-A; some nagging injuries over past two summers, including hamstring and hamate.

Bret Sayre's Fantasy Take: While the potential high-end defense in center field will likely inflate his value, in a fantasy context, Almora still has the upside at the plate to reach OF3 status. A much more valuable proposition in AVG leagues than OBP formats, Almora could be a .290 hitter with 15-20 homers and a small but not insignificant contribution in steals.

The Year Ahead: Almora is a complicated assortment of high-level baseball skills, natural ability, and unrefined approach. The strengths of his game—outfield play and bat-to-ball ability—are already ingrained in the profile, while the target areas of improvement—approach at the plate and ability to manifest in-game power—have shown development at a slower pace than one might have expected at acquisition. All that said, this is a 21-year-old with a month of Double-A ball under his belt and solid foundational value built into his profile as a plus defender up the middle who will serve as an asset on the bases. The materials are here for a true two-hole hitter with elite contact rates, plus-to-better hit, and average-to-better pop to emerge, and a more nuanced game plan could unlock that potential in short order. Almora should begin 2015 back in Double-A, with a chance to surprise and reach Wrigley by the end of the summer if everything comes together.

5. Kyle Schwarber   C/OF

Born: 3/5/93   **Age:** 22   **Bats:** L   **Throws:** R   **Height:** 6'0"   **Weight:** 235

MLB ETA	Hit	Power	Run	Glove	Arm	OFP	Realistic
2016	55	60	–	–	–	60 1ST DIVISION PLAYER	50 ML REGULAR

YEAR	TEAM	LVL	AGE	PA	R	2B	3B	HR	RBI	BB	SO	SB	CS	AVG/OBP/SLG	TAv	BABIP	BRR	FRAA	WARP
2014	DAY	A+	21	191	31	9	1	10	28	26	38	4	0	.302/.393/.560	.323	.328	-0.7	LF(26): 1.5, C(9): 0.1	2.0
2014	KNC	A	21	96	17	8	0	4	15	11	17	1	1	.361/.448/.602	.295	.419	-0.1	LF(2): -0.0, C(1): -0.0	0.2
2014	BOI	A-	21	24	7	1	1	4	10	2	2	0	1	.600/.625/1.350	.612	.533			0.0
2015	CHN	MLB	22	250	26	10	1	8	30	22	68	1	0	.227/.300/.382	.257	.285	-0.3	LF 2, C 0	0.7
2016	CHN	MLB	23	250	28	10	1	7	26	21	73	1	0	.218/.289/.357	.243	.287	-0.3	LF 1, C 0	0.6

Breakout: 2%   **Improve:** 20%   **Collapse:** 0%   **Attrition:** 13%   **MLB:** 36%   **Upside:** 22   *Comparables: Thomas Neal, Jaff Decker, Jamie Romak*

#77
BP Top
101
Prospects

Drafted/Acquired: 1st round, 2014 draft, Indiana University (Bloomington, IN)

Previous Ranking: NR

What Happened in 2014: Schwarber was selected fourth overall in the 2014 first-year player draft, then raked his way through the low minors slashing .341/.427/.636 over 71 games against overmatched arms.

Strengths: Advanced bat; plus-to-better raw power that plays in game thanks to plate coverage and strike zone awareness; solid bat speed and good bat-to-ball skills should help hit tool play average or better; strong leader and big makeup; lauded for work ethic; positive reviews from instructs on progress behind the plate.

Weaknesses: Below-average run and throw; long transfer and release hinders ability to control running game; unrefined receiver has struggled with advanced stuff in the past; limited defensive profile; below-average outfield breaks reduce range in left; failure of bat to play to potential could significantly eat into overall value.

Risk Factor/Injury History: Moderate; yet to reach Double-A; uncertainty surrounding defensive profile.

Bret Sayre's Fantasy Take: The best-case scenario for Schwarber's fantasy value is that he plays enough catcher to qualify in fantasy leagues, but isn't the everyday guy—allowing him to rack up at-bats that other fantasy catchers can't. But even without catcher eligibility, a .275 hitter with 25 homers is pretty valuable anywhere. He's an easy top-five pick in dynasty drafts this offseason—even with Rusney Castillo and Yasmani Tomas included.

The Year Ahead: Schwarber was eased into pro ball after a long collegiate season and the bat proved far too advanced for the likes of Single-A ball. The true test for the former Hoosier should come in 2015 on both sides of the ball, as he gets his first taste of advanced pro arms while simultaneously working to grow his game behind the dish. It's unlikely Schwarber ever develops into a true everyday catcher, capable of notching 100-plus games behind the plate. However, if he proves able to handle even a 60-game workload while providing passable defense in left field the remaining two-thirds of the time, it will be a boon to the overall value of the profile. Even skeptics of Schwarber's ability to catch long term rave about his on-field presence and ability to lead. He should be a favorite among teammates and fans alike, regardless of whether he settles as an impact talent or simply a solid everyday major leaguer.

6. Billy McKinney LF

Born: 8/23/94   **Age:** 20   **Bats:** L   **Throws:** L   **Height:** 6'1"   **Weight:** 195

MLB ETA	Hit	Power	Run	Glove	Arm	OFP	Realistic
2017	65	50	–	–	–	60 1ST DIVISION PLAYER	50 ML REGULAR

YEAR	TEAM	LVL	AGE	PA	R	2B	3B	HR	RBI	BB	SO	SB	CS	AVG/OBP/SLG	TAv	BABIP	BRR	FRAA	WARP
2014	DAY	A+	19	210	30	12	4	1	36	25	42	1	0	.301/.390/.432	.306	.377	2.4	RF(29): 2.6, CF(4): -0.1	1.8
2014	STO	A+	19	333	42	12	2	10	33	36	58	5	3	.241/.330/.400	.252	.267	0.1	CF(65): -2.9, RF(7): 0.3	0.3
2015	CHN	MLB	20	250	23	9	1	2	18	19	61	0	0	.214/.280/.301	.225	.276	-0.2	CF -2, RF 1	-0.4
2016	CHN	MLB	21	250	25	11	2	3	21	24	61	0	0	.220/.301/.328	.238	.285	-0.2	CF -2, RF 1	0.0

Breakout: 0%   Improve: 0%   Collapse: 0%   Attrition: 0%   MLB: 0%   Upside: 11   *Comparables: Aaron Hicks, Cedric Hunter, Che-Hsuan Lin*

Drafted/Acquired: 1st round, 2013 draft, Plano West Senior HS (Plano, TX)

Previous Ranking: #5 (Org – OAK)

What Happened in 2014: McKinney sputtered some in the hitter-friendly Cal League before being traded to the Cubs in early July and finishing the 2014 campaign with a strong offensive showing with High-A Daytona.

Strengths: Natural feel for contact; good bat speed; oppo capable; will flash some natural lift to pull; puts together mature at-bats; adequate glove and foot speed should play in left field.

Weaknesses: Evaluators divided on overall power potential; offensive profile could ultimately prove light for outfield corner; fringy arm with some length; has added size, reducing run and solidifying future left-field-only profile; bat path can create some coverage holes on inner half.

Risk Factor/Injury History: Moderate; yet to achieve Double-A; limited defensive profile.

Bret Sayre's Fantasy Take: The fantasy profile is strong in this one, as McKinney doesn't offer the defensive prowess to skyrocket up national lists. A potential .300 hitter in his prime, McKinney won't hit for a ton of power or add much speed, but will do enough of each to make fantasy owners happy.

The Year Ahead: McKinney drew mixed reviews from scouts throughout the summer and during instructs. Supporters believe the hit tool and on-base skill set will carry the profile, while less enthusiastic appraisals depict a power-shy corner bat that will see the hit tool play down as more advanced sequencing and consistent execution expose some coverage blips on the inner half. McKinney should join Almora and Schwarber in Double-A next April, with evaluators inside and outside the organization looking for developments on the power front. He'll play the bulk of his 2015 season as a 20-year-old, placing little urgency on the developmental horizon and affording McKinney some time to marinate before he's asked to produce at the major-league level. He tops out as a top-of-the-order stick thanks to his on-base abilities and at minimum should hit enough to provide value as a fourth outfielder with some pinch-hit utility.

#81

BP Top 101 Prospects

7. Pierce Johnson   RHP

Born: 5/10/91   **Age:** 24   **Bats:** R   **Throws:** R   **Height:** 6'3"   **Weight:** 170

MLB ETA	CT	FB	CH	CB	SL	OFP	Realistic
2016	55	60	55	65	–	60 NO. 3 STARTER	50 NO. 4 STARTER

YEAR	TEAM	LVL	AGE	W	L	SV	G	GS	IP	H	HR	BB	K	BB9	SO9	GB%	BABIP	WHIP	ERA	FIP	FRA	WARP
2014	TEN	AA	23	5	4	0	18	17	91.7	60	8	54	91	5.3	8.9	44%	.242	1.24	2.55	4.27	4.51	0.5
2014	KNC	A	23	0	1	0	2	2	11.0	4	1	3	8	2.5	6.5	63%	.115	0.64	2.45	4.30	5.83	0.0
2015	CHN	MLB	24	4	7	0	18	18	86.3	77	8	42	79	4.4	8.2	45%	.313	1.39	4.23	4.32	4.60	0.1
2016	CHN	MLB	25	9	10	0	30	30	190.7	171	19	87	192	4.1	9.1	45%	.322	1.36	4.24	3.93	4.60	-0.3

Breakout: 17%   **Improve:** 31%   **Collapse:** 8%   **Attrition:** 27%   **MLB:** 42%   **Upside:** 12   *Comparables: Jose Cisnero, Chris Dwyer, Andre Rienzo*

Drafted/Acquired: 1st round, 2012 draft, Missouri State University (Springfield, MO)

Previous Ranking: #7 (Org), #91 (Top 101)

What Happened in 2014: The Missouri State product racked up both strikeouts and walks while limiting hard contact through 17 Southern League starts. Johnson finished the year in dominant fashion, allowing just 13 earned runs over his final 65 innings while cutting his walk rate and increasing his strikeout rate over that same period.

Strengths: Loud stuff led by lively, low-90s fastball and sharp, low-80s hammer; can dial up to mid-90s with regularity; capable of cutting fastball for different look, counterbalance to two-seamer; some deception; traditional starter's build; good present strength; will flash above-average change piece with fade mirroring fastball action; showed improvement in consistency of pitch execution and command over final two months.

Weaknesses: Still working to find consistency in release, with arm path complicating efforts; missed release can cause secondaries to spin and hang; cutter is potential weapon but can ride swing plane to contact when not properly finished; below-average command at present; loose control in zone could negate effectiveness of stuff against major-league bats; stuff can drop a half to full grade deeper in game.

Risk Factor/Injury History: Moderate; yet to surpass 120 innings in a season; hamstring/calf injuries in 2014; forearm strains in amateur file.

Bret Sayre's Fantasy Take: Wait, the Cubs have arms, too? That just seems unfair. Johnson has the stuff to miss bats at the major-league level—especially on the strength of his curve—and even though he may give back some of that value in WHIP, he could one day find his way as a SP3 in mixed leagues.

The Year Ahead: Johnson struggled mightily with his mechanics in April and May but found his stride after returning from his second DL stint, putting together 65 highly impressive innings over his final 12 starts of the year. The key to unlocking a future spot in the Cubs rotation will be continued growth in his command profile and, most importantly, more consistency in working the lower "U" of the strike zone with the heater. Supporters saw Johnson flirt with that potential through multiple starts last August, and if he can build off that progress in 2015 he could find a spot in the Cubs' rotation by 2016. Depending on offseason moves and spring training showing, Johnson may or may not start the season back in Double-A, but in any event should get significant exposure to Triple-A bats over the course of the summer, with a focus on staying healthy, logging innings, and finding consistency in execution.

#83

BP Top 101 Prospects

8. Gleyber Torres   SS

Born: 12/13/96   **Age:** 18   **Bats:** R   **Throws:** R   **Height:** 6'1"   **Weight:** 175

MLB ETA	Hit	Power	Run	Glove	Arm	OFP	Realistic
2019	60	–	50	55	60	65 1ST DIV/ALL STAR	45 <AVG ML PLAYER

YEAR	TEAM	LVL	AGE	PA	R	2B	3B	HR	RBI	BB	SO	SB	CS	AVG/OBP/SLG	TAv	BABIP	BRR	FRAA	WARP
2014	BOI	A-	17	32	4	2	3	1	4	4	7	2	0	.393/.469/.786	.374	.500	0.6	SS(7): 0.5	0.7
2014	CUB	Rk	17	183	33	6	3	1	29	25	33	8	7	.279/.372/.377	.282	.339	2.3	SS(17): 0.9	0.8
2015	CHN	MLB	18	250	24	9	1	2	16	14	72	4	2	.199/.248/.275	.202	.272	-0.2	SS 3	-0.1
2016	CHN	MLB	19	250	23	10	1	3	21	14	70	5	3	.222/.269/.314	.219	.299	0.1	SS 2	-0.3

Breakout: 0%   **Improve:** 0%   **Collapse:** 0%   **Attrition:** 0%   **MLB:** 0%   **Upside:** 6   *Comparables: Jonathan Schoop, Argenis Diaz, Adrian Cardenas*

Drafted/Acquired: International Free Agent, 2013, Venezuela

Previous Ranking: NR

What Happened in 2014: In his stateside debut, the $1.7 million 2013 signee impressed at the complex before wrapping the year with a quick two-series stint in the Northwest League and a strong showing at fall instructs.

Strengths: Mature approach at the plate; keeps compact to contact and shows ability to work line to line; good hands and left-side arm; lower half works and allows profile to project to six-spot long term; completed first stateside season at age 17; game projects across the board; efficient barrel delivery produces hard contact and some power projection; high grades for work ethic and makeup.

Weaknesses: Lacks pro reps, experience; game can speed up on him in the field and on the bases; comfort in box exceeds comfort in other facets; average foot speed, first step could limit range at maturity.

Risk Factor/Injury History: High; yet to achieve full-season ball; hit may be only potential impact tool.

Bret Sayre's Fantasy Take: There's certainly fantasy potential in Torres, but the upside is not so lofty that dynasty leaguers should say, "ETA, be damned." The power may yet develop, and he could be a five-category threat, but there's so much distance between now and fantasy viability that it takes a toll on his overall value.

The Year Ahead: It's not often you see this blend of upside, probability, and feel in a player this age and at this level, let alone at the shortstop position. With present power his only below-average tool, he has already begun to add some strength and it would not be a surprise to see him begin driving the ball with more regularity as early as this year. Torres is advanced enough to be challenged with a South Bend assignment to start the season, though the Cubs could opt to keep him in extended to wait out the worst of the weather while continuing to work with him on the finer points of his game. The young Venezuelan will play all of 2015 as an 18-year-old, so there is some flexibility as to how Chicago opts to move forward with his development. Further, the wave of young infield talent currently descending on Wrigley should permit Torres the luxury of progressing through the system at his own pace. The bat is impressive enough, however, that he could force his way into the major-league picture much quicker than any expected at this time last year.

9. Dan Vogelbach   1B

Born: 12/17/92   **Age:** 22   **Bats:** L   **Throws:** R   **Height:** 6'0"   **Weight:** 250

MLB ETA	Hit	Power	Run	Glove	Arm	OFP	Realistic
2016	55	65	–	–	–	60 1ST DIVISION PLAYER	50 ML REGULAR

YEAR	TEAM	LVL	AGE	PA	R	2B	3B	HR	RBI	BB	SO	SB	CS	AVG/OBP/SLG	TAv	BABIP	BRR	FRAA	WARP
2014	DAY	A+	21	560	71	28	1	16	76	66	91	4	4	.268/.357/.429	.280	.296	-3.1	1B(103): -9.0	0.5
2015	CHN	MLB	22	250	25	10	0	7	28	23	60	0	0	.226/.298/.367	.252	.272	-0.5	1B -3	-0.3
2016	CHN	MLB	23	250	29	10	0	6	26	26	57	0	0	.224/.305/.363	.252	.269	-0.6	1B -3	0.3

Breakout: 0%   Improve: 0%   Collapse: 0%   Attrition: 0%   MLB: 0%   Upside: 11   *Comparables: Mike Carp, Chris Marrero, Logan Morrison*

Drafted/Acquired: 2nd round, 2011 draft, Bishop Verot HS (Fort Myers, FL)

Previous Ranking: #8 (Org)

What Happened in 2014: The 2011 second rounder continued his steady climb through the Cubs' system with a solid showing in the pitcher-friendly Florida State League, highlighted by regular jaw-dropping power displays both in game and during batting practice.

Strengths: Natural feel for contact and easy power to all fields; double-plus raw; professional approach; capable of extending at-bats and working to find pitches to drive; loose hands with impactful barrel delivery.

Weaknesses: Bad body with nonexistent value on the basepaths and in the field; DH profile in NL org; still learning to unpack advanced arms; can get caught guessing behind in count; some evaluators question ability to consistently identify spin.

Risk Factor/Injury History: Moderate; value tied exclusively to bat; yet to achieve Double-A.

Bret Sayre's Fantasy Take: Yes, he's guaranteed to be first-base-only (at best) and he'll offer zero value on the basepaths, but Vogelbach is a power hitter and we care about power hitters. After all, Albert Pujols hit .272 with 28 homers last year and was the 21st ranked fantasy hitter for the season—and that's attainable for the big man.

The Year Ahead: Vogelbach will join a talented lineup at Double-A Tennessee, leaving him a stone's throw from Wrigley where his bat-only profile will demand loud offensive performance to justify a roster spot. With Anthony Rizzo's 2014 breakout and wonderfully reasonable contract locked in through 2021 (including team options), most outside the organization have tabbed Vogelbach as a likely trade piece to be wielded this summer or next offseason, depending on his progress and needs of likely AL suitors. If a spot were to eventually open up on the 25-man in Chicago, Vogelbach possesses enough upside with the stick to account for the negative value he will bring to the table in the field, with a chance to slot in behind Bryant, Soler, Baez, Schwarber, and Russell as yet another impact power bat.

10. Carson Sands   LHP

Born: 3/28/95   **Age:** 20   **Bats:** L   **Throws:** L   **Height:** 6'3"   **Weight:** 195

MLB ETA	CT	FB	CH	CB	SL	OFP	Realistic
2019	–	60	55	55	–	65 NO. 2/3 STARTER	45 NO. 4/5 STARTER

YEAR	TEAM	LVL	AGE	W	L	SV	G	GS	IP	H	HR	BB	K	BB9	SO9	GB%	BABIP	WHIP	ERA	FIP	FRA	WARP
2014	CUB	Rk	19	3	1	0	9	4	19.0	15	0	7	20	3.3	9.5	43%	.306	1.16	1.89	3.19	4.94	0.3

Drafted/Acquired: 4th round, 2014 draft, North Florida Christian HS (Tallahassee, FL)

Previous Ranking: NR

What Happened in 2014: Sands saw a steady growth in stuff over the past 18 months, highlighted by a marked step forward his senior year at North Florida Christian and culminating in a seven-figure bonus and fourth-round selection in June's first-year player draft. He capped off a whirlwind 2014 with impressive showings in the Arizona Complex League and fall instructs.

Strengths: Balanced repertoire featuring three above-average offerings and above-average command; reports of improved consistency in mechanics and arm action through instructs; comfortable pitching to all four quadrants; some room to bump velo band to firm plus in comfort zone; already showing feel for sequencing; sturdy build; solid presence and even demeanor.

Weaknesses: Curve can flash but lacks consistent requisite snap for present plus grades; some knocks for arm action; more conservative evals see arsenal settling in as average across the board with solid command and back-end profile; needs to demonstrate ability to maintain quality of stuff on pro schedule.

Risk Factor/Injury History: High; yet to achieve full-season ball; standard proximity/probability risk for prep arm.

Bret Sayre's Fantasy Take: Do not overlook Sands in dynasty drafts this year, as he deserves to be drafted much earlier than his status as a fourth rounder indicates and is a top-50 name in a deep draft class. It would not be a surprise at all to see him make top-100 fantasy lists next offseason.

The Year Ahead: Sands is advanced enough to tackle the Midwest League in 2015, and some reports outside the organization maintain he could hold his own against High-A bats while conceding that would be an unnecessary stress for an arm yet to be challenged with a pro workload. His balanced arsenal, feel, strength, and maturity on the bump all suggest a future as a major-league starter, while history serves as a constant reminder that the path from acquisition to realization of major-league value is seldom linear for teenage arms. Provided he proves capable of weathering a full season's load in 2015, he could begin to move quickly thereafter, with his name prominently placed on prospect and acquisition lists alike.

Prospects on the Rise

1. LHP Justin Steele: Steele had evaluators flocking to the Magnolia State last spring when word got out that the projectable lefty was hitting the mid-90s with his fastball, and the Cubs wound up popping the Southern Miss

---

FROM THE FIELD

Kyle Schwarber

Team: Chicago Cubs

Evaluator: Jeff Moore

Dates seen: July 21–23, 2014

Affiliate: Daytona Cubs (High-A, Cubs)

Physical/health: Thick body, strong upper half; build not an issue now but should slow him down as he ages; broad shoulders.

MLB ETA	Risk factor	OFP	Realistic role
2015	Low	60	50, first-division regular

Tool	Future grade	Report
Hit	55	Open stance, starts in slight squat; keeps hands low and away from his body; short swing path, slight uppercut; can get rotational and pull off of outer half; good, patient approach, good idea of the strike zone; wants the ball up, balls down will be routine groundballs.
Power	55	Plus bat speed, ball jumps on good contact; good combination of size, strength and bat speed/hitting ability will lead to above-average power; understands how to drive the ball; plus power to pull side.
Baserunning/ speed	40	Below-average runner, slow first step; not station-to-station yet but will eventually be a base-clogger.
Glove	40	Below-average defensive catcher; lateral movement on balls in the dirt is below-average; stiff hips keep him from getting side to side; quiet hands receiving pitches; pitch framing isn't perfect but isn't terribly sloppy either—won't buy his pitchers a lot of extra pitches but won't cost them too many either; fundamentally sound enough to get the job done but not athletic enough to be an asset; effective enough to play position presently, especially in part-time role, but will eventually have to move off position.
Arm	50	Average arm strength, enough to make the throws behind the plate; arm is accurate to second base; fundamentally sound with throws; above-average accuracy helps throws play up; 2.00-2.10 to second base; won't throw out a ton of baserunners but shouldn't get taken advantage of either; arm is good enough to play behind the plate.

Overall: The Cubs drafted Schwarber for his bat, which doesn't have the high-ceiling talent of some of their current top prospects, but does profile to be that of a solid, major-league contributor. Schwarber's long-term home isn't behind the plate, but he can handle the responsibility for the time being, perhaps even catching everyday during the early part of his career. He'll always be below average behind the plate, but he's capable enough to remain back there for the time being given the asset that his offensive production would be from that position.

A realistic scenario could see the Cubs using him in the majors the same way they are using him in the minors, where he is catching a few days a week while splitting time in the outfield. That would allow his bat to continue to be an asset while keeping him from being overexposed at the position.

Overall, the bat is going to have to carry Schwarber no matter where he ends up. The longer he can stay behind the plate, the more valuable his bat will be, but it will always be a stretch defensively. He'll end up in left field full time before he turns 30, but he has enough bat to be an everyday player out there as well.

commit in the fifth round, inking him to a $1-million bonus. Steele lacks the physicality at present to maintain his velocity late into starts and most comfortably operated in the 88-91 mph band while piggybacking with Sands in his pro debut. His breaking ball is a second potential plus offering that should settle as a consistent swing-and-miss weapon at maturity, and he shows enough feel for his changeup to project average or better, giving him a potential weapon against righties. His frame should allow for the additional strength necessary to handle the rigors of rotation work. There's number 3 starter upside here, with a chance for late-inning work should he shift to the 'pen at some point along the developmental journey.

2. RHP Jake Stinnett: Stinnett wowed last spring in ACC play, showcasing a plus fastball-slider combo, serviceable change, and aggressive demeanor on the mound. A relatively low-mileage arm, the Terrapins' ace endured a long college season while maintaining his stuff late into starts, but showed significant signs of fatigue in his pro debut, including a sizeable velo dip and softer breaking ball. Stinnett throws with effort in generating his power stuff, leaving evaluators split as to whether he fits best as a power reliever or in a rotation, where he could provide mid-rotation upside. The Cubs could ease him into full-season ball with a Low-A assignment in 2015, but if the fastball and slider return to form, he could quickly prove too advanced for Midwest League bats.

3. C Mark Zagunis: Though he lacks a current defensive home, Zagunis possesses above-average athleticism and the work ethic to build up his proficiency at a number of positions, including behind the dish, where he drew solid reviews internally during instructs and mixed grades from outside evaluators. Where the former Hokie will shine, however, is in the box, consistently putting together solid at-bats thanks to an advanced ability to track and good feel for contact. He projects to hit for average and gap-to-gap pop, and could fill a super-utility role at maturity that includes a time share between catcher, left field, and third base. Expect Zagunis to hit the ground running in 2015 and to quickly establish himself as another Cubby bat for the Wrigleyville faithful to monitor closely.

Factors on the Farm
Prospects likely to contribute at the major-league level in 2015

1. RHP C.J. Edwards: Edwards was shelved for three months last summer thanks to a shoulder strain and fatigue, adding to the narrative that the slender righty lacks the durability to hold up to a starter's workload and is destined for the 'pen. Upon returning to action in late July, Edwards showcased impressive swing-and-miss stuff over six starts, with his fastball and curve each grading out as plus offerings and his change showing promise to boot. Were there more certainty that Edwards could maintain the quality of his stuff over the course of a full season at the upper levels, he would fit comfortably as one of the top 10 prospects in the system. But despite mid-rotation upside and solid athleticism and feel, signs continue to point to a late-inning fit, where his arsenal could play up and durability concerns would play down. He'll start 2015 back in Double-A and could be ready to provide useful major-league innings in short order if the opportunity should arise.

2. 3B Christian Villanueva: Were it not for the logjam of potential impact infielders populating the organization, Villanueva might have an opportunity to prove himself as a worthy everyday contributor at the major-league level. The glove plays to plus at the hot corner, and there is plus raw pop in the stick, but Villanueva's contact issues were magnified between Double- and Triple-A in 2014, calling into question whether the profile is ultimately that of a regular or corner backup with some pinch-hit utility. The timetable for Russell and Bryant could eat into Villanueva's opportunity to see time in Wrigley next summer, making him an obvious candidate to figure into any offseason discussions involving trade partners in search of an inexpensive upside play at third.

3. RHP Corey Black: The former fourth rounder logged 124 innings over 25 starts (and a relief appearance) for Double-A Tennessee, though he did so while struggling to limit free passes and showing continued fly-ball proclivities. Black can come at hitters with four or five different looks, including two distinct breaking balls, a change piece, and a fastball that can show two- or four-seam action, with the fastball being the most effective offering by a wide margin. While the Faulkner University product was able to keep the heater in the low- to mid-90s as a starter, he has shown the ability to dial it up to the upper-90s in shorter stints, making him an enticing relief option for a Cubs club increasing its pitching depth at the upper levels, and perhaps as early as this summer.

CHICAGO WHITE SOX

1.   Tim Anderson   SS

Born: 6/23/93   **Age:** 22   **Bats:** R   **Throws:** R   **Height:** 6'1"   **Weight:** 180

MLB ETA	Hit	Power	Run	Glove	Arm		OFP	Realistic
2016	60	55	70	55	50		65 1ST DIV/ OCC ALL STAR	50 AVG ML PLAYER

YEAR	TEAM	LVL	AGE	PA	R	2B	3B	HR	RBI	BB	SO	SB	CS	AVG/OBP/SLG	TAv	BABIP	BRR	FRAA	WARP
2014	BIR	AA	21	45	7	3	0	1	7	0	9	0	1	.364/.364/.500	.327	.441	-0.1	SS(10): 0.5	0.5
2014	WNS	A+	21	300	48	18	7	6	31	7	68	10	3	.297/.323/.472	.264	.369	3.6	SS(66): 0.1	1.7
2014	WSX	Rk	21	17	2	0	0	2	2	2	5	0	1	.200/.294/.600	.305	.125	-0.4	SS(6): 1.0	0.2
2015	CHA	MLB	22	250	26	9	2	3	19	8	75	6	2	.229/.262/.329	.219	.315	0.6	SS 2	0.3
2016	CHA	MLB	23	250	27	11	3	5	27	12	71	7	2	.256/.298/.395	.257	.340	0.9	SS 1	1.9

Breakout: 0%   Improve: 0%   Collapse: 0%   Attrition: 0%   MLB: 0%   Upside: 67   *Comparables: Zach Walters, Chris Nelson, Danny Santana*

#39
BP Top
101
Prospects

Drafted/Acquired: 1st round, 2013 draft, East Central Community College (Decatur, MS)

Previous Ranking: #2 (Org), Just Missed The Cut (Top 101)

What Happened in 2014: Anderson more than held his own during an assignment in High-A before a fractured wrist ate into the second half of his season, but the shortstop didn't miss a beat in a brief taste of Double-A after returning and continued to rip in the Arizona Fall League.

Strengths: Impact athlete; oozes fluidity; easy stroke with natural lift; loose and explosive hands; well-above-average bat speed; barrels fastballs well; turns around velocity with ease; contact is loud; thunder in the stick; shows pull-side power potential; double-plus run; puts it in an extra gear quickly; soft hands; good footwork; quick transfers when throwing.

Weaknesses: Raw overall game; plays on ability over polish; questions on instincts at short; doesn't get the best of reads off the bat; range plays down; arm comes up a bit short on left side when making long throws; may ultimately end up at second base or in outfield; approach and plate discipline are unrefined; can struggle handling secondary stuff; gets out on front foot often; still learning how to cover all four quadrants of zone with swing.

Risk Factor/Injury History: High; limited upper-level experience; wrist fracture (2014); refinement of strike zone management.

Bret Sayre's Fantasy Take: There's so much fantasy potential in Anderson's game here as a five-category threat who could steal north of 30 bases at the major-league level. He's going to be slightly more attractive in AVG leagues than OBP or points formats, but Anderson is a potential first-round fantasy pick, even if he doesn't stick at shortstop (or the infield, for that matter).

The Year Ahead: Anderson is a true five-tool talent who can be absolutely electric on the diamond when everything is flowing in unison. The athleticism is the fast-twitch type that fuels explosiveness with all of his actions, while the stroke shows a high level of ease and control due to the strength of his wrists and forearms. It's easy to fall in love with the 22-year-old when watching him on the field, and a strong showing in 2014 has continued to reinforce that the initial refinement of his overall game has begun to take. The future has the potential to be very bright, with all-star caliber seasons not out of the question, though there's still a high level of rawness in the player's game, especially when it comes to the defense and strike zone management skills. Opinions are mixed as to whether Anderson can stick on the left side of the infield, with his arm and fringy instincts drawing the most concerns from sources. Given the athleticism, the Alabama native could keep his value as an up-the-middle defender with a move out to center field or transition well to second base, where the arm is a better fit. It's ultimately going to come down to the refinement of the aforementioned offensive secondary skills to reach the peak potential. They'll be tested heavily in an assignment in the Southern League this season, with the belief here that the prospect can make the necessary adjustments and prove he's trending toward rounding into a future impact major leaguer.

2. Carlos Rodon LHP

Born: 12/10/92 **Age:** 22 **Bats:** L **Throws:** L **Height:** 6'3" **Weight:** 235

MLB ETA		CT	FB	CH	CB	SL		OFP	Realistic
2015		–	65	55	–	70		65 NO. 2 STARTER	55 NO. 3 STARTER

YEAR	TEAM	LVL	AGE	W	L	SV	G	GS	IP	H	HR	BB	K	BB9	SO9	GB%	BABIP	WHIP	ERA	FIP	FRA	WARP
2014	CHR	AAA	21	0	0	0	3	3	12.0	9	0	8	18	6.0	13.5	42%	.346	1.42	3.00	2.61	3.03	0.5
2014	WNS	A+	21	0	0	0	4	2	9.7	7	0	5	15	4.7	14.0	59%	.318	1.24	1.86	1.97	0.84	0.5
2014	WSX	Rk	21	0	0	0	2	1	3.0	4	0	0	5	0.0	15.0	50%	.500	1.33	6.00	0.70	2.70	0.1
2015	CHA	MLB	22	2	2	0	12	6	34.7	31	3	15	40	3.9	10.4	46%	.312	1.34	3.75	3.74	4.07	0.5
2016	CHA	MLB	23	6	4	0	72	9	120.3	104	11	57	133	4.3	10.0	46%	.298	1.34	3.71	3.82	4.03	1.3

Breakout: 19%   Improve: 25%   Collapse: 4%   Attrition: 13%   MLB: 34%   Upside: 38   *Comparables: Tommy Hanson, Fautino De Los Santos, Zach Braddock*

Drafted/Acquired: 1st round, 2014 draft, North Carolina State University (Raleigh, NC)

Previous Ranking: NR

What Happened in 2014: Seen as the consensus first overall pick in the June draft for most of the spring, Rodon fell to the third overall slot due to some inconsistencies during the season and signing concerns; the White Sox stepped up to the table to meet the price and then tracked him all the way up to Triple-A by season's end.

Strengths: Good size; thick lower half; muscular legs; excellent strength; good arm action; fastball works 92-96 with big late life and tailing action; attacks hitters with heater; snaps slider with a loose wrist; wipeout break at 85-88; bat-misser; changes shape when needed; throws for a strike; flashes feel for changeup; moderate fading action; competitive mentality; mature on the mound.

Weaknesses: Little projection left in body; some concerns about maintenance going forward; aggressive delivery with some effort; pace gets inconsistent; runs into ruts of releasing fastball early; command can come and go; leans heavily on slider; changeup is distant third in arsenal; tends to stay elevated and float; needs to throw with more trust and conviction.

Risk Factor/Injury History: Moderate; limited pro experience; emergence of third offering.

Bret Sayre's Fantasy Take: There's probably not a safer pick to take in dynasty drafts this year than Rodon, who has a low SP3 floor and the potential to border on SP1 status (with near-impact performance in all four categories) if he plays up to the potential he flashed so often at NC State. He'll be one of the first players from the 2014 draft to make the majors, which will make him a popular target among teams who fancy themselves reloaders, rather than rebuilders.

The Year Ahead: Rodon has been a much-talked-about name on the radar dating back to his freshman season at North Carolina State, and for good reason. The big left-hander features a very lively heater that consistently reaches the mid-90s and snaps off an extremely devastating slider. Both pitches may very well end up playing as plus-plus weapons at the 22-year-old's disposal when all is said and done. Toss in his mentality to come right after hitters, and this arm can be downright nasty on opposing bats in extended stretches. The White Sox aggressively pushed Rodon to Triple-A to finish out last season, with all signs pointing to the lefty making his debut this year, which could possibly come as early as right out of spring training. The most likely scenario is that the prospect spends some time in the International League to get into the cadence of starting as a pro and on a roll before coming up around midseason. Despite the proximity to The Show, though, the North Carolina native is still a work in progress when it comes to his fastball command and execution of the changeup. Both aspects may lead to some early career inconsistencies, but there should be enough growth with both to make a mid-rotation starter role well within his reach.

> **#41**
> BP Top 101 Prospects

3. Tyler Danish RHP

Born: 9/12/94 **Age:** 20 **Bats:** R **Throws:** R **Height:** 6'0" **Weight:** 205

MLB ETA		CT	FB	CH	CB	SL		OFP	Realistic
Late 2016		–	60	55	–	65		60 NO. 3 STARTER	50 NO. 4 STARTER

YEAR	TEAM	LVL	AGE	W	L	SV	G	GS	IP	H	HR	BB	K	BB9	SO9	GB%	BABIP	WHIP	ERA	FIP	FRA	WARP
2014	WNS	A+	19	5	3	0	18	18	91.7	87	7	23	78	2.3	7.7	62%	.301	1.20	2.65	3.69	4.63	1.1
2014	KAN	A	19	3	0	0	7	7	38.0	28	0	10	25	2.4	5.9	66%	.252	1.00	0.71	3.06	4.09	0.7
2015	CHA	MLB	20	4	6	0	21	14	86.7	96	10	35	58	3.6	6.0	56%	.306	1.51	4.98	5.12	5.42	-0.2
2016	CHA	MLB	21	7	8	1	37	23	167.0	173	19	53	123	2.9	6.6	56%	.298	1.36	4.38	4.41	4.76	0.2

Breakout: 0%   Improve: 0%   Collapse: 0%   Attrition: 0%   MLB: 0%   Upside: 3   *Comparables: Jacob Turner, Casey Kelly, Ian Krol*

Drafted/Acquired: 2nd round, 2013 draft, Duran HS (Plant City, FL)

Previous Ranking: #5 (Org)

What Happened in 2014: The former second-round pick put together a strong first full professional season across two levels, where he flashed advancing stuff and proved to be more than capable of handling low-minors hitters.

Strengths: Improving strength; has begun filling into body; strong competitive streak; creates angle on hitters via lower slot; repeats arm action well; fastball works 88-92 with strong sink and late life; can reach for more when needs it (94-95); tough to square up when in lower tier; slider flashes good tilt and bite; delivers from same angle as heater; can be very nasty on right-handed hitters; turns over changeup with drop and tumble; plays off of fastball well; plus pitchability; finishes well to throw strikes; rubber arm.

Weaknesses: Unconventional delivery with low three-quarters slot; lefties get a good look out of hand; change will come and go; still learning how to feel consistently; slider can sweep and spin across the plate; tends to have trouble throwing glove side due to arm angle; relies on movement and location with heater; more strike throwing than command at present.

Risk Factor/Injury History: Moderate; yet to reach Double-A; emergence of changeup to neutralize left-handed hitters.

Bret Sayre's Fantasy Take: Danish has been overlooked in fantasy since being drafted last year due to a combination of non-elite stuff and a funky delivery. However, there are no pictures in 5x5 valuations, so we have to look past that. Danish could be a workhorse who puts up good ratios and could strike out 160-170 batters a year if he can make it work—and we'll have a much better idea of that after 2015.

The Year Ahead: There are times when we can dwell on an aspect of a player's game because it is unconventional or not in line with the perceived norm. Danish's delivery certainly falls into this realm, but too much focus on it will only lead to losing sight that there is some nasty stuff coming out of this right-hander's hand. Armed with a low-90s sinking fastball, darting slider, and deceptive change, the 20-year-old loves to attack opposing bats and wears a noticeable competitive streak on his sleeve. The heater and slide piece are the more advanced offerings at present, which was evident last season while he carved up two levels of the low minors. The slope will get more slippery for Danish in Double-A this year, especially when it comes to pushing the consistency of his change to aid in attacking left-handed hitters. Are there concerns about how the delivery may limit the ultimate role? Sure. Is it possible the slider and change don't reach their on-paper potential? Absolutely. But the realistic role speaks to the belief here that this arm has what it takes to make it work in the rotation in the long run, with the expectation that this year will represent another developmental step in the right direction.

4. Spencer Adams RHP

Born: 4/13/96 **Age:** 19 **Bats:** R **Throws:** R **Height:** 6'3" **Weight:** 171

MLB ETA	CT	FB	CH	CB	SL	OFP	Realistic
2018	–	70	55	–	60	60 NO. 3 STARTER	50 NO. 4 STARTER

YEAR	TEAM	LVL	AGE	W	L	SV	G	GS	IP	H	HR	BB	K	BB9	SO9	GB%	BABIP	WHIP	ERA	FIP	FRA	WARP
2014	WSX	Rk	18	3	3	0	10	9	41.7	49	4	4	59	0.9	12.7	58%	.417	1.27	3.67	2.73	4.24	0.2
2015	CHA	MLB	19	0	0	0	6	1	31.3	38	4	19	20	5.5	5.8	47%	.319	1.83	6.33	5.95	6.88	-0.4
2016	CHA	MLB	20	0	0	0	8	1	44.7	47	6	23	39	4.6	7.9	47%	.307	1.56	5.11	5.00	5.55	-0.3

Breakout: 0% **Improve:** 0% **Collapse:** 0% **Attrition:** 0% **MLB:** 0% **Upside:** 1 *Comparables: Daniel Corcino, Joe Ortiz, Melvin Mercedes*

Drafted/Acquired: 2nd round, 2014 draft, White County HS (Cleveland, GA)

Previous Ranking: NR

What Happened in 2014: The three-sport prep star out of Georgia only lasted until the 44th overall pick in the June draft before being selected by the White Sox, with the early returns after signing offering a good clue that a quick assimilation into pro ball is likely.

Strengths: Very athletic; long and lean with a high waist; easy delivery; repeatable; loose arm; deceptive release; fastball presently sits low-90s with late life; can touch higher when reaching (95); potential for sitting velocity gains as physically matures; slider flashes tight spin and bite; horizontal movement; potential swing-and-miss offering; shows feel for low- to mid-80s change; mild fading action at present; delivers with solid arm speed; finishes delivery well; plus command profile; very projectable arm.

Weaknesses: Immature physically; needs added strength to enhance stuff and stamina; shorter arm action; can get around the ball; delivery presently lacks lower-body explosion; some cleanup needed to maximize overall package; slider gets on the loose and slurvy side when wrist wraps; inconsistent with release of changeup; offering tends to float within the strike zone; fastball straightens out in higher velocity band; long way to go developmentally.

Risk Factor/Injury History: Extreme; 19 years old; complex-league résumé; large gap between present and future.

Bret Sayre's Fantasy Take: There's no shortage of talent and risk here, but the projectable right-hander is a very viable third-round pick in medium-sized dynasty leagues this year—assuming you don't mind a long burn. Adams has the stuff to get strikeouts and the control/command projection to get the most out of it, making him a great flier.

The Year Ahead: This right-hander is basically an on-paper sketch at the present, but all of the ingredients are here for the arm to really start to take off now that he's in a structured environment. Adams is a former three-sport star in high school who oozes athleticism and looseness with a legit chance for big developmental gains with the overall package now that the focus is solely on baseball. The 19-year-old already comfortably sits in the low-90s with his lively heater and shows the early feel for reeling the offering in. Evaluators are bullish that as the 6-foot-3 frame starts to fill out and the prospect gains more "man-strength" velocity gains can take to potentially push the fastball into the double-plus range. While the secondaries are on the inconsistent side and Adams is in the early stages of finding an identity with them, it's not hard to see them rounding into average-to-better pitches down the line. The future potential listed here may end up looking a little light down the road, though there's a healthy serving of risk and variability on the plate. The next 12-18 months should see a focus on building the righty's stamina and sharpening the secondary arsenal, especially the changeup. This is a very good-looking arm, and one that can start to gain both developmental traction and a boost in status by season's end.

5. Francellis Montas RHP

Born: 3/21/93 **Age:** 22 **Bats:** R **Throws:** R **Height:** 6'2" **Weight:** 185

MLB ETA		CT		FB		CH		CB		SL		OFP		Realistic
2016		–		80		–		–		65		60 UPPER TIER CLOSER		50 SETUP

YEAR	TEAM	LVL	AGE	W	L	SV	G	GS	IP	H	HR	BB	K	BB9	SO9	GB%	BABIP	WHIP	ERA	FIP	FRA	WARP
2014	BIR	AA	21	0	0	0	1	1	5.0	1	0	1	1	1.8	1.8	47%	.067	0.40	0.00	3.39	3.60	0.1
2014	WNS	A+	21	4	0	0	10	10	62.0	45	2	14	56	2.0	8.1	54%	.256	0.95	1.60	2.90	3.56	1.5
2014	WSX	Rk	21	1	0	0	4	4	14.0	6	1	7	23	4.5	14.8	62%	.217	0.93	1.29	3.17	3.99	0.3
2015	CHA	MLB	22	3	6	0	14	14	65.7	72	8	33	51	4.5	7.0	43%	.312	1.60	5.32	5.29	5.79	-0.3
2016	CHA	MLB	23	2	1	0	39	0	41.3	45	5	19	34	4.1	7.4	43%	.314	1.55	5.16	4.78	5.61	-0.3

Breakout: 0%   Improve: 0%   Collapse: 0%   Attrition: 0%   MLB: 0%   Upside: 3   *Comparables: Matt Magill, Dan Straily, Andrew Heaney*

Drafted/Acquired: International Free Agent, 2009, Dominican Republic

Previous Ranking: #10 (Org)

What Happened in 2014: The Dominican flamethrower showed improving crispness with his arsenal and more fluidity in the delivery when on the mound during the year, but dealt with meniscus injuries to both knees that took a chunk of time out from the season and kept him from a full-fledged breakout year.

Strengths: Elite arm strength; very strong lower half; fastball comfortably works 94-98 with ride in upper velocity band and good life in lower tier; can reach for triple digits; explosive offering; snaps slider with loose wrist; shows tight rotation with depth and dart at 86-89; pitch made good progress since turning pro; improving strike-throwing ability; showing progress spotting in all four quadrants.

Weaknesses: Delivery can get messy and loose; mechanics aren't the smoothest; fastball gets flat when elevated; lacks good plane in upper tier; can get hurt in that area despite velocity; slider can get slurvy and lose bite; needs to throw for a strike more in sequences against advanced bats; changeup is more of a "show-me" piece; carries extra weight; conditioning will need to be consistent focus.

Risk Factor/Injury History: High; limited Double-A experience; multiple knee injuries (2013/2014); continued delivery refinement.

Bret Sayre's Fantasy Take: Montas has to be projected for fantasy as a reliever, but fortunately for him, he projects as one of the top relief prospects in the game. The arm can rack up strikeouts with a nasty one-two punch, but the usual caveats apply for reliever investments.

The Year Ahead: For those who have seen Montas since his early career stateside, the elite arm strength and intensity of the fastball have always stood out as strong positives, while the effort and nature of the mechanics have led to thoughts that the bullpen was going to be the ultimate home. The developmental hurdles to reaching his potential centered on whether any other pieces of the arsenal would emerge as a viable offering and whether the delivery could smooth out enough to boost the command. The 22-year-old has taken the initial steps toward answering those questions over the course of the past season or so, especially when it comes to the tightening of his slider and getting a bit more loose with his delivery to aid in throwing strikes. The big test for Montas will come with an assignment in Double-A this year. It's a twofold exercise for the prospect to prove that he can continue to push those improvements and also stay on the field for an entire season after battling knee injuries in 2014. The view here sees this prospect poised for a true breakout if the latter holds true, with an impact back-of-the-bullpen arm coming that much clearer into focus as a result.

6. Chris Beck RHP

Born: 9/4/90 **Age:** 24 **Bats:** R **Throws:** R **Height:** 6'3" **Weight:** 225

MLB ETA	CT	FB	CH	CB	SL	OFP	Realistic
2015	–	60	50	50	50	50 NO. 4 STARTER	50 NO. 5 SP/SWING MAN

YEAR	TEAM	LVL	AGE	W	L	SV	G	GS	IP	H	HR	BB	K	BB9	SO9	GB%	BABIP	WHIP	ERA	FIP	FRA	WARP
2014	CHR	AAA	23	1	3	0	7	7	33.3	36	1	13	28	3.5	7.6	49%	.324	1.47	4.05	3.42	4.45	0.7
2014	BIR	AA	23	5	8	0	20	20	116.7	116	7	31	57	2.4	4.4	49%	.278	1.26	3.39	3.92	4.71	0.5
2015	CHA	MLB	24	6	9	0	23	23	123.7	142	14	43	67	3.1	4.9	49%	.304	1.50	4.99	5.17	5.42	-0.3
2016	CHA	MLB	25	8	8	0	24	24	139.0	149	12	41	89	2.7	5.8	49%	.303	1.37	4.23	4.18	4.60	0.4

Breakout: 0% **Improve:** 0% **Collapse:** 0% **Attrition:** 0% **MLB:** 0% **Upside:** 3 *Comparables: T.J. McFarland, Brandon Cumpton, Zeke Spruill*

Drafted/Acquired: 2nd round, 2012 draft, Georgia Southern University (Statesboro, GA)

Previous Ranking: #4 (Org)

What Happened in 2014: The right-hander out of Georgia Southern University continued to prove he's capable of logging heavy workloads deep into a season, though the bat-missing concerns still loom as he approaches the major-league level.

Strengths: Big and strong frame; durable; flashes feel for craft; fastball operates 90-93 with good sink; can reach for more when ahead in the count; slider shows late cutting action; will induce weak contact; plays well off angle of fastball; capable of dropping curveball in for strikes and changing eye levels; can turn over average changeup; moderate arm-side fade; throws strikes; capable of holding stuff deep into games.

Weaknesses: Stuff is more average to solid-average across the board; relies heavily on pitching to weak contact; concerns on lack of bat-missing ability; lacks a wipeout secondary offering; fastball flattens out from middle of thighs and up; conditioning has been an issue in the past; delivery gets on the stiff and rigid side in stretches.

Risk Factor/Injury History: Low; 32 starts in the upper levels; mature arsenal; pedestrian secondary stuff.

Bret Sayre's Fantasy Take: There's really no reason to own Beck in a mixed league. There's just not enough in the profile that spells a fantasy return, whether it's the extremely weak strikeout rates or the hittable nature of his repertoire.

The Year Ahead: Beck has done little to bring any doubts toward the notion that he's an arm trending toward reaching the major leagues, which appears likely to happen at some point in 2015 if he continues to prove he can handle the upper levels like he displayed last season. The right-hander from Georgia shows feel for a four-pitch mix that he uses to keep hitters off-balance and has also demonstrated the ability to handle a meaty workload as a starter the past two full seasons since turning pro. The 24-year-old will set his sights on the International League this season, where the big test will be whether he can squeeze anything more out of his secondary arsenal to miss bats with more frequency. A brief taste of the level to close out 2014 offered an uptick in this department, but at the end of the day Beck is likely who he has always been—an arm that can eat innings and limit damage by changing speeds and that looks to induce weak contact. While it's not a high or sexy ceiling, and there's pressure on the more limited margin of error, things can play in the back of the rotation or in a swingman role out of the 'pen on a deeper pitching staff.

7. Courtney Hawkins OF

Born: 11/12/93 **Age:** 21 **Bats:** R **Throws:** R **Height:** 6'3" **Weight:** 220

MLB ETA	Hit	Power	Run	Glove	Arm	OFP	Realistic
Late 2016	–	60	–	50	60	55 >AVG REGULAR	40 <AVG ML PLAYER

YEAR	TEAM	LVL	AGE	PA	R	2B	3B	HR	RBI	BB	SO	SB	CS	AVG/OBP/SLG	TAv	BABIP	BRR	FRAA	WARP
2014	WNS	A+	20	515	65	25	4	19	84	53	143	11	3	.249/.331/.450	.272	.316	2.0	LF(108): -2.8, CF(6): -0.0	1.4
2015	CHA	MLB	21	250	25	8	1	9	29	14	94	3	1	.194/.246/.349	.222	.274	0.0	LF -0, CF -0	-0.4
2016	CHA	MLB	22	250	29	10	1	9	30	17	89	3	1	.208/.269/.383	.243	.290	0.1	LF -1, CF 0	0.4

Breakout: 0% **Improve:** 0% **Collapse:** 0% **Attrition:** 0% **MLB:** 0% **Upside:** 18 *Comparables: Chris Davis, Michael Choice, Marcell Ozuna*

Drafted/Acquired: 1st round, 2012 draft, Mary Carroll HS (Corpus Christi, TX)

Previous Ranking: #3 (Org)

What Happened in 2014: Hawkins rebounded from a disappointing first season in High-A, where the 21-year-old smacked 48 extra-base hits, but also continued to flash big swing-and-miss and offer concerns on the translation of the hit tool.

Strengths: Plus athlete; muscular build; thick lower half; well-above-average raw power; excellent bat speed; creates strong leverage with swing; power plays to all fields; punishes mistake fastballs middle-in; runs well for size; arm for right field; strong makeup.

Weaknesses: Actions can be on the stiff side; some restriction in upper body due to bulk; shows too much swing-and-miss; swing gets long when trying to cover outer third; pitch recognition needs considerable refinement;

approach is ultra-aggressive; lacks a plan at the plate; defense in center is below average (corner profile).

Risk Factor/Injury History: High; yet to reach upper levels; huge gap between present and future.

Bret Sayre's Fantasy Take: The power may be tempting, but even if he makes it as a major-league starter, the batting average is going to really ugly up the overall value he provides. In an OBP league, it's more palatable, but the name recognition far outpaces what he's actually worth in dynasty leagues right now.

The Year Ahead: There were definitely improvements for Hawkins last season in a return to the Carolina League that saw the outfielder produce more consistent hard contact and more of his natural raw power translate into game action. Still, the swing-and-miss as a result of his subpar pitch recognition and a crude approach at the plate leave strong concerns as to whether the hit tool is going to totally spoil the party against the more advanced arms at the next level and beyond. An assignment in Double-A awaits the muscular right-handed hitter in 2015, where the rubber is likely going to meet the road for the prospect in terms of making tangible adjustments to tone things down at the plate and better combat breaking stuff. A typical plate appearance from Hawkins usually sees him pick on a fastball early in the count, and if it's not put into play things start to spiral downhill once arms have the advantage of changing their looks. There's plenty of raw power here and an ability to impact the ball when getting into favorable hitting conditions that suggest a power hitter can emerge with further honing of the secondary skills. It's just becoming a tall order that the gap can be closed and evident that the shortcomings are likely to limit the overall end product.

---

8. Carlos Sanchez 2B

Born: 6/29/92 **Age:** 23 **Bats:** B **Throws:** R **Height:** 5'11" **Weight:** 195

MLB ETA	Hit	Power	Run	Glove	Arm		OFP	Realistic
Debuted in 2014	60	–	–	65	–		50 AVG ML PLAYER	45 UT/2ND DIV PLAYER

YEAR	TEAM	LVL	AGE	PA	R	2B	3B	HR	RBI	BB	SO	SB	CS	AVG/OBP/SLG	TAv	BABIP	BRR	FRAA	WARP
2014	CHA	MLB	22	104	6	5	0	0	5	3	25	1	1	.250/.269/.300	.220	.329	-1.5	2B(27): -1.9, SS(1): 0.1	-0.7
2014	CHR	AAA	22	494	60	19	6	7	57	36	84	16	4	.293/.349/.412	.251	.344	1.8	2B(64): -0.7, SS(44): 1.6	1.4
2015	CHA	MLB	23	250	26	10	2	2	18	12	52	6	3	.258/.298/.336	.238	.315	0.3	2B -2, SS 0	0.2
2016	CHA	MLB	24	442	45	16	3	5	39	24	88	11	4	.255/.302/.349	.243	.305	1.0	2B -4	0.5

Breakout: 6%   Improve: 22%   Collapse: 3%   Attrition: 10%   MLB: 31%   Upside: 31   *Comparables: Jose Pirela, Luis Valbuena, Alexi Amarista*

Drafted/Acquired: International Free Agent, 2009, Venezuela

Previous Ranking: #7 (Org)

What Happened in 2014: Sanchez rebounded well in his second tour at Triple-A, where he flashed more of his trademark contact ability and continued showing his above-average defensive game, before a call to the big club began the learning process at the highest level.

Strengths: Advanced skills for age; feel for making contact; good bat speed from both sides; controls head of the bat well; loose hands; willing to use the whole field; picks up spin well; soft glove; fluid actions; always engaged in the game; strong makeup reports.

Weaknesses: Limited physical projection; average size; well-below-average power; swing is geared to line-drive contact; impact of the bat is on the light side; arm comes up short at times on left side of infield; fits best at second base; profile is mostly glove.

Risk Factor/Injury History: Low; major-league ready; glove-first player.

Bret Sayre's Fantasy Take: If you loved Freddy Sanchez, you might like Carlos Sanchez a little at first. But then you'll realize that he's not as natural of a hitter and he has far too much competition for near-term playing time and you'll hit the trade market or free agency.

The Year Ahead: After a down 2013 campaign, the Venezuelan infielder showed much more comfort at the plate last season in the International League, which culminated with Sanchez earning a look with the White Sox to close out the year. The overall results during his 28-game foray in the bigs are fairly indicative of what to expect from the 23-year-old as a whole. While the bat is on the light side when it comes to the power department, there's feel for the barrel and good contact ability as a result of hands that stay nicely inside of the baseball. The defense is the calling card here for the prospect, which can easily play as plus at second base thanks to soft hands, strong instincts, and clean actions all around. Sanchez also has the ability to slide over to the left side of the infield, though the arm limits things to more of a fill-in type. It's second base if this player is to carve out a role as a regular. Prior to the acquisition of Emilio Bonifacio, it was believed that this season would see the youngster enter camp in a competition with fellow infield prospect Micah Johnson for the nod as the Opening Day second baseman. Further work proving he can manage plate appearances better against elite competition will go a long way toward Sanchez winning the spot and also proving there's enough consistency with the bat to hold down the position for the extended future.

9. Micah Johnson 2B

Born: 12/18/90 **Age:** 24 **Bats:** L **Throws:** R **Height:** 6'0" **Weight:** 190

MLB ETA	Hit	Power	Run	Glove	Arm		OFP	Realistic
2015	50	–	70	–	–		50 2ND DIV PLAYER	45 BENCH/<AVG PLAYER

YEAR	TEAM	LVL	AGE	PA	R	2B	3B	HR	RBI	BB	SO	SB	CS	AVG/OBP/SLG	TAv	BABIP	BRR	FRAA	WARP
2014	CHR	AAA	23	302	30	10	5	2	28	16	42	12	6	.275/.314/.370	.242	.315	1.5	2B(58): -4.6	-0.4
2014	BIR	AA	23	170	18	9	1	3	16	21	27	10	7	.329/.414/.466	.318	.385	1.1	2B(30): -1.2	1.5
2015	CHA	MLB	24	250	31	8	3	3	18	15	56	13	6	.251/.298/.347	.240	.309	0.8	2B 1	0.5
2016	CHA	MLB	25	432	44	14	4	5	39	28	93	23	10	.252/.302/.348	.243	.308	2.6	2B 3	1.2

Breakout: 7% **Improve:** 15% **Collapse:** 8% **Attrition:** 29% **MLB:** 41% **Upside:** 9 *Comparables: Eric Young, Cesar Hernandez, Jose Pirela*

Drafted/Acquired: 9th round, 2012 draft, Indiana University-Bloomington (Bloomington, IN)

Previous Ranking: #8 (Org)

What Happened in 2014: Johnson's game continued to round toward major-league-ready status in the system's upper levels, though a hamstring injury nagged the player for much of the season before he was ultimately shut down in mid-August, missing out on a chance for a call-up in the process with the trade of former incumbent Gordon Beckham.

Strengths: Excellent athlete; fast-twitch actions; plus-plus run; accelerates well out of the box; capable of impacting the game once on base; puts pressure on fielders; easy stroke; can square up velocity; will work the count; up-the-middle approach; shows some gap pop.

Weaknesses: Glove is below average; can struggle with reads at second; tends to rush; questions on future as infielder; may ultimately move to outfield; arm fits at keystone, but not enough for left side of infield or a corner; well-below-average power; contact tends to be empty; can be neutralized with soft stuff; will lunge on front foot; fringy overall instincts.

Risk Factor/Injury History: Low; major-league ready; elbow surgery on résumé (amateur); questions on glove.

Bret Sayre's Fantasy Take: Johnson has actual speed, and is better from a fantasy standpoint than the four names ahead of him, but there's a fair chance that he is going to lose the second base job to Emilio Bonifacio before he ever got it in the first place. He makes for a more interesting redraft reserve play than dynasty grab, given his ability to jump in and steal 30 bases at a moment's notice.

The Year Ahead: If it weren't for a lingering hamstring injury that dogged Johnson since a May stint on the disabled list, there's a very real possibility that the 24-year-old infielder would have spent the last six weeks of 2014 auditioning for the team's second base position. While the speedy prospect was hampered in the field by the leg injury, with his range and actions affected at times, evaluators have been mixed on whether Johnson's presently below-average glove is going to be up to par for handling the position full time. Some sources are more bullish on the player being a better fit in the outfield. Given the limited potential value of the glove, there's a fair amount of pressure on the bat to perform, and subsequently the speed to really impact the game. It'll come down to the player continuing to show that he can manage plate appearances and put offerings into play hard enough as a result. The ceiling isn't overly high here, with the likely outcome a utility player in the long run, but 2015 will serve as a chance to prove that things can play a bit higher for the next few seasons.

10. Jacob May CF

Born: 1/23/92 **Age:** 23 **Bats:** B **Throws:** R **Height:** 5'10" **Weight:** 180

MLB ETA	Hit	Power	Run	Glove	Arm		OFP	Realistic
2017	50	–	70	60	–		50 ML REGULAR	45 4TH OF/<AVG PLAYER

YEAR	TEAM	LVL	AGE	PA	R	2B	3B	HR	RBI	BB	SO	SB	CS	AVG/OBP/SLG	TAv	BABIP	BRR	FRAA	WARP
2014	WNS	A+	22	472	66	31	10	2	27	42	71	37	8	.258/.326/.395	.252	.305	5.3	CF(92): -7.2, LF(2): -0.0	0.7
2015	CHA	MLB	23	250	30	10	2	3	17	15	59	14	4	.224/.274/.325	.221	.277	1.7	CF -5, LF -0	-0.7
2016	CHA	MLB	24	250	27	10	2	5	25	19	60	15	4	.240/.305/.372	.249	.296	2.4	CF -5, LF 0	0.6

Breakout: 0% **Improve:** 0% **Collapse:** 0% **Attrition:** 0% **MLB:** 0% **Upside:** 21 *Comparables: Blake Tekotte, Jacoby Ellsbury, Shane Robinson*

Drafted/Acquired: 3rd round, 2013 draft, Coast Carolina University (Conway, SC)

Previous Ranking: On The Rise

What Happened in 2014: The speedster spent the year in the pitcher-friendly Carolina League, where the overall line was a bit mixed, but the outfielder flashed improvement managing counts and handling center field.

Strengths: Very good athlete; double-plus runner; speed shows in all aspects of the game; chance to impact on the bases; closes on the ball well in center; roams into both gaps well; plus range; compact stroke from both sides of the plate; feel for barrel; hands work well; flashes the makings of a patient approach; big-league bloodlines.

Weaknesses: Lacks physical projection; routes and judgment in center need work; arm is below average; won't play in a corner; below-average power ceiling; will need to learn how to pick spots to combat quality arms; expands zone and chases stuff with break at times; left-handed stroke gets loose; reads off pitchers need work; effort and pace can play down.

Risk Factor/Injury History: High; yet to reach upper levels; development of glove.

Bret Sayre's Fantasy Take: Any time you have a prospect with 70 speed, fantasy owners perk up their ears, but while May is an intriguing flier in deep leagues, there's a ways to go here before we can consider him in anything remotely shallow. He's a name to keep an eye on in 2015, though.

The Year Ahead: May is an intriguing prospect mainly based on his speed and defensive potential, but the switch-hitter does flash the type of stroke that lends thoughts to being capable of rounding into a line-drive contact bat down the line. At the peak, the 23-year-old offers potential as a top-of-the-order burner who can set the table for the thumpers that follow, disrupt on the bases, and become a favorite to the pitching staff for his ability to go get the ball in center field. It isn't a potential impact profile, but helps set the offensive tone and provides strong defense at a premium position. There is some work to go for May to make the vision a reality though. While the routes and reads in center have been improving, the prospect can lapse for stretches and drift around rather than crisply hunt fly balls down. Technique consistency is imperative as the arm falls well short in a corner, and the future prospects for achieving status as a regular hinge on sticking in center. A likely assignment in Double-A to start 2015 will also be a strong test for the player to prove his approach is up to the task of handling higher quality arms, and that the stick is trending toward producing enough true contact to get on-base at an acceptable clip. There's a major leaguer here, with some work, and one who can stick around for a while if the level of polish really starts to come with experience.

Prospects on the Rise

1. 3B Trey Michalczewski: The Oklahoma native possess the prototypical frame and size that tend to draw attention when discussing potential power-hitting third baseman. There's also plenty of natural strength here just

---

FROM THE FIELD

Tim Anderson

Team: Chicago White Sox

Evaluator: CJ Wittmann

Dates seen: April 11–14, 2014

Affiliate: Winston-Salem Dash (High-A, White Sox)

Physical/health: Shorter than listed 6'1"; very athletic build; filled out well in lower half presently with more room for growth; plus-plus athlete; just started playing baseball junior year of high school; super raw.

MLB ETA	Risk factor	OFP	Realistic role
2016	Extreme	65	50; major-league regular

Tool	Future grade	Report
Hit	60	Wide setup; loose, easy hands; Brandon Phillips-like preswing setup (bat wiggle); small wrist lock before starting swing; explosive hands; plus-plus bat speed; swing has natural lift; has some natural bat-to-ball skills; great strength in wrists and hands giving him good barrel control; exceptional hand-eye coordination; presently still learning to use the right side; often makes hard contact and can square velocity; needs refinement in approach and plate discipline; presently will expand the zone; recognizes spin but unable to barrel it presently; has trouble with anything down in the zone; hasn't shown the ability to adjust presently but still super raw.
Power	55	Sneaky plus raw pop; has present gap-to-gap pop; more pull-side power presently; raw pop comes from natural lift and plus-plus bat speed; has the ability to backspin the ball; will be plenty of doubles, with home-run potential.
Baserunning/ speed	70	Consistently in 4.04-4.07 range from right side; gets out of the box quickly and accelerates; still raw on bases; instinctive baserunner but needs work reading pickoff moves; will be a threat on the basepaths.
Glove	55	Has soft hands; exceptional hand-eye coordination; good footwork around bag; doesn't react well off the bat; instincts are lacking but has speed to make up for it; range is limited; couldn't get to ball in deep shortstop hole; collects and gathers himself well up the middle; has the hands to stay in the infield; needs repetition; presently below average at shortstop but with reps could play to average; would feel more comfortable with a move to second base. He'll get every opportunity to stay at shortstop and it will be interesting to see his progress later in the year. I need more convincing.
Arm	50	Makes throws on a line to first; fast, clean arm; quick transfers to throwing hand and quick release; has trouble making throw from shortstop hole; arm is not a strength on left side; will be plenty for second base.

Overall: There's extreme, extreme risk here because Anderson is a different kind of raw. He has probably played fewer games than everyone he's playing against. He needs reps and reps and reps. He has electric hands that could let him stay in the infield, but I don't love his range at shortstop and his arm lacked the strength to make the throw in the hole. At the plate, this is probably the first time Anderson has seen consistent breaking balls. He recognizes spin early and tracks the ball but hasn't shown the ability to barrel it. Presently, he still loves to pull the ball and is learning the use the right side. He makes consistent hard contact when balls are put into play, though. I am confident he can make the necessary adjustments to adjust to spin and barrel it. He's not off-balance when he's swinging; Anderson just doesn't look used to them yet. He's super raw and a long way away, but if he puts it all together, he has an electric profile.

waiting to be tapped into. Last season was relatively mixed from a performance standpoint, but youth and a pretty swing from both sides of the plate represent strong allies for Michalczewski as the level of experience starts to build. The main aspect of near-term focus resides with the 20-year-old's ability to pick up spin more quickly. This prospect will once again be age-advanced for his league in 2015, which makes this a careful study of experience level versus physical limitations in assessing the progress with the aforementioned need. A good showing in terms of being quicker with his trigger, along with not overcommitting his weight at the sight of every offering, will be a solid sign that things are starting to take and will push the status to a firm top-10 prospect in this system by next offseason.

2. RHP Nolan Sanburn: Acquired from Oakland in exchange for Adam Dunn at last year's waiver-deal deadline, this right-hander offers a potential power arsenal highlighted by a fastball that will work in the mid-90s and hard-breaking curveball that can miss bats. Sanburn also will throw the breaking ball harder for a slider look, while altering hitters' timing via turning over a changeup with arm-side action as well. The profile would get a present status boost if the 23-year-old could sustain things in a starter's role, but the lack of size is a concern when assessing whether he can handle the rigors of the long season in that capacity; a shoulder injury in early 2013 has led the former starter to work exclusively from the 'pen since returning that season. The organization may very well be inclined to give Sanburn an extended shot in the rotation again, with a quicker-tracking late-inning reliever as a definitive fall back if the stuff proves to play down too much. Either way, the Double-A litmus test awaits in 2015, and the feel here is that he passes it with flying colors.

3. OF Micker Adolfo: While the stateside debut on paper wasn't overly impressive, it is important to put into context that the Dominican import was playing in rookie ball last summer at the ripe old age of 17, when most are gearing up for senior-year glory and to grace the halls as the "big man on campus." Adolfo's 6-foot-3 frame already shows signs of filling out, with a solid amount of present strength that makes for batting practice sessions filled with towering fly balls and rising drives that land over the fence. The typical concerns exist for a player of this nature, including whether there is going to be progression with the hit tool for enough contact to happen and the associated gains needed with developing a pro approach. Adolfo is a lottery ticket for sure, but one with the type of fluid swing from the right side and early feel for the game to start showing the type of progress to affirm top-10 status in the near future.

Factors on the Farm

Prospects likely to contribute at the major-league level in 2015

1. 3B Matt Davidson: The wheels completely fell off the tracks for the third baseman last season in an ugly display at Triple-A that saw him fail to hit above the Mendoza line and fan at an accelerated clip. Davidson did flash some of the home-run power he is known for, but it's tough seeing anything other than a return trip to the International League to start this year. Still, if the 24-year-old can channel prior form during the early portion of the season and regain offensive traction in the process, the chance very well exists that he can push right back into the picture at the hot corner for the big club. There are times when the difference between failure and success is only the slightest adjustment, especially in a grinding mental game like this. The swing-and-miss may very well be the limiting factor here, but based on prior track record and solid reports on the work ethic a reemergence as a potential average regular is achievable.

2. C Kevan Smith: It's been a modest progression in terms of speed through the chain for the backstop despite coming out of the University of Pittsburgh back in 2011, but Smith will enter Triple-A this season looking to build off of a strong 2014 campaign that saw him finish out the year in the prospect-rich Arizona Fall League. The ceiling isn't overly high here, with the profile in line with a potential backup, but with the overall nature of the position, there is a chance he can stick in that type of role for some time. Given his background as a former college quarterback, the expectation that the 27-year-old can throw is an accurate one. The arm plays as about plus behind the dish, with a quicker release and solid accuracy down to second. The overall defense is still a bit unrefined and inconsistent, though, so some improvement shown this season will go a long way toward instilling confidence that he can handle the position should the need arise for the team during the summer.

3. RHP Michael Ynoa: The developmental road hasn't gone quite as planned for this former multimillion-dollar Dominican signee, with the majority of the career to date dotted with injuries and struggles in putting any type of consistent string of positive results together. A change of scenery can go a long way as a jump start for a player, and that's exactly what Ynoa now has after being acquired by the White Sox as part of the deal that brought Jeff Samardzija to the south side of the city. It may be more of longer shot that the right-hander gets an extended chance to contribute in 2015, but don't rule out that the 23-year-old can't ride the wave all the way up to the big club's bullpen on the strength of his mid-90s heater and more consistently plus curveball. It certainly wouldn't be the outcome that the promise suggested years ago, and there are still concerns about the player's level of buy-in, but the chance taken by the organization may pay off with a late-innings fixture for a handful of seasons.

CINCINNATI REDS

1. Robert Stephenson RHP

Born: 2/24/93   **Age:** 22   **Bats:** R   **Throws:** R   **Height:** 6'2"   **Weight:** 200

MLB ETA	CT	FB	CH	CB	SL	OFP	Realistic
2015	–	75	55	70	–	70 NO.2 STARTER	60 NO 3 SP/CLOSER

YEAR	TEAM	LVL	AGE	W	L	SV	G	GS	IP	H	HR	BB	K	BB9	SO9	GB%	BABIP	WHIP	ERA	FIP	FRA	WARP
2014	PEN	AA	21	7	10	0	27	26	136.7	114	18	74	140	4.9	9.2	38%	.264	1.38	4.74	4.58	5.43	0.3
2015	CIN	MLB	22	6	9	0	23	23	114.7	103	15	53	107	4.2	8.4	41%	.299	1.36	4.48	4.70	4.87	-0.2
2016	CIN	MLB	23	10	9	0	31	31	197.7	159	24	77	192	3.5	8.7	41%	.277	1.20	3.57	4.01	3.88	1.4

Breakout: 0%   Improve: 0%   Collapse: 0%   Attrition: 0%   MLB: 0%   Upside: 24   *Comparables: Yordano Ventura, Robbie Ray, Jake Odorizzi*

Drafted/Acquired: 1st round, 2011 draft, Alhambra HS (Martinez, CA)

Previous Ranking: #1 (Org), #22 (Top 101)

What Happened in 2014: Stephenson had an uneven first run at the Southern League but continues to show swing-and-miss stuff while retaining further projection in body and stuff.

#16 BP Top 101 Prospects

Strengths: Athletic and projectable; loose and easy power arm; solid extension; generates torque through upper/lower-half separation; fastball already plays to double-plus; operates comfortably in the mid-90s velocity band and regularly flirts in the upper-90s; hard curve with utility in and out of zone; sharp bite with plus-plus potential at maturity; changeup will flash; easy arm and athleticism give foundation for solid control and command; competitive; attack mentality on the bump with aggressive approach; already showing loud stuff with room for additional growth across the board.

Weaknesses: Yet to transition from thrower to pitcher; adversity too often met with "grip and rip" mentality; needs to work to unpack the craft and become less predictable, particularly with runners on or when struggling; control took a step back at Double-A with fewer bats chasing and Stephenson overthrowing when behind; changeup still budding, and can come deliberate and firm; needs off-speed to effectively neutralize righty bats, especially if command doesn't fully manifest.

Risk Factor/Injury History: Moderate; limited success at Double-A; overall refinement required

Bret Sayre's Fantasy Take: There's no questioning the potential in Stephenson, as it's among the highest in the minors, but his 2014 showed what the shortfalls could be in his fantasy profile—and they could take a big hit out of his value. The strikeouts are fantastic, and he could whiff 200 over a full year, but just look at 2014 Zack Wheeler, who struck out more than a batter per inning but walked 79 en route to a 1.33 WHIP and a 65th place ranking among starting pitchers in mixed leagues. And like Wheeler, he can take that next step forward to be a high-end SP2.

The Year Ahead: Stephenson survived the year at Double-A Pensacola, but in the process showed there is work to be done before tackling the next set of developmental challenges. Almost all of the righty's issues can be traced back to a propensity to try to throw through his on-field obstacles, rather than negotiate them via more precise execution of his craft. The fastball-curve combo has the potential to miss bats at every level, but to fully tap into that potential, Stephenson is going to have to rein things in and place a higher premium on spotting and execution. It's dangerous to scout the stat line when putting together a prospect profile, but in Stephenson's case, last year's numbers point to a profile confirmed by reports: struggles maintaining a handle on his power arsenal, lack of a present weapon against right-handed bats, and discomfort operating with runners on. While his problems caused evaluators in and out of the organization to pump their brakes, the road to major-league impact is still wide open for the former first rounder thanks to an impressive arsenal. Stephenson has the athleticism, projectable strength, and body control to grow into a solid command profile, and an enticing bit of room left in projecting his secondaries. It's likely he starts 2015 back in Double-A and remains on track to debut in Cincinnati at some point in the next two years with an eye to assuming Opening Day duties in the not-too-distant future.

2. Jesse Winker   OF

Born: 8/17/93   **Age:** 21   **Bats:** L   **Throws:** L   **Height:** 6'3"   **Weight:** 210

MLB ETA	Hit	Power	Run	Glove	Arm	OFP	Realistic
2016	60	55	50	50	–	60 1ST DIV REGULAR	50 AVG ML PLAYER

YEAR	TEAM	LVL	AGE	PA	R	2B	3B	HR	RBI	BB	SO	SB	CS	AVG/OBP/SLG	TAv	BABIP	BRR	FRAA	WARP
2014	PEN	AA	20	92	15	5	0	2	8	14	22	0	0	.208/.326/.351	.260	.259	0.4	LF(20): 0.9	0.4
2014	BAK	A+	20	249	42	15	0	13	49	40	46	5	1	.317/.426/.580	.324	.349	-2.2	LF(46): -2.8, LF(2): -2.8	1.8
2015	CIN	MLB	21	250	26	9	1	7	28	26	62	0	0	.220/.305/.363	.254	.269	-0.3	LF -1, RF -0	0.1
2016	CIN	MLB	22	250	31	10	1	8	28	28	59	0	0	.221/.313/.380	.260	.264	-0.4	LF -2, RF 0	1.2

Breakout: 0%   **Improve:** 0%   **Collapse:** 0%   **Attrition:** 0%   **MLB:** 0%   **Upside:** 39   *Comparables: Wil Myers, Jaff Decker, Joc Pederson*

#44
BP Top 101 Prospects

Drafted/Acquired: 1st round, 2012 draft, Olympia HS (Olympia, FL)

Previous Ranking: #5 (Org)

What Happened in 2014: After raking his way through 53 California League games, the former sandwich pick was promoted to Double-A Pensacola, where his season was cut short after a car accident left him with a partially torn tendon in his right wrist.

Strengths: Natural hitter; efficient barrel delivery with easy extension through contact; capable of squaring up with regularity across the quadrants; solid plate coverage; advanced approach; comfort hitting in all counts; can spray line to line; good present strength; power could play above average thanks to regular hard contact and some natural loft; capable defender in a corner; solid feel across his game; good makeup and positive presence on the field and in the locker room.

Weaknesses: Average at best athleticism; below-average runner; arm plays fringe-average; likely limited to left field; can expand zone some away when down in count; some issue with quality spin; pitch identification could limit impact of natural bat-to-ball ability and strike zone command; power derivation skewed slightly to strength over bat speed, enhancing risk profile associated with pitch identification.

Risk Factor/Injury History: Moderate; limited exposure to Double-A; danger hit utility drops at upper levels; 2014 checkered with injuries, including early-season concussion and partially torn tendon in right wrist.

Bret Sayre's Fantasy Take: It's easy to overlook the guy whose hit tool is his strongest in fantasy, but like your parents always told you, just because it's easy doesn't make it right. Winker could be a points league darling who hits .290 with 20-plus homers (especially in that park)—and even without much speed to speak of, it's a solid OF2 profile.

The Year Ahead: Winker is an interesting case study, with a feel for the barrel that sticks out at the lower levels but may play down some once exposed to more advanced arms. The combination of less-than-impactful bat speed and some issues with identifying the soft stuff have led to slightly higher whiff rates than you'd expect from a player with an advanced approach and a comfortable and loving relationship with the strike zone. As Winker is more regularly challenged with pitchers wielding quality secondaries and displaying more precision with their arsenal, there is a chance the strikeout rate increases to the point it starts to eat into the hit-tool production (and transitively the power production). Still, Winker has displayed a strong work ethic at the professional level, and there is little doubt he will put in the requisite time and effort to continue making adjustments as he progresses toward Cincy. This season should find him back in Double-A, hopefully fully healthy, and ready to make his first earnest run at the upper levels. The upside is a solid number two or three bat that won't be a drain in the field, and he should hit enough in any event to be a regular producer at the major-league level even if it happens to be a bit further down the lineup card.

3. Michael Lorenzen   RHP

Born: 1/4/92   **Age:** 23   **Bats:** R   **Throws:** R   **Height:** 6'3"   **Weight:** 205

MLB ETA	CT	FB	CH	CB	SL	OFP	Realistic
2016	–	65	60	–	55	60 NO. 3 STARTER	50 NO. 4 STARTER

YEAR	TEAM	LVL	AGE	W	L	SV	G	GS	IP	H	HR	BB	K	BB9	SO9	GB%	BABIP	WHIP	ERA	FIP	FRA	WARP
2014	PEN	AA	22	4	6	0	24	24	120.7	112	9	44	84	3.3	6.3	53%	.285	1.29	3.13	4.01	5.05	1.0
2015	CIN	MLB	23	4	6	1	27	15	84.7	85	10	35	56	3.7	6.0	49%	.304	1.42	4.80	4.99	5.22	-0.6
2016	CIN	MLB	24	8	9	1	50	24	174.0	173	18	64	134	3.3	6.9	49%	.316	1.36	4.55	4.16	4.95	-0.8

Breakout: 0%   **Improve:** 0%   **Collapse:** 0%   **Attrition:** 0%   **MLB:** 0%   **Upside:** 2   *Comparables: John Gast, Lance Broadway, Chaz Roe*

Drafted/Acquired: 1st round, 2013 draft, California State University Fullerton (Fullerton, CA)

Previous Ranking: #8 (Org)

What Happened in 2014: The former Fullerton Titan completed his first full season as a starter, logging 120 2/3 innings and dealing power stuff along the way before fading noticeably through the second half.

Strengths: Top-shelf arm strength; fastball capable of reaching the upper-90s up in the zone; operates comfortably 91-94 mph and can mix two- and four-seam looks to miss barrels; works effectively at the base of the zone; impressive comfort with changeup; will flash good fade and late drop; weapon against lefties; slider shows plus potential thanks to release and plane deception with fastball; can be tough to pick up with tilt and bite to draw empty swings; can drop a "show-me" curve with 12-to-6 action to keep bats off plane; excellent athlete with firm physique; improved consistency in mechanics; command projects; intense competitor; mental fortitude to close if shifted back to relief.

#63

BP Top
101
Prospects

Weaknesses: Faded significantly down the stretch; stuff tends to decrease over the course of a start; best fit may be in 'pen, where fastball and slider would both play up in shorter stints; changeup still a work in progress, with misfires often up and over the plate; can overthrow, particularly when working behind; still learning to pace through starts and season; lacks present durability and endurance to weather full season as a starter; arsenal consistently played a full grade lower late in season, and a half grade lower through later innings.

Risk Factor/Injury History: Low; needs to build up endurance for starter's slog; precipitous drop in quality stuff across innings/starts; safe bet to contribute in some form.

Bret Sayre's Fantasy Take: Lorenzen has a little too much bullpen risk to be a top-50 fantasy prospect, despite his proximity—which is a strange thing to say given that in a vacuum he has more fantasy potential in the bullpen than in the rotation. As a starter, he could look quite similar to 2014 Mike Leake on the stat page, contributing across the board without being dominant anywhere.

The Year Ahead: It was a hugely successful summer for the one-time two-way standout, as Lorenzen showed he could hold his own in a starter capacity while sprinkling in flashes of dominance. The big question is whether the strong-armed righty will be able to build up the arm and the body to the point where he is consistently delivering a power arsenal later into his starts, and more importantly later in the season. If a more conservative pacing causes the stuff to tick down, then this profile moves closer to a solid number 4 starter with three potential above-average offerings but not enough snap, crackle, and pop to be a true impact arm. At that point, it is likely team need would determine whether Lorenzen is more valuable as a solid contributor in the rotation or a true shutdown arm in the 'pen, where the fastball and slider could both play to double-plus in short bursts. Lorenzen could start back in Double-A with a more deliberate approach to his pacing and a chance to finish the level off on a strong note before continuing his ascent.

---

4. Yorman Rodriguez   OF

Born: 8/15/92   **Age:** 22   **Bats:** R   **Throws:** R   **Height:** 6'2"   **Weight:** 210

MLB ETA	Hit	Power	Run	Glove	Arm	OFP	Realistic
2016	–	65	60	55	70	60 1ST DIV REGULAR	50 AVG ML PLAYER

YEAR	TEAM	LVL	AGE	PA	R	2B	3B	HR	RBI	BB	SO	SB	CS	AVG/OBP/SLG	TAv	BABIP	BRR	FRAA	WARP
2014	CIN	MLB	21	29	3	0	0	0	2	1	12	0	1	.222/.276/.222	.194	.400	0.5	RF(4): 0.1, CF(2): -0.1	0.0
2014	PEN	AA	21	502	69	20	5	9	40	47	117	12	5	.262/.331/.389	.269	.333	2.7	CF(88): -3.0, RF(20): 0.2	2.2
2015	CIN	MLB	22	250	22	10	1	4	23	13	78	3	1	.217/.261/.324	.224	.301	-0.1	CF -3, RF -1	-0.8
2016	CIN	MLB	23	250	25	10	1	5	24	17	75	3	1	.217/.273/.336	.230	.296	0.0	CF -3, RF -1	-0.8

Breakout: 0%   Improve: 0%   Collapse: 0%   Attrition: 0%   MLB: 0%   Upside: 39   *Comparables: Felix Pie, Elijah Dukes, Michael Saunders*

Drafted/Acquired: International Free Agent, 2008, Venezuela

Previous Ranking: #4 (Org)

What Happened in 2014: Rodriguez made a brief debut in Cincinnati after putting together a solid Southern League showing over 119 games with Pensacola.

Strengths: Strength and athleticism; quality glove, plus speed, and plus-plus arm complete impressive defensive foundation for center or right; closes well; arm comes with accuracy and smooth release; loose hands and whippy bat; raw power displays about double-plus; quick-twitch with some natural lift and carry; solid feel for strike zone; improving approach and ability to make in-game adjustments.

Weaknesses: Reads and routes still a work in progress; some hitch and length to swing; susceptible to mature sequencing; can be led out of the zone up top and away; could rack up empty swings against major-league arms; in-game power could play down due to inconsistencies in lower-half weight transfer and merely average barrel control; second-gear runner with slight ramp-up delay.

Risk Factor/Injury History: Moderate; hit utility has potential to eat into value at major-league level; solid but unspectacular Double-A performance.

Bret Sayre's Fantasy Take: The power and speed are appealing, as his natural tools whisper 20/20, but he's far riskier than a prospect with a full season of upper-minors experience (and an MLB cup of coffee) should be. He's likely to give the type of roto value we've seen from Danny Espinosa (both the good and bad), but without the middle infield eligibility.

The Year Ahead: Rodriguez remains an interesting upside play, with the requisite physicality and athleticism to allow for some dream and daring in projection. Despite quality bat speed and big raw power buoying the offensive profile, there is a fair amount of risk anchored to the right-swinging outfielder as well. The swing violence, while producing impactful contact, limits Rodriguez's barrel control and, when paired with strike zone restraint that can fray at the margins both up and out, forms a dangerous combination that could be regularly exploited by major-league arms. While Rodriguez has shown an improved ability to make in-game adjustments, it remains likely that robust strikeout totals will be a fixture in his major-league game. That won't in and of itself sink him, but any significant struggles to make regular hard contact could limit the overall upside in the offensive profile, with added negative impact if a full-time switch to right occurs and a larger slice of the "value pie" is tied to the stick. Rodriguez would benefit from a stint in Louisville to start 2015, where the Venezuelan product could continue to log reps against advanced minor-league competition in the hopes of making the incremental progress necessary, both in the field and at the plate, to bridge the gap between present skill set and the proficiency required to contribute on the game's brightest stage.

5.   Nick Howard   RHP

Born: 4/6/93   **Age:** 22   **Bats:** R   **Throws:** R   **Height:** 6'3"   **Weight:** 215

MLB ETA	CT	FB	CH	CB	SL	OFP	Realistic
2017	–	65	–	55	60	60 NO.3 STARTER	50 NO. 4 STARTER

YEAR	TEAM	LVL	AGE	W	L	SV	G	GS	IP	H	HR	BB	K	BB9	SO9	GB%	BABIP	WHIP	ERA	FIP	FRA	WARP
2014	DYT	A	21	2	1	0	11	5	33.7	28	4	11	23	2.9	6.1	53%	.274	1.16	3.74	4.73	5.67	-0.3
2015	CIN	MLB	22	1	3	0	9	6	34.7	38	5	17	19	4.4	4.9	46%	.310	1.59	5.57	5.86	6.06	-0.5
2016	CIN	MLB	23	7	8	0	36	23	168.7	169	20	65	123	3.5	6.6	46%	.309	1.38	4.52	4.49	4.91	-0.7

Breakout: 0%   **Improve:** 0%   **Collapse:** 0%   **Attrition:** 0%   **MLB:** 0%   **Upside:** 2   *Comparables: Maikel Cleto, Ivan Nova, T.J. McFarland*

Drafted/Acquired: 1st round, 2014 draft, University of Virginia (Charlottesville, VA)

Previous Ranking: NR

What Happened in 2014: The Wahoo closer helped push UVA to its first ever College World Series Finals appearance before logging 54 professional innings between the Midwest League and Arizona Fall League.

Strengths: Power arm; fastball can reach as high as 98 mph in relief; could sit comfortably in 92-94 mph velocity band as a starter; works both sides of the plate effectively; slider and curve show distinct shape and action; low- to mid-80s slide piece comes with tilt and can be true swing-and-miss offering; 11-to-5 curve gives solid vertical look with depth and bite; changeup progressing and could be average in time; good balance throughout motion; hint of crossfire; sturdy build; short circle and quick arm helps ball to jump on hitters.

Weaknesses: Needs to build up stamina and arm to hold quality of stuff and control/command across starter's load; can slow arm with curve and change; will occasionally flash "hooked" wrist on the backside with curve; fastball-reliant working inner half against same-side bats; lacks effective weapon to handle lefties; stuff was slightly down in pro debut after long season.

Risk Factor/Injury History: Moderate; yet to complete full pro season; conversion to starter still theoretical.

Bret Sayre's Fantasy Take: Howard, given his usage at UVA, is going to take some time to build up to a true starter's workload even if the conversion is successful. This places a strain on his fantasy value, given the extension of his ETA. Without high-end starter potential, Howard is someone who should not be targeted in the first two rounds of dynasty drafts this year.

The Year Ahead: As was the case with Lorenzen, the Reds popped Howard in the draft with the intent to transition the college closer to a pro rotation. Howard shares a number of similarities with Lorenzen, including big velocity, sturdy build, a power breaking ball, and solid athleticism, providing on-the-surface comfort that there is a firm foundation from which to build up a quality pro starting pitcher. Howard comes with the additional advantage of having some experience starting in the past, though he has further to go in developing a quality off-speed pitch with which to disrupt timing and help set up the plus or better heater. At the outset this year, the curve should give Howard a reprieve from lower-level bats sitting on the fastball-slider velo and plane, but he will need to find a workable off-speed to consistently turn over lineups at the upper levels. Perhaps more importantly, the former Cavalier needs to find a pitch to help neutralize lefty bats if he's to prove effective over multiple innings. Virginia's deep run in the collegiate playoffs ate into Howard's time in pro ball, though the righty was able to get some work in during the Arizona Fall League, pushing him above 90 in-game innings for the calendar year. He's advanced enough to start 2015 in High-A, with hopes that he can follow in Lorenzen's footsteps in reaching 120 or so innings and perhaps a promotion to Double-A by year end. Again, like Lorenzen, there is late-inning potential in the arm should Howard shift back to the 'pen at some point.

6. Anthony DeSclafani RHP

Born: 4/18/90 **Age:** 25 **Bats:** R **Throws:** R **Height:** 6'1" **Weight:** 190

MLB ETA		CT	FB	CH	CB	SL		OFP	Realistic
Debuted in 2014		–	60	50	–	60		50 NO. 4 STARTER	50 LATE INN RP

YEAR	TEAM	LVL	AGE	W	L	SV	G	GS	IP	H	HR	BB	K	BB9	SO9	GB%	BABIP	WHIP	ERA	FIP	FRA	WARP
2014	MIA	MLB	24	2	2	0	13	5	33.0	40	4	5	26	1.4	7.1	42%	.330	1.36	6.27	3.74	4.65	-0.1
2014	NWO	AAA	24	3	3	0	12	11	59.3	48	2	21	59	3.2	8.9	45%	.284	1.16	3.49	3.41	3.68	1.2
2014	JAX	AA	24	3	4	0	8	8	43.0	45	4	10	38	2.1	8.0	46%	.333	1.28	4.19	3.33	4.77	0.3
2015	CIN	MLB	25	6	8	0	23	23	114.7	116	13	32	91	2.5	7.1	48%	.319	1.29	4.13	4.20	4.49	0.3
2016	CIN	MLB	26	9	9	0	29	29	178.7	182	20	46	144	2.3	7.3	48%	.323	1.28	4.13	3.84	4.48	0.0

Breakout: 23%   Improve: 44%   Collapse: 13%   Attrition: 33%   MLB: 73%   Upside: 9   *Comparables: Dillon Gee, Jeff Locke, Brandon Workman*

Drafted/Acquired: 6th round, 2011 draft, University of Florida (Gainesville, FL)

Previous Ranking: #8 (Org – MIA)

What Happened in 2014: DeSclafani handled the upper levels of the minors before getting his first taste of The Show, which proved to be challenging as a starter, but offered some promise coming out of the bullpen.

Strengths: Repeatable delivery; athletic; keeps arm in slot; sits low-90s with fastball, but reaches when needs it; late life to offering; creates hard snap with slider; sharp, late break; flashes feel for changeup; confident using it at any point in count; solid-average to better overall command of arsenal; aggressive mentality.

Weaknesses: At times gets into too much of a challenge mode; falls into ruts of trying to elevate fastball past hitters; needs more focus on pounding lower tier consistently; changeup lacks high-quality action; tends to float; slider will lose shape and get loose in stretches; lacks true bat-missing pitch.

Risk Factor/Injury History: Low risk; achieved major leagues; mature stuff.

Bret Sayre's Fantasy Take: Unless you're in a 16-team league or deeper, DeSclafani probably shouldn't be on your radar. Even if he's a starter, he's going to be replacement level at best in mixed leagues.

The Year Ahead: DeSclafani consistently pitches with a high level of confidence in his stuff. He isn't afraid to come right after and challenge hitters, avoiding spells of nibbling and trying to be too fine. When the stuff is more solid-average than well above average, however, there needs to be some element of finesse to avoid working in spots that usually result in ringing contact around the yard. The right-hander ran into this during his call-up in 2014, especially when working as a starter. DeSclafani's mentality and fastball-slider combo likely slot him into a relief role over the long run, where his heater can play up a tick in short bursts and his aggressive approach fits with getting two or three concentrated outs before handing the ball over to someone else. There is a chance that the 25-year-old can tone things down a bit and get enough out of the changeup to hang as a starter on a second-division team for the early portion of his career. The righty should be in line to log major-league time in 2015, with ample opportunity to serve as a swingman providing starter innings or coming out of Cincinnati's bullpen depending on team need.

7. Alex Blandino SS

Born: 11/6/92 **Age:** 22 **Bats:** R **Throws:** R **Height:** 6'0" **Weight:** 190

MLB ETA		Hit	Power	Run	Glove	Arm		OFP	Realistic
2016		55	50	–	55	55		60 1ST DIVISION REGULAR	50 AVG ML PLAYER

YEAR	TEAM	LVL	AGE	PA	R	2B	3B	HR	RBI	BB	SO	SB	CS	AVG/OBP/SLG	TAv	BABIP	BRR	FRAA	WARP
2014	DYT	A	21	152	20	10	1	4	16	13	42	1	2	.261/.329/.440	.289	.341	0.3	SS(34): 3.7	1.7
2014	BIL	Rk	21	131	20	10	1	4	16	16	18	6	3	.309/.412/.527	.348	.337	-2.1	SS(25): -1.5	1.6
2015	CIN	MLB	22	250	24	9	0	5	20	16	77	1	1	.197/.254/.304	.214	.268	-0.5	SS 4	0.3
2016	CIN	MLB	23	250	26	10	1	5	24	18	68	1	1	.217/.280/.336	.232	.280	-0.6	SS 4	0.5

Breakout: 0%   Improve: 0%   Collapse: 0%   Attrition: 0%   MLB: 0%   Upside: 23   *Comparables: Todd Frazier, Ryan Flaherty, Zach Walters*

Drafted/Acquired: 1st round, 2014 draft, Stanford University (Palo Alto, CA)

Previous Ranking: NR

What Happened in 2014: Blandino rode a strong 2013 summer performance on the Cape to a prominent place on follow lists, and a better-than-the-stats-show spring to selection in the back of the first round of the June draft.

Strengths: Compact swing produces regular loud contact across the diamond; has shown the ability to drop the barrel and drive the ball with wood; solid approach at present with ability to work deep into counts; good balance at the plate and quick wrists; very good with the glove; lower half works well and sets up above-average arm; throws play from all the angles and on the run; solid first step and clean actions help profile to play across three skill spots on the dirt despite fringy foot speed; chance to handle short, and glove could play above average at both third and second base.

Weaknesses: Below-average run; over-the-fence power is not natural part of game, so he'll need to learn when to look for pitches to try and drive; questions as to ultimate power output; hands can get too low in load, leading to coverage issues on inner half; can be beat with velocity up in the zone; at times too passive early in count; limited range; doubts as to long-term fit at shortstop, placing added pressure on offensive development.

Risk Factor/Injury History: Moderate; yet to reach High-A

Bret Sayre's Fantasy Take: Another prospect on this list far more suited to points leagues, Blandino should be the first Red taken in dynasty drafts—though he's a better use of a pick in deeper mixed leagues. The governor on his tools means he's not likely to be a consistent top-10 performer at whatever position he ends up at, but he could have Asdrubal Cabrera-type value (minus the fluky power season).

The Year Ahead: Blandino impressed pro evaluators with his actions at shortstop over a limited look last summer, showing enough aptitude to keep hope alive that that he could stick at the six-spot through at least the start of his pro career. With a good feel for contact and advanced approach, the Stanford product proved far too advanced for the Pioneer League and was bumped up to Low-A Dayton, where he showed some signs of fatigue and an uncharacteristic willingness to expand the zone. The range of possible outcomes varies widely for Blandino, which is not generally the case for a well-baked collegiate first rounder. Supporters see a first-division regular with the bat to hit at the top of a contender's lineup and the chops to provide adequate defense at short or flash above-average leather at the hot corner or keystone. One evaluator even compared Blandino to a poor man's Anthony Rendon, envisioning an above-average glove at third and solid arm to go with a .275/.350/.425 slash at maturity. Skeptics see a future utility player whose power will play light for third and whose limited range will keep him from a full-time gig up-the-middle. The most realistic outcome lies somewhere in between, potentially as a solid second-base glove whose baseball IQ will make up for below-average speed on the bases and range in the field, and whose solid but unspectacular bat could provide enough gap-to-gap pop and on-base ability to slot in as a number two hitter on a solid club. Blandino is ready to start 2015 with High-A Daytona and could move quickly depending on how he looks at short and the level of import the Reds place on his sticking there. If the bat progresses as most expect he could push his way to Cincy before long.

8. Nick Travieso RHP

Born: 1/31/94   **Age:** 21   **Bats:** R   **Throws:** R   **Height:** 6'2"   **Weight:** 215

MLB ETA	CT	FB	CH	CB	SL	OFP	Realistic
2017	–	60	50	–	55	60 NO. 3 STARTER	45 NO. 5 STARTER

YEAR	TEAM	LVL	AGE	W	L	SV	G	GS	IP	H	HR	BB	K	BB9	SO9	GB%	BABIP	WHIP	ERA	FIP	FRA	WARP
2014	DYT	A	20	14	5	0	26	26	142.7	123	10	44	114	2.8	7.2	50%	.272	1.17	3.03	3.93	5.04	-0.4
2015	CIN	MLB	21	5	10	0	23	23	111.7	119	15	50	62	4.0	5.0	42%	.302	1.51	5.30	5.56	5.77	-1.3
2016	CIN	MLB	22	7	9	0	27	27	160.3	161	19	58	104	3.3	5.8	42%	.300	1.36	4.60	4.61	5.00	-0.9

Breakout: 0%   Improve: 0%   Collapse: 0%   Attrition: 0%   MLB: 0%   Upside: 1   *Comparables: Brett Marshall, T.J. House, Mike Foltynewicz*

Drafted/Acquired: 1st round, 2012 draft, Archbishop McCarthy HS (Southwest Ranches, FL)

Previous Ranking: On The Rise

What Happened in 2014: After a disappointing 2013, Travieso took steps toward righting the ship in his second spin through the Midwest League, averaging just under six innings per start and finishing the year with nine impressive starts in which he held opponents to a .164 batting average and .048 ISO to go along with 38 strikeouts over those 51 2/3 innings.

Strengths: Relatively low-mileage arm; logged 142 2/3 innings in tough Midwest League, showing solid durability and improved stamina through starts; fastball reached the mid-90s periodically, sitting regularly in the 88-92 mph velocity band; slider will flash above average with short bite and tilt; shows some feel for changeup; can produce plane with the fastball; some deception, ability to hide ball; repeatable mechanics; should continue to throw strikes as he moves up the ranks.

Weaknesses: Still working to get mechanics to be second nature; deliberate in action; deep stab on back side; arm path not yet uniform and can hamper execution; slider can show below average when searching for release, with soft, slurvy action; changeup often too firm; in-zone command below average; still learning how to throw good strikes; can overthrow, leaving fastball flat and elevated; will need to stay on top of body and conditioning; fastball velocity and overall effectiveness of pitches fluctuates with regularity.

Risk Factor/Injury History: High; yet to reach High-A; volatility throughout profile.

Bret Sayre's Fantasy Take: There's an awful lot of risk in Travieso's fantasy profile, which places him closer in value to a short-season arm than one who spent all of 2014 in Low-A. The secondaries don't project strongly enough to suggest that Travieso will be able to generate the kind of strikeouts mixed leaguers need at the highest level, so he's a wait-and-see guy in dynasty formats.

The Year Ahead: While Travieso has not yet established himself as even a moderate risk asset, the developmental progress shown over the past 12 months has been encouraging. The former first rounder saw his stuff, and body, take a step back during his first pro season in 2013 but showed improvement on both fronts this past year. While not entirely back to where he flashed on longer rest in high school, the fastball did climb back into the mid-90s with regularity, and he was more effective in finding the strike zone with the offering, as well. Similarly, his slider has yet to realize the potential flashed predraft, most frequently showing short, cutter-like action, albeit with bite and tilt. The hope remains that as Travieso continues to build up pro experience and more effectively implement instruction, both pitches will consistently grade out as plus. He'll need to make conditioning a priority to keep the body in check and prevent physical fluctuations that could hamper efforts to solidify his mechanical foundation. While his second trip through the Midwest League fell shy of a true breakout season, the fact that Travieso saw growth in the arsenal and showed enough durability and effectiveness to work over 140 innings was a significant step in the right direction. This season should see a High-A assignment and the potential for Travieso to firmly establish himself as an arm of interest on the prospecting scape.

9.   Phil Ervin   OF

Born: 7/15/92   **Age:** 22   **Bats:** R   **Throws:** R   **Height:** 5'10"   **Weight:** 205

MLB ETA	Hit	Power	Run	Glove	Arm	OFP	Realistic
2018	55	50	55	50	60	55 >AVG ML PLAYER	45 4TH OF/<AVG PLAYER

YEAR	TEAM	LVL	AGE	PA	R	2B	3B	HR	RBI	BB	SO	SB	CS	AVG/OBP/SLG	TAv	BABIP	BRR	FRAA	WARP
2014	DYT	A	21	562	68	34	7	7	68	46	110	30	5	.237/.305/.376	.263	.284	3.1	CF(68): -2.9, LF(38): -1.9	1.1
2015	CIN	MLB	22	250	23	10	1	4	21	16	66	7	2	.205/.260/.302	.219	.265	0.6	CF -1, LF -1	-0.6
2016	CIN	MLB	23	250	25	10	1	4	23	17	66	8	2	.220/.281/.331	.233	.286	1.0	CF -1, LF -1	-0.3

Breakout: 0%   **Improve:** 0%   **Collapse:** 0%   **Attrition:** 0%   **MLB:** 0%   **Upside:** 26   *Comparables: Xavier Avery, J.B. Shuck, Trayvon Robinson*

Drafted/Acquired: 1st round, 2013 draft, Samford University (Birmingham, AL)

Previous Ranking: #3 (Org), #63 (Top 101)

What Happened in 2014: It was a rough year all around for Ervin, as he struggled to find any rhythm in the box and found himself stumbling through a season's worth of games at Low-A Dayton.

Strengths: Solid athleticism; strong build; chance to realize solid-average in-game power; ability to drive the ball middle in; has shown impact bat speed; at his best can stay short to contact and utilize full field; nose for the ball; routes continue to improve; arm should play in right field, with solid carry and accuracy; has shown plus foot speed underway.

Weaknesses: Can extend early, sapping power and complicating contact against spin; can get pull-happy; consistent struggles with soft stuff away; swing got upper-body centric through year, with choppy barrel delivery and limited swing plane/pitch plane overlap; slowing foot speed trending toward average; lacks physical projection; concerns injury history could negatively impact physical tools.

Risk Factor/Injury History: High; significant struggles at Low-A; robust injury history in file.

Bret Sayre's Fantasy Take: Buying low on Ervin is not a bad idea right about now, as his miserable 2014 season is far more fresh in fantasy owners' heads than his strong predraft profile. It's still possible that Ervin develops into a .275 hitter with 15/15 potential, but that "safe college bat" tag is long gone.

The Year Ahead: Ervin's assignment to Low-A Dayton in 2014, after he cruised through a quick 12-game stint to close 2013, was intended to ease the former first rounder into the year after he underwent surgery on his wrist during the offseason. While wrist injuries can often linger, the extent to which Ervin looked lost was shocking. In his pro debut the Samford product stood out for his contact-oriented approach, compact swing, bat speed, and ability to make loud contact across the zone. To a T, these attributes abandoned the former Cape Cod MVP, as his 2014 swing came with early extension and pull-side heave, slowing the barrel through the zone and limiting his ability to adequately cover the plate. The hope is that an offseason's worth of rest and continued strengthening of the wrist will see Ervin return to his presurgery form, when the first rounder looked the part of potential impact bat capable of wielding above-average hit and power tools. Outside of the box, Ervin appeared to slow some last year, with many viewing him as a lock for right field as early as 2015, putting even more pressure on the bat coming around. There is still an impact player buried in the profile, but the struggles were severe enough in Dayton that he could be approaching make-or-break territory despite having just 762 pro plate appearances to his name. A hot start this year would go a long way toward getting evaluators to shrug off 2014 as a developmental hiccup and putting Ervin back on developmental track.

10. Gavin LaValley 3B

Born: 12/28/94 **Age:** 20 **Bats:** R **Throws:** R **Height:** 6'3" **Weight:** 235

MLB ETA	Hit	Power	Run	Glove	Arm	OFP	Realistic
2019	50	60	–	–	–	55 >AVG ML PLAYER	45 BENCH BAT

YEAR	TEAM	LVL	AGE	PA	R	2B	3B	HR	RBI	BB	SO	SB	CS	AVG/OBP/SLG	TAv	BABIP	BRR	FRAA	WARP
2014	BIL	Rk	19	22	2	0	0	1	2	0	10	0	0	.190/.227/.333	.188	.300	0.0	3B(2): -0.3	-0.2
2014	CIN	Rk	19	219	29	10	2	5	30	26	44	3	0	.286/.374/.439	.258	.345	-0.1	3B(14): -2.4	0.0
2015	CIN	MLB	20	250	18	7	0	4	21	12	80	0	0	.181/.226/.267	.189	.254	-0.4	3B -5	-1.9
2016	CIN	MLB	21	250	25	10	1	6	24	15	80	0	0	.204/.258/.328	.220	.280	-0.5	3B -5	-1.7

Breakout: 0%   Improve: 0%   Collapse: 0%   Attrition: 0%   MLB: 0%   Upside: 11   *Comparables: Mat Gamel, Josh Bell, Alex Liddi*

Drafted/Acquired: 4th round, 2014 draft, Carl Albert HS (Midwest City, OK)

Previous Ranking: NR

What Happened in 2014: LaValley mashed his way through Oklahoma high school ball, hitting 18 home runs and finishing with 54 career dingers at the prep ranks. He was popped in the fourth round by the Reds, showing well in his pro debut.

Strengths: Big strength, massive size; plus or better raw power; will flash snap in the wrists; solid strike zone awareness; highly confident in attacking ball across zone; oppo-capable, with willingness to let the ball travel; easy lift in swing; moves well in field, considering size; some projection remains via firming of physique; impact potential at the plate.

Weaknesses: Limited reps against advanced competition; power is strength-derived; bat speed can fluctuate due to inconsistent weight transfer; body soft at present; will shift to first base; value tied exclusively to the bat; could struggle with velocity, particularly on the hands; swing can get uphill; doesn't backspin naturally, limiting carry; can get front-of-center, putting onus on arms and upper body; needs to better incorporate core in swing; well-below-average run.

Risk Factor/Injury History: High; yet to reach full-season ball; significant questions due to limited competition as amateur.

Bret Sayre's Fantasy Take: It's no secret that this type of profile—big power potential bat with very little defensive value—is attractive in fantasy, but LaValley is still a long ways away from being someone owned across most dynasty formats. He's a fun flier if your league rosters 300-plus minor leaguers, but that's about it.

The Year Ahead: There is no mistaking LaValley's carrying tool, as he is capable of putting big-time power on display regularly during batting practice and showed some in-game ability as well during his brief pro debut. There is a fair amount of work to do in growing the offensive profile, including cleaning up the weight transfer and adding efficiency to the swing, but it's a testament to his overall feel that LaValley was able to step right into complex ball and thrive despite the limited competition he faced during his prep years. Though he logged time exclusively at the hot corner in 2014, his future home is across the diamond, where he should move well enough to hold his own. There is a lot of risk inherent in the profile given the limited weapons and lack of evaluative history, but if the power plays it has the chance to be impactful. He's 20, so there is some urgency in getting him moving through the minors, with the Reds ideally starting him off in the Midwest League in 2015 provided his showings in camp indicate he is up to the challenge. It's a high-bust potential, but it comes with the chance for a very loud boom.

Notable Omission

RHP Raisel Iglesias: Due to his pro résumé, age, and proximity to majors, Iglesias was not considered a prospect for purposes of these rankings, but is a noteworthy addition to the Reds organization that would have ranked easily in the top five of the above list. His bread and butter is a hard low- to mid-90s heater, which he complements with multilook breakers and an improving changeup that will flash some late drop. Iglesias comes with some deception and shifting arm slot that ranges from almost true sidearm to high three-quarters, depending on the pitch and the shape he's reaching for. He delivers a lively fastball, showing the ability to throw it to both sides of the plate while possessing a true slider with wipeout action and a hard 11-to-5 curve out of a high release. The Reds have indicated they believe he can start, but the general take outside of the organization is that he is a likely late-inning arm, due to his 5-foot-11, 170 pound frame and questionable command profile. Regardless of ultimate role, he could provide innings for the Reds as early as this summer.

Prospects on the Rise

1. LHP Amir Garrett: With basketball firmly in the rearview, Garrett took a nice step forward in 2014, logging 133 innings in the Midwest League while showcasing a plus fastball and improving slider. The lefty has size and arm strength, and has shown some aptitude on the bump, but his secondaries remain a work in progress. Garrett struggles to find consistency with the slider, leading to frequent misses in and out of the zone, and the changeup is very much in the nascent stages, lacking much in the way of deception or action. Because of his two-sport past, the fact that Garrett was able to make his way through 27 starts is encouraging, likely buying him at least another year's worth of rotation work, where he'll need to start showing a little more feel. The upside is a mid-rotation arm, but he's a long way off at present and could be a better fit coming out of the 'pen and letting it fly.

2. OF Aristides Aquino: In his second year stateside, Aquino impressed over 71 Pioneer League games with Billings, showing good raw power out of a leveraged swing and a decent feel for contact. The Dominican outfielder continues to add strength to a projectable frame and could settle in as a true middle-of-the-order power threat if he is able to hone his approach. Progress was made in that department in 2014, with Aquino doing a better job of laying off soft stuff, but the true test will come when he is faced with more advanced spin. He is capable in right field and has the athleticism to grow into an average or better defender at maturity with continued reps and work. A strong 2015 showing could see Aquino's stock take off, and rocket him firmly into the top 10 by this time next year.

3. OF Sebastian Elizalde: Elizalde logged 300 Mexican League at-bats over parts of four seasons before being inked by the Reds in 2013 and immediately undergoing Tommy John surgery. He debuted in the system last summer, splitting time between Low-A Dayton and High-A Bakersfield, impressing at both stops. The lefty bat is well put together, bringing a solid approach to the plate with natural loft and lift in his swing that generates surprising raw power and allows him to drive the ball from oppo-gap to pull-side line. There's a strong enough feel for the barrel that his hit and in-game pop could both grade to average despite a bat path that can get uphill and limit contact opportunities across certain sections of the zone. Elizalde struggles with same-side stuff at present, and in particular soft stuff away. For the hit tool to play up, and for the power to fully manifest, he'll need to improve upon his plate coverage and pitch identification, and even then the swing could make him a specific-zone hitter that needs to pick his spots to drive. He shows solid breaks, above-average speed, and a reliable, accurate arm in the outfield, giving him a chance to log time across the grass depending on team needs. There's interesting upside here, and a 2015 Double-A assignment for the 23-year-old should provide a better indicator as to just

FROM THE FIELD

Robert Stephenson

Team: Cincinnati Reds

Evaluator: Ethan Purser

Dates seen: June 27, 2014

Affiliate: Pensacola Blue Wahoos (Double-A, Reds)

OFP: 60

Realistic role: 55; no. 3/4 starter

Mechanics: Tall, lanky frame with some upper-body development throughout torso; legs up to his neck; frame built to withstand 200-plus innings of work; arm action is compact after an initial deep plunge on the back side; hides the ball well; high three-quarters arm slot; drop-and-drive delivery with good momentum throughout; great separation between his two halves achieved by a slight upper-body dip over the rubber after reaching his balance point; lands square on a bent front leg and achieves some extension out front; can be a little upright at times; head displays some violence in follow-through. Pitcher generates good momentum throughout delivery and possesses an incredibly quick arm.

Pitch type	Present grade	Future grade	Sitting velocity	Peak velocity	Report
FB	55	65	92-94	96	Velocity: plus; sat comfortably in the plus range throughout the outing, touching higher. Command: below average; struggled to find the zone early in counts and throw quality strikes; worked from behind in the count a majority of the evening. Movement: plus arm-side bore, specifically in the low-90s; pitch can flatten out a bit due to delivery but pitcher creates good angle with higher slot; difficult to square when located in the lower quadrants; becomes hittable up in the zone. Comments: Stephenson relied on the fastball heavily in this outing and hitters jumped on it early in counts, forcing him to make a secondary adjustment with his sequencing. The offering was very hittable up in the zone, and Stephenson seemed to focus more on blowing pitches by hitters rather than locating effectively within the zone. With that being said, Stephenson's frame and the potential for added mass, in combination with his mechanics and lightning-quick arm, lead me to believe there could be a little more velocity in the tank.
CB	55	65	78-82	83	Command: fringe-average; flashed ability to bury the pitch for whiffs and drop it in the zone for weak contact/whiffs; struggled to consistently get over the curveball, leaving it hanging up in the zone; feel for pitch comes and goes. Movement: flashes plus or better 11/5 break late in pitch's trajectory with sharp two-plane slice; bat-missing break when snapped off effectively; pitch displays great shape; break can be elongated/not as sharp when pitcher gets around offering. Comments: Stephenson's curveball is legit and flashes plus-plus potential, but command concerns with the offering and with the entire arsenal downplay the pitch's overall future utility.
CH	40	45	85-88	89	Command: below average; left pitch up and to the arm side frequently; lacked feel for pitch; struggled to harness it; pitcher was very deliberate with the offering. Movement: straight; flashed the slightest bit of run but was mostly flat up and out of the zone; elicited a whiff from a right-handed hitter under his hands, flashing some sink. Comments: It was obvious that Stephenson was working on this pitch throughout the outing, but it was too firm and he showed little ability to spot it in this look. I do not envision this pitch becoming a weapon at the highest level.

Overall: Stephenson is a special arm, one with the potential to have two high-end pitches with the fastball and curveball. Along with the below-average changeup, the command profile is the bugaboo currently and will very likely be an issue going forward. It's easy to see the enormous potential in the arsenal, but in this outing, Stephenson looked the part of a mid-rotation starter who flashes front-of-the-rotation stuff but lacks the command profile to anchor a rotation. Though he's currently at Double-A, Stephenson needs a good bit of time to develop and refine his arsenal. An appearance at the highest level in the latter part of 2015 would not be a surprise, with a shot at a rotation spot the following season fully in his sights.

how good this bat might be. It's a low-probability profile, but he showed enough this summer and fall to warrant close attention next year.

Factors on the Farm
Prospects likely to contribute at the major-league level in 2015

1. RHP Daniel Corcino: Corcino held his own during a brief stint in Cincy last summer, but continues to run into bouts of wildness, lessening the effectiveness of his heavy upper-80s to low-90s fastball and average slider. Though the righty has spent the bulk of his career in the rotation, he fits best as a sinker/slider relief arm capable of handling the seventh or eighth inning depending on his ability to rein in his command and limit free passes. When he is clicking and hitting his release, his sinker comes with solid bore, making him tough to lift, with an average slider leading to further soft contact thanks to some plane deception. He could be an asset in the 'pen next year and may still get a shot to break into the rotation if he shows some improved feel come spring.

2. C Tucker Barnhart: It's not exciting, but Barnhart will provide useful innings at the major-league level in a backup capacity, and some evaluators still give him a shot at hitting just enough for the profile to play as a second-division starter. Make no mistake, the value is in the glove and the arm, with a defensive package that will add positive value when called upon, including limiting the running game and providing a dependable backstop capable of handling a diverse staff. He got a taste of the bigs last year and should enter the spring with a chance to break camp as the backup for 2014 breakout Devin Mesoraco.

3. LHP Ismael Guillon: Guillon comes with a big fastball that could play up in relief, perhaps as "up" as the mid-90s with arm-side life. His changeup is a swing-and-miss pitch that comes with disappearing action and good deception, giving him a one-two punch capable of neutralizing lefties and righties alike. The breaking ball is inconsistent, but has its moments, providing a third potential major-league-caliber weapon. Guillon is running out of options, which could force Cincy to shift him to the 'pen despite a foundation that could allow for starter development in time. If that shift to the 'pen does come, the Venezuelan could move quickly to Cincy and eventually grow into a late-inning option.

CLEVELAND INDIANS

1. Francisco Lindor   SS

Born: 11/14/93   **Age:** 21   **Bats:** B   **Throws:** R   **Height:** 5'11"   **Weight:** 175

MLB ETA	Hit	Power	Run	Glove	Arm		OFP	Realistic
2015	65	–	–	70	60		70 ALL-STAR	60 1ST DIVISION PLAYER

YEAR	TEAM	LVL	AGE	PA	R	2B	3B	HR	RBI	BB	SO	SB	CS	AVG/OBP/SLG	TAv	BABIP	BRR	FRAA	WARP
2014	COH	AAA	20	180	24	4	0	5	14	9	36	3	7	.273/.307/.388	.231	.317	0.7	SS(38): 0.9	0.5
2014	AKR	AA	20	387	51	12	4	6	48	40	61	25	9	.278/.352/.389	.274	.320	0.1	SS(88): 5.4	3.1
2015	CLE	MLB	21	250	29	9	1	3	18	18	51	9	4	.240/.298/.329	.239	.291	0.2	SS 1	0.7
2016	CLE	MLB	22	250	28	10	1	4	25	19	46	9	4	.266/.326/.377	.263	.312	0.6	SS 1	2.3

Breakout: 0%   **Improve:** 0%   **Collapse:** 0%   **Attrition:** 0%   **MLB:** 0%   **Upside:** 27   *Comparables: Tyler Pastornicky, Jose Pirela, Carlos Sanchez*

#4

BP Top
101
Prospects

Drafted/Acquired: 1st round, 2011 draft, Montverde HS (Montverde, FL)
Previous Ranking: #1 (Org), #6 (Top 101)
What Happened in 2014: The slick-fielding shortstop spent his age-20 season in the upper levels of the system, where he continued to play up to the level of competition despite consistently being one of the youngest in his league.
Strengths: Outstanding baseball instincts; extremely natural player; silky smooth actions; lightning-quick hands; soft glove; well-above-average range; arm to make all of the throws; impact defender; easy stroke from both sides of the plate; stays back well; efficient swing path; controls barrel well; advanced approach; picks up spin; heady and smart on the bases; makeup is plus.
Weaknesses: Bat is likely to be a bit on the empty side; contact can be soft; tends to slap when going the other way; will need to learn to do some occasional damage to keep arms honest; overswings at times; can lunge against stuff with break on outer third; well-below-average power; speed isn't of the impact variety.
Risk Factor/Injury History: Low; near major-league ready; consistency of creating hard contact.
Bret Sayre's Fantasy Take: The heights of Lindor's glove push his fantasy value both up (for those just watching standard prospect lists) and down (for those who think he's all leather), so it's important to make sure he's properly valued in your league. This is not an Austin Hedges situation, as Lindor is a top-25 fantasy prospect handily, as he is nearly ready and could hit .290 with 20-25 steals while scraping double-digit homers. His value also ticks up in points leagues.
The Year Ahead: When it comes to sure bets, Lindor's defense at shortstop easily falls into this category, with the glove pretty much being plug-and-play in terms of inserting it into a major-league lineup in the near future. There's going to be no assembly or waiting period required here. The 21-year-old is one of the more natural players you will see in the field, where he consistently flashes all the attributes to hold status as one of the premier defenders at the position for an extended portion of his career. It's a true impact glove. All of the near-term focus will continue to reside with polishing the bat, with the signs pointing to a likely return assignment in Triple-A to start 2015 for further offensive seasoning and simmering before a first taste of The Show. Lindor is far from a slouch with the stick, but the switch-hitter should not be mistaken for a potential impact bat in the making. The offensive game is going to need to heavily lean on high contact rates, utilizing the whole field from both sides of the plate, and finding the necessary balance to keep high-end arms from unmercifully attacking him within the zone. The maturity level and innate feel for the game speak volumes that the player can more than rise to the challenge and begin putting a foothold on owning the franchise's shortstop position for the foreseeable future as soon as this season.

2. Francisco Mejia   C

Born: 10/27/95   **Age:** 19   **Bats:** B   **Throws:** R   **Height:** 5'10"   **Weight:** 175

MLB ETA	Hit	Power	Run	Glove	Arm		OFP	Realistic
2018	60	55	–	55	70		70 ALL STAR	50 ML REGULAR

YEAR	TEAM	LVL	AGE	PA	R	2B	3B	HR	RBI	BB	SO	SB	CS	AVG/OBP/SLG	TAv	BABIP	BRR	FRAA	WARP
2014	MHV	A-	18	274	32	17	4	2	36	18	47	2	4	.282/.339/.407	.277	.337	0.0	C(52): 0.1	1.9
2015	CLE	MLB	19	250	17	10	1	3	22	8	71	0	0	.207/.238/.294	.200	.277	-0.4	C 0, LF 0	-0.7
2016	CLE	MLB	20	250	23	10	1	4	23	6	64	0	0	.229/.253/.328	.215	.289	-0.6	C 0, LF 0	-1.2

Breakout: 0%   **Improve:** 0%   **Collapse:** 0%   **Attrition:** 0%   **MLB:** 0%   **Upside:** 12   *Comparables: Tomas Telis, Miguel Gonzalez, Wilson Ramos*

Drafted/Acquired: International Free Agent, 2012, Dominican Republic

Previous Ranking: #5 (Org)

What Happened in 2014: The Dominican backstop continued to show impressive talent on both sides of the ball, while also proving to be more than up to the task of handling much more experienced competition in the college-heavy New York-Penn League.

Strengths: Athletic; explosive hands; plus-to-better bat speed from both sides of the plate; easy stroke; creates natural loft; contact is very loud; can turn around velocity; barrels up with backspin; thunder in stick; drives with carry; plus raw power; borderline elite arm strength; ball comes out of hand on a line; quick feet and reflexes; instinctive feel for position; embraces the game; good makeup reports.

Weaknesses: Overall game is unrefined; ultra-aggressive approach; extremely wide strike zone; fishes for breaking stuff; gets out front; footwork is choppy; ball control needs work; still learning how to get big with body; glove hand stabs; release gets long; body is very lean; plays at an accelerated pace.

Risk Factor/Injury History: Extreme; short-season résumé; dual-threat development; big gap between present and future.

Bret Sayre's Fantasy Take: Mejia has an appealing package for a fantasy catcher, but the fact that he is a catcher and he is years away puts a governor on his value for now. The upside is that of an easy top-five catcher in his prime, but that may not happen in reality until 2020 given the developmental challenges for young catchers. Be excited, but be sensible here.

The Year Ahead: The dual-threat development path often offers more bumps in the road than extended peaks during the early stages of the journey, but Mejia impressively hit the ground running against much more experienced competition last season. The tools are extremely loud for this 19-year-old, highlighted by unteachable bat speed, surprising pop for his size, and an arm that can be the type of weapon that halts opposing team's running games. All of the ingredients are here for impact on both sides of the ball, which in combination can lead to a very high payout and perennial upper-echelon player at the position. Make no mistake, though, the game is very unrefined, and it's likely going to be a longer developmental soak to polish away the rough edges. The healthy serving of risk due to the age and nature of the catcher position makes the achievement of the on-paper potential of each tool very volatile, but at the same time there is a strong feel here that Mejia is a special player in the making. It won't be surprising to see the player perform ahead of the curve this season in the Midwest League, and if the aggressive approach is beginning to show signs of maturation, it's a leading indicator that a passage into the upper levels will come with little resistance.

---

3. Clint Frazier   OF

Born: 9/6/94   **Age:** 20   **Bats:** R   **Throws:** R   **Height:** 6'1"   **Weight:** 190

MLB ETA	Hit	Power	Run	Glove	Arm	OFP 65 1ST DIV/OCC ALL STAR	Realistic 55 >AVG REGULAR
2017	60	65	60	50	55		

YEAR	TEAM	LVL	AGE	PA	R	2B	3B	HR	RBI	BB	SO	SB	CS	AVG/OBP/SLG	TAv	BABIP	BRR	FRAA	WARP
2014	LKC	A	19	542	70	18	6	13	50	56	161	12	6	.266/.349/.411	.276	.372	0.8	CF(111): -13.7, RF(1): 0.1	1.0
2015	CLE	MLB	20	250	24	8	1	4	20	17	92	2	1	.197/.256/.299	.212	.299	-0.2	CF -6, RF 0	-1.2
2016	CLE	MLB	21	250	27	10	2	6	25	20	86	2	1	.223/.290/.357	.241	.327	-0.2	CF -6, RF 0	-0.2

Breakout: 0%   Improve: 0%   Collapse: 0%   Attrition: 0%   MLB: 0%   Upside: 3   *Comparables: Oswaldo Arcia, Robbie Grossman, Chris Parmelee*

Drafted/Acquired: 1st round, 2013 draft, Loganville HS (Loganville, GA)

Previous Ranking: #2 (Org), #36 (Top 101)

What Happened in 2014: Frazier's season in the Midwest League can be divided into two distinct parts: a first half that saw the highly regarded outfielder struggle to find his footing out of the gate, and then a second half filled with plenty of solid contact and pop.

Strengths: Fast-twitch athlete; excellent strength; plus-plus bat speed; very strong hands and wrists; swing shows plenty of lift; can impact the baseball, especially on inner third; will time as plus runner down the line; arm works in all three outfield spots; improving reads and routes in center; competitor.

Weaknesses: Questions on ability to stick up the middle; can be slow with jumps; instincts more in line with corner outfielder; has in-zone swing-and-miss; aggressive at the plate; very wide strike zone; can lack swing coverage on outer third; hit tool may ultimately play down.

Risk Factor/Injury History: High; yet to reach Double-A; development of glove.

Bret Sayre's Fantasy Take: Speaking as the resident Frazier fanboy, he remains one of the highest upside prospects in the minors—and now is the perfect time to check in on the Frazier owner in your league and see if they are down on him even slightly. The potential is there for him to hit .280-plus with 30 homers and 20 steals, and no, that's not a typo.

The Year Ahead: There's nothing that really jumps off the page in regards to Frazier's composite line for 2014, but the year was marked with a strong second half ramp-up and improvement by season's end that left optimism heading into the offseason that firm developmental traction was made. It wasn't pretty for the outfielder early on, as he consistently expanded his strike zone and had a tendency to exhibit the thinking he could hit anything thrown his way regardless of pitch type or location. As the year wore on, though, there was a tightening of his strike zone and a more cognizant approach to utilize both gaps that led to much more consistent loud contact. Frazier possesses the type of bat speed, swing path, and raw power to really impact the baseball, making .280s averages and 25-plus home runs at peak possibly within reach. The questions come in as to whether he can limit the swing-and-miss, along with continuing to hone the approach against the rising competition. This year in the eight-team Carolina League will be a good litmus test as to whether the aggressiveness at the plate is becoming more controlled. A lot of eyes will also be on how the glove is refining in center, where there's a fighting chance he can stick. The clues point to the profile progressing to a potential power-hitting corner outfielder, with a good chance at another round of tangible steps forward by this season's end.

4. Bradley Zimmer   OF

Born: 11/27/92   **Age:** 22   **Bats:** L   **Throws:** R   **Height:** 6'4"   **Weight:** 185

MLB ETA	Hit	Power	Run	Glove	Arm	OFP	Realistic
2017	55	50	50	55	60	55 >AVG REGULAR	50 ML REGULAR

YEAR	TEAM	LVL	AGE	PA	R	2B	3B	HR	RBI	BB	SO	SB	CS	AVG/OBP/SLG	TAv	BABIP	BRR	FRAA	WARP
2014	LKC	A	21	13	4	1	0	2	2	2	3	1	0	.273/.385/.909	.392	.167	0.1	RF(1): -0.0, CF(1): 0.0	0.2
2014	MHV	A-	21	197	32	11	2	4	30	19	30	11	4	.304/.401/.464	.326	.348	2.4	CF(42): 1.9	2.4
2015	CLE	MLB	22	250	25	9	1	5	24	15	70	6	2	.211/.268/.324	.225	.273	0.3	CF 1, RF -0	-0.1
2016	CLE	MLB	23	250	27	9	1	6	26	15	68	7	2	.219/.277/.350	.236	.278	0.6	CF 1, RF 0	0.3

Breakout: 0%   **Improve:** 0%   **Collapse:** 0%   **Attrition:** 0%   **MLB:** 0%   **Upside:** 34   *Comparables: Nick Markakis, Felix Pie, Trayvon Robinson*

Drafted/Acquired: 1st round, 2014 draft, University of San Francisco (San Francisco, CA)

Previous Ranking: NR

What Happened in 2014: After being selected 21st overall, Zimmer quickly assimilated into professional ball, where the outfielder easily handled the New York-Penn League and then got a brief taste of full-season ball to finish out the year.

Strengths: Athletic frame; room for continued filling out; good present strength; easy stroke; loose hands; works to stay inside of baseball; goes the other way well; patient in the box; all-fields approach; picks up ball out of hand quickly; long strides cover ground in outfield; takes good routes; solid fundamentals; easy-plus arm—fits in all three spots; carries himself well on the field.

Weaknesses: Swing is on the flat side; more geared toward line-drive contact; questions on translation of power; will chase soft stuff down and away; can have trouble with velocity on inner third; at times looks clunky and awkward in center; may ultimately end up in a corner; slow with reads off pitchers when on the bases.

Risk Factor/Injury History: Moderate; limited pro experience; polished overall game.

Bret Sayre's Fantasy Take: Zimmer projects as the prototypical five-category player who doesn't excel in any single one. Of course, that still translates into OF2 potential if everything clicks, but it gives him multiple paths to value. He is a worthy selection toward the end of the first round in dynasty drafts this year.

The Year Ahead: Zimmer didn't miss a beat in transitioning from college to the professional ranks last summer, which wasn't overly surprising given the advanced nature of the player's game. There's a chance here that all five tools can play at least average at full bloom, though the swing lacks good lift and is more geared to contact than producing home-run power. The mature approach at the plate and solid pitch recognition are strong clues that the prospect can track relatively quickly through the low minors. The 22-year-old should prove to be ahead of the curve in A-Ball, with the reasonable expectation of seeing time in the Carolina League before the 2015 season ends. If you believe Zimmer capable of sticking in center field, then the profile can play up to borderline first-division status even if the power ends up playing down due to the nature of the swing. If you see the California native more likely to slide into a corner, then the production of power becomes more of a premium, and the role is ultimately going to play down. The feel here based on our looks is that there's a pretty good shot for a regular to emerge, but it's likely to come in a corner.

5. Tyler Naquin   CF

Born: 4/24/91   **Age:** 24   **Bats:** L   **Throws:** R   **Height:** 6'2"   **Weight:** 190

MLB ETA	Hit	Power	Run	Glove	Arm	OFP	Realistic
Late 2015	55	–	50	55	70	50 ML REGULAR	50 <AVG REG/PLATOON

YEAR	TEAM	LVL	AGE	PA	R	2B	3B	HR	RBI	BB	SO	SB	CS	AVG/OBP/SLG	TAv	BABIP	BRR	FRAA	WARP
2014	AKR	AA	23	341	54	12	5	4	30	29	71	14	3	.312/.371/.424	.292	.389	-0.1	CF(73): 0.7, RF(1): 0.1	2.6
2015	CLE	MLB	24	250	26	10	2	3	19	15	69	5	2	.234/.283/.330	.233	.316	0.2	CF 0, RF 0	0.0
2016	CLE	MLB	25	250	26	10	1	4	23	16	67	5	2	.235/.292/.345	.240	.312	0.4	CF 0, RF 0	0.4

Breakout: 8%   **Improve:** 12%   **Collapse:** 17%   **Attrition:** 24%   **MLB:** 34%   **Upside:** 13   *Comparables: Lane Adams, James Jones, Lorenzo Cain*

Drafted/Acquired: 1st round, 2012 draft, Texas A&M University (College Station, TX)

Previous Ranking: #3 (Org)

What Happened in 2014: The Texan put together a strong first half in the Eastern League, with a potential promotion to the next level just around the corner, before a pitch off the hand required surgery, putting an early end to his season.

Strengths: Good athlete; fluid actions; solid defensive instincts; improved reads and routes; enough glove to handle position; impact arm; adept at getting into position to unleash throws; shows more speed once getting into gear; simple stroke; solid-average bat speed; creates line-drive contact into both gaps; high baseball IQ.

Weaknesses: Some concerns on ability to consistently hit high-quality pitching; can be beat with high velocity middle-in; some swing-and-miss in the zone; will lunge against off-speed; needs work keeping weight back more frequently; below-average power; gets into stretches of being too defensive; hit tool may end up playing down due to lack of consistent hard contact.

Risk Factor/Injury History: Moderate; 94 games at Double-A; hand surgery (2014); hit tool utility.

Bret Sayre's Fantasy Take: Those in shallow leagues are better off skipping over Naquin and moving on to some of the names here with more fantasy juice. In deep leagues, he could be an undervalued asset, but as someone likely to top out at around a .270 hitter with 15-20 steals and little over-the-fence power to speak of, his utility on a dynasty roster is limited.

The Year Ahead: The 2014 season turned out to be bittersweet for the then-23-year-old, who definitely offered a round of positive progress toward rounding out his overall game but saw further momentum dashed in the second half by a broken bone in his right hand. The setback will likely cost Naquin a chance to begin the year in the International League, but if he gets off to a similar start it likely won't be long before he finds himself roaming center field in Triple-A. At his best, the lefty is a gap-to-gap hitter who is more than capable of producing hard line drives with backspin. There's been tangible improvement on both sides of the ball over the course of the last two seasons as well, and a future big-leaguer has come into focus. Evaluators have some concerns about the profile, mainly in regards to how well he can consistently handle high-quality pitching and whether he'll be able to hit enough to maintain status as a regular as a result, but the Texas native has shown the knack for making adjustments fairly quickly at each stop so far. A good showing this season will likely earn Naquin a call in some capacity by season's end. The athleticism and arm at the very least give the prospect the chance to stick around on a roster in a bench capacity over the long term, with further offensive upswing making it a very real possibility that he could compete for an outfield spot as a regular in 2016.

6. Justus Sheffield   LHP

Born: 5/13/96   **Age:** 19   **Bats:** L   **Throws:** L   **Height:** 5'10"   **Weight:** 196

MLB ETA	CT	FB	CH	CB	SL	OFP	Realistic
2018	–	60	55	55	–	60 NO. 3 STARTER	50 NO. 5 SP/LONG RP

YEAR	TEAM	LVL	AGE	W	L	SV	G	GS	IP	H	HR	BB	K	BB9	SO9	GB%	BABIP	WHIP	ERA	FIP	FRA	WARP
2014	CLE	Rk	18	3	1	0	8	4	20.7	24	0	9	29	3.9	12.6	50%	.458	1.60	4.79	2.67	3.57	0.4
2015	CLE	MLB	19	1	1	0	8	2	31.7	37	4	20	20	5.7	5.7	45%	.315	1.79	6.10	6.02	6.63	-0.4
2016	CLE	MLB	20	2	2	1	20	5	80.7	87	11	40	63	4.5	7.0	45%	.307	1.58	5.38	5.17	5.85	-0.8

Breakout: 0%   Improve: 0%   Collapse: 0%   Attrition: 0%   MLB: 0%   Upside: 0   *Comparables: Matt Moore, Michael Blazek, Joe Wieland*

Bats/Throws: L/L

Drafted/Acquired: 1st round, 2014 draft, Tullahoma HS (Tullahoma, TN)

Previous Ranking: NR

What Happened in 2014: Though the senior season was inconsistent and the left-hander owned a commitment to Vanderbilt, the organization made Sheffield the 31st overall selection in the June draft and then sent him to the Arizona League to begin his entry into pro ball.

Strengths: Very athletic; clean and repeatable delivery; low energy expending; arm works well; strong, filled-out lower half; fastball works 91-93 with some arm-side run; can reach back for more occasionally (94-95); lively in lower tier; snaps off mid-70s curveball that flashes strong depth and bite; early feel for throwing curve for strikes; loose wrist action; turns over promising change; flashes fading arm-side action; good arm speed; plus command profile.

Weaknesses: Limited physical projection; has to pitch down to create angle; heater can play down in high-80s at times; will need to build arm strength to handle rigors of the long season; has a tendency to wrap wrist when delivering curve; will sweep at present; can get deliberate with change; command is on the loose side; maturity concerns stemming from a recent arrest.

Risk Factor/Injury History: Extreme; complex-level résumé; 19 years old; large gap between present and future; legal issues (2015).

Bret Sayre's Fantasy Take: The 19-year old left-hander was the last arm cut from the Top 50 list for dynasty drafts, but it really was due to depth (especially of prep arms) and not talent. There may not be huge upside in Sheffield, but he makes for a nice flier at the end of drafts this year.

The Year Ahead: An off-field incident that has resulted in aggravated burglary and underage drinking charges puts a damper on the immediate future. When on the diamond, Sheffield is an intriguing young arm who, despite his lack of size, offers solid projection due to his athleticism and extremely loose, efficient delivery. While there isn't an expectation that the heater is going to see much uptick in velocity or that there will be massive gains with the overall stuff, the potential growth with the command and crispness of the secondary arsenal offer a three-pitch mix that can play above average to push the overall role to that of a mid-rotation starter at the peak. Of course, like most arms of this age, there is a healthy serving of risk and variability, with the near term—after the results of his pending legal issue—likely to be focused on building arm strength and repetition to start stimulating the professional journey one step at a time. Sheffield isn't likely to burst onto the scene in 2015, but the lefty is more than capable of stringing together positive results and showing the initial steps of polishing the overall command, which should come in a short-season assignment. All of the ingredients are here for a major-league arm, though expect ample development time and some seasoning in the lower levels over the next few seasons.

7. Mike Papi   OF/1B

Born: 9/19/92   **Age:** 22   **Bats:** L   **Throws:** R   **Height:** 6'2"   **Weight:** 190

MLB ETA	Hit	Power	Run	Glove	Arm		OFP	Realistic
Late 2017	60	50	–	50	–		55 >AVG REGULAR	45 BENCH BAT/PT PLAYER

YEAR	TEAM	LVL	AGE	PA	R	2B	3B	HR	RBI	BB	SO	SB	CS	AVG/OBP/SLG	TAv	BABIP	BRR	FRAA	WARP
2014	LKC	A	21	166	21	4	0	3	15	26	32	2	0	.178/.305/.274	.232	.204	0.7	RF(33): -1.8, 1B(2): 0.0	-0.4
2014	MHV	A-	21	9	2	0	0	0	3	0	0	0	0	.222/.222/.222	.160	.222	0.5	RF(1): -0.0	0.0
2015	CLE	MLB	22	250	20	8	1	3	21	23	67	1	0	.195/.271/.282	.215	.258	-0.3	RF -3, 1B 0	-1.1
2016	CLE	MLB	23	250	25	8	1	4	21	23	71	1	0	.190/.268/.288	.212	.253	-0.3	RF -3, 1B 0	-2.0

Breakout: 0%   Improve: 0%   Collapse: 0%   Attrition: 0%   MLB: 0%   Upside: 4   *Comparables: Rene Tosoni, Lorenzo Cain, Brandon Jones*

Drafted/Acquired: 1st round, 2014 draft, University of Virginia (Charlottesville, VA)
Previous Ranking: NR
What Happened in 2014: After a brief stop at Mahoning Valley, the University of Virginia product struggled to find his footing during a 39-game stint in the Midwest League, where he hit a paltry .178.
Strengths: Lean, wiry muscle; room for a bit more weight; shows a feel for hitting; loose hands; quick trigger with shorter stroke; plus bat speed; brings a plan to the plate; line-to-line hitter; can turn on offerings with carry; power can play as average; drives ball well into opposite field gap; plays with intensity.
Weaknesses: Average athlete; fringy foot speed in the field; flat with routes at times; fringe-average range; not enough arm for right; needs to learn how to get more lift and leverage out of swing; path on the flat side presently; hit tool may end up playing down in favor of increased power; limited defensive profile.
Risk Factor/Injury History: High; limited professional experience; bat-first player.
Bret Sayre's Fantasy Take: Another player, like Sheffield, who will get overlooked because of the depth of the 2014 draft class, Papi has the potential to be a .280-hitting first baseman with 15-20 homers—which in this offensively depressed environment would still be good enough to be a top-20 first baseman.
The Year Ahead: It wasn't pretty for Papi during his transitional stint in the professional ranks after signing with the org, but the left-handed hitter showed a technically sound swing and methodical approach in the box, which bodes well for offensive progress as he comes up to speed with seeing more advanced pitching on a consistent basis and begins to find his timing as a result. The 22-year-old was also pushed a bit with a more aggressive placement in the Midwest League, where most of the opposing arms had the benefit of a full season at the level. The draw here is the stick, as the outfielder flashes a solid feel for controlling the head of the bat and a swing that is more than capable of covering all four quadrants of the zone. The near-term work for Papi resides with adjusting more to the speed of the game and building further trust with his pitch recognition. These aspects of the prospect's game should have a much better showing in a return to A-Ball for the 2015 season given his level of experience coming from the college ranks, with the view here seeing much higher contact rates and a bat beginning to show that a quicker ascent into the upper levels of the system is highly likely.

8. Giovanny Urshela   3B

Born: 10/11/91   **Age:** 23   **Bats:** R   **Throws:** R   **Height:** 6'0"   **Weight:** 197

MLB ETA	Hit	Power	Run	Glove	Arm		OFP	Realistic
2015	55	–	–	60	60		55 >AVG REGULAR	45 2ND DIV REG/BENCH

YEAR	TEAM	LVL	AGE	PA	R	2B	3B	HR	RBI	BB	SO	SB	CS	AVG/OBP/SLG	TAv	BABIP	BRR	FRAA	WARP
2014	COH	AAA	22	430	63	27	6	13	65	30	51	0	2	.276/.331/.473	.268	.289	-0.6	3B(98): -0.6, SS(1): -0.1	1.7
2014	AKR	AA	22	98	15	9	0	5	19	6	16	1	1	.300/.347/.567	.305	.314	2.2	3B(23): 1.1	1.1
2015	CLE	MLB	23	250	22	12	1	6	28	7	42	0	0	.246/.270/.384	.244	.271	-0.4	3B -1, SS -0	0.0
2016	CLE	MLB	24	250	26	12	1	6	27	9	43	0	0	.242/.271/.378	.240	.267	-0.6	3B -2, SS 0	0.1

Breakout: 4%   Improve: 17%   Collapse: 9%   Attrition: 19%   MLB: 34%   Upside: 20   *Comparables: Henry Rodriguez, Brent Morel, Cody Asche*

Drafted/Acquired: International Free Agent, 2008, Colombia

Previous Ranking: NR

What Happened in 2014: Urshela made quick work of the Eastern League and then settled in nicely at Triple-A, where he continued to show the ability to make contact at a frequent clip and flashed his trademark above-average defense.

Strengths: Athletic actions; excellent defensive instincts; quick reactions; soft glove; plus range; can pick it at the hot corner; plenty of arm for deep throws; line-drive stroke; improved efficiency to ball; feel for controlling the barrel; looks gap to gap; doesn't overswing; shows ability to adjust.

Weaknesses: Swing is more geared to contact; power likely to be doubles more than consistent over-the-fence pop; hit tool lacks impact potential; some limitations covering outer third consistently; contact can play soft; aggressive early in the count; prone to spin away; pitch selection needs improvement against high-quality arms; defense may ultimately carry profile.

Risk Factor/Injury History: Low; 240 games in upper levels; near major-league ready; emergence of power.

Bret Sayre's Fantasy Take: Really not much here for fantasy, as Urshela made this top-10 on the strength of his defense. He could make for an interesting reserve pick in AL-only leagues this year, as a hedge for Lonnie Chisenhall, but he doesn't carry very much dynasty-league value.

The Year Ahead: The progression has been slow and steady since signing with the organization back in 2008, but Urshela now sits on the cusp of The Show, with a legit chance at getting a look as a potential regular in the near future. The slick-fielding third baseman brings an above-average glove to the table, which, paired with his plus arm, is the lead aspect of his overall game. The 23-year-old can easily provide defensive stability to the position. The questions in the past have centered on the capabilities of the bat and whether there's enough with the stick to provide sufficient offense at the position. The Colombian has made improvements getting more efficient with his stroke and has a knack for putting the barrel on the ball, but at times the contact plays weak and light against arms that are more indicative of what is seen in the majors on a regular basis. The offense can be boosted by further maturation of Urshela's pitch selection and subsequent tightening of his strike zone to drive offerings with more consistency. A return trip to Triple-A is likely to start 2015, with a good chance that the prospect can earn a call at some point in the summer if the offensive momentum continues.

---

9. Bobby Bradley 1B

Born: 5/29/96 **Age:** 19 **Bats:** L **Throws:** R **Height:** 6'1" **Weight:** 225

MLB ETA	Hit	Power	Run	Glove	Arm	OFP	Realistic
2018	55	60	–	50	–	60 1ST DIVISION PLAYER	45 <AVG REG/BENCH BAT

YEAR	TEAM	LVL	AGE	PA	R	2B	3B	HR	RBI	BB	SO	SB	CS	AVG/OBP/SLG	TAv	BABIP	BRR	FRAA	WARP
2014	CLE	Rk	18	176	39	13	4	8	50	16	36	3	0	.361/.426/.652	.369	.425	0.3	1B(29): 0.8	2.0
2015	CLE	MLB	19	250	21	9	1	6	25	10	77	0	0	.208/.244/.324	.213	.277	-0.3	1B 1	-0.9
2016	CLE	MLB	20	250	27	10	1	7	27	12	74	0	0	.226/.269/.368	.235	.294	-0.5	1B 1	-0.3

Breakout: 0%   **Improve:** 0%   **Collapse:** 0%   **Attrition:** 0%   **MLB:** 0%   **Upside:** 26   *Comparables: Kyle Blanks, Travis Snider, Freddie Freeman*

Drafted/Acquired: 3rd round, 2014 draft, Harrison Central HS (Gulfport, MS)

Previous Ranking: NR

What Happened in 2014: Cleveland lured the big, prep first baseman away from a Louisiana State University commit with a large six-figure, over-slot bonus, and then saw immediate returns as Bradley torched the Arizona League in 39 games.

Strengths: Sturdy frame; big body; excellent present strength; efficient swing path with upward plane; drives offerings with lift and loft; life in hands; plus bat speed; advanced feel for strike zone; plus-to-better raw power; uses lower body well in swing mechanics; willing to use the whole field; mature approach to the game.

Weaknesses: Will have to keep body from becoming too muscle bound; swing can get loose; on the aggressive side; uppercut in stroke leads to swing-and-miss above belt; will reach for stuff with break away; swing presently favors pulling the ball; limited defensive profile; first-base-only player.

Risk Factor/Injury History: High; complex-league résumé; early advancements with hit tool; bat-first profile.

Bret Sayre's Fantasy Take: The high school first-base profile can be a good shield for fantasy hype, as I'd take Bradley fifth in this system for a dynasty-league team, behind just the top four players on this list. With a strong 2015 season, he could solidify himself as a top-100 dynasty prospect capable of hitting .275 with 25-plus homers at the highest level.

The Year Ahead: Bradley's quick assimilation into professional ball last summer was a pleasant surprise and lent further credence to predraft reports that the bat was on the advanced side for a player of this age. The stick is the main draw here, as the 19-year-old possesses plenty of raw power and an early feel for consistently barreling up offerings thanks to a shorter swing path. The first baseman is also willing to work through sequences, which bodes well for his continuing to smoothly transition during the early career stages. It's not out of the question for Bradley to receive a placement in full-season ball this year, though the organization may be inclined to keep him back in extended spring training to work with the swing a bit to go the other way with more ease before fully letting him loose in 2015. Regardless, this is a good-looking hitter, who can very well round into a middle-of-the-order type when all is said and done, and provide strong offensive production on a consistent basis. There's a long developmental road ahead for the prospect, and the first-base-only profile puts pressure on the bat to fully play, but with a strong showing in 2015 this will be a rising player in status within this system by next offseason.

10. Mitch Brown   RHP

Born: 4/13/94   **Age:** 21   **Bats:** R   **Throws:** R   **Height:** 6'1"   **Weight:** 195

MLB ETA	CT	FB	CH	CB	SL	OFP	Realistic
Late 2017	60	60	–	55	–	55 NO. 3/4 STARTER	50 NO. 5 SP/LONG RP

YEAR	TEAM	LVL	AGE	W	L	SV	G	GS	IP	H	HR	BB	K	BB9	SO9	GB%	BABIP	WHIP	ERA	FIP	FRA	WARP
2014	LKC	A	20	8	8	0	27	27	138.7	113	6	55	127	3.6	8.2	55%	.286	1.21	3.31	3.64	4.51	1.6
2015	CLE	MLB	21	5	8	0	22	22	97.7	109	11	56	66	5.2	6.1	48%	.309	1.69	5.71	5.69	6.21	-1.0
2016	CLE	MLB	22	7	9	0	27	27	158.7	164	17	77	130	4.4	7.4	48%	.307	1.52	4.92	4.72	5.35	-1.0

Breakout: 0%   **Improve:** 0%   **Collapse:** 0%   **Attrition:** 0%   **MLB:** 0%   **Upside:** 19   *Comparables: Carlos Carrasco, Jose A. Ramirez, Jeurys Familia*

Drafted/Acquired: 2nd round, 2012 draft, Century HS (Rochester, MN)

Previous Ranking: NR

What Happened in 2014: The former second-round pick bounced back from a disappointing 2013 in a big way, as he logged a strong workload in the Midwest League and flashed improving fastball command throughout the year.

Strengths: Athletic; improved consistency repeating mechanics; good arm strength; strong body; fastball operates 91-95 with some downward action; difficult to lift in lower tier; learning to spot heater east/west with more ease; snaps off cutter with late horizontal action; will miss barrels; potential out pitch; curve flashes two-plane break; changes eye levels with offering; improving feel for overall arsenal; excellent makeup reports.

Weaknesses: Runs into ruts of inconsistent command; heater flattens out above top of the thighs; must selectively elevate; curveball is presently fringe-average; will cast and break early; command needs a step forward to solidify starter potential; shows changeup, but lacks quality action; not likely to be more than "show-me" offering.

Risk Factor/Injury History: High; yet to reach upper levels; command consistency.

Bret Sayre's Fantasy Take: There's not a ton of upside with Brown, but the former cold-weather prep pitcher is finally starting to warm up in the professional setting—making him a name to remember in deeper leagues if he has been dropped over the last year and a half.

The Year Ahead: After a rebound season in 2014, Brown has proven that he is ready for the next step up the chain this year and that his development is beginning to gather steam. The 21-year-old's fastball command has taken a nice step forward over the past 12 months, which has allowed the offering to play much better in the lower tier of the strike zone on a consistent basis as opposed to running wild above the belt as previously seen. The improvement in repeating his delivery has also translated to more ease in snapping off the cutter and curveball, though the latter offering will still come and go, with further refinement needed to stay above the ball on a consistent basis. At the minimum Brown can see both his fastball and cutter play as lead pieces in the arsenal, and paired with further command improvements through repetition, this arm possesses solid major-league potential. Given the loose wrist action when snapping his curve, and strong reports on the work ethic, there's belief with evaluators that the offering can also play as better than average at full bloom. A strong showing in the Carolina League this season will go a long way toward cementing this prospect's stock, potentially pushing him up into the top half of this system in the process.

Prospects on the Rise

1. SS/3B Yu-Cheng Chang: The 2013 import from Taiwan had a solid stateside debut in the Arizona League, where his overall game showed more refinement than initially expected. Chang possesses loose hands that enable him to quickly get the head of the bat through the hitting zone and also pull them inside of the ball well to control the head of the bat. The frame offers solid physical projection to where average-to-better power can continue to show down the line as strength gains further take. It would be the perfect-world scenario for the 19-year-old to stick up the middle at shortstop, but it's more likely that he transitions to the hot corner at some point in the future. A good showing with his hit tool against more seasoned competition in 2015 will put this prospect discussions as one of the 10 best here in short order.

2. RHP Dylan Baker: A broken ankle put a major dent into this right-hander's season, but when he was on the field in limited action, both the plus, lively fastball and hard breaking ball continued to show strong potential. The long pole for Baker remains the emergence of a third offering, as there's questionable feel for his changeup and thoughts that the pitch has too far to go to become a viable piece of his repertoire. Reaching the majors as a starter may not ultimately be in the cards, but the arm could end up very effective in a set-up role given the power nature of the fastball/breaking-ball combination. The 23-year-old has a good shot to track into Double-A by the end of the year, with traction gaining as a more solidified arm within this system and firm top-10 status in conjunction.

3. SS Willi Castro: The 2013 international signee out of the Dominican Republic made his stateside debut last year in the Arizona League with middling results, but it was a fairly advanced assignment for the then-17-year-old and offered some promise that he can handle another aggressive placement in short-season ball this year. Castro's game is all projection at present, with this just a collection of raw tools, but he flashes a compact stroke and solid potential with the glove on the infield. The bat will get a boost if the body begins to fill into the athletic 6-foot-1 frame and the increasing strength level starts to enhance the quality of contact. It's a rough sketch at present for sure, but one that can start putting a little more color to it as soon as this season.

Factors on the Farm

Prospects likely to contribute at the major-league level in 2015

1. OF James Ramsey: Acquired from the Cardinals in exchange for Justin Masterson at the end of July, the 25-year-old outfielder is likely to initially provide depth for the organization at Triple-A to start 2015, with a good chance to be one of the first called if an outfield spot opens up. Ramsey flashes a smooth stroke from the left side of the plate, along with the ability to handle center field and an arm that can play in all three outfield slots. He offers the type of versatility to profile as a fourth outfielder off the bench, with the potential for the role to play up a bit for a few seasons. The Florida State product gives the organization a near-term-ready outfielder in the upper levels and an option to turn to this season for a legit look if he keeps things rolling with the bat in the International League.

2. RHP Cody Anderson: The right-hander may be a deeper option to start the season given his struggles in Double-A last year, but with a few adjustments, Anderson has the potential to quickly get back on track and offer the organization depth within the rotation should the need arise at some point in the summer. When the 24-year-old has his low-90s sinker and biting slider working, he can successfully keep hitters at bay and navigate deep into games. The fastball command is a concern, though, as it deserted the big righty to the point last year where the pitch was elevated way too often and batted around with ease. It may ultimately limit things to the back of a rotation or relief role, but major-league potential is here, with a chance to get on a role and help in 2015.

FROM THE FIELD

Francisco Lindor

Team: Cleveland Indians

Evaluator: CJ Wittmann

Dates seen: April 18, 21, and 22, 2014

Affiliate: Akron RubberDucks (Double-A, Indians)

Physical/health: Short, stocky frame; noticeable added weight since last season; nice lower half and filled-out upper body; durability issues no longer a concern; could be heavier than listed weight; plus-plus look in his RubberDucks uniform.

Makeup: 70 grade; always is involved and interacting with teammates; shows willingness to work at craft; raved about work ethic.

MLB ETA	Risk factor	OFP	Realistic role
2014	Moderate	70	All-Star-caliber shortstop

Tool	Future grade	Report
Hit	65	Wide stance with loose hands; sweet, short path to the ball; plus-plus bat speed with slight lift in swing; barrel comes through hitting zone at slight angle; excellent balance; innate bat-to-ball skills; recognizes spin early; tracks ball deep into hitting zone; can barrel velocity and quality spin; gets great post-contact extension; swing is mirrored from both sides of the plate; small wrist lock before starting swing creates torque as hips get involved; excellent strength in wrists and hands giving him very good barrel control; makes consistent hard contact; shows advanced feel for strike zone; comes up with approach and will adjust to the situation; has a knack for hitting.
Power	50	Power will come from plus-plus bat speed and lift; natural bat-to-ball skills allow him to barrel everything; showed ability to backspin ball in BP; sneaky raw power; in game, hit two to the wall to right-center from the right side. Also launched one foul deep pull-side; added weight and strength has helped; will be plenty of doubles power, with home-run potential as he matures; gets very good extension with pitches out over the plate; presently below average.
Baserunning/ speed	55	Instinctive on the basepaths; reads pitchers and balls in play well; 4.1-4.17 range to first left side; swing allows him to get out of the box quickly and accelerate; second gear is average; not a burner.
Glove	80	Unbelievable; silky, smooth actions; unmatched instincts and reactions on the field; despite solid-average runner, quick first step and reactions allow range to play plus-plus; makes backhand pick look easy; extremely soft hands and smooth transfers to throw; stays low and has quick turn on double play; excellent footwork around second-base bag when turned double play; shows all traits of elite-level shortstop.
Arm	60	Strong, accurate throws from all places; made throw from deep shortstop hole on a line as well as spinning throw up the middle.

Overall: Francisco Lindor can do it all. Not only is he an elite defender at shortstop, but the bat will have impact too. Noticeable added weight and strength along with his natural ability will allow his power to play a little higher than most expect. I was mostly impressed with Lindor's advanced approach and ability to adjust to the situation. He is so advanced for his age and it shows. He's a special player.

3. RHP Shawn Armstrong: Fueled by a high-octane fastball that consistently works in the mid-90s and power breaking stuff, this right-hander profiles as a late-innings reliever and can arrive as soon as this season to contribute out of the 'pen. Armstrong runs into ruts of overthrowing and has a lot of effort in his delivery, but he made strides last year throwing strikes on a more consistent basis. If the trend continues to hold, the 24-year-old has a very good shot at emerging as a legit eighth-inning arm tasked with getting outs in key spots. Look for him to start in the International League and get the first look when an opportunity in the bullpen opens up.

1. Jonathan Gray   RHP

Born: 11/5/91   **Age:** 23   **Bats:** R   **Throws:** R   **Height:** 6'4"   **Weight:** 235

MLB ETA	CT	FB	CH	CB	SL	OFP	Realistic
2015	–	80	60	–	70	70 NO. 2 STARTER	60 NO. 3 STARTER

YEAR	TEAM	LVL	AGE	W	L	SV	G	GS	IP	H	HR	BB	K	BB9	SO9	GB%	BABIP	WHIP	ERA	FIP	FRA	WARP
2014	TUL	AA	22	10	5	0	24	24	124.3	107	10	41	113	3.0	8.2	40%	.285	1.19	3.91	3.43	4.42	0.7
2015	COL	MLB	23	5	6	0	19	19	91.3	94	10	32	76	3.2	7.5	41%	.327	1.37	4.52	4.26	4.91	0.7
2016	COL	MLB	24	10	10	0	31	31	193.7	194	23	56	179	2.6	8.3	41%	.330	1.29	4.24	3.77	4.61	1.8

Breakout: 19%   Improve: 29%   Collapse: 8%   Attrition: 26%   MLB: 44%   Upside: 51   *Comparables: Matt Barnes, Chad Bettis, Drew Smyly*

Drafted/Acquired: 1st round, 2013 draft, University of Oklahoma (Norman, OK)

Previous Ranking: #1 (Org), #16 (Top 101)

What Happened in 2014: Even with the raw stuff outdistancing the production, Gray put together a solid showing in the Texas League and continued to progress toward a Denver debut.

Strengths: Workhorse build with physicality and aggressiveness on the bump; confident pounding the zone with upper-90s heater; triple-digit capable; fastball plays across quadrants; wipeout slider works in and out of zone; elite two-pitch combo with parallel plane and release; developmental focus on change piece, flashing hard fade and deception; frontline offerings so good even average changeup will miss bats and barrels; can flip script with change-of-pace curve.

Weaknesses: Changeup still lags relative to fastball/slider; can struggle on both ends, implementing too firm or alternatively slowing arm and tipping; content pitching to contact and limited pitch count leave some question as to how dominant the stuff might be against top-tier bats; some stiffness in landing likely limits command ceiling.

Risk Factor/Injury History: Low; Double-A success; near major-league ready.

Bret Sayre's Fantasy Take: The only thing standing in the way of Gray projecting as a potential SP1 is Coors Field, and that's something that is going to be embedded in a lot of these pitcher write-ups throughout this list. The fastball/slider combo could lead to 220 strikeouts at the major-league level, but while he should pitch well enough on the road to act as a de facto ace, the home starts mixed in will leave his ratios closer to the 3.50/1.20 range.

The Year Ahead: Observing Gray in 2014 was akin to witnessing a bartender utilize a bottle of Lagavulin 16 to pour you a glass of Johnny Black—the result was perfectly satisfying, but lacked the impact and finish you anticipated upon spying the distinctive glass. The body, control, and quality of weaponry are everything you'd expect in an elite power arm, but Colorado's conservative guidance last summer left evaluators more reliant on projection than typical when grading out an advanced Double-A arm with loud present stuff. Even with a focus on developing his third-best offering and pitching to contact, the former Sooner still found success, regularly inducing soft contact from Texas League bats thanks to his ability to generally live around the zone with two double-plus offerings, and it's tough to envision him failing to rack up strikeouts once permitted a slightly longer leash via pitch count and pitch selection. There is little doubt that Gray will be a valuable major-league asset, and anything shy of number three production, even in the challenging Coors environs, would come as a surprise. He should start 2015 in Triple-A, but may not face the requisite resistance to truly refine until he faces major-league lineups capable of handling his electric arsenal.

> #13
> BP Top 101 Prospects

2. David Dahl   CF

Born: 4/1/94   **Age:** 21   **Bats:** L   **Throws:** R   **Height:** 6'2"   **Weight:** 195

MLB ETA	Hit	Power	Run	Glove	Arm	OFP	Realistic
2017	65	50	60	60	65	70 ALL STAR CF	60 1ST DIVISION REGULAR

YEAR	TEAM	LVL	AGE	PA	R	2B	3B	HR	RBI	BB	SO	SB	CS	AVG/OBP/SLG	TAv	BABIP	BRR	FRAA	WARP
2014	MOD	A+	20	125	14	8	2	4	14	5	27	3	0	.267/.296/.467	.274	.315	1.7	CF(25): 3.2, CF(4): 3.2	1.1
2014	ASH	A	20	422	69	33	6	10	41	23	65	18	0	.309/.347/.500	.280	.348	3.3	CF(70): 8.0, LF(7): 0.3	3.5
2015	COL	MLB	21	250	27	12	2	5	22	7	58	5	1	.247/.269/.372	.219	.302	0.5	CF 3, LF 0	0.0
2016	COL	MLB	22	250	26	13	3	4	26	12	54	6	2	.263/.300/.397	.256	.321	0.7	CF 2, LF 0	1.7

Breakout: 0%   Improve: 0%   Collapse: 0%   Attrition: 0%   MLB: 0%   Upside: 79   *Comparables: Felix Pie, Jordan Schafer, Austin Jackson*

Drafted/Acquired: 1st round, 2012 draft, Oak Mountain HS (Birmingham, AL)

Previous Ranking: #4 (Org), #100 (Top 101)

What Happened in 2014: After a tumultuous 2013, Dahl put his five-tool ability on display during an impressive run through the Sally League and solid showing in limited Cal League exposure, firmly establishing himself as one of the top center-field prospects in the game.

Strengths: Easy barrel delivery with extended pitch plane overlap; regular hard contact and comfort spraying line to line; good athleticism boosts the aggregate skill set; run is legit plus, showing up on the grass and rounding the bases; glove could play to plus at maturity with continued improvement in reads off the bat; already shows understanding of how to let power manifest naturally; arm plays across the outfield with carry and solid accuracy.

Weaknesses: Lacks leverage in swing, so power will be reliant on ability to barrel ball and might be limited to pull; routes are improving, but still limit full utilization of natural speed; can get aggressive, particularly early in count when hunting fastballs; advanced arms will work to expose with spin.

Risk Factor/Injury History: High; Low-A experience dominates résumé; hamstring and back injuries in 2013 not long-term concerns.

Bret Sayre's Fantasy Take: On the other side of the coin: hitters who might call Coors home. It doesn't get much better in fantasy leagues—and when you take a five-category talent like Dahl and put him at altitude, you could get a top-10 outfielder in his prime. If he stays with the organization, it's not unrealistic for him to hit .300 with 15 homers and 25 steals. That could make him a borderline first-round pick.

The Year Ahead: Last season, Dahl officially stepped into the bright lights of the national prospect scene thanks to a strong showing in the South Atlantic League and brief swing through the Cal League. The Alabama prep product's true five-tool potential alone provides enough reason for evaluators to lock in, but it's the combination of athleticism and baseball acumen characteristic of impact major leaguers that could see the profile emerge as one of the elite talents in the game. Dahl missed much of 2013 due to injury and some disciplinary issues, neither of which pose any concern moving forward, and it is highly encouraging to see the talented center fielder slide into the full-season routine with nary a missed step. There is work to be done smoothing out the reads and routes in the outfield, and the approach at the plate will need to be focused, but most of these potential issues reside in developmental areas commonly addressed through reps. Dahl should return to High-A Modesto in 2015, with a chance for in-season promotion if the hitter-friendly collection of California parks proves overly nurturing.

> **#24**
> BP Top 101 Prospects

---

3. Raimel Tapia OF

Born: 2/4/94 **Age:** 21 **Bats:** L **Throws:** L **Height:** 6'2" **Weight:** 160

MLB ETA	Hit	Power	Run	Glove	Arm	OFP	Realistic
2018	65	50	55	55	60	65 1ST DIV/ALL STAR	55 >AVG REGULAR

YEAR	TEAM	LVL	AGE	PA	R	2B	3B	HR	RBI	BB	SO	SB	CS	AVG/OBP/SLG	TAv	BABIP	BRR	FRAA	WARP
2014	ASH	A	20	539	93	32	1	9	72	35	90	33	16	.326/.382/.453	.289	.383	3.1	LF(43): -1.4, CF(42): 2.0	2.7
2015	COL	MLB	21	250	24	11	1	3	22	9	59	8	4	.251/.285/.346	.219	.315	-0.2	CF 1, RF -1	-0.6
2016	COL	MLB	22	250	27	11	2	4	25	13	54	8	5	.273/.319/.387	.259	.334	0.5	CF 1, RF -1	1.4

Breakout: 0%   Improve: 0%   Collapse: 0%   Attrition: 0%   MLB: 0%   Upside: 33   *Comparables: Xavier Avery, Peter Bourjos, Dexter Fowler*

Drafted/Acquired: International Free Agent, 2010, Dominican Republic

Previous Ranking: #3 (Org), #97 (Top 101)

What Happened in 2014: Tapia continued to put up impressive offensive numbers, slashing .326/.382/.453 as a 20-year-old with Low-A Asheville.

Strengths: Excellent feel for contact; above-average bat speed; malleable barrel delivery allows for consistent contact through variable planes; high level of comfort working across the diamond; good balance throughout; see-ball-hit-ball approach; some pop to pull with bat speed allowing for turn and burn on the inner half; above-average foot speed can play up underway thanks to solid feel on the basepaths; present arm strength; precocious five-tool talent in nascent stages of development.

Weaknesses: Speed can play down out of box depending on finish swing to swing; lots of uncertainty in first step limits range in the outfield; not a natural track-and-close defender; can come around throws, losing carry and accuracy; aggressive approach is bat-to-ball-reliant, leaving open possibility that quality sequencing will disrupt timing and ability to barrel; needs to add strength.

Risk Factor/Injury History: High

Bret Sayre's Fantasy Take: You can pretty much copy the blurb about Dahl and place it here for Tapia as well. The upside is substantial, even though Dahl gets a slight advantage in power potential and speed. While Asheville is conducive to left-handed hitters putting up big numbers, expect even more fantasy hype after spending a good chunk of 2015 in the California League.

The Year Ahead: Tapia utilizes an unconventional setup and variable swing that doesn't sit well with evaluators who prefer their hit tools wrapped in more traditional packaging. For those who can work past the optical quirks, what remains is an innate ability to find the ball with the barrel, regardless of quadrant or pitch type. The secret to Tapia's success is the ability of the native Dominican to meld natural bat speed and hand-eye coordination with consistent balance throughout multilook swings, resulting in a borderline unsettling level of comfort

> **#45**
> BP Top 101 Prospects

and confidence in the box. There is still a great deal to be determined as far as Tapia's ultimate offensive game, and time will tell whether more advanced arms will force the gifted batsman to alter his approach. Even with added strength through maturation of the body, the power could ultimately play below average if Tapia elects to keep a contact-centric approach to hitting that places a higher level of import on utilizing the whole field and putting the ball in play than finding spots and offerings to drive. Regardless, there may be enough in the hit tool to carry the profile, even if Tapia is forced to remain in a corner either through deference to Dahl or lack of requisite up-the-middle chops. He'll tackle High-A in 2015 with an eye to a third straight stateside season on the happy side of .320.

4. Eddie Butler   RHP

Born: 3/13/91   **Age:** 24   **Bats:** R   **Throws:** R   **Height:** 6'2"   **Weight:** 180

MLB ETA	CT	FB	CH	CB	SL	OFP	Realistic
2015	–	75	65	–	55	60 NO. 3 STARTER	55 LATE INN RP/CLOSER

YEAR	TEAM	LVL	AGE	W	L	SV	G	GS	IP	H	HR	BB	K	BB9	SO9	GB%	BABIP	WHIP	ERA	FIP	FRA	WARP
2014	COL	MLB	23	1	1	0	3	3	16.0	23	2	7	3	3.9	1.7	56%	.328	1.88	6.75	5.67	6.50	-0.2
2014	CSP	AAA	23	0	1	0	1	1	5.3	8	0	3	4	5.1	6.8	58%	.421	2.06	10.12	3.89	4.74	0.1
2014	TUL	AA	23	6	9	0	18	18	108.0	104	10	32	63	2.7	5.2	47%	.274	1.26	3.58	4.10	4.76	0.2
2014	MOD	A+	23	0	0	0	1	1	4.0	2	0	2	2	4.5	4.5	36%	.143	1.00	6.75	4.24	6.87	0.0
2015	COL	MLB	24	6	8	0	21	21	114.3	125	14	44	63	3.5	5.0	51%	.312	1.48	5.20	5.15	5.65	-0.1
2016	COL	MLB	25	10	11	0	31	31	196.7	192	21	71	133	3.2	6.1	51%	.299	1.33	4.40	4.32	4.78	1.4

Breakout: 11%   Improve: 15%   Collapse: 7%   Attrition: 18%   MLB: 27%   Upside: 10   *Comparables: Ivan Nova, Daryl Thompson, Troy Patton*

Drafted/Acquired: 1st round, 2012, Radford University (Radford, VA)

Previous Ranking: #2 (Org), #26 (Top 101)

What Happened in 2014: After a solid start to the season, Butler saw a downtick in the effectiveness and consistency of his stuff, likely due at least in part to shoulder ailments that flared up in the summer and fall, leaving open the possibility that the power arm could be best suited for high-leverage relief work.

Strengths: Mid- to upper-90s fastball that comes with arm-side dip and dance; change has shown double-plus potential in the past, mirroring two-seam fastball action and coming with arm speed and slot deception; long limbs with projection remaining in frame; slider can play above average off fastball plane; arsenal heavy across the board; has shown solid feel for zone with all offerings.

Weaknesses: Stuff backed up in 2014, with slider often showing flat and change losing some bite and handle; inconsistent timing and release exacerbated inconsistencies tied to crossfire release and regularly birthed choppy secondaries and loosened command; shoulder issues and lagging physical maturation strengthen case for future fit in the bullpen.

Risk Factor/Injury History: Moderate; uncertainty surrounding shoulder; missed time in-season and skipped Arizona Fall League.

Bret Sayre's Fantasy Take: There's a growing amount of doubt in the fantasy community with Butler, and for good reason. It's bad enough when a pitcher sees a big strikeout/velocity dip, suffers a shoulder injury, or is developing in a system where the final destination is an intense hitters' park—but when one has all three, it tends to put a dent in his value. He will still factor in the Dynasty 101, but the floor and ceiling have dropped since last year.

The Year Ahead: After breaking out with a dominant 2013, Butler saw the ugly side of the prospect coin last season, with injury and discomfort with mechanical tweaks combining to sap some of the pop from his arsenal and leaving him hittable. Because of the weight of Butler's multilook fastball and quality change, the lanky righty remained difficult to lift even when his stuff found too much of the plate. But the incendiary arsenal that was a mainstay two summers prior played tepid in 2014, and the Rockies' attempts to soften his finish and regulate his tempo did little to assist Butler in finding more ease in his arm action or precision with his pitches. Should Butler shift to the 'pen, his fastball and changeup could allow him to handle high-leverage situations with aplomb, particularly if he can get back to pounding the bottom of the strike zone, where both pitches are most effective. Butler could begin 2015 back in Double-A provided he returns to camp with his shoulder issues firmly in the rearview. A return to Colorado this summer isn't out of the question if he can rediscover the explosive stuff that captivated evaluators just 18 short months ago.

#64

BP Top 101 Prospects

5. Kyle Freeland LHP

Born: 5/14/93 **Age:** 22 **Bats:** L **Throws:** L **Height:** 6'3" **Weight:** 170

MLB ETA	CT	FB	CH	CB	SL	OFP	Realistic
2016	55	60	60	–	60	65	50
						NO. 2/3 STARTER	NO. 4 STARTER

YEAR	TEAM	LVL	AGE	W	L	SV	G	GS	IP	H	HR	BB	K	BB9	SO9	GB%	BABIP	WHIP	ERA	FIP	FRA	WARP
2014	ASH	A	21	2	0	0	5	5	21.7	14	1	4	18	1.7	7.5	52%	.220	0.83	0.83	3.08	3.74	0.6
2014	GJR	Rk	21	1	0	0	5	5	17.3	16	0	2	15	1.0	7.8	65%	.333	1.04	1.56	2.82	4.82	0.5
2015	COL	MLB	22	2	3	0	8	8	34.3	40	4	16	20	4.2	5.2	48%	.332	1.63	5.88	5.33	6.39	-0.2
2016	COL	MLB	23	7	10	0	30	30	185.3	198	19	70	133	3.4	6.5	48%	.328	1.45	4.87	4.27	5.30	0.3

Breakout: 0%   Improve: 0%   Collapse: 0%   Attrition: 0%   MLB: 0%   Upside: 8   *Comparables: Alex Cobb, Robbie Ross, Zach Phillips*

#76

BP Top 101 Prospects

Drafted/Acquired: 1st round, 2014 draft, University of Evansville (Evansville, IN)
Previous Ranking: NR

What Happened in 2014: Freeland enjoyed a dominant junior season leading up to the draft, racking up 128 strikeouts to just 13 walks over 99 2/3 innings pitched and holding opposition bats to a sub-1.00 WHIP and a .214 average. After coming off the board as a top 10 overall pick in June, the versatile lefty breezed through his first 39 professional innings, split between short-season and Low-A ball.

Strengths: All three foundational pitches show above-average potential and come with multiple looks and deception; fastball sits in low-90s velo band with ability to sink, cut, and run; four-seamer can reach mid-90s; slider comes with late sweep and can tighten to upper-80s cutter; change sits in mid-80s with late tumble; can cut change for different look; plus control; can live on the periphery with comfort; advanced feel for sequencing and ability to vary look and approach.

Weaknesses: Delivery comes with effort and some herk and jerk; low slot limits downhill plane and can hold fastball on swing path; potential to live too fully in the zone; elbow surgery already in the file; yet to show durability required of pro starter; stuff could play down over course of longer season.

Risk Factor/Injury History: High; durability yet to be tested; elbow surgery on record (2007); nontraditional starter mechanics.

Bret Sayre's Fantasy Take: A future FIP darling, Freeland is going to be a better play in points leagues due to the potential for him to put up pretty epic strikeout-to-walk rates. Unfortunately, as someone who will be in the strike zone a lot, his ratios are likely to suffer at the fate of Coors; he could see an ERA closer to 4.00, while maintaining a very good WHIP. The home park and his injury history will keep him toward the back of the top 20 in dynasty drafts.

The Year Ahead: One could argue that from the time Freeland saw his stuff tick up on the Cape in 2013 he has yet to be challenged for any significant stretch, easily overmatching collegiate competition and low-minors bats alike in 2014. The southpaw is distinctive both for his chameleonic arsenal and the adroit manner in which he wields it, with a uniform release and trajectory capable of resulting in seven-plus alternate finishes over a velocity band stretching cleanly from the low-80s to the mid-90s. Provided Freeland can maintain that quality of stuff over a long pro season, the former Purple Ace could force a speedy ascension through the minor-league ranks thanks to his advanced arsenal, plus command, and aggressive approach. Assuming no significant setbacks, the Rockies could see their 2014 first rounder logging major-league innings by 2016 as an impressive left-handed complement to the two power righties ranked first and fourth on this list.

6. Ryan McMahon 3B

Born: 12/14/94 **Age:** 20 **Bats:** L **Throws:** R **Height:** 6'2" **Weight:** 185

MLB ETA	Hit	Power	Run	Glove	Arm	OFP	Realistic
2017	55	60	–	55	55	60	50
						1ST DIVISION REGULAR	AVG ML PLAYER

YEAR	TEAM	LVL	AGE	PA	R	2B	3B	HR	RBI	BB	SO	SB	CS	AVG/OBP/SLG	TAv	BABIP	BRR	FRAA	WARP
2014	ASH	A	19	552	93	46	3	18	102	54	143	8	5	.282/.358/.502	.284	.360	-0.3	3B(118): 8.1	4.0
2015	COL	MLB	20	250	23	11	1	7	28	17	80	1	1	.221/.277/.364	.222	.303	-0.4	3B 3	-0.1
2016	COL	MLB	21	250	30	14	1	8	31	19	73	1	1	.243/.306/.422	.267	.315	-0.5	3B 3	2.2

Breakout: 0%   Improve: 0%   Collapse: 0%   Attrition: 0%   MLB: 0%   Upside: 15   *Comparables: Matt Davidson, Matt Dominguez, Mike Moustakas*

Drafted/Acquired: 2nd round, 2013 draft, Mater Dei HS (Santa Ana, CA)
Previous Ranking: #5 (Org)

What Happened in 2014: In his first full season of pro ball the Mater Dei alum showed flashes of offensive brilliance mixed with periodic struggles to find balance in his approach, culminating in a solid Sally League debut that fell short of a true breakout.

Strengths: Loose, whippy swing with above-average bat speed; natural lift and carry pole to pole; can be very difficult bat to unpack thanks to bat speed and solid plate coverage; good athlete; glove and arm can both play above average at the hot corner; lateral agility; hands work; strong competitor.

Weaknesses: Approach still developing; can slip into extended periods where he expands zone and gives away at-bats; needs continued reps to improve tracking and strengthen offensive foundation; particularly susceptible to same-side spin; thickening body could lead to loss of fluidity, particularly in field; gets deliberate in footwork; inconsistent setup can force throws off course.

Risk Factor/Injury History: High; limited full-season exposure; two-sport prep product with limited time focused on baseball development.

Bret Sayre's Fantasy Take: A power hitter in Coors is a beautiful thing. McMahon could launch 25-plus homers with a .270 average at sea level—which would make his potential in the thin air near elite for the position. He's unlikely to contribute more than a handful of steals at peak, but given the state of third base, it won't matter.

The Year Ahead: McMahon's calling card is going to be his raw power, which he comes by honestly thanks to good bat speed, solid strength, and wrists capable of producing whip in the barrel. The approach is still loose, but more as a result of inconsistent implementation of a plan and limited exposure to quality spin. When locked in and comfortable he comes by hard contact with ease, demonstrating an organic ability to use the whole field and giving some reason to project the hit tool aggressively despite the delta between present ability and requisite major-league baseline. While a thickening body carries with it the risk of limiting his actions at third, his overall athleticism and arm strength should allow him to stick at the five-spot long term. McMahon could put up big numbers in the California League this year, and if he continues to progress in smoothing out his game across the board, there is potential for the SoCal native to establish himself as one of the better corner talents in the minors.

---

7. Forrest Wall   2B

Born: 11/20/95 **Age:** 19 **Bats:** L **Throws:** R **Height:** 6'0" **Weight:** 176

MLB ETA	Hit	Power	Run	Glove	Arm	OFP	Realistic
2018	65	–	70	60	–	60	50
						1ST DIVISION REGULAR	AVG ML PLAYER

YEAR	TEAM	LVL	AGE	PA	R	2B	3B	HR	RBI	BB	SO	SB	CS	AVG/OBP/SLG	TAv	BABIP	BRR	FRAA	WARP
2014	GJR	Rk	18	188	48	6	6	3	24	27	32	18	5	.318/.416/.490	.300	.382	2.5	2B(20): -1.0	1.0
2015	COL	MLB	19	250	27	9	1	3	17	14	72	9	3	.209/.255/.299	.193	.283	0.8	2B -2	-1.1
2016	COL	MLB	20	250	24	9	2	3	21	15	62	10	3	.235/.283/.332	.230	.302	1.4	2B -1	-0.2

Breakout: 0%   Improve: 0%   Collapse: 0%   Attrition: 0%   MLB: 0%   Upside: 14   *Comparables: Ozzie Martinez, Starlin Castro, L.J. Hoes*

Drafted/Acquired: 1st round, 2014 draft, Orangewood Christian HS (Maitland, FL)

Previous Ranking: NR

What Happened in 2014: Wall tore through the showcase and travel-ball circuit, seeding fields across the country en route to a 35th-overall selection in the June draft and an over-slot signing bonus, capping the year with a juicy .318/.416/.490 slash line over his first 41 pro games with Rookie Grand Junction.

Strengths: Premium contact ability; natural ability to match swing plane to pitch plane, producing regular hard contact and allowing for maximum force at impact regardless of quadrant or pitch type; pure hitter in every sense; solid approach and comfort working deep or attacking early; average raw pop; double-plus speed plays out of the box and on the dirt; range spans from shallow right to behind the bag; sure hands.

Weaknesses: Below-average arm resultant from labrum surgery; arm could limit defensive impact, particularly around the bag; playable pop may top out to the gaps due to swing; limited defensive profile and capped power ceiling place pressure on the hit tool.

Risk Factor/Injury History: High; sub-200 pro plate appearances to his name; labrum surgery limiting arm strength.

Bret Sayre's Fantasy Take: The fantasy potential is strong enough for Wall to push him above Freeland on dynasty draft boards, despite the extended ETA, and making him a borderline first-round pick. As a left-handed hitter headed to Asheville, he could make a huge jump in fantasy value during 2015, but there is injury risk attached to his profile. Wall could be a .300 hitter with 30 steals from the keystone in time, but there will likely not be much power to speak of.

The Year Ahead: It's not often you see a pure second-base profile nab a $2 million signing bonus in the draft, but Wall is an exception to the rule, with his presence at the keystone tied solely to his below-average arm strength. The sturdy, sweet-swinging lefty has the hands and athleticism to handle the six-spot, as well as the speed and instincts for center field, and the case can be made that had Wall's arm permitted him to profile comfortably at either spot, his enticing hit tool could have garnered attention as early as the middle of the first round. While the hit tool is the crown jewel of the profile, Wall's speed and savvy should likewise allow him to impact the game on the bases and in the field, providing a broad baseline skill set to go with what could very well wind up being the best pure stick in the 2014 draft class. Wall could follow in the footsteps of Dahl, Tapia, and McMahon with an Asheville assignment to begin his first full season, and just might be advanced enough to catch up to that trio before the season concludes.

8. Tyler Anderson   LHP

Born: 12/30/89   **Age:** 25   **Bats:** L   **Throws:** L   **Height:** 6'4"   **Weight:** 215

MLB ETA	CT	FB	CH	CB	SL	OFP	Realistic
2015	50	50	60	50	–	50 NO. 4 STARTER	45 NO. 5 SP/SWINGMAN

YEAR	TEAM	LVL	AGE	W	L	SV	G	GS	IP	H	HR	BB	K	BB9	SO9	GB%	BABIP	WHIP	ERA	FIP	FRA	WARP
2014	TUL	AA	24	7	4	0	23	23	118.3	91	3	40	106	3.0	8.1	52%	.274	1.11	1.98	2.77	3.47	2.7
2015	COL	MLB	25	5	7	0	17	17	93.0	100	11	34	59	3.3	5.7	49%	.316	1.44	4.96	4.84	5.39	0.1
2016	COL	MLB	26	9	11	0	31	31	196.7	203	23	51	132	2.3	6.0	49%	.309	1.29	4.51	4.20	4.90	1.2

Breakout: 20%   Improve: 24%   Collapse: 6%   Attrition: 26%   MLB: 34%   Upside: 10   *Comparables: Rob Scahill, Chris Heston, Gus Schlosser*

Drafted/Acquired: 1st round, 2011 draft, University of Oregon (Eugene, OR)

Previous Ranking: Factor on the Farm

What Happened in 2014: Anderson completed a much needed full season of work with Double-A Tulsa, leading the Texas League in ERA (1.98), WHIP (1.107), and batting average against (.216), before leaving the last game of the season early with elbow soreness.

Strengths: Pitchability lefty; comfortable working in and out with average arsenal; mechanics come with some funk, adding deception and allowing average fastball velocity to play up; plus low-80s changeup projects heater through bulk of journey before late tumble; short slider/cutter is a weapon, regularly sliding up handles and off barrels; curve is serviceable as change of pace; hitchy motion and arm action disrupt hitter timing.

Weaknesses: Lacks durability; stuff is fringy on paper; deception and quirks may not be enough to keep major-league bats off center; razor-thin margin for error in zone; lacks go-to swing-and-miss offering for same-side bats.

Risk Factor/Injury History: Moderate; feel and approach to tackle major-league bats but limited upside; extensive injury history (shoulder/elbow) could force shift to 'pen.

Bret Sayre's Fantasy Take: There should be very little fantasy interest in Anderson, who at best could be a nondescript starter pitching in Coors. Even in a perfect world, he likely ends up as a streamer on the road in non-shallow mixed leagues.

The Year Ahead: After a shoulder injury limited Anderson to just 89 2/3 innings in 2013, last year's 118 1/3 innings pitched with Double-A Tulsa seemed to represent an important step toward an overdue audition with the big club. Unfortunately, the goodwill earned over those innings was lessened when elbow soreness resulted in Anderson's early exit from the final game of the season, once again casting doubt as to whether the former first rounder will be able to handle the rigors of starter workload. When healthy, Anderson relies on guile and deception in implementing a vanilla collection of pitches to surprising effect. The changeup is an equalizer, particularly nasty against oppo-side bats thanks to late fade and tumble, and he continues to improve upon his sequencing and placement to get the most out of an average fastball and short slider. Anderson could join Gray in a Triple-A assignment to start 2015 and should be available to help out in Colorado as soon as an opportunity arises, be it in the rotation or as a lefty arm out of the 'pen. The upside isn't great, but there's value in a steady, back-end arm provided he can stay healthy long enough to rack up some innings.

9. Trevor Story   SS

Born: 11/15/92   **Age:** 22   **Bats:** R   **Throws:** R   **Height:** 6'1"   **Weight:** 175

MLB ETA	Hit	Power	Run	Glove	Arm	OFP	Realistic
2017	–	50	50	–	60	55 >AVG ML REGULAR	45 PLATOON BAT/UT

YEAR	TEAM	LVL	AGE	PA	R	2B	3B	HR	RBI	BB	SO	SB	CS	AVG/OBP/SLG	TAv	BABIP	BRR	FRAA	WARP
2014	TUL	AA	21	237	29	8	1	9	20	28	82	3	1	.200/.302/.380	.250	.281	0.8	SS(43): -7.6, 3B(6): 0.7	-0.2
2014	MOD	A+	21	218	38	17	7	5	28	31	59	20	4	.332/.436/.582	.349	.467	2.8	SS(39): 0.2, 3B(8): -0.3	3.2
2014	TRI	A-	21	8	2	1	0	0	0	1	3	0	0	.286/.375/.429	.256	.500	0.4	SS(2): -0.3	0.2
2015	COL	MLB	22	250	26	11	2	6	27	19	82	6	1	.225/.289/.375	.232	.316	0.7	SS -2, 3B 0	0.2
2016	COL	MLB	23	250	30	12	2	8	30	20	77	6	1	.235/.302/.411	.265	.316	0.8	SS -3, 3B 0	2.0

Breakout: 0%   Improve: 0%   Collapse: 0%   Attrition: 0%   MLB: 0%   Upside: 30   *Comparables: Brandon Wood, Derek Dietrich, Mark Reynolds*

Drafted/Acquired: 1st round, 2011 draft, Irving HS (Irving, TX)

Previous Ranking: #10 (Org)

What Happened in 2014: The friendly confines of the Cal League were much kinder to Story in his half-season return, with the shortstop posting a .332/.436/.582 slash line before stumbling into a downward spiral upon promotion to Double-A Tulsa, where he hit just .200 over 237 Texas League plate appearances and struck out every third trip to the box.

Strengths: Shows potential for average or better pop; good strength; can punish mistakes up and over; solid athlete; left-side arm with zip; capable of making the throws from multiple angles; proficient pivots; feel for the game; enough versatility to develop into utility role.

Weaknesses: Lacks balance and fluidity in stroke; barrel comes off plane with regularity; advanced spin can brutalize; stark left/right splits with significant struggles against same-side arms; hit-tool utility likely to limit playable pop; actions adequate at short but not impactful; lacks carrying tool.

Risk Factor/Injury History: High; swing-and-miss could prevent advancement out of high minors.

Bret Sayre's Fantasy Take: The 2014 season saw a rebound in Story's value after he completely fell on his face in 2013, but his contact struggles will both hurt his value in that category and depress the home-run potential out of his bat. At this point, the best you can hope for is a shortstop with a .250 average with 20 homers and 15 steals—and that's with Coors factored in. Of course, that's still pretty good.

The Year Ahead: Story spent the first half of his year laying waste to the dreadful memories of a 2013 Cal League tour fraught with failures. Even in the midst of his first-half offensive outburst, evaluators pointed to still-present holes in his coverage and a hitchy swing that could put a hurt on fastballs on the fat, but left Story largely tooth-less against more precise arms and quality soft stuff. Those concerns proved valid, as Story was utterly domi-nated upon promotion to Double-A Tulsa, whiffing every third plate appearance and seeming all but helpless against same-side arms. There is a silver lining to the dark cloud, however, as Story continues to show an ability to punish mistakes, and his feel for the strike zone may be firm enough that a future as a useful three-outcome bat is not out of the question. At a minimum, Story is going to have to get more direct to contact and more uni-formity in his swing to keep his head above water in major-league seas. But the raw pop and capable glovework could come together to provide solid defensive value across the dirt and average offensive production in the aggregate, skewed to power and on base. Story will return to Double-A this year as a 22-year-old with time ever so slightly on his side, but he'll need to show significant improvements to win back the hearts of evaluators and reestablish himself as a potential building block for the organization.

10. Dom Nunez   C

Born: 1/17/95　**Age:** 20　**Bats:** L　**Throws:** R　**Height:** 6'0"　**Weight:** 175

MLB ETA	Hit	Power	Run	Glove	Arm	OFP	Realistic
2019	50	–	–	50	55	55 >AVG REGULAR	40 <AVG BACKUP

YEAR	TEAM	LVL	AGE	PA	R	2B	3B	HR	RBI	BB	SO	SB	CS	AVG/OBP/SLG	TAv	BABIP	BRR	FRAA	WARP
2014	GJR	Rk	19	198	30	12	0	8	40	21	28	5	7	.312/.384/.517	.300	.333	-1.2	C(37): -0.1	2.1
2015	COL	MLB	20	250	22	9	1	4	21	13	66	4	4	.207/.248/.301	.191	.265	-0.6	C -0, 2B -0	-1.1
2016	COL	MLB	21	250	25	10	1	5	24	15	56	5	4	.222/.269/.336	.226	.265	-0.3	C 0, 2B 0	-0.6

Breakout: 0%　**Improve:** 0%　**Collapse:** 0%　**Attrition:** 0%　**MLB:** 0%　**Upside:** 11　　*Comparables: Christian Vazquez, Luis Exposito, Tucker Barnhart*

Drafted/Acquired: 6th round, 2013 draft, Elk Grove HS (Elk Grove, CA)

Previous Ranking: NR

What Happened in 2014: After converting behind the plate full time, Nunez put together a strong performance during a return trip to the Pioneer League, impressing scouts equally with his growing skill set behind the plate and solid feel for the stick.

Strengths: Stays compact to contact with efficient lefty swing; can stay inside the ball or drop the barrel and turn on it; in-game pop can surprise; high-level makeup; big strides in development behind the plate; hands are soft-ening; comfortable as field general; quick and efficient transfer; throws come with carry and quick release.

Weaknesses: Still new to catching; glove can float and be carried out of zone; limited upside with bat; no standout tool at present; lacks physical projection; will need to rely on work ethic and makeup to get most out of average physical tools.

Risk Factor/Injury History: High; rookie-level résumé; dual-development risk (hit/catch).

Bret Sayre's Fantasy Take: Nunez is certainly interesting from a fantasy perspective, but the burn is going to be so long for him that it's barely worth worrying about in fantasy leagues right now. He's very much a guy to watch in 2015, though—and if that breakout starts early, jump on board.

The Year Ahead: Nunez shrugged off a rough 2013 and established himself as a legit prospect last year, quickly taking to his new role donning the tools of ignorance. The NorCal prep product has a traditional catcher's frame, compact and sturdy, with more than enough athleticism and lateral quickness to grow into a solid defender in time. Nunez's years as a middle infielder have no doubt helped him to transition behind the dish, particularly in the catch-and-throw department, where he displays a quick and clean transfer and impressive accuracy. Offen-sively, the young backstop stood out in the Pioneer League for his ability to get to pitches across the hit zone, utilizing a compact and efficient swing to spray line drives across the field. Nunez should graduate to full-season ball in 2015 and look to continue building on the momentum gained last year.

Prospects on the Rise

1. C Jose Briceno: The Venezuelan native didn't enter the season with the same fanfare as Asheville teammates David Dahl, Raimel Tapia, or Ryan McMahon, but his arm and his power both carry impact potential. Briceno had both tools on ready display over the course of the summer, posting a .193 ISO and gunning down 43 percent of would-be basestealers while simultaneously drawing praise for improved lateral actions and receiving. He should start this year at Modesto and will progress as quickly as his glove will carry him, with a chance to grow into an everyday backstop with above-average pop if things break right.

2. 3B Kevin Padlo: The 2014 fifth rounder utilizes a high-effort swing that generates above-average pop, but has also limited his ability to handle quality secondary offerings. Fortunately for Padlo, quality secondary offerings were in short supply in the Pioneer League, and the former San Diego commit capitalized on that fact, slashing .300/.420/.594 over his 48-game professional debut. Because Padlo's game comes with effort across the board, there is an extreme amount of risk tied to the profile. Still, the strong debut and presence of above-average raw power makes for an enticing 2015 follow. He should join Forrest Wall in Low-A Asheville as a worthy follow-up act to this year's talented trio of Dahl, Tapia, and McMahon.

3. SS Pedro Gonzalez: Gonzalez was inked to a seven-figure bonus last summer as part of the 2014 J2 class, with the long and projectable shortstop offering up a balanced profile that could flourish in any number of developmental directions. Gonzalez showed well in workouts and is roundly considered to have a solid handle at the plate despite his long limbs, with generous comps drawing similarities to Manny Machado as a steady, rangy shortstop who could fit best at the hot corner as he slowly fills out his frame. His actions in the field are clean, with the potential for significant added mass being the largest hurdle to his staying on the dirt. Gonzalez is advanced enough not only to handle a stateside debut in 2015 at the age of 17, but to impress upon arrival.

FROM THE FIELD

Raimel Tapia

Team: Colorado Rockies

Evaluator: Ryan Parker

Dates seen: Spring training, May 28–31, and June 27, 2014

Affiliate: Asheville Tourists (Low-A, Rockies)

Physical/health: Extremely thin frame. High waisted. Will add weight but hard to imagine breaking 200 lbs.

Makeup: Very energetic and focused player. Never appears to be stressed. Very competitive on everything from BP, to not giving away at-bats, to taking the extra base.

MLB ETA	Risk factor	OFP	Realistic role
2016	Moderate	65	First-division regular/all-star

Tool	Future grade	Report
Hit	70	It takes time to appreciate the hitting ability Tapia has. You can get thrown off by the body, the stance, or what he is working on in BP that day. Some days in BP you will see him do nothing but hit line drives up the middle or to the left side. Other days he will put on a show and let it fly. No matter what he is doing, his swing is very easy, well timed, and balanced. In games he sprays the ball to all fields. His swing is fluid and the ball is coming off his bat hot. His goal is simple at the plate: get the barrel on the ball. He accomplishes this more often than not thanks to an innate ability to manipulate himself and/or his bat to make sure he's squaring up the baseball.
Power	50	The power could actually play higher as Tapia fills out and adds strength. That being said, Tapia will never be known for power and that's almost a compliment. He can put on a show in BP but in games he saves those type of swings for when he is sitting 2-0 or 3-1. He won't give away an at-bat seeking to hit a home run and end up flying out. You make a mistake and he will punish it. Tapia is going to hit .300, but if he goes a month without seeing a pitch he can put over the fence then so be it.
Baserunning/speed	70	From a pure foot speed view Tapia is a 6.4 seconds down to first base with a solid first step out of the box. His grade gets raised thanks to his baserunning skills. He is a pest when he's on base. He stealing percentage isn't great currently, as he is very hit-and-miss on his ability to get good jumps. He's at his best when the ball is in play and he's running. He picks up the third base coach early, doesn't waste motion trying to jerk his head around to spot fielders, and can slide around tags. Instincts are incredible.
Glove	60	On any other club he would be a center fielder but will work in left field for Rockies. He is coming through the minors with David Dahl, who is better in center field. Tapia gets good jumps, but sometimes you will see him take slow small steps but breaking out into a full run. This could be him just getting used to reading the ball at a corner spot. Doesn't have great top end speed. Everything is good defensively and Tapia's natural athleticism carries him to a 6 grade but nothing is elite.
Arm	50	Quick arm but can get on the side of the ball at times and throw sinkers from the outfield. Arm is just fringe right now but I like the mechanics and I like the arm speed. Gets rid of the ball quick for an outfielder. Will never be strong enough for right field but plays well in left and center.

Overall: Tapia can straight up hit. First 7 I've ever put down on a hitter, and I did so with confidence. He makes adjustments during at-bats and during his own swings that are usually unseen at this level of minor league ball. Great instincts all around. Hopefully he can add some weight and strength to his frame. Could handle center easily. Top-of-the-order hitter who could either be a table-setter or clear the table himself. Special bat.

Factors on the Farm
Prospects likely to contribute at the major-league level in 2015

1. RHP Jairo Diaz: Proud owner of an elite, upper-90s fastball and upper-80s slide piece, Diaz and his power arsenal found their way to Colorado in exchange for middle infielder Josh Rutledge in December 2014. In addition to the borderline double-plus fastball/slider combo, Diaz can drop an occasional split change with late dive, most effective as a chase pitch ahead in the count. Diaz should compete for a spot in the big-league 'pen this spring and could begin logging high-leverage innings in short order.

2. 1B/OF Kyle Parker: Parker didn't dazzle in his brief major-league stints last summer, but there is still enough pop in the profile to warrant a look in 2015. The Clemson product is unlikely to hit for average thanks to pull-happy tendencies that yank his barrel off line and provide significant hurdles to proper plate coverage on the outer half. Still, Parker could prove useful as a power bat off the bench capable of spot starts at first base and either outfield corner, albeit with limited defensive value.

3. SS/2B Cristhian Adames: Adames provides steady hands, smooth actions, and adequate range at the six-spot, making him a worthy utility option should the need arise at the big-league level this year. The bat likely plays subpar, even considering the position, but the former international signee shows a solid feel for contact from both sides of the plate and could be serviceable as a down-order option if forced into regular action.

DETROIT TIGERS

1. Derek Hill CF

Born: 12/31/95 **Age:** 19 **Bats:** R **Throws:** R **Height:** 6'2" **Weight:** 195

MLB ETA	Hit	Power	Run	Glove	Arm	OFP	Realistic
Late 2018	55	–	70	70	50	60 1ST DIVISION PLAYER	50 AVG ML PLAYER

YEAR	TEAM	LVL	AGE	PA	R	2B	3B	HR	RBI	BB	SO	SB	CS	AVG/OBP/SLG	TAv	BABIP	BRR	FRAA	WARP
2014	ONE	A-	18	78	8	1	1	0	3	2	26	2	1	.203/.244/.243	.178	.312	0.0	-	0.0
2014	TGR	Rk	18	119	12	2	2	2	11	16	19	9	1	.212/.331/.333	.242	.241	0.0	-	0.0

Drafted/Acquired: 1st round, 2014 draft, Elk Grove HS (Elk Grove, CA)

Previous Ranking: NR

What Happened in 2014: The organization tabbed the speedy outfielder from California in the first round and then began his initiation to professional ball in the bottom rung of the chain.

Strengths: Excellent athlete; frame to physically mature into; feel for the barrel; loose hands; capable of driving offerings into both gaps; gets out of box extremely well; double-plus runner; potential to impact game on bases; gets good jumps off the bat; covers plenty of ground into both gaps; good fundamentals; impact glove; strong work ethic; good makeup reports.

Weaknesses: In the early stages of developing a professional approach; very aggressive hitter; needs to learn how to better dictate plate appearances; likes to expand strike zone; will chase spin; development of pitch recognition will take some time; contact-oriented stroke with little present lift; below-average power potential; bat could end up on the empty side; glove may ultimately carry profile.

Risk Factor/Injury History: Extreme; limited professional experience; progression of hit tool.

Bret Sayre's Fantasy Take: There's always interest in players with plus-plus run grades, but Hill has a chance to be a near-average fantasy contributor even without the speed. Despite the extended ETA, Hill shouldn't last beyond the top 25 picks in dynasty drafts this year—and if everything breaks right, he could look like the good version of former Tigers' center fielder Austin Jackson.

The Year Ahead: The speed and defense are attractive aspects of Hill's game, with both offering impact potential and a solid foundation for this prospect to begin building upon as a pro. It's not a leap to project the 19-year-old as a double-plus defender in center based on the way he already handles the position, especially when it comes to his ability to read balls off the bat and cover plenty of ground into both gaps. There's a strong floor here when considering the value of a true up-the-middle defender. The variability comes into play when evaluating the potential of the bat, with an overwhelming majority of the early-career focus centering on building both the approach and pitch recognition to enhance the strong feel for the barrel. It's likely to be on the slow and steady side for Hill out of the gate. Look for more subtle clues during what should be an assignment in the Midwest League in 2015 and for success to be a gradual ramp of controlling plate appearances better, with increased contact as a result. The major-league prospects here are bright, with the chance that a first-division player starts to come into focus as the offensive prowess develops with repetition and experience.

> **#98**
> BP Top 101 Prospects

2. James McCann C

Born: 6/13/90 **Age:** 25 **Bats:** R **Throws:** R **Height:** 6'2" **Weight:** 210

MLB ETA	Hit	Power	Run	Glove	Arm	OFP	Realistic
Debuted in 2014	50	–	–	55	60	55 >AVG REGULAR	50 AVG ML PLAYER

YEAR	TEAM	LVL	AGE	PA	R	2B	3B	HR	RBI	BB	SO	SB	CS	AVG/OBP/SLG	TAv	BABIP	BRR	FRAA	WARP
2014	DET	MLB	24	12	2	1	0	0	0	0	2	1	0	.250/.250/.333	.211	.300	0.1	C(6): -0.0	0.0
2014	TOL	AAA	24	460	49	34	0	7	54	25	90	9	2	.295/.343/.427	.265	.355	0.7	C(98): -1.0, 3B(1): 0.0	2.3
2015	DET	MLB	25	250	21	13	1	3	24	9	54	2	1	.246/.278/.349	.231	.300	-0.2	C -0, 3B 0	0.1
2016	DET	MLB	26	445	47	23	1	8	44	24	93	4	1	.241/.291/.364	.246	.287	-0.4	C -1	0.6

Breakout: 4% **Improve:** 6% **Collapse:** 14% **Attrition:** 19% **MLB:** 25% **Upside:** 4 *Comparables:* Caleb Joseph, Miguel Perez, Josh Phegley

Drafted/Acquired: 2nd round, 2011 draft, University of Arkansas (Fayetteville, AR)

Previous Ranking: #3 (Org)

What Happened in 2014: Always known for his defensive potential, McCann continued to build upon his offensive progress after arriving in the upper levels, where he carried the success of the season into a September call-up with the big club.

Strengths: Athletic behind the dish; sturdy and strong frame; shows solid receiving technique; firm glove hand; good game-calling skills; quick release; accurate to the bases; fires feet well when blocking; necessary intangibles for position; hands to control head of the bat; capable of driving offerings into the gaps; handles left-handed pitching well.

Weaknesses: Glove-first profile; tends to make weaker contact against arm-side pitching; can be beat with good velocity; hands at times have trouble staying above the ball; hit tool most likely to play below average; power is below average.

Risk Factor/Injury History: Low; achieved major leagues; quality of contact.

Bret Sayre's Fantasy Take: And we hope you enjoyed the portion of this list that is interesting for fantasy purposes (see Hill, Derek). McCann is best left for deep two-catcher leagues, as he's unlikely to produce enough to be more than waiver-wire fodder in one-catcher formats. On the plus side, he'll probably actually stay at the position.

The Year Ahead: McCann enters the year poised to leave Florida as a member of the 25-man roster and push for regular playing time alongside fellow catcher Alex Avila. The given here for the 25-year-old is the defense, which showed the makings of playing at a better-than-average level during his call-up in 2014. The California native has always demonstrated the knack for handling a pitching staff, along with flashing solid fundamentals and the ability to challenge the opposition's running game. At the very least, the rookie should provide the team with steady performance behind the dish and little drop-off in that department should he be pressed into or earn extended playing time during the season. The question mark for McCann has always been the stick, which over the last couple of seasons has shown progress in regards to chipping in at the bottom of a lineup. The power isn't likely to be much of a factor, but there's gap pop and the potential for .260s averages with continued adjustments in fine-tuning his strike zone. A major-league regular can very much emerge, with those prospects coming into focus as early as 2015.

---

3. Steven Moya OF

Born: 8/9/91 **Age:** 23 **Bats:** L **Throws:** R **Height:** 6'6" **Weight:** 230

MLB ETA	Hit	Power	Run	Glove	Arm		OFP	Realistic
Debuted in 2014	–	60	–	50	50		60 1ST DIVISION PLAYER	45 PLATOON/<AVG REG

YEAR	TEAM	LVL	AGE	PA	R	2B	3B	HR	RBI	BB	SO	SB	CS	AVG/OBP/SLG	TAv	BABIP	BRR	FRAA	WARP
2014	DET	MLB	22	8	2	0	0	0	0	0	2	0	0	.375/.375/.375	.289	.500	0.0	RF(5): 0.0	0.0
2014	ERI	AA	22	549	81	33	3	35	105	23	161	16	4	.276/.306/.555	.298	.327	1.4	RF(131): 2.8	3.5
2015	DET	MLB	23	250	28	11	1	11	33	7	81	4	1	.235/.257/.424	.246	.303	0.4	RF -0	0.1
2016	DET	MLB	24	250	28	13	2	9	32	8	75	4	1	.248/.274/.427	.260	.321	0.5	RF 0	1.4

Breakout: 1%   Improve: 15%   Collapse: 1%   Attrition: 7%   MLB: 24%   Upside: 39   *Comparables: Bryce Brentz, Carlos Peguero, Matt LaPorta*

Drafted/Acquired: International Free Agent, 2008, Dominican Republic

Previous Ranking: #8 (Org)

What Happened in 2014: Moya entered the upper levels of the system, where he was previously known more for his batting practice displays than game-action translation, but turned some heads in dropping 35 bombs on Eastern League arms before a brief call to The Show.

Strengths: Very large man; muscular body; good athlete for size; elite raw power; capable of driving offerings out to all fields; creates big lift and loft; punishes mistakes; 20-25 home-run potential; arm strength for corner spot; dedicated to defensive craft.

Weaknesses: Long swing; big leverage leads to holes; plenty of swing-and-miss; issues with pitch recognition; can struggle with good arm-side stuff; hit tool will play well below average; game power can fall down as result; glove needs work to get to average; power is only carrying tool.

Risk Factor/Injury History: Moderate; 133 games at Double-A; hit-tool utility.

Bret Sayre's Fantasy Take: The power makes Moya an interesting gamble, but considering how close he is to a regular role, he remains a huge risk in dynasty leagues. There's always a chance he could hit .250 with 25-30 homers at the major-league level, but if you can sell him based on his gaudy 2014 home-run total, I would do that immediately.

The Year Ahead: Moya took a tangible step forward last year in regards to translating his well-above-average raw power into game action, with the result being an onslaught of home runs during his tour in the Eastern League, and most importantly, a higher quality of contact consistently put into play. There's still plenty of swing-and-miss in his game, though, along with an approach that is still relatively crude and lacks the patience to lure opposing arms into giving in the deeper the sequence goes. If last summer's outburst is to be a long-term reality, Moya will need to further hone his secondary skills at the plate to combat what's more of a strength-fueled swing than one enhanced by bat speed. Triple-A will be the next stop for the Puerto Rican outfielder, where the step up in competition will serve as a litmus test for whether he can prove that the holes in his swing are not going to be outright exploited, especially by high-quality arm-side pitching that presently tends to give him fits. Things will fall well short here if the hit-tool utility spoils the continued translation of power, and this view sees something more of a bench player profile, but he is still young and, despite the proximity to the majors, can see further growth.

4. Buck Farmer   RHP

Born: 2/20/91   **Age:** 24   **Bats:** L   **Throws:** R   **Height:** 6'4"   **Weight:** 225

MLB ETA	CT	FB	CH	CB	SL	OFP	Realistic
Debuted in 2014	–	60	50	–	55	50 NO. 4 STARTER	50 NO. 4 SP/LONG RP

YEAR	TEAM	LVL	AGE	W	L	SV	G	GS	IP	H	HR	BB	K	BB9	SO9	GB%	BABIP	WHIP	ERA	FIP	FRA	WARP
2014	DET	MLB	23	0	1	0	4	2	9.3	12	2	5	11	4.8	10.6	32%	.385	1.82	11.57	5.84	6.14	-0.1
2014	TOL	AAA	23	1	1	0	2	2	7.3	11	1	4	2	4.9	2.5	53%	.345	2.05	9.82	6.22	8.37	-0.1
2014	ERI	AA	23	1	0	0	2	2	12.0	10	1	4	11	3.0	8.2	50%	.273	1.17	3.00	3.60	3.59	0.3
2014	WMI	A	23	10	5	0	18	18	103.7	91	6	24	116	2.1	10.1	48%	.314	1.11	2.60	2.78	3.62	1.4
2015	DET	MLB	24	5	7	0	20	20	92.0	101	11	38	72	3.7	7.0	44%	.315	1.52	5.07	4.96	5.51	0.0
2016	DET	MLB	25	7	8	0	53	20	153.3	160	17	60	116	3.5	6.8	44%	.300	1.43	4.59	4.54	4.99	0.1

Breakout: 20%   Improve: 41%   Collapse: 8%   Attrition: 23%   MLB: 55%   Upside: 12   *Comparables: Felix Doubront, Matt Magill, Travis Blackley*

Drafted/Acquired: 5th round, 2013 draft, Georgia Institute of Technology (Atlanta, GA)
Previous Ranking: NR

What Happened in 2014: The former fifth-round pick rocketed through three levels of the system, including a dominating stint in the Midwest League, before getting a four-game taste of the majors at the end of the year.

Strengths: Filled-out frame; sturdy lower half; durable arm; fastball comfortably operates 90-94; shows sinking action in lower-velocity band; ability to spot east/west; throws with life to glove side; snaps slider with loose wrist; flashes late bite and tilt in mid-80s; bat-missing potential; feel for turning over changeup; shows sinking, arm-side fading action; can round into weak-contact-inducing offering; not afraid to pound zone with fastball.

Weaknesses: Fastball can play down at times; tends to flatten out when above the thighs; must selectively elevate; more strike-throwing ability than command; slider will get slurvy and loose in low-80s; runs into stretches of wrapping wrist; inconsistent identity; change on the firm side; more deception and arm angle than consistent quality action; secondary stuff lacks knockout potential.

Risk Factor/Injury History: Low; achieved major leagues; mature arsenal; emergence of consistent third offering.

Bret Sayre's Fantasy Take: Another deep-league-only option, Farmer doesn't have the type of secondary offerings to be a big factor in the strikeout category. And for a pitcher who is unlikely to offer ratios that are anything to write home about (think 4.00 ERA, 1.30 WHIP), he really needs those strikeouts to be mixed-league relevant.

The Year Ahead: This right-hander's bread and butter is a plus fastball that at its best is consistently spotted in the lower tier of the strike zone, where it shows solid sinking action and difficulty in being elevated. Farmer's strike-throwing ability with the offering also stands out, as the 24-year-old likes to come out early in sequences with it to get ahead in the count before going to his secondary arsenal to start changing the looks on opposing batters. It was a quick ascent through the system last year for the Georgia Tech product, with solid progress shown that the arm is trending toward a potential back-of-the-rotation piece at peak. This season will likely see Farmer get a chance to continue the momentum in the upper levels of the system, before a longer look in the rotation is potentially in the cards at some point during the summer. One key development point to watch for will be improved crispness of his secondary stuff. The slider can be on the inconsistent side, while the changeup lags a bit behind the other two pitches. Advancement here will go a long way toward solidifying the prospect as a definitive starter at the major-league level, as otherwise things will end up playing better in a bullpen role. Regardless, this is a big-league arm, and one who can start proving to be a mainstay as early as 2015.

5. Kevin Ziomek   LHP

Born: 3/21/92   **Age:** 23   **Bats:** R   **Throws:** L   **Height:** 6'3"   **Weight:** 200

MLB ETA	CT	FB	CH	CB	SL	OFP	Realistic
Late 2016	–	55	50	–	55	50 NO. 4 STARTER	50 NO. 5 SP/LONG RP

YEAR	TEAM	LVL	AGE	W	L	SV	G	GS	IP	H	HR	BB	K	BB9	SO9	GB%	BABIP	WHIP	ERA	FIP	FRA	WARP
2014	WMI	A	22	10	6	0	23	23	123.0	89	5	53	152	3.9	11.1	47%	.286	1.15	2.27	2.98	3.27	2.5
2015	DET	MLB	23	4	6	0	17	17	80.7	82	9	44	74	4.9	8.3	44%	.310	1.55	4.88	5.01	5.30	0.1
2016	DET	MLB	24	8	10	0	29	29	182.7	183	17	88	172	4.3	8.5	44%	.313	1.48	4.51	4.23	4.90	0.3

Breakout: 0%   Improve: 0%   Collapse: 0%   Attrition: 0%   MLB: 0%   Upside: 23   *Comparables: Jake Arrieta, Jose Cisnero, Tyler Thornburg*

Drafted/Acquired: 2nd round, 2013 draft, Vanderbilt University (Nashville, TN)
Previous Ranking: NR

What Happened in 2014: The left-hander put together a solid season in A-Ball, where he showed improving command over the course of the year and an overall arsenal that is beginning to trend forward.

Strengths: Good athlete; long arms and limbs; deceptive release; fastball operates 89-93 with occasional arm-side run; can stay above heater to throw downhill and create angle on hitters; slider flashes tilt and late bite;

shows wipeout break in mid-80s; turns over changeup with loose wrist; throws with good arm speed and slot in sync with fastball; stuff tends to jump on hitters; hard worker.

Weaknesses: Doesn't presently repeat well; some jerk in delivery; command plays down; fastball grabs a lot of white; tends to straighten out in higher-velocity band; slider is on the loose side; tends to sweep rather than dart; will need to tighten and create more hard snap to play average to better; change comes and goes; seems to lack trust and confidence using it fully in sequences.

Risk Factor/Injury History: Moderate; yet to reach upper levels; command progression.

Bret Sayre's Fantasy Take: The only thing worse in a dynasty context than a pitcher with back-of-the-rotation potential is one that has back-of-the-rotation potential and is years away from the majors. The deception is great, but the stuff is unlikely to be good enough to warrant ownership in mixed leagues.

The Year Ahead: After a successful first full season as a pro, Ziomek is set to take the next step up the ranks of the system and prove that his stuff is quickly becoming too advanced for the low minors. The big theme from last season was improving command for the left-hander, especially in regards to throwing higher quality strikes with his fastball. The size and diversity of the arsenal put the on-paper potential in line with a starter's role, with further progress harnessing the stuff going a long way toward achieving it. Though there's a bit of jerk in the delivery that leads to some inconsistencies with his arm slot, Ziomek's a good enough athlete and loose when throwing that it's reasonable to believe more command growth can come over the course of the next season or two. The clues point to his being able to transition quickly to High-A this season, with a taste of the Eastern League well within the sights before year end, and a projection as back-end starter further solidifying in the process.

---

6. Kyle Lobstein   LHP

Born: 8/12/89   **Age:** 25   **Bats:** L   **Throws:** L   **Height:** 6'3"   **Weight:** 200

MLB ETA	CT	FB	CH	CB	SL	OFP	Realistic
Debuted in 2014	–	50	55	50	–	50 NO. 5 SP/SWINGMAN	45 LONG RP/6TH INN RP

YEAR	TEAM	LVL	AGE	W	L	SV	G	GS	IP	H	HR	BB	K	BB9	SO9	GB%	BABIP	WHIP	ERA	FIP	FRA	WARP
2014	DET	MLB	24	1	2	0	7	6	39.3	35	3	14	27	3.2	6.2	46%	.267	1.25	4.35	3.85	4.83	0.2
2014	TOL	AAA	24	9	11	0	26	25	146.0	174	10	42	127	2.6	7.8	49%	.360	1.48	4.07	3.45	4.34	1.7
2015	DET	MLB	25	8	11	0	27	27	153.0	175	18	55	107	3.2	6.3	42%	.317	1.50	5.04	4.88	5.48	-0.3
2016	DET	MLB	26	8	10	0	27	27	164.7	185	19	52	121	2.8	6.6	42%	.316	1.44	4.77	4.36	5.18	-0.2

Breakout: 18%   Improve: 33%   Collapse: 12%   Attrition: 35%   MLB: 55%   Upside: 7   *Comparables: Chris Schwinden, Philip Humber, Daryl Thompson*

Drafted/Acquired: 2nd round, 2008 draft, Coconino HS (Flagstaff, AZ)

Previous Ranking: Factor on the Farm

What Happened in 2014: Lobstein once again handled a meaty workload in the minors, where the left-hander changed speeds and spotted his arsenal to keep International League hitters at bay, and then held his own during six big-league starts down the stretch run.

Strengths: Body to withstand rigors of the position; capable of logging strong workloads; repeats arm slot well; fastball works 89-91 with occasional tail; throws strikes; moves offering around zone; turns over changeup with quality action; fading action in low-80s; throws from same angle as fastball; deceptive pitch; uses curveball to change eye levels; flashes depth and downward bite in mid-70s; understands how to execute craft.

Weaknesses: Fastball is pedestrian; lacks ability to throw past batters; prone to contact; command can be on the loose side; small margin of error with offering; lacks impact secondary pitch; curve can play too soft and lack sharp bite; hitters able to wait back to make contact; pressure on change to consistently play up; heavy overall reliance on inducing weak contact.

Risk Factor/Injury History: Low; 83 appearances in upper levels; mature arsenal.

Bret Sayre's Fantasy Take: Lobstein is a valuable asset for the Tigers to have, but if he's on your dynasty roster, you play in either a deep AL-only format or a Kyle-only format.

The Year Ahead: There isn't much that jumps off the page for Lobstein in terms of shiny tools or impact stuff, but the left-hander shows feel for his overall arsenal and a mind-set in line with how he needs to execute to be successful. It's all about changing speeds, looks, and eye levels for the 25-year-old. Though the ceiling is on the limited side, he is durable and possesses enough depth in the repertoire to where things can work as a fifth starter, especially if he can harness a bit more fastball command. Expect him to continue to be stretched out this season in Triple-A, where he'll serve as depth for the big club should it need to reach down for an injury replacement or want to make a change due to poor performance. The likely long-run scenario for Lobstein points to a role as a lefty out of the bullpen who hangs around for an extended major-league career, but he should get looks in the rotation until he proves otherwise or the transition just makes sense.

7. Spencer Turnbull   RHP

Born: 9/18/92 **Age:** 22 **Bats:** R **Throws:** R **Height:** 6'3" **Weight:** 215

MLB ETA	CT	FB	CH	CB	SL	OFP	Realistic
Late 2017	–	65	50	–	55	55 NO. 3/4 STARTER	50 LATE INN RP (7TH/8TH)

YEAR	TEAM	LVL	AGE	W	L	SV	G	GS	IP	H	HR	BB	K	BB9	SO9	GB%	BABIP	WHIP	ERA	FIP	FRA	WARP
2014	ONE	A-	21	0	2	0	11	11	28.3	31	1	14	19	4.4	6.0	68%	.347	1.59	4.45	4.14	5.34	0.0
2014	TGR	Rk	21	0	0	0	1	1	3.0	2	1	1	4	3.0	12.0	-	.200	1.00	3.00	6.17	6.71	-
2015	DET	MLB	22	1	3	0	8	8	31.3	40	4	17	16	4.9	4.6	47%	.318	1.82	6.45	6.02	7.01	-0.4
2016	DET	MLB	23	5	8	0	29	29	178.3	195	20	68	115	3.4	5.8	47%	.300	1.47	4.84	4.77	5.26	-0.4

Breakout: 0%   Improve: 0%   Collapse: 0%   Attrition: 0%   MLB: 0%   Upside: 5   *Comparables: Buddy Boshers, Chad Bettis, Preston Guilmet*

Drafted/Acquired: 2nd round, 2014 draft, University of Alabama (Tuscaloosa, AL)

Previous Ranking: NR

What Happened in 2014: The organization tabbed Alabama's Friday night starter in the second round and then began his introduction to life in the pro rotation in the New York-Penn League.

Strengths: Sturdy frame; strong lower half; above-average arm strength; fastball comfortably works 92-95; late life to offering; tough to square in lower tier; can reach for more when needs it (97); potential for heater to play up in shorter stints; snaps slider with tilt and late bite; can miss bats; change flashes parachuting action; average potential with repetition; likes to come after hitters.

Weaknesses: Slider on the inconsistent side; will get slurvy and spin when drops arm slot; needs some work staying above ball when delivering; change presently plays distant third in arsenal; at times similar to taking something off of fastball; may ultimately only get to fringe-average; still learning importance of pitching east/ west; heater will work too elevated.

Risk Factor/Injury History: High; limited pro résumé; emergence of third pitch.

Bret Sayre's Fantasy Take: Finally, a player on this list with at least some potential in mixed leagues. Turnbull isn't likely to be taken in the top 50 in drafts this offseason (and was only a fringy consideration for my list), but could miss bats eventually. He's a name to tuck away in the back of your head for leagues with large farm systems.

The Year Ahead: The Tigers eased Turnbull into pro ball during his time in short-season after signing, but the live-liness of his fastball and his mentality to come right after hitters definitely stood out. Look for the 22-year-old to begin this year in the Midwest League, where we should get a much better read on how the righty is stacking up in a starting role. The long pole for the arm is the development of his changeup, which presently lags behind his heater and slider. It makes sense for the organization to stretch him out as much as possible to see if continued repetition can push it to a more viable offering in sequences. Though the slide piece can be on the inconsistent side, it offers Turnbull a potential above-average weapon with some further tightening to pair with a fastball that can work in the mid-90s and touch higher when he's reaching back. The most likely scenario sees this righty profiling as a late-innings reliever due to the gap with the change, but he should pass into the upper levels in a starting role, where the true test of his stuff will come.

8. Grayson Greiner   C

Born: 10/11/92 **Age:** 22 **Bats:** R **Throws:** R **Height:** 6'6" **Weight:** 215

MLB ETA	Hit	Power	Run	Glove	Arm	OFP	Realistic
2018	–	50	–	60	60	50 ML REGULAR	45 BACKUP C/<AVG REG

YEAR	TEAM	LVL	AGE	PA	R	2B	3B	HR	RBI	BB	SO	SB	CS	AVG/OBP/SLG	TAv	BABIP	BRR	FRAA	WARP
2014	WMI	A	21	104	11	5	0	2	16	11	18	0	0	.322/.394/.444	.299	.375	0.0	-	0.0

Drafted/Acquired: 3rd round, 2014 draft, University of South Carolina (Columbia, SC)

Previous Ranking: NR

What Happened in 2014: The organization accelerated the former Gamecock into A-Ball after signing, where he got off to a hot start in his first 26 games as a pro before a pitch off the left wrist put him on the operating table to repair a broken hamate bone.

Strengths: Large frame; physical player; above-average arm strength; throws come out of hand with power; po-tential to control the running game; firm glove hand; quick feet for size; soft hands; can move laterally to swal-low up offerings; big target; easy swing; ability to square stuff up on a line; above-average raw; high baseball IQ; engaged in nuances of craft.

Weaknesses: Long arms create length in swing; concerns on ability to handle good velocity; hit tool likely to play below to fringe-average; limited zones for doing damage; release can be slow at times; ball control needs work; still learning how to fully use body to advantage when blocking.

Risk Factor/Injury History: High; limited pro experience; hit-tool utility.

Bret Sayre's Fantasy Take: Defense-first catchers don't do a whole lot for us, but he has a chance to hit for enough power to be deep-league relevant in a year or two. That's about all we can hope for with this profile in dynasty leagues.

The Year Ahead: Greiner's main value stems from his defensive ability, which has a bona fide chance to offer both a plus glove behind the dish and plus arm to control the running game. Despite his 6-foot-6 frame, the 22-year-old moves well laterally and flashes quick feet to go along with a firm glove hand that serves him well when receiving. It's a defensive game that ultimately can carry him to the majors with further refinement in regards to the nuances of the position. The wild card is the bat. Though the stick has made progress each season as an amateur, long arms that cause early extension and the overall limited nature of the bat speed lead to pause when projecting the hit tool to play higher than fringe-average as a pro at peak. There is some raw power that can manifest into game action if Greiner can work into favorable hitting conditions consistently, but it's likely a modest potential payout with the bat. Look for the backstop to return to the Midwest League to start 2015, where it bears watching for any lingering effects of the hamate injury suffered last August. The clues suggest he isn't in for a ton of resistance at the level, but it's a good first extended opportunity to begin polishing off some of the rough edges.

---

9. Joe Jimenez RHP

Born: 1/17/95 **Age:** 20 **Bats:** R **Throws:** R **Height:** 6'3" **Weight:** 220

MLB ETA	CT	FB	CH	CB	SL	OFP	Realistic
2018	–	70	50	–	60	55 2ND TIER CL/SETUP	50 SETUP

YEAR	TEAM	LVL	AGE	W	L	SV	G	GS	IP	H	HR	BB	K	BB9	SO9	GB%	BABIP	WHIP	ERA	FIP	FRA	WARP
2014	ONE	A-	19	3	2	4	23	0	26.7	22	1	6	41	2.0	13.8	44%	.350	1.05	2.70	1.75	3.22	0.6
2015	DET	MLB	20	1	0	1	23	0	32.7	35	4	18	28	5.0	7.7	43%	.316	1.63	5.27	5.24	5.72	-0.2
2016	DET	MLB	21	2	1	2	36	0	52.3	49	5	23	55	4.0	9.5	43%	.305	1.38	4.12	3.90	4.48	0.3

Breakout: 0% **Improve:** 0% **Collapse:** 0% **Attrition:** 0% **MLB:** 0% **Upside:** 6 *Comparables: Joe Ortiz, Eduardo Sanchez, Bruce Rondon*

Drafted/Acquired: Undrafted Free Agent, 2013, Puerto Rico Baseball Academy (Gurabo, PR)

Previous Ranking: NR

What Happened in 2014: The Puerto Rico native took the New York-Penn League by storm, as he fanned an impressive 41 batters in 26 2/3 innings and showed the makings of a budding late-innings power arm.

Strengths: Strong body; filled into frame, especially in trunk; near-elite arm strength; fastball comfortably sits 94-96 with some arm-side run; can reach for more when needs it (97-98); has hit triple digits; snaps slider with loose wrist; flashes tight rotation and hard bite; wipeout potential; will sprinkle in changeup; shows some feel for creating fade.

Weaknesses: Delivery can be rigid; will need to loosen up some to enhance command; arm can be late; body maxed out; gets deliberate with changeup; tends to slow body and arm down; will spike slider out in front; likes to work up with heater; presently a thrower.

Risk Factor/Injury History: High; short-season résumé; large gap between present and future.

Bret Sayre's Fantasy Take: You know the caveats of relief prospects in dynasty leagues—especially ones who haven't even reached full-season ball. He's not worth owning at this point, no matter what relief categories your league counts.

The Year Ahead: An intriguing arm with a high-octane fastball and hard slider, Jimenez has all of the ingredients of a potential late-innings piece who can miss bats and bring the power element to the back of a bullpen. Of course, the developmental road is still a long one for the 20-year-old, mainly driven by a need to squeeze out more fastball command and work in all four quadrants of the strike zone more consistently, but the right-hander proved to be far too much for the competition to handle last season. An assignment in A-Ball awaits the Puerto Rican this year, where things can very much play the same in terms of shutdown results. The telltale signs of success will reside with showing progress with the aforementioned needs, along with getting more consistency in changing the shape of his slider, to both bury it and pick up strikes, thus altering the look of sequences. This is a good-looking arm, and despite being limited in terms of versatility to the 'pen can offer nice value down the line.

10. Dixon Machado SS

Born: 2/22/92 **Age:** 23 **Bats:** R **Throws:** R **Height:** 6'1" **Weight:** 170

MLB ETA	Hit	Power	Run	Glove	Arm		OFP	Realistic
2015	–	–	55	60	70		45 UT/2ND DIV PLAYER	40 <AVG PLAYER

YEAR	TEAM	LVL	AGE	PA	R	2B	3B	HR	RBI	BB	SO	SB	CS	AVG/OBP/SLG	TAv	BABIP	BRR	FRAA	WARP
2014	ERI	AA	22	342	45	23	1	5	32	40	36	8	5	.305/.391/.442	.297	.331	2.4	SS(90): -1.3	3.1
2014	LAK	A+	22	187	30	8	1	1	8	23	34	2	1	.252/.348/.333	.253	.312	0.8	SS(41): -1.8	0.4
2015	DET	MLB	23	250	25	10	1	2	17	20	44	3	1	.222/.287/.305	.222	.259	-0.1	SS -1	0.0
2016	DET	MLB	24	425	43	17	1	5	35	37	70	6	2	.227/.298/.316	.233	.258	-0.1	SS -2	0.3

Breakout: 0%   Improve: 0%   Collapse: 0%   Attrition: 0%   MLB: 0%   Upside: 7   *Comparables: Christian Colon, Justin Sellers, Nick Noonan*

Drafted/Acquired: International Free Agent, 2008, Venezuela

Previous Ranking: NR

What Happened in 2014: After a stint in the Florida State League, the defensive-minded player caught fire during a promotion to Double-A and showed that, at the very least, a future in the majors is very much in the cards.

Strengths: Instinctive defender; smooth actions; plus range; excellent reads and first step; positions glove well; makes it look easy; plenty of arm for left side of infield; true weapon at his disposal; sound approach in the box; picks up ball out of hand quickly; willing to go deep into counts; gets out of box well; will take extra base; won't run into outs.

Weaknesses: Contact is weak and soft; ball lacks thump off the bat; hit tool is below average at best; strength isn't part of game; minimal power potential; typically overmatched by good velocity; will get casual in the field; can struggle with routine plays from time to time; glove-only profile.

Overall Future Potential: High 4; utility player/second-division player

Bret Sayre's Fantasy Take: If you've enjoyed owning Jose Iglesias, you're going to love Machado. But if you're not a masochist, you're better off leaving him on the waiver wire. There's no fantasy future here.

The Year Ahead: Machado can pick it with the best of them at shortstop, often making spectacular plays look routine, while turning heads in the process with the ease with which he pulls it all off. This is a highly instinctive player in the field. The glove is very much the draw here and it's one that can propel the 23-year-old to a fairly long career in some capacity. Further progress with the bat will go a long way toward solidifying those thoughts into a reality. We should not expect the prospect to suddenly morph into something he's not with the stick, but the approach and ability to pick up offerings quickly give him a fighting chance to at least push things past automatic-out status if he can continue to build upon the momentum of last season. This year will be a good test for Machado to prove he can make the necessary adjustments to handle the upper levels in a full season of action, with a debut in Detroit very much in reach to potentially boost the bench at some point in the summer. That's likely how things are going to play at potential peak in the long run, but defense is always an asset for teams looking to go deep into October.

Prospects on the Rise

1. RHP Anthony Castro: It's no secret: the Tigers love Venezuelans. Castro hails from Caracas, and he enjoyed some success in his debut stateside. It would not be a surprise if Castro threw close to triple-digit innings in full-season ball this year, as his arsenal is certainly advanced. The mechanical profile still needs some refinement, but his arm action is relatively clean. He features a fastball that has good life and some arm-side run in the 90-93 range, with some ability to command the offering. His slider in the 79-82 velocity band features sharp bite, showing the ability to miss bats as he moves up the chain. In addition, he has a feel for a change up in the mid-80s, which could also be solid-average down the line. Clearly, there is a big risk profile in a teenage, complex-league arm. However, this is a pitcher who could firmly place himself on next year's top 10 with a strong 2015 campaign.

2. 2B Javier Betancourt: Betancourt's plus-plus makeup, coupled with high baseball IQ and advanced approach at the plate, makes him an easy prospect to captivate attention on the diamond. Baseball runs in his blood: Edgardo Alfonso is his uncle. In the second baseman's first year of full-season ball, he came out hot in the first half, but struggled after the All-Star break. The hit tool is the carrying tool, as the rest of Betancourt's profile projects as average or a tick below. With soft hands, excellent positioning, and a major-league-average arm, Betancourt profiles as a solid defender, but he'll have to hit his way up the chain to reach his ceiling of a grinder-type second-division keystone.

3. 3B Zach Shepherd: Signed in 2012 for $325,000, the equivalent of fifth-round money in the Rule 4 draft, the Australian-born Shepherd opened up a few eyes via his bat in short-season ball last summer. He has natural feel for the barrel and the potential for big-league-average pop, making hard contact with regularity. While the 6-foot-2, 180 pound teenager has played infield since coming stateside, there is the distinct possibility that he'll have to transition to a corner outfield spot. With that being the case, Shepherd profiles as a bat-first 'tweener, although one who has steadily improved in every aspect of his game since turning pro. He'll likely stay in extended spring training for the beginning of the season, then get a taste of the New York Penn league—still an advanced assignment for someone in his age-19 season.

FROM THE FIELD

Dixon Machado

Team: Detroit Tigers

Evaluator: Mark Anderson

Dates seen: June 6–8, 2014

Affiliate: Erie SeaWolves (Double-A, Tigers)

Physical/health: Tall and thin; has added weight in recent years but still very thin; noticeably stronger with added muscle definition; well proportioned; good athlete.

Makeup: Quiet; shows minimal emotion on the field; puts in pregame work with diligence; carries himself with confidence.

MLB ETA	Risk factor	OFP	Realistic role
2015	Low	45	40; utility player

Tool	Future grade	Report
Hit	35	Excellent approach; knows the zone and recognizes pitches right out of the hand; decides what he wants to do quickly; barrel control is average; contact lacks punch and results in lots of weak groundballs and soft liners; won't hit much but can hit enough for bench role; will walk more than he strikes out thanks to approach and willingness to get deep in counts; .235-.245 hitter with some OBP if he can keep pitchers from blowing him away.
Power	20	Ball is sluggish off the bat; lacks strength; below-average bat speed; doesn't impact the ball; will find rare juice and drive one to the gaps; power is nonfactor in game.
Baserunning/speed	55	Good athlete with quality running technique; gets out of the box quickly and hustles down the line; 4.25-4.30 times; frequently at lower end of that range; speed really plays when he looks for extra bases; potential for 8-10 steals per year; not an aggressive baserunner.
Glove	60	True shortstop defender; easy actions; makes everything looks simple; instincts are off the charts; reads the ball extremely well and always takes the correct first step; positions himself like a veteran; plus range to both sides; gets to everything up the middle; extra soft hands; quick transfer; aggressive with double-play turns; loves to make a play; knows his capabilities; simple plays look mind-numbingly boring for him; makes impossible plays look easy; glove could play beyond plus.
Arm	70	Never really let it fly during series; shown better in the past; easy velocity with quick release; lasers across the field; ball carries and has excellent accuracy; velocity is evident on the move as well; can show near-elite arm strength on plant and throw from the hole.

Overall: Excellent left side glove that can carry him to MLB; arm is near-elite at times and plus-plus at all times; defensive profile is beyond impressive; speed plays above-average consistently; well-below-average hitter; approach is good; bottom-of-the-scale power; minimal offensive profile; quality makeup; highly instinctual player.

Factors on the Farm

Prospects likely to contribute at the major-league level in 2015

1. RHP Drew VerHagen: Narrowly missing the top 10, VerHagen took three steps forward and two steps back in development in 2014. While the right-hander put up solid stats in Triple-A, and even filled in nicely for a spot start with the big club, his secondary offerings have not refined as evaluators hoped. A mountain of a man, standing at 6-foot-6 and 230 pounds, the Vanderbilt product could without question chew through 200 innings a year. However, he only has one pitch that grades out above a 5—his sinker—with the breaking ball and changeup lagging behind. To fulfill that promise of taking the ball every fifth day, VerHagen will have to generate more swings and misses; the five per nine he's currently sporting will not be enough.

2. RHP Angel Nesbitt: Yet another Venezuelan pitcher—big surprise. Nesbitt has flown through the minor-league ranks, appearing at four levels in two seasons. Last summer was his coming-out party, however, as the squatly built right-hander vastly improved over the previous year's performance. He added some arm-side wiggle to his mid-90s fastball, made a stride forward in command, and tightened his short slider. Nesbitt was added to the 40-man roster this winter and, with the dearth of bullpen options, should see some action with the big club as soon as a right-handed reliever falters. The stuff isn't overly loud or bat-missing, but if the command continues to improve, he profiles as a seventh-inning reliever at the highest level.

3. LHP Kyle Ryan: Ryan comes at you with a deceptive delivery—all arms and legs, with arm action reminiscent of Madison Bumgarner. Don't let the funkiness fool you; his mechanics are repeatable, and his command has improved every year in pro ball. He didn't add the extra tick of velocity that the Tigers hoped for when he was drafted, but has combated that with a new offering for 2014—his cutter, a pitch that helped him achieve the major-league level. In fact, he started an integral game for the Tigers in September, helping them secure a playoff spot. His arsenal is built on finesse, deception, and command, leaving small margin for error. However, he wouldn't be the first tall left-hander to utilize the cutter on his way to big-league success. In the end, his profile is likely that of a long man or a LOOGY, but he has a chance to impact the big club in 2015 and beyond.

HOUSTON ASTROS

1. Carlos Correa   SS

Born: 9/22/94   **Age:** 20   **Bats:** R   **Throws:** R   **Height:** 6'4"   **Weight:** 205

MLB ETA	Hit	Power	Run	Glove	Arm		OFP	Realistic
2016	65	65	–	60	70		70 ALL STAR	60 1ST DIVISION PLAYER

YEAR	TEAM	LVL	AGE	PA	R	2B	3B	HR	RBI	BB	SO	SB	CS	AVG/OBP/SLG	TAv	BABIP	BRR	FRAA	WARP
2014	LNC	A+	19	293	50	16	6	6	57	36	45	20	4	.325/.416/.510	.320	.373	0.7	SS(48): 8.0, SS(7): 8.0	3.6
2015	HOU	MLB	20	250	23	11	1	3	23	17	58	5	2	.238/.294/.337	.243	.301	0.0	SS 1	0.7
2016	HOU	MLB	21	250	28	12	2	4	25	17	55	5	2	.262/.320/.385	.265	.324	0.3	SS 0	2.3

Breakout: 0%   **Improve:** 0%   **Collapse:** 0%   **Attrition:** 0%   **MLB:** 0%   **Upside:** 63   *Comparables: Brad Harman, Starlin Castro, Jonathan Schoop*

#3

BP Top 101 Prospects

Drafted/Acquired: 1st round, 2012 draft, Puerto Rican Baseball Academy (Gurabo, PR)

Previous Ranking: #1 (Org), #5 (Top 101)

What Happened in 2014: The expeditious development of Correa was dealt its first major blow, as a broken fibula cut short an up-until-then impressive 2014 that likely would have seen the former first rounder finish in Double-A at the age of 19.

Strengths: Advanced approach at the plate; top-shelf offensive skill set; broad frame filling in nicely; emerging strength in swing; good balance and barrel delivery; compact to contact but can flash more leveraged swing depending on situation; arm is a weapon; soft hands and clean actions; big makeup; elite talent.

Weaknesses: Fringy average run, could continue to decline; body could eventually push profile to third base at maturity; will occasionally fall into early extension, adding length to swing.

Risk Factor/Injury History: Moderate; high floor; if he can show full bounce-back from broken fibula, this drops to low risk quickly.

Bret Sayre's Fantasy Take: Correa is a top-three fantasy prospect and could be an absolute monster at a notoriously weak position. Sure, there's risk that he may have to move to third base long term, but the bat contains so much upside that it just doesn't matter. Correa could be a .300 hitter with 30 homers if the bat plays up to capacity, which would be a first-round pick at almost any position.

The Year Ahead: Correa was well on his way to staking a claim to title of best prospect in the game before an ill-fated slide into third abruptly ended his 2014 season 62 games into the campaign. There is impact potential on both sides of the ball, including the possibility for plus or better grades offensively and soft hands, clean actions, and a double-plus arm that could help him to stick at the six-spot. The Puerto Rican prep product has a natural feel for the game that has allowed him to progress quickly over his short pro career, as a healthy Correa would have been all but certain to reach Double-A last summer at the age of 19 and with fewer than two full pro seasons under his belt. Looking ahead, Correa's developmental trajectory will be wholly tied to whether there are lingering effects stemming from his broken fibula. The prevailing belief seems to be that little should change from a value standpoint, with the bat projecting to impact regardless of defensive position, and his high grades for makeup and work ethic give comfort that Correa will put in the requisite time and effort to get himself back up to speed. He could get a short return trip to the Cal League to build momentum, but should spend a nice chunk of 2015 in Double-A with a late-season cup of coffee possible and a 2016 extended Houston debut all but certain.

2. Mark Appel   RHP

Born: 7/15/91   **Age:** 23   **Bats:** R   **Throws:** R   **Height:** 6'5"   **Weight:** 220

MLB ETA	CT	FB	CH	CB	SL		OFP	Realistic
2016	–	70	60	–	60		65 NO. 2/3 STARTER	55 NO. 3/4 STARTER

YEAR	TEAM	LVL	AGE	W	L	SV	G	GS	IP	H	HR	BB	K	BB9	SO9	GB%	BABIP	WHIP	ERA	FIP	FRA	WARP
2014	CCH	AA	22	1	2	0	7	6	39.0	35	2	13	38	3.0	8.8	46%	.300	1.23	3.69	2.99	3.36	0.6
2014	LNC	A+	22	2	5	0	12	12	44.3	74	9	11	40	2.2	8.1	54%	.373	1.92	9.74	5.32	6.35	0.3
2015	HOU	MLB	23	3	5	0	14	14	60.0	67	7	22	42	3.3	6.3	47%	.310	1.49	4.97	4.97	5.40	-0.2
2016	HOU	MLB	24	9	10	0	30	30	187.0	199	21	61	147	2.9	7.1	47%	.308	1.39	4.41	4.30	4.80	-0.1

Breakout: 0%   **Improve:** 0%   **Collapse:** 0%   **Attrition:** 0%   **MLB:** 0%   **Upside:** 1   *Comparables: Kyle Lobstein, Brandon Workman, Anthony Swarzak*

Drafted/Acquired: 1st Round, 2013 draft, Stanford University (Palo Alto, CA)

Previous Ranking: #3 (Org), #21 (Top 101)

What Happened in 2014: Appel was shockingly hittable over 44 1/3 innings with High-A Lancaster, righting the ship some after a mechanical tune-up and promotion to Double-A Corpus Christi.

Strengths: Fastball can play to double-plus, sitting 93-96 and touching 98 mph; occasional bore; at best, low- to mid-80s slider can be a weapon, with depth, bite and tilt; low- to mid-80s change plays with solid arm-speed deception and tumble; can mix and match arsenal; durable build; shows ability to create angles on pitches.

Weaknesses: Slider and change can show inconsistencies across starts; control outdistances command at present; passive demeanor on mound can rub evaluators the wrong way; profile plays lower in the aggregate than sum of the grades; High-A bats had little trouble tracking and squaring offerings, even when executed.

Risk Factor/Injury History: Low; even with 2014 stumbles it's a high floor, high probability profile.

Bret Sayre's Fantasy Take: There may not have been a prospect whose perceived fantasy value changed so much over the course of the 2014 season without actually changing all that much in the end. Those who sold low after he bottomed out in the Cal League should regret their decision right about now, and the right-hander still possesses SP2 upside with the ability to impact all four categories.

The Year Ahead: Appel serves as an interesting Rorschach test for evaluators. The cross-section of scouts that like to see fire and a mean streak in their future front-enders have roundly dinged the former Stanford Cardinal for being soft and lacking the mental fortitude to thrive as an impact starter at the major-league level. Other evaluators see three plus or better offerings, a good body, easy arm action, and impressive pedigree and have no concerns projecting the emergence of a legit number-two starter from this amalgamation of attributes. It's unusual for an arm with such lofty grades across the profile to draw the level of vitriol and distrust that Appel has received from a vocal portion of the scouting community, but it's likewise unusual for such a refined and experienced talent to flounder to this degree 28 pro starts (22 of them coming in the lower levels) into his career. This is an important year for the two-time first rounder, as a strong showing in his return to the Texas League will all but erase a problematic 2014 from the minds of most. If inconsistencies and underperformance persist it will add fuel to the fast-burning narrative that places Appel's demeanor as a roadblock standing between frontline raw stuff and front-end production. The stuff is near major-league ready, but he'll have to wield it with more consistency and precision if he's to navigate his way through upper-level lineups.

3. Vincent Velasquez RHP

Born: 6/7/92   **Age:** 23   **Bats:** B   **Throws:** R   **Height:** 6'3"   **Weight:** 203

MLB ETA	CT	FB	CH	CB	SL	OFP	Realistic
2016	–	65	65	50	–	60 NO.3 STARTER	55 NO. 4 STARTER/SETUP

YEAR	TEAM	LVL	AGE	W	L	SV	G	GS	IP	H	HR	BB	K	BB9	SO9	GB%	BABIP	WHIP	ERA	FIP	FRA	WARP
2014	LNC	A+	22	7	4	0	15	10	55.3	45	6	23	72	3.7	11.7	44%	.243	1.23	3.74	3.96	3.65	1.8
2014	AST	Rk	22	0	1	0	3	3	8.7	5	0	2	19	2.1	19.7	80%	.400	0.81	2.08	0.85	1.57	0.4
2015	HOU	MLB	23	3	3	0	13	10	56.0	55	6	27	51	4.3	8.2	44%	.302	1.45	4.51	4.76	4.91	0.1
2016	HOU	MLB	24	8	7	0	34	24	177.3	157	16	68	170	3.5	8.6	44%	.287	1.27	3.58	3.88	3.89	1.9

Breakout: 0%   Improve: 0%   Collapse: 0%   Attrition: 0%   MLB: 0%   Upside: 27   *Comparables: Thomas Diamond, Bud Norris, Henry Sosa*

Drafted/Acquired: 2nd round, 2010 draft, Garey HS (Garey, CA)

Previous Ranking: #6 (Org)

What Happened in 2014: Velasquez followed up a strong post-Tommy John showing in 2013 with a near-breakout performance last summer, with two missed months (groin) preventing the potent power arm from firmly establishing himself as one of the top-tier arms in the minors.

Strengths: Fastball induces evaluative butterflies, showing neat plus velocity with ease and precision; some arm-side life; holds velo past 50-pitch mark and into later innings; changeup comes with big deception and abrupt dive; swing-and-miss offering low- to mid-80s; curve will flash average with solid shape; good competitor; not afraid to attack bats and stake claim to inner half.

Weaknesses: Trouble staying on field; curve is inconsistent offering and can come soft, lacking bite; if breaking ball never fully materializes, fastball/change combo probably not enough to turn over major-league lineups with regularity.

Risk Factor/Injury History: Moderate; Tommy John in 2010; missed two months in 2014 (groin).

Bret Sayre's Fantasy Take: Often overlooked among starting pitching prospects in fantasy, Velasquez could make himself into a high-end dynasty asset on the verge of the majors in the next 12 months. He'll need to take a better weapon with him to fight right-handed batters if he wants to really rack up the strikeouts, but even without it, there's SP4—or high-end relief—potential here.

The Year Ahead: A full season of Velasquez could have been a revelation, as the 23-year-old continues to display one of the most impressive all-around fastballs in the minors, thanks to a smooth implementation, good velocity, some late action, and an ability to command it to the quadrants. Aside from building up innings and showing the durability to weather a long major-league season, Velasquez needs to stay on the field if he is going to log the necessary reps to beef up the breaking ball. At present it's a lightweight fighter who will soon be asked to take on middle- and heavyweight pugilists from Double-A on. Thus far his plus off-speed offering has been enough to keep both lefty and righty bats at bay, serving to disrupt timing and draft soft and empty contact alike. Were Velasquez to ultimately prove incapable of sticking in a rotation, due to durability or lack of a requisite third offering, he could thrive in the late innings. That potential conversion is still a ways away, however, and Velasquez enters 2015 moving toward a future in the Astros' rotation. Even a half-grade bump on the curve could be enough to propel him onto the national prospect scene, and a full season's workload could line him up for consideration as a major-league contributor come 2016.

4. Brett Phillips   OF

Born: 5/30/94   **Age:** 21   **Bats:** L   **Throws:** R   **Height:** 6'0"   **Weight:** 175

MLB ETA	Hit	Power	Run	Glove	Arm	OFP	Realistic
2017	50	50	55	55	65	60 1ST DIVISION PLAYER	50 AVG ML PLAYER

YEAR	TEAM	LVL	AGE	PA	R	2B	3B	HR	RBI	BB	SO	SB	CS	AVG/OBP/SLG	TAv	BABIP	BRR	FRAA	WARP
2014	LNC	A+	20	128	19	8	2	4	10	14	20	5	4	.339/.421/.560	.324	.384	0.3	CF(20): -2.5, CF(4): -2.5	0.9
2014	QUD	A	20	443	68	21	12	13	58	36	76	18	10	.302/.362/.521	.320	.341	2.3	RF(60): 5.3, CF(44): -2.1	4.5
2015	HOU	MLB	21	250	27	9	2	4	20	13	62	5	3	.226/.271/.343	.229	.278	0.0	CF -1, RF 2	-0.1
2016	HOU	MLB	22	250	27	9	3	5	25	19	61	6	4	.241/.305/.374	.247	.301	0.4	CF -1, RF 2	0.9

Breakout: 0%   Improve: 0%   Collapse: 0%   Attrition: 0%   MLB: 0%   Upside: 95   *Comparables: Austin Jackson, Andrew McCutchen, Melky Cabrera*

Drafted/Acquired: 6th round, 2012 draft, Seminole HS (Seminole, FL)

Previous Ranking: NR

What Happened in 2014: The former sixth rounder impressed from the drop in an inhospitable Midwest League, ramping up his on-field production upon midseason promotion to High-A Lancaster, and culminating in a breakout year for the well-rounded outfielder.

Strengths: Five-tool potential, highlighted by an impact-outfield skill set; above-average runner; speed can play to plus thanks to acceleration and ability to close; right-field arm with glove and coverage to stick up the middle; improved strength throughout core; consistent hard contact across lower levels; good feel for barrel; evaluators note comfort in the box; loose and easy; already displays ability to track spin; oppo-capable.

Weaknesses: Can have trouble making impactful contact middle-in against same-side arms; still working to shorten path; tendency to bar front arm can leak back into swing periodically; can lose handle on barrel with overswings; proper in/out sequencing can keep barrel off ball; power could fall well short of potential.

Risk Factor/Injury History: High; yet to reach upper minors; bat still a work in progress.

Bret Sayre's Fantasy Take: A five-category profile is always a good one to invest in, and Phillips will likely only raise his stock, as he is expected to rack up more California League at-bats in 2015. Unfortunately, it's a weak across-the-board profile, with no carrying tools for fantasy. A .270 hitter with 10-15 homers and 15-20 steals is attractive, but don't invest in the stat line.

The Year Ahead: Early-season Midwest League looks at Phillips immediately pointed to a profile that had taken a firm step forward. A stronger body and more consistent barrel path helped Phillips to unlock more explosion at contact, and he built upon that progress throughout three months of impressive play with Quad Cities prior to finishing the season strong with Lancaster. Defensively, Phillips can fit in center or right, depending on team need, and can be a valuable producer at either spot thanks to his combination of arm strength, accuracy, speed, and ability to finish on the run. There are still questions as to where the bat tops out, but after seeing the results of a little added strength and continued reps and instruction, the developmental trajectory is definitively pointing upward and onward, with a real chance for the 2012 draftee to emerge from his minor-league journey as a top-of-the-order bat. Even if he falls shy of that upside, his value in the field and on the bases could make him a useful everyday player. He'll likely start 2015 back in Lancaster, with an eye toward an in-season bump to Double-A Corpus Christi.

5. Derek Fisher   OF

Born: 8/21/93   **Age:** 21   **Bats:** L   **Throws:** R   **Height:** 6'1"   **Weight:** 207

MLB ETA	Hit	Power	Run	Glove	Arm	OFP	Realistic
2017	60	60	60	50	–	60 1ST DIVISION PLAYER	50 AVG ML PLAYER

YEAR	TEAM	LVL	AGE	PA	R	2B	3B	HR	RBI	BB	SO	SB	CS	AVG/OBP/SLG	TAv	BABIP	BRR	FRAA	WARP
2014	TCV	A-	20	172	31	4	3	2	18	16	35	17	4	.303/.378/.408	.299	.379	-0.6	LF(38): 0.0, CF(1): -0.0	1.1
2014	AST	Rk	20	4	0	1	0	0	0	1	0	0	0	.667/.750/1.000	.583	.667	-0.3	LF(1): 0.0	0.1
2015	HOU	MLB	21	250	23	8	1	2	18	13	73	9	3	.200/.249/.273	.203	.277	0.8	LF 0	-0.8
2016	HOU	MLB	22	250	26	9	1	4	23	18	70	11	3	.224/.287/.329	.231	.301	1.3	LF 0	-0.2

Breakout: 0%   Improve: 0%   Collapse: 0%   Attrition: 0%   MLB: 0%   Upside: 5   *Comparables: Aaron Cunningham, Xavier Paul, Shane Peterson*

Drafted/Acquired: 1st round, 2014 draft, University of Virginia (Charlottesville, VA)

Previous Ranking: NR

What Happened in 2014: A potential top-10 pick in the 2014 draft, Fisher lost six weeks of his spring to a broken hamate bone, dropped to Houston as the 37th overall selection last June, and immediately stood out as one of the better bats in the New York-Penn League as a key member of the runner-up Tri-City squad.

Strengths: Athletic build; smooth left-handed swing; solid bat speed; easy power to pull; handles barrel well; can drive oppo; understands zone and comes with impressive approach; plus runner on the grass and the dirt; fringe-average arm strength can play up at times with occasional carry and solid accuracy; solid reads on the bases.

Weaknesses: Plus or better raw not yet a consistent in-game weapon; routes and reads can eat into speed utility in the field; lines on the basepaths can add distance between bases; occasionally dinged as low-energy during collegiate career.

Overall Future Potential: 6; first-division player

Realistic Role: 5; average major leaguer

Risk Factor/Injury History: Moderate; solid pedigree and refinement but limited pro experience.

Bret Sayre's Fantasy Take: One of my favorite fantasy targets in dynasty drafts this year, Fisher fell to the supplemental round, but mostly due to the deficiencies in his glovework. At the plate, Fisher could be a 20/20 option with the ability to hit for a strong average to boot. He shouldn't last beyond the first 20 picks in your draft.

The Year Ahead: In a draft many Astros fans would like to forget, Fisher stands out as a potential steal in the supplemental first round and could develop quickly into the top positional talent in the system behind Correa. All the makings are here for a quality number-two bat capable of serving the dual role of catalyst and run producer. When Fisher gets a hold of the ball, he has the ability to launch tape-measure shots, but his swing and approach are better geared toward hard line-drive contact at present. Time will tell whether he can work an approach that will allow him to tap into both facets of his game, and he possesses the comfort and fluidity in the box to eventually walk that line. Defensively, Fisher has the raw tools of a potential center fielder but lacks feel for the craft. With Minute Maid offering unique challenges for even the best in the business, he is a better fit in left, where he could grow into an average or better defender. The former Wahoo is advanced enough to jump right to Lancaster and could reach Double-A by the end of 2015 if the Astros decide to fast-track his development.

6. Michael Feliz RHP

Born: 6/28/93 **Age:** 22 **Bats:** R **Throws:** R **Height:** 6'4" **Weight:** 225

MLB ETA	CT	FB	CH	CB	SL	OFP	Realistic
2017	–	65	50	–	60	60 NO. 3 STARTER	55 LATE INN RP/CLOSER

YEAR	TEAM	LVL	AGE	W	L	SV	G	GS	IP	H	HR	BB	K	BB9	SO9	GB%	BABIP	WHIP	ERA	FIP	FRA	WARP
2014	QUD	A	21	8	6	0	25	19	102.7	104	6	37	111	3.2	9.7	41%	.348	1.37	4.03	3.31	3.88	1.7
2015	HOU	MLB	22	3	5	0	17	13	77.0	88	9	39	54	4.6	6.3	44%	.316	1.64	5.54	5.42	6.02	-0.8
2016	HOU	MLB	23	6	8	0	28	20	148.3	163	19	61	114	3.7	6.9	44%	.311	1.51	5.13	4.85	5.57	-1.2

Breakout: 0%   Improve: 0%   Collapse: 0%   Attrition: 0%   MLB: 0%   Upside: 29   *Comparables: Charlie Furbush, Jo-Jo Reyes, Shane Greene*

Drafted/Acquired: International free agent, 2010, Dominican Republic

Previous Ranking: #10 (Org)

What Happened in 2014: The burly righty made steady progress in his first taste of full-season ball, showing growth in his power slider and changeup while improving his approach across longer outings.

Strengths: Loud arm; arm speed to produce velo and spin; sits 92-94 mph with solid life, reaching as high as 98 mph up in the zone; good downward angle; most effective working down and can elevate ahead in count; slider is second potential plus offering with fastball trajectory out of the hand and hard, late, sweeping action; built for the long haul; thick lower half helps generate power without overexertion.

Weaknesses: Can get stiff in landing, impacting command in the zone; some length on the back side, causing inconsistencies in path and release; changeup lags as below-average offering; too firm and can float up in the zone; can tip pitch on arm swing and deceleration; will come around slider, softening bite and leaving hittable; can lean too heavily on fastball from stretch; fastball can leak back across plate against oppo bats.

Risk Factor/Injury History: High; low-minors résumé.

Bret Sayre's Fantasy Take: Another year closer and Feliz is still lingering in flier territory in most leagues. If your league rosters 200 minor leaguers, he should likely be owned, but the risk of his ending up a reliever is real and he's got an assignment in Lancaster staring him in the face—which is bad for business.

The Year Ahead: There is still a fair amount of work to be done before Feliz reaches his upside as a solid mid-rotation starter at the highest level, but the progress made in 2014 was encouraging. By the end of the year, Feliz looked much more comfortable his second time through the order, and there was more consistency in his secondary execution. More than anything, Feliz has to find a suitable option for tripping up lefty bats. His changeup doesn't offer enough trajectory variance or deception at present, and he can't yet command his fastball consistently enough to the inner half to lefty hitters to jump the offering. Should he transition to the 'pen, his fastball/slider combo could play as presently constituted, and he could even see an uptick in velocity letting it air out in short stints. The hitter-friendly California League will pose a challenge for Feliz and place increased import on his ability to disrupt timing and deal with more precision. With continued incremental improvement, Feliz could be competing for a rotation spot two springs from now, with a rapid ascent possible should Houston decide they want his big right arm as a late-inning option.

7. Lance McCullers   RHP

Born: 10/2/93   **Age:** 21   **Bats:** L   **Throws:** R   **Height:** 6'2"   **Weight:** 205

MLB ETA	CT	FB	CH	CB	SL	OFP	Realistic
2016	–	70	–	70	–	60 NO. 3 SP/ELITE CLOSER	50 LATE INN RP

YEAR	TEAM	LVL	AGE	W	L	SV	G	GS	IP	H	HR	BB	K	BB9	SO9	GB%	BABIP	WHIP	ERA	FIP	FRA	WARP
2014	LNC	A+	20	3	6	4	25	18	97.0	95	18	56	115	5.2	10.7	48%	.311	1.56	5.47	5.73	6.98	0.3
2015	HOU	MLB	21	3	5	0	18	14	71.0	73	8	41	64	5.2	8.1	48%	.309	1.59	5.11	5.18	5.56	-0.3
2016	HOU	MLB	22	6	7	0	31	22	163.3	142	16	83	155	4.6	8.5	48%	.281	1.38	4.03	4.41	4.38	0.8

Breakout: 0%   Improve: 0%   Collapse: 0%   Attrition: 0%   MLB: 0%   Upside: 52   *Comparables: Enny Romero, Gio Gonzalez, Casey Crosby*

Drafted/Acquired: 1st round, 2012 draft, Jesuit High School (Tampa, FL)

Previous Ranking: #7 (Org)

What Happened in 2014: The live-armed McCullers had no issue missing bats with High-A Lancaster thanks to a pair of potential double-plus power offerings, but was too often undone by his below-average command and erratic execution.

Strengths: Low- to mid-90s fastball shows giddy-up; can reach back for more; breaking ball is a true hammer; low-80s velo with big depth and sharp 11-to-5 action; some feel to vary shape; works to freeze and as a chase pitch; high-octane approach; bulldog; attacks hitters head on.

Weaknesses: High-effort, crossfire delivery; well-below-average command; arm action can lack fluidity; struggles to maintain consistent timing and release; crossfire complicates ability to reach both sides of the plate with consistency; breaking ball can play fringe-average due to inconsistent execution; can come soft and slurvy and can overthrow and bury; changeup clear third offering; lacks feel for the pitch.

Risk Factor/Injury History: Moderate; low-minors résumé.

Bret Sayre's Fantasy Take: There may be some who still hold out higher hope than others as to whether McCullers can cut it in a rotation, but he looks like an awfully strong relief prospect at this point. That said, we know where relief prospects end up in the grand scheme of farm systems, and if you can sell him on name value, I would.

The Year Ahead: The high-effort delivery, spotty execution, below-average command, and two-pitch repertoire still point to McCullers as a future relief arm. The possibility persists, however, that the former over-slot signee could find his way as an early A.J. Burnett-style mid-rotation arm capable of front-end gems and fringe-starter stinkers alike, with the effectiveness of his breaking ball on a given night being the primary determinant. Even that outcome will require a more consistent implementation of his curve and for his off-speed to grow to at least a fringe-average offering. McCullers will escape the High-A hitters' haven of the Cal League in 2015, advancing to the more inviting environs of Corpus Christi, where he will need to place an emphasis on improving his execution and working deeper into games with more frequency to continue to build up his arm. A solid showing should put him in line for a big-league call-up at some point in 2016.

8. Domingo Santana   RF

Born: 8/5/92   **Age:** 22   **Bats:** R   **Throws:** R   **Height:** 6'5"   **Weight:** 225

MLB ETA	Hit	Power	Run	Glove	Arm	OFP	Realistic
Debuted in 2014	–	65	–	–	65	55 >AVG REGULAR	45 <AVG REGULAR

YEAR	TEAM	LVL	AGE	PA	R	2B	3B	HR	RBI	BB	SO	SB	CS	AVG/OBP/SLG	TAv	BABIP	BRR	FRAA	WARP
2014	HOU	MLB	21	18	1	0	0	0	0	1	14	0	0	.000/.056/.000	.065	.000	0.1	LF(3): -0.4, RF(2): -0.1	-0.4
2014	OKL	AAA	21	513	63	27	2	16	81	64	149	6	4	.296/.384/.474	.302	.408	0.7	RF(59): 0.6, LF(49): 2.3	3.5
2015	HOU	MLB	22	250	28	10	1	8	30	21	85	2	1	.229/.302/.392	.265	.324	-0.2	RF -2, LF 0	0.4
2016	HOU	MLB	23	495	59	20	1	16	57	41	157	5	2	.230/.303/.386	.261	.317	-0.5	RF -4	0.5

Breakout: 2%   Improve: 28%   Collapse: 1%   Attrition: 14%   MLB: 50%   Upside: 69   *Comparables: Michael Choice, Oswaldo Arcia, Chris Carter*

Drafted/Acquired: International free agent, 2009, Dominican Republic

Previous Ranking: #8 (Org)

What Happened in 2014: Santana produced as a 21-year-old in Triple-A before running into a buzz saw in his first taste of major-league action, whiffing in 14 of his 18 plate appearances over two brief call-ups.

Strengths: Big raw pop; strength in leverage produces easy power to all fields; solid extension through contact; gets everything out of big boy body; strong enough to drive the ball without centering on barrel; power can force pitchers to margins, has ability to grow into solid on-base threat; impact arm plays well in right; solid athlete.

Weaknesses: Deep load and length to his swing; barrel can take long path to ball; average bat speed coupled with length can force early commit and exposure to spin away and velo in; significant swing-and-miss; struggles with same-side arms, and particularly same-side spin away; needs to improve breaks to maximize coverage in right.

Risk Factor/Injury History: Moderate; swing and overall approach stand as barrier to major-league transition.

Bret Sayre's Fantasy Take: Thirty-homer power does not grow on trees, but unfortunately his hit tool does. In an OBP league, Santana makes a better investment, but in roto and points leagues, he leaves a lot to be desired and likely tops out as an OF4 if he hits his ceiling.

The Year Ahead: Santana is an understandably divisive talent, with the heft of his raw pop outdistanced only by the weight of coverage issues. The result is a dangerous mistake hitter who can punish fringy stuff but who lacks the physical ability to get to certain pitches, both straight up and in sequence. The native Dominican has shown in the past a willingness to permit wary arms to work around him, resulting in a solid foundation for on-base production. If he can continue to develop that restraint in concert with a better approach to seeking out balls in his kill zone, there is a path here to a productive major-league career as a three-outcome corner bat that would fit comfortably in the six-hole on a contending lineup. Despite 513 productive Triple-A plate appearances last summer, Santana could be well served by a return to the PCL to start 2015. He was not ready for his first taste of major-league competition and further saw his approach loosen upon his return to Omaha after each of his brief stints with the big club. He'll play the bulk of 2015 at the age of 22, so there's little reason to force the issue at this point. His star may have dimmed some, but there is still plenty reason for the Astros to consider Santana a potential contributor on the next competitive squad they field.

9. Colin Moran 3B

Born: 10/1/92   **Age:** 22   **Bats:** L   **Throws:** R   **Height:** 6'4"   **Weight:** 215

MLB ETA	Hit	Power	Run	Glove	Arm	OFP	Realistic
2016	**55**	**50**	**–**	**50**	**55**	**55** >AVG REGULAR	**45** <AVG PLAYER

YEAR	TEAM	LVL	AGE	PA	R	2B	3B	HR	RBI	BB	SO	SB	CS	AVG/OBP/SLG	TAv	BABIP	BRR	FRAA	WARP
2014	CCH	AA	21	123	12	6	0	2	22	9	23	0	1	.304/.350/.411	.269	.360	-0.7	3B(28): 0.4	0.5
2014	JUP	A+	21	392	34	21	0	5	33	28	53	1	2	.294/.342/.393	.271	.330	-2.2	3B(86): -4.0	1.2
2015	HOU	MLB	22	250	20	11	1	4	24	13	56	0	0	.239/.280/.336	.235	.294	-0.5	3B -2	-0.3
2016	HOU	MLB	23	250	27	12	1	5	25	19	55	0	0	.242/.299/.367	.248	.293	-0.6	3B -2	0.5

Breakout: 0%   Improve: 0%   Collapse: 0%   Attrition: 0%   MLB: 0%   Upside: 35   *Comparables: Neil Walker, Ryan Wheeler, Jake Smolinski*

Drafted/Acquired: 1st round, 2013 draft, University of North Carolina (Chapel Hill, NC)

Previous Ranking: #2 (Org)

What Happened in 2014: The sixth overall selection in the 2013 draft was unspectacular in his first full season of pro ball (split between High-A with the Marlins and Double-A with Houston), showing a solid feel for contact but in-game power well shy of desired corner production.

Strengths: Natural feel to hit; good balance and willingness to utilize full field; above-average bat-to-ball skills; will flash leverage and some pop to pull; left-side arm; hands play at third; improved defensive consistency; punch-the-clock approach to his game with even demeanor regardless of situation.

Weaknesses: Dispassionate approach can come off as disinterested at times; lacks impact across his tools; average bat speed; infrequent hard contact despite solid production; kill zone much smaller than coverage area; needs to continue to add strength and more frequently manifest in-game power; lower half can hold back range at third and accuracy on throws; could be limited to first base long term.

Risk Factor/Injury History: Low; major leaguer in some form but profile could lack impact.

Bret Sayre's Fantasy Take: Two men entered the steel cage. One emerged victorious and the other is probably visiting the Coca-Cola Museum right now. Moran should be able to hit .280 at the major-league level, but there are enough questions surrounding it that his fantasy value is very much up in the air. If he hits 15 homers and sticks at third, that's great. If one of the two doesn't happen, dynasty leaguers can move on.

The Year Ahead: Moran is going to hit enough to have a major-league career in some form. The question remains whether there is enough in the profile to back up his bat-to-ball ability or whether the former Tar Heel will be limited to a hollow-average corner bat. His defense and baserunning are unlikely to provide significant value at the highest level, so he'll have to either max out his hit tool to impact levels or develop at least average power to warrant everyday consideration on the lineup card. Moran was one of the youngest collegiate players in his draft class, and his broad frame still affords room for additional strength. Still, if Moran is to grow that aspect of his game he will have to focus his approach and improve his hard contact rate. He should return to Double-A to start 2015, with his eye on an in-season jump to Fresno. The upside is that of a Pablo Sandoval type, capable of steady actions at third, a solid hit tool, and average power production. If Moran is forced off the hot corner, the likelihood of his growing into an average or better major leaguer will decrease significantly.

10. Teoscar Hernandez   OF

Born: 10/15/92 **Age:** 22 **Bats:** R **Throws:** R **Height:** 6'2" **Weight:** 180

MLB ETA	Hit	Power	Run	Glove	Arm	OFP	Realistic
2017	50	50	65	50	55	60 1ST DIVISION PLAYER	45 4TH OF/<AVG REG

YEAR	TEAM	LVL	AGE	PA	R	2B	3B	HR	RBI	BB	SO	SB	CS	AVG/OBP/SLG	TAv	BABIP	BRR	FRAA	WARP
2014	CCH	AA	21	98	12	4	1	4	10	2	36	2	3	.284/.299/.474	.284	.418	-1.0	CF(21): -0.3, RF(2): 0.1	0.4
2014	LNC	A+	21	455	72	33	8	17	75	49	117	31	6	.294/.376/.550	.329	.374	3.2	CF(82): 4.3, CF(10): 4.3	5.4
2015	HOU	MLB	22	250	29	10	2	6	22	13	81	8	3	.223/.265/.355	.234	.305	0.6	CF -2, RF 0	-0.1
2016	HOU	MLB	23	250	24	10	2	5	23	15	79	8	3	.211/.261/.333	.225	.291	0.9	CF -2, RF 0	-0.7

Breakout: 3%   **Improve:** 16%   **Collapse:** 1%   **Attrition:** 11%   **MLB:** 32%   **Upside:** 63   *Comparables: Jordan Schafer, Felix Pie, Michael Saunders*

Drafted/Acquired: International free agent, 2011, Dominican Republic

Previous Ranking: On the Rise

What Happened in 2014: Hernandez made the most of his run through Lancaster, showing solid pop and impact speed before struggling to adjust to more advanced Texas League arms late in the season.

Strengths: Natural hitter with aggressive approach; loves to swing it; capable of putting a charge into the ball; above-average raw; solid athlete; likely average defender with a chance to exceed that as he continues to gain confidence in his reads and improve his effective coverage; above-average arm can be an asset in center, allows for right-field fallback.

Weaknesses: Prone to mistakes of aggression in the box; lacks much in the way of approach; reliant on bat speed and feel for contact; swing-and-miss could limit power output at upper levels; doesn't fully leverage speed in outfield; can be timid at outset of routes; decrease in speed as body matures could force to a corner.

Risk Factor/Injury History: Moderate; limited upper-level exposure and significant contact questions.

Bret Sayre's Fantasy Take: The upside is certainly there to attract dynasty owners, especially in the speed department, but as has been a theme across the players on this list, his expectations have moved in lock step with the elevation he's played at. He could hit 15 homers and steal 30 bases, or never make the majors in any significant capacity.

The Year Ahead: The benefit of Hernandez's well-rounded skill set is that he doesn't need to max out any single aspect of his game to be a useful piece for the 'Stros. At present, his contact ability stands as a lynchpin to an everyday profile, with his ability to generate hard contact via solid bat speed his best weapon in the fight. If Hernandez can rein in his aggressiveness enough so as not to leave himself susceptible to regular early-count holes and forced contact out of the zone, he has a chance to produce an average-driven on-base profile with enough foot speed to leg out extra bases, even if the playable over-the-fence pop tops out at fringe-average. He should start 2015 back in Double-A and could benefit from a season's worth of at-bats in the eight-team league, where he'll be forced to adjust to advanced arms with enough exposure to build a book on him. Refinement of his jumps and reads on the bases will further bolster his foundational value by improving the frequency with which he can swipe an extra bag, be it by steal or off contact, and limit the outs he makes in the process.

Prospects on the Rise

1. RHP Joe Musgrove: A former supplemental first rounder in a stacked 2011 draft class, Musgrove has taken some time to get going on the developmental side. Last season was a coming-out party of sorts for the big and broad righty, as he was able to put together over 75 innings of high-quality ball for Tri-City, spearheaded by a solid plus fastball that can sit 91-95 mph with good life down in the zone. His curve is a second potential swing-and-miss pitch, and there is some feel for a change piece, which he worked in with more comfort as the season progressed. It's not an elite package, but Musgrove has a chance to develop into a solid number-three or -four starter in time, and could potentially handle late-inning work should Houston so require. He'll step up to full-season ball in 2015 and should be in play for next year's top-10 list assuming continued growth over the next year.

2. 3B/1B J.D. Davis: Davis led Cal State Fullerton in all three slash categories last spring, posting a .338/.425/.521 line in just over 250 plate appearances. The former Titan wound up coming off the board to Houston with the 75th overall selection last June and hit well upon arrival in the New York-Penn League, as well as with Low-A Quad Cities. There is plus power here to pull and enough strength to muscle the ball out to all fields. Defensively it's an adequate glove with big-time arm strength (Davis also served as the closer for Fullerton), though his limited range could see him shift across the diamond to first base in the not-too-distant future.

3. LHP Josh Hader: The long and lanky lefty enjoyed a season to build upon with High-A Lancaster, working with an upper-80s to low-90s fastball with lots of dance out of a tough low three-quarters slot. He can reach as high as 95 mph and could sit closer to that mark in shorter bursts should he wind up in the 'pen as some evaluators suggest. His slider is a second potential above-average offering that can make lefty bats highly uncomfortable due to the angle of approach. His change is a third usable weapon, though both it and the slider regularly play fringe-average or below, as Hader is still working to find a consistent release that allows him to work the totality of the zone with each. He will need more precision in execution to continue his run of success against stiffer Texas League competition and could find a home as a useful lefty relief arm should he prove incapable of turning over upper-level lineups with his fastball-heavy approach.

Factors on the Farm
Prospects likely to contribute at the major-league level in 2015

1. 2B Tony Kemp: Kemp's calling card is a compact stroke that plays well gap to gap and facilitates elite bat-to-ball rates. He regularly produces firm line-drive contact, with his plus speed helping to turn singles into doubles while keeping infielders' feet to the fire on anything requiring three or more steps to convert. The power is well below average, and he has a tendency to get front-of-center in his weight transfer, exposing him to soft stuff away, particularly from same-side arms. If he can sort out his splits there's enough thump to keep upper-level arms honest, and it's a tight enough approach to rack up a solid on-base percentage as pitchers try to work the black. Defensively, Kemp is a safe and solid glove at the keystone, with enough arm strength to push his functional range beyond the bag. He's not far from helping out in Houston and could wind up anywhere from a solid everyday bat with some on-base chops to a super-utility/platoon option with pinch-run utility.

2. UT Ronald Torreyes: Another undersized second baseman, Torreyes doesn't have Kemp's offensive upside, though he does offer more in the way of defensive versatility. The Venezuelan product logged time at every position on the field last year outside of first base and right field, with the bulk of his efforts coming at the keystone. His speed is average, which limits some of his extra-base opportunities and eats into his overall offensive profile. Torreyes likely tops out as a super-utility option, capable of logging time across the dirt as well as in left field and center. He could provide value in that capacity as early as 2015.

3. OF Preston Tucker: The thick-bodied former Gator continued to progress toward the majors in 2014, putting together another productive year—this time split between Double-A Corpus Christi and Triple-A Oklahoma City. Tucker is a solid and steady producer with the stick, showing natural loft and a good feel for the barrel. While the bat doesn't project to impact levels, there is solid 20-home-run upside in the stick if everything comes together, and at minimum he should carry with him some utility as a lefty power bat off the bench. Tucker is ready to take a cut at big-league arms, and the Astros should give him a chance to show his stuff in Houston at some point in 2015.

FROM THE FIELD

Carlos Correa

Team: Houston Astros
Evaluator: Chris Rodriguez
Dates seen: April 8, 10, 12, 17, 18, 22, and 24, 2014
Affiliate: Lancaster JetHawks (High-A, Astros)
Physical/health: Every bit of 6'4", 205 lbs.; a body to dream on; super athlete; tons of strength potential; already gaining some muscle; looks like an 18-year-old Alex Rodriguez.
Makeup: Elite makeup; he's into every single play; bounces around between pitches; baseball rat; loves to compete; makes adjustment in-game and game-to-game; the type of confidence to make his potential a reality.

MLB ETA	Risk factor	OFP	Realistic role
2015	Low	70	60; first-division starter

Tool	Future grade	Report
Hit	60	Wide, square stance; small leg kick for timing mechanism; hands drift into hitting position; well-above-average bat speed; lots of present strength in his wrists and arms; will only get stronger; generates plenty of leverage; fluid mechanics; hips fire and arms follow quickly behind; can allow the pitcher to dictate the at-bat; some swing-and-miss; swing can get long; struggled with his swing in early looks, but already has made improvements and shortened his path to the baseball; more aggressive recently as well; tracks pitches well; on-base could be above-average at the highest level; all the pieces to have impact potential.
Power	60	Present strength is plus, and when he adds 20 or so pounds his raw power could become a 7; hits bombs in batting practice; slight uppercut swing plus bat speed equals power potential; generates lots of torque very easily with good swing mechanics; dependent on how the hit tool actualizes; may take a while to fulfill the power potential due to adjustments to the majors at such a young age, but it's all there.
Baserunning/speed	40	Fringe-average speed currently; clocked anywhere from 4.33 to 4.43 down the line; hustles out of box; once his body fills out, he'll slow to below-average; good instincts on the basepaths; turned a single into a double when he saw the left fielder come in slowly for the ball.
Glove	50	Plus-plus instincts; has quick-twitch muscles to have a fast first step and plenty of athleticism to set his feet and make all the throws; range is average; very solid at the bag and with the turn; can be a league-average shortstop for the foreseeable future; will most likely move to third later in his career, where he has a much higher upside.
Arm	70	Cannon of an arm; a joy to watch even during warm-ups; plus carry and on a line; there isn't a throw he can't make; left side of the infield all the way.

Overall: Correa struggled early in the season with his bat, but he never took it on the field with him. That just shows you the type of makeup he has. He'll make a highlight-reel play and run back to the dugout without a smile on his face because that's what he's supposed to do. The bat will take some time, but you could make the case he's already the best shortstop in the organization. Combine the tools and the ability to make quick adjustments as a 19-year-old, the sky is the limit.

KANSAS CITY ROYALS

1. Raul Mondesi SS

Born: 7/27/95   **Age:** 19   **Bats:** B   **Throws:** R   **Height:** 6'1"   **Weight:** 165

MLB ETA	Hit	Power	Run	Glove	Arm		OFP	Realistic
2017	55	50	65	60	60		65 1ST DIV/ALL STAR	50 ML REGULAR

YEAR	TEAM	LVL	AGE	PA	R	2B	3B	HR	RBI	BB	SO	SB	CS	AVG/OBP/SLG	TAv	BABIP	BRR	FRAA	WARP
2014	WIL	A+	18	472	54	14	12	8	33	24	122	17	4	.211/.256/.354	.229	.274	1.4	SS(106): -0.5	0.8
2015	KCA	MLB	19	250	24	8	3	3	18	7	71	6	2	.217/.239/.308	.202	.285	0.8	SS 1	-0.3
2016	KCA	MLB	20	250	22	7	3	3	22	5	64	6	2	.237/.253/.337	.215	.297	1.1	SS 0	-0.8

Breakout: 0%   **Improve:** 0%   **Collapse:** 0%   **Attrition:** 0%   **MLB:** 0%   **Upside:** 11   *Comparables: Eduardo Nunez, Arismendy Alcantara, Chris Owings*

Drafted/Acquired: International free agent, 2011, Dominican Republic

Previous Ranking: #2 (Org), #29 (Top 101)

What Happened in 2014: The precocious six-spotter flashed impact potential on all sides of the ball despite underwhelming production as the third youngest player in the High-A Carolina League.

Strengths: Shows flash and substance with the leather; fluid actions, soft hands, and left-side arm; spry lower half; swing works short and direct from both sides; capable of producing impactful contact across zone; easy 6+ straight-line speed with quick acceleration; improving reads on the bases; could boast solid-average power buoyed by doubles/triples.

Weaknesses: Undisciplined approach at the plate; can be led out of the zone; lacks ability to conform approach to game situations; pitch identification has not advanced as hoped; often overmatched by quality sequencing; over-the-fence pop could play solidly below average.

Risk Factor/Injury History: High; teenager still transitioning to high minors.

Bret Sayre's Fantasy Take: There is plenty to like about Mondesi from a fantasy standpoint, but the usable ETA and home-run power diminish his shine a little. In roto leagues, he'll likely play similarly to Erick Aybar with a touch more power at peak, but likely topping out in the 10-12 range annually. He's a good prospect to shop in dynasty leagues because his lofty value on prospect lists is buoyed by his defense.

The Year Ahead: Mondesi has been pushed aggressively by the Royals, debuting stateside in 2012 as a 16-year-old and advancing one level each season thanks to an advanced glove and immense natural ability that has allowed him to keep his head above water while regularly competing against players two, three, and four years his senior. Evaluators who catch him on the right day have seen signs of an emerging star, but much of Mondesi's game remains understandably unrefined. Carolina League arms were often able to draw empty swings and disrupt timing with quality secondaries and by moving the ball around the zone, and the young Dominican has yet to display an ability to regularly put together a coherent approach in the box. To Mondesi's credit, he has shown a high degree of consistency in his swing and solid balance to go with a compact stroke, all of which could add up to a plus hit tool if he can prove capable of tightening his attack and forcing pitchers to work more frequently in the zone. The time may have come for Kansas City to let Mondesi repeat a level, and another year in the eight-team Carolina League would afford him the luxury of working on his approach while getting multiple looks at a relatively limited universe of High-A arms. Despite an underwhelming 2014 slash line, this remains one of the top shortstops in the game, and even if the bat never fully emerges, he should provide value at the major-league level in some capacity thanks to the plus or better grades across the balance of his game.

> #27
> BP Top 101 Prospects

2. Miguel Almonte RHP

Born: 4/4/93   **Age:** 22   **Bats:** R   **Throws:** R   **Height:** 6'2"   **Weight:** 180

MLB ETA	CT	FB	CH	CB	SL		OFP	Realistic
2016	–	65	65	50	–		60 NO. 3 STARTER	55 LATE INN RP/CLOSER

YEAR	TEAM	LVL	AGE	W	L	SV	G	GS	IP	H	HR	BB	K	BB9	SO9	GB%	BABIP	WHIP	ERA	FIP	FRA	WARP
2014	WIL	A+	21	6	8	0	23	22	110.3	107	9	32	101	2.6	8.2	48%	.316	1.26	4.49	3.92	4.41	0.7
2015	KCA	MLB	22	5	7	0	18	18	91.0	104	11	36	58	3.6	5.7	45%	.313	1.54	5.20	5.26	5.65	-0.5
2016	KCA	MLB	23	8	10	0	28	28	171.0	183	17	62	124	3.3	6.5	45%	.307	1.43	4.54	4.41	4.93	-0.3

Breakout: 0%   **Improve:** 0%   **Collapse:** 0%   **Attrition:** 0%   **MLB:** 0%   **Upside:** 8   *Comparables: Kyle Drabek, Andrew Heaney, Adam Wilk*

Drafted/Acquired: International Free Agent, 2010, Dominican Republic

Previous Ranking: #4 (Org), #46 (Top 101)

What Happened in 2014: Almonte endured an uneven run through the Carolina League but finished the year with six strong outings before shipping out to the Arizona Fall League and showing well.

Strengths: Loose arm with good extension produces lively low- to mid-90s fastball that jumps; can throw by hitters and elevate to chase; mid-80s changeup comes with significant arm-speed deception and fastball trajectory with disappearing action; comfortable working off of the pitch to set up fastball; swing-and-miss offering; curve can show two-plane action with solid shape and is best at natural 11-to-5 axis; fits well with three-quarters slot; maturing physique showing sturdier in lower half; more strength to come; chance to grow into workhorse.

Weaknesses: Command profile below average at present; body can get out front; arm will drag, forcing ball up in the zone; fastball has tendency to run back over the plate and can be particularly hittable for lefty bats; curve still inconsistent and will get soft, losing bite; can come around breaking ball, causing it to drift between horizontal and vertical action; overreliance on changeup can limit utility of pitch once hitters have had a look; needs to improve sequencing; needs to spot better to arm side with fastball; hasn't yet shown proficiency claiming inner half against lefties.

Risk Factor/Injury History: Moderate; yet to reach Double-A, but high likelihood of major-league utility in some capacity.

Bret Sayre's Fantasy Take: Despite coming off a rough season, Almonte still shows plenty of fantasy promise. However, with his fastball/change profile from the right side, he's going to have a hard time getting the strikeouts he needs to be anything more than a usable SP3. His future environment will likely help him keep his ratios in check, but Almonte is going to be more of a 4x4 target than 5x5.

The Year Ahead: Almonte saw mechanical inconsistencies hamper his day-to-day execution on the bump throughout the summer, and particularly during a rough July, when his in-zone command and execution both abandoned him, resulting in lots of hard contact. The live-armed righty seemed to find his stride as the calendar flipped to August and maintained that momentum through 19 innings of Arizona Fall League action. From the last week of July through the Arizona Fall League season, Almonte logged 36 2/3 innings, allowing just 30 hits and 14 walks (1.20 WHIP) while striking out 34 and holding the opposition to a .160 batting average. To take the next developmental step forward, Almonte is going to have to find more consistency in his breaking ball and better spot his fastball, which has a tendency to run into lefty barrels over the fat. There's a comfy floor thanks to a fastball/changeup combo that could flirt with double-plus and play to impact in the late innings should the Royals elect to go that route. Almonte will tackle Double-A to start 2015, with a chance to earn a cup of coffee later in the season. He could compete for a rotation spot in Kansas City as early as 2016.

#56

BP Top 101 Prospects

---

3. Sean Manaea   LHP

Born: 2/1/92   **Age:** 23   **Bats:** L   **Throws:** L   **Height:** 6'5"   **Weight:** 235

MLB ETA		CT	FB	CH	CB	SL	OFP	Realistic
2016		–	65	60	–	60	60 NO.3 STARTER	50 NO. 4 STARTER

YEAR	TEAM	LVL	AGE	W	L	SV	G	GS	IP	H	HR	BB	K	BB9	SO9	GB%	BABIP	WHIP	ERA	FIP	FRA	WARP
2014	WIL	A+	22	7	8	0	25	25	121.7	102	5	54	146	4.0	10.8	45%	.319	1.28	3.11	3.11	4.00	1.3
2015	KCA	MLB	23	5	6	0	17	17	81.7	84	8	38	74	4.2	8.2	43%	.316	1.49	4.57	4.54	4.97	0.2
2016	KCA	MLB	24	9	10	0	30	30	187.0	190	16	74	171	3.6	8.2	43%	.316	1.41	4.24	3.94	4.60	0.3

Breakout: 17%   **Improve:** 23%   **Collapse:** 5%   **Attrition:** 24%   **MLB:** 34%   **Upside:** 75   *Comparables: Jake McGee, Christian Friedrich, Chris Dwyer*

Drafted/Acquired: 1st round, 2013 draft, Indiana State University (Terre Haute, IN)

Previous Ranking: #5 (Org), #78 (Top 101)

What Happened in 2014: In his full-season debut, the former first rounder showed loose control and execution through the first half before running off a dominant final 11 starts, racking up 68 strikeouts over 62 innings while allowing just 37 hits, 25 walks, and 10 earned runs, all while holding opponents to a .175 average.

Strengths: Long-limbed lefty creates tough angles and solid downhill plane through crossfire delivery and three-quarters release; fastball can reach mid-90s and plays comfortably in the 91-93 mph velocity band by the middle innings; low- to mid-70s changeup shows arm-side action and is most effective as a chase pitch to righties; slider flashes plus with tilt and solid shape; can be devastating pitch to same-side arms due to tough angle and release point; flashes ability to drop on back foot of righties; control improved with mechanical consistency as season stretched on; finished season on strong note while reaching 120-plus innings, alleviating some durability concerns; improved balance and line to plate by season's end.

Weaknesses: Control is average and outdistances command at present; fastball can get straight, reliant on plane and angle to avoid barrels; can lose release on slider, leading to soft frisbee that can stick on swing plane; trouble working in to righties with consistency; slider lacks track record and could top out as average offering; motion doesn't come naturally to him, and command profile may always be an issue; multitude of injuries on résumé.

#85

BP Top 101 Prospects

Risk Factor/Injury History: Moderate; yet to reach Double-A; injury/durability concerns.

Bret Sayre's Fantasy Take: If I could own any Royals prospect in a dynasty league right now, it would be Manaea, who will look to keep the gains he made down the stretch last year and fulfill the promise that made him a potential top-five pick in the 2013 draft prior to his injury. He will likely always fight his WHIP a little, but with the potential for a 3.25 ERA or lower and a strikeout per inning, he has the upside of an SP2 in all leagues.

The Year Ahead: Manaea made good progress in 2014, most significantly in showing an ability to stay on the field and take the ball every fifth day. There is still a fair amount of inconsistency in his pitch execution, which periodically leaves both his slider and changeup as fringy offerings, but at his best he can show three legit major-league weapons with plus or better upside. He is still learning how to reach both sides of the plate with his arsenal, and one evaluator commented that he would like to see Manaea closer to the third-base side of the rubber to allow for a broader collection of entry points into the strike zone. If the former Sycamore can continue to build on the mechanical improvements he saw in the second half, he could emerge in 2015 as a true potential impact arm, though most see him as a future mid-rotation talent that will give you a blend of front- to back-end production from start to start.

---

4. Brandon Finnegan LHP

Born: 4/14/93 **Age:** 22 **Bats:** L **Throws:** L **Height:** 5'11" **Weight:** 185

MLB ETA		CT	FB	CH	CB	SL		OFP	Realistic
Debuted in 2014		–	65	50	–	60		60 1ST TIER CLOSER	55 LATE INN RP/CLOSER

YEAR	TEAM	LVL	AGE	W	L	SV	G	GS	IP	H	HR	BB	K	BB9	SO9	GB%	BABIP	WHIP	ERA	FIP	FRA	WARP
2014	KCA	MLB	21	0	1	0	7	0	7.0	6	0	1	10	1.3	12.9	59%	.353	1.00	1.29	0.73	1.95	0.2
2014	NWA	AA	21	0	3	0	8	0	12.0	15	2	2	13	1.5	9.8	52%	.342	1.42	2.25	3.87	4.63	0.1
2014	WIL	A+	21	0	1	0	5	5	15.0	5	1	2	13	1.2	7.8	50%	.121	0.47	0.60	3.05	3.65	0.2
2015	KCA	MLB	22	2	1	1	19	4	35.3	35	3	10	31	2.5	7.9	47%	.308	1.30	3.90	3.82	4.24	0.3
2016	KCA	MLB	23	6	5	0	65	11	122.7	124	12	30	111	2.2	8.1	47%	.311	1.25	3.92	3.64	4.26	0.9

Breakout: 24% **Improve:** 38% **Collapse:** 8% **Attrition:** 12% **MLB:** 53% **Upside:** 45 *Comparables: Carter Capps, Zach Putnam, Mat Latos*

Drafted/Acquired: 1st round, 2014 draft, Texas Christian University (Fort Worth, TX)

Previous Ranking: NR

What Happened in 2014: Finnegan was one of the most impressive arms at the collegiate ranks last spring, showing power stuff out of the TCU rotation and earning a first-round selection in the June draft before speeding through the minors as a reliever and eventually becoming the first pitcher ever to throw in both the College and MLB World Series in the same season.

Strengths: Strong three-pitch mix led by low- to mid-90s fastball with some late explosion; can pound the quadrants with the heater, reaching as high as 96-97 mph in short stints; low-80s slider can flash plus with sharp break and good deception off the fastball trajectory; changeup is solid-average offering with some tumble; solid feel across the arsenal; aggressive demeanor on mound; attacks hitters with fastball and slider; comfortable working across the zone and out of it; sturdy build; repeats well.

Weaknesses: Nontraditional starter height; fastball lacks plane and become hittable when velo dips; showed clear step down in stuff and effectiveness second and third time through order as starter; missed time in spring due to shoulder stiffness; throws with fair amount of effort; arm drag starts to show later in starts, pushing fastball up and out and causing decrease in slider utility.

Risk Factor/Injury History: Low; major-league ready as reliever; shoulder issues in 2014; has yet to demonstrate durability.

Bret Sayre's Fantasy Take: We saw what Finnegan was capable of at the major-league level down the stretch in 2014, but he'll give back some of that performance if he does successfully make it to the Royals rotation. With a strong chance of moving to the bullpen and recent injury concerns, his value is tied to multiple risks, but there is enough talent to make him an SP3 who can strike out nearly a batter an inning, with an ERA that is more valuable than his WHIP. As a reliever, he'd be very strong across the board, but would be much less attractive in dynasty leagues.

The Year Ahead: Finnegan looked like a potential top-10 arm in the 2014 draft class before missing time due to shoulder stiffness, showing comfort with three quality offerings, two of which could play to plus at the major-league level. While the raw stuff is there to turn over major-league lineups, his sub-six-foot stature, high-effort delivery, and a clear downward trend in effectiveness later in his starts last spring all seem to point to a much better fit in the back of the Royals 'pen. He would likely need to be stretched out some to transition to the rotation, with no guarantee he would be ready to contribute at the big-league level in such capacity in 2015. With Kansas City coming off of a World Series appearance, the Royals may opt for the bird in the hand, keeping Finnegan in the 'pen, where he can provide a powerful late-inning lefty arm throughout the 2015 campaign, with an opportunity to eventually step into the team's closer role down the line.

#87

BP Top
101
Prospects

5. Hunter Dozier 3B

Born: 8/22/91   **Age:** 23   **Bats:** R   **Throws:** R   **Height:** 6'4"   **Weight:** 220

MLB ETA	Hit	Power	Run	Glove	Arm	OFP	Realistic
2016	50	60	50	50	60	60 1ST DIVISION PLAYER	50 ML REGULAR

YEAR	TEAM	LVL	AGE	PA	R	2B	3B	HR	RBI	BB	SO	SB	CS	AVG/OBP/SLG	TAv	BABIP	BRR	FRAA	WARP
2014	NWA	AA	22	267	33	12	0	4	21	31	70	3	2	.209/.303/.312	.218	.280	0.9	3B(61): -4.0	-0.9
2014	WIL	A+	22	267	36	18	0	4	39	35	56	7	3	.295/.397/.429	.318	.371	2.2	3B(62): -5.8	2.0
2015	KCA	MLB	23	250	22	11	0	3	22	21	65	2	1	.221/.291/.314	.231	.294	-0.4	3B -4, SS -0	-0.7
2016	KCA	MLB	24	250	27	13	0	5	24	22	66	2	1	.225/.294/.349	.242	.291	-0.4	3B -5, SS 0	-0.2

Breakout: 0%   **Improve:** 0%   **Collapse:** 0%   **Attrition:** 0%   **MLB:** 0%   **Upside:** 14   *Comparables: Chris Gimenez, Zelous Wheeler, Jesus Guzman*

Drafted/Acquired: 1st round, 2013 draft, Stephen F. Austin State University (Nacogdoches, TX)

Previous Ranking: #6 (Org), #96 (Top 101)

What Happened in 2014: It was a tale of two seasons for Dozier, as the former first rounder feasted on Carolina League arms for two months before being eaten up by the Texas League upon promotion.

Strengths: Leveraged swing; strength to produce hard contact to all fields; core is an asset; feel for barrel; sound strike zone awareness; ability to put together quality at-bats; solid hands at hot corner; lower half and arm should play to five-spot; exhibits adequate body control; better runner than size would indicate; nose for the game; mature approach to all facets; handles successes and failures with even demeanor; plus makeup.

Weaknesses: Still learning to lift the ball; swing can get long; hitchy trigger; contact ability could be a question at upper levels; issues with velocity; can get caught cheating to get to inner half; bat could fall short of impact; still refining actions at third base.

Risk Factor/Injury History: Moderate; significant struggles in first taste of upper minors.

Bret Sayre's Fantasy Take: The power is certainly tempting to fantasy owners, but the rest of the profile does a good job of slowing rolls. Dozier is going to struggle to hit for the type of average that won't hurt you in mixed leagues, and he'll need to bring that power to the 20-25 range to be a top-10 third baseman one day. He's more valuable in OBP and points formats to boot.

The Year Ahead: After a 2013 campaign that exceeded all expectations, Dozier looked well on his way to a true breakout season through the first half of 2014. The wheels came off after his midseason promotion to Northwest Arkansas, where the Stephen F. Austin product struggled to keep pace with Double-A arms capable of better implementing quality secondaries while spotting velocity up and on the inner half. Too often, Dozier would get tripped up by off-speed early in the count, slowing down his bat and allowing pitchers to exploit his coverage holes with the heater. He showed some signs of adjustment during his stint in the Arizona Fall League, where he continued to display a strong feel for the zone and ability to track, though issues with sequencing and velocity in the zone persisted. Dozier may always struggle to hit for significant average given some of his coverage issues, so it will be important for him to manifest in-game power with more regularity if he is to grow into a legit first-division talent. He has just enough raw to keep pitchers honest when working the zone, and he'll have to continue to grow on that front if he's to fully leverage his advanced eye to produce a strong on-base/average delta. Dozier should return to Double-A in 2015 in the hope of proving last year's struggles to be nothing more than a developmental blip on his climb toward Kansas City.

#95

BP Top 101 Prospects

6. Kyle Zimmer RHP

Born: 9/13/91   **Age:** 23   **Bats:** R   **Throws:** R   **Height:** 6'3"   **Weight:** 215

MLB ETA	CT	FB	CH	CB	SL	OFP	Realistic
2016	–	70	50	65	55	60 NO. 3 STARTER	55 LATE INN RP/CLOSER

YEAR	TEAM	LVL	AGE	W	L	SV	G	GS	IP	H	HR	BB	K	BB9	SO9	GB%	BABIP	WHIP	ERA	FIP	FRA	WARP
2014	IDA	Rk	22	0	0	0	6	5	4.7	5	0	4	5	7.7	9.6	50%	.357	1.93	1.93	4.46	4.70	0.2
2015	KCA	MLB	23	2	3	0	8	8	34.3	35	4	13	32	3.4	8.4	51%	.315	1.41	4.41	4.54	4.79	0.2
2016	KCA	MLB	24	8	9	0	30	30	190.0	189	20	65	176	3.1	8.3	51%	.307	1.34	4.12	3.99	4.48	0.6

Breakout: 0%   **Improve:** 0%   **Collapse:** 0%   **Attrition:** 0%   **MLB:** 0%   **Upside:** 9   *Comparables: Christian Friedrich, Eric Surkamp, Matt Barnes*

Drafted/Acquired: 1st round, 2012 draft, University of San Francisco (San Francisco, CA)

Previous Ranking: #3 (Org), #34 (Top 101)

What Happened in 2014: It was a lost year for Zimmer, whose continued battle with various ailments kept him off the field for all but a handful of regular-season innings and three Arizona Fall League starts totaling an additional 9 2/3 innings.

Strengths: Frontline stuff when healthy and clicking; fastball can play comfortably in the mid-90s, reaching as high as 99 mph; multilook curve can come as a 12-to-6 hammer or a softer two-plane breaker bridging the axis gap with his slider; short slider is power offering in mid- to upper-80s with tilt and late action; can turn over change with some arm-side sink and will also utilize a cut variation for another look; strong and sturdy from trunk through core; solid command and feel.

Weaknesses: Lengthy medical sheet, including biceps, shoulder, lat, and elbow over past two seasons; offseason surgery to clean up shoulder; ball can be visible out of the hand; still looking to solidify feel for off-speed; missed developmental time in 2014 and to start 2015 will complicate ability to build up innings and continue to refine feel.

Risk Factor/Injury History: High; robust injury history; yet to log significant innings in upper minors.

Bret Sayre's Fantasy Take: If you know what to expect from Zimmer going forward, then I'd like to either borrow your time machine or take whatever you're on. There continues to be SP2 potential with large strikeout numbers looming, but his health may never permit that type of fantasy future.

The Year Ahead: While Zimmer's collection of power offerings brings the balance and bite of an exquisitely crafted fine-dining entree, a season's worth of injuries limited evaluators to but an amuse-bouche sampling of the righty's goods. It's difficult to nail down expectations for the USF product entering 2015, given the uncertain status of his shoulder and fluid timetable for his return to action. When healthy, Zimmer shows true front-end potential. He's an obvious late-inning candidate if his arm proves incapable of shouldering a pro starter's load, but the Royals will likely continue to work with Zimmer in a rotation until circumstances demand a change in roles. This season is all about getting back on the field and logging reps, though even that first step remains an uncertainty at this point following his offseason exploratory surgery. Zimmer was near major-league ready before being shelved, so the Royals could push him quickly as soon as he is back up and running.

7. Christian Binford   RHP

Born: 12/20/92   **Age:** 22   **Bats:** R   **Throws:** R   **Height:** 6'6"   **Weight:** 220

MLB ETA	CT	FB	CH	CB	SL	OFP	Realistic
2016	–	55	55	–	–	55 NO. 3/4 STARTER	45 NO. 4/5 STARTER

YEAR	TEAM	LVL	AGE	W	L	SV	G	GS	IP	H	HR	BB	K	BB9	SO9	GB%	BABIP	WHIP	ERA	FIP	FRA	WARP
2014	OMA	AAA	21	0	1	0	4	0	10.0	16	1	5	9	4.5	8.1	46%	.417	2.10	5.40	5.00	4.75	0.1
2014	NWA	AA	21	3	2	0	8	8	48.0	45	7	6	38	1.1	7.1	51%	.270	1.06	3.19	3.93	4.85	0.3
2014	WIL	A+	21	5	4	0	14	14	82.7	72	2	11	92	1.2	10.0	45%	.315	1.00	2.40	2.08	2.83	1.9
2015	KCA	MLB	22	6	7	0	20	20	112.0	131	12	31	72	2.5	5.8	47%	.318	1.45	4.76	4.66	5.17	-0.1
2016	KCA	MLB	23	10	10	0	28	28	169.3	183	18	37	128	2.0	6.8	47%	.310	1.30	4.09	3.99	4.45	0.6

Breakout: 0%   Improve: 0%   Collapse: 0%   Attrition: 0%   MLB: 0%   Upside: 16   *Comparables: Patrick Corbin, David Holmberg, Joe Wieland*

Drafted/Acquired: 30th round, 2011 draft, Mercersburg Academy (Mercersburg, PA)

Previous Ranking: NR

What Happened in 2014: The command righty relied on guile and execution in navigating his way from High-A Wilmington to Triple-A Omaha over the course of the season, leaving Binford a hop, skip, and a jump from his major-league debut.

Strengths: Plus command profile; extremely heavy fastball with late dive across 88-92 mph velocity range; spots pitch well to the corners and across the knees; difficult offering to lift; cambio mirrors fastball action with pronounced tumble keeping bats on the upper half of the ball; maturing frame still has room for additional strength; repeats well and shows firm handle wielding fastball and change piece; will rotate fastball and change as lead offerings, providing different looks while turning over lineups.

Weaknesses: Curve is fringy offering at present; inconsistent bite limits utility; "show-me" pitch; needs to firm up breaking ball to push toward ceiling; fastball can flatten up in zone; thin margin for error across repertoire; stuff lacks impact; reliant on command and sequencing to disrupt timing and keep balls off of barrels.

Risk Factor/Injury History: Low; lacks plus offering; will need to prove capable of keeping upper-minors bats at bay.

Bret Sayre's Fantasy Take: When you see words like "crafty" and "fringy" littered throughout scouting reports, you know you're looking at a pitching prospect who should be avoided in most mixed leagues. If you're in AL-only leagues, Binford is a nice name to track in the back of your head over the next 18 months or so.

The Year Ahead: Binford doesn't wow with his stuff, but extended exposure to his ability to work his craft has a way of winning over evaluators. Because there isn't a "go-to" weapon in his cache, it is tough to buy into the limby righty as a surefire major-league starter. At the same, ignoring Binford's steady execution and surgical command through last season does a disservice to the profile. Without question, the native Keystone-stater will need to work in a more dependable breaking ball to maintain his strikeout rates through the upper minors and at the major-league level, and a case can be made that he will need to lean on his command to more effectively work outside of the zone against those upper-tier sticks. There's still a chance Binford sees a half-grade uptick in velocity as he continues to mature, and there is enough strength and durability for him to accrue value via innings logged, so long as he can remain effective while dealing to big-league lineups. He'll likely begin 2015 as part of the Double-A Northwest Arkansas rotation with an eye toward an in-season promotion to Omaha and, perhaps, a late-season call-up to the big club, depending on need. Binford's combination of deception, command, and groundball tendencies gives him a chance to beat the odds as a command righty without a standout offering.

8. Chase Vallot   C

Born: 8/21/96   **Age:** 18   **Bats:** R   **Throws:** R   **Height:** 6'0"   **Weight:** 215

MLB ETA	Hit	Power	Run	Glove	Arm	OFP	Realistic
2018	50	60	–	50	60	60 1ST DIVISION PLAYER	45 OFF 2ND TIER C/BAT

YEAR	TEAM	LVL	AGE	PA	R	2B	3B	HR	RBI	BB	SO	SB	CS	AVG/OBP/SLG	TAv	BABIP	BRR	FRAA	WARP
2014	BNC	Rk	17	222	29	14	0	7	27	26	81	0	1	.215/.329/.403	.221	.327	-1.3	C(18): 0.0	-0.3
2015	KCA	MLB	18	250	17	8	1	3	20	11	89	0	0	.182/.223/.261	.183	.271	-0.4	C 0	-1.3
2016	KCA	MLB	19	250	23	9	1	5	23	11	90	0	0	.196/.238/.303	.203	.286	-0.5	C 0	-2.0

Breakout: 0%   Improve: 0%   Collapse: 0%   Attrition: 0%   MLB: 0%   Upside: 14   *Comparables: Kyle Skipworth, Brandon Snyder, Wilson Ramos*

Drafted/Acquired: 1st round, 2014 draft, St. Thomas More (Lafayette, LA)

Previous Ranking: NR

What Happened in 2014: Vallot followed a strong showing on the showcase circuit with a productive spring that included a slimmed-down and tightened physique, earning him a supplemental first-round selection in the June draft. He then went on to hold his own in his pro debut, despite not turning 18 until the second-to-last week of the season.

Strengths: Plus raw power that plays in game; big strength with natural lift and loft; easy power to the oppo gap; nice feel for the barrel; lots of leverage and solid bat speed; plus arm strength; moves reasonably well for size; big makeup; on-field leader; evaluators point to work ethic and progress behind plate as evidence of his likelihood to stick behind the dish; one of the younger talents in the draft class.

Weaknesses: Below-average runner; swing can move quickly in and out of zone, limiting points of impact; below-average receiver at present; actions can get stiff; needs to improve transfer and release for arm strength to play to potential.

Risk Factor/Injury History: High; limited pro exposure.

Bret Sayre's Fantasy Take: The upside is certainly fun to dream on in fantasy leagues, but prep catchers make for relatively poor investments due to their incredibly distant usable ETAs. Sure, Vallot could be a 25-plus homer catcher in time, but if it doesn't happen until 2020, that isn't all that useful right now.

The Year Ahead: Vallot's youth, work ethic, plus arm, and plus power make for an intriguing low-minors catching prospect, as the former Mississippi State commit has the tools to develop into a solid all-around backstop with impact potential in the middle of a lineup. Vallot struggled some to make consistent contact in his debut, though evaluators with a deeper history with Vallot aren't turned off by his high-strikeout rate over his first 200 pro plate appearances. The powerful righty bat displayed a solid approach, the willingness to work deep into a count and take a walk, and an ability to put a hurt on the ball when he gets it where he wants it. Vallot will play almost his entire 2015 season at the age of 18 and is advanced enough to be challenged with a full-season assignment. If he can continue to demonstrate an ability and a willingness to work the count and find his pitches, there is enough hand-eye ability for the average to play up and more than enough power for the profile to grow into a middle-of-the-order run producer.

9. Foster Griffin   LHP

Born: 7/27/95   **Age:** 19   **Bats:** R   **Throws:** L   **Height:** 6'3"   **Weight:** 200

MLB ETA	CT	FB	CH	CB	SL	OFP	Realistic
2019	–	60	60	55	–	60 NO. 3 STARTER	45 NO. 4/5 STARTER

YEAR	TEAM	LVL	AGE	W	L	SV	G	GS	IP	H	HR	BB	K	BB9	SO9	GB%	BABIP	WHIP	ERA	FIP	FRA	WARP
2014	BNC	Rk	18	0	2	0	11	11	28.0	19	2	12	19	3.9	6.1	58%	.216	1.11	3.21	4.53	6.77	0.0
2015	KCA	MLB	19	1	3	0	8	8	30.7	40	4	19	12	5.6	3.5	47%	.315	1.92	6.77	6.66	7.36	-0.6
2016	KCA	MLB	20	4	8	0	28	28	169.0	183	18	82	93	4.4	5.0	47%	.292	1.57	5.15	5.24	5.60	-1.5

Breakout: 0%   Improve: 0%   Collapse: 0%   Attrition: 0%   MLB: 0%   Upside: 1   *Comparables: Kyle Ryan, Mike Foltynewicz, Brandon Maurer*

Drafted/Acquired: 1st round, 2014 draft, The First Academy (Orlando, FL)

Previous Ranking: NR

What Happened in 2014: The projectable Griffin spiked mid-90s velocity early in the spring before settling in as an upper-80s to low-90s lefty arm capable of flashing a plus change and above-average curve from time to time—enough to get him off the board at 28th overall in the June draft.

Strengths: Good athlete; projectable frame; solid body control and some feel for repeatability and execution; fastball plays well from 88 to 92 mph and comes with some downhill plane; long arms can create angles; changeup shows regular 8-12 mph delta off of the fastball with good arm speed and slot deception; works as swing-and-miss offering or to draw soft contact; curve will flash average depth and above-average downer bite; lots of room to add strength; projects as innings-eater with upside arsenal.

Weaknesses: Velocity can drop off later in game; faded some during pro debut; ball can be easy to pick up out of the hand; can get loose in the zone; fastball lacks life; will need to further develop breaking ball to miss bats with consistency.

Risk Factor/Injury History: High; limited pro exposure.

Bret Sayre's Fantasy Take: The 2014 first rounder has a good base to work with from a fantasy standpoint, though the depth of prep arms in his class will push him down in dynasty drafts this year. Look for him to come off the board in the fourth round in most leagues.

The Year Ahead: Griffin provides a solid foundation for a pro developmental staff to work with. While projectable and broad with long limbs, Griffin does not struggle to implement instruction and make adjustments without throwing the remainder of his game out of whack. If things break right for the southpaw, he could finish with three plus offerings and a spot in the middle of the Royals rotation when all is said and done. First, the former Ole Miss commit will need to build up innings and improve upon his stamina and durability. He could start 2015 in extended to better manage his workload, and could see innings in short-season ball or with the Low-A affiliate, depending on system needs and opportunity.

10. Jorge Bonifacio   OF

Born: 6/4/93   **Age:** 22   **Bats:** R   **Throws:** R   **Height:** 6'1"   **Weight:** 195

MLB ETA	Hit	Power	Run	Glove	Arm		OFP	Realistic
2016	50	60	–	50	70		55 >AVG REGULAR	45 <AVG REG/BENCH BAT

YEAR	TEAM	LVL	AGE	PA	R	2B	3B	HR	RBI	BB	SO	SB	CS	AVG/OBP/SLG	TAv	BABIP	BRR	FRAA	WARP
2014	NWA	AA	21	566	49	20	4	4	51	50	127	8	3	.230/.302/.309	.227	.295	3.3	RF(125): -9.4, LF(2): -0.1	-1.8
2015	KCA	MLB	22	250	20	10	2	2	21	14	62	1	1	.230/.276/.317	.224	.300	-0.1	RF -3, LF -0	-0.9
2016	KCA	MLB	23	386	38	15	3	4	32	25	96	2	1	.234/.288/.326	.232	.305	-0.2	RF -5, LF 0	-1.0

Breakout: 0%   Improve: 0%   Collapse: 0%   Attrition: 0%   MLB: 0%   Upside: 5   *Comparables: Moises Sierra, Brandon Jones, Rene Tosoni*

Drafted/Acquired: International free agent, 2009, Dominican Republic

Previous Ranking: #7 (Org), #99 (Top 101)

What Happened in 2014: Bonifacio returned to Double-A Northwest Arkansas and found the confines to be not so cozy, as the young power bat failed to make regular hard contact and struggled to keep pace with more advanced velocity and secondaries.

Strengths: Will show impressive raw power; capable of driving oppo; some idea as to approach at the plate; right-field arm; moves well enough for size to grow into average defender; good bat speed; willing to let the ball travel and rely on quick hands to find the ball with the barrel.

Weaknesses: High-maintenance body; wide base can limit ability to tap into strong trunk; can get out front through weight transfer; swing can get long; bat speed to catch up to velocity but early trigger exposes swing against secondaries.

Risk Factor/Injury History: Moderate; yet to find upper-minors success.

Bret Sayre's Fantasy Take: It was tough to take any positives away from his 2014 season, but Bonifacio still has the potential to be an OF3 who can hit 25-plus homers annually at the major-league level. Of course, the risk is much greater at this point, though this is more of a real-life concern than a dynasty-league one.

The Year Ahead: Bonifacio has the raw tools to develop into an above-average right-field producer, but there is still a wide gulf between present skill set and where he needs to be to reach that ceiling. At this stage in his development, Bonifacio is going to have to show an ability to start making adjustments to how he is pitched instead of relying on a reactive approach predicated on solid tracking, strike zone awareness, and bat speed. There is also a question as to whether his swing needs to be retooled some to help him better tap into his raw power, though the Royals would settle for average pop if it comes with an average hit tool and on-base production. Still young for his level, Bonifacio will repeat Double-A in 2015 after hovering in a developmental holding pattern last season. He represents the best bet at present to provide a long-term solution in right field and, with incremental improvements, could put himself back on track to debut in Kansas City by 2016.

Prospects on the Rise

1. RHP Scott Blewett: As a projectable, cold-weather arm, Blewett saw his stock yo-yo throughout the evaluative process leading up to the 2014 draft, ultimately coming off the board to Kansas City in the second round. Blewett has reached 96 mph in the past, but saw his velocity generally fall off through the course of his starts and the spring season. At his best he'll leverage his 6-foot-6 stature and reach to produce a low-90s fastball on a steep downhill plane, with an ability to bump to the mid-90s with a flatter heater up in the zone. His curve has shown solid growth since the start of his senior year and could round into an above-average pitch with a more consistent release. Blewett is a long way off, but there is significant upside in the profile. He could be challenged with a jump to full-season ball if he looks ready come spring and should slide comfortably into the top 10 next year.

2. OF Brandon Downes: Downes started strong last spring, including a two-home-run performance against one of the top collegiate arms in the country, East Carolina's Jeff Hoffman. As UVA worked its way through conference play, however, Downes got roughed up both physically and metaphorically, struggling with minor injuries and an unraveling approach. The Royals were able to pop him in the seventh round, and the former Wahoo rewarded the selection with a solid Pioneer League debut at the plate. He runs well enough to stick in center, where his arm is an asset, and the bat carries with it 5/5 hit/power upside. Through his spring struggles Downes had trouble getting his barrel started, with his hands lagging behind the rest of his swing. He showed some of those same proclivities in pro ball, and he'll need to tighten things up some moving forward, as advanced arms will be able to more easily exploit the added length and further disrupt his timing. The hope is that as he puts more distance between himself and the wrist injury that hampered him last spring, the natural bat-to-ball and above-average raw will take over.

3. OF Elier Hernandez: Hernandez flirted with the top 10 for the second straight year, and once again warrants mention as an up-and-comer capable of breaking out this year. There is plus bat speed providing ample juice for hard contact, and Hernandez showed flashes of emerging pop throughout the summer, and most noticeably during an impressive August that saw the then-19-year-old put together a .340/.365/.490 slash line over 106 plate appearances. Hernandez is still too aggressive and will need to start refining the approach as he ascends to the Carolina League in 2015, where the book gets out on players quickly. With Jorge Bonifacio stumbling some at Double-A, Hernandez has a chance to close the gap and potentially usurp him as the Royals right fielder of the future with a strong showing at High-A Wilmington.

Factors on the Farm
Prospects likely to contribute at the major-league level in 2015

1. 2B/INF Christian Colon: The former first rounder—and fourth overall selection—finally made his major-league debut in 2014 after a long four-plus-year slog through the system and more than held his own in limited action. The former Cal State Fullerton Titan has a balanced profile, with no standout tool but a lot of baseball acumen and good overall feel. He should be able to hit for solid-average with little in the way of pop, while providing steady defense as an everyday second baseman or in a limited capacity at short and third. He could excel in a utility role and will add value off the bench as a contact-oriented bat who can lay down a bunt when needed and run the bases well despite fringe-average straight-line speed.

FROM THE FIELD

Hunter Dozier

Team: Kansas City Royals
Evaluator: Tucker Blair
Dates seen: April 26, May 30, and June 2, 2014
Affiliate: Wilmington Blue Rocks (High-A, Royals)
Physical/health: Great body; big, broad, and tall; powerful legs; built; muscular top; probably maxed out at this point; hard to imagine he ever played shortstop.
Makeup: Good makeup; takes his strikeouts and learns from them; keeps it on the bench and does not bring bad plays/at-bats with him to the other side of the game.

MLB ETA	Risk factor	OFP	Realistic role
2016	Medium	60	50: second-division player

Tool	Future grade	Report
Hit	60	Natural bat-to-ball skills; swing is exquisite; barrel control is evident; shows length and extension with hands; ability to pull them in on the hard stuff inside; strength is evident in swing; hands are a tad higher for my liking but he is able to get away with it due to plus bat speed; load is moderate; approach is plus; shows ability to understand a pitcher's arsenal and adapt in-game; lays off changeup away and looks for a more suitable pitch to hit.
Power	60	Plus bat speed; brute strength; slight lift; hips provide above-average torque; ball jumps off the bat in BP and in games; hitting more liners currently than flies; more doubles power right now; the homers are going to come soon; pure bat-to-ball skills with the brute strength are huge indicators.
Baserunning/ speed	50	Clocked 4.24, 4.27 home to first; speed is simply average all around; athletic player, but speed is not a true weapon here; good speed for how large he is.
Glove	50	Defense is currently fringe-average; footwork can become choppy; does not always set them; needs work on positioning his body defensively; hips are not fluid enough for my liking at the corner; struggles at times to rotate and will have to backhand some plays that another plus defender might field in a proper throwing position; range is average; has instincts but needs more reps; defense will be fine, just needs more reps at third base.
Arm	60	Arm is plus; can handle most throws; occasionally will struggle when does not set his feet; accuracy is solid when he does not rush.

Overall: Dozier has three future plus tools, but they are slumbering some at the current time. The most important part of Dozier's game is his approach at the plate and how he is able to conduct his at-bats. The barrel skills are tremendous and he will hit at the higher levels. While he is honing these skills, the home-run power might slumber more, but it should arise shortly. The defense is not an issue to me, as he still looks to be learning the craft of third base. It might take some time, but the bat should allow him to stick at the hot corner either way.

2. LHP Brian Flynn: Flynn came over to the Royals in exchange for Aaron Crow in November 2014 and should have the opportunity to compete for a rotation spot this spring. The big lefty will show four average pitches, each of which he can wield with solid feel. His best offering is an upper-80s to low-90s heater that he can throw effectively to both sides of the plate, while his worst is a fringy curve that lacks bite and serves best as a surprise, early-count offering. There is limited upside but plenty of value to be found in a left-handed, back-end starter capable of giving you 160 to 180 innings.

3. LHP Sam Selman: Selman has officially transitioned to relief, where his fastball and slider can both play up in shorter stints. More importantly, the adverse effects of his well-below-average command are lessened in limited one-inning exposure, and through his 11 Arizona Fall League relief appearances the former Vandy Commodore was much better able to keep the ball in and around the zone, totaling 12 strikeouts to just 3 walks over his 13 innings pitched. Selman is likely to start the year with Triple-A Omaha, but has an outside shot at breaking camp with the big club if he can continue to build upon his solid Arizona Fall League showing. If Selman proves ready for the bright lights of Kansas City, he would provide coverage as a lefty arm out of the 'pen should the Royals attempt to transition Brandon Finnegan into a starting role, likely through a high-minors assignment where his innings could be managed to start the season.

1. Andrew Heaney   LHP

Born: 6/5/91   **Age:** 24   **Bats:** L   **Throws:** L   **Height:** 6'2"   **Weight:** 185

MLB ETA	CT	FB	CH	CB	SL	OFP	Realistic
Debuted in 2014	–	65	55	–	65	65 NO. 2/3 STARTER	60 NO. 3 STARTER

YEAR	TEAM	LVL	AGE	W	L	SV	G	GS	IP	H	HR	BB	K	BB9	SO9	GB%	BABIP	WHIP	ERA	FIP	FRA	WARP
2014	MIA	MLB	23	0	3	0	7	5	29.3	32	6	7	20	2.1	6.1	48%	.289	1.33	5.83	5.42	5.94	-0.4
2014	NWO	AAA	23	5	4	0	15	15	83.7	75	9	23	91	2.5	9.8	45%	.296	1.17	3.87	3.89	4.25	1.6
2014	JAX	AA	23	4	2	0	9	8	53.7	45	2	13	52	2.2	8.7	47%	.285	1.08	2.35	2.46	3.13	1.4
2015	ANA	MLB	24	8	7	0	24	24	124.7	122	13	34	105	2.5	7.6	45%	.295	1.25	3.75	4.19	4.08	1.1
2016	ANA	MLB	25	9	6	0	69	19	167.7	150	15	39	145	2.1	7.8	45%	.282	1.13	3.11	3.60	3.38	2.7

Breakout: 23%   **Improve:** 53%   **Collapse:** 15%   **Attrition:** 25%   **MLB:** 75%   **Upside:** 34   *Comparables: Jake Odorizzi, Alex Cobb, Brett Oberholtzer*

Drafted/Acquired: 1st round, 2012 draft, Oklahoma State University (Stillwater, OK)

Previous Ranking: #1 (Org – MIA), #30 (Top 101)

What Happened in 2014: Heaney pitched 137 1/3 innings across two levels, striking out a batter an inning in the process, but hit some resistance in his first taste of The Show.

Strengths: Repeatable delivery; athletic; easy arm action; fastball jumps on hitters due to deceptive release; comfortably operates in low-90s with arm-side run; will reach for more when needs it; can throw heater to both sides of the plate; snaps slider with a loose wrist; capable of changing shape; buries for chases and shortens for strikes; grades as present plus; flashes feel for change; displays bottom-dropping action.

Weaknesses: Fastball can grab a lot of plate; more of a strike-thrower than spotter with offering; command can get loose; velocity ticks up and down; can stand to add more strength to withstand rigors of position; at times struggles to maintain release of slider; starts too low for consistent chases; change lags behind other offerings; lacks turnover and high-quality action.

Risk Factor/Injury History: Low risk; achieved major leagues; command progression.

Bret Sayre's Fantasy Take: The clear top fantasy prospect in the Angels' system, Heaney will get another crack at fantasy viability in 2015. He's likely to be more of a contributor in the ratios than in strikeouts, but don't sell him short on the latter—he has the potential to miss more bats with sharpened command. He should be a strong SP3 for a long time.

The Year Ahead: Heaney should have the inside track on a rotation spot with the big club this spring, and there's little left for him to prove in the minors. When the left-hander is on, he flashes three major-league-caliber offerings and the ability to work hitters in a variety of ways. The 24-year-old's easy, balanced delivery allows the overall stuff to play up, and there is some deception baked in, with the ball seemingly jumping out of his uniform, especially when he's delivering his heater. While Heaney's athleticism and fluid actions allow him to repeat his mechanics, he can get into trouble working too much of the white and he'll need to improve upon the fastball command to limit solid contact against elite hitters. Fortunately, he has some potential command growth in front of him thanks to the ease with which he delivers the ball and his overall athleticism, so this hopefully will not linger as a long-term issue. The profile is solid, and 2015 should serve as the first step in earnest toward Heaney establishing himself as a mid-rotation mainstay. He's the clear-cut headliner in this system and one of the better left-handed arms percolating through the ranks across baseball.

#37
BP Top 101 Prospects

2. Sean Newcomb   LHP

Born: 6/12/93   **Age:** 22   **Bats:** L   **Throws:** L   **Height:** 6'5"   **Weight:** 240

MLB ETA	CT	FB	CH	CB	SL	OFP	Realistic
2016	–	65	50	55	60	60 NO. 3 STARTER	50 NO. 4 STARTER

YEAR	TEAM	LVL	AGE	W	L	SV	G	GS	IP	H	HR	BB	K	BB9	SO9	GB%	BABIP	WHIP	ERA	FIP	FRA	WARP
2014	BUR	A	21	0	1	0	4	4	11.7	13	1	5	15	3.9	11.6	28%	.387	1.54	6.94	3.31	4.75	0.2
2014	ANG	Rk	21	0	0	0	2	2	3.0	3	1	1	3	3.0	9.0	20%	.250	1.33	3.00	7.36	11.45	-0.1
2015	ANA	MLB	22	2	3	0	8	8	33.0	36	4	16	23	4.4	6.3	42%	.310	1.58	5.12	5.44	5.57	-0.2
2016	ANA	MLB	23	5	8	0	29	29	182.7	189	20	78	143	3.8	7.0	42%	.303	1.46	4.54	4.61	4.93	-0.8

Breakout: 0%   **Improve:** 0%   **Collapse:** 0%   **Attrition:** 0%   **MLB:** 0%   **Upside:** 0   *Comparables: Andrew Heaney, Justin Wilson, Jose A. Ramirez*

Drafted/Acquired: 1st Round, 2014 draft, University of Hartford (West Hartford, CT)

Previous Ranking: NR

What Happened in 2014: Newcomb showed off a workhorse build and four average or better major-league offerings during a strong spring for Hartford before being selected by the Angels in the first round of the draft.

Strengths: Big man; durable build; very easy arm; fastball jumps; heater works comfortably 90-94 mph and can reach 97; low-80s slider will flash plus with tilt; one-to-seven curve comes with solid depth in mid- to upper-70s; changeup will flash average with fade; can fill up strike zone with fastball; projects as innings-eater; lots of room for growth given limited track record and exposure to advanced instruction.

Weaknesses: Limited track record; control profile well ahead of command; can throw fastball to both sides but catches a lot of white and doesn't command to quadrants; trouble finding consistent release with curve; will alter arm slot between curve/slider; changeup not yet in heavy rotation; can struggle to repeat mechanics and keep handle on big body; upper and lower half can get out of sync.

Risk Factor/Injury History: Moderate; strong baseline but more development/refinement required than typical first-round collegiate arm.

Bret Sayre's Fantasy Take: Though he may be a slower mover than other college arms, Newcomb still could claim a well-rounded SP3 ceiling for fantasy. The strikeouts could be tough to get unless a couple of secondaries play up to their potential, but the park will help him once he gets to the major-league level. He's a strong third-round choice in dynasty drafts this year.

The Year Ahead: Newcomb's profile is atypical for a first rounder. The brawny lefty is a cold-weather collegiate arm with the body and raw stuff to warrant first-round selection, but his limited track record and inconsistent execution carry with them a fair amount of risk. Evaluators all agree the raw materials are here for developing a 200-plus-inning mid-rotation arm, and Newcomb's more fervent supporters insist that the stuff will jump across the board once he has a year of pro instruction under his belt. He needs to tighten up his game, starting with better repeating his mechanics and showing capacity to spot his curve and changeup to both sides of the plate. If he can pull himself into alignment mechanically such that he is working with a consistent batch of offerings, there is potential for Newcomb to take off quickly thereafter. He will likely jump to the High-A California League this spring and will progress as quickly as his stuff and performance allow, with a 2016 Anaheim debut attainable.

3. Joe Gatto RHP

Born: 6/14/95 **Age:** 20 **Bats:** R **Throws:** R **Height:** 6'3" **Weight:** 204

MLB ETA	CT	FB	CH	CB	SL	OFP	Realistic
2018	–	60	55	55	–	60	50
						NO. 3 STARTER	NO. 4 STARTER

YEAR	TEAM	LVL	AGE	W	L	SV	G	GS	IP	H	HR	BB	K	BB9	SO9	GB%	BABIP	WHIP	ERA	FIP	FRA	WARP
2014	ANG	Rk	19	2	1	0	10	6	25.0	33	1	9	15	3.2	5.4	62%	.303	1.68	5.40	4.55	8.30	-0.1
2014	ORM	Rk	19	0	0	0	1	1	2.0	3	1	0	1	0.0	4.5	14%	.333	1.50	4.50	9.53	10.04	0.0
2015	ANA	MLB	20	1	2	0	9	4	31.0	39	4	19	13	5.5	3.8	46%	.310	1.88	6.59	6.56	7.16	-0.6
2016	ANA	MLB	21	3	3	1	31	12	116.7	128	13	54	64	4.2	4.9	46%	.294	1.56	5.19	5.24	5.64	-1.2

Breakout: 0%   Improve: 0%   Collapse: 0%   Attrition: 0%   MLB: 0%   Upside: 0   *Comparables: Hunter Strickland, Jake Odorizzi, Allen Webster*

Drafted/Acquired: 2nd round, 2014 draft, St. Augustine Prep (Richland, NJ)

Previous Ranking: NR

What Happened in 2014: Gatto put together inconsistent but promising performances between the showcase circuit and a cold-weather spring, and continued in that vein at the pro ranks with softer stuff in season but a solid showing through instructs.

Strengths: Pro body; room for more strength; stuff projects; easy arm, repeats well; upper-80s to low-90s fastball can reach mid-90s at present; curve will flash above average with downer action; shows feel for changeup in nascent stages; solid athleticism; steady demeanor; low-mileage arm.

Weaknesses: Present stuff lacks consistent pop; fastball can come flat and hittable over the meat of the plate; still developing feel for secondaries; inconsistent release can leave curve soft and slurvy; change can get firm, losing fade mid-80s and up; still learning the craft; needs to build up durability and hold stuff later into outings.

Risk Factor/Injury History: High; rookie-level résumé.

Bret Sayre's Fantasy Take: This is exactly how sad the Angels system is these days. Gatto shouldn't be more than a periphery arm in dynasty drafts, as his upside isn't huge and he's very far away from the majors.

The Year Ahead: Gatto joined Newcomb as the top two 2014 arms out of the northeast, and the Angels were happy to pop the duo with their first two picks in the June draft. The former UNC commit has shown flashes of future mid-rotation stuff, including a plus fastball and two above-average secondaries in his curve and change piece. There is a fair amount of room for growth with Gatto, which is good because the present profile remains a good bit off from where he needs to be to realize his potential as a future number three. His ability to better maintain his stuff should increase as he continues to add strength through natural maturation, and his easy motion and solid athleticism should aid him in implementing pro instruction en route to solidifying his mechanics and finding consistency in execution. He should see significant innings in the Midwest League this year, where he will look to lay a sound developmental foundation from which to work.

4. Chris Ellis   RHP

Born: 9/22/92   **Age:** 22   **Bats:** R   **Throws:** R   **Height:** 6'4"   **Weight:** 190

MLB ETA	CT	FB	CH	CB	SL	OFP	Realistic
2017	–	55	60	55	–	60 NO. 3 STARTER	50 NO. 4 SP/LATE INN RP

YEAR	TEAM	LVL	AGE	W	L	SV	G	GS	IP	H	HR	BB	K	BB9	SO9	GB%	BABIP	WHIP	ERA	FIP	FRA	WARP
2014	ORM	Rk	21	0	1	0	9	2	15.7	17	2	8	16	4.6	9.2	36%	.405	1.60	6.89	5.56	6.25	-0.1
2015	ANA	MLB	22	1	1	0	16	2	31.3	37	4	20	18	5.8	5.2	43%	.312	1.81	6.12	6.29	6.65	-0.6
2016	ANA	MLB	23	2	1	1	38	3	77.7	77	7	40	56	4.6	6.5	43%	.292	1.50	4.60	4.75	5.00	-0.1

Breakout: 0%   **Improve:** 0%   **Collapse:** 0%   **Attrition:** 0%   **MLB:** 0%   **Upside:** 1   *Comparables: Chase Anderson, Joe Kelly, Bobby Cassevah*

Drafted/Acquired: 3rd round, 2014 draft, University of Mississippi (Oxford, MS)

Previous Ranking: NR

What Happened in 2014: The converted reliever logged 116 innings for Ole Miss, putting together a solid spring despite not missing many bats along the way, and was eased into pro ball via limited action at rookie-level Orem.

Strengths: Three-way fastball plays above average in the 88-93 mph velocity band, coming with sink, cut, and run; upper-80s cutter can miss barrels and tie up oppo bats; off-speed comes with some arm-speed deception and works well off heater, drawing soft contact; power curve will flash average to a tick above, with solid bite; high-waisted with solid extension to home; recent convert to starting with limited mileage.

Weaknesses: Saw stuff back up some in pro debut; may lack consistency in breaking ball to miss bats with regularity; can struggle to spot curve; lacks impact velocity; reliant on moving fastball around zone and altering finish; thin frame does not portend significant increase in bulk; limited track record as starter; some issue maintaining quality of stuff later in games.

Risk Factor/Injury History: High; limited track record as starter and 15-inning pro résumé.

Bret Sayre's Fantasy Take: Ellis is like Gatto, but worse. Unless your league rosters more than 300 prospects, he shouldn't even hit your radar.

The Year Ahead: Ellis is an interesting projection case, as the rangy frame comes with narrow hips and does not necessarily point to a significant increase in bulk. Still, Ellis handled a significant jump in innings (over 130 total innings pitched between amateur and pro ball), and while there was some downtick later in games and over his pro appearances, the former Rebel looks to have initially taken well to his conversion from the 'pen. To turn over pro lineups consistently, Ellis will need to continue to develop his breaking ball to the point where it is a dependable offering that can help to change hitters' eye level and keep bats off the fastball/changeup plane. If that development never manifests, the fastball and changeup might be enough to keep hitters honest, and in any event could play well out of the 'pen. The Angels should continue to ease Ellis into rotation work, as the righty will be taxed for the first time with starting on less than a full week's rest. He should see mostly sub-Double-A time in 2015, with an eye toward a full season of upper-level ball in 2016 with continued development.

5. Nick Tropeano   RHP

Born: 8/27/90   **Age:** 24   **Bats:** R   **Throws:** R   **Height:** 6'4"   **Weight:** 200

MLB ETA	CT	FB	CH	CB	SL	OFP	Realistic
Debuted in 2014	–	55	60	–	50	55 NO. 3/4 STARTER	50 NO. 4 STARTER

YEAR	TEAM	LVL	AGE	W	L	SV	G	GS	IP	H	HR	BB	K	BB9	SO9	GB%	BABIP	WHIP	ERA	FIP	FRA	WARP
2014	HOU	MLB	23	1	3	0	4	4	21.7	19	0	9	13	3.7	5.4	43%	.279	1.29	4.57	3.34	3.92	0.2
2014	OKL	AAA	23	9	5	0	23	20	124.7	90	11	33	120	2.4	8.7	40%	.248	0.99	3.03	3.81	4.27	1.8
2015	ANA	MLB	24	8	6	0	22	22	118.0	112	11	39	101	3.0	7.7	43%	.296	1.28	3.66	4.15	3.98	1.1
2016	ANA	MLB	25	4	2	0	69	0	73.7	59	5	19	68	2.3	8.3	43%	.272	1.07	2.54	3.22	2.76	1.9

Breakout: 18%   **Improve:** 43%   **Collapse:** 13%   **Attrition:** 25%   **MLB:** 63%   **Upside:** 35   *Comparables: Jake Odorizzi, Eric Surkamp, Garrett Richards*

Drafted/Acquired: 5th round, 2011 draft, Stony Brook University (Stony Brook, NY)

Previous Ranking: Factor on the Farm (Houston Astros)

What Happened in 2014: Tropeano put together a strong PCL campaign, leading the league in ERA and WHIP while striking out almost a batter per inning, before receiving a four-start September cup of coffee.

Strengths: Solid strength; built to shoulder a major-league workload; low-90s fastball effective down in the zone; works effectively to both sides of the dish; changeup is plus offering with arm speed and slot deception, late tumble; natural deception in delivery with some jerkiness serving to disrupt hitters' timing; solid control profile; improved sequencing and comfort working forward and back.

Weaknesses: Breaking ball is fringe-average at present; not a consistent weapon; slider can lack bite and has tendency to hug swing plane; will run into trouble repeating release; can get imprecise in the zone; fastball lacks impactful velocity; reliant on deception and location; thin margin for error against major-league lineups; needs consistent breaking ball to turn over major-league lineups.

Risk Factor/Injury History: Low; major-league ready.

Bret Sayre's Fantasy Take: Before the Heaney trade, Tropeano was an interesting AL-only and deep-league target for 2015, but now he looks to be on the outside looking in for this year. Still, he should be on the near-term radar for deep leaguers as a boring option who could get a few starts and put up decent ratios.

The Year Ahead: It's not a sexy profile, but Tropeano offers plenty of value as a solid bet to provide 175-plus innings in the back of a big-league rotation. The command profile isn't yet where it needs to be for him to find consistent success at the highest level, but he is far enough along in his development that he could finish this refinement with the big club if he earns a spot in the Opening Day rotation. Should he return to Triple-A it shouldn't take long for Tropeano to find his way to the Halos, be it in a spot start/swingman capacity or as a rotation member. The overall stuff probably limits his ceiling to that of a fringy number three, but the floor is reasonably high and the progress he has shown over the past year with respect to improved comfort in sequencing and pounding the lower "U" of the strike zone with his fastball are both solid indicators that he has the ability to make the final adjustments necessary to stick in the bigs long term.

6.　Kyle Kubitza　3B

Born: 7/15/90　**Age:** 24　**Bats:** L　**Throws:** R　**Height:** 6'3"　**Weight:** 215

MLB ETA	Hit	Power	Run	Glove	Arm		OFP	Realistic
2015	50	55	–	50	60		55 >AVG REGULAR	45 BENCH/<AVG REG.

YEAR	TEAM	LVL	AGE	PA	R	2B	3B	HR	RBI	BB	SO	SB	CS	AVG/OBP/SLG	TAv	BABIP	BRR	FRAA	WARP
2014	MIS	AA	23	529	76	31	11	8	55	77	133	21	6	.295/.405/.470	.335	.401	3.7	3B(120): -5.2, LF(1): -0.0	5.8
2015	ANA	MLB	24	250	25	9	2	4	23	27	81	5	2	.215/.305/.334	.249	.316	0.1	3B -2	0.1
2016	ANA	MLB	25	250	28	10	2	5	24	28	82	5	2	.217/.307/.346	.247	.319	0.3	3B -2	0.5

Breakout: 0%　Improve: 7%　Collapse: 10%　Attrition: 12%　MLB: 24%　Upside: 28　*Comparables: Matt Tuiasosopo, Josh Fields, Adam Duvall*

Drafted/Acquired: 3rd round, 2011 draft, Texas State University (San Marcos, TX)

Previous Ranking: NR

What Happened in 2014: The third baseman spent the 2014 season in the Southern League, where he hit .295 with 50 extra-base hits, and made his way to Anaheim in January 2015 as part of a package exchanged for Ricardo Sanchez.

Strengths: Strong body; good size; quick stroke; strong wrists and forearms; can barrel up offerings with backspin; power to tap into; drives ball into both gaps well; willing to use the whole field; patience at the plate; not afraid to hit with a strike or two; will methodically look for pitch; plus arm; plenty of arm for hot corner; quick feet; soft hands.

Weaknesses: Can be awkward with footwork in field; will needlessly rush plays; average reactions; can miss in the zone; clear spots to work to—chases up and away in the dirt; hit tool will likely play fringe-average; swing more geared toward line drives; over-the-fence power a question; no real lead offensive tool; not much growth left.

Risk Factor/Injury History: Low; 132 games at Double-A; defensive profile.

Bret Sayre's Fantasy Take: The recently acquired third baseman ranks as the second-best fantasy profile in this system, which is a statement as much about the Angels as about Kubitza. There's a chance he could hit .260 with 15-20 homers, which would make him a usable third baseman in most nonshallow formats.

The Year Ahead: Kubitza took his biggest step forward as a pro last season in Double-A, proving he could handle advanced competition and continuing an upward developmental trend toward a big-league debut. That debut could very well come at some point in 2015 with a similar showing in Triple-A, with Kubitza stepping in as the top third-base prospect in the Angels system. Nothing truly pops off the page for Kubitza outside of the arm, but the bat, power, and glove can all play right around average, forming a solid baseline for major-league production. The aesthetics of the third baseman's games don't sing to observers, but he makes it work and should at minimum provide a decent option as a limited utility type. The perfect-world scenario is that Kubitza continues to blossom to the point where a solid-average hit/power profile and average defense come together to provide an above-average everyday profile in the aggregate.

7. Cam Bedrosian RHP

Born: 10/2/91 **Age:** 23 **Bats:** R **Throws:** R **Height:** 6'0" **Weight:** 205

MLB ETA	CT	FB	CH	CB	SL		OFP	Realistic
Debuted in 2014	–	60	–	–	55		55 2ND TIER CLOSER	50 LATE INN RP

YEAR	TEAM	LVL	AGE	W	L	SV	G	GS	IP	H	HR	BB	K	BB9	SO9	GB%	BABIP	WHIP	ERA	FIP	FRA	WARP
2014	ANA	MLB	22	0	1	0	17	0	19.3	23	2	12	20	5.6	9.3	43%	.356	1.81	6.52	4.30	3.67	0.1
2014	SLC	AAA	22	1	1	2	8	0	7.0	5	0	6	10	7.7	12.9	56%	.312	1.57	7.71	4.70	4.52	0.1
2014	ARK	AA	22	1	0	15	30	0	32.3	10	1	10	57	2.8	15.9	57%	.196	0.62	1.11	0.92	1.96	1.0
2014	INL	A+	22	0	0	1	5	0	5.7	1	0	2	15	3.2	23.8	-	.333	0.53	0.00	-0.50	-0.54	-
2015	ANA	MLB	23	2	2	0	28	5	47.7	47	4	26	44	4.9	8.3	48%	.308	1.54	4.68	4.65	5.09	-0.2
2016	ANA	MLB	24	2	1	0	41	0	43.7	43	3	25	42	5.1	8.6	48%	.320	1.58	4.82	4.22	5.24	-0.1

Breakout: 16% **Improve:** 22% **Collapse:** 10% **Attrition:** 19% **MLB:** 33% **Upside:** 5 *Comparables: Jose Dominguez, Scott Elbert, Phillippe Aumont*

Drafted/Acquired: 1st round, 2010 draft, East Coweta HS (Sharpsburg, GA)

Previous Ranking: Factor on the Farm

What Happened in 2014: Bedrosian opened the year with two dominant months between High-A Inland Empire and Double-A Arkansas, holding opposition bats to a .079 batting average while striking out almost two batters per inning over 24 frames, and sped through seven Triple-A innings before an uneven 19-plus inning stint out of the Angels' 'pen to close the year.

Strengths: Power pairing in mid-90s fastball and mid-80s slider; fastball features a little giddy-up; pitches aggressively with offering, including on the inner half and up in the zone; slider flashes plus with late bite; will occasionally drop a fringy curve as a change-of-pace pitch; late-inning mind-set; fortitude for high-leverage work.

Weaknesses: Can get loose in the zone with the fastball; slider isn't yet a consistent plus offering; can overthrow out of the zone and come around on occasion; change is often too firm, coming flat up in the zone.

Risk Factor/Injury History: Moderate; major-league ready but power-reliever volatility; Tommy John in the file.

Bret Sayre's Fantasy Take: Any time you have a high-end relief prospect in a good park, there's a temptation to invest, but he's at best third in line for saves, so even if he's very good, there's no guarantee he ever gets there.

The Year Ahead: It's tough to envision a better start to a season than Bedrosian spun off, and despite less-than-attractive pure production between Triple-A Salt Lake and Anaheim, a lot of the characteristics that contributed to Bedrosian's early-month domination remained with him over the balance of the season. He is a traditional power arm that relishes the opportunity to challenge hitters with his fastball, and at his best can deploy his slider with great effect thanks to its fastball-like trajectory and late action. He was roughed up a bit against more advanced bats, but through further exposure the former Georgia-prep product should be able to tease out the nuance in approach necessary to unwrap major-league hitters, including proper in/out sequencing and better picking his spots to challenge hitters up in the zone. He could break camp with the Angels, but a return to Salt Lake to continue to hone his craft could do him some good as well. Either way he stands a good chance of providing solid value for the Angels in 2015 and could ultimately compete for the ninth-inning job.

8. Taylor Featherston 2B/SS

Born: 10/8/89 **Age:** 25 **Bats:** R **Throws:** R **Height:** 6'1" **Weight:** 185

MLB ETA	Hit	Power	Run	Glove	Arm		OFP	Realistic
2015	50	–	50	50	50		50 AVG ML PLAYER	45 <AVG REGULAR

YEAR	TEAM	LVL	AGE	PA	R	2B	3B	HR	RBI	BB	SO	SB	CS	AVG/OBP/SLG	TAv	BABIP	BRR	FRAA	WARP
2014	TUL	AA	24	550	69	33	4	16	57	38	114	14	6	.260/.322/.439	.273	.305	-2.1	2B(72): 8.1, SS(39): 0.1	3.2
2015	ANA	MLB	25	250	24	11	1	5	25	12	64	4	1	.233/.278/.359	.246	.296	0.2	2B 3, SS -0	0.8
2016	ANA	MLB	26	450	47	20	3	10	46	22	107	8	3	.244/.286/.372	.245	.300	0.5	2B 5, SS -1	1.4

Breakout: 2% **Improve:** 11% **Collapse:** 6% **Attrition:** 17% **MLB:** 25% **Upside:** 9 *Comparables: Ryan Flaherty, Ryan Adams, Craig Stansberry*

Drafted/Acquired: 5th round, 2011 draft, Texas Christian University (Forth Worth, TX)

Previous Ranking: NR

What Happened in 2014: Featherston put together a solid all-around showing over 127 Texas League games before impressing evaluators with steady hands and an advanced approach during the Arizona Fall League.

Strengths: Balanced profile; compact stroke with slightly above-average bat speed; generates hard contact with carry; solid power to gaps with over-the-fence strength to pull; feel for strike zone; chance to grow on-base profile; clean actions in field; steady defender; arm to turn two and handle left-side action; lower half works across dirt; good feel for game.

Weaknesses: Profile lacks impact; limited ceiling; lacks carrying tool; can be beat up in the zone; can struggle to adjust behind in count; vulnerable to same-side spin and off-speed, particularly behind in count; bat can be led out of zone.

Risk Factor/Injury History: Low; high-minors success.

Bret Sayre's Fantasy Take: Feel free to ignore Featherston in anything other than 18-team leagues and deeper. If you play in a format that fits into that category, he could be usable as an unexciting middle-infield option. I mean, he is behind Josh Rutledge on the depth chart.

The Year Ahead: Featherston has the potential to grow into a useful everyday player and could thrive in a utility role or as the right-handed half of a platoon. His compact stroke works well across the zone, and he shows a high level of comfort in the box, particularly against oppo-side arms. There is enough juice in the barrel to keep pitchers honest, and low double-digit home-run totals are attainable. Defensively, the TCU product has the actions and arm to handle short, but the range is shy of ideal for an everyday gig. He profiles as a quality utility glove who can provide positive value across the dirt and whose defensive versatility could be further expanded to include an outfield corner should the Angels so desire. Featherston will have an opportunity to break camp in a utility capacity and figures to see action in Anaheim one way or another in the near future.

---

9. Roberto Baldoquin SS

Born: 5/14/94 **Age:** 21 **Bats:** R **Throws:** R **Height:** 5'11" **Weight:** 185

MLB ETA	Hit	Power	Run	Glove	Arm	OFP	Realistic
2016	55	50	–	55	50	55 >AVG REGULAR	45 <AVG PLAYER/UT

Drafted/Acquired: International free agent, 2015, Cuba

Previous Ranking: NR

What Happened in 2014: Baldoquin defected from Cuba in pursuit of a major-league gig and inked with the Angels for $8 million in January 2015.

Strengths: Tracks well for age and experience; shows feel for the strike zone and the foundation for on-base production; can produce hard contact to the gaps across the hit zone; room to grow into some over-the-fence power; hands play up the middle; quick hands; smooth transfer; clean from receipt to release, helping arm play up.

Weaknesses: Some length from load to contact; inconsistent launch can pull barrel off plane and out of zone; swing length could lead to adjustment issues, particularly against more advanced secondaries; lateral quickness may be a step slow for shortstop long term, particularly if lower half fills in further; inconsistent international competition; limited relevant track record.

Risk Factor/Injury History: High; yet to debut; uneven international competition.

Bret Sayre's Fantasy Take: There are going to be owners in all leagues who reach for Baldoquin in dynasty drafts this year just because he's a Cuban guy who signed for a large amount of money. Don't let that fool you, though; this isn't a special talent. While he could be a middle-infield option in time, and a stronger one in points leagues, taking him before the middle of the third round is a poor decision.

The Year Ahead: The investment made in signing Baldoquin says everything that need be said with respect to the Angels' belief in his ability to develop into their shortstop of the future. Should the body and range ultimately force the Cuban native off of the six-spot, he should find a home across the bag at the keystone, where his quick release and firm carry on his throws would serve him well at the margins and turning two. With solid foundational value in the glove, the ultimate ceiling on the profile will be tied to Baldoquin's feel to hit. There is enough bat speed and projected strength to dream on an impactful bat, with his contact ability determining the extent to which he is able to tap into that potential. The upside is an above-average hit and on-base profile with average aggregate power production skewed to doubles, all wrapped in an up-the-middle defensive profile. He should spend the bulk of 2015 in Double-A, though the Angels will not shy away from challenging him should he prove worthy of an accelerated development plan.

---

10. Trevor Gott RHP

Born: 8/26/92 **Age:** 22 **Bats:** R **Throws:** R **Height:** 6'0" **Weight:** 190

MLB ETA	CT	FB	CH	CB	SL	OFP	Realistic
2015	–	60	–	–	50	55 2ND TIER CLOSER	50 LATE INNING RP

YEAR	TEAM	LVL	AGE	W	L	SV	G	GS	IP	H	HR	BB	K	BB9	SO9	GB%	BABIP	WHIP	ERA	FIP	FRA	WARP
2014	ARK	AA	21	2	1	2	13	0	17.7	11	0	7	18	3.6	9.2	58%	.256	1.02	1.53	2.27	3.55	0.2
2014	SAN	AA	21	0	0	0	10	0	11.7	11	0	9	11	6.9	8.5	60%	.314	1.71	4.63	3.55	4.79	0.0
2014	LEL	A+	21	2	4	16	29	0	31.3	28	3	9	31	2.6	8.9	58%	.288	1.18	3.16	3.96	5.01	0.2
2015	ANA	MLB	22	2	1	2	36	0	41.3	41	4	19	35	4.1	7.6	51%	.302	1.45	4.29	4.67	4.67	0.0
2016	ANA	MLB	23	2	1	2	45	0	52.0	51	4	20	49	3.5	8.5	51%	.306	1.37	3.93	3.77	4.27	0.4

Breakout: 0% **Improve:** 0% **Collapse:** 0% **Attrition:** 0% **MLB:** 0% **Upside:** 12 *Comparables: Dominic Leone, Marcus Stroman, Kyle Crockett*

Drafted/Acquired: 6th round, 2013 draft, University of Kentucky (Lexington, KY)

Previous Ranking: NR

What Happened in 2014: The former Kentucky closer had no issue navigating his way through a hitter-friendly Cal League through the first half of the season or handling advanced Double-A bats in the second half, leaving him a step away from his major-league debut.

Strengths: Plus fastball sits low-90s with lots of weight; very difficult to lift down in zone; flat trajectory coupled with sink draws lots of soft contact; slider can be swing-and-miss offering when properly set up; shows some feel for changeup; willing to throw change and slider early in count; maintains focus and mechanics with runners on; brain and stomach for high-leverage situations.

Weaknesses: Slightly undersized; fastball can lack plane and angle; can be hittable waist and up; has tendency to overthrow slider; when slider and change are not effective, fastball can lose effectiveness; bat-missing ability could be limited against major-league bats without more consistency and precision with slider.

Risk Factor/Injury History: Moderate; fewer than 100 pro innings; reliever-volatility risk.

Bret Sayre's Fantasy Take: Take everything that I said about Bedrosian, but tone down the excitement a notch. Gott has the stuff to be a good major-league reliever, but there's just no reason to own him in fantasy leagues right now.

The Year Ahead: It was a strong 2014 campaign for the former sixth rounder, with Gott pounding his way through two levels, reaching Double-A after just 67 professional innings. Because the righty lacks significant plane and angle on his heater, the pitch relies heavily on late sink and an ability to throw to both sides of the plate to avoid hard contact. The slider is an adequate partner for the fastball and could grow into a true swing-and-miss offering once he finds a slightly tighter handle on the pitch and is better able to utilize it with precision and consistency. While he doesn't need the changeup to succeed out of the 'pen, there is enough feel for the pitch to project it to fringe-average or better with continued developmental focus. Gott is ready for Triple-A and should be afforded the opportunity to further refine his arsenal at that level, as the Angels are armed with adequate right-handed relief options at present. He profiles as a capable late-inning arm long term and could see some time in Anaheim this summer should the need arise.

Prospects on the Rise

1. RHP Victor Alcantara: While the likely future for Alcantara and his double-plus fastball remains in the 'pen, 2014 represented an encouraging step forward in the power righty's efforts to grow into a viable starter. His mid- to upper-90s heater proved too much for Midwest League bats to handle, allowing him to power through 125 innings despite a slider and split-change that both continue to register as below-average offerings. Further, the control likewise remains below average at present, though the Dominican native found a little more consistency in his execution last year, helping him to find the strike zone with a little more regularity than in years past.

FROM THE FIELD

Trevor Gott

Team: Los Angeles Angels of Anaheim

Evaluator: Chris Rodriguez

Dates seen: April 15 and May 22, 2014

Affiliate: Lake Elsinore Storm (High-A, Padres)

OFP: 55

Realistic role: 50; late-innings reliever

Mechanics: Smaller than listed height; probably 5'10", 5'11"; 190 lbs. is accurate; strong, lean body; plus athleticism; quick rock-and-turn delivery; shows his back to the hitter on occasion; three-quarters arm slot; super quick arm; creates deception because of his arm speed; easy plus arm strength; follows through well; closer mentality.

Pitch type	Present grade	Future grade	Sitting velocity	Peak velocity	Report
FB	65	70	92-96	97	Easy plus pitch; Worked 95-96 T97 in first appearance; 93-95 from the stretch; pitch features very good arm-side run; bores into right-handed hitters; can also sink the pitch; arm speed and quick delivery give the pitch deception; little plane due to short stature; was a tick down in second appearance but still had plus movement; pounded the zone with it; plays down; command was a little loose; control got away from him and walked a batter on four pitches; can be plus-plus offering with more command.
CB	60	65	79-82	83	Severe two-plane break; plus offering; 11-5 shape; snaps his wrist and gets on top of the pitch well; arm slot and speed work off the fastball; can lengthen horizontal break away from right-handed hitters; throws it for strikes and for chase; can be wild in the zone; can be plus-plus with better command/control.

Overall: Gott has a super quick arm that can touch the high-90s. He's already at Double-A following an appearance in the High-A All-Star Game, where he reportedly sat 94-98. The plane on his fastball isn't great because of his size, but the movement is plus-plus and I love the way he challenges hitters with it. Looks like he can make a contribution to the bullpen sometime next season, with a very good fastball/curveball mix that plays well at the back end.

While the ramp up in innings and overall production were positive signs for Alcantara, he will need to show more progress in 2015 in building his secondaries up to fighting weight while finding more pitch-to-pitch uniformity in his choppy mechanics if he's to find a long-term home in a rotation.

2. RHP Jeremy Rhoades: The Illinois State standout enjoyed a loud spring, with time spent both in the rotation and in the 'pen. After being selected by the Angels in the fourth round of the June draft, Rhoades worked three-inning stints at rookie-level Orem, alternating between starting and relief work, bringing his aggregate innings total for the year above 115 innings between amateur and pro ball. Rhoades's go-to pitch is a mid-80s slider that he wields with precision to both sides of the plate against lefty and righty bats alike. He can tighten the pitch up to a shorter upper-80s breaker with cutter action as well and does a good job using that variation to bridge the gap to his low-90s fastball. Despite a big pro body capable of handling a starter's load, Rhoades doesn't maintain his stuff particularly well late into his outings, and he likely profiles best as a reliever, where his fastball can regularly reach the 94-95 mph range and his slider could better play as a primary offering. He should start 2015 in Low-A, and could move quickly if and when the Angels opt to shift him into relief full time.

3. LHP Greg Mahle: Mahle racked up 70 innings for UC Santa Barbara last spring, almost exclusively in relief, and logged another 37 for Angels affiliates after being drafted. Despite the hefty workload, Mahle continued to show well throughout the summer and into fall instructs, keeping hitters off-balance with a fastball/changeup/curveball mix dealt from multiple arm slots ranging from true sidearm all the way to a three-quarters release. It isn't overpowering stuff, but it comes with a deceptive, fast-paced motion that is difficult to time and that can lead to a high level of unease in the box. His fastball and changeup grade out as average offerings that play up due to his quirks, and while the curve is inconsistent in both shape and bite there is potential for it to ultimately settle in as a reliable third weapon. Mahle should step into the 'pen for High-A Inland Empire to start 2015 and could speed through the system in short order if he can find a little more consistency in execution.

Factors on the Farm
Prospects likely to contribute at the major-league level in 2015

1. C Carlos Perez: An advanced glove with strong catch-and-throw skills, Perez could break camp as the reserve backstop for the Halos and has the defensive chops to settle into that role long term. He will flash occasional pop at the plate and has enough feel for the barrel to make use of his strike zone awareness, giving him a chance to provide some offensive value, albeit as a down-order stick. If he proves capable of leveraging his feel for the zone and occasional power, he could eventually develop into an everyday backstop at the major-league level.

2. LHP Nate Smith: Smith carved his way to Double-A Arkansas last year despite an average fastball and just 35 innings of pro experience entering the year. His bread and butter is an above-average to plus changeup that comes with deception and late dive. His curve comes and goes, and will need to be tightened up to consistently play against top-tier righty bats, but Smith's overall feel and ability to work forward and back with three offerings should be enough to allow him to operate as a back-end arm or swing man in the near future.

3. 2B Alex Yarbrough: It's a ho-hum profile outside of the hit tool, which some evaluators grade out as high as plus. The utility of his barrel awareness and feel for contact is somewhat limited by an aggressive approach that eats into his on-base profile, but provided Yarbrough is able to maintain a high enough hard-contact rate he should prove an asset with the bat at the major-league level in some capacity. He is a fringy defender at the keystone and lacks the range or arm to profile well in a utility role, so his bat will need to shoulder the load.

1. Corey Seager SS

Born: 4/27/94 **Age:** 21 **Bats:** L **Throws:** R **Height:** 6'4" **Weight:** 215

MLB ETA	Hit	Power	Run	Glove	Arm		OFP	Realistic
2015	**60**	**60**	**50**	**–**	**65**		**70** ALL STAR	**60** 1ST DIVISION PLAYER

YEAR	TEAM	LVL	AGE	PA	R	2B	3B	HR	RBI	BB	SO	SB	CS	AVG/OBP/SLG	TAv	BABIP	BRR	FRAA	WARP
2014	CHT	AA	20	161	28	16	3	2	27	10	39	1	1	.345/.381/.534	.310	.450	1.4	SS(35): -2.2	1.6
2014	RCU	A+	20	365	61	34	2	18	70	30	76	5	1	.352/.411/.633	.358	.411	2.4	SS(64): 9.5, SS(7): 9.5	6.4
2015	LAN	MLB	21	250	25	12	1	8	30	13	69	1	0	.240/.281/.397	.256	.302	-0.3	SS -2, 3B -0	0.7
2016	LAN	MLB	22	250	29	12	1	7	28	17	66	1	0	.245/.299/.397	.259	.309	-0.4	SS -3, 3B 0	1.5

Breakout: 4% **Improve:** 13% **Collapse:** 7% **Attrition:** 11% **MLB:** 29% **Upside:** 44 *Comparables: Reid Brignac, Xander Bogaerts, Joel Guzman*

Drafted/Acquired: 1st round, 2012 draft, Northwest Cabarrus HS (Concord, NC)

Previous Ranking: #2 (Org), #44 (Top 101)

What Happened in 2014: Seager served as a beautifully destructive offensive force for High Rancho Cucamonga and Double-A Chattanooga while holding his own on the defensive front as an oversized six-spotter, emerging as one of the game's elite prospect talents.

Strengths: Excellent strength; fluid and functional swing that produces line drives to all fields; steady hands through launch and steady head throughout swing; proficient tracker; solid plate coverage, including improved coverage on the inner half and high level of comfort hitting across the quadrants; easy, natural lift; increasingly produces backspin and carry; hands and arm play well on the dirt; has shown ability to make most out of limited range; if shifted to third, has the makings of a plus defender.

Weaknesses: Still learning to temper over-aggression, particularly early in count; lower half can get clunky and stiff in the field; defense unlikely to surpass fringe-average at shortstop; highly likely to settle in to below-average straight-line speed at maturity.

Risk Factor/Injury History: Low; successful in extended Double-A debut and developmental trajectory pointing up across the board.

Craig Goldstein's Fantasy Take: There is always risk in prospects, especially ones who have the potential to slide down the defensive spectrum. Seager is a special case, though, having experienced upper-minors success at a young age, and receiving near-universal praise for his bat. He might slide to third base down the line, but the state of that position isn't so glamorous in fantasy circles that it would significantly dent his value. He should contribute to the four major categories as a future middle-of-the-order hitter and will sprinkle in a steal here or there.

The Year Ahead: Seager entered 2014 ranked by Baseball Prospectus as the 44th best prospect in the game and by midseason had climbed to 19th. The former first rounder has solidified a spot among the elite position prospects in the game, thanks to a 2014 season that provided evaluators almost everything they could have asked for, from gaudy offensive production across two levels to improved plate coverage and strength to enough in the way of defensive chops to keep the door open to his logging major-league innings at the six-spot. All of this came with Seager turning just 20 years old last April, and there is still additional physicality yet to manifest in the Tar Heel Stater's projectable and athletic build. Seager falls shy of a true five-tool threat, but the bat, power, and arm could all mature to plus, and were he to shift to the hot corner his glove could bring the plus tool tally to four. Seager is near major-league ready, though there is not a present pressing need for his services in Los Angeles. He possesses the feel and maturity to make an impact upon arrival, and the potential to emerge as one of the game's elite overall talents.

> **#7**
> BP Top 101 Prospects

2. Julio Urias LHP

Born: 8/12/96 **Age:** 18 **Bats:** L **Throws:** L **Height:** 5'11" **Weight:** 160

MLB ETA	CT	FB	CH	CB	SL		OFP	Realistic
2016	**–**	**65**	**60**	**60**	**–**		**75** NO. 1/2 STARTER	**60** NO. 3 STARTER

YEAR	TEAM	LVL	AGE	W	L	SV	G	GS	IP	H	HR	BB	K	BB9	SO9	GB%	BABIP	WHIP	ERA	FIP	FRA	WARP
2014	RCU	A+	17	2	2	0	25	20	87.7	60	4	37	109	3.8	11.2	46%	.314	1.11	2.36	3.35	3.73	1.6
2015	LAN	MLB	18	3	4	0	16	14	56.7	50	6	23	55	3.7	8.7	46%	.309	1.27	3.78	4.10	4.11	0.5
2016	LAN	MLB	19	7	7	0	38	29	212.3	171	19	58	217	2.5	9.2	46%	.298	1.08	2.99	3.13	3.25	3.2

Breakout: 0% **Improve:** 0% **Collapse:** 0% **Attrition:** 0% **MLB:** 0% **Upside:** 43 *Comparables: Taijuan Walker, Madison Bumgarner, Jordan Lyles*

Drafted/Acquired: International Free Agent, 2012, Mexico

Previous Ranking: #1 (Org), #35 (Top 101)

What Happened in 2014: Neither a bump in level nor a 33-inning jump in workload could sidetrack the teenage pitching savant, who completed a full year of impressive work in the High-A California League, with all but four of his appearances coming at the age of 17.

Strengths: Advanced feel and pitchability; three-way fastball can run, sink, and cut across low-90s velocity band, reaching mid-90s; curveball plays average or better at present from upper-70s to and through low-80s, with a slider-like variation that can reach 83-84 mph without losing depth; chance to parse into two distinct breaking balls with continued refinement, each of which could grade out as above average to plus; low-80s changeup with arm-speed deception and abrupt fade down in the zone; mechanics work free and easy; creates solid angles through three-quarters release and solid posture; appears taller than listed 5-foot-11.

Weaknesses: Command and control can loosen with fastball at upper velocities; changeup comes and goes, sits flat and hittable up in the zone; can get predictable with runners on, relying on variations of fastball or breaking ball rather than full utilization of arsenal; still refining execution across arsenal; command lags behind control; body lacks projection and could become high maintenance based on present physique and body type; maintains stuff well but has yet to be tested by heavier workload.

Risk Factor/Injury History: Moderate; yet to reach Double-A; needs to reproduce current effectiveness while more than doubling innings load to play as major-league starter.

Craig Goldstein's Fantasy Take: While there's argument over whether Urias could be an ace at the major-league level, he's talented enough to carry a fantasy rotation no matter what the designation. It might take some time for him to carry a full season's workload, but he's got an arsenal designed to miss bats, with the potential to be a strikeout-per-inning guy. He's presently walking more guys than preferable, but at only 18 years old, he has time to fine-tune his control.

The Year Ahead: Urias presents an interesting case study for evaluators, as the stuff, approach, and maturity all belie his age and experience, and have allowed for an aggressive set of assignments through his first two seasons. Add to that the fact that the Dodgers have been appropriately conservative in scheduling the workload for the uniquely talented lefty, and you are left with the profile of a dominant teenage arm with the stuff and the results to warrant additional promotion, but lacking the established durability to quell concerns about overuse or botched developmental refinement, and the dangers of potential long-term negative impacts resulting therefrom. It's possible Urias could handle major-league bats as early as 2015, and it would not be a shock to see him in Dodger Blue this season, particularly later in the year as part of a playoff push. For now, Los Angeles is not lacking in quality arms, and the current regime has historically taken a fairly conservative approach to building innings and deliberately checking off developmental boxes when it comes to young pitching. However Urias is implemented in 2015, there is little doubt that he will be a part of the Dodgers' plans in the near future and could quickly establish himself as a foundational talent.

#10
BP Top 101 Prospects

3. Joc Pederson CF

Born: 4/21/92 **Age:** 23 **Bats:** L **Throws:** L **Height:** 6'1" **Weight:** 185

MLB ETA	Hit	Power	Run	Glove	Arm	OFP	Realistic
Debuted in 2014	55	60	55	55	55	65 1ST DIV/ALL STAR	55 >AVG REGULAR

YEAR	TEAM	LVL	AGE	PA	R	2B	3B	HR	RBI	BB	SO	SB	CS	AVG/OBP/SLG	TAv	BABIP	BRR	FRAA	WARP
2014	LAN	MLB	22	38	1	0	0	0	0	9	11	0	0	.143/.351/.143	.210	.235	-0.4	CF(7): 0.0, RF(5): -0.0	0.0
2014	ABQ	AAA	22	553	106	17	4	33	78	100	149	30	13	.303/.435/.582	.325	.385	3.7	CF(99): -0.4, LF(12): -0.5	5.9
2015	LAN	MLB	23	250	38	9	1	10	29	29	68	10	3	.244/.336/.433	.289	.302	0.4	CF -1, LF 0	1.4
2016	LAN	MLB	24	607	76	23	2	20	72	64	171	22	8	.234/.318/.397	.268	.301	2.1	CF -3	2.1

Breakout: 2% Improve: 23% Collapse: 6% Attrition: 17% MLB: 63% Upside: 93 *Comparables: Brett Jackson, Michael Choice, Brandon Belt*

Drafted/Acquired: 11th round, 2010 draft, Palo Alto HS (Palo Alto, CA)

Previous Ranking: #3 (Org), #50 (Top 101)

What Happened in 2014: Pederson produced the PCL's first 30 home-run/30 stolen-base season in over 80 years while continuing to display potential for five above-average tools, earning a September cup of coffee with the big club.

Strengths: Well-rounded, above-average athlete with baseball skill set to match; plus bat speed, balance, and strong feel for zone could allow hit tool to play above average despite some coverage holes; comfortable working deep into count; improved approach against same-side arms; forces pitchers to beat him with quality offerings; chance for above-average leather up the middle; covers ground; arm strength and accuracy should produce kills and holds; shows feel on the bases to go with foot speed; should be an asset in all facets of the game.

Weaknesses: May lack impact tool if swing-and-miss eats into playable power; natural bat-to-ball, but doesn't always find the barrel, particularly swinging from the heels; can be tripped up by sequencing and is at times slow to adjust to being pitched backward; solid feel in center, but reads need improvement for glove to reach potential; may ultimately fit best in an outfield corner (arm for right).

#18
BP Top 101 Prospects

Risk Factor/Injury History: Low; received call-up and showed very well in full season at Triple-A.

Craig Goldstein's Fantasy Take: While his 30/30 campaign in Triple-A might be a bit misleading thanks to the inflated offensive environment of the PCL, Pederson could well be fantasy gold. He's a potential five-category contributor, and whether his defensive prowess holds up in center is of less of a concern to fantasy owners. There's the potential for big volatility in his batting average, but he has the ability to be a 20/20 guy in relatively short order given a full slate of at-bats.

The Year Ahead: Pederson is ready to take his well-rounded game to The Show after proving there is little left for him to work on at the minor-league level. The Palo Alto prep product has blossomed into a dynamic talent, capable of affecting the game in all areas; he just has to continue his refinement at the major-league level to establish a foothold as a steady, everyday contributor. Pederson's strikeout rates continue to float at a level higher than one would expect from a fairly sound and balanced swing, not to mention an advanced feel for the strike zone, though evaluators point to his improvement against same-side arms in 2014 as evidence of his ability to adjust and are generally comfortable with the extra swing-and-miss as part of his offensive profile, so long as the power production continues. It was a good year for the system's top two positional prospects, with Seager and Pederson each poised to offer significant production at pre-arbitration prices in the coming years, and giving the deep-pocketed Dodgers flexibility to place their financial focus on other aspects of the 25-man roster.

---

4. Grant Holmes   RHP

Born: 3/22/96   **Age:** 19   **Bats:** L   **Throws:** R   **Height:** 6'1"   **Weight:** 215

MLB ETA	CT	FB	CH	CB	SL	OFP	Realistic
2018	–	70	60	65	–	70 NO. 2 STARTER	55 CLOSER

YEAR	TEAM	LVL	AGE	W	L	SV	G	GS	IP	H	HR	BB	K	BB9	SO9	GB%	BABIP	WHIP	ERA	FIP	FRA	WARP
2014	DOD	Rk	18	1	2	0	7	6	30.0	20	2	7	33	2.1	9.9	69%	.276	0.90	3.00	3.60	4.99	0.1
2014	OGD	Rk	18	1	1	0	4	4	18.3	19	1	6	25	2.9	12.3	74%	.400	1.36	4.91	3.16	4.94	0.5
2015	LAN	MLB	19	2	3	0	7	7	34.7	37	4	19	22	4.9	5.7	51%	.316	1.61	5.47	5.37	5.95	-0.5
2016	LAN	MLB	20	9	10	0	31	31	199.7	185	21	78	150	3.5	6.8	51%	.294	1.32	4.12	4.25	4.47	-0.3

Breakout: 0%   Improve: 0%   Collapse: 0%   Attrition: 0%   MLB: 0%   Upside: 1   *Comparables: Edwin Escobar, Jonathan Pettibone, Jenrry Mejia*

Drafted/Acquired: 1st round, 2014 draft, Conway HS (Conway, SC)

Previous Ranking: NR

What Happened in 2014: The former Florida commit impressed on the showcase circuit and throughout the spring, coming off the board as the 22nd overall selection in the June draft; he then proceeded to light up radar guns with his heater and drop jaws with his hammer in his professional debut.

#79

BP Top 101 Prospects

Strengths: Big, strong, durable build; prototypical power stuff, headlined by plus or better fastball/curveball combo; fastball will kiss the upper-90s while working comfortably 93-95 mph, showing quality life; power curve draws wobbly knees and empty swings alike, operating low- to mid-80s; feel for a changeup and has flashed ability to turn over plus-level offering with arm-speed deception and fade; can hold velocity to and through 75 pitches; aggressive demeanor; solid control profile at present, and command could improve to above average at maturity; repeats well.

Weaknesses: Body lacks projection; growth in stuff will likely be reliant upon improved tightening of physique and flexibility, adding to ability to execute with more precision; changeup still work in progress; fastball/curve too advanced for low-level bats, so will have to place purposeful developmental focus on off-speed; high-effort delivery; stuff saw downtick in power and effectiveness at end of long showcase circuit before returning in the fall and spring; yet to be tested on shorter rest and over long haul of full pro season.

Risk Factor/Injury History: High; limited pro exposure.

Craig Goldstein's Fantasy Take: As with Urias, no matter where Holmes slots in the rotation for you, be it a mid-rotation arm or higher, he'll play up in fantasy thanks to dynamic stuff and the ability to chew innings. There's not a ton of growth left thanks to his barrel-chested frame, but he could burn through the lower minors quickly, providing immediate name value and the chance to sell high early. This is a first-round talent in dynasty drafts and arguably the top prep arm on the board if you're too impatient for Tyler Kolek.

The Year Ahead: Holmes was arguably the best overall prep power arm in the 2014 draft class, considering the quality of his top two offerings and a lengthy track record that displayed an ability to replicate those offerings over multiple innings from appearance to appearance. The body is not projectable, and he is a bit undersized compared to your prototypical hard thrower, but the profile doesn't require much in the way of projection to reach the requisite level to provide major-league value. Even assuming health, because of the effort in the delivery, the untested ability to maintain effectiveness over the course of a full pro season, and the still-developing third pitch, there is a risk that the arm tops out as a high-end relief option. Leading up to and during his pro debut, however, the South Carolina native repeatedly showed an ability to effectively wield two, and at times three, above-average offerings with feel and control, and stands as one of the leading candidates to make a jump into the top tier of minor-league arms with a strong full-season debut.

5. Zach Lee   RHP

Born: 9/13/91   **Age:** 23   **Bats:** R   **Throws:** R   **Height:** 6'3"   **Weight:** 195

MLB ETA	CT	FB	CH	CB	SL	OFP	Realistic
2015	–	55	55	50	50	55 NO. 3/4 STARTER	50 NO. 4 STARTER

YEAR	TEAM	LVL	AGE	W	L	SV	G	GS	IP	H	HR	BB	K	BB9	SO9	GB%	BABIP	WHIP	ERA	FIP	FRA	WARP
2014	ABQ	AAA	22	7	13	0	28	27	150.7	177	18	54	97	3.2	5.8	52%	.323	1.53	5.38	5.16	5.91	1.9
2015	LAN	MLB	23	7	9	0	26	26	133.3	136	17	38	92	2.6	6.2	47%	.308	1.30	4.51	4.58	4.90	-0.4
2016	LAN	MLB	24	11	10	0	32	32	209.0	202	22	45	165	1.9	7.1	47%	.309	1.18	3.77	3.63	4.10	0.6

Breakout: 0%   Improve: 0%   Collapse: 0%   Attrition: 0%   MLB: 0%   Upside: 10   *Comparables: Brett Oberholtzer, Kyle Lobstein, Anthony Swarzak*

Drafted/Acquired: 1st round, 2010 draft, McKinney HS (McKinney, TX)

Previous Ranking: #4 (Org), #84 (Top 101)

What Happened in 2014: Lee advanced to Triple-A in 2014, logging 150 innings and continuing to show solid feel for four offerings, with the reports outdistancing the less-than-impressive production.

Strengths: Strong and athletic build; mechanics facilitate uniform release across arsenal; repeats well; fastball sits low-90s and can reach back for more when elevating ahead in the count; changeup flashes above average with solid deception and dive; slider serves as most dependable breaking ball, with solid shape and ability to throw to both sides of the plate; generally capable of working in the zone at will with all four offerings.

Weaknesses: Repertoire lacks impact; needs changeup to take consistent step forward to keep top-tier bats off fastball/slider; curve can get loopy and may be limited to occasional change-of-pace offering at highest level; while comfortable dropping all four pitches into the zone for strikes, command is generally loose and can get in trouble over the heart of the plate; slider may be more effective missing barrels than drawing swings and misses without quality changeup as a staple disrupting timing; can get more deliberate in his execution from the stretch, occasionally tipping pitches.

Risk Factor/Injury History: Low; reached upper levels and possesses feel and versatile arsenal to carve out major-league role.

Craig Goldstein's Fantasy Take: With a likely role as a back-end starter and a lack of a true bat-missing offering, Lee can safely be ignored in standard or shallow leagues outside of a streaming option once he does crack the majors. In deeper leagues he's a fine SP6 or so, but the upside isn't there to invest with any vigor.

The Year Ahead: When the Dodgers drafted Lee in 2010 and dropped a $5.25 million signing bonus on the two-sport LSU commit, the expectation was that the Dodgers were buying an elite talent to be molded into a front-end fixture in the LA rotation. Those expectations have softened as the Texan has traversed the minor-league developmental landscape, with the athletic righty now profiling more as a solid back-end option with enough feel and developmental room remaining to reach number three upside, which in and of itself would be a success on the acquisition and developmental front. Lee did not look overmatched at Triple-A, but likewise did not stand out, taking the ball each time out and showing the makings of a solid future major-league contributor but little in the way of impact. He struggled to handle same-side bats, in large part due to an inability to produce a consistent putaway breaking ball, and while there is some feel for sequencing, the command and consistency are not yet there for his average stuff to regularly dismantle more advanced sticks. He should return to the PCL to start 2015 where a continued focus will be placed on finding more precision within the zone and more consistency in effectively setting up and implementing his slider and changeup. A 2015 major-league debut is likely, and provided he continues to fine-tune his game, Lee should be in line to compete for a rotation spot no later than 2016.

6. Chris Anderson   RHP

Born: 7/29/92   **Age:** 22   **Bats:** R   **Throws:** R   **Height:** 6'4"   **Weight:** 215

MLB ETA	CT	FB	CH	CB	SL	OFP	Realistic
2016	–	60	60	–	60	55 NO. 3/4 STARTER	50 NO. 4 STARTER

YEAR	TEAM	LVL	AGE	W	L	SV	G	GS	IP	H	HR	BB	K	BB9	SO9	GB%	BABIP	WHIP	ERA	FIP	FRA	WARP
2014	RCU	A+	21	7	7	0	27	25	134.3	147	11	63	146	4.2	9.8	45%	.370	1.56	4.62	4.26	4.95	1.7
2015	LAN	MLB	22	5	7	0	19	19	88.0	87	9	42	71	4.3	7.3	41%	.322	1.46	4.66	4.65	5.06	-0.4
2016	LAN	MLB	23	9	9	0	32	32	203.3	173	17	79	176	3.5	7.8	41%	.295	1.24	3.52	3.75	3.83	1.3

Breakout: 0%   Improve: 0%   Collapse: 0%   Attrition: 0%   MLB: 0%   Upside: 12   *Comparables: Jeurys Familia, Anthony Ranaudo, Dan Cortes*

Drafted/Acquired: 1st round, 2013 draft, Jacksonville University (Jacksonville, FL)

Previous Ranking: #5 (Org)

What Happened in 2014: The 2013 first rounder overcame early-season struggles with control and execution to lead the California League in strikeouts (146) while routinely working five or more innings in his first full professional season.

Strengths: Looks the part of a big and durable innings-eater; creates good plane on fastball and leverages size to create tough angles; low-90s fastball can reach 94-95 mph and comes with heft; tilted slider will flash plus and can be legit swing-and-miss offering with solid depth and bite; changeup will play above average down in the zone with fading action on trajectory parallel to fastball; desire and ability to reach back for something extra when situation calls to put someone away.

Weaknesses: Overall approach and mentality in 2014 seemed defined by desire to try and overpower hitters; needs to improve ability to maneuver around challenges rather than trying to throw through them; arsenal is impactful at highest setting, but comes with erratic control (league-leading strikeout tally came hand in hand with league's third highest walk totals); durability and breadth of weaponry to hang as a starter long term, but stuff could play down some as he learns to rein in and execute pitches with more precision.

Risk Factor/Injury History: Low; size/strength and quality of arsenal will play in some capacity at major league level.

Craig Goldstein's Fantasy Take: Getting Anderson out of the California League will be the first step toward figuring out his ultimate role. While he didn't have any trouble missing bats and has the frame to log plenty of innings, there are still rumors of a future role in the bullpen. Anderson has the stuff to post SP3 numbers, but there's enough risk here that he's more appropriately valued as an SP4/5 going forward.

The Year Ahead: The Dodgers took it easy with Anderson in 2014, affording the former Jacksonville Friday night ace a full season in one locale, where he showed equal parts dominance and ineffectiveness. The impact nature of the stuff is undeniable, but it is still an open question as to whether the potential workhorse can keep a handle on the high-octane stuff while mashing the pedal firmly to the floor. Los Angeles is not without options in the rotation, so there is time to continue to take things slow with Anderson to allow him the opportunity to figure out the ebb and flow of pacing, both throughout the course of a start and over the span of the season. There's mid-rotation upside here, with a fairly high floor as a durable number four starter whose start-to-start production may very well be tied directly to his volatile strike-throwing ability on any given day.

7. Jose De Leon RHP

Born: 8/7/92   **Age:** 22   **Bats:** R   **Throws:** R   **Height:** 6'2"   **Weight:** 185

MLB ETA	CT	FB	CH	CB	SL	OFP	Realistic
2018	–	65	50	–	55	60 NO. 3 STARTER	50 LATE INN RP

YEAR	TEAM	LVL	AGE	W	L	SV	G	GS	IP	H	HR	BB	K	BB9	SO9	GB%	BABIP	WHIP	ERA	FIP	FRA	WARP
2014	GRL	A	21	2	0	0	4	4	22.7	14	1	2	42	0.8	16.7	31%	.317	0.71	1.19	0.62	1.12	1.2
2014	OGD	Rk	21	5	0	0	10	8	54.3	44	2	19	77	3.1	12.8	51%	.333	1.16	2.65	2.95	3.88	1.6
2015	LAN	MLB	22	3	4	0	13	13	62.7	59	7	29	60	4.2	8.6	44%	.321	1.41	4.41	4.43	4.80	-0.1
2016	LAN	MLB	23	8	9	0	30	30	184.7	164	20	84	182	4.1	8.9	44%	.309	1.34	4.22	4.07	4.59	-0.5

Breakout: 0%   Improve: 0%   Collapse: 0%   Attrition: 0%   MLB: 0%   Upside: 16   *Comparables: Michael Stutes, Tony Cingrani, Clay Buchholz*

Drafted/Acquired: 24th round, 2013 draft, Southern University and A&M College (Baton Rouge, LA)

Previous Ranking: NR

What Happened in 2014: The former 24th rounder took a nice developmental step forward, parlaying improved consistency with his slider and a mid-90s velocity bump into 77 whiff-laden, low-minors innings while posting a quality aggregate walk rate of 2.5 walks per nine.

Strengths: Fastball is plus offering at present and could mature a half grade higher with continued command refinement; will sit 92-94 mph and can touch 96-97; improved comfort working in/out; low-80s slider has gained consistency in shape and bite; changeup lags but foundation there for a third future average or better offering; soft body has firmed some; ability to maintain velocity through middle innings; herky-jerky deception; ball comes out quickly and jumps on hitters.

Weaknesses: Body still soft; will need to stay on top of conditioning; showed well deeper in games but yet to be tested over course of full season; changeup not yet a dependable third offering; fastball overpowered low-level hitters but will need to demonstrate more sophistication in pitch implementation as competition improves; can get formulaic in mixing fastball/slider.

Risk Factor/Injury History: High; yet to reach High-A.

Craig Goldstein's Fantasy Take: There's a ton of risk involved in a guy who has only thrown 22 2/3 innings of full-season ball, but De Leon might be a guy to target toward the back end of dynasty drafts. The mostly anonymous hurler struck out 49 percent of the batters he faced in Low-A (small sample size warning) and walked just over two percent. He is old for the level, but has the stuff and control to warrant a closer look, and could see his stock explode if he returns to Low-A to start 2015.

The Year Ahead: With an improved slider and developing feel with the fastball, De Leon took two important developmental steps in 2014, looking much more the part of a potential big-league starter while retaining a comforting safety net as a late-inning power arm. The bulky righty is now regularly filling up the strike zone with a plus heater, and the emergence of a solid breaking ball in the form of a slider gives De Leon the requisite one-two punch to solidify some foundational value; more importantly, it gives him ample firepower to work through low-level lineups as he continues to log reps and work to improve his off-speed and overall command. This season should serve as a solid indicator as to where De Leon currently sits on his developmental journey, testing his ability to both maintain his stuff over a longer haul and implement it effectively against more disciplined lineups. If it all comes together the result could be a plus-command, mid-rotation arm leaning heavily on an impact fastball.

8. Darnell Sweeney 2B

Born: 2/1/91   **Age:** 24   **Bats:** B   **Throws:** R   **Height:** 6'1"   **Weight:** 180

MLB ETA	Hit	Power	Run	Glove	Arm	OFP	Realistic
2015	–	–	60	50	50	55 >AVG REGULAR	45 UTILITY OPTION

YEAR	TEAM	LVL	AGE	PA	R	2B	3B	HR	RBI	BB	SO	SB	CS	AVG/OBP/SLG	TAv	BABIP	BRR	FRAA	WARP
2014	CHT	AA	23	586	88	34	5	14	57	77	117	15	16	.288/.387/.463	.297	.350	3.2	2B(81): -1.1, SS(28): -4.1	3.6
2015	LAN	MLB	24	250	29	10	2	4	20	18	68	7	4	.228/.286/.346	.238	.296	-0.1	SS -4, 2B 0	0.0
2016	LAN	MLB	25	250	26	10	2	5	25	19	70	7	4	.221/.283/.354	.233	.286	0.4	SS -4, 2B 0	-0.2

Breakout: 2%   Improve: 6%   Collapse: 3%   Attrition: 13%   MLB: 18%   Upside: 12   *Comparables: Ryan Flaherty, Kevin Melillo, Ryan Adams*

Drafted/Acquired: 13th round, 2012 draft, University of Central Florida (Orlando, FL)

Previous Ranking: NR

What Happened in 2014: The then-23-year-old put together a strong showing with Double-A Chattanooga, demonstrating an advanced feel for contact, on-base ability, and a workable glove at all three up-the-middle positions.

Strengths: Athletic build and actions; good balance at plate; rotates well through core and generates solid bat speed, natural loft from left side, resulting in surprising pop; right-side swing geared more to contact with flatter plane and earlier extension; can put together professional at-bats; willing to take a walk; plus speed should allow for increased on-base production; decent lines on the bases allow speed to play up in grabbing extra bases; glove works up the middle; chance to fill super-utility role as a capable shortstop, second baseman, and center fielder.

Weaknesses: Outfield feel lags well behind actions on the dirt; lacks feel on the bases; poor reads and jumps off pitchers; makes too many outs attempting steals, negatively impacting value as pinch-run option; hit and power could both max out as fringe-average; will fall into ruts where he tries too hard to drive the ball, resulting in empty swings and zone expansion; can be led out of zone with competent sequencing.

Risk Factor/Injury History: Low; achieved Double-A success; versatile skill set should find a major-league role.

Craig Goldstein's Fantasy Take: While he generates good pop for the position, Sweeney's defensive issues make him more of an offense-first backup and thus lacking in fantasy value. He's not someone to roster outside of extremely deep leagues with minor-league depth. If he's starting for a major-league team it's likely that something has gone wrong, but he'd still be worth rostering were that the case.

The Year Ahead: The ceiling is limited for the UCF product, but there is much value to be realized in a cost-controlled, versatile, up-the-middle asset with some feel for contact and enough pop to keep pitchers from pounding the middle of the zone. If Sweeney can tame some of his aggressive tendencies that lead him to give away at-bats via swing-and-miss there is an opportunity for him to develop into an above-average option at the keystone. He isn't quite steady enough at short to profile well there in an everyday capacity, but his ability to handle the position with limited exposure improves his stock, as does his ability to handle himself in center if needed. He should make the jump to Triple-A in 2015 and is close to being ready to contribute to the big club. As his game continues to grow across the board, so too grow the odds of Sweeney carving out a long-term niche for himself at Chavez Ravine.

9. Alex Verdugo OF

Born: 5/15/96   **Age:** 19   **Bats:** L   **Throws:** L   **Height:** 6'0"   **Weight:** 200

MLB ETA	Hit	Power	Run	Glove	Arm	OFP	Realistic
2018	55	55	50	50	60	60 1ST DIVISION PLAYER	40 4TH OF/<AVG REG

YEAR	TEAM	LVL	AGE	PA	R	2B	3B	HR	RBI	BB	SO	SB	CS	AVG/OBP/SLG	TAv	BABIP	BRR	FRAA	WARP
2014	DOD	Rk	18	196	28	14	3	3	33	20	14	8	0	.347/.423/.518	.412	.361	1.3	CF(16): -0.1, LF(2): 0.1	1.7
2014	OGD	Rk	18	20	3	1	0	0	8	0	4	3	0	.400/.400/.450	.288	.500	-0.3	RF(2): -0.2, CF(1): -0.1	0.1
2015	LAN	MLB	19	250	18	9	1	3	20	8	69	2	0	.204/.234/.280	.199	.270	0.0	CF -1, LF 0	-1.0
2016	LAN	MLB	20	250	23	10	1	4	22	10	63	2	0	.222/.258/.326	.219	.283	0.1	CF -1, LF 0	-1.1

Breakout: 0%   Improve: 0%   Collapse: 0%   Attrition: 0%   MLB: 0%   Upside: 50   *Comparables: Oscar Taveras, Che-Hsuan Lin, Joe Benson*

Drafted/Acquired: 2nd round, 2014 draft, Sahuaro HS (Tuscon, AZ)

Previous Ranking: NR

What Happened in 2014: After an inconsistent spring on the bump, at the plate, and in the field, Verdugo came off the board to Los Angeles in the second round of the June draft and proceeded to square up everything he saw in 54 games between the Arizona Rookie League and short-season Ogden, slashing a combined .353/.421/.511 over both stops.

Strengths: Gets the barrel to the ball consistently; plus raw power to pull, with strength and swing to drive the ball oppo; hard contact plays well to the gaps and could produce 20-plus home runs annually at maturity; in pro debut greatly improved discipline and implemented selectively aggressive approach with aplomb; moves well enough to cover the requisite ground in center at present, but may project best in right field, where plus arm would be an asset and overall defensive package could play to plus; good jumps and reads on the grass and on the bases.

Weaknesses: Has shown tendency to get frustrated on field; will let mental slipups snowball; agitation will carry over in game and can impact performance, including abandoning of approach at the plate; will need to demonstrate mental fortitude to work through struggles when they come; in the field, better coming in on the ball than ranging back to either side; as body matures, foot speed to slip to below average.

Risk Factor/Injury History: High; short-season résumé.

Craig Goldstein's Fantasy Take: Power will be the key determinant as to whether Verdugo can secure a role as an everyday player, and thus fantasy value, or be relegated to fourth-outfielder status. He's a worthy flier after the middle rounds in dynasty drafts, as there's a chance you'll get a solid five-category contributor, but expectations should be light on the power front, and thus realistic regarding his future playing time.

The Year Ahead: To say Verdugo's pro debut came as a surprise would be an understatement. The Arizona native has always been known to evaluators as a talented two-way player, but his performance through the spring leading up to the draft was peppered with inconsistencies and at times sloppy and borderline disinterested play. While reports will still note some questions as to makeup and on-field demeanor, Verdugo handled his in-game business through his first 216 professional plate appearances, and has taken a step toward winning the LA decision-makers over a as a future position player (at the time of the draft there were rampant rumors that the Dodgers would allow Verdugo to begin his career in the field to induce his signing, but that his ultimate developmental track was most likely to come on the mound). There is still a lot of work to be done before Verdugo steps onto to the field at Dodger Stadium for his first major-league game, but the early returns have been encouraging. He should make the jump to Low-A Great Lakes for the 2015 season, and a similarly loud showing could see the 2014 second rounder jump up the rankings, both organizationally and nationally, next year.

---

10. Scott Schebler OF

Born: 10/6/90 **Age:** 24 **Bats:** L **Throws:** R **Height:** 6'1" **Weight:** 208

MLB ETA		Hit	Power	Run	Glove	Arm		OFP	Realistic
2015		50	55	–	–	–		50 AVG ML PLAYER	45 <AVG REGULAR

YEAR	TEAM	LVL	AGE	PA	R	2B	3B	HR	RBI	BB	SO	SB	CS	AVG/OBP/SLG	TAv	BABIP	BRR	FRAA	WARP
2014	CHT	AA	23	560	82	23	14	28	73	45	110	10	4	.280/.365/.556	.312	.308	0.8	LF(87): 1.2, RF(45): -2.5	4.5
2015	LAN	MLB	24	250	26	10	2	8	30	10	69	3	1	.229/.273/.399	.252	.283	0.2	LF -1, RF -1	0.1
2016	LAN	MLB	25	250	29	10	2	9	31	13	70	3	1	.238/.290/.417	.259	.298	0.3	LF -1, RF -1	1.2

Breakout: 0%   Improve: 14%   Collapse: 9%   Attrition: 15%   MLB: 35%   Upside: 24   *Comparables: Eric Thames, Corey Dickerson, Kyle Parker*

Drafted/Acquired: 26th round, 2010 draft, Des Moines Area Community College (Boone, IA)

Previous Ranking: NR

What Happened in 2014: Schebler continued to defy the scouting reports, displaying impactful power with Double-A Chattanooga, including a Southern League leading 28 home runs over 560 plate appearances, with almost half of his hits (65 of 137) going for extra bases.

Strengths: Powerful build and leveraged swing produce plus raw pop; bat speed to turn on inner half or let ball get deep away before uncorking; strength and feel for the barrel allow him to drive ball to all fields; has paired power production with improved command of the strike zone, growing on-base profile; tracks well out of lefty and righty arms alike; continues to improve approach and shows ability to make adjustments game to game and across multiple looks at pitchers over course of season; could play as useful number five or six bat on a first-division club; potential run producer.

Weaknesses: Value tied almost exclusively to the bat; below-average arm likely limits to left field long term; fringe-average straight-line speed that plays down due to jumps in the field and on the bases; liberal approach to contact limits hit utility, with hard and soft contact both coming regularly; aggressive nature can force to work behind in the count; can let bats get away from him once behind.

Risk Factor/Injury History: Low; profile close to maturity with Double-A success under his belt.

Craig Goldstein's Fantasy Take: If you could combine Schebler's power with Verdugo's hitting ability, you'd really have something. Not that Schebler is shabby in his own right. He's shown a surprising ability to hit for average the last few seasons, though that's still expected to be an issue at the major-league level. He does have real pop, though, and in another organization could be a useful platoon outfielder, if not more. Given LA's outfield depth, it's going to take a trade to give him near-term fantasy value.

The Year Ahead: Schebler has led his league in extra bases in each of the last two seasons, tallying 55 home runs over 260 games during that same span. It isn't a dynamic profile, but Schebler has enough feel for the stick and raw strength to continue to rack up extra bases as he completes his ascension to The Show. Because the former

26th rounder is unlikely to impact the game outside of his bat, there will be a lot of pressure on his reaching his full potential in that department. This year should see Schebler taking on Triple-A arms, and should an opportunity arise at an outfield corner in LA, Schebler could find his way to the big-league club sooner rather than later.

Prospects on the Rise

1. C Julian Leon: The Mexican catcher flashed his talents in the Pioneer League last season, demonstrating the ability to hit for average and power. Leon displays good bat speed along with ample strength, potentially developing into a solid all-around hitter at the plate. Defensively, Leon displays a fringe glove at present, and while he boasts a plus arm he will need to improve upon his footwork and transfer and release—challenges exacerbated by a thick lower half—to avoid seeing his catch-and-throw game play down. The overall value will be tied primarily to the progression of his defense, but the bat could make the profile and already looks to be on the right developmental track.

2. RHP A.J. Vanegas: An extensive injury history and a high-effort delivery dimmed the allure for some within the industry heading into the draft, but the over-slot Stanford graduate retains a solid ceiling, tooled with a fast arm and a high-powered heater that tops out at 97 mph, rounding out the arsenal with a quality slider and cutter. At its best, the slider shows bite and tilt, but it can become loose and fluctuate in its effectiveness. The cutter may be more accurately described as a short slider, coming with slightly more horizontal action. While the role is a pure relief profile, Vanegas has enough talent to potentially provide innings in the back end of a bullpen. Consistency gained in normalizing his arm path and release points will go a long way in helping to play up the deception of his fastball and slider.

3. RHP Kam Uter: The righty was a two-sport standout in high school (football) and now brings his full attention to developing on the mound. With a sturdy build and broad shoulders, Uter has the physicality to develop into a workhorse. His low-90s fastball has arm-side run, and he pairs this with a potentially above-average curveball that flashes good shape and bite. Uter's development has just begun, as he only threw in five games after being signed for $200,000 in the 12th round last season. While the main focus in development will be tied into repeating his mechanics and finding a comfort zone with his arm path, he has a loose and quick arm that can generate velocity and spin. This season will shed further light on the talents, and ultimate ceiling, of the Georgia native.

FROM THE FIELD

Julio Urias

Team: Los Angeles Dodgers

Evaluator: Chris Rodriguez

Dates seen: April 6 and May 10, 2014

Affiliate: Rancho Cucamonga Quakes (High-A, Dodgers)

OFP: 70

Realistic role: 60; no. 3 starter

Mechanics: Closer to 6'1" and definitely not 160 lbs.; closer to 180; medium sized frame; solid lower half and midsection; don't see it being a problem until he reaches his thirties; three-quarters slot; plus arm speed; looks easy; very repeatable; extends stride leg and lands soft; turns away from the batter like Felix Hernandez at times; can land stiff; struggles with release point from the stretch on occasion; pitches have good shape due to arm slot; solid move to first; picked a guy in the first game.

Pitch type	Present grade	Future grade	Sitting velocity	Peak velocity	Report
FB	60	70	91-95	96	Present plus pitch; features natural arm-side run; very tough to square down in the zone due to tough plane; can cut it as well; pumps up the velocity with runners on base; several 94s and 95s late in both games; mostly 92-93; loose command early in both games; some noticeable frustration on the mound; settled down and began hitting his spots; can move the pitch up and down, in and out; pitch can be plus-plus with better control and command.
CB	60	65	77-81	82	Advanced offering; thrown very easy/natural with the same arm speed, which gives it extra deception; two-plane break; very good manipulation of the pitch; can lengthen the horizontal break to make it a slider; most pitches had more vertical drop; varies shapes often; can drop it for strikes and for chase; thrown to both left- and right-handed hitters; command was solid; can throw it in any count; love the projection for this pitch.
CH	50	65	78-82	83	Flashes plus; already an average pitch due to good glove-side fade/sink and velocity difference; plays off his fastball very well; can slow delivery a little, which can tip the pitch; bat-missing offering; often went to this pitch to get back into counts; wouldn't count this pitch out to become plus-plus due to feel for the craft.

Overall: Urias is the uber rare combination of raw stuff, extremely young age, and pitchability. It's a package that doesn't come around often, and one that can be special with the right molding and coaching. Urias already has two plus pitches and one on the way, all with crispness and plus movement. The overall command is fringe at the moment, but the profile is there to at least be above-average (repeatable delivery, ability to add/subtract, athleticism). Arguably the most impressive thing about Urias is his feel for the craft at such a young age. Normally with a young pitcher you have high or even extreme risk, but Urias is a different animal. I believe he can make a contribution by 2016, with the innings limit coming off next season at Double-A. If he finds success and improves on his command the rest of this season and next, there's nothing else holding him back.

Factors on the Farm
Prospects likely to contribute at the major-league level in 2015

1. C/2B Austin Barnes: Acquired in a December 2014 deal with Miami, Barnes brings a flexible profile capable of filling a super-utility role at the highest level. Barnes displays capable defense behind the plate, but is likely not a full-time starter at the position. His quality footwork and hands help his defense play up at the keystone. While Barnes may not boast impact tools, his average hit tool, good approach, and grinder mentality allow for him to provide value in versatility. With time spent at Double-A, the 25-year-old is close to the majors and could see time this season as a depth piece.

2. RHP Yimi Garcia: The 6-foot-1 Dominican spent the majority of 2014 with Triple-A Albuquerque, while also receiving a cup of coffee with the big-league club, showing solid command and deception with his arsenal. Garcia has a pure relief profile, and possesses a heavy fastball and split change that some industry sources believe could induce groundballs at an efficient rate. Garcia's breaking ball plays best when it is short and sharp like a cutter, but he can loosen it at times to provide the look of a more natural slider. Overall, he has the ability to provide value in the bullpen for the Dodgers this season, especially if he can keep working down and reduce the number of pitches left flat and fat up in the zone.

3. LHP Chris Reed: The southpaw logged more than 150 innings for the first time in his professional career, and signs of fatigue cropped up toward the end of the season. Reed possesses a heavy low-90s fastball, which can be tough to lift and drive when down in the zone. His low-80s slider can be efficient at drawing empty swings and soft contact when showing tilt and crispness. Reed flashes more control than command currently, but both tend to slip the further he goes in an outing. While the durability and fatigue issues may push Reed into a relief role down the road, the change can play to average and there is still a glimmer of hope that he may stick in the back end of a rotation. Regardless, his heavy fastball and tight slider are potential weapons in the bullpen.

MIAMI MARLINS

1. Tyler Kolek   RHP

Born: 12/15/95   **Age:** 19   **Bats:** R   **Throws:** R   **Height:** 6'5"   **Weight:** 260

MLB ETA	CT	FB	CH	CB	SL	OFP	Realistic
Late 2018	–	80	50	–	65	**65** NO. 2/3 STARTER	**50** LATE INN RP (7TH/8TH)

YEAR	TEAM	LVL	AGE	W	L	SV	G	GS	IP	H	HR	BB	K	BB9	SO9	GB%	BABIP	WHIP	ERA	FIP	FRA	WARP
2014	MRL	Rk	18	0	3	0	9	8	22.0	22	0	13	18	5.3	7.4	55%	.250	1.59	4.50	3.91	7.11	-0.2
2015	MIA	MLB	19	1	2	0	8	6	33.3	39	3	20	16	5.4	4.3	46%	.323	1.75	6.02	5.52	6.54	-0.6
2016	MIA	MLB	20	3	5	0	25	16	131.0	131	12	67	85	4.6	5.8	46%	.306	1.51	4.84	4.70	5.26	-0.9

Breakout: 0%   Improve: 0%   Collapse: 0%   Attrition: 0%   MLB: 0%   Upside: 9   *Comparables: David Holmberg, Roman Mendez, Kelvin Herrera*

Drafted/Acquired: 1st round, 2014 draft, Shepherd HS (Shepherd, TX)

Previous Ranking: NR

What Happened in 2014: Kolek's big arm and potential led to his being selected with the second overall pick by Miami, and then the right-hander threw his first professional innings in the Gulf Coast League.

Strengths: Large frame; very well filled out for age; elite arm strength; fastball routinely works in high-90s; capable of hitting triple digits; uses size to create plane with heater; explosive offering; feel for spinning breaking ball; flashes power break; learning how to turn over change; raw ingredients to round into power arm near the front of a rotation; takes to instruction.

Weaknesses: Max-effort type; little present concept of pacing; definition of a thrower; fastball can tick down deeper into games; breaking ball will sweep and lose shape; not overly loose wrist; changeup in infancy stages; command and pitchability have a ways to go; secondary arsenal is all projection.

Risk Factor/Injury History: High risk; minimal professional experience; huge gap between present and future.

Bret Sayre's Fantasy Take: There is no one in the system with more sheer fantasy upside than Kolek. However, the risk is great, and while he's a great piece to hold (and likely a top-7 pick in dynasty drafts), he's still in the flier category.

The Year Ahead: Kolek's arm strength grades off the charts, and when the right-hander reaches back to deliver his fastball, the end result generates a buzz from everyone watching. A heater consistently popping in the high-90s and touching triple digits will have that effect. Combined with his size, the overall raw ingredients here have the potential to come together into something special. But after the aura of the velocity dissipates, the reality is that Kolek is presently at the starting line of a developmental marathon, especially when it comes to the secondary stuff. Both his breaking ball and change have big gaps to close, as do the 19-year-old's pitchability and approach to his craft. There are concerns about how the max-effort approach is going to play and what things are going to look like in the long run. A couple of external sources spoken to for this list wondered if a third pitch (changeup) logistically is going to emerge. There is no question this arm is legit, but there are more questions than answers on what the future looks like. The realistic role reflects the large gap and rawness in the overall game. How quickly that gap can close gets clearer when Kolek takes the mound in a likely full-season assignment to start 2015.

2. J.T. Realmuto   C

Born: 3/18/91   **Age:** 24   **Bats:** R   **Throws:** R   **Height:** 6'1"   **Weight:** 215

MLB ETA	Hit	Power	Run	Glove	Arm	OFP	Realistic
Debuted in 2014	55	50	–	55	55	**55** >AVG REGULAR	**50** AVG ML PLAYER

YEAR	TEAM	LVL	AGE	PA	R	2B	3B	HR	RBI	BB	SO	SB	CS	AVG/OBP/SLG	TAv	BABIP	BRR	FRAA	WARP
2014	MIA	MLB	23	30	4	1	1	0	9	1	8	0	0	.241/.267/.345	.227	.333	0.0	C(9): -0.2	0.0
2014	JAX	AA	23	423	66	25	6	8	62	41	59	18	5	.299/.369/.461	.308	.333	5.6	C(88): -1.3	4.8
2015	MIA	MLB	24	250	22	11	2	3	22	15	49	5	1	.238/.287/.336	.241	.286	0.4	C -0, 1B -0	0.5
2016	MIA	MLB	25	420	42	19	2	6	38	30	88	8	2	.230/.289/.338	.236	.280	0.8	C -1	0.4

Breakout: 7%   Improve: 11%   Collapse: 6%   Attrition: 16%   MLB: 30%   Upside: 14   *Comparables: Austin Romine, Curtis Casali, Tim Federowicz*

Drafted/Acquired: 3rd round, 2010 draft, Carl Albert HS (Midwest City, OK)

Previous Ranking: NR

What Happened in 2014: The backstop made some adjustments in Double-A, posting an 830 OPS, before a brief call to The Show.

Strengths: Well-filled-out frame; good strength; athletic—former middle infielder; solid-average bat speed; feel for getting the barrel on the ball; line-drive stroke; mature approach; willing to go deep into counts and wait for pitch; arm is an asset; can control running game; fluid with footwork when popping out of crouch; moves well behind the dish; has quickly picked up nuances of position; soaks up instruction.

Weaknesses: Approach can be pull heavy; needs more willingness to use opposite field against high-quality arms; must continue to show selectivity; power likely to play down in favor of contact; can be beat on inner third by velocity; overall catching skills still in refinement stages; struggles getting big with body at times; ball control and blocking suffer as a result.

Risk Factor/Injury History: Low risk; achieved major leagues; further development of catching skills.

Bret Sayre's Fantasy Take: Shallow leaguers with one catcher spot don't need to concern themselves with Realmuto, as his offensive potential at the plate is not projected to be much more than what is available on the waiver wires (think .265 and 12 homers). However, if the bad version of Miguel Montero was valuable in your league, then Realmuto can provide return on your investment.

The Year Ahead: Much to Realmuto's credit, he's turned himself into a legit defensive catcher after transitioning to the position only a few years ago. That speaks to his athleticism as a former middle infielder and also gives a look into the makeup of the player. The key strength behind the dish is the arm, which should be good enough to control opposing teams' running games. Realmuto could still stand to improve some with his receiving skills, but there's no reason to believe that forward progress has stopped. When bringing the bat into the equation, this is the profile of a regular. Success at the highest level relies on the contact-heavy swing, with the raw power likely to play down, but enough pop for 10-15 home runs and 25 or so doubles. If his approach improves and he develops the ability to go the other way, the overall body of work could play up to the potential role, but Realmuto most likely settles in as an average major leaguer, and one that can stick around for a while. He may have to bide his time in Triple-A for 2015 depending on how the Marlins choose to handle their catching situation, but it won't be long in the grand scheme of things before a chance to stick comes his way.

3. Trevor Williams   RHP

Born: 4/25/92   **Age:** 23   **Bats:** R   **Throws:** R   **Height:** 6'3"   **Weight:** 228

MLB ETA	CT	FB	CH	CB	SL	OFP	Realistic
Late 2015	–	60	50	50	55	55 NO. 3/4 STARTER	50 NO. 4 STARTER

YEAR	TEAM	LVL	AGE	W	L	SV	G	GS	IP	H	HR	BB	K	BB9	SO9	GB%	BABIP	WHIP	ERA	FIP	FRA	WARP
2014	JAX	AA	22	0	1	0	3	3	15.0	22	0	6	14	3.6	8.4	69%	.431	1.87	6.00	2.52	3.53	0.2
2014	JUP	A+	22	8	6	0	23	23	129.0	138	5	29	90	2.0	6.3	52%	.322	1.29	2.79	3.17	4.48	0.9
2015	MIA	MLB	23	6	7	0	23	23	107.7	119	9	36	64	3.0	5.3	50%	.326	1.44	4.65	4.34	5.05	-0.5
2016	MIA	MLB	24	9	10	0	31	31	196.7	205	15	63	140	2.9	6.4	50%	.325	1.36	4.26	3.72	4.63	-0.4

Breakout: 0%   Improve: 0%   Collapse: 0%   Attrition: 0%   MLB: 0%   Upside: 1   *Comparables: Brandon Workman, Adam Wilk, Robbie Ross*

Drafted/Acquired: 2nd round, 2013 draft, Arizona State University (Tempe, AZ)

Previous Ranking: #4 (Org)

What Happened in 2014: Williams handled the Florida State League as expected, fanning three batters for every one walked, and reached Double-A for a quick taste of the upper minors.

Strengths: Uses big frame to advantage; creates leverage to throw downhill; will mix fastball; throws low-90s two-seamer with heavy downward action; can reach back with four-seamer look at 94-95; capable of pounding zone with heater for strikes; changes shape of breaking ball; curveball action in mid-70s; slider look in low-80s; flashes feel for changeup; fades off table at same release angle as fastball; not afraid to work both sides of the plate and come after hitters.

Weaknesses: Not the loosest of deliveries; has some rigidness; tends to work around the plate often with repertoire; fastball will grab a lot of white; lacks true chase pitch; will need to mix and match secondary stuff to induce weak contact against high-caliber hitters; not much growth left for overall stuff.

Risk Factor/Injury History: Moderate risk; limited upper-minors experience; limited growth potential.

Bret Sayre's Fantasy Take: A much better prospect in deeper leagues than shallower ones, Williams does not project highly enough in the strikeout department to warrant getting too excited about in fantasy. However, with a good division and ballpark in his back pocket, he could max out as a slightly lesser Kyle Lohse.

The Year Ahead: Williams may not be the flashiest of arms or offer top-shelf stuff, but he has a mature arsenal and shows a strong aptitude for his craft. Everything flows off of the right-hander's 90-95 mph fastball, which he'll manipulate between a heavy two-seamer in the lower tier of the zone and four-seamer in the upper reaches of his velocity that he looks to elevate past bats. Williams flashes feel for his secondary stuff across the board, but they project more average to solid-average than plus. He'll need to be mindful of changing speeds and shapes as he continues to advance. The risk here is that the repertoire is stretched too thin in the upper levels when higher quality hitters potentially can wait the righty out deeper into counts or are not apt to chase his breaking stuff. Williams's mentality and approach offer some clues that he's capable of adjusting sequences accordingly. Look for the 23-year-old to get his first big test in Double-A to start the season, and if all goes well, there's a strong chance he can ride the wave to the majors at some point in 2015.

4. Jose Urena RHP

Born: 9/12/91 **Age:** 23 **Bats:** R **Throws:** R **Height:** 6'2" **Weight:** 195

MLB ETA	CT	FB	CH	CB	SL		OFP	Realistic
2015	–	70	65	–	50		60 NO. 3 STARTER	50 LATE INN RP (SETUP)

YEAR	TEAM	LVL	AGE	W	L	SV	G	GS	IP	H	HR	BB	K	BB9	SO9	GB%	BABIP	WHIP	ERA	FIP	FRA	WARP
2014	JAX	AA	22	13	8	0	26	25	162.0	155	14	29	121	1.6	6.7	48%	.290	1.14	3.33	3.39	4.73	0.7
2015	MIA	MLB	23	8	8	0	23	23	131.3	139	13	37	79	2.5	5.4	46%	.313	1.34	4.40	4.35	4.79	-0.4
2016	MIA	MLB	24	8	8	0	23	23	133.3	137	14	34	88	2.3	5.9	46%	.311	1.28	4.05	3.97	4.41	0.1

Breakout: 0% **Improve:** 0% **Collapse:** 0% **Attrition:** 0% **MLB:** 0% **Upside:** 2 *Comparables: Dallas Keuchel, Adam Wilk, Elih Villanueva*

Drafted/Acquired: International Free Agent, 2008, Dominican Republic
Previous Ranking: #6 (Org)

What Happened in 2014: Urena passed the Double-A test, making 25 starts and logging a sound 162 innings.

Strengths: Easy delivery; loose, fast arm; fastball operates 92-95 regularly; can reach back for more when needs it; creates good angle on hitters with heater; shows feel for changeup; throws with similar arm speed to fastball; flashes strong arm-side fade; slider has shown signs of tightening and improvement; capable of throwing for a strike; still filling into body; demonstrates strike-throwing ability.

Weaknesses: Stuff can play down deeper into games; will wear himself out with pace; slider has a tendency to roll; lacks sharp bite off the table; distant third in arsenal; command more of the area variety; needs improvement working through sequences; lacks strong feel of craft.

Risk Factor/Injury History: Low risk; 25 starts in Double-A; breaking ball progression.

Bret Sayre's Fantasy Take: The right-hander/bad-breaking-ball profile is not a good one, unless the change is just dynamic. There's closer potential if he's in the bullpen and moderate strikeout potential if the slider can take a step forward. I'd rather roll the dice on a high-upside short-season arm.

The Year Ahead: The clues point toward Urena ultimately ending up in the back of a bullpen, but the right-hander has continued to climb the ranks in a starting role, and is likely ready to take the next step to the highest level of the minors this season. The realistic view sees an arm with a fastball that can play to plus-plus in spurts, with a fading changeup and slider to help change the angle on batters. It's a profile that leans heavily on two pitches (fastball/change) and a third (slider) sprinkled in to keep hitters honest. That's usually best suited for one-inning blasts. If you really squint with Urena, and believe the slider and pitchability can progress moderately forward, a potential mid-rotation starter slowly comes into focus. The safe bet is that the 23-year-old ends up a late-innings reliever over the long haul. The breaking ball will need to get more bats moving early, but the pitch has a significant gap to close, putting pressure on the precision of the other two pitches against elite hitters when going multiple times through a lineup. Still, it wouldn't be wise to rule out Urena getting a chance to start until he proves otherwise, which could include some major-league action at some point in 2015 if all continues to go well in Triple-A.

5. Avery Romero 2B

Born: 5/11/93 **Age:** 22 **Bats:** R **Throws:** R **Height:** 5'8" **Weight:** 190

MLB ETA	Hit	Power	Run	Glove	Arm		OFP	Realistic
Late 2017	60	55	–	50	60		60 1ST DIVISION PLAYER	50 AVG ML PLAYER

YEAR	TEAM	LVL	AGE	PA	R	2B	3B	HR	RBI	BB	SO	SB	CS	AVG/OBP/SLG	TAv	BABIP	BRR	FRAA	WARP
2014	JUP	A+	21	108	12	8	0	0	10	7	13	4	1	.320/.370/.400	.285	.368	0.9	2B(16): 0.3, 3B(6): -0.5	0.7
2014	GRB	A	21	399	51	23	1	5	46	25	47	6	4	.320/.366/.429	.287	.354	-0.2	2B(77): -3.0	1.8
2015	MIA	MLB	22	250	18	11	1	1	19	11	51	1	1	.234/.272/.300	.223	.290	-0.4	2B -0, 3B -0	-0.3
2016	MIA	MLB	23	250	23	12	1	2	21	12	46	1	1	.245/.283/.329	.230	.291	-0.4	2B 0, 3B 0	-0.3

Breakout: 0% **Improve:** 0% **Collapse:** 0% **Attrition:** 0% **MLB:** 0% **Upside:** 34 *Comparables: Luis Valbuena, Daniel Descalso, Enrique Hernandez*

Drafted/Acquired: 3rd round, 2012 draft, Pedro Menendez HS (St. Augustine, FL)
Previous Ranking: NR

What Happened in 2014: The then-21-year-old more than held his own in the South Atlantic League, hitting .320 prior to his promotion to High-A, where he continued to flash similar contact ability.

Strengths: Strong body despite smaller frame; quick bat; loose hands that stay inside of the ball; flashes ability to barrel offerings with backspin; strength to tap into to produce more carry; some leverage in swing; flashes the foundation of an approach; arm for the left side of the diamond; asset at second base; excellent work ethic; strong makeup; possesses feel for the game.

Weaknesses: Hit tool more projection than present; needs work toning down at the plate; must develop better selectivity—likes to get aggressive with fastballs early; may ultimately end up too prone to secondary stuff; will have to find balance in swing when trying to tap into power; fringe-average present defensive reactions; can be stiff and clunky with footwork; bat carries profile.

Risk Factor/Injury History: High risk; no upper-minors experience; pitch selection progression.

Bret Sayre's Fantasy Take: Speed will not be an asset from this middle infielder, but Romero has the potential to hit .280 with 12-15 homers down the road. The fantasy upside may not be sexy, but a solid contributor at a weak position can go a long way.

The Year Ahead: Romero is a solid prospect who flashes feel for the barrel and has the potential to develop some juice in the stick as he continues to mature as a hitter. The infielder possesses loose hands that enable him to stay inside of offerings and can adjust the head of the bat to the point of contact. He also shows the makings of a gap-to-gap approach, though presently Romero is on the aggressive side early in counts, which draws some concerns of growing pains upon reaching more advanced levels. The defense here isn't a calling card or carrying tool. Romero has the arm for the left side of the infield, but his reactions can be slow and the instincts are just average. The 22-year-old has been making progress at second base, but there's still lead time on becoming adequate with the glove. Romero should handle High-A well, with the big test being when he reaches Double-A, which could come around mid-summer. If the forward progress continues to show, he'll shoot up into the top half of this list in short order.

6. Justin Nicolino   LHP

Born: 11/22/91 **Age:** 23 **Bats:** L **Throws:** L **Height:** 6'3" **Weight:** 190

MLB ETA	CT	FB	CH	CB	SL	OFP	Realistic
2015	–	50	65	50	–	50 NO. 4 STARTER	50 NO. 5 SP/MIDDLE RP

YEAR	TEAM	LVL	AGE	W	L	SV	G	GS	IP	H	HR	BB	K	BB9	SO9	GB%	BABIP	WHIP	ERA	FIP	FRA	WARP
2014	JAX	AA	22	14	4	0	28	28	170.3	162	10	20	81	1.1	4.3	49%	.267	1.07	2.85	3.44	4.55	1.2
2015	MIA	MLB	23	9	8	0	26	26	137.7	147	11	32	77	2.1	5.0	48%	.315	1.30	4.15	4.04	4.51	0.1
2016	MIA	MLB	24	8	9	0	26	26	153.0	161	14	35	110	2.1	6.5	48%	.324	1.28	4.18	3.65	4.54	-0.1

Breakout: 0%   Improve: 0%   Collapse: 0%   Attrition: 0%   MLB: 0%   Upside: 13   *Comparables: Adam Wilk, Zach McAllister, Dallas Keuchel*

Drafted/Acquired: 2nd round, 2010 draft, University HS (Orlando, FL)

Previous Ranking: #7 (Org)

What Happened in 2014: Nicolino made some adjustments after his first pass in Double-A, logging an impressive 170 1/3 innings while only issuing 20 free passes on the season.

Strengths: Body to withstand the rigors of the long season; easy, repeatable mechanics; finishes delivery well with fastball to hit spots on both sides of the plate; can reach 90-91 with late tail; delivers changeup with excellent arm speed; very deceptive offering; turns over with loose wrist; shows late drop; understands how to execute craft; plus command profile.

Weaknesses: Fastball is only an average offering; lacks explosiveness; walks a very fine line with spotting offering consistently against highly advanced bats; must live in lower tier; curve can get loopy and lack good bite; finds a lot of barrels with stuff; works with a limited overall margin of error.

Risk Factor/Injury History: Low risk; over 200 innings at Double-A.

Bret Sayre's Fantasy Take: There's very little fantasy upside left with Nicolino, who could back his way into a few Jason Vargas-type seasons in that ballpark. Then again, how many of you owned Jason Vargas proudly, even this year?

The Year Ahead: Much to Nicolino's credit, he made some adjustments after his initial taste of Double-A to find sustained success in 2014. This is one of those arms, though, where the lack of bat-missing ability is likely to catch up at the next level or upon reaching the bigs. There's a chance the command can play up into the plus-plus range to push the future role, but the clues point more toward the left-hander having good, but not exceptional overall command in the long haul. This is a major-league arm, and one that can carve out a successful career. It's unlikely that Nicolino will churn easily through unforgiving lineups like he has in the minors, but as a back-end guy at peak or middle reliever for a handful of seasons there's value here filling out a roster.

7. Nick Wittgren   RHP

Born: 5/29/91 **Age:** 24 **Bats:** R **Throws:** R **Height:** 6'2" **Weight:** 215

MLB ETA	CT	FB	CH	CB	SL	OFP	Realistic
2015	–	60	50	60	–	50 LATE INN RP (SU/CL)	50 7TH INN RP

YEAR	TEAM	LVL	AGE	W	L	SV	G	GS	IP	H	HR	BB	K	BB9	SO9	GB%	BABIP	WHIP	ERA	FIP	FRA	WARP
2014	JAX	AA	23	5	5	20	52	0	66.0	73	6	14	56	1.9	7.6	42%	.332	1.32	3.55	3.40	3.86	0.9
2015	MIA	MLB	24	3	1	2	48	0	58.7	56	5	16	51	2.5	7.8	44%	.321	1.23	3.61	3.60	3.92	0.3
2016	MIA	MLB	25	1	0	1	28	0	34.7	39	4	11	31	2.9	8.0	44%	.361	1.45	5.11	3.95	5.55	-0.2

Breakout: 0%   Improve: 0%   Collapse: 0%   Attrition: 0%   MLB: 0%   Upside: 7   *Comparables: Matt Stites, Mark Melancon, Chase Whitley*

Drafted/Acquired: 9th round, 2012 draft, Purdue University (West Lafayette, IN)

Previous Ranking: #5 (Org)

What Happened in 2014: Wittgren took somewhat of a step back in Double-A, finding more barrels with his stuff, but still flashed control and pitchability.

Strengths: Deceptive release; hides ball well; repeatable delivery; good feel for fastball; capable of throwing to both sides of the plate; low-90s velocity plays up because of deception; curveball shows tight rotation and teeth; element of power to pitch; throws change with loose wrist; good separation to fastball; advanced command; aggressive approach.

Weaknesses: Walks a fine line with fastball; lacks big-time velocity; heater can play down; pressure on consistent command; effort in delivery leads to overthrowing; limited growth potential with stuff.

Risk Factor/Injury History: Low risk; upper-minors experience; mature arsenal.

Bret Sayre's Fantasy Take: Relief profiles are rarely target-worthy in fantasy because the nature of closers is so role dependent and there are always relievers on the waiver wire. Wittgren is not the exception to the rule.

The Year Ahead: The intrigue here is the ability to pitch, command profile, and deception that allows Wittgren's solid-average stuff to play up well in relief stints. The low-90s fastball is far from what's expected when tagging someone as a potential closer, but the right-hander is more than capable of moving his heater around all four quadrants of the zone to set up his secondary stuff. Hitters get a somewhat late look at Wittgren, which causes his fastball to jump a little bit more as well. There is heavy pressure on this arm to maintain the command in long stretches to achieve his ceiling at the highest level. It cracked a bit at Double-A last season and the test of the next level this season will be telling. Wittgren realistically profiles as a later-innings option who can bridge key outs, but the 24-year-old could hold down a closer role in the right situation. This isn't a glamorous arm or profile, but one with strong potential to carve out a big-league career in the bullpen while bringing value when constructing a roster.

8. Michael Mader LHP

Born: 2/18/94 **Age:** 21 **Bats:** L **Throws:** L **Height:** 6'2" **Weight:** 195

MLB ETA	CT	FB	CH	CB	SL	OFP	Realistic
Late 2017	–	65	50	–	55	55 NO. 3/4 STARTER	45 6TH INN RP

YEAR	TEAM	LVL	AGE	W	L	SV	G	GS	IP	H	HR	BB	K	BB9	SO9	GB%	BABIP	WHIP	ERA	FIP	FRA	WARP
2014	BAT	A-	20	1	0	0	12	12	45.0	31	3	16	28	3.2	5.6	51%	.228	1.04	2.00	4.46	5.83	-0.2
2015	MIA	MLB	21	2	3	0	8	8	34.0	40	3	17	15	4.5	4.0	45%	.321	1.67	5.77	5.35	6.27	-0.6
2016	MIA	MLB	22	7	10	0	29	29	181.0	197	16	73	104	3.6	5.2	45%	.320	1.49	5.02	4.49	5.46	-2.0

Breakout: 0%　Improve: 0%　Collapse: 0%　Attrition: 0%　MLB: 0%　Upside: 1　*Comparables: Jairo Diaz, Jake Buchanan, Robert Carson*

Drafted/Acquired: 3rd round, 2014 draft, Chipola College (Marianna, FL)

Previous Ranking: NR

What Happened in 2014: The JUCO signing immediately started showing dividends for Miami, firing 45 innings and posting a 2.00 ERA in the New York-Penn League.

Strengths: Sturdy frame; body to withstand rigors of position; filled out lower half; smooth, fluid delivery; hides ball well; fastball works 90-93, with late tail; capable of reaching for a little more; flashes feel for changeup; shows solid separation to fastball—works in low-80s; can spin slider with depth; projection for overall command growth.

Weaknesses: Slider gets slurvy and loose; will wrap wrist; can telegraph release of offering; change presently lacks quality action; tends to float; needs to get comfortable throwing secondary stuff for strikes more often in sequences; will release fastball early; hinders ability to spot glove side; stuff can wear down deeper into outings.

Risk Factor/Injury History: High risk; short-season résumé; development of secondary stuff.

Bret Sayre's Fantasy Take: Only an option in deep leagues with huge farm systems, Mader's combination of a low-ish ceiling and longish ETA is not the best use of a roster spot.

The Year Ahead: Mader is an intriguing arm whose main assets are his size and present plus fastball. The left-hander is also on the deceptive side, hiding the ball deeper into his delivery, which gives the heater some late jump on hitters. The secondary stuff is presently on the underdeveloped side, but the 21-year-old shows feel for both his slider and changeup. An assignment in full-season ball this season is going to be a big test for Mader. It'll be interesting to see how the deception plays against more experienced hitters and what the stuff looks like deeper into the season. Those are two big questions to be answered in the near-term that will go a long way toward further establishing the lefty on a starter's path.

9.   Jarlin Garcia   LHP

Born: 1/18/93   **Age:** 22   **Bats:** L   **Throws:** L   **Height:** 6'2"   **Weight:** 170

MLB ETA		CT	FB	CH	CB	SL		OFP	Realistic
2017		–	**60**	**50**	**55**	**55**		**55** NO. 3/4 STARTER	**50** LATE INN RP

YEAR	TEAM	LVL	AGE	W	L	SV	G	GS	IP	H	HR	BB	K	BB9	SO9	GB%	BABIP	WHIP	ERA	FIP	FRA	WARP
2014	GRB	A	21	10	5	0	25	25	133.7	152	13	21	111	1.4	7.5	49%	.332	1.29	4.38	3.77	4.62	1.7
2015	MIA	MLB	22	5	7	0	23	19	105.3	119	11	40	62	3.4	5.3	44%	.326	1.51	5.22	4.81	5.68	-1.3
2016	MIA	MLB	23	6	7	0	27	20	137.3	155	14	43	90	2.8	5.9	44%	.331	1.44	4.93	4.15	5.36	-1.2

Breakout: 0%   **Improve:** 0%   **Collapse:** 0%   **Attrition:** 0%   **MLB:** 0%   **Upside:** 5   *Comparables: Wilking Rodriguez, Ricky Romero, Jeff Locke*

Drafted/Acquired: International free agent, 2010, Dominican Republic

Previous Ranking: On the Rise

What Happened in 2014: It was an uneven season for the then-21-year-old in his first taste of full-season ball, but the projectable lefty finished strong over his final seven starts spanning 35 innings, holding the opposition to a .232 average while posting a 1.03 ERA and 28 strikeouts to just 5 walks.

Strengths: Athletic delivery; easy arm with clean release out of three-quarters slot; simple and repeatable step-in through deceleration; projection in body and stuff; heater plays in the low-90s with dance, touching as high as 95 mph with regularity; curve is a one-to-seven bender with some depth and occasional bite; matches fastball trajectory; early-stage low- to mid-80s short slider with tilt; can drop an occasional change.

Weaknesses: Heavy spine tilt with third-base pull-off; lacking in command, in-zone precision; occasional drag can push fastball back over plate against righties; change is too firm at present and too often traverses the upper half of the zone; curve can lack sharpness; below-average fielding the position due to exaggerated fall-off; velo and execution diminish later in starts.

Risk Factor/Injury History: High risk; low-level minors résumé.

The Year Ahead: Garcia has developed a nice developmental foundation to facilitate further growth, including proven durability over the course of a full season. His athleticism allows him to repeat a less-than-textbook delivery with regularity, though his posture and finish can lead to a fair amount of imprecision within the zone, and can reduce the effectiveness of his changeup and curve. Garcia should make the jump to High-A in 2015, where he will continue to work on refining his arsenal while working within the confines of his delivery. The stuff is solid, but may not prove up to the task of turning over higher-level lineups without a little more precision in implementation. Should he eventually switch to the 'pen he could provide value as a late-inning arm off the strength of his heater and emerging short slider, with the curve serving as a workable change-of-pace weapon. For now, all signs still point to a future in the rotation.

10.   Justin Twine   SS

Born: 10/7/95   **Age:** 19   **Bats:** R   **Throws:** R   **Height:** 5'11"   **Weight:** 205

MLB ETA		Hit	Power	Run	Glove	Arm		OFP	Realistic
2019		**50**	**50**	**65**	**–**	**55**		**60** 1ST DIVISION REGULAR	**45** <AVG REG/UTILITY

YEAR	TEAM	LVL	AGE	PA	R	2B	3B	HR	RBI	BB	SO	SB	CS	AVG/OBP/SLG	TAv	BABIP	BRR	FRAA	WARP
2014	MRL	Rk	18	179	19	8	5	1	16	6	52	5	1	.229/.285/.355	.249	.327	1.3	SS(18): 0.7	0.6
2015	MIA	MLB	19	250	16	8	1	2	18	9	79	2	1	.189/.223/.252	.185	.270	-0.1	SS 1	-0.7
2016	MIA	MLB	20	250	21	9	1	2	19	11	72	2	1	.215/.252/.290	.205	.295	0.0	SS 1	-1.5

Breakout: 0%   **Improve:** 0%   **Collapse:** 0%   **Attrition:** 0%   **MLB:** 0%   **Upside:** 4   *Comparables: Adrian Cardenas, Carlos Rivero, Neftali Soto*

Drafted/Acquired: 2nd round, 2014 draft, Falls City HS (Falls City, TX)

Previous Ranking: NR

What Happened in 2014: The ultra-athletic Texas prep shortstop crept all the way into the second round of the 2014 draft, struggling some to adjust to the pro game during his 44-game spin through the Gulf Coast League.

Strengths: Elite athlete; impressive strength; foot speed plays as high as double-plus with a solid second gear; above-average bat speed with good extension through contact; ball jumps when barreled; lower-half agility projects on the dirt; raw materials for an above-average glove in center field; good competitor.

Weaknesses: Game is raw; inconsistent and undisciplined approach in the box; contact ability could limit future power output; some length in load; footwork and hands play below average defensively; game can speed up on him.

Risk Factor/Injury History: High risk; complex level résumé.

The Year Ahead: The prospect landscape is littered with elite athletes who fell short of mastering the skill set necessary to make the transition from upside to on-field production. The physically gifted Twine faces just that challenge as he begins his developmental journey at the pro ranks, with the native Texan emerging from the prep scene as a standout performer on the gridiron, the track, and the diamond. Twine is an explosive talent, showcasing quick-twitch actions and the potential to grow into a game-changer across the full scope of his game. He's a borderline double-plus runner with a three-step ramp-up that should keep pressure on infielders and outfielders alike; as he continues to be exposed to pro instruction and further reps on the basepaths he could develop into a solid stolen-base threat as well. He can hit for power but to do so will need to make his load

FROM THE FIELD

Jose Urena

Team: Miami Marlins

Evaluator: Ethan Purser

Dates seen: August 12, 2014

Affiliate: Jacksonville Suns (Double-A, Marlins)

OFP: 50

Realistic role: 50; late-innings relief (7th/8th inning)

Mechanics: Very slender frame; thin lower half; broad shoulders; frame could hold more weight down the line; quick-paced drop-and-drive delivery; plane can suffer as a result; arm action is very quick; breaks hands at the letters and gets arm up too early, showing it to hitters for an extended period; increases visibility and decreases deception; arm action is very similar to Randall Delgado's; three-quarters arm slot; loose, whippy arm decelerates well; plus arm speed; long stride down the mound; front leg steps over an imaginary block during stride (aids in velocity); plus momentum; lands on heel; landing can be a bit loud on occasion; back leg is off the rubber at release; pitches over front side decently; falls off toward third base—slightly rotational. Urena is a quick-twitch athlete who shows plenty of fluidity and repeatability in his delivery. The delivery features some effort post-release as he falls off toward first base, but the arm itself is very clean.

Pitch type	Present grade	Future grade	Sitting velocity	Peak velocity	Report
FB	55	60	91-94	95	Velocity: plus. Command: average; projects to above-average; shows ability to work both sides of the plate with ease; elevates his four-seam to get whiffs; works two-seam low in the zone to elicit weak contact; elevated pitch far too frequently in this outing, allowing hard contact up and over the plate; threw strikes and flashed ability to get ahead of hitters with the pitch, but command was merely average; command should improve with repetitions given repeatable mechanics mixed with present strike-throwing ability. Movement: average; standard two-seam life low in the zone; will also show a short cut look in the high-80s that isn't particularly effective; drop-and-drive limits downhill plane. Comments: This projects to be a plus pitch at the highest level. Urena can pump mid-90s with ease and projects to have above-average command of the pitch. He shows different looks with the offering (two-seam, four-seam, cut) and can manipulate the two-seam in particular to miss barrels down in the zone and generate whiffs with the four-seam above the belt.
CH	45	50	85-87	88	Command: fringe-average; projects to average; buried a few too many in the dirt; flashed ability to work the outer half versus lefties; can get in trouble by elevating the pitch over the plate. Movement: fringe-average; projects to average; shows above-average arm-side fade at times, but the movement is inconsistent overall; will cut it at times; will also flatten out and become too firm up in the zone and in the upper-80s. Comments: At its best, this pitch can elicit weak pull-side contact from hitters who are caught on their front foot. There is not enough velocity separation for this to be a consistent swing-and-miss pitch, but he projects to have enough feel to be able to get the most out of this weak-contact offering.
SL	40	45	82-86	87	Command: fringe-average; projects to average; able to generate a few whiffs out of the zone but not a swing-and-miss pitch in the zone; struggled to accumulate quality strikes with pitch; will often choke pitch in the dirt. Movement: below-average; projects to fringe-average; decent three-quarters tilt; more lateral break than vertical depth in the mid-80s; more depth in the low-80s; snap on pitch is inconsistent; will get around the pitch and cause it to merely spin and not break; will also muscle up on pitch and lose sharp break/depth. Comments: This pitch has a tendency to flatten out and doesn't consistently display sharp break, leaving it as a fringy future offering against upper-level bats. It is a playable pitch and should generate some weak contact, but it will not be a swing-and-miss weapon.
CB	40	40	79		Command: average; shows ability to get the pitch over the plate early in counts. Movement: below-average; 11-to-5 break; break is soft; shows more vertical action than the slider. Comments: Show-me/get-me-over offering at the highest level; will be able to steal a strike early in counts but will never be a swing-and-miss offering either in the zone or out of the zone.

Overall: Urena is a live-armed right-handed pitching prospect who projects to have above-average command/control with a plus fastball, but a lack of swing-and-miss secondaries will likely limit his ability to stay in the rotation long-term. Urena's delivery is relatively free and easy with few, if any, red flags, helping with the overall command projection. His arm gets vertical very quickly in his motion, however, giving hitters a very long look at the ball and decreasing the overall deception therein. The fastball is easy gas, and he can pump a lively mid-90s heater with regularity and shows an ability to spot it up on the corners or blow it by hitters up in the zone. Despite a lack of plane, this pitch should be a plus offering at the highest level. The changeup headlines the secondary arsenal and should play to average at the highest level, while the slider and curveball are fringy to below average, respectively. The current lack of big strikeout numbers should continue as he reaches the big leagues due to an underwhelming secondary arsenal.

As a player who has seen success at Double-A, Urena's risk of reaching his no. 4 starter potential is moderate and is tempered by the concern that he ends up in the bullpen with the lack of a swing-and-miss secondary pitch. If the secondaries improve slightly (new grips, etc.), Urena has a better chance of sticking in the rotation. If not, he will slot in nicely as a late-innings relief reliever due to a fastball that will likely tick up beyond the mid-90s in short stints and an average changeup that will work in his favor against lefties.

and swing path more uniform and continue to refine his ability to identify spin and track from release to contact. Above all else he needs time on the field and in the box. Initial reviews on pro exposure have been solid, but have also reinforced the belief that there is likely a long developmental lead ahead of the second rounder. He should continue in extended spring training with a step-up to short-season ball in June with the hope that he will be ready to tackle a full-season assignment in 2016.

Prospects on the Rise

1. OF Casey Soltis: The former Oregon commit came off the board to Miami in the fifth round of the 2014 draft after enjoying a productive spring that saw his draft stock rise from likely college kid to upside target who some clubs valued as highly as a third-round asset. Soltis hits out of a balanced, open stance, showing good barrel acceleration through the zone and a compact cut that allows him access to all four quadrants. Given the efficient nature of his swing, solid bat speed, and growing strength, he could develop into an average or better hit tool with average power at maturity. Soltis runs well enough to handle center at present and possesses the arm strength to hold down right field should he lose a step as his body continues to pack on additional mass, though at either spot he will need to continue to improve his reads off the bat.

2. RHP Kendry Flores: Flores doesn't wow with raw stuff, but he shows feel for a solid four-pitch mix and wields his weapons with precision, fathering a 3.99 strikeout-to-walk ratio over his 458 professional innings. His fastball anchors the repertoire, sitting in the low-90s and working effectively to the quadrants, and he utilizes both a curve and a short slider (or cutter, depending on who's writing the report) to keep the ball off of barrels. His changeup is a fourth solid-average offering, which he executes with some arm speed and slot deception, helping to disrupt timing and boost the overall effectiveness of the heater. He'll advance to Double-A Jacksonville in 2015, where continued success could leave him a stone's throw from a big-league debut.

3. 2B/3B Brian Anderson: The Marlins' third-round selection in the 2014 draft enjoyed a strong professional debut, albeit against low-minors competition. The former Razorback cleaned up his bat path over the course of his spring and summer, helping him to more regular hard contact, though his timing can be disrupted by quality secondaries. Anderson has learned to get the most out of his wiry frame, producing good bat speed and a little bit of pop through a quick-twitch core and efficient barrel delivery, and has a chance to develop into an average hit/power bat. With above-average straight-line speed, adequate hands, and above-average arm strength, he could grow into a useful utility option, capable of holding down second base, third base, left field, and (in a pinch) center, and if things break right there's everyday upside in the profile. He will join High-A Jupiter in 2015 with an eye toward continuing the momentum he built up over the course of the 2014 season.

Factors on the Farm
Prospects likely to contribute at the major-league level in 2015

1. RHP Matthew Ramsey: On the plus side, Ramsey brings a mid-90s fastball and power curve to the bump that give the arm a leg up for missing bats in short blasts. It's stuff that lines up with a potential late-inning type in a major-league bullpen. The downside is that Ramsey struggles with the consistency of his control, often creating his own messes and making outings a high-wire act. If the righty can sharpen his control and navigate more crisply through his appearances, he could get a chance to prove he can get key outs in the later innings at some point in 2015.

2. LHP Adam Conley: The former second-round pick was unable to carry a good spring with the big club into the season, struggling early in Triple-A prior to missing time with elbow tendinitis, and then never getting back on track before being shut down in July. There's promise with the arsenal, highlighted by a low-90s fastball and fading, low-80s changeup that bring into focus the potential as a big-league arm. Given the limitation of the overall arsenal, Conley more likely is best suited for the bullpen at the highest level, where his stuff can potentially play up in short bursts. If the prospect can get back on track this year, there's a strong chance a call will be waiting.

3. 1B Justin Bour: The massive George Mason product got a taste of big-league action in 2014 during two separate call-ups, with the balance of his season spent at Triple-A New Orleans, where he slashed an impressive .306/.372/.517 over 103 contests. Bour has fringe-average bat speed and gets to his above-average raw pop through brute strength and a lengthy leveraged swing. He profiles as a lefty bat off the bench with some pop and could also fit in a platoon setup at first base. He'll compete for a spot on the 25-man this spring and, regardless of where he reports come April, could see significant time in South Beach over the course of the 2015 season.

MILWAUKEE BREWERS

1. Orlando Arcia   SS

Born: 8/4/94   **Age:** 20   **Bats:** R   **Throws:** R   **Height:** 6'0"   **Weight:** 165

MLB ETA	Hit	Power	Run	Glove	Arm	OFP	Realistic
2016	55	–	50	60	60	60 1ST DIVISION PLAYER	50 ML REGULAR

YEAR	TEAM	LVL	AGE	PA	R	2B	3B	HR	RBI	BB	SO	SB	CS	AVG/OBP/SLG	TAv	BABIP	BRR	FRAA	WARP
2014	BRV	A+	19	546	65	29	5	4	50	42	65	31	11	.289/.346/.392	.263	.326	4.3	SS(90): 9.8, 2B(36): 1.3	3.5
2015	MIL	MLB	20	250	26	10	1	2	17	12	45	7	3	.229/.270/.312	.223	.270	0.3	SS 4, 2B 0	0.6
2016	MIL	MLB	21	250	25	10	2	3	22	13	40	8	3	.249/.293/.344	.242	.285	0.7	SS 4, 2B 0	1.3

Breakout: 0%   **Improve:** 0%   **Collapse:** 0%   **Attrition:** 0%   **MLB:** 0%   **Upside:** 33   *Comparables: Ruben Tejada, Tyler Pastornicky, Wilfredo Tovar*

Drafted/Acquired: International Free Agent, 2010, Venezuela

Previous Ranking: #4 (Org)

What Happened in 2014: Arcia played most of the year as a 19-year-old in the Florida State League, where he stood out for his slick actions at the six-spot and more than held his own at the plate.

Strengths: Instinctual actions in the field; solid range to both sides; good hands and body control allow him to finish at the margins; smooth lower half and plus arm complete plus-defensive profile; comfortable throwing across his zone and doesn't sacrifice carry while delivering on the run; good bat-to-ball ability; on-base reads help average speed play up; will be asset on the basepaths.

Weaknesses: Below-average power; needs to continue to add strength; glove-first profile; might be limited to down-the-order bat without improved ability to produce more consistent hard contact; can get overly aggressive at the plate; regularly led to soft contact by advanced sequencing and spin.

Risk Factor/Injury History: Moderate risk; high-floor glove but questions linger with bat.

Bret Sayre's Fantasy Take: The Brewers system may be improved, but Arcia is one of the weakest number one prospects in this series from a fantasy perspective. Sure, a .270 hitting shortstop capable of stealing 20 bases is usable in fantasy, but when it's accompanied by single-digit homers, it's just not an attractive investment—especially in shallower leagues.

The Year Ahead: Over the past two seasons, Arcia has done well to establish a profile with a firm foundational value thanks to a major-league quality glove at a high-value position and an advanced feel for the game both on the dirt and on the bases. The approach at the plate is improving, but there is still much work to be done before Arcia can begin to realize his full potential. Continued added strength should help his frequent contact become more productive, but it's reining in his approach that could help Arcia truly push his offensive game from interesting to impactful. In the field, the Venezuelan product continues to refine and should provide a steady presence at shortstop at the highest level when the time comes. Arcia's impressive feel helps the whole profile play up, and while the tools don't scream, "elite talent," there is a high floor and enough projection in the stick and body for a legit first-division ceiling to be realized.

> **#93**
> BP Top
> 101
> Prospects

2. Tyrone Taylor   OF

Born: 1/22/94   **Age:** 21   **Bats:** R   **Throws:** R   **Height:** 6'0"   **Weight:** 185

MLB ETA	Hit	Power	Run	Glove	Arm	OFP	Realistic
2016	55	50	65	60	55	60 1ST DIVISION PLAYER	50 AVG ML PLAYER

YEAR	TEAM	LVL	AGE	PA	R	2B	3B	HR	RBI	BB	SO	SB	CS	AVG/OBP/SLG	TAv	BABIP	BRR	FRAA	WARP
2014	HUN	AA	20	14	0	0	0	0	0	1	5	1	0	.077/.143/.077	.082	.125	0.1	CF(5): 0.2	-0.2
2014	BRV	A+	20	559	69	36	3	6	68	39	58	22	6	.278/.331/.396	.267	.301	1.5	CF(128): 13.0, LF(1): 0.0	3.9
2015	MIL	MLB	21	250	22	12	0	3	22	10	47	5	2	.230/.268/.326	.225	.268	0.1	CF 5, LF 0	0.3
2016	MIL	MLB	22	250	26	10	1	3	23	14	42	6	2	.245/.296/.343	.240	.280	0.4	CF 5, LF 0	1.0

Breakout: 0%   **Improve:** 0%   **Collapse:** 0%   **Attrition:** 0%   **MLB:** 0%   **Upside:** 63   *Comparables: Ben Revere, Desmond Jennings, Melky Cabrera*

Drafted/Acquired: 2nd round, 2012 draft, Torrance HS (Torrance, CA)

Previous Ranking: #1 (Org)

What Happened in 2014: Taylor impressed through 130 High-A games and a brief taste of the Southern League, showing advanced barrel control and contact ability to go with the potential to impact the game with the glove and on the bases.

Strengths: Good athleticism; advanced feel for contact and nose for the ball despite limited number of years focused on baseball; athleticism and foot speed play well on defense, where the glove projects to plus with continued route refinement and reps; good jumps on the bases and reads the ball well in front of him; solid natural strength leaves the door open for average power at maturity; capable of racking up doubles.

Weaknesses: Defensive game still refining; lower half doesn't do as much work as it should in swing, limiting ability to leverage natural strength; in-game, over-the-fence pop may top out below average; struggles with same-side stuff, particularly off-speed and spin; production tailed off toward end of season; Arizona Fall League reports point to fatigue; aggressive approach limits ability to draw walks and may restrict potential as true top-of-the-order threat at the highest level.

Risk Factor/Injury History: Moderate risk; yet to achieve Double-A success

Bret Sayre's Fantasy Take: If it works, Taylor's skill set will make him a valuable fantasy commodity, as he has the raw tools to hit 15 homers and steal up to 25 bags without hurting your batting average. He becomes a less attractive proposition in OBP or points leagues, as plate discipline stats may not be his best friend.

The Year Ahead: Taylor surprised many in 2013 by taking to the pro game so quickly despite operating as an amateur with a bifurcated athletic focus. With his attention turned solely to baseball, the SoCal prep product has quickly built up a sturdy framework across his game, showing steady progress on both sides of the ball. Because Taylor has proven adept at slowing the pro game down, his natural talents have been allowed to flash with regularity, making it easy for evaluators to project impact potential in the profile. The quick developmental progress, however, has also worked against Taylor's stock, with the rapid improvements in the field and natural bat-to-ball ability leaving scouts wanting more when considering the minimal positive growth in the power department. While Taylor remains an interesting talent with the chance to grow into a five-tool major leaguer, he will need to start driving the ball more regularly while continuing to sharpen the finer points of his game. This season should find him making his first true go at the Southern League, with steady progress pointing him to solid-average, major-league production in the near future. A developmental jump with the stick could see his profile blossom and would move him squarely into the upper tier of outfield prospects.

3. Devin Williams   RHP

Born: 9/21/94   **Age:** 20   **Bats:** R   **Throws:** R   **Height:** 6'3"   **Weight:** 165

MLB ETA	CT	FB	CH	CB	SL	OFP	Realistic
2018	–	65	60		55	65 NO. 2/3 STARTER	50 NO. 4 STARTER

YEAR	TEAM	LVL	AGE	W	L	SV	G	GS	IP	H	HR	BB	K	BB9	SO9	GB%	BABIP	WHIP	ERA	FIP	FRA	WARP
2014	HEL	Rk	19	4	7	0	15	8	66.3	74	5	20	66	2.7	9.0	48%	.359	1.42	4.48	4.02	5.83	1.0
2015	MIL	MLB	20	2	3	0	14	7	51.0	56	6	31	32	5.5	5.6	48%	.318	1.69	5.87	5.71	6.38	-0.8
2016	MIL	MLB	21	4	5	1	30	12	123.7	126	14	59	84	4.3	6.1	48%	.309	1.49	5.04	4.82	5.47	-1.0

Breakout: 0%   Improve: 0%   Collapse: 0%   Attrition: 0%   MLB: 0%   Upside: 1   *Comparables: Rafael Dolis, Jarred Cosart, Daniel Corcino*

Drafted/Acquired: 2nd round, 2013 draft, Hazelwood West HS (Hazelwood, MO)

Previous Ranking: #7 (Org)

What Happened in 2014: Williams showed growth both on and off the field, with the former including a slow start and strong finish for short-season Helena and a positive showing during fall instructs, leaving the projectable righty poised for a full-season debut in 2015.

Strengths: Loose and easy arm; fastball projects to plus or better at maturity, with two- and four-seam variations; fastball regularly draws empty swings; athletic actions; improved consistency in mechanics; potential to grow into solid command profile; body projects well, particularly in lower half; should fill out to strong, durable build; changeup flashes plus at present, mirroring two-seam action; slider will flash with two-plane break; improved approach to conditioning and game prep.

Weaknesses: Still working to make repeatable mechanics a fixture; can lose release; slider and changeup can each come and go; seldom has all three offerings working on same day; profile reliant on projection, both body and stuff.

Risk Factor/Injury History: High risk; short-season résumé.

Bret Sayre's Fantasy Take: The list of arms who haven't reached full-season ball and rank ahead of Williams for fantasy purposes has gotten pretty small. With the chance for two secondary pitches that can miss bats, his strikeout potential is the calling card here and could lead to 180-plus in his prime. Of course, the risk inherent in his profile goes without saying.

The Year Ahead: It was a positive year for the former second rounder—one that saw him make developmental strides both on the field and off with his approach and preparation. Williams joined the organization as a developmental project with the potential to grow into a front-end starter, and that upside is still very much intact. He will need to work at maintaining his mechanics and timing to make his execution more uniform across his arsenal. With his body in flux and his impressive frame en route to maturing, the righty will need to rely on his athleticism and focus on instruction to continue progressing at a steady rate. With a full-season assignment looming in 2015, Williams will look to continue to log innings, build up his arm strength, and work to find more consistency with his secondaries. He is still on the outside looking in, as far as the premium, young prospect starters are concerned. But twelve more months of progress similar to the previous twelve could accelerate his development and elevate his profile in a hurry.

4. Corey Knebel   RHP

Born: 11/26/91   **Age:** 23   **Bats:** R   **Throws:** R   **Height:** 6'3"   **Weight:** 195

MLB ETA	CT	FB	CH	CB	SL	OFP	Realistic
Debuted in 2014	–	65	–	65	–	60 TIER 1 CLOSER	55 LATE INN RP/TIER 2 CL

YEAR	TEAM	LVL	AGE	W	L	SV	G	GS	IP	H	HR	BB	K	BB9	SO9	GB%	BABIP	WHIP	ERA	FIP	FRA	WARP
2014	DET	MLB	22	0	0	0	8	0	8.7	11	0	3	11	3.1	11.4	56%	.440	1.62	6.23	1.66	3.07	0.2
2014	ROU	AAA	22	1	0	0	9	0	12.0	9	2	5	20	3.8	15.0	42%	.318	1.17	3.75	4.03	3.70	0.3
2014	TOL	AAA	22	1	1	2	14	0	18.3	6	0	9	20	4.4	9.8	55%	.158	0.82	1.96	2.98	3.86	0.3
2014	ERI	AA	22	3	0	1	11	0	15.0	8	1	8	23	4.8	13.8	53%	.241	1.07	1.20	2.75	2.65	0.5
2015	MIL	MLB	23	2	1	0	36	0	41.7	33	3	17	50	3.7	10.8	48%	.297	1.21	3.09	3.42	3.35	0.7
2016	MIL	MLB	24	4	2	1	73	0	77.3	53	7	28	88	3.3	10.2	48%	.269	1.04	2.51	3.47	2.72	2.1

Breakout: 18%   Improve: 20%   Collapse: 12%   Attrition: 20%   MLB: 35%   Upside: 64   *Comparables: Eduardo Sanchez, Stephen Pryor, Bruce Rondon*

Drafted/Acquired: 1st round, 2013 draft, University of Texas (Austin, TX)
Previous Ranking: #6 (Org – DET)

What Happened in 2014: Knebel blew through the upper minors off the strength of a pair of power offerings in his fastball and curveball, earning his first taste of big-league action in Detroit before being shipped off to the Rangers as part of the package for Joakim Soria, then flipped to Milwaukee in the offseason in the deal that brought Yovani Gallardo to Arlington.

Strengths: Fastball flirts with double-plus, sitting easily in the mid-90s with downhill plane and reaching as high as 98 mph up in the zone; curve is a power offering; low-80s hammer with tight rotation and sharp action; effective as a drop-in weapon or burying as when ahead; lots of funk and deception; generally works well in the zone.

Weaknesses: Can overthrow the curve, unintentionally burying; fastball and curve both lose some effectiveness when arm slot drops, turning the bender slurvy and keeping the heater on plane; fastball is plane reliant and can be hittable from a lower angle; in-zone command below average and could leave susceptible to long ball at major-league level.

Risk Factor/Injury History: Low; major-league ready and stuff plays.

The Year Ahead: Knebel is an impressive relief prospect capable of lighting up the radar gun and buckling knees with a nasty curve. The stuff is major-league ready, with the remainder of the former Longhorn's development to come in the form of adjustments and refinement in execution. Knebel's stuff is explosive enough that he can get away with a little bit of imprecision, but to reach his ceiling as a true shutdown arm he'll need to limit the mistakes up in the zone and over the meat of the plate, where major-league bats will be well positioned to take advantage. He should have the inside track on a spot in the Brewers 'pen this spring and stands as a likely candidate to eventually take over the closer role for Milwaukee.

5. Taylor Williams   RHP

Born: 7/21/91   **Age:** 23   **Bats:** B   **Throws:** R   **Height:** 5'11"   **Weight:** 165

MLB ETA	CT	FB	CH	CB	SL	OFP	Realistic
2016	–	65	–	–	55	60 NO. 3 STARTER	50 LATE INN RP

YEAR	TEAM	LVL	AGE	W	L	SV	G	GS	IP	H	HR	BB	K	BB9	SO9	GB%	BABIP	WHIP	ERA	FIP	FRA	WARP
2014	BRV	A+	22	1	2	0	5	5	25.3	29	4	5	25	1.8	8.9	45%	.342	1.34	4.26	4.18	4.90	0.2
2014	WIS	A	22	8	1	4	22	12	107.0	78	4	23	112	1.9	9.4	52%	.264	0.94	2.36	2.69	3.75	1.8
2015	MIL	MLB	23	4	5	0	22	13	98.0	98	11	36	75	3.3	6.9	46%	.310	1.37	4.53	4.54	4.92	-0.3
2016	MIL	MLB	24	7	6	1	33	19	159.7	147	16	52	129	2.9	7.3	46%	.299	1.25	3.90	3.92	4.24	0.9

Breakout: 0%   Improve: 0%   Collapse: 0%   Attrition: 0%   MLB: 0%   Upside: 3   *Comparables: Stephen Fife, Hector Noesi, Jeff Manship*

Drafted/Acquired: 4th round, 2013 draft, Kent State University (Kent, OH)
Previous Ranking: NR

What Happened in 2014: Showed above-average command of a plus fastball and above-average slider while carving through the Midwest League before fading some upon a late-season promotion to High-A Brevard County.

Strengths: Fastball plays comfortably in the 90-94 mph range and can reach the upper-90s in relief; commands to both sides of the plate and can elevate to miss bats; impact-potential heater that could play a half to full grade higher if limited to short bursts from the 'pen; slider is second above-average offering; matches arm slot with breaker, adding deception; shows feel for a changeup that can tease with some late dip; good athleticism on the mound; potential plus-command profile; attacks strike zone; continually challenges hitters; logged over 130 innings through regular season and continued strong showings in fall instructs.

Weaknesses: Some durability concerns tied to size; power stuff comes with effort in mechanics; off-speed lags well behind fastball and slider; struggles to soften action on changeup; may struggle to turn over more advanced lineups without reliable third offering; some trouble working downhill with fastball; can be hittable up in the zone, where fastball gets flat.

Risk Factor/Injury History: Moderate risk; solid floor as potential late-inning arm; Single-A résumé.

Bret Sayre's Fantasy Take: The bullpen risk with Williams is high, which makes owning him in dynasty leagues a tricky proposition. Throw in the fact that he will likely be a fly-ball pitcher in a home-run-friendly park, and it's even trickier. At best, Williams is likely a league-average ERA pitcher with a good WHIP and fewer strikeouts than his raw velocity would portend.

The Year Ahead: Williams enjoyed a highly productive 2014, taking significant steps forward in better executing and commanding his fastball and slider. Midwest League bats were regularly overmatched, with Williams impressing evaluators with the consistency of his outings whether starting or entering from the 'pen (Wisconsin would generally fit 10 to 13 days between starts, with multi-inning relief appearances in between). The biggest question facing Williams is whether he can bring the changeup to a level where it can be a serviceable weapon against more advanced hitters. Without it, he will likely struggle to turn over high-end lineups with regularity, which in turn could push him to the 'pen. In a relief role, Williams has the mentality, the command, and the power pairing to handle high-leverage situations, and could be fast tracked if at any point Milwaukee elects that developmental path. For now, the Brewers will continue to run Williams out as a starter until he gives them reason to believe he cannot succeed in that role. He'll likely start 2015 back in Brevard County with an eye toward Double-A if he can continue to build upon last season's successes.

6.   Monte Harrison   OF

Born: 8/10/95   **Age:** 19   **Bats:** R   **Throws:** R   **Height:** 6'3"   **Weight:** 200

MLB ETA	Hit	Power	Run	Glove	Arm		OFP	Realistic
2019	–	55	55	55	70		**65** 1ST DIV REG/ALL-STAR	**50** AVG PLAYER

YEAR	TEAM	LVL	AGE	PA	R	2B	3B	HR	RBI	BB	SO	SB	CS	AVG/OBP/SLG	TAv	BABIP	BRR	FRAA	WARP
2014	BRR	Rk	18	224	37	7	2	1	20	31	48	32	2	.261/.402/.339	.294	.348	1.2	RF(12): -1.6, CF(6): 0.7	0.5
2015	MIL	MLB	19	250	27	8	0	2	14	13	74	13	2	.191/.240/.258	.192	.264	1.8	RF -3, CF 1	-1.3
2016	MIL	MLB	20	250	25	9	1	5	23	15	70	14	2	.214/.266/.324	.224	.280	2.4	RF -3, CF 1	-0.8

Breakout: 0%   Improve: 0%   Collapse: 0%   Attrition: 0%   MLB: 0%   Upside: 10   *Comparables: Caleb Gindl, Oswaldo Arcia, Marcell Ozuna*

Drafted/Acquired: 2nd round, 2014 draft, Lee's Summit West HS (Lee's Summit, MO)

Previous Ranking: NR

What Happened in 2014: Largely viewed by Midwest area scouts as a highly athletic but raw talent, Harrison drew rave reviews in his pro debut at the complexes after slipping to the Brewers in the second round, where he signed for first-round money.

Strengths: Three-sport standout in high school displays top-tier athleticism; showed more advanced feel than expected upon entry into pro game; speed plays up due to big acceleration; plus makeup; quick-twitch muscles with projectable and physical frame; should grow into impact strength; efficient weight transfer and forceful barrel delivery; power should play; raw tools to fit in center field long term, drawing one Adam Jones comp for body and future defensive package; double-plus arm could play as weapon in right if body ultimately forces shift from center; good jumps and reads on the bases; very high grades for work ethic and ability to absorb instruction.

Weaknesses: Overall game needs refinement; lacks reps against advanced competition; underdeveloped pitch identification; can get too aggressive and expand zone; reads and routes in center still a work in progress; overall feel for contact at the plate lags; hit utility could ultimately limit ability of power to play to full potential; plus speed underway plays down out of the box; body could go a lot of different ways, including enough added bulk to force a move from center field.

Risk Factor/Injury History: High risk; complex-level résumé and limited exposure to advanced competition.

Bret Sayre's Fantasy Take: Thirty-two steals in a 50-game debut will whet any roto owner's appetite, but as you can tell above, Harrison isn't a burner and his skill set is far more complex. The upside is there for a 20/20 outfielder, but he has forever to go before we can say that with any modicum of confidence. Harrison has the explosiveness to go within the first 30 picks in dynasty drafts this year, despite the second-round tag.

The Year Ahead: Harrison stood out in the Arizona complexes for his loud physical tools, but it was the eagerness with which he took to his initial round of pro instruction that has evaluators excited to see what the future has in store for the former two-sport Nebraska commit. It's a big and physical frame sure to be donned with significant added strength in the coming years, allowing the raw power to project to plus or better given the barrel acceleration already in place. While there is risk that Harrison could eventually out grow center, his plus-plus arm strength and the current ease with which he glides through the grass leave little question that he could slide over to right without missing a beat, and would project as an above-average defender in that role. Harrison has shown enough maturity and present comfort in his brief pro career for the Brewers to entertain jumping him straight to full-season ball in 2015. He is currently staring down a long developmental road, but elite raw materials and a willingness to put them to work have a way of easing the load along the way, if not shortening the trek altogether.

7. Gilbert Lara 3B

Born: 10/30/97 **Age:** 17 **Bats:** R **Throws:** R **Height:** 6'3" **Weight:** 205

MLB ETA	Hit	Power	Run	Glove	Arm		OFP	Realistic
2019	50	65	–	–	55		65 1ST DIV/ALL STAR	50 ML REGULAR

Drafted/Acquired: International Free Agent, 2014, Dominican Republic

Previous Ranking: NR

What Happened in 2014: After being awarded the highest bonus in franchise history for an international signee ($3.1 million), Lara put on a show during fall instructs centered on jaw-dropping power displays.

Strengths: Incredibly loud raw power; some project in-game pop as high as double-plus; easy extension with natural loft and carry; lots of leverage and violence in swing; showed solid pitch identification for age during instructs, allowing for more projection in hit tool than previously expected; solid hands and left-side arm give profile chance to stick on the dirt; arm would play in right field if forced to the grass; projectable frame should hold strapping build at maturity; swagger to hold up to normal course of developmental setbacks.

Weaknesses: Louder swing doesn't lend itself to high contact rates; feel for barrel will need to prove effective through the ranks for raw power to play to potential; still very raw and offensive success hinges on lengthy developmental road; lower half limits range in the infield; while currently working at short, certain to move off the position; may lack footwork to handle third base long term; run is well below average and could drop more as body matures.

Risk Factor/Injury History: High risk; stateside exposure limited to fall instructs.

Bret Sayre's Fantasy Take: There are draft classes in which to take chances somewhat early on current-year J2 signings, and then there's the 2014 draft class—which was as deep as any since dynasty leagues spiked in popularity. Lara's power potential is intense, and it's very easy to get excited about, but he's barely 17 years old.

The Year Ahead: Lara was so impressive last fall that the Brewers could challenge him with a stateside assignment in 2015 despite the fact he will not turn 18 until October. The bat could be a game changer, with the raw pop to eventually develop into a regular 30-plus home-run threat and middle-of-the-order force. There is enough fuzziness in the profile to project the hit tool anywhere from below to above average, though supporters point to Lara's ability to track and his impact power as a strong foundation for a solid on-base profile regardless of the existence of some swing-and-miss. Lara has received positive reports for his hands in the field, as well as his fluid transition from receipt to release, but a slow lower half and likely-to-thicken trunk could end up pushing him to right field and maybe even first base as he works his way toward Milwaukee. Assuming Lara does log time in the rookie-level Arizona League next summer, he could rack up homers, as well as strikeouts, in short order. This may be one of the most exciting young bats in baseball's lower levels, capable of emerging as an elite prospect in the near future despite a profile skewed almost exclusively to power.

8. Jorge Lopez RHP

Born: 2/10/93 **Age:** 22 **Bats:** R **Throws:** R **Height:** 6'4" **Weight:** 165

MLB ETA	CT	FB	CH	CB	SL		OFP	Realistic
2016	–	55	50	50	–		55 NO. 3/4 STARTER	45 NO. 5 SP/SWINGMAN

YEAR	TEAM	LVL	AGE	W	L	SV	G	GS	IP	H	HR	BB	K	BB9	SO9	GB%	BABIP	WHIP	ERA	FIP	FRA	WARP
2014	BRV	A+	21	10	10	0	25	25	137.7	144	12	46	119	3.0	7.8	50%	.328	1.38	4.58	3.88	5.37	-0.2
2015	MIL	MLB	22	5	8	0	24	21	115.7	125	15	52	77	4.0	6.0	46%	.318	1.53	5.40	5.26	5.87	-1.4
2016	MIL	MLB	23	5	7	0	23	19	124.3	132	16	49	91	3.5	6.6	46%	.320	1.46	5.09	4.62	5.53	-1.2

Breakout: 0%   Improve: 0%   Collapse: 0%   Attrition: 0%   MLB: 0%   Upside: 3   *Comparables: Jose A. Ramirez, Daryl Thompson, Wilking Rodriguez*

Drafted/Acquired: 2nd round, 2011 draft, Caguas Military Academy (Caguas, PR)

Previous Ranking: On The Rise

What Happened in 2014: Despite a trying year off the field, Lopez logged 25 starts for High-A Brevard County, averaging over five innings per start while showing feel for a solid three-pitch mix.

Strengths: Fastball sits comfortably in the low-90s with arm-side life; curve took a step forward, showing more consistent shape and solid depth; changeup can get firm, but at best serves as third average or better weapon; projectable build and room in frame to add strength; maintains stuff through starts; should show solid command profile at maturity thanks to improving consistency in mechanics; capable of driving his fastball downhill; impressive mound presence and resiliency; strong makeup.

Weaknesses: Arsenal lacks impact; has yet to realize previously projected velocity jump; changeup still in developmental stages; present command is loose in the zone; tendency to catch the fat of the plate; lacks pure swing-and-miss stuff; despite progress, can struggle to maintain timing, leading to inconsistent release and execution.

Risk Factor/Injury History: Moderate risk; yet to reach Double-A.

Bret Sayre's Fantasy Take: Lopez doesn't have the upside to warrant shallow-mixed investing, but in deep-mixed and NL-only formats, he should still be on radars. The Brewers have had some success as an organization in developing pitchers with less than frightening repertoires, but expectations should be low.

The Year Ahead: Lopez somehow achieved another solid developmental year while simultaneously dealing with the serious illness of his son, Maikel, who has struggled with a number of ailments since birth. On the diamond, Lopez saw peaks and valleys and everything in between. The struggles most often came when he failed to maintain consistent timing, leading to walks, soft secondaries, and too many hittable balls over the fat of the plate. While the arsenal hasn't taken the significant step forward that the Brewers hoped to see when selecting the projectable Puerto Rican in the second round of a talent-rich 2011 draft, the body and stuff continue to show room for growth, and steady progress is being made. He'll tackle Double-A in 2015, with his future in the Brewers rotation tied directly to his ability to close the loop on his mechanical inconsistencies.

9. Tyler Wagner RHP

Born: 1/24/91 **Age:** 24 **Bats:** R **Throws:** R **Height:** 6'3" **Weight:** 195

MLB ETA	CT	FB	CH	CB	SL	OFP	Realistic
2016	–	60	–	–	50	55 NO. 3/4 STARTER	45 GB SPECIALIST RP

YEAR	TEAM	LVL	AGE	W	L	SV	G	GS	IP	H	HR	BB	K	BB9	SO9	GB%	BABIP	WHIP	ERA	FIP	FRA	WARP
2014	BRV	A+	23	13	6	0	25	25	150.0	118	10	48	118	2.9	7.1	54%	.259	1.11	1.86	3.66	4.54	0.9
2015	MIL	MLB	24	7	9	0	23	23	125.0	124	15	55	80	4.0	5.8	54%	.300	1.43	4.66	5.09	5.07	-0.5
2016	MIL	MLB	25	8	8	0	24	24	143.3	134	14	52	107	3.3	6.7	54%	.303	1.30	3.96	4.08	4.30	0.5

Breakout: 0%   Improve: 0%   Collapse: 0%   Attrition: 0%   MLB: 0%   Upside: 4   *Comparables: Ryan Cook, Jake Petricka, Scott Snodgress*

Drafted/Acquired: 4th round, 2012 draft, University of Utah (Salt Lake City, UT)

Previous Ranking: NR

What Happened in 2014: Wagner logged 150 innings, averaging six innings per start for High-A Brevard County while posting a groundout/flyout rate over two and showing incremental progress toward an above-average command profile.

Strengths: Big, heavy fastball that can reach the mid-90s and works comfortably in the 90-93 mph range; low- to mid-80s slider can miss barrels with average bite; mechanics facilitate solid command; can work fastball and slider to both sides of the plate; followed 148 2/3 innings in 2013 with 150 innings in 2014; proven durability.

Weaknesses: Changeup primarily a "show-me" offering that could lack utility at upper levels; success as starter reliant upon ability to draw soft contact with sinker-slider combo; thin margin for error in execution; unlikely to miss bats consistently at upper levels.

Risk Factor/Injury History: Moderate risk; yet to reach Double-A; profile likely to offer sinker/slider-reliever floor.

Bret Sayre's Fantasy Take: The belly of the system, Wagner shouldn't be on fantasy radars, outside of obnoxiously deep leagues. When a pitcher has this many signs pointing at a bullpen future, the ceiling needs to be worth the investment, and it is not in Wagner's profile.

The Year Ahead: Wagner's ability to draw groundball contact should benefit him regardless of whether he ultimately reaches Milwaukee as a starter or as part of the relief corps. As with Taylor Williams, Wagner is a legitimate third offering away from projecting comfortably into a major-league rotation, though the former Ute is generally considered a safer bet to hold up to a starter's workload (albeit with less electric stuff). Wagner should join Lopez in Double-A this year, where more advanced lineups could provide a stiff challenge. An average off-speed would give Wagner more sequencing options—a necessity if he is to turn over major-league lineups in time. Conversely, Wagner's sinker could play up enough in one-inning runs to make him a late-inning option in the mold of a Zach Britton.

10. Kodi Medeiros LHP

Born: 5/25/96 **Age:** 19 **Bats:** L **Throws:** L **Height:** 6'2" **Weight:** 180

MLB ETA	CT	FB	CH	CB	SL	OFP	Realistic
2019	–	65	55	–	65	60 NO. 3 STARTER	45 MIDDLE RELIEF

YEAR	TEAM	LVL	AGE	W	L	SV	G	GS	IP	H	HR	BB	K	BB9	SO9	GB%	BABIP	WHIP	ERA	FIP	FRA	WARP
2014	BRR	Rk	18	0	2	1	9	4	17.7	24	2	13	26	6.6	13.2	48%	.467	2.09	7.13	4.93	4.34	0.3
2015	MIL	MLB	19	1	2	0	14	4	34.0	37	4	20	20	5.3	5.3	45%	.317	1.68	5.85	5.72	6.36	-0.5
2016	MIL	MLB	20	3	3	1	41	9	108.0	107	14	49	79	4.1	6.6	45%	.302	1.44	4.92	4.83	5.35	-0.7

Breakout: 0%   Improve: 0%   Collapse: 0%   Attrition: 0%   MLB: 0%   Upside: 0   *Comparables: Joe Wieland, Patrick McCoy, Jake Odorizzi*

Drafted/Acquired: 1st round, 2014 draft, Waiakea HS (Waiakea, HI)

Previous Ranking: NR

What Happened in 2014: Medeiros put together some of the most dominant innings of the entire high school showcase circuit, ultimately earning a seven-figure bonus after being popped by Milwaukee with the 12th overall pick in the 2014 draft.

Strengths: Full arsenal comes with lots of dance; at best, fastball shows big arm-side life and can sit low- to mid-90s in the early innings; heater can play above plus grade thanks to life and tough angle; slider has flashed double-plus with video-game bite and depth; true wipeout breaker; changeup will flash disappearing action with some deception; when everything is clicking, there's so much life across the arsenal it's tough to find someone who can catch the ball, let alone square it up; solid build; carries air of confidence to the mound.

Weaknesses: Though well put together, not overly physical; stuff can quickly fall off across the board as he works deeper into games; velocity down in short pro stint; can get under ball, causing arsenal to flatten; inconsistent arm slot holds present control and command below average; execution is inconsistent; arm slot and angle can limit ability to work both sides of the plate effectively.

Risk Factor/Injury History: High risk; complex-level résumé.

Bret Sayre's Fantasy Take: Unlike Wagner, Medeiros has the ceiling to warrant fantasy investment, although he's very likely to be overdrafted this winter due to his lofty draft spot—he should fall out of the top 30 picks, but that's mostly risk-related and not stuff-related.

The Year Ahead: Much will depend on what Medeiros looks like next spring after resting up and undergoing his first offseason pro training regimen. If the slinger from Hawaii shows up with the explosive stuff that pushed him into the top half of the first round, he could prove too advanced for short-season bats. It will be a delicate developmental line to walk for the Brewers, who will need to challenge Medeiros with innings if they are to determine whether he will be able to handle the rigors of starting. To log those innings, however, Medeiros has to establish a firm baseline that allows him to throw strikes with consistency. This is likely to be a slow burn, but the profile comes with mid-rotation upside and the chance to fast track the arm in relief provided the drop in velocity over the last four months of 2014 does not prove to be the new normal. A Helena assignment seems most likely, with a 2016 full-season debut the target. If Medeiros's stint out west proves as productive as Devin Williams's, he should climb these rankings next fall.

Prospects on the Rise

1. RHP Miguel Diaz: Diaz impressed in his stateside debut, tantalizing evaluators at the Arizona complexes with a big fastball, regularly sitting 92-94 mph and touching 96, and promising low-80s slider. The young Dominican followed up a solid summer by taking a step forward with his breaking ball during fall instructs, throwing his slider with more consistent shape and bite. He also began mixing in a mid-to-upper-80s short slider/cutter variation, giving him another look and a potential weapon for missing left-handed barrels should he fail to fully develop the cambio. Diaz gets good extension on his offerings, pushing the ball in on hitters quickly and allowing his

---

FROM THE FIELD

Jorge Lopez

Team: Milwaukee Brewers
Evaluator: Jeff Moore
Dates seen: May 21, 2014
Affiliate: Brevard County Manatees (High-A, Brewers)
OFP: 50
Realistic role: 45, middle reliever
Mechanics: Good, fluid motion and arm action; creates easy velo. Quick arm speed. Tends to get on top of the ball too much, causing him to miss down.

Pitch type	Present grade	Future grade	Sitting velocity	Peak velocity	Report
FB	45	55	92-94	94	Four-seam variety is relatively straight. Consistent velocity. Thrown with good control but not command. Player throws a lot of bad strikes with the pitch. Can be an above-average pitch with improved command.
CB	50	60	78-79		Pitch features true 12-6 movement, straight down. Player generates good spin on the ball. Does a good job of keeping it down. Not a big swing-and-miss pitch but will generate groundballs when low in the zone.
CH	30	40	87-89		Gets a low grade because, essentially, it's not a changeup. Looks and moves like a two-seamer, but was told by a teammate it's his changeup grip. Has arm-side fade consistent with both pitches, but thrown way too hard. Not nearly enough differential between fastball and changeup. If classified as a two-seamer, it's still below average, but a usable pitch. As a changeup, it's virtually nonexistent.

Overall: Lopez has a good arm and is still learning how to use it. He's throwing strikes much more consistently now than in his past, and as they begin to become better strikes, he'll be more effective. The curveball is a second potential above-average, maybe even a plus, pitch. The changeup, or lack thereof, was puzzling. I had it classified as a two-seam fastball for the first few innings until I asked his teammate if he threw a changeup and was informed that he had been throwing it all along. Regardless of pitch classification, Lopez didn't throw anything off-speed to keep hitters honest or combat left-handed hitters. The fastball/curveball combo gives him the start of a mid-rotation starter package, but until he comes up with something soft to throw, it's a middle-relief profile.

fastball to play above its plus velocity grade. The Brewers will likely take things slowly with Diaz in 2015, with a focus on continuing to build up arm strength and durability while refining the secondaries. A Helena assignment seems most likely and would put him in line for a full-season debut in 2016 at the age of 21.

2. OF Clint Coulter: After dropping off the top 10 rankings last year due to significant struggles at the plate and behind it, Coulter put together a loud 2014 in his second spin through the Midwest League that included a .287/.410/.520 slash line and 22 big flies. During fall instructs Coulter made the full-time switch to right field, which should be his home for the immediate future. The Washington native is never going to look smooth and sexy on the field—his game is all about brute force, and last summer he wielded that force admirably. Evaluators point to below-average athleticism, average bat speed, and a hitch-and-jerk swing as reasons to be cautious, and the transition to right field is still very much a high-risk proposition. Still, it's not often you see a 21-year-old put up the numbers that Coulter did in the tough Midwest League environs. He'll enter 2015 with an inside track on next year's top 10 list and could climb to a prominent position with a strong showing in the Florida State League, whose vast outfields will challenge both his power and his glove.

3. LHP Wei-Chung Wang: The Brewers nabbed Wang in the December 2013 Rule 5 draft and, despite the pressures of a playoff push, showed the fortitude to take the 25-man roster hit for the requisite time to ensure the young lefty remained a Brewer past 2014. Wang was clearly not ready to contribute at the major-league level, with a majority of his in-season work in Milwaukee accomplished through side sessions. August afforded the organization the ability to send Wang to the minors for a rehab assignment that spanned three levels, seven appearances, and 27 innings, where he very much looked the part of a future major-league starter thanks to a fastball and curve that each project to above-average offerings and a quality off-speed with splitter action. He needs to add strength, first and foremost, to aid him in repeating his mechanics deep into starts, and there is some cleanup to be done on the arm action, which at present includes a hook and inconsistent path. Arizona Fall League reports were largely positive, with the consensus generally that his stuff could play at Double-A this summer provided he's able to handle the innings. More likely he is eased into the lower levels to help control innings early on, and could move as quickly as his stuff permits.

Factors on the Farm
Prospects likely to contribute at the major-league level in 2015

1. RHP Taylor Jungmann: Jungmann split his 2014 between Huntsville and Nashville, showing well at each stop, leaving the former Longhorn ace ready for his first taste of major-league action. It's an average four-pitch mix, with the fastball and slider each capable of playing a half grade above, but the command isn't quite sharp enough for Jungmann to fully leverage the varied collection of offerings. There's a fit in the back end of the rotation, where he'll provide solid value taking the ball every five days and eating innings. Whenever the opportunity presents itself, Jungmann should log his first major-league start in 2015.

2. RHP Ariel Pena: Pena's best offering is a low-to-mid-90s fastball that evaluators feel could be a consistent plus or better weapon out of the 'pen, where he could air it out and let his natural arm-side run do its thing. The heater brings a usable slider and splitter in tow, but a stiff landing and high slot often prevent Pena from driving down in the zone and make uniformity in his release an issue. Though he amassed 24 starts for Triple-A Nashville in 2014 and was very difficult for hitters to square up, the walks and pitch counts ate into his overall effectiveness and cast big questions as to whether he has a real chance to succeed as a starter at the major-league level. This year could see a transition to the 'pen for the big righty, and the fastball alone could miss big-league bats from day one. There's risk tied to below-average command and control, but also late-inning upside.

3. RHP David Goforth: With a big fastball and workable slider/cutter combo, Goforth projects well to the back of a major-league bullpen, but first needs to find a little more precision and a lesser proclivity for blowups when his feel escapes him. Last summer saw his command come and go, with dozens of dominant outings checkered by some truly uncomfortable meltdowns. On the whole, he took care of business in the late innings over 54 Southern League appearances, and is not far off from being able to provide some value in the Milwaukee 'pen. Whether he will earn enough trust to handle the high-leverage situations in the bigs will depend entirely upon his ability to limit free passes and secondary "misfires" out and over the plate, which have had a tendency to get hit often and hard. He should start his season in Colorado Springs with a 2015 Milwaukee debut likely.

MINNESOTA TWINS

1. Byron Buxton   CF

Born: 12/18/93   **Age:** 21   **Bats:** R   **Throws:** R   **Height:** 6'2"   **Weight:** 190

MLB ETA	Hit	Power	Run	Glove	Arm	OFP	Realistic
Late 2015	60	60	80	70	60	80 ELITE ML PLAYER	65 1ST DIV/OCC ALL STAR

YEAR	TEAM	LVL	AGE	PA	R	2B	3B	HR	RBI	BB	SO	SB	CS	AVG/OBP/SLG	TAv	BABIP	BRR	FRAA	WARP
2014	NBR	AA	20	3	0	0	0	0	0	0	3	0	0	.000/.000/.000	.001	.000	0.0	CF(1): 0.0	-0.1
2014	FTM	A+	20	134	19	4	2	4	16	10	33	6	2	.240/.313/.405	.254	.298	1.5	CF(28): 4.6, RF(2): -0.2	1.0
2015	MIN	MLB	21	250	33	8	3	5	21	22	66	13	5	.248/.316/.376	.256	.324	1.1	CF 5, RF -0	1.3
2016	MIN	MLB	22	597	74	19	9	13	67	59	149	33	12	.273/.349/.422	.285	.352	4.6	CF 13	4.7

Breakout: 14%   Improve: 24%   Collapse: 2%   Attrition: 8%   MLB: 36%   Upside: 108   *Comparables: Christian Yelich, Anthony Gose, Jake Marisnick*

Drafted/Acquired: 1st round, 2012 draft, Appling County HS (Baxley, GA)

Previous Ranking: #1 (Org), #1 (Top 101)

What Happened in 2014: A wrist injury put a major dent in the season of the crown jewel of the system. The 21-year-old was limited to just 31 games and then had his time in the Arizona Fall League come to a crashing halt due to a concussion and a dislocated finger.

Strengths: Well-above-average athlete; elite run; endless range; superb instincts; gracefully moves from gap to gap; right-fielder's arm; advanced feel for hitting; lets balls travel deep into the zone; explosive hands; plus-plus bat speed; barrels offerings with authority; well-above-average raw; advanced approach at the plate.

Weaknesses: Still transitioning from raw athlete to skilled player; presently plays on ability; needs to learn to further slow the game down; swing at present more geared toward line-drive contact; can stand to create more lift and postcontact extension for power to play to full potential; has struggled against high-quality breaking stuff; tends to lunge and overcommit hands; will guess with some frequency.

Risk Factor/Injury History: Moderate; limited upper-level experience; wrist injury/concussion (2014).

Bret Sayre's Fantasy Take: It's really very hard to undersell Buxton's fantasy potential, and he's one of the few players in baseball with the potential to supplant Mike Trout as the number one pick overall one day. The rough 2014 and push back in his ETA are the only things keeping him from being the top fantasy prospect in the game, and he could be a 25-homer, 50-steal roto monster if it all comes to pass.

The Year Ahead: Despite essentially a lost season in 2014 and delay in development time, Buxton remains the headliner of this system and the premier prospect in all of the minor leagues. This is a true five-tool talent that oozes naturalness and the type of ability that makes even the most conservative of evaluators drop lofty projections for what the future holds. This space could be filled with superlatives and flowing language waxing poetically about the Georgia native, but it really boils down to one word: "easy." That's the way the 21-year-old makes this game look, which is a testament to the talent and the way it has come together so quickly since signing. This season will see Buxton return to the field, where a string of good health should lead to an uninterrupted foray into the upper levels and could very well culminate in a big-league debut during the latter stages of the season. We should expect that the uber-prospect will likely need to shake some off rust in the early going, but once he hits his stride look for the train to continue barreling down the tracks on a collision course for stardom at the highest level in the not-so-distant future.

> **#1**
> BP Top
> 101
> Prospects

2. Miguel Sano   3B

Born: 5/11/93   **Age:** 22   **Bats:** R   **Throws:** R   **Height:** 6'4"   **Weight:** 235

MLB ETA	Hit	Power	Run	Glove	Arm	OFP	Realistic
Late 2015	–	80	50	55	70	70 ALL STAR	60 1ST DIVISION PLAYER

YEAR	TEAM	LVL	AGE	PA	R	2B	3B	HR	RBI	BB	SO	SB	CS	AVG/OBP/SLG	TAv	BABIP	BRR	FRAA	WARP
2015	MIN	MLB	22	250	32	10	1	13	38	25	79	2	1	.231/.315/.464	.278	.289	-0.1	3B 0, 1B -0	1.1
2016	MIN	MLB	23	556	78	20	2	29	82	59	171	4	1	.226/.315/.454	.280	.278	-0.4	3B -1	1.5

Breakout: 3%   Improve: 31%   Collapse: 2%   Attrition: 10%   MLB: 55%   Upside: 156   *Comparables: Chris Carter, Chris Davis, Evan Longoria*

Drafted/Acquired: International Free Agent, 2009, Dominican Republic

Previous Ranking: #2 (Org), #14 (Top 101)

What Happened in 2014: The dreaded Tommy John struck the budding slugger, turning the year into a rehabilitation exercise instead of a return to Double-A to attempt to iron out key developmental needs.

Strengths: Massive man; extremely strong body; moves well for size; elite raw power; generates excellent extension and lift; drives offerings with loft to all fields; punishes stuff middle-away; can get out of box well; double-plus arm prior to surgery; charges balls well at third; aptitude for the game.

Weaknesses: Long, leveraged swing; will overextend with frequency; tendency to get tied up against good velocity on inner third; has swing-and-miss in the zone; easily fooled against off-speed stuff; needs work staying back; hit tool may ultimately play below average; defensive fundamentals and consistency need work; on the slow side laterally; arm strength may not fully return.

Risk Factor/Injury History: Moderate; 67 games at Double-A; Tommy John surgery (2014); handing of secondary stuff.

Bret Sayre's Fantasy Take: The year missed really hurt fantasy owners who were hoping he'd be in the majors in 2015 and hitting bombs left and right. But it did little to quiet his 40-homer potential. Of course, that power is likely to come with a batting average that hurts (think .250-.260 at the high end), but in an OBP league, he reverses course (think .340-.350 at the low end) given his eye at the plate.

The Year Ahead: There's never a good time for a major injury during the course of any player's career, but the hit to Sano's development time came at a critical juncture during his transition into the upper levels and put a hard stop on any type of traction the prospect could have made after the initial test at Double-A. The Dominican's massive power and potential impact in the middle of a lineup have been well documented around here, as has the big need for tightening things up when it comes to handling high-quality secondary stuff. The theme remains the same heading into this season, with the added task of having to navigate back up to speed after a year off from game action. It should stand as a highly interesting case study to evaluate whether there are signs of progress after the initial rust has dusted off. There isn't much doubt that the power is going to translate in some shape or form, but whether Sano rounds into the true middle-of-the-order monster the potential indicates will be directly tied into learning how to control plate appearances better. The belief here is that said ability resides inside the player, ready to be unlocked with continued experience, and that a first look at the highest level should come by the end of the summer.

#12

BP Top
101
Prospects

3. Alex Meyer RHP

Born: 1/3/90 **Age:** 25 **Bats:** R **Throws:** R **Height:** 6'9" **Weight:** 220

MLB ETA	CT	FB	CH	CB	SL	OFP	Realistic
2015	–	80	55	–	65	65 NO. 2/3 STARTER	60 LATE INN RP (CLOSER)

YEAR	TEAM	LVL	AGE	W	L	SV	G	GS	IP	H	HR	BB	K	BB9	SO9	GB%	BABIP	WHIP	ERA	FIP	FRA	WARP
2014	ROC	AAA	24	7	7	0	27	27	130.3	116	10	64	153	4.4	10.6	49%	.321	1.38	3.52	3.66	3.74	2.8
2015	MIN	MLB	25	6	7	0	21	21	103.0	100	10	47	103	4.1	9.0	50%	.314	1.43	4.22	4.34	4.59	1.0
2016	MIN	MLB	26	10	10	0	30	30	190.3	175	21	74	204	3.5	9.6	50%	.301	1.31	3.90	3.92	4.24	1.8

Breakout: 24% Improve: 36% Collapse: 17% Attrition: 39% MLB: 59% Upside: 25 *Comparables: Dellin Betances, Nate Karns, Scott Barnes*

Drafted/Acquired: 1st round, 2011 draft, University of Kentucky (Lexington, KY)

Previous Ranking: #3 (Org), #32 (Top 101)

What Happened in 2014: The University of Kentucky product proved he could handle a full workload in the upper levels, where he flashed the stuff to miss advanced bats and now sits on the cusp of The Show.

Strengths: Long limbed and extreme length; good athlete for size; coordinated; elite arm strength; fastball routinely works 94-96 with downward plane; can reach for more when needs to (97-100); explosive offering; snaps slider with loose wrist; wipeout break in mid-80s; throws from same angle as heater; bat-misser; change can flash quality arm-side fade.

Weaknesses: Lot of body to control; inconsistent with mechanics—loses delivery for stretches; command plays down as a result (below to fringe-average); slider will sweep when arm slot drops to mid-three-quarters; tends to drift toward first base during landing; can slow body on secondary offerings; change typically on the firm side.

Risk Factor/Injury History: Low; 27 starts at Triple-A; shoulder weakness (2013); emergence of consistent third offering.

Bret Sayre's Fantasy Take: It was surprising to some dynasty leaguers that Meyer was not called up in 2014 to hone his craft a bit at the major-league level, but barring something catastrophic, we should see that happen in 2015. Don't expect high performance out of the gate with Meyer, who is likely to struggle with his WHIP and win potential (due to racking up high pitch counts), but there's also a real chance he ends up in the bullpen—where he could be a dominant closer with big strikeout totals.

#14

BP Top
101
Prospects

The Year Ahead: An imposing figure on the mound, the 6-foot-9 right-hander continues to take strides toward rounding into a legit major-league power arm that can be downright nasty on opposing batters. The fastball and slider stand out in the front of this package, while the changeup has made tangible improvement since turning pro. However, evaluators are mixed on the ultimate role. Some see further growth with the change and point to improving body control as leading factors that things can work as a starter in the long term. Others feel the two-pitch nature and maintenance in the delivery indicate short bursts out of the back of a bullpen will be a better fit. The latter seems more likely over the long haul given the overall composition of the package, though Meyer should get an extended shot to prove otherwise as early as this season. The ingredients are here for an impact arm no matter which way you slice it. This year should serve as a chance for the prospect to put his minor-league career in the rearview mirror and begin putting a foothold as a long-term fixture on Minnesota's pitching staff.

4. Kohl Stewart   RHP

Born: 10/7/94   **Age:** 20   **Bats:** R   **Throws:** R   **Height:** 6'3"   **Weight:** 195

MLB ETA	CT	FB	CH	CB	SL	OFP	Realistic
Late 2016	–	70	55	55	70	70 NO. 2 STARTER	55 NO. 3/4 STARTER

YEAR	TEAM	LVL	AGE	W	L	SV	G	GS	IP	H	HR	BB	K	BB9	SO9	GB%	BABIP	WHIP	ERA	FIP	FRA	WARP
2014	CDR	A	19	3	5	0	19	19	87.0	75	4	24	62	2.5	6.4	57%	.270	1.14	2.59	3.73	5.26	0.2
2015	MIN	MLB	20	3	5	0	13	13	57.0	71	7	27	26	4.3	4.1	49%	.311	1.71	5.99	5.92	6.51	-0.5
2016	MIN	MLB	21	7	9	0	28	28	173.7	184	17	67	106	3.5	5.5	49%	.293	1.45	4.57	4.67	4.97	0.2

Breakout: 0%   Improve: 0%   Collapse: 0%   Attrition: 0%   MLB: 0%   Upside: 7   *Comparables: Jonathan Pettibone, Kyle Ryan, T.J. House*

Drafted/Acquired: 1st round, 2013 draft, St. Pius X HS (Houston, TX)

Previous Ranking: #4 (Org), #54 (Top 101)

What Happened in 2014: The highly regarded Texas native flashed the type of stuff and promise that made him the fourth overall pick in 2013, but some shoulder issues prevented Stewart from logging a full workload in his full-season debut.

Strengths: Athletic build; easy delivery; fast arm; fastball sits 92-95, with arm-side run; creates good downward angle; velocity has potential to tick up a bit; hard bite to slider in mid-80s; bat-missing potential; curveball flashes tight two-plane break; changes eye levels well with offering; turns over change with arm-side fade and some drop; plus command profile; high competitive nature.

Weaknesses: Body is on the mature side for age; physical gains likely to be more limited; still learning how to throw secondary stuff for strikes; tends to consistently try to bury curveball and slider; will cast curve; can get too soft and lose teeth; change is presently more like a fastball pitcher is taking something off of; too firm and lacks finish at times.

Risk Factor/Injury History: High; yet to reach upper levels; health concerns (type 1 diabetes/shoulder impingement in 2014); command progression.

Bret Sayre's Fantasy Take: Stewart has the highest fantasy upside of any starting pitcher in this system, including the closer names ahead of him and the younger guys behind him. At peak, he could come close to 200 strikeouts with that fastball/slider combination and, with a strong control profile, could throw a ton of innings to boot. If the shoulder soreness is nothing major, Stewart could pitch himself into a top-five fantasy pitching prospect by season's end.

The Year Ahead: Stewart did little to disappoint during his debut season, outside of offer some mild durability concerns after missing some time in the middle of the season due to a shoulder impingement and having things shut down early in mid-August after having trouble getting loose in a start. All indications were that the organization was taking precautionary measures with one of their prized assets and that the 20-year-old is at full health heading into this season. This right-hander features four pitches that all flash the potential to round to better than average, with both the fastball and slider already consistently playing right around plus. Toss in extremely easy arm action with a high level of athleticism and the peak payout can be of the frontline variety. The near term for Stewart resides with improving his command, which has a good chance to take steps forward with repetition due to his overall looseness and ease. An assignment in the Florida State League to start the season will be a challenge for the young arm, but the present quality of the stuff points to his being able to adjust and assimilate quickly. Don't rule out the possibility of the prospect finishing out 2015 in Double-A, in the process showing that the gap to the on-paper potential is quickly closing.

#28

BP Top
101
Prospects

5. Jose Berrios   RHP

Born: 5/27/94   **Age:** 21   **Bats:** R   **Throws:** R   **Height:** 6'0"   **Weight:** 185

MLB ETA	CT	FB	CH	CB	SL	OFP	Realistic
Late 2015	–	60	65	60	–	**60** NO. 3 STARTER	**50** LATE INN RP (SETUP)

YEAR	TEAM	LVL	AGE	W	L	SV	G	GS	IP	H	HR	BB	K	BB9	SO9	GB%	BABIP	WHIP	ERA	FIP	FRA	WARP
2014	ROC	AAA	20	0	1	0	1	1	3.0	7	0	3	3	9.0	9.0	38%	.538	3.33	18.00	4.36	3.84	0.0
2014	NBR	AA	20	3	4	0	8	8	40.7	33	2	12	28	2.7	6.2	45%	.261	1.11	3.54	3.65	4.41	0.6
2014	FTM	A+	20	9	3	0	16	16	96.3	78	4	23	109	2.1	10.2	38%	.297	1.05	1.96	2.51	3.33	2.0
2015	MIN	MLB	21	6	8	0	20	20	106.3	115	11	45	84	3.8	7.1	40%	.316	1.51	4.85	4.76	5.28	0.1
2016	MIN	MLB	22	8	10	0	26	26	154.0	179	19	51	116	3.0	6.8	40%	.323	1.49	5.13	4.57	5.58	-0.8

Breakout: 0%   Improve: 0%   Collapse: 0%   Attrition: 0%   MLB: 0%   Upside: 21   *Comparables: Jarrod Parker, Carlos Martinez, Drew Hutchison*

#48

BP Top
101
Prospects

Drafted/Acquired: 1st round, 2012 draft, Papa Juan HS (Bayamon, PR)

Previous Ranking: #6 (Org), #75 (Top 101)

What Happened in 2014: The right-hander took a strong step forward, with his electric stuff leading to a quick mastery of High-A as 20-year-old, pushing him into the upper levels a bit earlier than expected.

Strengths: Extremely fast arm; athletic delivery; fastball comfortably works 92-95; good life when thrown in lower tier of strike zone; snaps curveball with tight rotation and strong depth; hard downward break through zone; future out pitch; turns over quality changeup; flashes arm-side fade and occasional bottom-out action; throws with arm speed in sync with fastball; shows as present plus offering; likes to come after hitters on the mound; competitive nature; excellent makeup.

Weaknesses: Has to consistently work in the lower tier to create angle on hitters; limited size; fastball gets flat when from middle of thighs and up; prone to hard contact when stuff is elevated; wraps wrist when delivering curveball at times; can roll and sweep; still learning how to throw good strikes; can struggle spotting heater to glove side.

Risk Factor/Injury History: Moderate; limited Double-A experience; command progression.

Bret Sayre's Fantasy Take: There isn't ace potential here, despite how good his lower minors' stats were, but Berrios can be a strong contributor in all four categories at the major-league level. Of course, he'll have to prove he can throw 200 innings in a season, but he keeps getting closer to doing so. If it happens, he can have a future as a solid SP3 who can strikeout 170 batters and keep his ratios strong.

The Year Ahead: Berrios certainly made some noise last season as a rising arm within this system, as the right-hander showed tangible developmental progress, continuing to refine his arsenal and sharpen the overall package. The stuff can be downright electric in outings, and he flashed much more consistency over the course of the long season as well. The road will get tougher for the native of Puerto Rico this year in the upper levels, with how well he can consistently spot in the lower tier of the strike zone with the heater and change the eye levels of hitters in conjunction as key aspects to look for. While the realistic role lists a late-innings reliever—and there are sentiments from evaluators that the profile may fit the best there over the long haul—the view here sees Berrios having a good chance to make things work in the rotation and push up close to the overall future potential. This is a prospect with the mentality, work ethic, and feel for his craft to continue to make the necessary improvements. If adjustments click quickly for Berrios in this full tour in Double-A, there's a good chance he's going to roll to a major-league debut at some point before season's end and have a legit chance to win spot in 2016.

6. Nick Gordon   SS

Born: 10/24/95   **Age:** 19   **Bats:** L   **Throws:** R   **Height:** 6'0"   **Weight:** 160

MLB ETA	Hit	Power	Run	Glove	Arm	OFP	Realistic
Late 2018	60	–	55	60	60	**60** 1ST DIV PLAYER	**50** ML REGULAR

YEAR	TEAM	LVL	AGE	PA	R	2B	3B	HR	RBI	BB	SO	SB	CS	AVG/OBP/SLG	TAv	BABIP	BRR	FRAA	WARP
2014	ELZ	Rk	18	256	46	6	4	1	28	11	45	11	7	.294/.333/.366	.250	.352	2.4	SS(49): 9.8	1.9
2015	MIN	MLB	19	250	21	9	1	1	15	7	69	3	2	.207/.233/.270	.185	.280	-0.2	SS 8	-0.1
2016	MIN	MLB	20	250	20	7	1	2	18	5	65	4	2	.218/.237/.275	.192	.284	0.1	SS 7	-1.6

Breakout: 0%   Improve: 0%   Collapse: 0%   Attrition: 0%   MLB: 0%   Upside: 4   *Comparables: Danny Santana, Hector Gomez, Hernan Perez*

#70

BP Top
101
Prospects

Drafted/Acquired: 1st round, 2014 draft, Olympia HS (Orlando, FL)

Previous Ranking: NR

What Happened in 2014: Considered the top infield talent in the 2014 draft, the Florida native was quickly snatched up at fifth overall and proceeded to get a solid introduction to professional ball in the Appalachian League in preparation for ramping into the developmental journey.

Strengths: Above-average athlete; good feel for the game; shows fluid overall actions; quick hands; compact stroke from left side; barrels offerings well into both gaps; looks foul line to foul line; can put a charge into ball when turning on fastballs; soft glove; gets feet and body in position well; arm for left side of the infield; high potential to stick up the middle; gets out of box well; high baseball IQ.

Weaknesses: Limited physical projection; swing is more line-drive oriented; power likely to play below to fringe-average; will need to learn when to take chances to make pitchers pay; can lunge and reach at off-speed stuff; in early stages of developing understanding of strike zone; can struggle with reads in field; will get caught flat footed, limiting range; needs to rein arm in.

Risk Factor/Injury History: High; short-season résumé; hit tool progression.

Bret Sayre's Fantasy Take: The ability to stick at shortstop, while a nice bonus in fantasy, isn't as important as it is for the Twins. The combination of a distant ETA and the lack of a carrying fantasy tool (despite a potentially strong contribution in batting average) leaves Gordon on the outside looking in at the first round in most dynasty drafts this year.

The Year Ahead: Gordon represents yet another front-of-the-draft talent procured by the Twins in recent years, which speaks volumes to both the stockpile of top prospects in this system and the plights of the big club. The 19-year-old is a natural defender at shortstop, with a projectable hit tool highlighted by quick hands and a compact stroke. Despite the young age and inexperience as a pro, this prospect offers a higher floor and less (to a certain extent) variability in the overall outcome given the value in a legit up-the-middle defender, where things can comfortably play as a first-division player for a long stretch of his career. Gordon is likely set for an assignment in the Midwest League this season, with the objective to be heavily focused on building the offensive foundation and getting ample reps in the field to begin smoothing out the rough edges with his reads. There's strong feel for the game here, with the belief that strides and improvements will begin to take as the experience grows. A massive acceleration with the skill set during 2015 is a low-probability expectation, but by season's end the shortstop should be showing tangible progress forward and offering the promise that he can join the headliner of this list as a strong up-the-middle backbone for future seasons to come.

7. Lewis Thorpe LHP

Born: 11/23/95 **Age:** 19 **Bats:** R **Throws:** L **Height:** 6'1" **Weight:** 160

MLB ETA	CT	FB	CH	CB	SL	OFP	Realistic
Late 2017	–	70	65	60	55	70 NO. 2 STARTER	50 NO. 4 STARTER

YEAR	TEAM	LVL	AGE	W	L	SV	G	GS	IP	H	HR	BB	K	BB9	SO9	GB%	BABIP	WHIP	ERA	FIP	FRA	WARP
2014	CDR	A	18	3	2	0	16	16	71.7	62	7	36	80	4.5	10.0	44%	.297	1.37	3.52	4.24	4.43	0.9
2015	MIN	MLB	19	3	5	0	12	12	53.7	59	7	30	43	5.0	7.2	42%	.315	1.65	5.48	5.52	5.95	-0.2
2016	MIN	MLB	20	7	9	0	28	28	169.0	176	20	68	138	3.6	7.3	42%	.303	1.44	4.70	4.56	5.11	0.0

Breakout: 0%   Improve: 0%   Collapse: 0%   Attrition: 0%   MLB: 0%   Upside: 13   *Comparables: Jordan Lyles, Taijuan Walker, Martin Perez*

Drafted/Acquired: International Free Agent, 2012, Australia

Previous Ranking: #8 (Org), #101 (Top 101)

What Happened in 2014: The teenage Aussie left-hander hit full-season ball earlier than expected, where he more than held his own during a half a season of action and showed an overall package that is beginning to take the initial steps forward.

Strengths: Very projectable body; delivery is loose, easy, and repeatable; keeps arm in slot well; fastball works 91-94 with arm-side run; potential for more velocity gains; spins curve with good snap; flashes tight rotation and knee-bending depth; will change shape; can turn over changeup with high-quality action; flashes feel for slider with short, tight break; plus overall command profile; advanced pitchability for age.

Weaknesses: Still maturing physically; needs more strength to handle rigors of position; mechanics can get loose deeper into outings; velocity will dip at times; in the process of building arm strength; curve will get soft and big; fastball tends to flatten out in upper tier; will need to sharpen ability to spot east/west in lower tier; slider least mature of secondary offerings; tends to sweep more than dart.

Risk Factor/Injury History: High; limited full-season experience; 19 years old; ability to withstand workload.

Bret Sayre's Fantasy Take: Thorpe is a very exciting arm in our circles, as he has the potential for three bat-missing pitches—which gives him the potential for elite strikeout numbers. The control and command are things to watch, as those affect his overall upside, but with reasonable steps forward there, he could work his way to SP2 standing.

The Year Ahead: Last season shouldn't be considered a full-fledged breakout for Thorpe, but it's definitely an early sign that this arm is starting to gain developmental traction and that a larger outburst can be achieved in the not-so-distant future. While the 19-year-old left-hander is still on the raw side and has a ways to go, the arm has shown progress tightening up his stuff in the last twelve months and has begun to experience physical gains that are helping to push advancements quicker. There really isn't any rush here with the prospect, so a return to the Midwest League in 2015 to build more innings before being bumped up to the next level shouldn't be seen as a negative development. One area of unknown for Thorpe is how well the stuff is going to play over the course of a full season. The Aussie has seen an uptick in velocity, but it hasn't been tested as to whether it is something that can be maintained. This season will be about establishing a full year of workload, and there's a good chance that this arm can take a legit jump forward.

#91
BP Top 101 Prospects

8. Nick Burdi RHP

Born: 1/19/93 **Age:** 22 **Bats:** R **Throws:** R **Height:** 6'5" **Weight:** 215

MLB ETA	CT	FB	CH	CB	SL	OFP	Realistic
2015	–	80	50	–	60	60 TIER 1 CLOSER	55 CLOSER/SETUP

YEAR	TEAM	LVL	AGE	W	L	SV	G	GS	IP	H	HR	BB	K	BB9	SO9	GB%	BABIP	WHIP	ERA	FIP	FRA	WARP
2014	FTM	A+	21	2	0	1	7	0	7.3	5	0	2	12	2.5	14.7	46%	.385	0.95	0.00	1.35	2.07	0.2
2014	CDR	A	21	0	0	4	13	0	13.0	8	0	8	26	5.5	18.0	55%	.400	1.23	4.15	1.33	2.50	0.4
2015	MIN	MLB	22	2	1	1	34	0	34.3	32	3	17	38	4.5	10.0	46%	.321	1.42	4.12	4.14	4.48	0.3
2016	MIN	MLB	23	3	1	3	58	0	58.7	50	5	28	65	4.3	10.0	46%	.299	1.34	3.59	3.80	3.90	0.7

Breakout: 0%   **Improve:** 0%   **Collapse:** 0%   **Attrition:** 0%   **MLB:** 0%   **Upside:** 26   *Comparables: Stephen Pryor, Tommy Kahnle, Drew Storen*

#99

BP Top 101 Prospects

Drafted/Acquired: 2nd round, 2014 draft, University of Louisville (Louisville, KY)

Previous Ranking: NR

What Happened in 2014: The fireballer out of the University of Louisville didn't disappoint with the radar gun readings after signing with the organization and continued to add fuel to the thoughts during his initial transition to professional ball that a fast track to the majors is likely.

Strengths: Elite arm strength; sturdy build; can use body to advantage; fastball easily operates 96-100; capable of touching higher; explosive offering; hitters must gear up; generates late swings; can be very overpowering; snaps slider with loose wrist; hard, off-the-table break with downward action; bat-misser; turns over changeup with arm-side fade; competitor; likes to come right after hitters.

Weaknesses: Effort in delivery; landing can be inconsistent; not the cleanest of footwork; rushes at times; command and control can come and go; fastball will work too elevated and in the middle of the plate; will need to spot more against advanced bats; change can be too firm and blend in with slider; needs to throw more strikes overall.

Risk Factor/Injury History: Low; mature arsenal; command consistency.

Bret Sayre's Fantasy Take: The thought of having a future closer in your farm team is certainly an admirable one, but with the historical inconsistencies of "safe" college relievers and difficulty in predicting role outcomes, Burdi remains a difficult sell to dynasty leaguers. He should not be taken in the first 30 picks of drafts this offseason.

The Year Ahead: When it comes to high-octane fastballs and lighting up the radar gun at or near triple digits consistently, Burdi has the market cornered. But this right-hander isn't just all about the heater, as he can snap off a mid-to-upper-80s slider with wipeout break and sprinkle in a fading changeup when needed. Make no mistake about the profile here; this is a reliever all the way, but one who can provide considerable impact at the back of a bullpen and take ownership of the ninth inning. This is more of a finished product, though Burdi can stand to fine-tune his fastball command and throw more strikes overall. There's also a tendency to work a bit too elevated, but he can challenge often due to the quality of the fastball. The 22-year-old should start the season in the upper levels, where the power stuff will likely overmatch opposing hitters in short order. It'll be a good sign to see the righty tightening up on the aforementioned needs, which will point to a smoother assimilation into the majors and go a long way toward solidifying him as a top-flight closer over the long haul.

9. Jorge Polanco 2B/SS

Born: 7/5/93 **Age:** 21 **Bats:** B **Throws:** R **Height:** 5'11" **Weight:** 165

MLB ETA	Hit	Power	Run	Glove	Arm	OFP	Realistic
Debuted in 2014	60	–	60	55	–	55 >AVG REGULAR	50 AVG ML PLAYER

YEAR	TEAM	LVL	AGE	PA	R	2B	3B	HR	RBI	BB	SO	SB	CS	AVG/OBP/SLG	TAv	BABIP	BRR	FRAA	WARP
2014	MIN	MLB	20	8	2	1	1	0	3	2	2	0	0	.333/.500/.833	.455	.500	0.1	SS(4): 0.0	0.2
2014	NBR	AA	20	157	13	6	0	1	16	9	28	7	3	.281/.323/.342	.246	.342	0.8	SS(33): 1.6, 2B(4): -0.1	0.6
2014	FTM	A+	20	432	61	17	6	6	45	46	60	10	8	.291/.364/.415	.282	.327	1.0	SS(86): -0.6, 2B(6): -1.0	2.8
2015	MIN	MLB	21	250	26	11	2	2	19	15	50	3	2	.251/.297/.347	.236	.304	-0.1	SS -1, 2B -0	0.2
2016	MIN	MLB	22	535	58	26	4	7	52	37	95	7	4	.274/.323/.388	.265	.320	-0.1	SS -4	1.5

Breakout: 0%   **Improve:** 0%   **Collapse:** 0%   **Attrition:** 0%   **MLB:** 0%   **Upside:** 26   *Comparables: Tyler Pastornicky, Carlos Sanchez, Jose Pirela*

Drafted/Acquired: International Free Agent, 2009, Dominican Republic

Previous Ranking: #10 (Org)

What Happened in 2014: The smooth-swinging infielder created a lot of contact across two levels of the minors, with a brief call-up to The Show sandwiched between, serving as a taste of life with the big club.

Strengths: Quick hands; type that easily stay inside of ball; gets barrel on offerings consistently from both sides of the plate; line-drive stroke; gap power; all-fields approach—consistently looks up the middle; easy-plus runner; soft hands; quick first step; good glove technique; intelligent player.

Weaknesses: Body can stand to add strength to handle grind of long season; lacks arm strength to make play from deep in the hole; better fit for second base; defense can be on the loose side; power is more doubles than over the fence; could stand to look to muscle up more to keep arms honest; offensive profile hinges on hit tool playing to full utility; runs well, but jumps need work to round into stolen-base threat.

Risk Factor/Injury History: Moderate; limited Double-A experience; hit tool will need to carry the profile.

Bret Sayre's Fantasy Take: In a system of enormous upside, Polanco is an exception—though as a potential .290 hitter who could steal 20 bases (despite the minor-league totals), there's some heat to the profile. Of course, he's more of a MI play even at best.

The Year Ahead: Polanco's brief call to the majors from High-A last year was a move made more out of necessity, but spoke to the belief in the 21-year-old's makeup and ability to handle such a transition. The mind is also an asset for the Dominican when it comes to his offensive approach. The switch-hitter is more than willing to use the whole field and take what is given to him from opposing arms; he rarely tries to sell out or overswing. These attributes allow his quick hands and plus bat speed to do the rest. A full go-around in Double-A this season should further test Polanco's ability to make consistent contact and begin to challenge him as a hitter to do a little more damage in situations that dictate it. While the actions and glove in the field have been getting better, the arm isn't really suited for the left side of the infield, and second base is the likely home at the major-league level. There's a utility floor in the profile, with the translation of the hit tool as the leading factor to achieving status as a regular.

10. Stephen Gonsalves   LHP

Born: 7/8/94   **Age:** 20   **Bats:** L   **Throws:** L   **Height:** 6'5"   **Weight:** 190

MLB ETA	CT	FB	CH	CB	SL	OFP	Realistic
2018	–	65	65	55	–	65 NO. 2/3 STARTER	50 NO. 4 STARTER

YEAR	TEAM	LVL	AGE	W	L	SV	G	GS	IP	H	HR	BB	K	BB9	SO9	GB%	BABIP	WHIP	ERA	FIP	FRA	WARP
2014	CDR	A	19	2	3	0	8	8	36.7	31	1	11	44	2.7	10.8	35%	.326	1.15	3.19	2.50	3.32	0.9
2014	ELZ	Rk	19	2	0	0	6	6	29.0	23	1	10	26	3.1	8.1	45%	.289	1.14	2.79	3.36	6.05	0.1
2015	MIN	MLB	20	2	4	0	10	10	44.0	49	5	24	34	4.9	7.0	42%	.319	1.66	5.44	5.33	5.91	-0.2
2016	MIN	MLB	21	7	9	0	27	27	166.0	177	17	70	126	3.8	6.8	42%	.309	1.49	4.75	4.55	5.17	-0.1

Breakout: 0%   **Improve:** 0%   **Collapse:** 0%   **Attrition:** 0%   **MLB:** 0%   **Upside:** 29   *Comparables: Trevor Cahill, Chris Tillman, Jenrry Mejia*

Drafted/Acquired: 4th round, 2013 draft, Cathedral Catholic HS (San Diego, CA)

Previous Ranking: On The Rise

What Happened in 2014: The left-hander impressed during his first full professional season, with the shine and early feel for the raw stuff pushing him to a one-month stint in full-season ball to close out the year.

Strengths: Very projectable arm; frame to grow into; feel for craft; easy, repeatable delivery; capable of creating good angle and plane; fastball works 91-93 with late arm-side life; touches up higher in short spurts (95); potential to add sitting velocity with physical maturation; turns over quality changeup; present plus offering; excellent parachuting action; swing-and-miss offering; flashes feel for spinning curveball; spike break; high potential for command growth.

Weaknesses: On the lean and wiry side; body is immature; needs added strength to enhance overall package and hold up over long run; delivery can come and go in stretches; not a great present finisher; fastball command is below average; will work in dangerous spots elevated; curve is inconsistent; often gets loose and slurvy; still learning how to create consistent snap; at times deliberate delivering change.

Risk Factor/Injury History: High; limited pro experience; large gap between present and future.

Bret Sayre's Fantasy Take: Sure, the Twins really need another big upside arm. Gonsalves is a name that is likely unowned in plenty of leagues that roster 250-plus prospects, but shouldn't be. The fastball/change combo from the left side is one that can be fantasy friendly from a strikeout perspective.

The Year Ahead: Gonsalves is one of those arms to really dream on, with both the raw stuff and size to round into a highly effective starter down the line. The left-hander gave a glimpse of how things can look during a brief taste of full-season ball last August, when both the quality of the fastball and changeup stood at the forefront. Each offering shows the promise to evolve into a legit weapon at his disposal. While the curveball is on the inconsistent side, there's already been good progress since signing, with one evaluator spoken to when putting this list together expressing the belief that it is only a matter of time before the offering is on a similar level to the other two. The potential for three above-average-to-better pitches speaks loudly to what this arm can become. At the center of Gonsalves' near-term development is the need for added strength and more consistency finishing his delivery, which will serve as a strong jolt for really pushing this package forward. Expect some ebb and flow during the season at A-Ball, mainly in regards to holding his stamina over the grind of the year and working to lock in the delivery, but it's a prospect who can really start to make waves at this time next offseason and push as yet another riser in this deep system.

Prospects on the Rise

1. RHP Michael Cederoth: When the Twins took this right-hander out of San Diego State in the third round, it gave them the nod for landing the two hardest throwers in this year's draft. Like new system-mate Nick Burdi, Cederoth routinely dials his heater up to the triple digits and served as a closer in college last season. The 22-year-old still possesses the depth of a starter's arsenal (he converted to the bullpen last season), and he'll also feature a slider, changeup, and curve into sequences. The slider and change are regarded as the lead secondary pieces, though the curve will flash solid depth at times. Look for him to keep getting stretched out in a starter's role to help smooth out the delivery more and further sharpen the secondary stuff in 2015. The smart money says the end outcome is a high-leverage reliever, but don't rule out that chance the organization lets it marinate for a bit as a starter to see if some adjustments take.

2. 1B Lewin Diaz: The 2013 international signee out of the Dominican Republic brings plus-plus raw power to the diamond, where the strength level and already filled-out nature of the body stand out considerably for an 18-year-old. There's very little projection needed for drawing a physical conclusion with this prospect. Chatter from sources during last year's Fall Instructional League highlighted the ease with which Diaz creates power and the natural loft in his swing. Each source spoken to was also quick to point out the "five o'clock" nature of his hit tool presently and unevenness with the speed of the game. Both of these are aspects to be expected from a player with this experience level, but signs that point to a more modest early-career translation. The first-base-only nature always brings pause, but the power here can play and end up playing big. A stateside debut in 2015 should be in the cards, and a showing that proves the hit tool is more in line with the competition will start pushing the stock considerably in short order. You have been warned.

3. LHP Cameron Booser: Injuries have been a reoccurring theme for the 23-year-old left-hander since high school. He dealt with Tommy John, a torn ACL, and other elbow discomforts along the way before finding himself signed into the organization as an undrafted free agent in 2013. This arm is a deep sleeper in a thick system, but an extended clean bill of health and opportunity to throw consistently may just prove there's more than initially met the eye. Reports from sources highlighted a fastball that was up to 96-99 mph by late season, paired with

---

FROM THE FIELD

Kohl Stewart

Team: Minnesota Twins

Evaluator: Jordan Gorosh

Dates seen: June 9, 2014

Affiliate: Cedar Rapids Kernels (Low-A, Twins)

OFP: 65

Realistic role: no. 3 starter

Mechanics: Prototypical pitcher's build. Ultra athlete with strong, thick legs. High three-quarters with slow leg lift and clean arm action. Simple, repeatable delivery. Great posture. Stride length is excellent; finishes well over his front foot, generates solid hip torque. Not much effort, ball jumps out of hand.

Pitch type	Present grade	Future grade	Sitting velocity	Peak velocity	Report
FB	55	65	93-96	96	Big life up and down in zone; really explodes at times. Natural arm-side run. Command is high schoolish and loose at present, but delivery is extremely repeatable, and command could improve the pitch by a full grade. Lost half a tick in the later innings and averaged 91-93, but could reach back for mid-90s if he needed it. Went to a two-seamer late, which possessed even more arm-side run. Keeps the pitch off barrels, often yielding weak contact or broken bats.
SL	55	65	82-84	85	Hard snap with horizontal movement. 11-5 action that veers away from right-handed hitters. Looks like a fastball and makes left turn about 30 feet out of hand. Not an offering that's thrown for a strike at present, more of a chase pitch. Often keeps it low and away from righties, and can back foot to lefties. Swing-and-miss pitch to either-handed hitters, will be out pitch at major-league level. Can flash plus-plus.
CH	40	50	83-85	85	Shows feel for change. Arm speed lets pitch play up to major-league average. Not a pitch he throws with conviction yet, but turns it over nicely. Not thrown for a strike at this time. Throws predominantly to left-handed hitters and has some depth and fade. Feel for pitching will help refine this offering and make it an average pitch in time.
CB	40	50	76-78	78	Amateurish offering at present. Slurvy and high out of hand. Used it the least of any pitch. Slower than slider, with more vertical movement. Shows ability to generate spin and loose wrist, offering the ability to let it become major-league average. Inconsistent; could hang high and arm side, then flash major-league qualities.

Overall: Stewart's ceiling is that of a no. 2 starter who can log innings. May have four major-league-quality offerings. Due to big-time athleticism and the ability to repeat his delivery, the fastball command profile is outstanding and will also allow other pitches to play up. The gap between what the pitcher is now and what he will be is fairly large, but he's very polished for a teenager. The slider has wipeout potential and could miss bats at the major-league level right now. Showed ability to move the ball around to all quadrants and keep the ball off the barrel.

Does little things well on the mound. 1.15-1.27 times to home plate, and neutralized running game. Often would pause for a beat longer and give multiple looks to baserunners. Gold Glove-caliber fielder, and very aware of game situations. Usually would tag high school arms in Low-A with "high" risk proposition, but athleticism and polish give him a higher probability of reaching ceiling.

a hard-breaking slider and change he can turn over with some feel. One evaluator spoken to expressed strong thoughts that this may just be the type of late-blooming arm that seems to come out of nowhere to cement himself on the map. The ability to stay healthy is obviously a concern and will be closely watched this season, along with whether the uptick in stuff is just a short-term mirage, but don't rule out that further traction can make this more of a known name at this point next year.

Factors on the Farm

Prospects likely to contribute at the major-league level in 2015

1. RHP Jake Reed: If it seems like a theme here, it is. Last year's fifth-round pick out of Oregon is another freshly acquired arm that can track quickly through the system and potentially reach the bigs this year. Like his peers, Reed is a power arm with an aggressive mentality and the ability to get nasty in short spurts. The lively mid-90s fastball and hard breaking ball headline this package. The 22-year-old also comes from more of a low-to-mid three-quarters look that creates an uncomfortable angle and solid run with the heater. The advanced stuff should carve hitters up into the upper levels, where if Reed continues to hit little resistance, he can get a look as a seventh- or eighth-inning arm and start bridging innings as the summer months heat up.

2. RHP Trevor May: The overall output has never really lined up with the talent, but the right-hander put together a solid 2014 in Triple-A, although the call-up to The Show left a lot to be desired. May should get a chance to put his name into the hat for a look in the rotation this year; if he can place his fastball down in the zone more and stay out of the thick of the plate, the results can be indicative of a back-end starter over the long run. It's a big-league arm, and one who can help in some capacity if called upon and gain legs as a late-bloomer.

3. 2B/OF Eddie Rosario: After Rosario missed time to start the year (suspension for a drug of abuse), inconsistency plagued the left-handed hitter before a strong run in the Arizona Fall League, where he ended up second in the league in batting average. Rosario certainly has talent with the stick, as he flashes a smooth stroke with some leverage and the ability to impact offerings with backspin. Too often, though, the 23-year-old loses his identity as a hitter and tries to play the over-the-fence masher role instead of the gap-to-gap hitter with some pop. There's a good chance Rosario gets a look in 2015 if the late-season momentum keeps going, where adjustments with his mind-set will need to be a reality versus tease for this profile to maintain status as a regular as opposed to an up-and-down type filling spots on a roster as needed over the long run.

1. Noah Syndergaard   RHP

Born: 8/29/92   **Age:** 22   **Bats:** L   **Throws:** R   **Height:** 6'6"   **Weight:** 240

MLB ETA	CT	FB	CH	CB	SL		OFP	Realistic
2015	–	80	65	70	–		70 NO. 2 STARTER	65 NO. 2/3 STARTER

YEAR	TEAM	LVL	AGE	W	L	SV	G	GS	IP	H	HR	BB	K	BB9	SO9	GB%	BABIP	WHIP	ERA	FIP	FRA	WARP
2014	LVG	AAA	21	9	7	0	26	26	133.0	154	11	43	145	2.9	9.8	47%	.378	1.48	4.60	3.70	4.22	3.2
2015	NYN	MLB	22	7	8	0	25	25	120.3	108	11	36	118	2.7	8.8	48%	.317	1.20	3.50	3.54	3.81	1.1
2016	NYN	MLB	23	11	10	0	32	32	207.7	191	19	59	199	2.6	8.6	48%	.318	1.20	3.62	3.31	3.94	1.0

Breakout: 14%   **Improve:** 28%   **Collapse:** 2%   **Attrition:** 10%   **MLB:** 37%   **Upside:** 52   *Comparables: Gerrit Cole, Robbie Erlin, Danny Duffy*

Drafted/Acquired: 1st round, 2010 draft, Legacy HS (Mansfield, TX)

Previous Ranking: #1 (Org), #11 (Top 101)

What Happened in 2014: Syndergaard proved to be mortal in Triple-A, giving up 154 hits in 133 innings, but still fanned more than a batter an inning.

Strengths: Excellent size; uses frame to advantage; downhill thrower; elite fastball; routinely works mid-to-high-90s, with arm-side life; can overpower with offering; strong feel for curve; throws with a loose wrist; stays on top of pitch to create deep, downward break; already a mature piece of arsenal (present plus); will miss bats at highest level; change shows guise to fastball; throws with similar arm speed and angle; fades arm side aggressively; room for more growth; very athletic for size; projection for command improvement.

Weaknesses: Command presently more of the area variety; needs to throw quality strikes more often; falls into ruts of working elevated and in challenge mode; still learning the ins and outs of craft; at times wraps with curveball and will roll; change can be on the firm side and lack enough separation.

Risk Factor/Injury History: Low; 133 innings at Triple-A; further command polishing.

Bret Sayre's Fantasy Take: The big right-hander will enter 2015 as the top fantasy pitching prospect in baseball, and if he's being undervalued due to his struggles during the first half of 2014, this may be the best time to deal for him. He has the makings of a lower-tier fantasy ace who can support strong ratios and 200-plus strikeouts.

The Year Ahead: After a rapid rise into the upper minors, Syndergaard experienced growing pains last year. Not that uncommon really, but for a player with lofty expectations it can cause some ripples. The stuff here is absolutely legit. The big right-hander is a classic power pitcher, with an explosive, high-octane fastball that can blow away hitters and the type of curveball to leave heads shaking. Add in a progressing changeup and it's almost unfair. This is a monster in the making. The command and mind-set are where the growth needs to occur to reach his frontline potential. Syndergaard fills the zone with strikes, but throws too many meaty ones and likes to pitch more north than south with his fastball. Reports from later in the year indicated the 22-year-old was adjusting and it is expected that will continue. Getting whacked around consistently is usually humbling. With some finishing touches, Syndergaard gives the Mets another power arm toward the front of their rotation, and a glimpse of what the long-term production can look like should come in 2015.

> #9
> BP Top 101 Prospects

2. Steven Matz   LHP

Born: 5/29/91   **Age:** 24   **Bats:** R   **Throws:** L   **Height:** 6'2"   **Weight:** 200

MLB ETA	CT	FB	CH	CB	SL		OFP	Realistic
2015	–	65	60	65	–		65 NO. 2/3 STARTER	60 NO. 3 STARTER

YEAR	TEAM	LVL	AGE	W	L	SV	G	GS	IP	H	HR	BB	K	BB9	SO9	GB%	BABIP	WHIP	ERA	FIP	FRA	WARP
2014	BIN	AA	23	6	5	0	12	12	71.3	66	3	14	69	1.8	8.7	48%	.317	1.12	2.27	2.64	3.07	1.9
2014	SLU	A+	23	4	4	0	12	12	69.3	66	0	21	62	2.7	8.0	59%	.328	1.25	2.21	2.73	3.98	1.0
2015	NYN	MLB	24	6	8	0	22	22	116.3	107	10	43	101	3.3	7.8	49%	.313	1.29	3.87	3.95	4.21	0.4
2016	NYN	MLB	25	11	10	0	32	32	206.7	188	18	65	187	2.8	8.1	49%	.313	1.22	3.65	3.51	3.97	0.9

Breakout: 16%   **Improve:** 31%   **Collapse:** 14%   **Attrition:** 25%   **MLB:** 47%   **Upside:** 4   *Comparables: Chad Bettis, Andre Rienzo, Charles Brewer*

Drafted/Acquired: 2nd round, 2009 draft, Ward Melville HS (East Setauket, NY)

Previous Ranking: NR

What Happened in 2014: Matz continued to show that his injury history is in the past, logging 140 2/3 innings across two levels and posting a 2.24 ERA.

> #33
> BP Top 101 Prospects

Strengths: Clean, balanced delivery; soft landing; fast arm; hides ball well out of delivery; fastball works 91-94, at times with tail and sink; capable of reaching for more; curve flashes solid shape; tight rotation and depth at 76-79; projects to miss bats; flashes feel for changeup; able to turn over; displays fade, with occasional late tail (screwball action); throws secondary stuff with loose wrist; improving pitchability.

Weaknesses: Fastball can be straight; hittable when elevated despite velocity and deception; needs to fill lower tier of zone more often; can cast curve, which leaves it loopy and soft; tries to overthrow change; loses fading action; would be better served working to cut velocity a bit (84-86 at present); command needs more growth to round into better than average.

Risk Factor/Injury History: Low; achieved upper levels; arm injuries on résumé; playing catch-up due to late start.

Bret Sayre's Fantasy Take: This was the year that Matz began to surface on fantasy radars, as there have always been reasons not to believe, whether they were health or performance related. It's time to move on from that now, as Matz has the potential to be a SP4 as soon as 2016, with SP2 upside down the road, though impact will be tough to come by in 2015 due to the Mets' rotation depth. The left-hander should now be owned in nearly all dynasty formats.

The Year Ahead: Matz has now had two full seasons of good health and is showing the stuff that made him a second-round pick back in 2009. It all starts with the fastball for the left-hander, which jumps out of his delivery at velocities up to the mid-90s. Matz pairs his heater with a tight, breaking curve and fading changeup to keep opposing hitters at bay. The curve is presently the more advanced pitch, but the change has the potential to be right behind it. Those who believe in Matz see an arm that is blossoming into a potential fixture within the Mets' rotation. Reports from 2014 were extremely strong, with a lot of positive chatter on the pitcher's potential. The key area of improvement for his reaching that potential rests with polishing off the pitchability. It's more area command now for the lefty, but there is potential for growth. There's a good chance Matz makes his debut this season and begins putting a foothold on a rotation spot for a while.

3. Brandon Nimmo   CF

Born: 3/27/93   **Age:** 22   **Bats:** L   **Throws:** R   **Height:** 6'3"   **Weight:** 205

MLB ETA	Hit	Power	Run	Glove	Arm	OFP	Realistic
2016	50	55	50	50	60	55 >AVG REGULAR	50 AVG ML PLAYER

YEAR	TEAM	LVL	AGE	PA	R	2B	3B	HR	RBI	BB	SO	SB	CS	AVG/OBP/SLG	TAv	BABIP	BRR	FRAA	WARP
2014	BIN	AA	21	279	38	12	4	6	26	36	54	5	1	.238/.339/.396	.260	.283	0.1	CF(44): 0.9, LF(21): -1.3	0.5
2014	SLU	A+	21	279	59	9	5	4	25	50	51	9	3	.322/.448/.458	.320	.401	1.5	CF(56): -1.6	2.6
2015	NYN	MLB	22	250	27	8	2	3	19	29	72	2	1	.212/.311/.308	.245	.297	0.0	CF -0, LF -0	0.2
2016	NYN	MLB	23	250	27	8	2	4	22	28	74	2	1	.210/.306/.319	.241	.295	0.1	CF 0, LF 0	0.3

Breakout: 0%   Improve: 0%   Collapse: 0%   Attrition: 0%   MLB: 0%   Upside: 75   *Comparables: Aaron Hicks, Ryan Kalish, Brett Jackson*

Drafted/Acquired: 1st round, 2011 draft, East HS (Cheyenne, WY)

Previous Ranking: #9 (Org)

What Happened in 2014: The outfielder more than handled the Florida State League, posting a 906 OPS, but found the Eastern League much tougher, hitting .238 in 65 games.

Strengths: Smooth, fluid swing; hands to stay inside of baseball; stroke designed to hit from gap to gap; produces good backspin; improved physical strength could help tap into power; solid athlete; fundamentally sound in center; arm plays at all three outfield positions; shows instincts for the game; has made strong progress since turning pro.

Weaknesses: Average bat speed; concerns that hit tool will ceiling against high-quality stuff; may be more of a guess/cheat hitter; struggles against arm-side pitching; tends to lose backside and cave; average foot speed; corner spot may be the better fit if slows down further; needs more loft in swing to fully tap into power.

Risk Factor/Injury History: Low; upper-minors experience; hit tool utility.

Bret Sayre's Fantasy Take: Usually the "better in real life than fantasy" players are middle infielders, but Nimmo's skill set puts him in that camp as well. Of course, things change a bit in OBP leagues, as that's where he can make the biggest impact. However, an outfielder who can hit .260-.270 with around 15 homers and 15 steals is usable in just about every format.

The Year Ahead: Nimmo has definitely made strong strides since turning pro, which have been showing more and more on the field. There isn't anything high-end in the outfielder's game, but he does plenty well, suggesting this profile can work as a regular for a chunk of seasons. The 22-year-old shows good instincts out in center and works hard at his craft. Sources are mixed, though, as to whether he's going to stick at the position over the long haul. A slide over to a corner will put more pressure on the development of the stick. Nimmo is fairly sound with his swing, getting to the ball in an efficient path, and flashes loose hands that enable him to control the head of the bat. The bat speed against higher-end competition will bring about questions and he'll be tasked with proving he can rise to that challenge. There's still a good amount of work here to go and Nimmo will need ample time in the high minors, with the initial task of trying to implement adjustments against Double-A arms at the start of 2015.

#69
BP Top 101 Prospects

4. Amed Rosario   SS

Born: 11/20/95   **Age:** 19   **Bats:** R   **Throws:** R   **Height:** 6'2"   **Weight:** 170

MLB ETA	Hit	Power	Run	Glove	Arm	OFP	Realistic
2018	60	55	55	60	55	65 1ST DIV/OCC ALL-STAR	50 ML REGULAR

YEAR	TEAM	LVL	AGE	PA	R	2B	3B	HR	RBI	BB	SO	SB	CS	AVG/OBP/SLG	TAv	BABIP	BRR	FRAA	WARP
2014	SAV	A	18	31	2	0	1	1	4	1	11	0	0	.133/.161/.300	.157	.167	-0.1	SS(2): -0.1, 3B(1): -0.1	-0.3
2014	BRO	A-	18	290	39	11	5	1	23	17	47	7	3	.289/.337/.380	.274	.345	0.7	SS(64): 3.2	2.0
2015	NYN	MLB	19	250	20	8	1	2	16	8	74	1	1	.193/.220/.265	.191	.263	-0.2	SS -0, 3B -0	-0.8
2016	NYN	MLB	20	250	20	8	1	2	19	6	68	1	1	.207/.227/.283	.191	.271	-0.2	SS -1, 3B 0	-2.6

Breakout: 0%   **Improve:** 0%   **Collapse:** 0%   **Attrition:** 0%   **MLB:** 0%   **Upside:** 4   *Comparables: Hernan Perez, Danny Santana, Arismendy Alcantara*

Drafted/Acquired: International Free Agent, 2012, Dominican Republic

Previous Ranking: #5 (Org)

What Happened in 2014: The 2012 international signee took his talents to the New York-Penn League and flashed solid contact skills despite being only 18 years old.

Strengths: Fluid actions; good athlete; soft hands; strong defensive instincts; quick first step; decisive reads; solid-average to better range; arm to stick on left side of infield; quick, explosive wrists; feel for barreling the ball; loose hands; shows willingness to use the whole field; plus bat speed; room for power growth; body to continue to add strength; mind for the game.

Weaknesses: Overly aggressive hitter; will chase and get himself out; control of zone needs a lot of work; immature pitch recognition; swing can get loose; presently has some maintenance; large gap to reach power projection; loss of foot speed may hinder range; work to go with shoring up technique at short; plays on athleticism presently.

Risk Factor/Injury History: High; short-season résumé; large gap between present and future.

Bret Sayre's Fantasy Take: The ETA is what really hurts Rosario in terms of his fantasy value, as his fantasy upside is right there among the non-Syndergaard members of this organization. If you have the patience and the roster spot, he's a great long-term hold as the tools turn into skills, but in the time it takes to wait on Rosario, you could churn two or three prospects through that one spot.

The Year Ahead: Rosario is a long-lead player in terms of development time, but the tools point toward an impressive potential payout. He more than held his own as an 18-year-old in the college-heavy New York-Penn League, which speaks to his feel for the game and high baseball IQ. There is plenty of refinement needed with Rosario's game. It starts with toning down his approach at the plate and learning how to develop more of a plan during plate appearances. An assignment in full-season ball is going to challenge him to start adjusting immediately with this aspect of his game. All of the ingredients are here offensively to round into a contact hitter with some pop if the secondary skills continue to come along. There are some thoughts that physical development will slow Rosario down a bit and limit some of his range, but opinions are firm on his sticking at the position up to the highest level. It's going to take time, but this is a good-looking prospect and one that can jump into the upper tier with a good showing this season.

#78

BP Top
101
Prospects

5. Kevin Plawecki   C

Born: 2/26/91   **Age:** 24   **Bats:** R   **Throws:** R   **Height:** 6'2"   **Weight:** 225

MLB ETA	Hit	Power	Run	Glove	Arm	OFP	Realistic
2015	55	50	–	50	50	55 >AVG REGULAR	50 AVG ML PLAYER

YEAR	TEAM	LVL	AGE	PA	R	2B	3B	HR	RBI	BB	SO	SB	CS	AVG/OBP/SLG	TAv	BABIP	BRR	FRAA	WARP
2014	LVG	AAA	23	170	25	6	0	5	21	14	21	0	0	.283/.345/.421	.264	.299	-0.3	C(40): 0.6, 1B(1): -0.0	0.7
2014	BIN	AA	23	249	33	18	0	6	43	16	27	0	0	.326/.378/.487	.307	.344	0.8	C(54): -0.1	2.4
2015	NYN	MLB	24	250	23	12	0	5	26	14	43	0	0	.246/.304/.360	.260	.280	-0.5	C 0, 1B 0	0.8
2016	NYN	MLB	25	250	27	12	0	5	25	16	47	0	0	.239/.304/.357	.252	.279	-0.7	C 0, 1B 0	1.1

Breakout: 5%   **Improve:** 11%   **Collapse:** 18%   **Attrition:** 22%   **MLB:** 38%   **Upside:** 52   *Comparables: John Jaso, Curtis Casali, Jonathan Lucroy*

Drafted/Acquired: 1st round, 2012 draft, Purdue University (West Lafayette, IN)

Previous Ranking: #8 (Org)

What Happened in 2014: The catcher proved to be more advanced than Double-A arms, ripping .326, and then held his own after a promotion to Triple-A.

Strengths: Strong, filled-out frame; body to handle the rigors of the position; solid receiver; firm glove; uses body well; fundamentally sound; quicker release helps average arm strength play up; easy swing; quiet; direct to the point of contact; ability to get barrel on the ball; mature approach; gap power, with opportunity to muscle up in spots because of bat control.

#80

BP Top
101
Prospects

Weaknesses: Not much more tool growth left overall; no real leading tool; can be pitched to by high-quality arms; power likely to play down in favor of contact at highest level; defense projects as average; below-average speed; station-to-station runner.

Risk Factor/Injury History: Low; 43 games in Triple-A; consistency with bat.

Bret Sayre's Fantasy Take: The bar is set pretty low for catchers to be fantasy relevant, and with Plawecki's strong contact rate and potential for 12-15 homers, he has a good chance to be above that bar. However, the value proposition for stashing him in dynasty leagues now is different, given the difficult transition catchers have to make at the major-league level and the presence of Travis d'Arnaud ahead of him.

The Year Ahead: Plawecki proved to be more than up to the challenge posed by Double-A arms and passed a major test in the process. His contact ability and a mature approach serve him well at the plate. The 24-year-old is more than willing to grind through plate appearances, with a knack for getting into favorable hitting situations. That's going to have to continue for the catcher to do enough damage against the unforgiving arms in The Show. There's a chance the bat plateaus during his second tour of duty in the PCL, but the offensive profile likely rounds into a hitter who is a tough out in the lower portion of a big-league lineup. Add in Plawecki's potential for steady defense behind the dish, and this is a solid prospect with the overall game to be a contributing regular for a stretch of seasons.

6. Dilson Herrera 2B

Born: 3/3/94 **Age:** 21 **Bats:** R **Throws:** R **Height:** 5'10" **Weight:** 150

MLB ETA	Hit	Power	Run	Glove	Arm	OFP	Realistic
Debuted in 2014	55	55	60	55	50	60 1ST DIVISION PLAYER	50 AVG REGULAR

YEAR	TEAM	LVL	AGE	PA	R	2B	3B	HR	RBI	BB	SO	SB	CS	AVG/OBP/SLG	TAv	BABIP	BRR	FRAA	WARP
2014	NYN	MLB	20	66	6	0	1	3	11	7	17	0	0	.220/.303/.407	.255	.256	-0.9	2B(17): 0.1	0.0
2014	BIN	AA	20	278	50	17	3	10	48	29	52	9	4	.340/.406/.560	.333	.389	0.9	2B(55): -0.6, SS(8): -0.2	2.9
2014	SLU	A+	20	309	48	16	2	3	23	18	44	14	3	.307/.355/.410	.273	.353	0.3	2B(43): -2.0, SS(19): 1.4	1.2
2015	NYN	MLB	21	250	29	10	1	6	23	15	63	4	1	.239/.289/.368	.253	.298	0.1	2B 0, SS 0	0.7
2016	NYN	MLB	22	512	60	21	2	14	58	35	125	9	3	.250/.308/.395	.262	.307	0.3	2B 1	1.8

Breakout: 7% **Improve:** 17% **Collapse:** 4% **Attrition:** 12% **MLB:** 31% **Upside:** 54   *Comparables: Brett Lawrie, Jonathan Schoop, Lonnie Chisenhall*

Drafted/Acquired: International Free Agent, 2010, Colombia

Previous Ranking: NR

What Happened in 2014: Herrera busted out and rode the wave in a big way from High-A all the way to The Show, racking up 51 extra-base hits and posting an 858 OPS overall in the minors.

Strengths: Excellent athlete; fast-twitch muscle; plus bat speed; quick wrists, with strong hands for size; gap-to-gap power; drives through the ball; can put a charge into it for over-the-fence pop; quick feet in the field; ranges well at second; strong reactions; flashes defensive instincts for the position; plus runner; ability to impact the game on the bases.

Weaknesses: Aggressive approach; will try to sell out for power; swing loses fluidity in those instances; likes to get the head out in front of the ball; leaves him prone to off-speed stuff; swing on the long side; hit tool can play down as a result; learning how to slow the game down on both sides of the ball; needlessly rushes plays in the field; still raw overall.

Risk Factor/Injury History: Moderate; reached majors; polishing still needed on both sides of ball.

Bret Sayre's Fantasy Take: We saw flashes of the fantasy potential here in his cup of coffee in 2014, but the real fun will come when the Mets move on from Daniel Murphy, as there's currently not a place for him in New York. The specter of a .275 hitting second baseman with double-digit power and speed is very tempting, especially considering the near 100 percent ownership level of post-peak Ben Zobrist.

The Year Ahead: Herrera came out of relatively nowhere last season, fast-tracking to the highest level and putting himself on the map within the system in the process. The big draws here are the athleticism and plus bat speed, which give him the chance to do some nice things over the long haul at the plate and in the field. His game is rawer and rougher overall than the season line may indicate, though. Herrera is presently a free swinger who is still finding an identity as a hitter and learning the importance of being selective. Extended time in the upper levels leaves the chance he'll be exposed some against high-quality secondary stuff, though given his age he has a good chance to come along. A second baseman with the ability to hit in the .280s with pop and better-than-average defense is valuable. Just expect some more lead time and growing pains before reaching that potential outcome.

#82

BP Top 101 Prospects

7. Marcos Molina RHP

Born: 3/8/95 **Age:** 20 **Bats:** R **Throws:** R **Height:** 6'3" **Weight:** 188

MLB ETA	CT	FB	CH	CB	SL	OFP	Realistic
Late 2017	–	70	60	50	–	60 NO. 3 STARTER	50 NO. 4 STARTER

YEAR	TEAM	LVL	AGE	W	L	SV	G	GS	IP	H	HR	BB	K	BB9	SO9	GB%	BABIP	WHIP	ERA	FIP	FRA	WARP
2014	BRO	A-	19	7	3	0	12	12	76.3	46	2	18	91	2.1	10.7	52%	.246	0.84	1.77	2.33	3.41	1.2
2015	NYN	MLB	20	2	4	0	12	10	57.3	59	6	29	38	4.6	6.0	45%	.310	1.52	5.12	5.10	5.56	-0.7
2016	NYN	MLB	21	8	9	0	32	26	181.0	170	20	64	130	3.2	6.5	45%	.293	1.30	4.26	4.35	4.63	-0.4

Breakout: 0% Improve: 0% Collapse: 0% Attrition: 0% MLB: 0% Upside: 1   *Comparables: Kyle Lobstein, Roman Mendez, J.C. Ramirez*

Drafted/Acquired: International Free Agent, 2012, Dominican Republic

Previous Ranking: #10 (Org)

What Happened in 2014: Molina took the competition by storm in the New York-Penn League, fanning 91 batters in 76 1/3 innings, while giving up only 46 hits, and cemented himself as a prospect trending forward in the system.

Strengths: Excellent athlete; strong physical projection; repeatable delivery; live arm; potential to routinely work in mid-90s with fastball down the line; late life to pitch; early feel for spotting up; loose wrist action with change; arm-side fade, with some bottoming-out action; flashes of depth to breaking ball; can round into bat-misser with continued tightening up; aggressive approach on mound; not afraid to challenge and come after hitters.

Weaknesses: Command growth needed; loose with fastball in zone; learning importance of throwing secondary stuff for strikes; gives away changeup at times; breaking ball still finding identity; more of a slurve; loopy break at times; presently a thrower; gets away with mistakes; likes to pitch up.

Risk Factor/Injury History: High; short-season résumé; pitchability/command progress.

Bret Sayre's Fantasy Take: The numbers are eye-popping, but Molina is extremely unlikely to claim future fantasy ace status. The strikeout numbers will slide back as he moves up unless the breaker takes the necessary step forward, but his fantasy floor is higher than almost any pitcher who has yet to pitch in full-season ball. His trade value could go through the roof calling Savannah home in 2015.

The Year Ahead: Molina will take his talents to full-season baseball, where the quality of stuff will likely continue to play up and carry him to successful outings. The developmental goal here will be to start improving his pitch-ability, which may be a bit tough in the near term because the 20-year-old can likely live off his high-end stuff and mask mistakes. The athleticism, repeatable delivery, and personality intangibles all point toward Molina having strong growth potential with his command. It just may take some time to manifest. Early progress in his highlighted areas of need will serve as the trigger for pushing him up further. By the end of the season, Molina has the potential to be challenging for a spot toward the front of this system. The future is extremely bright for this right-hander, so sit back and enjoy the ride.

8. Dominic Smith 1B

Born: 6/15/95 **Age:** 20 **Bats:** L **Throws:** L **Height:** 6'0" **Weight:** 185

MLB ETA	Hit	Power	Run	Glove	Arm	OFP	Realistic
Late 2017	65	50	–	65	65	60 1ST DIVISION PLAYER	50 AVG REGULAR

YEAR	TEAM	LVL	AGE	PA	R	2B	3B	HR	RBI	BB	SO	SB	CS	AVG/OBP/SLG	TAv	BABIP	BRR	FRAA	WARP
2014	SAV	A	19	518	52	26	1	1	44	51	77	5	4	.271/.344/.338	.262	.321	-4.8	1B(110): -1.8	-0.1
2015	NYN	MLB	20	250	17	10	0	1	19	15	60	0	0	.210/.260/.273	.213	.274	-0.5	1B -1	-1.1
2016	NYN	MLB	21	250	27	12	0	5	24	19	59	0	0	.233/.297/.348	.246	.292	-0.6	1B -1	0.2

Breakout: 0% Improve: 0% Collapse: 0% Attrition: 0% MLB: 0% Upside: 36   *Comparables: Eric Hosmer, Joc Pederson, Pablo Sandoval*

Drafted/Acquired: 1st round, 2013 draft, Junipero Serra HS (Gardena, CA)

Previous Ranking: #6 (Org)

What Happened in 2014: The former first-round pick made his full-season debut, flashing contact ability paired with some control of the strike zone, but falling short on power.

Strengths: Innate bat-to-ball ability; shows strong separation with hands; waits back on the ball; feel for controlling the head of the bat; fluid, pretty left-handed swing; willing to use the whole field; brings a plan to the plate; quick feet around the bag at first; soft hands; good athleticism; fundamentally sound at position; excellent arm strength; shows strong overall baseball instincts.

Weaknesses: Questions on ultimate power ceiling; swing is geared more toward line-drive contact; limited present loft; tapping into power may come at the expense of the hit tool; limited to first base defensively; pressure on hit to play to full potential.

Risk Factor/Injury History: Moderate; yet to achieve upper minors; first-base-only profile.

Bret Sayre's Fantasy Take: Whether the 20-homer power comes or not, Smith is not going to be a fantasy star. But the hit tool can carry a long way, even at a power-laden position—which makes Smith a good bet to be fantasy useful, compared to other teenage prospects.

The Year Ahead: Smith has been a much-debated player both internally and externally on what he is exactly going to be in the long-term. There are no questions or disputes on the hit tool. The first baseman has one of those picture-perfect swings with the type of loose hands that leads to the player stinging hard contact to all fields right up through the ranks. But there are more questions than answers when it comes to his power potential and what that exactly means for the overall profile. There is a lot of pressure on Smith's hit tool to perform season in and season out if power is going to be a secondary piece of his game. There's a chance for some productive seasons along the lines of a first-division player, but in the long run the body of work leans more along the lines of an average regular.

9. Michael Conforto   OF

Born: 3/1/93   **Age:** 22   **Bats:** L   **Throws:** R   **Height:** 6'1"   **Weight:** 211

MLB ETA	Hit	Power	Run	Glove	Arm	OFP	Realistic
2016	50	60	–	50	–	60 1ST DIVISION REGULAR	50 AVG REGULAR

YEAR	TEAM	LVL	AGE	PA	R	2B	3B	HR	RBI	BB	SO	SB	CS	AVG/OBP/SLG	TAv	BABIP	BRR	FRAA	WARP
2014	BRO	A-	21	186	30	10	0	3	19	16	29	3	0	.331/.403/.448	.314	.383	1.9	LF(41): -1.7	1.8
2015	NYN	MLB	22	250	18	9	0	3	21	13	68	0	0	.200/.250/.278	.208	.265	-0.4	LF -2	-1.1
2016	NYN	MLB	23	250	27	10	1	6	25	16	67	0	0	.212/.272/.342	.231	.267	-0.4	LF -3	-0.7

Breakout: 0%   Improve: 0%   Collapse: 0%   Attrition: 0%   MLB: 0%   Upside: 10   *Comparables: Corey Dickerson, Michael Taylor, Adron Chambers*

Drafted/Acquired: 1st round, 2014 draft, Oregon State University (Corvallis, OR)

Previous Ranking: NR

What Happened in 2014: Conforto was drafted tenth overall, and then proceeded to rip in short-season ball after signing, offering clues that he can handle the lower levels fairly quickly.

Strengths: Well filled out; physical player; excellent strength; quiet load; produces a lot of leverage in swing; hits the ball with loft and carry; power plays to all fields; mid-20s home-run potential; mature approach; waits for pitch to drive; comfortable hitting with a strike or two; contact is loud and hard; potential to round into legit threat in lineup.

Weaknesses: Uppercut in swing leads to in-zone misses; can be beat above the thighs with velocity; needs work keeping hands above baseball; maintenance in swing; can fall into mechanical ruts; below-average speed; fringe-average range; limited to left field defensively; bat-first player.

Risk Factor/Injury History: High; yet to play in full-season ball; bat-first player.

Bret Sayre's Fantasy Take: There's no question that Conforto is a top-five fantasy prospect in this system, but sits down in the bottom half of the list due to his shortcomings everywhere else. He could be a strong OF3 in time, hitting around .260ish with 25 homers.

The Year Ahead: Conforto will take his talents to the low minors, where his power should immediately show and ultimately prove to be ahead of the competition in relatively short time. The left-handed hitter is big and strong, with a swing designed for getting max lift and extension. The power is here for the outfielder to project for home-run totals into the 20s and to evolve into a consistent threat to go deep. Conforto sacrifices contact ability with his extremely upward swing path, but also doesn't get himself out. He'll likely strike out with frequency against high-caliber arms, while projecting for more modest averages. The defense is nothing special either. The range is limited and paired with about an average arm, but as a left fielder it's passable. The bat is the main draw here, which puts pressure on Conforto to develop to his potential and then perform year in and year out. It's not a star player here, but as a solid-average regular who hits fifth or sixth in a lineup it can work.

10. Jhoan Urena   3B

Born: 9/1/94   **Age:** 20   **Bats:** B   **Throws:** R   **Height:** 6'1"   **Weight:** 200

MLB ETA	Hit	Power	Run	Glove	Arm	OFP	Realistic
2018	55	55	–	50	60	60 1ST DIVISION REGULAR	45 BENCH/<AVG REGULAR

YEAR	TEAM	LVL	AGE	PA	R	2B	3B	HR	RBI	BB	SO	SB	CS	AVG/OBP/SLG	TAv	BABIP	BRR	FRAA	WARP
2014	BRO	A-	19	315	30	20	1	5	47	27	58	7	9	.300/.356/.431	.303	.356	-2.1	3B(75): -3.5	2.3
2015	NYN	MLB	20	250	18	9	1	3	21	10	71	2	1	.203/.235/.285	.204	.272	-0.5	3B -3	-1.2
2016	NYN	MLB	21	250	25	11	1	5	24	13	64	2	2	.227/.267/.341	.229	.287	-0.5	3B -3	-0.8

Breakout: 0%   Improve: 0%   Collapse: 0%   Attrition: 0%   MLB: 0%   Upside: 14   *Comparables: Brandon Laird, Blake DeWitt, Alex Liddi*

Drafted/Acquired: International Free Agent, 2011, Dominican Republic

Previous Ranking: NR

What Happened in 2014: The Dominican third baseman more than held his own in the New York-Penn League as a 19-year-old, suggesting the organization has more than meets the eye here.

Strengths: Strong player; improving muscle composition; athletic for size; loose hands; ability to barrel up ball with backspin from both sides of plate; shows hand separation during stride; some present loft in swing; raw power to tap into; gap-to-gap approach; early makings of patience and plan at the plate; picks up offerings out of pitchers' hand well; arm for left side of infield; soft hands; instincts for third; strong work ethic.

Weaknesses: Fringe-average foot speed; fringy present range at third; a bit on awkward and stiff side; gap to close defensively to stick at position; concerns on how body will progress physically; needs to get more lift out of swing for power to play to full potential; hit tool may play down as a result; swing has some prepitch timing; can get into ruts of over-pulling; bat may not be enough to carry move across the diamond.

Risk Factor/Injury History: High risk; short-season résumé; questions on profile.

Bret Sayre's Fantasy Take: Where there's potential in the hit tool and power, fantasy owners will be interested. And when it comes in the package of a player who doesn't quite have a position they fit well at long term, it creates a value proposition. Urena could hit .280 with 20-plus homers at the major-league level, and if that happens, fantasy owners won't care what eligibility it comes with.

The Year Ahead: The knock on Urena is a body that doesn't really look the part and offers some concerns on how it is going to progress into his mid-twenties, but when peeling back the onion this is a very intriguing player. The 20-year-old flashes excellent hand-eye, along with the ability to consistently barrel up with authority. It's also a swing that already shows some loft and offers projection that there is power to grow into as the level of strength continues to mature. There's definite upside to develop into a run-producing bat. Where Urena is ultimately going to play remains to be seen, but for now the infielder has been making progress at the hot corner, with the body firming up a lot since signing with the organization. The work ethic also draws praise from sources who have observed the prospect closely. This is a player to keep a close eye on moving forward and one who will garner more attention this season if he passes some markers in Low-A, mainly proving the approach is as advanced as it appeared. Urena is the definition of sleeper prospect.

Prospects on the Rise

1. RHP Casey Meisner: This highly projectable arm may have a case for being included within the Top 10, but right now he's still a lot more vision than present, especially with his heater. Meisner is a tall, lanky 6-foot-7 right-hander, but shows surprising body control and the ability to keep balanced, which bodes well for his command profile. The key for the 20-year-old is adding strength to both squeeze out more velocity and enable him to

FROM THE FIELD

Brandon Nimmo

Team: New York Mets

Evaluator: Jeff Moore

Dates seen: April 5, 9, and 24, 2014

Affiliate: St. Lucie Mets (High-A, Mets)

Physical/health: Tall frame, strong and well developed for a 21-year-old, but with broad shoulders that still allow for some room to fill out.

MLB ETA	Risk factor	OFP	Realistic role
2016	Moderate	60	50; major-league regular

Tool	Future grade	Report
Hit	55	Classic left-handed stance with quiet hands and a slight knee bend. Features a short swing, especially for a tall player, with a slight natural uppercut. Not an ultra-quick bat, but enough to handle anything but the highest velocity. Has natural ability to put the barrel on the ball and is willing to use the whole field. Hits with a line-drive approach and is extremely patient at the plate, even in RBI situations. Hit tool will play up because of patience, which helps him get into hitter's counts.
Power	55	Does not have the premium bat speed needed to generate plus power, but does have good size and strength, a slight uppercut and creates natural backspin to help the ball carry. Still learning how to drive the ball, and his in-game power is limited by his all-fields/line-drive approach.
Baserunning/speed	55	Does not have quick acceleration but runs well underway; long-strider.
Glove	50	Good route runner, makes the most of his speed in the outfield. Can play adequate defense in center field or plus defense on the corners.
Arm	50	Average arm strength. Will play in center or left; below average in right field but won't be a liability.

Overall: Nimmo is still figuring out what kind of player he is going to be. He's built like a power hitter but approaches his at-bats like a table-setter, and his game fits that mold. While none of his traditional tools stand out, he does have one premium ability—plate discipline. He refuses to expand the strike zone, even when he has an easy run-producing opportunity. He can be an above-average hitter, but the hit tool will play up because of the plate discipline. He could be a plus on-base player. His defensive profile is still a question, but if he gets on base and provides plus defense in an outfield corner, he could start on a first-division team.

handle the rigors of the professional season better. If he shows some more growth with his stuff this year in full-season ball, he's firmly planted as a top-10 guy this time next year.

2. OF Champ Stuart: The former sixth-round pick brings an element of speed to the diamond, along with the potential for solid-average to better defense in center and gap power offensively. Stuart is intriguing given the potential growth in front of his tools and relatively young age for entering the professional ranks after coming out of a Division II college program. Make no mistake here, this is a risky prospect with the potential for the skills to level off quickly, but reports on the 22-year-old indicated solid progress across the board and the work ethic to maximize all his talent. It's a player than can bring a projection as a potential regular into more focus and challenge for higher status within the system next season.

3. RHP Gabriel Ynoa: This isn't a flashy profile like some of the arms in front of him, but the 22-year-old right-hander has progressed steadily into the upper minors. Ynoa features a low-90s fastball with some sink, along with a slider and changeup that both flash solid-average potential. The change is presently the better of the two offerings, showing strong arm-side fade at times and the ability to keep opposing hitters off-balance. The question is whether this arm will be able to miss enough bats as opposed to running consistently into barrels, but he offers further projection at improving his overall pitchability. This arm can take a jump in status by proving he can effectively churn through lineups and throw better strikes against Double-A competition this season.

Factors on the Farm

Prospects likely to contribute at the major-league level in 2015

1. RHP Rafael Montero: The 24-year-old has achieved the majors, where it's going to be about demonstrating he's capable of being consistent. Otherwise, this arm will fall more into the up-and-down category. Montero has solid-average overall stuff, but lacks an offering that he can lean on against the highest level of competition. His game on the mound is about mixing and matching, spotting from side to side, and changing eye levels often. It seemed like he lost some of that mind-set during his call-up, but that can also be expected the first time around. The righty will likely get another shot during 2015, where he can show that he can stick in a rotation. The likely role is toward the back of one, but that offers good value when constructing a team.

2. LHP Jack Leathersich: The University of Massachusetts-Lowell product continues to show bat-missing ability, though his results at the highest level of the minors have left something to be desired. The lefty pairs a low-90s fastball with a hard biting curveball to attack hitters with an aggressive pitching style. Leathersich is most likely best suited for getting an out or two toward the later stages of a ballgame before handing the ball over to the back of the 'pen, but if he can throw the curve for more strikes to take the dependency off his fastball, there's a chance for a little more.

3. OF Cesar Puello: This prospect offers some loud tools, but they tend to play down because of an overly aggressive approach at the plate. There's also the issue of his suspension for being linked with the Biogenesis scandal, which casts doubt on the authenticity of his prior performance. Puello has plus raw power, lift in his swing, and the ability to play up the middle, but his hit tool suffers as a result of a crude approach for his age. With some adjustments in Triple-A, the likely outcome over the long-haul can offer a bench bat or contributor over stretches as a regular. It's not what the tools suggest, but he offers value in the depth department for an organization.

NEW YORK YANKEES

1. Aaron Judge   OF

Born: 4/26/92   **Age:** 23   **Bats:** R   **Throws:** R   **Height:** 6'7"   **Weight:** 230

MLB ETA		Hit	Power	Run	Glove	Arm		OFP	Realistic
2016		50	65	–	–	60		60 1ST DIVISION PLAYER	50 AVG ML PLAYER

YEAR	TEAM	LVL	AGE	PA	R	2B	3B	HR	RBI	BB	SO	SB	CS	AVG/OBP/SLG	TAv	BABIP	BRR	FRAA	WARP
2014	TAM	A+	22	285	44	9	2	8	33	50	72	0	0	.283/.411/.442	.302	.377	1.8	RF(61): 6.5	2.9
2014	CSC	A	22	278	36	15	2	9	45	39	59	1	0	.333/.428/.530	.343	.408	-2.8	RF(55): 4.1	3.1
2015	NYA	MLB	23	250	26	8	1	7	28	28	76	0	0	.223/.314/.357	.256	.303	-0.3	RF 5	0.8
2016	NYA	MLB	24	250	29	10	0	6	26	25	72	0	0	.224/.306/.356	.252	.301	-0.6	RF 5	1.3

Breakout: 3%   **Improve:** 11%   **Collapse:** 7%   **Attrition:** 9%   **MLB:** 27%   **Upside:** 19   *Comparables: Nolan Reimold, Kyle Parker, Wladimir Balentien*

Drafted/Acquired: 1st round, 2013 draft, California State University Fresno (Fresno, Ca)

Previous Ranking: #10 (Org)

What Happened in 2014: Judge took on two levels of baseball in his debut season, where the 6-foot-7 monster of a man created plenty of hard contract and showed good on-base skills, but also flashed the expected swing-and-miss.

Strengths: Massive body; bottomless raw strength; moves well for his size; works to keep hands inside of offerings; generates solid bat speed; can barrel up balls hard to all fields; drives pitches with carry when arms get extended; able to hit ball out to any part of ballpark; just scratching the surface of power; arm plays well in right field; quick release; picks up ball well off the bat.

Weaknesses: Long arms lead to some holes in swing; concerns on ability to handle high velocity on inner third; bat speed comes from strength over hands; likes to extend early; leaves him prone to stuff with spin away; still learning how to get more leverage out of swing; power can play down due to hit tool; will miss in zone; defense likely to just be passable down the line.

Risk Factor/Injury History: Moderate; yet to reach Double-A; hit tool utility.

Bret Sayre's Fantasy Take: It seems uncommon that a Yankee prospect would be undervalued in a dynasty context, but here we are. Judge is unlikely to be a high contributor in batting average and won't offer much on the basepaths, but the potential 30-homer power without negative value elsewhere is what makes him a big riser in fantasy. And if you're in an OBP league, he's even better.

The Year Ahead: Despite a strong offensive output in the lower levels last season, Judge is still fairly unrefined with some aspects of his offensive game, including learning how to fully tap into his raw power and finding a balance with his extension to help mitigate some of his holes. Given the size and the nature of his long arms, there's inherently going to be maintenance needed, along with the cognizance to recognize when things are getting out of whack. The hulking outfielder shows advancement with his approach at the plate, typically bringing a plan of execution and, most importantly, the willingness to grind through plate appearances. This aspect of the 23-year-old's game bodes well for when he reaches the upper minors, likely at some point this season, which will be a strong test for the bat. There are concerns from evaluators that Judge's hit tool will reach a plateau against more advanced competition. The potential power output is the main draw and his status as a regular hinges on being able to produce at acceptable levels. The view here sees some bumps in the road in the near term, but at the end of the day a future regular emerging.

#49

BP Top
101
Prospects

2. Luis Severino   RHP

Born: 2/20/94   **Age:** 21   **Bats:** R   **Throws:** R   **Height:** 6'0"   **Weight:** 195

MLB ETA		CT	FB	CH	CB	SL		OFP	Realistic
Late 2015		–	70	60	–	50		65 NO. 2/3 STARTER	50 LATE INN RP (SETUP)

YEAR	TEAM	LVL	AGE	W	L	SV	G	GS	IP	H	HR	BB	K	BB9	SO9	GB%	BABIP	WHIP	ERA	FIP	FRA	WARP
2014	TRN	AA	20	2	2	0	6	6	25.0	20	1	6	29	2.2	10.4	48%	.297	1.04	2.52	2.27	3.05	0.8
2014	TAM	A+	20	1	1	0	4	4	20.7	11	0	6	28	2.6	12.2	59%	.239	0.82	1.31	1.55	1.81	0.9
2014	CSC	A	20	3	2	0	14	14	67.7	62	2	15	70	2.0	9.3	53%	.321	1.14	2.79	2.70	3.90	1.4
2015	NYA	MLB	21	5	5	0	17	17	80.3	81	9	31	69	3.5	7.7	49%	.303	1.40	4.40	4.63	4.79	0.3
2016	NYA	MLB	22	2	1	0	46	0	49.0	51	6	17	40	3.1	7.3	49%	.303	1.39	4.62	4.45	5.03	0.0

Breakout: 0%   **Improve:** 0%   **Collapse:** 0%   **Attrition:** 0%   **MLB:** 0%   **Upside:** 24   *Comparables: Drew Hutchison, Danny Duffy, Jarrod Parker*

Drafted/Acquired: International Free Agent, 2011, Dominican Republic

Previous Ranking: On The Rise

What Happened in 2014: The hard-throwing right-hander fully emerged onto the prospect landscape, firing 113 1/3 high-octane innings across three levels, flashing legit power-arm stuff in the process.

Strengths: Fast-twitch muscle; very fast arm; loose, whippy arm action; generates easy velocity; fastball comfortably sits 93-96; touches higher in short bursts (97); late, explosive arm-side life with some sink; can be an overpowering offering; turns over quality changeup; flashes bottom-dropping action and some late tumble; throws from same arm slot as heater; deceptive to hitter's eye; slider displays short, late break; barrel-missing bite in upper-velocity band (85-87); power-arm potential.

Weaknesses: Added strength needed to withstand rigors of position; inconsistent with landing; tends to be stiff on front foot; leads to opening early; finish suffers, which drives inconsistent command; change is firm at higher velocities; action flattens out; wrist will wrap when delivering slider; loose in lower-velocity band (83-84); concerns mechanics and size will push to bullpen.

Risk Factor/Injury History: Moderate; 6 Double-A starts; durability concerns.

Bret Sayre's Fantasy Take: The fastball is great, but Severino isn't as destined for fantasy stardom as his numbers may suggest. Right now, he's worked his way into the Dynasty 101, but with a high probability of a bullpen future, the ceiling gets muddied by risk. If he's a starter, the strikeouts may not come in bushels without a big step forward in his slider.

The Year Ahead: On the strength of his mid-90s fastball and complementary secondary arsenal, Severino rocketed into the upper levels last season and is now set for an extended tour with Trenton to start 2015. This arm generates extremely easy velocity, with the heater exploding out of his hand, and with early feel to fill the ledger with strike after strike. The 21-year-old isn't solely focused on trying to challenge with a constant barrage of heat to flat out beat opposing hitters. He will move the pitch around the zone and has the potential to continue developing into a knowledgeable executor of his craft. The changeup is the lead piece of the secondary repertoire right now, flashing good deception and the type of bottom-dropping action to miss bats at the highest level. Pairing it with the potential double-plus fastball, the righty has an excellent foundation for being able to get big-league outs down the road. There are concerns about the nature of this prospect's mechanics and whether the stuff is going to hold up over the course of the long season in a starter's role. Add in that the slider needs a good amount of tightening to churn through lineups deep into games, and things may end up more along the lines of a late-inning power arm. However, there is plenty of development time in front of Severino to continue pushing the package closer to the overall potential, with a cup of coffee at the end of 2015 not out of the question.

3. Gary Sanchez C

Born: 12/2/92 **Age:** 22 **Bats:** R **Throws:** R **Height:** 6'2" **Weight:** 235

MLB ETA	Hit	Power	Run	Glove	Arm	OFP	Realistic
Late 2015	–	65	–	–	70	55 >AVG REGULAR	50 AVG REGULAR (1B/DH)

YEAR	TEAM	LVL	AGE	PA	R	2B	3B	HR	RBI	BB	SO	SB	CS	AVG/OBP/SLG	TAv	BABIP	BRR	FRAA	WARP
2014	TRN	AA	21	477	48	19	0	13	65	43	91	1	1	.270/.338/.406	.283	.314	-2.6	C(93): 1.7	2.9
2015	NYA	MLB	22	250	25	10	0	8	29	14	64	0	0	.231/.280/.374	.249	.281	-0.5	C 0	0.6
2016	NYA	MLB	23	491	58	19	0	17	58	35	122	1	0	.229/.290/.383	.255	.274	-1.2	C 0	0.9

Breakout: 4%   Improve: 19%   Collapse: 3%   Attrition: 27%   MLB: 37%   Upside: 45   *Comparables: Hank Conger, Wilin Rosario, Tony Sanchez*

Drafted/Acquired: International Free Agent, 2009, Dominican Republic

Previous Ranking: #1 (Org), #85 (Top 101)

What Happened in 2014: The backstop made some strides in the Eastern League as a 21-year-old, creating more consistent contact, but it came at the expense of his overall power output, and the defense was very much touch and go.

Strengths: Excellent strength; well-filled-out body; lower half to tap into for power; leveraged swing that generates extension; can jump all over fastballs out and over the plate; punishes mistakes; displays home-run power to all fields; has idea of strike zone; learning how to shorten up and take what is given to him; fluid release; near-elite arm strength; pops out of crouch well; arm to control the running game.

Weaknesses: Engagement and in-game focus drift; tends to neglect defensive game; seems like treated as an afterthought; receiving skills lag behind; gets too loose with swing, leading to in-zone miss; struggles with stuff breaking across line of sight; power may play down due lack of consistent contact; well-below-average run; may ultimately move off position (first base).

Risk Factor/Injury History: Low; 133 games at Double-A; dual-threat development.

Bret Sayre's Fantasy Take: The shine is certainly starting to come off Sanchez in fantasy leagues, but it's important to remember that even if he doesn't have the defensive chops to be a full-time catcher, he could still play the position enough to claim eligibility (which is all we care about). If that happens, we could be looking at Evan Gattis-type value—and he was a top-10 catcher in 2014. Without the eligibility, he's more of a deeper mixed-league target.

The Year Ahead: It may seem like Sanchez has been around for a long time and has graced prospect lists forever, but the backstop is just 22. Still, the Dominican has lost some of the shine from the early stages of his career, which speaks to the difficulties of dual-threat development and the intensity of the process when polishing both aspects of a player's game in unison. The raw power here is undeniable, as the right-handed hitter has plenty to tap into and could hit 20-plus bombs on a regular basis. At times in 2014 he seemed to be making more of a concerted effort to navigate plate appearances more methodically and take what was given to him rather than just wildly sell out for a big payout. There were stretches, though, of inconsistency and what appeared to be a lack of engagement, especially behind the dish. Outside of the ability to throw, Sanchez is still rough with his receiving, and opinions are mixed on whether the defense just is what it is at this point. The stock is heavily tied to the potential production with the stick, which will face the next test at Triple-A this season. Some think that the closer he gets to the bright lights of the big stage, the more the intensity will ratchet up, and the offensive tools will begin to translate more consistently on the field. It's just more likely that it doesn't come from behind the plate.

4. Ian Clarkin   LHP

Born: 2/14/95   **Age:** 20   **Bats:** L   **Throws:** L   **Height:** 6'2"   **Weight:** 190

MLB ETA		CT	FB	CH	CB	SL		OFP		Realistic	
2017		–	**60**	**55**	**60**	–		**60** NO. 3 STARTER		**50** NO. 4 STARTER	

YEAR	TEAM	LVL	AGE	W	L	SV	G	GS	IP	H	HR	BB	K	BB9	SO9	GB%	BABIP	WHIP	ERA	FIP	FRA	WARP
2014	TAM	A+	19	1	0	0	1	1	5.0	7	0	1	4	1.8	7.2	47%	.467	1.60	1.80	2.39	2.98	0.1
2014	CSC	A	19	3	3	0	16	15	70.0	64	6	22	71	2.8	9.1	44%	.319	1.23	3.21	3.74	4.64	0.9
2015	NYA	MLB	20	3	4	0	12	12	48.7	53	6	22	37	4.1	6.8	43%	.306	1.53	5.10	5.24	5.55	-0.2
2016	NYA	MLB	21	7	9	0	29	29	182.0	189	22	63	145	3.1	7.2	43%	.303	1.38	4.46	4.51	4.84	-0.2

Breakout: 0%   Improve: 0%   Collapse: 0%   Attrition: 0%   MLB: 0%   Upside: 13   *Comparables: Jarrod Parker, Julio Teheran, Jordan Lyles*

Drafted/Acquired: 1st round, 2013 draft, Madison HS (San Diego, CA)

Previous Ranking: #9 (Org)

What Happened in 2014: The projectable left-hander bypassed short-season ball and received an advanced assignment in the South Atlantic League, where the stuff proved to be more than up to the challenge, fanning a batter per inning as he demonstrated good strike-throwing ability.

Strengths: Athletic; room for added strength; good arm speed; stays tall and creates downward plane with delivery; fastball works 89-92 with late life in lower tier of zone; potential to sit a tick higher with physical maturity; spins curveball with loose wrist; flashes deep break and teeth; can turn over change; arm-side fading action; deceptive release; throws for strikes; plus command profile.

Weaknesses: Lot of moving parts to delivery; big leg kick and exaggerated hands above head; can struggle keeping arm in slot; inconsistent timing and pace; command needs grade jump; fastball lacks east/west movement; velocity will play down; curve can get too soft and float; deliberate at times with changeup.

Risk Factor/Injury History: High; yet to reach upper levels; development of command.

Bret Sayre's Fantasy Take: Pitching in Tampa this season will likely do wonders for his perceived value, which makes Clarkin an interesting flier. In reality, he projects to be more of an SP4 with good all-around numbers, but no dominant categories.

The Year Ahead: Clarkin began his professional journey last season in a more aggressive setting than expected and showed that the stuff has taken an initial step forward. The projectable left-hander's potential solid-average-to-better three-pitch mix bodes well for his prospects of sticking in the rotation over the long term. With another season of tangible progress, there's enough ceiling to suggest that he is on the cusp of establishing himself as the top arm in the system. Those potential next steps will likely come in an assignment in the Florida State League, which will challenge Clarkin's ability to spot his arsenal more finely and repeat his delivery on a more consistent basis. Despite less than overpowering velocity, the 20-year-old's athleticism and looseness point to command growth being achievable, and the pitcher already flashes strike-throwing ability. There may be some initial growing pains, but this is an arm that, by the end of the year, could close the gap between the ceiling and reality.

5. Jorge Mateo   SS

Born: 6/23/95   **Age:** 20   **Bats:** R   **Throws:** R   **Height:** 6'0"   **Weight:** 188

MLB ETA		Hit	Power	Run	Glove	Arm		OFP		Realistic	
2018		**55**	**50**	**80**	**50**	**55**		**65** 1ST DIV ST/OCC AS		**50** AVG ML PLAYER	

YEAR	TEAM	LVL	AGE	PA	R	2B	3B	HR	RBI	BB	SO	SB	CS	AVG/OBP/SLG	TAv	BABIP	BRR	FRAA	WARP
2014	YAN	Rk	19	65	14	5	1	0	1	7	17	11	1	.276/.354/.397	.264	.390	0.8	SS(12): 2.8	0.7
2015	NYA	MLB	20	250	27	8	0	3	15	15	79	11	3	.185/.236/.259	.191	.260	1.3	SS 4	-0.3
2016	NYA	MLB	21	250	22	8	1	3	19	17	76	12	3	.195/.252/.272	.202	.273	1.9	SS 3	-1.3

Breakout: 0%   Improve: 0%   Collapse: 0%   Attrition: 0%   MLB: 0%   Upside: 2   *Comparables: Pedro Florimon, Pete Kozma, Michael Taylor*

Drafted/Acquired: International Free Agent, 2012, Dominican Republic

Previous Ranking: NR

What Happened in 2014: A broken finger limited the Dominican international signee to 15 games, but he impressed evaluators during the season and at fall instructs with his overall feel for the game and elite running ability.

Strengths: Very athletic; feel for the game; generates above-average bat speed; loose hands; flashes barrel control; gap pop; elite runner; high potential to impact the game on the bases; speed enables him to be disruptive and leg out hits; soft hands; moves well side to side; solid-average-to-better range; arm for left side of the infield.

Weaknesses: Limited exposure to quality arms; in the infancy stages of building approach and pitch recognition; gets caught lunging with timing; not a lock to stick at short; lacks high level of fluidity; raw fundamentals.

Risk Factor/Injury History: High; complex-league résumé; secondary skill progression.

Bret Sayre's Fantasy Take: Anytime a dynasty owner sees "8 run" in the tools line, they're going to get overly excited, and it's warranted in Mateo's case. There's enough in the rest of the profile to start dreaming, and it's not difficult to get carried away. For now, he'll have to settle as a 50-steal dream, but one that could come much more into focus during 2015.

The Year Ahead: There were limited looks at the then-19-year-old due to a finger injury during the year, but there's strong buzz surrounding him, especially from a few sources at fall instructs. The huge draw, and what first comes up in conversations, is the legit 80-grade speed from the right side of the plate. Mateo accelerates extremely well both in his times down to first and when making the turn on the bases. The speed also translates in the field, where the player shows a quick first step and good foot speed ranging to both sides. The Dominican isn't just all about speed, as there's also some nice feel for hitting at an early age and fluidity in the swing. It isn't a stroke just geared toward slapping or slashing. Mateo has good life in his hands, with a bit of present leverage and ability to barrel hard pull side. There are plenty of unknowns here and a ways to go, but it's a good-looking prospect and one who can gain considerable traction within the industry when the exposure increases this season, along with putting a projection as a future regular into focus.

---

6. Rob Refsnyder 2B/OF

Born: 3/26/91 **Age:** 24 **Bats:** R **Throws:** R **Height:** 6'1" **Weight:** 205

MLB ETA	Hit	Power	Run	Glove	Arm	OFP	Realistic
2015	55	50	–	50	–	55 >AVG REGULAR	45 UT/<AVG REGULAR

YEAR	TEAM	LVL	AGE	PA	R	2B	3B	HR	RBI	BB	SO	SB	CS	AVG/OBP/SLG	TAv	BABIP	BRR	FRAA	WARP
2014	SWB	AAA	23	333	47	19	1	8	33	41	67	4	4	.300/.389/.456	.291	.364	-0.8	2B(64): -5.4, RF(9): -0.6	1.4
2014	TRN	AA	23	244	35	19	5	6	30	14	38	5	5	.342/.385/.548	.329	.391	-2.2	2B(58): 3.8	2.8
2015	NYA	MLB	24	250	27	12	1	5	26	22	55	4	2	.252/.326/.382	.270	.309	-0.3	2B -2, RF -0	0.7
2016	NYA	MLB	25	538	65	22	1	13	58	52	112	8	4	.253/.333/.388	.271	.301	-0.4	2B -6	1.2

Breakout: 4%   Improve: 19%   Collapse: 9%   Attrition: 19%   MLB: 46%   Upside: 73   *Comparables: Ian Kinsler, Corban Joseph, Jason Kipnis*

Drafted/Acquired: 5th round, 2012 draft, University of Arizona (Tuscon, AZ)

Previous Ranking: NR

What Happened in 2014: The former fifth-round pick came on strong in the upper levels of the organization to push further onto the prospect landscape, where he barreled a lot of offerings up hard and continued to flash strong on-base ability.

Strengths: Athletic; quick hands; line-drive stroke; flashes bat control; relaxed approach; likes to go deep into the count; strong knowledge of strike zone; willing to use the whole field; gap-to-gap power; can muscle up in spots; solid-average range; improving footwork; high baseball IQ.

Weaknesses: Swing has some in-zone miss; tends to get out early on front foot against stuff with spin; will chase fastballs up; footwork can get choppy around the bag; fringe-average defender (present); stroke more linear; power may ultimately play down in favor of contact; limited defensively on infield.

Risk Factor/Injury History: Low; 77 games at Triple-A; bat-first profile

Bret Sayre's Fantasy Take: Dynasty leaguers love ceiling, which is why most are hands-off when it comes to Refsnyder. But given the dearth of reliable position players on the Yankees, he could find himself with plenty of opportunity in 2015 and produce surprisingly well in deeper leagues—with the potential to hit .260 with 10-12 homers. Long term, there's more ceiling in the average, but not much more to the fantasy profile.

The Year Ahead: Another tour at Triple-A awaits Refsnyder to start the season, where the main focus will be to continue polishing his defense at the keystone. It might not be long before the 24-year-old forces himself into the major-league discussion if the bat keeps trending forward like it did last season, but the reports on the glove indicate that he could definitely stand more reps before being pressed into extended action. The right-handed hitter's easy stroke and advanced control of the strike zone are strong assets for him at the plate. The offensive profile can push .270s averages with solid on-base ability and home-run pop that can approach 15 or so at peak. There are some concerns that the swing-and-miss can creep too much into Refsnyder's game against high-quality arms and sabotage the contact rates. Given this player's nature of going deep into counts and seeing a lot of pitches, he gives himself a good chance of getting into favorable hitting conditions and having plenty of opportunities to do damage. This is more of a bat-first profile, as the defense likely peaks as average, but it's a player who can carve out a regular role and maintain that status for a run of seasons, with the entry point potentially occurring at some point this season.

7. Greg Bird   1B

Born: 11/9/92   **Age:** 22   **Bats:** L   **Throws:** R   **Height:** 6'3"   **Weight:** 215

MLB ETA	Hit	Power	Run	Glove	Arm	OFP	Realistic
2016	55	60	–	–	–	50 ML REGULAR	45 PLATOON/<AVG REG

YEAR	TEAM	LVL	AGE	PA	R	2B	3B	HR	RBI	BB	SO	SB	CS	AVG/OBP/SLG	TAv	BABIP	BRR	FRAA	WARP
2014	TRN	AA	21	116	16	8	0	7	11	18	27	0	0	.253/.379/.558	.330	.274	-1.0	1B(24): -1.5	0.8
2014	TAM	A+	21	325	36	22	1	7	32	45	70	1	0	.277/.375/.442	.297	.342	-1.2	1B(61): -1.0	1.7
2015	NYA	MLB	22	250	28	10	0	8	30	31	71	0	0	.227/.327/.391	.270	.294	-0.5	1B -3, C -0	0.2
2016	NYA	MLB	23	250	32	11	0	8	30	33	69	0	0	.228/.331/.399	.271	.292	-0.6	1B -3, C 0	1.5

Breakout: 2%   **Improve:** 22%   **Collapse:** 0%   **Attrition:** 10%   **MLB:** 44%   **Upside:** 107   *Comparables: Jon Singleton, Anthony Rizzo, Jaff Decker*

Drafted/Acquired: 5th round, 2011 draft, Grandview HS (Aurora, CO)

Previous Ranking: #7 (Org)

What Happened in 2014: The left-handed swinging first baseman played across two levels of baseball, where he posted an 848 OPS, and then turned things up by clubbing 12 extra-base hits in 26 games out in the Arizona Fall League.

Strengths: Good strength; physical player; swing unfolds smoothly; generates solid bat speed through the zone; creates lift with swing; power plays to all fields; flashes bat control; good batting eye; willing to hit with a strike or two; up-the-middle approach; tireless worker.

Weaknesses: Fringe-average athlete; limited defensively to first; fringy range; below-average run; swing can get tangled and long; tends to reach for breaking stuff away to weakly put into play; too passive at the plate at times; bat-first profile.

Risk Factor/Injury History: Moderate; limited upper-level experience; bat-first profile.

Bret Sayre's Fantasy Take: Now this is a prospect built for fantasy. In this offensive environment, a potential .270 hitter with 25 homers is deceivingly valuable—which is driven home by the fact that Adam LaRoche did similar things this year and was a top-15 first baseman. And, like Judge, Bird gets a boost in OBP leagues because of his strong approach.

The Year Ahead: Bird is now set to fully enter the upper levels and see his skill set put to the test in the tough Eastern League. For a prospect like this, all eyes will be fully engaged on how quickly he can adjust and prove that the bat has what it takes to combat the step up in competition. The 22-year-old flashed a nice sampling out in Arizona, suggesting that things could transition smoothly in his extended tour at Double-A, but it's also important to keep in mind that was in a hitter's league at the end of the season. It comes down to the bat for Bird, and more specifically the swing. The player possesses the mind-set and approach to grind through plate appearances and work himself into favorable hitting conditions. It's what he can consistently do in those situations that will dictate whether he reaches the potential. There's hitting talent here, with power to tap into, and also reports that speak very highly of the makeup. The swing does get long and loose, which drives some inability to get the fat part on offerings in all four zones. The ceiling isn't huge, and the profile is tough given the defensive limitations, but it's a player who can sneak up and should be a big leaguer in some capacity.

8. Leonardo Molina   CF

Born: 7/31/97   **Age:** 17   **Bats:** R   **Throws:** R   **Height:** 6'2"   **Weight:** 180

MLB ETA	Hit	Power	Run	Glove	Arm	OFP	Realistic
2019	55	60	60	60	60	65 1ST DIV/OCC ALL STAR	45 4TH OF/<AVG REG

YEAR	TEAM	LVL	AGE	PA	R	2B	3B	HR	RBI	BB	SO	SB	CS	AVG/OBP/SLG	TAv	BABIP	BRR	FRAA	WARP
2014	YAN	Rk	16	217	18	10	0	1	21	19	51	6	1	.193/.267/.260	.178	.250	1.2	CF(20): -1.6	-0.4
2015	NYA	MLB	17	250	18	8	0	2	18	8	80	1	0	.184/.215/.252	.179	.259	-0.2	CF -3	-1.8
2016	NYA	MLB	18	250	22	9	2	3	21	9	71	2	0	.218/.253/.312	.210	.291	0.0	CF -3	-1.9

Breakout: 0%   **Improve:** 0%   **Collapse:** 0%   **Attrition:** 0%   **MLB:** 0%   **Upside:** 22   *Comparables: Austin Jackson, Xavier Avery, Reymond Fuentes*

Drafted/Acquired: International Free Agent, 2013, Dominican Republic

Previous Ranking: NR

What Happened in 2014: The line wasn't pretty overall, but this 17-year-old international signee was pushed with an extremely aggressive stateside assignment and possesses the raw tools to start turning heads in the near future.

Strengths: Plus athlete; excellent frame; fast-twitch muscle; room to pack on size and strength; strong hands and forearms; generates plus bat speed; stroke already shows leverage; plus-to-better raw power; flashes early makings of pro approach; easy-plus run; accelerates well; instincts and feel to stick in center; arm to challenge runners.

Weaknesses: Extremely raw; loose with swing; has some mechanical adjustments to make; needs toning down at plate; can be on the aggressive side; plays fast in the field; tools are all projection.

Risk Factor/Injury History: Extreme; limited pro experience; 17 years old; long developmental road ahead.

Bret Sayre's Fantasy Take: The fantasy ceiling is just plain stupid for Molina, but he remains forever and a half away. In shallow leagues with deep rosters, this is exactly the type of player for whom you should be reaching. It's both unnecessary and unhelpful to put numbers on someone this distant, but he has the tools necessary to be an elite fantasy talent one day.

The Year Ahead: It might be a tad early and on the aggressive side ranking Molina this high right now, but a couple of sources were adamant that the outfielder's potential was high and gushed about the overall feel for the game, while reports passed along suggested this is a special player in the making. The line was unassuming and points to his being overmatched, but it's hard to expect much more out of what's equivalently a high school sophomore playing in the Gulf Coast League. The tools are very loud, though far from being polished and playing together collectively as a group. The arm and speed immediately show, along with the raw power during practice sessions. His instincts, fluidity, and early feel for judgment in center point to a player who can stick up the middle and round into a solid-average-to-better defender. A year of experience like Molina received can be a strong trigger for pushing early career progress, but don't expect a large breakout this season. It should be more subtle, with steps forward coming in the form of settling down at the plate and showing more comfort. It's a boom-or-bust prospect, for sure, with a heavy serving of risk on the plate, but there's a feel this one is going to start emerging over the next couple of seasons.

9. Jacob Lindgren   LHP

Born: 3/12/93   **Age:** 22   **Bats:** L   **Throws:** L   **Height:** 5'11"   **Weight:** 180

MLB ETA	CT	FB	CH	CB	SL	OFP	Realistic
2015	–	60	–	–	60	55 MID TIER CLOSER	50 SETUP

YEAR	TEAM	LVL	AGE	W	L	SV	G	GS	IP	H	HR	BB	K	BB9	SO9	GB%	BABIP	WHIP	ERA	FIP	FRA	WARP
2014	TRN	AA	21	1	1	0	8	0	11.7	6	0	9	18	6.9	13.9	73%	.273	1.29	3.86	2.58	4.27	0.1
2014	TAM	A+	21	0	0	0	6	0	7.3	3	0	4	17	4.9	20.9	100%	.300	0.95	0.00	0.39	1.18	0.4
2014	CSC	A	21	1	0	1	4	0	5.0	1	0	0	11	0.0	19.8	71%	.143	0.20	1.80	-0.21	0.69	0.3
2014	YAN	Rk	21	0	0	0	1	0	1.0	2	0	0	2	0.0	18.0	100%	.667	2.00	0.00	-0.50	3.07	0.0
2015	NYA	MLB	22	1	1	1	27	0	35.7	28	3	16	46	4.0	11.6	53%	.302	1.24	3.21	3.55	3.48	0.5
2016	NYA	MLB	23	2	1	2	45	0	59.7	44	5	28	71	4.2	10.7	53%	.273	1.20	2.87	3.59	3.12	1.3

Breakout: 0%   Improve: 0%   Collapse: 0%   Attrition: 0%   MLB: 0%   Upside: 37   *Comparables: Andrew Carignan, Chris Perez, Craig Kimbrel*

Drafted/Acquired: 2nd round, 2014 draft, Mississippi State University (Mississippi State, MS)

Previous Ranking: NR

What Happened in 2014: The southpaw reliever tore up the Southeastern Conference in spring before being nabbed by the Yankees in the second round, and then proceeded to immediately make his presence in this system felt by fanning 48 batters in 25 innings.

Strengths: Loose arm; creates easy velocity; fastball works 91-95; strong movement; some late wiggle; cutting action when thrown glove side; aggressive with pitch; snaps slider at 82-86; late bite in mid-80s; wipeout break; bat-misser; likes to attack zone.

Weaknesses: Command is fringe-average; releases early with fastball (misses arm side and up); can struggle to spot east/west; will start slider too low; needs to throw more for strikes; pace can get uneven; gets overamped.

Risk Factor/Injury History: Moderate; eight appearances at Double-A; tightening of command; mature arsenal.

Bret Sayre's Fantasy Take: The left-handed reliever is coming, and coming soon—but with the uneasiness of investing in relievers and the big names ahead of him (Betances, Miller), he makes for a poor dynasty investment. In deep leagues, he can be plenty valuable without registering a single save, but you need to know your format to decide whether he's worth taking in drafts this spring.

The Year Ahead: Lindgren profiles as a reliever all the way, and one who can begin to make an impact in the majors as soon as this season. This isn't a high-ceiling arm or sexy profile, but in all likelihood should round into a valuable major leaguer. Both the fastball and slider are legit weapons, often overpowering batters and getting a lot of weak swings. The 22-year-old needs some fine-tuning with his command, which will bear watching in the upper levels and beyond. Without being reminded that he can fill the strike zone consistently, higher quality hitters are going to be less apt to chase his pitches out of the zone, especially the slider. The athleticism and ease in the arm action point to progress being achievable, especially if Lindgren can slow the game down a tad further and smooth out his pace. This arm has all the makings of a solid set-up guy, with closer potential at peak. Expect the lefty to be part of the Yankees' bullpen during the stretch run this season.

10. Luis Torrens C

Born: 5/2/96   **Age:** 19   **Bats:** R   **Throws:** R   **Height:** 6'0"   **Weight:** 175

MLB ETA	Hit	Power	Run	Glove	Arm	OFP	Realistic
2018	55	50	–	60	65	60 1ST DIVISION PLAYER	45 BACKUP/<AVG STARTER

YEAR	TEAM	LVL	AGE	PA	R	2B	3B	HR	RBI	BB	SO	SB	CS	AVG/OBP/SLG	TAv	BABIP	BRR	FRAA	WARP
2014	CSC	A	18	34	4	0	0	1	3	6	7	0	0	.154/.353/.269	.222	.167	0.3	C(9): 0.2	0.0
2014	STA	A-	18	202	27	13	3	2	18	14	41	1	2	.270/.327/.405	.260	.336	0.2	C(39): 0.3	1.1
2014	YAN	Rk	18	18	1	1	0	0	1	0	2	0	0	.250/.333/.312	.232	.286	0.0	C(4): -0.0	0.0
2015	NYA	MLB	19	250	22	8	1	3	18	15	74	0	0	.193/.248/.278	.202	.264	-0.4	C 1	-0.6
2016	NYA	MLB	20	250	24	8	1	4	22	13	69	0	0	.215/.263/.315	.217	.281	-0.6	C 1	-1.0

Breakout: 0%   **Improve:** 0%   **Collapse:** 0%   **Attrition:** 0%   **MLB:** 0%   **Upside:** 13   *Comparables: Miguel Gonzalez, Brandon Snyder, Tomas Telis*

Drafted/Acquired: International Free Agent, 2012, Venezuela

Previous Ranking: On The Rise

What Happened in 2014: The Venezuelan backstop showed promise on both sides of the ball in the New York-Penn League, impressing with his feel for the stick and big arm behind the dish.

Strengths: Well-proportioned frame; room to add more strength and mass; good present strength despite leanness; excellent arm strength; fires feet well; smooth release; has the foundation of a future above-average receiver; fluid stroke; good bat speed; loose hands; willing to use the whole field; plus raw.

Weaknesses: Raw overall game; needs added strength to withstand rigors of position; learning how to use body to get big; tends to come up early; glove hand needs work; struggles picking up stuff with spin; gets out on front foot too much; swing more geared to contact; power may ultimately play below to fringe-average; below-average run; large developmental gap to go.

Risk Factor/Injury History: Extreme; short-season résumé; 19 years old; dual-threat development.

Bret Sayre's Fantasy Take: The ETA and the fact that he's a catcher—and catching prospects turn into fantasy contributors at a slower rate than other positions—put a big governor on his value, despite the upside here. Unless you're in a league that rosters two catchers, or more than 300 prospects, he's more of a wait-and-see. But be ready to jump on him if he starts off hot in Low-A.

The Year Ahead: Torrens took a nice step forward last year, showing that both sides of his game are beginning to sharpen. This is one of those profiles where patience will be required and it may take a few years for considerable traction to show, but there's a strong foundation to work with here. The arm strength, fluid swing, and overall feel for the game all jump out as present leading assets for the 19-year-old. The ease and efficiency of the stroke give Torrens the potential to make a lot of hard contact as he begins to learn the strike zone. It's going to be some time before the bat really starts to come into focus, but the talent to produce .270s averages with 15-to-18 home runs is there. Even if the bat falls somewhat short, the Venezuelan's defense—especially the arm—has a chance to carry the profile as a regular. This is a true dual-threat talent, with a legit chance to develop on both sides of the ball. The next steps will come in full-season ball in 2015, where the improvements are likely to be subtle, but the expectation is this prospect can push considerably higher in the system by year end..

Prospects on the Rise

1. 3B Miguel Andujar: The 20-year-old Dominican's season was a bit on the inconsistent side, but he finished off the final two months strong to bring a lot of positives into the offseason. Andujar's strong wrists and forearms enable him to create plus bat speed through the hitting zone and barrel up offerings well, especially to the pull side. Sources spoken to were also complimentary of the quickness in which the prospect recognizes offerings out of the hand at his age. While the swing is presently a bit flat and more geared toward hitting line drives, the strength level and ability to drive the ball with backspin point to plus-power potential down the line. The defense is presently rough and on the choppy side, but there's athleticism and instincts that lend clues that the prospect could improve. The developmental path will take Andujar to High-A in 2015, where the bat will be challenged by the ability of the competition to be finer within the strike zone. It might not be a coming-out party, but this is a prospect with the ingredients to round into a regular at the highest level and start gaining more traction within the industry as a top name within the system.

2. RHP Austin DeCarr: The Massachusetts native brings an arsenal with projection and good size to the table, which led the organization to sign the third rounder to a seven-figure, over-slot bonus. DeCarr's low-90s fastball and hard-breaking curveball are presently the two best offerings at his disposal. The curve shows good downward bite and bat-missing potential, while there's a chance his heater can tick up a bit further in sitting velocity as the right-hander builds more stamina and arm strength. The changeup has a good ways to go and could ultimately push the profile into a relief role, but there's low mileage on the 20-year-old's arm, and proving that the stuff can play over the long season will push this prospect into top-10 discussion in short order.

3. RHP Ty Hensley: Surgery to repair labrum damage in both hips sidelined the former first-round pick for all of 2013 and put a halt to the start of the career, but the right-hander made it back to the mound in 2014 and has begun showing the form that made him an intriguing arm prior to the injury. This arm's lively low-to-mid-90s fastball and potential bat-missing curveball give him an excellent foundation to build upon as both the arm strength and experience move forward. Hensley's overall command and changeup need good steps forward, but as the 21-year-old gets his feet firmly on the ground and is set loose this year, he can make some waves within the system and reestablish himself as one of the better arms percolating up through the ranks.

Factors on the Farm
Prospects likely to contribute at the major-league level in 2015

1. RHP Jose Ramirez: Things didn't go as planned for the right-hander in 2014, first dealing with an oblique injury that delayed the start to his season, an uneven brief call-up to The Show, and then ultimately having his year end in July due to injury. It's been a run of injury-plagued seasons since 2012 for Ramirez. The mid-to-high-90s fastball and crisply fading changeup are the highlights of the arsenal. Both offerings give the arm strong pieces to attack hitters with, while also mixing in a slider than can flash solid-average. Difficulties repeating his delivery lead to subpar command, but the stuff is here to profile as a set-up guy or even potentially push as a closer. The opportunity should be there for the 26-year-old to earn a spot in the bullpen this season, where with good health he can begin to show that a high-leverage reliever is emerging.

2. OF Tyler Austin: Hand injuries have hampered the former 13th-round pick the last two seasons and put his progression through the system in neutral. Austin's solid bat speed and shorter stroke allow him to get the barrel on a lot of offerings, as he typically shows a knack for squaring the ball up with backspin. The 23-year-old's all-fields approach and relaxed nature in the box are also strong assets that enhance the offensive game. Though the right-handed hitter is strong and has nice size, the lack of big leverage in his swing leads evaluators to see a more average overall power projection. Last season, the prospect began getting some defensive work at first and third base in an effort to increase his versatility. A strong close to 2014 in the Eastern League and subsequent solid showing in the Arizona Fall League has left optimism that Austin is getting back on track after the hand injuries. If it holds true into 2015, and proves to be more trend than flash, the outfielder has a good chance to get a shot to help should a need arise.

FROM THE FIELD

Gary Sanchez

Team: New York Yankees
Evaluator: Tucker Blair
Dates seen: August 15–17, 2014
Affiliate: Trenton Thunder (Double-A, Yankees)
Physical/health: Stocky build; thicker body that looks like a catcher mold; slight room left to grow into frame; does not need that growth and could actually slim down some to provide more athleticism.
Makeup: Looks lazy out there; no hustle; knows he is slow and almost plays the game this way; does not look like a high-energy player.

MLB ETA	Risk factor	OFP	Realistic role
2015	High	50	40; C/1B/bench role

Tool	Future grade	Report
Hit	40	Inconsistent swing; plus bat speed; quick wrists; able to control the bat head efficiently but will not always put the ball in play; swing can become too handsy; sometimes fails to use his bottom half; generates efficient hip torque but swings can become lazy at times; very slight hitch at times; great extension and able to cover a lot of the zone; loves to push the ball to the right-center gap; ability to drive ball to all parts of the field; will get under the ball at times and backspin a popup; average pitch recognition; can handle high-end velocity but will cheat sometimes.
Power	60	Easy plus raw power; power is a big part of his game; hits the ball hard when he makes contact; slight lift in swing; plus bat speed and quick wrists; body is built for power and has the hip torque to hit balls hard.
Baserunning/ speed	20	Lacks any form of speed; home-to-first times are constantly over 4.6 seconds; poor second gear.
Glove	40	Defense has improved since my viewing last season; feet are still slow and he lacks the necessary movement to block pitches; really struggles to block pitches in the dirt; footwork is still largest issue; does show ability to bounce out in front of home plate and set himself for a throw to first or second; no feel for pitch framing; lacks the fluidity in his wrists and hands to catch; he can hold his own behind the dish but will not be an asset; sluggish movement added to below-average receiving skills hinder his defensive value.
Arm	70	Did not record a pop time in-game; 1.97 on a warmup; displays an excellent arm in-game; terrific arm strength; laser throws; able to throw with force and made two bullet throws to first on bunts; plus-plus tool that will help him behind the plate and might play up the defense.

Overall: Sanchez is an intriguing player with a hit-first style. His bat will likely work at catcher, but the defense is not at the level needed to stick defensively at the highest level. He is not reliable behind the plate currently, although there have been slight improvements in his horizontal movement since my last viewing in 2013.

The bat may play at first base, but it takes away his best value as a prospect—the arm. Sanchez is still a high-risk player even with significant time at the Double-A level. His defensive game is not ready for the majors and could significantly alter his value as a prospect. With fringe defense at catcher, he is a bat-first prospect that will need to crush the ball to stick as a consistent starter as a first base/DH hybrid that can play catcher in a pinch. I think he is closer to the realistic role than the OFP.

3. RHP Danny Burawa: Though 2014 was a struggle for the right-hander in Triple-A, there's a power arsenal here that can play up nicely in a seventh-inning role. Burawa features a 94-96 mph fastball, with hard arm-side run and some sinking action when thrown in the lower tier of the strike zone. The 26-year-old also utilizes an 83-87 mph slider that flashes late break off the table and wipeout potential when thrown in the upper band of its velocity. The nature of the prospect's slinging arm action from a mid-three-quarters slot and positioning on the third-base side of the rubber make him a fairly uncomfortable look for right-handed batters. There is jerkiness and high effort to Burawa's delivery, though, which lead to an inconsistent release. It comes down to whether this righty can consistently throw strikes, with a good chance for a look in the 'pen at some point in 2015 if that aspect of his game trends in the right direction.

OAKLAND ATHLETICS

1. Franklin Barreto   SS

Born: 2/27/96   **Age:** 19   **Bats:** R   **Throws:** R   **Height:** 5'9"   **Weight:** 175

MLB ETA	Hit	Power	Run	Glove	Arm	OFP	Realistic
2018	55	50	60	–	60	65 1ST DIV/OCC ALL STAR	50 AVG ML PLAYER

YEAR	TEAM	LVL	AGE	PA	R	2B	3B	HR	RBI	BB	SO	SB	CS	AVG/OBP/SLG	TAv	BABIP	BRR	FRAA	WARP
2014	VAN	A-	18	328	65	23	4	6	61	26	64	29	5	.311/.384/.481	.314	.378	2.9	SS(68): -5.9	3.1
2015	OAK	MLB	19	250	23	9	1	3	20	9	75	9	3	.204/.240/.295	.208	.278	0.9	SS -4	-0.6
2016	OAK	MLB	20	250	24	10	2	4	23	9	70	9	3	.226/.261/.331	.220	.297	1.3	SS -4	-0.9

Breakout: 0%   Improve: 0%   Collapse: 0%   Attrition: 0%   MLB: 0%   Upside: 4   *Comparables: Chris Owings, Arismendy Alcantara, Hernan Perez*

#74

BP Top
101
Prospects

Drafted/Acquired: International Free Agent, 2012, Venezuela

Previous Ranking: #7 (Jays)

What Happened in 2014: The then-18-year-old more than held his own in a short-season assignment, offering an impressive glimpse into what the distant future can hold and showing a bit more advancement than expected in the process.

Strengths: Strong athleticism; lot of life in hands; quick and explosive stroke; barrels up fastballs with authority; innate bat-to-ball ability; sneaky present strength; power projection; drives offerings into pull-side gap well; arm for left side of infield; arm would play in center field; easy-plus run; likely to maintain speed as continues to mature physically.

Weaknesses: Frame for added growth; wide present strike zone; very aggressive in the box; zealous nature; can be taken advantage of by good arms; fishes against stuff with spin; actions aren't overly natural at short; defensive fundamentals have a ways to go; loose with setting feet; likely to move to third or outfield; game is raw in general.

Risk Factor/Injury History: High risk; short-season résumé; 19 years old; large gap between present and future.

Bret Sayre's Fantasy Take: The excitement with Barreto is pretty obvious, but before getting carried away, let's not forget that he's at least three years away from contributing to fantasy rosters. There's no elite fantasy tool, but regardless of position, it's tough to knock a player who could hit .280 with 15 homers and 20 steals.

The Year Ahead: Barreto is a long-legged player with high variability in the overall outcome, but the raw tools are extremely impressive. Last season he showed early progress and began to display refinement. The shortstop's explosive hands create plenty of bat speed and drive, with the ability to get the fat part of the barrel consistently on offerings. The offensive question currently resides with the approach, as the 19-year-old is extremely aggressive in the box, often reacting to what is delivered to him regardless of the spot rather than bringing a definitive plan to the plate. While Barreto is very young and has room to improve this aspect, the nature of the ability to get the bat on a lot of balls can lead to being rewarded for less than ideal execution, especially at lower levels, and delay the realization that evolution is necessary. The short term will focus on continuing to hone all aspects of Barreto's game in a full-season assignment in 2015, where the natural ability with the bat has a good chance to mitigate extended resistance, while subtle progress in shaping the secondary skills will be the true indicator of a step forward. Some evaluators even think the end result of his development could lead him to center field.

2. Matt Olson   1B

Born: 3/29/94   **Age:** 21   **Bats:** L   **Throws:** R   **Height:** 6'5"   **Weight:** 230

MLB ETA	Hit	Power	Run	Glove	Arm	OFP	Realistic
2016	50	60	–	50	60	55 >AVG REGULAR	50 AVG ML PLAYER

YEAR	TEAM	LVL	AGE	PA	R	2B	3B	HR	RBI	BB	SO	SB	CS	AVG/OBP/SLG	TAv	BABIP	BRR	FRAA	WARP
2014	STO	A+	20	634	111	31	1	37	97	117	137	2	0	.262/.404/.543	.332	.287	0.3	1B(102): -1.4, RF(6): -0.4	5.4
2015	OAK	MLB	21	250	27	9	0	9	31	29	74	0	0	.203/.297/.377	.258	.253	-0.5	1B 1, RF -0	0.2
2016	OAK	MLB	22	250	33	9	0	11	32	32	71	0	0	.210/.313/.403	.267	.255	-0.6	1B 1, RF 0	1.7

Breakout: 2%   Improve: 11%   Collapse: 3%   Attrition: 5%   MLB: 19%   Upside: 58   *Comparables: Jon Singleton, Kyle Blanks, Anthony Rizzo*

Drafted/Acquired: 1st round, 2012, Parkview HS (Lilburn, GA)

Previous Ranking: #8 (2012 Org)

What Happened in 2014: The first basemen rebounded well from his mediocre 2013 season, putting together a loud season for Stockton en route to leading the league in home runs.

Strengths: Patient approach at the plate; pairs well with short swing to the ball; big and strong build; plus raw power, which can play up at times in game; overall defensive game is solid at first base.

Weaknesses: Swing can become long; stiff and lacks fluidity at times; athletic player but does not run well; plate patience can shift to overly passive; already limited to a first-base profile.

Risk Factor/Injury History: Moderate risk; yet to reach Double-A.

Bret Sayre's Fantasy Take: It's easy to run back to the "oh, it's just the Cal League" adage when a player puts up a season like Olson did in 2014, but there were some real gains made here—and they shouldn't be held against him because of the environment. Keeping the strikeouts reasonable may always be a challenge, but Olson has 30-homer power and makes an even better investment in OBP leagues.

The Year Ahead: Olson put his name back on the map after his loud campaign in the California League. Before the 2014 season, Olson was described as stiff and too bulky for his swing to provide the efficiency needed at the plate. Fast forward to the end of last season and the same industry sources had changed their tune. They now see a hitter who has regained some athleticism while finding consistency in his swing path. Olson has the power and plate approach to yield damage in the majors, and last season he took the correct steps to iron out his issues. There are still concerns shared whether the hit tool can play enough for the power to be implemented, and he will likely be a player who whiffs at high rates. However, Olson's feel in the box is advanced, which could help soften the extreme strikeout rates. Having proven the lower minors are no real challenge for him, the first basemen is ready for an introduction to Double-A. While this will be Olson's first big test at the higher levels, he isn't far off from the majors and could really see his stock jump if he can piece together another promising season at the next level.

---

3. Sean Nolin LHP

Born: 12/26/89 **Age:** 25 **Bats:** L **Throws:** L **Height:** 6'4" **Weight:** 230

MLB ETA	CT	FB	CH	CB	SL	OFP	Realistic
Debuted in 2013	–	50	60	50	50	50 NO. 4 STARTER	50 NO. 5 STARTER

YEAR	TEAM	LVL	AGE	W	L	SV	G	GS	IP	H	HR	BB	K	BB9	SO9	GB%	BABIP	WHIP	ERA	FIP	FRA	WARP
2014	TOR	MLB	24	0	0	0	1	0	1.0	1	1	0	0	0.0	0.0	25%	.000	1.00	9.00	16.16	16.46	-0.1
2014	BUF	AAA	24	4	6	0	17	17	87.3	74	6	35	74	3.6	7.6	42%	.270	1.25	3.50	3.86	4.30	1.0
2014	DUN	A+	24	0	1	0	2	2	7.3	4	0	4	9	4.9	11.0	42%	.211	1.09	3.68	2.57	2.80	0.3
2014	BLJ	Rk	24	0	0	0	1	1	2.3	1	0	0	5	0.0	19.3	67%	.333	0.43	0.00	-0.78	1.65	0.1
2015	OAK	MLB	25	5	6	0	17	17	85.0	83	9	32	71	3.4	7.5	41%	.297	1.36	4.05	4.52	4.40	0.5
2016	OAK	MLB	26	10	10	0	30	30	191.3	190	18	62	159	2.9	7.5	41%	.300	1.32	3.96	3.97	4.31	0.6

Breakout: 20%   Improve: 36%   Collapse: 11%   Attrition: 36%   MLB: 53%   Upside: 11   *Comparables: Matt Maloney, Brad Peacock, Alex Wilson*

Drafted/Acquired: 6th round, 2010 draft, San Jacinto Junior College (Pasadena, TX)

Previous Ranking: #5 (Jays)

What Happened in 2014: Two stints on the disabled list with a groin injury were a hit to the left-hander's season. In return, he lost a chunk of time and the ability to get into a rhythm of throwing consistently to push for an extended look at the big-league level.

Strengths: Body to withstand rigors of long season; smooth delivery; downhill thrower; commands fastball to both sides of the plate; shows tailing action; deceptive changeup; delivers with good arm speed; spins both curve and slider with loose wrist; throws each offering for strikes; understands how to execute craft; mixes and matches arsenal well.

Weaknesses: Fastball will play down; flattens; typically only scrapes above 90; needs to be fine consistently; neither breaking ball shows better than average; curve tends to be loopy and soft; change loses luster without other offerings starting bats; limited margin of error.

Risk Factor/Injury History: Low risk; achieved major leagues; mature arsenal.

Bret Sayre's Fantasy Take: Talk about a good change. Nolin was dealt from Toronto to Oakland in November 2014 and his fantasy outlook took a big step forward. Being a close-to-the-majors, fly-ball pitcher, Nolin should see opportunity in 2015 and could be a strong streamer at home in mixed leagues. Long term, the strikeouts are likely to underwhelm, but a SP4 profile is possible in the right park.

The Year Ahead: While Nolin's overall repertoire is on the bland side, the left-hander displays solid command of his arsenal and the ability to set up hitters by consistently changing angles. Both aspects give this arm's stuff the chance to play up further as a collection than the individual grades indicate, but the margin of error will be very tight against the best competition. There are concerns that the heavy reliance on inducing weak contact and effectively changing speeds will lead to uneven work as a starter over the long run. The 25-year-old's changeup is his best asset, and when the other offerings are working, it enables him to consistently keep hitters off-balance. Nolin runs into trouble at times with his fastball, especially when working above the thighs, as the better hitters can sit around and wait for it without having to fully respect the breaking stuff. It's not a flashy or exciting profile as a back-of-the-rotation arm, but the goal of any system is to produce major leaguers and Nolin fits that bill.

4. Renato Nunez   3B

Born: 4/4/94   **Age:** 21   **Bats:** R   **Throws:** R   **Height:** 6'1"   **Weight:** 200

MLB ETA	Hit	Power	Run	Glove	Arm		OFP	Realistic
2017	–	60	–	–	50		55 >AVG REGULAR	45 2ND DIV ST/BENCH BAT

YEAR	TEAM	LVL	AGE	PA	R	2B	3B	HR	RBI	BB	SO	SB	CS	AVG/OBP/SLG	TAv	BABIP	BRR	FRAA	WARP
2014	STO	A+	20	563	75	28	3	29	96	34	113	2	0	.279/.336/.517	.284	.303	-1.6	3B(80): 1.6, 3B(3): 1.6	2.7
2015	OAK	MLB	21	250	21	9	1	7	28	7	72	0	0	.211/.241/.345	.224	.266	-0.4	3B 1	-0.3
2016	OAK	MLB	22	250	27	11	1	8	28	11	70	0	0	.219/.264/.371	.237	.277	-0.6	3B 1	0.1

Breakout: 0%   Improve: 0%   Collapse: 0%   Attrition: 0%   MLB: 0%   Upside: 9   *Comparables: Josh Bell, Mike Moustakas, Josh Vitters*

Drafted/Acquired: International Free Agent, 2010, Venezuela

Previous Ranking: #10 (Org)

What Happened in 2014: After stumbling in his first shot at full-season ball, Nunez rebounded with Stockton, posting big power numbers at the hot corner.

Strengths: Plus power potential; plus bat speed; ability to extend hands and drive ball with backspin; feasts on fastballs; above-average arm strength from third base.

Weaknesses: Struggles to make contact; ultra-aggressive approach which leads to poor swings; footwork is choppy at third; lacks sufficient range; likely a first baseman down the road.

Risk Factor/Injury History: High; swing-and-miss causes concern; positional value is in question; yet to reach Double-A.

Bret Sayre's Fantasy Take: The raw power is real here, but Nunez makes for a very shaky fantasy investment because even if he stays at third base, which is anything but a given, his lack of a hit tool will drag down his earnings to near replacement-level in mixed leagues. And that's the positive spin.

The Year Ahead: Nunez flashed his big raw power this year, proving that he can cause damage with his ultra-aggressive approach. That being said, the concerns are still very real when it comes to his future. The approach lends itself to bad at-bats and poor swings on major-league average or higher secondary offerings. While there is still time for him to refine the approach, Nunez is about to journey into the Double-A level and face pitchers with more advanced repertoires. The defensive aspect of his game is very much in question as well, with the Athletics taking a wait-and-see approach to his ultimate defensive home. His footwork slightly improved last season, but not enough for scouts and industry members to feel comfortable about his ability to stick at third. Nunez has clear holes in his game, but the power might be enough to hide some of these deficiencies moving forward.

5. Kendall Graveman   RHP

Born: 12/21/90   **Age:** 24   **Bats:** R   **Throws:** R   **Height:** 6'2"   **Weight:** 185

MLB ETA	CT	FB	CH	CB	SL		OFP	Realistic
Debuted in 2014	50	55	–	–	50		50 NO. 4 STARTER	45 NO. 5 SP/LONG/MID RP

YEAR	TEAM	LVL	AGE	W	L	SV	G	GS	IP	H	HR	BB	K	BB9	SO9	GB%	BABIP	WHIP	ERA	FIP	FRA	WARP
2014	TOR	MLB	23	0	0	0	5	0	4.7	4	0	0	4	0.0	7.7	64%	.286	0.86	3.86	1.45	2.59	0.1
2014	BUF	AAA	23	3	2	0	6	6	38.3	34	1	5	22	1.2	5.2	66%	.282	1.02	1.88	2.94	4.09	0.4
2014	NHP	AA	23	1	0	0	1	1	6.0	8	0	2	4	3.0	6.0	53%	.421	1.67	1.50	3.02	4.41	0.1
2014	DUN	A+	23	8	4	0	16	16	96.7	89	1	18	64	1.7	6.0	59%	.287	1.11	2.23	2.88	4.35	0.9
2014	LNS	A	23	2	0	0	4	4	26.3	11	0	6	25	2.1	8.5	68%	.175	0.65	0.34	2.27	3.47	0.5
2015	OAK	MLB	24	6	8	0	21	21	118.3	124	10	36	65	2.7	4.9	55%	.292	1.35	4.04	4.60	4.39	0.5
2016	OAK	MLB	25	9	11	0	29	29	182.7	217	19	47	95	2.3	4.7	55%	.313	1.45	4.83	4.52	5.25	-1.4

Breakout: 17%   Improve: 28%   Collapse: 11%   Attrition: 28%   MLB: 46%   Upside: 19   *Comparables: Dallas Keuchel, Jake Buchanan, Adam Warren*

Drafted/Acquired: 8th round, 2013, Mississippi State University

Previous Ranking: NR

What Happened in 2014: The former eighth-round pick out of Mississippi State made a stop at each level in his first full professional season, beginning the year at Lansing and finding himself in the bigs with Toronto to close the summer out.

Strengths: 90-93 mph fastball with heavy downward action that makes it tough for hitters to elevate the offering; present pitchability; cutter is weapon against left-handed hitters and has helped his case to starting games.

Weaknesses: Lacks plus offering; questions about ability to miss bats and take pressure off the fastball having to induce weak contact to consistently get outs.

Risk Factor/Injury History: Low; achieved major leagues; mature arsenal.

Bret Sayre's Fantasy Take: Graveman's fantasy profile is like an even more pedestrian version of Nolin's, which makes his value almost nonexistent in mixed leagues. It's a good name to file away in AL-only formats, though, as Oakland doesn't have a ton of rotation depth.

The Year Ahead: The Mississippi State alum soared through the minors after adding a cutter to his arsenal. This helped alleviate some stress against left-handed hitters and mitigate the severity of an arsenal with a sinker-heavy approach. The cutter is mixed along with a slider and changeup, but his bread and butter is still the sinking fastball. While the pure stuff isn't overwhelming, Graveman shows poise and pitchability and shocked many within the industry with his ability to churn through the opposition and get outs. There are concerns moving forward in regards to his lacking a plus offering and his ability to efficiently maneuver through a major-league lineup multiple times, but the arsenal has enough juice to be a surefire bet in the bullpen at the very least.

---

6. Yairo Munoz   SS

Born: 1/23/95   **Age:** 20   **Bats:** R   **Throws:** R   **Height:** 6'1"   **Weight:** 165

MLB ETA	Hit	Power	Run	Glove	Arm	OFP	Realistic
2018	50	60	50	–	60	55 >AVG REGULAR	45 2ND DIV STARTER

YEAR	TEAM	LVL	AGE	PA	R	2B	3B	HR	RBI	BB	SO	SB	CS	AVG/OBP/SLG	TAv	BABIP	BRR	FRAA	WARP
2014	VER	A-	19	265	29	17	3	5	20	7	42	14	6	.298/.319/.448	.289	.338	0.9	SS(53): 4.0, 3B(8): 1.2	2.7
2015	OAK	MLB	20	250	21	9	1	2	18	8	66	6	3	.201/.229/.277	.198	.262	0.1	SS 1, 3B 1	-0.4
2016	OAK	MLB	21	250	22	10	1	3	20	11	62	6	3	.207/.245/.290	.202	.263	0.4	SS 1, 3B 1	-1.7

Breakout: 0%   Improve: 0%   Collapse: 0%   Attrition: 0%   MLB: 0%   Upside: 14   *Comparables: Trevor Plouffe, Charlie Culberson, Arismendy Alcantara*

Drafted/Acquired: International Free Agent, 2011, Dominican Republic

Previous Ranking: NR

What Happened in 2014: Munoz held his own in the college-heavy New York-Penn League, making the all-star game and enjoying a solid season overall.

Strengths: Big raw power, potentially impact at shortstop; above-average bat speed; ability to extend hands and drive ball; plus arm strength.

Weaknesses: Lacks high-end athleticism; body could fill out some; might move off shortstop down the road; footwork and hands are just average; difficulty recognizing spin; still marinating the tools and approach together.

Risk Factor/Injury History: High; short-season résumé; large gap between present and future.

Bret Sayre's Fantasy Take: On this list, it can get tough to find guys to have some excitement about in fantasy leagues, but Munoz fits the bill. There's a long way to go here, but even the distant light of a potential five-category infielder is worth paying attention to. If you are in a deep league that rosters 300-plus prospects, Munoz might be available and worth grabbing.

The Year Ahead: After signing Munoz for $280,000 in 2011, the Athletics have taken development slowly with the Dominican talent. He has legitimate raw power, impressing scouts and industry members in batting practice. While Munoz's body is not fully matured and the power is more of the five o'clock variety at this time, the flashes are enough to provide optimism. Munoz displays advanced feel for the barrel and has a good swing through the zone, although he is still susceptible to spin. His defense has a chance to be average at shortstop, but some evaluators believe he may be a better fit for third base down the road. At this current time, Munoz has an outside chance to stick at shortstop, although it is likely he never becomes an asset defensively at the position. It remains to be seen how future growth into his frame will limit the speed and agility in the field and on the basepaths, but this year will shed further light on Munoz as he treks into his first campaign of full-season ball. In a system lacking prodigious talent, Munoz is certainly a player to keep an eye on.

---

7. Dillon Overton   LHP

Born: 8/17/91   **Age:** 23   **Bats:** L   **Throws:** L   **Height:** 6'2"   **Weight:** 172

MLB ETA	CT	FB	CH	CB	SL	OFP	Realistic
2017	–	50	50	55	–	55 NO. 3 STARTER	50 NO. 5 SP/7TH INN RP

YEAR	TEAM	LVL	AGE	W	L	SV	G	GS	IP	H	HR	BB	K	BB9	SO9	GB%	BABIP	WHIP	ERA	FIP	FRA	WARP
2014	VER	A-	22	0	1	0	5	5	15.0	11	0	1	22	0.6	13.2	47%	.324	0.80	2.40	0.90	1.29	0.7
2014	ATH	Rk	22	0	2	0	7	7	22.0	19	0	3	31	1.2	12.7	40%	.365	1.00	1.64	1.89	3.32	0.8
2015	OAK	MLB	23	2	3	0	9	9	32.7	35	3	18	24	5.0	6.6	43%	.309	1.62	5.18	5.18	5.63	-0.2
2016	OAK	MLB	24	6	8	0	29	29	182.7	181	16	90	159	4.4	7.8	43%	.306	1.49	4.42	4.32	4.80	-0.5

Breakout: 0%   Improve: 0%   Collapse: 0%   Attrition: 0%   MLB: 0%   Upside: 5   *Comparables: Jesse Hahn, Alex Wilson, Jimmy Barthmaier*

Drafted/Acquired: 2nd round, 2013, University of Oklahoma

Previous Ranking: OTR

What Happened in 2014: Overton finally made some progress on the mound after missing a year (July 2013-June 2014) due to Tommy John surgery.

Strengths: Present feel for pitching; fastball has arm-side run low in the zone; quick and loose arm; athletic build with potential for minor gains in projection; changeup has fade and deception; mature presence on mound.

Weaknesses: Stuff is down from college; high-80s fastball, which is still progressing back from injury; curveball lacks consistency and depth at higher velo bands; mechanics are mostly smooth but will pitch across body at times; some sources believe this could sap velocity.

Risk Factor/Injury History: High; Tommy John surgery on résumé, limited pro action in the past two years; still regaining past form.

Bret Sayre's Fantasy Take: There is some upside here, given both his amateur track record and the command profile, but gambling on a starting-pitching prospect with an average fastball and Tommy John surgery on his résumé isn't the greatest idea.

The Year Ahead: Overton has an interesting story, as he was abused and injured during his college years, which led to surgery and a large portion of time missed. Last season was all about regaining his form and working his stuff back to its potential. While the arsenal is clearly not 100 percent quite yet, Overton received optimistic reviews and has shown more feel than anticipated after surgery. When healthy, Overton is one of the better arms in this system, with a potential plus changeup and the ability to spot his fastball low in the zone. The risk remains high with the lefty, but there is still room for rehabilitation and projection, with a chance of the latter coming into focus this season.

8. Chad Pinder   2B

Born: 3/29/92   **Age:** 23   **Bats:** R   **Throws:** R   **Height:** 6'2"   **Weight:** 195

MLB ETA	Hit	Power	Run	Glove	Arm	OFP	Realistic
2017	50	50	50	50	50	55 >AVG REGULAR	45 2ND DIV/UTILITY

YEAR	TEAM	LVL	AGE	PA	R	2B	3B	HR	RBI	BB	SO	SB	CS	AVG/OBP/SLG	TAv	BABIP	BRR	FRAA	WARP
2014	STO	A+	22	436	61	32	5	13	55	22	99	12	9	.288/.336/.489	.290	.352	-1.0	2B(70): -6.3, SS(12): 2.0	2.2
2015	OAK	MLB	23	250	21	10	1	4	22	10	71	4	3	.213/.252/.310	.223	.284	-0.3	2B -3, SS 1	-0.4
2016	OAK	MLB	24	250	24	11	1	5	23	10	67	4	2	.217/.256/.331	.224	.281	0.0	2B -3, SS 1	-0.7

Breakout: 0%   Improve: 0%   Collapse: 0%   Attrition: 0%   MLB: 0%   Upside: 4   *Comparables: Charlie Culberson, Luke Hughes, Josh Barfield*

Drafted/Acquired: 2nd round, 2013, Virginia Tech

Previous Ranking: NR

What Happened in 2014: The Hokie alum put his short-season struggles in the rearview mirror, showing an all-around display of talent at Stockton.

Strengths: Athletic build; solid bat speed; approach is sound; shows feel for the game; adept at spraying ball around field; versatile mold that can play as a utility option.

Weaknesses: Lacks a standout or carrying tool; insufficient athleticism and range to consistently play left side of the infield; mild bat wrap; occasional struggle to extend and reach pitches low and outside.

Risk Factor/Injury History: Moderate; yet to reach Double-A; concerns regarding lack of a carrying tool.

Bret Sayre's Fantasy Take: Pinder is a deep-league special, as he's overlooked and can do a bit of everything. It's extremely unlikely that he'll do enough at the major-league level to be shallow-mixed worthy, but if he can survive up the chain, he can do enough to get playing time—which is half the battle if you're currently rostering players like Yunel Escobar or Eric Sogard.

The Year Ahead: Pinder is the definition of an average Joe. There is a lack of sexiness in the profile, which causes some allure to be lost in the grand scheme. However, he provides an all-around profile that has gone somewhat under the radar. While he lacks the pure athleticism and range to play on the left side of the diamond, Pinder offers enough versatility to give the Athletics a utility option. The hit tool has enough to keep Pinder afloat and potentially provide second-division ability down the road, but he will need to prove more to scouts in his first test at Double-A. These types of players are never going to gain national attention or much buzz, but Pinder has a chance to turn more heads as he moves up the chain.

9. Joe Wendle   2B

Born: 4/26/90   **Age:** 25   **Bats:** L   **Throws:** R   **Height:** 6'1"   **Weight:** 190

MLB ETA	Hit	Power	Run	Glove	Arm	OFP	Realistic
2015	55	–	–	50	50	50 AVG ML PLAYER	45 2ND DIV/UT/BENCH

YEAR	TEAM	LVL	AGE	PA	R	2B	3B	HR	RBI	BB	SO	SB	CS	AVG/OBP/SLG	TAv	BABIP	BRR	FRAA	WARP
2014	AKR	AA	24	370	46	20	5	8	50	26	56	4	2	.253/.311/.414	.262	.279	1.3	2B(80): 10.2	2.7
2014	CLE	Rk	24	26	8	1	1	0	4	4	4	1	1	.455/.538/.591	.381	.556	1.2	2B(5): -0.6	0.4
2015	OAK	MLB	25	250	23	11	2	5	26	14	53	2	1	.231/.281/.358	.247	.275	-0.1	2B 4, 3B 0	1.0
2016	OAK	MLB	26	250	27	10	1	6	26	14	53	2	1	.239/.290/.369	.247	.284	-0.1	2B 5, 3B 0	1.4

Breakout: 0%   Improve: 6%   Collapse: 9%   Attrition: 21%   MLB: 36%   Upside: 6   *Comparables: Ryan Flaherty, David Adams, Steve Tolleson*

Drafted/Acquired: 6th round, 2012, West Chester University of Pennsylvania

Previous Ranking: #10 (Indians)

What Happened in 2014: After a rough start and time missed due to a broken hamate bone, Wendle was shipped to Oakland in the Brandon Moss deal.

Strengths: Natural bat-to-ball ability; smooth swing; compact through zone with loose hands and minimal noise; potential for above-average hit tool; agile in the field with decent footwork; good feel for the game.

Weaknesses: Fringe power; lacks a plus tool; grinder more than toolsy; bat speed is average; lacks range to be true utility option; more agility than speed (fringe).

Risk Factor/Injury History: Low; significant time in Double-A; tools are matured; hamate injury is no longer a concern.

Bret Sayre's Fantasy Take: There's little of consequence for fantasy leagues here, as Wendle likely tops out as a poor man's Scooter Gennett. If that's valuable in your league, blink twice and we will send help.

The Year Ahead: Wendle's 2014 season would not be classified as sexy, but he displayed his value midseason after the rough April start. Wendle brings a solid approach to the plate, where he understands his strengths and takes his at-bats in a manner conducive to success. While his fringe power is likely not an asset, Wendle can provide enough power to potentially hit 8-10 homers at the highest level, with a good share of doubles. His gap-to-gap style of hitting has been displayed at every level throughout the minors, and he was able to put some of the questions about being too old for his current level behind him. The Athletics are comfortable keeping him at second base, with Wendle lacking the pure athleticism and range to play as a utility option on the left side of the diamond. Overall, Wendle's OFP hinges on the hit tool, but the second baseman has shown encouraging signs throughout his development. Oakland will have Wendle as depth heading into this season, with potential for him to become a larger piece down the road.

10. Matt Chapman   3B

Born: 4/28/93   **Age:** 22   **Bats:** R   **Throws:** R   **Height:** 6'2"   **Weight:** 205

MLB ETA	Hit	Power	Run	Glove	Arm	OFP	Realistic
2018	–	60	–	60	70	50 AVG ML PLAYER	45 <AVG ML PLAYER

YEAR	TEAM	LVL	AGE	PA	R	2B	3B	HR	RBI	BB	SO	SB	CS	AVG/OBP/SLG	TAv	BABIP	BRR	FRAA	WARP
2014	MID	AA	21	3	0	0	0	0	0	0	0	0	0	.000/.000/.000	.015	.000	0.0	3B(1): -0.0	-0.1
2014	BLT	A	21	202	22	8	3	5	20	7	46	2	1	.237/.282/.389	.220	.288	0.4	3B(21): 1.1	0.2
2014	ATH	Rk	21	15	1	1	1	0	0	1	1	0	0	.429/.467/.643	.490	.462	0.0	3B(1): -0.1	0.1
2015	OAK	MLB	22	250	17	9	1	3	20	9	72	0	0	.194/.228/.272	.196	.262	-0.3	3B 2	-0.9
2016	OAK	MLB	23	250	24	11	1	4	22	13	68	1	0	.210/.261/.319	.220	.275	-0.4	3B 1	-0.9

Breakout: 0%   Improve: 0%   Collapse: 0%   Attrition: 0%   MLB: 0%   Upside: 7   *Comparables: Alex Castellanos, Brad Emaus, Ryan Rua*

Drafted/Acquired: 1st round, 2014, California State University Fullerton

Previous Ranking: NR

What Happened in 2014: The Athletics drafted Chapman in the first round out of Cal State Fullerton and he spent most of his time in Low-A Beloit. The results of his assignment were below-average numbers and mixed reviews from scouts.

Strengths: Cannon arm at the hot corner; hands and actions are smooth; range down the line; big raw power; has feel for an approach at the plate.

Weaknesses: Swing has holes and can become elongated; drops elbow/shoulder on low pitches; can get out on front foot against good off-speed; raw power is often underutilized due to weak contact and not barreling pitches.

Risk Factor/Injury History: High; struggled in Beloit; hit tool underwhelming in first pro stint; needs to refine swing before realizing potential.

Bret Sayre's Fantasy Take: For a college bat, it's going to be a long burn for Chapman to tap into his 25-plus-homer potential power. Despite his appearance on the Top 50 from earlier this offseason in dynasty drafts, he's someone I'd try to avoid this offseason.

The Year Ahead: It was a rude awakening to pro ball for the Cal State Fullerton alum, as he struggled through 200 at-bats with Beloit. The glove and arm are weapons at third, but the bat holds many question marks. The swing has too many holes right now, and there was a note of inconsistency from every source talked to. The raw power is nice, but the hit tool may leave a less-than-desired outcome for the third basemen. His feel and approach are evident when he's in the box, which leaves some optimism moving forward. Chapman still has time to rekindle the flame that scouts were attracted to while in college, but the hit tool is the serious question mark at this point. If all else fails, Chapman can hit the upper-90s with his fastball off the mound, but that's probably putting the cart before the horse at this stage of his development.

Prospects on the Rise

1. RHP Daniel Gossett: Drafted last year in the second round out of Clemson, Gossett carries a three-pitch arsenal consisting of a fastball, slider, and changeup. While some sources are not sold on the overall profile, Gossett has produced results at every level. The questions moving forward will be whether the arsenal has enough firepower to turn over lineups multiple times and whether his body can hit the mechanical checkpoints necessary to keep efficient stamina after a decent amount of pitches thrown. Gossett passed his initial test at Vermont with flying colors and will look to continue his progression in full-season ball this season.

2. RHP Bobby Wahl: The development has been volatile and erratic, but Wahl possesses too much talent to simply be a forgotten man. The likely profile is a max-effort reliever who could potentially pitch in the late innings. While his command has been spotty, Wahl possesses heat in the mid- to upper-90s along with a decent breaking ball. The righty will need to establish health and consistency before more within the industry jump back on the bandwagon, but Wahl still has enough potential to revitalize his pro career and provide value to a major-league club.

3. 2B/SS Jesus Lopez: After signing for $950,000 in 2013, the slender Nicaraguan held his head above water in the Arizona Rookie League. The switch-hitting middle infielder has a smooth swing from both sides of the plate and could piece together enough of a hit tool to push his way through the lower minors with ease. Scouts are pessimistic about his chances to stick at shortstop, as he lacks fast-twitch athleticism and his actions in the field are merely adequate at this point. Lopez is a decent prospect to keep an eye on for now, with this season potentially boosting his stock in a barren system full of volatility in its rankings.

FROM THE FIELD

Franklin Barreto

Team: Oakland Athletics

Evaluator: Chris King

Dates seen: June 27–August 14, 2013

Affiliate: Bluefield Blue Jays (Rookie, Blue Jays)

Physical/health: No major injuries; body still young and developing strength; strong lower half; upper body has room to grow; strong wrists; physically mature for his age; could be a beast once fully mature.

MLB ETA	Risk factor	OFP	Realistic role
2017	Extreme	60	

Tool	Future grade	Report
Hit	60	Has some swing-and-miss due to aggressiveness; fast hands; good bat speed; swing is short and compact; makes loud contact; uses the entire field; opposite field is a strength; handles pitching from either side; excellent hand-eye coordination.
Power	50	Mostly gap to gap; extra-base-hit machine; opposite field power is already showing; strong wrists and quick bat allow him to drive ball; swing has some uppercut and will generate loft.
Baserunning/speed	65	Easy natural speed; consistent plus times to first; shows occasional plus-plus times; top end he can fly; needs work with stolen-base game; lacks some natural instincts; 25-30 stolen-base potential.
Glove	50	Still rough; unnatural looking at shortstop; decent range; will struggle with routine plays; better going up the middle than to his right; glove won't play at current position.
Arm	65	Above average; plenty strong for current position or outfield; will drop arm angle, affecting accuracy; still plus strength while on the move.

Overall: Has good pitch recognition but will expand the zone at times; vulnerable to fastball up in the zone; destroys any pitch down and away; very advanced bat for his age; aggressive style on both sides of the field.

Shortstop is not his future; bat will play at almost any position; will make a tough play look easy, then make an easy one look tough; too inconsistent with his glove and arm accuracy. Barreto's future is bright: a high-impact bat that seems destined for center field. Seeing him drive the ball to the opposite field is a thing of beauty. Wherever he ends up defensively, the bat will play. Future impact bat at top of the order.

Factors on the Farm
Prospects likely to contribute at the major-league level in 2015

1. RHP Chris Bassitt: Acquired in the deal that sent Jeff Samardzija to the White Sox, Bassitt has already pitched a handful of innings in the majors. As a starter, the stuff is mostly 89-93 mph with heavy movement and life, but the fastball has ticked up to 94-97 mph out of the 'pen. He also owns an average slider and a lollipop curveball that comes in around 72 mph and tends to get hitters out on their front foot. While Bassitt still has a chance to start due to his ability to throw strikes and decent arsenal, the stuff should really play up in short-inning spurts out of the 'pen.

2. RHP R.J. Alvarez: The 24-year-old pitched in 10 games for San Diego before being shipped to Oakland in the Derek Norris deal. The righty brings a fierce fastball/slider combo to the mound, with potential to pump both by hitters. He flashes more stuff than command due to iffy mechanics, which leaves speculation regarding whether he is a late-inning arm or leaning more toward middle relief. The overall arm is certainly major-league caliber, but there is enough risk involved here to leave questions about the overall ceiling moving forward.

3. RHP Raul Alcantara: 2014 was a lost year for the 22-year-old Dominican, as he underwent Tommy John surgery early in the season. While he will likely miss some time heading into the 2015 season, Alcantara has a live arm with a fastball gleaming with movement and velocity. His overall arsenal has the projection to work in a rotation, but the development path might have changed now with the arm injury and lost time on the mound. Either way, Alcantara is a Double-A arm that might not take too long in his development process moving forward, depending on a healthy recovery.

PHILADELPHIA PHILLIES

1. J.P. Crawford   SS

Born: 1/11/95   **Age:** 20   **Bats:** L   **Throws:** R   **Height:** 6'2"   **Weight:** 180

MLB ETA		Hit	Power	Run	Glove	Arm	OFP	Realistic
2017		55	–	60	60	55	**60** 1ST DIVISION PLAYER	**50** ML REGULAR

YEAR	TEAM	LVL	AGE	PA	R	2B	3B	HR	RBI	BB	SO	SB	CS	AVG/OBP/SLG	TAv	BABIP	BRR	FRAA	WARP
2014	CLR	A+	19	271	32	7	0	8	29	28	37	10	7	.275/.352/.407	.284	.292	-2.9	SS(62): 0.4	1.6
2014	LWD	A	19	267	37	16	0	3	19	37	37	14	7	.295/.398/.405	.291	.342	1.2	SS(59): 2.3	2.3
2015	PHI	MLB	20	250	28	9	0	4	19	21	55	6	4	.226/.296/.319	.240	.278	-0.4	SS 1	0.6
2016	PHI	MLB	21	250	28	9	1	4	24	22	51	6	4	.243/.313/.350	.253	.291	0.0	SS 0	1.5

Breakout: 0%   **Improve:** 0%   **Collapse:** 0%   **Attrition:** 0%   **MLB:** 0%   **Upside:** 37   *Comparables: Jurickson Profar, Brad Harman, Ruben Tejada*

Drafted/Acquired: 1st round, 2013 draft, Lakewood HS (Lakewood, CA)

Previous Ranking: #3 (Org), Just Missed the Cut (101)

What Happened in 2014: Crawford was all systems go in his full-season debut, hitting .285 in 123 games, including spending half the year in High-A as a 19-year-old.

Strengths: Smooth and agile body actions; athletic player; arm for left side of the infield; instincts for position; can range well to both right and left; soft glove; plus run; loose, quick hands enable barrel control; solid-average bat speed; ability to stay inside of ball.

Weaknesses: In the early stages of learning the ins and outs of being a pro and slowing the game down; engagement in field can drift; glove technique needs work; power likely to play to fringe-average at best; will presently lunge at spin; needs to continue to add strength to handle rigors of long season.

Risk Factor/Injury History: Moderate risk; yet to reach upper levels; gap between present and future.

Bret Sayre's Fantasy Take: At first glance, Crawford's scouting report reads like a player who's a good bit more valuable in real life than fantasy, but similar to Francisco Lindor (in theory, not practice), this undersells the fantasy potential here. Crawford's power can play up to the mid-teens in Philadelphia and with 20-plus steal potential at an extremely tough fantasy position, he's someone to be excited about in our world as well.

The Year Ahead: Crawford will likely return to High-A for further experience before getting a taste of Double-A at some point this season. The 20-year-old will dictate his own pace, though. Crawford's swing is geared toward high contact, which bodes well for his hit tool projection, but don't expect high power output to be a large part of the ultimate game. Some sources suggested the shortstop might experience some growing pains as he continues to learn to slow the game down against the rising competition. There are still plenty of rough edges to polish in Crawford's game, making what he could look like in his mid-20s quite different than the current product. This will be a developmental journey, with plenty of lead time before reaching peak totals, but all the ingredients are here to round into a first-division talent with continued repetition of his overall game.

> **#36**
>
> BP Top 101 Prospects

2. Aaron Nola   RHP

Born: 6/4/93   **Age:** 22   **Bats:** R   **Throws:** R   **Height:** 6'1"   **Weight:** 195

MLB ETA		CT	FB	CH	CB	SL	OFP	Realistic
2015		–	60	55	60	–	**55** NO. 3 STARTER	**50** NO. 4 STARTER

YEAR	TEAM	LVL	AGE	W	L	SV	G	GS	IP	H	HR	BB	K	BB9	SO9	GB%	BABIP	WHIP	ERA	FIP	FRA	WARP
2014	REA	AA	21	2	0	0	5	5	24.0	25	4	5	15	1.9	5.6	49%	.284	1.25	2.62	4.90	4.90	0.3
2014	CLR	A+	21	2	3	0	7	6	31.3	24	4	5	30	1.4	8.6	34%	.247	0.93	3.16	3.61	5.02	0.2
2015	PHI	MLB	22	2	3	0	8	8	37.7	37	4	12	28	2.9	6.7	42%	.309	1.31	4.28	4.28	4.65	0.0
2016	PHI	MLB	23	10	10	0	32	32	206.7	196	22	56	173	2.4	7.5	42%	.309	1.22	3.80	3.72	4.13	0.8

Breakout: 0%   **Improve:** 0%   **Collapse:** 0%   **Attrition:** 0%   **MLB:** 0%   **Upside:** 18   *Comparables: Joe Wieland, Patrick Corbin, Will Smith*

Drafted/Acquired: 1st round, 2014 draft, Louisiana State University (Baton Rouge, LA)

Previous Ranking: NR

What Happened in 2014: Nola was drafted seventh overall, and then proceeded to throw 55 1/3 professional innings, including five starts at Double-A.

Strengths: Easy delivery; repeatable mechanics; low-90s fastball displays strong movement; can reach back for more; creates deception via changing angles on hitters; feel for turning over change; curve flashes deep break and tight rotation; plus-to-better command of arsenal; understands how to execute craft; comes after hitters.

> **#60**
>
> BP Top 101 Prospects

Weaknesses: Doesn't have prototypical size; can wrap and have trouble staying on top of curveball; becomes loose and loopy; needs to throw changeup more in sequences; fastball is flat when above middle of the thighs; needs one of the secondary offerings to emerge as consistent bat-misser; more polish than projection.

Risk Factor/Injury History: Low risk; reached upper levels; limited experience against advanced pro bats.

Bret Sayre's Fantasy Take: Nola is much more about safety than upside in fantasy leagues, as he currently projects to be a helpful starter in all four categories, who can rack up enough innings to be a roto compiler—his aggressiveness and control can lead to 220 innings a year down the road. Even if he tops out, Nola is unlikely to push past solid SP3 status.

The Year Ahead: Nola's stuff is likely to be advanced past minor-league hitters and ready for the bigs this season. The right-hander brings a polished three-pitch arsenal, with strong command and solid deception via a low three-quarters delivery. Nola needs at least one of his secondary offerings to fully emerge to complement his fastball against high-quality hitters. There are concerns that if neither the curve nor change reach potential, batters will sit on his heater, which is around the plate often. The concerns are somewhat mitigated by Nola's advanced mind-set, but it's something to keep on the radar. The ceiling isn't enormous, but it's likely he develops into a quality middle-of-the-rotation arm for a number of years with a bit more development going forward.

---

3. Maikel Franco 1B/3B

Born: 8/26/92   **Age:** 22   **Bats:** R   **Throws:** R   **Height:** 6'1"   **Weight:** 180

MLB ETA	Hit	Power	Run	Glove	Arm		OFP	Realistic
Debuted in 2014	55	65	–	50	65		55 >AVG REGULAR	50 ML REGULAR

YEAR	TEAM	LVL	AGE	PA	R	2B	3B	HR	RBI	BB	SO	SB	CS	AVG/OBP/SLG	TAv	BABIP	BRR	FRAA	WARP
2014	PHI	MLB	21	58	5	2	0	0	5	1	13	0	0	.179/.190/.214	.147	.227	0.5	3B(12): 0.7, 1B(5): 0.2	-0.3
2014	LEH	AAA	21	556	64	33	4	16	78	30	81	3	1	.257/.299/.428	.249	.276	2.4	3B(107): -3.8, 1B(23): 0.6	0.9
2015	PHI	MLB	22	250	24	12	1	8	30	8	47	0	0	.248/.273/.403	.257	.275	-0.4	3B -2, 1B 0	0.3
2016	PHI	MLB	23	601	68	29	1	19	71	26	117	1	0	.245/.281/.402	.253	.276	-1.3	3B -3, 1B 1	0.5

Breakout: 4%   Improve: 27%   Collapse: 6%   Attrition: 26%   MLB: 50%   Upside: 46   *Comparables: Josh Vitters, Brandon Laird, Lonnie Chisenhall*

#96
BP Top 101 Prospects

Drafted/Acquired: International Free Agent, 2010, Dominican Republic

Previous Ranking: #1 (Org), #52 (Top 101)

What Happened in 2014: Franco experienced resistance out of the gate in his jump to Triple-A, but came on strong in the second half of the year, culminating in a call-up to The Show.

Strengths: Excellent fastball hitter; explosive hands; lightning-quick swing; feel for barreling the ball up with backspin; thunder in the stick; knows how to create lift; can adjust swing in zone; plenty of arm for left side of infield; soft hands and glove.

Weaknesses: Extremely aggressive approach; will guess, leading to misses or weak contact against soft stuff; gets out in front of ball often—creates hole with breaking stuff away; despite excellent hand-eye and bat speed, hit tool may end up playing down due to approach; lacks quick reactions and instincts at hot corner.

Risk Factor/Injury History: Low risk; achieved major-league level; concerns with exploitable aggressiveness and glove.

Bret Sayre's Fantasy Take: Some players are just built for standard 5x5 roto leagues, and Franco is one of them. Franco's third-base eligibility will linger for longer than his skill or playing time at the hot corner, but even if that passes, he could hit .275 with 25-plus homers and more RBI than you'd expect, due to his free-swinging nature. He's still the top fantasy prospect in this system.

The Year Ahead: While Franco might end up starting the year in Triple-A for another tour of duty, the 22-year-old is in line to get an extended chance to show what he can do in the majors at some point this season. Franco is a talented hitter, with top-shelf bat speed and the power to crack 25-plus bombs. While the early Triple-A struggles proved to be a transition period, the overzealousness in the box casts some doubts as to whether the hit tool will translate consistently, possibly leading to extended valleys at the highest level. If there were stronger feeling about his ability to stick at the hot corner, the role would play up a little, but it's still a potential regular at first who can hit down a bit in the order with some pop.

4. Zach Eflin   RHP

Born: 4/8/94   **Age:** 21   **Bats:** R   **Throws:** R   **Height:** 6'4"   **Weight:** 200

MLB ETA	CT	FB	CH	CB	SL	OFP	Realistic
2016	–	55	60	–	55	60 NO. 3 STARTER	50 NO. 4 STARTER

YEAR	TEAM	LVL	AGE	W	L	SV	G	GS	IP	H	HR	BB	K	BB9	SO9	GB%	BABIP	WHIP	ERA	FIP	FRA	WARP
2014	LEL	A+	20	10	7	0	24	24	128.0	138	9	31	93	2.2	6.5	52%	.338	1.32	3.80	4.02	4.91	1.1
2015	PHI	MLB	21	4	7	0	17	17	88.3	93	9	32	51	3.3	5.2	44%	.308	1.42	4.67	4.73	5.07	-0.7
2016	PHI	MLB	22	10	10	0	32	32	207.0	191	18	60	147	2.6	6.4	44%	.294	1.21	3.61	3.79	3.92	0.7

Breakout: 0%   Improve: 0%   Collapse: 0%   Attrition: 0%   MLB: 0%   Upside: 2   *Comparables: Kyle Ryan, Erasmo Ramirez, Jonathan Pettibone*

Drafted/Acquired: 1st round, 2012 draft, Paul J. Hagerty HS (Orlando, FL)

Previous Ranking: On the Rise – SD

What Happened in 2014: Eflin put together a solid campaign with High-A Lake Elsinore, showing improved consistency across his arsenal and averaging over five innings per start.

Strengths: Good size; still filling in frame; high waist; gets solid extension and leverages long limbs to create tough angles; shields ball very well; good deception; fastball comes upper-80s to low-90s, routinely topping 94 mph; two-seamer shows lots of arm-side action and weight; changeup is a potential weapon; action mirrors two-seamer; at best comes with arm-speed deception; low-80s tilted slider flashes above average with some bite and depth; fills up the zone; confident air on the bump; developmental progress across arsenal bodes well for continued growth.

Weaknesses: Can get deliberate in mechanics; fastball can get flat up in the zone; change can come too firm in the mid-80s; slider is inconsistent, often lacking bite or backing up; still developing feel for sequencing; can get formulaic in approach.

Risk Factor/Injury History: Moderate; yet to reach Double-A; lacks swing-and-miss profile at present.

The Year Ahead: 2014 was an encouraging year for the former Hagerty High product, as Eflin saw the body, stuff, and feel all take a solid step forward. Despite long limbs and a continually thickening build, Eflin has done a solid job of keeping his mechanics generally in line, which in turn has facilitated a better control profile than you generally see in big-bodied arms with long levers. To reach his mid-rotation upside, Eflin will need to continue to refine his in-zone command as well as better implement his arsenal. As he learns to work both sides of the plate and better utilize his offerings to set each other up, he should be able to keep pace with the advanced bats he'll face at the upper levels and could also see an uptick in strikeouts. He'll spend 2015 in Double-A as a 21-year-old and is positioned to earn himself a taste of the bigs as early as 2016.

5. Yoel Mecias   LHP

Born: 10/11/93   **Age:** 21   **Bats:** L   **Throws:** L   **Height:** 6'2"   **Weight:** 160

MLB ETA	CT	FB	CH	CB	SL	OFP	Realistic
2017	–	60	65	–	50	60 NO. 3 STARTER	50 NO. 4 STARTER

YEAR	TEAM	LVL	AGE	W	L	SV	G	GS	IP	H	HR	BB	K	BB9	SO9	GB%	BABIP	WHIP	ERA	FIP	FRA	WARP
2014	LWD	A	20	3	3	0	7	7	33.7	29	2	9	23	2.4	6.1	43%	.270	1.13	3.21	3.97	4.92	0.3
2014	PHL	Rk	20	0	1	0	4	4	17.0	19	0	8	10	4.2	5.3	34%	.328	1.59	4.76	3.74	5.47	0.0
2015	PHI	MLB	21	2	3	0	11	8	44.0	46	5	21	30	4.3	6.1	44%	.315	1.54	5.21	5.07	5.67	-0.5
2016	PHI	MLB	22	6	7	0	32	20	148.7	145	17	76	107	4.6	6.5	44%	.300	1.49	4.97	4.81	5.40	-1.4

Breakout: 0%   Improve: 0%   Collapse: 0%   Attrition: 0%   MLB: 0%   Upside: 6   *Comparables: Jose A. Ramirez, Anthony Swarzak, Carlos Carrasco*

Drafted/Acquired: International Free Agent, 2010, Venezuela

Previous Ranking: #9 (Org)

What Happened in 2014: Mecias returned to the mound after Tommy John surgery in 2013 to log 50 2/3 innings, while also showing that his stuff is coming back to presurgery form.

Strengths: Loose arm; frame to continue filling out and add strength; balanced delivery; late life to fastball; works 89- 92, with potential to sit higher; can touch up to 95; feel for changeup; shows arm-side fade and fastball guise; more grow in offering; flashes ability to snap tight slider; solid foundation of raw pitching tools to work with.

Weaknesses: Immature body; must improve strength levels to handle grind of professional season year in and year out; learning how to approach pitching; some delivery cleanup needed to enhance command; presently below average; tends to spin slider with more slurvy than true break; lacks hard bite.

Risk Factor/Injury History: High risk; Tommy John on résumé; limited professional experience.

Bret Sayre's Fantasy Take: Once you get beyond the top-50 fantasy pitching prospects or so, the sound strategy is often grabbing guys who could see short-term value bursts and then looking to package them in a trade immediately. With a strong change and the Florida State League in his future, Mecias is a strong choice for the strategy.

The Year Ahead: This may seem a little aggressive with Mecias considering he still isn't too far into his return from surgery and has fairly limited professional experience, but this is a prospect with an excellent foundation, who is likely to start turning some heads. Both the fastball and changeup show the makings of plus pitches at the left-hander's disposal, with the change having the most room for growth. With added strength to Mecias' lanky frame, the heater also has a good chance to tick up in velocity. The long pole is the slider, which needs tightening and to emerge as a legit piece of the arsenal for the projection to come into full focus. Look for Mecias to further sharpen his skills in High-A this year and for the whispers of a potential future mid-rotation starter to get louder.

6.   Ben Lively   RHP

Born: 3/5/92   **Age:** 23   **Bats:** R   **Throws:** R   **Height:** 6'4"   **Weight:** 190

MLB ETA	CT	FB	CH	CB	SL	OFP	Realistic
2015	–	55	55	50	60	60 NO. 3 STARTER	50 NO. 4 STARTER

YEAR	TEAM	LVL	AGE	W	L	SV	G	GS	IP	H	HR	BB	K	BB9	SO9	GB%	BABIP	WHIP	ERA	FIP	FRA	WARP
2014	PEN	AA	22	3	6	0	13	13	72.0	60	7	36	76	4.5	9.5	37%	.290	1.33	3.88	4.01	4.19	1.2
2014	BAK	A+	22	10	1	0	13	13	79.0	57	6	16	95	1.8	10.8	35%	.281	0.92	2.28	2.97	3.08	2.8
2015	PHI	MLB	23	6	7	0	22	22	106.0	91	11	43	105	3.7	8.9	39%	.302	1.26	3.74	4.03	4.06	0.8
2016	PHI	MLB	24	10	10	0	32	32	203.3	177	23	75	197	3.3	8.7	39%	.299	1.24	3.79	3.88	4.12	0.8

Breakout: 20%   Improve: 29%   Collapse: 4%   Attrition: 23%   MLB: 40%   Upside: 59   *Comparables: Matt Barnes, Matt Harvey, Jake McGee*

Drafted/Acquired: 4th round, 2013 draft, University of Central Florida (Orlando, FL)

Previous Ranking: #7 (Org – CIN)

What Happened in 2014: Lively split 2014 between High-A Bakersfield and Double-A Pensacola, dominating the California League and continuing to look the part against Southern League competition.

Strengths: Strong, durable build; big-time deception across arsenal; shields ball from hitter, with fastball and slider particularly difficult to pick up/differentiate; excellent balance and consistent timing; plus control and above-average command; fastball ranges comfortably 88-92 and reaches 94 with regularity; some arm-side run; low- to mid-80s slider capable of missing bats and barrels alike; improving feel for changeup; can flash above-average fade; mid-70s curve serves as change-of-pace offering that is most effective as a freeze pitch; can mix all four offerings; little trouble maintaining effectiveness throughout starts.

Weaknesses: Still working to make changeup a consistent weapon; can struggle to put away lefty bats when off-speed not clicking; slider will back up on him when struggling to find release; curve is a limited-use weapon and can be tracked if not properly sequenced; faded some in August; some questions as to whether effort and unorthodox delivery will allow for enough consistency in execution over course of a major-league season; fastball flattens out, particularly up in the zone; could be susceptible to the long ball if in-zone command doesn't fully develop.

Risk Factor/Injury History: Moderate; limited exposure to Double-A.

Bret Sayre's Fantasy Take: Lively became a very popular name in dynasty leagues as the 2014 season kicked off, and frankly it's not his fault that owners got far too excited. The right-hander isn't a great bet to hold a ton of value in mixed leagues, as he projects for only average ratios and strikeout numbers—and that's if he sticks as a starter.

The Year Ahead: Lively cruised through the first half of 2014, overwhelming High-A bats with four pitches that all showed major-league average or better over the course of his 13 Bakersfield starts. The transition to Double-A fell short of seamless, but the powerful righty continued to show mid-rotation potential thanks to the quality of his fastball and slider, and willingness to mix in the curve and change as needed. Any time you run into a nontraditional mechanical package you will get evaluators entrenched on either side, and Lively is no different. Critics of the arm action and effort continue to insist that Lively will struggle to establish enough command and consistency to thrive against major-league bats, fitting best in the late innings pumping his fastball and slide piece. Supporters point to Lively's solid 150-plus innings last year and believe the steady progress he has shown in refining his four-pitch mix and overall feel bodes well for a future as a number 3 or 4 starter. Whether the former Central Florida Knight starts 2015 in Double- or Triple-A, he is on the cusp of beginning his big-league career, with a chance to debut in Philly at some point next summer.

7. Tom Windle   LHP

Born: 3/10/92   **Age:** 23   **Bats:** L   **Throws:** L   **Height:** 6'4"   **Weight:** 215

MLB ETA	CT	FB	CH	CB	SL	OFP	Realistic
2016	–	55	55	–	60	55 NO. 3/4 STARTER	50 LATE INN RP

YEAR	TEAM	LVL	AGE	W	L	SV	G	GS	IP	H	HR	BB	K	BB9	SO9	GB%	BABIP	WHIP	ERA	FIP	FRA	WARP
2014	RCU	A+	22	12	8	0	26	25	139.3	147	14	44	111	2.8	7.2	57%	.315	1.37	4.26	4.53	5.83	0.9
2015	PHI	MLB	23	5	7	0	20	20	99.3	104	10	38	59	3.4	5.3	48%	.310	1.43	4.75	4.76	5.16	-0.6
2016	PHI	MLB	24	9	9	0	28	28	174.7	164	17	59	130	3.0	6.7	48%	.298	1.28	4.04	4.00	4.39	0.0

Breakout: 0%   Improve: 0%   Collapse: 0%   Attrition: 0%   MLB: 0%   Upside: 5   *Comparables: T.J. House, Anthony Ortega, John Gast*

Drafted/Acquired: 2nd round, 2013 draft, University of Minnesota (Minneapolis, MN)

Previous Ranking: NR

What Happened in 2014: Windle was a steady force but seldom dominant as an advanced collegiate product in his first full season of pro ball, working in the zone with regularity and at times showing three above-average offerings.

Strengths: Solid size; durable build; sturdy trunk and high waist; leans on long limbs, high release, and slight crossfire to create tough angle on offerings and some deception; low-90s fastball with some heft and tail; can cut for a different look; low-to-mid-80s slider is heavily tilted, approaching one-to-seven action; short and crisp; changeup works 78-83 mph with similar action to two-seamer; at best shows late dive and is tough to lift.

Weaknesses: Command still loose in the zone; stiff landing can force ball up into zone and reduce effectiveness of downhill trajectory; overall lack of fluidity in arm and motion can complicate release, precision, and consistency in execution; changeup lacks feel at present; can tip with retarded arm speed or come too firm and flat; can lose slot, leaving slider short and on plane, very hittable; can get overly reliant on the slider.

Risk Factor/Injury History: Moderate risk; yet to reach Double-A; some shoulder woes during amateur career.

The Year Ahead: Windle's profile comes with the benefit of a high-floored reliever safety net thanks to his deception, tough angles, and a fastball/slider combo that could play up in shorter stints. His progress out of a rotation in his first full pro season, however, should permit him to continue to work as a starter until upper-level lineups prove him incapable of succeeding in that role. He may lack the looseness in actions and athleticism to fully develop his command or his off-speed, though he has found enough consistency to at least work with regularity in the zone. He will step up to the Eastern League in 2015, where Double-A bats should serve as a solid gauge as to the overall effectiveness of his raw stuff while forcing him to further refine and better mix his arsenal.

8.   Jesse Biddle   LHP

Born: 10/22/91   **Age:** 23   **Bats:** L   **Throws:** L   **Height:** 6'5"   **Weight:** 220

MLB ETA	CT	FB	CH	CB	SL	OFP	Realistic
2015	–	55	55	50	–	55 NO. 3/4 STARTER	50 NO. 4 STARTER

YEAR	TEAM	LVL	AGE	W	L	SV	G	GS	IP	H	HR	BB	K	BB9	SO9	GB%	BABIP	WHIP	ERA	FIP	FRA	WARP
2014	REA	AA	22	3	10	0	16	16	82.3	78	11	44	80	4.8	8.7	44%	.291	1.48	5.03	4.93	6.09	-0.1
2014	CLR	A+	22	2	0	0	2	2	10.0	3	0	6	9	5.4	8.1	59%	.136	0.90	0.90	3.39	4.35	0.1
2014	PHL	Rk	22	0	0	0	1	1	2.0	1	1	1	3	4.5	13.5	25%	.000	1.00	4.50	8.50	9.53	-0.1
2015	PHI	MLB	23	5	7	0	17	17	89.7	82	9	47	79	4.7	7.9	41%	.306	1.44	4.42	4.58	4.81	-0.2
2016	PHI	MLB	24	9	11	0	30	30	190.0	176	19	104	182	4.9	8.6	41%	.321	1.48	4.53	4.20	4.92	-1.0

Breakout: 0%   Improve: 0%   Collapse: 0%   Attrition: 0%   MLB: 0%   Upside: 37   *Comparables: Casey Crosby, Chris Archer, Dan Cortes*

Drafted/Acquired: 1st round, 2010 draft, Germantown Friends HS (Philadelphia, PA)

Previous Ranking: #2 (Org), #94 (Top 101)

What Happened in 2014: In a repeat of Double-A, the wheels suddenly fell off the tracks for Biddle during a disastrous June stretch where the left-hander posted a 12.64 ERA over four starts that heavily contributed to an ugly overall season line.

Strengths: Smooth, fluid delivery; size and strength to handle rigors of starting; able to throw 89-92 heater downhill; shows feel for creating fade with change—potential for more growth; loose wrist when throwing both curve and change; depth and teeth to curve when throwing from same spot as fastball; athletic on mound.

Weaknesses: Inconsistent fastball command; struggles to finish pitch across the plate (glove side); runs into stretches of wavering release point—stuff becomes bland; changeup will float up in zone; slow and loopy break (69-74) to curve allows good hitters to wait; up-and-down confidence shows in body language on the mound.

Risk Factor/Injury History: Low risk; upper-minors experience; concerns about confidence level and ability to manage expectations.

Bret Sayre's Fantasy Take: While there's still a modicum of name value left here, Biddle is not someone who should be relied upon in anything but deep mixed and NL-only formats. A left-hander without an out pitch in a ballpark that significantly aids right-handed power is not a recipe for fantasy value.

The Year Ahead: Biddle will look to use his late-season success as a stepping stone into 2015. The assignment could be a third stint in Double-A or a bump up to the next level. There have always been questions centering on the left-hander's fastball command and lack of a true plus pitch. Can the command grow enough to allow him to fulfill a role near the back of a rotation? Well, that's even more muddied now, as some concerns over Biddle's ability to manage the peaks and valleys of the game have crept in. The mental side of the game can always be interesting, as both good and bad results tend to snowball. It's not time to bury Biddle, but the stock here has definitely dropped and this is a pivotal season.

9. Deivi Grullon C

Born: 2/17/96   **Age:** 19   **Bats:** R   **Throws:** R   **Height:** 6'1"   **Weight:** 180

MLB ETA	Hit	Power	Run	Glove	Arm	OFP	Realistic
2018	50	–	–	65	80	60 1ST DIVISION PLAYER	45 BACKUP/PLATOON C

YEAR	TEAM	LVL	AGE	PA	R	2B	3B	HR	RBI	BB	SO	SB	CS	AVG/OBP/SLG	TAv	BABIP	BRR	FRAA	WARP
2014	CLR	A+	18	10	0	0	0	0	1	0	1	0	0	.200/.200/.200	.129	.222	0.0	C(2): 0.1	-0.1
2014	LWD	A	18	81	9	5	0	1	7	3	13	0	0	.237/.275/.342	.221	.274	0.1	C(24): 0.1	0.0
2014	WPT	A-	18	199	14	9	1	0	18	9	39	3	0	.225/.268/.283	.213	.284	-2.1	C(53): 0.2	-0.4
2015	PHI	MLB	19	250	17	9	1	2	18	7	68	0	0	.199/.226/.266	.191	.264	-0.4	C 0	-0.8
2016	PHI	MLB	20	250	22	10	0	3	21	6	60	0	0	.224/.245/.305	.207	.280	-0.5	C 0	-1.6

Breakout: 0%   Improve: 0%   Collapse: 0%   Attrition: 0%   MLB: 0%   Upside: 13   *Comparables: Tomas Telis, Wilson Ramos, Francisco Pena*

Drafted/Acquired: International Free Agent, 2012, Dominican Republic

Previous Ranking: #6 (Org)

What Happened in 2014: Grullon continued to flash his elite arm and defensive promise behind the dish, but the then-18-year-old showed that there's a ways to go on the other side of the ball, hitting a combined .227 on the season and slugging under .300.

Strengths: Elite arm strength; crisp with release; accurate when throwing with power; frame to handle rigors of position—already filled out in trunk; flashes high growth potential with glove; solid footwork and movements; whip-like swing generates some bat speed.

Weaknesses: In the early stages of learning how to catch; more vision than polish presently; ball control needs work; likes to come up early with body; hit tool potential plays to average at best; tends to break wrists early; lunges at stuff with spin; below-average power; well-below-average run.

Risk Factor/Injury History: Extreme risk; 19 years old; dual development profile.

Bret Sayre's Fantasy Take: He's really fun to watch behind the plate, but Grullon should not be owned in any fantasy leagues.

The Year Ahead: It's easy to like Grullon's defensive potential, as he does some things well now that you don't typically see yet from catchers his age. Toss in the elite arm strength with a quick release, and this can develop into a monster behind the plate. Of course, the hit tool is a little on the light side, but Grullon shows some ability to hit the ball hard when he squares it up. This is a player who is going to require patience and will slowly marinate. The bat likely isn't going to do much in a full-season assignment this season, but it's about a steady progression offensively over the next handful of years to fulfill a projection of a regular.

10. Kelly Dugan RF

Born: 9/18/90   **Age:** 24   **Bats:** L   **Throws:** R   **Height:** 6'3"   **Weight:** 215

MLB ETA	Hit	Power	Run	Glove	Arm	OFP	Realistic
2015	50	55	–	55	60	50 ML REGULAR	45 <AVG REG/BENCH OF

YEAR	TEAM	LVL	AGE	PA	R	2B	3B	HR	RBI	BB	SO	SB	CS	AVG/OBP/SLG	TAv	BABIP	BRR	FRAA	WARP
2014	REA	AA	23	290	43	18	1	5	34	28	56	1	0	.296/.383/.435	.286	.363	-0.1	RF(53): -0.2, LF(11): 0.5	1.1
2015	PHI	MLB	24	250	23	11	1	6	27	13	72	0	0	.238/.292/.369	.251	.315	-0.5	RF 1, LF 1	0.4
2016	PHI	MLB	25	250	28	11	0	7	27	14	73	0	0	.238/.295/.375	.251	.316	-0.7	RF 1, LF 1	1.0

Breakout: 1%   Improve: 9%   Collapse: 3%   Attrition: 11%   MLB: 20%   Upside: 21   *Comparables: Casper Wells, Steven Souza, John Bowker*

Drafted/Acquired: 2nd round, 2009 draft, Notre Dame HS (Sherman Oaks, CA)

Previous Ranking: #4 (Org)

What Happened in 2014: Dugan once again showed that he can hit when on the field, but missed two months with an oblique injury, which ate into some development time and adds another injury to the résumé.

Strengths: Solid frame; athletic; shows feel for barreling up balls consistently; brings a plan to the plate; some leverage in swing; solid-average bat speed; filled out chest and shoulders; arm for right field; fundamentally sound in the outfield.

Weaknesses: More of an upper-body hitter; power doesn't play up to strength level; doesn't have the loosest of hands; reaches out on front foot against off-speed stuff; questions on how bat will play up against high-quality stuff; below-average runner.

Risk Factor/Injury History: Moderate risk; has missed development time with injuries.

Bret Sayre's Fantasy Take: An underrated option in deep leagues, Dugan is close to the major-league level in an organization that has very little outfield help or depth. In that respect, he's similar to what future teammate Cody Asche was last year, though whether they are teammates in Philadelphia or Lehigh Valley speaks to the risk.

The Year Ahead: Dugan is a bit of a bland profile, as the ceiling here isn't all that high, but if he can stay on the field and continue to polish the offensive skills, he has a chance to carve out an extended career. These types can fool you because nothing really jumps off the page. The 24-year-old's bat speed will be tested by a step up in competition and, ultimately, the unforgiving, merciless arms in the majors. If the contact can remain consistent, Dugan should drive some balls out of the ballpark, especially as he gets comfortable muscling up in his spots. It comes down to the outfielder staying healthy and taking advantage of an opportunity, which could come this season if the former holds up. The end result is likely a big leaguer who can put up some productive seasons.

Prospects on the Rise

1. LHP Elniery Garcia: Garcia put together a solid effort last season, primarily at the Florida complexes, highlighted by a continuing uptick in velocity and flashes of potential with each of his secondaries. The undersized lefty has a loose arm that allows for solid projection across the arsenal, with his two-plane curve showing the most potential at present and a lively upper-80s to low-90s fastball providing an interesting complement. He'll play the entirety of 2015 at the age of 20 and could find himself returning to the New York-Penn League, where he could breach the 70-innings mark and set himself up for a full-season assignment in 2016.

2. OF Cord Sandberg: It's clear that the former Mississippi State football recruit is a bit of a project, but there are baseball skills that can be teased out. The easiness of the swing sticks out, though the heavy pull nature to his

---

FROM THE FIELD

J.P. Crawford

Team: Philadelphia Phillies
Evaluator: Chris King
Dates seen: June 23 and July 1–2, 2014
Affiliate: Clearwater Threshers (High-A, Phillies)
Physical/health: Very lean build; athletic and lanky; room to add strength; projection left, but could be tricky; long legs; lower half is ahead of the upper body when it comes to maturity; no major injury history.
Makeup: Plus makeup; good work ethic on and off the field; able to put bad plays/at-bats behind him; can make adjustments on the fly; shows leadership skills at every level he's been.

MLB ETA	Risk factor	OFP	Realistic role
2016	High	60	High 5; major-league regular

Tool	Future grade	Report
Hit	60	Slightly open stance; high hands; fairly quiet preswing; bat-to-ball-oriented swing; advanced approach; two-strike approach is very mature; pitch-recognition skills are evident; willing and able to use the entire field; shifts weight early at times and rolls over on front foot; bat speed is there; nice hands allow for sound bat control; contact getting louder.
Power	40	Current gap-to-gap pop; flashed in-game power to pull side only; swing is built for contact and line drives; not a lot of lift and lacks backspin to help the ball carry; don't see a future average grade in this department.
Baserunning/speed	60	First step out of the box can be slow; once he gets going he's a plus runner; long and effortless strides; home-to-first times in the 4.1-4.2 range; not a blazer, but effective speed with solid instincts on the bases and in the field.
Glove	65	Silky smooth hands and actions; very polished glove for his age; ranges well to both sides; very comfortable with the backhand; transfers are quick on either end of a double play; quick, soft hands; overall actions are crisp and fluid; easy plus glove that will stick at current position.
Arm	60	Currently above-average, but fringe-plus; can make any throw with accuracy; has a pretty quick release and gets nice carry on throws; release gets sloppy when rushed; maintains accuracy when moving in or on the run to either side.

Overall: Crawford is one of the most defensively polished players I've seen come through the Gulf Coast League and Florida State League. He's a no-doubt future big-league shortstop with an offensive game that won't put up eye-popping numbers, but will be playable at the top of a lineup. With positive makeup and a strong work ethic, Crawford should steadily show improvements in all phases of his game. There are legitimate questions about his bat in the future, so risks remain high, as he's yet to be tested by the polished pitching that players don't encounter until the Double-A level. Even with those concerns not yet being answered, Crawford shows a high baseball IQ, with instincts that will help his tools play up as he advances. Defense will always be his calling card, but with his contact-based approach, he should be able to hit for good average. Couple that with his glove and you have yourself a nice big-league player that plays a premium position at a high level. That's a combination that can make you live with the lack of power.

approach and off-balanced attacking of secondary offerings are equally visible. It's a longer developmental road for Sandberg, but one that can lead to a projection as a regular with the unlocking of his hit tool potential as experience builds.

3. OF Aaron Brown: The former two-way star at Pepperdine is an intriguing prospect, mainly because of the growth potential in the bat with his attention now fully turned to hitting. There are questions about Brown's ability to stick in center field, but the raw power is impressive, with some feel for the barrel. If the 23-year-old can fine-tune his pitch selection to compensate for the swing-and-miss in his game, it's a player who can rise up in status within the system relative quickly.

Factors on the Farm
Prospects likely to contribute at the major-league level in 2015

1. RHP Nefi Ogando: It's been a winding developmental road for Ogando, but one that has always featured a high-octane fastball. Anyone who has followed Ogando's career can tell you that his command has always been the big issue. The right-hander can crank his heater up to 98-99 out of the bullpen and flashes a power, mid-80s slider. If he can consistently slow the game down, it's an arm that can click, leading him right into the back of the major-league bullpen.

2. OF Cameron Perkins: The former sixth-round pick found his way to Triple-A in 2014 after quickly proving he had advanced past the Eastern League. The highest level of the minors was a challenge to Perkins as he struggled to adjust to the caliber of secondary stuff. If he can prove his hit tool is up to snuff, the 24-year-old has a chance to provide outfield help should the organization have a need for him. The profile is more of a bench outfielder or up-and-down player, but Perkins does some things well and can hit his way into contention for a look.

3. RHP Ethan Martin: The lack of command has never enabled Martin to reach the level that his stuff should have gotten him too, but as a potential late-inning reliever there is some promise. The righty's fastball has shown to tick up close to the mid-90s in relief appearances; that and the late-breaking version of his slider can be a tough two-pitch combo. It's not the most exciting profile, and the former mid-first-round pick could be labeled a disappointment, but he can help the club in getting key outs in a seventh-inning role.

1. Tyler Glasnow RHP

Born: 8/23/93   **Age:** 21   **Bats:** L   **Throws:** R   **Height:** 6'8"   **Weight:** 225

MLB ETA	CT	FB	CH	CB	SL	OFP	Realistic
Late 2015	–	65	55	60	–	65 NO.2/3 STARTER	55 NO.3/4 STARTER

YEAR	TEAM	LVL	AGE	W	L	SV	G	GS	IP	H	HR	BB	K	BB9	SO9	GB%	BABIP	WHIP	ERA	FIP	FRA	WARP
2014	BRD	A+	20	12	5	0	23	23	124.3	74	3	57	157	4.1	11.4	40%	.260	1.05	1.74	2.63	3.03	3.1
2015	PIT	MLB	21	6	7	0	22	22	102.3	79	8	57	114	5.0	10.0	42%	.303	1.33	3.67	3.94	3.99	0.9
2016	PIT	MLB	22	9	9	0	30	30	185.0	146	18	101	200	4.9	9.7	42%	.298	1.34	3.85	4.01	4.19	0.7

Breakout: 0%   Improve: 0%   Collapse: 0%   Attrition: 0%   MLB: 0%   Upside: 15   *Comparables: Trevor May, Joel Zumaya, Matt Moore*

#21
BP Top 101 Prospects

Drafted/Acquired: 5th round, 2011 draft, Hart HS, (Santa Clarita, CA)

Previous Ranking: #3 (Org), #42 (Top 101)

What Happened in 2014: Glasnow proved to be well ahead of the curve in the Florida State League, fanning an impressive 157 batters in 124 1/3 innings and allowing only 74 hits.

Strengths: Outstanding size; creates good angle on hitters; throws downhill; fast arm; heater easily operates 93-95 with late life; capable of reaching for more; aggressive with fastball; snaps curveball with loose wrist; creates excellent snap; deep break and teeth at 77-79; bat-missing potential; flashes feel for changeup; improving action; power-arm potential.

Weaknesses: Lot of body to control due to size; loses feel for delivery; consistency of release point suffers; will overthrow fastball when reaching back; can hold onto curve too long; change lags behind other offerings; too firm at times; lacks finish out of the strike zone; overall command needs a grade jump; gets away with mistakes in the zone; still learning finer points of craft.

Risk Factor/Injury History: Moderate risk; yet to pitch in upper levels; pitchability progression.

Bret Sayre's Fantasy Take: The WHIP will likely always be an issue, outside of any extreme BABIP-depressing seasons, but it's a small price to pay for the strikeout potential. He's exciting from a statistical standpoint, but for fantasy owners, he's still a big risk—and even the payoff may look a little like Lance Lynn. I'd still take the next guy on this list as the top fantasy arm in this system.

The Year Ahead: There is no doubt Glasnow is ready for an assignment in Double-A as he gets set to take the next step in his developmental journey this season. The raw stuff here shines on the mound. The right-hander's fastball-curveball combination gives him a distinct leg up on the competition. It's typically a barrage of mid-90s fastballs and hammer curves aimed at churning quickly through opposing lineups. The vision is of Glasnow pushing to the front of a big-league rotation at peak, with the ability to have a solid string of successful seasons. The future is without a doubt bright, but there are some underlying concerns that the big righty needs to address to reach his potential. The feel for the craft—notably command—and utility of the changeup presently lag behind. Currently, the other weapons help mask these weaknesses, but once in the majors, their development will be big factors in making the ceiling a reality. It'll be interesting to see how Glasnow transitions into the Eastern League and whether he is pushed right off the bat to be finer with the heater, along with incorporating his change more in sequences. If he can show similar success to previous campaigns, he'll ride the wave to a 2015 debut.

2. Jameson Taillon RHP

Born: 11/18/91   **Age:** 23   **Bats:** R   **Throws:** R   **Height:** 6'5"   **Weight:** 245

MLB ETA	CT	FB	CH	CB	SL	OFP	Realistic
Late 2015	–	70	55	65	–	70 NO. 2 STARTER	60 NO. 3 STARTER

YEAR	TEAM	LVL	AGE	W	L	SV	G	GS	IP	H	HR	BB	K	BB9	SO9	GB%	BABIP	WHIP	ERA	FIP	FRA	WARP
2015	PIT	MLB	23	2	3	0	7	7	36.3	36	3	13	28	3.2	6.9	44%	.313	1.34	4.31	4.11	4.68	0.0
2016	PIT	MLB	24	9	10	0	31	31	196.7	192	16	67	154	3.1	7.0	44%	.314	1.32	4.19	3.79	4.55	-0.1

Breakout: 0%   Improve: 0%   Collapse: 0%   Attrition: 0%   MLB: 0%   Upside: 32   *Comparables: Burch Smith, Nick Tropeano, Matt Magill*

Drafted/Acquired: 1st round, 2010 draft, The Woodlands HS (The Woodlands, TX)

Previous Ranking: #1 (Org), #19 (Top 101)

What Happened in 2014: Tommy John surgery struck the right-hander in the spring, and a season of development was washed away in favor of the rehab process.

Strengths: Big frame; physical player; excellent arm strength; body to withstand the rigors of the season; mid-90s (to more) fastball with outstanding arm-side life; runs in on right-handed hitters' hands; can be very heavy; power curve in the low-80s range; two-plane break; bat-missing ability; comes right after hitters.

Weaknesses: Command already needed work prior to injury; can be late with arm; fastball operates in dangerous spots; elevated often; has trouble consistently throwing curve for strikes; change lags behind other offerings; more like a fastball he takes something off of; lacks quality action; arsenal recovery from injury.

Risk Factor/Injury History: Moderate risk; Tommy John on résumé; regaining feel for stuff/command.

Bret Sayre's Fantasy Take: Forget about Taillon at your own peril. It's been out of sight, out of mind for the 23-year-old, but his combination of strikeout stuff and frame for a ton of innings makes him plenty valuable to fantasy owners. It will likely be 2017 before he's really let loose, but 200 strikeouts is possible down the road, and he could help this season.

The Year Ahead: Taillon's path this season starts with proving he's healthy and ready for game action, which should come this spring. It remains to be seen how the right-hander's arsenal will look in the early stages making it back to the mound after surgery, but this was top-shelf stuff prior to the injury. Assuming Taillon shows signs of regaining his feel and progresses into the middle stages relatively quickly, the attention turns to how the command profile is shaping up. The 23-year-old had lost some of his shine at the national level due to command inconsistencies, but these were questions the prospect had upon entering the pro ranks. The injury definitely clouds things more for Taillon, but it's not time to say a ceiling as a number 2 starter is out of the equation. This is a big arm with an extremely lively fastball and curveball that can straighten up high-quality hitters. Toss in the potential to squeeze more out of the change and the focus an injury rehab brings overall, and this arm can comfortably settle into a role as a strong mid-rotation starter, with the chance for some seasons higher.

#26
BP Top
101
Prospects

---

3. Josh Bell   RF/1B

Born: 8/14/92   **Age:** 22   **Bats:** B   **Throws:** R   **Height:** 6'2"   **Weight:** 235

MLB ETA	Hit	Power	Run	Glove	Arm	OFP	Realistic
Late 2015	**55**	**60**	**–**	**50**	**55**	**60** 1ST DIVISION REGULAR	**50** AVG ML PLAYER

YEAR	TEAM	LVL	AGE	PA	R	2B	3B	HR	RBI	BB	SO	SB	CS	AVG/OBP/SLG	TAv	BABIP	BRR	FRAA	WARP
2014	ALT	AA	21	102	13	2	0	0	7	8	12	4	1	.287/.343/.309	.251	.329	0.3	RF(19): 0.4	0.3
2014	BRD	A+	21	363	45	20	4	9	53	25	43	5	4	.335/.384/.502	.309	.364	-1.8	RF(62): -6.6	1.7
2015	PIT	MLB	22	250	23	11	1	4	25	14	51	2	1	.251/.296/.359	.250	.300	-0.3	RF -2	0.0
2016	PIT	MLB	23	250	27	12	1	5	25	18	53	2	1	.251/.308/.378	.257	.303	-0.3	RF -1	1.0

Breakout: 2%   Improve: 24%   Collapse: 2%   Attrition: 23%   MLB: 38%   Upside: 36   *Comparables: Domonic Brown, Brandon Moss, Shane Peterson*

Drafted/Acquired: 2nd round, 2011 draft, Dallas Jesuit College Prep (Dallas, TX)

Previous Ranking: #5 (Org), #77 (Top 101)

What Happened in 2014: Bell played at two levels, including a taste of Double-A, and hit .325 overall with 35 extra-base hits.

#58
BP Top
101
Prospects

Strengths: Strong player; athletic; physical specimen; feel for hitting; displays ability to get barrel on the ball from both sides of the plate; good lift in left-handed stroke; simpler swing right-handed; squares up with backspin; plus bat speed; raw power to tap into; strength to hit home runs to both fields; arm for right field; shows acceleration and closing speed in the field when getting good reads.

Weaknesses: A bit long with swing left-handed; still learning how to balance lift; can be susceptible to breaking balls; likes to get head of bat out front; power is there, but needs some development lead time; chance hit tool plays down to maximize power potential; will take bad routes in outfield; reads aren't the best; makes it look difficult when it shouldn't be; upper body thickness can hinder arm.

Risk Factor/Injury History: Moderate risk; only 23 games in Double-A; knee injury in 2012.

Bret Sayre's Fantasy Take: With two pitchers ahead of Bell, there's a good argument to be made that he's the top fantasy prospect in this system. And as a potential .275 hitter with 25 homers, it's no real surprise as to why. With a full outfield in Pittsburgh, the ability to play first base will make him move more quickly to the majors—as that was a weakness of the team last season.

The Year Ahead: Bell continued to take steps forward in 2014, firmly cementing himself within this system and in all of baseball in the process. He's a physically imposing player, built like a bruising fullback, who will surprise with his athleticism when watching him in the field. There's more than enough here for the 22-year-old to stick in the outfield, but his curious routes at times and slow reads bring in some doubts. If Bell dedicates himself more to this side of the game, it's not hard to see him bringing adequate defense to the table in right field. His commitment has paid off in other areas, as the outfielder has made some strong strides in the box, particularly with his patience and working through sequences to find pitches he can drive. Double-A will be a test for Bell to stay back on the ball more frequently, as the switch-hitter can get too far out in front from the left side, trying to load up to hit the ball in the air. An adjustment in mind-set against good breaking balls will be key in preventing the bat from getting stuck in neutral this season. This is a prospect who can post .270s averages with 20-plus home runs in the majors at peak. There's lead time to reaching that projection, and we may start finding out if it's possible to get there, with a late-season call-up a definite possibility.

4. Reese McGuire   C

Born: 3/2/95   **Age:** 20   **Bats:** L   **Throws:** R   **Height:** 6'0"   **Weight:** 181

MLB ETA	Hit	Power	Run	Glove	Arm	OFP	Realistic
Late 2017	55	50	–	65	70	60 1ST DIVISION PLAYER	50 AVG REGULAR

YEAR	TEAM	LVL	AGE	PA	R	2B	3B	HR	RBI	BB	SO	SB	CS	AVG/OBP/SLG	TAv	BABIP	BRR	FRAA	WARP
2014	WVA	A	19	428	46	11	4	3	45	24	44	7	2	.262/.307/.334	.232	.284	0.2	C(84): 0.4	1.2
2015	PIT	MLB	20	250	15	9	1	0	18	8	46	0	0	.218/.248/.265	.199	.264	-0.3	C 0	-0.7
2016	PIT	MLB	21	250	22	9	1	2	19	10	35	0	0	.227/.261/.299	.212	.254	-0.4	C 0	-1.3

Breakout: 0%   Improve: 0%   Collapse: 0%   Attrition: 0%   MLB: 0%   Upside: 18   *Comparables: Miguel Gonzalez, Salvador Perez, Christian Vazquez*

Drafted/Acquired: 1st round, 2013 draft, Kentwood HS (Covington, WA)

Previous Ranking: #4 (Org), #59 (Top 101)

What Happened in 2014: The overall line was unassuming in A-Ball, but the then-19-year-old more than held his own on both sides of the ball, including nailing 39 percent of would-be basestealers.

Strengths: Athletic; light on his feet; good present overall strength; potential to add more; plus-to-better raw arm strength; crisp arm action; fires feet quickly coming out of crouch; arm projects to control the running game; moves well laterally; knows how to use body to get big; firm glove hand; easy stroke; displays separation with hands; plus bat speed; ability to create solid contact consistently; excellent makeup; shows early makings of taking control of the game.

Weaknesses: More of a line-drive stroke; a bit on the flat side; power may play below average in favor of contact; aggressive early in the count; will chase breakers out of zone; concerns on hit tool playing light; questions on what swing will look like against good velocity; overall receiving skills in early refinement stages; will get over-zealous with arm; footwork can get sloppy.

Risk Factor/Injury History: High risk; Low-A experience; dual-threat development.

Bret Sayre's Fantasy Take: The one thing that overrates prospects from a fantasy perspective more than anything else is extreme catcher defense—and McGuire is the latest example. That's not to say he doesn't have offensive potential, but in one-catcher mixed leagues, the payoff isn't likely to be worth using a roster spot for this long (unless it's a deep league).

The Year Ahead: McGuire has the type of potential with the glove to ride it all the way to the big leagues. The combination of arm strength, athleticism, and polished receiving skills point to a defender who can easily settle in as an above-average backstop down the line. A tireless worker, the 20-year-old exhibits both drive and desire when executing his defensive craft, making it easy to see a player capable of maximizing all of his talent. With the stick, there's bat speed, a feel for the barrel, promise with the approach, and strength to tap into. Extrapolating far forward, the potential for a .275-.280 hitter with 12-15 annual home runs comes into focus, especially when factoring the makeup into the equation. It's going to take time, though, and the conservative view sees something less than those projections. It's likely that 2015 will be something similar in terms of a line for McGuire in High-A, as a huge offensive breakout isn't expected, but more subtle progress toward putting things together. He's likely the type that suddenly sneaks up with the stick a couple of seasons from now, with the foundation being put in place during these early seasons.

#59
BP Top 101 Prospects

5. Nick Kingham   RHP

Born: 11/8/91   **Age:** 23   **Bats:** R   **Throws:** R   **Height:** 6'5"   **Weight:** 220

MLB ETA	CT	FB	CH	CB	SL	OFP	Realistic
2015	–	60	50	60	–	55 NO. 3/4 STARTER	50 NO. 4 STARTER

YEAR	TEAM	LVL	AGE	W	L	SV	G	GS	IP	H	HR	BB	K	BB9	SO9	GB%	BABIP	WHIP	ERA	FIP	FRA	WARP
2014	IND	AAA	22	5	4	0	14	14	88.0	70	6	27	65	2.8	6.6	45%	.244	1.10	3.58	3.72	5.03	0.2
2014	ALT	AA	22	1	7	0	12	12	71.0	71	3	25	54	3.2	6.8	46%	.305	1.35	3.04	3.52	4.32	0.6
2015	PIT	MLB	23	7	9	0	26	26	134.7	129	12	47	99	3.1	6.6	44%	.303	1.31	4.16	4.24	4.53	0.2
2016	PIT	MLB	24	7	5	0	70	11	128.0	128	13	39	99	2.7	7.0	44%	.314	1.31	4.33	3.92	4.71	0.1

Breakout: 0%   Improve: 0%   Collapse: 0%   Attrition: 0%   MLB: 0%   Upside: 17   *Comparables: Andrew Heaney, Kyle Gibson, Erik Johnson*

Drafted/Acquired: 4th round, 2010 draft, Sierra Vista HS (Las Vegas, NV)

Previous Ranking: #6 (Org), #80 (Top 101)

What Happened in 2014: The big right-hander pushed toward the cusp of The Show in 2014, firing 159 innings and proving he can handle upper-minors' lineups in the process.

Strengths: Fluid delivery; repeats well; excellent size; utilizes body and strength; downhill thrower; stays above fastball; plays 91-94, with ability to reach for more in spots; flashes arm-side life; strong downward break to

#67
BP Top 101 Prospects

curveball; buries off the table; creates hard snap; turns over change with loose wrist; improving look to pitch; potential for continued command progress due to ease of delivery.

Weaknesses: Loose with fastball in the zone; can be forced into smaller spots, which puts pressure on control; struggles at times to throw curve and change for strikes; good hitters will lay off; lacks legit out pitch presently; will hold onto curve too long and bounce with frequency; change can float; finds barrels with offering.

Risk Factor/Injury History: Low risk; 14 Triple-A starts under belt; secondary stuff consistency.

Bret Sayre's Fantasy Take: There's not much excitement here for shallow leaguers, but Kingham is close and should be able to provide good ratios and the backbone for wins and quality starts. The big missing piece is the strikeouts, and without consistent secondaries, we're looking at a 140-strikeout-per-year pitcher at best.

The Year Ahead: Kingham projects as a potential workhorse who can pitch somewhere from the middle to back of a rotation, depending on the depth. Despite his size, the right-hander presently displays solid control of his body and clean mechanics that enable him to repeat his arm slot consistently. The bread and butter is the lively fastball that, when on, the 23-year-old slices down through the strike zone and spots to both sides of the plate. Kingham can also lean heavily on the curve and change, though the spottier command with the two limits the amount of chases right now. If the righty can push his pitchability with the secondary stuff and force hitters to commit earlier, especially with the hard-breaking curveball, the profile can play up close to the peak potential or even outkick it as a firm mid-rotation starter. It wouldn't be surprising to see the secondary arsenal take a step forward, but whether it can get to the level necessary on a consistent basis over the long run remains to be seen. Kingham more likely settles in as an innings-eater toward the back of a rotation, with a good chance at some point in 2015 to begin cutting his teeth against big-league hitters.

---

6. Mitch Keller   RHP

Born: 4/4/96   **Age:** 19   **Bats:** R   **Throws:** R   **Height:** 6'3"   **Weight:** 195

MLB ETA	CT	FB	CH	CB	SL	OFP	Realistic
2018	–	65	55	60	–	60 NO. 3 STARTER	50 NO. 4 STARTER

YEAR	TEAM	LVL	AGE	W	L	SV	G	GS	IP	H	HR	BB	K	BB9	SO9	GB%	BABIP	WHIP	ERA	FIP	FRA	WARP
2014	PIR	Rk	18	0	0	0	9	8	27.3	19	0	13	29	4.3	9.5	56%	.268	1.17	1.98	3.14	5.38	0.0
2015	PIT	MLB	19	1	3	0	8	8	33.7	37	3	21	20	5.6	5.3	47%	.321	1.70	5.71	5.43	6.21	-0.5
2016	PIT	MLB	20	7	8	0	30	30	192.7	180	17	89	138	4.2	6.4	47%	.298	1.40	4.33	4.37	4.70	-0.5

Breakout: 0%   Improve: 0%   Collapse: 0%   Attrition: 0%   MLB: 0%   Upside: 1   *Comparables: Edwin Escobar, Jenrry Mejia, Jonathan Pettibone*

Drafted/Acquired: 2nd round, 2014 draft, Xavier HS (Cedar Rapids, IA)

Previous Ranking: NR

What Happened in 2014: The second-round pick signed for a seven-figure bonus, then went out and struck out slightly more than a batter an inning in the Gulf Coast League.

Strengths: Good frame; room to carry more mass and add strength; loose arm; easy, low energy expending delivery; good balance; fastball already works 90-93 with arm-side life; potential to add more velocity; shows feel for curveball; spins with a loose wrist; depth and teeth in mid-70s; potential bat-missing pitch; learning how to turn over change; flashes better-than-average potential; low-mileage arm; high growth potential.

Weaknesses: Can be erratic with release; not a great present finisher of delivery; needs to learn how to use size to advantage; below-average present fastball command; curve needs more tightening to add power; will roll with some frequency; in early stages of honing changeup; offering tends to float; must learn how to throw secondary stuff for strikes; can use more strength to avoid wearing down.

Risk Factor/Injury History: High risk; complex-league résumé; command progression.

Bret Sayre's Fantasy Take: There are places on dynasty teams for short-season arms, but the risk and ETA associated with them will keep Keller down dynasty draft lists this year, despite strong potential. Look for him to come off the board after the first 25 players have been taken—likely by a Baseball Prospectus subscriber.

The Year Ahead: Keller drew solid reviews both pre- and postdraft as an arm with a chance to really take off once fully within the confines of the professional environment. The Iowa native's fastball velocity has ticked up over the course of the last year, mainly driven by increased strength and some natural filling out into his 6-foot-3 frame. It's not hard to envision the right-hander being able to squeeze out a little more velocity as he continues to physically mature while getting plenty of repetitions in a more structured throwing program. Keller pairs his low-90s fastball with a potential knee-bending curveball and developing changeup. The curve shows the highest potential of the two and with tightening can round into a legit bat-missing offering. The current long pole is the command of the entire arsenal, especially the fastball. Keller has some work in front of him getting more consistent with finishing his delivery, which isn't uncommon for an arm his age, but can lead to inconsistencies early in the career. This may seem like an aggressive placement for a relatively inexperienced player in a deeper system, but it speaks to the belief in the righty's overall package and feeling that the stuff will show well out of the gate in 2015, with the arsenal taking the initial steps toward developing into a mid-rotation starter.

7. Austin Meadows   OF

Born: 5/3/95   **Age:** 20   **Bats:** L   **Throws:** L   **Height:** 6'3"   **Weight:** 200

MLB ETA	Hit	Power	Run	Glove	Arm		OFP	Realistic
Late 2017	55	55	60	55	–		60 1ST DIVISION REGULAR	50 ML REGULAR

YEAR	TEAM	LVL	AGE	PA	R	2B	3B	HR	RBI	BB	SO	SB	CS	AVG/OBP/SLG	TAv	BABIP	BRR	FRAA	WARP
2014	WVA	A	19	167	18	13	1	3	15	14	30	2	3	.322/.388/.486	.293	.383	-0.3	CF(38): -0.0	1.2
2014	BRI	Rk	19	18	2	0	0	0	0	3	3	0	0	.071/.235/.071	.138	.091	0.1	CF(5): -0.5	-0.1
2014	PIR	Rk	19	6	1	2	1	0	1	2	0	0	0	1.000/1.000/2.000	.827	1.000	0.0	CF(2): -0.3	0.4
2015	PIT	MLB	20	250	21	10	1	3	23	17	67	1	1	.218/.278/.313	.226	.288	-0.5	CF -1	-0.3
2016	PIT	MLB	21	250	27	11	1	3	23	23	61	1	1	.238/.314/.344	.250	.308	-0.5	CF -1	0.9

Breakout: 0%   Improve: 0%   Collapse: 0%   Attrition: 0%   MLB: 0%   Upside: 60   *Comparables: Fernando Martinez, Aaron Hicks, Oswaldo Arcia*

Drafted/Acquired: 1st round, 2013 draft, Grayson HS (Loganville, GA)

Previous Ranking: #7 (Org), #89 (Top 101)

What Happened in 2014: The outfielder missed a good chunk of time with a hamstring injury, but when he made it back to the field, Meadows posted an 874 OPS in 38 games at Low-A.

Strengths: Good size and strength; athletic; frame that can continue to add strength pulling hands inside of ball; plus raw power; plenty of strength to tap into for home-run ability down the line; gets out of box well; shows good acceleration; above-average wheels; improving with reads off the bat.

Weaknesses: Questions on ultimate power potential; may come at expense of hit tool; increased leverage in swing over natural bat speed; concerns on added mass decreasing speed; not overly natural in center; could slide to a corner; doesn't have the arm for right; pressure on bat to develop to full potential.

Risk Factor/Injury History: High risk; limited full-season résumé; questions on profile.

Bret Sayre's Fantasy Take: The outfielder has the tools you want to see in a fantasy performer, but lacks impact in any of them. Of course, individual impact isn't a requirement for fantasy impact, but it requires a lot more co-alescence. If he settles in as a 15/15 guy, which is certainly realistic, shallow leaguers may be left wanting more.

The Year Ahead: Meadows certainly looks the part in the field, with an already developed body that has more room, a picture-perfect stroke, and an easy-plus run. What would have been an initial look at really gauging the young outfielder's chops in the professional ranks fell flat in 2014 due to a hamstring injury. What's interesting is that when on the field so far as a pro, though briefly, the 20-year-old has performed well. The lack of looks makes it tough to discern whether this is a more presently advanced hitter that's better than the relatively inex-perienced competition or whether there's been progress with some of the initial offensive concerns. Those con-cerns do hang loudly over Meadows at the moment. The body has a good chance to add more bulk, but it's likely to come at the expense of his speed and he already isn't the most natural in center. The arm is short of right-field caliber, so the potential destination is left field, which puts a lot of pressure on the bat. Some sources don't see the type of offensive thump to support that profile. The only real certainty surrounding Meadows in 2015 is that a lot of people will be zoned in on getting good looks at him to start putting the development trends together.

8. Alen Hanson   2B/SS

Born: 10/22/92   **Age:** 22   **Bats:** B   **Throws:** R   **Height:** 5'11"   **Weight:** 170

MLB ETA	Hit	Power	Run	Glove	Arm		OFP	Realistic
2015	55	55	60	55	–		55 >AVG REGULAR	50 2ND DIV STARTER

YEAR	TEAM	LVL	AGE	PA	R	2B	3B	HR	RBI	BB	SO	SB	CS	AVG/OBP/SLG	TAv	BABIP	BRR	FRAA	WARP
2014	ALT	AA	21	527	64	21	12	11	58	31	88	25	11	.280/.326/.442	.283	.321	-0.9	SS(100): -0.6, 2B(17): 1.3	3.5
2015	PIT	MLB	22	250	30	10	3	4	20	14	56	9	4	.245/.289/.367	.246	.297	0.7	SS -2, 2B 0	0.5
2016	PIT	MLB	23	516	56	21	7	10	54	33	108	21	9	.255/.308/.393	.259	.304	2.5	2B 2, SS -3	1.7

Breakout: 5%   Improve: 32%   Collapse: 4%   Attrition: 18%   MLB: 46%   Upside: 49   *Comparables: Tim Beckham, Junior Lake, Arismendy Alcantara*

Drafted/Acquired: International Free Agent, 2009, Dominican Republic

Previous Ranking: #8 (Org), Just Missed The Cut (Top 101)

What Happened in 2014: Hanson put together a solid campaign in the Eastern League, hitting .280 and ripping 44 extra-base hits, but struggled maintaining consistency defensively at shortstop.

Strengths: Athletic player; fluid actions; quick, strong hands; generates good bat speed; smooth swing from both sides of the plate; feel for controlling the barrel; some thunder in the stick; makes hard contact; can drive the ball with loft; speed to make an impact on the bases; quick first step in the field; ability to play better than average at second.

Weaknesses: Needlessly rushes plays at short; makes unforced mistakes; lacks consistency at the position; not likely to stick in the long run; approach will get aggressive; likes to get head out in front of ball early; leaves him prone to secondary stuff; can yank with bat; still learning situations to muscle up; power may play more gap than over the fence; reads off pitchers need some work.

Risk Factor/Injury History: Low risk; 153 Double-A games; profile questions.

Bret Sayre's Fantasy Take: While there's a big difference between a shortstop and a second baseman in real life, in fantasy leagues, it's minimal at best. Prospect fatigue may be setting in with Hanson, but we'd all take .270 with 15 homers and 20 steals from a middle infielder any day—after all, even the 2014 version of Daniel Murphy was a top-10 second baseman.

The Year Ahead: Most evaluators saw Hanson sliding over to second base at some point prior to reaching, or very early on in, the major leagues, so it didn't come as a surprise to see the prospect get work there during the last month of 2014. Whether it's sold as increasing the infielder's versatility or what-have-you, this long-term view sees Hanson at second. There's still defensive work for the 22-year-old to round into a better-than-average defender, but the position just seems to fit better and will likely alleviate some of the overall defensive stress that plagues him. There is pressure on the bat to play to full potential and produce consistently season in and season out. It's more of a solid-average offensive profile, which is a hit to the overall value due to not sticking up the middle, but there's good contact ability and some pop here. A key factor to Hanson reaching his potential offensive grades rests with further development of the approach. He'll continue to be tested in Triple-A this season to stay back longer and not get caught out in front of breaking stuff, which drives weak contact and swings and misses. If all goes well, look for the infielder to make his debut toward the end of the summer.

---

9. Cole Tucker   SS

Born: 7/3/96   **Age:** 18   **Bats:** B   **Throws:** R   **Height:** 6'3"   **Weight:** 185

MLB ETA	Hit	Power	Run	Glove	Arm	OFP	Realistic
2019	50	55	60	55	60	60 1ST DIVISION PLAYER	45 2ND DIV/UTILITY

YEAR	TEAM	LVL	AGE	PA	R	2B	3B	HR	RBI	BB	SO	SB	CS	AVG/OBP/SLG	TAv	BABIP	BRR	FRAA	WARP
2014	PIR	Rk	17	217	39	6	2	2	13	26	38	13	5	.267/.368/.356	.278	.329	2.7	SS(20): -0.2	1.0
2015	PIT	MLB	18	250	23	8	0	2	15	12	72	5	2	.196/.240/.259	.193	.269	0.0	SS -1	-0.8
2016	PIT	MLB	19	250	23	9	1	3	20	12	66	6	2	.231/.270/.310	.218	.304	0.2	SS -1	-0.9

Breakout: 0%   Improve: 0%   Collapse: 0%   Attrition: 0%   MLB: 0%   Upside: 6   *Comparables: Adrian Cardenas, Argenis Diaz, Carlos Rivero*

Drafted/Acquired: 1st round, 2014 draft, Mountain Pointe HS (Phoenix, AZ)

Previous Ranking: NR

What Happened in 2014: The Pirates selected Tucker with the 24th overall pick, and then after signing, the shortstop more than held his own in the Gulf Coast League as an 18-year-old.

Strengths: Frame to continue adding size and strength; light on feet; fluid actions; reads ball off the bat well; soft hands; quick stroke from left side; loose hands; flashes ability to barrel up offerings with backspin; body to grow into power with physical maturity; high baseball IQ; shows instincts for the game.

Weaknesses: Swing gets loose right-handed; on the long side; needs more strength to enhance bat speed; stroke is more contact oriented at present; will need to learn how to tease more lift and postcontact extension out to hit with power; foot speed likely to decrease with physical maturation; runs risk of losing range with added mass; in the early stages of developing a professional approach.

Risk Factor/Injury History: High risk; limited professional experience; big gap between present and future.

Bret Sayre's Fantasy Take: The list of potential exciting fantasy contributors in this system continues, as Tucker could end up a power/speed combo at a very weak position—which holds true even if he shifts to the hot corner. For all the talk of him being an overdraft for the Pirates, he could be nicely undervalued in dynasty drafts this offseason.

The Year Ahead: Tucker is one of those players where the vision of the future leads to gazing fairly far off into the horizon and heavily projecting out the tools at present. But as they start to become more polished skills, the potential finished product really comes into focus. The body also has strong potential to evolve over the course of the next few years, as the 18-year-old's frame and wiry muscle type lend strong clues that there can be plenty of strength gains on the way. The progression is likely going to be on the slower side, though, as Tucker is a bit raw, and a lot of it is tied into strength and experience gains. There are some concerns that the prospect's natural physical development is going to lead to his being pushed off the shortstop position, but the arm plays up on the left side of the infield and the defensive tools are there. It's currently "wait and see" as to exactly how it all unfolds given that Tucker is just entering the stage of larger physical gains. It'll be interesting to see whether he goes to short- or full-season ball in 2015 given that he was on the young side for the draft class, but there's a good chance the first developmental steps forward will happen at whichever level he begins.

10. Harold Ramirez OF

Born: 9/6/94 **Age:** 20 **Bats:** R **Throws:** R **Height:** 5'10" **Weight:** 210

MLB ETA	Hit	Power	Run	Glove	Arm		OFP	Realistic
Late 2017	55	50	65	50	50		60 1ST DIVISION PLAYER	45 BENCH OF/2ND DIV ST

YEAR	TEAM	LVL	AGE	PA	R	2B	3B	HR	RBI	BB	SO	SB	CS	AVG/OBP/SLG	TAv	BABIP	BRR	FRAA	WARP
2014	WVA	A	19	226	30	14	1	1	24	11	35	12	3	.309/.364/.402	.283	.365	2.5	CF(24): -0.0, RF(23): -2.3	1.3
2015	PIT	MLB	20	250	21	10	1	1	18	9	59	7	3	.219/.260/.284	.210	.282	0.2	CF -1, RF -1	-0.8
2016	PIT	MLB	21	250	23	8	1	1	18	11	49	8	3	.234/.282/.295	.218	.288	0.7	CF -1, RF -1	-1.2

Breakout: 0%   Improve: 0%   Collapse: 0%   Attrition: 0%   MLB: 0%   Upside: 11   *Comparables: Abraham Almonte, Cedric Hunter, Eury Perez*

Drafted/Acquired: International Free Agent, 2011, Colombia

Previous Ranking: #10 (Org)

What Happened in 2014: Ramirez dealt with leg injuries that hampered his overall season, but the outfielder was able to hit .309 and post a 766 OPS when on the field.

Strengths: Good present strength; strong lower half; excellent athlete; strong wrists and forearms; life in hands; ability to control the barrel; squares up offerings with good backspin; raw power to tap into down the line; accelerates well out of the box; speed is an asset; covers good ground into both gaps in center; shows closing speed; arm plays in position.

Weaknesses: Approach is on the crude side; needs work bringing a plan to the plate; gets aggressive early with fastballs regardless of location; prone to breaking balls across line of sight; will commit hands early; bat can drag; on the rough side in center; can be slow with reads and take flat-angled routes; arm doesn't play in right; further added mass can cut into speed.

Risk Factor/Injury History: High risk; limited full-season experience; gap between now and future.

Bret Sayre's Fantasy Take: There's a long way to go here, but Ramirez could be a fantasy performer in the mold of Starling Marte—a player who is speed-based, but can contribute across the board regardless. Even if the power never materializes, Rotisserie owners aren't likely to get too up in arms.

The Year Ahead: Ramirez is presently a work in progress and crude as a player, but the overall tools are here and if things click, the outcome can be a solid payout. The combination of a projectable hit tool, playable potential power, and speed make the 20-year-old an attractive prospect if you believe he can stick up the middle. The latter aspect is where the initial concerns creep in, as there are mixed opinions as to whether Ramirez is going to be able to stick in center over the long haul. Despite the athleticism and plus speed, he's not the most natural and fluid at the position, often getting slower reads and seemingly lacking high-caliber instincts. The arm is only average, so it's likely left field if he can't refine the defense enough, which makes the offensive tools developing to their potential grades all the more important. Ramirez possesses the type of hitting talent that will probably allow him to get by until the upper minors, but his pitch selection and overall approach will need to start showing progress to ease concerns of his weaknesses being exposed upon reaching Double-A. This is a long-lead development player, with a sizable gap between the present and future, but one who can take some steps forward with consistent repetitions in 2015.

Prospects on the Rise

1. RHP Trey Supak: The 6-foot-5 right-hander shows starter upside, which led to the Pirates selecting him in the Competitive Balance portion after the second round of the 2014 draft. Supak possesses a loose arm and the type of frame that can pack on a good amount more strength as he physically matures. The 19-year-old already dials his fastball into the low-90s and can occasionally touch higher. The view is that with added strength, this player's entire arsenal can take a step forward, including a curveball and changeup that can play average to better. There's a longer developmental curve here, but if some of the gains start to show out of the gate, Supak has a chance to be firmly in this system's top-10 discussion next season.

2. RHP Gage Hinsz: The Pirates signed the 11th rounder out of Montana to an over-slot deal last year and will likely slowly begin his developmental journey. Another projectable arm, Hinsz is on the raw side, but his easy delivery, ability to work his fastball up into the low-90s, and early feel for the secondary stuff stand out. It's likely going to be longer lead with the 19-year-old, considering that he isn't exactly coming from a baseball hotbed and there are plenty of rough edges to polish. It may be a bit early with Hinsz, but the feeling is this a player with a good chance to make some strong gains once he gets going in the pro structure, and a rise in status will quickly follow suit.

3. OF Tito Polo: A true five-tool talent, the 20-year-old outfielder spent his first season stateside in the Gulf Coast League, drawing some high marks on the overall skill set. Polo already shows good present strength—with a frame that can still pack on a little more to further enhance his overall game—and a feel for barreling up the ball with backspin. A potential assignment in full-season ball will likely be a good test for the Colombian's approach. Early clues pointed to the ability to stay back on the ball and let it travel deeper, but it remains to be seen whether the step up in competition will have a neutralizing effect. Polo has a chance to start really generating buzz this season if the tools continue to show progress and a projection as a regular comes into focus.

Factors on the Farm
Prospects likely to contribute at the major-league level in 2015

1. C Elias Diaz: The defensive skills carry this profile, though Diaz flashes the ability to control the head of the bat and get the barrel on the ball. The 24-year-old Venezuelan is polished behind the dish, with solid footwork, a firm glove, and a plus-to-better arm highlighting the package. Diaz has also made strong strides with his game management and leadership skills since reaching the upper minors, which puts his defense at near major-league ready. Feedback on the bat was mixed as to whether there will be enough consistent hard contact against high-caliber arms to hit enough in extended stretches. It's a likely solid backup profile in The Show, with the chance to play a little higher if he can squeeze more out with the bat.

2. OF Willy Garcia: The 22-year-old outfielder's strike zone management skills can still use some refinement, and there's a chance that his overaggressiveness will expose the hit tool a level up and beyond, but Garcia flashes in-game power and the ability to impact the baseball. If the right-handed hitter can learn to work himself into more favorable hitting conditions while showing more trust to use the whole field, there's potential here to ride it to a look at the big-league level should the situation present itself. Given Pittsburgh's already crowded outfield picture, Garcia may be more of a long shot in 2015, but a good showing in Triple-A can force the issue and give the organization that many more options during the summer.

FROM THE FIELD

Josh Bell

Team: Pittsburgh Pirates

Evaluator: Tucker Blair

Dates seen: July 24–26, 2014

Affiliate: Altoona Curve (Double-A, Pirates)

Physical/health: Thicker build; mild room left for growth; should settle into a power body that looks like a major-league power hitter; thick thighs and broad shoulders; looks like a right fielder.

MLB ETA	Risk factor	OFP	Realistic role
2016	Moderate	60	50; major-league regular

Tool	Future grade	Report
Hit	50	Wide stance with slight front foot open; helps to keep him balanced and minimize noise from load; replicates stance from both sides of the plate; plus bat speed; ability to recognize spin is average; will get tied up on the really good stuff but can recognize the fringe to solid-average stuff; needs to cut back on the preswing noise from both sides; leaks into the actual swing sometimes and is completely unnecessary.
		Left-handed hitter: swing is more natural; keeps balance better; feet are mostly fine; will occasionally fly open with his shoulder, which causes him to put a slight loop in swing and slow down bat; gets under and is late on pitches when this occurs; hands can become noisy and shoulder is too noisy; swing has slightly more lift and shows better ability to barrel pitches than as right-handed hitter.
		Right-handed hitter: swing has more noise; balance is an issue; jumps out of his shoes at times; hands move around too much; drops his shoulder more than as left-handed hitter; hands will drift and he sometimes will overextend; same tools as from other side but swing is generally less refined and has further to go before seeing true in-game success.
Power	60	Tick above plus raw power; hands explode through zone; has brute strength; plus bat speed and slight lift in swing make for a swing conducive to power; ball screams off his bat when barreled; he's going to hit the ball hard when he makes contact; ball carries off his bat well; power as left-handed hitter is more evident; shows power from both sides but as left-handed hitter has a cleaner natural swing and likely translates to more in-game success.
Baserunning/speed	45	4.43 from home to first; decent second gear; takes a while to start his body into full motion; first gear is poor; not a high amount of initial agility; looks faster in the outfield than on the basepaths; might actually be an average runner right now; will settle in at fringe-average with slight growth and maturity as he gets older.
Glove	40	Adventurous; instincts are not terrific; reads are average; first step is delayed at times; feet can become sloppy or staggered; has trouble twisting body and moving laterally after balls behind him; shows some inconsistencies with footwork moving backward; route running is a large aspect of this issue; routes are not clean and takes incorrect angles; footwork is clearly what is being worked on; practiced footwork in pregame and was able to replicate and refine the issues there; need to see in-game now.
Arm	60	Cannon arm; shows ability to throw on a line from long distance in outfield; made a line throw from the pole to second base in excellent time; ball hovered off ground; good arm strength and accurate throws; easily enough arm for right field.

Overall: Bell has two plus tools that will provide positional value due to being a right fielder. The swing is currently inconsistent, but he shows ability to hit the ball to all fields, and the barrel-to-ball ability is solid. The skills are still lagging in-game, but the raw tools are all there and he is showing some of them. The ball jumps off his bat when he makes contact, but he still needs to learn and grow as a hitter when it comes to situational hitting and his general approach at the plate. He has a decent eye, but there were a few at-bats where he did not have the most logical approach for the situation at hand.

Overall, I like Bell and think there is enough talent to be a very talented right fielder. However, the swing still needs some refinement and he looks like a player that will need at least another year at the Double-A level.

3. RHP Casey Sadler: The former 25th-round pick has steadily climbed the ranks of the system since signing, culminating in a call to The Show last September. The right-hander's main weapons are a low-90s sinking fastball and hard-biting slider that he leans on to miss bats. The 24-year-old displays confidence in utilizing his entire arsenal at any point in the count, which also includes about an average changeup. Sadler could serve as starting depth at Triple-A in 2015 should the organization be inclined to keep him stretched out as protection to the rotation. The power nature of his fastball-slider combination also leaves the door open for the righty to be utilized in a bullpen role as early as the start of the season should Pittsburgh be inclined to expedite his arrival.

SAN DIEGO PADRES

1. Austin Hedges   C

Born: 8/18/92   **Age:** 22   **Bats:** R   **Throws:** R   **Height:** 6'1"   **Weight:** 190

MLB ETA	Hit	Power	Run	Glove	Arm	OFP	Realistic
2016	50	–	–	75	65	65 1ST DIV / ALL STAR	60 1ST DIV REGULAR

YEAR	TEAM	LVL	AGE	PA	R	2B	3B	HR	RBI	BB	SO	SB	CS	AVG/OBP/SLG	TAv	BABIP	BRR	FRAA	WARP
2014	SAN	AA	21	457	31	19	2	6	44	23	89	1	3	.225/.268/.321	.207	.269	-1.7	C(106): -2.6	-0.7
2015	SDN	MLB	22	250	19	11	1	3	22	11	59	2	1	.211/.249/.304	.218	.263	-0.5	C -0	-0.2
2016	SDN	MLB	23	250	24	12	0	4	23	13	57	2	1	.218/.263/.328	.223	.267	-0.5	C 0	-0.7

Breakout: 0%   **Improve:** 0%   **Collapse:** 0%   **Attrition:** 0%   **MLB:** 0%   **Upside:** 23   *Comparables: Josmil Pinto, Miguel Montero, Rob Brantly*

#23

BP Top 101 Prospects

Drafted/Acquired: 2nd round, 2011 draft, Junipero Serra Catholic HS (San Juan Capistrano, CA)

Previous Ranking: #1 (Org), #18 (Top 101)

What Happened in 2014: While his glove and arm remain impact weapons in every sense of the term, Hedges struggled to find any level of comfort or success at the plate against Texas League arms.

Strengths: Defensive chops and catch-and-throw game play to borderline elite levels at present; seamless actions from reception through transfer and release; advanced footwork; throws come with regular precision; improved decision-making on field (e.g., back picks); tracks well at the plate; swing works; strength and leverage to develop playable pop; high makeup; field general.

Weaknesses: Bat unlikely to play to impact levels; approach unraveled through summer; average bat speed magnifies negative impact of regressed approach; power ceiling limited; needs to produce more regular impactful contact to force advanced arms to work the margins; if hit/power play down, strike zone command and tracking lose value/utility.

Risk Factor/Injury History: Low; even with hit concerns the glove and arm will carry profile.

Bret Sayre's Fantasy Take: The future Padre backstop will be the highest ranked player in the Top 101 who does not factor into the Dynasty 101—and it won't be particularly close. There's really no point in shallow mixed leaguers owning him at all, as his best-case scenario looks similar to what Wilin Rosario did in 2014 (.267 average and 13 homers), and he was not a top-10 fantasy catcher. In deep mixed and NL-only leagues, there's still something here, but if you own him, sell him on name value.

The Year Ahead: On the heels of Hedges's 2013 offensive struggles in the Texas League, which could be easily written off as a small sample size from an aggressively promoted 20-year-old, the continued trials and tribulations that defined his full year of Double-A exposure last summer did little to bolster confidence in the stick. The good news is that there is still a solid offensive producer tucked into the profile. Dating back to his days as an amateur, the JSerra prep product has displayed the solid strike zone command you would expect from an advanced backstop, as well as the balance and swing path to produce solid contact across the quadrants. Hedges got away from that sound mechanical foundation during his tumultuous 2014, with opposing arms challenging him more regularly in the zone as the resultant swing proved less and less capable of squaring up offerings with any degree of frequency. It's unlikely Hedges will ever produce impact level power numbers, but there is plenty of strength in the body and leverage in the swing to keep pitchers honest provided he can work his way back to the approach and swing that served him so well as an amateur and through the start of his pro career. Supporters are banking on just that, with an additional note that San Antonio's home park is particularly rough on right-handed power and may have been at least partly responsible for Hedges's departure from a contact-friendly swing to a pull-happy cut. He'll play the bulk of 2015 at the age of 22, leaving plenty of flexibility as to how the organization wants to handle his assignment, with an interesting option being a month of High-A ball to build momentum with the stick and subsequent promotion directly to El Paso. The glove and arm are major-league ready, and Hedges should make his debut in San Diego as soon as the organization is comfortable that there is no additional developmental value in logging minor-league at-bats.

2. Hunter Renfroe OF

Born: 1/28/92 **Age:** 23 **Bats:** R **Throws:** R **Height:** 6'1" **Weight:** 200

MLB ETA	Hit	Power	Run	Glove	Arm	OFP 65 1ST DIV / ALL STAR	Realistic 55 >AVG REGULAR
2016	50	70	55	55	60		

YEAR	TEAM	LVL	AGE	PA	R	2B	3B	HR	RBI	BB	SO	SB	CS	AVG/OBP/SLG	TAv	BABIP	BRR	FRAA	WARP
2014	SAN	AA	22	251	17	12	0	5	23	25	53	2	1	.232/.307/.353	.239	.280	-0.5	LF(30): -2.7, CF(22): -1.8	-0.2
2014	LEL	A+	22	316	46	21	3	16	52	28	81	9	3	.295/.370/.565	.342	.359	-0.3	RF(49): -4.1, RF(7): -4.1	3.1
2015	SDN	MLB	23	250	24	10	1	7	27	17	74	2	1	.212/.268/.351	.240	.276	-0.3	RF -1, LF -1	-0.3
2016	SDN	MLB	24	250	25	12	0	4	22	18	75	2	1	.208/.270/.317	.223	.286	-0.4	RF -1, LF -1	-1.2

Breakout: 1%   Improve: 5%   Collapse: 1%   Attrition: 1%   MLB: 8%   Upside: 10   *Comparables: Kyle Parker, Roger Kieschnick, Rene Tosoni*

Drafted/Acquired: 1st round, 2013 draft, Mississippi State University (Mississippi State, MS)

Previous Ranking: #4 (Org), Just Missed The Cut (Top 101)

What Happened in 2014: After punishing High-A arms through the first half of the season, Renfroe sputtered in 60 Texas League contests, ultimately reasserting himself as an alpha power bat via a strong Arizona Fall League showing in which he paced the league in slugging (.569) and tied for the league lead in home runs (6).

Strengths: High-level athlete; big raw that plays in game; swing brings natural loft and carry; easy backspin; above-average run and aggressive implementation of tool; arm can be a weapon; covers ground and capable of the flashy finish; strong competitor; swagger.

Weaknesses: Aggressive approach can limit power utility; Double-A pitching further exposed holes in approach, particularly with respect to same-side secondaries; failure to shrink coverage holes could soften profile to one-dimensional power bat with limited kill zone.

Risk Factor/Injury History: Low; achieved Double-A; high floor through broad value base with impact power potential.

Bret Sayre's Fantasy Take: With some of Renfroe's contact troubles, he's more attractive in an OBP format, but that certainly doesn't mean he should be undersold in standard 5x5. A potential .260 hitter who could hit 25-30 homers, even in Petco, Renfroe could sweeten the pot with 15-20 steal ability. The odds are low he'll get to that point, but he has many paths to value.

The Year Ahead: Despite some choppy stretches with Double-A San Antonio, Renfroe ended 2014 on a high note, impressing evaluators throughout his Arizona Fall League stint with loud BP showings and in-game at-bats demonstrative of a solid overall approach and power that plays. With the bat speed to turn on premium velocity, Renfroe revels in rising to fastball challenges, which can get him in to trouble when he locks into his search for heaters, something Double-A arms were able to exploit. To his credit, the former Mississippi State Bulldog was able to somewhat tame those urges in the fall, and the positive results were apparent. Whether he can continue to maintain a more focused and methodical plan of attack has yet to be seen, and will be the ultimate determinant as to whether he is able to maximize his opportunities for hard contact and fully tap into that double-plus raw. With an influx of major-league outfielders making their way to San Diego this winter, the organization has the latitude to afford Renfroe more developmental time in Double-A to start the 2015 campaign. He could debut as early the end of this season and should in any event by ready to contribute in earnest by 2016.

#50
BP Top 101 Prospects

3. Matt Wisler RHP

Born: 9/12/92 **Age:** 22 **Bats:** R **Throws:** R **Height:** 6'3" **Weight:** 195

MLB ETA	CT	FB	CH	CB	SL	OFP 60 NO. 3 STARTER	Realistic 50 NO. 4 STARTER
2015	–	60	60	–	55		

YEAR	TEAM	LVL	AGE	W	L	SV	G	GS	IP	H	HR	BB	K	BB9	SO9	GB%	BABIP	WHIP	ERA	FIP	FRA	WARP
2014	ELP	AAA	21	9	5	0	22	22	116.7	131	19	36	101	2.8	7.8	44%	.317	1.43	5.01	5.14	5.11	0.8
2014	SAN	AA	21	1	0	0	6	6	30.0	26	2	6	35	1.8	10.5	47%	.312	1.07	2.10	2.25	3.33	0.6
2015	SDN	MLB	22	5	7	0	26	19	130.7	118	13	39	112	2.7	7.7	42%	.302	1.21	3.67	3.90	3.98	0.6
2016	SDN	MLB	23	5	5	0	22	15	122.7	113	12	35	107	2.6	7.8	42%	.310	1.21	3.65	3.57	3.97	0.7

Breakout: 12%   Improve: 27%   Collapse: 5%   Attrition: 17%   MLB: 37%   Upside: 16   *Comparables: Cesar Carrillo, Eric Hurley, Michael Pineda*

Drafted/Acquired: 7th round, 2011 draft, Bryan HS (Bryan, OH)

Previous Ranking: #2 (Org), #47 (Top 101)

What Happened in 2014: Wisler played most of his 2014 season as a 21-year-old in Triple-A, holding his own in an oft-challenging PCL while continuing to refine his command and execution.

Strengths: Lively fastball with good life down in the zone; sits comfortably 91-93 mph with the heater, and can reach back for the mid-90s with regularity; low- to mid-80s slider comes with good tilt and bat-missing ability; at best, change flashes late fade and deception; good deception; physicality to hang innings.

Weaknesses: Control outdistances command; fastball flattens up in the zone and can lend itself to hard fly-ball contact; lacks consistency in secondary execution; can work too often to the fat of the plate; can drop slot with

#53
BP Top 101 Prospects

slider, keeping break on swing plane; can spin a curve, but offering lacks present bite to play past fringe.

Risk Factor/Injury History: Low; near major-league ready.

Bret Sayre's Fantasy Take: The ongoing gentrification of Petco Park makes mid-rotation types like Wisler slightly less attractive than they used to be, but there's still plenty to like here. The strikeout numbers may top out at around 160-170 over the course of a full season, but strong ratios could accompany those whiffs, and he's ready to contribute this year—especially with the injury-prone arms ahead of him.

The Year Ahead: While Wisler's stats from last season do not jump off the page, it was a very strong showing for a young arm regularly challenged with hitter-friendly parks and savvy bats. At its best, Wisler's arsenal can flirt with a front-end projection, but the nonuniform implementation of his mechanics, and in particular his arm slot and release, can complicate execution and holds back the playable command. The spacious outfield plains of Petco should help mitigate the risk inherent in a profile with fly-ball tendencies. Perhaps more importantly, the Ohio native is athletic enough to leave open the possibility that he finds the consistency in execution to deploy his cache of major-league offerings with the requisite precision to lean on his fastball and changeup down in the zone to generate more groundballs. Wisler should enter the spring with an outside shot at breaking camp with the big club, though a return trip to El Paso seems most likely. Either way he'll undoubtedly log major-league innings this year and should be a rotation mainstay by 2016.

---

4. Rymer Liriano   OF

Born: 6/20/91   **Age:** 24   **Bats:** R   **Throws:** R   **Height:** 6'0"   **Weight:** 230

MLB ETA	Hit	Power	Run	Glove	Arm	OFP	Realistic
Debuted in 2014	–	60	60	55	60	60 1ST DIV REGULAR	50 ML REGULAR

YEAR	TEAM	LVL	AGE	PA	R	2B	3B	HR	RBI	BB	SO	SB	CS	AVG/OBP/SLG	TAv	BABIP	BRR	FRAA	WARP
2014	SDN	MLB	23	121	13	2	0	1	6	9	39	4	1	.220/.289/.266	.211	.329	1.1	RF(34): -0.7	-0.3
2014	ELP	AAA	23	71	14	11	1	0	13	8	14	3	1	.452/.521/.661	.368	.583	-1.3	RF(11): -1.1, CF(5): 0.1	0.1
2014	SAN	AA	23	415	55	20	2	14	53	35	102	17	7	.264/.335/.442	.270	.326	5.3	LF(55): 2.6, CF(37): -0.1	2.9
2015	SDN	MLB	24	250	26	11	1	4	23	17	72	8	2	.228/.288/.341	.246	.310	0.5	RF -1, LF 1	0.2
2016	SDN	MLB	25	250	26	11	1	4	23	19	71	8	2	.223/.291/.336	.238	.304	0.8	RF -1, LF 1	0.1

Breakout: 1%   Improve: 14%   Collapse: 9%   Attrition: 13%   MLB: 32%   Upside: 26   *Comparables: Kelly Johnson, Justin Huber, Matt Murton*

Drafted/Acquired: International Free Agent, 2007, Dominican Republic

Previous Ranking: #5 (Org)

What Happened in 2014: The immensely talented outfielder slashed a combined .291/.362/.473 between Double-A San Antonio and Triple-A El Paso before being overwhelmed by big-league arms over his first 121 plate appearances with the Pads.

Strengths: Strong and athletic; wields tools forcefully, leveraging plus power, speed, and arm strength; plus bat speed allows for some confidence in hit utility despite present swing-and-miss; potential elite corner talent, capable of impacting the game in all facets.

Weaknesses: Tools at present play below lofty paper presentation; not an instinctual player; natural bat-to-ball is adequate, but not supportive of consistent barreling, preventing maximization of raw; power might manifest more to gaps than over the fence at maturity; early extension can further sap playable pop and minimize inner half coverage.

Risk Factor/Injury History: Moderate; Tommy John surgery in file; underdeveloped feel can force flashy tools to play down.

Bret Sayre's Fantasy Take: Over the course of two weeks, Liriano went from a good fantasy sleeper in 2015 to buried under a mountain of corner outfielders in the depth chart. When he does get back to The Show, he can be a 20/20 outfielder with a batting average somewhere between "hey that's not so bad" and "oh god really."

The Year Ahead: Liriano surprised in 2014 by forcing his way to the majors for an extended debut, though the results of that debut were as one would expect given the aggressive promotion of an exciting but presently flawed profile. The former J2 signee oozes with impact potential, consistently enticing evaluators to loosen their evaluative inhibitions and submit to the ecstasy of a clean five-tool projection. The raw materials with which Liriano is working could certainly justify such a generous proclamation, and those backing Liriano as a future force at the highest level are quick to point to excellent makeup and work ethic in their insistence that the present developmental obstacles will eventually be overcome. Liriano's refinement would benefit more from daily Triple-A reps than irregular major-league game action off the bench to start 2015, though he could provide good value in a limited role should the opportunity arise. He'll return to San Diego at some point this year, likely better equipped to establish firm footing at the game's highest level.

5. Michael Gettys   OF

Born: 10/22/95 **Age:** 19 **Bats:** R **Throws:** R **Height:** 6'1" **Weight:** 203

MLB ETA	Hit	Power	Run	Glove	Arm	OFP	Realistic
2019	–	55	70	65	70	65 1ST DIV REG / ALL STAR	45 4TH OF/PNCH RUN UTL

YEAR	TEAM	LVL	AGE	PA	R	2B	3B	HR	RBI	BB	SO	SB	CS	AVG/OBP/SLG	TAv	BABIP	BRR	FRAA	WARP
2014	PDR	Rk	18	233	29	8	5	3	38	15	66	14	2	.310/.353/.437	.275	.429	0.2	CF(19): 2.0, RF(1): 0.2	0.8
2015	SDN	MLB	19	250	19	8	1	3	19	9	81	4	1	.187/.218/.261	.189	.266	0.4	CF 3, RF 0	-0.8
2016	SDN	MLB	20	250	24	11	2	4	23	11	71	5	1	.223/.263/.334	.222	.297	0.6	CF 3, RF 0	-0.4

Breakout: 0%   Improve: 0%   Collapse: 0%   Attrition: 0%   MLB: 0%   Upside: 20   *Comparables: Oscar Taveras, Joe Benson, Gorkys Hernandez*

Drafted/Acquired: 2nd round, 2014 draft, Gainesville HS (Gainesville, GA)

Previous Ranking: NR

What Happened in 2014: Despite consistent struggles at the plate through the showcase circuit and high school spring, Gettys landed a significant seven-figure bonus after being selected 51st overall by San Diego in the June draft and proceeded to put together a solid pro debut at the complexes.

Strengths: Top-tier athlete with natural strength and explosiveness; double-plus speed plays even higher out of the box and in the field thanks to rapid acceleration to top speed; will show plus raw in batting practice; covers large swaths of ground in center and is comfortable leaving his feet to finish; arm can play to impact; staggering upside.

Weaknesses: Hit tool comes with huge question marks; extended struggles with contact, including versus marginal high school competition; during extended slumps can expand zone, compounding negative swing-and-miss effects; penchant for showing off arm can lead to ill-advised throws and baserunner advancement.

Risk Factor/Injury History: High; immense contact issues and complex level résumé.

Bret Sayre's Fantasy Take: If you're a big-time risk taker, then Gettys is your man in the late second/early third round of dynasty drafts. The lack of a good hit tool grade is the crux of the problem here, as all the tools in the world won't matter if he can't make contact. But if he does, watch out.

The Year Ahead: Gettys may have more upside than any position player in the 2014 draft class, but with that upside comes significant risk tied to near-jarring struggles with contact throughout the 12 months leading up to the draft. While the pro production was solid over 52 complex-level games, the impressive slash line was accompanied by a strikeout every four plate appearances, and reports pointed to little in the way of tangible adjustments to indicate progress had been made in smoothing the barrel delivery and improving pitch selection. It's seldom that a player with Gettys' upside is available 50-plus picks into the draft, and it's almost unheard of when the profile comes with the potential for plus or better up-the-middle defense and impact speed on the bases. That in and of itself says all that needs be said with respect to confidence the amateur scouting circuit has in the hit tool playing to the minimal level necessary for the former Georgia commit to be an everyday major-league contributor. The Padres could ease Gettys into short-season ball with a trip through extended, eyeing a Midwest League assignment in 2016 once confident he is adequately prepared to tackle full-season arms.

6. Jose Rondon   SS

Born: 3/3/94 **Age:** 21 **Bats:** R **Throws:** R **Height:** 6'1" **Weight:** 160

MLB ETA	Hit	Power	Run	Glove	Arm	OFP	Realistic
2016	55	–	50	50	50	55 >AVG REGULAR	45 UTLITY GLOVE

YEAR	TEAM	LVL	AGE	PA	R	2B	3B	HR	RBI	BB	SO	SB	CS	AVG/OBP/SLG	TAv	BABIP	BRR	FRAA	WARP
2014	INL	A+	20	324	40	17	5	0	24	17	50	8	6	.327/.362/.418	.276	.391	0.0		0.0
2014	LEL	A+	20	154	18	9	0	1	12	13	23	3	1	.301/.371/.390	.278	.357	-0.3	SS(30): -0.3, SS(3): -0.3	0.8
2014	ANG	Rk	20	10	3	0	0	0	0	1	0	2	1	.125/.300/.125	.252	.125	0.6	SS(2): 0.1	0.1
2015	SDN	MLB	21	250	21	9	1	1	14	13	60	2	2	.198/.242/.253	.197	.256	-0.4	SS 1, 3B 0	-0.5
2016	SDN	MLB	22	250	21	9	1	1	17	13	52	3	2	.212/.257/.271	.200	.260	-0.3	SS 0, 3B 0	-1.9

Breakout: 0%   Improve: 0%   Collapse: 0%   Attrition: 0%   MLB: 0%   Upside: 19   *Comparables: Andrelton Simmons, Cristhian Adames, Donovan Solano*

Drafted/Acquired: International Free Agent, 2011, Venezuela

Previous Ranking: #8 (Org – LAA)

What Happened in 2014: Rondon bypassed the dreary Midwest League and split his first full season between High-A leaguemates Inland Empire and Lake Elsinore, impressing with both clubs.

Strengths: Solid contact bat with good feel for the barrel and sound approach; should grow into gap-to-gap threat as body matures; hands and arm play at the six-spot; speed plays average to tick above; firm foundational value in profile thanks to glovework and overall baseball acumen; impressive refinement to game for age/level.

Weaknesses: Profile lacks impact across the board; if strength doesn't fully manifest, hit tool could play to hollow average; footwork can get sloppy, negatively impact throws and ability to finish; limited range at present; profile could be pushed off of shortstop with any future decrease in speed.

Risk Factor/Injury History: Moderate; glove and feel for contact provide stable floor; yet to reach upper minors.

Bret Sayre's Fantasy Take: Value is in the eye of the beholder, but a .275-hitting shortstop with 15-20 steals, while useful in deeper leagues, is not a worthy aspiration for most mixed leaguers. If you can sell high on his inflated Cal League stats, I would.

The Year Ahead: Rondon's full-season debut was a terrific success, with a well-balanced profile regularly playing to its full potential. Advanced strike zone awareness, ability to track multiple pitch types, and contact ability all combine to help the hit tool project to average or better, and Rondon's ability to consistently display those skills gives comfort that he possesses the skill set necessary to make adjustments as he continues to face increasingly more advanced arms and arsenals. The ultimate ceiling remains limited, as there is no single aspect of the game in which Rondon figures to provide impact-level production. Nevertheless, there is unquestionable value in a steady performer versatile enough to fill a utility role if needed, but also capable enough with the bat to produce in an everyday capacity. Rondon should start 2015 with Double-A San Antonio and will play the full year as a 21-year-old. Despite logging fewer than 500 full-season at-bats thus far, he could be ready to offer assistance at the major-league level within the next two years.

---

7. Franchy Cordero SS

Born: 9/2/94   **Age:** 20   **Bats:** L   **Throws:** R   **Height:** 6'3"   **Weight:** 175

MLB ETA	Hit	Power	Run	Glove	Arm	OFP	Realistic
2018	**50**	**55**	**55**	**50**	**60**	**55** >AVG REGULAR	**45** BENCH BAT / PWR UTL

YEAR	TEAM	LVL	AGE	PA	R	2B	3B	HR	RBI	BB	SO	SB	CS	AVG/OBP/SLG	TAv	BABIP	BRR	FRAA	WARP
2014	FTW	A	19	94	5	2	1	0	9	4	36	3	3	.188/.237/.235	.206	.314	-0.9	SS(20): -5.0	-0.7
2014	EUG	A-	19	259	40	8	4	9	35	14	75	13	5	.279/.329/.458	.291	.372	1.4	SS(36): -4.8, 3B(1): 0.0	1.0
2015	SDN	MLB	20	250	23	7	1	3	16	9	94	5	3	.182/.216/.262	.189	.279	0.2	SS -10, 3B 0	-1.9
2016	SDN	MLB	21	250	21	7	2	3	20	10	86	5	3	.198/.233/.283	.196	.287	0.4	SS -10, 3B 0	-3.3

Breakout: 0%   Improve: 0%   Collapse: 0%   Attrition: 0%   MLB: 0%   Upside: 7   *Comparables: Jonathan Villar, Reid Brignac, Junior Lake*

Drafted/Acquired: International Free Agent, 2011, Dominican Republic

Previous Ranking: On The Rise

What Happened in 2014: After stumbling in his first taste of full-season ball, Cordero was able to put together an encouraging short-season campaign that included regular displays of potent power interspersed with empty swings.

Strengths: Impressive raw pop that can already play above average in game; ability to let ball travel and drive oppo; can drop barrel and lift with ease to pull; lots of leverage, and room for added strength to push power past current projections; good balance; natural comfort in the box; arm could be molded into a left-side or right-field weapon; above-average run at present; good feel on bases should allow for run utility even if thickening body drags down foot speed.

Weaknesses: Lower half can get stiff and deliberate in the infield; battles footwork when closing and during setup for throws; infield actions don't come naturally, with frequent lapses in arm action and imprecise glovework; still working to find consistency in swing; can load low and open up holes in plate coverage.

Risk Factor/Injury History: High; yet to graduate short-season.

Bret Sayre's Fantasy Take: The fantasy upside for Cordero is the selling point, as the probability of him being a roto asset is relatively low. If it all breaks right, he could be a five-category contributor, but not an impact performer in any of them (unless the power really shows up and maxes out, in which case he could hit 25).

The Year Ahead: The high-waisted infielder has already started to thicken in the lower half, lending credence to the thought that a shift off shortstop might soon be in the cards. While Cordero regularly displays above-average athleticism in the form of strength, explosiveness, and speed, the aggregate result of those physical gifts doesn't always translate to clean baseball actions. Accordingly, Cordero can struggle with the little things, such as footwork and a firm defensive hand to finish in the field, and consistent load, launch, and barrel delivery at the plate. As one would expect, the result is a high degree of inconsistency in performance from viewing to viewing, though even the ugly outings are underscored by the allure of a power-based tool set that could slot well into the middle of a lineup and a corner defensive home. While the young Dominican currently faces a long developmental road, it's impossible to ignore the ease with which he can impact the baseball at the plate, and the ultimate upside is that of a solid power bat who will hit for some average and provide enough corner defense to allow the offensive game to keep the overall production comfortably in the green. He will make another run at full-season ball in 2015, with an eye toward firmly establishing himself as prospect worthy of inclusion in the organization's long-term plans.

8. Zech Lemond RHP

Born: 10/9/92 **Age:** 22 **Bats:** R **Throws:** R **Height:** 6'1" **Weight:** 170

MLB ETA	CT	FB	CH	CB	SL	OFP	Realistic
2017	–	60	50	60	–	55 NO. 3/4 STARTER	50 LATE-INN RP

YEAR	TEAM	LVL	AGE	W	L	SV	G	GS	IP	H	HR	BB	K	BB9	SO9	GB%	BABIP	WHIP	ERA	FIP	FRA	WARP
2014	SAN	AA	21	0	0	0	1	0	4.0	1	0	0	2	0.0	4.5	42%	.083	0.25	0.00	2.12	2.98	0.1
2014	EUG	A-	21	2	3	0	11	8	38.0	39	1	5	34	1.2	8.1	66%	.330	1.16	3.79	3.08	3.92	0.7
2015	SDN	MLB	22	1	3	0	10	6	35.3	38	4	15	21	3.8	5.4	49%	.311	1.49	5.03	5.03	5.46	-0.4
2016	SDN	MLB	23	7	7	1	40	23	173.7	167	16	60	135	3.1	7.0	49%	.310	1.31	4.13	3.91	4.49	-0.3

Breakout: 0%   Improve: 0%   Collapse: 0%   Attrition: 0%   MLB: 0%   Upside: 8   *Comparables: Chad Bettis, Tommy Milone, Juan Gutierrez*

Drafted/Acquired: 3rd round, 2014 draft, Rice University (Houston, TX)

Previous Ranking: NR

What Happened in 2014: After effectively wielding a plus fastball and hard spike curve both in the rotation and out of the 'pen last spring for Rice, the 2014 third-round signee breezed through 36 short-season innings and a four-inning relief outing with Double-A San Antonio.

Strengths: Fastball works with arm-side life in the low-90s and regularly registers 94-96 mph in short stints; sharp low-80s curve plays both in and out of the zone, with late bite and impressive depth; shows feel for change piece, presenting a third potential average or better major-league weapon; steady demeanor on the bump; mind-set to handle starter slog and high-leverage relief work alike; good physicality.

Weaknesses: Durability is a big question; can get predictable in implementation of fastball/curve combo; needs to improve in-zone command; long, sweeping arm action on the back side can complicate release and timing; can come around breaking ball when arm dips; can flash curve grip entering arm circle; changeup can come firm, flat, and hittable.

Risk Factor/Injury History: High; elbow inflammation last spring; limited pro experience; yet to demonstrate durability at any level.

Bret Sayre's Fantasy Take: The likelihood is that Lemond ends up in the bullpen, which docks him from our standpoint, as he doesn't profile as an impact reliever. He's an interesting name to stash in very deep leagues, or to roster if your dynasty draft goes 100 deep, but otherwise, he's all wait and see.

The Year Ahead: With a wave of arm ailments sweeping through the organization over the past few seasons, the thought of a Rice pitching product with recent elbow issues joining the system might not be particularly comforting for Padres fans. Fortunately, Lemond brings with him two power offerings that are near major-league ready, providing a welcome safety net in the form of late-inning relief work should the former Owl prove ill-suited for a starter's workload. For the time being, San Diego is expected to continue to develop the strapping righty in the rotation, with a gradual ramp-up in innings over the course of the summer laying the groundwork for a loosening of the reins in 2016. His changeup should receive the lion's share of his developmental focus at the outset, with an overarching theme of improved precision and comfort utilizing his full complement of pitches across variable game situations.

9. Taylor Lindsey 2B

Born: 12/2/91 **Age:** 23 **Bats:** L **Throws:** R **Height:** 6'0" **Weight:** 195

MLB ETA	Hit	Power	Run	Glove	Arm	OFP	Realistic
2015	60	–	–	50	–	50 ML REGULAR	45 <AVG ML PLAYER

YEAR	TEAM	LVL	AGE	PA	R	2B	3B	HR	RBI	BB	SO	SB	CS	AVG/OBP/SLG	TAv	BABIP	BRR	FRAA	WARP
2014	ELP	AAA	22	159	18	6	1	2	17	9	15	0	2	.219/.270/.315	.203	.229	-0.8	2B(33): -3.6, 3B(6): 0.1	-0.8
2014	SLC	AAA	22	334	50	13	4	8	30	31	44	7	2	.247/.323/.400	.257	.267	0.8	2B(71): -10.6	-0.4
2014	ANG	Rk	22	4	1	0	0	0	0	1	0	0	0	.333/.500/.333	.319	.333	0.0	2B(1): -0.1	0.0
2014	ORM	Rk	22	5	0	1	0	0	1	0	0	0	0	.200/.200/.400	.193	.200	0.0	2B(1): -0.2	-0.1
2015	SDN	MLB	23	250	25	9	2	4	20	14	45	2	1	.224/.269/.328	.235	.257	-0.2	2B -2, 3B 0	-0.1
2016	SDN	MLB	24	250	27	9	2	5	25	18	42	2	1	.238/.295/.359	.246	.268	-0.1	2B -2, 3B 0	0.7

Breakout: 8%   Improve: 20%   Collapse: 0%   Attrition: 9%   MLB: 22%   Upside: 49   *Comparables: Daniel Descalso, Brad Emaus, Kyle Seager*

Drafted/Acquired: 1st round, 2010 draft, Desert Mountain HS (Scottsdale, AZ)

Previous Ranking: #1 (Org – LAA)

What Happened in 2014: Lindsey put up less-than-inspiring numbers across two Triple-A affiliates, but nevertheless continues to display top-shelf bat-to-ball ability.

Strengths: Excels at finding the ball with the barrel; quick hands allow unorthodox swing mechanics to play; when clicking can utilize the full field to great effect; will flash fringe-average power to pull side; quick hands are good fit for the keystone, producing speedy release that helps fringy arm to play up, particularly turning two.

Weaknesses: Elongated leg lift through stride complicates timing; gifted hands often work more to mitigate issues from swing irregularities than to consistently advance hit tool; inconsistent load and launch; intricate swing mechanics can come unglued, leading to pronounced bouts of soft contact; below-average run.

Risk Factor/Injury History: Low; modest upside with minimal refinement remaining.

Bret Sayre's Fantasy Take: This is about as boring of a fantasy profile as you can get, but one that will likely hold value in deeper formats. Lindsey has the benefit of San Diego's questionable infield, as far as short-term value is concerned, but in the long run, he could peak by hitting .280 with 10 homers and a handful of steals—essentially making him another Scooter Gennett in fantasy.

The Year Ahead: While the back of the baseball card tells the story of a prospect whose stock is trending the wrong way, the scouting book on Lindsey hasn't changed much over the past 12 months. Last year's top prospect in the Angels system remains a good bet to make lots of contact while providing adequate second-base defense, and while that collection of words isn't likely to get your heart racing, there is potentially solid value to be found in a cost-controlled asset with some upside in the hit tool. In years prior, the former supplemental first rounder had relied almost exclusively on his preternatural contact ability to serve the ball to all fields despite a swing that features a hitchy load, inconsistent stride, and volatile timing. His first foray in Triple-A ball last summer saw a decrease in production, in part due to bad luck and in part due to multiple periods of discomfort in the box. Throughout it all, Lindsey continued to do the one thing he has always done, regardless of experience or competition—make contact. He'll take another stab at the PCL in 2015 and, provided he can more frequently find his rhythm at the plate, should get a chance to test his skills as a batsman against major-league arms at some point this year.

10. Tayron Guerrero   RHP

Born: 1/9/91   **Age:** 24   **Bats:** R   **Throws:** R   **Height:** 6'7"   **Weight:** 190

MLB ETA	CT	FB	CH	CB	SL	OFP	Realistic
2016	–	70	–	–	55	55 LATE-INN RP	45 MID RP

YEAR	TEAM	LVL	AGE	W	L	SV	G	GS	IP	H	HR	BB	K	BB9	SO9	GB%	BABIP	WHIP	ERA	FIP	FRA	WARP
2014	LEL	A+	23	0	0	3	14	0	13.7	10	1	8	14	5.3	9.2	45%	.267	1.32	2.63	4.62	5.84	-0.1
2014	FTW	A	23	6	1	1	25	0	36.0	22	2	12	42	3.0	10.5	51%	.233	0.94	1.00	2.87	3.77	0.7
2015	SDN	MLB	24	1	1	1	21	3	38.3	37	4	24	29	5.6	6.8	49%	.311	1.60	5.10	5.28	5.54	-0.5
2016	SDN	MLB	25	3	2	2	43	4	82.0	73	7	46	70	5.0	7.7	49%	.302	1.45	4.30	4.34	4.68	0.1

Breakout: 0%   Improve: 0%   Collapse: 0%   Attrition: 0%   MLB: 0%   Upside: 2   *Comparables: Jay Sborz, Vic Black, Aaron Barrett*

Drafted/Acquired: International Free Agent, 2009, Colombia

Previous Ranking: NR

What Happened in 2014: Things started to come together for the rangy righty, as Guerrero yielded little in the way of impactful contact, challenging hitters with a double-plus heater and rapidly improving slide piece over 50 innings split between High- and Low-A.

Strengths: Fastball and slider can overwhelm; mid- to upper-90s heater comes downhill; slider works consistently in the mid-80s and can miss bats with regularity; should continue to add strength as body matures; very quick arm; solid extension adds to hitters' discomfort; at best can use low-effort mechanics to produce high octane stuff.

Weaknesses: Lacks consistent balance, leading to variable release and swings in control and secondary execution; has tendency to increase effort in mechanics throughout the course of his appearance, including an exaggerated finish and fall-off at the extremes; can struggle to keep a handle on long limbs; command and control could both max out at subpar; changeup plays firm and below average; lack of adequate off-speed can leave arsenal one-note; overthrew slider in Arizona Fall League, reducing velo delta off fastball and lessening depth.

Risk Factor/Injury History: High; yet to reach Double-A; standard reliever volatility risk.

Bret Sayre's Fantasy Take: The rule about relievers in dynasty leagues is that you don't want them unless they could be special from a strikeout perspective, and Guerrero likely doesn't have the secondary offering to make that a reality.

The Year Ahead: Guerrero made good developmental progress last year, navigating two levels of full-season ball before being overmatched by advanced Arizona Fall League bats. This is your typical high-risk/high-reward power arm, complete with requisite mechanical inconsistencies and physical projection. In a perfect world Guerrero develops enough comfort with his body and motion to successfully execute his fastball and slider, with a focus on working down in the zone and elevating as needed. Even if the control and consistency never fully come around, Guerrero should provide major-league value in some capacity, if only pumping an inning's worth of upper-90s heat in low-leverage situations. Upper-minors bats should pose a formidable challenge for the late-inning hopeful, and another strong developmental year could leave him a stone's throw from the Padres 'pen

Notable Omission

Trea Turner, SS: In an odd twist, Turner finds himself a member of the Padres system with an expiration date on his affiliation with the organization set at just over six months. This is a result of the present limitation on trading draftees prior to the one-year anniversary of their signing, which as a matter of process requires the Nationals and Padres to wait until June 13, 2015, to formalize his inclusion in their December 2014 trade as a "player to be named later." The 2014 first rounder would have come in as the number 5 prospect in the San Diego system, with the potential to stick at the six-spot long term while providing some offensive value through his plus-plus speed and average hit tool. The former NC State standout has solid range to the glove side and is comfortable both coming across and behind the bag, but needs to improve his focus and execution to cut down on unforced errors. At the plate, Turner features a lengthy swing that sweeps in and out of the hit zone with little pitch plane overlap, leading to more swing-and-miss than you'd like to see from a top-of-the-order stick. There's first-division upside here, with a likely outcome settling somewhere between utility glove and second-division shortstop.

Prospects on the Rise

1. RHP Ryan Butler: At 6-foot-4, 230 pounds, Butler projects an intimidating presence on the mound even before uncorking a plus to double-plus fastball that can reach triple digits. Both his slider and changeup play below average, though the latter has flashed average periodically between the spring and summer, showing some arm-side fade and deception. With one Tommy John surgery already in his pocket and a limited collection of effective secondaries, the most obvious developmental path would be in relief, where the seventh rounder could progress quickly with even minimal growth in his off-speed.

2. OF Jordan Paroubeck: The 2013 third rounder failed to gain in-game experience his draft year due to a shoulder ailment, but rebounded nicely this summer with a noteworthy performance in the Arizona Rookie League. There is a level of controlled violence to the switch-hitter's swings that a pro developmental team could shape into

FROM THE FIELD

Hunter Renfroe

Team: San Diego Padres
Evaluator: Chris Rodriguez
Dates seen: Spring training; April 10, 12, and 15; and May 10 and 12, 2014
Affiliate: Lake Elsinore Storm (High-A, Padres)
Physical/health: Big-man strength; imposing size; heavier than listed weight; thick legs and rear; plenty of muscle up top as well; very good athlete; major-league body; he's what a right fielder should look like.

MLB ETA	Risk factor	OFP	Realistic role
2016	High	60	50; league-average right fielder

Tool	Future grade	Report
Hit	50	Slightly open stance; rocks at the plate; looks very comfortable; extremely strong hands/wrists; clears his hips well; unleashes the bat with authority; uppercut stroke with leverage; swing is short and compact for a power bat; bat speed is plus; loves fastballs; approach was questionable early; hyper-aggressive; in early looks, he sat fastball all game and was fooled by change of speed and spin; out on his front foot; made some adjustments; better swings/takes vs. quality off-speed; swing-and-miss will always be a part of his game; I like the outlook because of his improved approach, bat speed, and strength.
Power	65	Raw power is plus-plus; overall strength flows through the bat well; his BP was a home-run show; shows power to the opposite field; uppercut swing creates leverage and balls have a ton of carry; game power is present; hit two home runs in my looks, one on a spinning slider and one on a fastball on the inner half; hits a ton of fly balls, which bears well for his power output; hit tool needs to reach close to an average level for power to flow.
Baserunning/speed	35	Clocked 4.46; shut it down the last step; moves well in the outfield; corner profile; better runner when he gets a head of steam; present below average; will settle slightly lower as he gets older.
Glove	55	Athleticism allows him to get some good breaks in right field; routes are solid; range is about average, but once he gets going he can move well; makes all the routine plays; above-average coordination should allow him to become a plus defender down the line.
Arm	60	Arm is a weapon; gets behind the throw; threw a guy out at the plate from medium-deep right field, but the catcher couldn't handle the ball; will play in either corner.

Overall: Renfroe has the chance to become a big-time power bat on a team that is itching for offense. It's important that they let him marinate at Double-A until he refines his approach even more so and finds some consistent success. It was very simple to beat him early on. Fastball outer half, then slider/curve outer half, and then off the plate to get him to chase. The hit tool did not grade out well in the first couple of looks, but the bat speed was evident, and as the season went on he started knocking balls out of the park with more regularity. Adjustments were made; he showed the ability to spit on pitches that he was chasing early and attack pitches in the zone more often. His power is tied to the hit tool, of course, and for him to become a game-changing bat he must continue to adjust to the pitchers tendencies.

Hitters hit, and Renfroe did enough mashing to get to Double-A at the All-Star break. He's struggling a little now, which could be just adjusting to the level and getting a feel (which he seemed to do well at High-A), so I'd keep him there the rest of this season and the majority of next before seeing what he can do at the major-league level.

a 30-plus home-run threat, and the former Fresno State commit also brings above-average speed and some defensive projection to the table. Paramount to Paroubeck's development at this point is logging in-game reps, and with a developmental step forward in 2015 the NorCal native could establish himself as one of the more interesting talents in the system.

3. INF Fernando Perez: After sputtering through short-season ball in 2013, Perez emerged as a potent weapon in the middle of the Fort Wayne lineup last summer, tallying 18 home runs while cutting down on empty swings and generally showing a higher level of comfort in the box. The 2012 third rounder is not a natural fit in the infield, lacking ideal range for second and the footwork or first-step quickness for the hot corner. For the time being, the Padres will take whatever defense they can get so long as the bat continues to progress. With the welcoming confines of the California League awaiting Perez in 2015, there's a good chance his bat forces strong top 10 consideration when this list is assembled next winter.

Factors on the Farm
Prospects likely to contribute at the major-league level in 2015

1. 2B Cory Spangenberg: The former Indian River standout has progressed through the system at a pace belying his lofty draft status as the 10th overall pick in a loaded 2011 draft class. There isn't much in the way of impact here, but as a lefty bat with good speed and an adequate glove at second there is very likely a spot for him on a National League roster, if only as a late-inning bat off the bench with some pinch-run utility. Spangenberg showed well in limited major-league action last summer, and he should enter the spring with a chance to break camp with the big club.

2. OF Alex Dickerson: Despite his size and strength, Dickerson does not offer the playable power expected out of an everyday corner bat. While he shows balance and fluidity throughout his swing, the path of the barrel plays best to line-drive contact, and particularly so against same-side arms. While the former Indiana Hoosier missed much of 2014 after undergoing surgery on his left foot, he impressed at the plate during his short late-season stint at Double-A and could be in line for a cup of coffee at some point in 2015. It's a bat-only profile, and the ceiling on that bat isn't particularly lofty. Still, as a capable lefty stick with a knack for contact he could carve out a role as a bench bat capable of plugging a hole in an outfield corner or at first base as needed.

3. RHP Aaron Northcraft: After a solid start to 2014 things unraveled quickly for the right-hander after a midseason promotion to Triple-A in the second half, where his 89-92 mph fastball was frequently and forcefully put into play, and the lack of a third viable pitch caught up to him. It's long been thought that Northcraft's sinking fastball and breaking ball are better suited for the bullpen, which brings us to the reason for his inclusion in this section. An arm coming out of the 'pen capable of getting groundballs and missing some bats is a nice asset to have. There's a chance the 25-year-old can be just that at some point in 2015.

SAN FRANCISCO GIANTS

1. Adalberto Mejia   LHP

Born: 6/20/93   **Age:** 22   **Bats:** R   **Throws:** L   **Height:** 6'3"   **Weight:** 195

MLB ETA	CT	FB	CH	CB	SL	OFP	Realistic
2016	c	55	60	–	55	60 NO. 3 STARTER	50 NO. 4 STARTER

YEAR	TEAM	LVL	AGE	W	L	SV	G	GS	IP	H	HR	BB	K	BB9	SO9	GB%	BABIP	WHIP	ERA	FIP	FRA	WARP
2014	RIC	AA	21	7	9	0	22	21	108.0	119	9	31	82	2.6	6.8	36%	.326	1.39	4.67	3.78	4.38	1.3
2015	SFN	MLB	22	4	7	0	17	17	90.7	98	10	29	59	2.9	5.9	39%	.319	1.40	4.72	4.52	5.13	-0.6
2016	SFN	MLB	23	10	10	0	30	30	189.0	192	16	51	136	2.4	6.5	39%	.319	1.29	4.06	3.66	4.42	-0.1

Breakout: 0%   **Improve:** 0%   **Collapse:** 0%   **Attrition:** 0%   **MLB:** 0%   **Upside:** 2   *Comparables: Jeanmar Gomez, Vance Worley, Will Smith*

Drafted/Acquired: International Free Agent, 2011, Dominican Republic

Previous Ranking: #2 (Org)

What Happened in 2014: Mejia logged 108 Double-A innings, around 60 percent of them as a 20-year-old, averaging around five innings per start and showing good feel for three potential above-average to plus major-league offerings.

Strengths: Loose and easy arm; big and sturdy frame; all three offerings play in the zone; shows comfort mixing offerings in different game situations; can create tough angles, particularly with changeup against righty bats and slider against lefties; fastball is low-90s offering with arm-side action and some late giddy-up; low- to mid-80s slider can play at different depths; changeup has deception at best and turns over with late screwball action; good control at present and projects to good command down the line.

Weaknesses: Command can play soft; arm slot will leave fastball flat up in the zone and will keep slider on swing planes; arm can drag, forcing ball up; will spin off finish, impacting precision of execution; some "soft body" concerns, particularly in lower half; mechanics are smooth but require further refinement and uniformity for command and execution to take next step; doesn't always stay on top and on line; slider and changeup both rely more on deception than snap; profile could top as a soft-contact arm at maturity rather than consistent strikeout generator; tested positive for Sibutramine and will serve a 50-game suspension to start 2015 season.

Risk Factor/Injury History: Moderate; young with Double-A résumé but will miss developmental time in 2015.

Bret Sayre's Fantasy Take: Despite the ballpark he is likely to call home in the future, Mejia fell off the Dynasty 101, leaving the Giants as one of three teams without a resident this year. Mejia could top out as a decent SP4 in time, but his strikeout numbers are likely to be more in the 140-150 range and he looks unlikely to contribute in 2015 at this point.

The Year Ahead: Mejia continued his impressive march to the Bay Area with a strong 2014 showing as one of the younger arms in the Eastern League. His solid three-pitch mix continues to interest and entice evaluators, and while the overall arsenal can comfortably turn over lineups, the lack of a true knockout offering regularly prevented the big-bodied lefty from putting away more advanced Double-A bats. The body is still maturing, and it's possible that Mejia sees additional growth in each of his offerings by the time he finishes filling out and firming up. While the suspension will retard the developmental progress, Mejia is young enough and advanced enough to handle the challenge without getting sidetracked. After working himself back up to speed with some low-minors tune-ups, expect Mejia to tackle the Eastern League again in the hope of tightening up the bolts on his overall game. He is in line for a 2016 major-league debut and projects well as a solid mid-rotation arm.

2. Kyle Crick   RHP

Born: 11/30/92   **Age:** 22   **Bats:** L   **Throws:** R   **Height:** 6'4"   **Weight:** 220

MLB ETA	CT	FB	CH	CB	SL	OFP	Realistic
2016	–	70	60	60	60	60 NO. 3 STARTER	55 2ND TIER CLOSER

YEAR	TEAM	LVL	AGE	W	L	SV	G	GS	IP	H	HR	BB	K	BB9	SO9	GB%	BABIP	WHIP	ERA	FIP	FRA	WARP
2014	RIC	AA	21	6	7	0	23	22	90.3	78	7	61	111	6.1	11.1	47%	.326	1.54	3.79	3.96	3.53	2.0
2015	SFN	MLB	22	4	6	0	16	16	75.3	64	5	45	81	5.4	9.7	45%	.322	1.44	4.07	3.95	4.42	0.2
2016	SFN	MLB	23	9	9	0	31	31	201.7	157	13	110	225	4.9	10.0	45%	.308	1.32	3.47	3.44	3.77	1.6

Breakout: 0%   **Improve:** 0%   **Collapse:** 0%   **Attrition:** 0%   **MLB:** 0%   **Upside:** 14   *Comparables: Trevor May, Zack Wheeler, Mauricio Robles*

Drafted/Acquired: 1st round, 2011 draft, Sherman HS (Sherman, TX)

Previous Ranking: #1 (Org), #38 (Top 101)

What Happened in 2014: Crick racked up 11.1 strikeouts per nine innings pitched in his Double-A debut, but an inability to find any consistency or command limited his innings tally and led to far too many walks.

Strengths: Very loud, pure stuff; fastball plays to double-plus despite marginal control and borderline nonexistent command; lots of late life and easy mid-90s velocity that will climb higher; maintains velo past 75-pitch mark; excellent arm speed; maintains arm speed on changeup, producing solid deception; tight slider with cutter action, works mid-80s to and through 90 mph; two-plane curve will flash depth and bite; good size; strength to hold stuff deep into starts; arsenal has top-tier potential.

Weaknesses: Throws with effort; inconsistent timing disrupts balance and release; arm drag; dramatic inconsistencies in execution regularly force stuff to play down; changeup ineffective off-trajectory, tips early when release is off; slider will frisbee and play as a soft cutter when overthrown; control is fringy and well outdistances command.

Risk Factor/Injury History: Moderate; extreme control issues hold back floor despite demonstrated bat-missing ability at Double-A.

Bret Sayre's Fantasy Take: The stuff is generally unquestioned with Crick, but then again, so is his inability to throw strikes. For fantasy purposes, he looks to be more valuable with a move to the bullpen, which is unusual for a pitching prospect. In the rotation, he's a high-WHIP, low-win probability pitcher who can strike out 180 batters a year despite the shortcomings. In the bullpen, there are more interesting relief prospects.

The Year Ahead: Throughout 2014 Crick continued to display high-octane, swing-and-miss stuff, but his inability to wield that stuff with consistency drove down its effectiveness and limited the powerful righty to just 90 1/3 innings due to elevated pitch counts. The stat sheet points to a future in relief, but there is more than enough pure stuff and durability for the former supplemental first rounder to turn over major-league lineups with regularity. Further, all four of Crick's offerings can play above average or better, so there is room to ease the foot off the gas to try and find an operating speed that better facilitates more stable mechanics and consistent execution. In the end, it may come down to whether Crick is willing to make the conscious decision to sacrifice some stuff to give him a better chance to work more regularly in the zone and last deeper into games. The fallback is that of a late-inning power arm, with strike-throwing ability the determinant as to whether the Giants will be able to trust him with true high-leverage situations. Overall, this remains one of the most explosive arms in the minors, and incremental improvements could get him back on track in short order.

#88
BP Top
101
Prospects

3. Andrew Susac C

Born: 3/22/90 **Age:** 25 **Bats:** R **Throws:** R **Height:** 6'1" **Weight:** 215

MLB ETA	Hit	Power	Run	Glove	Arm
Debuted in 2014	50	60	–	50	55

OFP	Realistic
55	50
>AVG REGULAR	AVG ML PLAYER

YEAR	TEAM	LVL	AGE	PA	R	2B	3B	HR	RBI	BB	SO	SB	CS	AVG/OBP/SLG	TAv	BABIP	BRR	FRAA	WARP
2014	SFN	MLB	24	95	13	8	0	3	19	7	28	0	0	.273/.326/.466	.291	.368	0.5	C(29): -0.1	0.8
2014	FRE	AAA	24	253	34	9	0	10	32	34	50	0	0	.268/.379/.451	.292	.305	0.4	C(56): 1.2	2.3
2015	SFN	MLB	25	250	25	10	1	6	28	25	66	0	0	.227/.311/.367	.261	.289	-0.3	C 0, 1B -0	0.9
2016	SFN	MLB	26	444	50	17	1	10	44	44	115	0	0	.215/.300/.344	.245	.274	-0.9	C 0	0.7

Breakout: 7% **Improve:** 23% **Collapse:** 8% **Attrition:** 27% **MLB:** 52% **Upside:** 71 *Comparables: Geovany Soto, Chris Gimenez, Josmil Pinto*

Drafted/Acquired: 2nd round, 2011 draft, Oregon State University (Corvallis, OR)

Previous Ranking: #6 (Org)

What Happened in 2014: Susac continued to show a power-centric approach with Triple-A Fresno before making his major-league debut and affording the Giants the freedom to rest all-world backstop Buster Posey without ceding offensive production from the catcher position.

#97
BP Top
101
Prospects

Strengths: Advanced approach with good feel for zone; solid plus power plays in game at present; good strength; balanced swing stays on plane and allows for hard contact pole to pole; natural backspin and carry; improving actions behind the plate; capable defender who could refine to average overall producer with glove; above-average arm with solid release and accuracy.

Weaknesses: Average bat speed and coverage holes; can be beat by sequencing and elevated heat; danger that overexposure at big-league level will eat into contact and power utility once book gets out; well-below-average runner; likely tops out as average defender.

Risk Factor/Injury History: Low; solid major-league debut in 2014.

Bret Sayre's Fantasy Take: In an organization that would see him getting real playing time in 2015, Susac would be a more interesting fantasy name. However, given that he'll likely get used sparingly, his fantasy ETA remains unknown. Given a full complement of at-bats, Susac could hit .260 with 20 homers, making him a potential top-10 catcher.

The Year Ahead: Given the risks associated with the two names ahead of him, a pretty strong case could be made for Susac as the top prospect in the system, and there are undoubtedly a number of teams out there that would be willing to take on the limited defensive ceiling and swing-and-miss risk to roll the dice with Susac as their everyday backstop to start 2015. Don't expect that trade to come any time soon, however, as the fit with San

Francisco is tight and comfy, with the Giants able to rest Posey more regularly without ceding impact at-bats from their backstop. Susac has the opportunity to gradually earn more regular time behind the dish over the coming years as Posey continues to age and the Giants look to maximize the number of quality at-bats their soon-to-be $20 million man will log

4. Tyler Beede   RHP

Born: 5/23/93   **Age:** 22   **Bats:** R   **Throws:** R   **Height:** 6'4"   **Weight:** 200

MLB ETA		CT	FB	CH	CB	SL		OFP	Realistic
2017		–	65	55	55	–		60 NO. 3 STARTER	50 NO. 4 STARTER

YEAR	TEAM	LVL	AGE	W	L	SV	G	GS	IP	H	HR	BB	K	BB9	SO9	GB%	BABIP	WHIP	ERA	FIP	FRA	WARP
2014	SLO	A-	21	0	0	0	2	2	6.7	8	0	3	7	4.1	9.4	65%	.400	1.65	2.70	3.06	4.04	0.2
2014	GIA	Rk	21	0	1	0	4	4	8.7	8	0	4	11	4.2	11.4	65%	.348	1.38	3.12	2.87	4.34	0.2
2015	SFN	MLB	22	1	4	0	9	9	34.0	38	3	19	21	5.0	5.6	48%	.326	1.65	5.59	5.17	6.07	-0.5
2016	SFN	MLB	23	6	7	0	31	31	193.3	183	17	75	147	3.5	6.8	48%	.305	1.33	4.04	4.02	4.39	0.0

Breakout: 0%   Improve: 0%   Collapse: 0%   Attrition: 0%   MLB: 0%   Upside: 5   *Comparables: Nick Maronde, Buddy Boshers, Adam Warren*

Drafted/Acquired: 1st round, 2014 draft, Vanderbilt University (Nashville, TN)

Previous Ranking: NR

What Happened in 2014: Beede capped an inconsistent career at Vandy with an up-and-down spring that included equal part flashes of brilliance and hints at a future relief role, culminating in his selection 14th overall in the June draft—a seven-spot improvement from 2011, when the Blue Jays popped him with the 21st overall pick.

Strengths: Will flash front-end stuff, including a plus or better heater and two swing-and-miss secondaries; fastball is lively and sits comfortably 91-94 mph, regularly reaching 96-97; low-80s power curve shows plus bite and solid depth at its best; can manipulate low-80s changeup, showing straight drop and cutting action depending on situation; good present strength; aggressive approach, attack mentality.

Weaknesses: Large inconsistencies across profile with only minimal growth over past three seasons; irregular timing produces volatile release and often results in curve playing soft and fastball spraying; yet to show ability to hold together mechanics consistently across starts; inability to regularly dominate overmatched opponents; can fight himself on the mound, particularly when struggling.

Risk Factor/Injury History: Moderate; limited pro showings and spotty collegiate résumé.

Bret Sayre's Fantasy Take: For those of you who can own amateur talent in your leagues, you've notice Beede's fantasy value slipping almost daily over the last 18 months. The Giants were a good organization for him to land in, both for ballpark reasons and development ones, but there's enough risk to push him outside the top 20 in drafts this year.

The Year Ahead: The Vandy ace entered the 2014 season as a candidate to go first overall, but the volatility that had underscored his profile as an underclassman continued to define his junior year performances. As a result, Beede slipped to the middle of the first round, where San Francisco jumped at the opportunity to grab "Kyle Crick light." The pure stuff isn't as explosive as Crick's, but Beede shows the potential to wield three above-average or better weapons, and the body and arm upon which 180 innings could regularly be hung. First, the two-time first rounder will need to clean up his timing and release to bring his true offerings to the surface, at which point Beede and the Giants developmental staff should have plenty to work with in crafting a future rotation mainstay. He'll likely ease into A-ball in 2015 and could don the orange and black as soon as 2017 if things break right.

5. Keury Mella   RHP

Born: 8/2/93   **Age:** 21   **Bats:** R   **Throws:** R   **Height:** 6'2"   **Weight:** 200

MLB ETA		CT	FB	CH	CB	SL		OFP	Realistic
2017		–	70	50	60	–		65 NO. 2/3 STARTER	50 LATE INN RP

YEAR	TEAM	LVL	AGE	W	L	SV	G	GS	IP	H	HR	BB	K	BB9	SO9	GB%	BABIP	WHIP	ERA	FIP	FRA	WARP
2014	AUG	A	20	3	3	0	12	12	66.3	69	1	13	63	1.8	8.5	62%	.337	1.24	3.93	2.79	3.49	
2014	SLO	A-	20	1	1	0	6	6	19.7	16	0	6	20	2.7	9.2	47%	.302	1.12	1.83	3.00	3.82	1.3
2015	SFN	MLB	21	3	6	0	14	14	66.3	71	6	29	47	3.9	6.4	51%	.326	1.50	4.93	4.57	5.36	-0.7
2016	SFN	MLB	22	8	10	0	30	30	191.3	190	16	76	152	3.6	7.2	51%	.321	1.39	4.34	3.94	4.72	-0.7

Breakout: 0%   Improve: 0%   Collapse: 0%   Attrition: 0%   MLB: 0%   Upside: 15   *Comparables: Edwin Escobar, Jordan Walden, Kyle Lobstein*

Drafted/Acquired: International Free Agent, 2011, Dominican Republic

Previous Ranking: #7 (Org)

What Happened in 2014: The talented Dominican showed bat-missing velocity and a promising breaker before being sidelined by a rotator cuff strain, costing him a couple of months in the middle of the season.

Strengths: Big arm speed generates easy-plus velocity and life; weighty two-seamer works effectively in low-90s, four-seam heater plays in 92-95 mph velo band and can touch higher; curve flashes hard bite and comes with solid depth; future plus offering that will play in the zone and as bury pitch; some feel for cambio and is increasing comfort level with offering; solid build and present strength.

Weaknesses: Missed time due to rotator cuff sidetracked innings buildup; has yet to prove durable over full season; changeup is below-average offering more often than not; can fall back on fastball when curve isn't there; needs to improve quality of offerings out of zone, can live too freely on the fat; control outdistances command.

Risk Factor/Injury History: High; low-level résumé; rotator cuff issues in 2014.

Bret Sayre's Fantasy Take: There may not be a player in this system with more usable fantasy potential than Mella, whose huge arm could lead to a potential SP2 future if he can make it through the gauntlet. If the change can keep lefties off kilter, he can put up strong ratios (particularly WHIP) and run up near 180 strikeouts in the long run. Keep an eye out as to whether Mella is owned in your league.

The Year Ahead: Had Mella put together 24 starts on par with the aggregate of his 12 Augusta showings there is a good chance he would have found himself at or near the top of this prospect list, and comfortably within the top 100 prospects in the game. The quick-armed righty produces easy velocity through low-maintenance mechanics, adding a power breaker to the mix that provides a one-two punch that could project to the front of a major-league rotation. The shoulder issues cloud the picture some, and there is still a fair amount of work to be done to get the changeup to fighting weight against more capable bats. Still, Mella possesses some of the highest upside in the system and even if relegated to relief, the profile carries impact potential. He should get a shot at High-A in 2015 and could earn a midseason promotion if the fastball-curve pairing proves too much for Cal League lineups.

---

6. Christian Arroyo SS/2B

Born: 5/30/95 **Age:** 20 **Bats:** R **Throws:** R **Height:** 6'1" **Weight:** 180

MLB ETA		Hit		Power		Run		Glove		Arm			OFP	Realistic
2018		55		–		50		50		–			60 1ST DIV REGULAR	50 AVG ML PLAYER

YEAR	TEAM	LVL	AGE	PA	R	2B	3B	HR	RBI	BB	SO	SB	CS	AVG/OBP/SLG	TAv	BABIP	BRR	FRAA	WARP
2014	AUG	A	19	125	10	3	1	1	14	4	22	1	2	.203/.226/.271	.189	.237	-0.8	2B(26): 5.7, SS(5): -0.2	0.0
2014	SLO	A-	19	267	39	14	2	5	48	18	31	6	1	.333/.378/.469	.310	.360	0.1	SS(58): 5.9	3.0
2015	SFN	MLB	20	250	17	9	1	2	20	7	61	1	0	.214/.237/.292	.205	.272	-0.3	SS 5, 2B 2	0.3
2016	SFN	MLB	21	250	22	10	1	3	20	11	54	1	1	.213/.248/.301	.208	.260	-0.4	SS 4, 2B 2	-0.8

Breakout: 0% **Improve:** 0% **Collapse:** 0% **Attrition:** 0% **MLB:** 0% **Upside:** 15 *Comparables:* Trevor Plouffe, Lonnie Chisenhall, Charlie Culberson

Drafted/Acquired: 1st round, 2013 draft, Hernando HS (Brooksville, FL)

Previous Ranking: On The Rise

What Happened in 2014: The former first rounder followed up his loud professional debut with a slow start at Low-A Augusta, where a sprained thumb shelved him for much of May. Arroyo returned to action in short-season ball, where he raked his way through the Northwest League over the final three months of the season.

Strengths: Simple and balanced swing produces regular contact across the diamond; solid leverage; contact-friendly path that seeks out pitch plane; above-average bat-to-ball ability; shows feel for strike zone and solid plan of attack; solid strength; could grow into average power down the line; hands work well up the middle; arm strength can play on the left side; solid footwork around the bag.

Weaknesses: Average runner at present and could lose a step or two as body matures; may fit best at keystone long term; can get front-of-center in weight transfer, causing rollover and soft contact; reliant on reads to add value on bases; bat could fall short of impact; lacks carrying tool outside of hit potential.

Risk Factor/Injury History: High; yet to establish footing in full-season ball.

Bret Sayre's Fantasy Take: The combination of ETA and lack of upside makes Arroyo a bad bet in most fantasy leagues. In very deep formats, he could be an interesting late roster guy, but we're really talking about a pretty empty .280 hitter—at least for fantasy owners.

The Year Ahead: It isn't a sexy profile, but Arroyo has the raw materials in place to help him grind his way to the majors and establish himself as an offensive-minded middle infielder with pull-side pop and steady hands. Even if the bat doesn't reach its ceiling, there is enough glove and arm for the Hernando High School prep product to provide ample value as a versatile utility option capable of logging innings across the dirt. Arroyo should get another shot at Low-A Augusta in 2015 and could break out in a big way thanks to a strengthening physique, balanced swing, and advanced approach. There is still a long developmental lead here, but the payout could be well worth the wait.

7.   Steven Okert   LHP

Born: 7/9/91   **Age:** 23   **Bats:** L   **Throws:** L   **Height:** 6'3"   **Weight:** 210

MLB ETA	CT	FB	CH	CB	SL	OFP	Realistic
2015	–	60	50	–	60	60 1ST DIV CLOSER	55 2ND TIER CLOSER

YEAR	TEAM	LVL	AGE	W	L	SV	G	GS	IP	H	HR	BB	K	BB9	SO9	GB%	BABIP	WHIP	ERA	FIP	FRA	WARP
2014	RIC	AA	22	1	0	5	24	0	33.0	24	3	11	38	3.0	10.4	43%	.266	1.06	2.73	3.23	3.83	0.5
2014	SJO	A+	22	1	2	19	33	0	35.3	33	2	11	54	2.8	13.8	46%	.308	1.25	1.53	2.52	1.72	1.6
2015	SFN	MLB	23	2	1	2	40	0	53.7	50	5	23	48	3.9	8.0	46%	.318	1.36	4.18	4.16	4.54	-0.1
2016	SFN	MLB	24	2	1	2	47	0	62.7	52	5	24	55	3.4	7.9	46%	.291	1.22	3.30	3.64	3.59	1.0

Breakout: 0%   Improve: 0%   Collapse: 0%   Attrition: 0%   MLB: 0%   Upside: 5   *Comparables: Daniel Stange, Gus Schlosser, C.C. Lee*

Drafted/Acquired: 4th round, 2012 draft, University of Oklahoma (Norman, OK)

Previous Ranking: NR

What Happened in 2014: Okert carved through the California and Eastern Leagues before putting the Arizona Fall League on lockdown over his 12 innings of relief work, in which he tallied 17 strikeouts to just five hits and one walk.

Strengths: Low-angle heater works easily low- to mid-90s with arm-side life; sharp, tilted low- to mid-80s slide piece is second plus offering; capable of working the quadrants with both offerings; can pitch off fastball or slider with ease; shows some feel for changeup; comes with some funk; uniform release and trajectory on fastball and slider adds to deception.

Weaknesses: Lacks consistent offering against right-handed bats despite high-quality pairing at top of arsenal; slider can flatten out of lower slot and stay on plane for righty bats; if stuff doesn't play to same impact level as in Arizona Fall League, could top out as late-inning matchup arm.

Risk Factor/Injury History: Moderate; standard relief arm volatility risk; some potential left/right split issues.

Bret Sayre's Fantasy Take: If you're into relievers, Okert is easily a top-20 dynasty relief prospect out there. Of course, you shouldn't be into relievers.

The Year Ahead: Okert's dominant showing in the Arizona Fall League elevated his stock from that of a potential late-inning arm to a near major-league ready contributor with shutdown potential. At their best, Okert's slider and fastball are true high-leverage weapons, capable of neutralizing left- and right-handed sticks alike, thanks to a parallel trajectory that camouflages the offerings and prevents early identification. The changeup is a "show-me" offering that has some utility against righty bats and will be necessary if his primary offerings aren't quite as crisp when he returns to action this spring. If last fall was an indication of a true step forward, the Giants could have a future closer candidate ready to join an impressive collection of power arms in the big-league 'pen. Even if Okert falls short of that lofty upside, he should be a valuable lefty arm ready to help the big club sooner rather than later

8.   Hunter Strickland   RHP

Born: 9/24/88   **Age:** 26   **Bats:** R   **Throws:** R   **Height:** 6'4"   **Weight:** 220

MLB ETA	CT	FB	CH	CB	SL	OFP	Realistic
Debuted in 2014	–	75	–	–	60	60 1ST DIV CLOSER	55 2ND TIER CLOSER

YEAR	TEAM	LVL	AGE	W	L	SV	G	GS	IP	H	HR	BB	K	BB9	SO9	GB%	BABIP	WHIP	ERA	FIP	FRA	WARP
2014	SFN	MLB	25	1	0	1	9	0	7.0	5	0	0	9	0.0	11.6	56%	.312	0.71	0.00	0.53	1.49	0.2
2014	RIC	AA	25	1	1	11	38	0	35.7	25	3	4	48	1.0	12.1	41%	.275	0.81	2.02	2.09	2.86	0.9
2014	SJO	A+	25	0	0	0	3	0	3.0	2	0	0	7	0.0	21.0	25%	.500	0.67	3.00	-0.93	1.37	0.1
2015	SFN	MLB	26	2	1	1	25	2	37.3	37	4	11	29	2.7	7.0	45%	.320	1.28	4.19	4.22	4.56	0.0
2016	SFN	MLB	27	2	1	0	45	0	47.7	46	5	12	40	2.3	7.5	45%	.315	1.23	4.05	3.68	4.40	0.3

Breakout: 13%   Improve: 16%   Collapse: 3%   Attrition: 9%   MLB: 21%   Upside: 3   *Comparables: Jeremy Horst, Sandy Rosario, Bryan Price*

Drafted/Acquired: 18th round, 2007 draft, Pike County HS (Zebulon, GA)

Previous Ranking: NR

What Happened in 2014: Strickland blew away High-A, Double-A, and major-league bats alike through September before allowing a jaw-dropping six home runs over eight postseason appearances.

Strengths: Borderline elite fastball sits comfortably in the upper-90s; pounds the strike zone; comfortable working the inner half; mid-80s slider shows late bite and can miss bats and barrels alike; late-inning mentality; prototypical late-inning power pairing.

Weaknesses: Fastball and slider can both be flat and hittable when arm drops; lefty bats do not seem to struggle picking up offerings out of the hand; can lack deception; can get fastball heavy and predictable; lacks consistent offering to disrupt oppo bats; command is loose.

Risk Factor/Injury History: Moderate; standard reliever volatility risk.

Bret Sayre's Fantasy Take: Being right-handed, Strickland is more likely to end up with a closer job than Okert is, but the same comment still applies. Friends don't let friends invest in relief prospects, but at least Strickland has seen the majors.

The Year Ahead: Strickland enjoyed a dominant season and was riding a euphoric wave before crashing in spectacular fashion during the Giants' world championship march. While the shocking nature of Strickland's postseason home-run binge was largely blown out of proportion due to the stage, it underscores the concern evaluators have envisioning the big righty as an impact closer. To reach his potential heights as a true shutdown relief arm, Strickland will need to develop either a vertical offering to get bats (and particularly lefty bats) off his fastball/slider plane or a usable off-speed pitch capable of disrupting timing. Short of that, this is still a late-inning arm capable of racking up whiffs and doing so from the jump in 2015.

9. Clayton Blackburn   RHP

Born: 1/6/93 **Age:** 22 **Bats:** L **Throws:** R **Height:** 6'2" **Weight:** 260

MLB ETA	CT	FB	CH	CB	SL	OFP	Realistic
2016	–	55	50	–	50	55 NO. 4 STARTER	45 SWINGMAN /MID RP

YEAR	TEAM	LVL	AGE	W	L	SV	G	GS	IP	H	HR	BB	K	BB9	SO9	GB%	BABIP	WHIP	ERA	FIP	FRA	WARP
2014	RIC	AA	21	5	6	0	18	18	93.0	94	1	20	85	1.9	8.2	57%	.341	1.23	3.29	2.54	3.33	2.2
2014	GIA	Rk	21	0	1	0	2	2	5.0	4	0	0	9	0.0	16.2	70%	.400	0.80	3.60	1.03	3.01	0.2
2015	SFN	MLB	22	4	7	0	17	17	91.0	89	7	26	73	2.6	7.2	52%	.319	1.26	3.90	3.71	4.24	0.4
2016	SFN	MLB	23	11	9	0	32	32	209.7	179	15	58	180	2.5	7.7	52%	.298	1.13	3.20	3.31	3.48	2.4

Breakout: 14%   Improve: 27%   Collapse: 3%   Attrition: 20%   MLB: 38%   Upside: 18   *Comparables: Patrick Corbin, Nick Tropeano, David Holmberg*

Drafted/Acquired: 16th round, 2011 draft, Edmond Santa Fe HS (Edmond, OK)

Previous Ranking: #5 (Org)

What Happened in 2014: The big-bodied righty posted impressive 4.3 and 9.0 strikeout-to-walk rates over 93 Double-A innings and 11 Arizona Fall League innings, but allowed more than a hit per inning along the way.

Strengths: Will show three major-league-caliber offerings and a fringy curve, and can work the zone with all four; strong frame and durable build; plus control; can pound the lower third of the zone with a heavy upper-80s to low-90s fastball; slider and changeup play well off the heater with similar path and varying finish; as feel for sequencing continues to develop could regularly produce soft contact; enough life on fastball to garner empty swings, particularly when set up by secondaries.

Weaknesses: Arsenal lacks impact; body was soft in 2014 and will work to profile's detriment if not monitored; low-70s curve is loopy and only effective when bat is properly prepped; will be reliant on steady defense to keep batters off base; needs to be more judicious as to when and where to work his stuff; could benefit from working more effectively out of the zone.

Risk Factor/Injury History: Low; solid Double-A showing.

Bret Sayre's Fantasy Take: Blackburn is a very undervalued arm in deep leagues (think more than 16-team mixed), as he has a good chance to be a back-end starter in a park that makes back-end starters look better than they really are—sort of like Chris Young's 2014 season.

The Year Ahead: Blackburn is the epitome of a high-floor, low-ceiling arm. While that label in and of itself can fail to capture the imagination of evaluators, Blackburn further did himself a disservice by sporting a soft body and low-energy approach on the diamond, resulting in more evaluative vitriol than was probably warranted. This is never going to be a front-end arm, and in fact, Blackburn is unlikely to wield the requisite stuff to approach consistent mid-rotation production. But provided the former 16th rounder can keep his body and mechanics in check, there is more than enough feel and quality of stuff for Blackburn to carve out a productive career in the back of a big-league rotation. He should make the jump to Fresno in 2015 and could compete for a spot in the big-league rotation a year from now.

10. Ty Blach   LHP

Born: 10/20/90 **Age:** 24 **Bats:** R **Throws:** L **Height:** 6'1" **Weight:** 210

MLB ETA	CT	FB	CH	CB	SL	OFP	Realistic
2015	–	55	60	50	50	50 NO. 4/5 STARTER	45 SWINGMAN /MID RP

YEAR	TEAM	LVL	AGE	W	L	SV	G	GS	IP	H	HR	BB	K	BB9	SO9	GB%	BABIP	WHIP	ERA	FIP	FRA	WARP
2014	RIC	AA	23	8	8	0	25	25	141.0	142	8	39	91	2.5	5.8	47%	.295	1.28	3.13	3.70	3.95	2.4
2015	SFN	MLB	24	6	9	0	21	21	121.3	126	10	32	75	2.4	5.6	46%	.312	1.30	4.11	4.03	4.47	0.1
2016	SFN	MLB	25	10	9	0	29	29	176.3	169	12	41	130	2.1	6.6	46%	.311	1.19	3.46	3.30	3.76	1.4

Breakout: 23%   Improve: 31%   Collapse: 7%   Attrition: 29%   MLB: 44%   Upside: 11   *Comparables: Dallas Keuchel, Elih Villanueva, Seth Maness*

FROM THE FIELD

Keury Mella

Team: San Francisco Giants
Evaluator: Ethan Purser
Dates seen: June 10, 2014
Affiliate: Augusta GreenJackets (Low-A, Giants)
OFP: 65
Realistic role: 55; no. 3/4 starter

Mechanics: Looks a hair shorter than 6-foot-2; athletic frame; plenty of present strength in lower body; pitches from the first-base side of the rubber; stays tall into balance point then shows a big upper-body lean toward third base during stride, harming the pitcher's overall balance; lands closed and throws across his body; delayed trunk rotation; arm action is on the long side with a bit of a hook in the back and a high back elbow; releases the ball from a three-quarters slot; exhibits some arm recoil and violence, spinning off wildly toward first base. Despite some mechanical oddities, Mella repeats the delivery fairly well and should continue to harness the intricacies going forward.

Pitch type	Present grade	Future grade	Sitting velocity	Peak velocity	Report
FB	60	70	94-96	97	Velocity: plus-plus; held velocity throughout start. Command: fringe-average; flashed ability to live low in the zone and get grounders and go up and out of the zone for whiffs; missed high too often in this look and was loose within the zone, but further repetitions should iron out minor control concerns; above-average future command profile. Movement: plus-plus; incredibly heavy fastball with explosive arm-side life; generates great plane when he works low in the zone. Comments: This is a plus-plus future offering, with plus-plus life and velocity. The command profile needs work, but the pitch has the ability to be a major weapon at the major-league level as both a barrel-missing offering and one that can generate whiffs.
CH	45	60	82-84	85	Command: below average; around the plate with the pitch but left it up and hanging too often. Movement: plus arm-side sink and fade; bat-missing pitch vs. left-handed batters; falls off the table at the front of the plate and elicits awkward swings. Comments: The changeup was ahead of the curveball in this particular outing. He showed major confidence in the pitch and threw it with conviction. Command of the offering will be refined with time and further repetitions.
CB	40	55	76-80	82	Command: below average; choked it in the dirt and left it up in the zone with frequency; struggled with feel and release point throughout the entire start. Movement: flashed sharp 11/5 break a handful of times; was a spinner/cement mixer at its worst. Comments: The curveball was behind the other two pitches in this viewing and requires projection, but the pitch flashes above-average with sharp break and should be harnessed with further iterations. He showed enough with the pitch in this offering for it to be considered a future above-average offering at the major-league level.

Overall: While there are some delivery concerns with Mella, he flashes the repeatability and the required command of his pitches to make it work in a starting role despite some funkiness. This is a legitimate three-pitch mix, and the soon-to-be 21-year-old shows the necessary ability to sequence and pitch off of his future double-plus fastball. Both secondaries require projection in terms of consistency and command, but each flashes above-average to plus potential and should play well off of the potentially dominant fastball.

Some will see the funky, somewhat violent delivery and immediately slot Mella into a future bullpen role, but the repertoire is well-rounded and would work beautifully in the rotation if each pitch reaches its potential. I have enough confidence in the total package to say that he sticks in the rotation long-term with the ceiling of a no. 2 starter on a first-division club. This is an arm that will shoot up lists this offseason.

Drafted/Acquired: 5th round, 2012 draft, Creighton University (Omaha, NE)

Previous Ranking: #10 (Org)

What Happened in 2014: Blach showed durability and pitchability over 140-plus Double-A innings, while keeping the ball in the park and maintaining his developmental trajectory as a solid future back-end starter.

Strengths: Good feel for four major-league-quality offerings; fastball can work heavy in the upper-80s to low-90s (two-seam) and will reach as high as 94 mph up in the zone (four-seam); changeup is a legit weapon with arm speed and arm-slot deception, showing late tumble; slider and curve show distinct shape, and both serve as potential average offerings at maturity; good balance; repeats mechanics; can fill up strike zone with full complement of pitches; some herky-jerky deception, does not affect execution.

Weaknesses: Stuff falls well shy of impact; will be high-contact arm at highest level; arsenal loses effectiveness up in zone; very slim margin for error; fastball command can get loose in the zone, opening up possibility for extensive damage at highest level; ho-hum velocity combined with lack of quality breaking ball could limit major-league utility to swingman/middle-relief role.

Risk Factor/Injury History: Low; near major-league ready.

Bret Sayre's Fantasy Take: Blach really shouldn't be owned in mixed dynasty leagues, but if he somehow squeezes his way into a rotation spot in 2015 for the Giants, there are worse players to spend some FAAB on in NL-only leagues.

The Year Ahead: Blach's floor mirrors that of Blackburn's, with the latter offering a shade more upside thanks to a slightly greater ability to miss bats. Evaluators seem to prefer Blach at present, however, in large part due to his mound presence and professional approach to attacking hitters. At the end of the day, the lefty will need to continue to operate at the same high level of precision if he's to survive turning over major-league lineups with regularity, and even then there simply may not be enough here for him to stick as a fixture in the San Fran rotation. His penchant for producing soft contact would play very well out of the 'pen—should he end up there—and at a minimum he should be a useful asset as a swingman capable of stepping into a starter's role as needed over the long haul of the major-league season. Blach should tackle Triple-A in 2015 and is ready for the challenge of big-league bats as soon as the opportunity presents itself.

Prospects on the Rise

1. RHP Michael Santos: Santos is the latest projectable low-level arm to emerge for the Giants, with the 2012 international signee making his stateside debut in the Arizona Rookie League at the age of 19. Santos boasts a broad frame and developing trunk and core that should be able to pack on significant bulk as he matures and continues to build strength. The young righty utilizes a simple step-in to kick off his up-tempo and limby mechanics. There's a fair amount of deception, and he hides the ball well, helping his low-90s heater to play up at present and preventing hitters from getting clean early looks at the secondaries—a solid low-70s, 12-to-6 curve with good shape and a budding low-80s change with fade. Santos figures to continue to add velocity and could stand with three true plus offerings when all is said and done. He should see some time in full-season ball this year and could start the season with Low-A Augusta if the organization feels he's physically prepared to handle the load.

2. C Aramis Garcia: Garcia came off the board to San Francisco in the second round of the 2014 draft, as the 52nd overall pick. The Florida International product hit his way into the hearts of Florida area scouts and national evaluators alike last spring, slashing .368/.442/.626 with 25 walks to just 23 strikeouts over his 199 plate appearances. Garcia does a good job keeping the barrel in the hit zone, enabling hard contact to all fields, though he can get pull-happy at times and particularly when seeking out fastballs. With continued development he could blossom into a solid bat for average with on-base ability, capable of working the count to find his pitches and possessing enough feel to turn tough offerings into hits. Defensively, Garcia gets the job done and could grow into an average receiver with a solid catch-and-throw game. He already shows some feel for blocking and deadening the ball, though his lower half is a tick slower than evaluators generally like to see. He should be ticketed for Augusta to start 2015 and could emerge as an easy top-10 prospect in the system by this time next year.

3. LHP Luis Ysla: The native Venezuelan enjoyed a solid full-season debut with Low-A Augusta, logging over 120 innings and averaging more than 5 innings per start. The hard-throwing lefty generates above-average velocity out of a sturdy lower half and core and does a solid job of consistently hitting his low arm slot with the slider and changeup, as well. There is a fair amount of effort involved, and the up-tempo mechanics paired with a longish arm on the backside can often lead to drag and an inconsistent release, forcing fastballs up and to the arm side and leaving his slider ineffective. Still, the fastball and changeup could both grow to plus offerings, and the slider isn't far behind given its late bite and tilt. With incremental improvements and more consistency in his execution, Ysla should step comfortably into the top 10 next year and looks the part of a potential mid-rotation arm or late-inning asset.

Factors on the Farm

Prospects likely to contribute at the major-league level in 2015

1. RHP Chris Stratton: The Mississippi State product continued his steady climb through the system, logging over 120 innings last year and finishing the season with five starts at Double-A Richmond. Stratton will show four distinct offerings, anchored by a heavy upper-80s to low-90s fastball and 82-84 mph short slider with borderline cutter action. He is often too loose with his low-80s change and upper-70s curve, and will need to focus on firming up each if he is to survive in a rotation long term. There is a solid case to be made for converting Stratton into a sinker/slider relief arm that could air it out in shorter spurts, potentially with his four-seamer playing to mid-90s heat. He could help out the Giants in short order should the organization go that route and could provide added value as a spot starter or multi-inning option out of the 'pen as needed.

2. RHP Erik Cordier: Cordier is yet another big velo arm that will be competing for quality innings out of the 'pen in 2015, bringing to the table a prototypical late-inning fastball/slider combo and intimidating presence on the bump. Cordier sits comfortably in the mid- to upper-90s with his fastball, showing some late life down and a truer trajectory when elevating. The slider is a hard mid-80s offering that grades out as plus with sharp bite. Control can come and go, though he did a solid job staying on line and pounding the zone during his brief 2014 call-up. He lacks the feel of San Fran's other late-inning options, but nevertheless could prove an important contributor along the way, while also providing a safety net should one or two of the arms ahead of him on the depth chart slip or miss time due to injury.

3. SS/2B Matt Duffy: The former Long Beach Stater probably lacks the defensive chops to hang as an everyday big-league shortstop, and the gap power is far from ideal elsewhere on the infield. Still, Duffy could prove a useful utility option for the Giants this season, with steady hands that work up the middle and enough arm to play across the diamond. The glovework is much more dependable than flashy, and his range is stretched at the margins when occupying the six-spot, but he can get the job done across the infield and will do so while posting solid contact rates at the plate. Though the former 18th rounder has below-average straight-line speed, Duffy handles himself well on the bases and could chip in as an additional contributor in a pinch-run capacity.

SEATTLE MARINERS

1. D.J. Peterson 1B/3B

Born: 12/31/91 **Age:** 23 **Bats:** R **Throws:** R **Height:** 6'1" **Weight:** 205

MLB ETA	Hit	Power	Run	Glove	Arm		OFP	Realistic
2015	60	60	–	–	–		60 1ST DIV 3B	50 2ND DIV 1B

YEAR	TEAM	LVL	AGE	PA	R	2B	3B	HR	RBI	BB	SO	SB	CS	AVG/OBP/SLG	TAv	BABIP	BRR	FRAA	WARP
2014	WTN	AA	22	248	32	8	0	13	38	22	51	1	1	.261/.335/.473	.291	.283	-0.8	3B(45): -3.0, 1B(9): 0.5	1.4
2014	HDS	A+	22	299	51	23	1	18	73	23	65	6	0	.326/.381/.615	.323	.372	1.3	3B(37): -0.3, 1B(8): 0.8	2.7
2015	SEA	MLB	23	250	27	9	0	11	34	12	69	0	0	.231/.273/.412	.266	.277	-0.4	3B -3, 1B 0	0.3
2016	SEA	MLB	24	250	30	9	0	10	32	14	69	0	0	.224/.272/.395	.249	.273	-0.5	3B -3, 1B 0	0.4

Breakout: 1% **Improve:** 22% **Collapse:** 2% **Attrition:** 14% **MLB:** 51% **Upside:** 76 *Comparables: Alex Liddi, Alex Gordon, Allen Craig*

#62
BP Top
101
Prospects

Drafted/Acquired: 1st round, 2013 draft, University of New Mexico (Albuquerque, NM)

Previous Ranking: #2 (Org), #65 (Top 101)

What Happened in 2014: Peterson clobbered his way through two levels, accumulating 61 extra-base hits in 547 plate appearances

Strengths: Masher; barrels up with frequency; strong hands/wrists; hard contact to all fields; line-drive swing with ability to backspin; home runs look like well struck four irons; goes gap to gap; excellent extension; keeps barrel in hitting zone; massive raw; long, high finish; attacks pitches he can hit early in the count; looks to do damage in every plate appearance.

Weaknesses: Likely will have to move to first base long term; stabs at balls; limited quickness and agility for third base; can be overly aggressive at the plate; tendency to lunge on off-speed pitches; pitch recognition needs improvement; stiff in field; takes time to get out of batter's box.

Risk Factor/Injury History: Medium; position switch possible.

Bret Sayre's Fantasy Take: It's such a shame when a right-handed power hitting prospect ends up in Safeco, but Peterson is a good enough hitter that it shouldn't empty out his fantasy value much. Even with the ballpark working against him, he can still be a high-end CI option in time, though his eligibility may hurt given that Kyle Seager should man the hot corner in Seattle for a while.

The Year Ahead: The former first rounder has a propensity for hurting baseballs and has done so since arriving on the scene. This season will be another year of refinement in the high minors, with the potential for a taste of the major leagues. He's going to stick at third for the time being, but evaluators believe that first base will be his final landing spot. While Peterson may not have the athleticism for the hot corner, he certainly is more athletic than most first basemen and would play solid-average defense upon moving. With excellent feel for the barrel and the ability to make adjustments at the plate in short order, the bat should be a weapon, regardless of the defensive home. He'll always have some swing-and-miss in his game, but he also possesses the potential to hit .280 with 25 bombs at the highest level. The stick is certainly ahead of the glove at present, and with the lack of right-handed power in the game—especially with the Mariners of late—he'll be a sight for sore eyes in the middle of the lineup.

2. Alex Jackson RF

Born: 12/25/95 **Age:** 19 **Bats:** R **Throws:** R **Height:** 6'2" **Weight:** 215

MLB ETA	Hit	Power	Run	Glove	Arm		OFP	Realistic
2018	55	65	–	–	60		65 OCC ALL STAR/1ST DIV	50 ML REGULAR

YEAR	TEAM	LVL	AGE	PA	R	2B	3B	HR	RBI	BB	SO	SB	CS	AVG/OBP/SLG	TAv	BABIP	BRR	FRAA	WARP
2014	MRN	Rk	18	94	11	6	2	2	16	9	24	0	1	.280/.344/.476	.224	.362	-0.3	RF(1): -0.0	-0.1
2015	SEA	MLB	19	250	16	7	0	2	19	11	80	1	0	.181/.220/.243	.189	.259	-0.4	RF -0	-1.5
2016	SEA	MLB	20	250	22	6	0	4	20	13	71	1	0	.185/.229/.266	.190	.242	-0.5	RF 0	-3.2

Breakout: 0% **Improve:** 0% **Collapse:** 0% **Attrition:** 0% **MLB:** 0% **Upside:** 7 *Comparables: Cedric Hunter, Matt Davidson, Caleb Gindl*

#68
BP Top
101
Prospects

Drafted/Acquired: 6th overall, 2014 draft, Rancho Bernardo HS (San Diego, CA)

Previous Ranking: NR

What Happened in 2014: Jackson got a small taste of professional ball and put up nice numbers in the fastball-heavy Arizona League.

Strengths: Muscular build; strong base at the plate; ability to drive the ball pull side; excellent bat speed; uses the middle of the field; produces backspin; plus-plus raw; advanced feel for barrel; has plenty of reps against high-level amateur competition; athletic for size; plus arm strength with carry.

Weaknesses: Can struggle with horizontal spin; could put on bad weight; needs to improve reading ball off the bat in right field; needs to clean up outfield throwing motion and improve arm accuracy; swing can get leveraged; has struggled against plus-plus velo; profile is based on hit-tool manifestation.

Risk Factor/Injury History: High; hasn't played full-season ball.

Bret Sayre's Fantasy Take: If you're looking for fantasy upside in the non-speed division, Jackson may have the highest potential of anyone in the 2014 draft class. However, the long lead time and the risk drop them just outside the top 50 dynasty prospects overall. He should go in the top half of the first round in dynasty drafts, even with the international signees mixed in, as a potential 30-homer outfielder with a hit tool.

The Year Ahead: The converted catcher is primed for reps in full-season ball. There's the chance that he starts in extended spring training, but he could accumulate 400-plus plate appearances in Low-A Clinton during the 2015 campaign. Jackson drew rave reviews as the most polished high school hitter of last year's draft class, although some evaluators are split on his ultimate ceiling as an outfielder. There have been some whisperings of work-ethic concerns, stemming from his position switch from behind the plate. The college-heavy Midwest League, with its pitcher-friendly environment and cold weather, will be a nice test for the teenage power hitter's development. There is no question that Jackson possesses the innate bat-to-ball ability and strength to drive a baseball over the fence to be a consistent force in the middle of a big league lineup.

---

3. Ketel Marte   2B/SS

Born: 10/12/93   **Age:** 21   **Bats:** B   **Throws:** R   **Height:** 6'1"   **Weight:** 180

MLB ETA	Hit	Power	Run	Glove	Arm	OFP	Realistic
Late 2015	55	–	60	60	–	55 >AVG REGULAR	50 <AVG STARTER/UTILITY

YEAR	TEAM	LVL	AGE	PA	R	2B	3B	HR	RBI	BB	SO	SB	CS	AVG/OBP/SLG	TAv	BABIP	BRR	FRAA	WARP
2014	TAC	AAA	20	90	16	5	0	2	9	8	13	6	0	.312/.367/.450	.293	.343	1.2	SS(19): 0.8	1.2
2014	WTN	AA	20	472	63	27	6	2	46	19	65	23	10	.302/.329/.404	.269	.346	0.2	SS(102): -2.3, 2B(7): 1.4	2.2
2015	SEA	MLB	21	250	24	9	1	1	15	4	49	8	3	.243/.255/.304	.223	.292	0.6	SS 1, 2B 1	0.3
2016	SEA	MLB	22	250	23	10	2	2	21	8	45	9	3	.266/.290/.347	.235	.313	1.0	SS 0, 2B 1	0.5

Breakout: 0%   Improve: 0%   Collapse: 0%   Attrition: 0%   MLB: 0%   Upside: 5   *Comparables: Joaquin Arias, Alcides Escobar, Carlos Triunfel*

Drafted/Acquired: International Free Agent, 2010, Dominican Republic

Previous Ranking: On the Rise

What Happened in 2014: After a relatively pedestrian 2013 season in the Midwest and Cal Leagues, Marte took a step forward in development in the high minors. Some of his tools are starting to realize—slowly closing the gap between present and future.

Strengths: Sharp line-drive hitter; plenty of topspin on hard-hit balls; recognizes offerings out of the hand; natural bat-to-ball skills; major-league-quality bat speed; fastball hitter; sprays balls all over the field; natural instincts; soft hands; steady around the bag; accelerates quickly out of the box; stretches singles into doubles; base-stealing instincts.

Weaknesses: Aggressive nature at the plate; limited over-the-fence power; likely will have to move to second base due to weak arm; lack of carry on throws can make immature plays; needs to get stronger; must develop approach from right side of the plate.

Risk Factor/Injury History: Medium; has had upper-minors success.

Bret Sayre's Fantasy Take: It may be a slight problem when your best position is the one at which Robinson Cano is signed for a billion years for a trillion dollars, but if Marte can hit, he should find a place in the lineup. At peak, Marte could be a .280 hitter capable of stealing 25 bases annually—but that type of player is more valuable as a middle infielder.

The Year Ahead: Marte's game started to come together in 2014, and he rewarded the Mariners for an aggressive assignment to Double-A. He mastered the level and got a taste of Triple-A, where he'll start in 2015. Evaluators were extremely impressed with Marte's feel for the barrel in addition to his game speed and quickness. There's no reason to push the Dominican middle infielder off shortstop until absolutely necessary, especially with Robinson Cano manning the keystone in Seattle. However, scouts feel that the arm will ultimately deter him from playing shortstop on an everyday basis, and he'll be a defensive weapon at second base. Marte will be waiting in the wings this season, so if he improves as much as he did during the 2014 campaign, Seattle will have a nice problem on their hands. At minimum, he figures to get a September call-up, as he's already on the 40-man roster.

4. Gabriel Guerrero   RF

Born: 12/11/93   **Age:** 21   **Bats:** R   **Throws:** R   **Height:** 6'3"   **Weight:** 190

MLB ETA	Hit	Power	Run	Glove	Arm	OFP	Realistic
2017	–	60	50	50	65	60 1ST DIV REGULAR	45 PWR PLATOON BAT

YEAR	TEAM	LVL	AGE	PA	R	2B	3B	HR	RBI	BB	SO	SB	CS	AVG/OBP/SLG	TAv	BABIP	BRR	FRAA	WARP
2014	HDS	A+	20	580	97	28	2	18	96	34	131	18	6	.307/.347/.467	.269	.373	3.6	RF(94): 1.7, CF(9): -1.4	1.6
2015	SEA	MLB	21	250	19	8	1	3	21	6	74	3	1	.215/.232/.295	.211	.290	-0.1	RF 1, CF -0	-0.7
2016	SEA	MLB	22	250	23	8	1	4	22	7	71	3	1	.235/.257/.322	.217	.313	0.1	RF 1, CF 0	-1.2

Breakout: 0%   Improve: 0%   Collapse: 0%   Attrition: 0%   MLB: 0%   Upside: 30   *Comparables: Avisail Garcia, Francisco Peguero, Yorman Rodriguez*

Drafted/Acquired: International Free Agent, 2011, Dominican Republic

Previous Ranking: #10 (Org)

What Happened in 2014: Guerrero put up solid numbers in the hitter-friendly Cal League and is primed for a Double-A challenge.

Strengths: Long limbs; the highest of butts, possibility of adding more muscle as he fills out; wiry strong; smooth actions; loose hands/wrists; big-time bat speed; aesthetically pleasing at the plate; excellent hand-eye; baseball background/bloodlines; impressive arm strength that will be a weapon in either corner; can drive baseballs a mile in batting practice.

Weaknesses: BP power doesn't always show up in games; dead-red hitter; struggles against off-speed offerings; limited plan of attack at the plate; gets behind in counts; expands the zone; approach could prevent raw power from playing at big-league level; thinks he can drive everything; risk to flame out in high minors.

Risk Factor/Injury History: High; approach concerns, no high-minors success.

Bret Sayre's Fantasy Take: There's plenty of risk here, but Guerrero also has plenty of what fantasy owners desire most: power. The odds of his turning into a 25-plus-homer bat at the major-league level are small, and that's not even including the chance of his turning into one that hits .220. He has more name/stat value than actual value at this point.

The Year Ahead: Guerrero took advantage of favorable Cal League conditions and put up impressive numbers for someone two-plus years below the median league age. However, Double-A will be a monstrous challenge for the 21-year-old outfielder. Not only will the hitting conditions worsen, but the High-A to Double-A talent jump is the second largest behind the major-league leap. Guerrero may hit a snag in development during this time, and it will be interesting to see how he reacts to failure. Pitchers will look to exploit his aggressive approach, and it may take some time to adjust, but when your uncle is Vladimir Guerrero and you have one of the best bodies in the minor leagues coupled with impact power potential, it's easy to imagine that Gabby will have plenty of chances to achieve major-league success

5. Edwin Diaz   RHP

Born: 3/22/94   **Age:** 21   **Bats:** R   **Throws:** R   **Height:** 6'2"   **Weight:** 178

MLB ETA	CT	FB	CH	CB	SL	OFP	Realistic
2017	–	65	–	–	60	55 NO. 3/4 STARTER	50 NO. 4/5/LATE INN RP

YEAR	TEAM	LVL	AGE	W	L	SV	G	GS	IP	H	HR	BB	K	BB9	SO9	GB%	BABIP	WHIP	ERA	FIP	FRA	WARP
2014	CLN	A	20	6	8	0	24	24	116.3	96	5	42	111	3.2	8.6	44%	.289	1.19	3.33	3.48	4.21	1.3
2015	SEA	MLB	21	5	6	0	17	17	85.0	89	9	42	59	4.4	6.2	43%	.297	1.54	4.88	5.26	5.30	-0.7
2016	SEA	MLB	22	8	9	0	28	28	174.3	167	17	82	142	4.2	7.3	43%	.291	1.43	4.31	4.56	4.69	-0.7

Breakout: 0%   Improve: 0%   Collapse: 0%   Attrition: 0%   MLB: 0%   Upside: 9   *Comparables: Jordan Walden, Jeremy Hellickson, Jose A. Ramirez*

Drafted/Acquired: 3rd round, 2012 draft, Caguas Military Academy (Caguas, PR)

Previous Ranking: #5 (Org)

What Happened in 2014: Diaz enjoyed success in his first taste of full-season ball—making 24 starts and enjoying a 3.34 ERA over 116 innings.

Strengths: Easy arm action with extension; long fingers for pronation; loose wrist; fastball explodes at 91-95 mph, darting in on right-handed hitters; boring arm-side run; snaps 80-84 mph slider with two-plane movement—pitch has depth and bat-missing ability; some room to fill out and increase fastball velo; improving feel for changeup.

Weaknesses: Big gap between present changeup and future, feel for pitch is limited at present; command comes and goes; needs to add strength; must spot fastballs to all four quadrants; has nagging injuries; inconsistent mechanical profile with inconsistent release point and crossfire.

Risk Factor/Injury History: High; low-minors arm.

Bret Sayre's Fantasy Take: Oh hey, look, it's a pitcher in the Mariners' system. That's good for fantasy value. The downside is glaringly obvious with Diaz, as he has a long way to go to get a third pitch—and frankly, even with Safeco at his back, the upside isn't much more than an SP4. He's a worthy own if your league rosters 200 prospects.

The Year Ahead: Diaz will be tasked with a Cal League assignment—a pitcher's nightmare. If he continues to keep the ball down and work off the fastball, he may not be as negatively impacted as other hurlers. The 21-year-old still offers a sizeable risk profile, as the changeup still lags firmly behind the other two offerings. There are recent examples of a two-pitch starter sustaining major-league success; however, the odds are stacked against the former third rounder without the advent of the third pitch. The ingredients are apparent, and some evaluators preferred Diaz to virtually any arm in the Midwest League last season. But the gap between present and future utility remains, and he'll have to take another step forward with command and the progression of the changeup in 2015.

6. Tyler Marlette C

Born: 1/23/93 **Age:** 22 **Bats:** R **Throws:** R **Height:** 5'11" **Weight:** 195

MLB ETA	Hit	Power	Run	Glove	Arm	OFP	Realistic
Late 2016	50	55	–	–	60	55 >AVG ML PLAYER	45 BAT-1ST BACKUP C

YEAR	TEAM	LVL	AGE	PA	R	2B	3B	HR	RBI	BB	SO	SB	CS	AVG/OBP/SLG	TAv	BABIP	BRR	FRAA	WARP
2014	WTN	AA	21	36	3	2	0	2	2	4	10	0	1	.250/.333/.500	.294	.300	-0.4	C(9): -0.1	0.2
2014	HDS	A+	21	339	51	23	0	15	49	24	61	9	2	.301/.351/.519	.292	.332	0.0	C(70): 0.3, C(7): 0.3	2.8
2015	SEA	MLB	22	250	23	10	0	5	25	12	67	3	1	.224/.261/.338	.238	.284	-0.2	C 0	0.4
2016	SEA	MLB	23	250	27	10	0	6	26	16	63	3	1	.228/.280/.356	.239	.283	-0.2	C 0	0.5

Breakout: 0%   Improve: 0%   Collapse: 0%   Attrition: 0%   MLB: 0%   Upside: 51   *Comparables: Austin Romine, Wilson Ramos, Max Stassi*

Drafted/Acquired: 5th round, 2011 draft, Hagerty HS (Oviedo, FL)

Previous Ranking: #9 (Org)

What Happened in 2014: The backstop had a strong offensive season in the Cal League and finished with a taste of high-minors ball for the last couple weeks of the season.

Strengths: Highly competitive player; good makeup; solid-average power potential; whips bat through zone; improving receiving skills; creates backspin; thick legs, prototypical catcher build.

Weaknesses: Not a finished product defensively; must improve receiving/framing skills; aggressive at the plate; needs to make more regular hard contact; gap between present and future hit tool; swing can get long; sells out for power.

Risk Factor/Injury History: High; hit tool/defensive risk.

Bret Sayre's Fantasy Take: Marlette was one of the last cuts from the dynasty catcher list, mostly because the odds of his sticking behind the plate are lower than I want to see in fantasy catching prospects. The bat has enough to play in deeper leagues even if he has to move off the position, but he'll have Safeco working against him. Expecting .260 with 15-18 homers is reasonable at peak.

The Year Ahead: Marlette has improved his stock in each of the last two years, as his raw tools have started to manifest into a potential major-league backstop. A converted infielder by trade, the former fifth-round pick has made strides picking up the intricacies of the catcher position. Catchers typically take more time to develop defensively, and learning a very difficult defensive position can often slow the development of the bat. Impressively enough for Marlette, he has mastered the low minors with the stick and will begin the challenge of an everyday assignment at Double-A Jackson in 2015. The high minors will present somewhat of a different obstacle, as pitchers will look to take advantage of his aggressive approach, while he'll experience the physical demands that come with 100-plus games behind the plate. Even if Marlette stumbles in development this season he's ahead of most catchers his age, giving him plenty of time to recoup his prospect stock.

7. Luiz Gohara LHP

Born: 7/31/96 **Age:** 18 **Bats:** L **Throws:** L **Height:** 6'3" **Weight:** 210

MLB ETA	CT	FB	CH	CB	SL	OFP	Realistic
2019	–	60	60	55	–	60 NO. 3 STARTER	50 NO. 4/5 STARTER

YEAR	TEAM	LVL	AGE	W	L	SV	G	GS	IP	H	HR	BB	K	BB9	SO9	GB%	BABIP	WHIP	ERA	FIP	FRA	WARP
2014	EVE	A-	17	0	6	0	11	11	37.3	46	6	24	37	5.8	8.9	60%	.348	1.88	8.20	6.25	6.75	-0.1
2014	MRN	Rk	17	1	1	0	2	2	12.7	11	0	2	16	1.4	11.4	67%	.333	1.03	2.13	1.98	3.05	0.4
2015	SEA	MLB	18	2	4	0	10	10	39.7	45	5	22	22	5.0	5.0	51%	.302	1.69	5.70	6.00	6.19	-0.6
2016	SEA	MLB	19	7	9	0	30	30	189.7	185	19	75	126	3.6	6.0	51%	.280	1.37	4.22	4.61	4.59	-0.6

Breakout: 0%   Improve: 0%   Collapse: 0%   Attrition: 0%   MLB: 0%   Upside: 3   *Comparables: Edwin Escobar, Julio Teheran, Jonathan Pettibone*

Drafted/Acquired: International Free Agent, 2012, Brazil

Previous Ranking: #6 (Org)

What Happened in 2014: Gohara took a step backward in development, posting forgettable numbers in the Northwest League.

Strengths: Loose arm; fastball gets into the mid-90s; natural arm-side wiggle; can generate downward plane; life down in the zone; feel for changeup, rolls off his fingers; ability to snap off nice curve or slider, but will have to pick one moving forward.

Weaknesses: Mechanical inconsistencies; hardly any repetition against competition that can handle his raw stuff; body could get out of control; command needs to improve mightily; already a very large man at 18; huge gap between present and future; extremely raw.

Risk Factor/Injury History: Extreme; no full-season ball experience.

Bret Sayre's Fantasy Take: The southpaw had a rough statistical season, but it was a tough assignment. Still, with many owners possibly cutting him to make room for the next big thing, Gohara remains worth tracking in deeper dynasty leagues even though it will take a while for him to climb the developmental ladder.

The Year Ahead: Gohara hails from Brazil and received $880,000, the largest amateur bonus of all time for a player from that country. He doesn't have the polish and requisite experience that many teenagers from other Latin American countries like the Dominican and Venezuela have. The left-hander is more of a project than originally anticipated, especially from a body standpoint; in fact, keeping his build under control may be his biggest hurdle. At this point in time, Gohara is an extremely raw teenage arm that touches 96—not a bad foundation for a big-league starter. However, the Brazilian comes with plenty of inherent risk, and will likely go through crests and troughs in development before he comes to fruition.

8. Victor Sanchez RHP

Born: 1/30/95 **Age:** 20 **Bats:** R **Throws:** R **Height:** 6'0" **Weight:** 255

MLB ETA	CT	FB	CH	CB	SL	OFP	Realistic
2016	–	50	60	55	55	55 NO. 3/4 STARTER	50 BACK-END STARTER

YEAR	TEAM	LVL	AGE	W	L	SV	G	GS	IP	H	HR	BB	K	BB9	SO9	GB%	BABIP	WHIP	ERA	FIP	FRA	WARP
2014	WTN	AA	19	7	6	0	23	23	124.7	128	17	34	97	2.5	7.0	39%	.294	1.30	4.19	4.39	5.21	0.0
2015	SEA	MLB	20	6	7	0	19	19	104.3	111	13	31	65	2.7	5.6	41%	.290	1.36	4.43	5.01	4.81	-0.3
2016	SEA	MLB	21	10	10	0	31	31	194.3	203	24	41	140	1.9	6.5	41%	.295	1.25	4.01	4.28	4.36	-0.1

Breakout: 0%   Improve: 0%   Collapse: 0%   Attrition: 0%   MLB: 0%   Upside: 9   *Comparables: Casey Kelly, Jacob Turner, Ian Krol*

Drafted/Acquired: International Free Agent, 2011, Venezuela

Previous Ranking: #4 (Org)

What Happened in 2014: Sanchez skipped the Cal League and pitched at Double-A as a 19-year-old, having modest success and solid ratios.

Strengths: Plus fastball command potential; throws both two- and four-seam fastball for strikes; arm-side run on fastball; works 88-93, often adding and subtracting; can manipulate within the zone; slider is just a harder version of curveball, slurvy-type pitch that can miss barrels; excellent feel and fade on change; plus feel for a teenager; short, quick, repeatable arm swing and delivery; advanced sequencing; stays within himself; has plan of attack; nice posture at release.

Weaknesses: Weight is an obvious concern; rotund build; not much room for error with offerings; doesn't have live arsenal; fastball can flatten when up; needs to continue to hold velocity late into games; can sometimes lose angle due to height; work ethic often questioned.

Risk Factor/Injury History: Medium; bad body, advanced pitchability.

Bret Sayre's Fantasy Take: Sanchez has a profile built for Safeco, as he won't be the type to rack up large strikeout numbers at the major-league level and a big park will suppress what will likely be home-run tendencies. He's a better roster spot in deep leagues at this point, but he's also a name for AL-only owners to remember.

The Year Ahead: Sanchez will likely see plenty of time in the hitter-friendly PCL, where his fly-ball tendencies may adversely affect his numbers and he'll look to improve on modest success from 2014, when he took a step forward with control and command. While he doesn't have any offerings that project to baffle major-league hitters, he also doesn't have many weaknesses either. An adept comparison would be Livan Hernandez—from both a physical standpoint and a results-oriented standpoint. He projects to be a pitcher who can provide a steady but unassuming performance every fifth day. Even though Sanchez is often downgraded for his body, his delivery is simple and repeatable, with a short arm swing that allows him to command the fastball with regularity. While it's not the prototypical major-league starter kit, Sanchez has all the ingredients to become a successful big-league arm.

9. Carson Smith   RHP

Born: 10/19/89   **Age:** 25   **Bats:** R   **Throws:** R   **Height:** 6'6"   **Weight:** 215

MLB ETA	CT	FB	CH	CB	SL	OFP	Realistic
Debuted in 2014	–	65	–	–	60	55 LATE-INN RP	50 7TH INN RP

YEAR	TEAM	LVL	AGE	W	L	SV	G	GS	IP	H	HR	BB	K	BB9	SO9	GB%	BABIP	WHIP	ERA	FIP	FRA	WARP
2014	SEA	MLB	24	1	0	0	9	0	8.3	2	0	3	10	3.2	10.8	81%	.125	0.60	0.00	1.84	1.86	0.2
2014	TAC	AAA	24	1	3	10	39	0	43.0	44	1	13	45	2.7	9.4	70%	.352	1.33	2.93	2.89	3.49	0.9
2015	SEA	MLB	25	2	1	0	38	0	43.7	37	3	15	47	3.1	9.7	59%	.298	1.20	2.88	3.42	3.13	0.7
2016	SEA	MLB	26	4	2	1	67	0	70.7	59	5	22	77	2.8	9.8	59%	.295	1.14	2.71	3.13	2.95	1.7

Breakout: 20%   **Improve:** 23%   **Collapse:** 16%   **Attrition:** 35%   **MLB:** 48%   **Upside:** 26   *Comparables: Kevin Quackenbush, C.C. Lee, Louis Coleman*

Drafted/Acquired: 8th round, 2011 draft, Texas State University (San Marcos, TX)

Previous Ranking: Factor on the Farm

What Happened in 2014: Smith started slowly, while eventually adding velocity and crispness as the season wore on. He achieved the major-league level and projects to begin this season in the Mariners bullpen.

Strengths: Fastball has life, thrown in the 94-97 mph range; low three-quarters delivery is very difficult for right-handed hitters to pick up; fastball bores in on same-side hitters; very difficult to square; can manipulate speed on slider from 82-88 mph; hard, two-plane break; mixes in a changeup that fades away from lefties for different look.

Weaknesses: Often starts season slowly, velocity was 90-93 in first two months; can get on side of slider for frisbee-like action; propensity to lose fastball command; lefties can pick him up from current arm angle.

Risk Factor/Injury History: Low; already achieved major-league level.

Bret Sayre's Fantasy Take: Relief profiles and fantasy leagues make poor bedfellows. Smith could find himself racking up holds as soon as this season, but saves are unlikely to be in his near future.

The Year Ahead: A safe bet to play a large role in the Mariners 2015 bullpen, Smith has nothing left to prove at the minor-league level. He's simply too overpowering at this point, and it's time to get a taste of The Show. Smith is 6-foot-6 with long limbs, and his ball can jump on opposing hitters. If he can continue to improve his command while manipulating the fastball around the zone, he'll wreak havoc on righties going forward. His slider will cause problems for same-side hitters, and at the very least, he'll be asked to attack opponent's best right-handed options in the late innings. Smith sports mostly a two-pitch arsenal—his fastball and slider comprise 90 percent of his offerings, with his changeup rounding out the remaining 10 percent according to Brooks Baseball. The righty looks like a solid bet to strike out better than a batter an inning in his prime and could boast impressive ratios out of the bullpen.

10. Austin Wilson   OF

Born: 2/7/92   **Age:** 23   **Bats:** R   **Throws:** R   **Height:** 6'4"   **Weight:** 249

MLB ETA	Hit	Power	Run	Glove	Arm	OFP	Realistic
2017	–	65	–	50	60	60 1ST DIV PLAYER	45 PLAT BAT/EXTRA OF

YEAR	TEAM	LVL	AGE	PA	R	2B	3B	HR	RBI	BB	SO	SB	CS	AVG/OBP/SLG	TAv	BABIP	BRR	FRAA	WARP
2014	CLN	A	22	299	38	17	3	12	54	26	65	1	1	.291/.376/.517	.321	.346	1.0	RF(51): 1.2, LF(9): 0.1	2.7
2014	MRN	Rk	22	9	3	1	1	1	1	2	1	1	0	.625/.667/1.375	.661	.800	0.3	RF(2): 0.0	0.4
2015	SEA	MLB	23	250	22	9	1	7	27	11	70	0	0	.212/.259/.343	.238	.269	-0.4	RF 0, LF 0	-0.2
2016	SEA	MLB	24	250	27	9	1	7	27	14	72	0	0	.220/.276/.357	.237	.286	-0.5	RF 0, LF 0	-0.1

Breakout: 0%   **Improve:** 0%   **Collapse:** 0%   **Attrition:** 0%   **MLB:** 0%   **Upside:** 25   *Comparables: Roger Kieschnick, Andrew Lambo, J.D. Martinez*

Drafted/Acquired: 2nd round, 2013 draft, Stanford University (Palo Alto, CA)

Previous Ranking: NR

What Happened in 2014: Wilson missed time due to injuries but accumulated 299 plate appearances in a league where he performed as expected, brutalizing pitchers with the type of arsenal that he can handle.

Strengths: Giant human; brute strength; decent athlete for size; plus raw power, swing is geared to loft balls out of the park; hard contact when he connects; pull-side power; plus arm strength, can make all the throws; aptitude for the game.

Weaknesses: Maintaining large body may be difficult going forward; issues with pitch recognition against arm-side pitching; susceptible to spin; converting strength and raw pop to usable game power; high swing-and-miss rate; swing can get long, leveraged; inconsistent swing path via long levers; feasts on mistakes; run will slow as he ages; needs to stay on the field.

Risk: High; big gap between present and future hit-tool utility.

Bret Sayre's Fantasy Take: If it feels like there's a lot of power in this system that may or may not ever see the major leagues in a meaningful capacity, it's because there is. Wilson has plenty of upside and will likely boost his stock in the Cal League this year, but his 30-homer potential is legitimate—and could make for a good value stock at this point.

The Year Ahead: When Wilson was on the field, he put up impressive statistics in a league not conducive to offense. However, he was only able to accrue about 300 plate appearances, so at this point, it's getting late early for the former second rounder. Already entering his age-23 season without having played above Low-A, the outfielder is going to have to make adjustments, and in a hurry, to get to the major-league level while he is still in his physical prime. Unfortunately for prospect evaluators and Wilson, short of falling on his face, his Cal League stop does nothing to make his future less murky. If the prospect goes to the hitting paradise and succeeds, it's expected, but if he performs just slightly above league average, he won't receive credit. Essentially, a fly-ball-oriented college power hitter is dropped in a no-win situation. As it has for many other right-handed corner power-hitting prospects before him, it all hinges on the hit tool and the ability to make adjustments against high-level arms, especially arm side.

Prospects on the Rise

1. OF Tyler O'Neill: O'Neill posted a superb .466 slugging percentage in the pitcher-friendly Midwest League, although he did whiff 32 percent of the time. A very strong player with thick forearms and chest, the outfielder's power comes from both bat speed and leverage. The ball jumps off his bat, especially to the pull side. An aggressive competitor, he'll have to let the game come to him a bit more and not become frustrated with failure. O'Neill missed a chunk of 2014 due to a self-inflicted injury—punching a wall—and needless to say, the wall won. His hit tool will act as the gatekeeper between a career as a regular and up-and-down bat. The Canadian-born outfielder plays with a balls-to-the-wall mentality on every play. Sometimes that can be detrimental to his development, though, as evidenced by his hand injury. He'll need to cut down on the swing-and-miss going forward, and look for better pitches to drive to the gaps. A taste of the Cal League may be a hindrance to his development if he's not careful, as the strong corner outfielder will likely lift 25-plus home runs in the light air. Double-A will be the ultimate test for O'Neill, as it is for many prospects, but that won't come until 2016.

2. 3B Greifer Andrade: On name tool alone, this is a plus-plus prospect. I know this may shock you, but he'd be the first Greifer to ever play in the major leagues. In fact, he may be the only Greifer to ever have Greifered.

FROM THE FIELD

Gabriel Guerrero

Team: Seattle Mariners

Evaluator: Chris Rodriguez

Dates seen: April 17 and 18, and May 6 and 22, 2014

Affiliate: High Desert Mavericks (High-A, Mariners)

Physical/health: Height and weight are accurate; good athlete; high waist; tree-trunk legs; body resembles his uncle Vlad's; strength throughout; physically mature at 20; could see him gaining some bad weight in a couple years.

MLB ETA	Risk factor	OFP	Realistic role
2017	High	60	50; second-division right fielder

Tool	Future grade	Report
Hit	55	Closed stance; very loose hands/arms; bat speed is plus; hand-eye coordination is very good; can put the barrel on the ball in any quadrant in the strike zone and even outside the zone; has a knack for hard contact; enjoys fastballs; pitch recognition and approach are getting better; chases often still; doesn't like to keep the bat on his shoulder; plus bat-to-ball skills, strength, and a better feel for hitting (which will come with time) should allow him to hit around .275-.285 at the highest level.
Power	55	Raw power is above-average; doesn't display it in BP often, but he's capable of hitting tape measure blasts; creates leverage and backspin; slight uppercut; mostly line-drive hitter at the moment; plus strength; back leg can slip out of the box (lunging) while he swings which can sap some power; don't see a ton of homers like his uncle, but mid-20s in home runs isn't out of the question.
Baserunning/speed	50	Clocked 4.25 to first; moves well for his size on the bases and in the field; good baserunner; 14 for 16 in steal attempts; can go first to third; will slow a step in a few years, but speed can be a factor.
Glove	50	Shows good range in right field; athleticism is clear; routes can be a bit of a journey, but he can make the adjustment; can boot a ball on the ground at times; don't think it would work in center field because he'll only slow down with age; corner guy only.
Arm	60	Arm is a weapon; throws are on a line and accurate with good carry; gets behind the ball before a throw to a base.

Overall: Guerrero has what you look for in an corner-outfield prospect: a large body with plus raw power and an above-average arm, especially one with a lineage as rich as his. He's impressed in my couple of looks this season, hitting the ball all over the field and on a line. He tends to expand the zone, and because of that still has a high risk tied to his name. The approach is getting better from previous reports, though, which is promising. The next test is Double-A, which will probably be late this season and all of next. If he can continue to refine his plate discipline during that time, a first-division bat will start to look a little clearer on the horizon. I like his chances.

While names are important, Andrade's on-the-field tools are the second most intriguing thing about him. Signed for just over $1 million in the 2013 class, the barely-18-year-old Venezuelan has innate bat-to-ball ability and solid-average regular potential—likely at third base, despite his time spent at short in Venezuelan Summer League last season. A converted outfielder, he projects to hit enough to warrant a gig at the hot corner, and his line-drive swing coupled with gap power could move him into the top 10 in 2015.

3. LHP Ryan Yarbrough: Baseball seems to run in the Yarbrough family, as Ryan's brother Alex is a second-base prospect in the Angels organization. Selected in the fourth round of the 2014 draft, the 6-foot-5 left-hander was a senior sign out of Old Dominion after the Mariners went over slot with their first two picks. He proceeded to put up inappropriate numbers in short-season ball, delivering 58 strikeouts and just five walks over 42 2/3 innings of work. Inexperienced hitters were overmatched by his deceptive 87-92 mph fastball and potential big-league-quality breaking ball. The advent of a changeup will help round out the arsenal, but at the very least, Yarbrough could be an interesting left-handed relief option down the line.

Factors on the Farm

Prospects likely to contribute at the major-league level in 2015

1. C John Hicks: Though the Mariners look to be relatively set at catcher this season, it's never a bad thing to have a capable backstop waiting in the wings. Hicks's bat has steadily improved since he was selected in 2011, but the calling card is solid-average defense behind the plate. While he only has fringy arm strength, a quick transfer and quick feet keep his pop times below 2.0 seconds consistently. His receiving and blocking skills grade out as potential major-league average—enough to keep a job in the big leagues for a few years. Backup catchers are never sexy but can be valuable pieces to an organization, and Hicks may play that role with Seattle in short order.

2. 1B/OF Patrick Kivlehan: A former football player at Rutgers, Kivlehan decided to try his hand at professional baseball and has made himself into a potential major-league player. While he doesn't have much natural feel for the game, that's not unexpected, as he's only focused solely on baseball for the last three years. An extremely strong kid with plus raw power, Kivlehan has an aggressive approach and stiff actions, preventing him from making regular hard contact. His swing is flat, leading him to only hit balls up in the zone with any authority. He primarily feasts on mistakes at this time, typically consisting of thigh-high fastballs, cement-mixing sliders, and hanging changeups. The arm strength is impressive, but he's unable to provide utility, as it's often inaccurate. Kivlehan seems primed for a bench corner-outfield/first-base role, and he may provide some pop along the way.

3. OF Leon Landry: Small sample size, but Seattle sure does love its converted football players, huh? What with Austin Wilson built like one, Tyler O'Neill acting like one, plus Kivlehan and Landry, we're only seven guys away from a competitive squad. Landry is a superb athlete, but is just starting to refine his quick-twitch nature into his baseball game. He has more than enough speed and quickness to play center field, and is beginning to take better routes to the ball, especially going back over his head. Coming in on balls is not a problem at this time, as he's able to instinctually react. A left-handed hitter, Landry has a contact-oriented approach at the plate, and he looks to spray the ball and leg out hits. His baserunning is a work in progress, but he routinely clocks 4.0-second times to first, putting pressure on the opposing defense. While the three-sport prep star will never hit enough to be a regular, he may contribute as an extra outfielder who can provide speed and solid-average center-field defense.

ST. LOUIS CARDINALS

1. Stephen Piscotty   RF

Born: 1/14/91   **Age:** 24   **Bats:** R   **Throws:** R   **Height:** 6'3"   **Weight:** 210

MLB ETA	Hit	Power	Run	Glove	Arm	OFP	Realistic
2015	65	50	–	50	65	60 1ST DIVISION PLAYER	55 >AVG REGULAR

YEAR	TEAM	LVL	AGE	PA	R	2B	3B	HR	RBI	BB	SO	SB	CS	AVG/OBP/SLG	TAv	BABIP	BRR	FRAA	WARP
2014	MEM	AAA	23	556	70	32	0	9	69	43	61	11	5	.288/.355/.406	.276	.312	-1.0	RF(113): 7.0, LF(8): 0.3	3.7
2015	SLN	MLB	24	250	24	13	0	4	25	16	36	4	2	.256/.312/.366	.258	.285	-0.3	RF 1, 3B -0	0.2
2016	SLN	MLB	25	250	27	12	0	4	23	17	40	4	2	.249/.313/.354	.253	.285	-0.2	RF 1, 3B 0	1.2

Breakout: 5%   Improve: 19%   Collapse: 12%   Attrition: 30%   MLB: 44%   Upside: 17   *Comparables: Alex Romero, Caleb Gindl, Adrian Cardenas*

Drafted/Acquired: 1st round, 2012 draft, Stanford University (Palo Alto, CA)

Previous Ranking: #3 (Org), #66 (Top 101)

What Happened in 2014: The former first rounder continued his steady rise through the system, putting together a solid showing in the PCL while displaying the advanced feel for contact that has thus far defined his prospect profile.

Strengths: Advanced hit tool, ability to barrel; good balance; high level of comfort in box; high-contact bat capable of working line to line; patient approach, not afraid to work deep into counts; will flash loft and pop, particularly against oppo arms; improved actions in outfield; athleticism, work ethic, and progress thus far allows to project glove to average or tick above; easy right-field arm; glowing reports on effort put in and progress made on defensive front.

Weaknesses: Over-the-fence pop yet to manifest with regularity; power profile could be doubles dependent with added import to hit tool/on-base; lacks impact bat speed; continued ability to barrel balls against top-tier arms will hinge on approach and ability to make adjustments; susceptible to lapses in the field; limited foot speed will make further refinement of reads and routes in the field a necessity.

Risk Factor/Injury History: Low; success through all minor-league levels; advanced feel and approach.

Bret Sayre's Fantasy Take: The Cardinals seem to have a never-ending supply of prospects who hit first and do everything else second, and Piscotty fits right in. He's a stronger play in points and OBP leagues than standard 5x5 formats, due to the potential for strong plate discipline and extra-base potential, but he is ready to contribute in 2015 across most leagues and could hit .290 with 15 homers in time.

The Year Ahead: Regular hard contact is a fixture in Piscotty's game, though his ability to rack up extra bases, be it by home run or double, will determine whether he reaches his upside as a true first-division right fielder. There is no question the former Stanford Cardinal has the raw strength to drive the ball, and his power will have to be strength and leverage derived since the bat speed isn't special. That places an increased level of importance on Piscotty's ability to continue to refine his approach and learn which situations allow for some added length and leverage in the swing. Based on his feel for the craft and the professional manner in which he already puts together at-bats, it would not be a surprise to see him make the requisite adjustments in short order as he finishes baking in St. Louis. The addition of Jason Heyward fills the void in right field left by the tragic loss of Oscar Taveras. Prior to Heyward's arrival, Piscotty had progressed enough on defense to put himself into the discussion for the Opening Day gig in right field, and he has the chops to take hold of the job if the former Brave departs via free agency after 2015

> **#32**
> BP Top 101 Prospects

2. Marco Gonzales   LHP

Born: 2/16/92   **Age:** 23   **Bats:** L   **Throws:** L   **Height:** 6'1"   **Weight:** 195

MLB ETA	CT	FB	CH	CB	SL	OFP	Realistic
2015	-	55	75	50	-	60 NO. 3 STARTER	50 NO. 4 STARTER

YEAR	TEAM	LVL	AGE	W	L	SV	G	GS	IP	H	HR	BB	K	BB9	SO9	GB%	BABIP	WHIP	ERA	FIP	FRA	WARP
2014	SLN	MLB	22	4	2	0	10	5	34.7	32	4	21	31	5.5	8.0	39%	.283	1.53	4.15	4.72	4.57	0.4
2014	MEM	AAA	22	4	1	0	8	8	45.7	43	7	9	39	1.8	7.7	43%	.279	1.14	3.35	4.77	5.01	0.5
2014	SFD	AA	22	3	2	0	7	7	38.7	33	2	10	46	2.3	10.7	45%	.304	1.11	2.33	2.19	3.28	1.0
2014	PMB	A+	22	2	2	0	6	6	37.7	34	1	8	32	1.9	7.6	53%	.303	1.12	1.43	2.67	3.34	0.6
2015	SLN	MLB	23	7	7	0	22	22	114.0	105	11	40	95	3.2	7.5	43%	.304	1.27	3.95	4.11	4.29	0.7
2016	SLN	MLB	24	9	9	0	29	29	177.3	158	16	57	157	2.9	8.0	43%	.303	1.22	3.70	3.60	4.02	1.4

Breakout: 23%   Improve: 58%   Collapse: 7%   Attrition: 26%   MLB: 85%   Upside: 55   *Comparables: Chris Tillman, Randall Delgado, Alex White*

Drafted/Acquired: 1st round, 2013 draft, Gonzaga University (Spokane, WA)

Previous Ranking: #5 (Org), Just Missed The Cut (101)

What Happened in 2014: It took Gonzales just 21 starts to breeze through three minor-league levels before making his major-league debut in St. Louis at the ripe old age of 22.

Strengths: Swing-and-miss changeup with silly drop and arm-slot/arm-speed deception; "any count" pitch that elevates effectiveness of overall arsenal; average fastball velocity plays up due to late action and ability to spot; comfortable working both sides of the plate and solid feel for sequencing displayed through minors; curveball en route to solid-average status; can mix in a short slider that should miss barrels; even demeanor, stolid presence on bump; repeatable mechanics and feel should allow for plus command profile; plus makeup.

Weaknesses: Struggled with consistent execution during major-league debut; at times predictable use of changeup, particularly against right-handed hitters; fastball velocity leaves slim margin for error; aggregate package places premium on command profile and precision in execution; limited ceiling; not overly physical; lacks putaway breaking ball.

Risk Factor/Injury History: Low

Bret Sayre's Fantasy Take: Development will be less of an issue for Gonzales' short-term fantasy value than the traffic jam that is the Cardinals' rotation. The lefty will likely spend most of 2015 in the bullpen, where he'll likely be just an NL-only option, but were he to make the rotation in 2016 or beyond, he could provide strong ratios (especially WHIP) with a modest contribution in strikeouts.

The Year Ahead: Gonzales had his share of ups and downs during his cup of coffee, but generally impressed both as a starter and out of the 'pen. Despite lacking an impact breaking ball, Gonzales has been able to keep left- and right-handed hitters at bay throughout his short pro career thanks to advanced feel and a prime change piece. Gonzales will have the opportunity to compete for a spot in the St. Louis rotation to start 2015, but with a robust collection of starters set to return next spring, the lefty could be forced to the 'pen or back down to Memphis to begin the season. To firmly establish himself as a reliable option in a major-league rotation, Gonzales will need to find more consistency in his curveball and become less predictable in certain counts and situations. There is enough balance to the arsenal, and enough command in the profile, for evaluators in and out of the organization to continue to peg him as a future rotation mainstay. The consensus view is that the remaining open items left on the developmental front should be addressed over the natural course as he logs major-league reps. The ease with which Gonzales took to relief work at the end of 2014 affords the Cardinals organization the luxury of considering him for a bullpen assignment if there isn't room in the rotation to start the 2015 season, a role in which he could continue to smooth out the edges while providing value to the big club.

---

3. Alexander Reyes RHP

Born: 8/29/94 **Age:** 20 **Bats:** R **Throws:** R **Height:** 6'3" **Weight:** 185

MLB ETA	CT	FB	CH	CB	SL	OFP	Realistic
2017	-	70	55	65	-	70 NO. 2 STARTER	55 NO. 3/4 / LATE INN RP

YEAR	TEAM	LVL	AGE	W	L	SV	G	GS	IP	H	HR	BB	K	BB9	SO9	GB%	BABIP	WHIP	ERA	FIP	FRA	WARP
2014	PEO	A	19	7	7	0	21	21	109.3	82	6	61	137	5.0	11.3	40%	.295	1.31	3.62	3.45	3.84	1.7
2015	SLN	MLB	20	5	6	0	17	17	86.0	81	8	51	75	5.3	7.8	40%	.315	1.54	4.87	4.75	5.30	-0.5
2016	SLN	MLB	21	9	10	0	31	31	194.3	175	17	96	179	4.4	8.3	40%	.312	1.39	4.23	4.03	4.60	0.1

Breakout: 0%   Improve: 0%   Collapse: 0%   Attrition: 0%   MLB: 0%   Upside: 8   *Comparables: Trevor May, Tyler Matzek, Trevor Cahill*

Drafted/Acquired: International Free Agent, 2012, Dominican Republic

Previous Ranking: #4 (Org), #98 (Top 101)

What Happened in 2014: Reyes surprised Midwest League evaluators with erratic stuff and a larger-than-expected trunk when he showed up in Peoria, but ended the season in dominant fashion, holding hitters to a .195 average over his final 11 starts while racking up 11.7 strikeouts per nine over that same span.

Strengths: Power arsenal that could fit comfortably into the front of a big-league rotation; potential double-plus fastball that comfortably works in mid-90s velo band at present; elite arm speed; power curve that often played to plus in second half; improved feel for changeup; easy arm and second-half repeatability allow for fringe-plus to plus command projection.

Weaknesses: Body went backward between 2013 and 2014; needs to embrace full spectrum of development, including conditioning and non-arsenal-related mound work (fielding/controlling running game); erratic first-half performance reinforced delta between present profile and realization of potential; changeup still lags behind other offerings; foundation for good command but needs to prove second-half strides represent true step forward.

Risk Factor/Injury History: High; yet to advance past Low-A ball; early-season struggles add to risk profile.

Bret Sayre's Fantasy Take: Dynasty leaguers are always higher on low-minors arms with sharp risk/reward profiles than they should be, and Reyes is just another example of this. Sure, the ceiling is there for a SP2 with big strikeout totals if things break right, but Reyes still falls into the flier category given his lead time and potential pitfalls.

The Year Ahead: Depending on when you caught Reyes last season you might have seen a future bullpen arm, a future Opening Day starter, and everything in between. The good news is that you could not ask for a more encouraging end to the season than he provided, with the young power arm running off 11 strong starts that blended top-shelf swing-and-miss stuff and drastically improved control, if not command. Had that caliber of performance defined his 2014 there would be a strong case for his being the top prospect profile in the organization. He will be tasked with improved conditioning in the offseason and a continued focus on rounding out all aspects of his game this spring. Next up on the developmental journey is a High-A assignment in 2015, where another step forward could see Reyes establish himself as one of the minors' truly elite arms.

4. Jack Flaherty RHP

Born: 10/15/95 **Age:** 19 **Bats:** R **Throws:** R **Height:** 6'4" **Weight:** 205

MLB ETA	CT	FB	CH	CB	SL	OFP	Realistic
2019	-	60	60	50	60	65 NO. 2/3 STARTER	50 NO. 4 STARTER

YEAR	TEAM	LVL	AGE	W	L	SV	G	GS	IP	H	HR	BB	K	BB9	SO9	GB%	BABIP	WHIP	ERA	FIP	FRA	WARP
2014	CRD	Rk	18	1	1	0	8	6	22.7	18	1	4	28	1.6	11.1	53%	.318	0.97	1.59	2.53	4.63	0.1
2015	SLN	MLB	19	2	3	0	8	8	33.7	37	4	20	19	5.3	5.1	46%	.317	1.70	5.91	5.81	6.42	-0.5
2016	SLN	MLB	20	6	9	0	29	29	179.7	176	17	80	120	4.0	6.0	46%	.301	1.42	4.61	4.51	5.01	-0.7

Breakout: 0%   Improve: 0%   Collapse: 0%   Attrition: 0%   MLB: 0%   Upside: 2   *Comparables: Jenrry Mejia, Edwin Escobar, Jonathan Pettibone*

Drafted/Acquired: 1st round, 2014 draft, Harvard-Westlake HS (Los Angeles, CA)
Previous Ranking: NR

What Happened in 2014: After winning over SoCal area scouts on the bump thanks to a broad arsenal and advanced feel, the former North Carolina commit was popped 34th overall in the June draft and impressed in limited pro exposure.

Strengths: Advanced feel for four-pitch repertoire; ability to execute and command offerings that belies his age and experience level; fastball plays to average velocity at present but comes with projection and good present command; good feel for off-speed and will flash plus already; comfort with two distinct breaking balls; repeats extremely well; good athleticism; displays aptitude on the bump and takes well to instruction; firm foundation for development puts profile in rarified air for prep arm.

Weaknesses: Profile is heavily reliant on projection to reach lofty ceiling; fastball velocity often dipped to below-average range during spring; needs to build up arm strength and durability; highly enticing collection of attributes for developmental staff to work with, but still very much a developmental project; if stuff doesn't tick forward as expected, will need to fully realize command profile for average arsenal to play at highest level.

Risk Factor/Injury History: High; complex-level résumé; standard proximity risk for prep arm.

Bret Sayre's Fantasy Take: Given the lack of predraft hype around Flaherty, he's a name that could be undervalued in dynasty drafts this year and someone who should be off the board within the first 30 picks. His advanced approach could lead to strong initial performance and increased trade value in 2015.

The Year Ahead: Though the presence of Appy and New York-Penn League affiliates affords St. Louis the opportunity to bring players along conservatively, Flaherty may be advanced enough to step right into full-season ball at the outset this year. While lacking in loud present stuff, the value of the profile is predicated on the idea that this core set of attributes serves as a foundation upon which an impact, major-league arm can be built. Evaluators are comfortable projecting at least some growth in the arsenal due to the natural maturation of the body and benefits of pro instruction alone. What sets him apart is the athleticism, body control, and feel that he already displays, all of which should help him implement instruction and tweaks without throwing off other aspects of his game. It is a unique profile for a top prospect to be sure. If you had five of him in your system you could very well be looking simultaneously at a collection of arms that will give you a 2015 Low-A staff without a plus fastball, and one of the most productive 2020 major-league staffs in the game.

5. Rob Kaminsky LHP

Born: 9/2/94 **Age:** 20 **Bats:** R **Throws:** L **Height:** 5'11" **Weight:** 191

MLB ETA	CT	FB	CH	CB	SL	OFP	Realistic
2018		60	55	70	-	65 NO. 2/3 STARTER	50 NO. 4 / LATE INN RP

YEAR	TEAM	LVL	AGE	W	L	SV	G	GS	IP	H	HR	BB	K	BB9	SO9	GB%	BABIP	WHIP	ERA	FIP	FRA	WARP
2014	PEO	A	19	8	2	0	18	18	100.7	71	2	31	79	2.8	7.1	53%	.239	1.01	1.88	3.28	4.07	0.9
2015	SLN	MLB	20	4	5	0	14	14	71.0	75	7	34	38	4.3	4.8	48%	.305	1.52	5.08	5.22	5.52	-0.6
2016	SLN	MLB	21	9	10	0	30	30	191.3	178	16	75	128	3.5	6.0	48%	.292	1.32	4.01	4.19	4.36	0.6

Breakout: 0%   Improve: 0%   Collapse: 0%   Attrition: 0%   MLB: 0%   Upside: 10   *Comparables: Jeurys Familia, T.J. House, Ian Krol*

Drafted/Acquired: 1st round, 2013 draft, St. Joseph Regional HS (Montvale, NJ)

Previous Ranking: #7 (Org)

What Happened in 2014: Kaminsky handled a challenging full-season assignment with aplomb, logging 100-plus innings in the Midwest League and averaging over five innings per start while leading all starters in ERA (1.88) and finishing in the top five in WHIP (1.013, fourth).

Strengths: Already capable of filling up the strike zone; fastball can scrape mid-90s and works comfortably in 88-92 velocity band with some arm-side action; curve is a weapon at present, with potential to reach double-plus at maturity; tight downward action with heavy spin and depth; changeup showed signs of progress and projects to above average with some fade; competitor on the mound; not tall, but very sturdily built; maintained stuff through starts and over course of season.

Weaknesses: In-zone command can play loose; depth and break on curve can limit entry points for strikes and may be less effective as chase pitch against advanced bats; changeup still a work in progress and needs developmental focus; creates some angle, but fastball generally lacks plane, putting added pressure on curve to change eye level of hitters.

Risk Factor/Injury History: High; Low-A résumé.

Bret Sayre's Fantasy Take: The fantasy potential is high with Kaminsky if he can take the next step with his changeup, but fantasy owners should realistically view him as an inconsistent SP4 who will get enough strikeouts to tempt you, but give up enough hard contact to frustrate you. Anything on top of that is gravy.

The Year Ahead: Kaminsky sailed through his first full-season test without issue, thanks in large part to the quality of his fastball-curveball tandem. Midwest League bats were generally overwhelmed by the two offerings, as well as the Garden State product's ability to consistently spot each in the zone, with lots of soft contact resulting. As Kaminsky advances to High-A in 2015 he will need to show further development in his off-speed and a lesser reliance on the curve if he is to continue to prove capable of keeping pro bats off-balance through multiple lineup turns. Changeup savant Marco Gonzales has already provided the young southpaw with some pointers regarding the former, and as Kaminsky's comfort level with the pitch increases he should feel less reliant on the breaker as his go-to change-of-pace pitch. The fastball has a chance to reach consistent plus velocity, but the lack of plane could cause the pitch to play down some even when delivered with precision. In the aggregate, the parts all add up to a potentially valuable asset in a major-league rotation, with just enough projection to leave the door open for an impact outcome. It was a strong full-season campaign for the lefty, but much work remains to bridge the gap between present skill set and rotation stalwart at the highest level.

6. Charlie Tilson   CF

Born: 12/2/92   **Age:** 22   **Bats:** L   **Throws:** L   **Height:** 5'11"   **Weight:** 175

MLB ETA	Hit	Power	Run	Glove	Arm	OFP 60 1ST DIVISION PLAYER	Realistic 50 AVG MLB PLAYER
2017	50	-	60	60	55		

YEAR	TEAM	LVL	AGE	PA	R	2B	3B	HR	RBI	BB	SO	SB	CS	AVG/OBP/SLG	TAv	BABIP	BRR	FRAA	WARP
2014	SFD	AA	21	145	19	4	1	2	17	6	28	2	3	.237/.269/.324	.217	.284	2.8	CF(26): -1.0, LF(6): 0.3	0.0
2014	PMB	A+	21	402	54	8	8	5	36	24	76	10	7	.308/.357/.414	.281	.377	3.8	CF(83): -8.6	1.4
2015	SLN	MLB	22	250	25	7	2	3	19	11	57	3	2	.240/.277/.326	.225	.300	0.0	CF -4, LF 0	-0.7
2016	SLN	MLB	23	250	26	7	3	3	23	14	52	3	2	.253/.304/.354	.244	.308	0.3	CF -4, LF 0	0.2

Breakout: 2%   Improve: 7%   Collapse: 7%   Attrition: 12%   MLB: 18%   Upside: 35   *Comparables: Peter Bourjos, Gorkys Hernandez, Eury Perez*

Drafted/Acquired: 2nd round, 2011 draft, New Trier HS (Winnetka, IL)

Previous Ranking: On The Rise

What Happened in 2014: Tilson showed well in the Florida State League, including notable added strength, before being promoted to Double-A Springfield and struggling some while pressing at the plate.

Strengths: Speed is a weapon; ability to leverage speed in the field and on the bases; covers good ground on the grass; arm is an asset in center; hit tool progressing with potential to play at the top of a big-league lineup; power projects to play from gap to line, pull side; speed to rack up doubles; impressive developmental progress over relatively short time frame after missing significant time early in career.

Weaknesses: At present speed serves as masking agent for underdeveloped reads in the field and on the bases; needs to refine overall approach to max out raw tools; limited power projection; at times overly aggressive at the plate, particularly in second half and after promotion; needs to continue to refine approach to more effectively grow hit tool.

Risk Factor/Injury History: Moderate; reached Double-A; unrefined game; significant injury to nonthrowing shoulder caused missed season in 2012.

Bret Sayre's Fantasy Take: No one will confuse Tilson with a fantasy superstar, but speed is valuable, and although he hasn't put up gaudy stolen-base numbers in the minors, there's potential for him to be a 25-30 steal guy in full-time action. There just won't be much that accompanies it.

The Year Ahead: Tilson continues to make developmental progress as he works his way toward St. Louis. There is a lot to like in the profile, with the in-game improvements realized over the past two seasons the most encouraging aspect of the center fielder's game. As a cold weather amateur, it would have been easy for a missed full season, and all the pro reps that go with it, to sidetrack Tilson's development. But the physically gifted former second rounder has worked hard to maintain an admirable pace, with positive reports manifesting from evaluators both inside and outside of the organization. He'll start 2015 back in Springfield, where the focus will remain on incremental improvements across the board. Improved reads and routes in the field, as well as reads and jumps on the bases, will bolster his foundational value, while an improved ability to drive soft stuff away to the opposite field with more regular authority will simultaneously strengthen the hit tool and allow for a more robust tally of two-baggers via the gap and the line. While the home-run power might be limited to the pull side, it should be more than enough to keep arms honest. Tilson is one developmental step away from solidifying himself as a safe bet to provide major-league value, and there is enough upside here to envision a future two-hole bat with potential to impact the game in every facet.

7. Tim Cooney   LHP

Born: 12/19/90 **Age:** 24 **Bats:** L **Throws:** L **Height:** 6'3" **Weight:** 195

MLB ETA	CT	FB	CH	CB	SL	OFP	Realistic
2015	50	50	55	50	-	50 NO. 4 STARTER	45 NO. 5 STARTER

YEAR	TEAM	LVL	AGE	W	L	SV	G	GS	IP	H	HR	BB	K	BB9	SO9	GB%	BABIP	WHIP	ERA	FIP	FRA	WARP
2014	MEM	AAA	23	14	6	0	26	25	158.0	158	21	47	119	2.7	6.8	48%	.291	1.30	3.47	4.93	4.67	2.0
2015	SLN	MLB	24	9	8	0	24	24	136.3	140	14	35	98	2.3	6.5	47%	.317	1.29	4.16	4.14	4.52	0.3
2016	SLN	MLB	25	9	9	0	27	27	161.7	162	15	39	121	2.2	6.7	47%	.318	1.24	3.86	3.67	4.20	0.9

Breakout: 19%   Improve: 30%   Collapse: 7%   Attrition: 26%   MLB: 44%   Upside: 3   *Comparables: Kyle Gibson, Tommy Milone, Rudy Owens*

Drafted/Acquired: 3rd round, 2012 draft, Wake Forest University (Winston-Salem, NC)

Previous Ranking: #9 (Org)

What Happened in 2014: Another year, another level, and another solid showing for the former Demon Deacon, who averaged over six innings per start for Triple-A Memphis despite striking out almost two fewer batters per nine.

Strengths: Big and durable; broad arsenal with solid command profile and feel for each offering; changeup can play above average; fastball has some life and works to all quadrants despite average velocity; can create angles; mechanics work and repeat well; mature approach.

Weaknesses: Aggregate arsenal lacks impact; fly-ball tendencies and average arsenal will leave small margin for error against major-league bats; sequencing and command less effective in producing strikeouts at Triple-A than in previous pro showings; lacks deception; strikeout rate likely to tick down further at major-league level.

Risk Factor/Injury History: Low

Bret Sayre's Fantasy Take: Cooney lacks the upside to be of interest in most mixed-league formats, as even in 14-16 team leagues he's likely to be near replacement level at best. One of these years, though, he'll be an NL-only FAAB superstar.

The Year Ahead: Cooney is ready for the challenge of major-league lineups but finds himself queued up behind a full complement of capable arms at the major-league level and an equally refined and more impactful profile in fellow lefty prospect Marco Gonzales. That makes the 'pen the most likely point of entry, where Cooney's ability to eat innings could provide value in a swingman capacity and his success against same-side bats could make him an option as a lefty-centric, middle-inning option. While the feel and the command are impressive, Cooney allows too much contact to project more than a back-end future. All the same, it's a profile certain to provide major-league value in some capacity and he is ready to start the final phase of his development at the major-league level. The odds have Cooney returning to Memphis to start the 2015 season, but there's a chance he breaks camp with a bullpen assignment in St. Louis and in any event should begin his major-league career at some point this year.

8. Sam Tuivailala   RHP

Born: 10/19/92 **Age:** 22 **Bats:** R **Throws:** R **Height:** 6'3" **Weight:** 195

MLB ETA	CT	FB	CH	CB	SL	OFP	Realistic
2015	-	75	-	60	-	60 >AVG CLOSER	55 HIGH LEV LATE-INN RP

YEAR	TEAM	LVL	AGE	W	L	SV	G	GS	IP	H	HR	BB	K	BB9	SO9	GB%	BABIP	WHIP	ERA	FIP	FRA	WARP
2014	SLN	MLB	21	0	0	0	2	0	1.0	5	2	2	1	18.0	9.0	0%	.600	7.00	36.00	33.10	22.34	-0.3
2014	MEM	AAA	21	0	0	1	2	0	1.3	1	0	0	3	0.0	20.2	0%	.500	0.75	0.00	1.45	-1.43	0.1
2014	SFD	AA	21	2	1	1	17	0	21.0	18	0	9	30	3.9	12.9	56%	.375	1.29	2.57	1.69	1.44	0.9
2014	PMB	A+	21	0	1	3	29	0	37.7	29	1	18	64	4.3	15.3	47%	.364	1.25	3.58	1.93	2.15	1.3
2015	SLN	MLB	22	2	1	1	42	0	52.0	43	4	26	62	4.5	10.7	45%	.327	1.33	3.80	3.60	4.13	0.3
2016	SLN	MLB	23	3	2	1	63	0	67.3	49	5	30	81	4.0	10.8	45%	.303	1.18	3.04	3.18	3.31	1.3

Breakout: 0%   Improve: 0%   Collapse: 0%   Attrition: 0%   MLB: 0%   Upside: 36   *Comparables: Jhan Marinez, Andrew Carignan, Tommy Kahnle*

Drafted/Acquired: 3rd round, 2010 draft, Aragon HS (San Mateo, CA)

Previous Ranking: On The Rise

What Happened in 2014: The infielder-turned-reliever overpowered hitters with premium gas across three minor-league levels, earning a brief two-appearance major-league debut to close his 2014 campaign.

Strengths: Borderline elite fastball with regular upper-90s velocity and life; only command keeps pitch shy of true "elite" grade; power curve flashes plus and could settle there at maturity; solid development in brief career on the mound; should miss bats immediately; mind-set to handle high-leverage situations.

Weaknesses: Two-pitch arm; control and command profile is below average; fastball can flatten when he loses his slot; mechanics not yet second nature; curve can play average or lower when mechanics out of whack; lacks consistency to handle innings of import at present.

Risk Factor/Injury History: Moderate; standard reliever volatility risk.

Bret Sayre's Fantasy Take: Tuivailala is a perfect example of why investing in relief prospects in dynasty leagues is inadvisable. In a vacuum, he'd likely be one of the five best "future closer" prospects in the minors, but with guys like Trevor Rosenthal, Carlos Martinez, and the recently acquired Jordan Walden ahead of him, even if he develops perfectly, saves still likely are not in his near future.

The Year Ahead: After showing progress in his new role in 2013, "Tui" took off last summer, showing increased comfort on the mound en route to taking a significant developmental step forward. Because he is still working to maintain consistency in his execution, there is an ever-present risk he can fall out of his mechanics, leading to significant bouts of wildness and a steep falloff in curveball effectiveness. As he continues to work to refine his craft, he should see a plus curve show up for him with more regularity, which could pair with his upper-90s heater to give him a closer-worthy one-two punch. There is some risk of a regression in stuff, since it is still relatively early in Tuivailala's career on the mound and evaluators don't have a deep history to draw upon for the file. But 2014 represents a noteworthy transition from "arm-strength lotto ticket" to "potential shutdown reliever." With a little faith and projection, you can see "dominant, high-leverage arm" sitting patiently on the horizon.

9. Luke Weaver RHP

Born: 8/21/93 **Age:** 21 **Bats:** R **Throws:** R **Height:** 6'2" **Weight:** 170

MLB ETA	CT	FB	CH	CB	SL	OFP	Realistic
2018	-	60	60	50	-	60 NO. 3 STARTER	50 LATE INN RP

YEAR	TEAM	LVL	AGE	W	L	SV	G	GS	IP	H	HR	BB	K	BB9	SO9	GB%	BABIP	WHIP	ERA	FIP	FRA	WARP
2014	PMB	A+	20	0	1	0	2	2	3.3	11	1	4	3	10.8	8.1	24%	.625	4.50	21.60	9.09	6.90	0.0
2014	CRD	Rk	20	0	0	0	4	4	6.0	4	0	0	9	0.0	13.5	67%	.333	0.67	0.00	1.00	3.19	0.2
2015	SLN	MLB	21	2	3	0	9	9	34.7	37	4	17	22	4.4	5.7	45%	.318	1.56	5.29	5.28	5.75	-0.3
2016	SLN	MLB	22	4	6	0	30	30	191.0	186	20	82	138	3.9	6.5	45%	.303	1.40	4.54	4.47	4.94	-0.7

Breakout: 0%   Improve: 0%   Collapse: 0%   Attrition: 0%   MLB: 0%   Upside: 2   *Comparables: Edwin Escobar, Kyle Lobstein, Jose A. Ramirez*

Drafted/Acquired: 1st round, 2014, Florida State University (Tallahassee, FL)

Previous Ranking: NR

What Happened in 2014: Weaver saw a downtick in stuff during his junior year, leading him to fall to the Cardinals in the back of the first round, with the lanky righty showing some flashes of his former self in limited pro looks.

Strengths: At its best, fastball can reach the mid-90s with boring action; changeup comes with deception and hard, late action; after working upper-80s to low-90s through the spring, saw a slight bump in velocity during short pro outings; repeats well and projects to above-average command; advanced feel for setting up hitters with fastball-change combo.

Weaknesses: Though slight in present build, frame doesn't project to add much additional bulk; breaking ball has not seen much growth through collegiate career; might not have enough spin in the wrist to get the pitch to play to major-league average; fastball might only play to average or tick above with pro starter's workload.

Risk Factor/Injury History: Moderate; has flashed advanced stuff at collegiate level; near null pro résumé.

Bret Sayre's Fantasy Take: Even with being selected first and being a college arm, Weaver falls behind Flaherty in dynasty drafts as well. In fact, he may be the least attractive fantasy commodity among all true first-round picks in 2014.

The Year Ahead: Weaver's advanced feel for his changeup was an attractive selling point for a Cardinals organization that places a premium on the offering. Further, evaluators have enough history with Weaver to project a step up in velocity if he is forced to the 'pen, giving him a relatively high floor and providing some intrinsic foundational value to the profile. For now, the plan is still very much to develop the FSU product as a starter, with the effectiveness of Weaver's breaking ball and fastball likely to dictate the pace and trajectory of his development. The return of his low-to-mid-90s velocity and the establishment of even an average curve could put Weaver on the fast track toward realizing his mid-rotation upside, but at present each of those outcomes continues to exist in the abstract. As much as any profile in the system, 2015 will serve as a opportunity for Weaver to show the Cardinals' developmental staff exactly what it is they have to work with.

10. Carson Kelly C

Born: 7/14/94 **Age:** 20 **Bats:** R **Throws:** R **Height:** 6'2" **Weight:** 200

MLB ETA	Hit	Power	Run	Glove	Arm	OFP	Realistic
2018	-	55	-	55	65	55 >AVG REGULAR	45 BACKUP C

YEAR	TEAM	LVL	AGE	PA	R	2B	3B	HR	RBI	BB	SO	SB	CS	AVG/OBP/SLG	TAv	BABIP	BRR	FRAA	WARP
2014	PEO	A	19	415	41	17	4	6	49	37	54	1	0	.248/.326/.366	.264	.274	-2.2	C(79): -0.5	1.5
2015	SLN	MLB	20	250	19	10	1	3	22	13	50	0	0	.208/.258/.297	.211	.247	-0.4	C -0, 3B -4	-1.0
2016	SLN	MLB	21	250	24	11	1	4	23	13	41	0	0	.219/.265/.328	.223	.242	-0.5	C 0, 3B -4	-1.3

Breakout: 0%   Improve: 0%   Collapse: 0%   Attrition: 0%   MLB: 0%   Upside: 17   *Comparables: Travis d'Arnaud, J.R. Murphy, Christian Vazquez*

Drafted/Acquired: 2nd round, 2012 draft, Westview HS (Portland, OR)

Previous Ranking: #6 (Org)

What Happened in 2014: In his second spin through the Midwest League, Kelly held his own at the plate and, more importantly, behind it, as the former second rounder made a successful transition from third base to backstop.

Strengths: Good athleticism; significant positive strides made during transitional year behind the plate; arm can be a weapon; raw power could play above average at maturity; shows feel and comfort in the box; puts together solid at-bats with regularity; comfortable leader and plus grades for work ethic and presence.

Weaknesses: Even with strong developmental year, a fair amount of refinement remains to push defensive profile to major-league ready; game calling in nascent stage; some length to release could limit impact of arm strength; raw strength doesn't show up in game; fails to make regular impactful contact at plate; lacks advanced feel for contact; swing comes with effort and some heave and could limit ability for power to emerge.

Risk Factor/Injury History: High; dual development of hit tool and defensive profile could limit full realization of profile.

Bret Sayre's Fantasy Take: With the lead time of developing into a catcher and the questions around his offensive game, Kelly is just someone worth monitoring, and not owning, in fantasy leagues right now.

The Year Ahead: Kelly did everything he had to in 2014, proving the shift behind the plate could work while showing some incremental growth in the rest of his game. With the pressure of the initial position shift behind him, and behind the developmental staff, the focus will now be on developing Kelly's offensive and defensive profile in tandem. While this challenge is not unique to catchers, the amount of effort generally required to get a prep-level profile from typical entry-level to major-league adequate is far greater on the defensive side for those donning the tools of ignorance. There is inherent risk that while Kelly could project to above-average production both behind the plate and with the stick, the toll of trying to develop both could prevent either aspect of his game from reaching full potential, and at minimum is likely to require a slow and deliberate march up the minor-league ladder. That march should continue with a High-A assignment in 2015.

Prospects on the Rise

1. CF Magneuris Sierra: One of the more entertaining prospects to populate the complex-level GCL, Sierra drew rave reviews for his actions in center field and knack for bringing barrel to ball. The precocious lefty torched Gulf Coast arms to the tune of a .386/.434/.505 slash line with an aggressive approach at the plate. He could see a full-season assignment in 2015, where even a fraction of his 2014 production could firmly plant his name on prospect lists and acquire lists alike. The upside is a plus-glove, plus-run, plus-hit center fielder with the arm to rack up assists if tested. Grab your seat on the Sierra train now; by this time next year it might be standing room only.

2. SS Edmundo Sosa: The young Panamanian shortstop put together a solid showing this summer in the Gulf Coast League at the age of 18, displaying smooth actions in the field and an advanced feel for contact. He has shown some ability to drive the gaps on occasion, but the offensive profile will be average- and on-base-centric, which will require continued refinement in pitch selection and strike zone awareness. Defensively, Sosa is a strong bet to stick at the six-spot with a clean and quick transfer, good footwork, and sure hands, though his arm can be stretched at the margins. He is advanced enough defensively to bypass the New York-Penn League and jump straight to Peoria, where his prospect status could take a significant step forward if he proves capable of holding his own at the plate.

3. 2B Malik Collymore: Collymore was a 10th-round selection out of high school in the 2013 draft and has spent the past two summers in the complexes refining his game. The Canadian prep product took a significant step forward at the plate in 2014, showing much more comfort in the box while better identifying spin and more regularly producing hard contact through his compact right-handed swing. Collymore has natural strength and athleticism, and through his first 16 months of pro ball has made strides improving his overall feel and on-field IQ. There is still a question as to his ultimate defensive home, with opinions ranging from second base, to center field, to left field. Regardless of where he sets up shop in the field, the bat could be impactful if he continues on this developmental trajectory. The Cardinals will likely continue to take it slowly with Collymore, who won't turn 20 until after the start of the 2015 season, but there is breakout potential here. If you are looking for a sleeper to monitor with regularity next season, this is your guy.

FROM THE FIELD

Marco Gonzales

Team: St. Louis Cardinals

Evaluator: Jeff Moore

Dates seen: April 28, 2014

Affiliate: Palm Beach Cardinals (High-A, Cardinals)

OFP: 60

Realistic role: 55, no. 3/4 starter

Mechanics: Clean arm action, above-average arm speed. Thick lower half helps keep him steady and repeat his mechanics well. Not overly athletic but enough so to repeat his delivery and get off the mound to field his position.

Pitch type	Present grade	Future grade	Sitting velocity	Peak velocity	Report
FB	50	55	88-90	91	Works down in the zone; command was better to arm side of plate; missed frequently on inner half but made a concerted effort to work inside on right-handed hitters to keep them from diving out onto outer half. Does not have velocity or movement to miss bats with fastball in fastball counts. Must command pitch to be effective.
CB	50	55	75-77		Not a power curve; big sweeping pitch with downward bite; plus command of pitch; will throw it to both sides of the plate against hitters of either handedness. Will definitely keep left-handed hitters off balance at the major-league level. Major-league righties may square it up if he leaves it in the zone. Better to righties when he buries it at their feet with two strikes.
CH	65	70	78-81		Definitely plus pitch with even more potential as fastball command improves. Will throw it to any batter at any time. Has plus arm-side fade and some had diving action. Will be a 70 pitch as soon as he can consistently make it dive as well as fade.

Overall: Gonzales will go as far as his changeup will take him, which should be pretty far. His fastball isn't overpowering, but it also may be his third-best pitch. He's not going to overpower hitters, but being a lefty with a great changeup should be enough to make him a mid-rotation starter. Now that he's in full-season ball, he should move quickly and is clearly too advanced for the Florida State League.

Factors on the Farm

Prospects likely to contribute at the major-league level in 2015

1. RHP Zach Petrick: The stuff isn't loud, but there is a solid baseline here with three average or better major-league offerings including a boring fastball, change, and slide piece, as well as some evidence that there is more in the tank when airing it out in relief. With a full season of Triple-A ball under his belt and no apparent opening for Petrick in the rotation, he could make for an intriguing option out of the 'pen, where his heavy fastball has flirted with the mid-90s in the past.

2. OF Randal Grichuk: Grichuk's calling card is his plus raw power, and the Texas prep product has shown some ability to get to it in game at the upper levels over the past two seasons. He continues to struggle with same-side stuff, and there is a risk that his aggressiveness could be further exploited at the major-league level to the point that there just isn't enough in the stick to warrant regular time. Defensively it's a corner profile, though there is enough glove and arm to envision average production out of right field. Grichuk likely fits as a bench bat/platoon option, albeit one with some interesting juice in the barrel. With Piscotty still not on the 40-man, the Cards could elect to delay his promotion long enough to gain the extra control year, leaving Grichuk as an easy favorite to break camp with the big club, where he'll look to build upon a strong finish to his 2014 campaign. He should serve as a capable righty bat off the bench with periodic spot starts when favorable matchups arise.

3. 2B Jacob Wilson: Wilson's carrying tool is his bat, and throughout his pro career he has hit at every stop along the way. He missed significant time in 2014 following surgery on his left knee, but reports last fall had him fully recovered and comfortable, with no expected lingering effects. With fewer than 70 games logged in 2014, Wilson utilized the Arizona Fall League to get in his work, including reps at the plate and across the infield. He is still viewed primarily as a second baseman, but his ability to adequately handle the corners could bolster his profile and allow him to carve out playing time in St. Louis in a utility capacity as early as this summer.

TAMPA BAY RAYS

1. Daniel Robertson   SS

Born: 3/22/94   **Age:** 21   **Bats:** R   **Throws:** R   **Height:** 6'1"   **Weight:** 205

MLB ETA		Hit	Power	Run	Glove	Arm		OFP	Realistic
2016		**60**	**–**	**–**	**50**	**55**		**60** 1ST DIVISION PLAYER	**50** AVG ML PLAYER

YEAR	TEAM	LVL	AGE	PA	R	2B	3B	HR	RBI	BB	SO	SB	CS	AVG/OBP/SLG	TAv	BABIP	BRR	FRAA	WARP
2014	STO	A+	20	642	110	37	3	15	60	72	94	4	4	.310/.402/.471	.313	.349	3.0	SS(115): -2.2, 2B(7): -0.8	6.5
2015	TBA	MLB	21	250	24	10	1	3	19	18	56	0	0	.227/.291/.316	.241	.283	-0.5	SS -2, 3B -0	0.3
2016	TBA	MLB	22	250	28	11	0	4	24	20	52	0	0	.246/.315/.356	.256	.296	-0.7	SS -3, 3B 0	1.3

Breakout: 0%   **Improve:** 0%   **Collapse:** 0%   **Attrition:** 0%   **MLB:** 0%   **Upside:** 17   *Comparables: Eugenio Suarez, Jose Pirela, Tyler Pastornicky*

Drafted/Acquired: 1st round, 2012 draft, Upland HS (Upland, CA)

Previous Ranking: #4 (Org – OAK)

What Happened in 2014: Robertson took a firm developmental step forward in the California League, showing improved actions in the field and a more efficient swing at the plate, which allowed both his approach and bat speed to play up.

Strengths: Contact-friendly stroke; barrel stays on plane; some natural lift and ability to backspin; firm front side and efficient use of body, strength; good balance; comfortable using full field; bat speed to turn on velocity as well as allow the ball to get deeper and drive off outer half; improved fluidity in field; arm strength plays on left side and would be an asset turning two or behind the bag at the keystone; hands and lower half work up the middle; chance to stick at short long term; good overall approach; positive makeup mentions.

Weaknesses: Below-average run; fringy value on the bases; lacks ideal range for short; reliant on reads to convert at the margins; could struggle to make all the plays as the game continues to speed up; power projects to fringe-average.

Risk Factor/Injury History: Moderate risk; yet to reach Double-A.

The Year Ahead: 2014 was a coming-out party of sorts for Robertson, as the former first rounder began to win over evaluators on both sides of the ball. The offensive promise that flashed in the Midwest League more regularly manifested in his time with Stockton, with added strength through a maturing body allowing Robertson to shorten his load some and providing for more consistency and efficiency across his swing. Defensively, Robertson has improved enough for the hands, arm, and overall feel to play well at the six-spot, though his limited speed will make him reliant on good reads and positioning to continue to hold down short at the upper levels. Should he eventually shift to another defensive home, the skill set would fit at second or third. Robertson will step up to Double-A in 2015 and could be ready to contribute to a retooling Tampa club as early as 2016, profiling as a top-of-the-order table setter.

> **#66**
> BP Top 101 Prospects

2. Willy Adames   SS

Born: 9/2/95   **Age:** 19   **Bats:** R   **Throws:** R   **Height:** 6'1"   **Weight:** 180

MLB ETA		Hit	Power	Run	Glove	Arm		OFP	Realistic
Late 2017		**55**	**55**	**–**	**50**	**55**		**60** 1ST DIVISION PLAYER	**50** AVG ML PLAYER

YEAR	TEAM	LVL	AGE	PA	R	2B	3B	HR	RBI	BB	SO	SB	CS	AVG/OBP/SLG	TAv	BABIP	BRR	FRAA	WARP
2014	BGR	A	18	114	15	5	2	2	11	15	30	3	0	.278/.377/.433	.291	.379	2.1	SS(25): -1.2	0.8
2014	WMI	A	18	400	40	14	12	6	50	39	96	3	6	.269/.346/.428	.307	.353	0.7	SS(97): -0.4	3.8
2015	TBA	MLB	19	250	21	8	2	3	21	18	77	0	0	.211/.272/.311	.227	.296	-0.1	SS -1	0.1
2016	TBA	MLB	20	250	25	10	3	4	23	18	68	0	0	.234/.293/.348	.242	.313	-0.2	SS -2	0.6

Breakout: 0%   **Improve:** 0%   **Collapse:** 0%   **Attrition:** 0%   **MLB:** 0%   **Upside:** 39   *Comparables: Manny Machado, Xander Bogaerts, Dilson Herrera*

Drafted/Acquired: International Free Agent, 2012, Dominican Republic

Previous Ranking: NR

What Happened in 2014: The teenage shortstop put together a solid debut season stateside in A-Ball, where he held his own against more advanced competition, and also added being traded for David Price to his résumé.

Strengths: Lean muscle; maturing body; strong legs; keeps hands in good hitting position during stride; generates plus bat speed; barrels up offerings into both gaps; flashes solid bat control; stays inside of ball; can learn how to muscle up and tap into strength; arm for left side of the infield; soft hands; shows feel for game at early age.

> **#94**
> BP Top 101 Prospects

Weaknesses: Agility and quickness are only average; not the most natural player at shortstop; likely to lose some foot speed as he matures physically; could potentially slide to third or second; lunges at secondary offerings; tends to guess in counts leading to in-zone miss; may need to sacrifice power to sustain contact against higher quality arms; overall tool set is more solid-average than plus.

Risk Factor/Injury History: High; yet to reach upper levels; hit-tool translation.

Bret Sayre's Fantasy Take: Adames had a coming-out party in fantasy leagues when he was the only prospect piece in the David Price deal, and it's only continuing every time he's ranked atop this admittedly weak system. Now might be a good time to cash in on him, as his fantasy upside could be similar to Jhonny Peralta, at peak, and he's a good three years away from contributing, with a lot of development ahead of him.

The Year Ahead: It was a successful stateside debut for the Dominican international signee, but also one that saw change midstream. Adames was the lone prospect acquired in the deadline deal that saw Tampa send long-time ace David Price to Detroit, and the 19-year-old immediately ascends to the forefront of this system. While the on-paper potential of each individual tool is more average to solid-average, the composition of the skill set and the way it meshes together make this profile a potential first-division player. Adames flashes feel for hitting at an early age, largely driven by his plus bat speed and the looseness of his hands. The shortstop gets the head of the bat to the point of contact efficiently to barrel up offerings hard into both gaps. His approach and the manner in which he attacks breaking balls need refinement, but there's already maturity in his game that points to the ability to continue to adjust. The potential of the package hinges on the premise that the prospect can stick up the middle, which isn't a foregone conclusion. Evaluators are mixed on whether further physical gains—especially in the lower body—are going to slow him down enough to where a move makes the most sense, but for now he's showing to be capable of handling the position and getting better. Adames is ready for the next step up the ranks, where an assignment in the Florida State League will be a good test to show that both the bat and glove are taking the next step forward.

3. Justin O'Conner C

Born: 03/31/92 **Age:** 23 **Bats:** R **Throws:** R **Height:** 6'0" **Weight:** 190

MLB ETA	Hit	Power	Run	Glove	Arm	OFP	Realistic
2016	50	50	–	55	80	55 >AVG REGULAR	50 SOMETIME STARTER

YEAR	TEAM	LVL	AGE	PA	R	2B	3B	HR	RBI	BB	SO	SB	CS	AVG/OBP/SLG	TAv	BABIP	BRR	FRAA	WARP
2014	MNT	AA	22	84	9	4	0	2	3	1	20	0	0	.262/.298/.388	.249	.328	0.6	C(14): 0.2	0.4
2014	PCH	A+	22	340	40	31	2	10	44	15	78	0	0	.282/.321/.486	.269	.343	-1.4	C(68): -0.2	1.9
2015	TBA	MLB	23	250	20	10	0	6	26	9	79	0	0	.205/.239/.327	.215	.275	-0.4	C 0	-0.4
2016	TBA	MLB	24	250	26	11	0	7	26	12	75	0	0	.218/.262/.353	.230	.287	-0.6	C 0	-0.4

Breakout: 0%   Improve: 0%   Collapse: 0%   Attrition: 0%   MLB: 0%   Upside: 29   *Comparables: Josh Phegley, Welington Castillo, Yan Gomes*

Drafted/Acquired: 1st round, 2010 draft, Cowan HS (Muncie, IN)

Previous Ranking: NR

What Happened in 2014: O'Conner continued to flash the eye-popping arm strength and promise to control the running game at the highest level, while also showing some improvement making consistent contact and with his receiving skills.

Strengths: Elite arm strength; excellent throwing mechanics; lightning quick release; fires feet effectively; agile in crouch; improving receiving skills; using body more to advantage; developing leadership skills; plus bat speed; quick hands; ability to backspin the ball; some present lift in stroke; plus raw power; strong makeup.

Weaknesses: Gets loose and casual behind dish; glove hand isn't overly firm; runs into trouble squeezing; ball control needs work; pulls up often; aggressive approach; likes to swing early and often; lacks plan at the plate; reluctant to go deep into counts; bat control is fringe; susceptible to spin away; power likely to play at fringe-average; streaky-hitter profile.

Risk Factor/Injury History: Moderate; limited Double-A experience; dual-threat development.

Bret Sayre's Fantasy Take: Catching prospects are not great bets in general, and O'Conner offers the potential for solid mixed-league value only if everything clicks at the plate. Unless you're in a 16-team or two-catcher format, he's best left on either the waiver wire or someone else's roster.

The Year Ahead: When discussing O'Conner in industry circles, after getting past the initial comments on the well-documented arm strength, the theme from the past year or so is "improvement." The backstop has pushed both his offensive and defensive games to the point where a major leaguer is coming into clearer focus. The question is, in what capacity? Evaluators who feel that there's more progress to come into his mid-twenties, especially offensively, see a player who can hold down a regular job and hit in the bottom third of the lineup. The feel on impacting the running game is universal, with those more optimistic on the stick seeing the both the potential for average power and hitting outputs. A .250s-.260s hitting catcher with 15 or so home-run pop and better-than-average defense is valuable. The main issue is whether O'Conner can tone things down at the plate to the point that high-quality arms are not going to exploit his aggressiveness. The less than bullish on the bat touch on how much work he has to go in that aspect and see a backup in the long run. A good showing in the 2014 Arizona Fall League gives optimism that the 23-year-old can make adjustments when pushed by the level of competition, and a placement in Double-A to start 2015 will serve as the next test for the prospect. It's there where O'Conner will try to prove the bat is up to the challenge that higher quality arms pose and will attempt to show a legit big-league regular is emerging.

4. Alex Colome   RHP

Born: 12/31/88   **Age:** 26   **Bats:** R   **Throws:** R   **Height:** 6'2"   **Weight:** 220

MLB ETA	CT	FB	CH	CB	SL	OFP	Realistic
Debuted in 2013	60	70	60	60	–	55 NO. 3/4 STARTER	50 LATE INN RP (SETUP)

YEAR	TEAM	LVL	AGE	W	L	SV	G	GS	IP	H	HR	BB	K	BB9	SO9	GB%	BABIP	WHIP	ERA	FIP	FRA	WARP
2014	TBA	MLB	25	2	0	0	5	3	23.7	19	1	10	13	3.8	4.9	41%	.247	1.23	2.66	3.88	4.81	0.1
2014	DUR	AAA	25	7	6	0	15	15	86.0	84	2	30	73	3.1	7.6	42%	.319	1.33	3.77	3.25	4.18	1.3
2014	PCH	A+	25	0	1	0	3	3	11.0	7	0	5	10	4.1	8.2	45%	.241	1.09	1.64	2.94	2.87	0.3
2015	TBA	MLB	26	5	7	0	18	18	95.7	92	9	44	73	4.1	6.9	43%	.288	1.42	4.26	4.83	4.63	0.3
2016	TBA	MLB	27	8	11	0	28	28	173.3	182	23	83	131	4.3	6.8	43%	.299	1.53	5.14	5.18	5.58	-1.9

Breakout: 19%   Improve: 32%   Collapse: 15%   Attrition: 38%   MLB: 57%   Upside: 11   *Comparables: Kyle Weiland, Eric Surkamp, Jeff Niemann*

Drafted/Acquired: International Free Agent, 2007, Dominican Republic
Previous Ranking: #3 (Org)

What Happened in 2014: A 50-game suspension for testing positive for a performance-enhancing substance delayed the start of Colome's season and likely cost the right-hander a shot at cementing himself on the major-league roster, but the stuff played up on par with previous looks and has him knocking on the door.

Strengths: Loose arm; generates easy velocity; fastball will work 93-96, with late life; heavy, sinking action in lower velocity band; ride in upper reaches; can touch higher in short bursts; snaps cutter with late bite and slicing break; difficult to barrel; curveball flashes teeth and deep bend through strike zone; potential bat-misser; turns over deceptive changeup; good guise to fastball.

Weaknesses: Struggles keeping delivery together in stretches; inconsistent release; command plays down as a result; gets too much into challenge mind-set with heater; changeup can get too firm; body and arm will slow down when delivering; casts curve on occasion, leading to early break; questions on ability to execute consistently in line with stuff's potential.

Risk Factor/Injury History: Low; achieved major leagues; delivery consistency

Bret Sayre's Fantasy Take: The near-term upside is there, especially in light of the Jeremy Hellickson trade, but despite the raw stuff, Colome is unlikely to be better than a spot starter in mixed leagues—and that's if he sticks in the rotation, which is anything but a lock. In the bullpen, he's just another arm with potential trolling for saves.

The Year Ahead: When Colome has things going, the right-hander can be extremely tough on opposing batters, typically unleashing a barrage of mid-90s fastballs and mixing in an assortment of secondary stuff. He is very much a rhythm pitcher who feeds off of early count success and getting into a groove right off the bat. In these instances, the 26-year-old arm can look every bit the part of a mid-rotation starter, slicing and dicing his way through lineups or just plain overpowering them. Reality sets in when assessing Colome's command over the grind of the season. It comes and goes, primarily driven by ruts of inconsistency with his delivery, which stem from flying open early and a lack of being able to adjust quickly. There can be flashes or even stretches in a starting role where success is achievable, but this view sees the arm profiling the best in the bullpen, where short bursts will allow him to focus on keeping things together in a concentrated setting. The stuff also has a very good chance to play up further, especially the heater and cutter, as he can let loose without worry of pacing. Barring any type of major setbacks like last season, and because he is out of options, Colome is in line to break camp this season as part of the 25-man roster. A crack at holding down the fifth spot in the rotation is likely his to grasp, with the long term pointing to a potential bullpen fixture if performance is uneven.

5. Adrian Rondon   SS

Born: 7/7/98   **Age:** 16   **Bats:** R   **Throws:** R   **Height:** 6'2"   **Weight:** 180

MLB ETA	Hit	Power	Run	Glove	Arm	OFP	Realistic
Late 2018	65	50	55	55	50	70 ALL STAR	50 AVG ML PLAYER

Drafted/Acquired: International Free Agent, 2014, Dominican Republic
Previous Ranking: NR

What Happened in 2014: The Rays broke the bank to the tune of an almost $3 million bonus for the highly touted international prospect, who draws rave reviews for his feel for hitting and potential to stick up the middle.

Strengths: Highly athletic; fluid with actions; natural on the field; plus bat speed; compact stroke; feel for barreling up offerings; can turn around velocity; loose hands; bat head hangs within the zone; flashes gap power; instincts to stick at the position; soft hands; quick first step; good foundation to build fundamentals; strong feel for the game.

Weaknesses: Raw overall game; in the early stages of building professional approach; limited experience against quality breaking stuff; on the wild side with swing; power is all projection; line-drive stroke may play more to contact as game develops; crude footwork in field; arm can presently play a little hollow; projection player.

Risk Factor/Injury History: Extreme; no professional experience; 16 years old; large gap between present and future.

Bret Sayre's Fantasy Take: In a year with a shallower draft class, Rondon has enough fantasy potential to be a top-30 pick in dynasty drafts. But unfortunately for him, this is an absurdly deep class and he remains a very strong flier for the late rounds of drafts—though his advanced hit tool could play a role in shortening his ETA.

The Year Ahead: Rondon generated a ton of buzz during the international signing period, mainly due to the advanced nature of his offensive game for a player his age and strong potential to stick at a premium position. The life in his hands and early feel for controlling the head of the bat bode well for the shortstop to begin developing into a hitter who creates plenty of hard contact as his experience builds. The compactness of the 16-year-old's swing also lends strong clues that this player can evolve into a high-average hitter when all is said and done. The development of the power is a bit of a wild card at present, though Rondon possesses some lift in his stroke and stings offerings with authority into both gaps. At minimum, given the projection of the hit tool, the Dominican stands a good chance to bring extra-base pop to the table, and very well may surprise with the over-the-fence power as he progresses into his twenties. In the field this is very much a shortstop all the way. Despite some expected rawness with his technique, mainly the footwork, Rondon oozes the natural ability and fluidity seen in major-league defenders at the position in the same age bracket. There's a lot of projection here, and the associated risk that comes with it, but the view here is of a player that can quickly start to eat into those gaps as early as this season.

6. Steven Souza   OF

Born: 4/24/89   **Age:** 26   **Bats:** R   **Throws:** R   **Height:** 6'4"   **Weight:** 225

MLB ETA	Hit	Power	Run	Glove	Arm	OFP	Realistic
Debuted in 2014	50	60	55	–	65	55 >AVG REGULAR	45 4TH OF/<AVG REGULAR

YEAR	TEAM	LVL	AGE	PA	R	2B	3B	HR	RBI	BB	SO	SB	CS	AVG/OBP/SLG	TAv	BABIP	BRR	FRAA	WARP
2014	WAS	MLB	25	26	2	0	0	2	2	3	7	0	0	.130/.231/.391	.225	.071	0.0	RF(8): 0.1, LF(4): -0.0	0.0
2014	SYR	AAA	25	407	62	25	2	18	75	52	75	26	7	.350/.432/.590	.351	.398	0.0	RF(63): 6.5, CF(27): 3.3	6.1
2014	POT	A+	25	10	0	0	0	0	1	0	4	1	0	.111/.200/.111	.133	.200	0.1	RF(2): -0.0, LF(1): 0.1	-0.1
2014	HAG	A	25	2	0	0	0	0	1	0	1	1	0	.500/.500/.500	.319	1.000	-0.1	RF(1): 0.1	0.0
2015	TBA	MLB	26	250	35	11	0	10	33	23	62	11	3	.270/.340/.460	.299	.325	0.7	RF 1, CF 1	1.8
2016	TBA	MLB	27	622	82	25	2	23	81	62	157	27	8	.254/.333/.435	.284	.309	2.9	LF -1	3.2

Breakout: 5%   Improve: 26%   Collapse: 15%   Attrition: 29%   MLB: 68%   Upside: 45   *Comparables: Russ Canzler, Justin Ruggiano, Ryan Shealy*

Drafted/Acquired: 3rd round, 2007 draft, Cascade HS (Everett, WA)

Previous Ranking: NR

What Happened in 2014: The outfielder continued to show that his career is back on track, unleashing an onslaught of power and speed on the International League and getting his first taste of The Show.

Strengths: Strong body; well-filled-out frame; athletic for size; above-average foot speed; quiet swing setup; keeps balance; taps into core and lower body well; above-average bat speed; can drive ball with carry and loft to all fields; plus-to-better raw power; willing to use the whole field; punishes mistakes out and over the plate; easy-plus arm; can challenge runners; has overcome early-career issues.

Weaknesses: Highly leveraged swing; shows in-zone miss; hands lose timing and come under the ball; can be beat by good stuff middle-in; questions on hit translation against elite competition; contact may ultimately end up playing down and limit power output; defense on the limited side; reads off pitchers need improvement to utilize speed on bases.

Risk Factor/Injury History: Low risk; achieved major leagues; hit tool translation.

Bret Sayre's Fantasy Take: He turns 26 in April. If given the playing time, Souza could hit .260 with 20 homers and 15 steals.

The Year Ahead: After a variety of issues during the early part of his career that seemingly had him down and out, Souza has been able to put things together on and off the field the last few seasons to get back on track, culminating with an opportunity in the majors last year. The highlight of the outfielder's game is power. He unleashes a stroke that is designed to do damage, and when an opposing arm makes a mistake they typically pay. The 26-year-old has the type of power to translate into around 20-25 home runs provided a full complement of plate appearances over the course of a season, and that's the big key. Souza's swing has some timing where his hands can get a little late, which leads to swing-and-miss or getting himself tied up. How well he can adjust and keep his stroke fluid against elite arms will be the driving force to maintaining enough contact to profile as a regular over the long run. To reach the potential role, Souza will have to continue his recent adjustments sharpening his approach and keeping the swing together. If the contact plays down, the profile points more to a bench player over the entire body of work. Souza will likely get an extended chance in 2015 to show what he can do and try to prove he's up to the task against quality stuff consistently.

7. Brent Honeywell   RHP

Born: 3/31/95   **Age:** 20   **Bats:** R   **Throws:** R   **Height:** 6'2"   **Weight:** 180

MLB ETA	CT	FB	CH	CB	SL	OFP	Realistic
2018	–	65	55	50	60	60 NO. 3 STARTER	50 NO. 4 STARTER

YEAR	TEAM	LVL	AGE	W	L	SV	G	GS	IP	H	HR	BB	K	BB9	SO9	GB%	BABIP	WHIP	ERA	FIP	FRA	WARP
2014	PRI	Rk	19	2	1	0	9	8	33.7	19	1	6	40	1.6	10.7	52%	.230	0.74	1.07	2.20	4.92	0.3
2015	TBA	MLB	20	1	3	0	7	6	31.3	37	4	20	17	5.8	4.9	46%	.306	1.80	6.11	6.36	6.64	-0.5
2016	TBA	MLB	21	5	7	0	26	20	147.3	154	17	70	105	4.3	6.4	46%	.295	1.52	4.97	5.01	5.41	-1.2

Breakout: 0%   Improve: 0%   Collapse: 0%   Attrition: 0%   MLB: 0%   Upside: 1   *Comparables: Steve Johnson, Jose A. Ramirez, Enny Romero*

Drafted/Acquired: 2nd round, 2014 draft, Walters State Community College (Morristown, TN)

Previous Ranking: NR

What Happened in 2014: Honeywell began to make some waves during the JUCO season, which led to Tampa Bay tabbing him in the second round, and then really turned heads during his professional debut in the Appalachian League.

Strengths: Good frame; room to continue filling out and add strength; clean arm action; fastball comfortably works 90-94, with some sink; can reach for more (95-96) when needs it; potential to sit in plus-to-better range; turns over screwball with quality action; excellent deception with offering; flashes feel for change; arm-side fade with drop; curve can show two-plane break; feel for craft; projectable arm.

Weaknesses: Strength levels need improvement to withstand rigors of position; fastball velocity can yo-yo from outing to outing; presently more control than command; learning how to spot to both sides of the plate; inconsistent delivering change; tends to be on the deliberate side; slows body and arm down; curve is presently below average; tends to cast and break early; more projection than polish.

Risk Factor/Injury History: High; limited pro experience; emergence of consistent third offering.

Bret Sayre's Fantasy Take: Honeywell is a perfect example of why dynasty drafts are going to be so deep this year. The collection of talent in the supplemental and second rounds of the 2014 draft put a bigger-than-usual value on non-first-round picks this spring. The fact that Honeywell, one of the better short-season arms for fantasy purposes, will be there in the third or fourth round is your proof.

The Year Ahead: A very intriguing arm, this right-hander has come on strong since right before the draft and was able to sustain the buzz through a professional debut that left many impressed with the potential for considerable gains now that the arm is entrenched in a more structured environment. Honeywell is an easy thrower who generates good present velocity via solid arm speed and possesses mechanics that point to some increase in this area with natural strength progression. The 20-year-old does throw meaty strikes and frequently works in the fat part of the plate, but the overall looseness points to the potential for progress in this department as he builds experience through repetition. Honeywell's screwball is the best offering in his repertoire, as the consistency and deception of the pitch gets bats started early and can play as a true weapon against advanced hitters. His other secondary pieces—a curveball and changeup—presently lag behind and are unrefined. Honing at least one of these offerings into a viable option to consistently mix into sequences will be key in reaching the overall potential. This season will offer a look as to how well Honeywell can hold his stuff during a likely full-season assignment and whether the gains witnessed last summer were just a short-term spike. There's definitely something brewing here, with a good chance that he further solidifies himself as a top arm within this system by season's end.

8. Nate Karns   RHP

Born: 11/25/87   **Age:** 27   **Bats:** R   **Throws:** R   **Height:** 6'3"   **Weight:** 230

MLB ETA	CT	FB	CH	CB	SL	OFP	Realistic
Debuted in 2013	–	70	–	65	–	55 NO.3/4 STARTER	50 LATE INN RP (SETUP)

YEAR	TEAM	LVL	AGE	W	L	SV	G	GS	IP	H	HR	BB	K	BB9	SO9	GB%	BABIP	WHIP	ERA	FIP	FRA	WARP
2014	TBA	MLB	26	1	1	0	2	2	12.0	7	3	4	13	3.0	9.8	47%	.148	0.92	4.50	5.74	6.34	-0.1
2014	DUR	AAA	26	9	9	0	27	27	145.3	142	16	62	153	3.8	9.5	47%	.323	1.40	5.08	4.03	5.00	1.0
2015	TBA	MLB	27	7	9	0	25	25	132.3	122	15	57	129	3.9	8.8	46%	.294	1.35	4.07	4.53	4.42	0.7
2016	TBA	MLB	28	9	9	0	29	29	176.7	161	18	73	176	3.7	9.0	46%	.296	1.32	3.91	4.07	4.25	0.7

Breakout: 28%   Improve: 31%   Collapse: 11%   Attrition: 24%   MLB: 49%   Upside: 33   *Comparables: Corey Kluber, Joel Carreno, P.J. Walters*

Drafted/Acquired: 12st round, 2009 draft, Texas Tech University (Lubbock, TX)

Previous Ranking: NR

What Happened in 2014: Karns logged a heavy workload as a starter in Triple-A, where the results were on the inconsistent side, but the bat-missing ability continued to play up and the loud front two pitches offer promise in a short-burst role.

Strengths: Well filled out; strong and physical player; quick arm; fastball comfortably works 93-95 as starter; capable of reaching for more (96-97) and sitting there in short bursts; snaps off power curveball at 84-86; hard break, with depth and teeth through strike zone; bat-missing ability; will throw for a strike; average command of arsenal; competitive demeanor; high potential for stuff to play up a tick in relief role.

Weaknesses: Changeup lags behind other offerings; presently fringe-average; more of a show-me pitch than complementary piece; not overly loose with wrist when turning over; aggressive nature on mound; can get too amped up; inconsistent with landing; lacks feel for craft as a starter.

Risk Factor/Injury History: Low; achieved major leagues; mature arsenal.

Bret Sayre's Fantasy Take: You can look at the fact that there are only two pitches in his tools line above and think, "yep, he must be a reliever," but he's not entirely in that bucket yet. But with his concentrated arsenal, he could have more fantasy value in a bullpen role than a starting one.

The Year Ahead: There are times when we can allow the age to influence how we see players, and though Karns is on the older side, this is a legit prospect. Both the fastball and curveball are weapons at the right-hander's disposal. The offerings bring a high element of power to the arm's game, lending both bat-missing ability and the option to slice up the strike zone. There's also a strong competitive nature that shows in the way the pitcher goes about his business on the mound. Despite reaching the highest level in a starting capacity, sources see Karns fitting best in a relief role, fitting nicely at the back of a bullpen. His aggressive nature and lack of a true third offering make it tough to envision sustainment of the consistency necessary to churn through multiple lineups over the long run. The 27-year-old may continue to be stretched out as depth to start 2015, but when he's officially let loose in the later stages of games, look out.

9. Taylor Guerrieri RHP

Born: 12/1/92 **Age:** 22 **Bats:** R **Throws:** R **Height:** 6'3" **Weight:** 195

MLB ETA	CT	FB	CH	CB	SL	OFP	Realistic
2017	–	70	–	70	–	65 NO. 2 STARTER	50 NO. 4 STARTER

YEAR	TEAM	LVL	AGE	W	L	SV	G	GS	IP	H	HR	BB	K	BB9	SO9	GB%	BABIP	WHIP	ERA	FIP	FRA	WARP
2014	RAY	Rk	21	0	0	0	5	5	9.3	7	0	2	10	1.9	9.6	84%	.280	0.96	0.00	2.00	5.06	0.1
2015	TBA	MLB	22	2	3	0	8	8	33.7	37	4	14	20	3.7	5.3	56%	.300	1.51	5.06	5.41	5.50	-0.2
2016	TBA	MLB	23	8	9	0	30	30	191.3	192	16	64	139	3.0	6.5	56%	.298	1.34	4.08	4.15	4.43	0.3

Breakout: 0%   Improve: 0%   Collapse: 0%   Attrition: 0%   MLB: 0%   Upside: 9   *Comparables: Robbie Ross, Alex Cobb, Andrew Heaney*

Drafted/Acquired: 1st round, 2011 draft, Spring Valley HS (Columbia, SC)

Previous Ranking: #7 (Org)

What Happened in 2014: The right-hander made his return to the mound late in the season, and the stuff showed flashes of pre-Tommy John form, but questions still linger on keeping himself in check off the field.

Strengths: Excellent size; good present strength; repeatable delivery; smooth arm action; fastball works 91-93 with strong movement; arm-side run and sink with late life; can reach to mid-90s; snaps curveball with loose wrist; bends deeply with tight rotation; bat-missing offering; command growth potential.

Weaknesses: Still regaining feel for stuff postsurgery; can hold onto change too long when throwing; lacks quality action; often telegraphs secondary stuff; loose with fastball within the zone; works too elevated; makeup concerns (two drug of abuse violations).

Risk Factor/Injury History: High; Tommy John on résumé (2013); progression of viable third pitch.

Bret Sayre's Fantasy Take: It's impossible to ignore the risks with Guerrieri, but he checks in as the second-best fantasy prospect in this system (behind Adames) because the payoff could be closer to impact than anyone mentioned thus far. If he was dropped or forgotten about in your dynasty league, grab him now before he reminds owners why he was a first-round pick in the first place.

The Year Ahead: Guerrieri has the makings of a legit power arm, with the stuff to firmly cement himself in a rotation for many seasons to come. The 22-year-old right-hander brings to the table a lively heater and curveball that can be downright nasty on batters. His size, present strength, and athleticism lend strong clues that the pitcher can continue to physically develop to handle the rigors of the long season, and that there is also command growth that can be unlocked with further repetition. It's a solid package that can emerge. The injury was a developmental setback, though, and the second violation last offseason for a drug of abuse leaves questions as to whether the player can stay on course. Reports from Guerrieri's rehab and his return to the mound suggested there was the required focus and dedication to overcome the injury obstacle. This summer will provide a deeper look at this young arm's progression out of surgery, likely ramping in full-season ball, with a strong chance that once momentum starts to build the prior shine will return.

10. Casey Gillaspie   1B

Born: 1/25/93   **Age:** 22   **Bats:** B   **Throws:** L   **Height:** 6'4"   **Weight:** 240

MLB ETA	Hit	Power	Run	Glove	Arm	OFP	Realistic
2017	50	55	–	50	–	55 >AVG REGULAR	50 AVG ML PLAYER

YEAR	TEAM	LVL	AGE	PA	R	2B	3B	HR	RBI	BB	SO	SB	CS	AVG/OBP/SLG	TAv	BABIP	BRR	FRAA	WARP
2014	HUD	A-	21	308	27	16	1	7	42	42	65	2	3	.262/.364/.411	.267	.321	-2.5	1B(63): 3.0	0.3
2015	TBA	MLB	22	250	19	8	0	3	21	21	73	0	0	.189/.261/.270	.209	.259	-0.5	1B 2	-0.9
2016	TBA	MLB	23	250	28	10	0	6	25	21	71	0	0	.222/.295/.350	.242	.293	-0.6	1B 2	0.2

Breakout: 0%   Improve: 0%   Collapse: 0%   Attrition: 0%   MLB: 0%   Upside: 8   *Comparables: Matt Clark, Lucas Duda, Brock Peterson*

Drafted/Acquired: 1st round, 2014 draft, Wichita State University (Wichita, KS)

Previous Ranking: NR

What Happened in 2014: The big first baseman mashed his way through the Missouri Valley Conference in the spring to a video-game-like 1202 OPS before being selected by Tampa 20th overall and embarking on his professional journey in the New York-Penn League.

Strengths: Excellent present strength; well-filled-out body; powerful lower half; defined knowledge of strike zone; willing to go deep into counts; not afraid to hit with a strike or two; grinds through plate appearances looking for pitch to drive; generates loft with left-handed stroke; barrels up offerings hard; quick and efficient right-handed; uses the whole field from right side; potential for 20-plus home runs annually; soft hands; handles himself around bag well; shows ability to adjust.

Weaknesses: Tends to yank head of the bat, especially left-handed; deeper hand load from left side leads to concerns against high velocity on inner third; likely to see more swing-and-miss in game against premium stuff; will sell out for power; more of a contact hitter right-handed; needs improvement tapping into lower body for power to play to full potential; presently relies on upper body; limited range at first; lacks defensive versatility; first-base/DH type.

Risk Factor/Injury History: Moderate; limited professional experience; mature secondary skill set; first-base-only profile.

Bret Sayre's Fantasy Take: You'd expect a first-base profile who can move quickly to be a positive for fantasy value, and it is, but Gillaspie doesn't provide the type of upside you need in a 1B/UT in shallow mixed formats. In deeper leagues, he makes for a solid value pick in dynasty drafts, but not among the first 30 picks.

The Year Ahead: Gillaspie is an advanced bat, with the type of secondary skills at the plate and well-rounded approach that point to a quicker assimilation into full-season ball, along with the potential to track fairly quickly into the upper minors and beyond. The 22-year-old's ability to control plate appearances and grind through sequences is very noticeable. It's hard not to envision the first baseman taking advantage of inexperienced arms in the near term and doing some serious damage as he finds his footing in pro ball. This is also player oozing strength, with a body already built for handling the grind of the long season. There's plenty of power for the switch-hitter to tap into, though opinions see the game power not playing up to the strength level unless Gillaspie can get more out of his lower half in the swing mechanics. The rubber is likely to meet the road when the prospect reaches Double-A, where the quality of arms will be more of a match for his skill set and some evaluators feel the lack of premium bat speed will start to catch up in the form of reduced contact. This isn't an overly high-ceiling prospect, but one with a shorter lead time and high probability of major-league payout.

Prospects on the Rise

1. OF Justin Williams: Williams came to the Tampa Bay organization as half of the return for Jeremy Hellickson, fresh off of a productive 2014 split between Rookie and Low-A ball. After being frequently pitched around in high school, and often struggling against premium stuff on the prep showcase circuit, Williams has been a pleasant surprise from the drop in pro ball. The lefty wields the barrel with confidence and accuracy in the box, with his feel for contact exceeding evaluator expectations thus far. Previously viewed as a power-based lotto ticket, over 500-plus pro plate appearances Williams has displayed the characteristics of a bat with a chance to hit for average at the highest level, thanks to his bat speed and natural bat-to-ball skills. Questions remain regarding his ability to spot quality spin and maintain a tight enough attack zone to ensure quality hitters counts and balls to drive, however, and until the raw power translates to regular in-game production the profile will be miscast as a 'tweener of sorts. The raw goods are present, and it would be a mistake to undersell the import of his impressive showings at the plate and the progress he has made defensively after shifting to the outfield. There's a wide spread between upside and likely outcome, but the combination of youth, raw ability, physicality, and aptitude is a quality jumping-off point for Tampa Bay's development staff. He could begin 2015 back in the Midwest League, where he will look to build on his success at the plate and continue to improve his execution both in the outfield and on the bases, and will play the bulk of this season at the age of 19.

2. LHP Blake Snell: The 22-year-old left-hander is one of those intriguing arms that may end up taking bigger strides toward the end of his minor-league developmental cycle due to the nature of the rough edges he still needs to polish. Snell showed some improvement last season repeating his delivery, which aided in keeping his arm in a more consistent slot and allowed the low-90s fastball to be thrown downhill more often, and his slider and change to more frequently flash above average. His struggles with finding a uniform release have historically led to frequent arm-side misses and a general lack of ability to execute consistently in all four quadrants of the strike zone, and those issue still persist— albeit it to a lesser extent than in years past. While the former first rounder still has a ways to go to push the command to where it needs to be if he's to stick in a rotation long term, the raw stuff will play, and his athleticism should help him continue to build toward a future as a starter. He should start 2015 back in High-A, with a good chance to crack the next level at some point in the middle of the summer, elevating his status in the system in the process.

3. C Nick Ciuffo: It was a mixed overall season for the former first-round pick, with the gap to go being a bit larger than previously identified, but the talent and potential remain. The stroke from the left side is pretty and smooth, while the defensive ability points to a backstop that can round into an above-average defender down the line. Dual-threat development can be tricky though. The pressure on both aspects of the game, along with the delicate balance that comes with splitting focus, can lead to unevenness or one side lagging in stretches while the other gets the attention. It may seem like being down on the 19-year-old, which isn't the case, as reassessments and resetting the baseline are important. With progress showing the rough edges are starting to give way to more polish, especially in regards to picking up stuff with spin better at the plate and handling offerings more firmly behind the dish, Ciuffo has the potential to quickly shoot back up this system next offseason.

Factors on the Farm
Prospects likely to contribute at the major-league level in 2015

1. OF Mikie Mahtook: The ceiling isn't huge for the Louisiana State University product, but the prospect enters the season with a chance to be in the major-league mix at some point in 2015. Mahtook is capable of playing all three outfield positions, and while he profiles best in a corner, the 25-year-old can spell center in stretches. The development of power has been an area of question for the outfielder since signing with the organization. The right-handed hitter showed more last season in Triple-A, but it also came with some added swing-and-miss in his offensive game, which leaves many to suggest that a balance between contact and power will be a difficult line for the player to find against the highest competition. It's a fourth-outfielder profile, with some below-average regular upside at peak, and brings value to a bench in the long run. Look for Mahtook to make his debut in 2015 and get a chance to begin carving out a role.

2. LHP Enny Romero: The 24-year-old took a bit of a step backward, or at least remained in neutral, during 2014, primarily driven by very inconsistent command. Romero can certainly crank up his fastball, often popping into the mid-90s, and snaps off a tightly breaking power curveball. Both offerings can flash double-plus in stretches,

---

FROM THE FIELD

Casey Gillaspie

Team: Tampa Bay Rays
Evaluator: Tucker Blair
Dates seen: June 27–29, August 31, and September 1, 2014
Affiliate: Hudson Valley Renegades (Short-Season A, Rays)
Physical/health: Body likely maxed; similar frame to his brother Connor; thicker frame; likely needs to stay in shape; thicker legs and power lower half.
Makeup: Good makeup; team-oriented player that handles himself professionally.

MLB ETA	Risk factor	OFP	Realistic role
2016	Moderate	50	45; second-division/bench player

Tool	Future grade	Report
Hit	50	Left-handed hitter: Slight loft; better power side; more swing-and-miss; hands and feet move slightly more from this side; more pull than spray; load is bigger from this side; less contact but more impact.
		Right-handed hitter: Linear swing; bat is quick through zone; minimal movement in hands; very soft load that lacks drive; more contact oriented; sprays the ball all over field from this side.
		Plus bat speed; does not use hips enough; lacks true torque; great approach; ability to lay off close pitches and work counts into his favor; terrific batting eye; moderate ability to recognize spin.
Power	50	Most power derives from left side; lofted swing with bigger load; plus raw power; plays down in-game and especially from right side; power could display more down the road once he begins to establish himself within pro ball.
Baserunning/ speed	40	4.47 home to first; below-average speed; lacks a good first or second gear; slow-paced speed; not a weapon; looks like a first baseman.
Glove	50	First-base profile; soft hands; able to get good extension off the base; good pick; works well around the base; lacks large range; not highly athletic but can handle first base with ease.
Arm	50	Average arm; did not display it much playing first base; looks to have enough strength for the arm to work in corner outfield spots.

Overall: Gillaspie is the younger brother of Connor Gillaspie.

He lacks true impact at first base, but can handle the bat efficiently enough to play as a second division mold. The bat is consistent from the right side, showing a linear swing that is able to produce more efficiently. However, the left side is where all his power impact will likely come.

The overall package is not impact, but Gillaspie should be a fast moving prospect that displays a great approach and excellent maturity. This is a floor prospect rather than ceiling.

especially when the left-hander is using his size to stay tall and above the baseball. The well-below-average command is problematic as a starter, typically forcing Romero into long, drawn-out sequences and leaving his heater in dangerous areas where good hitters are waiting to pounce. The stuff and size lead to dreams of what might happen if things click, but the smart money says this is a reliever, and one who can play up as a power arm toward the back of a bullpen as soon as this season.

3. RHP Jose Dominguez: Acquired from the Dodgers in November 2014, the 24-year-old right-hander offers the organization another potential late-inning arm at its disposal and enters the season in the mix to earn a spot in the bullpen. Dominguez is known for his high-90s heat that can downright overpower hitters when he's staying above the baseball and creating leverage. The knock on the arm has been his ability to be consistent with his release, along with staying on the field over the course of the last few seasons. There is nothing tricky about this arm. He primarily leans on his fastball, where the secondary stuff is more of a quick look before turning right back to it. He lives and dies with the pitch. It's an arm that can begin bridging the sixth or seventh innings as soon as this season.

1. Joey Gallo 3B

Born: 11/19/93 **Age:** 21 **Bats:** L **Throws:** R **Height:** 6'5" **Weight:** 205

	Hit	Power	Run	Glove	Arm		OFP	Realistic
MLB ETA							70	50
2016	–	80	–	50	70		ALL STAR	ML REGULAR

YEAR	TEAM	LVL	AGE	PA	R	2B	3B	HR	RBI	BB	SO	SB	CS	AVG/OBP/SLG	TAv	BABIP	BRR	FRAA	WARP
2014	FRI	AA	20	291	44	10	0	21	56	36	115	2	0	.232/.334/.524	.297	.322	-1.3	3B(53): 1.0, 1B(7): -0.0	0.5
2014	MYR	A+	20	246	53	9	3	21	50	51	64	5	3	.323/.463/.735	.391	.370	1.0	3B(54): 3.5	6.9
2015	TEX	MLB	21	250	35	7	1	17	43	26	98	1	0	.219/.303/.488	.288	.289	-0.1	3B 0, 1B -0	0.9
2016	TEX	MLB	22	250	38	7	1	17	43	27	98	1	0	.217/.306/.493	.291	.289	-0.1	3B 0, 1B 0	2.1

Breakout: 5% **Improve:** 24% **Collapse:** 8% **Attrition:** 7% **MLB:** 40% **Upside:** 306 *Comparables: Giancarlo Stanton, Javier Baez, Domingo Santana*

> #15
> BP Top 101 Prospects

Drafted/Acquired: 1st round, 2012 draft, Bishop Gorman HS (Las Vegas, NV)

Previous Ranking: #6 (Org), #95 (Top 101)

What Happened in 2014: The legend of Gallo and his Herculean power continued to grow, with the Las Vegas native launching 40 home runs between two levels (good for second in the minors) and putting on a batting practice performance at the 2014 Futures Game over All-Star weekend that overshadowed the MLB Home Run Derby held the next evening.

Strengths: Elite raw power; jaw-dropping displays both pregame and in game; huge leverage and extension through contact; showed improved ability to make in-game adjustments throughout summer; powerful trunk and core; thick, maturing body; good athlete for size; controls body; impressive bat speed; easy double-plus arm across the diamond; glove continues to improve, as does footwork at third.

Weaknesses: Big swing-and-miss; some coverage holes due to long levers; almost no ability to make in-swing adjustments due to swing path produced by heavy rotation through hips and long arms; still improving setup on throws; hit utility could eat into giant raw; can struggle to keep on line; below-average runner.

Risk Factor/Injury History: Moderate; swing-and-miss concerns persist as he works toward high minors.

Bret Sayre's Fantasy Take: There's little point in questioning Gallo's upside, as it's that of a perennial top-five option at the hot corner—even with a .250 average. The issue here is the risk, and it has significantly diminished since a year ago, clearing the way for Gallo to be one of the most exciting dynasty prospects around with his potential 40-plus homer power.

The Year Ahead: Forget watching a Gallo BP session or tracking the ball from the pitcher to contact to the far reaches beyond the outfield wall, the mere sound of Gallo making contact elicits feelings of majesty—the glorious Ninth, by Ludwig Van, angel trumpets, and devil trombones. There isn't a player in the game that outstrips Gallo in the raw power department, and while a year ago the promise of a generational slugger was very much something to dream on, Gallo's growth throughout the 2014 season, and particularly his demonstrated ability to begin making adjustments in game and more generally with respect to his level of competition, have pushed the profile closer to realization. He is far from out of the woods, as demonstrated by his struggles upon initial exposure to Double-A competition. But his progress, both at the plate and on the dirt, has been impressive, and he is nearing the point where even a low estimated outcome could see Gallo as a useful major-league piece. He will return to the Texas League to continue to refine his approach and adjust to more advanced arms. The safe money has Gallo splitting this season between Double- and Triple-A and reaching the majors at some point in 2016. Should Texas find itself in a position where Gallo's unique skill set has immediate utility to assist a push at the major-league level, however, he could easily find himself taking swings in Arlington sometime in the next seven months.

2. Chi Chi Gonzalez   RHP

Born: 1/15/92   **Age:** 23   **Bats:** R   **Throws:** R   **Height:** 6'2"   **Weight:** 195

MLB ETA	CT	FB	CH	CB	SL	OFP	Realistic
2015	–	70	60	–	60	65 NO. 2/3 STARTER	60 NO. 3 STARTER

YEAR	TEAM	LVL	AGE	W	L	SV	G	GS	IP	H	HR	BB	K	BB9	SO9	GB%	BABIP	WHIP	ERA	FIP	FRA	WARP
2014	FRI	AA	22	7	4	0	15	14	73.3	67	3	25	64	3.1	7.9	55%	.300	1.25	2.70	3.09	4.22	1.0
2014	MYR	A+	22	5	2	0	11	11	65.3	56	3	16	49	2.2	6.8	55%	.262	1.10	2.62	3.62	4.13	0.8
2015	TEX	MLB	23	5	8	0	22	22	100.3	108	9	37	65	3.3	5.8	52%	.302	1.44	4.62	4.71	5.02	0.2
2016	TEX	MLB	24	9	9	0	31	31	193.0	190	15	57	143	2.7	6.7	52%	.295	1.28	3.74	3.89	4.06	1.6

Breakout: 0%   **Improve:** 0%   **Collapse:** 0%   **Attrition:** 0%   **MLB:** 0%   **Upside:** 28   *Comparables: Robbie Ross, Jarred Cosart, Bobby Livingston*

Drafted/Acquired: 1st round, 2013 draft, Oral Roberts University (Tulsa, OK)

Previous Ranking: #3 (Org), #70 (Top 101)

What Happened in 2014: Gonzalez split his summer between Myrtle Beach and Frisco, flexing a potent four-pitch mix and impressive command.

Strengths: Three-way heater plays low- to mid-90s with run, sink, and cut action; commands pitch very well across and outside of the zone; plus slider comes with mid-80s velocity, tilt, and solid bite; swing-and-miss offering that plays well off the fastball; can back door and back foot to oppo bats and bury to same-side sticks; has made strides with the changeup, now showing consistent 8-11 mph velo delta off the fastball and coming with some tumble and occasional cut; third potential plus offering; will drop an occasional early-count curve to get ahead; good balance; high floor.

Weaknesses: Command can get a little loose in the zone; still working to effectively meld changeup into sequencing; curve can get borderline gimmicky, with deliberate release; delivery with some stiffness, which can negatively affect control if timing falls too far out of whack.

Risk Factor/Injury History: Low; could be big-league ready by mid-2015.

Bret Sayre's Fantasy Take: The 2013 draftee has often been cast as a lower upside starter in dynasty leagues due to the fact that he doesn't throw 100 or rack up huge strikeout numbers, but Gonzalez has the talent to be a strong SP3, even in shallower leagues, and a floor much higher than many of his peers. With a second-half debut possible, this is your last chance to get him at a reasonable price.

The Year Ahead: Gonzalez has enjoyed a rapid ascent through the Rangers system, with his fastball and slider paving the way. While the power tandem atop the arsenal does the heavy lifting, the development of a not only effective but potentially impactful changeup, as well as the chance for a useful fourth look in the form of a curve, could push the Oral Roberts product into front-end territory. He is still finding his way as he learns to more effectively incorporate his lesser secondary offerings, and if and when he is capable of wielding those weapons with the same level of comfort as his fastball and slider, he could see a rapid uptick in strikeouts and nasty looks from opposing hitters. Gonzalez could find himself with a brief return to Frisco, but is ready to take on Triple-A competition if the Rangers have the room in the Round Rock rotation and are so inclined. Either way, he should debut in 2015 and has the stuff and refinement to stick once he arrives.

#29
BP Top 101 Prospects

3. Jorge Alfaro   C

Born: 6/11/93   **Age:** 22   **Bats:** R   **Throws:** R   **Height:** 6'2"   **Weight:** 185

MLB ETA	Hit	Power	Run	Glove	Arm	OFP	Realistic
2016	–	60	55	50	80	65 1ST DIV/ALL STAR	55 > AVG REGULAR

YEAR	TEAM	LVL	AGE	PA	R	2B	3B	HR	RBI	BB	SO	SB	CS	AVG/OBP/SLG	TAv	BABIP	BRR	FRAA	WARP
2014	FRI	AA	21	99	12	4	0	4	14	6	23	0	0	.261/.343/.443	.264	.311	0.1	C(15): 0.1, 1B(1): 0.1	0.4
2014	MYR	A+	21	437	63	22	5	13	73	23	100	6	5	.261/.318/.440	.263	.315	-1.7	C(75): 1.6, 1B(17): 0.2	1.7
2015	TEX	MLB	22	250	22	10	1	6	26	8	77	2	1	.214/.257/.341	.227	.287	-0.1	C 1, 1B -0	0.0
2016	TEX	MLB	23	250	26	10	1	6	26	9	73	2	1	.217/.265/.355	.233	.284	-0.2	C 1, 1B 0	0.0

Breakout: 0%   **Improve:** 0%   **Collapse:** 0%   **Attrition:** 0%   **MLB:** 0%   **Upside:** 23   *Comparables: Max Stassi, Luke Montz, Wilin Rosario*

Drafted/Acquired: International free agent, 2010, Colombia

Previous Ranking: #2 (Org), #41 (Top 101)

What Happened in 2014: Alfaro earned a midseason promotion to Double-A Frisco shortly after turning 21 and continued to showcase prime-time power and elite arm strength to go with a well-rounded skill set that carries with it potential to impact the game in all facets.

Strengths: Strong; big athleticism; moves very well for a catcher, recording home-to-first times in 4.15 to 4.30 range; double-plus raw that could manifest in game as a true plus weapon; slowly refining as a receiver and technical defender, including transfer and release and blocking; elite arm strength; improving approach at the plate leaves door open for an average hit tool at maturity.

#31
BP Top 101 Prospects

Weaknesses: Aggregate defense below average at present; can vacillate between too loose and too stiff in the wrist; can give away strikes on the margins; transfer and release limit impact of arm strength; high-effort swing can be managed with solid off-speed; some trouble making in-game adjustments; can get overly aggressive and lock in looking fastball, exasperating swing-and-miss issues.

Risk Factor/Injury History: Moderate; reached Double-A and held his own; still carries risk associated with dual development of catcher skill set and hit-tool refinement.

Bret Sayre's Fantasy Take: Catchers who can hit .260 with 25-plus homers and a slew of RBI don't exactly grow on trees, so the excitement that has followed Alfaro around for years is warranted. There's little standing in the way for Alfaro in Texas, and despite the boom-or-bust reputation he's been saddled with, he's safer with the stick than most assume.

The Year Ahead: Alfaro continues to stand out for his premium athleticism and strength-based impact tools. Progress was made last year in incrementally improving his approach, and he continues to work to find a balance between leveraging his impact power through aggressively attacking the ball and being willing to let pitchers throw around him. Alfaro has started to identify situations where he is unlikely to get a ball to drive and has been more willing to adjust his approach accordingly than in the past. That said, he is still an overly aggressive swinger and upper-level arms are going to continue to try and lead him out of the zone in playing to that aggressiveness. Alfaro continues to struggle with identifying and handling same-side spin down and away, and needs to do a better job of letting his power come naturally rather than looking to yank and drive. He'll return to Frisco to start 2015, with a continued focus on refining his defense and tightening up his approach enough to blossom into a power/on-base bat capable of holding down a spot in the middle of a major-league order.

4. Nomar Mazara RF

Born: 4/26/95   **Age:** 20   **Bats:** L   **Throws:** L   **Height:** 6'4"   **Weight:** 195

MLB ETA	Hit	Power	Run	Glove	Arm	OFP	Realistic
2016	60	60	–	50	60	65 1ST DIV/ALL STAR	55 > AVG REGULAR

YEAR	TEAM	LVL	AGE	PA	R	2B	3B	HR	RBI	BB	SO	SB	CS	AVG/OBP/SLG	TAv	BABIP	BRR	FRAA	WARP
2014	FRI	AA	19	97	10	7	1	3	16	9	22	0	0	.306/.381/.518	.305	.377	-3.1	RF(23): -0.7	0.1
2014	HIC	A	19	461	68	21	2	19	73	57	99	4	3	.264/.358/.470	.291	.304	-3.5	RF(91): -11.2	0.9
2015	TEX	MLB	20	250	22	9	1	6	26	18	74	0	0	.210/.271/.336	.231	.277	-0.4	RF -4	-0.8
2016	TEX	MLB	21	250	29	11	1	6	27	23	66	0	0	.232/.306/.375	.256	.296	-0.5	RF -4	0.7

Breakout: 0%   Improve: 0%   Collapse: 0%   Attrition: 0%   MLB: 0%   Upside: 15   *Comparables: Caleb Gindl, Chris Parmelee, Travis Snider*

Drafted/Acquired: International free agent, 2011, Dominican Republic

Previous Ranking: #8 (Org)

What Happened in 2014: The then-19-year-old enjoyed a breakout year between Low-A Hickory and Double-A Frisco, tallying 22 bombs and posting a plump 90-point on-base delta over his average.

Strengths: Advanced approach; big raw power has a chance to play thanks to bat speed, barrel control, and ability to track; quick trigger; prototypical corner profile; chance for hit to play to plus; plus arm; improved actions on the grass; enough progress to project glove to fringe-average or better; improved release and carry on throws; strong with more to come; very high ceiling bat.

Weaknesses: Big issues with same-side stuff; trouble consistently covering outer half against lefties; defense below average at present; needs to improve routes; below-average runner who will slow more as the body matures.

Risk Factor/Injury History: High; significant split issues; swing-and-miss has potential to limit impact of bat.

Bret Sayre's Fantasy Take: Another name, another slam-dunk top-50 dynasty prospect. Mazara made huge strides in 2014, making him one of the fastest risers in fantasy leagues. The potential is there for a .290-hitting outfielder with 25 homers—which would make him a pretty easy OF2 in most formats.

The Year Ahead: Last season was highly impressive for the then-teenage Dominican and leaves him ready to emerge as one of the top bats in the minors. Mazara possesses the bat speed and hand/eye to handle pitches across the quadrants, though he tracks much better out of righty arms. It's a broad frame that's already filling in and should continue to hang more "good" mass along the way, particularly in the trunk. If Mazara is able to put together a more effective approach against same-side arms, there is potential for the bat to emerge as a true plus hit/plus power package, which paired with a fringe-average glove and well-above-average arm would put him comfortably in the upper tier of right fielders in the game at maturity. Mazara won't turn 20 until April and will benefit from an extended spin through the Texas League. Steady progress should see him in Texas by 2017, though it would surprise no one if he forces the issue with his bat much sooner than that. If he can repeat his efforts from 2014, Mazara should solidify his status as the Rangers' right fielder of the future and a potential fixture in the middle of the lineup for years to come.

#40

BP Top
101
Prospects

5. Jake Thompson RHP

Born: 1/31/94 **Age:** 21 **Bats:** R **Throws:** R **Height:** 6'4" **Weight:** 235

MLB ETA	CT	FB	CH	CB	SL	OFP	Realistic
2016	–	60	50	–	65	65 NO.2/3 STARTER	55 NO.3/4 STARTER

YEAR	TEAM	LVL	AGE	W	L	SV	G	GS	IP	H	HR	BB	K	BB9	SO9	GB%	BABIP	WHIP	ERA	FIP	FRA	WARP
2014	FRI	AA	20	3	1	0	7	6	35.7	28	3	18	44	4.5	11.1	46%	.305	1.29	3.28	3.34	5.35	0.3
2014	ERI	AA	20	1	0	0	2	2	11.0	10	0	4	7	3.3	5.7	40%	.286	1.27	2.45	3.45	4.00	0.2
2014	LAK	A+	20	6	4	0	16	16	83.0	75	3	25	79	2.7	8.6	44%	.316	1.20	3.14	3.11	3.61	1.5
2015	TEX	MLB	21	5	7	0	20	20	98.7	101	10	44	83	4.0	7.6	43%	.308	1.47	4.56	4.78	4.96	0.1
2016	TEX	MLB	22	8	10	0	29	29	177.0	181	17	75	143	3.8	7.3	43%	.306	1.44	4.46	4.43	4.85	-0.1

Breakout: 0%   Improve: 0%   Collapse: 0%   Attrition: 0%   MLB: 0%   Upside: 17   *Comparables: Jarrod Parker, Carlos Martinez, Chris Tillman*

Drafted/Acquired: 2nd round, 2012 draft, Rock Wall-Heath HS (Heath, TX)

Previous Ranking: #4 (Org)

#47 BP Top 101 Prospects

What Happened in 2014: Thompson reached Double-A as a 20-year-old and emerged from 2014 better able to maintain his velocity through his starts and more comfortable utilizing his changeup and curve, strengthening his chances of not only sticking in a rotation long term, but thriving in that role.

Strengths: Hard and heavy heater; two-seamer shows arm-side action in the 89-92 mph velo band; can dial four-seamer up to the mid-90s; mid-80s slider comes with tilt and sharp, late bite; can throw to both sides of the plate and pitch off of offering; very high level of comfort; improved feel for low- to mid-80s changeup; solid innings jump without stuff backing up; projects to handle major-league starters workload without issue; not afraid to work inside aggressively; tough downward plane on fastball out of three-quarters slot.

Weaknesses: Lacks consistent weapon against lefties; can drop arm on slider, causing pitch to ride along swing plane; still developing feel for changeup; can get too firm, losing fade; inconsistent timing; lower half can get out front, causing drag; curve still plays below average; command still inconsistent and, when struggling with timing, can slip into bouts of wildness; can rely too heavily on slider.

Risk Factor/Injury History: Moderate; limited upper-minors experience.

Bret Sayre's Fantasy Take: During the 2014 season, Thompson went from interesting flier to bona fide dynasty target. He has the profile of a starter capable of striking out 180-plus batters and throwing a slew of innings. The right-hander has borderline SP2 upside, but will likely top out as a solid SP3.

The Year Ahead: Thompson's 2014 began with a two-month run during which he held opposing hitters to a .200 average and .237 slugging while striking out just under a batter an inning. His High-A dominance earned him a midseason promotion to Double-A Erie at the age of 20 and just over 200 pro innings to his name. Thompson continued to dominate through his first two Double-A starts before finding himself shipped to the Rangers organization as part of a package traded for Joakim Soria. Thompson took the change of scenery in stride, finishing the season strongly and completing a highly successful developmental campaign. As impressive as Thompson's fastball and slider are, he will need to more frequently and effectively tap into his changeup if he's to continue working toward his immense potential. He's a prime candidate to return to the Texas League to continue refining his third and fourth offerings. With concerns about his ability to maintain velocity seemingly behind him, Thompson is looking more and more the part of a mid-rotation starter, with an outside shot of producing at an even higher rate should he continue to refine the frequency with which he is able to repeat his mechanics and execute his offerings.

6. Luis Ortiz RHP

Born: 9/22/95 **Age:** 19 **Bats:** R **Throws:** R **Height:** 6'3" **Weight:** 230

MLB ETA	CT	FB	CH	CB	SL	OFP	Realistic
2018	–	65	55	–	60	65 NO. 2/3 STARTER	50 NO. 4 STARTER

YEAR	TEAM	LVL	AGE	W	L	SV	G	GS	IP	H	HR	BB	K	BB9	SO9	GB%	BABIP	WHIP	ERA	FIP	FRA	WARP
2014	HIC	A	18	0	0	1	3	1	7.0	4	1	3	4	3.9	5.1	-%	.143	1.00	1.29	5.59	6.07	\N
2014	RNG	Rk	18	1	1	0	6	5	13.3	12	0	3	15	2.0	10.1	-%	.343	1.12	2.03	2.68	2.91	\N

Drafted/Acquired: 1st round, 2014 draft, Sanger HS (Sanger, CA)

Previous Ranking: NR

What Happened in 2014: Ortiz lit up the showcase circuit and was named MVP on the USA Baseball Gold Medal 18U team before coming off the board to Texas at the end of the first round of the 2014 draft and pounding complex- and rookie-league bats during his 20-inning pro debut.

Strengths: Pure power arsenal; fastball plays from the low-90s all the way up to 97 mph with regularity; slider is a future plus offering with sharp action in the low- to mid-80s; slider comes with enough bite and deception to miss bats in and out of the zone; ability to lead with slider or fastball in setting up hitters; changeup shows promise, with some arm speed deception and fade; big, sturdy build; repeats mechanics consistently; good competitor; advanced ability to throw strikes with regularity.

Weaknesses: Lacks projection; missed time in spring due to forearm tightness; high effort; changeup isn't a go-to pitch yet; needs to build up confidence in offering; curve still in nascent stages; tired some toward end of season/fall.

Risk Factor/Injury History: High; yet to reach full-season ball; missed time in spring with forearm tightness.

Bret Sayre's Fantasy Take: The enigmatic prep pitcher has plenty of upside and talent to reach the SP2 level, but has a long way to go to get there—both developmentally and chronologically. It's a risk, but Ortiz would be a smart pick late in the second round of dynasty drafts.

The Year Ahead: Ortiz was one of the more electric arms in the 2014 draft class and, had he not missed three weeks in the spring with elbow issues, almost certainly would have been off the board well before the 30th pick. The former Fresno State commit has no issue maintaining velocity into the middle innings and has the physicality to shoulder a heavy pro workload. There's always some trepidation when a young power arm is shelved with forearm tightness, but thus far Ortiz has shown no ill effects from the missed time. A full-season assignment seems likely in 2015, as his fastball/slider combo is too advanced for rookie-level competition. Assuming he's healthy, Ortiz could move quickly through the system and projects well as a mid-rotation innings-eater with a nice fallback as a late-inning power arm.

---

7. Nick Williams LF

Born: 9/8/93   **Age:** 21   **Bats:** L   **Throws:** L   **Height:** 6'3"   **Weight:** 195

MLB ETA	Hit	Power	Run	Glove	Arm	OFP	Realistic
2017	**65**	**55**	**60**	–	–	**60** 1ST DIVISION PLAYER	**50** AVG ML PLAYER

YEAR	TEAM	LVL	AGE	PA	R	2B	3B	HR	RBI	BB	SO	SB	CS	AVG/OBP/SLG	TAv	BABIP	BRR	FRAA	WARP
2014	FRI	AA	20	64	4	2	1	0	4	2	21	1	1	.226/.250/.290	.201	.341	0.1	LF(11): -0.4, CF(4): -0.1	-0.3
2014	MYR	A+	20	408	61	28	4	13	68	19	117	5	7	.292/.343/.491	.281	.391	-1.3	LF(44): -0.5, CF(25): -2.1	1.6
2014	RNG	Rk	20	14	3	0	1	0	2	1	2	0	0	.308/.357/.462	.278	.364	0.4	CF(3): 0.6	0.2
2015	TEX	MLB	21	250	22	10	2	6	27	5	83	2	2	.226/.252/.360	.227	.313	-0.2	LF -1, CF -1	-0.7
2016	TEX	MLB	22	250	26	11	2	6	27	7	80	2	2	.236/.270/.384	.241	.326	-0.2	LF -2, CF -1	-0.1

Breakout: 0%   Improve: 0%   Collapse: 0%   Attrition: 0%   MLB: 0%   Upside: 23   *Comparables: Chris Davis, Marcell Ozuna, Greg Halman*

Drafted/Acquired: 2nd round, 2012 draft, Ball HS (Galveston, TX)

Previous Ranking: #5 (Org), #88 (Top 101)

What Happened in 2014: Williams had his innate bat-to-ball skills on display through 94 games with High-A Myrtle Beach before earning a late-season promotion to Double-A at the age of 20.

#71
BP Top 101 Prospects

Strengths: Natural feel for the barrel; tracks spin; very good bat speed; compact delivery; good plate coverage and ability to make hard contact across the hit zone, utilizing entire field; plus raw power; ability to both turn on velocity and drive the other way; improving strength; bat projects to impact; plus runner underway.

Weaknesses: Lacks feel; instincts in field and on bases are poor; speed plays down due to reads/jumps; overly aggressive at the plate; still formulating an approach; locked into see-ball-hit-ball mentality; propensity to give away at-bats once behind; arm plays below average.

Risk Factor/Injury History: Moderate; limited Double-A exposure; profile heavily reliant on natural hit ability.

Bret Sayre's Fantasy Take: Just when you thought we couldn't find any more top-shelf fantasy assets on this list, here comes Williams. The risks are well known and detailed here, but Williams could end up as a near-.300 hitter with 25-home-run power if everything clicks. Of course, the odds of his turning into an OF1 are small, and the flameout risk is high, but dynasty leagues are won by the bold. Sometimes.

The Year Ahead: Williams provides an interesting juxtaposition of top-shelf feel for contact and excessive swing-and-miss in his game. The good news is that even a moderate tightening of his approach could lead to a huge breakout at the plate. Unfortunately, there are enough questions about Williams's overall feel for the game to call into question whether he will ever be able to fully leverage his preternatural ability to track baseballs out of the hand and find them with the barrel. There isn't much value to be teased out in the field or on the bases, so everything is riding on Williams's ability to focus his kill zone and limit the number of at-bats he gives away once he falls behind. There are precious few ballplayers that come with the potential to grow into a true plus-plus hit tool, and fewer still that pair that upside with above-average power potential. The former Texas prep product checks both of those boxes and will return to Double-A Frisco in 2015 looking to tap into that potential with more regularity.

8. Luke Jackson RHP

Born: 8/24/91 **Age:** 23 **Bats:** R **Throws:** R **Height:** 6'2" **Weight:** 205

MLB ETA	CT	FB	CH	CB	SL	OFP	Realistic
2015	–	65	55	60	50	55 NO.3/4 STARTER	50 LATE-INN RP

YEAR	TEAM	LVL	AGE	W	L	SV	G	GS	IP	H	HR	BB	K	BB9	SO9	GB%	BABIP	WHIP	ERA	FIP	FRA	WARP
2014	ROU	AAA	22	1	3	0	11	10	40.0	56	9	28	43	6.3	9.7	45%	.395	2.10	10.35	6.72	8.20	-0.7
2014	FRI	AA	22	8	2	1	15	14	83.3	58	5	24	83	2.6	9.0	44%	.242	0.98	3.02	2.92	3.24	1.7
2015	TEX	MLB	23	5	8	0	21	21	102.0	105	11	53	88	4.7	7.8	43%	.307	1.54	4.92	4.99	5.35	-0.3
2016	TEX	MLB	24	8	8	0	27	27	162.0	149	13	73	158	4.1	8.8	43%	.299	1.37	3.93	3.90	4.27	1.0

Breakout: 0%   Improve: 0%   Collapse: 0%   Attrition: 0%   MLB: 0%   Upside: 43   *Comparables: Chris Withrow, Scott Barnes, Jered Weaver*

Drafted/Acquired: 1st round, 2010 draft, Calvary Christian HS (Fort Lauderdale, FL)

Previous Ranking: #7 (Org)

What Happened in 2014: After a solid 83 innings with Double-A Frisco, Jackson jumped to Triple-A Round Rock, where he immediately ran into issues both in and out of the zone, leaving evaluators still split as to whether his future lies in a rotation or at the back of a bullpen.

Strengths: Big arm; fastball can play low- to mid-90s with late life, regularly topping 97 mph up in the zone; high release creates angle; can hold velo late into starts; curve is second potential plus weapon; clean and deep 12-to-6 action, flashing bite; changeup will tease with tumble; some arm-speed deception; solid job hitting uniform release with fastball; will mix in a slider with some vertical action; sturdy build; likes to challenge hitters.

Weaknesses: Struggles to maintain mechanics, leading to inconsistent execution and frequent bouts of wildness; command is very loose in the zone; fastball flattens up and can be easy to square from front to back of hit zone; can struggle to spot curve with consistency; changeup often comes too firm; slider plays below average, not pure fit for slot; can get predictable with fastball; mechanical issues can snowball with runners on as a result of speeding up to the plate and forcing lower half further out front.

Risk Factor/Injury History: Low; should contribute in some capacity; achieved Double-A success.

Bret Sayre's Fantasy Take: There will always be Luke Jackson Stuff Apologists in every deep league, and for good reason. However, his inconsistencies push Jackson to a frustrating SP4 level if he sticks in the rotation (though with more strikeouts than most other SP4s), and someone who is likely off the radar—barring saves—if he's a reliever.

The Year Ahead: Jackson has the raw stuff to dominate, but lacks the feel and precision to leverage that stuff into dominant production. He is most effective establishing his fastball, though inconsistencies in his secondaries can result in an overreliance on the heater, allowing hitters to sit on the pitch. Further complicating the matter is Jackson's preference to chase the strikeout and challenge hitters in the zone, as opposed to pushing the development of the changeup and relying on the livelier low-90s rendition of the fastball, each of which could be useful tools in drawing soft contact and helping to keep pitch counts down. Jackson should get another shot at Triple-A to start 2015 and will be on the short list of arms to get a call to the big club as need arises. His fastball and curve could play well in a late-inning role should he prove incapable of finding enough consistency in his mechanics to effectively turn over upper-level lineups.

9. Lewis Brinson CF

Born: 5/8/94 **Age:** 21 **Bats:** R **Throws:** R **Height:** 6'3" **Weight:** 170

MLB ETA	Hit	Power	Run	Glove	Arm	OFP	Realistic
2017	–	60	65	60	60	60 1ST DIV REGULAR	45 4TH/5TH OUTFIELD

YEAR	TEAM	LVL	AGE	PA	R	2B	3B	HR	RBI	BB	SO	SB	CS	AVG/OBP/SLG	TAv	BABIP	BRR	FRAA	WARP
2014	MYR	A+	20	199	17	8	1	3	22	15	50	5	5	.246/.307/.350	.248	.323	-0.9	CF(33): 2.8, LF(3): -0.1	0.5
2014	HIC	A	20	186	36	8	1	10	28	18	46	7	4	.335/.405/.579	.329	.413	3.0	CF(43): 3.7	3.0
2015	TEX	MLB	21	250	29	8	1	7	23	14	92	5	3	.205/.256/.336	.224	.299	-0.1	CF 2, LF -0	0.0
2016	TEX	MLB	22	250	28	9	1	7	27	18	86	5	3	.221/.281/.362	.241	.317	0.3	CF 2, LF 0	0.7

Breakout: 0%   Improve: 0%   Collapse: 0%   Attrition: 0%   MLB: 0%   Upside: 9   *Comparables: Michael Choice, Greg Halman, Brett Jackson*

Drafted/Acquired: 1st round, 2012 draft, Coral Springs HS (Coral Springs, FL)

Previous Ranking: #9 (Org)

What Happened in 2014: Brinson continued to rack up strikeouts at a troubling rate over 89 Single-A games, though he did so while showing an ability to impact the baseball with regularity and leverage his fringe double-plus speed both on the bases and out in center field.

Strengths: High upside skill set; chance for four plus or better tools with ability to provide impact in the field, at the plate, and on the bases; big raw pop, with ability to get to it in game; glove can be a difference maker up the middle; solid reads, with fine ability to close and finish; arm is a potential weapon; high scores for work ethic and makeup.

Weaknesses: Swing comes with noise; inconsistent barrel delivery; regular contact unlikely to be component of his game; power could play well below ceiling due to inconsistent ability to center on the barrel; athleticism out-distances feel and reads at present; speed and ability to finish anchor defensive value, but reads limit ultimate upside.

Risk Factor/Injury History: High; yet to reach Double-A; swing-and-miss could weigh down entire profile.

Bret Sayre's Fantasy Take: Yet another prospect on this list with huge fantasy ceiling, if Brinson could just hit .250 at the major-league level, he'd likely be a solid second outfielder in most mixed leagues. Unfortunately, the risk leaves him lingering as a great flier instead of a great fantasy prospect for now.

The Year Ahead: Brinson draws a wide range of opinions from evaluators, ranging from future impact player to up-and-down guy without the requisite skills to regularly hold down a 25-man spot. The strikeouts are a significant concern, but perhaps more troubling are the mechanical quirks in the swing that produce those strikeouts. Brinson doesn't provide a firm base with his lower half; that, combined with a hitchy load and inconsistent trigger and bat path, forms a significant barrier to regular hard contact. There is still time for Brinson to smooth out some of the rough edges, and because there's a fair amount of juice in the bat he may not have to increase his contact rate by much to provide the requisite offensive production to make him an everyday contributor. He'll provide value with his glove and legs in any event. Brinson would likely benefit from a return to High-A to start 2015, with a focus on finding a little more mechanical consistency and balance in the box. He won't turn 21 until the second month of the season, so the Rangers have some room to slow down Brinson's ascent until he has demonstrated a firm enough developmental foundation to give him the requisite tools to tackle more advanced competition.

10. Travis Demeritte 2B/3B

Born: 9/30/94 **Age:** 20 **Bats:** R **Throws:** R **Height:** 6'0" **Weight:** 178

MLB ETA		Hit	Power	Run	Glove	Arm	OFP	Realistic
2018		–	55	50	50	60	60 1ST DIV REGULAR	45 <AVG REGULAR

YEAR	TEAM	LVL	AGE	PA	R	2B	3B	HR	RBI	BB	SO	SB	CS	AVG/OBP/SLG	TAv	BABIP	BRR	FRAA	WARP
2014	HIC	A	19	466	77	16	2	25	66	50	171	6	2	.211/.310/.450	.262	.286	1.6	2B(92): 4.2, 3B(12): -0.3	1.9
2015	TEX	MLB	20	250	24	6	1	9	29	19	101	0	0	.180/.252/.335	.221	.266	-0.3	2B 1, 3B -0	0.0
2016	TEX	MLB	21	250	30	7	1	10	30	24	95	0	0	.196/.281/.368	.243	.281	-0.4	2B 2, 3B 0	0.8

Breakout: 0%   Improve: 0%   Collapse: 0%   Attrition: 0%   MLB: 0%   Upside: 60   *Comparables: Mike Carp, Domingo Santana, Travis Denker*

Drafted/Acquired: 1st round, 2013 draft, Winder-Barrow HS (Winder, GA)

Previous Ranking: NR

What Happened in 2014: In his first full season, Demeritte showcased plus raw power and big contact issues in the zone over 118 games with Low-A Hickory.

Strengths: Good strength and leverage; emerging power; bat speed plays; lots of torque through core and lower half; solid understanding of the strike zone; left-side arm; glove and lower half could play at hot corner or key-stone; solid athlete; projectable build.

Weaknesses: Lots of noise in load; open stance, can fail to properly close front side through load, cutting off coverage on the outer half; swing comes with length; can be tripped up with solid spin and sequencing; average present run likely to drop a half to full grade once body reaches maturity.

Risk Factor/Injury History: High; big strikeout concerns; only one full season under belt.

Bret Sayre's Fantasy Take: The ETA and swing-and-miss tendencies in Demeritte's game will leave him off radars in leagues rostering fewer than 200 minor leaguers, but he will be someone to keep an eye on, as Rangers' prospects seem to have an uncanny ability to take a step forward after racking up big strikeout numbers in Hickory.

The Year Ahead: Demeritte manifested more power than expected this early in his career, notching 25 round-trippers over the course of his 118 Sally League contests in 2014. The Peach State native generates good bat speed and impressive violence in his swing thanks to quick hips and a strong core, and is capable of producing hard contact across the diamond. He is more than capable of handling velocity and truly thrives on taking full advantage of mistakes left up and over the plate. Defensively, he lacks the lower-half quickness to handle shortstop at the highest level, but could grow into an average defender, perhaps more, at both second and third base. A return trip to Hickory might not be a bad idea as Demeritte works to improve his coverage on the outer half and limit his aggressiveness to the appropriate game situations. The ceiling is that of an impact bat wrapped in a solid-average defensive profile at second base, but there's lots of work to be done to get him from where he is to where he needs to be.

Prospects on the Rise

1. SS Ti'Quan Forbes: One of the youngest and most projectable talents in the 2014 draft class, Forbes routinely impressed with flashes of an impact skill. At his best, Forbes is quick and loose with the bat, capable of squaring velocity across the quadrants while utilizing the entire field. The load is inconsistent and can be hitchy at its worst, but the issue should subside as he continues to add strength and gain reps. The power plays below average at present, but projects well with a fair amount of maturation to come with the broad and projectable body, and it is easy to envision him growing into average or better pop in time. Defensively, Forbes shows loose actions at short, with plenty of arm strength for the left side, but is likely to shift off the position as he continues to add mass to his frame. Third seems like a natural fit, but the 2014 second rounder has enough lower-half agility to potentially handle the keystone as well. Either way he has a chance to quickly establish himself as yet another potential impact talent in a deep Rangers system and could fit comfortably in the top 10 at this time next year.

2. SS Josh Morgan: The former UCLA commit provides a well-rounded middle-infield profile that includes an advanced feel at the plate, steady hands and footwork in the field, and solid-average speed. He's comfortable working deep into counts and maintains a steady and comfortable focus regardless of game situation. It's a compact and efficient swing geared to line-drive production across the field and particularly adept at driving the ball up the middle and oppo. Defensively, Morgan is capable of making the outstanding play, and his game is underscored by crisp and refined actions. His hands are soft to receive and quick to transfer, making him a good fit at second base should he have to move off short down the line. Morgan put together a strong professional debut in 2014 and will look to build on that in full-season ball this year.

3. OF Ryan Cordell: Cordell came off the board to Texas in the 11th round of the 2013 draft and has since come into his own as a prospect, putting together a strong 2014 campaign between Low-A Hickory and High-A Myrtle Beach. The Liberty product is well put together and produces hard contact out of a leveraged swing, projecting to average power or a tick above. He runs well enough to handle center field at present and displays enough athleticism that some evaluators believe he can stick there long term, even if he loses a step at maturity. He'll

---

FROM THE FIELD

Joey Gallo

Team: Texas Rangers

Evaluator: CJ Wittmann

Dates seen: April 8–10 and 26–28, 2014

Affiliate: Myrtle Beach Pelicans (High-A, Rangers)

Physical/health: Massive, thick frame; all of 6'5"; thought he could add weight and he has; lower half is very sturdy and muscular; wide, broad shoulders with lean muscle upper half; very good athlete for how big he is; very good control of limbs and body.

MLB ETA	Risk factor	OFP	Realistic role
2015	High	70	50; major-league regular

Tool	Future grade	Report
Hit	45	Wide base stance, slightly open; slight front leg kick timing to come closed as pitch comes in; loose hands; has extreme strength and plus bat speed; swing has serious leverage; hips turn in then explode creating extreme torque when deciding to swing, but much improved from last season (calmer); he'll have trouble controlling the barrel and adjusting to quality off speed; swing is extremely long but makes loud contact often; loves to get hands extended; has made extremely noticeable improvements in pitch recognition and plate discipline; controlled the strike zone well all series and calmed approach in 2 strike counts; recognized spin much better and tracked the ball deep into hitting zone; still will be a lot of swing-and-miss, but hit tool could play to maximum potential after a lot of questions last year.
Power	80	Off-the-charts raw pop; creates extreme bat speed from body and has massive strength; has big lift in swing; has top of the scale power to all fields; great post-contact extension; improvements in hit tool quality will allow raw power to play at the highest level.
Baserunning/ speed	40	Aggressive but smart baserunner; takes the extra base and makes good reads with balls in play; long strides; 4.3 range to first base.
Glove	50	Robotic actions at third base; has okay reactions off the bat; can make backhand play down the line; still improving footwork; could see a move to outfield.
Arm	70	Elite arm strength; makes hard throws with ease and they stay on a line to first base; accuracy is a problem at times; has tuned down arm to improve accuracy.

Overall: Gallo hit massive shots in BP that we all have seen before, but that's not what impressed me. He struggled against Sean Manaea and arm-side stuff but made an adjustment each night. Gallo was sitting on breaking pitches and still driving fastballs. Against Miguel Almonte, he crushed a mistake to left-center field for a home run like he will usually do. His next at-bat, with runners at first and second, he laid off a plus-plus changeup (one of the best Almonte threw all night) just off the plate, fading away. I anticipated Gallo was going to swing out of his shoes, but he took it. He then took a strike on the outer part of the plate, which was a pitch he could have driven but chose to be patient. Almonte threw him a changeup down and Gallo sat on it and drove it through the hole between first and second base, hitting behind the runners. In his last at-bat against Almonte, Almonte tried to come inside with a 95-mph fastball. It had heavy sink and started at Gallo's hip and ended up on the inside corner. I saw Gallo shuffle out of the way of this pitch before. This time he opened the hips, kept hands inside the ball, and got extreme extension post-contact. The ball got lost in the night. The adjustments he's made have impressed me. And even if the hit tool never reaches my projected assumption, I still think he's Pedro Alvarez at the plate at least.

likely split time between the California and Texas Leagues in 2015, putting him on track for a potential big-league debut as early as 2016.

Factors on the Farm

Prospects likely to contribute at the major-league level in 2015

1. RHP Keone Kela: Kela's big right arm continued to chew through bats in 2014, regularly registering upper-90s velocity and kissing triple digits. He mixes in a power curve that serves as a second potential plus weapon, though he struggles at times to maintain a handle on both. It's a classic power reliever profile that could slot into the late innings in Arlington in short order. His ability to avoid too much trouble via bases on balls will determine how quickly the Rangers trust him with higher leverage situations. He could start the year in Triple-A Round Rock.

2. 3B Ryan Rua: Rua is a fringy corner glove with above-average pop out of a leveraged swing. He can get long through his load and trigger, hindering his ability to adjust to quality spin, but he should make enough contact to get to his power in game at the major-league level. Rua is a solid athlete who should settle in as a corner utility profile with a little bit of thump, and he showed well in his brief major-league debut in 2014. He'll enter the spring with a chance to break camp with the big club.

3. OF Delino DeShields: DeShields was plucked in the 2014 Rule 5 Draft and will get an opportunity to stick with the Rangers entering the 2015 season. While the former first rounder gets dinged for a low-energy approach, there is hope that a change of scenery will serve as a jump start for the profile. His double-plus speed and a solid glove will play well in a reserve outfielder role, giving him a good chance to stick with Texas throughout the season; if the Rangers can find a way to get DeShields to maintain his focus and efforts, they could wind up with a solid fourth outfielder with pinch-run utility and the upside of an everyday talent in center.

1. Aaron Sanchez   RHP

Born: 7/1/92   **Age:** 22   **Bats:** R   **Throws:** R   **Height:** 6'4"   **Weight:** 200

MLB ETA	CT	FB	CH	CB	SL	OFP	Realistic
Debuted in 2014	–	70	55	65	–	65 NO. 2/3 STARTER	60 NO. 3 STARTER

YEAR	TEAM	LVL	AGE	W	L	SV	G	GS	IP	H	HR	BB	K	BB9	SO9	GB%	BABIP	WHIP	ERA	FIP	FRA	WARP
2014	TOR	MLB	21	2	2	3	24	0	33.0	14	1	9	27	2.5	7.4	67%	.157	0.70	1.09	2.83	3.56	0.5
2014	BUF	AAA	21	0	3	0	8	6	34.3	36	4	17	27	4.5	7.1	62%	.317	1.54	4.19	4.87	6.15	-0.3
2014	NHP	AA	21	3	4	0	14	14	66.0	52	2	40	57	5.5	7.8	69%	.279	1.39	3.82	4.16	5.56	0.3
2015	TOR	MLB	22	6	5	0	29	18	100.7	95	10	57	84	5.1	7.5	56%	.289	1.50	4.52	5.10	4.91	0.5
2016	TOR	MLB	23	7	6	0	55	14	128.3	125	14	58	109	4.1	7.6	56%	.297	1.42	4.32	4.52	4.69	0.5

Breakout: 21%   **Improve:** 26%   **Collapse:** 5%   **Attrition:** 19%   **MLB:** 44%   **Upside:** 18   *Comparables Nathan Eovaldi, Franklin Morales, Sean Gallagher*

#25
BP Top 101 Prospects

Drafted/Acquired: 1st round, 2010 draft, Barstow HS (Barstow, CA)

Previous Ranking: #2 (Org), #31 (Top 101)

What Happened in 2014: Things were uneven for the former first rounder in the minors when starting, but after a conversion to the bullpen the top-notch stuff really played up to carry the right-hander to a dominant stint with the big club.

Strengths: Easy, efficient delivery; athletic on the bump; extremely loose arm; ball jumps out of hand; fastball comfortably sits 93-96; able to reach for more in short stints (98-99); displays hard arm-side movement and some sink; very difficult to square up in lower tier; creates excellent snap with curve via loose wrist; power two-plane break; can manipulate shape depending on situation; commands well for strikes; flashes ability to turn over change; late fading action.

Weaknesses: Delivery gets stiff and upright; has trouble staying above the ball; fastball command inconsistent as a result; has trouble consistently spotting in all four quadrants of the zone; heater flattens out above the thighs; occasionally wraps wrist and rolls curve arm side; change on the firm side (88-90); will blend with fastball and lack quality action; doesn't command well.

Risk Factor/Injury History: Low risk; achieved major leagues; command consistency over the long haul.

Bret Sayre's Fantasy Take: The 2014 season went a long way toward showing that Sanchez will have fantasy value, whether he makes it as a starter or not. But despite his impressive showing, the rotation remains his best bet for fantasy value going forward, especially given his strikeout ability. As a starter, he's a potential SP2 with WHIP risk, but not as much as you'd think given his walk rate—as he has the arsenal to sustain a lower hit rate than you'd be comfortable projecting. He's a great sleeper for 2015 redraft leagues, along with being a strong dynasty asset.

The Year Ahead: Sanchez is one of the loosest arms you'll see on the mound, with a fastball that absolutely explodes out of his hand and the type of tightly rotating curveball that can miss the best of bats. The heater not only consistently operates in the mid-90s as a starter, but is enhanced by hard arm-side run that makes it difficult for hitters to gauge and often leaves them in protection mode. The crispness of the curve gives the 23-year-old right-hander a legit power offering to attack batters with at any point in the count. When he's working his change into sequences with feel and confidence, the arm can consistently roll right through opposing lineups. Sanchez's struggles with his fastball command have been well documented around here, with the theme from last season being a Jekyll-and-Hyde-like story for those who watched him closely. The conversion to the bullpen, and subsequent success in the role, point to some developmental steps forward, but also lent a look at how things could play up on the other side of the fence for the young pitcher and allow thoughts to percolate as to whether relief is the best ultimate option. The roles reflect the belief that there's still plenty of time for growth and the fact that the developmental arc is an ongoing process at the highest level. This season should offer Sanchez the chance to prove that he is closing the gaps and can solidify a spot in Toronto's rotation for seasons to come.

2. Daniel Norris LHP

Born: 4/25/93   **Age:** 22   **Bats:** L   **Throws:** L   **Height:** 6'2"   **Weight:** 180

MLB ETA		CT	FB	CH	CB	SL		OFP	Realistic
Debuted in 2014		–	60	55	–	60		60 NO. 3 STARTER	55 NO. 3/4 STARTER

YEAR	TEAM	LVL	AGE	W	L	SV	G	GS	IP	H	HR	BB	K	BB9	SO9	GB%	BABIP	WHIP	ERA	FIP	FRA	WARP
2014	TOR	MLB	21	0	0	0	5	1	6.7	5	1	5	4	6.8	5.4	38%	.200	1.50	5.40	6.16	6.20	-0.1
2014	BUF	AAA	21	3	1	0	5	4	22.7	14	2	8	38	3.2	15.1	51%	.324	0.97	3.18	2.21	3.26	0.6
2014	NHP	AA	21	3	1	0	8	8	35.7	32	5	17	49	4.3	12.4	39%	.329	1.37	4.54	4.03	4.60	0.4
2014	DUN	A+	21	6	0	0	13	13	66.3	50	0	18	76	2.4	10.3	48%	.298	1.03	1.22	1.91	2.76	2.1
2015	TOR	MLB	22	7	7	0	24	24	99.3	96	11	49	104	4.4	9.4	44%	.311	1.46	4.49	4.52	4.88	0.6
2016	TOR	MLB	23	5	4	0	65	8	105.3	104	12	49	105	4.2	9.0	44%	.310	1.45	4.59	4.29	4.99	0.0

Breakout: 17%   Improve: 23%   Collapse: 3%   Attrition: 11%   MLB: 30%   Upside: 47   *Comparables* Tommy Hanson, Shelby Miller, Christian Friedrich

Drafted/Acquired: 2nd round, 2011 draft, Science Hill HS (Johnson City, TN)

Previous Ranking: #4 (Org), Just Missed The Cut (Top 101)

What Happened in 2014: The easy throwing left-hander gained considerable developmental traction with his arsenal during the season, blitzing through three levels of the minors before making his debut in The Show at the tail end of the year.

Strengths: Repeatable, balanced delivery; fast arm; athletic; smooth arm action; fastball operates 92-95 with late finish; spots offering east/west well; lively in lower tier; can selectively elevate; sharp break and bite to slider; will change shape; throws for strikes well; bat-missing potential; flashes feel for turning over change; late bottoming-out action; competitor on mound.

Weaknesses: Overall body of work needs polish; runs into ruts of releasing early and drifting with front foot; command plays down as a result; tends to nibble when in trouble; can wrap wrist with slider and sweep into middle of plate; changeup still finding identify; can be too firm and lack trust in offering; will float in strike zone; curve more of "show-me" pitch than weapon.

Risk Factor/Injury History: Low risk; achieved majors; bone spurs in elbow (2014); emergence of consistent third pitch.

Bret Sayre's Fantasy Take: Norris is the compressed version of Sanchez for fantasy purposes, as he's both lower upside and lower risk. That said, he's the more valuable player in dynasty leagues right now, given his own SP3 ceiling, with the potential for 180-plus strikeouts and above-average ratios (think 3.50/1.20). Norris, however, is a starter all the way and should be able to crack the rotation relatively quickly in 2015.

The Year Ahead: The left-hander rumbled along an accelerated developmental curve last year as a 21-year-old, with considerable tangible progress in proving that his ceiling can become a reality. Norris is a good-looking young arm, with an arsenal that can further bloom into a nasty combination for opposing hitters to deal with. There's a certain ease in how he delivers his lively fastball to begin setting the tone, and when the pitcher gets into a rhythm, the slider and changeup allow him to slice and dice the strike zone with a combination of finesse and power. Norris can get off kilter, though, especially when his pace is challenged in jams, where he can fall into a mode of trying to be too fine rather than fully trusting the process with his stuff, but that's all part of learning the finer points of the game for a young player. The surgery to remove bone spurs in his elbow after last season offers some concerns and will put focus on how his arm is returning to form during the spring. This is far from a finished product, and a player where the signs point to a gradual ramp at the big-league level as the rough edges continue to get smoothed over the next few seasons, but one that has all the ingredients to establish himself as a mid-rotation starter at peak.

#34
BP Top 101 Prospects

3. Dalton Pompey CF

Born: 12/11/92   **Age:** 22   **Bats:** B   **Throws:** R   **Height:** 6'2"   **Weight:** 195

MLB ETA		Hit	Power	Run	Glove	Arm		OFP	Realistic
Debuted in 2014		55	–	65	60	55		60 1ST DIV PLAYER	55 >AVG REGULAR

YEAR	TEAM	LVL	AGE	PA	R	2B	3B	HR	RBI	BB	SO	SB	CS	AVG/OBP/SLG	TAv	BABIP	BRR	FRAA	WARP
2014	TOR	MLB	21	43	5	1	2	1	4	4	12	1	0	.231/.302/.436	.253	.308	0.8	LF(9): -0.5, CF(5): -0.1	0.1
2014	BUF	AAA	21	56	15	5	0	0	5	3	10	6	0	.358/.393/.453	.302	.442	0.7	CF(11): 0.1	0.5
2014	NHP	AA	21	127	20	5	3	3	12	14	18	8	5	.295/.378/.473	.305	.330	2.3	CF(30): -2.1	1.1
2014	DUN	A+	21	317	49	12	6	6	34	35	56	29	2	.319/.397/.471	.307	.380	6.6	CF(70): 1.9	3.7
2015	TOR	MLB	22	250	31	10	3	4	19	21	64	12	3	.235/.303/.348	.244	.307	1.6	CF -2, LF -0	0.2
2016	TOR	MLB	23	629	67	26	8	9	59	56	152	31	7	.239/.311/.361	.252	.307	5.2	CF -5	1.2

Breakout: 4%   Improve: 27%   Collapse: 2%   Attrition: 14%   MLB: 42%   Upside: 105   *Comparables* Ryan Kalish, Austin Jackson, Nick Markakis

Drafted/Acquired: 16th round, 2010 draft, John Fraser SS (Mississauga, ON)

Previous Ranking: NR

What Happened in 2014: The fleet-of-foot Canadian center fielder breezed from an opening in High-A to a late look in the bigs, with an impressive display of contact ability and defense in the minors, firmly establishing himself on the prospect map.

Strengths: Very athletic; wiry muscle; still some room on frame; quick hands; line-drive stroke from left side; creates some lift from both sides; ability to muscle up for power in spots; loud present pull-side contact; gap-to-gap approach; easy-plus run; kicks it up a gear on the bases; good instincts in center; hunts balls into gaps; excellent closing speed; arm to keep runners honest.

Weaknesses: Will open hips early to pull left-handed; tends to sell out for power as righty; susceptible to soft stuff away; swing will get defensive; power likely to play as fringe-average; can get tied up above belt by velocity; still learning how to consistently use hands to go the other way; arm loses power to bases at times.

Risk Factor/Injury History: Low risk; achieved big-league level; full utility of hit tool.

Bret Sayre's Fantasy Take: The argument is certainly there to be made that Pompey is the top fantasy prospect in the Blue Jays system, given his stolen-base capabilities and his ability to surround that with some average and pop. Additionally, with Anthony Gose and Colby Rasmus out of town, Pompey should begin the march toward a 10-homer, 30-steal fantasy outfielder with a ton of runs scored in early 2015.

The Year Ahead: Pompey's meteoric rise last season was not only impressive in the sheer speed, but also lends a good look at how a player can ride the developmental wave and confidence that swells with positive results on the field. The carrying strengths are the defensive chops and ability to impact the game on the bases, both of which offer good value should the potential of the hit tool not come to fruition. That's not to say there isn't hitting ability here, but there is less pressure on the particular tool and the prospect could contribute in multiple facets to maintain his status as a regular in the long run. The big theme from last season in regards to the offense is the amount of improvement and increased comfort, allowing the natural skills to come to the surface. The swing from the left side has especially tightened, and while things right-handed can be messy at times, Pompey's loose hands point to continued overall growth as the secondary skills build with experience. The peak seasonal view sees .270s averages, with gap pop, and occasional home-run power. That talent set fits nicely at the top of a good lineup and things rout out with plus up-the-middle defense. That's a valuable player, and this season will likely serve as the chance to begin putting the foothold on the position for years to come.

#42

BP Top 101 Prospects

---

4. Jeff Hoffman RHP

Born: 1/8/93 **Age:** 22 **Bats:** R **Throws:** R **Height:** 6'4" **Weight:** 185

MLB ETA		CT	FB	CH	CB	SL		OFP	Realistic
2017		–	70	65	60	–		70 NO. 2 STARTER	55 NO. 3/4 STARTER

Drafted/Acquired: 1st round, 2014 draft, East Carolina University (Greenville, NC)

Previous Ranking: NR

What Happened in 2014: The power arm was cruising through the college season and pushing for a definitive chance at being selected first overall, but then the dreaded Tommy John struck and dropped him into Toronto's lap at 9th overall.

Strengths: Very athletic; loose arm and delivery; explosive fastball at 93-96; touches higher when needs it; can throw past hitters or pound the zone; turns over good changeup; true bat-missing ability; shows arm-side fade with quality tumbling action; high amount of confidence in offering; snaps breaking ball with loose wrist; shows power break in upper-velocity band (78-82); will vary shape; can throw for strikes; aggressive on the mound; projects a high amount of confidence in stuff; plus future command profile.

Weaknesses: Command presently plays down; lot of limbs and body to control; can stand to add strength to maintain stuff over long season; fastball can be on the straight side; present mentality to work in dangerous areas with offering; breaking ball can get slurvy and soft; will cast; gets predicable with change; heavily throws to arm side; needs to focus more on hitting all four quadrants with arsenal in general; developmental delay due to injury.

Risk Factor/Injury History: High risk; yet to pitch professionally; Tommy John on résumé (2014); return of arsenal to previous levels.

Bret Sayre's Fantasy Take: The ceiling for Hoffman is unquestioned as he's the one pitcher in this system with a nonminute chance at becoming a true SP1 in mixed leagues. Unfortunately, due to the surgery, his ETA is backed up and it has caused him to fall behind a few players in dynasty drafts. However, even with the international players factored in, Hoffman should go in the top five of all drafts this winter.

The Year Ahead: Hoffman would easily challenge for consideration at the front of this system if healthy, but it's also reasonable to expect that had injury not struck, the 22-year-old right-hander would never have gotten to Toronto in the first place. The potential of the arsenal and what the overall future role can look like are loud. The arm was already showing strong advancement in the college ranks, suggesting that the ascent as a professional could be on the quicker side. Of course, we have to consider the near-term hurdle of the injury rehab, combined with the fact that the arsenal must first return to form before taking any more steps forward, which was especially necessary in regards to the overall command. The likely view takes into consideration the risk and probability that the full picture of the stuff in the pro arena won't start to show until 2016. This season will focus

#73

BP Top 101 Prospects

on passing the early markers coming out of surgery, returning fully to the mound, and beginning to ramp the arm strength back up. Recent trends tell us there's a strong chance Hoffman can make a full return to form, with the organization's potential reward for taking on the risk and investment being a future front-of-the-rotation power arm for multiple seasons to come.

5. Max Pentecost   C

Born: 3/10/93   **Age:** 22   **Bats:** R   **Throws:** R   **Height:** 6'2"   **Weight:** 191

MLB ETA	Hit	Power	Run	Glove	Arm	OFP	Realistic
2017	55	50	–	55	55	55 >AVG REGULAR	50 AVG ML PLAYER

YEAR	TEAM	LVL	AGE	PA	R	2B	3B	HR	RBI	BB	SO	SB	CS	AVG/OBP/SLG	TAv	BABIP	BRR	FRAA	WARP
2014	TOR	MLB	21	43	5	1	2	1	4	4	12	1	0	.231/.302/.436	.253	.308	0.8	LF(9): -0.5, CF(5): -0.1	0.1
2014	BUF	AAA	21	56	15	5	0	0	5	3	10	6	0	.358/.393/.453	.302	.442	0.7	CF(11): 0.1	0.5
2014	NHP	AA	21	127	20	5	3	3	12	14	18	8	5	.295/.378/.473	.305	.330	2.3	CF(30): -2.1	1.1
2014	DUN	A+	21	317	49	12	6	6	34	35	56	29	2	.319/.397/.471	.307	.380	6.6	CF(70): 1.9	3.7
2015	TOR	MLB	22	250	31	10	3	4	19	21	64	12	3	.235/.303/.348	.244	.307	1.6	CF -2, LF -0	0.2
2016	TOR	MLB	23	629	67	26	8	9	59	56	152	31	7	.239/.311/.361	.252	.307	5.2	CF -5	1.2

Breakout: 4%   Improve: 27%   Collapse: 2%   Attrition: 14%   MLB: 42%   Upside: 105   *Comparables Ryan Kalish, Austin Jackson, Nick Markakis*

Drafted/Acquired: 1st round, 2014 draft, Kennesaw State University (Kennesaw, GA)

Previous Ranking: NR

What Happened in 2014: The highly regarded backstop was tabbed by the Jays with the 11th overall pick and got an early taste of professional competition before an injury ended his season.

Strengths: Solid athleticism; fluid actions; compact stroke from right side; efficient to the point of contact; plus bat speed; barrels up offerings with backspin; gap-to-gap approach; willing to use the whole field; can learn to muscle up in the right spot; recognizes stuff with spin well; agile behind the plate; fires feet well; solid-average arm strength; improving glove hand; high-energy player.

Weaknesses: Body presently a bit underdeveloped; added strength necessary to withstand demands of position; footwork can get choppy and tangled; release needs some cleaning up to enhance accuracy; still learning how to get big and use body to control offerings; glove angle can drift; contact-heavy swing; flatter through hitting zone; power may ultimately play below-average in favor of contact; bat can end up a bit empty.

Risk Factor/Injury History: High risk; limited professional experience; labrum surgery (2014); dual-threat development.

Bret Sayre's Fantasy Take: Pentecost not only has a near 80-grade name, but he comfortably sits above the line of offensive demarcation, which means we care about him as a fantasy catcher. His best-case scenario is a poor man's Jonathan Lucroy, which can still be an easy top-10 catcher in his prime by hitting .285 with 10-12 homers and providing strong counting stats for a backstop.

The Year Ahead: Similar to his fellow 2014 first rounder within the organization, Pentecost will spend a good chunk of 2015 rehabbing an injury as the backstop recently had surgery to repair his labrum. It comes as a blow to a player just starting out his career, but at the very least, he was fairly advanced with the bat entering the professional ranks. And those skills with the stick are this prospect's biggest present strength. Pentecost possesses an easy and simple stroke that's efficient to the point of contact. The 22-year-old's loose hands enable him to stay inside of the baseball and barrel up a lot of offerings hard. The swing is on the flat side, though, with home-run power most likely to be of the modest variety, but the right-handed hitter's all-fields approach and ability to drive the ball into both gaps lends credence to extra-base hits in the form of doubles having the potential to pile out. Tack on defense that has the potential to round into solid-average, and this is an attractive player beginning to percolate up the ranks. The injury puts a damper on things, but when the catcher returns to full health, look for some tangible strides forward to show fairly quickly.

6. Jairo Labourt   LHP

Born: 3/7/94   **Age:** 21   **Bats:** L   **Throws:** L   **Height:** 6'4"   **Weight:** 204

MLB ETA	CT	FB	CH	CB	SL	OFP	Realistic
Late 2017	–	65	55	–	60	60 NO. 3 STARTER	50 NO. 4 STARTER

YEAR	TEAM	LVL	AGE	W	L	SV	G	GS	IP	H	HR	BB	K	BB9	SO9	GB%	BABIP	WHIP	ERA	FIP	FRA	WARP
2014	LNS	A	20	0	0	0	6	3	14.0	15	1	20	11	12.9	7.1	43%	.359	2.50	6.43	7.77	9.20	-0.4
2014	VAN	A-	20	5	3	0	15	15	71.3	47	0	37	82	4.7	10.3	54%	.278	1.18	1.77	3.41	3.84	1.5
2015	TOR	MLB	21	3	6	0	16	16	61.0	70	8	43	39	6.3	5.8	45%	.311	1.86	6.45	6.42	7.01	-0.9
2016	TOR	MLB	22	5	9	0	26	26	152.0	152	16	109	127	6.5	7.5	45%	.300	1.71	5.46	5.39	5.94	-1.5

Breakout: 0%   Improve: 0%   Collapse: 0%   Attrition: 0%   MLB: 0%   Upside: 3   *Comparables Scott Elbert, Kevin Jepsen, Bryan Mitchell*

Drafted/Acquired: International Free Agent, 2011, Dominican Republic

Previous Ranking: #10 (Org)

What Happened in 2014: After a brief look in full-season to start the year, the big left-hander settled into the short-season ranks, where he dominated the competition, striking out over a batter an inning and limiting the opposition to 47 hits.

Strengths: Sturdy body; room to get stronger in lower half; uses body to throw downhill; creates easy velocity; fastball works 91-95; displays arm-side run and some sink; lively in lower tier of strike zone; capable of snapping hard slider; two-plane break with tilt (mid-80s); flashes feel for turning over change; arm-side action and drop; not afraid to come after hitters; good pitchability.

Weaknesses: Will need to watch body to avoid losing athleticism and looseness; overall command is below average; can release fastball early; pitch flattens out above thighs; slider will sweep in lower-velocity band (low-80s); still finding identity with offering; gets deliberate with changeup; can be too firm (85-86); needs more trust in grip when throwing; can stand to work more into sequences.

Risk Factor/Injury History: High risk; short-season résumé; development of third pitch.

Bret Sayre's Fantasy Take: With the potential to be a strikeout-inducing left-handed starter, Labourt is someone whose ownership you should be checking in your dynasty league this offseason. If he's available, he should be taken within the first three rounds of your draft, despite the depth of the 2014 draft class.

The Year Ahead: This Dominican left-hander possesses all of the necessary ingredients to round into a long-term starter at the major-league level. With a big body, budding three-pitch repertoire, and early feel for executing his craft, Labourt brings the starter kit of a potential mid-rotation starter to the table. The fastball already comfortably operates in the low-90s, with the 21-year-old capable of reaching for more consistently with improving command. The offering also displays solid movement and tends to jump on opposing batters due to the angle he creates. Labourt presently favors his slider more consistently in sequences, which can dart and break late off the table, but also flashes good feel for his changeup and can push the growth of the pitch as he develops more trust delivering it. The development of that third offering will be key for the prospect to achieve his on-paper potential. It'll be very important for him to be able to mix and match the two secondary offerings, especially against right-handed batters, as he percolates up through the ranks to prove the stuff is going to neutralize advanced bats. The next proving ground will take place at full season in 2015 for Labourt, where the trends point to a good chance the young arm can fully break out onto the scene as more get a look at the overall package.

7. Miguel Castro RHP

Born: 12/24/94 **Age:** 20 **Bats:** R **Throws:** R **Height:** 6'5" **Weight:** 190

MLB ETA	CT	FB	CH	CB	SL	OFP	Realistic
Late 2017	–	**70**	**50**	–	**60**	**60** NO. 3 STARTER	**50** LATE INN RP (SETUP)

YEAR	TEAM	LVL	AGE	W	L	SV	G	GS	IP	H	HR	BB	K	BB9	SO9	GB%	BABIP	WHIP	ERA	FIP	FRA	WARP
2014	DUN	A+	19	1	0	0	2	1	8.7	4	2	3	5	3.1	5.2	52%	.095	0.81	3.12	6.28	7.91	-0.2
2014	LNS	A	19	1	1	0	4	4	21.7	10	2	7	20	2.9	8.3	55%	.151	0.78	3.74	3.95	5.53	0.0
2014	VAN	A-	19	6	2	0	10	10	50.3	36	2	20	53	3.6	9.5	49%	.272	1.11	2.15	3.48	3.84	1.1
2015	TOR	MLB	20	3	3	0	12	9	51.0	54	7	28	38	4.9	6.7	44%	.300	1.61	5.40	5.76	5.87	-0.3
2016	TOR	MLB	21	7	8	0	33	22	159.0	166	20	68	116	3.8	6.6	44%	.296	1.47	4.85	4.93	5.28	-0.5

Breakout: 0%   Improve: 0%   Collapse: 0%   Attrition: 0%   MLB: 0%   Upside: 12   *Comparables Sean Gallagher, Chris Tillman, Christian Garcia*

Drafted/Acquired: International Free Agent, 2012, Dominican Republic

Previous Ranking: On The Rise

What Happened in 2014: The Dominican right-hander drew solid reviews in the lower levels, where his explosive fastball carried him to success at short-season and enabled him to get a taste of life in full-season ball in preparation for 2015.

Strengths: Large frame; plenty of room to fill into and add strength; excellent arm strength; fast arm; fastball easily works 93-95; able to reach for more in spurts (97); late life and explosiveness; flashes feel for slider; snaps with loose wrist; can break late and dart off the table; bat-missing potential; turns over change at 82-85; arm-side fading action.

Weaknesses: Some effort and jerk to delivery; inconsistent holding mechanics deeper into outings; below-average command; presently more of a thrower; good gap to close with secondary stuff; slider will sweep and spin; inconsistent creating tight rotation; deliberate at times delivering change; body and arm will slow down; floats in the strike zone.

Risk Factor/Injury History: High risk; limited professional experience; emergence of secondary stuff.

Bret Sayre's Fantasy Take: Of the final four arms on this list, Castro is most likely to end up in the bullpen, but he's still a ways away from his fantasy owners worrying about that. In the near term, Castro could ride his strong fastball to popup status in the Midwest League and create a lot of trade interest from other owners—if you're into that sort of thing.

The Year Ahead: An emerging name within this system, Castro's live arm and projectable nature shine when he is on the mound. Everything starts with the right-hander's explosive mid-90s heater, which has a legit chance to be a difference maker and round into a double-plus offering at his disposal. The sitting velocity has ticked up over the course of the last 12 months as the 20-year-old has begun to add strength and mature more physically. It's not out of the question that the fastball can consistently operate more closely to the present peak velocity (97) as this prospect matures further into his mid-twenties or works in more isolated short bursts. The secondary stuff flashes promise and the potential to reach at least average grades, but presently has a ways to go to become true staples in the repertoire. This aspect of his game, combined with some rigidness in the delivery, lend some clues as to why some believe that a late-innings role will be the ultimate outcome, but there's a long way to go here, with plenty of time for development. Steps forward are the most important factor in the short term. Castro is primed for an assignment in full-season ball in 2015, where if this lively arm is showing signs of more refinement, expect another jump in status to come with it.

8. Roberto Osuna   RHP

Born: 2/7/95   **Age:** 20   **Bats:** R   **Throws:** R   **Height:** 6'2"   **Weight:** 230

MLB ETA	CT	FB	CH	CB	SL	OFP	Realistic
2017	–	65	55	60	–	60 NO. 3 STARTER	50 LATE-INN RP (SETUP)

YEAR	TEAM	LVL	AGE	W	L	SV	G	GS	IP	H	HR	BB	K	BB9	SO9	GB%	BABIP	WHIP	ERA	FIP	FRA	WARP
2014	DUN	A+	19	0	2	0	7	7	22.0	28	3	9	30	3.7	12.3	37%	.446	1.68	6.55	4.07	5.54	0.2
2014	BLJ	Rk	19	0	0	0	1	1	1.0	0	0	0	2	0.0	18.0	100%	.000	0.00	0.00	-0.50	2.73	0.1
2015	TOR	MLB	20	2	3	0	9	9	33.7	34	4	16	31	4.3	8.3	44%	.311	1.51	5.00	4.90	5.43	0.0
2016	TOR	MLB	21	7	8	0	29	29	180.0	170	21	66	168	3.3	8.4	44%	.294	1.31	4.09	4.26	4.45	1.1

Breakout: 0%   Improve: 0%   Collapse: 0%   Attrition: 0%   MLB: 0%   Upside: 53   *Comparables Shelby Miller, Tyler Robertson, Danny Duffy*

Drafted/Acquired: International Free Agent, 2010, Mexico

Previous Ranking: Notable Omission (Tommy John)

What Happened in 2014: The Mexican right-hander returned to the mound after finishing his rehab from Tommy John, where the stuff began to show a return to previous form and lend clues that the arm is past the initial comeback hurdle.

Strengths: Well filled out for age; excellent present strength; repeatable delivery; fast arm; fastball works 92-95; can reach for more when needed (97); lively in lower tier of strike zone; difficult to square up; shows ability to create tight rotation and snap with curve; change flashes bottom-dropping action with late tumble.

Weaknesses: Lacks physical projection; body will need to be closely watched; has to stay on top of conditioning; works elevated and to the arm side with the fastball; overthrows heater with effort; doesn't finish and stay over the ball well; below-average command of arsenal (present); inconsistent keeping wrist above curveball; tends to wrap and roll; lacks strong identity (more of a slurve).

Risk Factor/Injury History: High risk; yet to reach upper levels; Tommy John on résumé (2013); emergence of third pitch.

Bret Sayre's Fantasy Take: It's like you can't fall down in this system without hitting a pitcher with SP3 potential. Osuna has both a strong track record and a big red mark in his injury history, but when you add them together, you get a pitcher who could consistently put up sub-4.00 ERAs with 160-plus strikeouts per season, and he certainly should be owned in all leagues that roster 200 or more prospects.

The Year Ahead: Osuna successfully made it back to the mound last season and was able to make some consistent appearances at the tail end of the year in the Florida State League. The right-hander should receive a return trip to High-A in 2015, where the stuff will get a good test in extended action. The 20-year-old is loose and easy when delivering his heater, which typically sits 92-95 mph with solid late life when thrown below the thighs. It's the type of fastball that can allow Osuna to control lineups with further command growth. The secondary stuff is presently on the inconsistent side, but both the curveball and changeup show promise to develop into at least average offerings. The curve does need strong strides to play up to its on-paper potential, primarily in the form of the prospect getting more consistent staying on top of the ball and producing more downward action with the pitch. There are concerns about the high maintenance nature to the body, but reports indicated that Osuna returned from injury in good shape. Still, it'll be something to keep a close eye on as he continues to mature. This is an arm that can really start to take off as he gets further and further removed from surgery, eventually making this placement seem too conservative in the process.

9. Sean Reid-Foley   RHP

Born: 8/30/95   **Age:** 19   **Bats:** R   **Throws:** R   **Height:** 6'3"   **Weight:** 220

MLB ETA	CT	FB	CH	CB	SL	OFP	Realistic
2018	–	70	50	–	60	60 NO. 3 STARTER	50 LATE-INN RP (SETUP)

YEAR	TEAM	LVL	AGE	W	L	SV	G	GS	IP	H	HR	BB	K	BB9	SO9	GB%	BABIP	WHIP	ERA	FIP	FRA	WARP
2014	BLJ	Rk	18	1	2	0	9	6	22.7	21	0	10	25	4.0	9.9	60%	.339	1.37	4.76	2.75	5.87	0.2
2015	TOR	MLB	19	1	2	0	9	5	31.3	37	4	20	19	5.8	5.5	48%	.312	1.83	6.37	6.23	6.93	-0.4
2016	TOR	MLB	20	3	4	1	31	14	129.7	133	16	61	97	4.2	6.7	48%	.294	1.50	4.86	4.98	5.28	-0.4

Breakout: 0%   Improve: 0%   Collapse: 0%   Attrition: 0%   MLB: 0%   Upside: 1   *Comparables Brad Hand, Stolmy Pimentel, Aaron Sanchez*

Drafted/Acquired: 2nd round, 2014 draft, Sandalwood HS (Jacksonville, FL)

Previous Ranking: NR

What Happened in 2014: The intriguing prep arm out of Florida had his name called by Toronto in the second round, then didn't have to travel too far from home to begin his professional assimilation in the Gulf Coast League.

Strengths: Athletic; strong frame; good arm strength; fastball works 91-95 with late life and explosiveness; runs hard arm side; potential to comfortably sit higher down the line; spins breaking stuff with loose wrist; slider flashes hard bite and tilt (84-85); bat-missing potential; turns over low-80s change; late, arm-side fade; shows early willingness to feature; plus command profile; power-arm foundation.

Weaknesses: Some moving parts to delivery; needs work ironing out pace; can get too quick; will wear himself down; command and control need grade step forward; wraps wrist at times delivering slider; spins and flattens out in lower band (81-82); learning how to get over for strike; change clear third pitch in effectiveness; tends to float and lack finish; mentality on hill will need to be shaped.

Risk Factor/Injury History: High risk; limited professional experience; emergence of true third offering (changeup).

Bret Sayre's Fantasy Take: Reid-Foley is one of those hidden gems in dynasty drafts, as he slipped all the way to the middle of the second round, but should be taken at least 15 spots higher than that this offseason. Strong velocity in complex-league arms is always a good deep-league investment strategy, and he fits the bill.

The Year Ahead: The ingredients are here for this right-hander to emerge as a legit power arm at full bloom, with the early feel for his repertoire to begin making strides as the experience builds within the professional structure. Though Reid-Foley presently works more low-90s with his heater, there's strong potential for his sitting velocity to tick up a bit due to his overall looseness and size that points to solid strength gains coming as he physically matures into his early-twenties. Toss in good movement with late life and this can be both a sequence-starting and -finishing pitch in the double-plus range. The secondary stuff also offers the type of promise to envision both evolving into crisp offerings down the line. The prospect feels his slider the best presently, but flashes good turnover with the change to create consistent, quality action. There are some concerns about the overall nature of the 19-year-old's delivery, but he shows the ability to repeat it and consistently get his arm into slot. Early career focus is likely to reside with smoothing out his pace and working to maintain a more steady rhythm. There's a nice package here, and one that should start to roll forward developmentally this season while offering flashes of what's potentially to come.

---

10. Alberto Tirado RHP

Born: 12/10/94 **Age:** 20 **Bats:** R **Throws:** R **Height:** 6'0" **Weight:** 180

MLB ETA	CT	FB	CH	CB	SL	OFP	Realistic
2018	–	70	65	–	60	65 NO. 2 STARTER	50 NO. 5 SP/MID RP

YEAR	TEAM	LVL	AGE	W	L	SV	G	GS	IP	H	HR	BB	K	BB9	SO9	GB%	BABIP	WHIP	ERA	FIP	FRA	WARP
2014	LNS	A	19	1	2	1	13	7	40.0	45	3	39	40	8.8	9.0	55%	.359	2.10	6.30	5.61	6.15	-0.1
2014	VAN	A-	19	1	0	0	17	3	35.7	25	1	28	36	7.1	9.1	58%	.255	1.49	3.53	4.77	5.89	0.1
2015	TOR	MLB	20	2	4	0	19	10	59.0	69	8	45	36	6.9	5.5	49%	.310	1.92	6.70	6.73	7.28	-1.1
2016	TOR	MLB	21	3	5	1	29	13	116.7	124	15	72	90	5.6	6.9	49%	.302	1.68	5.80	5.54	6.30	-1.6

Breakout: 0%   Improve: 0%   Collapse: 0%   Attrition: 0%   MLB: 0%   Upside: 19   *Comparables Daniel Corcino, Yovani Gallardo, Rafael Dolis*

Drafted/Acquired: International Free Agent, 2011, Dominican Republic

Previous Ranking: #3 (Org), #76 (Top 101)

2014 Stats: 6.30 ERA (40 IP, 45 H, 40 K, 39 BB) at Low-A Lansing, 3.53 ERA (35.2 IP, 25 H, 36 K, 28 BB) at short-season Vancouver

The Tools: 7 potential FB; 6+ potential CH; 6 potential SL

What Happened in 2014: The highly regarded right-hander took a step back in full-season ball, where his inconsistent command was too much to overcome, before being demoted to short-season to get him back on track.

Strengths: Loose arm; easy release; clean arm action; fastball operates 92-95 routinely; arm-side life with some sink; strong feel for changeup; deceptive release; late, diving action; snaps slider at 80-84 with bite and depth; flashes future plus; projectable stuff; room for good physical growth.

Weaknesses: Inconsistent mechanics; release point fluctuates; leads to difficulties finishing, with command suffering as a result; below average at present; will wrap with slider; can sweep and lack bite at times; body is on the lean side; needs strength to enhance overall package; learning how to handle ins and outs of craft.

Overall Future Potential: High 6; no. 2 starter

Realistic Role: Low 5; no. 5 starter/middle reliever

Risk Factor/Injury History: High; limited full-season experience; development of command.

Bret Sayre's Fantasy Take: Tirado was one of those short-season fantasy-league darlings that owners got super excited about, only to see everything go up in smoke last season. The upside is still there to be a high-strikeout, high-walk contributor, but he's both further away and riskier than when he exploded onto the scene. If he's been dropped or given up on, he makes for an interesting trade target.

The Year Ahead: The 20-year-old Dominican right-hander is a loose arm who generates easy velocity and flashes early feel for his secondary stuff, while possessing a very projectable body. When all is said and done, each piece of Tirado's arsenal can round out as plus to better and give the arm some nasty stuff with which to attack hitters. The hurdle for the prospect is developing more consistency with his mechanics, which presently drives a spotty release point and subsequent below-average command and control. Things weren't pretty overall for Tirado in 2014, but some reports indicated that subtle strides were starting to show toward the tail end of the year. The definitive markers to watch with this young arm in 2015 are progress with the aforementioned command and also the level of confidence. Bad results can snowball for young players and lead to overthinking or second guessing. Sources were high on the way Tirado handles himself and goes about his business, with the indication that it's a player who can bounce back and quickly go the other way with some positive traction out of the gate early. That, of course, remains to be seen pending what transpires this season, but the view here is that the arm gets past the initial early-career speed bump and will show tangible progress to polishing the rough edges in the very near future.

Prospects on the Rise

1. OF Anthony Alford: The previously part-time minor leaguer has officially given up college football to fully focus on his baseball career, where the final product can end up pretty big. Despite the lost development time, Alford is still only 20 years old and brings an element of power and speed to the table. The 6-foot-2 outfielder is extremely athletic and an outright physical specimen, possessing strong wrists and forearms that enable him to generate plus bat speed. The stroke is presently more designed to line-drive contact, but there's plenty of back-spin created and he has the potential to add more lift as hitting experience builds. This prospect is something of a wild card, though, with a lot of rough edges, gaps to close, and time to make up. There's a feel here that, as the body shapes into more of a baseball player and the level of experience builds, this is a prospect who is going to take some steps forward as quickly as this season.

2. LHP Matt Smoral: The 21-year-old native of Ohio started putting together some developmental traction last season, and if that trend continues with further gains in 2015, this arm can really take off. The left-hander's

FROM THE FIELD

Dalton Pompey

Team: Toronto Blue Jays

Evaluator: Chris Mellen

Dates seen: June 27 (doubleheader) and July 19, 2014

Affiliate: New Hampshire Fisher Cats (Double-A, Blue Jays)

Physical/health: Athletic; proportionate frame; room to fill out more; wiry muscle; should grow into more strength; agile and smooth with actions; body to withstand rigors of the grind with continued physical maturity.

Makeup: Brings energy to the field; focused on the task at hand; needs to learn to manage the ups and downs—a bit overemotional when a call or play isn't to his liking; need a read on ability to adjust.

MLB ETA	Risk factor	OFP	Realistic role
2016	Moderate	55	45; fourth outfielder

Tool	Future grade	Report
Hit	50	Solid-average bat speed right-handed; plus bat speed left-handed; quick hands; a bit of length to the swing due to early extension; inconsistent pulling hands inside of ball—swing can look stiff and choppy; more of a defensive hitter right-handed; tries to work count; presently on the indecisive side attacking the ball—looking to be too fine; see settling into an approach as experience in upper levels builds; line-drive stroke; swing to use the whole field; questions on the consistency of hard contact produced against high-quality arms over the long term.
Power	45	Strength to tap into; leverage in stroke left-handed; can turn on the ball; pull-side power from both sides of the plate; gap hitter when going the other way; not a big lift guy; see power being more occasional over-the-fence pop—8-10 home runs; chance to hit for fair share of doubles and a handful of triples.
Baserunning/speed	60	4.18-4.22 down line; shows extra gear on the bases and in the field; working to improve reading of pitchers—very engaged when reaching base; see 20-stolen-base potential; wheels to stretch hits in front of outfielders and push extra bases in the gaps; asset on the bases.
Glove	60	Excellent closing speed; long strides; hunts down balls into the gaps; sees the ball off the bat well; good outfield fundamentals; limits drifting; gets body in position to throw; charges and cuts ball off well; chops to stick in center over the long-run; ability to play all three outfield positions; defense best present aspect of game in terms of polish.
Arm	50	Longer throwing motion; average accuracy; throws lose some steam at the tail end; not afraid to throw; can possibly squeeze out a little more strength.

Overall: Excellent athlete; overall game is still on the raw side; type of player that can take a big step forward as experience against quality competition builds; swing left me a little flat in this look; have some questions as to whether ability to adjust swing is there; strong defensive skills—can add value to roster if bat falls short; potential to hold down a regular job if everything comes together, but see this player as a fourth outfielder over the long-run of the career.

low-to-mid-90s heater comes out of his hand easily, with some hard, arm-side action, and the secondary stuff has strong potential. Smoral's slider is the most advanced piece and flashes plus consistently, but there's also feel for the changeup that suggests it can approach above average at full utility. The long pole is the inconsistent mechanics, which are driven by the 6-foot-8 frame and extreme length. The effect on his release leads to struggles throwing strikes in stretches. Given the amount of body to control, this may very well always be an arm on the wild side, but further reining in the delivery is a must to keep a future outlook as a starter in the view. This name belongs on everyone's radar, and it may very well just be a matter of time before it is entrenched in the top 10.

3. OF Dwight Smith Jr.: The 22-year-old is a name to keep on the radar; the big asset is solid hitting ability fueled by quick hands and a mature approach that enables him to frequently work into favorable hitting conditions. Smith's compact stroke and knack for staying inside of the baseball also lead to high instances of contact. It will come down to whether the outfielder can maintain that contact as the hard line-drive variety into the upper levels (and beyond) given the power is likely to max around below average, and it's a bit of a 'tweener defensive profile. The prospect fits more into a corner spot, with an arm that's on the light side for right field. There's been some chatter that Smith may get some work on the infield (second base), which would aid the versatility. It's not the sexiest of profiles, but one with good major-league potential and the bat to push as a regular at full peak.

Factors on the Farm

Prospects likely to contribute at the major-league level in 2015

1. C A.J. Jimenez: The inability to stay on the field has been a consistent theme for the Puerto Rican backstop over the course of his career, with about a month spent on the disabled list last year, adding another injury to the résumé. The defense is the main asset here for Jimenez, as he is a solid receiver with smooth footwork and a plus arm. The 25-year-old also shows strong presence behind the dish and command of the various game-management situations. The bat is likely to play on the light side, as the prospect struggles to consistently get his hands above the baseball against good stuff, but there's a bit of pop that can play up. It's a backup or occasional regular profile, and one that can get a good look in 2015, provided good health.

2. 2B Devon Travis: Acquired from the Tigers in November 2014, the former 13th-round pick has cemented himself within the professional landscape and sits on the cusp for a chance in The Show. Travis flashes good bat-to-ball ability, which translates as hard contact into the gaps and lends a projection that the hit tool can play average to better. The 24-year-old is also the consummate worker who has shown a keen ability to adjust quickly to each new challenge. This is more of a second-division regular at peak, but Travis seems to keep outplaying the expectations. There's a strong chance the prospect will get a chance to push for the second-base job this spring and prove he can continue playing above what an initial glance at the package may suggest.

3. LHP Tyler Ybarra: It's been a steady climb into the upper levels for the former 43rd rounder. This profile is a reliever all the way, but there's stuff here that if harnessed a bit further can consistently get batters out in late-inning stints. The left-hander features a lively fastball that works in the mid-90s routinely and a mid-80s slider that can miss barrels. Ybarra's heater also shows good arm-side movement and sink. It's actually this aspect of the pitch that the arm needs to reel in, often working a bit too elevated with it where it runs down into the middle of the plate, something that bit him more in Double-A last season. There's nothing overly flashy here and the ceiling isn't that high, but as a piece bridging innings there's value to a bullpen, and a chance to prove he can do so at some point in the summer may very well be a reality.

WASHINGTON NATIONALS

1. Lucas Giolito   RHP

Born: 7/14/94   **Age:** 20   **Bats:** R   **Throws:** R   **Height:** 6'6"   **Weight:** 255

MLB ETA	CT	FB	CH	CB	SL	OFP	Realistic
2016	–	**80**	**65**	**80**	–	**80** NO.1 STARTER	**70** NO 1/2 STARTER

YEAR	TEAM	LVL	AGE	W	L	SV	G	GS	IP	H	HR	BB	K	BB9	SO9	GB%	BABIP	WHIP	ERA	FIP	FRA	WARP
2014	HAG	A	19	10	2	0	20	20	98.0	70	7	28	110	2.6	10.1	51%	.262	1.00	2.20	3.16	4.13	1.8
2015	WAS	MLB	20	4	5	0	16	16	72.0	69	7	31	62	3.9	7.8	47%	.319	1.39	4.30	4.31	4.68	0.1
2016	WAS	MLB	21	8	9	0	31	31	200.7	193	21	66	179	3.0	8.0	47%	.319	1.29	4.06	3.79	4.42	0.4

Breakout: 0%   **Improve:** 0%   **Collapse:** 0%   **Attrition:** 0%   **MLB:** 0%   **Upside:** 9   *Comparables: Julio Teheran, Robbie Ray, Jenrry Mejia*

> **#6**
>
> BP Top 101 Prospects

Drafted/Acquired: 1st round, 2012 draft, Harvard-Westlake HS (Los Angeles, CA)

Previous Ranking: #1 (Org), #13 (Top 101)

What Happened in 2014: The young right-hander made his much-anticipated full-season debut and took the South Atlantic League by storm, fanning a whopping 110 batters in 98 innings while allowing only 70 hits.

Strengths: Outstanding size; excellent present strength; proportionally filled out throughout frame; uses body well to create steep plane; stays tall above the ball; good balance; elite arm strength; fastball easily works 93-97; can reach back for more; big arm-side run in lower band (93-95); explosive offering; can already throw to all four quadrants; curve shows deep two-plane break; power pitch; adept at replicating arm slot and disguise to fast-ball; high confidence in offering; will use at any point in the count; commands to both sides of the plate; already plus to better; elite potential; flashes feel for change; turns over with a loose wrist; displays fade with late drop; early makings of strong pitchability; competes.

Weaknesses: Lot of body to control; can drift during landing and open early; diminishes fastball command at times; still in the early stages of building stamina; some effort in delivery wears him down; stuff can get loose and sloppy deeper into outings; velocity trails off third time through; will wrap wrist when delivering curve from time to time; change has gap to close to reach on-paper potential; loses action when throws too hard; doesn't presently command pitch well; leaves up in zone due to early release.

Risk Factor/Injury History: High risk; yet to reach upper levels; Tommy John on résumé; progression of changeup.

Bret Sayre's Fantasy Take: While it's true that no other arm rivals Giolito's pure fantasy upside, there are risk factors holding him back from being an elite fantasy prospect, other than just "he's a pitcher." The biggest is that with one Tommy John already behind him, but not wholly in the rearview mirror, his downside is increased. That sentence would read "increased compared to similar players" for almost anyone, but his lack of a peer group renders that meaningless. Beyond the nitpicking, this is a pitcher who could be the top fantasy arm in baseball one day, offering potentially elite contributions in all four categories.

The Year Ahead: Giolito is one of the premier pitchers rising up through the ranks, with a ceiling that highlights his potential to round into one of the best arms in the game for many seasons to come. The combination of size and elite raw stuff seems unfair at times. This is the total package: a power arm with explosive stuff who has shown early on that he has a feel for his craft and a mentality to use his arsenal to make hitters look feeble. The reports from last season all spoke glowingly of the 20-year-old, with a unified front that things can be very big. The next step for Giolito will be an assignment in High-A, where, with another year removed from surgery, the workload is likely to increase and the train can steamroll even further down the tracks. It's not out of the question that the right-hander reaches Double-A at some point in the summer should the Carolina League prove no match. The main developmental markers ahead are improvements with his stamina and progression with the change. The former should come naturally given more strength is likely to come into his early twenties and with the increased repetition he will see. The latter comes down to execution and focus. Sit back and enjoy the ride with this one.

2. A.J. Cole RHP

Born: 1/5/92 **Age:** 23 **Bats:** R **Throws:** R **Height:** 6'5" **Weight:** 200

MLB ETA	CT	FB	CH	CB	SL	OFP	Realistic
2015	–	70	60	–	50	60 NO. 3 STARTER	55 NO. 3/4 STARTER

YEAR	TEAM	LVL	AGE	W	L	SV	G	GS	IP	H	HR	BB	K	BB9	SO9	GB%	BABIP	WHIP	ERA	FIP	FRA	WARP
2014	SYR	AAA	22	7	0	0	11	11	63.0	69	9	17	50	2.4	7.1	40%	.316	1.37	3.43	4.48	5.36	-0.2
2014	HAR	AA	22	6	3	0	14	14	71.0	79	1	15	61	1.9	7.7	40%	.342	1.32	2.92	2.58	3.14	2.2
2015	WAS	MLB	23	7	8	0	23	23	119.7	124	12	35	100	2.6	7.5	39%	.329	1.32	4.29	3.94	4.66	0.0
2016	WAS	MLB	24	9	10	0	30	30	185.7	191	17	48	167	2.3	8.1	39%	.336	1.29	4.17	3.36	4.53	0.1

Breakout: 0%   **Improve:** 0%   **Collapse:** 0%   **Attrition:** 0%   **MLB:** 0%   **Upside:** 14   *Comparables Burch Smith, Hector Rondon, Jeremy Sowers*

Drafted/Acquired: 4th round, 2010 draft, Oviedo HS (Oviedo, FL)

Previous Ranking: #2 (Org), #53 (Top 101)

What Happened in 2014: Cole split his time across both levels of the upper minors, where the right-hander logged another strong workload and flashed his strike-throwing ability.

Strengths: Clean arm action; size to withstand rigors of position; uses body to advantage; fastball routinely works 92-96; adept at pounding zone with offering; capable of spotting to both sides of the plate; lively in lower tier of zone; seamless arm speed with changeup; plays well off of heater; arm-side fade with ability to command; spots slider well in sequences; has been tightening last few years; good command profile.

Weaknesses: Lacks clear bat-missing secondary offering; change is more of a contact-inducing offering; plays down on occasion; shape of breaking ball can be inconsistent; will get on the slurvy side; lacks bite off the table; hasn't been able to find definitive identity with offering; may end up too fastball dependent at highest level; pitch is often around plate.

Risk Factor/Injury History: Low risk; 11 games at Triple-A; utility of secondary arsenal.

Bret Sayre's Fantasy Take: The strikeouts are likely not going to get Cole to the point where he's much more than an SP3 at his peak, but with strong ratios (particularly WHIP, given his fastball control), he's worth rostering in even the shallowest of dynasty formats. Unfortunately, as of right now, there's no spot for him in Washington—though that can change on a dime.

The Year Ahead: Cole continued to march along in 2014 and now sits on the cusp of getting his chance in The Show. There's a lot to like with this arm, as both the size and power stuff are there to churn through opposing lineups on a consistent basis. The overall profile gets a boost from the right-hander's ability to effortlessly pound the zone with his fastball and fill up the ledger with a lot of strikes. Everything flows off of the heater for the 23-year-old. The plus command profile is a big reason there's a good chance the potential can become a reality, but the secondary stuff leaves some questions as to what the overall body of work will look like in the long run. The changeup is right there in terms of playing at a plus level, but is more of a contact-inducing pitch. If the breaking ball continues to have inconsistencies and can't find an identity, there's a lot of pressure on the fastball. High-caliber hitters may end up taking advantage of the fact that Cole's fastball is around the plate so often. This season will likely be the first look at how his stuff is going to play against big-league hitters, and a little more tightening of the slider would go a long way toward achieving true mid-rotation status.

#30
BP Top 101 Prospects

3. Michael Taylor CF

Born: 3/26/91 **Age:** 24 **Bats:** R **Throws:** R **Height:** 6'3" **Weight:** 210

MLB ETA	Hit	Power	Run	Glove	Arm	OFP	Realistic
Debuted in 2014	–	65	60	65	60	65 1ST DIV/OCC ALL STAR	50 AVG ML PLAYER

YEAR	TEAM	LVL	AGE	PA	R	2B	3B	HR	RBI	BB	SO	SB	CS	AVG/OBP/SLG	TAv	BABIP	BRR	FRAA	WARP
2014	WAS	MLB	23	43	5	3	0	1	5	3	17	0	2	.205/.279/.359	.235	.333	-0.8	CF(10): 0.0, RF(5): 0.8	0.0
2014	SYR	AAA	23	52	7	3	1	1	3	7	14	3	1	.227/.333/.409	.261	.310	0.8	CF(12): 1.4	0.5
2014	HAR	AA	23	441	74	17	2	22	61	50	130	34	8	.312/.396/.539	.327	.421	3.5	CF(87): 13.1, RF(1): 0.1	6.9
2015	WAS	MLB	24	250	32	11	1	5	21	19	79	13	3	.229/.292/.351	.245	.321	1.1	CF 4, RF 0	0.9
2016	WAS	MLB	25	476	53	19	2	10	49	38	150	26	7	.242/.306/.370	.254	.341	3.4	LF 4, CF 4	2.1

Breakout: 2%   **Improve:** 11%   **Collapse:** 5%   **Attrition:** 10%   **MLB:** 23%   **Upside:** 18   *Comparables Justin Maxwell, Melky Mesa, Matt Den Dekker*

Drafted/Acquired: 6th round, 2009 draft, Westminster Academy (Fort Lauderdale, FL)

Previous Ranking: #4 (Org)

What Happened in 2014: After some more middling seasons in the low minors, Taylor exploded in Double-A, where he posted a 935 OPS and dropped 22 bombs before a brief call-up to the majors.

Strengths: Plus athlete; great frame; has been adding size and strength; tools are loud; big raw power; leverage in swing to create lift and carry; drives balls with loft; shows power to all fields; punishes offerings out and over the plate; 25-plus home-run potential; plus runner; covers ground into both gaps; plus range; shows good closing

#57
BP Top 101 Prospects

speed; reads ball well off the bat; defense is an asset up the middle; can impact the game on the bases.

Weaknesses: Overly aggressive at the plate; has a wide strike zone; likes to swing early; gears up for fastball—leaves him prone to secondary stuff; gets off-balance chasing; leads to swing-and-miss or weak contact; brings hands forward early during stride; extends early with swing; has trouble barreling good fastballs inside; power may play down due to hit tool; could end up all-or-nothing, mistake hitter.

Risk Factor/Injury History: Moderate risk; achieved major leagues; questions on hit-tool utility.

Bret Sayre's Fantasy Take: Drool, drool, drool. That's what the Double-A numbers Taylor put up make fantasy owners do. Unfortunately, the contact issues are going to limit some of that usefulness and—like Cole above him—there's a full outfield in Washington that it will take an injury or trade for him to crack. There's certainly 20/20 possibility here, but it could be paired with a .240 average.

The Year Ahead: Taylor's tools are extremely loud, and when these types of skills start to show production, especially in the upper levels, we can get at times overly eager about what exactly it indicates. There is no doubt the 24-year-old outfielder took a step forward last season, when he worked himself into more favorable hitting conditions and punished offerings in his wheelhouse from Double-A arms. Not to splash cold water on a solid prospect entrenched in a good system, but it is important to illustrate there's still a wide range of potential outcomes, which the overall grades strive to reflect, despite the proximity to The Show. The defensive ability and value on the bases give Taylor a leg up at providing good value at an up-the-middle position even if the body of work falls short of the potential run producer the tool ceilings suggest. The scouting still indicates that the strike zone management skills and swing composition may limit the ultimate outcome. If the club is going to commit to him as regular early in his career, adjustments are needed to close a decent-sized gap against unforgiving arms. This season should provide more of a look at how the traits in question are trending at the highest level and whether the gap in outcomes is quickly closing.

4.   Reynaldo Lopez   RHP

Born: 1/4/94   **Age:** 21   **Bats:** R   **Throws:** R   **Height:** 6'0"   **Weight:** 185

MLB ETA	CT	FB	CH	CB	SL	OFP	Realistic
Late 2017	–	75	55	60	–	**65** NO. 2/3 STARTER	**50** NO. 4 STARTER

YEAR	TEAM	LVL	AGE	W	L	SV	G	GS	IP	H	HR	BB	K	BB9	SO9	GB%	BABIP	WHIP	ERA	FIP	FRA	WARP
2014	HAG	A	20	4	1	0	9	9	47.3	27	1	11	39	2.1	7.4	65%	.211	0.80	1.33	2.91	3.68	1.0
2014	AUB	A-	20	3	2	0	7	7	36.0	15	0	15	31	3.8	7.8	62%	.167	0.83	0.75	3.13	4.09	0.3
2015	WAS	MLB	21	3	4	0	12	10	53.0	56	5	24	35	4.1	5.9	51%	.320	1.52	4.90	4.75	5.33	-0.4
2016	WAS	MLB	22	8	9	0	34	26	176.3	175	15	70	137	3.6	7.0	51%	.318	1.39	4.34	3.99	4.71	-0.1

Breakout: 0%   Improve: 0%   Collapse: 0%   Attrition: 0%   MLB: 0%   Upside: 14   *Comparables Jhoulys Chacin, Jose A. Ramirez, Jordan Walden*

Drafted/Acquired: International Free Agent, 2012, Dominican Republic

Previous Ranking: NR

#72
BP Top 101 Prospects

What Happened in 2014: The previously unheralded Dominican busted onto the scene in 2014, when the right-hander fired 83 1/3 innings across two levels, limiting opposing hitters to 42 hits and fanning nearly eight batters per nine innings.

Strengths: Athletic; projectable body; easy delivery; fast arm; good present arm strength; fastball comfortably operates in mid-90s; capable of dialing up higher frequently; heavy downward action and late life; explosive offering; difficult to barrel in lower tier; early makings of ability to command; feel for spinning curve; shows best at 76-78; teeth and depth at ideal velocity; plus potential; future bat-missing look; change flashes quality action; arm-side fade; throws with loose wrist; overall command growth projection.

Weaknesses: Arm can get into slot late; some length in delivery; lands stiff on front leg at times; command has good gap to close; release with curve can be inconsistent; will roll at times; shape can be loose; needs improvement throwing for strikes; change presently lags behind; on the firm side (84-86); more like a fastball pitcher is taking something off of; arm speed and body will slow down; release will waver; in the early stages of building stamina; stuff drops off deeper into outings; some questions as to how it will sustain over long season.

Risk Factor/Injury History: High risk; limited full-season experience; progression of secondary stuff.

Bret Sayre's Fantasy Take: Lopez is going to be a hot name in dynasty drafts this year, because unless your league allows in-season minor-league pickups, he's extremely unlikely to be owned. That said, he's a borderline first rounder, as his risk and ETA are still limiting factors. It's easy to have your mind drift to Yordano Ventura's fantasy successes in 2014, but Lopez has a long way to go.

The Year Ahead: Lopez is the definition of a "pop-up prospect," as it would be revisionist history to suggest he was on the radar entering 2014. Fueled by both internal and external reports, the overall raw stuff and potential here is very legit. The right-hander's fastball is clearly his best present offering, with velocity that can approach elite and downward movement through the strike zone that makes it difficult to square up. While the secondary stuff lags a bit behind for the 21-year-old, the feel and potential growth exists for both the curveball and changeup to play at better-than-average levels when all is said and done. Like most young arms, Lopez has a gap between the present command and where it needs to be to effectively churn through lineups as a starter at the highest level, but his overall looseness and athleticism suggest growth can happen with continued repetition. His overall inexperience and limited workload across a full season also leave some questions as to how the stuff will hold over the grind of the season. A good showing in full-season ball, coupled with proof that the arsenal can sustain its high-octane look from start to finish, could potentially push this prospect's stock into upper-echelon territory.

5. Joe Ross RHP

Born: 5/21/93 **Age:** 22 **Bats:** R **Throws:** R **Height:** 6'4" **Weight:** 205

MLB ETA	CT	FB	CH	CB	SL	OFP	Realistic
2016	–	60	55	–	50	60 NO.3 STARTER	50 NO. 4 STARTER

YEAR	TEAM	LVL	AGE	W	L	SV	G	GS	IP	H	HR	BB	K	BB9	SO9	GB%	BABIP	WHIP	ERA	FIP	FRA	WARP
2014	SAN	AA	21	2	0	0	4	3	20.0	23	2	1	19	0.4	8.6	47%	.339	1.20	3.60	2.67	3.13	0.3
2014	LEL	A+	21	8	6	0	19	19	101.7	101	6	28	87	2.5	7.7	54%	.325	1.27	3.98	3.83	4.44	1.5
2015	WAS	MLB	22	4	9	0	21	21	100.3	105	10	39	63	3.5	5.7	48%	.312	1.43	4.72	4.70	5.13	-0.8
2016	WAS	MLB	23	8	10	0	30	30	189.3	193	16	73	137	3.5	6.5	48%	.321	1.41	4.45	4.03	4.83	-1.4

Breakout: 0%   Improve: 0%   Collapse: 0%   Attrition: 0%   MLB: 0%   Upside: 6   *Comparables: Brett Marshall, Collin Balester, Jeanmar Gomez*

Drafted/Acquired: 1st round, 2011 draft, Bishop O'Dowd HS (Oakland, CA)

Previous Ranking: #10 (Org – SD)

What Happened in 2014: After a 2013 campaign through the Midwest League, where the production far outdistanced the stuff, Ross took a solid step forward in 2014, holding Cal League bats at bay with a plus fastball and improving secondaries, and maintained that momentum through a late-season promotion to Double-A.

Strengths: Good body and strength; starter's build; retains some physical projection; minimalist motion with very quick arm; low-90s fastball reached as high as 97 last summer and regularly touched 94/95; maintains velo from the stretch and later into starts; solid late run; short slider plays 83-86 mph with tilted action; can flash some bite; turns over changeup well, working mid-80s with fade.

Weaknesses: Fastball often catches too much of the dish and gets straight at higher end of velocity band; hitters don't seem to have any trouble picking up the ball out of the hand; control well ahead of command; changeup can flutter up in the zone when he doesn't finish the pitch; slider lacks depth and is reliant on fastball speeding up bats; overall stuff might not play impactful against more advanced bats.

Risk Factor/Injury History: Low risk; reached Double-A; solid developmental progression.

The Year Ahead: Overall it was a very productive year for Ross, as he took a developmental step forward across his game, including more consistent execution of his secondaries and more effective implementation of his plus fastball. Ross effectively utilizes an easy, repeatable delivery to pound the zone with all three offerings, giving him a good chance to stick as a starter long term provided he continues to refine those offerings. As he transitions to the upper minors, Ross will need to work on the finer points of the craft, including knowing when to take some zip off the fastball to get more wiggle and how best to work to both sides of the plate to set up the secondaries. The repertoire still plays below where you would expect given the arm speed and raw velo, but there is a lot to work with here and 2014 saw Ross begin to tap into the potential the Padres saw when they popped him in the first round of a loaded 2011 draft. He'll return to Double-A in 2015, with the Nationals likely to take their time rounding out his development over the next 18 months.

6. Erick Fedde RHP

Born: 2/25/93 **Age:** 22 **Bats:** R **Throws:** R **Height:** 6'3" **Weight:** 170

MLB ETA	CT	FB	CH	CB	SL	OFP	Realistic
2018	–	65	55	–	60	60 NO. 3 STARTER	50 LATE INN RP (SETUP)

Drafted/Acquired: 1st round, 2014 draft, University of Nevada-Las Vegas (Las Vegas, NV)

Previous Ranking: NR

What Happened in 2014: The right-hander had his junior season cut short due to Tommy John, but Washington still saw enough during the year to tab Fedde with the 18th overall pick and take on the rehab process.

Strengths: Athletic; good frame; room to pack on more size; uses body to create leverage and throw downhill; fastball works 90-94; can touch into mid-90s frequently; displays strong sink and some run; slices downward through zone; difficult to square up in lower tier; capable of working both sides of plate; throws strikes; snaps slider with loose wrist; late breaker; throws from same angle as heater; gets bats started; presently solid-average; can turn over change; flashes arm-side fade; room for command growth.

Weaknesses: On the lean side; needs more strength to handle grind of long professional season; fastball velocity can fluctuate; flattens out above middle of thighs; has to selectively elevate to change eye level; more control than command presently; changeup still a work in progress; needs continued honing to get to playable level; inconsistent action; can wrap with slider; will occasionally get loose and sweep; uncertainty as to whether stuff returns to prior form.

Risk Factor/Injury History: High risk; Tommy John on résumé (2014); lost early-career development time; change-up progression.

Bret Sayre's Fantasy Take: There is something to be said about the trust factor in Washington drafting Fedde and guiding him through the recovery process when it comes to fantasy. Organizations have swings on value, and it's not just team or ballpark based, it can start in the developmental phase. Fedde likely falls outside the top 10 picks in dynasty drafts this year, and he's a strong value play in the second round who can contribute in all four categories.

The Year Ahead: Fedde was enjoying a strong junior season, with buzz building as a potential top-10 pick, prior to an elbow injury putting a halt to his campaign. It speaks to the belief in the talent and potential to see him only slip to 18th overall. The 22-year-old's bread and butter is a low-90s sinking fastball that generates plenty of groundballs and should continue to do so in the professional ranks. It's the type of heater that can both set the tone for sequences and also get him out of trouble when needed. The right-hander adds a late-breaking slider and improving changeup to the mix that both show better-than-average potential. The slider is presently the better of the two, with the change getting to a playable level being the big key in projecting him as a starter. Given that Fedde went down in May 2014, much of the near term will be focused on rehabbing and making a return to the mound. It likely won't be until 2016 that things start to come back into focus, with at the very least the floor pointing to a late-inning arm and prior upside indicating a mid-rotation starter.

---

7. Jakson Reetz   C

Born: 1/3/96   **Age:** 19   **Bats:** R   **Throws:** R   **Height:** 6'1"   **Weight:** 195

MLB ETA	Hit	Power	Run	Glove	Arm	OFP	Realistic
2019	55	60	–	55	65	60 1ST DIVISION PLAYER	45 BACKUP/<AVG REG

YEAR	TEAM	LVL	AGE	PA	R	2B	3B	HR	RBI	BB	SO	SB	CS	AVG/OBP/SLG	TAv	BABIP	BRR	FRAA	WARP
2014	NAT	Rk	18	155	20	6	1	1	15	26	30	6	3	.274/.429/.368	.282	.348	-1.5	C(17): -0.4	0.4
2015	WAS	MLB	19	250	18	8	0	2	19	13	75	2	1	.197/.246/.262	.197	.275	-0.3	C -0	-0.9
2016	WAS	MLB	20	250	23	8	0	3	20	12	69	2	1	.215/.256/.289	.208	.284	-0.3	C 0	-1.7

Breakout: 0%   Improve: 0%   Collapse: 0%   Attrition: 0%   MLB: 0%   Upside: 14   *Comparables Miguel Gonzalez, Wilson Ramos, Brandon Snyder*

Drafted/Acquired: 3rd round, 2014 draft, Norris HS (Firth, NE)

Previous Ranking: NR

What Happened in 2014: The Nationals signed the potential power-hitting backstop to an above-slot bonus after tabbing him in the third round and then sent him to the Gulf Coast League to begin his professional journey.

Strengths: Strong body; good present strength; athletic; loose hands; creates solid extension through point of contact; squares up ball with backspin; ability to hit gap-to-gap; plus-to-better raw power; 20-plus home run potential down the line; quick feet; moved well laterally behind the dish; body to smother offerings; plus-to-better arm strength; throws show good carry; intelligent player; high baseball IQ.

Weaknesses: Overall receiving skills on the raw side; glove hand will drift; catch-and-throw mechanics need work; release can get long and tangled; footwork can be choppy; stroke presently line-drive oriented; must learn how to create more loft to reach full power potential; in the infancy stages of developing approach; susceptible to offerings with spin; long-lead developmental path.

Risk Factor/Injury History: Extreme risk; 19 years old; limited pro experience; dual-threat development.

Bret Sayre's Fantasy Take: While the ETA makes a big dent in his fantasy value, Reetz is a very strong endgame option in dynasty drafts. Catchers are generally only worth gambling on if their fantasy upside gives them enough distance above replacement level, and Reetz has Brian McCann-type fantasy potential, portending a .270 average and 20-plus homers. So, yes.

The Year Ahead: Reetz is definitely one of those long-lead players that require a lot of projection to see the overall vision and patience while the raw tools start to marinate into more polished skills, but the ingredients are here to round into a first-division type down the line. The 19-year-old catcher brings a balanced skill set to the diamond, with the potential for impact on both sides of the ball. Offensively, the stroke is fluid and he possesses loose hands, allowing him to control the head of the bat within the strike zone. Reetz's swing is presently more geared to line-drive contact, but there's plenty of raw power to tap into to hit home runs if the prospect can learn to get more loft out of the stroke as he matures as a hitter. Defensively, the backstop moves well behind the dish and shows plus-to-better arm strength. Early on, the main areas of focus developmentally reside with cleaning up his footwork to enhance the throwing game and getting stronger with offerings in the dirt. Expect things for Reetz to be slow and steady early in his career, with signs of progress to be more subtle, but this is a player that should start to move forward in 2015 and show flashes of what the talent can do when it all comes together.

8. Jake Johansen   RHP

Born: 1/23/91   **Age:** 24   **Bats:** R   **Throws:** R   **Height:** 6'6"   **Weight:** 235

	MLB ETA			CT			FB			CH			CB			SL			OFP			Realistic	
	2016			–			70			50			–			60			55 NO.3/4 STARTER			50 LATE-INN RP (SETUP)	

YEAR	TEAM	LVL	AGE	W	L	SV	G	GS	IP	H	HR	BB	K	BB9	SO9	GB%	BABIP	WHIP	ERA	FIP	FRA	WARP
2014	HAG	A	23	5	6	0	29	18	100.7	120	3	55	89	4.9	8.0	62%	.376	1.74	5.19	4.05	5.69	0.5
2015	WAS	MLB	24	4	6	0	22	16	82.7	93	8	46	53	5.0	5.8	54%	.336	1.68	5.57	5.19	6.05	-1.2
2016	WAS	MLB	25	6	8	0	32	21	142.3	150	12	74	108	4.7	6.8	54%	.333	1.57	5.09	4.35	5.53	-1.4

Breakout: 0%   Improve: 0%   Collapse: 0%   Attrition: 0%   MLB: 0%   Upside: 1   *Comparables Tom Koehler, Humberto Sanchez, Josh Butler*

Drafted/Acquired: 2nd round, 2013 draft, Baptist University (Dallas, TX)

Previous Ranking: #5 (Org)

2014 Stats: 5.19 ERA (100.2 IP, 120 H, 89 K, 55 BB) at Low-A Hagerstown

The Tools: 7 potential FB; 6 potential SL; 5 potential CH

What Happened in 2014: The big right-hander's overall line wasn't pleasing to the eye, as he struggled to throw strikes and gave up a lot of contact at a level where the expectation would be otherwise.

Strengths: Excellent size; well filled out into frame; elite arm strength; physical presence on the mound; uses body to throw downhill; fastball operates 91-95 as starter; capable of reaching back for more; flashes cut in lower velocity band; shows feel for snapping and twisting breaking ball; acts as slider in upper present-velocity band (low-80s); can spot glove side; potential to further evolve into late breaker; change can show late drop; stuff can play up in shorter stints.

Weaknesses: Presently struggles with command; lot of body to control; not the best repeater of delivery; fastball works elevated often, where it is on the flat side; needs work spotting east/west; breaking ball lacks identity; more curve look with loose break in lower band (77-79); presently fringe-average; can be deliberate with change; average utility may ultimately be a stretch.

Risk Factor/Injury History: Moderate risk; yet to reach upper levels; command profile questions.

Bret Sayre's Fantasy Take: Valuing Johansen as a starter for fantasy purposes is not a great value proposition as there are many short-season arms with better chances of sticking. It will be tough for him to get the secondaries to the point where there's strikeout impact even if he does end up in a rotation.

The Year Ahead: Johansen is an enigmatic arm, where the size and potential of the stuff point to one set of results, but the execution and relative crudeness overall for the age hold it back. In all likelihood, the 24-year-old right-hander is probably best suited for the bullpen, where he can let loose with his fastball in short bursts and work to snap off the breaking ball with more true-slider tilt. A continued tour as a starter in the near term can squeeze more out developmentally in terms of sharpening the overall stuff. It's possible, though the far lean-forward, perfect-world scenario, that things can further click to achieve the overall potential. The overall belief is that Johansen can track quickly if fully converted to a relief role and round into one capable of bridging key outs in the late innings. It will be interesting to see what path 2015 brings for the prospect, and whether the 'pen option becomes the near-term reality to accelerate his developmental cycle.

9. Rafael Bautista   CF

Born: 3/8/93   **Age:** 22   **Bats:** R   **Throws:** R   **Height:** 6'2"   **Weight:** 165

	MLB ETA			Hit			Power			Run			Glove			Arm			OFP			Realistic	
	2017			55			–			70			65			50			55 >AVG REGULAR			45 BENCH/<AVG REGULAR	

YEAR	TEAM	LVL	AGE	PA	R	2B	3B	HR	RBI	BB	SO	SB	CS	AVG/OBP/SLG	TAv	BABIP	BRR	FRAA	WARP
2014	HAG	A	21	543	97	20	5	5	54	33	72	69	15	.290/.341/.382	.266	.328	8.5	CF(117): 5.5, RF(16): 1.6	3.7
2015	WAS	MLB	22	250	30	8	1	1	13	9	57	19	5	.229/.264/.283	.210	.290	2.0	CF 2, RF 0	-0.2
2016	WAS	MLB	23	250	24	7	1	2	19	11	54	22	6	.246/.288/.308	.225	.302	3.0	CF 2, RF 0	0.0

Breakout: 0%   Improve: 0%   Collapse: 0%   Attrition: 0%   MLB: 0%   Upside: 14   *Comparables Engel Beltre, Reymond Fuentes, Luis Durango*

Drafted/Acquired: International Free Agent, 2012, Dominican Republic

Previous Ranking: On The Rise

2014 Stats: .290/.341/.382 at Low-A Hagerstown (134 games)

The Tools: 7 run; 6+ potential glove; 5+ potential hit; 5 arm

What Happened in 2014: The Dominican outfielder transitioned well to full-season ball, where he flashed the ability to get the bat on the ball and continued to show better-than-average defense in center.

Strengths: Still room on frame to add size; good present strength; athletic; well-above-average runner; natural in center; displays strong instincts; takes sound routes to the ball; plus range; excellent closing speed; defense is an asset; life in hands and wrists; line-drive stroke built to use the whole field; good bat speed; high-contact potential; improving patience; can impact on bases.

Weaknesses: Power not likely to be a factor in game; below-average power ceiling; swing more geared to heavy contact; hands oriented over tapping into entire body; selectivity still has a ways to go; struggles with good breaking stuff; hit can play too light without enough hard contact; likely the type who will have to hit way on base consistently; still learning how to read pitchers on bases to get good jumps.

Risk Factor/Injury History: High risk; yet to reach upper levels; development of bat.

Bret Sayre's Fantasy Take: It's really hard to ignore 69 steals as a fantasy owner, even if it does come in Low-A. The profile may be a tough everyday sell, but a potential .270 hitter with 40-plus steals is a very valuable fantasy player—and Bautista's defense gives him a shot to let it play.

The Year Ahead: The carrying tool for Bautista is the defense, as it gives him a fairly good shot at being able to ride it up the ranks. The outfielder is very natural in center, with excellent instincts and the speed to cover ground swiftly into both gaps. The reports also indicate that he's solid with his judgment and route taking, which points to the fact he's not just living on raw speed at the position. The risk lies with the bat, and whether there's enough in the hit tool for it to play up and maintain status as a regular. The 22-year-old is strong, but the line-drive nature of his stroke likely means home-run power won't be a factor in the game and doubles into the gaps will be needed to keep opposing arms honest. This is a potential leadoff profile, with strong defense at a premium position. There may be some regression this season in the tough Carolina League, but if the scouting points to positive trends with the secondary skills, consider it a very good sign that the bat is continuing to inch its way forward.

---

10. Wilmer Difo SS/2B

Born: 4/2/92 **Age:** 23 **Bats:** B **Throws:** R **Height:** 6'0" **Weight:** 175

MLB ETA	Hit	Power	Run	Glove	Arm	OFP	Realistic
2017	55	–	70	55	60	55 >AVG REGULAR	45 UT/<AVG REGULAR

YEAR	TEAM	LVL	AGE	PA	R	2B	3B	HR	RBI	BB	SO	SB	CS	AVG/OBP/SLG	TAv	BABIP	BRR	FRAA	WARP
2014	HAG	A	22	610	91	31	7	14	90	37	65	49	9	.315/.360/.470	.293	.333	6.5	SS(70): 4.2, 2B(66): 4.3	5.6
2015	WAS	MLB	23	250	28	9	1	3	17	11	51	11	3	.232/.269/.318	.225	.281	1.1	SS 1, 2B 1	0.4
2016	WAS	MLB	24	250	25	9	2	3	22	14	48	11	3	.235/.284/.331	.231	.280	1.7	SS 1, 2B 1	0.5

Breakout: 11%   Improve: 30%   Collapse: 8%   Attrition: 25%   MLB: 45%   Upside: 30   *Comparables Trevor Plouffe, Carlos Triunfel, Adeiny Hechavarria*

Drafted/Acquired: International Free Agent, 2010, Dominican Republic

Previous Ranking: NR

What Happened in 2014: The then-22-year-old Dominican infielder exploded offensively in A-Ball, where he ripped 52 extra-base hits and swiped 49 bags in his first extended action since signing back in 2010. In the process, Difo quickly raised his status from relative unknown to on-the-radar.

Strengths: Excellent athlete; fluid baseball actions; has filled into body the last few years; improving strength; compact stroke from both sides of the plate; capable of pulling hands inside of the ball; good bat speed; gap-to-gap approach; some pop in stick; arm for left side of infield; improving fundamentals in field; potential position versatility; has matured emotionally over the past year.

Weaknesses: Can be on choppy side at shortstop; slower with reads; likely best suited for second base; will fish for stuff with spin away; can get out on front foot early and bring hands too far forward; power likely to play below average; has struggled with confidence and dealing with failure in the past.

Risk Factor/Injury History: High risk; yet to reach upper levels; progression of approach.

Bret Sayre's Fantasy Take: A better option for points leagues, Difo has a stat line that fantasy owners love, but beware the trapdoors here. The speed and contact skills are the most likely to follow Difo up the ladder, but there are plenty of developmental hurdles to cross before anointing him the new, old Jose Altuve (pre-breakout).

The Year Ahead: A relative unknown nationally entering the season, Difo rode the wave of early success out of the gate in a regular role and parlayed that into a breakout season. Confidence is always an interesting determining factor. In the past, the 23-year-old struggled to deal with early-season failure and it led to his skills playing down during the rest of the year. It was a more mature overall game for the prospect last season, and the end result was a coming-out party for the raw tools. Difo features a compact stroke from both sides of the plate that enables the switch-hitter to get the fat part of the barrel on a lot of offerings. The over-the-fence power is likely to play below average in the long run, but there's ability to plug gaps and use the double-plus speed to his advantage. While the defensive skills at shortstop aren't the most natural, the prospect shows promise at second base and likely can add more positions (third and outfield) to the résumé should the need for more versatility present itself. A placement at High-A in 2015 will challenge Difo's secondary skills and ability to stay back on the ball. With a passing of that test, the infielder can continue to track as a utility player at the floor, with upside as a regular.

Prospects on the Rise

1. RHP Jefry Rodriguez: Tendinitis limited the 6-foot-5 right-hander's workload last season, but the upside remains for this converted shortstop who signed back in 2012. Rodriguez's fastball works 92-95 mph with ease, showing downward action and some late explosiveness. He also flashes the ability to spin a tight curveball, with teeth and sharp overhand break. The long poles still remain the development of a viable third offering (changeup) and building the arm's stamina up to handle the grind of the season. Neither aspect was helped by the limited innings of 2014. Rodriguez has the potential to take some steps forward this season, with extended action helping to build experience and reaffirm himself as a top-10 prospect within the organization by next offseason.

2. C Pedro Severino: The calling card for the 2010 international signee is defense. Severino possesses an arm that can play at plus-plus and overall skills behind the dish that can round into above average. It's the type of defensive profile that can carry the 21-year-old to the majors without a whole lot from the bat. That's where the questions on the future role come in, with the bat presently light and not projecting to provide much overall impact. The jump into Double-A this season is going to be a huge test. If Severino can improve his contact skills

FROM THE FIELD

Lucas Giolito

Team: Washington Nationals

Evaluator: Tucker Blair

Dates seen: July 19, 2014

Affiliate: Hagerstown Suns (Low-A, Nationals)

OFP: 80

Realistic role: 65; no. 2 starter

Mechanics: Excellent frame; huge build with muscled top half; sturdy bottom half; proportionate throughout frame; high three-quarters arm slot; still shows mild arm stab; great arm speed; long extension due to long arms; terrific plane; shows excellent drive and ability to stay tall; delivery is slow and deliberate in windup; velocity and stuff hold in stretch; delivery times 1.37-1.43 range; toes right side of rubber with finish pointed toward right-handed hitters box; slightly higher leg kick than last view; shows ability to stay balanced even with mild exertion in delivery; drifted less this outing; showed ability to stay more compact.

Pitch type	Present grade	Future grade	Sitting velocity	Peak velocity	Report
FB	65	75	91-96	97	Sat mostly 92-95; fastball is explosive and looks faster than listed velocity; shows extreme arm-side run at 92-95 velo band; mild boring action; excellent plane plays up the velocity and movement from fastball; changes the eye level of the hitter; right-handed hitters have hard time picking pitch up out of his hand due to plane and movement; command is average; flashed better command in first 4 innings; flew open a few times in 5th and 6th innings; this caused a few fastballs to sail up in zone, but hitters could not make sufficient contact; overall, a near-elite potential offering that could be a terrific offering at the highest level; did not see the consistent elite pitch that was displayed in first time seeing, but still a plus-plus offering for most of the outing; command could still improve, and extra velocity could come with more stamina gained; trailed off in 6th inning.
CB	70	80	78-82	82	Elite offering; very tight spin; extreme depth; 11-5 with terrific movement and looks faster than the actual listed velocity; shows two-plane break; hitters had a difficult time recognizing the pitch out of hand; near perfection in terms of replicating arm speed and action relative to fastball; shows ability to pound outside half of plate to both sides; extreme confidence in this pitch and will throw at any time; clearly his go-to pitch and will challenge hitters with it in consecutive pitches; command was better than last viewing; currently solid-average; does not need to throw this for a strike to have effectiveness; casted only one out of a dozen thrown; release point showed better this outing.
CH	45	55	81-83	84	Flashed solid-average; arm speed is replicated from fastball; release points were an issue; was releasing too early and leaving up in zone; command is currently fringe; pitch has mild feel; becomes too firm at times and looks like a slower fastball without much fade; clearly a work-in-progress but has the ability to become at least an average offering and help counter the fastball/curveball combo; works best in the 81-82 velo band.

Overall: In my second viewing of Giolito this season, he flashed generally the same arsenal and displayed another outing of the near-elite fastball/curveball combo. The fastball did not quite reach the ceiling that was displayed in my first look, but it was still an excellent pitch capable of dominating at higher levels. The curveball is a true elite offering, with only slight release point issues as the main concern. The curveball is one of the best pitches in the minors, and he shows extreme confidence in the offering.

His changeup was thrown more in this outing, and it was clear he was working on this pitch throughout the entire outing. In certain cases, he went to the changeup instead of the curveball to finish off a batter. For progression as a pitcher, this was important for me to see. It is clear that the curveball is going to play at the higher levels, but Giolito was able to flash the changeup and show that this pitch can be effective when it is consistent. The changeup needs more refinement, but the ability is there and slight improvements were noted from my last viewing.

Giolito is a competitor on the mound, and you can generally see the emotions on the rubber. He wants to be perfect out there, but he does not let it faze him when something does not go his way. I like his pitchability and competitiveness, and I think once the training wheels completely come off, he will fly through the minors. He still has not built up his stamina, but remember, this is a pitcher coming off Tommy John surgery and it is the latter half of the season now.

Overall, this is a potential front-line starter with a chance to be one of the better pitchers in the game. The risk is there, but the package is one of the best I have seen.

by getting more comfortable staying back on stuff with spin, the outlook on the bat can point to a bottom-of-the-order hitter as a regular and boost his status within the system at this time next season.

3. 3B Drew Ward: The 20-year-old left-handed hitter flashes big raw power and the chance to stick on the left side of the infield. It's important to remember that Ward was given a fairly aggressive Sally League assignment last season, where his early development needs stuck out immediately. He's a hitter with some length and early extension in the swing that needs balancing to make consistent contact against good stuff. The power has a chance to really play up if the third baseman can make some adjustments and clean up the swing a bit. It remains to be seen whether he ends up outgrowing the hot corner, where the range is already on the fringy side. But don't sleep on Ward showing more—now that his experience is building—resulting in a rise in status.

Factors on the Farm
Prospects likely to contribute at the major-league level in 2015

1. OF Brian Goodwin: In what was expected to be a potential tune-up for getting time at the big-league level in 2014, the 24-year-old outfielder battled inconsistency and injury in Triple-A, which limited him to just 81 games. The tools and athleticism have always suggested things could reach an above-average role, but the overall execution and consistency have been lacking. If Goodwin can tone things down at the plate and stay within himself as a hitter, the bat can round into form to hit enough over the long run. The profile is looking more like a fourth outfielder for the projected career body of work, with the chance to contribute as a regular in stretches. Look for the prospect to get a shot at helping the club during the summer should he make the necessary offensive adjustments during his second stint in the International League.

2. 1B Matt Skole: The former fifth-round pick is a tough profile given the limited nature of the defense and the heavy focus on offensive production it brings. It's also important to keep in mind that there can be lingering effects from an entire season missed due to injury. Skole has power from the left side of the plate and a grinding approach that makes opposing arms work hard for an out. The hit tool is likely to play no better than average given the length and extension in the swing, but there's offense that can be squeezed out of this bat. The profile points to a potential bench bat in the long run, but it wouldn't be a surprise to see the first baseman show more life at the plate a year further removed from injury and get a chance to contribute in some form this summer.

3. LHP Felipe Rivero: After being acquired from the Rays in February 2014, the hard-throwing Venezuelan left-hander struggled with injuries and when he was on the field showed a lack of consistency. When on, Rivero brings a fastball that can work into the mid-90s, a sharp curveball, and a viable changeup. Command inconsistencies have plagued him in the past, but if the arm can show good health in 2015 and gets on a roll, don't rule out that he can emerge as an option should the organization need to dip down into its depth, especially for help out of the bullpen.

2015 Farm System Rankings

Note: Players mentioned in the "Prospects To See There" sections aren't necessarily starting the season at the "Must-See Affiliate." However, they may appear there at some point in 2015.

1. Chicago Cubs

Farm System Ranking in 2014: 2

Top Prospect: Addison Russell (2)

Prospects on the BP 101: 7

State of the System: Despite graduating infielders Arismendy Alcantara and Javier Baez, and mildly uninspiring years from former top-10 prospects like C.J. Edwards and Christian Villanueva, the Cubs are the proud owners of the game's top system. With the 2014 arrival of shortstop Addison Russell via trade, the explosive emergence of third baseman Kris Bryant, and the selection of a hit-first prospect like Kyle Schwarber, the Cubs remain absolutely loaded with impact talent. The arrival and emergence of those players don't even begin to touch on the continued presence of outfielders Jorge Soler and Albert Almora, as well as quality depth of high-ceiling players like Gleyber Torres, Eloy Jimenez, Carson Sands, and Mark Zagunis. The Cubs system is loaded to the gills with talent that could help their roster continue to improve internally or via trade.

Must-See Affiliate: Triple-A Iowa

Prospects to See There: Kris Bryant, Addison Russell, Pierce Johnson

2. Minnesota Twins

Farm System Ranking in 2014: 1

Top Prospect: Byron Buxton (1)

Prospects on the BP 101: 8

State of the System: After resting atop these rankings in 2014, the Twins managed to retain their lofty title despite injury-marred seasons from two of the game's elite prospects, Byron Buxton and Miguel Sano. Even with their arrivals delayed due to injury, both prospects headline an impressive crop of talent that was augmented by top picks Nick Gordon and Nick Burdi, both of whom offer impact potential. When combined with the continued progress of Alex Meyer, Kohl Stewart, Jose Berrios, and Lewis Thorpe, and depth provided by the likes of Eddie Rosario and Trevor May, the Twins boast an enviable collection of talent with the potential to push them back up the Central Division standings in the years to come.

Must-See Affiliate: Double-A Chattanooga

Prospects to See There: Jose Berrios, Nick Burdi, Byron Buxton, Miguel Sano

3. Los Angeles Dodgers

Farm System Ranking in 2014: 14

Top Prospect: Corey Seager (7)

Prospects on the BP 101: 4

State of the System: Bolstered by the continued rapid ascent of outfielder Joc Pederson, left-hander Julio Urias, and shortstop Corey Seager, the Dodgers offer a nearly unparalleled crop of talent with plus-plus ceilings. With a strong 2014 draft bringing arms like Grant Holmes and A.J. Vanegas, and a quality high school bat in Alex Verdugo, the Dodgers built on their depth previously anchored by mid-rotation arms such as Zach Lee, Chris Anderson, and Chris Reed. With such high-end impact talent at the top of the organization's top 10 and impressive depth throughout, the Dodgers should be able to augment their talent-laden roster through minor-league call-ups or trades without completely depleting the farm system.

Must-See Affiliate: Double-A Tulsa

Prospects to See There: Chris Anderson, Corey Seager, Julio Urias

4. Texas Rangers

Farm System Ranking in 2014: 9

Top Prospect: Joey Gallo (15)

Prospects on the BP 101: 6

State of the System: Your love for the Rangers system directly depends on how you feel about high-risk/high-reward prospects. If you're a ceiling junkie, you'll get your high off of players like Nick Williams, Jorge Alfaro, and Lewis Brinson. But if it's high floor you crave, they have that also in Chi Chi Gonzalez. Top prospect Joey Gallo has both—he's going to hit for massive power even if it only plays to 75 percent in major-league game power because of his off-the-charts raw ability, and if everything clicks right, he's got the potential to be the best power hitter in the game. There's a lot of talent throughout the system in a lot of different forms, but there is also a good deal of development to be done along the way.

Must-See Affiliate: Double-A Frisco

Prospects to See There: Most of the top hitting talent—Joey Gallo, Jorge Alfaro, Nomar Mazara, Nick Williams

5. New York Mets

Farm System Ranking in 2014: 8

Top Prospect: Noah Syndergaard (9)

Prospects on the BP 101: 6

State of the System: Not the best, but likely the most balanced farm system in all of baseball, the Mets have everything you could want from a group of minor-league players—a potential ace (Noah Syndergaard); a major-league-ready, everyday player (Dilson Herrera); an up-the-middle regular (Kevin Plawecki); a next wave of prospects coming behind them (Brandon Nimmo and Steven Matz); potential bats with a few years to go (Dominic Smith and Michael Conforto); and young, unproven, high-ceiling talent (Amed Rosario and Johan Urena). Not all of these players are going to work out, but the Mets, as an organizational whole, have enough safety nets to continue to refill their major-league roster for the next few years.

Must-See Affiliate: Triple-A Las Vegas

Prospects to See There: Noah Syndergaard, Dilson Herrera, Kevin Plawecki, Rafael Montero

6. Boston Red Sox

Farm System Ranking in 2014: 4

Top Prospect: Blake Swihart (17)

Prospects on the BP 101: 5

State of the System: The Red Sox have routinely rated as having a strong minor-league system, and while they are routinely criticized for having an overhyped collection of talent, this version of the Sox farm is legitimately full of big-league talent. Starting at the top with a loaded Triple-A roster that should make a difference in Boston over the course of the 2015 season and beyond, the Red Sox lack the impressive high-ceiling talent of some of the teams ranked ahead of them, but they offer more depth of talent than most organizations in the game. At the lower levels of the system, the Sox offer plenty of talent to dream on, including two fast-rising names in Manuel Margot and Rafael Devers, both of whom burst onto the scene with strong 2014 showings. All told, the Red Sox continue to maintain an impressive pipeline of future major-league players, with depth stretching from top to bottom in the organization.

Must-See Affiliate: Triple-A Pawtucket

Prospects to See There: Matt Barnes, Garin Cecchini, Brian Johnson, Deven Marrero, Henry Owens, Eduardo Rodriguez, Blake Swihart

7. Arizona Diamondbacks

Farm System Ranking in 2014: 15

Top Prospect: Archie Bradley (11)

Prospects on the BP 101: 3

State of the System: The Diamondbacks have a well-balanced system, featuring a potential ace in Archie Bradley (albeit one with some command issues to overcome), more starting pitching depth in Aaron Blair and Braden Shipley, and potential regular bats in Jake Lamb and Brandon Drury. They also have long-term developmental projects like 2014 first rounder Touki Toussaint and potential fast-moving bullpen assets like Jimmie Sherfy. As an organization, the Diamondbacks are well balanced to build for the future with players prepared to make an impact soon, but have enough depth to remain a strong organization even after some promotions.

Must-See Affiliate: Double-A Mobile

Prospects to See There: Aaron Blair, Braden Shipley, Brandon Drury

8. Pittsburgh Pirates

Farm System Ranking in 2014: 3

Top Prospect: Tyler Glasnow (21)

Prospects on the BP 101: 5

State of the System: While a pitcher of Jameson Taillon's caliber missing the entire 2014 season with Tommy John surgery would dramatically hurt the standing of many teams, the Pirates continued to display a loaded system that rates among the best in baseball. With Taillon on the shelf, right-hander Tyler Glasnow and outfielders Josh Bell and Austin Meadows picked up the slack by continuing to demonstrate impressive developmental progress. In addition, players like Alen Hanson, Nick Kingham, and Willy Garcia cemented themselves as potential big-league options, giving the Pirates the depth top teams typically demonstrate throughout the minor-league ladder. Though the Pirates get more credit for the upper-level talent discussed above, they do have young talent coming along in the form of shortstop Cole Tucker, right-hander Trey Supak, and outfielders Harold Ramirez and Tito Polo, giving the club another wave of quality talent to fill in behind the upcoming graduates.

Must-See Affiliate: Double-A Altoona

Prospects to See There: Josh Bell, Tyler Glasnow

9. Colorado Rockies

Farm System Ranking in 2014: 10

Top Prospect: Jonathan Gray (13)

Prospects on the BP 101: 6

State of the System: It's easy to nitpick the Rockies farm system after Jonathan Gray failed to dominate in his first full season and Eddie Butler came down with injuries, and with David Dahl's rough 2013 season still visible in the rearview mirror, but with an honest look, the Rox bring a strong group of talent to the table. Gray is still poised to help the Rockies rotation in short order and Dahl looks like an impact bat with monster potential. That doesn't even touch on outfielder Raimel Tapia or third baseman Ryan McMahon, both of whom have strong believers in the scouting community and potential role 6 futures. Though the Rockies system tapers off a bit after the upper-echelon talent, that top tier is enough to carry them to a high ranking.

Must-See Affiliate: High-A Modesto

Prospects to See There: Jose Briceno, David Dahl, Kyle Freeland, Ryan McMahon, Raimel Tapia

10. Toronto Blue Jays

Farm System Ranking in 2014: 12

Top Prospect: Aaron Sanchez (25)

Prospects on the BP 101: 4

State of the System: Consistently known for having a deep arsenal of boom-or-bust prospects, the Blue Jays continue to impress the scouting community with high-ceiling talents that are beginning to reach the major-league level. Led by big-league-ready prospects Aaron Sanchez, Daniel Norris, and Dalton Pompey, and the addition of first rounder and potential front-of-the-rotation arm Jeff Hoffman, the top of the Blue Jays system could offer some awe-inspiring talent. Coming behind that impressive group, Jays fans can look forward to the development of left-hander Jair Labourt; right-handers Miguel Castro, Roberto Osuna, and Alberto Tirado; and the wild card that is Anthony Alford. Even with the impending graduations of Sanchez, Norris, and Pompey, the Blue Jays still should have one of the top systems in the game.

Must-See Affiliate: Low-A Lansing

Prospects to See There: Jairo Labourt, Max Pentacost, Sean Reid-Foley, Matt Smoral, Alberto Tirado

11. Washington Nationals

Farm System Ranking in 2014: 18

Top Prospect: Lucas Giolito (6)

Prospects on the BP 101: 4

State of the System: Lucas Giolito. The Nationals system has built up some depth after a few years of quick promotions of top prospects, but Lucas Giolito. A.J. Cole is on the verge of the big leagues but is blocked and Reynaldo Lopez has gained a ton of traction in prospect circles, but Lucas Giolito. Additionally, Rafael Bautista and Wilmer Difo emerged last season as tantalizing offensive prospects, but again, Lucas Giolito. The big right-hander isn't the only prospect in this system worth mentioning, but he is the best pitching prospect in baseball and is worth more mentions than anyone else in this system. There is additional talent, but the drop-off between him and everyone else is great enough (mostly due to his talent) that his success could swing the future of this organization.

Must-See Affiliate: High-A Potomac

Prospects to See There: Lucas Giolito, Reynaldo Lopez, Trea Turner, Rafael Bautista, Wilmer Difo

12. Houston Astros

Farm System Ranking in 2014: 5

Top Prospect: Carlos Correa (3)

Prospects on the BP 101: 3

State of the System: Despite being weaker than it once was thanks to a few big-league promotions and a trade, any system with Carlos Correa atop it has some bragging rights. The reemergence of Mark Appel from a strange start to the 2014 season gives the Astros legitimate impact talent on the mound as well as up the middle of the field, something few systems can boast. After that, there is talent surrounded with question marks, but plenty of potential pieces for their future.

Must-See Affiliate: Double-A Corpus Christi

Prospects to See There: Carlos Correa, Mark Appel, Lance McCullers, Colin Moran, Teoscar Hernandez

13. St. Louis Cardinals

Farm System Ranking in 2014: 6

Top Prospect: Stephen Piscotty (32)

Prospects on the BP 101: 3

State of the System: A perennially strong system, the Cardinals don't have the impact talent at the top that they typically have to offer, but maintain their standard depth. At every level they feature future major leaguers, with prospects like Stephen Piscotty and Marco Gonzales ready when needed, while youngsters Alexander Reyes and Magneuris Sierra simmer lower in the minors. Once again, the Cardinals are able to find the balance between retaining major-league veterans and replacing

them with young, cheap talent from within their own system, continuing their run as one of the best organizations in the game, even during their down years.

Must-See Affiliate: High-A Palm Beach

Prospects to See There: Alexander Reyes, Rob Kaminsky, Luke Weaver, Carson Kelly

14. Kansas City Royals

Farm System Ranking in 2014: 7

Top Prospect: Raul Mondesi (27)

Prospects on the BP 101: 5

State of the System: Fans may be a bit sick of hearing about all the minor-league talent the Royals continue to bring to the table, after having what many considered the best minor-league system in recent memory as prospects like Eric Hosmer, Mike Moustakas, and Yordano Ventura were coming along. While that may be true, and while the Royals system doesn't have the luster of just a couple of years ago, that doesn't mean they are without impact talent ready to form the next wave of youth. As players like Sean Manaea, Miguel Almonte, and Raul Mondesi get closer to the major-league level—not to mention Brandon Finnegan, who had a taste of the spotlight last October, and Hunter Dozier, who has already reached the Double-A level—the Royals will have to hope their latest crew of intriguing low-level talent begins to develop to backfill the minor-league ladder and keep the pipeline flowing.

Must-See Affiliate: Double-A Northwest Arkansas

Prospects to See There: Miguel Almonte, Hunter Dozier, Sean Manaea, Raul Mondesi

15. Cincinnati Reds

Farm System Ranking in 2014: 16

Top Prospect: Robert Stephenson (16)

Prospects on the BP 101: 3

State of the System: Without the 2014 emergence of outfielder Jesse Winker and right-hander Michael Lorenzen, the Reds system would have a tough time rating in the game's middle tier. Despite Robert Stephenson headlining the farm system, the Reds lack the punch of most systems rated ahead of them. Beyond the top three talents, Cincinnati's prospects quickly begin to have substantial holes that could lead to big-league roles that are more middling than impact. One bright spot for the Reds could be outfielder Aristides Aquino, a power bat who could augment the top talent in the system to help boost the Reds rating come 2016.

Must-See Affiliate: Double-A Pensacola

Prospects to See There: Robert Stephenson, Jesse Winker

16. San Diego Padres

Farm System Ranking in 2014: 11

Top Prospect: Austin Hedges (23)

Prospects on the BP 101: 3

State of the System: The Padres feature a top-heavy system with some impact talent nearing major-league readiness, but there's a drop-off midway through the top 10. The trio of Austin Hedges, Hunter Renfroe, and Matt Wisler give the Padres a solid core for the future—or a solid trade package for a big-name veteran, with plenty of young talent still remaining after them, albeit with much development in front of them. Rymer Liriano is also on the brink of major-league contribution, though he is currently blocked by the Padres glut of major-league outfielders.

Must-See Affiliate: Triple-A El Paso

Prospects to See There: Austin Hedges, Matt Wisler, Rymer Liriano, Taylor Lindsey

17. Cleveland Indians

Farm System Ranking in 2014: 20

Top Prospect: Francisco Lindor (4)

Prospects on the BP 101: 3

State of the System: It's easy to fall in love with shortstop Francisco Lindor, catcher Francisco Mejia, and outfielders Clint Frazier and Bradley Zimmer, and begin believing that the Indians have a high-ceiling system, but there is a substantial gap in talent level between those four prospects and the rest of the system. When the focus shifts to players like Tyler Naquin, Giovanny Urshela, and Mitch Brown, the discussion begins to shift toward likely fringe- or below-average profiles that aren't enough to buoy the Indians system higher than the late teens. As right-hander Dylan Baker and shortstop Willi Castro get their feet under them in 2015, the Indians could see a little boost in their rating, though they will have to figure out a way to compensate for the likely loss of Lindor from the prospect ranks.

Must-See Affiliate: High-A Lynchburg

Prospects to See There: Dylan Baker, Mitch Brown, Clint Frazier, Mike Papi, Bradley Zimmer

18. Chicago White Sox

Farm System Ranking in 2014: 21

Top Prospect: Tim Anderson (39)

Prospects on the BP 101: 2

State of the System: As top-heavy as they come, the White Sox system features one of the largest gaps between their top guys and everyone else. The top two—Tim Anderson and Carlos Rodon—have the potential to be impact players and anchor the next great White Sox team (which may not be that far away). Anderson has major boom-or-bust potential and enters an important year for his development, but if it clicks, he could be a difference maker. Rodon won't need nearly as much time to reach the South Side and could make his impact felt this year. After those two, there is an interesting collection of high-ceiling guys with risk and low-ceiling guys with proximity to fill in the gaps.

Must-See Affiliate: Double-A Birmingham

Prospects to See There: Tim Anderson, Tyler Danish, Courtney Hawkins, Francelis Montas, Jacob May

19. Atlanta Braves

Farm System Ranking in 2014: 24

Top Prospect: Lucas Sims (54)

Prospects on the BP 101: 2

State of the System: Perhaps no system in baseball is more reliant on potential, but there is significant distance between current and future skill throughout the top 10. Players like top prospect Lucas Sims have significant work to do to get their production in line with their talent, while many members of the Braves top-10 list will be making their full-season debut in 2015. There is talent on the big-league horizon, however, as Christian Bethancourt and his howitzer arm are ready for a big-league test, and Jose Peraza and his blazing speed may not be too far behind. Over the course of the offseason, they've added Mike Foltynewicz and Arodys Vizcaino to that tier of prospects ready to see some time in Atlanta—and that's without even mentioning the pair of high-profile southpaws who have seen their careers slowed by Tommy John surgery, in Max Fried and Manny Banuelos. If talent trumps all, the Braves are now positioned strongly to move up this list.

Must-See Affiliate: Low-A Rome

Prospects to See There: Braxton Davidson, Garrett Fulenchek, Ozhaino Albies, Alec Grosser

20. Philadelphia Phillies

Farm System Ranking in 2014: 25

Top Prospect: J.P. Crawford (36)

Prospects on the BP 101: 3

State of the System: Recently decimated thanks to trades and poor drafts, the Phillies system is on the upswing thanks to the emergence of J.P. Crawford as an elite prospect and a 2014 draft that featured near-major-league-ready college picks like Aaron Nola. Trades have added depth to an organization in desperate need of it, especially in useable, major-league-caliber arms. Much of the system hinges on the ultimate success or failure of Maikel Franco and whether he can remain at third base or ultimately replaces Ryan Howard at first.

Must-See Affiliate: Double-A Reading

Prospects to See There: J.P. Crawford, Aaron Nola, Roman Quinn, Zach Eflin, Ben Lively, Tom Windle

21. New York Yankees

Farm System Ranking in 2014: 23

Top Prospect: Aaron Judge (49)

Prospects on the BP 101: 2

State of the System: A spending spree last summer in the international market, the depths of which might force a change in the international spending structure, has turned the Yankees system into one of the most balanced in the game. There isn't a ton of impact talent near the majors, though Aaron Judge is emerging as a key piece of the future, and Luis Severino is going to make an impact soon, though 10 different scouts will give you 10 different answers on how. Then there's the youth movement from last summer, most of whose participants are still teenagers and won't be seen in the big leagues for a half-decade, if at all, but could make for some of the most intriguing GCL teams in the league's history.

Must-See Affiliate: Double-A Trenton

Prospects to See There: Aaron Judge, Luis Severino, Greg Bird, Jacob Lindgren

22. Baltimore Orioles

Farm System Ranking in 2014: 13

Top Prospect: Dylan Bundy (8)

Prospects on the BP 101: 3

State of the System: One of the shallower systems in baseball, the Orioles do have some impact talent atop their system, which gives them a leg up on some of the teams below them on this list. Two years ago it seemed unlikely that Dylan Bundy would still have prospect eligibility remaining. He's one of two potential impact arms, along with Hunter Harvey, at the top of this system, but neither of the two has spent any significant time in the upper minors. Bundy, however, could see Camden Yards this season. Beyond the two big arms, the system is littered with low-ceiling guys near the majors and high-ceiling risks that have a long way to go.

Must-See Affiliate: High-A Frederick

Prospects to See There: Hunter Harvey is reason enough, but the Keys should also roster Chance Sisco and Josh Hart at some point during the year.

23. Seattle Mariners

Farm System Ranking in 2014: 17

Top Prospect: D.J. Peterson (62)

Prospects on the BP 101: 2

State of the System: The Mariners system took a small tumble in the rankings after graduating big-league arms like Taijuan Walker and James Paxton, and seeing left-hander Danny Hultzen continue to battle injuries and generally regress. Adding outfielder Alex Jackson and his impact bat, and seeing the continued development of shortstop Ketel Marte and outfielder Gabriel Guerrero, helps keep the system from falling too far, and if they make additional strides in 2015, the system could be back closer to the top half of the league in short order. Keep an eye on players like Tyler Marlette, Luiz Gohara, and Greifer Andrade as the next crop of young players who could bolster the Mariners system as they further establish their prospect standing.

Must-See Affiliate: Triple-A Tacoma

Prospects to See There: Patrick Kivlehan, Ketel Marte, D.J. Peterson, Victor Sanchez, Carson Smith

24. Tampa Bay Rays

Farm System Ranking in 2014: 26

Top Prospect: Daniel Robertson (66)

Prospects on the BP 101: 2

State of the System: Previously considered one of the gold standards for developing minor-league depth and augmenting the major-league roster with homegrown talent, the Rays minor-league system has fallen on hard times. Even after acquiring big-ticket items Daniel Robertson and Steven Souza (as the headliners returning for Ben Zobrist and Wil Myers, respectively) the system still lacks an anchor—a role not filled by Willy Adames, the system's top prospect before Matthew Silverman started putting his stamp on the organization. As far as holdovers from the 2014 season, the resurgence of the Rays system hinges on the development of Justin O'Conner and the reestablishment of Taylor Guerrieri, who will look to put his injuries and off-field issues behind him. With young talents like Brent Honeywell, Adrian Rondon, and Justin Williams, it's not difficult to see the system rebounding, but it's going to take some time, especially given the last half-decade of success the Rays have had at the major-league level.

Must-See Affiliate: Low-A Bowling Green

Prospects to See There: Nick Ciuffo, Casey Gillaspie, Brett Honeywell, Jamie Schultz, Justin Williams

25. San Francisco Giants

Farm System Ranking in 2014: 22

Top Prospect: Adalberto Mejia (86)

Prospects on the BP 101: 3

State of the System: We tend to question things that the Giants do, including the volume of potential major-league contributors bouncing around the minor-league levels, and yet they continue to foster talent that arrives in San Francisco and finds a way to make an impact. While the Giants lack standout depth and there are open questions about the future role or ultimate ceiling of arms like Adalberto Mejia, Kyle Crick, and Tyler Beede, at some point we have to believe the club can develop and get value out of a minor-league system that appears thin on talent. If the Giants can coax catcher Andrew Susac and right-hander Keury Mella to approach their raw ceilings, this ranking could look a touch low.

Must-See Affiliate: Triple-A Sacramento

Prospects to See There: Ty Blach, Clayton Blackburn, Erik Cordier, Kyle Crick, Adalberto Mejia, Steven Okert, Hunter Strickland, Andrew Susac

26. Milwaukee Brewers

Farm System Ranking in 2014: 29

Top Prospect: Orlando Arcia (93)

Prospects on the BP 101: 1

State of the System: The Brewers did little to augment a minor-league system that ranked near the bottom following the 2013 season, adding intriguing but unknown talents like Kodi Medeiros, Jacob Gatewood, and Monte Harrison through the draft, and third baseman Gilbert Lara via the international signing period. While those prospects represent upside, they also have serious extreme-risk profiles and are difficult to count on in a rating like this. Shortstop Orlando Arcia and outfield Tyrone Taylor represent the system's best chance to find impact big-league talent, and if the club is to rise in the organizational rankings, lower-level talent will need to step forward to fortify the upper reaches of the Brewers prospect list. The only member of the current top 10 who could impact the major-league club in 2015 is Corey Knebel, acquired in the Yovani Gallardo trade, and even that's assuming his elbow is healthy.

Must-See Affiliate: Double-A Biloxi

Prospects to See There: Orlando Arcia, Jorge Lopez, Tyrone Taylor, Tyler Wagner

27. Oakland Athletics

Farm System Ranking in 2014: 28

Top Prospect: Franklin Barreto (74)

Prospects on the BP 101: 1

State of the System: Perhaps no organization in baseball has used their top prospects to retool their big-league club more recently or more diligently than the A's have over the past 18 months. The charred remains, however, contain as many questions as answers. Top prospects Franklin Barreto and Yairo Munoz have yet to reach a full-season affiliate. Others, like Matt Olson and Renato Nunez, offer big power but potential holes and a lack of upper-minors track record. If you're looking for the upper-minors track record, the two names that stand out are Sean Nolin and Kendall Graveman—both picked up in the

Josh Donaldson trade—but they don't project to be impact players. Overall, it's a system with some interesting pieces, but the more certain pieces are not going to light the world on fire.

Must-See Affiliate: Double-A Midland.

Prospects to See There: Matt Olson, Renato Nunez, Chad Pinder

28. Los Angeles Angels

Farm System Ranking in 2014: 30

Top Prospect: Andrew Heaney (37)

Prospects on the BP 101: 1

State of the System: It's difficult to trade for a top prospect and still easily finish as a bottom-five system, but the Angels managed to accomplish that feat with relative ease. Adding left-hander Andrew Heaney from Miami, via the Dodgers, helps give the system at least one prospect that can be expected to provide substantial big-league value in short order, but there is little talent behind Heaney that inspires similar hope. Left-hander Sean Newcomb, third baseman Kyle Kubitza, and newly signed Cuban Roberto Baldoquin have some potential as solid big leaguers, but each comes with questions that remain unanswered. Barring significant changes at the major-league level that could lead to an infusion of minor-league talent, it is difficult to see the fortunes of the Angels' farm system changing anytime soon.

Must-See Affiliate: Triple-A Salt Lake

Prospects to See There: Cam Bedrosian, Kyle Kubitza, Eric Stamets, Nick Tropeano, Alex Yarbrough

29. Miami Marlins

Farm System Ranking in 2014: 11

Top Prospect: Tyler Kolek (NR)

Prospects on the BP 101: 0

State of the System: A system already weakened over the past year by aggressive promotions to the big-league club got even weaker with the trade of Andrew Heaney to the Dodgers (and subsequently, the Angels). The system, as it stands now, hinges on the developmental progress of 2014 second overall pick Tyler Kolek, which is just beginning and has a long way to go. After Kolek, the Marlins feature a muddle of middling talent that should result in some usable pieces, but lacks impact. Overall, this is one of the weaker systems in the game.

Must-See Affiliate: Triple-A New Orleans.

Prospects to See There: J.T. Realmuto, Jose Urena, Justin Nicolino, Nick Wittgren

30. Detroit Tigers

Farm System Ranking in 2014: 27

Top Prospect: Derek Hill (98)

Prospects on the BP 101: 1

State of the System: While the Tigers continue to dominate the American League Central, and they continue to find ways to make trades for big-league talent and fill small holes at the major-league level using their minor-league system, the scouting community continues to look at the talent on the farm with a curious stare. The club's 2014 first-round pick, Derek Hill, is the only talent truly worthy of top-101 consideration, and other than outfielder Steven Moya—who owns a controversial profile—the Tigers system lacks talent that projects as more than a fringe major leaguer. One of the few minor-league bright spots for Tiger fans may be the Tigers ongoing ability to find inexpensive international talent like Anthony Castro, Sandy Baez, Gerson Moreno, and Eduardo Jimenez that could become high-powered pitching prospects as they move up the ladder.

Must-See Affiliate: Triple-A Toledo

Prospects to See There: Buck Farmer, Kyle Lobstein, Dixon Machado, James McCann, Steven Moya, Angel Nesbitt, Kyle Ryan, Drew VerHagen ■

Top 101 Prospects

by Nick J. Faleris, Chris Mellen, Mark Anderson, Tucker Blair, Craig Goldstein, Jordan Gorosh, Jeff Moore, Ethan Purser, and Bret Sayre

1. Byron Buxton, OF, Minnesota Twins

2014 Ranking: 1

Dear Byron, Please stay on the field. Love, everyone who watches baseball. Buxton's health failed him last year—from a nagging wrist issue to a nasty collision in the outfield. When 2012's second overall pick did play, he flashed the same elite pre-injury skill set that made him our top prospect before the season, though his offense was clearly restricted by the wrist, and the need for continued refinement handling breaking stuff does stick out. The upside is a top-of-the-scale runner, a plus-plus glove in center, a plus hitter with power that can peak as above-average: a player who can take over the game in every situation. If Buxton can make up for lost time in 2015, he might see the majors before the year ends.

2. Addison Russell, SS, Chicago Cubs

2014 Ranking: 7

Russell is the current flag-bearer for a cadre of standout shortstops clustered atop the minor-league ranks, providing an elite blend of offensive upside, defensive stability at a high-value position, athleticism, and strength. Through his first 233 professional contests Russell has shown an ability to impact the game in all facets, hitting for average and power while providing steady defense at short and impressing on the bases. He's close to major-league ready and possesses the skill set, makeup, and natural ability to step in as a contributor immediately upon arrival.

3. Carlos Correa, SS, Houston Astros

2014 Ranking: 5

Though a broken right fibula ended his season prematurely, Correa showcased electrifying tools and impressive game awareness. The first overall selection in the 2012 draft has a well-rounded offensive package with an advanced approach, remarkable feel to hit, and projectable raw power. Even at 6-foot-4 he should have the ability to stick at shortstop for the foreseeable future. With elite makeup, he figures to be one of the main building blocks in Houston going forward.

4. Francisco Lindor, SS, Cleveland Indians

2014 Ranking: 6

Close your eyes for a second and imagine the ideal shortstop prospect. Without knowing it, you just conjured Lindor. Yes, we're positive. The 2011 first rounder is a switch-hitting contact-oriented batter who possesses an approach well beyond his years, and sneaky pop to boot. He's otherworldly in the field, a player whose elite skills are obvious even in pregame infield practice. Really, head out to Columbus this year and get to the game early: His youthful exuberance and pillow-quality hands are worth the price of admission.

5. Kris Bryant, 3B, Chicago Cubs

2014 Ranking: 17

Through his minor-league career, which covers a shade more than one full season's worth of plate appearances, Bryant has posted steroids-era numbers at the plate, with a slash line of .327/.428/.666 and a home run almost every three games. The former first rounder is ready to bring his act to The Show, where he should eventually settle in as a fixture in the middle of the Cubs lineup, joining Russell as foundational talents for the up-and-comer Cubbies. Both are set to debut in 2015 as the North Siders look to effect the transition from loveable losers to feared frontrunners.

6. Lucas Giolito, RHP, Washington Nationals

2014 Ranking: 13

There are major-league teams who don't currently have a better pitcher than Giolito, a 20-year-old who spent his summer pitching in front of three-digit hometown crowds at Hagerstown. The Nationals have paced his development slowly, a reasonable precaution for a pitcher with a Tommy John surgery on his résumé, but it created an unreasonable mismatch for Low-A hitters: Giolito flashed an elite fastball/curveball combination on his way to 10 strikeouts per nine innings and a 2.20 ERA. The changeup is still a work in progress, but he replicates arm speed and has shown steady improvement with it. Giolito is the full package, the best pitching prospect in baseball, and a future ace whose only red flag is his job title.

7. Corey Seager, SS, Los Angeles Dodgers

2014 Ranking: 44

While Seager's unrestricted offensive march through the California League seemed all but predetermined, it was his assault on Double-A arms upon promotion that pushed him firmly into the upper echelon of the prospectscape. Despite a placid setup featuring minimal load, the former first rounder excels at driving the ball and should supplement his solid over-the-fence pop with plenty of doubles. At present his advanced feel for the game offsets his limited range at short, and his soft hands and strong, accurate arm are left-side assets, be it at the six- or five-spot.

8. Dylan Bundy, RHP, Baltimore Orioles

2014 Ranking: 15

After missing all of 2013 following Tommy John surgery, Bundy took the mound again in June with the same exceptional shape on his up-and-down curveball, but without the full suite that had made him electric preinjury. He lacked feel for the rest of his arsenal, and his velocity was a bit slower to return (though he did notch 96 in his later starts). He still has the makeup and mentality to reestablish his frontline potential, so now he has to prove he still has the stuff.

9. Noah Syndergaard, RHP, New York Mets

2014 Ranking: 11

Spending too much time in Vegas can drag anyone down, but Syndergaard's 2014 stats belie his true talent. The big right-hander still flashes the same huge stuff, including a potential double-plus curve and a fastball that sits in the mid-90s while touching higher. The fact that his changeup is constantly improving and can miss major-league bats makes it hard not to envision a top-of-the-rotation workhorse. Even with a full rotation ahead of him in Queens, expect him to force the issue before the All-Star break.

10. Julio Urias, LHP, Los Angeles Dodgers

2014 Ranking: 35

There's no truth to the rumor that Urias, born in 1996, was inspired to pitch by Robert Rodriguez's 1995 masterpiece *Desperado*. There's every reason to believe it, though, as he packs multiple weapons into an unassuming frame and toys with hitters as deftly as El Mariachi plucks his guitar. Urias' impressive arsenal is further bolstered by his ability to cut, run, and sink his fastball, and vary the length and bite on his breaking ball. The cambio gives him a chance for three above-average pitches, and his feel for the craft at such a young age instills confidence he'll approach his overall future projection of a no. 2 starter.

11. Archie Bradley, RHP, Arizona Diamondbacks

2014 Ranking: 9

Bradley endured a bevy of challenges in 2014, including an extended DL stint and mechanical issues ranging from a variable arm slot to inconsistent posture, timing, and landing, all combining to throw off his release and complicate his execution. Evaluators remain bullish, however, and the Arizona Fall League found the Oklahoman showing renewed confidence and a notably impactful cutter, broadening a repertoire that already included some of the filthiest raw stuff in the game. Recent hiccups notwithstanding, this is an elite arm capable of bridging the gap between his lackluster 2014 performance and a front-end future in the blink of an eye.

12. Miguel Sano, 3B, Minnesota Twins

2014 Ranking: 14

Tommy John surgery took his 2014 season, but the good news is that Sano is not a pitcher and this injury is unlikely to negatively affect his long-term potential. If baseball held its own version of a "longest drive" contest, Sano would contend for the crown, with top-of-the-scale raw power that already shows up in games. The only thing that might prevent production is a lack of hit-tool refinement. It remains to be seen whether he can stick at third: The action and hands are major-league quality, but he has Tommy John surgery and size working against him. Even in right field or at the cold corner, he'd be an impact prospect.

13. Jonathan Gray, RHP, Colorado Rockies

2014 Ranking: 16

Gray continued to showcase power stuff in 2014, headlined by an elite fastball/slider combo and an emerging changeup that could give the former Oklahoma Sooner a third plus offering with which to attack major-league bats. The Rockies limited Gray in his pitch selection and counts, encouraging a pitch-to-contact approach that drew soft contact from Texas League bats and mild angst from evaluators longing to see the burly right-hander unleashed and unrestricted. Gray should provide major-league value in short order, with anything shy of no. 3 production, even in the challenging Coors environs, coming as a surprise.

14. Alex Meyer, RHP, Minnesota Twins

2014 Ranking: 32

It's easy to imagine Meyer, a 6-foot-9 flamethrower with a plus-plus slider, becoming an impact closer chasing 400 saves. He's abnormally large, with tree-trunk legs, and his stuff would play up in short bursts. But the fastball command started to take a step forward in 2014, and despite the lack of consistent changeup, Meyer's two main pitches add up to four plusses, so a ceiling as a no. 2 starter is not out of the question. Meyer is entering his age-25 season, but large pitchers take a longer time to develop.

15. Joey Gallo, 3B, Texas Rangers

2014 Ranking: 95

It's been some time since minor-league pitchers have seen natural raw power like this. More impressive is that Gallo has had no trouble putting that power into play in games; despite the swing-and-miss, he has hit 104 bombs in just 296 career minor-league games. (For context, Giancarlo Stanton hit 91 in 333 games, though Gallo *has* been a year or so behind Stanton's promotion schedule.) Power is the headliner, but Gallo's baseball IQ and work ethic have been praised since he was drafted in 2012, and he could stick at third or work in right field due to his huge arm. Just watch where you park when he's playing.

16. Robert Stephenson, RHP, Cincinnati Reds

2014 Ranking: 22

Stephenson survived the year at Double-A Pensacola, but in the process showed there is work to be done before he can tackle his next set of developmental challenges. Almost all of the righty's issues can be traced back to a propensity to go through on-field obstacles, rather than negotiating them via precise execution and craft. The fastball-curve combo has the potential to miss bats at every level, but to fully tap into that potential, Stephenson must rein things in and place a higher premium on spotting and execution.

17. Blake Swihart, C, Boston Red Sox

2014 Ranking: 73

Stumbles out of the gate by previous top Red Sox prospects should in no way factor into one's opinion of Swihart. The latest player bestowed with the honor has everything you want in a prospect, with plus defensive ability up the middle, a major-league-caliber bat, and elite makeup, the latter of which is extremely important given his position and home ballpark. While not necessarily a middle-of-the-order slugger, Swihart will hit enough to be a first-division regular, and the defensive profile grades out even better than his bat. He should be an everyday catcher for the better part of a decade and could be the best player on a contending team.

18. Joc Pederson, OF, Los Angeles Dodgers

2014 Ranking: 50

With a patient approach that borders on passive, Pederson pairs his stellar walk rate with a strikeout-heavy profile. It's a strategy that worked last year as he rode a 30/30 season in Triple-A all the way to his major-league debut, quelling concerns about his ability to hit same-side pitching in the process. While there's no carrying tool in his profile, he grades out as average or a tick above across the board and should be a starting-caliber player, whether he sticks in center or shifts to a corner down the line.

19. Jorge Soler, OF, Chicago Cubs

2014 Ranking: 45

Soler put together a solid but checkered showing in his first taste of major-league ball to close out 2014 and should be ready to step in full time for the Cubs on Opening Day. If he's to reach his upside as a true middle-of-the-order masher, he'll need to prove capable of adjusting to major-league arms who work with a book and a game plan. But even if the hit tool never fully materializes, Soler could thrive as a dangerous five- or six-hole bat capable of punishing mistakes en route to 25-plus home runs per season.

20. Hunter Harvey, RHP, Baltimore Orioles

2014 Ranking: 58

Harvey was shut down with shoulder soreness late in the season, which is the last thing one wants to read in the first sentence of a prospect write-up. But his season was otherwise impeccable, as he feasted on Low-A hitters in 17 starts at Delmarva. He can make his electric fastball cut or run, and his hammer curveball won't find a fair fight until he reaches the upper levels. Hunter showed mild improvements in arm-speed repetition and overall feel for his changeup. That pitch will struggle to keep up as the rest of his arsenal pushes him up the Orioles' system toward a possible 2016 debut.

21. Tyler Glasnow, RHP, Pittsburgh Pirates

2014 Ranking: 42

Glasnow's a huge guy with a huge fastball, and he racked up huge strikeout totals with High-A Bradenton. The heater is hard to square up due to his long limbs and extreme plane, and his hammer curve has deep break and plus potential. Taming such a big delivery will be a challenge, and for now he struggles with his release point and consistency. Glasnow needs to improve his command and the consistency of his secondaries, but the first signs of pitching-not-throwing are already flashing, and the upside is impressive.

22. Braden Shipley, RHP, Arizona Diamondbacks

2014 Ranking: 62

Shipley accomplished a great deal in 2014: He increased proficiency with his breaking ball, managed a solid jump in workload, and showed more comfort mixing and matching his offerings in variable game situations. His mechanics work for him and his repertoire. His athleticism is an asset, both in implementing tweaks suggested by player development staff and in self-correcting when his motion slides slightly out of whack within outings. With a chance for three plus or better offerings and the strength and arm to shoulder a major-league starter's workload, Shipley represents one of the more exciting profiles in the minors.

23. Austin Hedges, C, San Diego Padres

2014 Ranking: 18

When you are the best defensive catcher in the minor leagues, the expectations for big-league arrival are accelerated. Hedges is on track to debut in San Diego this year based on his glovework alone. It truly is his glovework alone, though: He hit .225/.268/.321 line in his first full exposure to Double-A, where his approach unraveled and pitchers challenged him with impunity. He has shown good strike-zone judgment, a balanced swing, and plenty of strength in the past, so some offensive development isn't out of the question, but Hedges' impact will almost certainly be limited to what he does behind the plate.

24. David Dahl, OF, Colorado Rockies

2014 Ranking: 100

After missing much of 2013 due to injury and some disciplinary issues (neither of which poses any concern moving forward), Dahl slid into the full-season routine last summer with nary a missed step, showcasing true five-tool talent and an impressive combination of athleticism and baseball acumen. There is work to be done smoothing out the reads and routes in the outfield, as well as the overall approach at the plate, but many of these concerns should abate with continued reps, leaving the talented center fielder poised to emerge as an elite talent.

25. Aaron Sanchez, RHP, Toronto Blue Jays

2014 Ranking: 31

After starting the year in Double-A, Sanchez climbed to the major leagues and spent the latter part of the season in Toronto's bullpen. He generates easy fastball velocity that can reach elite levels out of the bullpen with generous arm-side life. His low-80s curveball flashes late, hard bite and projects as at least a plus offering. Sanchez has made strides with the changeup, and though he rarely used it out of the bullpen, the pitch flashes above-average potential. His ultimate role has yet to be determined, but the talented righty has the requisite stuff to impact a staff in either capacity.

26. Jameson Taillon, RHP, Pittsburgh Pirates

2014 Ranking: 19

Though Taillon missed the entire season after Tommy John surgery and still hasn't thrown off a mound as the book goes to press, signs point toward a healthy return heading into the 2015 season. He offers a four-pitch arsenal and potentially dominant stuff, and was inching close to a major-league debut before Dr. Altchek cut him open. Development is rarely linear, but Taillon will be looking to prove good health this spring before reminding everybody why he was (and is) one of the premier pitching talents in the minors.

27. Raul Mondesi, SS, Kansas City Royals

2014 Ranking: 29

Last year's Top 101 stated that "it might take some time for [Mondesi's] numbers to catch up with the scouting," and so it remains. He started the year like a house on fire before turning into ash in May and June. He recovered toward season's end, curtailing his free-swinging ways in favor of a more patient approach. His plus-plus bat speed allows him to generate thump despite a frame that's more lithe than powerful. That pop is more evident from the left side, but hard contact is a constant from either side of the plate. He's a good defender who projects to average-or-better tools across the board, a valuable skill set in an up-the-middle package.

28. Kohl Stewart, RHP, Minnesota Twins

2014 Ranking: 54

Shoulder impingement, we abhor thee. Any time a pitcher's name is mentioned alongside the word "shoulder," sirens should start going off. The good news is that Stewart required no surgery and should resume a full workload at High-A. An excellent athlete and former Division I quarterback recruit, he features repeatable mechanics and plus fastball life. Backing up a low-to-mid-90s heater with a potential plus slider, average curve, and feel for a changeup, the ceiling is way up there.

29. Chi Chi Gonzalez, RHP, Texas Rangers
2014 Ranking: 70

The consistently underrated Gonzalez has done nothing but impress since being drafted late in the first round in 2013. It all starts with a fastball that he can cut and sink, and that he learned to command better over the course of the season. There's no wow pitch in the package, but he can miss bats from either side of the plate with his hard slider and developing change, both of which could be plus in time. Gonzalez might not face adversity until he reaches The Show, which could happen in the second half.

30. A.J. Cole, RHP, Washington Nationals
2014 Ranking: 53

It's been almost five years since Cole was drafted, and four since he first appeared on a BP Top 101, but he continues to make steady progress. He pounds the strike zone with an effortless mid-90s fastball, spotting the pitch on either side of the plate while mixing in two average-or-better secondaries. The command could still use refinement and the slider still needs to find a shape if he's to reach his mid-rotation upside. He handled Triple-A in 2014 and has logged at least 25 starts in each of the past three seasons, so he'll eat major-league innings soon.

31. Jorge Alfaro, C, Texas Rangers
2014 Ranking: 41

The tools have been legendary since he was an 18-year-old in the Northwest League, and slowly and steadily Alfaro has harnessed those tools. Gifted with a plus-plus arm that makes scouts recalibrate their stopwatches, Alfaro also has the athleticism to project to above-average defense behind the plate. Perhaps more impressive is what he does at the plate, where he boasts 70 raw power and the potential to regularly knock 25-plus homers. Catchers this dynamic are as rare in today's game as they were in previous eras, and it might be some time before we see this collection of tools and upside in a backstop again.

32. Stephen Piscotty, OF, St. Louis Cardinals
2014 Ranking: 66

Regular hard contact is a fixture in Piscotty's game, and his ability to rack up extra bases, be it by home run or double, will determine whether he reaches his first-division upside. The former Stanford Cardinal has the raw strength to drive the ball, but merely average bat speed will place increased importance on continued refinement of his approach. He must learn which situations allow for added length and leverage in the swing. His feel for the craft and a professional approach should aid Piscotty in making the requisite adjustments as he finishes baking in the majors.

33. Steven Matz, LHP, New York Mets
2014 Ranking: N/A

The southpaw from Long Island finally showed he could stay on the mound for a full season and saw his prospect status go through the roof. Drafted in the second round in 2009, he threw more innings in 2014 than he had in his entire career up to that point. He remains a health risk (with Tommy John already on

his résumé) who must work on sharpening his command and working down in the zone, but three potential plus pitches from the left-hand side and Double-A success breed excitement.

34. Daniel Norris, LHP, Toronto Blue Jays
2014 Ranking: N/A

Norris flew through three minor-league levels before making five appearances in the majors in September. The 22-year-old showcased a quality four-pitch mix at every stop, including a plus fastball/slider combination, a changeup that shows at least above-average potential, and an average curveball that can change sight lines. The 2011 second rounder showcased much better strike-throwing ability in 2014 and projects to have an average command/control profile, though the 6-foot-2, 180-pound lefty throws across his body and falls off significantly toward third base. He projects as a solid no. 3 starter and is nearly major-league ready.

35. Mark Appel, RHP, Houston Astros
2014 Ranking: 21

A year after being selected first overall by the Astros, Appel remains an enigma. With a durable 6-foot-5, 225-pound frame and a relatively clean delivery, the Stanford product *looks* the part of a front-end innings eater. At his best he flashes a double-plus fastball and a plus slider and changeup that can make hitters on either side of the plate look foolish. The command is often loose and the stuff has a tendency to play down, with the results not always backing the arsenal and some evaluators questioning the ultimate upside. The quality of the repertoire gives him a high floor, and he should be in line for a Houston debut in the near future.

36. J.P. Crawford, SS, Philadelphia Phillies
2014 Ranking: N/A

Crawford marries an exciting ceiling with a high floor. There are very few questions about his ability to remain at shortstop, and thus it's a near certainty that he'll be a big leaguer. He doesn't offer the power projection of some of the top shortstop prospects in the game, but he also doesn't have massive strikeout numbers burning a hole through his hit tool. Crawford still needs some polish, but his flaws are far from glaring and he's handled the Phillies' aggressive promotions with aplomb thus far. He should continue to be pushed this season.

37. Andrew Heaney, LHP, Los Angeles Angels
2014 Ranking: 30

The former Marlin (and Dodger for a half-hour) should snag a rotation spot with the Angels this season. Heaney had moved quickly through the Miami system, failing to find a challenge at any minor-league level before finally scuffling in the majors. He profiles as a mid-rotation starter whose fastball/slider combination could carry him into a no. 2 role. There's not much left for Heaney in the minors, and there's little reason to believe that his struggles will carry over. He's as major-league ready as pitching prospects come and should benefit from the Angels' pitcher-friendly ballpark.

38. Albert Almora, OF, Chicago Cubs
2014 Ranking: 25

Almora is a complicated assortment of high-level baseball skills, natural ability, and unrefined approach that has thus far resulted in uneven offensive production through his first two full seasons of pro ball. There is solid foundational value built into the profile, however, with the 21-year-old providing plus defense up the middle and serving as an asset on the bases. While there's work to be done on his approach, the bat-to-ball is top shelf, allowing Almora to post elite contact rates that should buoy the hit tool moving forward.

39. Tim Anderson, SS, Chicago White Sox

2014 Ranking: N/A

Potential drips off this former first rounder and puddles at his feet. Be patient with him, as he has fewer baseball reps than most do at his stage of development, but the tools are loud: Plus-plus run, potential plus hit tool wrapped up with some pop and dynamic athleticism offer mountainous upside. It'll fit at an up-the-middle position, more likely second base or center field than shortstop. This is one of the most naturally gifted players in the minor leagues, and Double-A will present an interesting challenge for his skill set.

40. Nomar Mazara, OF, Texas Rangers

2014 Ranking: N/A

Before A.J. Preller became San Diego's GM, he was the international scouting savant who gave Mazara $4.95 million in 2011; at the time, it was the largest amateur signing bonus ever. Mazara struggled in his full-season debut in 2013, but after making mechanical adjustments, he took off in 2014, reaching Double-A as a teenager. A prototypical right fielder, his presence looms large on both sides of the ball, with a plus arm and power potential to match. A plus work ethic and above-average hit tool could make him truly special.

41. Carlos Rodon, LHP, Chicago White Sox

2014 Ranking: N/A

Just a few months into his pro career, during which he struck out 14 batters per nine while reaching Triple-A, Rodon is already suffering from prospect fatigue. Despite having one of the game's best sliders, an electric fastball, and precocious feel for his changeup, Rodon reached Peak Prospect back in college and has since left scouts wanting to see more refinement. In the prospect world, staying the same can be viewed as taking a step backward, but Rodon could have a chance to impress anew with a big-league debut this year.

42. Dalton Pompey, OF, Toronto Blue Jays

2014 Ranking: N/A

Pompey is an impressive athlete who shows plus speed and instinctive routes in center field, utilizing an above-average arm to keep runners honest. He wields a line-drive stroke with above-average bat speed, particularly from the left side, controlling the zone well and projecting for low-teens home-run output with plenty of gap power. The former 16th-round pick jumped from High-A to the majors in 2014, making enough progress at the plate that he should be an above-average regular in short order.

43. Aaron Blair, RHP, Arizona Diamondbacks

2014 Ranking: N/A

Blair's deception, size, and ability to create a sharp plane despite a low three-quarters slot proved too much for low-minors bats last summer, especially once the Marshall University product was able to tap into his two-plane breaker with regularity. He releases each of his offerings with uniformity, and the well-shielded release complicates hitters' ability to pick up the secondaries. The improved consistency of the curve has given Blair a vertical weapon to pair with his already solid fastball/changeup combo. If the command tightens enough to avoid regular mistakes up in the zone, he could flirt with no. 2 status.

44. Jesse Winker, OF, Cincinnati Reds

2014 Ranking: N/A

Winker is a polarizing prospect with a bat-first profile. He has a feel for the barrel but less-than-impactful bat speed and some issues identifying soft stuff. The whiff rates have thus far exceeded what one would expect from a player with an advanced approach and a comfortable and loving relationship with the strike zone. Supporters, however, note Winker's strong work ethic at the professional level and count as a given that he will put in the requisite time and effort to continue making adjustments as he progresses toward Cincy.

45. Raimel Tapia, OF, Colorado Rockies

2014 Ranking: 97

Tapia utilizes an unconventional setup, variable swing, and innate ability to find the ball with the barrel regardless of quadrant or pitch type, producing one of the most interesting hit tools in the minors. The native Dominican possesses natural bat speed and hand-eye coordination, with steady balance throughout his swing serving as the foundation for regular impactful barrel delivery. Tapia lacks the same level of feel on the defensive side, though his foot speed and arm could make for average or better production in center or right with continued work.

46. Henry Owens, LHP, Boston Red Sox

2014 Ranking: 69

Much has been made of Owens' ascent through the Red Sox system, and while expectations seem to be trending toward frontline starter, it is far more likely Owens settles in as a mid-rotation arm. Owens' changeup is a standout pitch that earns easy plus grades, and it helps his average fastball play to a slightly more impressive level. Owens is continuing to develop both his curveball and command, two items that must step forward if he is to cement himself as a no. 3 starter; if he does, it could happen as early as the second half of this year.

47. Jake Thompson, RHP, Texas Rangers

2014 Ranking: N/A

A second rounder in 2012, Thompson returned home to Texas in the Joakim Soria trade and continued posting big strikeout totals, microscopic home-run rates, and an ERA in the low 3s. He is big-bodied and holds his velocity extremely well throughout his starts, but it's the slider that will launch a thousand GIFs. With eight starts already at Double-A, Thompson could force his way to Arlington before 2015 is over.

48. Jose Berrios, RHP, Minnesota Twins

2014 Ranking: 75

The word is "electric." Berrios took huge strides in 2014 and has put himself in position for a late-2015 arrival. As is said about many slight hurlers who have success at the lower levels, the 6-foot Dominican must show the requisite durability for a 200-inning role and continue to hold his velocity late in games. The stuff isn't in question: Berrios' three-pitch mix, including a filthy hard slider that sets him apart, is comparable to any in the minors today.

49. Aaron Judge, OF, New York Yankees

2014 Ranking: N/A

The first thing you notice about Judge is his massive size, but watching him reveals a portfolio of skills that go deeper. He doesn't have many of the same flaws that plague other behemoths, moving extremely well for his size and pretty well even for humans of normal dimensions. He keeps his swing as short as his long arms will allow. In right field, he's presently an average defender, aided by a strong, accurate arm that can be a true asset. He will hit for above-average power without even trying; he knows this and chooses not to sell out for power, lifting the entire offensive approach. The result is an advanced hitter who could jump from High-A to the majors within the year.

50. Hunter Renfroe, OF, San Diego Padres

2014 Ranking: N/A

The club's top pick in the 2013 draft, Renfroe is part of an increasingly rare group of prospects in the minor leagues with legitimate 70-grade raw power and the potential to post 25-plus home runs annually at his peak. Renfroe clearly needs refinement at the plate, and the degree to which his power plays in game situations will ultimately depend on how his approach develops and how he handles quality spin. If everything comes together, Renfroe could become a prototypical right-field bat with solid defense and a powerful arm.

51. Luis Severino, RHP, New York Yankees

2014 Ranking: N/A

Severino's fastball has the potential to be an elite pitch, and when paired with a potential plus changeup, he generates the swinging strikes that make scouts drool. Many of those evaluators are split, however, on whether he can remain a starter given his build and lack of a third pitch. It's far too early for the Yankees to have to make that decision; for now, he's simply the most exciting arm in the system, categories be damned. He will continue to start and should spend most of the season in Double-A. Regardless of his role, Severino has a big-league arm with impact potential.

52. Marco Gonzales, LHP, St. Louis Cardinals

2014 Ranking: N/A

Gonzales took his share of knocks during a 2014 cup of coffee, but generally impressed both as a starter and out of the 'pen. Despite lacking an impact breaking ball, the former Gonzaga Bulldog has been able to keep left- and right-handed hitters alike at bay thanks to advanced feel and a prime change piece. He'll have the opportunity to compete for a spot in the St. Louis rotation to start 2015, but with the Cardinals' robust collection of starters returning, the lefty could be forced to the bullpen or back down to Memphis to begin the season.

53. Matt Wisler, RHP, San Diego Padres

2014 Ranking: 47

Wisler didn't dominate in 2014, but maintains no. 3 upside and at a minimum should help in the back of a big-league rotation. He has enough fastball to avoid being labeled a finesse right-hander, and is at his best when he's filling up the bottom of the zone with the lively heater and secondaries. The slider earns some plus scores from scouts, giving him a pitch that can miss bats and induce weak contact, while the changeup might prove his most useful offering, flashing late fade and deception. Wisler

is a good bet to settle in as a solid no. 4 starter and with some incremental improvements could reach his mid-rotation ceiling.

54. Lucas Sims, RHP, Atlanta Braves

2014 Ranking: 40

Don't be scared off by a less-than-impressive stat line from 2014, as Sims still showed all the potential of a major-league starter. He shows the promise of three plus pitches, though command jumps are needed across the set. The most important developmental need, as with most young pitchers, is fastball command. Still, he's handled a workload that few pitchers his age can take on and he did so while maintaining a live arm all season. A few steps forward here and there and Sims will take off.

55. Alex Reyes, RHP, St. Louis Cardinals

2014 Ranking: 98

Reyes disappointed early in the year, arriving in the Midwest League with a bulky lower half and a jarring inability to repeat his mechanics and execute with any regularity. The young power arm self-corrected as the season progressed, crescendoing in his final 11 starts as he blended top-shelf swing-and-miss stuff with drastically improved control. Had that caliber of performance carried his entire 2014 season there would be a strong case for his ranking some 20 spots higher on this list. This is a potential front-end arm who will be on the way to elite status with improved conditioning and a sharper focus on game prep and execution.

56. Miguel Almonte, RHP, Kansas City Royals

2014 Ranking: 46

You rarely hear "fluid" mentioned this often outside of medical recovery scenarios, but Almonte's smooth, effortless delivery elicits the same assessment time and again. The ease with which he throws belies a mid-90s fastball that he carries deep into games. His changeup is a major-league-quality offering that features more fade than Patrick Ewing circa 1994. The curve lags at present but has shown considerable development already and projects to be an average third offering. Despite not lighting up A-ball, Almonte is ready for the rigors of the upper minors.

57. Michael Taylor, OF, Washington Nationals

2014 Ranking: N/A

After two years marinating quietly at High-A, Taylor sizzled at Double-A Harrisburg, flashing impact tools across the board. Propelled throughout his career by his toolsy athleticism, he finally lessened the noise in his swing, turning his plus bat speed and raw power into production. His defense alone provides a second-division floor in the majors, but the bat now gives hope for much more. A bit more contact, and a bit more *hard* contact, will make him a first-division center fielder.

58. Josh Bell, OF, Pittsburgh Pirates

2014 Ranking: 77

Bell had his second (mostly) healthy season, putting the knee injury that cost him almost all of 2012 further in the rearview mirror. He had been making up quickly for the lost time until reaching Double-A Altoona, where his power disappeared over 102 plate appearances. The physically mature outfielder has plenty of raw tools, including plus power and an arm that's plenty strong enough for right field. His swing has noise from both sides of the plate, which must be quieted before he consistently taps into his tools. The Pirates sent him to the AFL with instructions to play first base, which increases his flexibility moving forward but limits the value of his arm.

59. Reese McGuire, C, Pittsburgh Pirates

2014 Ranking: 59

McGuire is such a talented defensive catcher that some writer is probably already working on a "future major-league manager" profile about him. His polished receiving skills are paired with athletic movements behind the plate and a strong arm, which gunned down 39 percent of attempted basestealers. There were, and will be, hiccups at the plate, but the underlying skills are enough to expect a competent hitter in the long term: barrel feel, good bat speed. The defense creates a very high floor, but he'll look to prove that his value isn't entirely tied to what he does *behind* the plate.

60. Aaron Nola, RHP, Philadelphia Phillies

2014 Ranking: N/A

Perhaps the most major-league-ready arm in the 2014 draft, Nola was at Double-A within two months of draft day. The results were reassuring, as Nola handled advanced batters with the same aplomb he had in the SEC. His advanced skills make up for a moderate ceiling as a mid-rotation starter. His biggest strength is his ability to throw strikes at an elite level, but his future will depend on the development of at least one of his off-speed offerings as a legitimate weapon to keep hitters honest.

61. Manuel Margot, OF, Boston Red Sox

2014 Ranking: N/A

The Dominican center fielder's fast-twitch athleticism was on full display during his time split between Low-A Greenville and High-A Salem. He pairs loose hands and strong barrel skills with above-average bat speed and surprising pop. His strong defensive instincts suggest enough talent to provide impact with his glove at an up-the-middle position. The raw tools are not quite refined, but the skill set carries tremendous value at full potential.

62. D.J. Peterson, 3B, Seattle Mariners

2014 Ranking: 65

Eventually Peterson will be forced to the other side of the diamond by his limited quickness and poor range, so he must really slug if he's to maintain his prospect status. The 12th pick in the 2013 draft has the potential to develop into a plus hitter with plus power, and the gains should happen rapidly thanks to his solid approach and college experience. He already passed the Double-A test, showing a knack for hard contact to all fields and substantial in-game power.

63. Michael Lorenzen, RHP, Cincinnati Reds

2014 Ranking: N/A

It was a hugely successful summer for the one-time two-way standout, as Lorenzen showed he could hold his own as a starter while sprinkling in flashes of dominance. The big question is whether the strong-armed righty can build up the arm and the body to the point that he consistently delivers his power arsenal later into starts, and more importantly later into the season. If more conservative pacing causes the stuff to tick down, it's still a solid no. 4 starter profile, with a fallback in high-leverage relief.

64. Eddie Butler, RHP, Colorado Rockies

2014 Ranking: 26

After breaking out with a dominant 2013, Butler struggled through much of 2014 due to shoulder issues and discomfort with mechanical tweaks. At his best, the lanky righty wields a mid-to-upper-90s heater with multiple looks and lots of weight, and a plus or better change piece that aids in keeping balls off barrels and on the ground. If questions about Butler's ability to hold up to a major-league starter's workload prove valid, the Radford product could thrive in a late-innings role, pounding the bottom of the strike zone with his heavy fastball/changeup pairing.

65. Eduardo Rodriguez, LHP, Boston Red Sox

2014 Ranking: 61

The Venezuelan lefty dominated the Eastern League after Boston acquired him in the Andrew Miller trade. Rodriguez sits comfortably in the low-90s but topped out at 96 a few times down the stretch. While the delivery is smooth and repeatable, the inconsistent command, velocity, and secondary arsenal must improve if Rodriguez is to hit his mid-rotation ceiling. At his best, he flashes three above-average pitches and could be capable of working through a major-league lineup as early as this season.

66. Daniel Robertson, SS, Tampa Bay Rays

2014 Ranking: N/A

There was a brief moment, in between the Addison Russell and Josh Donaldson trades, when Robertson was the "shortstop of the future" for the Athletics. It was a tenuous title at best given his lack of lateral quickness, though his heady play and soft hands should work well at either the keystone or the hot corner if he can't stick at the six-spot. At the plate Robertson has solid contact skills that play up thanks to an advanced approach, and fringe power that could be major-league average at his peak.

67. Nick Kingham, RHP, Pittsburgh Pirates

2014 Ranking: 80

Kingham projects to be a workhorse who can eat innings in the middle or back of a rotation. The 6-foot-5 righty has good mechanics for somebody of his size, leading to above-average control and, when he's on, the ability to effortlessly command his fastball on both sides of the plate. That, combined with his poise on the mound, makes for a pitchability profile, though he'll need to improve his changeup to make it all work. There's no out pitch in his repertoire, and his strikeout rates were worse than his leagues' averages last year, but he should see time in the majors this season.

68. Alex Jackson, OF, Seattle Mariners

2014 Ranking: N/A

The Mariners moved the 2014 first rounder to the outfield permanently, rather than even attempt to develop him as a backstop, but Jackson's offensive potential is so vast that he still maintains his status as a very good prospect. Indeed, the simpler development path of an outfield prospect could help ensure that his offensive game flourishes. While evaluators are divided as to quality of the approach and ultimate contact ability, Jackson is roundly lauded for his 60- to 70-grade raw power, which can already flash in games. Through reps and instruction he could eventually develop into a dominant force in the middle of a major-league lineup.

69. Brandon Nimmo, OF, New York Mets

2014 Ranking: N/A

The Wyoming native's prospect package leaves plenty of room for doubt, but the weight of his overall tools still makes him an extremely strong prospect. Although he might not be a center fielder in the long term, he could be an easy plus defender in a corner. Even without the strongest hit tool he can get on base via a strong approach, and he flashes above-average power potential. More of the focus should be on what he can do, and Nimmo can do almost everything.

70. Nick Gordon, SS, Minnesota Twins

2014 Ranking: N/A

The top prep hitter in the 2014 draft, Gordon's great makeup and high baseball IQ—Did you know he has family who played in the majors? Totally new fact!—have given scouts reason to believe he's got an excellent chance to be a first-division big leaguer, or a tick more. While the tools are more solid-average across the board than impact, he's a "sum of his parts" prospect who could play a premium position for a decade and contribute in all facets of the game.

71. Nick Williams, OF, Texas Rangers

2014 Ranking: 88

Williams' ceiling is immense due to an aesthetically pleasing left-handed swing built for power and grace. Yet the approach is about two steps away from qualifying even as rudimentary. (At least his OBP gets a boost from plentiful HBPs.) To reach his ultimate ceiling, Williams must get himself into better hitting counts and find a way to be a nonliability in the field. Even if he never develops that baseball acumen or focus, he'll hit some big-league pitches a long way.

72. Reynaldo Lopez, RHP, Washington Nationals

2014 Ranking: N/A

The Dominican flamethrower entered the season with five stateside innings and virtually no prospect profile, but dominated two levels of the low minors. Beyond leading all Sally League starters in ERA (he was second in the New York-Penn League), he had scouts raving about his elite fastball, a mid-90s pitch with heavy sink and late life. Although the command isn't always there, he has the physical foundation to suggest it will come. It's a very long trek from Hagerstown to the majors, but Lopez displayed enough to forecast an impact arm who could front a rotation if everything breaks right.

73. Jeff Hoffman, RHP, Toronto Blue Jays

2014 Ranking: N/A

Hoffman emerged as a legitimate 1:1 candidate early last spring before Tommy John surgery in May caused him to fall to the ninth overall pick. Prior to the injury, Hoffman flashed a double-plus fastball, sitting comfortably in the mid-90s with arm-side life and sink. His secondary arsenal features a changeup and a hard curveball that flash at least plus potential, sometimes higher. The 6-foot-4, 185-pound East Carolina product is a lithe athlete, utilizing a drop-and-drive delivery with plenty of momentum throughout. He has a track record of throwing strikes and could eventually have a plus command profile, giving him the ceiling of frontline starter if his arm recovers to full strength.

74. Franklin Barreto, SS, Oakland Athletics

2014 Ranking: N/A

While the diminutive Barreto stands just 5-foot-9, he packs a punch at a physically maxed-out 175 pounds. Despite the solid frame, he isn't thick, and maintains plus speed on the basepaths and in the field. At the plate he features a swing smoother than your cool uncle and bat-to-ball skills significantly more natural than your uncle's second wife. Barreto could see double-digit home runs in his prime thanks to a fluid, powerful weight transfer. He has yet to reach full-season ball but has drawn plus hit-tool grades from scouts and is known to be a hard worker.

75. Vincent Velasquez, RHP, Houston Astros

2014 Ranking: N/A

A groin injury sidelined him for two months, but Velasquez showcased bat-missing stuff across 64 innings in the California League. The broad, athletic Californian possesses a fastball that comfortably works in the mid-90s to go along with a swing-and-miss changeup, a true plus offering. His curveball is inconsistent but flashes average, giving him three pitches he can throw for strikes with a solid command/control profile. He will likely begin the 2015 season in Double-A, giving him a legitimate shot at an extended look by 2016, with health being the most important caveat.

76. Kyle Freeland, LHP, Colorado Rockies

2014 Ranking: N/A

Freeland easily overmatched collegiate competition and low-minors bats alike in 2014 and could ascend quickly through the minor-league ranks. The southpaw is distinctive for the chameleonic manner in which he wields his three-pitch arsenal: He can give different looks or vary the cut and sink of the pitches, effectively turning the three pitches into seven, covering a velocity band that stretches cleanly from the low-80s to the mid-90s. Provided Freeland can maintain that quality of stuff over a long pro season, the former Purple Ace should provide an impressive left-handed complement to power righties Jonathan Gray and Eddie Butler, perhaps as early as 2016.

77. Kyle Schwarber, C/OF, Chicago Cubs

2014 Ranking: N/A

The former Hoosier had little trouble raking through three levels of A-ball, slashing .344/.428/.560 over his first 311 pro plate appearances (60 percent of which came in the pitcher-friendly Florida State League). The true test will come in 2015, when Schwarber gets his first taste of advanced pro arms on both sides of the ball. If the 2014 first rounder proves capable of handling even a 60-game workload behind the dish while also providing passable defense in left field, he could become an immensely valuable asset for Chicago, be it in the lineup or as a trade chip.

78. Amed Rosario, SS, New York Mets

2014 Ranking: N/A

He is still years away from reaching it, but Rosario has more upside than any position prospect in the Mets' system, and it starts with his glove. A strong bet to stay at shortstop, he could develop into a plus defender in time due to his high baseball IQ and fluid actions, though he's getting by on pure athleticism right now. At the plate, he shows a strong aptitude for contact and the foundation for average power projection, but he is overly aggressive and will chase. It will be a slow burn, but one with a possible All-Star payoff.

79. Grant Holmes, RHP, Los Angeles Dodgers

2014 Ranking: N/A

A last name isn't the only thing connecting Grant with John, given the former's X-rated breaking ball. Holmes' power curve generated rave reviews on top of copious whiffs and ranked as one of the best among prep products in the 2014 draft class. He's not a one-trick pony, as his long arm action begets a fastball that sits in the mid-90s and can touch 98, along with a developing changeup that flashes above-average potential. His growth will have to come from improved command and sequencing, as there isn't much projection in his 6-foot-1, 215-pound frame.

80. Kevin Plawecki, C, New York Mets

2014 Ranking: N/A

There's nothing overly exciting about Plawecki's game—he's the vanilla of catching prospects—but this downplays the delectability of said flavor. Four average tools (he's not going to be a threat on the basepaths) from a catcher is extremely valuable, and there's a chance he could bring that hit tool up over time. He's a grinder in all aspects of the game, and a tough out, which will likely endear him to fans and members of the media alike.

81. Billy McKinney, OF, Chicago Cubs

2014 Ranking: N/A

McKinney drew mixed reviews from scouts throughout the summer and during instructs, but supporters believe strongly in the hit tool and on-base skill set. As he ascends to the Southern League in 2015, more advanced sequencing and consistent execution could expose some coverage blips on the 20-year-old's inner half. But with a preternatural feel for both the barrel and the strike zone, there's good reason to bet on the sweet-swinging lefty making the necessary adjustments. Incremental developments on the power front could solidify McKinney as one of the minors' top corner bats, with some already putting him on par with Jesse Winker.

82. Dilson Herrera, 2B, New York Mets

2014 Ranking: N/A

The undersized second baseman flew through the Mets' system in 2014 before arriving in August as the youngest player in the majors, and even held his own with a .255 TAv in 18 games for the Metropolitans. Last season's success might lead to unrealistic short-term expectations for Herrera, who will too willingly chase breaking balls and who still needs to slow down the game on defense. Another year of development wouldn't hurt, which matches nicely with Daniel Murphy's impending free agency this winter.

83. Pierce Johnson, RHP, Chicago Cubs

2014 Ranking: 91

After struggling with his mechanics early in 2014, Johnson found his stride in the second half, putting together 65 highly impressive innings over his final 12 starts. The key to unlocking a future spot in the Cubs rotation will be continued growth in his command profile and more consistency working the lower "U" of the strike zone with the heater. The Missouri State product should get significant exposure to Triple-A bats over the course of this summer, with a focus on staying healthy, logging innings, and finding consistency in execution.

84. Francisco Mejia, C, Cleveland Indians

2014 Ranking: N/A

Mejia is a switch-hitting catcher with feel for the barrel and solid-average defensive chops, a profile that produces less risk than you'd typically associate with a 19-year-old in short-season ball. The Dominican signee could rank significantly higher on the 2016 list if his ultra-aggressive approach proves not to be a liability against Midwest League pitching, and if he continues to refine his receiving behind the plate. The raw skills jump off the field, but patience is key, as catchers typically take longer to develop. There will be some bumps ahead, but Mejia offers All-Star upside at a premium defensive position.

85. Sean Manaea, LHP, Kansas City Royals

2014 Ranking: 78

Manaea faced an adjustment period at High-A before taking command of the reins over the final three months of the season, as he simplified his delivery and was able to better limit the inconsistencies in his control and execution. Manipulation and deception feature into every facet of Manaea's game, as his ideal pitcher's frame (6-foot-5, 235 pounds) and slight crossfire delivery allow him to hide the ball until the last possible frame. His fastball features sink or run, depending on grip and velocity band, and his slider and change can both flash above-average with bat-missing ability. He could be a fast mover if he can hold his mechanics together.

86. Adalberto Mejia, RHP, San Francisco Giants

2014 Ranking: N/A

Arguably the most polished of the high-profile arms in the Giants system, Mejia has the fine skills to make his impressive arsenal play against advanced competition. Armed with a low-90s fastball from the left side, Mejia can induce plenty of weak contact just by mixing his two- and four-seam fastballs. Mejia's slider and changeup earn unanimous praise from scouts, with opinions divided as to which will settle as the most effective secondary. The promising lefty will miss developmental time in 2015 due to a 50-game suspension for a drug violation. Once back in the fold, Mejia should continue his progression toward San Francisco and could settle in as a no. 3 starter in short order.

87. Brandon Finnegan, LHP, Kansas City Royals

2014 Ranking: N/A

Finnegan was introduced to the world as a reliever, and that's a role many think he's destined for long term. Still, the only player to ever appear in the College and Major League World Series in the same season has the pure arsenal to hang as starter, provided he can maintain the quality of stuff through his second and third spins through the lineup. Despite a stocky 5-foot-11, 185-pound frame, Finnegan creates downhill plane from a high-three-quarters arm slot, and while his delivery features effort he repeats it well. His unproven durability is the only obstacle standing between him and a major-league rotation, but at present that obstacle looms large.

88. Kyle Crick, RHP, San Francisco Giants

2014 Ranking: 38

Crick represents the latest in a long line of high-end pitching prospects to pass through the Giants system. He offers extreme upside but also carries more risk than the typical high-minors arm. Crick's profile is headlined by a near-elite fastball that explodes on hitters and can be difficult to square. Both his breaking ball and changeup flash at an above-average level, but neither consistently shows in that range. Many scouts believe Crick is destined for the bullpen because of his lack of control, though some believe he can survive in a rotation thanks to his electric stuff alone.

89. Clint Frazier, OF, Cleveland Indians
2014 Ranking: 36

Frazier puts on a batting practice display like few others in the lower levels. He has preposterous wrists and power-lifter hand strength, which he uses to lift balls deep into or over the bleachers in left-center field. The hit tool and approach must take steps forward; otherwise, he'll struggle against breaking balls down and away as so many disappointing prospects before him have. Whether he sticks in center is not an existential issue, as the power and secondary skills could carry a corner.

90. Rafael Devers, 3B, Boston Red Sox
2014 Ranking: N/A

One of the prize signings of the 2013 J2 class, Devers commanded a bonus of $1.5 million that already looks like a bargain. The third baseman has quickly made a name for himself at the plate, drawing raves from evaluators for his effortless bat speed and a hit/power package that few in the minors match. With a physically maxed-out body, his defense needs to improve at the hot corner, particularly in his lateral quickness. But if the bat keeps coming it won't matter which position Devers plays; even a player with no defensive utility can provide elite value, as all Bostonians know.

91. Lewis Thorpe, LHP, Minnesota Twins
2014 Ranking: 101

Thorpe rounded out the Top 101 last offseason, with his projectable build, loose delivery, and versatile arsenal providing fertile ground for the development of an impact lefty starter. Through 72 Low-A innings across 16 starts last year, the teenaged Aussie saw an uptick in velocity to the 91-to-94-mph range, as well as further growth across his full complement of secondaries. Having gained firm developmental traction over the past 12 months, the southpaw can now set his sights on a true breakout this summer, likely to be split between Low- and High-A.

92. Jose Peraza, 2B, Atlanta Braves
2014 Ranking: N/A

To get away with having virtually no power, a prospect typically needs to have near-elite speed, as Peraza does. He embraces his small-ball role and makes contact at an incredibly high rate, giving his legs a chance to help get him on base. That speed, coupled with plus defense at second base, gives him a chance to be a valuable everyday player even if he never produces double-digit home-run totals. Peraza handled Double-A last season without missing a beat and should head straight to Triple-A to begin the 2015 season; from there, he could top the Braves' depth chart by this time next year.

93. Orlando Arcia, SS, Milwaukee Brewers
2014 Ranking: N/A

Arcia has established a profile with a firm foundational value thanks to a major-league-quality glove at a high-worth position and advanced feel for the game on the bases. The approach at the plate is improving, and as he continues to add strength it will help his frequent contact become more productive. Ultimately,

though, reining in his approach will most help Arcia push his offensive game from interesting to impactful. In the field, the Venezuelan product continues to refine and should provide a steady presence at shortstop when his time comes.

94. Willy Adames, SS, Tampa Bay Rays
2014 Ranking: N/A

Acquired in the David Price trade, Adames performed well for two teams in his Midwest League debut. He has an easy, balanced swing that allows for at least average projections on both his hit and power tools. At 6-foot-1 and 180 pounds, he is an average runner at present but projects to get bigger down the line, though most believe he'll retain the ability to stick at shortstop. If he is forced to slide off the position eventually, he has the requisite arm strength to profile at third base. It's a solid all-around skill set at a premium position.

95. Hunter Dozier, 3B, Kansas City Royals
2014 Ranking: 96

Grab your best Russian friend and take him to see Dozier, just so you can hear the phrase "strong like bull" as it's meant to be heard. His strength and tremendous hands enable him to barrel the ball with authority, though the swing plays more to doubles at present. While Dozier struggled upon his promotion to Double-A, the former first rounder displays an understanding of how opposing pitchers work him and he should be able to make adjustments with further exposure. In the field he shows good mobility for his size and a strong arm, and shouldn't have any trouble sticking at the hot corner.

96. Maikel Franco, 3B, Philadelphia Philies
2014 Ranking: 52

Franco made his major-league debut last year and figures to get regular playing time at both infield corners in Philly this year. His natural bat-to-ball skills are near elite, but his aggressive approach gets him in trouble and leads to extremely streaky production, especially when he gets long with his swing. When he's on, he can carry an offense. How he responds to a healthy dose of major-league off-speed stuff will determine where on that streaky spectrum he spends the majority of his career. He has plenty of arm to handle third base, and his range should be enough for a few years, though eventually he'll shift across the diamond.

97. Andrew Susac, C, San Francisco Giants
2014 Ranking: N/A

Often overlooked on the prospect scene, Susac nevertheless proved a welcome addition to the 2014 champions, affording the club the freedom to rest all-world backstop Buster Posey without ceding offensive production from the catcher position. While the former OSU Beaver is a capable receiver with enough catch-and-throw to keep baserunners honest, he makes his bones with above-average pop and a methodical approach at the plate, allowing for above-average on-base and power production out of a defensive spot traditionally light in both departments. There's first-division upside here, with a solid floor as an offensive-minded backup and bench bat.

98. Derek Hill, OF, Detroit Tigers
2014 Ranking: N/A

Premium defensive skills, plus-plus speed, and natural hand-eye coordination make for a wonderful starting point. Hill's hit tool is a work in progress, but he often makes sharp contact and is already driving balls to the gaps. Over-the-fence power might never come, but even without that he could produce extreme value with his run-saving in center field and top-of-the-lineup skill set. The Tigers will be aggressive with the high-IQ prospect.

99. Nick Burdi, RHP, Minnesota Twins
2014 Ranking: N/A
With an upper-90s fastball that can pop triple digits on the Stalker, mid- to upper-80s wipeout slider, and promising changeup, this 2014 draftee is already in possession of enough firepower to step into late-inning work and thrive in the majors. He'll need to refine aspects of his game, including improving his fastball command and picking better spots to elevate the heater, and evaluators would like to see him maintain his stuff better on back-to-back nights. Nevertheless, it shouldn't be long before Louisville's all-time saves leader starts making his case to rack up finishes in Minnesota.

100. Ryan McMahon, 3B, Colorado Rockies
2014 Ranking: N/A
McMahon's calling card is his raw power, which he comes by honestly thanks to good bat speed, solid strength, and wrists capable of producing whip in the barrel. The approach is still loose, and he remains particularly susceptible to same-side spin, but when McMahon is locked in and comfortable he comes by hard contact with ease and demonstrates an organic ability to use the whole field. While a thickening body carries with it the risk of limiting his actions at third, his overall athleticism and arm strength should allow him to stick at the five-spot.

101. Chance Sisco, C, Baltimore Orioles
2014 Ranking: N/A
The young catcher led the South Atlantic League in average and OBP in his full-season debut, and the 2013 second rounder now has a .345 batting average in 600 pro at-bats. His swing is relaxed and easy, with minimal movement in the hands and a quick stroke through the zone. The early consensus is that the power will likely come once he adds strength and durability to his frame, though the developmental demands placed on young catchers could challenge his offensive growth. His receiving and blocking skills do not match his athleticism, and he allowed a whopping 95 stolen bases in 74 games last year. ∎

2015 Top 100 Draft Rankings

compiled by Perfect Game USA

Rank	Player	POS	YR	B-T	HT	WT	School	Hometown	ST	Last Drafted	Commitment
1	Brendan Rodgers	SS	SR	R-R	6-2	190	Lake Mary	Longwood	FL		Florida State
2	Brady Aiken	LHP	NA	L-L	6-4	205	No School	Jamul	CA	Astros '14 (1)	
3	Michael Matuella	RHP	JR	R-R	6-6	220	Duke	Great Falls	VA	Never drafted	
4	Kyle Funkhouser	RHP	JR	R-R	6-2	225	Louisville	Oak Forest	IL	Never drafted	
5	Walker Buehler	RHP	JR	R-R	6-1	170	Vanderbilt	Lexington	KY	Pirates '12 (14)	
6	Dansby Swanson	SS	JR	R-R	6-1	190	Vanderbilt	Kennesaw	GA	Rockies '12 (38)	
7	Justin Hooper	LHP/1B	SR	R-L	6-7	230	De la Salle	San Ramon	CA		UCLA
8	Carson Fulmer	RHP	JR	R-R	6-1	190	Vanderbilt	Lakeland	FL	Red Sox '12 (15)	
9	Kolby Allard	LHP	SR	L-L	6-2	175	San Clemente	San Clemente	CA		UCLA
10	Phillip Bickford	RHP	SO	R-R	6-4	200	Southern Nevada	Westlake Village	CA	Blue Jays '13 (1)	
11	Cody Ponce	RHP	JR	R-R	6-5	235	Cal Poly Pomona	Upland	CA	Never drafted	
12	Dazmon Cameron	OF	SR	R-R	6-1	185	Eagles Landing	McDonough	GA		Florida State
13	Chris Betts	C	SR	L-R	6-2	220	Woodrow Wilson	Long Beach	CA		Tennessee
14	Nathan Kirby	LHP/OF	JR	L-L	6-2	185	Virginia	Richmond	VA	Never drafted	
15	Mike Nikorak	RHP	SR	R-R	6-5	205	Stroudsburg	Stroudsburg	PA		Alabama
16	Richie Martin	SS	JR	R-R	6-0	190	Florida	Brandon	FL	Mariners '12 (38)	
17	Alex Bregman	SS	JR	R-R	6-0	190	Louisiana State	Albuquerque	NM	Red Sox '12 (29)	
18	Kyle Cody	RHP	JR	R-R	6-7	245	Kentucky	Chippewa Falls	WI	Phillies '12 (33)	
19	Jacob Lemoine	RHP	JR	R-R	6-5	220	Houston	Orange	TX	Rangers '12 (21)	
20	Ian Happ	OF/2B	JR	B-R	6-0	190	Cincinnati	Pittsburgh	PA	Never drafted	
21	Riley Ferrell	RHP	JR	R-R	6-1	200	Texas Christian	College Station	TX	Never drafted	
22	Ashe Russell	RHP	SR	R-R	6-4	195	Cathedral	Fairland	IN		Texas A&M
23	Beau Burrows	RHP	SR	R-R	6-2	200	Weatherford	Weatherford	TX		Texas A&M
24	Trenton Clark	OF	SR	L-L	6-0	205	Richland	North Richland Hills	TX		Texas Tech
25	Christin Stewart	OF	JR	L-R	6-0	215	Tennessee	Lawrenceville	GA	Never drafted	
26	D.J. Stewart	OF	JR	L-R	6-0	230	Florida State	Yulee	FL	Yankees '12 (28)	
27	James Kaprelian	RHP	JR	R-R	6-4	200	UCLA	Irvine	CA	Mariners '12 (40)	
28	Nick Plummer	OF	SR	L-L	5-11	195	Brother Rice	Lathrup Village	MI		Kentucky
29	Dillon Tate	RHP	JR	R-R	6-2	180	UC Santa Barbara	Claremont	CA	Never drafted	
30	Jon Duplantier	RHP	SO	L-R	6-4	210	Rice	Katy	TX	Never drafted	
31	Alex Young	LHP	JR	L-L	6-3	190	Texas Christian	Hawthorn Woods	IL	Rangers '12 (32)	
32	Triston McKenzie	RHP	SR	R-R	6-5	160	Royal Palm Beach	Royal Palm Beach	FL		Vanderbilt
33	Tyler Jay	LHP	JR	L-L	6-1	175	Illinois	Lemont	IL	Never drafted	
34	Chris Shaw	OF/1B	JR	L-R	6-3	250	Boston College	Lexington	MA	Mets '12 (26)	
35	Juan Hillman	LHP	SR	L-L	6-2	185	Haines City	Haines City	FL		Central Florida
36	Brett Lilek	LHP	JR	L-L	6-4	190	Arizona State	South Holland	IL	Mariners '12 (37)	
37	Demi Orimoloye	OF	SR	R-R	6-2	225	St. Matthews	Orleans	ON		Oregon
38	Tyler Ferguson	RHP	JR	R-R	6-4	225	Vanderbilt	Fresno	CA	Giants '12 (40)	
39	Kep Brown	OF	SR	R-R	6-5	210	Wando	Mt. Pleasant	SC		Miami
40	Gio Brusa	OF	JR	B-R	6-4	205	Pacific	Stockton	CA	Braves '12 (37)	
41	Kyle Tucker	OF	SR	L-R	6-4	185	H.B. Plant	Tampa	FL		Florida
42	Austin Smith	RHP	SR	R-R	6-4	230	Park Vista Community	Boynton Beach	FL		Florida Atlantic
43	Marc Brakeman	RHP	JR	L-R	6-1	180	Stanford	Tierra Verde	FL	Never drafted	
44	Steven Duggar	OF	JR	L-R	6-2	190	Clemson	Moore	SC	Never drafted	
45	Cole McKay	RHP	SR	B-R	6-5	215	Smithson Valley	Spring Branch	TX		Louisiana State
46	Nick Neidert	RHP	SR	R-R	6-1	185	Peachtree Ridge	Lawrenceville	GA		South Carolina
47	Joe McCarthy	OF	JR	L-L	6-3	215	Virginia	Scranton	PA	Never drafted	
48	Cornelius Randolph	SS	SR	L-R	6-1	190	Griffin	Williamson	GA		Clemson
49	Garrett Whitley	OF	SR	R-R	6-2	195	Niskayuna	Niskayuna	NY		Wake Forest
50	Daniel Reyes	OF	SR	R-R	6-2	215	Mater Academy	Miami Springs	FL		Florida

Rank	Player	POS	YR	B-T	HT	WT	School	Hometown	ST	Last Drafted	Commitment
51	Kyle Molnar	RHP	SR	R-R	6-3	205	Aliso Niguel	Aliso Viejo	CA		UCLA
52	Donny Everett	RHP	SR	R-R	6-2	220	Clarksville	Clarksville	TN		Vanderbilt
53	Justin Garza	RHP	JR	R-R	5-11	180	Cal State Fullerton	Ontario	CA	Indians '12 (26)	
54	Chandler Day	RHP/OF	SR	R-R	6-4	160	Watkins Memorial	Granville	OH		Vanderbilt
55	Mikey White	SS	JR	R-R	6-1	200	Alabama	Hoover	AL	Mets '12 (34)	
56	Andrew Suarez	LHP	SR	L-L	6-2	205	Miami	Miami	FL	Nationals '14 (2)	
57	Mac Marshall	LHP	FR	R-L	6-2	180	Chipola (Fla.)	Lilburn	GA	Astros '14 (21)	
58	Luken Baker	RHP	SR	R-R	6-4	235	Oak Ridge	Spring Branch	TX		Texas Christian
59	Travis Lakins	RHP	SO	R-R	6-1	175	Ohio State	Franklin	OH	Never drafted	
60	Cole Irvin	LHP	SO	L-L	6-4	180	Oregon	Anaheimn	CA	Blue Jays '12 (29)	
61	Kyler Murray	SS	SR	R-R	6-1	170	Allen	Lewisville	TX		Texas A&M
62	Blake Trahan	SS	JR	R-R	5-9	180	Louisiana-Lafayette	Kinder	LA	Never drafted	
63	Nick Shumpert	SS	SR	R-R	6-0	175	Highlands Ranch	Lone Tree	CO		Kentucky
64	Tyler Stubblefield	LHP	SO	L-L	6-5	215	Texas A&M	Diboll	TX	Braves '13 (36)	
65	Jalen Miller	SS	SR	R-R	6-0	185	Riverwood International	Atlanta	GA		Clemson
66	Kevin Newman	SS	JR	L-R	6-1	175	Arizona	Poway	CA	Never drafted	
67	Kyle Wilcox	RHP	JR	R-R	6-4	185	Bryant	Newtown	CT	Never drafted	
68	Josh Naylor	1B/OF	SR	L-L	6-1	225	St. Joan of Arc Catholic	Mississauga	ON		Texas Tech
69	Jahmai Jones	OF/SS	SR	R-R	6-0	210	Wesleyan	Roswell	GA		North Carolina
70	Joe DeMers	RHP	SR	R-R	6-2	210	College Park	Martinez	CA		Washington
71	Jonathan Harris	RHP	JR	R-R	6-4	170	Missouri State	Florissant	MO	Blue Jays '12 (33)	
72	Mitchell Hansen	OF	SR	L-L	6-4	195	Plano	Plano	TX		Stanford
73	Ryan Burr	RHP	JR	R-R	6-4	215	Arizona State	Highlands Ranch	CO	Rangers '12 (33)	
74	Josh Staumont	RHP	JR	R-R	6-2	200	Azusa Pacific (Calif.)	La Habra Heights	CA	Never drafted	
75	Cadyn Grenier	SS	SR	R-R	5-11	180	Bishop Gorman	Henderson	NV		Oregon State
76	Cody Poteet	RHP	JR	R-R	6-1	190	UCLA	Bonita	CA	Nationals '12 (27)	
77	Cole Sands	RHP	SR	R-R	6-3	200	North Florida Christian	Tallahassee	FL		Florida State
78	A.J. Minter	LHP/OF	JR	L-L	6-0	210	Texas A&M	Whitehouse	TX	Tigers '12 (38)	
79	Wyatt Cross	C	SR	L-R	6-3	195	Legacy	Broomfield	CO		North Carolina
80	Alonzo Jones	SS	SR	B-R	5-10	190	Columbus	Columbus	GA		Vanderbilt
81	Trent Thornton	RHP	JR	B-R	6-0	185	North Carolina	Charlotte	NC	Never drafted	
82	Ke'Bryan Hayes	3B/OF	SR	R-R	6-2	210	Concordia Lutheran	Tomball	TX		Tennessee
83	Ryan Mountcastle	SS	SR	R-R	6-3	190	Hagerty	Winter Springs	FL		Central Florida
84	Tyler Williams	OF	SR	R-R	6-4	210	Raymond S. Kellis	Peoria	AZ		Arizona State
85	Greg Pickett	OF	SR	L-R	6-4	205	Legend	Aurora	CO		Mississippi State
86	Eric Jenkins	OF	SR	L-R	6-1	170	West Columbus	Chadbourn	NC		UNC Wilmington
87	John Aiello	SS/RHP	SR	B-R	6-2	200	Germantown Academy	Lansdale	PA		Wake Forest
88	Skye Bolt	OF	JR	B-R	6-3	175	North Carolina	Woodstock	GA	Nationals '12 (26)	
89	Tyler Krieger	SS	JR	B-R	6-2	180	Clemson	Johns Creek	GA	Mariners '12 (35)	
90	Antonio Santillan	RHP	SR	R-R	6-3	195	Seguin	Arlington	TX		Texas Tech
91	Matt McGarry	RHP	SR	R-R	6-3	185	Menlo-Atherton	Portola Valley	CA		Vanderbilt
92	Ryan McKenna	OF	SR	R-R	5-10	180	St. Thomas Aquinas	Dover	NH		Liberty
93	Doak Dozier	OF	SR	L-R	6-3	175	Arlington Heights	Fort Worth	TX		Virginia
94	Josh Sborz	RHP	JR	R-R	6-2	225	Virginia	McLean	VA	Never drafted	
95	Travis Blankenhorn	SS	SR	L-R	6-2	190	Pottsville Area	Pottsville	PA		Kentucky
96	Patrick Sandoval	LHP	SR	L-L	6-3	190	Mission Viejo	Mission Viejo	CA		Vanderbilt
97	Blake Hickman	RHP/C	JR	R-R	6-5	210	Iowa	Chicago	IL	Cubs '12 (20)	
98	Garrett Wolforth	C	SR	B-R	6-2	190	Concordia Lutheran	Spring	TX		Dallas Baptist
99	Travis Bergen	LHP	JR	L-L	6-0	195	Kennesaw State	McDonough	GA	Never drafted	
100	Riley Smith	RHP	SO	R-R	6-1	180	San Jacinto (Texas)	Lufkin	TX	Never drafted	Louisiana State

Perfect Game Presents:

Before They Were Pros

by David Rawnsley, Todd Gold, Patrick Ebert, and Frankie Piliere

As part of Perfect Game's partnership with Baseball Prospectus, David Rawnsley, Todd Gold, Patrick Ebert, and Frankie Piliere have conducted a "Before They Were Pros" series, providing scouting reports on some of the top prospects in baseball from when they were in high school attending PG events.

NL East

Philadelphia Phillies

J.P. Crawford – SS

Crawford made a name for himself at an early age and was considered one of the top class of 2013 prospects throughout the entirety of his prep career. He represented the alluring potential five-tool superstar scouts dream about signing and are inherently skeptical of. Throughout the draft process the conversation about Crawford centered around, "Sure, he could be a star, but is he really going to hit/stick at short/develop power?"

Crawford's profile had a narrow margin for error. If he didn't stick at shortstop, a lot would be riding on the offensive development. If the swing-and-miss issues never improved, his value would be tied strictly to his defense, and there were better present defensive shortstops available in the 2013 draft. Following the 2012 WWBA World Championship, amateur baseball's most intensely competitive draft evaluation environment, Crawford's profile was explained in the 2012 Jupiter Impact Players article:

> In some years, Crawford would be the top defensive shortstop in the class. As it stands, he has an edge on Oscar Mercado in arm strength and is similarly athletic. But beyond his defense, Crawford boasts an especially impressive upside with the bat. His smooth left-handed swing features plus bat speed and good contact ability. He flashes present power, and should develop average or above power as he gets stronger and continues to develop as a hitter. That power potential is rare to find in a prospect with a legitimate chance to stay at a defensive home up the middle. His overall upside is higher than that of Mercado, though he will need to work very hard and reach his lofty ceiling in order to become a more valuable asset. Crawford's floor appears to be that of an everyday corner outfielder with above-average tools across the board, but he has a shot at developing into the rarest and most valuable variety of prospect: a legitimate five-tool shortstop. If he can convince clubs with his performance this spring that there is a legitimate possibility of him achieving that upside, Crawford should come off the board early.

In hindsight, with enough effort a pessimistic scout can find a way to talk themselves out of any player. And when compared to the other top prospects in the 2013 draft, it becomes more understandable how such a high-ceiling prospect managed to fall to the Phillies and the 17th pick. SoCal had a very strong 2013 high school crop, headlined from the get-go by sweet-swinging first baseman Dominic Smith, who was Crawford's summer teammate for several years. While Smith didn't offer the same kind of upside as Crawford, he owned the best pure hit tool in the high school class and enough certainty to make scouts confident in his profile. Right-hander Phil Bickford shot up draft boards as the spring of 2013 went on, thanks to his rapid improvement that rounded out a profile that included a mid-90s fastball. Third baseman Ryan McMahon also drew some first-round interest before slipping to the sandwich round. At the time, Crawford was seen as having the most potential of that heady group, but also as the riskiest proposition.

With that risk, which chased off several organizations, comes tremendous reward potential. And after his first full season of pro ball, Crawford has begun to answer the questions about him that nagged scouts coming into the draft. He now appears to be on his way to realizing that potential, and the Phillies may be in line for a handsome reward. —*Todd Gold*

Ben Lively – RHP

At 6-foot-4, 180 pounds, Lively offered a lean, projectable frame with obvious growth potential. He frequently peaked in the low-90s, as he did at the 2009 WWBA World Championship, and was ranked the 235th high school prospect in the class of 2010 prior to being drafted in the 26th round by the Indians that year. That wasn't early enough to sign him away from UCF, although he didn't truly break out until the summer of 2012 during his time spent on the Cape.

However, during that time, he was often overshadowed by being part of what has to be looked back as one of the great pitching staffs in the history of the Cape Cod League. The Yarmouth-Dennis Red Sox staff staff included Andrew Thurman, Chris Anderson, Alex Gonzalez, and Aaron Blair—each of those pitchers was taken in the first 40 picks in the 2013 draft.

The impressive aspect of Lively's Cape emergence was how well he carried his stuff deep into the summer. In fact, his stuff ticked up somewhat by summer's end. He mostly worked at 91-93 mph with his sinking fastball and he relied very heavily on this pitch. His 76-78 mph curveball flashed solid action, but was fringy over stretches of the summer. His 81-84 mph changeup was a reliable offering, but if he got into trouble, it would still be his fastball that not only induced weak contact, but allowed him to miss bats as well. That ability to stay off the barrel on the strength of his fastball was what opened the eyes of many scouts during that summer.

The numbers spiked for Lively in his final spring at UCF, as the 6-foot-4 righty finished his collegiate career with a flourish. He posted a 2.04 ERA, allowed just 88 hits in 106 innings, and struck out 101 batters along the way. The velocity was closer to 89-92 mph at times during the spring, but he did top as high as 94 and consistently showed that heavy fastball life that put him on the map the summer prior. That led to the Reds taking him in the fourth round of the 2013 draft. —*Frankie Piliere*

Miami Marlins

Trevor Williams – RHP

Williams pitched for the late Mike Spiers and the ABD Bulldog teams in 2008-09 that rank among the best travel teams ever assembled. A typical lineup on a day that Williams started might have included Christian Yelich at first base, Jio Mier at shortstop, either Travis Harrison or Nolan Arenado at third base, and Henry Owens on the bench waiting for his turn on the mound. During the spring, he pitched for the legendary Rancho Bernardo High School program in northern San Diego. To say that Williams was surrounded by a winning environment in his developmental years as a player would be an understatement.

Williams was a command and control guy at that time who really wasn't a professional prospect. He pitched pretty consistently in the 86-88 mph range, topping out at 89, from his sophomore to his senior year in high school, with a long and loose arm action that was fairly projectable. He threw a big breaking, low-70s curveball for strikes and his changeup was advanced for a pitcher that age. Williams started and won many big games for ABD during that time, and it was a given that he'd be a solid Division I pitcher at Arizona State. He wasn't drafted out of high school.

Here's his report from the 2009 National Showcase:

> Nice athletic pitcher's build, long limbs, mature look. Side-step delivery, long, swinging arm action with high elbow. FB to 87 mph in Metrodome, cuts FB occ, slow, big CB with sweeping break, throws CB to spots, tries to work changeup down, mixes it up and tries to spot ball. Command type, follow for velo gain.

It wasn't until he got to Arizona State that Williams' velocity jumped up into the low- to mid-90s and he developed the heavy sinking action on his fastball that defines his pitching style. He went 12-2 with a 2.05 ERA as a sophomore to really put himself on the prospect map, although scouts were concerned about his lack of a swing-and-miss pitch. He did struggle a bit as a junior, going 5-6, 3.92, but was nonetheless picked in the second round (44th overall pick) by the Marlins.—*David Rawnsley*

Avery Romero – 2B

Romero played in his first national tournament days after finishing middle school and by the end of his prep career he had more than 20 under his belt. In the early days, Avery was seen as Jordan Romero's little brother, and the two would team up to form a double-play partnership on numerous travel ball teams. But that dynamic swapped fairly quickly. Jordan, who was a solid college player, quickly became the other Romero, despite being a decent player in his own right.

Avery's game developed early and was always centered around strength and effort. While that profile doesn't project

particularly well, there was enough present ability during his draft year that Romero's name was floated as a potential first-round surprise. In his 2012 MLB Draft Profile David Rawnsley explained:

> He's getting strong talk as a potential first-round pick, as in veteran scouts saying things like, "Don't be surprised at all when Avery Romero goes higher than lots of those other Florida high school guys you talk about so much." … He's a yard rat with floppy hair, a dirty uniform, and a smile on his face that hides his intense competitiveness boiling underneath. Romero is also much closer to 5-foot-10 than his listed 6-foot-0, 200-pound size, at least per the official measurements given at events such as the East Coast Pro and Area Code Games last summer. Not that scouts didn't know that already. Plus, Romero ran the 60 at two events during 2011 and recorded times of 7.43 and 7.51. Scouts knew that already as well.

Scouts liked Romero the player more than they liked Romero's raw tools. But there was one potential avenue to squeeze the requisite amount of value out of Romero's physical ability to justify a top two round selection: moving him behind the plate. His athleticism (or lack thereof) and arm strength were a natural fit, and his advanced hit tool would have been a huge asset for the position. Of course, it's a massive transition project to move a player behind the plate for the first time in pro ball, and one that would have likely impeded his ability to develop as a hitter. The latter was seen by most as too much of a risk given that his profile was carried by the hit tool. Diminishing the one carrying tool that fit well in an offensive-minded, second-base profile ultimately didn't make enough sense for the Marlins to follow through with on Romero, who they landed in the third round for a well-above-slot signing bonus.

One can look back on Romero's early pro career and wonder what might have been had he moved behind the plate and developed well there while still hitting as much as he has to this point. That would have added tremendous value to his prospect profile. But then, it's also hard to argue with the production he's given the Marlins thus far. —*Todd Gold*

Justin Nicolino – LHP

The first time left-handed pitcher Justin Nicolino took the mound at a Perfect Game event was at the 2008 18u WWBA National Championship. At the time he was throwing in the high-70s to low-80s, but did exhibit advanced pitchability by changing speeds well and throwing four pitches for strikes.

His stuff took a significant step up the following summer, pitching in the 85-89 range while peaking at 90 mph at the 17u WWBA National Championship, showing a well-rounded four-pitch mix that included a curveball, slider, and changeup. His changeup in particular stood out, as he threw a perfect "slowball" with the exact same arm speed and action as his fastball.

Here is a summation of his performance from the PG scouting database:

> Lanky, skinny, long limbs. Good mechanics. Easy delivery, arm really works, works downhill, online low effort 3/4 tall and fall delivery. Consistent arm speed with change, plus run on FB, above average high school 2-8 curveball. CH w/ fade from RHH. Good location on all pitches, fields position well. Decent pick-off, high ceiling.

As a 6-foot-2, 155-pound athlete, Nicolino had obvious room

for improvement as he continued to add strength to his lean and lanky frame. He also excelled at the plate at the high school level, playing at University High School in Orlando, Florida, and was committed to playing for the Virginia Cavaliers.

Nicolino's rapid improvement with plenty of room for added development at the next stage of his career was reflected in his being ranked the 122nd prospect in the high school class of 2010 prior to being selected in the second round of that year's draft by the Toronto Blue Jays. Those improvements continued in the lower levels of the minor leagues, and he was a key prospect included in the blockbuster trade between the Blue Jays and Marlins that sent Mark Buehrle, Josh Johnson, and Jose Reyes to Toronto. —*Patrick Ebert*

Atlanta Braves

Alec Grosser – RHP

Grosser didn't have extensive experience on the showcase and travel circuit prior to the summer before his senior year in high school, but he quickly made a strong impression, showing a tall and athletic build with plenty of signs that he was just starting to scratch the surface of his lofty potential. His relative inexperience made him somewhat of an unknown commodity, although he did a lot to change that with his breakout performance in Jupiter at the 2012 WWBA World Championship, where he worked at 89-92 mph. Grosser's athleticism also served him well on the left side of the infield and in the batter's box on days he didn't take the mound.

Here's a collection of scouting notes on Grosser from the summer and fall of 2012 from PG's internal database:

> Great athlete. Large XL frame. Lean, wiry, projectable. Room to fill. Arm works well, loose, long arm action. Outstanding arm speed. Armside run on FB w/ sink. Fields position well.

Grosser continued to improve between his standout performance in Jupiter at the WWBA World Championship in October of 2012 and the 2013 MLB draft. Prior to his senior year in high school he was named to the Rawlings/Perfect Game All-Region team in the Atlantic Region, and, as predicted, his velocity continued to climb. After sitting in the high-80s and peaking in the low-90s, Grosser frequently sat in the low-90s, peaking as high as 94 mph during the spring of his senior year at T.C. Williams High School in Alexandria, Virginia.

That rapid improvement pointed to a player whose stock was on the rise, even more so than his no. 191 PG prospect ranking in the high school class of 2013 would indicate. Here's the report on Grosser prior to the 2013 draft in which he was ranked the 140th player overall:

> Grosser's name has begun to come up more frequently this spring, as he's impressed scouts with improved velocity and consistency. His fastball has been up a tick this spring to 89-93 mph and he has reached as high as 94. His projectable 6-foot-4, 190-pound frame is also enticing to scouts, as he shows solid athleticism as well. He works out of a high three-quarters arm slot with outstanding arm speed and shows some consistency with his delivery. The secondary stuff is still going to need to come along, as the breaking ball is still somewhat slurvy at this point at 75-77 mph. He's had a strong spring and has seen the presence of scouts steadily grow at his outings. There's some disagreement among scouts as to where Grosser belongs in the

draft, but there are many that believe he's a candidate as high as the third round.

While he wasn't drafted as high as the third round, the Braves astutely plucked him up in the 11th round and were able to sign him away from his commitment to George Mason.
—*Patrick Ebert*

New York Mets

Steven Matz – LHP

A native of Long Island, Matz was pretty much a prototypical Northeast pitching prospect growing up, making his big push to top-prospect status during the spring of his senior year. He was a slender and projectable southpaw who made plenty of stops on the summer circuit in 2008, including the PG National, the 17u WWBA National Championship playing for Baseball U, and the East Coast Pro Showcase. He regularly pitched in the high-80s with good feel for his fastball location, a soft curveball that needed more power, and a workable changeup. The top velocity that PG ever saw from him was 91 mph that summer.

Here's his report from the PG National:

> Matz has a very loose arm and shows the potential to be a big-time power lefty. He used a high 3/4 arm angle with a fast, easy arm to produce a fastball that topped at 91 at the Metrodome. He showed good command of his fastball and also of a solid curveball and changeup. Hitters struggled picking the ball up out of his hand, as he hides the ball well in his delivery. Don't be surprised if Matz shoots up the charts because we think he has even more velocity in that left arm.

During his senior season, however, Matz ramped it up, sitting in the low-90s and topping out at 94 mph according to many reports. The Mets did not own a first-round pick in 2009, having sent it to the Angels as part of the price for signing closer Francisco Rodriguez on the free-agent market, but selected Matz in the second round with the 72nd overall pick and gave him a well-above-slot bonus of $895,000 to sign him away from a Coastal Carolina scholarship. The pick had some hometown flavor, as Matz grew up approximately 50 miles away from Citi Field/Shea Stadium, but was not warmly embraced by the New York media.

Matz signed too late to throw in rookie ball in 2009 and the rest of his story is well known. An almost complete tear in his elbow necessitated Tommy John surgery, which kept Matz out all of the 2010 and 2011 seasons, meaning he didn't make his professional debut until June 2012, nearly three years after he inked his original contract. —*David Rawnsley*

Dominic Smith – 1B

A favorite among most scouts who followed him closely, Smith was a bit of an acquired taste. The initial viewings of Smith generally leave scouts with some questions about his desire and work ethic, an odd contradiction with his actual personality, but a consistent phenomenon. It stems from the fact that Smith comes at the game, and life, with the type of laid-back approach that matches the stereotype of his demographic as a left-handed native of Southern California. His low-heart-rate game is also influenced by how naturally easy the game is for him, as there is no hint of panic to anything he does on the field, regardless of situation.

It takes an extended look to be able to discern the fact it's not about a disinterest in being on the field, but rather that the game unfolds more slowly to Smith than most. But the more feel scouts develop for Smith as a player and person, the more clear it becomes that he is an extremely hard worker. The strides he made during the course of his amateur career were remarkable. He debuted as a young outfielder with an extremely long and violent swing, complete with a "grip it and rip it" plate approach. A lot of scouts who were charged with making draft decisions on Smith never saw that underclass version. The Smith they saw was the matured, calm, and under control hitter who showed not only a willingness but almost a preference to drive the ball to the opposite field. As a result, there was concern over his ultimate ceiling as a first baseman who didn't show a lot of game power.

The fact that Smith came off the board at 11th overall despite being a 6-foot high school first baseman who had questions about his power speaks volumes about how highly regarded his other tools were. He was widely considered as having the best hit tool in the high school class and is frequently discussed by veteran scouts as being one of the best defensive high school first basemen they've ever evaluated. He was limited to first base because he throws with his left hand, not because of a lack of aptitude for other positions. He was a low-90s, left-handed pitcher and also played a significant amount of right field for his high school team. He even made an occasional cameo appearance behind the plate as a left-handed catcher. At the 2012 WWBA World Championship he caught two innings at the end of a consolation game and popped a 1.84 to second base and a 1.55 to third (with a coach standing in the right-handed batter's box).

Moreover, Smith wasn't just an elite player on the field, he was also his team's leader off of it. He took younger players under his wing and imparted lessons that he had just recently learned himself. He was an unofficial recruiting coordinator for his travel ball team and was well respected by both his teammates and players from other teams on the national showcase circuit. He could frequently be found holding court at the park with other top prospects from around the country before and after his games. The expectation on Smith wasn't just that he'd play in the Major Leagues someday, but rather that when he did play in the Major Leagues, he'd be a clubhouse leader. —*Todd Gold*

Washington Nationals

Michael Taylor – CF

Although Michael Taylor was ranked 370th in PG's class of 2009 high school player rankings, his athletic talents were evident. The Washington Nationals recognized those talents in taking him in the sixth round of that year's draft, as he has enjoyed a steady development on his way to the big leagues, making his debut in mid-August 2014.

Currently a center fielder, Taylor played shortstop and also pitched at Westminster Academy in Fort Lauderdale, Florida. He enjoyed a big growth spurt between his junior and senior years, going from 5-foot-10, 160 pounds to 6-foot-3, 185 pounds, with long, wiry, strong limbs, quickly passing the eye test for onlooking scouts.

On the mound his velocity saw a similar spike during that time, going from 77-80 mph at the 2007 WWBA Underclass World Championship to 87-90 with a sharp mid-70s curveball at the 2008 WWBA World Championship. However, his graceful infield actions and promising bat at the plate pointed to a future as a position prospect.

Here are some collective notes from his time spent at Perfect Game tournaments:

> Tall, very athletic body. Upton body. Good actions at SS, winds up to throw. Slick fielder, all over the field, plus arm. Quick through zone, good bat speed, good speed. Line drive swing, quick hands, can swing it. Long, loose arm action. Good arm speed, live arm. Good downhill plane, hard, sharp 11-to-5 curveball for strikes.

While he spent his first full season as a professional as an infielder, seeing time at all four infield positions in 2010, he was converted to an outfielder full time for the beginning of the 2011 season. —*Patrick Ebert*

Jake Johansen – RHP

Johansen has always been a "just wait, be patient, this guy has a chance to be really, really good if it all comes together" type of prospect.

Johansen first appeared at a PG event in 2007 following his sophomore season at Allen High School in North Texas. He was 6-foot-5, 215 pounds and was as much a power-hitting first baseman at that point as he was a pitcher. He took a turn on the mound, however, and was 80-83 while topping out at 85 mph from a high-energy delivery, while flashing a decent 74 mph slider.

At his next sighting at Jupiter in 2008, Johansen had grown to 6-foot-6, 240 pounds, was now in the high-80s, and showed a calmer delivery and good command of his fastball. His slider had developed real power, up to 81 mph, and had plus potential. The Mets made him a summer follow in the 45th round, but Johansen ended up at Dallas Baptist.

Johansen's first two years at Dallas Baptist showed how far away he was from competing at the college level. He redshirted during his first year, then threw only 13 innings in his first season seeing action, posting a 12.15 ERA while allowing 16 hits and 16 walks. His 2011-12 season showed progress, as Johansen appeared in 20 games, including four starts, posting a 5.48 ERA in 46 innings. He was still allowing lots of hits (47) and walks (32), but was competitive on a 41-19 NCAA regional team. The Pirates noticed and speculated a 27th-round pick on Johansen, but he decided to return for a fourth year at Dallas Baptist.

Johansen really came on during the 2012-13 season, mostly because he virtually eliminated his walks. He started 15 games for DBU, going 7-6 with a 5.40 ERA in 88 innings, walking only 26 hitters against 75 strikeouts, but allowing 109 hits. His overall stuff was top drawer, with a fastball that sat in the mid-90s and topped out at 98 mph, although the pitch was very straight and tended not to roam much from the middle of the plate. His mid-80s slider also flashed plus at times. It was a power-arm profile with two present pitches that could already be graded out on the plus side, although the changeup and command were still short. But it was impossible to mistake Johansen's progress.

The Nationals picked Johansen in the 2013 draft right about where the industry consensus had him pegged, in the second round with the 68th overall selection. —*David Rawnsley*

NL Central

Chicago Cubs

Kris Bryant – 3B

Baseball's top power hitting prospect, along with fellow Las Vegas native and former PG All-American, Joey Gallo, Bryant was a much scouted and debated player in high school without there being a consensus about any of his future tools or even his future role.

One thing that Bryant could do back at Bonanza High School was, not surprisingly, hit for power. He started his swing from a fairly high hand position for a long, power-oriented swing and generated tremendous backspin on the ball from his swing plane. My notes from the 2009 Perfect Game National Showcase evoked a comparison to Dave Kingman—who arguably hit the highest pop-up/fly balls in the game's history—for how high Bryant's balls went in the air and how long they stayed up there. There are no 7.0-plus second hang times recorded in the PG database, but they surely existed and were probably frequently repeated. It was a fairly calm and low-effort swing for such huge power and stood out more for its leverage than for the raw bat speed.

The rest of Bryant's tools, and his future position, along with his ability to make enough square contact to use his prodigious power, were the subject of debate. He had balanced actions at third base and even played some shortstop at times, but was a 7.0 runner in the 60-yard dash and had only average arm strength across the diamond. There was plenty of talk about first base and left field.

High school pitching wasn't much of a challenge for Bryant and he hit .489-22-51 as a high school senior, although scouts were still only lukewarm in their evaluations, similar to what Gallo was to go through two years later with similar performance numbers. Bryant was considered a very difficult sign with a strong desire to go to college at San Diego, and it was a surprise to no one when he was only picked in the 18th round by the Blue Jays as a speculation pick.

While Bryant's first two collegiate seasons were very strong (.365-9-36 as a freshman, .366-14-57 as a sophomore), they merely set the stage for his junior year. At a time in college baseball when players just weren't hitting home runs and entire teams barely broke double figures in long balls, Bryant hit 31 home runs all by himself despite getting walked 66 times in 57 games. In addition, Bryant had matured athletically as a defensive player at third base, and much of the doubt about his future at third base had been quieted.

Bryant, along with college right-handers Mark Appel and Jonathan Gray, were generally considered the top three prospects in the 2013 draft. When the Astros went with Appel with the first pick, the Cubs chose Bryant and signed him to a $6.7 million signing bonus. —*David Rawnsley*

Billy McKinney – OF

The most important tool for a position player is the hit tool. It is also the most difficult to accurately grade and just so happened to be Billy McKinney's carrying tool.

The Plano (Texas) High School product and 2012 PG All-American topped out at average or slightly below in every other tool category. That typically precludes a high school prospect from first-round draft consideration. In the case of McKinney, however, it led to a wide range of opinions among scouts. He was seen as a major wild card, with some scouts extolling his bat-to-ball virtues, and others suggesting he was a streaky hitter with a moderate power ceiling.

David Rawnsley broke down McKinney's offensive profile in his Pre-Draft Focus profile:

> He has very sound hitting mechanics, with a left-handed swing that is very quick and compact to the ball with outstanding raw bat speed. He is especially aggressive on

the inside half of the plate and can pull the highest velocity fastballs with authority. McKinney also has some lift in his swing plane and the ability to put backspin on balls and hit them deep to the gaps. The teams that are most interested in McKinney are going to likely grade him out at least as a 60 (MLB plus) in both the hitting and power categories.

While there was some question as to whether McKinney would be picked in the first round, there was rampant speculation as to which team would be the one to pull the trigger if given the opportunity. Organizations show tendencies as to which types of profiles they prefer and which tools they place highest priority upon. There were a small handful of organizations that seemed to fit the bill as potential suitors for McKinney who held picks in the late first round. The A's likely realized this and knew that he wouldn't be on the board when their second pick came around, even though he didn't look like a traditional first-round high school prospect.

Given his advanced hit tool it shouldn't come as a huge surprise in hindsight that McKinney was able to skip Low-A entirely and not miss a beat. The question about his ceiling remains as a corner outfielder with average present power production. But in terms of contributing on both sides of the ball, McKinney has hit the ground running as a professional and is justifying his draft position. —*Todd Gold*

Milwaukee Brewers

Devin Williams – RHP

Live-armed right-hander Devin Williams provided an interesting case study of a pitcher who, step by step, gradually improved as the 2013 MLB draft approached, something David Rawnsley explained in great detail in Williams' Draft Focus feature from April 2013.

Playing for the St. Louis Pirates travel ball organization, Williams performed at a high level at numerous high-profile tournament events across the country, beginning the summer after his sophomore year in high school. He first took the mound as a 6-foot-3, 165-pound right-hander at the 17u WWBA National Championship, where he peaked at 87 mph and threw four different pitches for strikes.

His stuff, and overall status, took a significant step up the following February at the 2012 Pitcher/Catcher Indoor Showcase, which he entered as the 306th high school prospect in the 2013 class, a ranking that shot up after he threw his fastball in the 88-90 mph range while peaking at 91.

That showing led to an invite to the 2012 National Showcase, where he flashed similar stuff but didn't take another step forward as hoped. That happened four months later in Jupiter, Florida at the WWBA World Championship where Williams' fastball was much firmer, up to 93 mph, with improved bite on his slider, now his go-to breaking pitch, and more polish to his changeup.

Williams once again took the mound at the Pitcher/Catcher Indoor Showcase in 2013, and amidst a group of several high-profile arms that included fellow St. Louis Pirates hurler Jake Brentz and PG All-American Clinton Hollon, Williams may have had the best performance. Throwing loose and easy, with an athletic, repeatable delivery, his fastball now peaked at 94, and his changeup, thrown with the exact same arm speed and overall action as his fastball, continued to be a very good secondary pitch for him.

Later that spring Williams, who grew to 6-foot-4, 190 pounds, appeared to have finally tabled his curveball for his slider, a pitch he seemed hesitant to throw, but when he did, showed very good potential. He could throw his slider, a hard-biting breaking pitch, as hard as 85 mph and also learned to take a little off of his fastball, now up to 95, for two-seam life in the upper-80s to low-90s, to go along with his usual low-80s change.

All of this led to Williams being ranked PG's 14th best high school prospect and 29th overall draft prospect prior to the 2013 draft, which put his name in the conversation for the first round. Although there were some indications that he could go as high as the middle of the first round, he slipped to the middle of the second, where the Brewers, who had lost their first-round pick after signing Kyle Lohse as a free agent the previous offseason, were thrilled to pick him up. –Patrick Ebert

Jorge Lopez – RHP

A lean, projectable, and well-coordinated 6-foot-4, 175-pound athlete in high school in Puerto Rico, Lopez was a gifted all-around athlete that excelled in numerous sports, including basketball, track and field, and volleyball. His volleyball talents in particular could have led to a promising collegiate career, but it was his progression as a pitcher as a converted shortstop that pointed to the best route for a professional career.

Lopez attended numerous PG tournament events stateside to make him a well enough known commodity, seeing a steady progression to his fastball velocity from the mid-80s in 2009 to his peak velocity of 91 at the WWBA World Championship in Jupiter, Florida in late October 2010. However, it was his appearance at the 2011 World Showcase in early January that may have ultimately led to him becoming such an early-round draft pick (second round) later that year.

Here is his report from that event:

> Slender, young build, should gain strength but not much weight. Slow-paced, low-effort delivery, high 3/4 release point, pulls off some on release, very long and loose arm, good use of his lower half. Fastball to 91 mph, velo comes easy. Flashes hard curveball spin when on top of the ball, changeup shows nice sink and should be thrown more. Very nice young pitching prospect who should keep improving.

That performance also led to Lopez being ranked the 83rd prospect in the high school class of 2011. With an upper-80s to low-90s fastball, a promising overall three-pitch mix, and a lean, projectable frame Lopez gave Puerto Rico, usually known more for producing toolsy middle infielders and strong-armed catchers, a rare top-flight pitching prospect who appeared to be just scratching the surface of his potential. Because of that, Lopez garnered predraft comparisons to 14-year MLB veteran Javier Vazquez, who coincidentally played his last year in the big leagues the same year Lopez was drafted. —Patrick Ebert

Tyler Wagner – RHP

Although Wagner had no shortage of opportunities to be seen playing for national powerhouse Bishop Gorman High School outside of Las Vegas, it wasn't until he made a permanent transition to the mound that he started to get noticed by scouts and recruiters. He also made the most of his appearance at the 2008 West Uncommitted Showcase, where he threw in the 86-89 range with a mid-70s curveball, which helped lead to his commitment to play for Utah. Here's the PG scouting report from that event:

> Tall athletic build, body projects well on the mound, long arm action, quick and easy, balls come out of his hand well, good feel for curveball, 11-to-5 curveball with tight break, stays tall, new to pitching, very good projection, strong student, plays for a very strong high school team.

As expected, his velocity continued to improve while pitching for the Utes, where he was used exclusively in short relief. He made only 10 appearances as a freshman, recording three saves and a 2.11 ERA prior to his breakout sophomore season, in which he saved 12 games with a 2.04 ERA in 35 1/3 innings of work.

By his junior year Wagner was peaking in the mid-90s with a relatively fresh and still-improving arm, although he didn't perform as well as he did during his sophomore year. Leading up to the 2012 draft he was ranked the 121st overall draft prospect, with many wondering how well he would fare in a starting role at the next level, and garnered this report:

> The rangy 6-foot-3, 195-pound Wagner has an explosive arm with a fastball that frequently touches 95 mph and gets on hitters quickly from a three-quarters slot. He also has a second plus pitch in a power slider, giving him two weapons needed to excel as a closer. Wagner had only two saves in 17 appearances in early May, though, as his opportunity to close out games was limited. At the same time, Wagner struggles to throw strikes consistently, which led to a 2-5, 3.98 record, while walking 21 and striking out 29 in 32 innings. Had he pitched more like he did in 2011, Wagner might have been a fit as early as the third round, though he is still expected to be the state's top pick.

Wagner was drafted almost exactly where he was ranked, going in the fourth round–155th overall–to the Brewers in the 2012 MLB draft. —Patrick Ebert

Pittsburgh Pirates

Reese McGuire – C

McGuire first appeared at a Perfect Game event in August 2011 after his sophomore year, traveling down to San Diego from his Washington home to play in the PG National Games following the Perfect Game All-American Classic. It was love at first site for this scout, as McGuire almost immediately pegged himself as a potential first-round candidate for 2013. Here are my notes from those first two days at the USD field:

> Low and flexible setup, + hands, + arm, easy actions, stud, hosed guy from knees on perfect release/throw, one of the best game blockers I've seen in ages, plays C like a shortstop. Solid build, square strong shoulders, thin waist, loose quick swing, lifts and shows power, good bat speed, aggressive swing, solid pull contact, HRs, tries to hit it hard, 4.38 Like!

That may be the only time that I've ever written "plays catcher like a shortstop" in my notes and it was a reoccurring theme with McGuire over the next two years. There was one sequence at the 2012 Tournament of Stars when McGuire was catching left-hander Stephen Gonsalves—a fourth-round pick of the Twins—in a late-inning, bases-loaded jam. The six-pitch sequence to the hitter was perfectly symmetrical: First pitch 59-foot curveball that McGuire blocks, second pitch 91-mph fastball for a strike, third pitch 59-foot curveball blocked again, fourth pitch 91-mph fastball for a strike, fifth pitch, etc. McGuire's ability to completely deaden pitches in the dirt, especially breaking balls, completely separated him from his peers behind the plate. He had an extremely rare combination of anticipation, catlike quickness, and polished, high-level technique to his blocking.

Of course, it didn't hurt his overall defensive profile that McGuire also had a plus arm and was regularly in the 1.90s during games on his pop times and in the low-1.80s during drills.

McGuire went on to star for the gold-medal-winning USA 18u National team, leading them in batting average (.400), runs scored (11), and walks (nine versus only three strikeouts) in 13 games while splitting the catching duties with fellow Perfect Game All-American Chris Okey.

That combination of defensive and offensive ability enabled McGuire to go 14th overall in the 2013 draft, the second highest a high school catcher has been selected, behind Kyle Skipworth (sixth overall pick, 2008/Marlins), in the last 10 years. The Pirates signed him out of a University San Diego commitment almost immediately after the draft, giving him a $2,369,000 bonus. —*David Rawnsley*

Austin Meadows – OF

2012 PG All-American outfielder Austin Meadows fit comfortably into two appealing draft demographics coming out of high school: the "performer" and the "jeans salesman."

The former is self-explanatory, as Meadows performed at a high level throughout his prep career. He burst onto the national scene by hitting .571 for Team USA's 16U National team in 2011. He put up big numbers in high school ball and made a lot of contact against quality pitching on the national showcase circuit. While scouts give very little weight to high school stats, performance track record is often a tiebreaker between two similarly talented prospects.

The latter is a term borrowed from Michael Lewis' bestseller *Moneyball*. Within the book, Oakland A's GM Billy Beane is quoted as telling his scouts in the draft room that "we're not selling jeans here," in regards to the importance placed on player body types. As a high school prospect, Meadows had the "prospect body," with a long, high-waisted 6-foot-3 frame and strong, lean 200-pound build with room to carry additional muscle mass.

The equation created by being a strong present contact hitter who would likely offer at least solid contributions in the average department, combined with his above-average speed and strength projection, hinted at the potential to be an impact player. His arm strength was the only tool that scouts were confident didn't have plus potential, giving them the opportunity to dream on a four-plus-tool player. The fact that he didn't show present power and had a swing that would require adjustments to tap into his raw power potential created some risk, but his solid floor was seen as relatively stable. Prospects who offer relative certainty tend to go high in the draft, but those whose security come with upside are the type that come off the board in the top half of the first round.

There was also some question as to his future defensive home. The straight-line speed he showed in the 60-yard dash suggested he had the potential to be an above-average defender in center field, though he didn't take that same speed into the outfield at the time, leading many to project him to wind up in left field long term. Had his speed translated from the 60-yard dash and his raw power converted from batting practice, Meadows might have been one of the first players selected in the 2013 draft. He didn't last very long regardless, going ninth overall. —*Todd Gold*

Cincinnati Reds

Michael Lorenzen – RHP

Big tools have always defined Lorenzen's game, which featured one of the best—if not the best—combinations of speed and arm strength of those eligible for the 2010 draft. His speed is shown by the 6.54 60-yard dash time he recorded at the 2009 West Coast Top Prospect Showcase, and his arm strength by the 99-mph throw he made from the outfield at the 2009 National Showcase, one of the best such throws at any Perfect Game event.

Here is the report he received from the National:

> Lean athletic build with sloped shoulders, loose actions. Two-way prospect because of special arm. Huge OF arm strength, 99 mph in drills, 6.80 speed. Balanced hitting approach, good clean swing, creates bat speed, gap to gap power, can handle the bat head, projects much more strength. Arm strength translates to mound, FB easy 91-93 mph, simple delivery with long arm stroke, low effort release, SL has good depth, CB spins hard, may have higher ceiling as RHP. Could explode by next June as a pitcher. Early draft possibilities, especially on the mound.

Lorenzen's performance led to his being selected to play in the PG All-American Classic that same summer, and despite being drafted by the Rays the following June in the seventh round as the 54th best high school prospect in the 2010 class, he decided to forego his pro career at the time and honor his commitment to Cal State Fullerton.

His career with the Titans, which initially began as a primary outfielder, got off to a good start as he hit .342 with a .427 on-base percentage and was 19-for-26 in stolen base attempts. He didn't take the mound his freshman year, but that changed during his sophomore season, when he recorded 16 saves in a two-way role. He never hit as well as he did during his freshman season, posting a .297 batting average as a sophomore and .335 as a junior, but he added 19 more saves during his final season at Cal State Fullerton, giving him 35 in two years while setting the school's all-time record.

Offensively, his profile was similar to that of another former college standout, Drew Stubbs—also a first-round pick of the Reds—with good speed, great range and instincts in center field, a strong arm, and intriguing power potential, especially to the right-center-field gap as a right-handed hitter. However, the more time Lorenzen got on the mound the more it became impossible to ignore his special arm strength, as noted in the showcase report shared above, peaking as high as 99 mph during his junior year and routinely working in the mid-90s in short relief stints to go along with a sharp breaking ball.

Ultimately the Reds selected Lorenzen in the supplemental first round of the 2013 draft. It was believed leading up to the draft, when he was ranked by PG as the 44th best overall prospect, that he might be allowed to begin his career as an outfielder, with pitching being a very realistic fallback option down the road. However, the Reds selected him with the intent of him pitching at the professional level from Day 1.
—*Patrick Ebert*

Nick Travieso – RHP

A native of Southeast Florida, Travieso put his name on prospect lists at an early age, as he was topping out at 92-93 mph the summer following his freshman year in high school. However, the 6-foot-3, 200-pound right-hander never saw his name near the top of those lists and wasn't selected as a Perfect Game All-American.

The reason for those snubs was that Travieso rarely pitched until his senior year in high school. He attended two powerhouse programs in American Heritage (freshman/sophomore) and Archbishop McCarthy (junior/senior) and was a middle-of-the-order, power-hitting corner infielder and occasional relief pitcher with those deep and talented programs. In fact, Travieso only threw 18 innings his junior year. It was much the same story for the South Florida Elite Squad team he played for in the summer and fall.

Travieso, who was committed to Miami, began working as a starter as a senior and regularly pitched in the 93-95 mph range while topping out at 98-99 mph on a consistent basis. There were even reports of him touching the magical 100 mph mark on some radar guns. Even with that type of velocity, Travieso wasn't getting across-the-board recognition as a probable first-round draft choice. While his lack of innings on the mound and his overall athleticism gave him the fresh arm and clean health résumé that scouts value, he had also spent very little time working on his secondary pitches. The PG database shows numerous events when Travieso didn't throw a single breaking ball and only a couple of rare changeups.

While Travieso's slider showed improvement with use and repetition during his senior year, it still was a hard pitch to project due to his delivery and arm action. This breakdown of Travieso's mechanics appeared on the PG website in his predraft report in May 2012:

> Travieso has a well-paced delivery with a compact and short high arm circle in back and gets very good use of his strong lower half to generate power and torque prior to release. He also leans off pretty severely on release and spins to the first-base side. The result is when Travieso releases the ball he's coming inside and over it in a pronounced way. That makes it very difficult for him (or any pitcher) to get on top of and out front of a breaking ball and create consistent quality spin on the ball and also presents somewhat of a tip to advanced hitters because he has to change his hand angle and position for a breaking ball.
>
> His breaking ball has gone from an upper-70s slurve-type curveball to a low- to mid-80s slider over the past year and reports out of Florida this spring seem to indicate that he's becoming more consistent throwing a true slider with more consistency as he gets more repetitions. He also throws a changeup that is in the developing stages, and pitchers with this type of arm action and mechanics have frequently been able to develop power split-finger fastballs as they mature.

The Reds, who scout Florida as heavily as any organization in baseball, knew all of this, of course. They also place a premium on high-ceiling, young, fresh arms and had seen virtually every one of Travieso's outings that spring. They surprised some of the industry by grabbing Travieso with the 14th overall pick and proceeded to sign him only a couple of days later for a $2 million signing bonus, $375,000 under the MLB recommended bonus for that slot. —*David Rawnsley*

Phil Ervin – OF

A gifted overall athlete and a three-sport star in high school, Ervin was a part of state championship teams in both baseball and football at Leroy High School in Alabama. Since he didn't focus on just one sport prior to attending Samford, Ervin wasn't

a well-known commodity on the travel circuit prior to his collegiate career. In fact, the only PG event he attended was in 2007 as a 14-year-old at the 15U WWBA National Championship.

That changed quickly in college, with Ervin hitting .371 during his freshman year on his way to being named a Freshman All-American. The productivity continued throughout his sophomore and junior years, as well as the summers between, as he was named the no. 22 prospect in the Northwoods League in 2011 only to earn MVP honors on the Cape the following summer.

Despite being 5-foot-10, 205 pounds coming out of college, Ervin showed true five-tool ability. Although you wouldn't think he could generate significant pop, his electric bat speed, among the best of those eligible for the 2013 draft, made up significant ground on sluggers with more prototypical statures. He also displayed good foot speed, routinely showing advanced instincts in the outfield, and his arm strength allowed him to take the mound occasionally, where he would peak in the 92-93 mph range.

Here's his PG draft report coming out of Samford, when he was ranked the 30th best overall prospect:

> The 5-foot-10, 195-pound Ervin established himself as a first rounder last summer in his first 15 games in the Cape Cod League, when he went deep eight times on his way to earning league MVP honors. He has continued to sting the ball at a steady clip this spring for Samford, hitting .364 with a team-high 10 homers, even as he has been pitched around extensively ... Though he isn't overly physical in his sub-6-foot frame, Ervin generates excellent bat speed with his lightning-quick hands and flashes raw power to all fields. More than just a power threat, Ervin has a solid all-around approach to hitting with good bat control and a patient approach, and stays inside the ball well while emphasizing going the other way. His speed and ability to run down balls in center field are also significant assets, and he has been clocked up to 93 mph off the mound in occasional stints as a pitcher.

A three-year starter in center field for the Bulldogs, Ervin finished his junior year hitting .337-11-40 with 21 stolen bases in 23 attempts and was selected by the Reds in the first round with the 27th overall selection in the 2013 draft. —*Patrick Ebert*

St. Louis Cardinals

Rob Kaminsky – LHP

Polish has always been a word scouts have heavily associated with Rob Kaminsky, and one that has been featured in his scouting reports dating back to his early years in high school. It's something he ultimately acquired through years of pitching at the highest tournament levels with the Tri-State Arsenal.

Despite his less-than-prototypical pitcher's frame, Kaminsky showed signs of precocious velocity as far back as 2010, coming off what was only his freshman year in high school. Pitching at the 15U WWBA National Championship, the young Kaminsky showed an 84-90 mph fastball, and perhaps more importantly already showed a tight and hard 75-mph curveball, a pitch that has come to define his game.

However, it was his absolutely dominant and eye-opening performance at the 2012 PG National Showcase that vaulted Kaminsky up the rankings, which he continued to climb thanks to a strong senior year, finishing his high school career as the number two prospect in his class.

Here's his report from the PG National:

Steady low-90s fastball, topped at 94 mph, mostly straight with occasional small run. Nasty curveball with velocity, hard spin and depth, can manipulate shape of CB and spot it to both sides of the plate, plus/plus pitch, one of the best seen at this level. Rare changeup but it was also plus with late diving action and good arm speed. Absolutely no contest vs. hitters.

Kaminsky went on to start the PG All-American Classic later that summer for the East squad. In a number of ways, the scouting community went into the spring of 2013 looking for ways to nitpick Kaminsky's game. There was a large degree of uncertainty at the top of the high school pitching crop, and despite his often electric displays of stuff and advanced command, it seemed that many remained skeptical of the hard-throwing lefty.

But, to his credit, Kaminsky battled the often frigid northern New Jersey spring conditions and put together an outstanding and consistent spring. And, on April 27 against rival Don Bosco, Kaminsky put together an outing that may have cemented his status and erased many remaining doubts scouts had voiced. Here is Perfect Game's account of that outing:

Rob Kaminsky is continuing to make a strong case as the best prep left-hander in the 2013 draft class. His velocity has jumped over his last two outings, and he showed two clear plus pitches against Don Bosco on Friday. Kaminsky pitched consistent at 91-94 mph over six innings of work and showed two variations of his plus breaking ball. The harder version topped at 85 mph, while the more traditional curveball we've seen from him in the past worked at 77-80. After having some minor command problems early, Kaminsky was able to locate his curveball with tremendous consistency throughout the game.

This mid-spring performance was as good as we've seen Kaminsky in terms of velocity and crispness to his breaking ball. But his value still lies in his ability to locate his elite-level, plus curveball. It's always been the equalizer for him, and even in outings where his velocity was closer to 88-91 as an amateur, he still left scouts impressed with his ability to dominate on the strength of that true hammer curveball. Some teams and scouts interpreted the use of his curveball differently, referring to it as a crutch.

That and his less-than-prototypical 5-foot-11 frame allowed him to fall to the Cardinals at 28th overall. The teams that looked past his frame saw the value in his plus makeup, ability to repeat his delivery, and advanced feel for pitching at a very young age. —*Frankie Piliere*

Charles Tilson – OF

Tilson grew up on the north side of Chicago near Wrigley Field, but was a virtual unknown outside of Illinois before August 5, 2010. His New Trier High School baseball team played together in the summer locally and Tilson played football in the fall. He never played at a Perfect Game event nor any other national level tournament or showcase prior to the 2010 Area Code Games.

Dan Durst, the White Sox scout (now with the Orioles) who organized the Midwest Area Code Games team, told me just before the event started, "Wait until you see this center fielder I have, you're going to love him. Nobody's ever seen him play outside of Illinois. He's even committed to Illinois because none of the southern schools know who he is."

Durst, of course, was correct. The 6-foot, 165-pound left-handed hitter was the star of the week, using his blazing speed to wreak havoc on the bases and track down everything in center field, then hitting the only home run spacious Blair Field allowed that week as a bonus. Scouts were left scrambling to figure out the new talent they had shooting up toward the top of their lists.

My notes from the event read as follows:

Outstanding prospect, strong athletic build, medium frame, quick hands at the plate, has deceiving pop, drives the ball, impact speed on bases, 3.18 steal, aggressive, 4.05, 6.54 in the sixty, drove 92 FB hard, plays at 100% speed/effort, center fielder with + range/quickness, solid average arm. Potential 1st round type.

Tilson went on to be the Illinois Gatorade Player of the Year as a senior when he hit .406 and stole 28 bases. The Cardinals drafted him in the second round (79th overall pick) and signed him to a $1,275,000 bonus right at the August 15th deadline. —*David Rawnsley*

NL West

Arizona Diamondbacks

Braden Shipley – RHP

If you read enough of the "Before They Were Pros" series or take the time to delve into enough player's backgrounds, you'll find perhaps a surprising number of top prospects and present major leaguers who are conversions from one position to another. Braden Shipley is another of the position player to pitcher conversions.

Shipley attended high school in Medford, Oregon, and was not a very heavily recruited high school player. In fact, he had no commitment when he attended the PG West Uncommitted Showcase in November of his senior year. He went to that event as a 6-foot-1, 170-pound primary shortstop and secondary pitcher and did both at the showcase. Shipley was a decent middle-infield prospect, although his 7.50 speed in the 60-yard dash was a drawback. He had smooth actions in the infield and enough arm strength, and he swung the bat well. There was no standout tool, but he knew how to play and was physically projectable. As strictly a position prospect he garnered a PG grade of 8.5.

But Shipley also took the mound and was much better than that. He had a short, quick, and very easy arm action off the mound and an upper-80s fastball that touched 90 mph that really jumped on hitters quickly. Shipley also threw a 74-mph curveball that had hard, tight spin and an occasional changeup. He received a PG grade of 9.5 off the mound and definitely profiled as a high D-I or even professional prospect. His overall report after the event read:

Projectable athletic body, some developing strength, young face. Quality 2-way prospect, best on mound this event. FB touches 90 mph, short/quick/clean arm action, FB jumps on hitters, hard spin on downer CB, very good sharpness at times, needs to learn to throw inside more. Velo/stuff projects. Solid infield actions, good bat speed, handles the barrel very well, short swing with consistent hard contact. Should keep getting better in all areas. Quality D1 type player, maybe more.

Shipley first committed to Western Nevada CC after the event, then later to the University of Nevada. He played almost exclusively at shortstop as a freshman for the Wolf Pack, hitting .287-1-19 in 44 starts and earning second-team All-WAC honors. Shipley did manage to work in 10 innings on the mound, posting an 8.71 ERA and allowing 27 baserunners.

A trip that summer to the Alaskan Summer League turned Shipley's career path around. He received more mound time, going 1-2 with seven saves and a 2.44 ERA, and was named the top overall prospect in the league by Perfect Game while featuring a consistent mid-90s fastball out of the bullpen. Shipley was a full-time pitcher when he returned to Nevada, going 9-4, 2.20 in 98 innings as a sophomore while getting only 12 at-bats. He virtually duplicated that performance as a junior, going 7-3, 2.77 in 107 innings while getting two token at-bats, both resulting in strikeouts.

Shipley was the third college pitcher selected in the 2013 draft and the 15th overall selection, signing with the Diamondbacks for a $2.25 million signing bonus. —*David Rawnsley*

Aaron Blair – RHP

Aaron Blair has one of the more unique development résumés one could find among top prospects today, and his continued improvement since signing with the Diamondbacks isn't surprising in context. He's gone from receiving a PG grade of 7.5 as a high school junior to being a lightly recruited high school senior to a good D-I starter in college to a top draft pick and present top prospect.

The now-22-year-old right-hander grew up in Las Vegas and went to the 2008 Jr. National Showcase. He was listed at 6-foot-1, 175 pounds at that point and did very little to either distinguish himself or even show that he was projectable. Blair pitched in the 79-81 mph area at that event, but just as notably in some ways ran the 60-yard dash in 8.67 seconds and was timed at 5.41 from home to first base. That's another way of saying that he wasn't that good of an athlete at that point in time.

But approximately a year later, at the beginning of his senior year, Blair was up to 88 mph and pitching for the Ohio Warhawks at the WWBA World Championship. He threw again for the Warhawks at the 2010 18u WWBA National Championship after graduating and being picked in the 21st round by the Houston Astros, where he topped out at 91 mph with a hard spinning mid-70s curveball. Blair was also now listed at 6-foot-5, 229 pounds, a huge improvement in size and strength.

Blair traveled across the country to attend Marshall in West Virginia and his record at Marshall was reflective of that program's record, as Blair went 9-16 in three seasons, including 5-5, 2.85 in 84 innings as a junior, while the Thundering Herd finished a combined 57-102 during that span.

Where Blair made his reputation with scouts was pitching for Yarmouth-Dennis in the Cape Cod League the summer before his junior season. He went 6-0, 1.17 during the regular season, then added two more wins during the playoffs to cap off a perfect summer that saw him win almost as many games in two months as he did in three college seasons. Blair pitched in the 91-94 mph area in the Cape, with a curveball that was now touching 80 mph and an outstanding changeup he'd developed at Marshall.

Blair was the 36th overall pick in the 2013 draft and signed for a $1,435,000 bonus. —*David Rawnsley*

Brandon Drury – 3B/2B

Ranked as the 493rd high school prospect in the class of 2010, Drury only got one extended look from Perfect Game, in 2008 at the NorCal Underclass Showcase. This was the summer before

Drury's junior year in high school, and he received this report after his performance:

> Brandon has a very athletic build, good hands and actions in the infield, soft hands, looks easy in the field, made plays in games, very good bat speed at the plate, ball flies off bat when centered, hard line-drive contact to all fields, very good juice in bat, can hit, very good game contact, very interesting player. He is also a good student.

At 6-feet, 175 pounds, Drury received a PG grade of 8.5 at the time, although he added another inch and 10 pounds of strength to his athletic frame prior to graduating in 2010. It was easy to see him improving across the board after throwing 82 mph across the infield and running the 60-yard dash in 7.42 seconds.

Hailing from Grants Pass, Oregon, Drury was expected to see his game take a step up in college, as he had committed to play in-state for national Division I powerhouse Oregon State, which was coming off of recent back-to-back College World Series championships in 2006 and 2007. Oregon State also had done (and continues to do) an excellent job recruiting in the Pacific Northwest, rarely letting their top recruits get away.

While Drury being drafted in the 13th round of the 2010 MLB draft wasn't a surprise, the Braves clearly did their homework to gauge his interest and sign him away from the Beavers.
—*Patrick Ebert*

Colorado Rockies

Jonathan Gray – RHP

Although it's hard to accurately predict a pitcher eventually recording triple digits on the radar gun some day, it wasn't that hard to believe for Gray. Already 6-foot-4 and 225 pounds coming out of high school, Gray peaked at 93 mph after participating at a pair of Perfect Game/WWBA tournament events in 2009, the second of which occurred in Jupiter, Florida, at the WWBA World Championship.

Gray opened the spring of 2013 as the 58th best overall draft prospect according to Perfect Game after being ranked the 177th high school prospect three years earlier. In the months that followed he not only established himself as a no-doubt first rounder, but also put himself squarely in the conversation for the first overall pick and was eventually named PG's top ranked prospect for the draft.

With an extra-large and powerful frame that evoked comparisons to big-league starter Josh Johnson, Gray routinely worked in the upper-90s and frequently touched 100 mph in his starts for the Sooners. He maintained that velocity exceptionally well deep into ballgames thanks to his workhorse build, and also changed speeds effectively between his upper-80s slider and surprisingly good changeup. He proved to be nearly untouchable, going 10-3 with a 1.64 ERA, striking out 147 and allowing only 83 hits and 24 walks in 126 innings of work.

Here's Gray's predraft report:

> A combination of better conditioning and improving mechanics have vaulted Gray from a potential first-round pick before the season to a potential first overall pick when the Houston Astros kick off the draft on June 6. Gray has been lighting up radar guns in the 95-100 range while peaking as high as 102 mph consistently all spring and maintaining his velocity deep into starts. His slider, which some scouts feel the Oklahoma coaching staff calls too frequently, is a second plus pitch in the mid to upper 80s with a hard and deep late

bite. Not only has Gray shown dominant stuff that has been compared to Justin Verlander, he's shown the ability to use it as well, posting a 8-1, 1.20 record in 89 innings, with only 51 hits and 16 walks allowed to go with 104 strikeouts. Batters are hitting .166-1-15 against Gray this year. Gray was a well-known prospect out of Chandler, Okla. as a high schooler, topping out at 93 mph, but was only picked in the 13th round (Royals) and again in the 10th round (Pirates) after attending Eastern Oklahoma JC in 2011 before transferring to Oklahoma.

After the Astros selected right-hander Mark Appel with the first pick of the 2013 draft and the Cubs took the Golden Spikes Award winner from that year, Kris Bryant, the Rockies were thrilled to have Gray fall in their lap with the third overall selection. —*Patrick Ebert*

Ryan McMahon – 3B

McMahon was a stranger to national level baseball scouts until late in the summer in 2012, prior to the start of his senior year in high school.

The reason for that was a combination of his playing quarterback and going to Mater Dei High School in Santa Ana, California. Mater Dei is a football powerhouse that produces future NFL players at almost every position, but is occasionally referred to as "Quarterback High." Five eventual NFL quarterbacks have attended the private Catholic school, including Heisman Trophy winners John Huarte and Matt Leinart.

While McMahon was never a potential NFL quarterback, he did start 15 games for Mater Dei between his junior and senior seasons, throwing for 1,863 yards and 16 touchdowns.

Mater Dei also has a very successful baseball program and boasts alumni such as Danny Espinosa, Sergio Santos, Matt Treanor, and Bobby Meacham. McMahon was a three-year starter for Mater Dei in baseball who hit .405-4-32 during his senior season and .376-10-73 over his career.

The only time McMahon appeared in a national level scouting event was at the 2012 Area Code Games. The AC Games are held annually in early August and McMahon was surely already deeply involved in football workouts. Despite that, he put on a very impressive performance and solidly put himself on the baseball prospect map as a potential high round draft choice. I recall turning to a SoCal-based scouting friend during a McMahon at-bat and asking him, "Do the area scouts here know they have a potential first rounder?" My own notes from that event were about as glowing as possible:

> All-American quality tools and athleticism, first-round potential. Sweet left-handed swing, bat speed, looseness, has everything. Very athletic at 3B. Top 50 player, resembles Corey Seager with a better swing.

The Rockies picked McMahon, who had a baseball commitment to Southern California, with the 42nd overall pick near the top of the second round and signed him to a $1,328,000 signing bonus that exactly matched the slot for that pick. It was considered a pretty aggressive selection at that time by the industry as a whole, but early indications are that it was a very wise one as well. —*David Rawnsley*

San Diego Padres

Hunter Renfroe – OF

A two-way talent whose tools were highlighted by an incredibly strong arm and power potential at the plate, Renfroe participated in back-to-back 18u WWBA National Championships in 2009 and 2010 playing for the Mississippi Bandits. He received high marks at the time for his defensive mechanics behind the plate, registering pop times in the 1.90 range while using a compact, balanced swing to drive the ball to the gaps.

He also threw in the 88-91 mph range on the mound, although he threw mostly fastballs in the process, and his two-way career didn't continue past his freshman season at Mississippi State, when he made six relief appearances for the Bulldogs.

Although Renfroe hit .154 and .252 during his first two years in college, he made an immediate impression the two summers that followed in the Cal Ripken Collegiate League, being named the top prospect of the league each year. During his second summer in the league Renfroe hit an eye-popping .366 with 16 home runs in just 134 at-bats.

Even though he touched the upper-90s on the mound and popped 1.7s from behind the plate, Renfroe continued to post big numbers during his junior year as an outfielder, with the prototypical power-bat/arm profile for right field. He recorded eight outfield assists while hitting .345 with 16 home runs, and proved to be a star on the big stage of the College World Series as well, hitting a booming three-run home run in a 4-1 victory over Oregon State that carried the Bulldogs to the championship round against the eventual champion UCLA Bruins.

Here's his report prior to the 2013 draft, when he was ranked PG's 11th overall prospect:

> The real Hunter Renfroe has stood up this spring, and there may not be a player in the 2013 draft class who has a better overall tool set than the powerful Mississippi State right fielder. After playing sparingly for the Bulldogs as a freshman and hitting a modest .252-4-25 as a sophomore, the 6-foot-3, 215-pound Renfroe has busted out with a monster junior season and leads his team with a .410 average, 14 homers and 45 RBIs ... Though he is viewed as a legitimate big-league prospect at any number of positions, Renfroe seemed to find a comfort zone this spring for the Bulldogs as a right fielder, and his easy transition to that position speaks to his superior athleticism and versatility. There isn't a tool in his bag that doesn't rate as above average but it's his prodigious power at the plate, both for distance and frequency, that truly sets him apart.

Renfroe's continued development in college led to his being selected with the 13th overall pick in the 2013 draft by the Padres. —*Patrick Ebert*

Taylor Lindsey – 2B

A well-known talent coming out of high school, Lindsey was ranked 76th in Perfect Game's high school class of 2010 player rankings. While Lindsey called shortstop home in high school, his future position on the field was somewhat in question, as he lacked the ideal range and at short. A high-level athlete, Lindsey could play almost anywhere else on the field, but his advanced left-handed bat and overall approach and the strength in his swing drew the most attention.

Although he wasn't a regular on the national travel circuit, Lindsey did attend both the 2009 Area Code Games and the WWBA World Championship in Jupiter, Florida, that same year.

Here is a collection of reports from his performance in Jupiter:

> Patient at plate, has pop on inner half, good bat speed ...
> aggressive hitter, rotational, swings uphill ... closed slightly,
> hands high, good approach, confident, very good quick
> hands, line-drive hitter with power potential, good drive off
> bat ... stands tall, simple approach.

And the Area Code Games:

> Very nice swing, big bat speed, has lift, drives the ball deep,
> projects more, squares up good stuff, looks and acts like a
> top-level hitter. Didn't stand out on defense, played some OF
> as well.

The Los Angeles Angels used a supplemental first-round pick on Lindsey in the 2010 MLB draft to steer him away from his home-state commitment to Arizona State. —*Patrick Ebert*

San Francisco Giants

Christian Arroyo – SS/2B

Arroyo was a well-known prospect at Hernando High School in Florida, playing in close to 20 Perfect Game events beginning in his freshman year, including the 2012 PG National Showcase, and also for the 2012 USA National 18u team. He received a PG Grade of 10 at the National Showcase, and this scout wrote the following glowing report on him:

> Medium athletic build, good present strength. Right-handed
> hitter, outstanding plate coverage and hand/eye coordina-
> tion, short crisp swing with bat speed, squares up every-
> thing, no problems against plus velocity, hard line drive
> contact to all fields, gap power, has special ability to square
> up the ball. Second base tools defensively, 7.10 runner, good
> hands, stays balanced and light on his feet, arm strength
> playable. Bat is special.

Despite his impressive résumé, Arroyo was generally not considered the type of prospect that would interest many pro teams as a high draft pick out of high school. While his bat was a special tool, his running speed and arm strength, two prospect barometers for a middle-of-the-field athlete, were simply average. Arroyo was seen by most as a player who would go to Florida (he was an excellent student) and be an immediate impact player for head coach Kevin O'Sullivan. In fact, O'Sullivan, in private conversations before the draft, expressed shock that he might lose Arroyo to the draft.

There was talk through the late spring that there were a couple of teams that were looking at Arroyo very high, but most of the industry believed he was more of a third- to fifth-round option and more likely going to Florida. Some even thought his best future position was behind the plate.

That the Giants were the team that snapped Arroyo up with a first-round pick, the 25th overall, shouldn't have been surprising in retrospect. The team selected high school middle infielder Nick Noonan with the 32nd overall pick in 2007 despite concerns about his ability to stay at short. They also famously picked Joe Panik out of St. John's with the 29th pick in 2011 despite concerns that the future playoff hero didn't have a true plus tool. Both players were very intelligent middle-of-the-field players whose best tool was their bat. The Giants valued those two, along with Arroyo, for their ability to play baseball and hit rather than their athleticism.

That formula seems to have worked well for them thus far.
—*David Rawnsley*

Steven Okert – LHP

Okert was a two-way talent in high school, performing at a high level both on the mound and at the plate for Rowlett High School in Texas. He didn't play at a Perfect Game event until the summer after he had already graduated from high school, the 2009 18u WWBA National Championship, playing with the Frozen Ropes travel team organization.

With a sturdy 6-foot-3, 195-pound build Okert offered intriguing power potential as a first baseman and a power arm on the mound. At the 18u WWBA National Championship he peaked at 88 mph, sitting comfortably in the 86-88 mph range while throwing both a curveball and a changeup in the mid-70s. It was noted at the event that his mechanics could be brushed up, as he threw across his body, and that he would need to make sure to keep his focus on conditioning given his strong lower half.

After two years at Grayson County College, a junior college located in Denison, Texas, Okert transferred to the University of Oklahoma thanks to a significant spike in velocity. He now had the ability to sit in the low to mid-90s when used in short relief, a role that seemed to suit him well despite having three pitches in his arsenal. Here's his predraft report in 2012:

> [Okert] started the 2012 season in the Sooners rotation,
> but was moved to the bullpen after five starts. Since then,
> Okert's stuff has been nothing short of outstanding, with a
> fastball consistently in the 94-96 mph range, touching 97,
> to go with a solid slider and changeup. A more confident
> presence on the mound speaks to the greater comfort zone
> he has achieved as a reliever. Okert has a smooth, easy
> delivery and demonstrates good command of his fastball
> to both sides of the plate, but it is still not refined overall,
> as he has served up 33 walks in 69 innings this spring,
> while striking out 65 and posting a 6-6, 3.26 record. Okert's
> overall package would seem to be a good fit in the third to
> fifth rounds, but the sheer power in his left arm has scouts
> talking him up as high as the second round.

Although he didn't go as high as the second round, the Giants did select Okert in the fourth round that year, which marked the third time he was drafted after being taken by the Brewers in the later rounds in both 2010 and 2011 after his freshman and sophomore years at Grayson County College. —*Patrick Ebert*

Clayton Blackburn – RHP

2011 was the year of the high school pitcher in the state of Oklahoma. Dylan Bundy was the fourth overall pick and had some scouts calling him the best high school right-hander they'd ever seen. Some didn't even think Bundy was the best high school pitcher in the state, believing Archie Bradley, who went with the seventh overall pick, had a higher ceiling. Then there was Mike Fulmer, who went 44th overall, and Adrian Houser, who was plucked up with the 69th overall pick. Mason Hope got into the act in the fifth round.

As perspective, there has been only one high school pitcher from Oklahoma selected in the first five rounds since 2011.

Blackburn was a known prospect in high school but certainly not a high profile one. He went to the 2009 Perfect Game Sunshine South Showcase as a 6-foot-2, 210-pound primary first baseman and received a PG grade of 7.5 at that position. However, his report from the event noted the following:

Also pitched, strong arm, 82-84 mph fastball from OH release, good extension, FB flashes hard boring action, hard CB spin, has potential on the mound.

Blackburn improved significantly over the course of the next year and was invited to the 2010 Area Code Games. He pitched in the 87-90 mph range with his characteristic feel for pitching. His notes from that outing read:

Soft build, young look, full delivery, full arm circle, pretty smooth delivery, loose out front, H 3/4 release. Has arm strength, FB straight, CB spin soft, nice changeup, knows how to work changeup well.

Blackburn was signed with Oklahoma when the Giants took a flier on him in that loaded 2011 Oklahoma draft class in the 16th round and were able to sign him for a surprisingly low $160,000 bonus. —*David Rawnsley*

Los Angeles Dodgers

Chris Anderson – RHP

Lightly recruited out of Centennial Park High School just northeast of the Twin Cities in Minnesota, Anderson participated in Perfect Game's Midwest Scout League during the fall of his senior season to gain additional exposure. Already a well-built athlete at 6-foot-3, 210 pounds, Anderson peaked at 91 mph during the fall, and then 92 the following spring, prior to attending Jacksonville University.

Anderson grew another inch and added 15-20 pounds to his already workhorse build while in college, and although he enjoyed two solid-yet-unspectacular seasons in his first two years at Jacksonville, he started to make a much bigger name for himself during the summer of 2012 when he pitched on the Cape. While his performance numbers may not reflect his success, he was throwing in the low-90s on a regular basis and started to find more consistency with his off-speed pitches.

Those pitches included a low- to mid-80s slider and a continually improving changeup. By his junior year Anderson opened the spring by sitting in the low- to mid-90s with his fastball, peaking a few ticks higher, and effectively changing speeds between his improving secondary pitches.

Frankie Piliere had this to say about Anderson as part of his Draft Focus report in the spring of 2013:

Flash forward to this spring and we find a very different pitcher. His velocity is up–he's now sitting 92-95 mph and reaching as high as 96-97 mph. He's also been locating exceptionally well. But the biggest difference has been with his secondary pitches. Anderson is throwing a plus slider, as well as a potential solid-average changeup, and he's missing a lot of bats in the process. His slider at 81-84 mph is becoming a legitimate above-average offering, and the changeup command is there in a way it hasn't been before. In other words, Anderson has gone from merely an intriguing power arm with a durable frame to a full-fledged three-pitch starter.

Anderson was a well enough known draft commodity for the Cubs to take him in the 35th round of the 2010 draft out of high school. That wasn't high enough to lure him away from college, but it stands as enough proof that he was on team's radars even before he exploded onto the prospect scene two years later. That explosion led to his being selected in the first round by the Dodgers in 2013. —*Patrick Ebert*

Scott Schebler – OF

The state of Iowa has had a steady trickle of high profile high school prospects over the years, helped significantly by the Perfect Game spring and fall leagues that give the state's young players a chance to play during more than just their summer high school seasons. Scott Schebler was definitely not one of those high-profile prospects, though.

Schebler went to school at Prairie High School just outside of Cedar Rapids, Perfect Game's home, and played five sports in high school and was all-state in three of them. He started playing in the spring and fall leagues immediately after he entered high school, along with attending numerous showcases, including the 2007 National Underclass, where he received a PG grade of 8. He had upped that grade to 9 by the end of senior year, when the comments on his 2009 Midwest Top Prospect Showcase report read:

Strong athletic build, fairly mature. Aggressive hitting style, looking to pull everything, has good bat speed, lift in swing, ball jumps hard on contact, will hit HRs at the next level. 6.91 runner, moves well in the outfield, raw arm strength, will improve throws with better fundamentals. Bat is a plus.

Still, Schebler was only the 719th ranked prospect on the PG Class of 2009 rankings and was signed to attend Des Moines Area Community College, a well-respected Division II junior college program.

At DMACC, Schebler continued to do what he'd always done which was hit. He posted a .446-20-82 line in 58 games as a freshman. When he ran the 60-yard dash in 6.52 seconds at the PG Pre-Draft Showcase in mid-May 2010, it was noted how he was getting stronger and more athletic, but teams still weren't excited. The Dodgers and area scout Mitch Webster liked Schebler the best but only ventured a 26th-round pick on him. The Dodgers stepped up, though, signing Schebler away from Wichita State with a $300,000 signing bonus. —*David Rawnsley*

AL East

Boston Red Sox

Rafael Devers – 3B

There was already a serious buzz in the international scouting community when Devers came to the PG World Showcase in early January 2013, with the thought being that the Dominican native might be the premium player in the 2013 international class that would become eligible to sign that July 2.

Devers was a couple months past his 16th birthday when he arrived in Fort Myers, Florida, meaning he would likely have been a sophomore in high school if he had been raised in the United States. He had a strong 6-foot, 185-pound build that was well filled out in the hips and thighs. Although he ran a respectable 7.00 and threw 88 mph across the infield in drills, it was obvious that Devers wasn't your typical tooled-up Dominican prospect. The buzz from the scouts was directed at Devers' left-handed bat, and the rest of the tools just had to be playable to support the buzz.

Devers' batting practice was what you might expect from a 16-year-old with all those eyes on him. He had a big coil and uppercut in his approach and spent the entire session trying to pull and lift the ball with only moderate success. The scouting notes in the PG database from BP specifically include the phrase "probably not his game swing."

Things changed entirely once live pitching took the mound. It was immediately obvious that Devers saw the ball exceptionally well for such a young hitter and had the ability not only to recognize what pitches he could drive to what part of the ballpark, but also to take close pitches and to foul off pitches he needed to in order to stay alive in counts. His swing was fluid and loose with plus raw bat speed and he hit the ball to left-center field as hard as he pulled it.

Devers had one very notable at-bat against Dustin Hagy, a 6-foot-6 right-hander who was later a 31st-round pick of the Orioles. Hagy was throwing 89-92 mph with a pretty nasty 77-mph curveball and it was pretty evident that he knew who was in the batter's box by the way he ratcheted up his stuff and focus with Devers in the box. The at-bat went at least a dozen pitches, with the 16-year-old continually fouling off pitches in every quadrant of the plate and Hagy not backing down a bit. The battle ended with Devers lining a hit to left-center field and scouts throughout the stands muttering a collective "wow" at the quality of performance of both players.

Devers went on to sign with the Red Sox for a $1.5 million signing bonus, one of the top bonuses given in the 2013 class. His exceptional performance between the Dominican Summer League and the Gulf Coast League in his first season (.322-7-57, 35 walks in 70 games) certainly seems to support the initial impressions of his offensive potential. —*David Rawnsley*

Matt Barnes – RHP

Although he was built super lean and lanky, the potential for growth and strength gains were obvious for the 6-foot-4, 180-pound Barnes in high school. He competed in a handful of Perfect Game tournament events and one showcase, the 2007 Northeast Top Prospect Showcase, where he earned a PG grade of 9 and garnered this report:

> He pitches from a 3/4 arm slot with long and loose arm action. Barnes has good arm speed and a live arm. He has good mechanics with some effort in his delivery. Matthew has an 88-mph fastball with arm-side run and good command. He has a sharp 11-5 curveball at 71 mph and a solid changeup at 75 mph. Barnes has a projectable body and arm and the ball comes out easy.

While the projectability and likelihood for increased fastball velocity were evident, it's nearly impossible to project a near 10-mph increase in his three years in college. But that's exactly what happened with Barnes, who attended UConn, playing alongside current Astros slugger George Springer, while dialing his fastball up to 97 mph by his junior year.

The velocity came largely thanks to the loose arm and arm speed that were noted in his showcase report above. It was easy to envision Barnes, still projectable at 205 pounds, maintaining that newfound velocity deep into games.

His curveball also gained more power in college, now thrown in the mid- to upper-70s, to go along with his changeup while picking up and developing a slider to give him a solid four-pitch repertoire. Here is a snippet of Barnes' predraft report in 2011:

> Along with a significant increase in velocity, his feel for pitching has also improved by leaps and bounds. He produces a good downhill angle on his fastball ... His hard, sharp 75-78 mph curve is his best off-speed pitch, though he still has a tendency to cut it off instead of snapping it off out front. His 79-80 mph slider continues to evolve, but often is

flat with a slurvy-shaped rotation. He can produce the same arm speed on his changeup as his fastball, and locates it well to both sides of the plate with late sink. Though Barnes uses minimal effort in his delivery, he still struggles at times with his mechanics, particularly in identifying a consistent release point, which mildly impacts his command.

At the time Barnes was expected to go off the board among the top eight to 15 overall picks, so it was a mild surprise that he fell to the Red Sox at 19. That was the first of four first-round picks for the Red Sox that year, a draft haul that included Blake Swihart, Henry Owens, Jackie Bradley Jr., and Mookie Betts. —*Patrick Ebert*

Brian Johnson – LHP

Selected by the Dodgers in the 27th round out of high school in 2009, Johnson opted to honor his commitment to play for the Florida Gators on a talent-laden squad. He served a crucial two-way role while in college, serving as one of the team's top starters while also batting in the middle of the Gators' lineup in the cleanup spot, usually behind his batterymate and Golden Spikes winner Mike Zunino, the no. 3 overall pick in the 2012 draft.

Here's the report written about him leading up to the 2012 draft, in which he was ranked the 37th overall prospect:

> Johnson has legitimate pro potential as both a hitter and pitcher, and brings to mind former two-way college stars and high-round picks such as Joe Savery (Rice) and Sean Doolittle (Virginia). Though he hasn't been quite as consistent across the board this spring as he was in 2011 (5-1, 3.88 with 11 BB/39 SO in 48 IP; .315-4-23 as a hitter), Johnson's stuff has been solid. His fastball normally has been in the 89-91 mph range, but will top out at 93, and he complements it with a big-breaking curve that he commands with maturity.

Prior to his time spent at Florida, Johnson was a well-known prospect from Cocoa Beach, Florida. He finished his high school career as the 119th high school prospect in the class of 2009, and although he didn't participate at any PG showcase events, he did appear in numerous tournaments, including two trips to the WWBA World Championship in Jupiter. His peak velocity at those events was 90 mph, routinely sitting in the mid- to upper-80s with a sharp curveball.

Johnson's velocity of course took a step up while in college, frequently sitting in the low-90s while peaking at 94 mph. His curveball continued to be his second best offering, a perfect complement to his fastball and overall command.

Although most lefties that have the ability to throw in the 90s are developed on the mound, Johnson could have been drafted early as a power-hitting first-base prospect, as noted in his report above. His 6-foot-4, 220-pound stature gave him intriguing power potential, and he routinely exhibited one of the more polished approaches at the plate in the college game and a smooth, left-handed swing with a natural uppercut path. However, his profile as a big, strong, and durable left-hander with the ability to eat up innings was too good to pass up. —*Patrick Ebert*

Tampa Bay Rays

Justin O'Conner – C

It hasn't been particularly surprising that Justin O'Conner has emerged as one of the best defensive catchers in minor-league baseball, except when you consider that he didn't catch until his senior year in high school. But then again, conversions from the middle infield to behind the plate are not unprecedented or even uncommon. Buster Posey played shortstop and pitched in high school, the same positions that O'Conner excelled at as a PG All-American prior to converting full time during his senior season at Cowen High School in Muncie, Indiana.

What was obvious was that O'Conner had the athletic ability to play just about any position on the field defensively, highlighted by a throwing arm that was one of the best to come along in many, many years. Here are his defensive notes from the 2009 PG National Showcase, before he'd started catching:

> ++ arm, extra step, overmatched the 1B/almost broke his wrist, everything works cleanly ... Very, very good defensive actions. 70/80 arm, 60 agility, very quick hands (65-70). Tools to become premium MIF at the major-league level. Made plays in the games. Has short release and is effectively one of the best HS infield throwers I've ever seen. Defensive ability will give teams plenty of patience with the bat. Can play anywhere on field and be above average.

O'Conner threw an absurd 95 mph across the infield in drills at the National and was also 91-93 off the mound. It wasn't effortless velocity but it wasn't contrived showcase velocity either. He had a top-of-the-scale hose to go with 6.7 speed and overall athleticism.

O'Conner's bat, as mentioned in the defensive notes, wasn't a polished tool, although he had lots of raw bat speed and plenty of power. In fact, he won the Rawlings Home Run Challenge at the PG National Showcase, held that year in the Metrodome in Minneapolis. O'Conner also hit .460-8-40 as a high school senior. But most of the concerns in scouts' minds were about how his offense would develop, and it was evident even then that O'Conner's aggressive nature would lead to walk and strikeout issues against high-level pitching.

There was a somewhat painful example of O'Conner's aggressive offensive approach that many scouts probably remember to this day. The right-handed hitter was at the plate at the 2009 Area Code Games facing a left-handed pitcher with a big-breaking curveball. O'Conner took his usual big swing at the breaking ball, came up empty, and was left completely open to the pitch hitting him square where all players fear to be hit. It may have been a fitting introduction to one of the unfortunate but regular pains of playing catcher.

However, the Rays believed in O'Conner enough to take him with the 31st pick in the 2010 draft, a selection they received for having not signed LeVon Washington the previous year, and signed him to a $1,025,000 bonus. —*David Rawnsley*

Nathan Karns – RHP

A well-known commodity coming out of high school, Karns was ranked 43rd in Perfect Game's final ranking of the high school class of 2006. After the Arlington, Texas native was drafted by the Astros in the 10th round of the draft that year, Karns decided to take his talents to North Carolina State.

Karns, who defined Texas heat with his strong 6-foot-4, 225-pound frame and heavy, low-90s fastballs, attended a trio of Perfect Game showcases while in high school. His peak velocity of 92 mph came at the 2005 National Showcase held at Turner Field, and here is his report from that event:

> He has a long arm action in back that works smoothly and smooth mechanics with a medium-effort release way out

front. Karns does a good job staying balanced over the rubber and letting his strong lower half drive him to the plate. His fastball topped out at 92 mph with some sinking and running action. Karns' breaking ball is a mid-70s slurve that has a late bite with good two-plane action. He also threw a couple of 76-mph changeups. With his frame, present velocity, and fast arm, Karns is one of the top pitching prospects in the country and one of the true power pitchers who might end up throwing in the mid- to upper-90s before everything is said and done.

After going 3-2 as a freshman with a 2.67 ERA in nine appearances, eight of which were starts, Karns opted to transfer to a school much closer to home at Texas Tech, but in the two years that followed he never enjoyed the same success. Although he did strike out 105 in 104 1/3 combined innings during his sophomore and junior years, he also allowed 116 hits and 69 walks, leading to a 6.90 cumulative ERA for the Red Raiders.

At the time there was some belief that Karns may be better suited to a short-relief role where he wouldn't have to worry about pacing himself, not to mention his swing-and-miss one-two punch, as his heavy fastball now peaked in the mid-90s to go along with his hard-biting breaking ball. Still recognizing his strong, sturdy build and powerful right arm, the Nationals took Karns in the 12th round of the 2009 draft. —*Patrick Ebert*

Taylor Guerrieri – RHP

Guerrieri was a late comer to the top-prospect ranks even though he threw at a number of WWBA events prior to his senior year for the Diamond Devils team out of South Carolina. That changed one day in early July 2010 at the 17u WWBA National Championship, with Guerrieri pitching for the Diamond Devils in a pool play game on East Cobb Field 1.

Guerrieri topped out at 94 mph that day, eclipsing his previous high at a Perfect Game event by five miles per hour. His curveball was his best pitch, showing big power up to 81 mph with sharp, biting action and lots of 11-to-5 depth. One of the more interesting parts of Guerrieri's performance that day was that he seemed to be able to reach back for his best stuff just about any time he wanted it, often pitching in the upper-80s until there was a threat, then dialing up the 93-94s with the big hammer. He was still touching 94 mph when he came out after six innings.

The rest of the summer was much of the same, including strong performances at the 18u WWBA National Championship and at the East Coast Pro Showcase.

The aspect of Guerrieri's talent from a scouting standpoint that really stood out was how well he synchronized his upper and lower halves when throwing. His arm came through at exactly the right time to maximize his leverage on release, making it look like he was throwing with no effort whatsoever. When you see someone with the ability to keep their lower half, upper half, and arm all in sync and make it look so easy, you can't help but think, "Why doesn't every pitcher just do that?" Of course, it's one of the hardest things to do and repeat in the game of baseball.

Guerrieri was even better in the spring prior to the draft, pitching in the 93-96 range and touching as high as 98 mph regularly. His curveball was more consistent as well, and he was even able to mix in some surprisingly good changeups, giving scouts the opportunity to project him with three potential-plus pitches. There is a note in Perfect Game's draft report on Guerrieri that says while fellow class of 2011 right-hander Dylan

Bundy was considered one of the best high school pitchers to come along in many years, there were a number of scouts who liked Guerrieri better.

The 2011 draft class was absolutely loaded, which was one reason that Guerrieri slid to the 24th overall pick, where he signed for a $1.6 million bonus. The other was a number of youthful off-the-field incidents that Guerrieri had reportedly been involved in that made some teams have second thoughts. —David Rawnsley

Justin Williams – OF

It is very rare for an athlete to pick up the game of baseball as a teenager and manage to make up for lost time quickly enough to develop into a legitimate prospect. It takes a special athlete to be able to develop the requisite muscle memory in relatively limited reps. Pitchers are more able to do so, but the odds are skewed very heavily against a position player.

Justin Williams didn't allow that to deter him, though. He was a nationally ranked wide receiver prospect before giving up football after his junior season at Terrabonne High School in Houma, Louisiana. The physically imposing outfielder put on jaw-dropping power displays during batting practice, highlighted by blasting a shot into the upper deck of the Metrodome during the 2012 PG National Showcase, and he also claimed the Rawlings Home Run Challenge as part of the 2012 PG All-American Classic.

Understandably, Williams was raw as a pure hitter during his high school days. And while he made tremendous strides and developed at a very rapid rate, he was still behind many of his prospect peers in the 2013 class. As a result, his raw power didn't translate to game swings. But given his background, that shouldn't have come as a surprise.

David Rawnsley touched on this topic in his Draft Focus article on Williams during the spring of 2013:

> How to hit for power is often the last skill that hitters learn. If you watch Williams hit in games and don't see it, don't be disappointed. It's there. Be patient. Appreciate what you are seeing now.

The Diamondbacks were patient, and they waited until the second round of the draft that year before snagging him with the 52nd overall pick. They were able to cash him in as a valuable trade chip last November after he continued his rapid development trajectory in the low levels of the minors. And if that development continues, he will be a very valuable player in the modern game in which power is scarce. —Todd Gold

Toronto Blue Jays

No new reports are provided for the Toronto Blue Jays top prospects this year. See Futures Guide 2014 *for prospect reports on Blue Jays top prospects Aaron Sanchez and Daniel Norris, as well as others.*

New York Yankees

Ian Clarkin – LHP

Ian Clarkin, a product of San Diego and a participant in the 2012 Perfect Game All-American Classic, was well known to scouts from an early age. While he was always on the radar as a prominent prospect, there was a wide range of opinions on his future potential.

The single most important factor in evaluating a teenage pitching prospect is the arm action. Everything else about a pitcher can be changed and improved, but arm action is not only the most important indicator of future potential, it is also the most difficult to change. The scouts who saw the good in Clarkin pointed to his arm action as what they liked most.

He had good velocity on his fastball for his age, though he wasn't elite in terms of peak fastball velocity. He steadily marched from the mid-80s to the low-90s during his high school career, which put him near the top of the class's left-handers. But an indicator that scouts often look to in order to predict fastball velocity increases is curveball spin, and Clarkin's curveball didn't quite meet the quality of his fastball and changeup during his underclass years, causing some to doubt his projection.

It is uncommon for a prominent pitching prospect to make a dramatic improvement in their breaking ball from their junior to senior year. Typically the pitchers who feature a plus curveball have shown the ability to spin the ball well from an early age, but Clarkin proved to be the exception and watched his curve jump a level in his final college season. In doing so, Clarkin answered his biggest question mark and put himself into the conversation as a first rounder. During the spring of his senior year at Madison High School in San Diego, his curveball showed sharpness and depth in the upper-70s and was arguably his best pitch.

All of this led to his being drafted in the first round by the Yankees, the third of three first-round picks they made that year, as the 33rd-overall selection. —Todd Gold

Rob Refsnyder – 2B/OF

Refsnyder's bat has carried him for quite a few years. As the 293rd ranked high school prospect in the class of 2009, his other tools didn't quite stack up with his bat, making him somewhat of a fringe player when it came to finding a set position for him to play. His fastest time in the 60-yard dash was 7.09 seconds and his best throw from across the infield was clocked at 85 mph.

Here is his report from the 2007 Sunshine West Showcase:

> Refsnyder has a lean and athletic frame with lively actions ... has nice footwork in the middle of the diamond moving very well allowing him to make all the plays. He also has very soft and sure hands ... Refsnyder uses a simple swing with a line-drive swing plane to make consistent contact. He stays balanced throughout his swing, and he keeps his hands inside the ball. Refsnyder tracks pitches well and keeps his hands back, allowing him to stay on the breaking ball well.

Refsnyder ended up at the University of Arizona and continued to show well at the plate. He used a big junior season to help propel the Wildcats to a College World Series championship in 2012 and was named a College All-American because of it. The summer before he was listed as the 39th prospect that played on the Cape, and leading up to the 2012 draft was ranked as Perfect Game's 177th best draft-eligible prospect.

Here is his predraft report:

> The 6-foot-1, 205-pound Refsnyder is the type of ballplayer scouts may need to see over the course of several games to truly appreciate his array of skills. He lacks flair in his approach to the game and none of his tools jump out as a matter of routine, but Refsnyder is a solid all-around talent who has juice in his bat (.320-6-55 in 2011, .375-4-39 in 2012 through games of mid-April) ... More than anything, scouts would like to see more speed and/or power out of Refsnyder, but his running times are often compromised by

his penchant for getting bad jumps out of the batter's box and his power is mitigated by his team playing in huge new home ballpark.

The overall report on Refsnyder remained the same; he was labeled as somewhat of an outfield 'tweener for not having the ideal power production of a corner outfielder and lacking the straight-line speed to play center. That said, he routinely quieted those concerns by hitting at every level he had played at prior to being drafted in the fifth round by the Yankees in the 2012 draft. —*Patrick Ebert*

Baltimore Orioles

Hunter Harvey – RHP

Harvey is the son of two-time All-Star, right-handed pitcher Bryan Harvey, but the Harvey family baseball background goes far deeper than just father and son. Bryan Harvey's late father, Stan, is regarded as one of the greatest hitters in softball history and was inducted into the ASA Hall of Fame in 1996. Bryan only played one year at UNC-Wilmington before returning home to work and play locally before being signed as an undrafted free agent and moving on to an unlikely MLB career. Hunter's brother, Kris, also played professionally for eight years, the first three years as an outfielder before switching to the mound and reaching Double-A.

Perhaps because of the family's baseball background, Hunter Harvey essentially disregarded the standard summer/fall circuit, playing for his local American Legion team, and very rarely traveled outside of North Carolina. Those connections made his name well circulated in the scouting community but mostly just as word of mouth that Bryan Harvey had a son who was very talented.

The only national level event Harvey ever threw at was the 2012 East Coast Professional Showcase. He had a very long and loose build at 6-foot-3, 175 pounds and a smooth delivery with a slight pause and gather at the top. His arm was fast and fluid, and it was immediately obvious that he was a high-ceiling talent. Harvey's fastball worked between 90 and 94 mph in that outing, with steep downhill angle from a high three-quarters arm slot. Harvey also threw a 75-mph curveball that had hard, tight spin, and a respectable upper-70s changeup.

Harvey was even better as a high school senior, going 8-0, 0.38 with 116 strikeouts and only 17 walks. He regularly topped out at 96-97 mph and also showed the Harvey family athleticism while playing shortstop. In a move that was unconventional–rare but totally in keeping with the Harveys' approach to the entire process with Hunter–he didn't commit to any college and clearly told everyone from teams to the media that he was going to sign and start his professional career immediately.

The Orioles selected him with the 22nd overall pick, just about where he was projected to be picked, and signed him for a $1,947,000 signing bonus. —*David Rawnsley*

Chance Sisco – C

A talented and versatile overall athlete, Sisco was ranked the 141st prospect in the high school class of 2013, and the 179th overall draft prospect. However, formerly a third baseman, Sisco saw his stock rise as the 2013 draft approached, as he took to catching fairly quickly, leading to his being taken in the second round of the draft that year.

Here's his predraft report:

> Another talented left-handed hitter with a commitment to Oregon, Sisco doesn't have quite the same offensive impact that Francis Christy (No. 38) does, but he is a better bet to stick behind the plate. He's somewhat new to catching and his footwork is still improving, but he has good catch-and-throw tools and the athleticism to eventually become a quality defensive catcher. He's also a talented defender at third, and his left-handed bat is plenty interesting in its own right. He's been a bit under the radar for most of his career, though that has begun to change over the past six months.

At 6-foot-1 and 180 pounds, Sisco wasn't overly physical, and no one tool stood out, but the sum of his parts created a well-rounded player. He positioned himself well, both behind the plate and at third base, and his arm played anywhere on the field.

Offensively, hitting left-handed worked in his favor, with a fluid swing and good extension. Sisco routinely showed the ability to stay inside the ball well while covering the plate, and his loose, strong wrists allowed him to hit the ball hard to the gaps with budding over-the-fence power. He made the most of his time spent at the one Perfect Game event he attended, the 2012 WWBA World Championship, where he was named to the All-Tournament team by going 6-for-10 with three doubles, a triple, and a home run as a member of the powerful Midland Redskins squad. —*Patrick Ebert*

Christian Walker – 1B

During his high school career Walker attended 13 Perfect Game events, including numerous showcases that help show the progression he made from his very first event as a 13-year-old in 2004 to his final event in the fall of 2008.

At the time Walker played third base and also spent time behind the plate, showing good speed (6.86 60-yard dash at the 2008 National Showcase) and overall athleticism for his 6-foot, 210-pound stature, but it was his bat that stood out the most.

After being drafted in the 49th round out of high school by the Dodgers, Walker attended the University of South Carolina, where he played in three consecutive College World Series championships. The Gamecocks won the first of those two in 2010 and 2011, with Walker being named to the College World Series All-Tournament Team all three years. He did so in 2011 while playing with a broken hamate bone in his left wrist, which caused him to miss the always-important summer travel season the year prior to his being eligible for the draft out of college.

He hit .336 with with 45 doubles and 30 home runs in those three years with the Gamecocks, proving time and time again that he was an offensive force to be reckoned with. During the 2011 College World Series, the first time the event was held at TD Ameritrade Park, Walker was the only player in attendance that had no problem consistently driving the ball to the park's deep and spacious outfield gaps.

After being ranked 88th in Perfect Game's high school class of 2009 rankings, he was ranked the 200th overall prospect leading up to the 2012 draft. Here's his predraft report:

> The 6-foot-1, 220-pound Walker has been a powerful presence in the middle of the order on consecutive national-championship teams. While he has very good plate discipline, sometimes he can be patient to a fault. As a first baseman, Walker is going to have to continue to hit at the

next level to move up the ladder, and most of his power at this point of his career is to the alleys.

Had Walker been 2-3 inches taller and hit left-handed, his draft stock may have been viewed significantly different, although the Orioles still liked his bat enough to take him in the fourth round with the 132nd overall pick of the 2012 draft. —*Patrick Ebert*

Josh Hart – OF

The prodigious East Cobb program has been a national powerhouse on the travel-ball circuit dating back to the late twentieth century. They have a rich tradition of winning, and Josh Hart enjoyed a healthy share of success as their leadoff hitter throughout his prep days.

His game was centered around speed and center-field defense. And while he wasn't quite a plus runner, his awareness of how to utilize that above-average speed allowed it to play up. While he wasn't an elite hitter, he combined good contact skills with a good approach that allowed him to utilize his speed well.

David Rawnsley commented on these attributes as part of Hart's Draft Focus article prior to the 2013 MLB draft:

> He's a speed player without blazing speed. He ran a 6.49 at the 2012 Perfect Game National, but that might have been an outlier for him. He ran 6.70 at the 2012 East Coast Pro and is usually around 4.15 down to first base from the left side. He's probably a 55 runner on the pro scale, with scouts that like him giving him a 60 and those who don't a 50 ... But Hart plays so much faster than his stopwatch times that it makes those numbers irrelevant.

As a result of his skill set there was a wide range of opinions on Hart among evaluators. Those that didn't think his speed-oriented game would have the same level of impact at the highest level had only lukewarm interest. But given the number of games that scouts saw him play during his East Cobb career and at talent-rich Parkview High School in suburban Atlanta, there were many who appreciated the nuanced ability he displayed in every phase of the game. He was an exceptional basestealer who read pitchers' moves very well for his age and wreaked havoc on the bases as a result.

Hart also made good decisions on the bases and showed steady development both at the plate and in center field. It all added up for some evaluators and as a result he was expected to be a top-50 pick in the 2013 draft, which he was. —*Todd Gold*

AL Central

Minnesota Twins

Kohl Stewart – RHP

Kohl Stewart's baseball career took off, not surprisingly, when he stopped playing football.

The Houston area native was best known as a prep high school quarterback at St. Pius X High School. He threw for 3,167 yards and 30 touchdowns as a junior and committed to play quarterback for Texas A&M. The thought of playing quarterback for the Aggies in 2012 was as good as it got. Their previous quarterback, Ryan Tannehill, had graduated to the Miami Dolphins. Their present quarterback was Johnny Manziel. They were moving to the all-hallowed SEC. That was heady stuff.

Stewart hadn't been seen much outside of the Houston area when he went to the 2012 PG National Showcase in Minnesota.

After throwing what PG's Ben Ford described as the best bullpen he'd ever seen a high school pitcher throw, Stewart's back tightened up and he was unable to take the Metrodome mound. He was able to recover from that mild setback and make a number of national appearances late in the summer, including the 2012 PG All-American Classic. Stewart would regularly top out at 94-95 mph at these events and flash his power mid-80s slider, although he tended to overthrow this pitch at times.

Stewart was enjoying another very successful football season in the fall of his senior year, throwing for 2,560 yards, 28 touchdowns, and adding another 483 yards on the ground before his season ended in early November when he landed awkwardly on his right shoulder after being tackled. There was significant concern in the scouting community, along with an overabundance of Texas-sized rumors, about Stewart's health as the baseball season started.

Stewart eased into the season slowly but ended up throwing so well and being so dominant that the shoulder injury became deep background by draft time. Stewart ended up posting a 5-1 record and a 0.18 ERA, allowing only one earned run and 13 hits in 40 innings while striking out 59 hitters. Stewart also hit .384-10-34 for good measure to remind scouts of his overall athletic ability. His stuff was consistent, with regular mid-90s velocity and his signature slider showing big depth to go along with its knee-buckling power. There was no doubt that Stewart was going to be a top-10 selection and with very little discussion about his potential football career, either.

The Twins grabbed him with the fourth overall pick, making him the first high school player selected, one pick ahead of Clint Frazier and the Indians. Stewart agreed to a $4,544,000 signing bonus almost immediately. —*David Rawnsley*

Stephen Gonsalves – LHP

Stephen Gonsalves' success in pro ball thus far is a testament to the often forgotten and nearly impossible-to-measure role of a team's minor-league coaches in his development.

A native of San Diego, Gonsalves was a well-known player nationally by the time he was a sophomore and was a highly ranked player from the first time the Perfect Game class of 2013 rankings were posted. He grew to his full 6-foot-5 height early and was always superbly coordinated. In fact, he was considered almost as much of a position prospect as a pitching prospect at one point, even playing as an outfielder at Cathedral Catholic, one of the top high school programs in the country, as a freshman.

But Gonsalves' ticket to the next level was his left arm, and velocity always came easily for him. He hit 90 mph for the first time at a Perfect Game event at the Sunshine West Showcase at the end of his sophomore year. With his athleticism, silky smooth arm action, and prototypical pitcher's build, the word "projectable" followed Gonsalves around like the number on the back of his uniform jersey.

Gonsalves backed it up on the mound as well, going 9-0, 1.03 for Cathedral Catholic as a sophomore and 10-0, 1.73 as a junior. He was frequently talked about as a potential first rounder when his draft year came around.

However, one thing was becoming increasingly worrisome to those who had tracked Gonsalves from early in his career. He really struggled throwing a curveball and it was getting worse, not better. He slowed his body significantly and had an early release on it that is universally known in the scouting world as "casting" the ball. On a pro grading scale it was a 20 pitch. The most worrisome aspect was that Gonsalves should have had at least a decent curveball; he was athletic, he played for top programs with well-respected coaches and it wasn't as if he was afraid to use the pitch—he probably threw it too often.

During his senior year Gonsalves and the entire Cathedral Catholic team struggled. Pegged by some as the top team in the country and featuring three PG All-Americans on its pitching staff in Gonsalves, junior Brady Aiken, and sophomore Drew Finley, the team finished 20-13. Gonsalves went 6-2, 2.19 with mediocre ratios compared to his previous two seasons. His draft stock was plummeting and it looked like the University of San Diego staff would get a chance at fixing his curveball before professional ball.

The Twins took a shot at buying low on Gonsalves and picked him in the fourth round, eventually signing him to a $700,000 bonus.

This scout had seen Gonsalves pitch at least six times as a high schooler. I ran into him by coincidence on a back field at the Red Sox Complex during the 2013 WWBA Underclass World Championship, where the Twins and Red Sox were playing an Instructional League game. I couldn't believe the difference in Gonsalves' curveball. Instead of being in the upper-60s, it was mid-70s and had some hair on it. If Gonsalves had thrown that pitch in high school, he would have been a lock-down first rounder. The Twins pitching coaches had done their job and done it very well. —*David Rawnsley*

Chicago White Sox

Chris Beck – RHP

Chris Beck's peak velocity at a Perfect Game event occurred the summer before his senior year, pitching for the powerful Georgia-based Team Elite program at the 2008 17u WWBA National Championship. There the projectable 6-foot-3, 190-pound right-hander worked at 82-88 mph, but the ease with which he threw and potential for additional velocity as he gained more strength to his frame were evident.

Like so many pitchers who blossom while in college, it was near impossible to project just how far the strength gains would allow Beck to improve. His talent was evident enough in high school for him to be ranked 326th in the 2009 class, but his game elevated to a much higher level at Georgia Southern.

Beck's game took off during his sophomore year in college and took another step forward during the following summer while playing on the Cape. He entered his junior year as a likely first-round pick, although he didn't carry the success from the previous year over. Beck was still good enough to be ranked the 41st overall prospect leading up to the 2012 draft.

Here's his predraft report from Allan Simpson:

> Beck's raw stuff has been consistent with where it was last spring, when he went 9-5, 3.23 with a Southern Conference-high 109 strikeouts in 103 innings, but it has not been as electric as it was last summer in the Cape Cod League (3-2, 2.12, 51 IP/41 SO), when he surged to prominence as one of the top arms in the 2012 college class by featuring three average to above-average major-league pitches in a 94-96 mph fastball, 80-83 mph slurve-like breaking ball, and 84-mph straight change. This spring Beck's fastball has been consistently 91-94 mph leading to a 4-4, 3.82 record and a 18-87 walk-to-strikeout ratio. Beck has altered his delivery to more of an overhanded slot, which may have led to the slight drop in velocity. Beck's slider has still been a solid pitch at 82-84 mph when he gets on top of it and

creates two-plane break, and he continues to throw a solid changeup.

Beck played alongside Victor Roache in college, giving Georgia Southern a rare dynamic duo for scouts to follow during the spring of 2012. Although Roche's junior season was cut short due to a broken wrist, he still was drafted late in the first round by the Brewers. Beck, who was also believed to be a potential first rounder, still went in the second round despite not being as sharp that spring. —*Patrick Ebert*

Micah Johnson – 2B

Prior to attending the University of Indiana, Johnson was lightly recruited out of an Indianapolis area high school. He showed the requisite tools to play at the Division I level, and received complimentary reports from the Perfect Game scouting staff at the tournament events he attended, playing mostly with the Lids Indiana Bulls travel program.

At the time Johnson hit from both sides of the plate, showing a line-drive swing path, quick hands, and good bat speed. His eventual defensive home was somewhat in question, but he was a good enough athlete to move between the infield and outfield relatively seamlessly.

It didn't take long for him to make an immediate impression in college, hitting .312 with 11 home runs for the Hoosiers his freshman year while playing third base, and .335 with three home runs playing second base as a sophomore. Johnson gave up switch-hitting to focus on his approach and swing from the left side of the plate, one more positive aspect of his prospective value.

Unfortunately, he never got into the full swing of things during his pivotal junior year due to an elbow injury that relegated him to serving as Indiana's designated hitter. Here's his predraft report from the spring of 2012:

> Johnson began the 2012 season as Indiana's DH, prior to having surgery on his throwing elbow in early March. He recently returned to action and understandably was a little rusty at the plate from his long layoff, and finished the regular season by hitting just .203-1-8 in 20 games. He may have to get on a hot streak at the plate in the Big Ten tournament in order to justify his current standing as a potential top-10-round pick. Nonetheless, Johnson's athleticism is readily evident with his quick-twitch actions and strong, well-proportioned build. He has good strength throughout his 5-foot-11, 190-pound frame, and his raw speed (6.65 second in the 60) is a critical part of his game ... While there is modest power in his quick left-handed swing, Johnson is at his best when driving balls gap-to-gap. He takes a lot of pitches, leading to his fair share of walks, but by working deep counts is also prone to higher strikeout totals than desired for a player with his skill set.

Johnson had made a strong enough impression during his first two years in college to be selected by the White Sox in the ninth round of the 2012 draft, which isn't too far off from where he was being projected to be taken prior to his injury. —*Patrick Ebert*

Jacob May – OF

Jacob May, the grandson of former big-league slugger Lee May, attended the 2009 PG National Showcase as a 5-foot-10, 175-pound switch-hitting shortstop. He earned a PG grade of 10 at the event, showing good foot speed by running the 60-yard dash in 6.69 seconds while throwing 85 mph from across the infield. His performance garnered this report:

Small but very athletic build, good present strength. Very good defensive actions, range to both sides, excellent body control, plus hands, 2B star potential at pro level, SS/2B at college level. Switch-hitter, similar approaches, better bat speed from left side, contact/high average approach, handles barrel well, will hit to all fields, line drive plane, hits with hands, 6.69 runner with quick first step. Could create some good draft interest, but maybe a lot more after college. He can really play!

That report proved to be a good prognostication for May's future career path, as he ended up attending Coastal Carolina after the Reds took him in the 39th round of the 2010 draft out of high school.

Players of May's size often have to prove themselves at every step along the way to get drafted where their talent, not their stature, may warrant. Although he hit only .206 his freshman year in college, he rebounded well the summer that followed in the Northwoods League, hitting .296 with 14 extra-base hits while proving to be a nuisance on the basepaths. That success carried over to his sophomore year, when he hit .306 with 27 stolen bases; the summer of 2012 on the Cape, where he was named the 25th best prospect on the circuit; and finally his junior year at Coastal Carolina, where he hit .324 while collecting 21 extra-base hits and 16 swipes.

Since he didn't possess the ideal arm strength for shortstop, it was determined that his speed and overall profile would fit best in the outfield as a prototypical top-of-the-order threat. Here is May's predraft report from 2013, when he was named the 183rd overall draft-eligible prospect:

Not only is May one of the fastest, most athletic players in the 2013 college class, but he looks as graceful as a deer running across a pasture at full gait ... Initially pegged as high as a possible second rounder, May now appears a better fit in rounds 4-6. The biggest area of concern to scouts remains his bat. A switch-hitter, May has a simple, contact-oriented approach at the plate, geared toward staying inside the ball and filling the gaps with line drives ... That said, May's game is predicated by his speed, as he has led Coastal in stolen bases the last two years.

His overall profile was similar to that of Phil Ervin, who May played with during the summer of 2011 in the Northwoods League. Ervin, considered the better, more consistent offensive threat, ended up being a first-round pick of the Reds in 2013. The White Sox, who always place a premium on dynamic, well-rounded athletes, plucked up May in the third round the same year. —Patrick Ebert

Cleveland Indians

Clint Frazier – OF

Frazier's ascension to the top high school position player selected in the 2013 draft came largely in two steps, with a mythical day attached prior to the draft.

Frazier was basically an unknown on the national stage when he came to the 2011 PG Junior National Showcase in Fort Myers, Florida, as a third baseman. He ran a 6.9 60-yard dash, threw 89 mph across the infield, and was probably the best hitter at the entire event during the games, although his funky hand-hitch swing did already raise some concerns. It was immediately obvious that not only did he have high-level tools, he also played the game with a passion and could perform up to those tools.

During the spring of his junior year, one started to hear rumblings about the kid in Georgia who was putting up video game numbers. That would have been Frazier, who hit 24 home runs that spring. So when he showed up at the 2012 PG National Showcase in Minnesota, Frazier was no longer a low-profile player.

He put on a show at the Metrodome that ranks with the best ever seen at a PG National. Frazier ran a 6.42 60-yard dash. Now an outfielder, he threw 98 mph during drills despite having a tender arm. He hit absolute bombs in batting practice, including one absurd one when he reached for an outside pitch and visibly only had one hand on the bat when he hooked it down the left field line. He played the game like his mane of red hair was on fire. PG's Todd Gold commented in his scout notes that, "He plays like he's in fast forward."

Despite his being a 6-foot, right-handed hitting outfielder with flawed hitting mechanics, it was easy to rank him as the top prospect in the country, although there was plenty of discussion and some anxiety about it. The tools, the personality, and the performance were just too loud.

Frazier went out the next spring and sealed the deal with a single performance. His March 12 matchup against fellow top prospect and 2012 PG All-American Austin Meadows was the most talked about and scouted game of the spring. Frazier hit two home runs, including an epic blast that was one of the longest observers had ever seen.

He went on to hit .485-17-45 his senior year and added 22 stolen bases. The Indians picked him with the fifth overall pick, giving him a $3.5 million signing bonus. —David Rawnsley

Tyler Naquin – OF

A talented two-way prospect in high school, Naquin's arm strength was evident early in his career. Playing for the Houston Heat travel ball club at the 2008 WWBA World Championship in Jupiter, Florida, Naquin dialed his fastball up to 92 mph from a low-effort delivery on the mound, working consistently in the 88-91 range while consistently making hard, line-drive contact. A high-energy player, Naquin got down the first-base line quickly, busting out of the box at contact, and was aggressive on the basepaths even though he wasn't a pure burner.

A 6-foot-1, 160-pound athlete, Naquin's talents were evident, but it was clear at the time that three years in college could go a long way for his prospective draft stock as he added strength and honed his left-handed swing, especially after he was drafted by the Orioles in the 33rd round of the 2009 draft.

That occurred at Texas A&M, although not initially, as he hit .244 as a freshman prior to his breakout sophomore campaign when he led the Big 12 with a .381 average and the entire nation in hits with 104. His numbers were nearly identical his junior year.

His overall profile was that of an outfield 'tweener. While he showed very good plate discipline and pitch-recognition skills, he never displayed the raw power potential to be an everyday fixture on an outfield corner. And while he showed good speed and instincts, center field wasn't a perfect fit either. For as good as he was as a hitter, his aforementioned arm strength remained his best pure tool, routinely showing off accurate, cannon-like throws from right field playing for the Aggies.

However, Naquin may have been ranked even higher than his PG predraft rank as the 20th overall prospect had he been the regular center fielder for Texas A&M. He played right field in college due to the presence of teammate Krey Bratsen, a more dynamic athlete who possessed true game-changing speed. Either way, Naquin's draft ranking was a good estimation for his eventual selection, as the Indians took him with the 15th overall pick in the 2013 draft when he was considered one of the safest bets to succeed at the professional level. —*Patrick Ebert*

Mitch Brown – RHP

Brown was a four-year veteran of Perfect Game events, pitching at 19 different tournaments and showcases starting with the 2009 WWBA National invitational. His notes from that event, where he topped out at 78 mph, read:

> Slender, athletic body, very young, smooth delivery, longer 2-piece arm action, sharp 11/5 CB, lands closed, across body, good shape on CB, can pitch a bit, has idea, body and arm project, throws easy, High 3/4.

Brown filled out to a strong 6-foot-2, 210 pounds over the next four years and saw his fastball grow into a 90-plus-mph pitch, but much of the rest of that initial scouting blueprint remained the same. He always had a long and fast arm action, he always had an advanced idea how to pitch despite his Minnesota roots, and he could always spin the ball.

The curveball was his out pitch early in his high school career, but he kept adding to his breaking-ball arsenal as he got older. Brown added a slider first, then eventually figured out how to throw a cutter off his fastball. He pitched at the 2012 PG Pitcher/Catcher Indoor Showcase prior to his senior high school season, and while he showed some understandable young confusion about his multiple breaking balls, there was no mistaking the quality. Brown's notes from that event, where he was 90-93 mph on his fastball, read:

> Mature well-proportioned build, good strength. On line hand drop delivery, fairly fast pace, quick easy arm, CB has hard tight spin, good life on Chg, very straight FB, will come inside with FB, H 3/4, throws downhill, more effort on CB than FB, good change mechanics/arm speed, tends to bury CB, works quickly, everything down in zone. Needs to ID breaking balls, threw 76 downer and 84 SL during warm-ups, 79 slurve and 88 cutter in games. Like the 76/84/88 progression and not the 79.

Brown was even better during the spring than he was on that cold, indoor February weekend. He was in the mid-90s right out of the gate and showed all the national-level scouts flocking to Minnesota the quality and variety of his breaking stuff.

One other aspect of Brown's overall résumé endeared him especially to the area scouts. Home visits are often the bane of the area scout's existence. The Brown family, although both parents are professionals and not farmers, live at the end of a series of dirt roads well outside of Rochester. Multiple area scouts told the story of visiting the Browns something like this: "That house is pretty much impossible to find; I think I drove past that last dirt road twice before finally convincing myself to try it. But once I got there, that might have been the nicest family I've ever visited." —*David Rawnsley*

Detroit Tigers

Buck Farmer – RHP

If it seemed to serious prospect fans as if George Runie "Buck" Farmer had been around forever when he made his MLB debut last summer, a scant 14 months after being signed out of Georgia Tech, there is good reason for it: He pretty much has.

Farmer made his debut with Perfect Game as a 15-year-old,

rising sophomore at the 2006 17u WWBA National Championship playing for the Ocee Stars. He was 6-foot-3, 190 pounds at that point and throwing in the mid-80s off the mound while gaining as much attention for his powerful left-handed bat. Farmer went on to become one of the better two-way performers in the high school and travel-ball circuits, including winning the MVP award for the East Cobb Yankees after they won the 2008 Connie Mack national championship. The hometown Braves picked him in the 46th round of the 2009 draft despite his commitment to Georgia Tech.

Farmer was a major contributor for four seasons at Georgia Tech, pitching out of the bullpen primarily as a freshman and as a weekend starter for his final three seasons. He went 8-4 with a 3.54 ERA and 115 strikeouts in 106 innings as a junior and was considered a potential high-round draft pick. However, Farmer slid in that 2012 draft, as clubs believed he wanted to return to Georgia Tech for his senior year, finally being picked by the Brewers with a 15th-round pick. He did return as a senior to post a 9-5, 2.78 record with 122 strikeouts in 113 innings.

Farmer's scouting reputation throughout his college career was much the same as it was when he was in high school. His fastball worked in the low-90s and would flash plus occasionally, as would his slider and changeup. But he didn't consistently show a plus pitch and depended as much on his durability (he's never had an injury concern or likely even missed a start) and his ability to pitch as his raw stuff. In scouts' eyes, Farmer was, and always had been, the consummate low-risk, back-of-the-rotation starter.

And that is what he is today, many years later.
—*David Rawnsley*

Kevin Ziomek – LHP

Vanderbilt recruits the Northeast as well as any other college, as left-handed pitcher Kevin Ziomek was a well-known talent coming out of high school. The Amherst, Mass. native was taken in the 2010 draft by the Diamondbacks in the 13th round, but as the 46th-best overall high school prospect in his class, he would have gone much higher if it weren't for his commitment to play for the Commodores.

Prior to attending college Ziomek worked comfortably in the upper-80s and frequently peaked at 91 mph while mixing in three quality off-speed pitches, with his power slider and advanced changeup standing out. He garnered a perfect PG grade of 10 at the 2009 National Showcase, and at 6-foot-2, 180 pounds, he offered a lean, projectable build with obvious potential gains in fastball velocity thanks to a fast, loose arm and fluid delivery.

Not surprisingly, Ziomek enjoyed immediate success during his freshman year at Vanderbilt as he was eased into SEC competition in a setup role out of the bullpen. However, he didn't enjoy the same success the summer that followed, and the same was true during his sophomore year. Ziomek rebounded well during his second stint on the Cape in 2012, leading to his breakout junior campaign.

Here's a part of Ziomek's predraft report in the spring of 2013 when he was ranked the 48th overall prospect:

> [Ziomek] was as dominant in his short stint as any pitcher on the Cape with the possible exception of Hyannis left-hander Sean Manaea, a top prospect for this year's draft, with his solid-average major league fastball, tight, downer breaking ball, and changeup all working in unison, all thrown with the same arm action. His changeup, in

particular, was outstanding and made his 91-93 mph fastball look even faster, and also enabled him to freeze hitters with his breaking ball. For the second straight year, Ziomek's performance in summer-league competition—good or bad—has largely carried over to the following spring, and he has gone a sparkling 9-2, 2.03 through his first 12 starts as Vanderbilt's Friday starter. In 89 innings, he has allowed just 53 hits, walked 29 and struck out 88—a significant upgrade from 2012. With a couple of minor exceptions when his velocity dipped, Ziomek has pitched every bit as impressively as a junior for the Commodores as he did in his five-game cameo on the Cape, with stuff and command to match. In the end, Ziomek has done pretty much everything this spring that he was supposed to do from the beginning of his career at Vanderbilt.

Ziomek's expected yet modest uptick in velocity, as well as his possessing one of the best changeups in the 2013 draft, led to his being selected by the Tigers in the second round with the 58th overall pick, which reflects his predraft ranking that year. —*Patrick Ebert*

Joe Jimenez – RHP

The thing that stands out immediately when you look at Jimenez and his top-10 prospect status with the Tigers is that he was signed as an undrafted free agent by the Tigers during the summer of 2013. One's reaction, without knowing the player's background, would be, "Wow, the Tigers did a great job of scouting there; they must have seen something that no one else did."

The Tigers obviously did do a good job, but it wasn't because Jimenez wasn't a well-known prospect. At draft time, Jimenez was the second-ranked prospect from Puerto Rico on the Perfect Game class of 2013 rankings behind PG All-American Jan Hernandez and was the 95th-ranked overall prospect in the entire class.

Multiple scouting industry contacts at the time, and media reports afterward, said that Jimenez, who was a very good student at Puerto Rico Baseball Academy and High School and had signed with Florida International, floated a large number as the bonus he needed to sign and didn't waver from that number through the draft. No team even ventured a mid-round or late-round pick on him, which in retrospect seems like 30 teams worth of mistakes, so he went completely undrafted and was thus a free agent when the draft ended.

Jimenez had made his big debut about 18 months prior to the draft when he pitched at the 2011 WWBA World Championship in Jupiter, Florida, for a Perfect Game team. He pitched in the 90-92 range at that heavily scouted event, although his big, strong body had some softness to it.

Over those 18 months, Jimenez did two things that made his prospect stock continue to rise. First, he worked on his conditioning and gradually turned some of that softness into mature muscle while maintaining the looseness and speed in his arm. Second, he developed a slider that was a legitimate second pitch to go with his steady low-90s fastball. Jimenez had started out throwing a soft, low-70s curveball that was strictly a get-me-over pitch that he commanded well, but that would be an easy target for barrels at the professional level.

Based on his build, his delivery while an amateur, and his pitches—Jimenez also threw a very serviceable changeup prior to signing—it seemed as if he would have a future as a starter. He's obviously blossomed thus far as a reliever, but maybe the

key part of the entire process was just the local Tigers scout sticking with the undrafted free agent and getting the deal done. —*David Rawnsley*

Kansas City Royals

Hunter Dozier – 3B

Like his fellow Royals' top prospects and first-round picks Kyle Zimmer and Sean Manaea, Dozier was an unheralded prospect out of high school who fell under the scouting radar and went to a less-than-prominent baseball school.

In Dozier's case, he attended Denton High School on the north side of the Dallas-Fort Worth Metroplex, where he was a three-year starter in baseball along with quarterbacking the football team. After breaking his collarbone his junior year he gave up football to concentrate on baseball. Dozier stood out as both a lanky middle infielder and as a right-handed pitcher on the baseball field. He only appeared in a couple of Perfect Game tournaments for the Dallas Tigers after his sophomore year and was listed at a slender 6-foot-3, 160 pounds. When he arrived at the Stephen F. Austin campus northeast of Houston for his freshman year, Dozier was listed at 6-foot-3, 195 pounds.

Dozier was a starter at shortstop for Stephen F. Austin from the beginning of his freshman year in 2011 and immediately stood out for his athleticism in the middle infield and for his right-handed power potential. Stephen F. Austin is usually not a homing beacon for scouts and cross-checkers, but they gave it plenty of attention in 2011 due to his teammate, outfielder Bryson Myles. Myles was eventually picked by the Indians in the sixth round and his presence helped put Dozier on the scouting map.

By Dozier's junior year, he had grown to 6-foot-4, 220 pounds. Although he still moved well at shortstop, scouts had already consigned him to third base at the professional level. What created the most interest was Dozier's power, as he hit .396-17-52 as a junior.

Most scouts and analysts believed Dozier to be a late first-round to early second-round pick leading up to the 2013 draft. The Royals, holding the eighth and 34th picks, didn't want to risk trying to let Dozier slide to their second pick. So they created and executed a plan to pick Dozier in the eighth slot while grabbing Manaea, a potential first overall pick prior to his injury-plagued junior season, with the 34th pick. Dozier signed almost immediately for a $2.2 million signing bonus, saving the Royals $937,800 on the assigned slot value that they then used to help sign Manaea. —*David Rawnsley*

Kyle Zimmer – RHP

Scouts often refer to a young pitcher who hasn't thrown much as having a fresh or low-mileage arm. It's almost always used as a positive term, translating to "he hasn't been abused or taught bad things yet."

It can also be a double-edged sword on occasion, as the Royals are finding out while trying to get Zimmer healthy enough to use his prodigious talent on the mound. And you won't find a top-prospect pitcher with much lower mileage on his arm than Zimmer.

Zimmer's high school baseball résumé at the end of his junior season at La Jolla High School consisted of one year of varsity play as a reserve position player, where he hit .191-1-2 in 47 at-bats, with no appearances on the mound. He blossomed as a third baseman as a senior, hitting .375-4-23, and was recruited by the University of San Francisco as a position player. Zimmer did pitch some as a senior, going 3-3, 4.69 and allowing 38 baserunnners in 22 innings.

Zimmer didn't get into a game as a freshman position player at USF his freshman year, but he did make five short-relief appearances on the mound totaling 5 1/3 innings (0-0, 8.44). He didn't become a full-time pitcher until his sophomore year, going 6-4, 3.73 in 91 innings for the Dons and helping them to an NCAA Regional berth. Still, Zimmer was a virtual unknown to scouts until he took the mound against UCLA's Gerrit Cole, the then-presumed first overall pick in the 2011 draft, in the first Regional game. With a capacity crowd watching, including plenty of scouts, Zimmer threw a complete game shutout to outduel Cole, striking out 11 Bruins with the combination of a 92-94 mph fastball and a plus curveball. Right there he went from an unknown to a potential first-round pick in nine innings.

The kind of stuff and the command that Zimmer surprisingly had despite his lack of experience continued through the summer in the Cape Cod League and through his junior year, where he went 5-3, 2.85 in 13 starts and 88 innings, striking out 107 hitters while only walking 17. He did miss a couple of late-season starts with a hamstring injury, which complicated his draft status a bit, as teams couldn't get that valuable final look at him before the draft.

The Royals jumped on Zimmer right away, grabbing him with the fifth overall pick, and signed him quickly with a $3 million signing bonus. —*David Rawnsley*

AL West

Texas Rangers

Alex Gonzalez – RHP

The Orioles selected and signed a number of late-round high school pitchers in the 2009-2011 period that were projectable physically and polished on the mound. A couple of them appear on their present top prospect list and could make their MLB debuts this year, including left-hander Tim Berry and right-hander Zach Davies.

The one that got away was Gonzalez, who the Orioles failed to sign after making him their 11th-round pick out of Boca Raton (Florida) High School in 2010.

In high school, Gonzalez was a 6-foot-3, 185 pounder who generally sat in the 86-88 mph range and occasionally touched a bit higher. His best pitch was a slurve-type curveball that often got up into the 75-77 mph area with hard biting action. Notes in the PG database indicate that Gonzalez threw his curveball perhaps too much but that he also showed lots of life on his fastball and had the present ability to work the outside corner to both right- and left-handed hitters.

Two things happened to Gonzalez while he attended Oral Roberts. The first was that Gonzalez got stronger and fulfilled his physical projection, thus seeing his fastball move from the upper-80s to the low-90s, usually working in the 91-93 mph range. The second was that Oral Roberts coach Rob Walton taught Gonzalez how to throw a cutter, and Gonzalez took to it like a natural, especially in the rare ability to throw it with pretty much the same velocity as his normal four-seam fastball.

Those two things combined enabled Gonzalez to post a 9-5, 1.83 mark as a junior in 2013, including 126 strikeouts and only 27 walks in 113 innings, and move himself into a solid first-round position. The Rangers took him with the 23rd overall pick.

Gonzalez is known throughout the baseball world, of course,

as "Chi Chi." When people of my generation think of that name, many of us think of the charismatic golfer Chi Chi Rodriguez and that is the first thing one sees when one types "Chi Chi" into a search engine. According to published reports, Gonzalez got the nickname from his grandfather, who called one of his sisters Nina, the other Nene, and Alex "Chi Chi." Perhaps in another 10 years, the first Chi Chi we'll think about and find on the Internet is the Rangers right-hander. —*David Rawnsley*

Lewis Brinson – OF

The 2012 draft class was loaded with high school outfielders and Brinson was the sixth high school outfielder taken despite being the 29th overall pick. He was preceded by Byron Buxton (second overall), Alberto Almora (sixth), David Dahl (10th), Courtney Hawkins (13th), and D.J. Davis (17th). But at draft time, the consensus was that of those half dozen young outfielders, only Buxton had a higher ceiling athletically than Brinson.

Brinson was a fun athlete to watch play, with a loose 6-foot-4, 180-pound build that was both graceful and quick-twitch. He also played the game happy and loose and outwardly enjoyed himself on the baseball field.

His jumps and routes in the outfield were raw at that point, but his high-end speed made anything hit to the middle of the field within his range. He ran a 6.39 at the Florida State High School All-Star game in Sebring two weeks prior to the draft, which certainly got everyone's attention.

Brinson's swing generated surprising power for such an angular athlete. He loaded his hands deep with somewhat of an arm-bar approach and had a big stride and shift into contact. But the raw bat speed was definitely there. A sentence in PG's predraft report on Brinson reads, "catching up to high-velocity fastballs will not be an issue with Brinson based on what he has shown thus far."

The issue virtually every scout acknowledged going into the draft was that Brinson was a four-tool player, with a big question mark on the hit tool. He could get very long at times, and the big shift into contact left him off balance as well. Brinson did hit .394-4-21 as a senior at Coral Springs High School but continued to show some swing-and-miss in his approach. —*David Rawnsley*

Travis Demeritte – 3B

Demeritte was a mainstay for the East Cobb Braves during his high school career and played in two dozen Perfect Game events, including the 2012 PG All-American Classic, and finished his high school career ranked no. 19 in the 2013 class rankings. It would be difficult to accurately count how many times this scout has seen Demeritte play in both tournament and showcase settings.

Two things stand out when looking back at Demeritte's pre-professional scouting résumé with what he's accomplished with the Rangers since being their first-round pick (30th overall) in 2013.

First, while Demeritte played shortstop and pitched at Winder-Barrow High School in Georgia, he only played third base (along with an occasional trip to the mound, where he was regularly 89-91 mph) for the Braves. And he was simply outstanding defensively, as good a defensive third baseman as one will find at that level. Demeritte showed all the ingredients of a potential Gold Glove defender at third–the catlike quickness, the soft hands, and the accurate cannon arm. He actually played third base like a shortstop, setting up deeper than the usual third baseman, and consistently made far-ranging plays that showed off his athletic gifts on defense.

As a professional, Demeritte has played 92 games at second base, 26 games at third base, and 25 games at shortstop. It goes without saying that if his offensive potential comes together he has more value in the middle infield. But he could be an impactful defensive third baseman as well.

Offensively, it should surprise no one who watched him extensively as an amateur that he has produced both power and copious strikeout totals. Demeritte hit from an open right-handed stance that he never closed about 90 percent of the time I saw him over a three-year period. He hunted inside fastballs and hanging breaking balls and crushed them. But because he was so open, not only with his feet but with his front side, he was easy prey to a pitcher who could spot his fastball outside and his breaking ball or changeup off the outside corner. He didn't have the balance or the reach to cover that part of the zone.

There was one event, the 2012 17u PG World Series, when Demeritte noticeably made the adjustment and closed off his stance, and he absolutely raked at that event. —David Rawnsley

Seattle Mariners

D.J. Peterson – 1B/3B

A handful of impressive hitters have emerged from the Southwest part of the nation in recent years, including Peterson, his younger brother Dustin (a second-round pick of the Padres in 2013), Boston Red Sox farmhand Blake Swihart, and soon-to-be professional hitter Alex Bregman, one of college baseball's biggest bats.

While Dustin Peterson, Swihart, and Bregman were all well-known and premium talents coming out of high school, D.J. Peterson fell to the 33rd round of the draft, getting a token selection by the Seattle Mariners in the 2010 draft before heading to play at the University of New Mexico.

In college Peterson developed into one of the most lethal bats eligible for the 2013 draft, with the ability to hit for both average and power while displaying a keen eye at the plate. It remained unclear whether he would be able to stay at third base long term, and others questioned the historical success of right-handed hitting power hitters coming out of college.

Here's his predraft report from 2013, when he was ranked the 13th overall draft-eligible player:

> [Peterson] hit a robust .419-17-78 (33 BB/29 SO) as a sophomore for the Lobos, led USA Baseball's college-national team in homers last summer and has continued to swing the bat at a fast clip this spring, as his .406 average, 20 doubles, 13 homers, and 53 RBI (as of late April) are all club-leading figures by wide margins. Peterson has a smooth, balanced, disciplined swing that transitions easily to wood and enables him to generate easy raw power. He has shown no difficulty turning around high-velocity fastballs or recognizing the best breaking stuff in the college game. He also has a very mature approach to hitting and has become very adept at grinding out at-bats in his quest to find a pitch he can drive, or simply draw a walk. The remainder of Peterson's tools aren't as strong, but he's a better runner underway than he is generally given credit for. Defensively, he has adequate actions and a playable arm at third, but his hands and footwork are a little short and he may not be long for that position, with first base or an outfield corner likely destinations. Where Peterson might end up in the field is almost incidental to where he might be drafted, as teams know they are buying an advanced bat with significant home-run potential.

As part of his Draft Focus report that same spring, Frankie Piliere compared Peterson's overall profile to that of Paul Konerko, an upside the Mariners had in mind when they picked him yet again, this time with the 12th overall selection, in the 2013 draft. —Patrick Ebert

Austin Wilson – OF

Wilson both looked and acted the part of the high-ceiling prospect at Harvard-Westlake High School in Los Angeles. He was listed at 6-foot-4, 200 pounds, and notes from the 2009 PG National Showcase reference "his Andre Dawson-look with the tapered waist, but the overall frame to hold 230 pounds in the future easily."

His tools spoke just as loudly, especially when it came to power tools. When Wilson squared up a ball, it exploded with that sound one rarely hears. He didn't have much lift in his swing, but often just overpowered the ball with strength and leverage at contact. Wilson's arm strength was also a power tool; he registered 98 mph from the outfield at that National Showcase with a long and fast, low-effort release. On top of it, Wilson also regularly ran in the 6.7s in the 60-yard dash.

Based on those tools, it was pretty clear that Wilson, who was also a Perfect Game All-American, was a likely first-round draft pick in 2010. But that wasn't going to happen without a team taking a big risk. Wilson's mother and father had undergraduate degrees from MIT and Stanford, respectively, and both had MBAs from Harvard. Education was paramount in the Wilson household and Austin was signed with Stanford. The Cardinals picked him in the 12th round and made a hard run at him to no avail.

Wilson had a solid three-year career at Stanford, hitting .311-5-30 as a freshman, .285-10-51 as a sophomore, and .288-5-26 as junior despite missing most of the first half of the season with an elbow injury.

That elbow injury and Wilson's drop in performance did impact his draft status a bit, leaving him still available for the Mariners with the 49th overall pick. Wilson signed for a $1.7 million bonus, $590,000 over the MLB recommendation for that slot.

It is worth noting that despite signing after his junior season at Stanford, Wilson did manage to graduate on time in four years, even getting to wear the cap and gown at the ceremony when it coincided with the Midwest League All-Star break last June. —David Rawnsley

Oakland Athletics

Matt Olson – 1B

That Olson has been a high-level performer for the A's from the start of his professional career should not come as a surprise, as that is precisely what he was at Parkview High School in North Atlanta. Olson led Parkview to two straight Georgia Class 5A titles as a two-way standout, hitting .407-11-51 as a senior and going 12-1, 1.64 on the mound.

What was actually a bit surprising was that the A's ventured the 47th overall pick in the 2012 draft on Olson, as he generally wasn't considered quite that level of prospect by the scouting community as a whole. A large part of that was Olson's profile. He was a 7.6 runner in the 60-yard dash, although he was agile and athletic around the bag on defense. And though he was able to produce steady upper-80s fastballs on the mound, his overall profile fit best at first base. In other words, you were betting on the bat and strictly the bat. Olson, who was an excellent student, also had a ride to Vanderbilt and the potential to be a two-way star at that top program.

The key to his being drafted that high, of course, was his performance. Olson was outstanding at the final national event he played the previous summer, wearing the gaps out at the 2011 East Coast Professional Showcase in front of a big crowd of scouting directors and cross-checkers. And as Oakland scouting director Eric Kubota noted in articles written immediately after the 2012 draft, Olson hit home runs off both Lucas Sims (the 21st overall pick) and Duane Underwood (67th) that spring in what were undoubtedly very heavily scouted matchups.

The moral of the story is that if you are going to bet big on a bat, you'd better not be projecting the ability to perform. That has to be a present skill. —*David Rawnsley*

Chad Pinder – 2B/3B

Pinder enjoyed a successful tour playing in Perfect Game-based tournament events during his high school career, leading to his being ranked 176th in the high school class of 2010. At 6-foot, 170 pounds, he wasn't overly physical, but was a gamer that always seemed to come through when his team needed him to, whether it be at the plate, on the basepaths, or defensively in the infield.

Here's a collection of some of the notes from PG's database from those events:

> Made hard contact, good hands ... quick, long stride, quick out of box, gets on base, avg power ... good approach, great top hand, rotational backside hitter, avg to good (bat speed) ... tall, narrow stance, toe-tap trigger, flat path, slight bat wrap.

At Virginia Tech, Pinder carried a similar profile leading all the way up to 2013, when the Athletics took him in the supplemental second round of the draft, with the usual "low-ceiling, high-floor" description accompanying his draft report.

So while he did pretty much everything well, nothing really stood out aside from the sum of his parts. He hit for a high average, including during his time spent in both the Coastal Plain and Cape Cod summer collegiate leagues swinging a wood bat. However, he didn't project for a ton of over-the-fence power, with most of his extra-base hits going to the alleys. While he was a versatile overall athlete, he lacked the ideal range for shortstop, although he profiled very well defensively at third base. He wasn't a burner, but he ran the bases well and showed an overall high baseball IQ.

Such players, or infield 'tweeners, seem destined for second base, and that's exactly where his value was deemed the highest coming out of college, when he was ranked the 53rd best draft-eligible player as the 2013 draft approached. —*Patrick Ebert*

Houston Astros

Brett Phillips – OF

The fact that Phillips was a sixth-round draft pick out of high school is notable because entering 2013 he wasn't even on the scouting radar. Although he'd gained enough attention to sign with North Carolina State, Phillips wasn't ranked in the Perfect Game top 500. He'd never appeared in a national-level showcase or played at the WWBA World Championship in Jupiter, and even took off most of his summer before his senior year from any baseball activities.

That fall, on a whim, Phillips decided to try to play high school football despite not having played yet in high school. He ended up playing in the Pinellas County All-Star game following the season. There is a video online (http://youtu.be/fOfyddYLox0) that is pretty instructive when you look at Phillips as an athlete. Just in the first three minutes there are highlights of him playing running back, wide receiver, quarterback, linebacker, and safety; blocking a kick; and kicking an extra point. It's impressive to watch, especially in the context of his having never played at that level before.

So when Phillips came to the PG World Showcase in Fort Myers, Florida, the first weekend in January, 2013, he not only wasn't on the radar, he hadn't played any real baseball in six to seven months.

All Phillips did there was light it up and immediately put his name on scouts' "must-see" list. He threw 96 mph, ran a 6.7 60-yard dash, and lined the ball all over the field with a short and strong left-handed swing. Here's his report from that event:

> Medium athletic build, some present strength. Excellent run/throw tools, 6.76 in the 60. 96 mph OF arm strength with on line carry, moves to the ball well, good overall actions. Left-handed hitter, spread stance, gets hands back, simple load and swing mechanics, hits off hard front side, short quick stroke, squares up well, line drive contact all fields, has some bat speed and gap power. High-energy player, defense really stands out and has a chance with the bat.

Getting a talent like Phillips for a sixth-round pick and a $300,000 signing bonus is quite a scouting coup. The Astros surely knew about the aptitude and athletic ability that Phillips showed with his football experiment as a senior, and those traits have served him well thus far in his baseball career. —*David Rawnsley*

Colin Moran – 3B

Pure hitter is a term reserved for players such as Colin Moran. You don't necessarily know, or even care, what else they may provide down the road, but you know they're going to hold their own and hit at the highest of levels.

Moran's talents were readily evident in high school, earning him a commitment to Division I college powerhouse North Carolina while being ranked among the top 500 players in the high school class of 2010. At an extremely slender 6-foot-4, 175 pounds, he made a positive impression at Perfect Game's 2009 Sunshine Northeast Showcase, garnering a PG grade of 9.0 and this report:

> Moran has a thin athletic build, this from a simple stance, smooth swing, stays inside baseball, gets barrel to baseball, future power, stays on pitch, good opposite approach, very smooth swing, sound defensive actions, arm works well.

The nephew of former big-leaguer B.J. Surhoff, Moran followed in his uncle's footsteps at North Carolina. Like Surhoff and another former Tar Heel, Dustin Ackley, Moran was a left-handed hitter who quickly proved he could hit at the college level, hitting .335 his freshman year, .365 as a sophomore, and .345 as a junior. His power production improved each season as well, as he added 40 pounds to his previously lanky frame, socking 13 home runs while driving in 91 runs prior to being taken with the sixth overall pick in the 2013 draft by the Miami Marlins.

However, observers questioned how well the bat, and more importantly, his power would translate to the next level playing a traditional run-producing position. He had the hand quickness, discipline, and bat speed to catch up with high-quality stuff, but his swing path and overall approach were geared more toward making hard contact to all parts of the field. His long-term ability to stick at the hot corner also was in question, but in the end, his left-handed swing and repeated production was too great to ignore. —*Patrick Ebert*

Los Angeles Angels

Nick Tropeano – RHP

Tropeano was a primary infielder in high school who also pitched, with a peak velocity of 87 mph at a Perfect Game event. That occurred the summer before his senior year in high school at the 2007 17u WWBA National Championship while playing for the Long Island Titans.

Although he wasn't ranked among the top 500 prospects coming out of high school, in PG's database his size, arm strength, and potential for more were noted. Here is a snippet of those notes:

> Looks good on mound, good live arm, IF arm action, tall and lanky build, looks better at RHP than at SS ... good body, quick arm, good velo projection, mid 3/4, balanced delivery, will add velo, more a thrower now than pitcher, very effective with good upside, held velo for 4 IP.

Tropeano continued his baseball career and honed his skills while playing at Stony Brook. Although his velocity did increase, peaking in the 90-91 range while mostly working in the mid- to upper-80s, he never was a flamethrower at the college level. He did possess one of the best changeups in the college game and used that pitch to tie for the Cape Cod League lead in strikeouts during the summer of 2010. Tropeano also provided 6 1/3 no-hit innings to lead Cotuit to the Cape title that same summer.

The following spring Tropeano went 12-1 with a 1.84 ERA for Stony Brook, which finished the year 42-14, and although his stuff alone didn't warrant an early selection, his command and repeated performance-based success led to him being drafted by the Astros in the fifth round of the 2011 draft. —*Patrick Ebert*

Cam Bedrosian – RHP

The son of 14-year big-league relief pitcher and 1987 National League Cy Young Award winner Steve Bedrosian, Cam Bedrosian had a repertoire similar to that of his father's while in high school growing up in Georgia, including a low- to mid-90s fastball and hammer curve.

The younger Bedrosian's career came to a peak during the summer of 2009 when he touched 95 mph with his fastball numerous times, including his time spent on the summer tournament circuit with the Homeplate Chilidogs as well as his appearance at the PG All-American Classic, where he was named the starter of the East squad.

Here's the report I wrote about Bedrosian after that appearance:

> The son of former big-league closer Steve Bedrosian took the mound for the East team opposite [Jameson] Taillon to start the game. He gave up a couple of runs on an odd play that involved a wild pitch, but overall his stuff looked sharp. He ran his fastball up to 95, but looked better pitching in the 90-91 range where his fastball appeared to have better, natural sinking movement. His curveball is a true hammer, and with a somewhat shorter, stockier build he reminded me a lot of Ben Sheets given his size and stuff. Bedrosian clearly has the big league aptitude, and is also hailed for his character off the field.

His size at 6-foot, 195 pounds, as noted in the report above, did draw the usual concerns that come with shorter right-handed pitchers, including his long-term durability in a starting role. Bedrosian had a strong enough repertoire to start, as he also threw a solid changeup, and he was ranked the 28th overall player in his class leading up to the 2010 draft.

Bedrosian was one of five first-round picks the Angels made that year–a year after their draft boon that landed them Mike Trout–with all five of them hailing from the high school ranks. —*Patrick Ebert* ∎

Friends Don't Let Friends Draft Mid-Rotation Prospects

by Ben Carsley

Prospects, more often than not, will break your heart. It's a concept that Baseball Prospectus has hammered home for many a year, simultaneously selling you on the dreams of young players while warning you that history suggests you're heading for disappointment.

This is true of all prospects, of course. From the "safest" top-10 shortstops to the 16-year-old flamethrowers who catch our attention as international signees, the bust rate among prospects is extraordinarily high. Fantasy owners know this, yet the allure of such players is irresistible, and keeper and dynasty leagues seem to be more popular than ever.

Yet there is one type of prospect fantasy owners should be especially leery of, a class of prospect that lures owners in with a false sense of security, only to let them down not by flaming out spectacularly, but by slowly fading: mid-rotation starters.

They seem innocent enough, what with their proximity to the majors and their relatively high floors. In fact, you might even convince yourself that trading upside for probability is the responsible thing to do in deeper leagues, leaving flashier players to greedier owners.

It's a sound strategy in theory, but in practice, it doesn't work. As the past few years have shown, mid-rotation starters offer little upside and often fail to meet even their modest projections. They litter top-100 lists because in real life, an average starter who can eat up 200 innings is quite valuable. But for fantasy purposes, they truly represent fool's gold.

Before you let history repeat itself in your next dynasty draft, take a look at the last five seasons alone.

Between 2009 and 2013, there were a total of 52 players who ranked on the Baseball Prospectus Top 101 lists classified as projecting as no. 3, no. 3/4, or no. 4/5 starters. These players ranked as high as Mike Minor (no. 26 in 2011) and as low as Tyler Thornburg (no. 100 in 2013).

Trying to package and present these players in neat little boxes is problematic, but we can create five different tiers of pitchers who:

- Exceeded their projections to become top-flight fantasy assets
- Lived up to their mid-to-back-end-rotation fantasy profiles
- Became moderately impactful major league relievers
- Still profile as relevant pitchers/prospects
- Never reached the majors or established themselves as fantasy assets

Yes, players within the tiers have seen varying levels of success or failure, but this is the best way to break down this group of 52 into digestible subsets.

With that in mind, let's assume we're evaluating these prospects in standard 5x5 formats, and in a league depth of 12-14 teams. In 10-team leagues, mid-rotation starters become even less valuable. In deeper leagues, they're more enticing, but still not a necessary evil.

If you think that's melodramatic, take a look at what the past five years have yielded from our supposed mid-rotation prospect stalwarts. Next to each player, you'll see in parentheses his ranking upon his initial 101 appearance, the organization with which he appeared, and the year in which he first appeared.

The Seducers

Jordan Zimmermann (no. 56, WAS, 2009),
Sonny Gray (no. 72, OAK, 2012)

Out of the 52 players, only two have surpassed their mid-rotation starter projections to become credible no. 1 or 2 fantasy arms. What you *should* hear is that gambling on mid-rotation guys in the hope that they truly blossom is a fool's errand. What you *probably* hear is that you need to get better at identifying which prospects you should target as buy-low candidates.

To illustrate what a waste of time that is and what a bad listener you are, let's take a brief look at how Zimmermann's and Gray's careers developed:

Zimmermann was a second-round draft pick back in 2007, making his way to the middle of BP's 2009 Top 101. In an article in late 2008, former BP prospect guru and current Astros front office member Kevin Goldstein referred to Zimmermann as "a potential mid-rotation starter by 2010," and his reputation slowly improved throughout the 2009 campaign. Tommy John surgery robbed Zimmermann of most of his 2010 campaign, but his recovery went according to plan, and he cemented himself as a well-above-average pitcher in 2011.

From 2011 to 2013, Zimmermann was excellent, routinely posting ERAs of 3.25 or better, winning a total of 39 games, and profiling as a solid if unspectacular resource in terms of strikeouts, too. Then, in 2014, Zimmermann's game took another step forward, as the 28-year-old fanned 182 batters in 199 2/3 innings. With a 2.66 ERA, matching FIP, and 14 wins, he was the 13th-best starter in fantasy baseball. If you drafted him when he projected as a mid-rotation starter, you'd be ecstatic.

Gray, meanwhile, was the 18th overall selection in the 2011 draft, and while he was a fairly high-profile collegiate pitcher, there were plenty of concerns in the scouting community that he'd need to transition to the bullpen professionally. The right-hander struggled at Double-A in 2012, but was much better when the A's decided to promote him to Triple-A in 2013 anyway, eventually making an impact in the majors later that year.

In Goldstein's breakdown of the A's farm system before the 2012 season, he ranked Gray as Oakland's fifth-best prospect, one spot behind Brad Peacock, and gave him a perfect world projection of a mid-rotation starter. Yet Gray kept inducing groundballs as he moved up the ranks, and his curveball became a truly elite pitch. Despite his small stature, he threw 219 innings in 2014, finishing as the 27th-best starter in standard 5x5 formats. If you drafted him when he projected as a mid-rotation starter, you'd be ecstatic.

"This isn't so bad," you may be thinking. "Two success stories right off the bat!"

Unfortunately, if you're looking to replicate that success, there are no real common threads we can look to that link Zimmermann's and Gray's success, and even if there were, we'd be dealing with a sample size of two. Plus, it's fair to say that Zimmermann and Gray really both project better as good no. 2 or very strong no. 3 fantasy starters in standard formats; neither profiles as a legit fantasy ace.

The take-home here is that if you draft a starter with a mid-rotation projection in the hopes that he's going to exceed your expectations, you're not planning well. No matter how enticing it is to have the next Zimmermann or Gray on your roster, the odds dictate that it won't happen if you value probability over upside, which is really what taking a mid-rotation prospect is all about.

Not convinced yet? Let's dig deeper.

They Are Who We Thought They Were

Carlos Carrasco (no. 43, PHI, 2009),
Jake Arietta (no. 52, BAL, 2009),
Nick Adenhart (no. 71, LAA, 2009),
Dan Hudson (no. 55, CHW, 2010),
Mike Leake (no. 59, CIN, 2010),
Kyle Gibson (no. 71, MIN, 2010),
Jordan Lyles (no. 59, HOU, 2011),
Mike Minor (no. 26, ATL, 2011),
Danny Duffy (no. 67, KC, 2011),
Chris Archer (no. 70, TB, 2011),
Jake Odorizzi (no. 77, KC, 2011),
Tyler Skaggs (no. 83, ARI, 2011),
James Paxton (no. 59, SEA, 2012),
Wily Peralta (no. 92, MIL, 2012),
Martin Perez (no. 59, TEX, 2013),
Michael Wacha (no. 56, STL, 2013),
Tony Cingrani (no. 91, CIN, 2013),
Dan Straily (no. 85, OAK, 2013)

Eighteen of the 52 eligible players fit into what is essentially the "you get what you paid for" category. Admittedly, that's a decent chunk. But, as you'll soon see, not every name here has continued to provide fantasy baseballers with value.

Really, only a few guys in this section classify as long-term, reliable no. 3/4 starters. I'd wager that only Leake, Duffy, Odorizzi, Paxton, and Peralta are solid bets to still be okay mid-rotation guys in, say, four years, health permitting. Skaggs and Perez are potentially set to join them, but given that both of those talented southpaws are currently recovering from Tommy John surgery, we can't give them the benefit of the doubt quite yet.

Last year, Leake, Duffy, Odorizzi, Paxton, and Peralta finished with respective overall starter ranks of 66, 38, 83, 113, and 55. That's the type of production you're going to have to be okay with potentially losing out on if you heed my advice and ignore mid-rotation prospects. Yes, you can argue that they didn't all get a full season's worth of playing time, but that only adds to my

point: there are too many variables in play, from organizational depth to contextual factors to player development and more, to bank on guys like these.

To be fair, that may paint too bleak a picture. The reason I haven't mentioned Carrasco, Arrieta, Minor, Archer, or Wacha yet is that they all have the upside to be something more than mid-rotation filler. Minor, Archer, and Wacha are young, good, and filled with upside. If you drafted 'em, you're playing with house money, and they're closer in value to Zimmermann and Gray than to the bottom half of the players on this list.

But if you drafted Carrasco or Arrieta way back in 2009, are you really happy with what you've received? Elevators have fewer ups and downs than Carrasco has had in his career. He finished as fantasy's 31st-best starting option in 2014, the first year he came even close to top-50 starter status. Arrieta's rises and falls haven't been quite so dramatic, but his 17th-best ranking from 2014 is far and away the best mark of his career, too.

Sure, Carrasco and Arrieta made owners very happy in 2014. But how many of those owners are the same guys who originally drafted them five seasons earlier? How many people held on to Carrasco when he missed all of 2012 with Tommy John? How many held on to Arrieta after he posted a 6.20 ERA in 2012? Odds are, the owners who originally invested in these arms weren't the ones reaping the rewards when the payday finally came. And while Carrasco and Arrieta both have the potential to serve as no. 2/3 fantasy starters moving forward, they both have plenty of red flags.

The next subset in this larger group consists of guys who are fringy back-end starters rather than legit fantasy options in 14-team leagues. I refer you in this instance to Lyles, Gibson, Cingrani, and Straily. I think the middle two still have a bit of upside left in them, but if you invested in any of these four, you could've made better use of a roster spot. Players like these are always available on the waiver wire.

Finally, the two players who don't fit into any other group are Hudson and Adenhart. Hudson was quite good before injuries totally derailed his career, and that's a risk with any pitcher. Adenhart's circumstances are more unfortunate, of course, and there's no fantasy lesson to be learned from his passing.

Thus, from these 18 names who are supposed to fill you with hope, there are really only a dozen who you'd be happy to own moving forward in 14-team leagues. If you like those odds, stay away from Vegas.

And if you like happy thoughts, stop reading before we get to this next group.

Fantasy-Relevant Relievers

Brett Cecil (no. 90, TOR, 2009),
Wade Davis (no. 34, KC 2010),
Neil Ramirez (no. 77, TEX, 2012),
Jeurys Familia (no. 89, NYM, 2012),
Tyler Thornburg (no. 100, MIL, 2013)

Quite often, when you read about a pitcher with a mid-rotation profile, you'll see "no. 3 starter" listed as their best possible outcome and "late-inning reliever" listed as their most likely outcome. In the real world, this isn't a bad thing; the Royals just showed what can be accomplished with a dominant bullpen. For fantasy owners in moderately deep leagues, though, non-closing relievers are often useless.

Still, there are plenty of you out there who play in 20-team leagues, AL- or NL-only leagues, and leagues that count holds, and so some of these relievers will matter to you. From a pure talent standpoint, the best of the bunch here is Davis. After floundering as a starter he turned into a lights-out bullpen weapon, and odds are he'll be closing some day. Even if he never closes, though, he's the rare middle reliever worth owning in standard leagues.

The rest of these guys are a mixed bag. Familia notched five saves in 2014 and had a very nice year, but he's not guaranteed to close moving forward. If you invested in him heavily as a prospect, you're probably not thrilled with the end result as of 2015. Thornburg, long a personal favorite, showed an ability to miss bats but also walked a ton of guys in the majors, then hit the DL with an elbow injury. If he comes back healthy I still think he could start or close, but you'd be justified in not retaining him long enough to find out.

Ramirez and Cecil still have fairly uncertain roles moving forward, but both play for teams with shoddy bullpens and could theoretically see some saves in 2015. They're a better bet to nab some holds, and while there's value in that, once again, there's not enough value to justify them sucking up an MiLB roster spot for a few seasons.

Even though there are only five players here, to me, I think they adequately represent the larger sample of starter-turned-reliever prospects. For every one pitcher who blossoms into the 'pen to become Davis, four more exist as eminently replaceable entities. Honestly, that's probably an optimistic ratio, even among prospects once considered the cream of the crop.

Don't ever let anyone tell you relief pitchers are cool or interesting. Relief pitchers are the worst.

Still Prospects... For Now

Jesse Biddle (no. 84, PHI, 2012),
Danny Hultzen (no. 50, SEA, 2013),
Justin Nicolino (no. 73, MIA, 2013),
Zach Lee (no. 87, LAD, 2013),
Clayton Blackburn (no. 95, SF, 2013),
Sean Nolin (no. 97, TOR, 2013),
Michael Fulmer (no. 98, NYM, 2013)

After reading the previous three groups, everyone must be super excited to read about middling starter prospects, and here we are. It's too early to truly make a judgment call on any of these guys, so in the interest of fairness, they're not falling to the "failed" category yet. Before you take that as a sign of optimism, let's check in on each prospect's status.

Nicolino, Lee, Blackburn, and Nolin are back-end guys through and through, all more valuable in real life than for our purposes. Lee plays for a team that should net him a ton of wins if he reaches the majors, and the A's work magic with guys like Nolin, but unless you roster 150-plus minor leaguers, most of these guys are waiver wire fodder.

Hultzen perfectly illustrates the hubris of assuming that any pitching prospect is "safe." When he came out of the draft as the no. 2 overall pick in 2011, he was billed as a fast-moving, mid-rotation arm with a very high floor. To this point, he has fewer than 200 innings pitched in the minors and missed all of 2014 with a shoulder injury. It's arguably more likely he never sees the majors than it is he reaches his projection.

Biddle and Fulmer probably offer the most hope out of this group, but the former battled concussion symptoms after getting stuck in a hailstorm, of all things, while the latter has already had surgeries on his knee and elbow. Such is life with

pitching prospects: a hailstorm can screw up your plans.

It's entirely possible one of these guys transforms himself and could be listed in the "They Are Who We Thought They Were" group if we repeat this exercise in three years. It's more likely that some, if not all, end up in the next section instead.

Failed or Failing

Michael Bowden (no. 31, BOS, 2009),
Tim Alderson (no. 60, SF, 2009),
James McDonald (no. 65, PIT, 2009),
Aaron Poreda (no. 74, CHW, 2009),
Alex White (no. 77, CLE, 2010),
Phillippe Aumont (no. 78, PHI, 2010),
Trevor Reckling (no. 92, LAA, 2010),
Tim Melville (no. 93, KC, 2010),
Randall Delgado (no. 58, ATL, 2011),
Simon Castro (no. 61, SD, 2011),
Chris Dwyer (no. 66, KC, 2011),
Trey McNutt (no. 68, CHC, 2011),
Andy Oliver (no. 87, DET, 2011),
Ian Krol (no. 89, OAK, 2011),
Trevor May (no. 51, PHI, 2012),
Robbie Erlin (no. 53, SD, 2012),
Brad Peacock (no. 64, OAK, 2012),
Joe Wieland (no. 74, SD, 2012),
Casey Kelly (no. 78, SD, 2012),
Allen Webster (no. 69, BOS, 2013)

And here is the piece de resistance: of the 52 players who projected as mid-rotation starters on BP Top 101 lists between 2009 and 2013, 20 of them have been of no use to fantasy owners whatsoever. In a way, this number is perhaps surprisingly low, but when you consider just how many of the pitchers in the first four tiers come with caveats, it should hammer home how futile chasing arms of this caliber truly is.

There's no need to dive too deep into the names on this list. Bowden, Alderson, Poreda, White, Reckling, Melville, Castro, Dwyer, McNutt, and Krol really deserve no further explanation at all: if there are two usable fantasy seasons combined for these 10 in their careers, it would be rather surprising.

There are some pitchers in this group who still have a modicum of fantasy potential. McDonald, Delgado, May, Peacock, Wieland, Erlin, Kelly, and Webster could all potentially see MLB starts in 2015, and there's a nonzero chance that one or two of those guys sticks. However, none of the players mentioned above comes with any type of real upside anymore, and it's likely that guys like May, Peacock, and Webster are headed toward permanent moves to the bullpen sooner rather than later.

The 20 players here all failed or are failing for a variety of reasons. Some got hurt and washed out. Some never developed the secondary pitches they needed to succeed, or never refined their command to the point where their arsenals became effective. A few will stick around as relievers or Quadruple-A depth. A few will leave the game altogether within the next few seasons.

Conclusion

There we have it: of the 52 players listed, fewer than half are worthy of retaining in 14-team leagues at this time, and depending on your personal evaluations of several of these players, that number could be as low as 12. Outlining the outcomes of the various members of the 52-player sample is useful in demonstrating the peril that comes with investing in such mediocre returns. What it doesn't entirely address, however, is opportunity cost.

Spending a draft pick or trading away a good player for a mid-rotation starter is bad if that mid-rotation starter doesn't pan out, yes. But you're not just losing that player plus that draft pick or the player you gave away; you're losing out on the chance to own someone better, too. Given the rate at which many of these pitchers—even the ultimately successful ones—toiled in the high-minors or at the MLB level, they likely cost you a roster spot for several seasons.

A big part of that is because of the elephant in the room, the one thing we haven't fully addressed yet that's an obvious factor when it comes to talking pitching prospects: injuries.

The lifeblood of the TINSTAAPP group, injuries can derail careers. But the more subtle ways they do damage—setting back timetables and changing projections—lead to even tougher decisions for fantasy owners. Sometimes, you cut a pitcher with a checkered medical history and he becomes Carrasco. More often than not, you miss out on the chance to capitalize on the development of a different player when you retain a pitcher suffering from a major arm injury.

Of the 52 players sampled, a whopping 27, or 52 percent, suffered at least one major arm injury—an injury resulting in missing at least about 50 percent of a season—at some point in his career. This doesn't count multiple injuries to the same pitcher, or specific instances of an injury; it's simply a hard count of the total number of pitchers impacted.

Twelve of the 27 pitchers who suffered from injures underwent Tommy John surgery. The other injuries include ailments such as rotator cuff tears and injuries, bone spur removals, finger problems, and more. A few of the players were unfortunate enough to suffer from both Tommy John and a second major injury. Pitching is a dangerous profession.

While there are plenty of success stories above involving pitchers who recovered from major injuries, it's also interesting that the proportion of "failed or failing" players is in line with the overall sample, as 10 of the 20 pitchers in the bottom rung had major injuries. That makes it obvious that, yes, injuries derail pitchers quite often. But there are plenty more ways for arms to betray fantasy owners.

It's true that all prospects will break your heart, and that targeting pitchers with top-of-the-rotation upside will also often lead to ruin. But when you truly hit on those guys, at least you get an anchor, an irreplaceable fantasy asset that can make the difference between a middling fantasy staff and one that pushes you to a title.

When you target mid-rotation starters, the odds are never in your favor. If you're lucky, you hit on a pretty good arm. Maybe you at least get what you pay for. But odds are, you end up with an arm that underwhelms or becomes useless to you altogether.

The next time you balk at an offer in which you're getting an established major leaguer in return for one or more mid-rotation pitchers, think of these 52 names. Don't be afraid of missing out on a Gray or a Wacha or an Arrieta. Be afraid of getting stuck with a waste of a roster space, like what ultimately became of 30-plus of the names above.

Just say no to mid-rotation fantasy prospects. ■

Special thanks to handsome gentleman and scholar, Baseball Prospectus intern Andrew Koo, for help pulling numbers for this piece.

Defensive Decision Making and Prospect Valuation:
How to Avoid Inviting Additional Error into an Already Impossible Task

by Jeff Quinton

Our indiscriminate enjoyment of being right is matched by an almost equally indiscriminate feeling that we are *right.*

–*Kathryn Schulz[1]*

Being right, being seen as being right, and having certainty about being right are things that we all want. Conversely, being wrong, being seen as wrong, and not having certainty about that which we hold to be true are all things that we try to avoid. People spend a lot of time and money to avoid being wrong—just look at the popularity of Yelp or rankings articles. In analyzing baseball as an analyst, writer, or fantasy baseball participant, we do the same. Even given the failure inherent in the game of baseball, and even given the unpredictability inherent in prospects, avoiding being wrong and avoiding uncertainties are two goals that we often cannot avoid striving toward while performing such valuations. The steps we take, which we will later describe as defensive decision making (borrowing the term from the great Gerd Gigerenzer), to accomplish these goals often add additional error to the process of prospect valuation.

The problem with placing value on being perceived as right and avoiding uncertainty is that these goals do not always play nicely with a more important, overarching goal: making the best decision. What exactly does making the best decision mean? As an analyst it means giving the most valuable insight possible; as a baseball team it means taking action that maximizes your chances at achieving your competitive or monetary goals; and as a fantasy baseball team it is the same as the real baseball team, but with different rules, much lower stakes, and no fans. Pretty much we want to inform, win, and profit. In regards to prospect valuation (using scouting and statistical information to determine the value of a prospect), making the best decision means having the most accurate forecasts possible. The solution at first seems pretty simple: just make the best decision/valuation and the being right part will follow. While this solution holds in theory, our own aversion to being wrong and attitudes toward uncertainty disallow us from fully buying into it. As noted earlier, while there will always be error in prospect valuation, we invite even more error to the equation through these misaligned goals. Luckily, this additional error often manifests itself in certain ways; thus, we can take a look at what is going wrong and what we can do to fix it.

Before we get into the fixin', we need to take a look at what exactly is needing a fix. For that we go back to our two misaligned goals: wanting to appear correct and avoiding uncertainty.

Right, Wrong, and Uncertainty

Projecting prospects is an exercise in failure. Scouts—our best resource for projecting prospects—have been doing their thing for over 100 years now and they still miss with regularity, which means that everything else misses with more regularity. It is therefore no surprise that making decisions based on this information often yields misses. Given all this, one could reasonably assume that we would take being wrong as part of the job, that we would obviously prefer to be right, but that we would trust that our process is sound. If only we could make life so easy for ourselves.

The reason we cannot make life easy on ourselves is that we worship right and wrong. Even if we know that we are following a good process, being viewed as wrong—and consequently unintelligent, undisciplined, and/or unprepared—by others still hurts. Bosses, fan bases, and, most importantly, our own inner critic can only tolerate being wrong so much. This is not merely an attempt at persuasive conjecture; rather, this is a part of how human beings are wired. The below is from the psychologists who published "Bad is Stronger Than Good" in the *Review of General Psychology* in 2001:

> The greater power of bad events over good ones is found in everyday events, major life events (e.g., trauma), close relationship outcomes, social network patterns, interpersonal interactions, and learning processes. Bad emotions, bad parents, and bad feedback have more impact than good ones, and bad information is processed more thoroughly than good. The self is more motivated to avoid bad self-definitions than to pursue good ones. Bad impressions and bad stereotypes are quicker to form and more resistant to disconfirmation than good ones. Various explanations such as diagnosticity and salience help explain some findings, but the greater power of bad events is still found when such variables are controlled. Hardly any exceptions (indicating greater power of good) can be found. Taken together, these findings suggest that bad is stronger than good, as a general principle across a broad range of psychological phenomena.[2]

More succinctly, the negative—in the case of prospect valuation, being wrong—hurts and we know it is going to hurt. As a result, we seek to avoid that future pain; and this is where the importance of uncertainty comes into play. If prospect valuation involved *risk*, where the outcome is unknown and the odds are known, we would be more comfortable following a system and shrugging off any errors as, to use a poker term, bad beats (bets that do not work out when the odds are in your favor). However, prospect valuation does not involve risk; it involves *uncertainty*, where the outcome *and* the odds are unknown. Consequently, we are not as comfortable using process or the odds as a crutch with prospects. Saying, "Well, I thought he had a 20 percent chance at being an impact middle infielder for a guy who flamed out," sounds a lot like being wrong to our outcome-obsessed minds because we are the ones making up the odds (as opposed to the people who decided to make a die six-sided).

Defensive Decision Making

Given all of this, we hedge. With an uncertain future ahead of us, we often act not in a way that gives us the best chances of accomplishing our goal, but rather in a way that gives us the best odds at defending our actions if wrong. The previously mentioned Gerd Gigerenzer, whose book *Risk Savvy: How to Make Good Decisions* was one of the main inspirations for this piece, calls this uncertainty-driven hedging "defensive decision making," which he explains via the following example: "A person or group ranks option A as the best for the situation, but chooses option B to protect itself in case something goes wrong."[3] This affects how we update our valuations for prospects. Instead of continuing to adjust our valuations as best we can based on the new information at hand, we are likely to adjust our valuations based on how we think our actions will be perceived in the future. This is especially true if we have made our original valuation public in some way (writing an article, publishing a list, making a fantasy baseball draft selection, etc.). Our minds have come up with many ways to add this extra layer of error to our decision-making process (either that, or our minds have come up with many different ways to describe this phenomenon). To succumb to this less frequently, we will now take a look at what these errors are, how they manifest themselves, and some strategies for battling them.

Valuation with all the Wrong Reasons

It is important to note here that this is not a discussion about errors in scouting, which is a skill in itself; rather, this is a discussion about errors in consuming scouting and statistical information, making decisions based on that information, and determining player value from that information. While the causes for these errors may be complex, the way in which they manifest themselves is straightforward: we either overreact or underreact. Overreacting is adjusting a valuation based on a false signal, on an indicator that does not exist (type I error). Underreacting is not adjusting a valuation because a legitimate signal is not detected (type II error). Defensive decision making causes us to fall into these errors in numerous ways.

Underreacting

To kick this all off, we have the disposition effect, which is probably the granddaddy of biases when it comes to underreacting to misevaluating an asset. The disposition effect, a theory of behavioral finance, shows the tendency of investors to keep their losers too long and sell their winners too quickly. In this case we are clearly discussing the "keeping their losers too long" portion of this phenomenon. We know this happens with investments of all kinds: bad stocks, bad boyfriends, and bad career decision; thus, it is not surprising that this happens when determining the value of prospects. While it may be easiest to chalk this up to sunk cost, this is really about being perceived as wrong and admitting error on our behalf. Put differently, this is not about initially incorrectly valuing prospect A over prospects B and C; rather, this is about continuing to value prospect A over prospects B and C only because of the initial valuation.

This is where Richard Thaler's endowment effect, which Thaler states is "the fact that people often demand much more to give up an object than they would be willing to pay to acquire

it," comes into play.[4] At its most extreme, we have the example of children; whereas most would look at having to care for a child who is not ours as a cost (and probably a significant one), once that child is yours the child becomes priceless. At a lesser extreme, Daniel Kahneman, Jack Knetsch, and Thaler "found that randomly assigned owners of a mug required significantly more money to part with their possession (around \$7) than randomly assigned buyers were willing to pay to acquire it (around \$3)".[5] What does this have to do with prospect valuation? Well, even front-office types will admit that teams overrate their own players. That said, we do not have to be part of a front office to have feelings of ownership toward players. Whether we are fans, writers, scouts, or fantasy baseball players, we all have *our* guys—the ones we have "been in on before everyone else was" and, ultimately, the ones whose performances on which we have staked our reputation.

The point of all this is that our valuations are overly sticky and they are so because we are afraid of changing our opinion only to see it backfire. This is the defensive decision-making aspect of our initial underreactions. We are not holding firm because we have not seen any additional predictive data; rather, we are clinging to our previous valuations because we imagine it being the easiest to defend should we end up being wrong. In example form, we anchor to our initial Mike Moustakas-like valuations, leading us to pay premiums for what should be a prospect fatigue discount. This is, of course, the case until it is not the case, but our overreacting (below) is driven by the same unhelpful factors.

Overreacting

Whereas underreacting allows us to proscriptively explain our valuation errors, overreacting allows us to prescriptively affect our ability to explain our valuation errors. By switching our beliefs to coincide with the most recent information available or prevailing trend, we are less likely to have our valuations questioned or criticized. Again, we are weighing factors that have nothing to do with making the best or most accurate valuation. We see this in prospect valuation in many ways:

- Going back and forth as to whether a pitcher will be a starter or a reliever with each start as opposed to just saying he has a percent chance of ending up in each role

- Dropping a post Tommy John surgery recipient down our rankings during recovery only to bounce the player back up upon their return (not that any of the time was going to be spent in the majors anyway)

- Bouncing our valuation up and down on a high-variability prospect (such as a toolsy player with a lot of swing-and-miss) based on how that variability plays year to year

In each of these scenarios we are overweighting the most recent information, not just because it is the most recent, but because it is the defensible line of logic.

Furthermore, there are reasons beyond defensive decision making that make us even more likely to change our valuations on prospects. These reasons are excitement and boredom. No one wants to read about how prospect X remains the same. No one pays money for firsthand scouting accounts to leave their valuations unchanged. That said, we thirst for new information and the excitement that new information can bring. This is a bit of a tangent but aligns with defensive decision making in that we are allowing nonpredictive factors to be a part of our valuations.

Getting out of Our Own (Valuations') Way

So we get it, we all have pride inside that's wrong, at least pride that is wrong for prospect valuation. The question worth asking then becomes, "How do we avoid bringing this additional error to our valuations?" While there is no panacea, there are two solutions that can certainly help us improve: (i) focusing on process instead of results and (ii) learning from the experts.

Focusing on Process Instead of Results

Focusing on process as opposed to results is not new or groundbreaking advice, but it does cut to the core of the problem in defensive decision making. By paying more attention to our valuation process (the information we are gathering, how we are weighing that information, finding our biases, and how all the information and biases are combined to form a valuation), we will pay less attention to how our decisions are viewed by others in the future. Additionally, the more we are analyzing our process, the more we are measuring the different ingredients in our valuation recipe, the more likely we are to be able to recognize defensive decision making creeping into our process. While focusing on process allows us to improve our prospect valuations over time, there are measures we can take to speed up this improvement process, namely, learning from the experts.

Learning from the Experts

While this may not sound like the most fun solution, it just might be the most helpful. For starters, when we say experts, we are really talking about people who have been there before, who have seen the illusions, who have made mistakes by not identifying those illusions, and who can now identify illusions as illusions. While we may not have ever been in a situation where we had to assess a particular player, there are those who have been. Should we therefore just take their position as our own? The short answer is maybe, but it should not be automatic. The longer and more helpful answer is that we should be looking for the logic in the experts' positions or valuations. We want to find out what they are considering that we are not considering and why they are doing so. The more we are able to weigh these factors, the more we get away from framing our valuations through how we can defend them if they turn out wrong.

In the end, improving our prospect valuations (and many other decisions in life) comes down to being able to properly frame each situation. We will never bat 1.000 because the future is unpredictable, but if we can frame our decisions to remove additional biases and errors, we will be a step ahead of most. ■

Notes

1. Kathryn Schulz, *Being Wrong: Adventures in the Margin of Error* (New York: Ecco, 2010).
2. Roy F. Baumeister, Ellen Bratslavsky, Catrin Finkenauer, and Kathleen D. Vohs, "Bad Is Stronger Than Good," *Review of General Psychology* 5, no.4 (2001): 323-370.
3. Gerd Gigerenzer, *Risk Savvy: How to Make Good Decisions* (London: Allen Lane, 2014).
4. Richard H. Thaler, *The Winner's Curse: Paradoxes and Anomalies of Economic Life* (New York: Free, 1992).
5. David Gal, "A Psychological Law of Inertia and the Illusion of Loss Aversion," *Judgment and Decision Making* 1, no.1 (2006): 23-32.

The Top 101 Dynasty League Prospects for 2015

by Bret Sayre

Being a self-proclaimed veteran of these lists, I've spent the introduction space here on plenty of topics—ranging from the benefits of reading scouting reports, to not giving up on guys too quickly, to reflecting on your own personal biases. There are always discussion points to jump into here that discuss how best to digest and use the information embedded in this article—possibly one for each of the over 9,000 words spread across these 101 players. This time, I'm going to focus on one that we all know, yet are often afraid to put into action.

As excited as we get about the top prospects in baseball, they represent a value. A number. A price point. And while so many owners, including the ones on this staff, can fall in love with their favorite prospects, the risk in holding onto the larvae of the fantasy world when they can be used best as currency is one that we don't often consider. If I own Tim Anderson (and believe me, I do), my first thought is always going to be on the type of player Anderson could be—when it should be equally on both that and what Anderson could return for me now in the trade market. Though the pull of drafting a player out of the amateur ranks or picking up a player when he was far from a top-101 prospect is strong, it's not the same way you'd generally view a financial investment. Not to get too Quinton on you, as that's best saved for the man himself (seriously, go read his chapter), but if you buy a share of stock at $20 and it goes up to $40, maybe it's time to cash it in for something that actually costs $40, rather than waiting for it to go up to $75.

It's both a truth and a fallacy that dynasty championships are won by building a strong farm system. The fallacy is that those players are the ones that will lead you to a string of trophies and jellybeans—the myth perpetuated best by the "constant rebuilder." The truth is that a strong farm system will grant you entrance into the area of the trade market you need to pass through to truly build a contender. Not all prospects are created with equal ETAs, and even the ones with equal ETAs have varying performance curves and eligibility. Waiting for the moon and stars to line up will often cause owners to bypass their window to win, so while it's important to be excited about the players we'll get to shortly, it's also okay to shed the fear that we associate with letting them go.

Now, the fine print…

First, there are a few disclaimers specific to the prospect list to go over before we jump in. Again, these rankings are for fantasy purposes only and do not directly take into account things like an outfielder's ability to stick in center or a catcher's pop time. Of course, these things do matter indirectly, as they affect a player's ability to either stay in the lineup or maintain eligibility. So, while Austin Hedges may be a top-25 prospect on BP's Top 101, this is due in large part to his defensive value; and you'll see that he's not on this list because his upside isn't nearly as great for fantasy. Additionally, home parks need to be factored in, just as when we are when talking about a major-

league player. If Nelson Cruz's fantasy potential shrinks on going from Baltimore to Seattle, we can't pretend that these prospects operate in a vacuum, unaffected by park factors. Of course, there's no guarantee that they will reach the majors with their current organization, so while it is not a heavy consideration, it is reflected. But most importantly, the intention of this list is to balance the upside, probability, and proximity of these players to an active fantasy lineup.

Within the list that follows, you'll find important information about each prospect, including his potential fantasy value (in dollars) at his peak and the risk factor associated with reaching that peak. Also, you will find a fantasy overview, which summarizes how many categories each player will be useful in, along with any that carry impact. For this exercise, we defined "impact" as having the potential to be in the top 15-20 players in a given category. For instance, impact in home runs is the potential to hit 30 and impact for strikeouts is the potential to punch out 200. Then you'll see a realistic ceiling and floor for each prospect, purely in terms of Rotisserie value, and a brief comment that adds a little extra color. The comments are specifically brief because I've already written fantasy-specific comments on each of these players in the individual top-10 lists (which are great and which you should read, if you haven't already).

So without any further ado, here is the newest batch of the best 101 prospects for dynasty leagues.

1. Kris Bryant, 3B, Chicago Cubs

Age: 23, Previous Rank: 10
Potential Earnings: $35+
Risk Factor: Low
Fantasy Overview: Four-category contributor; impact potential in HR, RBI, R
Realistic Ceiling: The guy everyone thinks Evan Longoria is
Realistic Floor: A 30-homer outfielder

It takes an awful lot of thump to unseat Buxton as the top fantasy prospect in the game, but Bryant has it. He has done nothing but hit since he entered pro ball, and though you can quibble about his contact rate, there's little standing in the way of him being a fantasy star and in short order.

2. Byron Buxton, OF, Minnesota Twins

Age: 21, Previous Rank: 2
Potential Earnings: $35+
Risk Factor: Medium
Fantasy Overview: Five-category contributor; impact potential in AVG, R, SB
Realistic Ceiling: A perennial first-round pick who contributes in all five categories
Realistic Floor: A strong speed-based OF2

There is a healthy debate to be had as to whether Buxton

or Bryant deserves top billing, but there should be no debate that they are the first two prospects on this list. Buxton's injury-plagued 2014 season pushed back his ETA (which contributed to his ranking), but did not diminish any of his upside.

3. Carlos Correa, SS, Houston Astros

Age: 20, Previous Rank: 5
Potential Earnings: $35+
Risk Factor: Low
Fantasy Overview: Four-category contributor; impact potential in AVG, HR, RBI
Realistic Ceiling: An elite fantasy shortstop
Realistic Floor: A top-10 fantasy third baseman

Sure, there's a chance he could move off the position and he's not going to make any major contribution in steals, but Correa has a chance to be the best average/power bat that we've seen at the position since Troy Tulowitzki. Like we've been hammering home, with talent like this, eligibility is very, very secondary.

4. Addison Russell, SS, Chicago Cubs

Age: 21, Previous Rank: 9
Potential Earnings: $25-30
Risk Factor: Low
Fantasy Overview: Five-category contributor; impact potential in RBI, R
Realistic Ceiling: A consistent top-five fantasy shortstop
Realistic Floor: A consistent top-10 fantasy shortstop

There's a level of certainty with Russell that pushes him up into the top five, even though organization depth could push him off shortstop in the short term. He's young and close to major-league ready, and although his ceiling isn't quite as high as Correa's, it's still more than enough to get very excited about.

5. Miguel Sano, 3B, Minnesota Twins

Age: 21, Previous Rank: 7
Potential Earnings: $30-35
Risk Factor: Medium
Fantasy Overview: Four-category contributor; impact potential in HR, RBI, R
Realistic Ceiling: Nelson Cruz with health and third-base eligibility
Realistic Floor: Pedro Alvarez

The missed season was certainly a bummer for Sano, but thankfully he's not a pitcher. One of the small handful of prospects in the minors with elite raw power, he will try to get back on track to hit Target Field in 2016. And it's a good thing the Twins are a team of the Twin Cities, since some of his bombs may wind up in St Paul.

6. Corey Seager, SS, Los Angeles Dodgers

Age: 20, Previous Rank: 36
Potential Earnings: $25-30
Risk Factor: Low
Fantasy Overview: Four-category contributor; impact potential in AVG, RBI
Realistic Ceiling: A .300 hitting shortstop with power
Realistic Floor: His brother, non-park-adjusted

The sweet-swinging still-a-shortstop continues to impress as he moves up the latter and could reach Los Angeles as soon as late 2015—though next year is more likely. There's still a very good chance he ends up at third base long term, but he may surprise many by keeping that shortstop eligibility for a few seasons.

7. Jorge Soler, OF, Chicago Cubs

Age: 23, Previous Rank: 46
Potential Earnings: $25-30
Risk Factor: Low
Fantasy Overview: Four-category contributor; impact potential in HR, RBI
Realistic Ceiling: An OF2 who can hit 30 homers
Realistic Floor: An OF3 who just doesn't quite make enough contact for OF2 status

Of all the players on this list, Soler is most guaranteed playing time in 2015, as he'll likely roll out as Chicago's opening day right fielder. Pitchers began to figure him out after a blazing start, and how quickly he can adjust back will dictate where his fantasy value goes in the near term.

8. Noah Syndergaard, RHP, New York Mets

Age: 22, Previous Rank: 13
Potential Earnings: $25-30
Risk Factor: Low
Fantasy Overview: Four-category contributor; impact potential in W, K, ERA, WHIP
Realistic Ceiling: A back-end SP1
Realistic Floor: A strong SP3 with lots of whiffs

Many, including myself, thought that Syndergaard would be ineligible for this list, but it should be no great surprise that he checks in as the top fantasy pitching prospect in baseball. His advantageous home park and division should be nice bedfellows for his top-shelf stuff, and he'll push through the Mets' rotation depth in short order.

9. Lucas Giolito, RHP, Washington Nationals

Age: 20, Previous Rank: 17
Potential Earnings: $30-35
Risk Factor: Medium
Fantasy Overview: Four-category contributor; impact potential in W, K, ERA, WHIP
Realistic Ceiling: A pitcher you'd take in the first round
Realistic Floor: A Tommy John cautionary tale

There's ceiling and then there's Giolito's ceiling. Have you ever seen the Sistine Chapel? Sort of like that, but on the mound. The fact that a pitcher who hasn't pitched above Low-A is a top-10 fantasy prospect is nearly unheard of, but there's something special brewing in that right arm of his.

10. Joc Pederson, OF, Los Angeles Dodgers

Age: 22, Previous Rank: 32
Potential Earnings: $20-25
Risk Factor: Low
Fantasy Overview: Five-category contributor
Realistic Ceiling: A 20/20 option who ticks up in OBP leagues
Realistic Floor: A 15/15 option who ticks up in OBP leagues

Similar to Soler, Pederson is staring ahead at a ton of playing time in 2015, mostly because the Dodgers don't really have anyone else they can play in center field. Pederson has been tagged as a grinder who gets the most out of his tools, and while that's correct, it sells the tools he does have short.

11. Joey Gallo, 3B, Texas Rangers

Age: 21, Previous Rank: 83
Potential Earnings: $25-30
Risk Factor: Medium
Fantasy Overview: Three-category contributor; impact potential

in HR, RBI, R
Realistic Ceiling: Peak Adam Dunn with third-base eligibility
Realistic Floor: Chris Carter with no third-base eligibility

The power is prodigious—and likely the best in all of the minors—but Gallo still has plenty of development ahead of him before he can hit at the major-league level. If you're expecting him to contribute in 2015, you'll likely be disappointed, but his strong work ethic and baseball IQ give him a good chance to put it all together.

12. Julio Urias, LHP, Los Angeles Dodgers

Age: 18, Previous Rank: 45
Potential Earnings: $25-30
Risk Factor: Medium
Fantasy Overview: Four-category contributor; impact potential in W, K, ERA, WHIP
Realistic Ceiling: A back-end fantasy ace, à la Cole Hamels
Realistic Floor: Leif Garrett

There's very little question that Urias is the top left-handed pitching prospect in baseball these days, and that excitement carries over to fantasy leagues. It's still incredible that he will pitch most of the 2015 season in the upper minors as an 18-year old, and his age gives him a leg up on some other arms with similar upside in the long term.

13. Archie Bradley, RHP, Arizona Diamondbacks

Age: 22, Previous Rank: 12
Potential Earnings: $25-30
Risk Factor: Medium
Fantasy Overview: Four-category contributor; impact potential in W, K, ERA, WHIP
Realistic Ceiling: An easy top-10 fantasy starter
Realistic Floor: A high variance SP4 who infuriates you with his inconsistency

There are no shortage of high-end pitching prospects who take steps back every year, but the developmental curve can be nastier than Bradley's. After poor performance and an elbow strain set him back, Bradley returned with a vengeance and a cutter in the Arizona Fall League. He'll look to do in 2015 what he couldn't last year, and make an impact in Arizona.

14. Dylan Bundy, RHP, Baltimore Orioles

Age: 22, Previous Rank: 18
Potential Earnings: $25-30
Risk Factor: Medium
Fantasy Overview: Four-category contributor; impact potential in W, K, ERA, WHIP
Realistic Ceiling: A Jordan Zimmermann type borderline SP1
Realistic Floor: The old Jordan Zimmermann before he got more awesome

It's unfortunate when people forget about, or are unnecessarily down on, a prospect with an elite amateur and minor-league track record because of injury. If the person who owns Bundy in your league is one of those people, now might be a good time to teach them a lesson.

15. Francisco Lindor, SS, Cleveland Indians

Age: 21, Previous Rank: 33
Potential Earnings: $20-25
Risk Factor: Low
Fantasy Overview: Five-category contributor; impact potential in AVG

Realistic Ceiling: A non-elite five-category shortstop
Realistic Floor: A non-elite five-category shortstop

We played this game last year, but Lindor is this high on a fantasy list because he's as much of a lock to be a contributing member of a mixed-league team as anyone on this list. His defense will keep him in the lineup and likely overrate him in dynasty leagues, but there is real top-10 shortstop potential here.

16. Jonathan Gray, RHP, Colorado Rockies

Age: 23, Previous Rank: 20
Potential Earnings: $25-30
Risk Factor: Medium
Fantasy Overview: Four-category contributor; impact potential in W, K
Realistic Ceiling: A high-end SP2, despite Coors
Realistic Floor: Another reason not to draft Colorado pitchers

We often talk about easy analysis being easy, and yes, Colorado pitchers should scare you as an entire group, but Gray's stuff is as good as the Rockies have seen since that time Ubaldo Jimenez was an absolute monster. Be wary of the park, but bet on the pitcher.

17. David Dahl, OF, Colorado Rockies

Age: 21, Previous Rank: 37
Potential Earnings: $30-35
Risk Factor: High
Fantasy Overview: Five-category contributor; impact potential in AVG, R, SB
Realistic Ceiling: Jacoby Ellsbury (not the 70-steal version) in Coors
Realistic Floor: Leonys Martin in Coors

Dahl gets the opposite movement as the player directly in front of him, just because of his nonpitcherness. The upside is tremendous, with Coors helping out in the one category he could be below-average in at sea level. It would not be a surprise if Dahl ended up as a top-five fantasy prospect at this time next year.

18. Tim Anderson, SS, Chicago White Sox

Age: 21, Previous Rank: 61
Potential Earnings: $30-35
Risk Factor: High
Fantasy Overview: Five-category contributor; impact potential in SB
Realistic Ceiling: A 20/30 monster at shortstop
Realistic Floor: A speed-based mixed-league 2B or OF option

It's easy to drool over the stats that Anderson could put up, especially with the ballpark helping him out, but despite having Double-A experience, he remains relatively raw and there are loud questions about his defense. However, his valued gets buoyed in roto leagues by that 30-plus-steal potential.

19. Carlos Rodon, LHP, Chicago White Sox

Age: 22, Previous Rank: NR
Potential Earnings: $25-30
Risk Factor: Medium
Fantasy Overview: Four-category contributor; impact potential in W, K, ERA, WHIP
Realistic Ceiling: A strong SP2 in relatively short order
Realistic Floor: A capable SP4 in relatively short order

The general belief is that we'll see Rodon at some point this summer for the Pale Hose, but the better question is which

Rodon we will actually see. If he's the pitcher he was last spring, it's more of a mid-rotation profile. But if he's the guy from his sophomore year and his pro debut, there's certainly more.

20. Dalton Pompey, OF, Toronto Blue Jays
Age: 22, Previous Rank: NR
Potential Earnings: $20-25
Risk Factor: Low
Fantasy Overview: Four-category contributor; impact potential in SB
Realistic Ceiling: A top-40 outfielder in 2015
Realistic Floor: Anthony Gose part deux

Alright, so the floor may be a little harsh, but Pompey ranks up here because he's here now and there's five-category potential in a loaded lineup. The 2014 fantasy pop-up darling may still have his nonbelievers, but I think they'll be thinned out by around midseason.

21. Andrew Heaney, LHP, Los Angeles Angels
Age: 23, Previous Rank: 34
Potential Earnings: $20-25
Risk Factor: Low
Fantasy Overview: Four-category contributor; impact potential in W, ERA
Realistic Ceiling: An SP3 with stronger ratios than strikeouts
Realistic Floor: Wade Miley in a better ballpark

If you're looking for sheer upside, Heaney's doesn't stand out amongst the players around him, but he's already made his major-league debut and looks to play a big role for the Angels this season. He has the profile and pitchability to step right in as an SP5 in mixed leagues this year.

22. Kyle Schwarber, C/OF, Chicago Cubs
Age: 22, Previous Rank: NR
Potential Earnings: $25-30
Risk Factor: Low
Fantasy Overview: Four-category contributor; impact potential in RBI
Realistic Ceiling: The best kind of fantasy catcher
Realistic Floor: A strong OF3

Schwarber shouldn't have earned much in the way of helium for destroying pitchers who stood little chance against a high-end college hitter, but he doesn't need much helium anyway. Schwarber can hit for average and power, so even if long-term catcher eligibility isn't in the cards, he'll still be a regular on mixed-league rosters.

23. Robert Stephenson, RHP, Cincinnati Reds
Age: 22, Previous Rank: 23
Potential Earnings: $25-30
Risk Factor: Medium
Fantasy Overview: Four-category contributor; impact potential in W, K, ERA
Realistic Ceiling: Garrett Richards
Realistic Floor: Nate Eovaldi

The Reds fireballer took a step back in 2014, but has the raw stuff to rack up strikeouts at the major-league level. The ballpark is unfortunate, as velocity begets velocity, but greater consistency in his command and secondary offerings could get him closer to an SP2 future.

24. Daniel Norris, LHP, Toronto Blue Jays
Age: 21, Previous Rank: NR
Potential Earnings: $20-25
Risk Factor: Low
Fantasy Overview: Four-category contributor; impact potential in W, WHIP
Realistic Ceiling: A solid SP3
Realistic Floor: A solid SP4

Norris took one big wrong turn out of the gate after being drafted, but it's been full steam ahead over the last couple of seasons. He's unlikely to rack up huge strikeout totals (think more in the 160-170 range), but his floor is higher than almost anyone on this list and he's ready now.

25. Josh Bell, 1B/OF, Pittsburgh Pirates
Age: 22, Previous Rank: 82
Potential Earnings: $20-25
Risk Factor: Low
Fantasy Overview: Four-category contributor; impact potential in RBI
Realistic Ceiling: A top-20 outfielder
Realistic Floor: Adam LaRoche with slightly less power

In the near term, Bell looks to get some chances at first base because of the crowded Pirates' outfield—and with those guys all locked up for a while, that won't clear up anytime soon. However, if the bat plays, it will play anywhere and there's no reason he can't get that OF back in-season.

26. Jorge Alfaro, C, Texas Rangers
Age: 21, Previous Rank: 27
Potential Earnings: $25-30
Risk Factor: Medium
Fantasy Overview: Three-category contributor; impact potential in HR, RBI
Realistic Ceiling: A middle-of-the-order catcher
Realistic Floor: A reason you don't invest in catching prospects

As Alfaro's ETA approaches, the volatility of his future value decreases, but catching prospects are always higher in risk than prospects at other positions. The 25-plus-homer power is very real, but he's already growing out of his double-digit steal ability and the plate discipline leaves a lot to be desired.

27. Rymer Liriano, OF, San Diego Padres
Age: 23, Previous Rank: 80
Potential Earnings: $20-25
Risk Factor: Low
Fantasy Overview: Five-category contributor
Realistic Ceiling: A poor man's George Springer
Realistic Floor: Will Venable part deux

Liriano started the offseason as a strong candidate to get 300-400 plate appearances for the Padres in 2015, but ended it under a mountain of high-profile corner outfielders. With a less certain ETA, Liriano's readiness becomes less important, but the power/speed potential remains.

28. Raimel Tapia, OF, Colorado Rockies
Age: 21, Previous Rank: 54
Potential Earnings: $30-35
Risk Factor: High
Fantasy Overview: Five-category contributor; impact potential in AVG, R

Realistic Ceiling: A Charlie Blackmon we can believe in

Realistic Floor: That guy who Mau used to pronounce awesomely

The dreams can be limitless when you put someone with a plus-plus hit tool in Coors and sprinkle in a healthy dose of speed and some power potential. And his minor-league numbers as he heads to the California League are unlikely to do much to pour water on those expectations.

29. Jesse Winker, OF, Cincinnati Reds

Age: 21, Previous Rank: NR
Potential Earnings: $20-25
Risk Factor: Low
Fantasy Overview: Four-category contributor; impact potential in AVG, RBI
Realistic Ceiling: Matt Holliday, non-park-adjusted version
Realistic Floor: A batting-average-based OF4

There's more ceiling around him on this list, but it doesn't mean that Winker should be overlooked or that he lacks upside of his own. There's nothing wrong with a hitter who could approach .300 with 20 homers annually.

30. Nomar Mazara, OF, Texas Rangers

Age: 19, Previous Rank: NR
Potential Earnings: $25-30
Risk Factor: Medium
Fantasy Overview: Four-category contributor; impact potential in HR, RBI
Realistic Ceiling: A .290 hitting, 30-homer outfielder
Realistic Floor: A perfectly viable OF4

Mazara took an unexpected jump up to Double-A in 2014, which helped facilitate a somewhat unexpected jump up the fantasy rankings. The prototypical right fielder could end up launching homers in a ballpark that helps induce them as soon as midseason 2016.

31. Blake Swihart, C, Boston Red Sox

Age: 22, Previous Rank: 96
Potential Earnings: $20-25
Risk Factor: Low
Fantasy Overview: Four-category contributor
Realistic Ceiling: A Jonathan Lucroy-type top fantasy catcher
Realistic Floor: Yadier Molina without the power spike

Having come a long way since he made his full season debut, Swihart is now considered just about a lock to stick at catcher long term and hit for a strong average. How much power he can tap into at the major-league level will determine whether he's a great fantasy option or just a middle-of-the-road one in mixed leagues.

32. Alex Gonzalez, RHP, Texas Rangers

Age: 23, Previous Rank: 85
Potential Earnings: $20-25
Risk Factor: Low
Fantasy Overview: Four-category contributor; impact potential in W, ERA
Realistic Ceiling: James Shields with slightly fewer innings
Realistic Floor: The good version of Mike Leake

I'm well aware that I'm the high guy on Gonzalez, but there's nothing in his stuff, performance, or development that has given me a reason not to be. He'll never be an SP1, even in deep leagues, but he can be a very strong SP3 for the better part of a decade, even in Texas.

33. Clint Frazier, OF, Cleveland Indians

Age: 20, Previous Rank: 19
Potential Earnings: $30-35
Risk Factor: High
Fantasy Overview: Five-category contributor; impact potential in HR, RBI
Realistic Ceiling: A no doubt OF1
Realistic Floor: Colby Rasmus

The fact that Frazier still ranks this high should shock absolutely no one, as he more than held his own in the Midwest League as a teenager. Just because he didn't put up disruptive numbers doesn't mean he's any less exciting for fantasy than he was at this time last year.

34. Jameson Taillon, RHP, Pittsburgh Pirates

Age: 23, Previous Rank: 21
Potential Earnings: $20-25
Risk Factor: Medium
Fantasy Overview: Four-category contributor; impact potential in W, ERA, WHIP
Realistic Ceiling: The reasonable SP2 he was projected as pre-surgery
Realistic Floor: That Texan pitcher who was on Team Canada in the WBC

Forget about Taillon at your own risk. He will return early in 2015 from Tommy John surgery and even if the Pirates take their time, he should be ready to fill A.J. Burnett's slot in the rotation next April. There may not be the upside many thought when he was taken second overall in the draft, but he's still a pitcher in Pittsburgh.

35. Maikel Franco, 3B, Philadelphia Phillies

Age: 22, Previous Rank: 35
Potential Earnings: $15-20
Risk Factor: Low
Fantasy Overview: Four-category contributor; impact potential in RBI
Realistic Ceiling: The good Marlon Byrd at third base
Realistic Floor: The bad Marlon Byrd at first base

Those who were ready to anoint Franco the Phillies third baseman of the future and an investable dynasty league asset at this time last year weren't wrong, but they were a little overenthusiastic. He remains a player built for 5x5 roto, with his defense and on-base partially sinking the overall package.

36. D.J. Peterson, 1B/3B, Seattle Mariners

Age: 23, Previous Rank: 67
Potential Earnings: $20-25
Risk Factor: Low
Fantasy Overview: Four-category contributor
Realistic Ceiling: Kyle Seager without the speed
Realistic Floor: A 20-homer first baseman

It really is a shame that Peterson had to wind up in Safeco, as we'd be drooling over him if we were in Philadelphia or Baltimore. The average and power should both be very helpful, but neither is likely to get to the point where he could turn into a top-five third baseman.

37. Braden Shipley, RHP, Arizona Diamondbacks

Age: 23, Previous Rank: 68
Potential Earnings: $20-25
Risk Factor: Medium
Fantasy Overview: Four-category contributor; impact potential in W, K
Realistic Ceiling: A top-25 starting pitcher
Realistic Floor: A SP4 who just gives up too many homers for his own good

It's alright to be skeptical of a right-handed pitching prospect who relies as much on his change as Shipley does, but that sells the rest of the profile short. With three pitches that could get major-league hitters to catch nothing but air, he could reach the 200-strikeout mark once he sharpens the curve.

38. Aaron Sanchez, RHP, Toronto Blue Jays

Age: 21, Previous Rank: 51
Potential Earnings: $20-25
Risk Factor: Low
Fantasy Overview: Four-category contributor; impact potential in K, ERA
Realistic Ceiling: A strikeout-laden SP2
Realistic Floor: A reliever capable of being a top-10 closer

During 2014, Sanchez showed what he could do coming out of a major-league bullpen—and it was nasty. What we don't want to see happen next is him get pigeonholed as a reliever because he was so good in his first stint, but he still holds a lot of upside in a rotation spot.

39. Hunter Harvey, RHP, Baltimore Orioles

Age: 20, Previous Rank: 65
Potential Earnings: $20-25
Risk Factor: Medium
Fantasy Overview: Four-category contributor; impact potential in K, WHIP
Realistic Ceiling: A usable SP2 despite the tough park
Realistic Floor: Chris Tillman

Harvey ended the 2014 season with an injury blip, but back at full health, he'll look to reach the upper minors in 2015. The fastball/curve combination is very legit and could lead to 200-plus strikeouts at the major-league level if everything breaks right.

40. Nick Williams, OF, Texas Rangers

Age: 21, Previous Rank: 94
Potential Earnings: $25-30
Risk Factor: High
Fantasy Overview: Five-category contributor; impact potential in AVG, RBI
Realistic Ceiling: Not quite peak Matt Kemp
Realistic Floor: A college football player in four years

For a player who has already reached the levels Williams has, there is still a ton of risk remaining because of his incredibly aggressive approach. However, his bat-to-ball skills are among the best in the minor leagues, and there's both power and speed to boot.

41. Mark Appel, RHP, Houston Astros

Age: 23, Previous Rank: 26
Potential Earnings: $20-25
Risk Factor: Medium
Fantasy Overview: Four-category contributor; impact potential in W

Realistic Ceiling: A good overall SP2
Realistic Floor: A frustrating SP5 in mixed leagues

Owning Appel in 2014 was like ending up on a roller coaster when you thought you were waiting in line for a carousel. But just like any fun ride, we're pretty much back in the same place we started at, despite any dizziness we might feel.

42. Tyler Glasnow, RHP, Pittsburgh Pirates

Age: 21, Previous Rank: 47
Potential Earnings: $25-30
Risk Factor: High
Fantasy Overview: Four-category contributor; impact potential in W, K, ERA
Realistic Ceiling: A back-end SP1 with huge strikeout numbers
Realistic Floor: A back-end reliever with huge walk numbers

There are going to be plenty of lists that have Glasnow higher based on upside alone, and I completely understand that, but Glasnow is a terrifying player to own and I would be selling him based on his current perceived value. The stuff is unquestioned, but so are the control issues.

43. Jose Peraza, 2B, Atlanta Braves

Age: 20, Previous Rank: NR
Potential Earnings: $15-20
Risk Factor: Low
Fantasy Overview: Three-category contributor; impact potential in SB
Realistic Ceiling: Jose Altuve 1.0 (pre-2014)
Realistic Floor: That, with less batting average

Peraza is on the radars of those in both redraft and dynasty formats, given the black hole that is second base on the Braves' depth chart. Don't expect too much in the current year, as it's still not all that likely he gets to Atlanta before July, but he should be a nice source of steals with a decent average moving forward.

44. Matt Wisler, RHP, San Diego Padres

Age: 22, Previous Rank: 38
Potential Earnings: $15-20
Risk Factor: Low
Fantasy Overview: Four-category contributor
Realistic Ceiling: A strong SP4
Realistic Floor: A strong SP4

Some guys just are who they are, and Wisler is a decent mid-rotation pitcher who will shortly wind up in a strong park for decent mid-rotation pitchers. And while Petco may not play as extremely as it used to, and A.J. Preller seems to have a disdain for defense, it's still an attractive place to find arms.

45. J.P. Crawford, SS, Philadelphia Phillies

Age: 20, Previous Rank: 81
Potential Earnings: $20-25
Risk Factor: Medium
Fantasy Overview: Five-category contributor
Realistic Ceiling: A 15/20 option at shortstop
Realistic Floor: The guy we think Francisco Lindor could be

Crawford is about to go through the same cycle that Lindor did two years ago. Right now, he'll be overvalued because he's being juiced up prospect lists—then next year, he'll be underrated because everyone will know him as a guy who is more valuable in real-life.

46. Aaron Judge, OF, New York Yankees

Age: 22, Previous Rank: NR
Potential Earnings: $20-25
Risk Factor: Medium
Fantasy Overview: Three-category contributor; impact potential in HR
Realistic Ceiling: A power-hitting OF2
Realistic Floor: Corey Hart with half the steals

Judge is the rare Yankees prospect who doesn't get overrated among the general public. He's a behemoth of a man, and his power is worthy of his size, but he's going to have to prove that he can make enough contact as he moves up for it to make a difference in fantasy leagues.

47. Jake Thompson, RHP, Texas Rangers

Age: 21, Previous Rank: NR
Potential Earnings: $20-25
Risk Factor: Medium
Fantasy Overview: Four-category contributor; impact potential in W, K
Realistic Ceiling: Mat Latos
Realistic Floor: The good side of Edwin Jackson

Those of you who know much affection I have for Edwin Jackson know that floor isn't a knock at all. Thompson could rack up large strikeout numbers given his frame and his fastball/slider combination. He could sneak into the majors as soon as late 2015.

48. Steven Matz, LHP, New York Mets

Age: 23, Previous Rank: NR
Potential Earnings: $20-25
Risk Factor: Medium
Fantasy Overview: Four-category contributor; impact potential in ERA
Realistic Ceiling: Clayton Kershaw
Realistic Floor: Madison Bumgarner

Did you know that they are all left-handers who throw off mounds? Sarcasm aside, Matz could turn out to be the version of Jonathon Niese that Mets fans always wanted to see—with solid SP3 valuations and the potential for a shiny ERA in that park.

49. Alex Meyer, RHP, Minnesota Twins

Age: 25, Previous Rank: 42
Potential Earnings: $15-20
Risk Factor: Low
Fantasy Overview: Three-category contributor; impact potential in K
Realistic Ceiling: A high-strikeout closer
Realistic Floor: A high-strikeout reliever

Don't take the ceiling/floor designations to mean he's destined for the bullpen. In fact, I think it's likely he remains a starter. However, I think we've gotten to the point with Meyer where he would be more valuable if he turns into a strong closer than if he tops out as a starter.

50. Michael Taylor, OF, Washington Nationals

Age: 24, Previous Rank: NR
Potential Earnings: $25-30
Risk Factor: High
Fantasy Overview: Four-category contributor; impact potential in SB
Realistic Ceiling: A compressed version of George Springer
Realistic Floor: A fourth outfielder

It may seem rough to throw a high risk factor on a player who has seen major-league time, but fantasy owners don't get extra credit for Taylor's defense. The power and speed are very attractive, but despite a shiny batting average in Double-A, he's got a ways to go to tap into them in Washington.

51. Jeff Hoffman, RHP, Toronto Blue Jays

Age: 22, Previous Rank: NR
Potential Earnings: $25-30
Risk Factor: High
Fantasy Overview: Four-category contributor; impact potential in W, K, ERA, WHIP
Realistic Ceiling: A back-end SP1
Realistic Floor: A nondescript mixed-league starter

The next two players on this list represent a difficult decision many owners are going to have to make in dynasty drafts this year. A healthy Hoffman would have been an easy top-four pick in the draft and a top-25 prospect in baseball, so here's your discount window.

52. Aaron Nola, RHP, Philadelphia Phillies

Age: 21, Previous Rank: NR
Potential Earnings: $15-20
Risk Factor: Low
Fantasy Overview: Four-category contributor; impact potential in W
Realistic Ceiling: A reliable SP3
Realistic Floor: A reliable SP4

The first boring and safe option toward the top of dynasty drafts this season, Nola is one of the most likely players to reach the majors in 2015. The ballpark will work against him, but it shouldn't keep him from being a mixed-league option for a long time.

53. Alex Jackson, OF, Seattle Mariners

Age: 19, Previous Rank: NR
Potential Earnings: $30-35
Risk Factor: Extreme
Fantasy Overview: Five-category contributor; impact potential in HR, RBI, R
Realistic Ceiling: Adam Jones with more OBP
Realistic Floor: A high-profile draft disappointment

While it may seem like a disappointment that Jackson was moved out from behind the plate before his pro career even took off, it's for the best as far as his fantasy value is concerned. He has more upside offensively than anyone available in dynasty drafts this year.

54. Kohl Stewart, RHP, Minnesota Twins

Age: 20, Previous Rank: 48
Potential Earnings: $25-30
Risk Factor: High
Fantasy Overview: Four-category contributor; impact potential in W, K, ERA, WHIP
Realistic Ceiling: Future Kevin Gausman
Realistic Floor: Present Kevin Gausman

Don't look at the strikeout rate in Low-A as any sort of cause for concern. Stewart has the stuff to be a strong number two fantasy starter at the major-league level with the ability to strike out 200 batters at peak, but is a few years away and was sidelined at the end of 2014 with a shoulder impingement.

55. Sean Manaea, LHP, Kansas City Royals

Age: 23, Previous Rank: 64
Potential Earnings: $20-25
Risk Factor: Medium
Fantasy Overview: Four-category contributor; impact potential in K, ERA
Realistic Ceiling: A back-end SP2
Realistic Floor: A poor man's C.J. Wilson

The former high-end college arm took some big steps forward over the last two months of the 2014 season, and if he continues that forward, he has the potential to take a big jump up this list in 2015.

56. Albert Almora, OF, Chicago Cubs

Age: 20, Previous Rank: 57
Potential Earnings: $20-25
Risk Factor: Medium
Fantasy Overview: Five-category contributor
Realistic Ceiling: Kole Calhoun in roto
Realistic Floor: Desmond Jennings with half the speed

While he's not the greatest selection in OBP leagues, Almora should hit enough to contribute everywhere. He may not have the type of speed you'd associate with a potential plus defensive center fielder, but his instincts should allow him to swipe enough.

57. Hunter Renfroe, OF, San Diego Padres

Age: 23, Previous Rank: 74
Potential Earnings: $20-25
Risk Factor: Medium
Fantasy Overview: Four-category contributor
Realistic Ceiling: A 25/15 OF whose average you put up with
Realistic Floor: The not-so-great Carlos Quentin

It's great when a hitter has enough power to really help in the category, and even better when they can provide value on the bases too, but Renfroe will have to fight his hit tool and Petco to get there.

58. Ryan McMahon, 3B, Colorado Rockies

Age: 20, Previous Rank: NR
Potential Earnings: $25-30
Risk Factor: High
Fantasy Overview: Four-category contributor; impact potential in HR, RBI, R
Realistic Ceiling: Evan Longoria (post-Coors effect)
Realistic Floor: A top-18 first baseman

Just for clarity, the equation for that ceiling isn't McMahon = Longoria + Coors. It's McMahon + Coors = Longoria. He's exactly the kind of hitter you love to see in Colorado for fantasy purposes, and we may only be a few years away from experiencing it.

59. Dan Vogelbach, 1B/DH, Chicago Cubs

Age: 22, Previous Rank: 39
Potential Earnings: $20-25
Risk Factor: Medium
Fantasy Overview: Four-category contributor; impact potential in HR, RBI, R
Realistic Ceiling: My boo
Realistic Floor: My boo

The defensive value is just about nil with Vogelbach, but the bat has the potential to make him quite well-liked in fantasy leagues. Of course, with Anthony Rizzo already in Chicago, he'll need a trade or a rule change to get playing time.

60. Jose Berrios, RHP, Minnesota Twins

Age: 20, Previous Rank: NR
Potential Earnings: $20-25
Risk Factor: Medium
Fantasy Overview: Four-category contributor; impact potential in ERA
Realistic Ceiling: Can't quite touch it, even if he jumps
Realistic Floor: A high-leverage reliever

The jokes just write themselves, people. Berrios has done nothing but get batters out since entering pro ball, yet he still hasn't fully shaken those who believe he won't hold up as a 200-inning starting pitcher. He'll seek to continue proving it in 2015.

61. Henry Owens, LHP, Boston Red Sox

Age: 22, Previous Rank: 55
Potential Earnings: $10-15
Risk Factor: Low
Fantasy Overview: Three-category contributor
Realistic Ceiling: A serviceable SP3
Realistic Floor: A replacement-level pitcher in shallow mixed

It's tough to be a strong fantasy starter when you reside in a tough American League ballpark without a plus fastball. The change and deception will help him generate strikeouts, but keeping his ratios down may always be a struggle.

62. Austin Meadows, OF, Pittsburgh Pirates

Age: 19, Previous Rank: 84
Potential Earnings: $20-25
Risk Factor: Medium
Fantasy Overview: Five-category contributor
Realistic Ceiling: A near 20/20 outfielder
Realistic Floor: A mixed-league OF5 in many possible combinations

The problem with Meadows' fantasy value is that since he doesn't have the potential to impact an individual category, he'll need to make them all work to hit his ceiling. If the power or average falters, he becomes more middling.

63. Daniel Robertson, SS, Tampa Bay Rays

Age: 21, Previous Rank: NR
Potential Earnings: $20-25
Risk Factor: Medium
Fantasy Overview: Four-category contributor
Realistic Ceiling: Neil Walker at shortstop
Realistic Floor: Stephen Drew (he wasn't always this bad)

Sometimes slow and steady really does win the race, and usually those situations involve the middle infield. Robertson may have his ETA held up by the Rays, but he is likely to be a reliable, but unexciting option at shortstop as soon as mid-2016.

64. Marco Gonzales, LHP, St Louis Cardinals

Age: 23, Previous Rank: NR
Potential Earnings: $10-15
Risk Factor: Low
Fantasy Overview: Four-category contributor
Realistic Ceiling: A solid SP4
Realistic Floor: A solid SP4

Gonzales is more or less a finished product at this point, although the Cardinals' rotation depth is going to push him either back to the minors or to the bullpen to start the 2015 season.

65. Gary Sanchez, C, New York Yankees

Age: 22, Previous Rank: 50
Potential Earnings: $15-20
Risk Factor: Medium
Fantasy Overview: Three-category contributor
Realistic Ceiling: A healthy Wilson Ramos
Realistic Floor: Replace the "R" in his name with a "B"

While certainly not the prospect he used to be, Sanchez still holds enough potential in his bat—especially in the power department—to be a good fantasy catcher (repeat after me) if he can stick behind the plate.

66. Dilson Herrera, 2B, New York Mets

Age: 21, Previous Rank: NR
Potential Earnings: $15-20
Risk Factor: Medium
Fantasy Overview: Five-category contributor
Realistic Ceiling: A top-12 second baseman
Realistic Floor: An all-around middle-infield option

Herrera will likely be looking at minor-league time in 2015, despite debuting last year; however, there are a few paths he has to near-term playing time. He has the ability to hit double digits in homers and steals.

67. Stephen Piscotty, OF, St Louis Cardinals

Age: 24, Previous Rank: 86
Potential Earnings: $10-15
Risk Factor: Low
Fantasy Overview: Four-category contributor
Realistic Ceiling: Matt Carpenter in the outfield
Realistic Floor: A continued bridesmaid

Despite being labeled as near-major-league ready for a while now, Piscotty keeps finding himself second in line for an outfield spot in St Louis. He'll need to hit .280-.290 in the bigs to be a realistic fantasy option in mixed leagues.

68. Reynaldo Lopez, RHP, Washington Nationals

Age: 21, Previous Rank: NR
Potential Earnings: $20-25
Risk Factor: High
Fantasy Overview: Four-category contributor; impact potential in K
Realistic Ceiling: Yordano Ventura
Realistic Floor: Kelvin Herrera

The comps are easy, but appropriate for right now. Lopez has easy velocity and a good idea of where it's going, which could lead to large strikeout totals if he can pair it with a plus secondary pitch.

69. Manuel Margot, OF, Boston Red Sox

Age: 20, Previous Rank: NR
Potential Earnings: $20-25
Risk Factor: High
Fantasy Overview: Five-category contributor; impact potential in SB
Realistic Ceiling: The 30-steal version of Brett Gardner
Realistic Floor: A SB-only OF5

The high risk factor is somewhat deceiving for Margot, as his defense and speed will keep his overall risk down. However, the average and power are still a work in progress and are what would make him an OF2 at peak.

70. Steven Souza, OF, Tampa Bay Rays

Age: 25, Previous Rank: NR
Potential Earnings: $15-20
Risk Factor: Medium
Fantasy Overview: Five-category contributor
Realistic Ceiling: A 15/15 outfielder with a touch of upside to boot
Realistic Floor: The new James Shields

As the biggest piece hitting Tampa Bay as part of the second Wil Myers trade, Souza will look to prove the projection systems right and take his place as the latest late-bloomer to become a valuable fantasy option.

71. Nick Kingham, RHP, Pittsburgh Pirates

Age: 23, Previous Rank: NR
Potential Earnings: $10-15
Risk Factor: Low
Fantasy Overview: Three-category contributor
Realistic Ceiling: A ratio-based SP4
Realistic Floor: A ratio-based SP4

See Gonzales, Marco. Kingham is boring and won't anchor a staff even in the deepest of leagues, but will be pitching in a strong home park and is likely to contribute in 2015.

72. Brandon Nimmo, OF, New York Mets

Age: 22, Previous Rank: NR
Potential Earnings: $15-20
Risk Factor: Medium
Fantasy Overview: Four-category contributor
Realistic Ceiling: Alex Gordon
Realistic Floor: The guy the Mets took ahead of Jose Fernandez

We know, we know. For a raw product out of high school, Nimmo has shown great instincts and approach at the plate, so while neither the power or speed will be difference makers, they're likely to exist.

73. Eduardo Rodriguez, LHP, Boston Red Sox

Age: 21, Previous Rank: 77
Potential Earnings: $10-15
Risk Factor: Low
Fantasy Overview: Two-category contributor; impact potential in W
Realistic Ceiling: John Danks
Realistic Floor: Waiver wire fodder in shallow mixed leagues

Rodriguez walks a fine line because of how his stuff has ticked up in both of the last two second halves. If he's the first-half guy, he's solely a deep league option. If not, he makes for a strong target.

74. Kyle Zimmer, RHP, Kansas City Royals

Age: 23, Previous Rank: 25
Potential Earnings: $20-25
Risk Factor: High
Fantasy Overview: Four-category contributor; impact potential in K
Realistic Ceiling: A solid SP2 in a good park
Realistic Floor: Luggage

One of the most disappointing prospect storylines over the last year has been Zimmer's inability to get his shoulder to cooperate, as on talent alone, he should have been in the top 30 on this list by now.

75. A.J. Cole, RHP, Washington Nationals

Age: 23, Previous Rank: 89
Potential Earnings: $10-15
Risk Factor: Low
Fantasy Overview: Three-category contributor
Realistic Ceiling: A strikeout-heavy SP4
Realistic Floor: A high-strikeout reliever

Being major-league ready doesn't really matter when your major-league club keeps adding superstars. In another org, Cole could get a look in the second half, but in Washington, that's unlikely.

76. Brandon Finnegan, LHP, Kansas City Royals

Age: 21, Previous Rank: NR
Potential Earnings: $15-20
Risk Factor: Medium
Fantasy Overview: Four-category contributor
Realistic Ceiling: Scott Kazmir
Realistic Floor: Finnegan, the reliever

We saw what the 2014 draftee was capable of coming out of the bullpen down the stretch in 2014, but he should be given a chance to start going forward.

77. Rafael Devers, 3B, Boston Red Sox

Age: 18, Previous Rank: NR
Potential Earnings: $25-30
Risk Factor: Extreme
Fantasy Overview: Four-category contributor; impact potential in AVG, HR, RBI
Realistic Ceiling: Oh my god
Realistic Floor: Oh dear lord

The 17-year old impressed with the bat during his stateside debut and while he may not be long for the hot corner, the bat should play at any position if it comes close to his lofty ceiling.

78. Franklin Barreto, SS, Oakland Athletics

Age: 19, Previous Rank: NR
Potential Earnings: $20-25
Risk Factor: High
Fantasy Overview: Five-category contributor; impact potential in AVG
Realistic Ceiling: A .300 hitter who can also go 15/15 at a middle infield spot
Realistic Floor: A boring fantasy outfielder

Barreto got some extra publicity during the offseason after being the big prospect chip in the Josh Donaldson trade, but while he's still a long ways away, there's enough here for fantasy owners to get excited.

79. Lucas Sims, RHP, Atlanta Braves

Age: 20, Previous Rank: 62
Potential Earnings: $15-20
Risk Factor: Medium
Fantasy Overview: Four-category contributor
Realistic Ceiling: A reasonable SP3
Realistic Floor: A guy who was ranked too high on this list

Despite not having the greatest 2014 season, Sims still projects to be a good fantasy starting pitcher, and he'll face the large test of rebounding at Double-A in 2015.

80. Trea Turner, SS, San Diego Padres/Washington Nationals

Age: 21, Previous Rank: NR
Potential Earnings: $20-25
Risk Factor: High
Fantasy Overview: Three-category contributor; impact potential in SB
Realistic Ceiling: Alcides Escobar with more speed
Realistic Floor: A utility guy who is still owned in deep leagues

The speed is very real, and Turner should be able to hit 40 steals per season over the first part of his career. How valuable he'll be will depend on whether he can hit .250 or .280.

81. Raul Mondesi, SS, Kansas City Royals

Age: 19, Previous Rank: 88
Potential Earnings: $15-20
Risk Factor: Medium
Fantasy Overview: Five-category contributor
Realistic Ceiling: The best version of Erick Aybar
Realistic Floor: A shortstop you're always looking to replace

The real-life package is much more attractive than the fantasy package at this point with Mondesi, and he continues to be a good source of prospect arbitrage on the trade market. The roto upside isn't substantial and he has a good amount of name value.

82. Dominic Smith, 1B, New York Mets

Age: 19, Previous Rank: 58
Potential Earnings: $20-25
Risk Factor: High
Fantasy Overview: Four-category contributor; impact potential in AVG
Realistic Ceiling: A .300 hitting, 20-homer first baseman
Realistic Floor: The current Joe Mauer

Did you know that Smith only hit one home run last year in Low-A? Well, he did. The in-game power that lays dormant in him at the moment may not really show up until he gets to Double-A, but it's there.

83. Eddie Butler, RHP, Colorado Rockies

Age: 24, Previous Rank: 41
Potential Earnings: $10-15
Risk Factor: Low
Fantasy Overview: Three-category contributor
Realistic Ceiling: A SP4 who rides the bench in tough matchups
Realistic Floor: Another Coors casualty

The Rockies have Butler working on keeping the ball down and inducing weak contact, but his raw stuff can fight through the Coors effect and still allow him to be a good mixed-league starter.

84. Tyler Kolek, RHP, Miami Marlins

Age: 19, Previous Rank: NR
Potential Earnings: $25-30
Risk Factor: Extreme
Fantasy Overview: Four-category contributor; impact potential in W, K, ERA
Realistic Ceiling: Nolan Ryan
Realistic Floor: Nolan Ryan's beef

Any time a prep pitcher is selected second overall in the draft, you can be certain there's both plenty of upside and waiting to go around. Kolek can hit 101 on the gun, so that's a good start.

85. Grant Holmes, RHP, Los Angeles Dodgers

Age: 19, Previous Rank: NR
Potential Earnings: $20-25
Risk Factor: High
Fantasy Overview: Four-category contributor; impact potential in W
Realistic Ceiling: A solid SP3
Realistic Floor: That kid with the awesome hair that never turned into anything

As far as prep pitchers go, Holmes is about as safe as they get, although with added safety comes diminished upside, so expecting him to carry your staff at the end of the decade is an unreasonable thought.

86. Alen Hanson, 2B/SS, Pittsburgh Pirates

Age: 22, Previous Rank: 63
Potential Earnings: $15-20
Risk Factor: Medium
Fantasy Overview: Five-category contributor
Realistic Ceiling: Daniel Murphy
Realistic Floor: A usable middle infielder in mixed leagues

Hanson has lost most of his prospect shine at this point, but he also hit .280 with double-digit homers and steals at Double-A. There are a lot of players ahead of him, but don't let that dissuade you.

87. Alexander Reyes, RHP, St Louis Cardinals

Age: 20, Previous Rank: 100
Potential Earnings: $25-30
Risk Factor: Extreme
Fantasy Overview: Four-category contributor; impact potential in W, K, ERA
Realistic Ceiling: A high-end SP2 with piles of strikeouts
Realistic Floor: Carlos Marmol, and not the good version

The stuff is rarely questioned when it comes to Reyes, but he needs to have a much better idea of where it's going if he wants to claim his frontline starter destiny.

88. Bradley Zimmer, OF, Cleveland Indians

Age: 22, Previous Rank: NR
Potential Earnings: $15-20
Risk Factor: Medium
Fantasy Overview: Five-category contributor
Realistic Ceiling: A poor man's Shin-Soo Choo
Realistic Floor: A 10/10 outfielder

There are few bats from the 2014 draft more likely to produce fantasy value at the major-league level than Zimmer. So while he can't match the upside of some of his peers, he should move fast.

89. Tyrone Taylor, OF, Milwaukee Brewers

Age: 21, Previous Rank: NR
Potential Earnings: $15-20
Risk Factor: Medium
Fantasy Overview: Three-category contributor
Realistic Ceiling: Carl Crawford, circa 2014 (but healthy)
Realistic Floor: A 15-steal fourth outfielder

Taylor hasn't put up much power production in the minor leagues, but his home park may help that a touch. His defense in center should give him plenty of chances to hit.

90. Michael Conforto, OF, New York Mets

Age: 22, Previous Rank: NR
Potential Earnings: $15-20
Risk Factor: Medium
Fantasy Overview: Three-category contributor
Realistic Ceiling: Marcell Ozuna
Realistic Floor: Matt Joyce

For a college draft pick whose value is based almost solely on his bat, you'd think Conforto would be a better fantasy option. Then again, it's the Mets.

91. Max Fried, LHP, Atlanta Braves

Age: 21, Previous Rank: 42
Potential Earnings: $20-25
Risk Factor: High
Fantasy Overview: Four-category contributor; impact potential in ERA, WHIP
Realistic Ceiling: An all-around borderline SP2
Realistic Floor: John Lamb

There's always risk with starters who lose as much developmental time as Fried is in the process of losing; however, if the stuff comes back strong, he's a bargain at his current value.

92. Joe Ross, RHP, Washington Nationals

Age: 21, Previous Rank: NR
Potential Earnings: $15-20
Risk Factor: Medium
Fantasy Overview: Four-category contributor
Realistic Ceiling: His brother, without the benefits of Petco
Realistic Floor: A guy you stream against bad lineups

A starting pitcher being dealt from San Diego to Washington isn't the optimal move, but unlike A.J. Cole, Ross is too far away right now to be considered blocked. He could sniff SP3 status in a few years if things break right.

93. Brandon Drury, 3B, Arizona Diamondbacks

Age: 22, Previous Rank: NR
Potential Earnings: $15-20
Risk Factor: Medium
Fantasy Overview: Three-category contributor
Realistic Ceiling: A .275 hitting, 20-homer third baseman
Realistic Floor: Luis Valbuena

After two seasons of very strong performance, prospects without big amateur pedigree generally get legitimate looks from fantasy owners. Drury should be there, but he's still overlooked.

94. Touki Toussaint, RHP, Arizona Diamondbacks

Age: 18, Previous Rank: NR
Potential Earnings: $25-30
Risk Factor: Extreme
Fantasy Overview: Four-category contributor; impact potential in W, K, ERA
Realistic Ceiling: Bob Gibson
Realistic Floor: ¯_(シ)_/¯

If you watched the 2014 draft coverage on MLB Network, you saw that comp dropped on the 18-year old. And while it's completely over-the-top, it's not the craziest thing I've ever seen.

95. Luis Severino, RHP, New York Yankees

Age: 21, Previous Rank: NR
Potential Earnings: $20-25
Risk Factor: High
Fantasy Overview: Four-category contributor; impact potential in K
Realistic Ceiling: A high-volatility SP3
Realistic Floor: A very strong source of holds

If you really believe Severino is a starting pitcher, he could be 40 spots higher on this list. The fact that he still made the list is a hedge, since we all know how to value relievers.

96. Matt Olson, 1B, Oakland Athletics

Age: 21, Previous Rank: NR
Potential Earnings: $15-20
Risk Factor: Medium
Fantasy Overview: Three-category contributor; impact potential in HR, RBI
Realistic Ceiling: Carlos Santana at first base
Realistic Floor: A Quadruple-A slugger

The California League has produced its fair share of mirages, but Olson had some real development in his time in Stockton. How much of it is real will be revealed at Double-A.

97. Marcos Molina, RHP, New York Mets

Age: 20, Previous Rank: NR
Potential Earnings: $20-25
Risk Factor: High
Fantasy Overview: Four-category contributor; impact potential in ERA, WHIP
Realistic Ceiling: A borderline SP2
Realistic Floor: A yearly xFIP breakout candidate

Molina's number were downright stupid in the New York-Penn League as a teenager, and they'll likely continue to stay that way at Savannah. He doesn't have ace upside, but the ratios could be great and those shiny numbers beget trade value.

98. Forrest Wall, 2B, Colorado Rockies

Age: 19, Previous Rank: NR
Potential Earnings: $25-30
Risk Factor: Extreme
Fantasy Overview: Three-category contributor; impact potential in AVG, R, SB
Realistic Ceiling: A top-five second baseman
Realistic Floor: A tear on Craig Goldstein's pillow

The upside is obvious with Wall, as he was one of the best pure hitters in the 2014 draft and he has 30-plus speed and Coors Field to go along with it. But let's not pretend there isn't plenty of risk here.

99. Miguel Almonte, RHP, Kansas City Royals

Age: 21, Previous Rank: 56
Potential Earnings: $15-20
Risk Factor: Medium
Fantasy Overview: Four-category contributor
Realistic Ceiling: A solid SP4
Realistic Floor: A middle reliever

It was a tough season for Almonte, especially when you factor in his environment (Wilmington is a glorious park for a pitcher). But with that cambio, there will always be potential here.

100. Erick Fedde, RHP, Washington Nationals

Age: 22, Previous Rank: NR
Potential Earnings: $20-25
Risk Factor: High
Fantasy Overview: Four-category contributor; impact potential in K, ERA
Realistic Ceiling: A passable SP2
Realistic Floor: Another TJ disappointment

The UNLV right-hander had Tommy John surgery the week of the 2014 draft and was taken by an organization with a lot of experience in the area. His slider was one of best secondaries in the draft class prior to his arm blowing out.

101. Hunter Dozier, 3B, Kansas City Royals

Age: 23, Previous Rank: NR
Potential Earnings: $15-20
Risk Factor: Medium
Fantasy Overview: Four-category contributor
Realistic Ceiling: A top-10 third baseman
Realistic Floor: Trevor Plouffe

Upon being promoted to Double-A, Dozier looked completely lost, which was a far cry from his pro career up to that point. He can still be a strong contributor in average and power at a tough position.

Honorable Mention (in alphabetical order):

Willy Adames, SS, Tampa Bay Rays
Greg Bird, 1B, New York Yankees
Aaron Blair, RHP, Arizona Diamondbacks
Garin Cecchini, 3B, Boston Red Sox
Derek Fisher, OF, Houston Astros
Kyle Freeland, LHP, Colorado Rockies
Mike Foltynewicz, RHP, Atlanta Braves
Nick Gordon, SS, Minnesota Twins
Pierce Johnson, RHP, Chicago Cubs
Michael Lorenzen, RHP, Cincinnati Reds
Billy McKinney, OF, Chicago Cubs
Rafael Montero, RHP, New York Mets
Eddie Rosario, OF, Minnesota Twins
Lewis Thorpe, LHP, Minnesota Twins
Vincent Velasquez, RHP, Houston Astros ■

The Ones Who Could Jump

by Craig Goldstein

Now in our second offseason as the People's Champion of List Making, the Baseball Prospectus Fantasy Team has endeavored to give you even more of what you wanted. To that end, we've generated what can be legitimately considered a sickening amount of online content. We average more than 15 fantasy articles per week starting in January—and that doesn't address the numerous questions sent to the Bat Signal—and still, we cannot stem the tide of questions that awaits at the bottom of each article.

The most common request we receive aside from, "Why isn't Javier Baez listed as a second baseman?" is, "Who isn't being talked about that has a chance to fly up this list next season?" Last year, I gave you 24 names in this space and hit a brutal .208 in actually finding names to land on the list. Even so, two of those names were Nomar Mazara and Ryan McMahon, and even getting a few people to pay attention to those guys ahead of time makes it well worth it.

This year I have another 20 names for you, and the goal is the same: to not only identify talent that isn't on the Dynasty 101, but also key you into names that you should be paying attention to. Many of these names won't crack the 2016 list, and you should be aware of that ahead of time. Pay attention to how far away the names are from the majors before investing heavily, but keep in mind that they're listed here because they might be guys worth getting in on early anyway.

As with last year, this list is not in an order of preference, but rather in alphabetical order. It is my sincere hope that it serves you well.

Ozhaino Albies, SS, Braves

Likely to get buried beneath the sudden influx of prospect depth, Albies was generating some buzz toward the end of the season. The next in the line of intriguing prospects from Curaçao, Albies sports plus-plus wheels and a potential above-average hit tool, and should be able to stick on the left side of the infield. With a complex-league résumé, Albies is more of a name to know than a legitimate contender for the 101, but could surprise if challenged by the Braves next season.

Jorge Bonifacio, RF, Royals

Bonifacio the Younger suffered through a brutal age-21 season at Double-A in 2014, slashing .230/.302/.309, generating weak contact against premium velocity. It's often said that the biggest jump in the minor leagues is from High-A to Double-A, and Bonifacio is a great example why. His tools remain intact, as he still boasts enough bat speed to warrant a potential plus power grade to go with an average hit tool. Still, a reactive hitter with good pitch identification skills before, Bonifacio struggled to adapt to the better stuff he saw in the upper minors. He maintained a solid walk rate and avoided striking out with alarming consistency, but instead failed to make hard contact, resulting in a slugging percentage and ISO that both represent his nadir as a professional. Young for the level, Bonifacio won't be dinged too hard if he can show a return to form at Northwest Arkansas this season. He still has the ceiling of a prototypical right fielder, although the risk level has changed after a rough season exposed his flaws.

Lewis Brinson, CF, Rangers

Last year I said, "There's a good chance Brinson repeats Low-A, and if he can cut down on the prodigious number of strikeouts, it will be hard to ignore his other tools." Brinson followed through on his end, slashing .335/.405/.579 at Low-A, while trimming his strikeout rate by 13 percentage points, but Benevolent Overlord Bret Sayre let me down on ranking him. Call me Trent from now on, because I'm doubling down on this prediction. Brinson struggled upon his promotion to High-A, but showed a promising ability to adjust given enough time. Ultimately, he put together a .288/.354/.458 slash line across the two levels with 13 home runs and 12 stolen bases in 385 plate appearances. With his prodigious tools, if Brinson can merely stay in a lineup at the major-league level, he'll be at worth at least a flier. Besides, having a list about guys who could jump and leaving someone with Brinson's athleticism off would just be a crime.

Sean Coyle, 2B, Red Sox

Bret has often said that a change in position belies an upcoming call-up. This isn't necessarily the case with the incredibly deep Red Sox, but Coyle did start to play third base last season, despite not having an arm normally befitting a left-side-of-the-infield player. While the angle and distance of his throws had changed, Coyle was his same old self at the plate, slugging .500+ for the second straight season, despite a 5-foot-8, 175-pound frame. A smaller player with a grinder attitude coming out of the Red Sox system, Coyle will draw countless comparisons to Dustin Pedroia, even though they're fairly different players, with Coyle shooting off fireworks (home runs) where Pedroia offers lasers (line drives, contact).

Jose De Leon, SP, Dodgers

It took De Leon fewer than 23 innings at Low-A to place himself firmly on the prospect radar, as he poured in more strikes than Pete Weber on a hot streak, though there's no word on whether he screams, "WHO DO YOU THINK YOU ARE? I AM!" after each whiff. In four starts, De Leon struck out 42 of the 86 batters he faced, walking only two. He attacks hitters with a fastball that already grades out as plus and has some room to grow as he refines his command. His slider has achieved more consistent shape just as De Leon did, though his body still could use some conditioning. The changeup isn't as advanced as his other offerings, but his ability to pitch off the fastball has allowed it to play up at times. De Leon profiles as a mid-rotation starter who could miss an ample number of bats if it all clicks—not bad for a 24th-round pick.

Miguel Diaz, RHP, Brewers

In all honesty, Diaz has little to no chance to crack the 2016 Dynasty 101, but rather he falls under the "guy to watch" category mentioned above. He's one of many pitchers who have yet to touch short- or full-season ball that have the potential for three average to above pitches. Divining the ones who will make it from the ones who won't is borderline impossible, but finding signs of an impending breakout is not. Diaz already boasts excellent extension on his release, and he started using that to his advantage in fall instructs, unleashing a slider/cutter that featured late break and gave hitters another offering to think about. All indications are that Diaz will progress to short-season this year, where he'll remain too far off for a list like the 101. That doesn't mean you shouldn't be monitoring his progress and making sure to pounce if he develops more quickly than anticipated.

Wilmer Difo, SS/2B, Nationals

Hands down the best Wilmer this side of Valderrama, Difo burst onto the scene as a 22-year-old shoving his Low-A competition into lockers and giving them swirlies. While his age relative to level isn't a separator, don't let it fool you—Difo has real tools. It starts with his double-plus speed, which enabled him to pilfer 49 bases. He displays above-average bat-to-ball skills as well, striking out in fewer than 11 percent of his plate appearances. While he did swat 14 home runs, power isn't a major part of Difo's game. He doesn't lack for muscle, but his swing just isn't geared for the long ball.

Taylor Guerrieri, SP, Rays

Everyone loves a comeback story, right? Guerrieri was once prominent on many a prospect list, but makeup concerns followed by Tommy John followed by a suspension for a drug of abuse (substantiating those makeup concerns for many) certainly will take the shine off one's apple. Guerrieri returned to the mound for 9 1/3 innings in 2014 and showcased his health. At his best, he has the potential for two plus-plus offerings, with a low-to-mid-90s fastball that features significant arm-side run. He complements that with a vicious curveball that can function as a major-league out pitch. Two-pitch starters are hard to come by, so the development of his changeup will be crucial, but if he can get it to passable, he should last as long as he stays on the mound. Guerrieri has suffered a bit from being out of sight and out of mind. When he returns to full-season baseball, he should remind everyone just how good he is.

Monte Harrison, CF, Brewers

The Brewers are hoping that persuading a premium athlete and Nebraska football commit to play baseball goes better for them than it did for the Royals with Bubba Starling. Like Starling, Harrison plays center field and draws some questions based on the lack of advanced competition he's faced thus far in his career. He runs well for his size (6-foot-3, 200 pounds) and has the potential for above-average power down the line. He showed a penchant to swing and miss in his first taste of pro ball, with a 21 percent whiff rate, but he balanced it with a patient approach that yielded a walk rate just shy of 14 percent. Harrison requires reps more than anything, as his multisport background means he's behind many of his colleagues in time spent on the field. Even if the hit tool fails to develop to it's utmost potential, there's hope that he could be molded into a power/speed-style player. High grades on his work ethic engender belief that he'll get the most out of whatever abilities he has.

Brent Honeywell, RHP, Rays

Drafted in the second supplemental round, Honeywell's stock soared following an impressive pro debut. In 33 2/3 innings, he whiffed 40 batters while walking only six, and allowing one home run. Largely unknown prior to the draft, and even then known mostly for his screwball, Honeywell is well more than a one-pitch wonder. He pounds the zone with a low-90s fastball that can touch 95 mph, and can mix in a curveball and changeup as well. The change flashes above average, and his screwball is a plus pitch that acts as a more dramatic version of the change. At 6-foot-2, 180 pounds, Honeywell has room to add velocity as he fills out. He doesn't lack for confidence, and it shows on the mound as he fills up the zone with all his pitches. Command in the zone is the next step for Honeywell, as better hitters will make him pay for being around the plate so often, but it was a promising first step. Don't be afraid to get aggressive in drafting Honeywell despite the late second-round draft tag.

Rob Kaminsky, SP, Cardinals

There are a few negatives that Kaminsky will have to fight all the way up the chain. First and foremost, he's an undersized lefty with a plus secondary, which will make people throw him in the reliever bin almost immediately. He's mature physically, so additional height/velo shouldn't be anticipated. He's also mature on the field, with an aggressive yet cerebral on-mound demeanor. Those high on Kaminsky tab his breaking ball with plus-plus potential, but his fastball remains mostly flat and in the low-90s. He's going to require some movement on the fastball and a little more depth on his change if he wants to avoid getting touched up in the upper minors. All this said, the 19-year-old recorded a 1.88 ERA in just over 100 innings of full-season ball.

Jorge Mateo, SS, Yankees

Top-of-the-scale speed should draw your attention to Mateo, but there's more there than future stolen bases to drool over. He has impressive baseball instincts, showing an advanced approach at the plate and on the basepaths. The potential remains for him to become a five-tool player, though it's likely that his power rests in the fringe-average range when it's all said and done. There's a lot of buzz about Mateo in scouting circles, but less so in the fantasy game. A broken finger limited him to 14 games in 2014, but a healthy season would go a long way toward making Jorge the most interesting Mateo since Ruben.

Francisco Mejia, C, Indians

It was an aggressive move to place Mejia in this space last year, but he more than justified it with his .282/.339/.407 slash line at short-season Mahoning Valley. Mejia is a fantasy hipster's dream, with a vaulted ceiling (role seven OFP) and exposed brick (raw tools)—you can say you saw him before he went mainstream. There are certainly flaws, as several tools lack refinement, but he shows more than enough promise to stay behind the dish, and could be the rare catcher that boasts above-average hit and power tools. Rare as they may be, it seems Cleveland fans have been spoiled in recent years, watching Yan Gomes, Carlos Santana, and Victor Martinez cycle through. Here's hoping Mejia can follow the same developmental path, offensively speaking.

Leonardo Molina, CF, Yankees

A fast Molina! Who knew it was possible? Granted, all it took was not being related to Jose, Bengie, or Yadier. A potential five-tool center fielder, Molina's struggles in the Gulf Coast League belie a gifted 17-year-old athlete with knowledge of the strike zone, feel for the game, and plus raw power. Molina carries an elite fantasy ceiling, but is eons away from it. He's unlikely to break out statistically while being aggressively placed, and even a tepid season while repeating the GCL shouldn't be perceived as a failure. Molina's ascendance should be a slow-burn (finally, something comfortable for a Molina), but the payoff could be well worth it.

Roman Quinn, CF, Phillies

Already a questionable bet to remain at shortstop, Quinn's broken ankle didn't help matters. He transitioned to the outfield in 2014, where his 80-grade speed could truly flourish, and quickly earned praise. At the plate he was the same as he ever was, pairing a solid walk rate with a strikeout rate right around 20 percent. Concern remains that he won't have the pop to punish pitchers who pound the zone with better stuff in the upper minors, but he was solid offensively in the pitcher-friendly Florida State League. Double-A will be a big test for him, but if he can earn regular at-bats on the strength of his defense, he'll be worth owning as a speed-only option.

Amed Rosario, SS, Mets

A precocious talent, Rosario struggled in a brief stint at Low-A (seven games) before being returned to short-season Brooklyn, where he proceeded to knock covers off balls, and socks off feet. Hyperbole aside, Rosario's .289/.337/.380 slash line in a league where most players are two or three years older has earned him numerous plaudits. In the mold of Raul (son of Raul, brother of Raul) Mondesi before him, don't let his stats guide you. The Mets will likely challenge Rosario with an assignment to Low-A Savannah, a park that crushes the stat lines of hitters. If he's merely surviving as a 19-year-old there, it's a wild success. Invest in the scouting reports and reap the rewards next offseason.

Magneuris Sierra, OF, Cardinals

Though he'll appear to be yet another Cardinals prospect who came out of nowhere to earn a ton of attention, Sierra actually signed for a six-figure bonus ($105,000) in the 2012 international free agent signing period. The sweet-swinging lefty has natural loft in his swing, though he's mostly focused on using his plus speed to get on base. He was too advanced for complex-level pitching, skewing the results on his .386/.434/.585 slash line. St. Louis could choose to challenge Sierra with an assignment to full-season ball this spring, and if he can hold his own there, his prospect stock should soar. He boasts a plus glove, plus speed, and the potential for a plus hit tool.

Chance Sisco, C, Orioles

As a converted shortstop, Sisco's athleticism behind the plate is apparent, as is the crude nature of his game. He has a good chance to continue donning the tools of ignorance, but unlike most catching prospects, a move from behind the plate wouldn't necessarily slide him to the wrong end of the defensive spectrum. Defensive questions affect his risk, but the real question is what of the reward. A premium hit tool earned Sisco the nickname "Uptown Funk," as he gave it to Sally League pitchers all season long, finishing with a .340/.406/.448 slash line. He'll never hit for a ton of power, but catchers who can come within spitting distance of .300 don't grow on trees.

Trevor Story, SS, Rockies

A strong half-season in the hitter's paradise that is Modesto gave way to a precipitous decline upon promotion to Double-A for Story. He succeeded despite himself in High-A, striking out 27 percent of the time, but countering that with a penchant for walks, an aspect of his game that has never left him. His struggles picking up spin mean the strikeouts are here to stay, but the sturdy infielder has enough power to warrant playing. Whether that's in a utility role or as a second-division player is TBD, but middle infielders with his power and a future home park of Coors are awfully attractive. If he can right the ship to the point that he's ready to contribute in 2016, it will be hard to ignore his fantasy potential given his position and home park.

Gleyber Torres, SS, Cubs

While he played second fiddle to Eloy Jimenez in the Cubs' 2013 international signing class, Torres has earned first chair when it comes to prospect status over the last year-plus. Both players came stateside during their age-17 seasons, but where Jimenez floundered, Torres flourished. Spending the majority of the season at the Cubs' Mesa complex, Torres slashed .279/.372/.377, walking nearly 14 percent of the time and swiping eight bases. He doesn't boast the most fantasy-friendly profile, but he projects to stick at the talent-starved shortstop position, and his OFP includes a plus hit tool and an average run. Fantasy shortstops have been valuable with less. ■

The Top 50 2014 Signees for Dynasty Drafts

by Bret Sayre

This list was originally published at BaseballProspectus.com on January 6, 2015

At this time of year, the focus in dynasty leagues is squarely on two things: the yearly draft and polishing off those last few keeper spots heading into the new season. Usually, these two are very intertwined, especially when it comes to offseason trading—and knowing both the depth and pressure points of the draft class can help you figure out the best course of action for your team. After all, not all draft picks or classes are created equally.

It's easy to look back at last year's class—specifically, last year's list—and see that this is a great year to have multiple draft picks. We've known for quite a while that the 2014 class was extremely deep, but when you look at the last five or so names from last year's list, it's no exaggeration to say that those players (at this time last year) might have struggled to fit into a top 75 now. In fact, while three members of the J2 class from 2013 made that list, no members of last year's made this one. Some of that may have been due to the talent of Rafael Devers, Eloy Jimenez, and Gleyber Torres; then again, it's not like Gilbert Lara, Adrian Rondon, and Juan De Leon are chumps either.

The problem comes at the top of the draft. We've been spoiled recently with the combination of draftees with elite potential and high-profile international signings. Here is what the top of my draft board has looked like the last four years:

2014	2013	2012	2011
Kris Bryant	Carlos Correa	Yu Darvish	Bryce Harper
Jose Abreu	Byron Buxton	Anthony Rendon	Manny Machado
Masahiro Tanaka	Mike Zunino	Gerrit Cole	Jameson Taillon
Clint Frazier	Jorge Soler	Trevor Bauer	Nick Castellanos
Jonathan Gray	Addison Russell	Dylan Bundy	Chris Sale
Mark Appel	Max Fried	Yoenis Cespedes	Nolan Arenado

As you can see, not only is the top spot significantly less valuable in 2015 drafts, it's weaker across the board in the first half of the first round. If you were drafting the 2013 and 2014 classes together (with values locked at time of each draft), you might be hard-pressed to squeeze anyone into the top six from the current crop.

And while the issues with the no. 1 slot may be talent-based, the rest of it isn't. There is a lot of upside scattered throughout these rankings, but there is more risk than usual—and mitigating circumstances that make the high end of the board look weaker. Things could have been slightly different had Jeff Hoffman not had Tommy John, or if Kenta Maeda had been posted and Yoan Moncada had signed (though this could still happen—and he'd rank in the top tier if he were eligible).

And 500 words is just about enough of an introduction here, so let's move things along. Here are the top 50 players available in 2015 dynasty league first-year player drafts:

1. **Yasmany Tomas, OF, Arizona Diamondbacks**
2. **Carlos Rodon, LHP, Chicago White Sox**
3. **Rusney Castillo, OF, Boston Red Sox**
4. **Kyle Schwarber, C/OF, Chicago Cubs**

So this is the top tier we get this year. If these four break right, we're looking at a 30-plus home-run threat in the desert, a perpetual borderline SP1 candidate, a five-category threat that calls Fenway home, and a catcher who can hit for average and eclipse 25 homers (something that's only been done five times in the last five seasons). Of course, we know that won't all happen. The trouble is, when you're deciding at the top of the draft this year, all four of these players are reasonably close to one another in value.

The incredible thing here is that I've spent so much time and effort over the past few years trying to get across the BPA (best player available) mentality in dynasty drafts. You've seen me write about it, and you've heard us talk about it on TINO (There Is No Offseason podcast, for the uninitiated). Yet this year, if you're picking in the top three (fourth doesn't matter, you'll take who comes to you), the top tier is so densely packed, your team composition actually matters. If you're built to win right now and need an outfielder, Castillo might be your guy. If pitchers are more valuable in your league and you're short an arm or two, Rodon might be your pick. Just don't get too used to me saying that it's okay not to go with the best player available.

There's no great pick at the top of the draft this year, and there's no inherently bad pick at the top of the draft this year. Whether you find comfort in that largely depends on your individual valuations and what your draft slot is. Tomas might not make enough contact to be a difference-maker in fantasy. Rodon could end up just being the guy from his junior season at North Carolina State. Castillo could be a center fielder better known for his defense than offense. Schwarber could be a generic almost-power-hitting outfielder. Such is life. Choose wisely or trade back.

5. **Jeff Hoffman, RHP, Toronto Blue Jays**
6. **Aaron Nola, RHP, Philadelphia Phillies**
7. **Alex Jackson, OF, Seattle Mariners**

Both Hoffman and Jackson have the talent to be in the first tier, but not only does each carry his own risk, they both have ended up in pretty unfavorable future home-park situations. In fact, it would not be surprising if either player ended up as the best dynasty-league asset from this draft class. Of course, if you're not much of a risk taker, Nola will probably top out as a good SP3, but he could be in the majors this year and pretty close to peak value by next.

8. **Brandon Finnegan, LHP, Kansas City Royals**
9. **Trea Turner, SS, San Diego Padres**
10. **Tyler Kolek, RHP, Miami Marlins**
11. **Grant Holmes, RHP, Los Angeles Dodgers**
12. **Bradley Zimmer, OF, Cleveland Indians**
13. **Michael Conforto, OF, New York Mets**

Here's where things start to get interesting. There's a slight line of demarcation at this point between the players who are surer bets and the ones who have more upside, with a small amount of crossover. Finnegan has already pitched in the big leagues, and though a rotation future is far from guaranteed, he's passed the first test. Turner, Zimmer, and Conforto should all be relatively fast movers in their systems—and they all may get to the majors as soon as 2016. For better or worse, Turner will lose two months of developmental time due to being a PTBNL in the Wil Myers trade. Where things get slightly divergent is with Kolek and Holmes, but for different reasons. Kolek has plenty of upside, and despite his ETA, the Marlins have a strong track record of developing power pitchers. Holmes is very polished and should be one of the first prep pitchers to reach the majors from this class.

14. **Touki Toussaint, RHP, Arizona Diamondbacks**
15. **Forrest Wall, 2B, Colorado Rockies**
16. **Erick Fedde, RHP, Washington Nationals**
17. **Nick Gordon, SS, Minnesota Twins**
18. **Derek Fisher, OF, Houston Astros**

And if you're less into safety, this is the tier that probably looks more attractive. From the mound, Toussaint may have the best fastball/breaking ball combination in this entire draft class, but he's got a lot of work to do before he can start to make good on his top-of-the-rotation potential. Wall has the whole sexy Coors angle going for him, and he's a natural hitter with speed. Fedde is the second player on this list recovering from Tommy John, and while his upside doesn't match Hoffman's, he would be on the edge of the top 10 if fully healthy. Gordon will get inflated slightly because of his draft spot, but it's not a true defense-first profile. Fisher remains one of my favorite targets, as a toolsy college guy who may not put it together but could approach five-category fantasy star territory if he does.

19. **Kyle Freeland, LHP, Colorado Rockies**

Where Freeland falls in drafts will be one of the more fascinating things to track. On one hand, he's a top-10 pick who put up ridiculous stats in his junior season, including strikeout-to-walk ratios that would make your mother blush. On the other hand, eww Colorado. Let's be honest, if Freeland had been drafted by the Mariners or the Mets, he would be right up near Nola and Finnegan, but the history of how pitchers fare in Coors can't be ignored.

20. **Michael Chavis, 2B/3B, Boston Red Sox**
21. **Derek Hill, OF, Detroit Tigers**
22. **Max Pentecost, C, Toronto Blue Jays**
23. **Luis Ortiz, RHP, Texas Rangers**
24. **Tyler Beede, RHP, San Francisco Giants**
25. **Jack Flaherty, RHP, St Louis Cardinals**

To show how deep this draft class is in this segment, all six of these players were dark-horse candidates for the Dynasty 101. Chavis has one of the most natural hit tools of the draft class, but his position is unknown and he's got a pretty long road ahead of him.

Hill's road may be even longer, but he could be a five-category contributor, in the mold of Austin Jackson—though his defense will make him more valuable in real life than fantasy. Pentecost doesn't have huge upside but should be a mixed-league starter for a while as an all-around contributor. Ortiz has as much talent as any pitcher in this draft class outside the top five of this list, with the possible exception of Toussaint. Beede had a mostly strong college résumé and landed with a good organization for his profile, but he has his work cut out for him if he wants to remain a starter. Flaherty flew under the radar because of perceived unsignability, but he is a first-round talent with athleticism, four offerings, and advanced feel for a prep arm.

26. **Roberto Baldoquin, 2B/3B, Los Angeles Angels**

Probably the biggest unknown in dynasty drafts this year, Baldoquin is a 21-year-old Cuban import who doesn't have the Serie Nacional experience to have name recognition among dynasty leaguers or the big-time tools of Moncada. He doesn't project to have a ton of power or speed, but could be ready in a year or two and provide some value everywhere.

27. **A.J. Reed, 1B, Houston Astros**
28. **Bobby Bradley, 1B, Cleveland Indians**

Two big guys. Two potentially big bats. Both Reed and Bradley had impressive debuts in 2014 and carry plenty of potential with the stick. The fact that they are both limited to first base in the long run will keep them off or down prospect lists, but not here.

29. **Alex Blandino, 2B/3B, Cincinnati Reds**
30. **Mitch Keller, RHP, Pittsburgh Pirates**
31. **Sean Newcomb, LHP, Los Angeles Angels**
32. **Braxton Davidson, 1B/OF, Atlanta Braves**
33. **Monte Harrison, OF, Milwaukee Brewers**
34. **Brent Honeywell, RHP, Tampa Bay Rays**

The depth continues, as this tier includes a nice collection of upside with some proximity sprinkled in. Blandino doesn't have much to offer in terms of speed, and his power is middling at best, but he should move quickly and can offer sneaky value in non-shallow mixed leagues. Keller and Honeywell aren't well known, especially given their draft position, but they are prep pitchers with exciting futures despite not carrying ace upside. Davidson was one of my favorite prep bats coming into the 2014 draft, and that hasn't changed despite a disappointing pro debut.

35. **Nick Burdi, RHP, Minnesota Twins**

The velocity out of Burdi's right arm is special, and he should be ready very quickly. Reliever investments in a dynasty context are still not a recommended strategy, but if you're not going to listen to that advice and take one anyway, it should be him.

36. **Michael Gettys, OF, San Diego Padres**
37. **Cole Tucker, SS/3B, Pittsburgh Pirates**
38. **Carson Sands, LHP, Chicago Cubs**
39. **Michael Kopech, RHP, Boston Red Sox**
40. **Nick Howard, RHP, Cincinnati Reds**
41. **Spencer Adams, RHP, Chicago White Sox**

The parade of upside continues, as all six of the names above have the potential to be strong fantasy contributors if they can overcome their weaknesses and ETAs. Gettys could be a fantasy star if he has just a fringy hit tool. Tucker was widely considered an overdraft by the Pirates but has the tools to be a five-category contributor—just likely not at shortstop. Sands, Kopech, and

Adams are another three in a long line of prep pitchers to watch from this draft class. Howard has similar upside, but his conversion from relief to starting pitcher will give him more risk and lead time than some of his fellow college first rounders.

42. **Alex Verdugo, OF Los Angeles Dodgers**
43. **Ti'Quan Forbes, SS/3B, Texas Rangers**
44. **Foster Griffin, LHP, Kansas City Royals**
45. **Sam Travis, 1B, Boston Red Sox**
46. **Kodi Medeiros, LHP, Milwaukee Brewers**
47. **Jacob Gatewood, SS, Milwaukee Brewers**
48. **Jakson Reetz, C, Washington Nationals**
49. **Sean Reid-Foley, RHP, Toronto Blue Jays**
50. **Luke Weaver, RHP, St Louis Cardinals**

There are some famous predraft names in this group, including the two back-to-back Brewers (though they both check in behind their third pick, Monte Harrison). Medeiros is very likely a reliever, but there's still a glimmer of hope that he could be a starter with high-strikeout potential. Prep catchers are the slowest of burns, but Reetz has the chops to stick and plenty in the bat. Travis and Weaver are likely to be quick movers, but are also unlikely to ever be fantasy stars.

Honorable Mention

- Marcus Wilson, OF, Arizona Diamondbacks
- Mike Papi, 1B/OF, Cleveland Indians
- Matt Chapman, 3B, Oakland Athletics
- Justus Sheffield, LHP, Cleveland Indians
- Gilbert Lara, OF, Milwaukee Brewers
- Casey Gillaspie, 1B, Tampa Bay Rays
- Gavin LaValley, 3B, Cincinnati Reds
- Chase Vallot, C, Kansas City Royals
- Adrian Rondon, SS, Tampa Bays Rays
- Jake Stinnett, RHP, Chicago Cubs

Look, I usually stop with the comments after the top 50 is over, but all 10 of these players would have made the list in almost any other year, so we'll continue. There are some interesting first-round bats (but not too interesting) in Chapman and Gillaspie—though they drop off the list because of a lack of upside. The two biggest J2 signings for fantasy purposes finally show up here in Lara and Rondon—Lara is the bigger bat, but Rondon is relatively advanced and should stick at shortstop. Also, I have mentioned Jake Stinnett again, so that I don't get punched in the neck by Mike Ferrin. He may seem harmless, but the man has a serious mean streak. ■

Top 50 Prospects for 2015 Fantasy Value Only

by Mike Gianella

When I started playing in competitive fantasy baseball leagues in the mid-1990s, there was plenty of viable prospect information available for fantasy players to review. Unfortunately, despite the tremendous amount of data, little was geared toward fantasy.

We have come a long way since those somewhat darker days. Toolsy players like Glenn Williams and Derrick Gibson are avoided in all but the deepest of dynasty leagues, and most prospect rankings provide a good deal of insight into what a player's fantasy impact will be throughout his career.

If there is a gap in today's fantasy landscape, it comes when fantasy owners try to balance present-day considerations with a player's long-term outlook. In keeper (non-dynasty) leagues, owners tend to overvalue rookies, but this tendency exists in redraft leagues as well.

To remedy this, Baseball Prospectus has put together a list of the top 50 prospects for one-year, non-keeper leagues. While it's obviously an inexact science, the list below attempts to value players based on what they might do this year only if they are called up.

1. Jorge Soler, OF, Chicago Cubs

Soler isn't the best prospect in baseball–he isn't even the best prospect on the Cubs–but for 2015 only, he is the safest bet to produce for the Northsiders, and for your fantasy team. A polished hitter, Soler produced at every level and didn't miss a beat upon his promotion, hitting .292 with five home runs and 20 RBI in a mere 89 at-bats. He won't keep up that pace in 2015, but 20 home runs with a decent batting average seems like a realistic proposition. The right field job is his barring a horrible spring, and Soler should produce consistently all season long.

2. Rusney Castillo, OF, Boston Red Sox

There are many possible outcomes for Castillo, but few disagree that he should stick in the major leagues all year long, even if the results are erratic on a week-by-week or even a game-by-game basis. Castillo's defense is worthless for fantasy, but it will play in center field, keeping him in the lineup through the slumps and likely giving him an opportunity to play a full season. Realistic expectations are along the lines of a .260 average with 15 home runs, but Castillo has some speed to go along with that and could be a 20/20 player if everything breaks right. He has a higher ceiling than Soler, but ranks just a tick behind him due to the overall uncertainty and lack of a minor-league record to review.

3. Yasmany Tomas, 3B, Arizona Diamondbacks

If Castillo is uncertain, Tomas is the great nothingness in the center of a black hole that will drive us to madness if we ever glimpse into its core. Tomas has tremendous power potential, but with that potential come questions about whether his swing will be exposed against major-league pitching and whether he can keep his batting average above .230. He is not viewed in the same class as Jose Abreu, but that is hardly a knock given the incredible season Abreu had out of the gate in 2014. The hope is that Tomas also exceeds expectations, but the ceiling seems lower and the risks far greater with Tomas. He has the greatest power potential for 2015 of anyone on this list with the possible exception of Kris Bryant, but unlike Bryant, Tomas' $68 million deal makes it extremely likely that the Cuban outfielder will be in the Opening Day lineup for the Snakes.

4. Kris Bryant, 3B, Chicago Cubs

In terms of identifiable and immediate impact, this year's list is much thinner than last year's Top 50. However, even if Bryant doesn't break camp with the Cubs, it is extremely likely that the young third baseman runs with the job whenever he is promoted. Bryant has demolished pitching at every level in his year and a half as a professional, smashing a ridiculous 43 home runs between Double-A and Triple-A last season. Bryant even stole 15 bases for good measure. His 2015 value hinges upon when he is promoted, but even if the call "only" comes in mid-May, a 20-25 home-run campaign with a .260 batting average isn't out of the question. Bryant's third-base eligibility pushes him a bit higher as well, particularly with power at a premium in the current, pitcher-friendly environment and with the plethora of outfielders on this list.

5. Joc Pederson, OF, Los Angeles Dodgers

The Dodgers' outfield was extremely crowded, but as they did in the past with Yasiel Puig, the organization found room for what they believe is a premium talent by trading Matt Kemp and eating a healthy chunk of Kemp's salary. Pederson has moved up a level per year, and even with the PCL boost his 33-home run, 30-steal, .435 OBP campaign at Triple-A tantalized fantasy owners with what might be. The power and speed both should translate to the major leagues, and a 20/20 pace is a realistic expectation.

6. Steven Souza, OF, Tampa Bay Rays

No single rookie on this list benefited more from a trade than Souza did after the Nationals shipped him to Tampa Bay and handed him a starting job. Souza was blocked in Washington, but now he gets a chance to unleash that 15/15 potential with an outside chance at 20 home runs. He isn't the player many on this list are, but the opportunity is significant and the fantasy toolbox cannot be denied.

7. Dalton Pompey, OF, Toronto Blue Jays

The Blue Jays were impressed enough with Pompey to move him across four levels in 2014, culminating in a healthy-sized cup of coffee and a 43 plate appearance call-up to Toronto to conclude the season. Pompey's game is mostly speed and defense at this point, but the Jays are likely to give him a crack at the center-field job, and he is capable enough to run with it with the glove. He won't show any power out of the gate, but if he can get on base at a decent enough clip, his speed should provide enough fantasy value to make Pompey an asset. The new and improved Blue Jays lineup should help Pompey's overall fantasy value by adding runs and/or RBI no matter where he hits in the order.

8. Noah Syndergaard, SP, New York Mets

Syndergaard appears to be stuck behind a significant logjam with the Mets and might have trouble breaking camp with the club. However, injuries and ineffectiveness have a way of decimating pitching staffs, and Syndergaard will be first in line for New York even if he doesn't make the club in April. Even with the fences at Citi Field moved in, the park is still likely to play pitcher-friendly, and Syndergaard's high strikeout potential can play in any venue. If the Mets take a step forward this year, Syndergaard could even provide the wins that Mets starters have been unable to give their fantasy owners in the past.

9. Andrew Heaney, SP, Los Angeles Angels of Anaheim

Heaney's terrible 29 1/3 innings for the Marlins in 2014 somewhat masks the fact that he is still a terrific prospect in his own right. He's not that far behind Syndergaard in terms of his ceiling (the Baseball Prospectus prospect team has Syndergaard as a 7/no. 2 starter, compared to a high 6/no. 2/3 for Heaney), and Heaney has a clearer path to the Opening Day rotation than his Mets counterpart. Heaney's 2014 can't be thrown out the window completely, but it is entirely possible that his second go 'round is much more successful than his first. He is an under-the-radar Rookie of the Year candidate and is easily the most likely rookie starter to rack up 30-plus starts in 2015.

10. Daniel Norris, SP, Toronto Blue Jays

Norris ripped through four levels in 2014, culminating in a cup of coffee for the Jays that included one late September start. His raw stuff is impressive, but command was a significant issue for the then-21-year-old left-hander. Immediately after the season, Norris had arthroscopic surgery to remove loose bodies from his elbow. It is possible that this could have contributed to Norris' command issues. If so, Norris could take another step forward next year, which is kind of scary considering the raw stuff. Aaron Sanchez and Marcus Stroman might be better bets at the moment, but Norris' ceiling is at least where theirs is and–if the injury was a definitive factor–it might be a little higher.

11. Matt Wisler, SP, San Diego Padres

After a strong start at Double-A, Wisler's numbers appeared to collapse at Triple-A in the second half of the season. However, a closer look reveals that much of this was due to a home-run spike, a common product of prolonged exposure to the Pacific Coast League. Most of the damage came in Wisler's first four Triple-A starts. Take those out and he put up a more acceptable 3.83 ERA in a little over 100 innings. Wisler changes speeds well, and while he doesn't project as an ace, he has done well making adjustments at every level. The Petco advantage is huge, and the competition ahead of him at the back end of the rotation is injury prone. Wisler is very likely to be in the Padres rotation at some point in 2015.

12. Archie Bradley, SP, Arizona Diamondbacks

This ranking is the optimistic outcome for Bradley, who many feel hurt his stock significantly in 2014 as he struggled and revealed some flaws for the first time in his career. Bradley dealt with elbow issues last year, but assuming health he still has a fairly strong arsenal, including a fastball he can dial up into the mid-90s and a slider he showed for the first time in the Arizona Fall League that hit 88-90 mph. Some are pointing to him as a future no. 4 starter, but this seems too reactionary to last year's struggles. Given full health, Bradley could at least be a mid-tier starter and possibly provide more than that.

13. Maikel Franco, 3B, Philadelphia Phillies

There are few bright spots in the near-term for the Phillies, but Franco is most definitely one of those little rays of sunshine. He struggled in the early going at Triple-A in 2014, but then picked it up and showed why he is viewed as one of the better prospects in the game. Franco doesn't quite possess the raw power of some of the prospects ahead of him on this list, but could still get to 25-30 home runs at his peak if everything breaks right. He might not be able to stick at third base as he gets older, but he should stick at the position early in his career. Cody Asche and Ryan Howard aren't significant roadblocks at the corners for the Phillies. If Franco breaks camp with the big club, he moves up a couple of ticks on this list.

14. Dylan Bundy, SP, Baltimore Orioles

Bundy struggled at Triple-A after dominating Double-A, but since the sample size is so small, you almost have to ignore both small sets of results entirely. A lot of Bundy's failure or success will be predicated on whether he can throw that cutter of his effectively and for strikes. The ceiling is sky high, but so is the risk, and added to this risk is the fact that the Orioles will probably bring him along slowly to mitigate further injuries. If the health questions are resolved in his favor this spring, Bundy has the potential to be a legitimate ace. It is doubtful, though, that this version of Bundy is what will be on display in 2015.

15. Cory Spangenberg, 2B, San Diego Padres

The ceiling here isn't extremely high and the Petco factor definitely will tamp down Spangenberg's fantasy impact. But speed is speed, and middle-infield speed cannot be ignored. Spangenberg's ceiling isn't nearly as high as that of some middle infielders lower on this list, but he transitioned almost seamlessly to the majors (albeit in a very limited number of at-bats). Assuming he can hold off Taylor Lindsey all year long, Spangenberg has the potential to be a Top 10 rookie in 2015 if he can find his way into the Padres lineup.

16. Alex Meyer, SP, Minnesota Twins

Meyer has some of the best raw stuff of anyone on this list. The problem he has is with repeatability and command. Some believe that Meyer's path to Minnesota will eventually be as a reliever due to these problems, but the Twins understandably don't want to give up completely on the idea of Meyer in the rotation. Meyer will probably start the year at Triple-A, but if he can get the walk rate down, he will be up at some point during

2015. That high strikeout rate combined with that home venue is incredibly appealing.

17. Jose Peraza, 2B, Atlanta Braves

Forget about those glittering batting averages in the minors last year. Peraza is on this list–and this high on this list–because of those 60 stolen bases. He also might have an open opportunity at the starting job at some point, with the weak competition in front of him at the keystone. However, while 60 steals from a second baseman get the salivary glands going, keep in mind that he's unlikely to carry most of those over and he has fewer than 200 plate appearances in the high minors. Stealing bases against Double-A catchers is much different than learning to get good reads and jumps off of major-league pitchers and catchers. Peraza will provide some value if he gets the call, but pencil in a 20-25 stolen-base pace and hope for more than that.

18. Rymer Liriano, OF, San Diego Padres

Coming off of Tommy John surgery, Liriano tore apart Double-A, ripped up Triple-A in a small sample size, and struggled in the majors at the end of the season. He has been compared to Raul Mondesi, which sounds great from a fantasy perspective, but Mondesi never had to play half of his home games in the depressing hitters' venue that is Petco. Liriano's power might not translate to Petco, but the speed should carry over and all he needs to do is hold down a starting job to produce fantasy value with his legs in any format. The Padres outfield is now crowded thanks to the acquisitions of Matt Kemp, Wil Myers, and Justin Upton, but Liriano still could find a way to make the team in 2015.

19. Brandon Finnegan, SP/RP, Kansas City Royals

If you don't know who Finnegan is, you're that awful kind of fantasy player who doesn't really care about baseball and is always shoulder-deep into fantasy football in mid-August. Finnegan could easily be a shutdown reliever, but with the Royals awash in bullpen arms, he will probably get a shot to start. He hardly has any professional experience, but the stuff will play in the majors in relatively quick order. The open question is whether Finnegan will have the durability for the rotation in the long-term. The Royals are likely to stretch him out in Triple-A in an attempt to find out.

20. Henry Owens, SP, Boston Red Sox

Owens lacks the ceiling that many of the pitchers on this list have, but he has been fairly successful throughout most of his minor-league career and should be able to slot in as a no. 4/no. 5 starter in the majors without too many struggles when he is eventually promoted. The strikeouts should translate fairly well to the majors, and the only thing that could keep Owens down in 2015 is if the Red Sox contend and are aggressive in the trade market. Owens should contribute at some point this year, and the high floor makes him worth monitoring even in non-keeper formats.

21. Devon Travis, 2B, Toronto Blue Jays

Travis's lack of a strong tool set has always turned off prospect watchers, but all he has done in the minors since signing with the Tigers in 2012 is hit. Traded to the Blue Jays last November in a deal for Anthony Gose, Travis has a pretty good shot at the second-base job. His power might not translate right away, but a 10- to 15-home-run pace wouldn't be shocking. Multiple people in the industry believe that Travis can be one of those players who defy the scouting reports and become a steady (if unspectacular) regular for 10-12 seasons.

22. Sean Nolin, SP, Oakland Athletics

Nolin might not have made this list had he stayed with the Blue Jays, but with the Athletics he benefits from a combination of opportunity and a huge park boost, particularly for a fly-ball pitcher whose mistakes will be hidden more easily in his new venue. The A's have many options entering the year, but Nolin is just about ready and should be one of the first arms called up if there is a need. Nolin projects as a no. 4 or no. 5 starter, but in Oakland that could still translate to some decent fantasy numbers.

23. Alex Colome, SP, Tampa Bay Rays

Colome will be 26 years old on Opening Day, so there is a good chance that 2015 is his last chance at establishing himself as a starting pitcher. The raw stuff is great, but Colome has always had problems with command and consistency, and there are no guarantees that these won't continue to be problems in 2015. He's an exciting player to take a flier on in deeper formats, but there is a lot of distance between the ceiling and the floor in this case. Colome has a good chance at starting the season in the Rays' rotation, so he is ranked a little higher than he might be if we were simply looking at raw potential.

24. Addison Russell, SS, Chicago Cubs

Russell is one of the best baseball players on this list, even though he might never be the best fantasy player in this group. The centerpiece to the Jeff Samardzija/Jason Hammel swap with the Athletics, Russell tore up the minors after the trade. He offers an all-around profile that suggests the potential for superstardom even if the fantasy numbers don't come all at once. Even the drop in steals in 2014 might not be a concern; Russell had a hamstring injury early in the year, and the Cubs exercised caution with him on the basepaths. Russell might not be up in 2015, but the overall potential could see him break through fairly quickly and succeed right out of the gate.

25. Nick Tropeano, SP, Los Angeles Angels of Anaheim

Tropeano was solid in a four-start trial for the Astros at the end of 2014 and now could get the opportunity to ply his craft in the pitching graveyard that is Angel Stadium. Tropeano lives off of deception and an above-average changeup; while he might struggle his second time around the majors, he is the kind of pitcher who could have a good deal of success in his initial go 'round. The competition in Anaheim isn't particularly stiff, so it's fairly likely that Tropeano gets the call at some point in 2015.

26. Michael Foltynewicz, RP/SP, Atlanta Braves

There is a lot of work that still needs to be done here, but if the Braves trade Craig Kimbrel as part of their rebuild, Folty could close at some point in 2015. The risk is high–and there might be some bumps in the road–but in fantasy, saves are saves. He could also return to starting, in which case you can cross him off for 2015 entirely barring a big leap forward on his secondary stuff as the season progresses.

27. Robbie Ray, SP, Arizona Diamondbacks

In this topsy-turvy, helter-skelter, fast-paced world we live in, you can be forgiven for believing that Ray is already a colossal failure. However, he is still very young and there is plenty of time for a turnaround. The potential the Tigers saw when they acquired him in December 2013 as part of a package for Doug Fister is still there, and now he gets to go to the weaker hitting league and potentially reinvent himself with the Diamondbacks. There are no guarantees—and maybe Ray won't even be up this year—but given Arizona's needs and depth chart, it is more likely than not he will be.

28. Eddie Rosario, OF, Minnesota Twins

Opinions are split on whether Rosario can be a viable major leaguer. In the near term, Rosario's strong AFL showing puts him on a faster trajectory to the majors than initially believed after a drug suspension and a poor minor-league showing last year. Some believe Rosario is going to be a batting-average-only player whose power and speed won't translate to Minnesota, while others think the fantastic offensive output he showed at one point in the minors will return. He is here because there might be opportunity on a transitional Twins team to carve out a role this year.

29. Francisco Lindor, SS, Cleveland Indians

Lindor fits in on this list the way that his counterpart Russell on the Cubs does. Extremely talented, Lindor is extremely likely to ply his trade in the majors for many years as an everyday player, and quite possibly as a high-impact player at a skill position. Lindor made it all the way to Triple-A last year, and while he didn't light up the world, he held his own as a 20-year-old against much older competition. The power likely won't come right away, but if Lindor can put up a five-home-run/20-steal pace upon promotion, he will provide plenty of value. The only thing keeping him this low on this list is that–for 2015 at least–it is still a question of if and not when.

30. Micah Johnson, 2B, Chicago White Sox

Carlos Sanchez might be the first rookie out of the gate for the Sox, but Johnson is the one with the upside for the White Sox. With Marcus Semien out the door, Johnson's path is pretty open to the job in Chicago, as he is only blocked by perennial utility type Emilio Bonifacio. Johnson lacks some polish in his overall game but has enough speed that he could steal 20-25 bases even if he does little else. His fantasy profile is likely better than his real-life prospects, but this is a fantasy list.

31. Aaron Sanchez, RP/SP, Toronto Blue Jays

Sanchez finished the season saving games for the Blue Jays, but many believe that he has too much talent and upside to waste in the bullpen. There were rumblings over the winter that Sanchez had a shot at cracking the rotation in spring training, but it appears that the Jays will follow the model of using Sanchez in the bullpen for a year before transitioning him to the rotation in 2016. Interestingly, Sanchez could still provide significant fantasy value if the Jays stand pat with their 'pen and don't bring in a free-agent closer.

32. Michael Taylor, OF, Washington Nationals

Taylor barely scraped the bottom of this list before an injury to Jayson Werth opened the door, at least for a little while. Taylor might not have much time to prove himself, but he has a nice power/speed combination and could stick as a fourth outfielder even after Werth returns. Taylor has the potential like his former teammate Souza to be a 15/15 player with even more potential upside if everything breaks right.

33. Nate Karns, SP, Tampa Bay Rays

At 27, Karns is the oldest player on this list. But Karns lost a season due to shoulder surgery and has been behind schedule ever since. His stuff might push him to the bullpen in the long-term, but the Rays will need someone to take the mound every fifth day, and if his teammate Colome can't do it, then Karns could pick up the slack. He already has two solid pitches; if Karns can refine his changeup he could stick as a no. 4 type in the rotation for the Rays.

34. Marco Gonzales, SP/RP, St. Louis Cardinals

There are a number of possible Opening Day outcomes for Gonzales, including starting the year at Triple-A. Even if that happens, the talent is likely to force the questions and get him back to St. Louis sooner rather than later. The Cardinals could take the Carlos Martinez route with him and stick Gonzales in the 'pen. If so, Gonzales could be one of those relievers who put up strong rate stats while gobbling up the occasional save when Trevor Rosenthal can't go. We might not see Gonzales at all this year, but this is the least likely outcome.

35. Jacob Lamb, 3B, Arizona Diamondbacks

Will Tomas work out at third-base for the Diamondbacks? This ranking for Lamb sits in the middle of the answer to that question. Lamb might have some holes in his game from a real-life perspective, but from a fantasy standpoint his strong power bat and third-base eligibility in that hitters' park has fantasy owners drooling. Lamb has 20- to 25-home-run potential. The strikeouts are likely to keep the batting average down, but Lamb should be able to hit for enough average to survive and provide value in all formats. A trade of Aaron Hill could open the door for Lamb at some point even if Tomas sticks at the hot corner.

36. Christian Walker, 1B, Baltimore Orioles

Walker gets nothing more than a lethargic shrug from many in the prospect community due to a somewhat low power ceiling, but Walker has done an excellent job making adjustments throughout his minor-league career and could be one of those players who exceed the scouts' modest expectations. He succeeded in adjusting his approach after pitchers figured out his pull-oriented style early last season, resulting in a .301 batting average with 20 home runs in 411 plate appearances at Double-A last year. Although 15-20 home runs is probably a more realistic expectation, Camden Yards will help. Walker might get stuck in the minors to start the year but should contribute at some point during the season.

37. Byron Buxton, OF, Minnesota Twins

Injuries derailed what was supposed to be Buxton's inevitable arrival to the major leagues in 2014, so now he is ranked on this list in the 30s just like last year. He is in the same position as he was a year ago: it is likely that he won't be in Minnesota this year, but elite prospects have a way of defying timetables when they are ready. Bryce Harper did it, Giancarlo Stanton did it, and there is no reason to believe that Buxton can't do it. He might provide mostly speed out of the gate without a lot of power, but if Buxton gets called up he shoots up to near the top of this list.

38. Domingo Santana, OF, Houston Astros

Santana's ceiling is the kind of thing that fantasy players dream on, but his inconsistency puts the range of outcomes at anything from Jay Bruce to Kyle Blanks. Santana can look completely baffled in one sequence and then hit a monster home run in another. Opportunity more than his current talent profile puts him on this list. The Astros' bevy of offseason outfield acquisitions pushes Santana's timetable back somewhat; on the other hand, the Astros have not been shy about remedying a crowded roster when talent forces the issue.

39. Nick Kingham, SP, Pittsburgh Pirates

Kingham isn't a particularly exciting prospect, but he has solid if not completely polished mechanics and gets the most out of his decent arsenal of pitches. He realistically slots in as a no. 4 at best, but the combination of a favorable pitchers' park and a great coaching staff in Pittsburgh elevates Kingham's fantasy value higher than his scouting profile. Pittsburgh continues to churn these types of pitchers out, and fantasy owners continue to gladly take advantage.

40. Dilson Herrera, 2B, New York Mets

Herrera was considered athletic but raw entering 2014, and the progress he made during the season with his swing was strong enough that he found himself in the majors for the last month of the season filling in for the injured Daniel Murphy. Herrera will likely return to the minors to ply his craft and doesn't have a position (even though he is arguably better than Wilmer Flores defensively at shortstop), but although the strikeouts were somewhat high, he more than held his own at the major-league level. He could be up, and a 10-home-run/20-steal pace if he nabs a starting job shouldn't shock anyone. The profile plays better in fantasy than reality, but if you're reading this, who really cares?

41. Miguel Gonzalez, RP/SP, Philadelphia Phillies

Gonzalez's long-term future is likely in the bullpen, but with the Phillies in a full-blown rebuild, they have almost nothing to lose by letting him start. He is a fairly high-risk proposition in fantasy, but if he makes the rotation he could be a back-end innings eater who puts up an ERA in the high 3s with a decent amount of strikeouts in a best-case scenario. The Phillies acquired a number of inning-eater arms to fill in the rotation, but they aren't world beaters, so Gonzalez could see some starts in Philadelphia this summer.

42. Miguel Sano, 3B, Minnesota Twins

Before Tommy John surgery derailed Sano's season last May, he was discussed as one of the best power hitting prospects in the game and was often mentioned with Bryant as a future 30- to 35-homer guy. Sano won't be rushed by the Twins, but he already had around 300 plate appearances at Double-A in 2013 and like his teammate Buxton could force the organization's hand with a strong start. Sano likely won't be up, but if he is it means that he realized his potential and could be a great August or September 2015 target for contending fantasy teams.

43. Eddie Butler, SP, Colorado Rockies

Butler would be a Top 15-20 pitcher on this list based on opportunity and talent if he pitched in any other ballpark. Alas, he pitches in Colorado and even though the ground-ball profile makes some swoon, Coors Field is a dangerous proposition in fantasy for all but the most elite strikeout pitchers. Butler could survive in Coors, but he could also put up a 4.30 ERA across a full season at a time when pitcher ERAs have been significantly lower than this. Butler will have his uses as a spot starter in mixed leagues with reserve lists, but despite the talent profile, he is a high-risk play in every format.

44. Jon Gray, SP, Colorado Rockies

Unlike Butler, Gray isn't penciled into the Rockies' Opening Day rotation, but the ceiling is arguably higher with Gray and he will put the theory that it is impossible for a rookie Rockies starter to provide fantasy value to the test when he is eventually promoted. Given the weak Colorado rotation, it is likely Gray is up in 2015. He will provide strikeouts, but the home venue combined with a rebuilding Rockies team that won't provide too many win opportunities keeps Gray low on this list.

45. Joey Gallo, 3B, Texas Rangers

Gallo's ridiculous power potential makes him fantasy relevant in keeper and dynasty leagues in any format, but for 2015 it is questionable whether he will make the Rangers. He is blocked at third base by future Hall of Famer Adrian Beltre. The Rangers sent Gallo to play outfield in instructional league this winter, and given that Jake Smolinski is penciled in as a starter for the big club, Gallo could be up by midseason and bringing that power to Arlington. The risk are those strikeouts. Gallo struck out nearly 40 percent of the time at Double-A, and this simply won't translate to the majors. The reality is that Gallo could be a 2016 or 2017 play.

46. Jorge Polanco, SS, Minnesota Twins

Polanco offers very little with the bat but profiles very similarly to last year's 2014 surprise, Danny Santana. Polanco will start in the minors, but if Santana falters, there is a good chance that Polanco will be next in line to replace him. It is a long shot, but on a list like this in a weak year for rookies, he is worth keeping an eye on.

47. Stephen Piscotty, OF, St. Louis Cardinals

Piscotty is talented and looks like he entered the world with a bat in his hand, but the crowded Cardinals outfield means that Piscotty must wait for an injury before he gets the call. In addition to the lack of opportunity, the fantasy numbers are extremely boring, so even if Piscotty does get the call he could be the offensive equivalent of teammate Jon Jay without the steals. Piscotty is a better long-term play than he is for 2015, but the talent is there and he is in an organization whose prospects perpetually exceed expectations.

48. Robert Refsnyder, 2B, New York Yankees

Refsnyder appeared to be on the cusp of getting an opportunity for the Yankees before they decided to bring back Stephen Drew and apparently push Refsnyder back to Triple-A. The Yankees are an ancient team, so Refsnyder could see some time in New York as a result of injuries. He won't fill up a box score, but Refsnyder's low double-digit home-run and steal potential combined with his middle-infield eligibility would make him viable in deeper fantasy formats.

49. Christian Bethancourt, C, Atlanta Braves

Bethancourt probably doesn't belong on this list as a catcher with little offensive upside, but he will play every day. As long as he doesn't kill the batting average he should be owned in all leagues that play two catchers. Bethancourt probably is no better than an 8- to 10-home-run guy; if you nab him, make sure that you have a catcher ahead of him who is better and can provide more counting stats than Bethancourt will.

50. Rafael Montero, SP, New York Mets

Montero is buried in the suddenly pitching-rich Mets organization, but despite his erratic numbers last year, Montero is still capable of being a decent fantasy pitcher in 2015. Although he will be completely ignored by owners in all but the deepest of leagues, Montero has an opportunity to make it back to the majors at some point and provide decent stats for fantasy teams that give him another chance. ■

The Top 40 Dynasty Prospects Outside Major League Baseball

by Bret Sayre

There's no question we've gotten spoiled by all the high-end talent that has come into the United States from Cuba and Japan over the course of this decade. In fact, if Masahiro Tanaka hadn't suffered an unfortunate elbow injury, players from those countries likely would have had an epic battle for Rookie of the Year in the American League—though even that sentence sells their talent level short. From Yasiel Puig to Aroldis Chapman to Yu Darvish, we're seeing a wave of immediate superstars that have changed our evaluation of the ones yet to come stateside.

And that's precisely why we're here. It's becoming more and more common for fantasy leagues to allow owners to scoop up amateur and foreign players before those players sign their first big MLB contract (or receive their draft bonus), and while this list is directly speaking to them, it's also a good introduction to those who play in more standard formats, but want to get a closer look at that next wave. There's nothing more alluring than upside, and if standard prospect lists are Oreos, this list is the piping bag full of cream filling.

You'll notice very quickly that the list below is not just of international professionals, waiting their turn to show their mettle against the best in the world, but is predominantly made up of potential fantasy studs from the next handful of draft classes—both from the prep and college ranks. However, some of the upside comes at a price, as ETAs of some players highlighted can run up to 2020 or 2021. It's not science fiction, we're just all getting old. How's that for harsh reality?

So let's jump in and see who these future Rookie of the Year candidates and 2025 first-round fantasy picks are.

1. Yoan Moncada, SS, Cuba

The unknowns outflank the knowns at this point, but Moncada's scouting reports read as though they were filmed in the Valley. It's rare enough that a player projects to have plus power and plus speed, but when you find that combination at a middle-infield spot (even if he has to slide over to second base in the end), you're looking at someone who could be a perennial first-round pick. Moncada, who doesn't turn 20 until the end of May, might be eligible for your standard dynasty drafts this year, depending on your rules or the generosity of your commissioner, and it's very reasonable to take him at number one overall. *Editor's note: Moncada signed with the Red Sox as we were going to press.*

2. Brendan Rodgers, SS, 2015 draft, prep

The top fantasy prospect from the 2015 draft class, Rodgers' game is built on upside. The combination of his excellent bat speed and ability to stick at shortstop offers the kind of potential that is a rare commodity in dynasty leagues. Rodgers has a long way to go, but if he can harness his raw tools, he can hit .280-plus at the major-league level with 25 homers and enough

stolen bases to be meaningful (whether that's 10 or 25 depends how his body develops). He could be special.

3. Kenta Maeda, RHP, Japan

There was talk of Maeda being posted this past offseason, but it looks like MLB teams will have to wait until at least next offseason to get their hands on the most intriguing near-term arm to make the jump. Maeda is unlikely to be anything more than a mid-rotation starter, but his safety is high. With a low-90s fastball that he can spot everywhere and a slider/change combo that could both be above average, he could be a solid SP4 in short order, with a strong WHIP and more strikeouts than you'd expect—and the upside for more, given his command profile.

4. Mike Matuella, RHP, 2015 draft, college

The big right-hander brought the heat at Duke during his sophomore season, but supports his mid-90s fastball with a curveball that conservatively projects as plus and a couple more potentially average pitches to boot. Unfortunately, Matuella was diagnosed with spondylolysis—a condition that affects the connection between vertebrae in the back—which was the likely underlying cause of a lat injury that bothered him in the spring. It's not a major long-term concern, but a full, healthy spring will go a long way toward putting that behind him.

5. Brady Aiken, LHP, 2015 draft, juco

Aiken would have been a top-three fantasy selection in dynasty drafts this year had he and the Astros agreed to terms. With junior college in his sights, Aiken will look to enter the 2015 draft in the hope of being a top pick once again. We are aware of his UCL issue by now—it's not damaged, just abnormal—but the stuff is still top-of-the-class worthy. He still projects to have three plus pitches with the potential for plus control/command and is barely older than many of the top prep players available in the 2015 draft.

6. Hector Olivera, 2B, Cuba

On the verge of being granted free agency, Olivera is the top player on this list if you're just projecting for the next two to three seasons. He turns 30 in April and was one of the best pure hitters in Cuba before defecting—hitting over .300 in each of his last seven seasons. Olivera missed significant time recently with a blood disorder, and that makes him slightly more risky in the short-term, but he could be a near .300 hitter at the major-league level with 10-15 homers.

7. Ian Happ, 2B/OF, 2015 draft, college

The University of Cincinnati product has an appealing fantasy future, as he could be a fast-moving five-category threat. He also doesn't really have a standout tool or a true defensive home, but if he threatens 20/20 with a .280 average, none of that will matter.

8. Kolby Allard, LHP, 2015 draft, prep

The top left-handed prep arm in the 2015 draft, Allard made a name for himself on the tournament circuit last summer, culminating in his MVP performance at the Perfect Game All-American Classic. The California southpaw has a fastball/curveball combination that will make him a potential top pick in 2015, but his advanced command may allow him to move faster than your typical prep arm.

9. Nathan Kirby, LHP, 2015 draft, college

Despite ranking very highly on this list, Kirby's stuff isn't out-of-this-world quality. With high-profile status, like Kirby has had at Virginia, comes a heavy focus—and often, nitpicking. The left-hander has the potential for three plus pitches, with the strongest being his slider. He also has the advantage of being a likely fast mover, and in dynasty leagues, that can be an important factor when drafts come around.

10. Yadier Alvarez, RHP, Cuba

We're all still in the very early stages of figuring out who Alvarez is, as he is an 18-year-old with no Serie Nacional experience who recently defected from Cuba and has only thrown a handful of times for scouts. However, with a mid-90s fastball and a slider that looks like it can miss all kinds of bats, he's a name that won't be unknown for long. Look for him to collect the largest amateur signing bonus for a pitcher later this year.

11. Andy Ibañez, 2B, Cuba

In some ways, Ibañez is overlooked strictly because he's nowhere near the prospect that Yoan Moncada is. But even without the top player on this list to compare to, he still doesn't rank as a standout fantasy prospect. He can hit, but has middling power potential and won't steal many bases. Then again, if he hits in the .280-.290 range with 10 homers and 10 steals, that's a valuable asset at second base.

12. Dansby Swanson, SS, 2015 draft, college

Swanson has a more stereotypical profile for a shortstop, in that he's average and speed based; however, even if he never hits more than 10-12 homers at the major-league level, he can still rack up plenty of fantasy value. The added benefit to Swanson, besides the team name pun possibilities, is that he should move quickly as an advanced college bat.

13. Walker Buehler, RHP, 2015 draft, college

It's tough to think about a smallish Vanderbilt starter with a strong fastball/curve combo and not have Sonny Gray come to mind. Right now, Buehler isn't the prospect Gray was, but he stands a good chance of sticking in the rotation and accumulating enough strikeouts at the major-league level to make a difference.

14. Chris Betts, C, 2015 draft, prep

There's always plenty of risk while investing in catching prospects, let alone predraft prep catching prospects, but he may not be long for the position anyway. The projection in his bat is exciting, with the potential for plus power and at least an average hit tool. Unfortunately, if he moves, the athleticism isn't there for a non-first-base future—though the bat would play there.

15. Alex Bregman, 2B, 2015 draft, college

Maybe the most well-known hitter in the college ranks today, Bregman projects to have one of the top hit tools in the class. And while he's a shortstop for LSU, it's highly unlikely he'll stick there in the pros—second base seems most likely, with whispers that some teams would like to try him at catcher. He should move fast and could be a slightly better version of Daniel Murphy for fantasy.

16. Shohei Otani, RHP, Japan

Almost everyone knows Otani at this point, as he famously considered circumventing the NPB draft at age 18 and coming to the United States out of high school. Ultimately it never happened, but he can touch the upper-90s with his fastball and could be an SP1 in time. The time, however, is up in the air. Otani can't be a free agent until 2020 (he'll still only be 25 then), but there have been rumors that the Nippon Ham Fighters agreed to post him early as an off-the-books term for signing. Oh, and he also hit .274/.338/.505 in 212 at-bats when he wasn't pitching. No big deal.

17. Carson Fulmer, RHP, 2015 draft, college

Take Walker Buehler, remove two inches off his head, and give him more risk/reward, and you get Fulmer. It can be argued that Fulmer has the most upside of any college arm outside of Matuella, as despite the knocks on him (size, delivery), he can consistently work in the mid-90s with a curve and change that could miss bats in pro ball.

18. Dazmon Cameron, OF, 2015 draft, prep

Two years ago, Cameron was the "next great thing" from this draft class, and while he's still an exciting fantasy prospect, it's more from a bulk perspective than an impact one. There's enough power and speed here for a 20/20 performer at peak, and unlike his dad (you may recall Mike Cameron), he should also be able to hit for some average.

19. Kyle Funkhouser, RHP, 2015 draft, college

Yeah, it's a great name. Funkhouser's slider is one of the best secondary pitches in this draft class among college arms, and while he profiles to be a WHIP risk at the major-league level (due to his struggles with command), he has the ability to make up for it in strikeouts. He could be one of the more volatile arms this spring in terms of draft projection.

20. Norge Ruiz, RHP, Cuba

The most exciting pitching prospect in Cuba, Ruiz is 21 years old and already shows the foundation for three plus pitches. He may not have perfect height or a superhuman fastball, like Aroldis Chapman, but he projects as a mid-rotation starting pitcher, with a touch of upside beyond that if his fastball can creep up closer to the mid-90s.

21. Skye Bolt, OF, 2015 draft, college

The North Carolina center fielder was much more highly regarded at this time last year than he is now, but the switch-hitter still projects as a five-category contributor—an increasingly rare trait for a college bat. A strong junior season would get him back to a first-round lock and strong dynasty pick in 2016.

22. Justin Hooper, LHP, 2015 draft, prep

Hooper stands out, not only for his fastball that can reach the upper-90s, but also because he's a very large human being. He'll have a long time to iron out the mechanical issues you'd expect from a very large human being, but an easy plus-plus fastball from the left side is a very good place to start.

23. Philip Bickford, RHP, 2015 draft, juco

The big right-hander was the 10th overall selection in the 2013 draft by the Toronto Blue Jays, but failed to agree to terms. After a year at Cal State Fullerton, Bickford took the juco route to get into the 2015 draft—and with a strong spring, he could find his way into the first half of the first round again. His fastball and slider can be a strong combination for strikeouts, but consistency is not his strong suit at this point.

24. Riley Ferrell, RHP, 2015 draft, college

The TCU right-hander is often labeled as a reliever all the way, although with the trend of teams transitioning pitchers from the college 'pen to a minor-league rotation, Ferrell could get a chance in the right organization. The stuff is electric, and even a small chance that he could make it work in the rotation is worth a gamble. That said, if he's a reliever, it's a tough fantasy profile, but he could be a top-tier closer who reaches the majors in 2016.

25. Nick Plummer, OF, 2015 draft, prep

Another potential 20/20 option down the road from the cold weather prep ranks, Plummer is undersized, but popped up on many radars during the 2014 showcase circuit. Of course, the exciting thing with Plummer is not just the power/speed ability (neither rates as much above average), but the pairing of sexy stats with an easy plus hit tool.

26. Nicholas Shumpert, SS, 2015 draft, prep

This will likely be the second year in a row that a prep shortstop with major-league bloodlines (you may *not* recall Terry Shumpert) gets drafted in the first round. Though while Nick Gordon relied on a projectable hit tool to strengthen his stock, Shumpert's is the question mark holding him back. The right-hander has 20-homer power potential and speed to match.

27. Sho Nakata, OF, Japan

One of the top power hitters in Japan, Nakata has hit 79 homers over his last three seasons and is roughly four seasons from being an international free agent. It's generally pitchers who are the more popular imports from the NPB, but Nakata was courted out of high school by numerous MLB teams and could come stateside via the posting process even earlier.

28. Kyle Cody, RHP, 2015 draft, college

A large, large man, Cody stands 6'7" and his mid-90s fastball offers plenty of plane to pair with the velocity, making it very difficult to square up. The secondaries will have to take a step forward, and he struggles with many of the same maladies that other tall pitchers do (which may cause ETA extension), but he could be a strikeout-laden SP3 in time. If not, he can fall back to being a high-end reliever.

29. Zack Collins, 1B, 2016 draft, college

After a very impressive freshman campaign, for which he was named *Baseball America*'s Freshman of the Year, Collins has a strong profile for fantasy. The Hurricane star has potential to approach 30 homers and both hit for average and get on base. If he even approaches that, he'll be very valuable, even with a 1B next to his name.

30. Jose Fernandez, 2B, Cuba

The long-rumored defector is similar to Andy Ibañez in profile, but he's older and has less potential for fantasy thump. There's little question that he could come over and hit at least .280 at the major-league level right now, but it comes in pretty empty, as he may not reach double digits in either homers or steals.

31. Kyle Tucker, OF, 2015 draft, prep

The younger brother of Astros prospect Preston Tucker, the left-hander has one of the sweetest looking swings among amateur hitters—though it's not without its questions. Despite projecting to hit for average and power, he has struggled against high-end competition on the showcase circuit, leading to questions about the usability of his tools.

32. Riley Pint, RHP, 2016 draft, prep

It's pretty uncommon for a prep pitcher who is 18 months out from even being drafted to make this list, but the tales of Pint are growing by the day. In fact, some believe that not only is he the best prep pitcher in the 2016 draft, but he would be the top prep arm in the 2015 class as well. Pint has a strong fastball, ranging 91-96 mph, and a high-end breaker in his curve.

33. Luis Yander La O, SS/3B, Cuba

Besides having an incredible name to fall back on, La O is one of the most natural contact hitters in Cuba, striking out in just seven of his 181 at-bats last season in Serie Nacional. Of course, if that was it, he wouldn't be worth gambling on—but he's also one of the faster players on the island. As a likely shortstop in MLB (if he comes over), he could be a better version of what Elvis Andrus is now in fantasy.

34. Blake Rutherford, OF, 2016 draft, prep

Rutherford may get a downgrade in prospect circles because he's unlikely to stick in center field, but fortunately that doesn't matter to us. What does matter is that he projects to be a five-category contributor, with the potential for plus power down the road. He's one of those guys you want to be a year early on in dynasty leagues.

35. Matt Krook, LHP, 2016 draft, college

The Oregon left-hander was on his way to making the Marlins look awfully foolish for not signing him after they popped him in the second round of the 2013 draft, but blew out his elbow in April and has been sidelined since due to Tommy John surgery. That said, the upside is high enough that he still sticks on the list and he has enough time to recover the SP2 upside in time for the 2016 draft.

36. Demi Orimoloye, OF, 2015 draft, prep

There are so many reasons to love Orimoloye. First of all, he's Canadian. Everyone loves a good Canadian. But most importantly, he has one of the best power/speed combinations in the draft class—and though being a cold weather kid means he's more raw than some of his counterparts, the upside here could be very fun.

37. Ryan Boldt, OF, 2016 draft, college

Boldt was one of my favorite prospects from the 2013 draft and showed the ability to be a five-category fantasy contributor despite the limited looks as a prep player in Minnesota. Now a sophomore at the University of Nebraska, he will be eligible as part of the 2016 draft class—and he'll look to build off his strong 2014, when he was named as a Freshman All-American.

38. Chihiro Kaneko, RHP, Japan

In the initial draft of this list, Kaneko was significantly higher, but then he signed a four-year contract to remain in Japan with the Orix Buffaloes—though he still has expressed interest in coming to the United States. He won the Sawamura Award (NPB's equivalent of the Cy Young Award) last season and backs a low-90s fastball with a wide array of strong secondary offerings.

39. Alfredo Despaigne, OF, Cuba

I believe I gave the same disclaimer last year, but if we knew Despaigne was coming to the United States in the next two years, he'd be in the top five of this list. He's the best power hitter in Cuba right now, and has taken those talents to Japan and Mexico recently. He could hit 30 homers at the major-league level right now, but the 29-year-old doesn't appear to be heading over any time soon.

40. Gio Brusa, OF, 2015 draft, college

Another college bat with some real power potential, Brusa doesn't project to contribute a ton in average or speed (though he's not a zero in either). He'll likely be a bit of a slower burn than a typical college bat, as he's been inconsistent in his college career—though his most impressive showing came in front of the most scouts in the Cape last summer.

Honorable Mention

- Lourdes Gourriel, SS, Cuba
- Shintaro Fujikawa, RHP, Japan
- Austin Bergner, RHP, 2016 draft, prep
- Hyeon-Jong Yang, LHP, Korea
- Mike Nikorak, RHP, 2015 draft, prep
- Takahiro Norimoto, RHP, Japan
- Ronald Washington, OF, 2017 draft, prep
- Jeong Choi, 3B, Korea
- Herbert Iser, C, 2016 draft, prep
- Alonzo Jones, OF, 2015 draft, prep

Notable Omission
Jung-Ho Kang, SS, Korea

Kang was ranked 16th when this list was originally compiled but signed with the Pirates in January, making him ineligible for inclusion. His profile is presented here because you should still know who he is.

If you just look at Kang's KBO stats, you'd think he was a superstar coming over in his prime, but it's an offensive league that became even more hitter-friendly in the last year partially due to a change in the ball. In an MLB setting, Kang is much more likely to settle in as a .260 hitter with 15-homer pop, not the hitter who hit .354/.457/.733 with 39 homers in 116 KBO games last season—after all, just look up what Eric Thames did in the same league last year. ■

Contributors

Nick J. Faleris is a practicing attorney and member of the Sports Industry Team with Foley & Lardner LLP. He has been involved in player evaluation at the amateur and professional ranks for eight years, including three seasons as an associate scout for a Major League organization. Nick has worked with Baseball Prospectus since 2012, authoring various articles relating to scouting and player evaluation, in addition to contributing to the Baseball Prospectus Annual Publication and the *Futures Guide*.

Chris Mellen joined Baseball Prospectus in 2012, specializing in scouting and player development. He spends the season in the field watching pro games across all levels to contribute first-hand reports and scouting updates throughout the year. Prior to joining BP, Chris was Director of Scouting and part owner of SoxProspects.com, where he authored the site's scouting reports on Red Sox prospects and collaborated on player rankings. In addition to spending the offseason assisting with BP's Top 10s and preseason rankings, he roots on his Boston Bruins as a loyal season ticket holder.

Bret Sayre is the Fantasy Manager and Prospect Coordinator at Baseball Prospectus. He's known to be a bit verbose, so he's really trying to keep this brief. By day, he is quite adept at telling investment professionals what not to do. By night, he is a full-time family man, part-time cook, part-time nurse, full-time baseball writer, and part-time musician. As an eight-year-old, he was knocked over by a grown man as he tried to catch a dead ball thrown by Kevin Mitchell at Shea Stadium. Now, he lives in New Jersey with his wife, Carolyn; his daughter, Alyson; and his son, Joshua, who learned to switch-hit before he could walk. And no, that's not a reflection of his plate discipline.

Craig Goldstein is an author at Baseball Prospectus and The Dynasty Guru. He formerly wrote for MLB Draft Insider and SB Nation's MLB News Desk, and Fake Teams. He lives outside Washington, DC, and spends just the right amount of time thinking about sandwiches.

Jordan Gorosh is a member of the Baseball Prospectus prospect team who resides in the Windy City. According to him, there is nothing better than sitting behind home plate, watching a backfield game with two stud teenage pitchers getting their early work in. He hates your favorite prospect, unless they're traded to a smart team, and then he'll move them up 50 spots in the rankings. Pineapple is the best fruit.

Tucker Blair was born and raised in Charm City, where he still resides. While he may not be the next Omar Little or Edgar Allan Poe, he is a craft beer connoisseur and a longstanding member of the elite arm speed bandwagon.

Ben Carsley is a senior fantasy writer at Baseball Prospectus, host of the TINO podcast and a bad influence at The Dynasty Guru. Born, raised, and living in Boston, his past work has appeared on NESN.com, Over the Monster, Fire Brand of the AL, Bleacher Report, and other sites. When he's not writing about baseball, Ben is generally cooking, sampling IPAs, arguing about sandwiches, and catering to his niche Twitter following of William Faulkner-loving Red Sox fans with a high tolerance for sarcasm.

Jeff Quinton is a supply chain analyst in the consumer packaged goods industry. He is also a writer for Baseball Prospectus, where he writes about strategy, human behavior, and decision making as they relate to baseball in his non-fantasy (Tools of Ignorance) and fantasy baseball (The Quinton) columns. Jeff is a proud Fightin' Blue Hen and recent MBA graduate from New York University who resides in his home state of New Jersey.

A fantasy baseball player for over 25 years, **Mike Gianella** was a frequent contributor to the comments section of fantasy baseball pioneer Alex Patton's Patton and Company website before starting his own fantasy baseball blog, Roto Think Tank, in 2007. Mike has contributed to Rotoman's Fantasy Baseball Guide since 2010. In 2013, Mike joined the staff of Baseball Prospectus as a Senior Fantasy Writer. Mike has participated in multiple expert leagues, including CBS, LABR, and Tout Wars. Mike is a four-time champion of the CBS expert leagues, including three consecutive titles from 2009 to 2011.

Mark Anderson pitched at the collegiate level for Division III Clarkson University in northern New York from 1998 to 2003. After college he began scouting and writing for TigsTown.com as Director of Scouting and Managing Editor, focusing on scouting and evaluation of Detroit Tigers prospects. His work for TigsTown.com continues today. Mark's scouting experience led him to work as a Senior Minor League Analyst for Scout.com from 2009 to 2011, developing prospect rankings and reports for the annual Scout.com Prospect Guide. From November 2011 through June 2013, Mark conducted scouting and analysis for his own site, BaseballProspectNation.com. Added to the Baseball Prospectus Prospect Team in September 2012, Mark has continued to refine his scouting skills as one of BP's national scouts with coverage focusing in the northeast.

Jeff Moore is a former college player and Division I coach who resides in Delray Beach, Florida. He primarily covers the Florida State and Gulf Coast Leagues for the Baseball Prospectus Prospect Team.

Geoff Young founded Ducksnorts, publishing articles and books about the Padres under that title from 1997 to 2011. He has written for Baseball Prospectus, The Hardball Times, and ESPN.com, and his words have appeared in many books. He has also been writing and editing technical documents for more than 20 years, which is every bit as glamorous as it sounds. A fan of craft beer, train trips, and stringed instruments, Geoff lives in San Diego with his patient wife, Sandra.

Additional contributors: CJ Wittmann, Chris Rodriguez, Ethan Purser, Ryan Parker, Chris King, Patrick Ebert, Frankie Piliere, Todd Gold, David Rawnsley.

Statistical Appendix

Why don't you get your nose out of those numbers and watch a game? It's a false dilemma, of course. Chances are, Baseball Prospectus readers watch more games than the typical fan. They also probably pay better attention when they do. The numbers do not replace observation, they supplement it. Having the numbers allows you to learn things not readily seen by mere watching and to keep up on many more players than any one person could.

So this book doesn't ask you to choose between the two. Instead, we combine numerical analysis with the observations of a lot of very bright people. They won't always agree. Just as the eyes don't always see what the numbers do, the reverse can be true. To get the most out of this book, however, it helps to understand the numbers we're presenting and why.

Offense

The core of our offense measurements is True Average, which attempts to quantify everything a player does at the plate—hitting for power, taking walks, striking out, and even "productive" outs—and scale it to batting average. A player with a TAv of .260 is average, .300 exceptional, .200 rather awful.

True Average also accounts for the context a player performs in. That means we adjust it based on the mix of parks a player plays in. Also, rather than use a blanket park adjustment for every player on a team, a player who plays a disproportionate amount of his games at home will see that reflected in his numbers. We also adjust based on league quality: The average player in the AL is better than the average player in the NL, and True Average accounts for this.

Because hitting runs isn't the entirety of scoring runs, we also look at a player's Baserunning Runs. BRR accounts for the value of a player's ability to steal bases, of course, but also for his ability to go first to third on a single, or advance on a fly ball.

Defense

Defense is a much thornier issue. The general move in the sabermetric community has been toward stats based on zone data, where human stringers record the type of batted ball (grounder, liner, fly ball) and its presumed landing location. That data is used to compile expected outs for comparing a fielder's actual performance.

The trouble with zone data is twofold. First, unlike the data that we use in the calculation of the statistics you see in this book, zone data wasn't made publicly available; it was recorded by commercial data providers who kept the raw data private, only disclosing it to a select few who paid for it. Second, as we've seen the field of zone-based defensive analysis open up—more data and more metrics based on that data coming to light—we see that the conclusions of zone-based defensive metrics don't hold up to outside scrutiny. Different data providers can reach very different conclusions about the same events. And even two metrics based on the same data set can reach radically different conclusions based on their starting assumptions—assumptions that haven't been tested, using methods that can't be duplicated or verified by outside analysts.

The quality of the fielder can bias the data: Zone-based fielding metrics will tend to attribute more expected outs to good fielders than bad fielders, irrespective of the distribution of batted balls. Scorers who work in parks with high press boxes will tend to score more line drives than scorers who work in parks with low press boxes.

Our FRAA incorporates play-by-play data, allowing us to study the issue of defense at a granular level, without resorting to the sorts of subjective data used in some other fielding metrics. We count how many plays a player made, as well as expected plays for the average player at that position based on a pitcher's estimated groundball tendencies and the handedness of the batter. There are also adjustments for park and the base-out situations.

Pitching

Of course, how we measure fielding influences how we measure pitching.

Most sabermetric analysis of pitching has been inspired by Voros McCracken, who stated, "There is little if any difference among major-league pitchers in their ability to prevent hits on balls hit in the field of play." When first published, this statement was extremely controversial, but later research has by and large validated it. McCracken (and others) went forth from that finding to create a variety of defense-independent pitching measures. One that you'll see in the book is FIP, Fielding Independent Pitching, which accounts for walks, strikeouts, hit by pitches, and homers accumulated by a pitcher and puts them into one number on an ERA scale.

The trouble is that many efforts to separate pitching from fielding have ended up separating pitching from *pitching*—looking at only a handful of variables in isolation from the situation in which they occurred. What we've done instead is take a pitcher's actual results—not just what happened, but when it happened—and adjust it for the quality of a pitcher's defensive support, as measured by FRAA.

Applying FRAA to pitchers in this sense is easier than applying it to fielders. We don't have to worry about figuring out which fielder is responsible for making an out, only identifying the likelihood of an out being made. So there is far less uncertainty here than there is in fielding analysis.

Note that Fair RA intentionally omits the "E"; looking only at earned runs tends over time to overrate three kinds of pitchers:

1. Pitchers who play in parks where scorers hand out more errors. Looking at error rates between parks tells us scorers differ significantly in how likely they are to score any given play as an error (as opposed to an infield hit);
2. Groundball pitchers, because a substantial proportion of errors occur on groundballs; and
3. Pitchers who aren't very good. Good pitchers tend to allow fewer unearned runs than bad pitchers, because good pitchers have more ways to get out of jams than bad pitchers. They're more likely to get a strikeout to end the inning, and less likely to give up a home run.

Projection

Of course, many of you aren't turning to this book just for a look at what a player has done, but a look at what a player is going to do—the PECOTA projections.

PECOTA, initially developed by Nate Silver (who has moved on to greater fame as a political analyst), consists of three parts:

1. Major league equivalencies, to allow us to use minor-league stats to project how a player will perform in the majors;
2. Baseline forecasts, which use weighted averages and regression to the mean to produce an estimate of a player's true talent level; and
3. A career-path adjustment, which incorporates information on how comparable players' stats changed over time.

Now that we've gone over the stats, let's go over what's in the book.

Position Players

As an example, take a look at the position player statistical block for minor-league home-run champion Kris Bryant.

YEAR	TEAM	LVL	AGE	PA	R	2B	3B	HR	RBI	BB	SO	SB	CS	AVG/OBP/SLG	TAv	BABIP	BRR	FRAA	WARP
2014	IOW	AAA	22	297	57	14	1	21	52	43	85	7	2	.295/.418/.619	.358	.367	-2.2	3B(67): 5.3	4.4
2014	TEN	AA	22	297	61	20	0	22	58	43	77	8	2	.355/.458/.702	.405	.440	0.1	3B(62): 1.5	6.0
2015	CHN	MLB	23	250	37	10	0	14	41	27	79	4	1	.261/.351/.514	.321	.336	0.0	3B 4	2.5
2016	CHN	MLB	24	627	96	27	1	32	97	74	195	10	3	.264/.363/.499	.315	.349	0.1	3B 8	4.1

The player-specific sections begin with biographical information before moving onto the column headers and actual data. The column headers begin with more standard information like year, team, level (majors or level of the minors), and the raw, untranslated tallies found on the back of a baseball card: PA (plate appearances), R (runs), 2B (doubles), 3B (triples), HR (home runs), RBI, (runs batted in), BB (walks), SO (strikeouts), SB (stolen bases), and CS (caught stealing). (While these stats and the similar ones for pitchers are easy to find in American organized baseball, stats from games played farther afield are harder. Thanks, then, to Clay Davenport for his site claydavenport.com, where we sourced the Cuban stats reported for certain players here.)

Following those are the untranslated "slash" statistics: batting average (AVG), on base percentage (OBP), and slugging percentage (SLG). The slash line is followed by True Average (TAv), which rolls all those things and more into one easy-to-digest number.

BABIP stands for Batting Average on Balls in Play and is what it sounds like: How often did a ball put in play by the hitter fall for a hit? An especially low or high BABIP may mean a hitter was especially lucky or unlucky. However, hitters who hit the ball hard tend to have especially high BABIPs from season to season; so do speedy hitters who are able to beat out more grounders for base hits.

Next is Baserunning Runs (BRR), which as mentioned earlier covers all sorts of baserunning accomplishments, not just stolen bases. Then comes Fielding Runs Above Average; for historical stats, we have the number of games played at each position in parentheses.

The last column is Wins Above Replacement Player. WARP is our total-value stat that combines a player's batting runs above average (derived from a player's True Average), BRR, FRAA, an adjustment based on position played, and a credit for plate appearances based on the difference between the "replacement level" (derived from looking at the quality of players added to a team's roster after the start of the season) and the league average.

Pitchers

Now let's look at how pitchers are presented, using PCL strikeout king Noah Syndergaard:

YEAR	TEAM	LVL	AGE	W	L	SV	G	GS	IP	H	HR	BB	K	BB9	SO9	GB%	BABIP	WHIP	ERA	FIP	FRA	WARP
2014	LVG	AAA	21	9	7	0	26	26	133.0	154	11	43	145	2.9	9.8	47%	.378	1.48	4.60	3.70	4.22	3.2
2015	NYN	MLB	22	7	8	0	25	25	120.3	108	11	36	118	2.7	8.8	48%	.317	1.20	3.50	3.54	3.81	1.1
2016	NYN	MLB	23	11	10	0	32	32	207.7	191	19	59	199	2.6	8.6	48%	.318	1.20	3.62	3.31	3.94	1.0

The first line and the YEAR, TM, LVL, and AGE columns are the same as in the hitters' example above. The next set of columns—W (wins), L (losses), SV (saves), G (games pitched), GS (games started), IP (innings pitched), H (hits), HR, BB, K, BB/9 (walks per nine innings), K/9 (strikeouts per nine innings)—are the actual, unadjusted cumulative stats compiled by the pitcher during each season.

Next is GB%, which is the percentage of all batted balls that were hit on the ground including both outs and hits. The average GB% for a major-league pitcher in 2007 was about 45%; a pitcher with a GB% anywhere north of 50% can be considered a good groundball pitcher. As mentioned above, this is based on the observation of human stringers and can be skewed based on a number of factors. We've included the number as a guide, but please approach it skeptically.

BABIP is the same statistic as for batters, but often tells you more in the case of pitchers, because most pitchers have very little control over their batting average on balls in play. A high BABIP is most likely due to a poor defense or bad luck rather than a pitcher's own abilities, and may be a good indicator of a potential rebound. A typical league-average BABIP is around .295–.300.

WHIP and ERA are common to most fans. The former measures the number of walks and hits allowed on a per-inning basis, while the latter prorates earned runs allowed on a per-nine-innings basis. Neither is translated or adjusted in any way.

FIP was discussed above. It puts onto an ERA scale a measurement of how the pitcher performed on the events that do not involve the fielders behind him.

Fair RA (FRA), as also described above, is the basis of WARP for pitchers. Incorporating play-by-play data allows us to set different replacement levels for starting pitchers and relievers. Relief pitchers have several advantages over starters: they can give their best effort on every pitch, and hitters have fewer chances to pick up on what they're doing. This means that it's significantly easier to find decent replacements for relief pitchers than it is for starting pitchers, and that's reflected in the replacement level for each.

We also credit starters for pitching deeper into games and "saving the 'pen"—a starting pitcher who can go deep in a game (while pitching effectively) allows a manager to keep his worst relievers in the 'pen and bring his best relievers out to preserve a lead.

All of this means that WARP values for relief pitchers (especially closers) will seem lower than what we've seen in the past and may conflict with how we feel about relief aces coming in and "saving" the game. Saves give extra credit to the closer for what his teammates did to put him in a save spot to begin with; WARP is incapable of feeling excitement over a successful save and judges them dispassionately.

PECOTA

Both pitchers and hitters have PECOTA projections for next season, as well as a set of biographical details that describe the performance of that player's comparable players according to PECOTA.

The 2015 line is the PECOTA projection for the player at the date we went to press. Note that the player is projected into the league and park context as indicated by his team abbreviation. All PECOTAs represent a player's projected major-league performance. The numbers beneath the player's name—Breakout, Improve, Collapse, and Attrition—are also a part of PECOTA. These estimate the likelihood of changes in performance relative to a player's previously established level of production, based on the performance of the comparable players:

- **Breakout Rate** is the percent chance that a player's production will improve by at least 20 percent relative to the weighted average of his performance over his most recent seasons.

- **Improve Rate** is the percent chance that a player's production will improve at all relative to his baseline performance. A player who is expected to perform just the same as he has in the recent past will have an Improve Rate of 50 percent.

- **Collapse Rate** is the percent chance that a position player's runs produced per plate appearance will decline by at least 25 percent relative to his baseline performance over his past three seasons.

- **Attrition Rate** operates on playing time rather than performance. Specifically, it measures the likelihood that a player's playing time will decrease by at least 50 percent relative to his established level.

Breakout Rate and Collapse Rate can sometimes be counterintuitive for players who have already experienced a radical change in their performance levels. It's also worth noting that the projected decline in a given player's rate performances might not be indicative of an expected decline in underlying ability or skill, but rather something of an anticipated correction following a breakout season.

MLB% is the percentage of similar players who played at the major-league level in the relevant season. Note that players who have an MLB% of 0 also have Breakout, Improve, Collapse, and Attrition Rates of 0.

UPSIDE is determined by evaluating the performance of a player's top-20 PECOTA comparables. If a comparable player turned in a performance better than league average, including both his batting and fielding performance, then his wins above average (WARP minus replacement value) are counted toward his UPSIDE. A base of two times wins above average is used for position players, and an adjustment is made to pitcher values such that they are comparable. If the player was worse than average in a given season, or he dropped out of the database, the performance is counted as zero.

The final pieces of information, listed just to the right of the player's UPSIDE, are his three highest scoring comparable players as determined by PECOTA. Occasionally, a player's top comparables will not be representative of the larger sample that PECOTA uses. All comparables represent a snapshot of how the listed player was performing at the same age as the current player, so if a 23-year-old hitter is compared to Sammy Sosa, he's actually being compared to a 23-year-old Sammy Sosa, not the decrepit Orioles version of Sosa, nor to Sosa's career as a whole.

Index of Names

Garcia, Willy	198	**J**		Marlette, Tyler	220		
Garcia, Yimi	132	Jackson, Alex	217, 281, 329	Marrero, Deven	45		
Garrett, Amir	70	Jackson, Luke	247	Marte, Ketel	218		
Gatto, Joe	117	Jenkins, Tyrell	27	Martin, Ethan	190		
Gettys, Michael	203	Jimenez, A.J.	259	Martinez, Jose	18		
Gillaspie, Casey	239	Jimenez, Joe	96, 310	Mateo, Jorge	168		
Giolito, Lucas	260, 267, 275, 324	Johansen, Jake	265, 292	Matz, Steven	158, 278, 291, 329		
Glasnow, Tyler	191, 277, 328	Johnson, Brian	43, 302	May, Jacob	60, 307		
Goforth, David	148	Johnson, Micah	60, 307	May, Trevor	157		
Gohara, Luiz	220	Johnson, Pierce	50, 283	Mazara, Nomar	244, 279, 327		
Gonsalves, Stephen	155, 306	Judge, Aaron	166, 280, 329	McCann, James	91		
Gonzales, Marco	225, 232, 280, 330	Jungmann, Taylor	148	McCullers, Lance	103		
Gonzalez, Chi Chi	243, 278, 311, 327	**K**		McGuire, Reese	193, 281, 294		
Gonzalez, Pedro	89	Kaminsky, Rob	227, 296	McKinney, Billy	49, 283, 293		
Goodwin, Brian	268	Karns, Nate	237, 303	McMahon, Ryan	85, 285, 299, 330		
Gordon, Nick	152, 282	Kela, Keone	250	Meadows, Austin	195, 295, 330		
Gossett, Daniel	181	Keller, Mitch	194	Mecias, Yoel	185		
Gott, Trevor	121, 122	Kelly, Carson	231	Medeiros, Kodi	146		
Graveman, Kendall	177	Kemp, Tony	106	Meisner, Casey	164		
Gray, Jonathan	82, 298, 325	Kingham, Nick	193, 281, 331	Mejia, Adalberto	209, 283		
Greiner, Grayson	95	Kivlehan, Patrick	224	Mejia, Francisco	73, 283		
Grichuk, Randal	232	Knebel, Corey	143	Mella, Keury	211, 215		
Griffin, Foster	112	Kolek, Tyler	133, 332	Meyer, Alex	150, 276, 329		
Grosser, Alec	25, 291	Kopech, Michael	43	Michalczewski, Trey	61		
Grullon, Deivi	188	Kubitza, Kyle	24, 119	Molina, Leonardo	170		
Guerra, Javier	44	**L**		Molina, Marcos	162, 334		
Guerrero, Gabriel	219, 223	Labourt, Jairo	254	Mondesi, Raul	107, 277, 332		
Guerrero, Tayron	206	Lamb, Jake	15	Montas, Francellis	57		
Guerrieri, Taylor	238, 303	Landry, Leon	224	Montero, Rafael	165		
Guillon, Ismael	72	Lara, Gilbert	145	Moran, Colin	104, 313		
H		LaValley, Gavin	70	Morgan, Josh	249		
Hader, Josh	105	Leathersich, Jack	165	Moya, Steven	92		
Hanson, Alen	195, 333	Lee, Zach	127	Munoz, Yairo	178		
Harrison, Monte	144	Lemond, Zech	205	Musgrove, Joe	105		
Hart, Josh	31, 306	Leon, Julian	131	**N**			
Harvey, Hunter	28, 277, 305, 328	Leyba, Domingo	19	Naquin, Tyler	75, 308		
Hawkins, Courtney	58	Lindgren, Jacob	171	Nesbitt, Angel	98		
Heaney, Andrew	116, 278, 326	Lindor, Francisco	73, 80, 275, 325	Newcomb, Sean	116		
Hedges, Austin	200, 277	Lindsey, Taylor	205, 299	Nicolino, Justin	136, 290		
Heim, Jonah	35	Liriano, Rymer	202, 326	Nimmo, Brandon	159, 164, 282, 331		
Hensley, Ty	172	Lively, Ben	186, 289	Nola, Aaron	183, 281, 329		
Hernandez, Elier	114	Lobstein, Kyle	94	Nolin, Sean	176		
Hernandez, Teoscar	105	Longhi, Nick	44	Norris, Daniel	252, 278, 326		
Herrera, Dilson	161, 283, 331	Lopez, Jesus	181	Northcraft, Aaron	208		
Hicks, John	224	Lopez, Jorge	145, 147, 294	Nunez, Dom	88		
Hill, Derek	91, 284	Lopez, Reynaldo	262, 282, 331	Nunez, Renato	177		
Hinsz, Gage	197	Lorenzen, Michael	64, 281, 295	**O**			
Hoffman, Jeff	253, 282, 329	**M**		O'Brien, Peter	19		
Holmes, Grant	126, 283, 333	Machado, Dixon	97, 98	O'Conner, Justin	234, 302		
Honeywell, Brent	237	Mader, Michael	137	O'Neill, Tyler	223		
Howard, Nick	66	Mahle, Greg	123	Ogando, Nefi	190		
Hursh, Jason	27	Mahtook, Mikie	240	Okert, Steven	213, 300		
I		Manaea, Sean	108, 283, 330	Olson, Matt	175, 312, 334		
Iglecias, Raisel	70	Margot, Manuel	38, 281, 331	Ortiz, Luis	245		